Mergent's
DIVIDEND
ACHIEVERS

Summer 2004

Mergent's
DIVIDEND
ACHIEVERS

Mergent, Inc.

JONATHAN WORRALL
Publisher

THOMAS WECERA
Associate Publisher

JOHN PEDERNALES
*Director of Global
Fundamental Data*

Index Department

ROBY MUNTONI
Director of Index Operations

KEVIN B. HECKERT
Manager, Equity Research

WILLIAM H. ROGERS
Manager, Equity Analysis

John Wiley & Sons, Inc.

SUE LEWIS
Publisher

JOAN O'NEIL
Publisher

JO-ANN WASSERMAN
Associate Publisher

DAVID PUGH
Editor

COLLEEN SCOLLANS
Associate Director, Marketing

MICHAEL GREGORY
*Director, Production &
Operations*

JENNIFER CHINWORTH
Production Editor

MERGENT'S DIVIDEND ACHIEVERS (ISSN 1547-8335; electronic ISSN 1548-2839) is published quarterly by Mergent, Inc. and Wiley Subscription Services, Inc., a Wiley Company, 111 River Street, Hoboken, NJ 07030-5774.

SUBSCRIPTION PRICE: Print only: $165.00 in U.S., Canada, and Mexico and $189.00 outside of North America for individuals, and $165.00 in U.S., $205.00 in Canada and Mexico, and $239.00 outside North America for institutions, agencies, and libraries. Prices subject to change. Payment must be made in U.S. dollars drawn on a U.S. bank. Claims for undelivered copies will be accepted only after the following issue has been received. Please enclose a copy of the mailing label. Missing copies will be supplied when losses have been sustained in transit and where reserve stock permits. Please allow four weeks for processing a change of address. Address subscription inquiries to Subscription Manager, Jossey-Bass, a Wiley Company, 989 Market Street, San Francisco, CA 94103-1741; Tel.: (888) 378-2537, (415) 433-1767 (International); E-mail: jbsubs@jbp.com.

POSTMASTER: Send address changes to *Mergent's Dividend Achievers*, Jossey-Bass, 989 Market Street, San Francisco, CA 94103-1741.

ADVERTISING SALES: Inquiries concerning advertising should be forwarded to the Advertising Sales Manager, c/o John Wiley & Sons, Inc., 111 River Street, Hoboken, NJ 07030-5774; (201) 748-8832. Advertising Sales, European Contact: Jackie Sibley, c/o John Wiley & Sons, Ltd., The Atrium, Southern Gate, Chichester, West Sussex, PO19 8SQ, England; Tel.: 44 1243 770 351; Fax: 44 1243 770 432; E-mail: adsales@wiley.co.uk.

www.wiley.com/go/mergent

TABLE OF CONTENTS

U.S. Dividend Achievers

Canadian Dividend Achievers

Notes From The Editor

In May 2004, Mergent, Inc. and PowerShares Capital Management, LLC, an asset management firm entered into a licensing agreement to offer an exchange-traded fund (ETF) based on the Mergent's Dividend Achievers 50™ Index and its independent third-party methodology. The Index contains the 50 highest yielding stocks from Mergent's Dividend Achievers Index. Further details on the product will be announced as they become available.

Also in 2004, Mergent identified 30 Canadian companies that have consistently increased their dividends for the last five or more consecutive years, the Canadian Dividend Achievers. In this edition Mergent is featuring full-page profiles of the Canadian Dividend Achievers. This elite group represents less than 1.0% of all Canadian companies. Canadian Utilities Ltd., a provider of natural gas and electric energy in the Province of Alberta, leads the group with 21 years of dividend increases.

As of April 30, 2004, the average yield for Mergent's Canadian Dividend Achievers was 2.3%. The highest yield of 4.6% belongs to Emera, Inc., an energy and services company with a five-year average annual compound dividend growth rate of 14.3%. BMTC Group, engaged in retail sales of furniture household goods and electronic appliances in Quebec, recorded the highest five-year average annual compound dividend growth rate of 26.2%.

In the U.S., despite improved corporate results, financial markets continue to be adversely affected by geo-political uncertainty and the possibility of an increase in the prime rate and the federal funds rate. The steady increase in the price of oil per barrel is also impacting the market.

Despite unfavorable market conditions, the Dividend Achievers Index is still showing positive results. The 303 companies included in the Index in 2004 are profiled in the Summer 2004 edition, expanded to include performance and statistical information on Mergent's Dividend Achievers Index.

This edition includes companies that have increased dividends for 50 years, such as Procter and Gamble, a manufacturer and marketer of nearly 300 products to more than five billion consumers in 140 countries, Diebold, Inc., a provider of self-service delivery systems such as automatic teller machines and electronic security, and American States Water Company, a supplier of water and electrical service to customers in California and Arizona. Newcomers to the Dividend Achievers include companies such as Harley-Davidson, Inc., Caterpillar Inc, and John Wiley and Sons, Inc.

At April 30, 2004, Mergent's Dividend Achievers Index price appreciation showed a year-to-date return of 1.61% compared to -2.18% for the Dow Jones Industrial Average (DJIA) and -0.42% for the S&P500.

Year-to-date, the Dividend Achievers Index total return was 2.31%, which is particularly striking when considering the tax legislation changes of 2003. With the new tax rate, investors gain up to an additional 30% on dividend income, making dividend-paying securities an attractive alternative to fixed-income securities. Total return for the DJIA fell 1.57%, while the S&P 500 posted a gain of 0.10%.

Mergent's Dividend Achievers Index uses a market-capitalization-weighted scheme. The real-time price appreciation performance is calculated and published by the American Stock Exchange under ticker symbol DAA. The Index is reconstituted annually and changes are effective on the last trading day of January. Visit www.DividendAchievers.com to find more information.

For the trailing ten years ended April 30, 2004, annualized total returns were as follows:

Mergent's Dividend Achievers	14.88%
Dow Jones Industrial Average	13.00%
S&P 500	11.36%

In 2004, Mergent, Inc. achieved another milestone through the successful licensing of its Dividend Achievers selection methodology to BlackRock, Inc., one of the largest investment management firms in the United States with more than $331 billion in assets under management (as of 3/31/04). The new closed-end fund named "BlackRock Strategic Dividend Achievers Trust," which began trading on the New York Stock Exchange (NYSE) under ticker symbol BDT on March 26, 2004, focuses on small to mid capitalized companies.

Mergent's foray into the closed-end market was achieved through the initial public offering of the BlackRock Dividend Achievers Trust on December 19, 2003. The closed-end fund, which raised more than $720 million and trades on the NYSE under ticker symbol BDV, reflects the top yielding constituents of Mergent's Dividend Achievers. Note worthy is the pre-tax yield for BDV, an impressive 6%, which excludes the new tax benefits associated with the reduced taxes on dividend income.

As of March 31, 2004, BlackRock, Inc. had more than $1.2 billion in assets under management on the Dividend Achievers selection methodology. Mergent plans to continue licensing the Dividend Achievers Index for the creation of additional investment products. For more information on the Fund visit www.Blackrock.com.

Kevin B. Heckert
Manager, Equity Research

Mergent Dividend Achievers Timeline

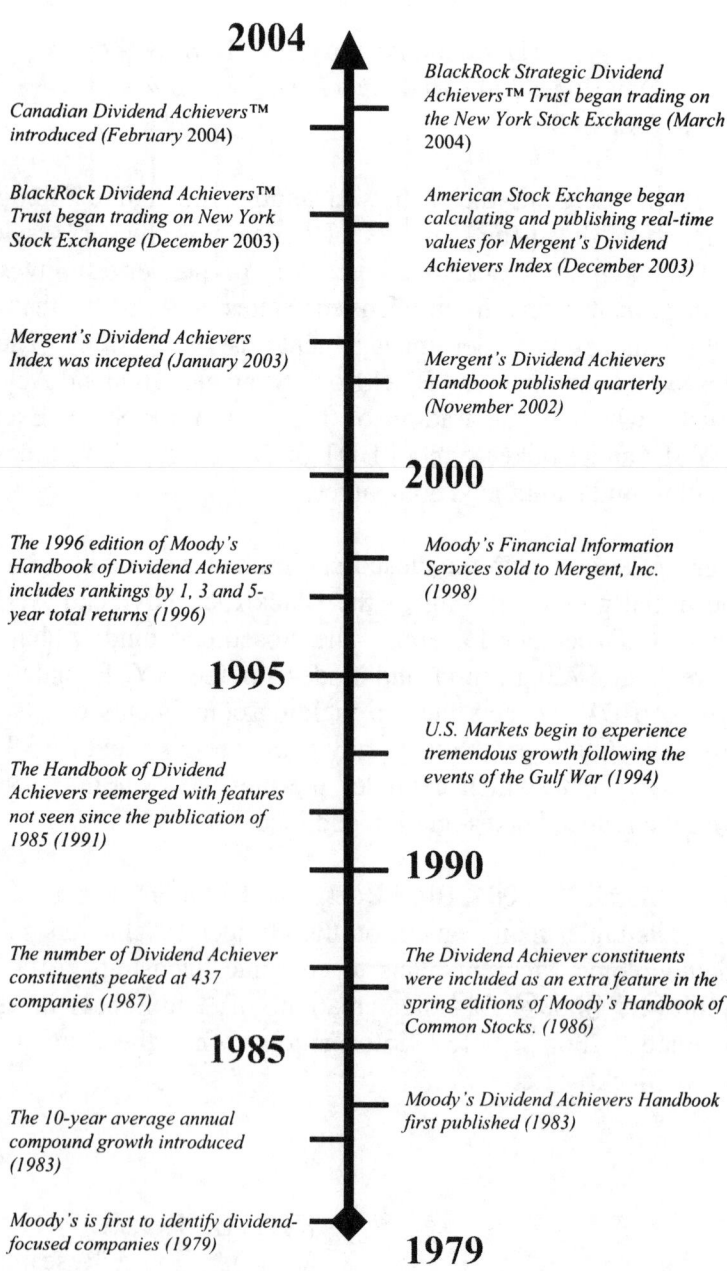

2004

Canadian Dividend Achievers™ introduced (February 2004)

BlackRock Strategic Dividend Achievers™ Trust began trading on the New York Stock Exchange (March 2004)

BlackRock Dividend Achievers™ Trust began trading on New York Stock Exchange (December 2003)

American Stock Exchange began calculating and publishing real-time values for Mergent's Dividend Achievers Index (December 2003)

Mergent's Dividend Achievers Index was incepted (January 2003)

Mergent's Dividend Achievers Handbook published quarterly (November 2002)

2000

The 1996 edition of Moody's Handbook of Dividend Achievers includes rankings by 1, 3 and 5-year total returns (1996)

Moody's Financial Information Services sold to Mergent, Inc. (1998)

1995

U.S. Markets begin to experience tremendous growth following the events of the Gulf War (1994)

The Handbook of Dividend Achievers reemerged with features not seen since the publication of 1985 (1991)

1990

The number of Dividend Achiever constituents peaked at 437 companies (1987)

The Dividend Achiever constituents were included as an extra feature in the spring editions of Moody's Handbook of Common Stocks. (1986)

1985

Moody's Dividend Achievers Handbook first published (1983)

The 10-year average annual compound growth introduced (1983)

Moody's is first to identify dividend-focused companies (1979)

1979

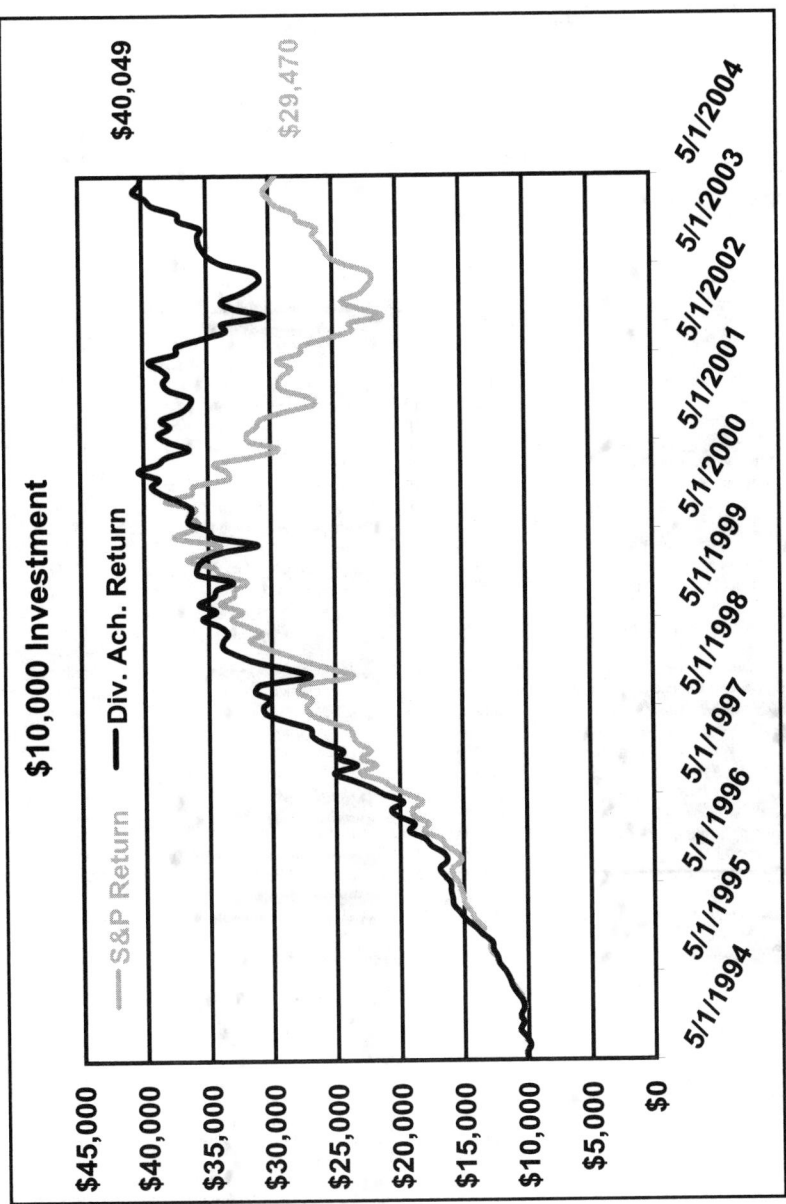

$10,000 Investment

Ranking The 2004 Dividend Achievers

Companies are listed by the 10-year average annual compound growth of their dividends.
Also shown are total numbers of consecutive years of dividend growth

Rank	Name	10-Year Growth Rate	Years	Rank	Name	10-Year Growth Rate	Years
1	People's Bank	43.967	10	52	Arrow International,Inc.	16.983	11
2	Paychex Inc	39.781	15	53	Superior Industries Intl.	16.917	18
3	Cullen/Frost Bankers, Inc.	38.010	10	54	Freddie Mac	16.805	13
4	Courier Corp.	35.649	10	55	Pacific Capital Bancorp	16.752	34
5	Hibernia Corp.	35.588	10	56	Commerce Bancorp, Inc	16.736	12
6	Citigroup Inc	29.698	17	57	Republic Bancorp, Inc.	16.710	11
7	Harley-Davidson, Inc.	29.239	10	58	Wells Fargo & Co.	16.706	16
8	Doral Financial Corp.	28.209	14	59	Hudson United Bancorp	16.644	13
9	Home Depot, Inc.	26.387	16	60	AFLAC Inc.	16.585	21
10	SWS Group, Inc.	26.202	11	61	Tanger Factory Outlet Cntrs.	16.470	10
11	Chittenden Corp.	25.346	11	62	Applebee's International	16.231	12
12	Caterpillar Inc.	25.204	10	63	General Growth Properties	16.231	10
13	BancFirst Corp.	24.711	10	63	Community First Bankshares	16.231	12
14	Camden Property Trust	24.672	10	65	Healthcare Realty Trust, Inc.	16.186	10
15	Linear Technology Corp.	24.240	11	66	Danaher Corp.	16.087	10
16	Anchor BanCorp Wisconsin	24.223	10	67	Popular Inc.	16.032	11
17	Pinnacle West Capital Corp.	24.044	10	68	Tootsie Roll Industries Inc	16.021	40
18	Stryker Corp.	23.114	11	69	Mercury General Corp.	15.970	17
18	SEI Investments Co.	23.114	12	70	State Street Corp.	15.757	23
20	CVB Financial Corp.	23.062	13	71	S & T Bancorp, Inc.	15.698	14
21	Roper Industries, Inc.	22.768	11	72	Pfizer Inc.	15.665	36
22	TCF Financial Corp.	22.426	12	73	Harleysville National Corp.	15.581	17
23	Fidelity National Financial	22.289	16	74	SouthTrust Corp.	15.326	33
24	Pier 1 Imports Inc.	22.076	12	75	First Indiana Corp.	15.224	12
25	Franklin Electric Co., Inc.	22.048	10	76	Sigma-Aldrich Corp.	15.066	22
26	National Commerce Financial	21.654	29	77	First Financial Holdings, Inc.	15.016	11
27	Medtronic, Inc.	21.425	26	78	McGrath RentCorp	14.870	13
28	Charter One Financial, Inc.	20.900	15	79	MBNA Corp.	14.866	12
29	Wolverine World Wide, Inc.	20.850	10	80	Glacier Bancorp, Inc.	14.762	12
30	Eaton Vance Corp	20.641	22	81	Golden West Financial Corp.	14.709	20
31	T Rowe Price Group Inc.	20.540	17	82	Gallagher (Arthur J.) & Co.	14.705	19
32	Washington Mutual Inc.	20.289	14	83	Leggett & Platt, Inc.	14.655	32
33	M & T Bank Corp	20.238	23	84	Brady Corp.	14.636	19
34	Sysco Corp.	20.181	27	85	Automatic Data Processing	14.633	28
35	Synovus Financial Corp.	19.673	27	86	Simmons First National Corp.	14.357	12
36	Meridian Bioscience Inc.	19.528	11	87	BB&T Corp.	14.320	32
37	Cintas Corporation	19.189	21	88	Illinois Tool Works, Inc.	14.270	41
38	Fifth Third Bancorp	18.854	31	89	McDonald's Corp	14.243	27
39	Wal-Mart Stores, Inc.	18.749	22	90	Legg Mason, Inc.	14.176	20
40	Archer Daniels Midland Co.	18.621	29	91	Irwin Financial Corp.	14.080	14
41	WestAmerica Bancorporation	18.488	14	92	Park National Corp.	13.883	16
42	Independent Bank Corp.	18.139	15	93	American International Group	13.872	18
43	AptarGroup Inc.	17.923	10	94	Johnson & Johnson	13.864	41
44	First Federal Capital Corp.	17.724	12	95	Praxair, Inc.	13.854	11
45	Nucor Corp.	17.687	31	96	Fannie Mae	13.830	18
46	Jack Henry & Associates, Inc.	17.669	12	97	Brown & Brown, Inc.	13.784	10
47	Sterling Bancshares, Inc.	17.608	10	98	General Electric Co.	13.726	28
48	SLM Corp.	17.424	23	99	Northern Trust Corp.	13.707	18
49	Corus Bankshares, Inc.	17.417	17	100	Trustmark Corp.	13.683	30
50	F.N.B. Corp (FL)	17.377	19	101	Bank of America Corp.	13.386	26
51	Whitney Holding Corp.	17.247	10	102	Teleflex Incorporated	13.238	26

Rank	Name	10-Year Growth Rate	Years	Rank	Name	10-Year Growth Rate	Years
103	Old Republic International	13.195	22	161	Dover Corp.	9.741	48
104	Artesian Resources Corp.	13.078	11	162	Valley National Bancorp	9.724	12
105	Transatlantic Holdings, Inc.	12.935	13	163	United Technologies Corp.	9.693	10
106	National Penn Bancshares	12.844	25	164	Nordson Corp.	9.687	23
107	Wiley (John) & Sons Inc.	12.835	10	165	Mine Safety Appliances Co	9.643	33
108	Compass Bancshares Inc.	12.780	22	166	Protective Life Corp.	9.574	14
109	Webster Financial Corp.	12.695	11	167	First Merchants Corp.	9.545	19
110	Badger Meter, Inc.	12.614	11	168	Carlisle Companies Inc.	9.533	27
111	Associated Banc-Corp.	12.468	33	169	Sherwin-Williams Co.	9.508	24
112	Heinz (H.J.) Co.	12.445	40	169	First Commonwealth Fin.	9.508	16
113	Alberto-Culver Co.	12.443	19	171	Regions Financial Corp.	9.420	32
114	Avery Dennison Corp.	12.413	28	172	Unizan Financial Corp	9.395	19
115	Franklin Resources, Inc.	12.385	14	173	Anheuser-Busch Cos., Inc.	9.335	29
116	Raven Industries, Inc.	12.335	16	174	Becton, Dickinson and Co.	9.259	31
117	Chemical Financial Corp.	12.126	28	175	Pentair, Inc.	9.203	27
118	Commerce Bancshares, Inc.	12.020	35	176	Meredith Corp.	9.035	10
119	ConAgra Foods, Inc.	12.010	26	177	Community Trust Bancorp	8.970	15
120	SunTrust Banks, Inc.	11.991	18	178	National City Corp	8.959	11
121	First Charter Corp.	11.938	11	179	Sterling Financial Corp.	8.942	16
122	Lancaster Colony Corp.	11.937	34	180	Vulcan Materials Co.	8.842	11
123	First Midwest Bancorp, Inc.	11.874	11	180	Community Bank System	8.842	12
124	Ecolab, Inc.	11.807	11	182	Wrigley (William) Jr. Co.	8.717	23
125	ABM Industries, Inc.	11.760	39	183	Citizens Banking Corp	8.664	20
126	Mercantile Bankshares Corp.	11.699	27	184	Federal Signal Corp.	8.657	16
127	First Financial Corp.	11.649	11	185	Hillenbrand Industries	8.527	33
128	Myers Industries Inc.	11.615	27	185	FirstMerit Corp	8.527	21
129	Altria Group Inc	11.612	38	187	TEPPCO Partners, L.P.	8.458	11
130	Nuveen Investments Inc	11.612	11	188	Sara Lee Corp.	8.447	27
131	Family Dollar Stores, Inc.	11.612	27	188	Alfa Corp	8.447	18
132	Procter & Gamble Co.	11.452	50	190	Washington Federal Inc.	8.427	20
133	Abbott Laboratories	11.385	31	191	RLI Corp.	8.402	27
134	Holly Corp.	11.362	10	192	Bemis, Inc.	8.399	20
135	Cincinnati Financial Corp.	11.327	43	193	Harleysville Group, Inc.	8.367	17
136	Jefferson-Pilot Corp.	11.192	36	194	Beckman Coulter, Inc.	8.313	12
137	Comerica, Inc.	11.010	20	195	Lilly (Eli) & Co.	8.277	36
138	1st Source Corp.	10.921	16	196	Clorox Co.	8.276	27
139	Merck & Co., Inc	10.906	20	197	Old National Bancorp	8.256	20
140	General Dynamics Corp.	10.845	12	198	Wilmington Trust Corp.	8.128	22
140	Ambac Financial Group, Inc.	10.845	12	199	KeyCorp (New)	8.098	24
142	United Mobile Homes, Inc.	10.784	13	200	United Bankshares, Inc.	8.075	22
143	Valspar Corp.	10.554	25	201	Weyco Group, Inc	8.061	23
144	BancorpSouth Inc.	10.548	17	202	Emerson Electric Co.	7.936	47
145	Rouse Co.	10.482	11	203	PepsiCo Inc.	7.895	32
146	Colgate-Palmolive Co.	10.387	41	204	Banta Corporation	7.811	25
147	AmSouth Bancorporation	10.347	33	205	Johnson Controls Inc	7.792	28
148	Pitney Bowes, Inc.	10.305	20	206	Midland Co.	7.745	17
149	State Auto Financial Corp.	10.224	12	207	Susquehanna Bancshares, Inc	7.695	33
150	Fulton Financial Corp.	10.135	16	208	McCormick & Co., Inc.	7.655	17
151	Lowe's Cos., Inc.	10.132	42	209	Grainger (W.W.) Inc.	7.625	32
152	Marsh & McLennan Cos., Inc.	10.120	42	210	Walgreen Co.	7.602	28
153	Pennichuck Corp.	10.104	10	211	Farmer Bros. Co.	7.329	15
154	Second Bancorp, Inc.	10.095	16	212	Air Products & Chemicals, Inc.	7.056	21
155	HNI Corporation	10.027	15	213	Avon Products, Inc.	7.051	13
156	MBIA Inc.	10.007	16	214	West Pharmaceutical Svcs.	7.046	11
157	Coca-Cola Co (The)	9.977	41	215	Bandag, Inc.	7.011	27
158	Kimco Realty Corp.	9.963	11	216	Target Corp	6.906	32
159	Marshall & Ilsley Corp.	9.927	31	217	La-Z-Boy Inc.	6.826	22
160	Hershey Foods Corp.	9.749	29	218	NACCO Industries Inc.	6.761	20

Rank	Name	10-Year Growth Rate	Years	Rank	Name	10-Year Growth Rate	Years
219	Bank of Hawaii Corp	6.755	26	262	Kimberly-Clark Corp.	4.500	29
220	Diebold, Inc.	6.699	50	263	Stanley Works	4.394	36
221	Hormel Foods Corp.	6.680	36	264	NICOR Inc.	4.365	16
222	National Security Group, Inc	6.651	13	265	Gannett Co., Inc.	4.165	32
223	Rohm & Haas Co.	6.612	26	266	Briggs & Stratton Corp.	4.138	12
224	McGraw-Hill Cos., Inc.	6.599	30	267	Progressive Corp.	4.138	34
225	Wesbanco, Inc.	6.544	18	268	Vectren Corp	3.964	28
226	Stepan Co.	6.532	37	269	MDU Resources Group Inc.	3.875	13
227	Frisch's Restaurants, Inc.	6.358	20	270	Questar Corp.	3.650	24
228	Cedar Fair, L.P.	6.309	16	271	SJW Corp.	3.616	37
229	EastGroup Properties, Inc.	6.280	11	272	Wesco Financial Corp.	3.609	32
230	Sonoco Products Co.	6.233	20	273	Gorman-Rupp Co.	3.544	31
231	SBC Communications, Inc.	6.208	19	274	Black Hills Corporation	3.468	32
232	Telephone and Data Systems	6.192	29	275	Atmos Energy Corp.	3.431	16
233	Health Care Property Investors	6.051	18	276	Quaker Chemical Corp.	3.422	32
234	Masco Corp.	5.963	45	277	National Fuel Gas Co. (NJ)	3.383	32
235	Aqua America Inc	5.901	12	278	Florida Public Utilities Co.	3.373	35
236	Haverty Furniture Cos., Inc.	5.897	33	279	Supervalu Inc.	3.315	31
237	Lincoln National Corp.	5.835	20	280	Energen Corp.	3.253	21
238	ALLTEL Corp.	5.756	43	281	Progress Energy, Inc.	3.167	15
239	Parker-Hannifin Corp.	5.661	47	282	Exxon Mobil Corp.	3.131	21
240	Piedmont Natural Gas Co., Inc.	5.478	24	283	Helmerich & Payne, Inc.	2.919	27
241	Chubb Corp.	5.402	39	284	Tennant Co.	2.757	31
242	RPM International Inc	5.388	30	285	Smith (A.O.) Corp	2.647	11
243	Genuine Parts Co.	5.366	47	286	Otter Tail Corp.	2.545	28
244	St. Paul Travelers Companies	5.256	17	287	UGI Corp. (New)	2.532	16
245	Bard (C.R.), Inc.	5.241	32	288	Middlesex Water Co.	2.511	31
246	PPG Industries, Inc.	5.221	32	289	Cleco Corp. (New)	2.472	22
247	Fuller (H.B.) Company	5.182	36	290	Federal Realty Investment Tr.	2.329	36
248	VF Corp.	5.172	31	291	WPS Resources Corp.	2.069	45
249	Brown-Forman Corp.	5.163	19	292	Clarcor Inc.	1.933	23
250	Washington REIT	5.146	33	293	Peoples Energy Corp.	1.744	20
251	Quixote Corp.	5.135	10	294	Universal Health Realty Inc. Tr.	1.675	16
252	United Dominion Realty Trust	5.080	18	295	WGL Holdings, Inc.	1.647	27
253	Universal Corp.	5.048	33	296	California Water Service Group	1.599	36
254	ChevronTexaco Corp.	5.035	16	297	Commercial Net Lease Realty	1.527	14
255	Hilb, Rogal and Hamilton Co.	5.029	17	298	EnergySouth, Inc.	1.462	26
256	Weingarten Realty Investors	4.975	15	299	Consolidated Edison, Inc.	1.448	29
257	May Department Stores Co.	4.841	28	300	Connecticut Water Service	1.246	28
258	CenturyTel, Inc.	4.791	30	301	American States Water Co.	1.109	50
259	ServiceMaster Co. (The)	4.764	33	302	MGE Energy Inc	0.950	28
260	3M Co	4.749	45	303	Donnelley (R.R.) & Sons Co.	0.820	34
261	Bowl America Inc.	4.739	31				

Longest Records Of Dividend Achievement

These Dividend Achievers boast the longest records of consecutive annual dividend increases.

Rank	Years	Name	Ticker	Rank	Years	Name	Ticker
1	50	American States Water Co.	AWR	40	33	AmSouth Bancorporation	ASO
	50	Diebold, Inc.	DBD		33	Associated Banc-Corp.	ASBC
	50	Procter & Gamble Co.	PG		33	Haverty Furniture Cos., Inc.	HVT
4	48	Dover Corp.	DOV		33	Hillenbrand Industries, Inc.	HB
5	47	Emerson Electric Co.	EMR		33	Mine Safety Appliances Co	MSA
	47	Genuine Parts Co.	GPC		33	ServiceMaster Co. (The)	SVM
	47	Parker-Hannifin Corp.	PH		33	SouthTrust Corp.	SOTR
8	45	3M Co	MMM		33	Susquehanna Bancshares, Inc	SUSQ
	45	Masco Corp.	MAS		33	Universal Corp.	UVV
	45	WPS Resources Corp.	WPS		33	Washington R.E.I.T	WRE
11	43	ALLTEL Corp.	AT	50	32	Bard (C.R.), Inc.	BCR
	43	Cincinnati Financial Corp.	CINF		32	BB&T Corp. (Lumberton, NC)	BBT
13	42	Lowe's Cos., Inc.	LOW		32	Black Hills Corporation	BKH
	42	Marsh & McLennan Cos., Inc.	MMC		32	Gannett Co., Inc.	GCI
15	41	Coca-Cola Co (The)	KO		32	Grainger (W.W.) Inc.	GWW
	41	Colgate-Palmolive Co.	CL		32	Leggett & Platt, Inc.	LEG
	41	Illinois Tool Works, Inc.	ITW		32	National Fuel Gas Co.	NFG
	41	Johnson & Johnson	JNJ		32	PepsiCo Inc.	PEP
19	40	Heinz (H.J.) Co.	HNZ		32	PPG Industries, Inc.	PPG
	40	Tootsie Roll Industries Inc	TR		32	Quaker Chemical Corp.	KWR
21	39	ABM Industries, Inc.	ABM		32	Regions Financial Corp.	RF
	39	Chubb Corp.	CB		32	Target Corp	TGT
23	38	Altria Group Inc	MO		32	Wesco Financial Corp.	WSC
24	37	SJW Corp.	SJW	63	31	Abbott Laboratories	ABT
	37	Stepan Co.	SCL		31	Becton, Dickinson and Co.	BDX
26	36	California Water Service Group	CWT		31	Bowl America Inc.	BWLA
	36	Federal Realty Investment Trust	FRT		31	Fifth Third Bancorp	FITB
	36	Fuller (H.B.) Company	FUL		31	Gorman-Rupp Co.	GRC
	36	Hormel Foods Corp.	HRL		31	Marshall & Ilsley Corp.	MI
	36	Jefferson-Pilot Corp.	JP		31	Middlesex Water Co.	MSEX
	36	Lilly (Eli) & Co.	LLY		31	Nucor Corp.	NUE
	36	Pfizer Inc.	PFE		31	Supervalu Inc.	SVU
	36	Stanley Works	SWK		31	Tennant Co.	TNC
34	35	Commerce Bancshares, Inc.	CBSH		31	VF Corp.	VFC
	35	Florida Public Utilities Co.	FPU	74	30	CenturyTel, Inc.	CTL
36	34	Donnelley (R.R.) & Sons Co.	RRD		30	Fulton Financial Corp.	FULT
	34	Lancaster Colony Corp.	LANC		30	McGraw-Hill Cos., Inc. (The)	MHP
	34	Pacific Capital Bancorp	PCBC		30	RPM International Inc	RPM
	34	Progressive Corp.	PGR		30	Trustmark Corp.	TRMK

Dividend Achievers Arrivals

The following companies, which recorded at least ten consecutive years of dividend increases in 2003, mark their debut as Dividend Achievers.

Anchor Bancorp Wisconsin, Inc.
AptarGroup Inc.
Artesian Resources Corp.
BancFirst Corp.
Brown & Brown, Inc.
Camden Property Trust
Caterpillar Inc.
Courier Corp.
Cullen/Frost Bankers, Inc.
Danaher Corp.
Farmer Bros. Co.
First Merchants Corp.
Franklin Electric Co., Inc.
General Growth Properties, Inc.
Harley-Davidson, Inc.
Healthcare Realty Trust, Inc.
Helmerich & Payne, Inc.
Hibernia Corp.

Holly Corp.
Independent Bank Corporation
Meredith Corp.
Meridian Bioscience Inc.
Parker-Hannifin Corp.
Pennichuck Corp.
People's Bank
Pinnacle West Capital Corp.
Quixote Corp.
Second Bancorp, Inc.
Simmons First National Corp.
Sterling Bancshares, Inc.
SWS Group, Inc.
Tanger Factory Outlet Centers, Inc.
United Technologies Corp.
Whitney Holding Corp.
Wiley (John) & Sons Inc.
Wolverine World Wide, Inc.

Dividend Achievers Departures

The following former Dividend Achievers have not increased their regular cash dividends in 2003.

American National Insurance Co.
Bank of New York Co., Inc.
Bristol-Myers Squibb Co.
Donegal Group Inc.
El Paso Corp.
Energy West Inc.
First Financial Bancorp
FleetBoston Financial Corp.

GATX Corp.
J.P. Morgan Chase & Co.
Northwestern Corp.
TECO Energy Inc.
Trustco Bank Corp. (N.Y.)
Unitrin, Inc.
Virco Mfg. Corp.

The following former Dividend Achievers have been acquired in 2003.

First Virginia Banks, Inc.

Household International, Inc.

The following former Canadian Dividend Achievers have been acquired in 2003.

Cara Operations Ltd.

Dividend Achievers Name Changes

The following Dividend Achiever companies have changed their name.

Old Name	New Name
HON Industries, Inc.	HNI Corporation
Investors Group Inc.	IGM Financial Inc.
Nuveen (John) Company (The)	Nuveen Investments, Inc.
Philadelphia Suburban Corporation	Aqua America, Inc.
Philip Morris Companies, Inc.	Altria Group, Inc.
St. Paul Companies, Inc.	St Paul Travelers Companies Inc.

Top 20 by Return on Equity

Based on latest available year-end information. Ratios determined using net income.

Rank	Company	R.O.E.	Rank	Company	R.O.E.
1	Avon Products, Inc.	179.05%	11	Altria Group Inc	36.70%
2	Colgate-Palmolive Co.	160.22%	12	Hershey Foods Corp.	35.75%
3	Anheuser-Busch Cos., Inc.	76.55%	13	Sysco Corp.	35.42%
4	Sara Lee Corp.	65.29%	14	Fannie Mae	35.33%
5	SLM Corp.	58.31%	15	Procter & Gamble Co.	32.04%
6	Heinz (H.J.) Co.	47.22%	16	Nuveen Investments Inc	31.04%
7	Pitney Bowes, Inc.	45.81%	17	Coca-Cola Co (The)	30.85%
8	Merck & Co., Inc	43.85%	18	3M Co	30.48%
9	Clorox Co.	40.58%	19	PepsiCo Inc.	29.99%
10	SEI Investments Co.	39.31%	20	Florida Public Utilities Co.	29.96%

Top 20 by Return on Assets

Based on latest available year-end information. Ratios determined using net income.

Rank	Company	R.O.A	Rank	Company	R.O.A
1	SEI Investments Co.	24.13%	11	Nuveen Investments Inc	15.09%
2	Colgate-Palmolive Co.	19.00%	12	Johnson & Johnson	14.91%
3	Avon Products, Inc.	18.66%	13	T Rowe Price Group Inc.	14.71%
4	Wrigley (William) Jr. Co.	17.69%	14	Applebee's International, Inc.	14.53%
5	Raven Industries, Inc.	17.40%	15	Stryker Corp.	14.36%
6	Lancaster Colony Corp.	16.86%	16	Anheuser-Busch Cos., Inc.	14.13%
7	Merck & Co., Inc	16.83%	17	PepsiCo Inc.	14.09%
8	Eaton Vance Corp	16.11%	18	3M Co	13.65%
9	Coca-Cola Co (The)	15.90%	19	Clorox Co.	13.50%
10	Harley-Davidson, Inc.	15.46%	20	Pier 1 Imports Inc.	13.37%

Top 20 by Current Yield

Based on closing prices at April 30, 2004

Rank	Company	Yield	Rank	Company	Yield
1	Commercial Net Lease Realty, Inc.	7.72%	11	Cedar Fair, L.P.	5.78%
2	Universal Health Realty Income Trust	7.56%	12	Weingarten Realty Investors	5.74%
3	Healthcare Realty Trust, Inc.	7.09%	13	Consolidated Edison, Inc.	5.48%
4	TEPPCO Partners, L.P.	7.05%	14	Washington Real Estate Investment T	5.48%
5	Health Care Property Investors, Inc.	6.99%	15	NICOR Inc.	5.47%
6	EastGroup Properties, Inc.	6.63%	16	Progress Energy, Inc.	5.38%
7	Tanger Factory Outlet Centers, Inc	6.54%	17	Kimco Realty Corp.	5.33%
8	United Mobile Homes, Inc.	6.52%	18	Federal Realty Investment Trust (MD	5.29%
9	United Dominion Realty Trust, Inc.	6.52%	19	Peoples Energy Corp.	5.17%
10	Camden Property Trust	6.00%	20	SBC Communications, Inc.	5.02%

Highest Price/Earnings Ratios

Based on latest available year-end information. Ratios determined using net income.
Based on closing prices at April 30, 2004

Rank	Company	P/E Ratio	Rank	Company	P/E Ratio
1	Meredith Corp.	509.40	11	Stepan Co.	53.44
2	Farmer Bros. Co.	280.34	12	Pennichuck Corp.	51.63
3	First Indiana Corp.	114.06	13	RPM International Inc	50.27
4	SWS Group, Inc.	95.53	14	Linear Technology Corp.	48.15
5	United Dominion Realty Trust	85.48	15	Paychex Inc	47.79
6	Helmerich & Payne, Inc.	77.11	16	Stryker Corp.	44.36
7	Nucor Corp.	74.25	17	First Charter Corp.	43.94
8	Pfizer Inc.	66.22	18	EastGroup Properties, Inc.	41.36
9	Telephone and Data Systems	62.82	19	People's Bank	40.98
10	Camden Property Trust	59.61	20	Medtronic, Inc.	38.82

Lowest Price/Earnings Ratios

Based on latest available year-end information. Ratios determined using net income.
Based on closing prices at April 30, 2004

Rank	Company	P/E Ratio	Rank	Company	P/E Ratio
1	Freddie Mac	4.12	11	MBIA Inc.	10.50
2	Florida Public Utilities Co.	6.39	12	National Fuel Gas Co.	11.13
3	Fidelity National Financial, Inc.	6.50	13	Weyco Group, Inc	11.15
4	Fannie Mae	8.69	14	Bank of America Corp.	11.29
5	Old Republic International Corp.	9.25	15	Sterling Bancshares, Inc.	11.55
6	Washington Mutual Inc.	9.36	16	Universal Corp.	11.58
7	Irwin Financial Corp.	9.65	17	SLM Corp.	11.64
8	SBC Communications, Inc.	9.73	18	Holly Corp.	11.66
9	National City Corp	10.11	19	Protective Life Corp.	11.71
10	ABM Industries, Inc.	10.20	20	ALLTEL Corp.	11.84

Highest Seven-Year Price Scores

Scores cover a seven-year period ending April 30, 2004

Rank	Company	Price Score	Rank	Company	Price Score
1	Raven Industries, Inc.	244.2	11	Lowe's Cos., Inc.	168.2
2	Doral Financial Corp.	238.6	12	Progressive Corp.	167.9
3	Courier Corp.	208.3	13	Frisch's Restaurants, Inc.	165.2
4	Applebee's International, Inc.	192.5	14	Clarcor Inc.	163.6
5	Independent Bank Corporation	187.2	15	Weyco Group, Inc	163.1
6	Golden West Financial Corp.	180.2	16	Harleysville National Corp.	163.1
7	General Growth Properties, Inc.	179.0	17	UGI Corp.	161.9
8	Fidelity National Financial, Inc.	178.8	18	Glacier Bancorp, Inc.	161.6
9	Legg Mason, Inc.	172.7	19	Commerce Bancorp, Inc.	161.6
10	SLM Corp.	172.3	20	CVB Financial Corp.	159.7

Highest Twelve-Month Price Scores

Scores cover a twelve-month period ending April 30, 2004

Rank	Company	Price Score	Rank	Company	Price Score
1	People's Bank	121.08	11	Nordson Corp.	110.98
2	Mine Safety Appliances	120.95	12	Florida Public Utilities Co.	110.68
3	National Security Group	118.81	13	Raven Industries, Inc.	110.42
4	Corus Bankshares, Inc.	117.80	14	Bandag, Inc.	110.29
5	Pentair, Inc.	116.73	15	Becton, Dickinson	110.28
6	Commerce Bancorp, Inc.	116.22	16	Legg Mason, Inc.	109.81
7	Stanley Works	115.00	17	Unizan Financial Corp	109.29
8	General Growth Prop.	114.54	18	May Department Stores	109.12
9	Bard (C.R.), Inc.	114.32	19	T Rowe Price Group Inc.	109.02
10	Fidelity National Fin.	111.71	20	SJW Corp.	108.52

Top 20 By Revenues

Based on latest available year-end information

Rank	Name	Revenues	Rank	Name	Revenues
1	Wal-Mart Stores, Inc.	$258,681,000,000	11	Bank of America Corp.	$48,065,000,000
2	Exxon Mobil Corp.	$242,365,000,000	12	Pfizer Inc.	$45,188,000,000
3	General Electric Co.	$132,797,000,000	13	Procter & Gamble Co.	$43,377,000,000
4	ChevronTexaco Corp.	$120,732,000,000	14	Johnson & Johnson	$41,862,000,000
5	Citigroup Inc	$94,713,000,000	15	SBC Communications	$40,843,000,000
6	American International	$82,736,000,000	16	Walgreen Co.	$32,505,400,000
7	Altria Group Inc	$81,832,000,000	17	Wells Fargo & Co.	$31,800,000,000
8	Home Depot, Inc.	$64,816,000,000	18	United Technologies	$31,034,000,000
9	Fannie Mae	$53,768,000,000	19	Lowe's Cos., Inc.	$30,838,000,000
10	Target Corp	$48,163,000,000	20	Archer Daniels Midland	$30,708,033,000

Top 20 By Net Income

Based on latest available year-end information

Rank	Name	Net Income	Rank	Name	Net Income
1	Exxon Mobil Corp.	$21,510,000,000	11	Johnson & Johnson	$7,197,000,000
2	Citigroup Inc	$17,853,000,000	12	Merck & Co., Inc	$6,830,900,000
3	General Electric Co.	$15,002,000,000	13	Wells Fargo & Co.	$6,202,000,000
4	Bank of America Corp.	$10,810,000,000	14	Procter & Gamble Co.	$5,186,000,000
5	American International	$9,274,000,000	15	Coca-Cola Co.	$4,347,000,000
6	Altria Group Inc	$9,204,000,000	16	Home Depot, Inc.	$4,304,000,000
7	Wal-Mart Stores, Inc.	$9,054,000,000	17	Pfizer Inc.	$3,910,000,000
8	SBC Communications	$8,505,000,000	18	Washington Mutual	$3,880,000,000
9	Fannie Mae	$7,905,000,000	19	PepsiCo Inc.	$3,568,000,000
10	ChevronTexaco Corp.	$7,230,000,000	20	Abbott Laboratories	$2,753,233,000

Top 20 by Market Capitalization

Based on closing prices at April 30, 2004

Rank	Name	Current Value	Rank	Name	Current Value
1	General Electric Co.	$300,723,746,458	11	Altria Group Inc	$112,486,303,588
2	Exxon Mobil Corp.	$281,246,998,170	12	Merck & Co., Inc	$104,574,864,640
3	Pfizer Inc.	$272,903,255,900	13	ChevronTexaco Corp.	$97,809,746,304
4	Citigroup Inc	$248,080,776,545	14	Wells Fargo & Co.	$95,531,960,502
5	Wal-Mart Stores, Inc.	$246,683,509,248	15	PepsiCo Inc.	$93,545,544,466
6	American International	$186,859,329,754	16	Lilly (Eli) & Co.	$82,881,548,964
7	Bank of America Corp.	$164,448,475,080	17	SBC Communications	$82,435,684,992
8	Johnson & Johnson	$160,368,771,909	18	Home Depot, Inc.	$80,064,846,536
9	Procter & Gamble Co.	$137,128,884,480	19	Abbott Laboratories	$68,818,797,299
10	Coca-Cola Co (The)	$123,972,965,076	20	3M Co	$67,876,682,532

Bottom 20 by Market Capitalization

Based on closing prices at April 30, 2004

Rank	Name	Current Value	Rank	Name	Current Value
1	National Security Group	$56,247,600	11	EnergySouth, Inc.	$186,016,740
2	Pennichuck Corp.	$64,520,550	12	Weyco Group, Inc	$191,552,350
3	Bowl America Inc.	$72,652,390	13	Connecticut Water Svc.	$218,299,750
4	Florida Public Utilities Co.	$79,218,000	14	Stepan Co.	$218,470,200
5	Artesian Resources	$108,515,535	15	Gorman-Rupp Co.	$224,707,200
6	United Mobile Homes, Inc.	$113,990,100	16	Quaker Chemical Corp.	$241,915,020
7	Badger Meter, Inc.	$137,862,900	17	SWS Group, Inc.	$277,947,600
8	Frisch's Restaurants, Inc.	$141,904,000	18	First Indiana Corp.	$287,510,500
9	Meridian Bioscience Inc.	$166,870,000	19	Second Bancorp, Inc.	$288,576,160
10	Quixote Corp.	$169,420,200	20	Raven Industries, Inc.	$300,072,500

Top 20 by Total Assets

Based on latest available year-end information

Rank	Name	Total Assets	Rank	Name	Total Assets
1	Citigroup Inc	$1,264,032,000,000	11	National City Corp	$113,933,460,000
2	Fannie Mae	$1,009,569,000,000	12	Lincoln National Corp.	$106,744,868,000
3	Bank of America Corp.	$736,445,000,000	13	Wal-Mart Stores, Inc.	$104,912,000,000
4	American International	$678,346,000,000	14	SBC Communications	$100,166,000,000
5	General Electric Co.	$647,483,000,000	15	Altria Group Inc	$96,175,000,000
6	Wells Fargo & Co.	$387,798,000,000	16	Fifth Third Bancorp	$91,143,000,000
7	Washington Mutual Inc.	$275,178,000,000	17	BB&T Corp.	$90,466,613,000
8	Exxon Mobil Corp.	$174,278,000,000	18	State Street Corp.	$87,534,000,000
9	SunTrust Banks, Inc.	$125,393,153,000	19	KeyCorp	$84,487,000,000
10	Pfizer Inc.	$116,775,000,000	20	Golden West Financial	$82,549,890,000

About Total Return

Total return represents one of the best measures of how well an investor of a given stock has fared as it reflects both dividend income and price appreciation. Mergent calculates total return for each Dividend Achievers company on the basis that cash dividends were reinvested on the ex-dividend date of each dividend payment. The following table demonstrates the effect of compounding as well as each stock's performance and the level of dividends paid. Total returns have been adjusted for splits, stock dividends and spin-offs. In the case of a spin-off, shares in the spun-off company were assumed to be converted to cash and reinvested in the original company's stock.

How to read the rankings: On the following pages, the Dividend Achievers companies are listed alphabetically with their respective total returns and rankings over trailing one, three and five year periods ending April 30, 2004. For example, an investor who purchased shares of 1st Source Corp. on April 30, 2003, and sold them on April 30, 2004, would have realized a total return of 96.377% on their original investment. Following each company's one-year total return are its three-year and five-year annualized total returns and their respective rankings for each period. The three-year annualized total return is based on an investment made on April 30, 2001, and the five-year annualized total return represents an investment made on April 30, 1999. Thus an investment made in 1st Source at April 30, 2001, would have generated an annualized total return of 11.694% during the three year period ended April 30, 2004. If an investor had bought shares in 1st Source on April 30, 1999, and sold them on April 30, 2004, their annualized total return would have been –0.339%.

Ranking The Dividend Achievers By Total Returns

Based on the 1, 3 & 5 year periods ending April 30, 2004.

Name	1-Year Tot. Ret.	1 Year Rank	3-Year Ann. Ret.	3-Year Rank	5-Year Ann. Ret.	5-Year Rank
1st Source Corp.	96.377%	3	11.694%	150	-0.339%	282
3M Co	38.972%	57	14.886%	112	15.784%	50
Abbott Laboratories	10.805%	241	0.322%	264	-0.029%	275
ABM Industries, Inc.	36.101%	68	8.166%	191	5.846%	191
AFLAC Inc.	30.113%	95	10.585%	163	9.817%	129
Air Products & Chemicals, Inc.	16.087%	204	6.800%	213	2.758%	242
Alberto-Culver Co.	-3.653%	297	5.756%	224	14.376%	69
Alfa Corp	7.591%	259	13.608%	124	12.159%	98
ALLTEL Corp.	10.499%	243	-0.067%	267	-3.291%	294
Altria Group Inc	88.752%	5	7.832%	196	13.388%	81
Ambac Financial Group, Inc.	18.989%	179	9.252%	179	11.948%	102
American International Group Inc	24.055%	142	-4.059%	284	3.049%	234
American States Water Co.	-7.005%	299	5.529%	225	10.141%	117
AmSouth Bancorporation	6.791%	268	12.961%	132	-3.687%	295
Anchor BanCorp Wisconsin, Inc	6.690%	269	18.044%	78	7.183%	170
Anheuser-Busch Cos., Inc.	4.451%	274	10.233%	168	8.431%	149
Applebee's International, Inc.	41.737%	44	27.901%	19	27.771%	9
AptarGroup Inc.	14.991%	214	8.251%	189	7.661%	162
Aqua America Inc	15.563%	209	13.722%	120	14.870%	62
Archer Daniels Midland Co.	51.017%	25	17.157%	84	7.493%	168
Arrow International,Inc.	41.632%	45	16.970%	89	22.251%	21
Artesian Resources Corp.	29.842%	96	23.172%	37	13.088%	83
Associated Banc-Corp.	20.120%	164	11.818%	148	9.084%	141
Atmos Energy Corp.	13.477%	221	7.560%	201	3.837%	221
Automatic Data Processing Inc.	31.817%	89	-5.878%	288	0.639%	269
Avery Dennison Corp.	23.710%	146	6.417%	220	0.648%	268
Avon Products, Inc.	45.969%	36	26.903%	24	10.124%	120
Badger Meter, Inc.	50.282%	27	15.872%	100	7.007%	175
BancFirst Corp. (Oklahoma City, Ok)	12.422%	230	13.386%	125	10.642%	109
BancorpSouth Inc.	4.030%	278	14.342%	115	6.839%	179
Bandag, Inc.	28.666%	102	16.469%	93	9.291%	136
Bank of America Corp.	12.121%	233	16.405%	94	5.233%	203
Bank of Hawaii Corp (DE)	35.619%	70	27.254%	23	16.938%	41
Banta Corporation	43.365%	40	21.167%	50	17.442%	39
Bard (C.R.), Inc.	69.123%	11	35.169%	6	17.672%	37
BB&T Corp. (Lumberton, NC)	9.724%	247	2.344%	252	-0.126%	276
Beckman Coulter, Inc.	44.739%	37	17.012%	87	19.051%	31
Becton, Dickinson and Co.	44.209%	39	17.013%	86	7.163%	172
Bemis, Inc.	20.850%	161	15.033%	111	10.445%	114
Black Hills Corporation	11.657%	236	-12.767%	299	9.875%	127
Bowl America Inc.	28.221%	106	18.199%	76	20.882%	27
Brady Corp.	18.442%	187	7.923%	194	10.487%	111
Briggs & Stratton Corp.	57.975%	18	22.165%	42	2.951%	236
Brown & Brown, Inc.	9.785%	245	23.202%	36	37.332%	3
Brown-Forman Corp.	24.536%	137	17.300%	83	6.431%	185
California Water Service Group (DE)	7.386%	261	6.985%	206	8.066%	157
Camden Property Trust	28.355%	103	14.406%	113	14.993%	57
Carlisle Companies Inc.	32.562%	84	18.708%	64	5.251%	201
Caterpillar Inc.	50.551%	26	17.766%	81	5.627%	194
Cedar Fair, L.P.	26.597%	120	19.356%	59	10.310%	115
CenturyTel, Inc.	-1.188%	291	2.788%	247	-5.778%	299
Charter One Financial, Inc.	16.576%	201	10.639%	162	7.651%	164
Chemical Financial Corp.	19.236%	175	18.676%	65	6.269%	186

Name	1-Year Tot. Ret.	1 Year Rank	3-Year Ann. Ret.	3-Year Rank	5-Year Ann. Ret.	5-Year Rank
ChevronTexaco Corp.	50.279%	28	1.137%	260	1.033%	263
Chittenden Corp. (Burlington, Vt.)	13.600%	219	11.203%	157	8.435%	148
Chubb Corp.	33.239%	82	3.146%	245	5.069%	208
Cincinnati Financial Corp.	19.573%	171	6.095%	222	3.224%	230
Cintas Corporation	26.220%	126	1.470%	258	0.152%	273
Citigroup Inc	26.854%	117	1.338%	259	6.799%	180
Citizens Banking Corp	36.940%	65	9.460%	175	2.052%	252
Clarcor Inc.	19.006%	178	22.570%	39	19.873%	29
Cleco Corp. (New)	27.200%	115	-2.503%	276	7.658%	163
Clorox Co.	16.895%	199	19.692%	57	-0.515%	284
Coca-Cola Co (The)	27.426%	111	4.717%	234	-4.548%	296
Colgate-Palmolive Co.	2.921%	281	2.611%	250	3.760%	223
Comerica, Inc.	23.305%	147	3.723%	244	-1.611%	289
Commerce Bancorp, Inc. (NJ)	41.923%	43	19.535%	58	23.306%	18
Commerce Bancshares, Inc.	26.824%	118	16.979%	88	8.339%	150
Commercial Net Lease Realty, Inc.	10.582%	242	18.229%	74	12.774%	89
Community Bank System, Inc.	21.004%	158	18.325%	72	12.781%	88
Community First Bankshares, Inc.	23.140%	148	17.968%	79	11.874%	103
Community Trust Bancorp, Inc.	22.803%	150	28.354%	17	14.884%	61
Compass Bancshares Inc.	17.589%	195	21.479%	48	9.649%	132
ConAgra Foods, Inc.	42.476%	42	15.483%	103	6.124%	188
Connecticut Water Service, Inc.	11.120%	239	10.256%	167	16.231%	47
Consolidated Edison, Inc.	11.809%	235	8.577%	185	2.820%	239
Corus Bankshares, Inc.	76.811%	8	15.461%	104	20.896%	26
Courier Corp.	25.053%	133	35.064%	7	35.927%	5
Cullen/Frost Bankers, Inc.	34.980%	73	12.859%	133	11.976%	100
CVB Financial Corp.	13.713%	218	33.565%	8	18.011%	35
Danaher Corp.	34.271%	78	18.264%	73	6.941%	176
Diebold, Inc.	17.034%	198	13.851%	119	14.902%	60
Donnelley (R.R.) & Sons Co.	51.042%	24	5.175%	231	-0.694%	286
Doral Financial Corp.	24.280%	139	32.841%	10	34.198%	6
Dover Corp.	41.336%	47	1.640%	257	2.907%	237
EastGroup Properties, Inc.	18.784%	183	17.051%	85	15.146%	55
Eaton Vance Corp	24.128%	141	5.176%	230	27.197%	10
Ecolab, Inc.	16.031%	205	17.456%	82	8.222%	151
Emerson Electric Co.	21.913%	156	-0.880%	271	0.988%	264
Energen Corp.	28.323%	104	5.397%	228	21.048%	25
EnergySouth, Inc.	46.374%	35	22.617%	38	16.619%	44
Exxon Mobil Corp.	23.722%	145	0.814%	261	2.420%	245
F.N.B. Corp (FL)	-29.089%	303	-2.022%	274	-0.216%	277
Family Dollar Stores, Inc.	-5.089%	298	8.922%	181	6.718%	182
Fannie Mae	-2.390%	293	-2.952%	277	1.286%	258
Farmer Bros. Co.	13.374%	222	20.424%	53	14.031%	74
Federal Realty Investment Trust	26.671%	119	30.039%	16	14.055%	73
Federal Signal Corp.	8.796%	251	-3.762%	282	-2.417%	292
Fidelity National Financial, Inc.	48.761%	30	39.053%	4	28.396%	8
Fifth Third Bancorp (Cincinnati, OH)	11.438%	238	1.803%	256	3.974%	218
First Charter Corp.	22.579%	151	12.605%	138	2.305%	247
First Commonwealth Financial Corp.	15.156%	211	9.988%	172	9.280%	137
First Federal Capital Corp.	35.699%	69	20.629%	52	14.456%	67
First Financial Corp. (IN)	17.693%	193	18.740%	62	9.987%	122
First Financial Holdings, Inc.	9.027%	249	15.093%	109	9.871%	128
First Indiana Corp.	13.234%	223	0.569%	263	6.115%	190
First Merchants Corp.	6.925%	265	10.084%	171	8.138%	155
First Midwest Bancorp, Inc.	24.892%	134	16.679%	92	11.737%	104
FirstMerit Corp	19.951%	167	2.426%	251	0.272%	271
Florida Public Utilities Co.	40.811%	49	23.493%	34	14.280%	72
Franklin Electric Co., Inc.	17.345%	196	19.861%	56	14.929%	59
Franklin Resources, Inc.	58.114%	17	8.472%	186	7.034%	174
Freddie Mac	2.729%	282	-2.376%	275	-0.026%	274
Frisch's Restaurants, Inc.	57.017%	19	31.880%	13	24.373%	15
Fuller (H.B.) Company	13.534%	220	11.597%	152	-2.794%	293

Name	1-Year Tot. Ret.	1 Year Rank	3-Year Ann. Ret.	3-Year Rank	5-Year Ann. Ret.	5-Year Rank
Fulton Financial Corp. (PA)	6.680%	270	13.320%	127	9.476%	133
Gallagher (Arthur J.) & Co.	32.133%	86	10.675%	161	24.179%	16
Gannett Co., Inc.	15.782%	207	11.521%	154	5.198%	205
General Dynamics Corp.	51.419%	23	7.740%	197	7.176%	171
General Electric Co.	4.346%	276	-12.825%	300	-1.094%	288
General Growth Properties, Inc.	52.373%	22	35.603%	5	20.652%	28
Genuine Parts Co.	15.702%	208	13.325%	126	6.685%	183
Glacier Bancorp, Inc. (New)	24.014%	143	31.654%	14	15.318%	52
Golden West Financial Corp.	39.857%	54	21.799%	44	26.114%	14
Gorman-Rupp Co.	34.900%	74	12.617%	137	13.744%	76
Grainger (W.W.) Inc.	15.146%	212	12.053%	143	2.171%	250
Harley-Davidson, Inc.	27.273%	114	6.605%	216	13.747%	75
Harleysville Group, Inc. (PA)	-16.610%	301	-8.133%	292	3.381%	226
Harleysville National Corp.	26.582%	121	24.243%	30	18.917%	32
Haverty Furniture Cos., Inc.	26.276%	125	10.218%	169	10.150%	118
Health Care Property Investors, Inc.	37.346%	62	16.822%	91	15.203%	53
Healthcare Realty Trust, Inc.	39.266%	55	21.531%	47	16.844%	43
Heinz (H.J.) Co.	31.426%	90	2.664%	249	-0.581%	285
Helmerich & Payne, Inc.	6.141%	272	-18.312%	303	2.050%	251
Hershey Foods Corp.	38.544%	59	15.415%	106	12.538%	91
Hibernia Corp.	24.890%	135	13.115%	129	12.952%	85
Hilb, Rogal and Hamilton Co.	1.885%	286	23.302%	35	32.205%	7
Hillenbrand Industries, Inc.	37.355%	63	11.619%	151	8.884%	143
Holly Corp.	19.516%	173	26.089%	26	38.309%	2
Home Depot, Inc.	26.058%	127	-8.688%	293	-1.920%	290
HNI Corporation	26.910%	116	15.572%	101	7.841%	159
Hormel Foods Corp.	33.896%	79	15.426%	105	12.013%	99
Hudson United Bancorp	10.858%	240	18.062%	77	5.571%	197
Illinois Tool Works, Inc.	36.230%	67	11.952%	144	3.261%	229
Independent Bank Corporation	17.977%	190	31.918%	11	26.567%	12
Irwin Financial Corp. (Columbus, IN)	1.013%	287	6.962%	207	0.864%	266
Jack Henry & Associates, Inc.	40.769%	50	-12.943%	301	17.895%	36
Jefferson-Pilot Corp.	24.474%	138	4.482%	237	4.166%	216
Johnson & Johnson	-2.431%	294	5.428%	227	3.439%	225
Johnson Controls Inc	35.384%	71	16.338%	96	9.769%	130
KeyCorp (New)	28.287%	105	12.852%	134	2.794%	240
Kimberly-Clark Corp.	34.358%	77	5.247%	229	3.091%	233
Kimco Realty Corp.	24.199%	140	18.717%	63	14.988%	56
Lancaster Colony Corp.	-1.357%	292	13.076%	130	8.764%	144
La-Z-Boy Inc.	8.756%	252	6.918%	211	2.859%	238
Legg Mason, Inc.	70.571%	9	24.975%	28	21.956%	23
Leggett & Platt, Inc.	12.107%	234	7.540%	202	1.093%	262
Lilly (Eli) & Co.	17.784%	192	-2.997%	278	1.571%	255
Lincoln National Corp. (ID)	44.712%	38	1.878%	255	1.141%	261
Linear Technology Corp.	4.268%	277	-9.152%	294	5.123%	206
Lowe's Cos., Inc.	18.888%	181	18.447%	70	14.748%	65
M & T Bank Corp	2.166%	284	7.304%	204	9.903%	126
Marsh & McLennan Cos., Inc.	-2.810%	295	0.207%	266	5.664%	193
Marshall & Ilsley Corp.	27.430%	110	15.337%	107	2.562%	243
Masco Corp.	31.935%	88	8.920%	182	0.883%	265
May Department Stores Co. (The)	46.901%	34	-3.324%	280	-2.271%	291
MBIA Inc.	33.624%	80	8.465%	187	6.755%	181
MBNA Corp.	31.111%	91	2.124%	253	6.625%	184
McCormick & Co., Inc.	39.895%	52	21.816%	43	19.061%	30
McDonald's Corp	61.579%	15	0.710%	262	-7.661%	301
McGrath RentCorp	29.212%	100	10.677%	160	12.632%	90
McGraw-Hill Cos., Inc. (The)	36.958%	64	8.172%	190	8.696%	145
MDU Resources Group Inc.	16.280%	203	-3.037%	279	12.353%	94
Medtronic, Inc.	6.305%	271	4.728%	233	7.479%	169
Mercantile Bankshares Corp.	15.389%	210	7.432%	203	5.588%	196
Merck & Co., Inc	-16.690%	302	-12.274%	298	-5.252%	297
Mercury General Corp.	18.977%	180	16.308%	97	9.366%	134
Meredith Corp.	18.811%	182	11.315%	156	7.507%	166

Name	1-Year Tot. Ret.	1 Year Rank	3-Year Ann. Ret.	3-Year Rank	5-Year Ann. Ret.	5-Year Rank
Meridian Bioscience Inc.	27.722%	108	45.952%	3	9.927%	124
MGE Energy Inc	12.392%	231	13.713%	122	15.183%	54
Middlesex Water Co.	29.736%	97	13.719%	121	16.876%	42
Midland Co.	30.897%	93	14.000%	118	14.677%	66
Mine Safety Appliances Co	126.118%	1	49.058%	2	37.058%	4
Myers Industries Inc.	37.596%	61	10.565%	164	2.006%	253
NACCO Industries Inc.	64.724%	14	9.298%	178	2.214%	249
National City Corp	19.993%	166	12.119%	141	2.503%	244
National Commerce Financial Corp.	34.513%	76	4.712%	235	3.359%	227
National Fuel Gas Co. (NJ)	8.994%	250	-0.573%	269	6.166%	187
National Penn Bancshares, Inc.	8.613%	254	18.333%	71	12.943%	86
National Security Group, Inc	81.628%	6	23.686%	33	22.138%	22
NICOR Inc.	17.157%	197	0.242%	265	3.280%	228
Nordson Corp.	39.272%	56	10.517%	165	4.401%	215
Northern Trust Corp.	22.437%	153	-12.112%	297	-0.495%	283
Nucor Corp.	47.393%	32	6.732%	214	1.376%	257
Nuveen Investments Inc	6.980%	263	14.373%	114	16.142%	48
Old National Bancorp	18.527%	185	6.857%	212	0.329%	270
Old Republic International Corp.	19.314%	174	9.325%	177	14.772%	64
Otter Tail Corp.	0.182%	289	3.060%	246	10.545%	110
Pacific Capital Bancorp	15.118%	213	23.760%	32	14.927%	58
Park National Corp. (Newark, Oh.)	20.692%	162	15.085%	110	7.152%	173
Parker-Hannifin Corp.	37.783%	60	7.242%	205	4.633%	214
Paychex Inc	21.188%	157	3.763%	242	11.288%	108
Pennichuck Corp.	21.004%	159	9.786%	174	15.528%	51
Pentair, Inc.	56.798%	20	26.258%	25	6.119%	189
People's Bank (Bridgeport, CT)	66.363%	12	27.452%	22	9.270%	138
Peoples Energy Corp.	13.076%	225	6.540%	219	6.846%	178
PepsiCo Inc.	27.380%	113	8.727%	183	9.219%	139
Pfizer Inc.	18.309%	188	-4.782%	287	-0.240%	279
Piedmont Natural Gas Co., Inc.	12.901%	227	8.450%	188	8.633%	147
Pier 1 Imports Inc.	12.931%	226	24.247%	29	23.959%	17
Pinnacle West Capital Corp.	22.938%	149	-4.231%	285	3.877%	220
Pitney Bowes, Inc.	28.055%	107	6.922%	210	-6.680%	300
Popular Inc.	17.963%	191	13.684%	123	8.185%	154
PPG Industries, Inc.	25.850%	131	6.631%	215	0.806%	267
Praxair, Inc.	26.020%	129	16.887%	90	8.211%	152
Procter & Gamble Co.	19.777%	169	22.338%	41	3.877%	219
Progress Energy, Inc.	7.803%	258	3.746%	243	4.981%	210
Progressive Corp. (OH)	28.853%	101	31.143%	15	12.966%	84
Protective Life Corp.	27.393%	112	8.066%	192	-0.220%	278
Quaker Chemical Corp.	16.823%	200	16.089%	99	13.179%	82
Questar Corp.	20.099%	165	5.439%	226	16.526%	46
Quixote Corp.	8.224%	257	-6.562%	290	11.384%	107
Raven Industries, Inc.	105.666%	2	76.250%	1	49.726%	1
Regions Financial Corp.	6.971%	264	8.003%	193	1.401%	256
Republic Bancorp, Inc. (MI)	13.029%	224	11.842%	146	12.815%	87
RLI Corp.	19.019%	177	21.469%	49	18.021%	34
Rohm & Haas Co.	19.752%	170	6.297%	221	-0.904%	287
Roper Industries, Inc.	59.922%	16	5.849%	223	11.957%	101
Rouse Co.	29.583%	99	21.748%	45	15.813%	49
RPM International Inc (DE)	26.456%	123	20.387%	54	3.801%	222
S & T Bancorp, Inc. (Indiana, PA.)	6.933%	266	11.727%	149	5.305%	199
Sara Lee Corp.	40.703%	51	7.610%	199	3.188%	231
SBC Communications, Inc.	12.543%	229	-11.625%	296	-11.381%	302
Second Bancorp, Inc. (OH)	29.612%	98	21.652%	46	7.760%	161
SEI Investments Co.	12.809%	228	-9.328%	295	13.677%	78
ServiceMaster Co. (The)	32.105%	87	6.947%	209	-5.751%	298
Sherwin-Williams Co.	38.773%	58	23.870%	31	5.621%	195
Sigma-Aldrich Corp.	14.853%	215	7.663%	198	12.486%	93
Simmons First National Corp.	41.020%	48	31.882%	12	9.897%	125
SJW Corp.	26.482%	122	11.441%	155	13.695%	77
SLM Corp.	4.447%	275	18.603%	67	22.752%	20
Smith (A.O.) Corp	2.280%	283	18.207%	75	5.230%	204

Name	1-Year Tot. Ret.	1 Year Rank	3-Year Ann. Ret.	3-Year Rank	5-Year Ann. Ret.	5-Year Rank
Sonoco Products Co.	17.620%	194	6.948%	208	2.287%	248
SouthTrust Corp.	18.509%	186	11.841%	147	11.435%	105
St. Paul Travelers Companies, Inc.	19.540%	172	-0.572%	268	10.126%	119
Stanley Works	79.218%	7	7.870%	195	9.211%	140
State Auto Financial Corp.	50.106%	29	22.560%	40	23.164%	19
State Street Corp.	39.887%	53	-1.032%	272	3.102%	232
Stepan Co.	-0.161%	290	4.176%	239	1.781%	254
Sterling Bancshares, Inc. (TX)	8.586%	255	2.687%	248	10.089%	121
Sterling Financial Corp. (PA)	32.704%	83	27.492%	20	10.477%	112
Stryker Corp.	47.645%	31	18.752%	61	26.589%	11
SunTrust Banks, Inc.	22.160%	154	4.886%	232	1.279%	259
Superior Industries International, Inc.	-12.462%	300	-4.037%	283	7.762%	160
Supervalu Inc.	90.468%	4	33.456%	9	9.969%	123
Susquehanna Bancshares, Inc	6.819%	267	11.074%	158	8.093%	156
SWS Group, Inc.	0.422%	288	-4.712%	286	-14.681%	303
Synovus Financial Corp.	26.040%	128	-3.733%	281	3.678%	224
Sysco Corp.	34.807%	75	11.947%	145	21.891%	24
T Rowe Price Group Inc.	70.380%	10	15.300%	108	7.576%	165
Tanger Factory Outlet Centers, Inc	26.304%	124	27.488%	21	14.384%	68
Target Corp	30.502%	94	4.680%	236	5.752%	192
TCF Financial Corp.	27.727%	109	11.524%	153	13.557%	79
Teleflex Incorporated	20.995%	160	-0.728%	270	2.369%	246
Telephone and Data Systems, Inc.	54.537%	21	-13.597%	302	2.789%	241
Tennant Co.	22.477%	152	-1.256%	273	5.004%	209
TEPPCO Partners, L.P.	23.814%	144	17.791%	80	12.487%	92
Tootsie Roll Industries Inc	24.769%	136	-6.970%	291	0.201%	272
Transatlantic Holdings, Inc.	32.250%	85	7.605%	200	12.262%	96
Trustmark Corp.	11.597%	237	10.931%	159	6.909%	177
UGI Corp. (New)	3.291%	280	25.454%	27	26.307%	13
United Bankshares, Inc.	7.375%	260	12.674%	136	5.073%	207
United Dominion Realty Trust, Inc.	14.440%	216	18.599%	68	16.591%	45
United Mobile Homes, Inc.	8.563%	256	16.215%	98	14.320%	71
United Technologies Corp.	41.563%	46	4.297%	238	4.675%	213
Universal Corp.	30.987%	92	12.061%	142	17.484%	38
Universal Health Realty Income Trust	7.228%	262	14.002%	117	12.173%	97
Unizan Financial Corp	42.882%	41	20.027%	55	5.305%	200
Valley National Bancorp	5.992%	273	12.440%	139	10.461%	113
Valspar Corp.	16.485%	202	18.517%	69	8.661%	146
Vectren Corp	8.688%	253	6.555%	217	-0.293%	281
VF Corp.	19.929%	168	6.550%	218	-0.250%	280
Vulcan Materials Co.	35.087%	72	2.024%	254	1.226%	260
Walgreen Co.	12.281%	232	-6.528%	289	5.547%	198
Wal-Mart Stores, Inc.	1.918%	285	3.880%	241	4.911%	211
Washington Federal, Inc.	21.959%	155	10.192%	170	12.285%	95
Washington Mutual Inc.	3.924%	279	9.053%	180	10.268%	116
Washington R.E.I.T.	9.755%	246	12.832%	135	14.849%	63
Webster Financial Corp.	18.727%	184	13.032%	131	8.925%	142
Weingarten Realty Investors	15.837%	206	21.060%	51	14.373%	70
Wells Fargo & Co. (New)	20.410%	163	8.666%	184	7.502%	167
Wesbanco, Inc.	18.211%	189	13.203%	128	2.957%	235
Wesco Financial Corp.	36.698%	66	10.332%	166	4.067%	217
West Pharmaceutical Services, Inc.	66.164%	13	14.328%	116	4.818%	212
WestAmerica Bancorporation	13.899%	217	12.181%	140	9.663%	131
Weyco Group, Inc	-3.383%	296	27.943%	18	17.060%	40
WGL Holdings, Inc.	9.600%	248	3.923%	240	7.970%	158
Whitney Holding Corp.	25.326%	132	18.661%	66	11.399%	106
Wiley (John) & Sons Inc.	25.908%	130	18.762%	60	9.299%	135
Wilmington Trust Corp. (DE)	33.296%	81	9.434%	176	5.236%	202
Wolverine World Wide, Inc.	47.017%	33	15.554%	102	18.246%	33
WPS Resources Corp.	19.057%	176	16.399%	95	13.446%	80
Wrigley (William) Jr. Co.	10.386%	244	9.945%	173	8.192%	153

Ranking the Dividend Achievers by Total Return

Based on the 1 year period ending April 30, 2004

Rank	Name	Ticker	1-Year Tot. Ret	Rank	Name	Ticker	1-Year Tot. Ret
1	Mine Safety Appliances	MSA	126.118%	11	Bard (C.R.), Inc.	BCR	69.123%
2	Raven Industries, Inc.	RAVN	105.666%	12	People's Bank	PBCT	66.363%
3	1st Source Corp.	SRCE	96.377%	13	West Pharmaceutical Svcs.	WST	66.164%
4	Supervalu Inc.	SVU	90.468%	14	NACCO Industries Inc.	NC	64.724%
5	Altria Group Inc	MO	88.752%	15	McDonald's Corp	MCD	61.579%
6	National Security Group	NSEC	81.628%	16	Roper Industries, Inc.	ROP	59.922%
7	Stanley Works	SWK	79.218%	17	Franklin Resources, Inc.	BEN	58.114%
8	Corus Bankshares, Inc.	CORS	76.811%	18	Briggs & Stratton Corp.	BGG	57.975%
9	Legg Mason, Inc.	LM	70.571%	19	Frisch's Restaurants, Inc.	FRS	57.017%
10	T Rowe Price Group Inc.	TROW	70.380%	20	Pentair, Inc.	PNR	56.798%

Based on the 1 year period ending April 30, 2004

Rank	Name	Ticker	3-Year Ann. Ret	Rank	Name	Ticker	3-Year Ann. Ret
1	Raven Industries, Inc.	RAVN	76.250%	11	Independent Bank Corp	IBCP	31.918%
2	Mine Safety Appliances	MSA	49.058%	12	Simmons First National Corp.	SFNC	31.882%
3	Meridian Bioscience Inc.	VIVO	45.952%	13	Frisch's Restaurants, Inc.	FRS	31.880%
4	Fidelity National Financial	FNF	39.053%	14	Glacier Bancorp, Inc.	GBCI	31.654%
5	General Growth Properties	GGP	35.603%	15	Progressive Corp.	PGR	31.143%
6	Bard (C.R.), Inc.	BCR	35.169%	16	Federal Realty Inv. Tr.	FRT	30.039%
7	Courier Corp.	CRRC	35.064%	17	Community Trust Bancorp	CTBI	28.354%
8	CVB Financial Corp.	CVBF	33.565%	18	Weyco Group, Inc	WEYS	27.943%
9	Supervalu Inc.	SVU	33.456%	19	Applebee's International, Inc.	APPB	27.901%
10	Doral Financial Corp.	DRL	32.841%	20	Sterling Financial Corp.	SLFI	27.492%

Based on the 1 year period ending April 30, 2004

Rank	Name	Ticker	5-Year Ann. Ret	Rank	Name	Ticker	5-Year Ann. Ret
1	Raven Industries, Inc.	RAVN	49.726%	11	Stryker Corp.	SYK	26.589%
2	Holly Corp.	HOC	38.309%	12	Independent Bank	IBCP	26.567%
3	Brown & Brown, Inc.	BRO	37.332%	13	UGI Corp.	UGI	26.307%
4	Mine Safety Appliances	MSA	37.058%	14	Golden West Financial Corp.	GDW	26.114%
5	Courier Corp.	CRRC	35.927%	15	Frisch's Restaurants, Inc.	FRS	24.373%
6	Doral Financial Corp.	DRL	34.198%	16	Gallagher (Arthur J.) & Co.	AJG	24.179%
7	Hilb, Rogal and Hamilton	HRH	32.205%	17	Pier 1 Imports Inc.	PIR	23.959%
8	Fidelity National Financial	FNF	28.396%	18	Commerce Bancorp, Inc.	CBH	23.306%
9	Applebee's International	APPB	27.771%	19	State Auto Financial Corp.	STFC	23.164%
10	Eaton Vance Corp	EV	27.197%	20	SLM Corp.	SLM	22.752%

Web Site & Dividend Reinvestment Plan Information

Company	Web Site	DRIP
1st Source Corp.	www.1stsource.com	No
3M Company	www.3m.com	Yes
Abbott Laboratories	www.abbott.com	Yes
ABM Industries Inc.	www.abm.com	No
AFLAC Inc.	www.aflac.com	Yes
Air Products & Chemicals	www.airproducts.com	Yes
Alberto-Culver Co.	www.alberto.com	No
Alfa Corp.	www.alfains.com	Yes
ALLTEL Corp.	www.alltel.com	Yes
Altria Group, Inc.	www.altria.com	Yes
Ambac Financial Group, Inc.	www.ambac.com	No
American International Group	www.aig.com	No
American States Water Co.	www.aswater.com	Yes
AmSouth Bancorporation	www.amsouth.com	Yes
Anchor BanCorp Wisconsin, Inc.	www.anchorbank.com	No
Anheuser-Busch Cos., Inc.	www.anheuser-busch.com	Yes
Applebee's International, Inc.	www.applebees.com	No
AptarGroup Inc.	www.aptargroup.com	No
Aqua America Inc	www.aquaamerica.com	Yes
Archer-Daniels-Midland Co.	www.admworld.com	Yes
Arrow International, Inc.	www.arrowintl.com	No
Artesian Resources Corp.	www.artesianwater.com	Yes
Associated Banc-Corp.	www.associatedbank.com	Yes
Atmos Energy Corp.	www.atmosenergy.com	Yes
Automatic Data Processing	www.adp.com	No
Avery Dennison Corp.	www.averydennison.com	Yes
Avon Products, Inc.	www.avon.com	Yes
Badger Meter, Inc.	www.badgermeter.com	Yes
BancFirst Corp.	www.bancfirst.com	No
BancorpSouth, Inc.	www.bancorpsouth.com	Yes
Bandag, Inc.	www.bandag.com	Yes
Bank of America Corp.	www.bankofamerica.com	Yes
Bank of Hawaii Corp.	www.boh.com	Yes
Banta Corp.	www.banta.com	Yes
Bard (C.R.) Inc.	www.crbard.com	Yes
BB&T Corp.	www.bbandt.com	Yes
Beckman Coulter, Inc.	www.beckmancoulter.com	Yes
Becton, Dickinson & Co.	www.bd.com	Yes
Bemis Co., Inc.	www.bemis.com	Yes
Black Hills Power, Inc.	www.blackhillscorp.com	Yes
Bowl America Inc.	----	No
Brady Corp.	www.bradycorp.com	Yes
Briggs & Stratton Corp.	www.briggsandstratton.com	Yes
Brown & Brown, Inc.	www.brown-n-brown.com	No
Brown-Forman Corp.	www.brown-forman.com	Yes
California Water Service Co.	www.calwater.com	Yes
Camden Property Trust	www.camdenliving.com	Yes
Carlisle Companies Inc.	www.carlisle.com	Yes
Caterpillar Inc.	www.cat.com	Yes
Cedar Fair, L.P.	www.cedarfair.com	Yes
CenturyTel, Inc.	www.centurytel.com	Yes
Charter One Financial, Inc.	www.charterone.com	Yes
Chemical Financial Corp.	www.chemicalbankmi.com	Yes
ChevronTexaco Corp.	www.chevrontexaco.com	Yes
Chittenden Corp.	www.chittenden.com	Yes
Chubb Corp.	www.chubb.com	Yes
Cincinnati Financial Corp.	www.cinfin.com	Yes
Cintas Corp.	www.cintas.com	No

Web Site & Dividend Reinvestment Plan Information

Company	Web Site	DRIP
Citigroup Inc.	www.citigroup.com	No
Citizens Banking Corp.	www.cbclientsfirst.com	Yes
Clarcor Inc.	www.clarcor.com	Yes
CLECO Corp.	www.cleco.com	Yes
Clorox Co. (The)	www.clorox.com	Yes
Coca-Cola Co. (The)	www.coca-cola.com	Yes
Colgate-Palmolive Co.	www.colgate.com	Yes
Comerica, Inc.	www.comerica.com	Yes
Commerce Bancorp, Inc.	www.commerceonline.com	No
Commerce Bancshares, Inc.	www.commercebank.com	Yes
Commercial Net Lease Realty	www.cnlreit.com	Yes
Community Bank System, Inc.	www.communitybankna.com	Yes
Community First Bankshares, Inc.	www.communityfirst.com	Yes
Community Trust Bancorp, Inc.	www.ctbi.com	No
Compass Bancshares, Inc.	www.compassweb.com	Yes
ConAgra Foods, Inc.	www.conagra.com	Yes
Connecticut Water Service, Inc.	www.ctwater.com	Yes
Consolidated Edison, Inc.	www.conedison.com	Yes
Corus Bankshares, Inc.	www.corusbank.com	No
Courier Corp.	www.courier.com	No
Cullen/Frost Bankers, Inc.	www.frostbank.com	No
CVB Financial Corp.	www.cvbcorp.com	No
Danaher Corp.	www.danaher.com	No
Diebold, Inc.	www.diebold.com	Yes
Donnelley (R.R.) & Sons Co.	www.rrdonnelley.com	Yes
Doral Financial Corp.	www.doralfinancial.com	No
Dover Corp.	www.dovercorporation.com	Yes
Eastgroup Properties, Inc.	www.eastgroup.net	No
Eaton Vance Corp.	www.eatonvance.com	No
Ecolab Inc.	www.ecolab.com	Yes
Emerson Electric Co.	www.gotoemerson.com	Yes
Energen Corp.	www.energen.com	Yes
EnergySouth, Inc.	www.energysouth.com	Yes
Exxon Mobil Corp.	www.exxonmobil.com	Yes
F.N.B. Corp.	www.fnbcorporation.com	Yes
Family Dollar Stores, Inc.	www.familydollar.com	No
Fannie Mae	www.fanniemae.com	Yes
Farmer Bros. Co.	----	No
Federal Realty Invest. Trust	www.federalrealty.com	Yes
Federal Signal Corp.	www.federalsignal.com	Yes
Fidelity National Financial, Inc.	www.fnf.com	No
Fifth Third Bancorp	www.53.com	Yes
First Charter Corp.	www.firstcharter.com	Yes
First Commonwealth Financial	www.fcfbank.com	Yes
First Federal Capital Corp	www.firstfed.com	Yes
First Financial Corp.	www.first-online.com	No
First Financial Holdings, Inc.	www.firstfinancialholdings.com	Yes
First Indiana Corp.	www.firstindiana.com	Yes
First Merchants Corp.	www.firstmerchants.com	Yes
First Midwest Bancorp, Inc.	www.firstmidwest.com	Yes
FirstMerit Corp.	www.firstmerit.com	Yes
Florida Public Utilities Co.	www.fpuc.com	Yes
Franklin Electric Co., Inc.	www.fele.com	No
Franklin Resources, Inc.	www.franklintempleton.com	Yes
Freddie Mac	www.freddiemac.com	Yes
Frisch's Restaurants, Inc.	www.frischs.com	No
Fuller (H.B.) Co.	www.hbfuller.com	Yes
Fulton Financial Corp.	www.fult.com	Yes
Gallagher (Arthur J.) & Co.	www.ajg.com	No
Gannett Co., Inc.	www.gannett.com	Yes
General Dynamics Corp.	www.generaldynamics.com	No
General Electric Co.	www.ge.com	Yes

Web Site & Dividend Reinvestment Plan Information

Company	Web Site	DRIP
General Growth Properties, Inc.	www.generalgrowth.com	Yes
Genuine Parts Co.	www.genpt.com	Yes
Glacier Bancorp, Inc.	www.glacierbancorp.com	Yes
Golden West Financial Corp.	www.worldsavings.com	No
Gorman-Rupp Co. (The)	www.gormanrupp.com	Yes
Grainger, (W.W.) Inc.	www.grainger.com	No
Harley-Davidson, Inc.	www.harley-davidson.com	Yes
Harleysville Group Inc.	www.harleysvillegroup.com	Yes
Harleysville National Corp.	www.hncbank.com	Yes
Haverty Furniture Cos., Inc.	www.havertys.com	No
Health Care Property Investors	www.hcpi.com	Yes
Healthcare Realty Trust, Inc.	www.healthcarerealty.com	Yes
Heinz (H.J.) Co.	www.heinz.com	Yes
Helmerich & Payne, Inc.	www.hpinc.com	No
Hershey Foods Corp.	www.hersheys.com	Yes
Hibernia Corp.	www.hibernia.com	No
Hilb, Rogal & Hamilton Co.	www.hrh.com	No
Hillenbrand Industries, Inc.	www.hillenbrand.com	Yes
Holly Corp.	www.hollycorp.com	No
Home Depot, Inc. (The)	www.homedepot.com	Yes
HNI Corporation	www. honi.com	No
Hormel Foods Corp.	www.hormel.com	Yes
Hudson United Bancorp	www.hudsonunitedbank.com	Yes
Illinois Tool Works Inc.	www.itw.com	Yes
Independent Bank Corporation	www.ibcp.com	Yes
Irwin Financial Corp.	www.irwinfinancial.com	Yes
Jack Henry & Associates, Inc.	www.jackhenry.com	Yes
Jefferson-Pilot Corp.	www.jpfinancial.com	Yes
Johnson & Johnson	www.jnj.com	Yes
Johnson Controls, Inc.	www.johnsoncontrols.com	Yes
KeyCorp	www.key.com	Yes
Kimberly-Clark Corp.	www.kimberly-clark.com	Yes
Kimco Realty Corp.	www.kimcorealty.com	Yes
Lancaster Colony Corp.	www.lancastercolony.com	Yes
La-Z-Boy Inc.	www.la-z-boy.com	Yes
Legg Mason, Inc.	www.leggmason.com	No
Leggett & Platt, Inc.	www.leggett.com	No
Lilly (Eli) & Co.	www.lilly.com	Yes
Lincoln National Corp.	www.lfg.com	Yes
Linear Technology Corp.	www.linear.com	No
Lowe's Cos., Inc.	www.lowes.com	Yes
M&T Bank Corp.	www.mandtbank.com	Yes
Marsh & McLennan Cos., Inc.	www.mmc.com	Yes
Marshall & Ilsley Corp.	www.micorp.com	Yes
Masco Corp.	www.masco.com	Yes
May Department Stores (The)	www.maycompany.com	Yes
MBIA Inc.	www.mbia.com	No
MBNA Corp.	www.mbna.com	No
McCormick & Co., Inc.	www.mccormick.com	Yes
McDonald's Corp.	www.mcdonalds.com	Yes
McGrath Rentcorp	www.mgrc.com	No
McGraw-Hill Cos., Inc. (The)	www.mcgraw-hill.com	Yes
MDU Resources Group, Inc.	www.mdu.com	Yes
Medtronic, Inc.	www.medtronic.com	Yes
Mercantile Bankshares Corp.	www.mrbk.com	Yes
Merck & Co., Inc.	www.merck.com	Yes
Mercury General Corp.	www.mercuryinsurance.com	No
Meredith Corp.	www.meredith.com	Yes
Meridian Bioscience Inc.	www.meridianbioscience.com	Yes
MGE Energy, Inc.	www.mge.com	Yes
Middlesex Water Co.	www.middlesexwater.com	Yes
Midland Co. (The)	www.midlandcompany.com	Yes
Mine Safety Appliances Co.	www.msanet.com	No

Web Site & Dividend Reinvestment Plan Information

Company	Web Site	DRIP
Myers Industries, Inc.	www.myersind.com	Yes
NACCO Industries, Inc.	www.nacco.com	No
National City Corp.	www.nationalcity.com	Yes
National Commerce Financial	www.ncbccorp.com	Yes
National Fuel Gas Co.	www.natfuel.com	Yes
National Penn Bancshares, Inc.	www.nationalpennbancshares.com	Yes
National Security Group (The)	www.nationalsecuritygroup.com	No
NICOR Inc.	www.nicorinc.com	Yes
Nordson Corp.	www.nordson.com	Yes
Northern Trust Corp.	www.northerntrust.com	No
Nucor Corp.	www.nucor.com	Yes
Nuveen Investments, Inc.	www.nuveen.com	No
Old National Bancorp	www.oldnational.com	Yes
Old Republic International Corp.	www.oldrepublic.com	Yes
Otter Tail Corp.	www.ottertail.com	Yes
Pacific Capital Bancorp	www.pcbancorp.com	No
Park National Corp.	www.parknationalcorp.com	Yes
Parker-Hannifin Corp.	www.parker.com	Yes
Paychex, Inc.	www.paychex.com	Yes
Pennichuck Corp.	www.pennichuck.com	Yes
Pentair, Inc.	www.pentair.com	Yes
People's Bank	www.peoples.com	Yes
Peoples Energy Corp.	www.pecorp.com	Yes
PepsiCo, Inc.	www.pepsico.com	Yes
Pfizer Inc.	www.pfizer.com	Yes
Piedmont Natural Gas Co., Inc.	www.piedmontng.com	Yes
Pier 1 Imports, Inc.	www.pier1.com	Yes
Pinnacle West Capital Corp.	www.pinnaclewest.com	Yes
Pitney Bowes Inc.	www.pb.com	Yes
Popular, Inc.	www.popularinc.com	Yes
PPG Industries, Inc.	www.ppg.com	Yes
Praxair, Inc.	www.praxair.com	Yes
Procter & Gamble Co. (The)	www.pg.com	Yes
Progress Energy, Inc.	www.progress-energy.com	Yes
Progressive Corp. (The)	www.progressive.com	No
Protective Life Corp.	www.protective.com	Yes
Quaker Chemical Corp.	www.quakerchem.com	Yes
Questar Corp.	www.questar.com	Yes
Quixote Corp.	www.quixotecorp.com	No
Raven Industries, Inc.	www.ravenind.com	Yes
Regions Financial Corp.	www.regionsbank.com	Yes
Republic Bancorp Inc.	www.republicbancorp.com	Yes
RLI Corp.	www.rlicorp.com	Yes
Rohm & Haas Co.	www.rohmhaas.com	Yes
Roper Industries, Inc.	www.roperind.com	No
Rouse Company (The)	www.therousecompany.com	Yes
RPM International Inc.	www.rpminc.com	Yes
S&T Bancorp, Inc.	www.stbank.com	Yes
Sara Lee Corp.	www.saralee.com	Yes
SBC Communications Inc.	www.sbc.com	Yes
Second Bancorp, Inc.	www.secondbancorp.com	Yes
SEI Investments Co.	www.seic.com	No
ServiceMaster Co. (The)	www.servicemaster.com	Yes
Sherwin-Williams Co. (The)	www.sherwin.com	Yes
Sigma-Aldrich Corp.	www.sigma-aldrich.com	No
Simmons First National Corp.	www.simmonsfirst.com	No
SJW Corp.	www.sjwater.com	No
SLM Corporation	www.salliemae.com	Yes
Smith (A.O.) Corp.	www.aosmith.com	Yes
Sonoco Products Co.	www.sonoco.com	Yes
SouthTrust Corp.	www.southtrust.com	Yes
St. Paul Traveler Cos., Inc.	www.stpaul.com	Yes
Stanley Works (The)	www.stanleyworks.com	Yes
State Auto Financial Corp.	www.stauto.com	Yes

Web Site & Dividend Reinvestment Plan Information

Company	Web Site	DRIP
State Street Corp.	www.statestreet.com	Yes
Stepan Co.	www.stephan.com	No
Sterling Bancshares, Inc.	www.banksterling.com	No
Sterling Financial Corp.	www.sterlingfi.com	Yes
Stryker Corp.	www.strykercorp.com	No
SunTrust Banks, Inc.	www.suntrust.com	Yes
Superior Industries Int'l, Inc.	www.supind.com	Yes
SuperValu Inc.	www.supervalu.com	Yes
Susquehanna Bancshares, Inc.	www.susqbanc.com	Yes
SWS Group, Inc.	www.swsgroupinc.com	No
Synovus Financial Corp.	www.synovus.com	Yes
Sysco Corp.	www.sysco.com	Yes
T. Rowe Price Group, Inc.	www.troweprice.com	No
Tanger Factory Outlet Centers, Inc.	www.tangeroutlet.com	Yes
Target Corp.	www.target.com	Yes
TCF Financial Corp.	www.tcfbank.com	Yes
Teleflex Inc.	www.teleflex.com	Yes
Telephone & Data Systems	www.teldta.com	Yes
Tennant Co.	www.tennantco.com	Yes
TEPPCO Partners, L.P.	www.teppco.com	No
Tootsie Roll Industries, Inc.	www.tootsie.com	No
Transatlantic Holdings, Inc.	www.transre.com	No
Trustmark Corp.	www.trustmark.com	Yes
UGI Corp.	www.ugicorp.com	Yes
United Bankshares, Inc.	www.ubsi-wv.com	Yes
United Dominion Realty Trust	www.udrt.com	Yes
United Mobile Homes, Inc.	www.umh.com	Yes
United Technologies Corp.	www.utc.com	Yes
Universal Corp.	www.universalcorp.com	Yes
Universal Health Realty Inc. Trust	www.uhrit.com	Yes
Unizan Financial Corp.	www.unbcorp.com	Yes
Valley National Bancorp	www.valleynationalbank.com	Yes
Valspar Corp. (The)	www.valspar.com	Yes
Vectren Corporation	www.vectren.com	Yes
VF Corp.	www.vfc.com	Yes
Vulcan Materials Co.	www.vulcanmaterials.com	Yes
Walgreen Co.	www.walgreens.com	Yes
Wal-Mart Stores, Inc.	www.wal-mart.com	Yes
Washington Federal, Inc.	www.washingtonfederal.com	No
Washington Mutual, Inc.	www.wamu.com	Yes
Washington R.E.I.T.	www.writ.com	Yes
Webster Financial Corp.	www.websterbank.com	Yes
Weingarten Realty Investors	www.weingarten.com	Yes
Wells Fargo & Co.	www.wellsfargo.com	Yes
WesBanco, Inc.	www.wesbanco.com	Yes
Wesco Financial Corp.	----	No
West Pharmaceutical Services	www.westpharma.com	Yes
WestAmerica Bancorporation	www.westamerica.com	Yes
Weyco Group, Inc.	www.weycogroup.com	No
WGL Holdings, Inc.	www.washgas.com	Yes
Whitney Holding Corp.	www.whitneybank.com	Yes
Wiley (John) & Sons Inc.	www.wiley.com	No
Wilmington Trust Corp.	www.wilmingtontrust.com	Yes
Wolverine World Wide, Inc.	www.wolverineworldwide.com	No
WPS Resources Corp.	www.wpsr.com	Yes
Wrigley (Wm.) Jr. Co.	www.wrigley.com	Yes

NAICS Classification of Companies By Industry

Accommodation and Food Services
Applebee's International, Inc.
Frisch's Restaurants, Inc.
* McDonald's Corporation

Administrative & Support and Waste Management
Administrative and Support Services
ServiceMaster Company (The)

Waste Management and Remediation Services
* Johnson Controls, Inc.

Arts, Entertainment, and Recreation
Bowl America Inc.
* Cedar Fair, L.P.

Construction
ABM Industries Incorporated
* MDU Resources Group, Inc.

Finance and Insurance
Commercial Banking

1st Source Corp.
* AmSouth Bancorporation
* Associated Banc-Corp.
BancFirst Corp.
* BancorpSouth, Inc.
* Bank of America Corporation
* Bank of Hawaii Corporation
* BB&T Corporation
* Chemical Financial Corp.
* Chittenden Corporation
* Citizens Banking Corp.
* Comerica, Inc.
* Commerce Bancorp, Inc.
* Commerce Bancshares, Inc.
* Community Bank System, Inc.
* Community First Bankshares, Inc.
Community Trust Bancorp, Inc.
* Compass Bancshares Inc.
Corus Bankshares, Inc.
Cullen/Frost Bankers, Inc.
CVB Financial Corp.
* F.N.B. Corp.
* Fifth Third Bancorp
* First Charter Corp.
* First Commonwealth Financial
First Financial Corp.
* First Merchants Corp.
* First Midwest Bancorp, Inc.
* FirstMerit Corp.
* Fulton Financial Corp.
* Harleysville National Corp.
* Hibernia Corporation
* Hudson United Bancorp
* Independent Bank Corporation
* Irwin Financial Corp.
* KeyCorp

* M&T Bank Corporation
* Marshall & Ilsley Corporation
MBNA Corporation
* Mercantile Bankshares Corp.
* National Commerce Financial
* National Penn Bancshares, Inc.
Northern Trust Corp.
* Old National Bancorp
Pacific Capital Bancorp
* Park National Corp.
* People's Bank
* Popular, Inc.
* Regions Financial Corporation
* Republic Bancorp, Inc.
* S&T Bancorp, Inc.
* Second Bancorp, Inc.
Simmons First National Corp.
* SouthTrust Corp.
* State Street Corporation
Sterling Bancshares, Inc.
* Sterling Financial Corp.
* SunTrust Banks, Inc.
* Susquehanna Bancshares, Inc.
SWS Group, Inc.
* Synovus Financial Corporation
* TCF Financial Corp.
* Trustmark Corp.
* United Bankshares, Inc.
* Unizan Financial Corp.
* Valley National Bancorp
* Wells Fargo & Company
* WesBanco, Inc.
* WestAmerica Bancorporation
* Whitney Holding Corp.
* Wilmington Trust Corporation

Direct Health and Medical Insurance Carriers
* AFLAC Incorporated

Direct Life Insurance Carriers
* Jefferson-Pilot Corp.
* Lincoln National Corporation
National Security Group, Inc.
* Protective Life Corporation

Direct Property and Casualty Insurance Carriers
* Alfa Corp.
American International Group
* Chubb Corporation (The)
* Cincinnati Financial Corp.
* Harleysville Group, Inc.
Mercury General Corporation
* Midland Company (The)
Progressive Corporation (The)
* RLI Corp.
* State Auto Financial Corp.
Transatlantic Holdings, Inc.
Wesco Financial Corp.

31a

NAICS Classification of Companies By Industry

Direct Title Insurance Carriers
Fidelity National Financial, Inc.

Insurance Agencies and Brokerages
Brown & Brown, Inc.
Gallagher (Arthur J.) & Company
Hilb, Rogal & Hamilton Company
* Marsh & McLennan Companies

Nondepository Credit Intermediation
Doral Financial Corporation
* Fannie Mae
* Freddie Mac
SLM Corporation

Real Estate Investment Trusts
Camden Property Trust
* Commercial Net Lease Realty
* EastGroup Properties, Inc.
* Federal Realty Investment Trust
* General Growth Properties, Inc.
* Health Care Property Investors
* Healthcare Realty Trust, Inc.
* Kimco Realty Corp.
* Tanger Factory Outlet Centers, Inc.
* United Dominion Realty Trust
* United Mobile Homes, Inc.
* Universal Health Realty Inc. Trust
* Washington Real Est. Invst Trust
* Weingarten Realty Investors

Reinsurance Carriers
Ambac Financial Group, Inc.
MBIA Inc.
* Old Republic International Corp.
* St. Paul Traveler Cos., Inc.

Savings Institutions
Anchor BanCorp Wisconsin, Inc.
* Charter One Financial, Inc.
* First Federal Capital Corp.
* First Financial Holdings, Inc.
* First Indiana Corp.
* Glacier Bancorp, Inc.
Golden West Financial Corp.
Washington Federal, Inc.
* Washington Mutual, Inc.
* Webster Financial Corp.

Securities and Other Financial Investments
* Citigroup Inc.
Eaton Vance Corporation
* Franklin Resources, Inc.
Legg Mason, Inc.
Nuveen Investments, Inc.
SEI Investments Co.
T. Rowe Price Group, Inc.

Information

Information Services and Data Processing
Automatic Data Processing, Inc.
* Jack Henry & Associates, Inc.
* Paychex, Inc.

Publishing Industries
Courier Corp.
* Gannett Co., Inc.
* McGraw-Hill Companies, Inc.
Meredith Corporation
Wiley (John) & Sons Inc.

Telecommunications
* ALLTEL Corporation
* CenturyTel, Inc.
* Telephone and Data Systems, Inc.

Management of Companies & Enterprises
* National City Corporation
* SBC Communications Inc.
* Universal Corporation

Manufacturing

Beverage and Tobacco Product Manufacturing
* Altria Group, Inc.
* Anheuser-Busch Companies
* Brown-Forman Corporation
* Coca-Cola Company (The)
Farmer Bros. Co.
* PepsiCo Inc.

Chemical Manufacturing
* 3M Company
* Air Products & Chemicals, Inc.
Alberto-Culver Company
* Avon Products, Inc.
* Clorox Company (The)
* Colgate-Palmolive Company
* Ecolab, Inc.
* Fuller (H.B.) Company
* PPG Industries, Inc.
* Praxair, Inc.
* Procter & Gamble Company
* Rohm & Haas Company
* RPM International Inc.
* Sherwin-Williams Company
Sigma-Aldrich Corp.
Stepan Company
* Valspar Corporation (The)

Computer and Electronic Product Manufacturing
* Badger Meter, Inc.
* Beckman Coulter, Inc.
* Emerson Electric Co.
Linear Technology Corp.
* Medtronic, Inc.

NAICS Classification of Companies By Industry

Elec. Eqpmt., Appliance, and Component Mfg.
Franklin Electric Co., Inc.
* General Electric Company
* Gorman-Rupp Co.
* Smith (A.O.) Corporation

Fabricated Metal Product Manufacturing
Danaher Corporation
* Parker-Hannifin Corp.
* Stanley Works

Food Manufacturing
* Archer Daniels Midland Co.
* ConAgra Foods, Inc.
* Heinz (H.J.) Company
* Hershey Foods Corporation
* Hormel Foods Corporation
* Lancaster Colony Corp.
* McCormick & Company, Inc.
* Sara Lee Corporation
Tootsie Roll Industries, Inc.
* Wrigley (Wm.) Jr. Company

Furniture and Related Product Manufacturing
HNI Corporation
* La-Z-Boy Incorporated
Leggett & Platt, Incorporated
* Masco Corporation

Machinery Manufacturing
* Briggs & Stratton Corporation
* Caterpillar Inc.
* Diebold, Inc.
* Dover Corporation
NACCO Industries, Inc.
* Nordson Corp.
* Pentair, Inc.
Roper Industries, Inc.
* Tennant Company

Medical Equipment and Supplies Manufacturing
Arrow International, Inc.
* Bard (C.R.), Inc.
* Becton, Dickinson and Company
* Meridian Bioscience Inc.
Stryker Corporation
* Teleflex Inc.

Paper and Wood Product Manufacturing
* Avery Dennison Corporation
* Bemis Company, Inc.
* Kimberly-Clark Corporation
* Sonoco Products Company

Petroleum and Coal Products Manufacturing
* ChevronTexaco Corp.
* Exxon Mobil Corporation
Holly Corp.
* Quaker Chemical Corporation

Pharmaceutical Preparation Manufacturing
* Abbott Laboratories
* Johnson & Johnson
* Lilly (Eli) & Company
* Merck & Co., Inc.
* Pfizer Inc.

Plastics and Rubber Products Manufacturing
AptarGroup Inc.
* Bandag, Inc.
* Carlisle Companies Incorporated
* Illinois Tool Works, Incorporated
* Myers Industries, Inc.
* West Pharmaceutical Services

Primary Metal Manufacturing
* Nucor Corporation

Printing and Related Support Activities
* Banta Corporation
* Donnelley (R.R.) & Sons Co.

Textiles, Apparel, and Leather Manufacturing
* VF Corporation
Weyco Group, Inc.
Wolverine World Wide, Inc.

Transportation Equipment Manufacturing
* Clarcor Inc.
* Federal Signal Corp.
General Dynamics Corporation
* Harley-Davidson, Inc.
Superior Industries International, Inc.
* United Technologies Corp.

Other Manufacturing
* Brady Corporation
* Hillenbrand Industries, Inc.
Mine Safety Appliances Co.
Quixote Corp.
* Raven Industries, Inc.

Mining
Helmerich & Payne, Inc.
* Vulcan Materials Company

Real Estate and Rental and Leasing
Real Estate
* Rouse Company (The)

Rental and Leasing Services
Cintas Corp.
McGrath RentCorp

Retail Trade
Building Material and Supplies Dealers
* Home Depot (The), Inc.
* Lowe's Companies, Inc.

NAICS Classification of Companies By Industry

Furniture and Consumer Electronics
Haverty Furniture Companies
* Pier 1 Imports, Inc.

General Merchandise Stores
Family Dollar Stores, Inc.
* May Department Stores Co.
* Target Corporation
* Wal-Mart Stores, Inc.

Health and Personal Care Stores
* Walgreen Co.

Transportation and Warehousing
* Atmos Energy Corporation
* EnergySouth, Inc.
TEPPCO Partners, L.P.

Utilities
Utilities - Electric
* Black Hills Corporation
* Cleco Corporation
* Consolidated Edison, Inc.
* MGE Energy Inc.
* Otter Tail Corp.
* Pinnacle West Capital Corp.
* Progress Energy, Inc.
* WPS Resources Corporation

Utilities - Natural Gas
* Energen Corporation
* Florida Public Utilities Co.
* National Fuel Gas Company
* NICOR Inc.
* Peoples Energy Corporation
* Piedmont Natural Gas Company, Inc.
* Questar Corporation
* UGI Corporation
* Vectren Corporation
* WGL Holdings, Inc.

Utilities - Water
* American States Water Co.
* Aqua America, Inc.
* Artesian Resources Corp.
* California Water Service Group
* Connecticut Water Service, Inc.
* Middlesex Water Co.
* Pennichuck Corp.
SJW Corp.

Wholesale Trade
* Genuine Parts Company
Grainger (W.W.), Inc.
* Pitney Bowes Inc.
* Supervalu Inc.
* Sysco Corporation

* Designates companies offering dividend reinvestment plans.

Ranking the 2004 Canadian Dividend Achievers

Companies are listed by the five-year average annual compound growth rate of their dividends.

Rank	Company	5-Year Growth Rate	Rank	Company	5-Year Growth Rate
1	BMTC Group Inc.	26.191	16	Atco Ltd.	13.485
2	Loblaw Cos. Ltd.	24.573	17	Thomson Corp.	12.939
3	Weston (George) Limited	24.356	18	Melcor Developments Ltd.	12.888
4	Empire Ltd.	22.698	19	Leon's Furniture Ltd.	12.196
5	IGM Financial Inc.	21.673	20	Toronto Dominion Bank	11.939
5	Jean Coutu Group (PJC) Inc.	21.673	21	Buhler Industries, Inc.	11.382
7	Great-West Lifeco Inc.	20.654	22	National Bank of Canada	10.351
8	Metro Inc.	20.546	23	Toromont Industries Ltd.	10.301
9	Power Financial Corp	19.551	24	Bank of Montreal	8.774
10	AGF Management Ltd.	17.808	25	Enbridge Inc.	8.188
11	Quebecor World Inc.	16.724	26	Terasen Inc.	7.017
12	Power Corp. du Canada	16.466	27	West Fraser Timber Co., Ltd.	4.554
13	Bank of Nova Scotia	15.996	28	Canadian Utilities Ltd.	4.462
14	Royal Bank of Canada	14.343	29	Imperial Oil Ltd.	3.144
15	Canadian National Railway Co.	13.539	30	Emera Inc.	0.957

Ranking the 2004 Canadian Dividend Achievers By Current Yield

Based on closing prices at April 30, 2004

Rank	Company	Yield	Rank	Company	Yield
1	Emera Inc.	4.56	16	Melcor Developments Ltd.	2.32
2	Enbridge Inc	3.65	17	Quebecor World Inc.	2.20
3	Canadian Utilities Ltd.	3.62	18	Buhler Industries, Inc.	1.98
4	Terasen Inc	3.50	19	Leon's Furniture Ltd.	1.85
5	Royal Bank of Canada	3.41	20	Power Corp. of Canada	1.80
5	IGM Financial Inc.	3.18	21	Metro Inc	1.62
7	Bank of Montreal	3.08	22	Weston (George) Limited	1.57
8	Toronto Dominion Bank	3.06	23	Canadian National Railway Co.	1.51
9	National Bank of Canada	2.97	24	Empire Co Ltd	1.50
10	Atco Ltd.	2.87	25	Imperial Oil Ltd.	1.46
11	Bank of Nova Scotia	2.84	26	Toromont Industries Ltd.	1.41
12	Great-West Lifeco Inc.	2.56	27	Loblaw Cos. Ltd.	1.29
13	Thomson Corp.	2.39	28	West Fraser Timber Co., Ltd.	1.29
14	AGF Management Ltd	2.38	29	BMTC Group Inc.	0.90
15	Power Financial Corp	2.33	30	Jean Coutu Group (PJC) Inc.	0.62

Ranking the 2004 Canadian Dividend Achievers By P/E Ratio

Based on closing prices at April 30, 2004

Rank	Company	P/E	Rank	Company	P/E
1	Jean Coutu Group (PJC) Inc.	26.74	16	Canadian Utilities Ltd.	14.37
2	Thomson Corp.	23.74	17	AGF Management Ltd	14.23
3	Emera Inc.	22.98	18	Royal Bank of Canada	13.88
4	Power Financial Corp	20.82	19	National Bank of Canada	13.32
5	Canadian National Railway Co.	20.46	20	Imperial Oil Ltd.	13.31
5	Great-West Lifeco Inc.	20.15	21	Buhler Industries, Inc.	12.84
7	Power Corp. of Canada	19.66	22	Enbridge Inc	12.54
8	Toromont Industries Ltd.	19.57	23	BMTC Group Inc.	12.20
9	Loblaw Cos. Ltd.	19.26	24	West Fraser Timber Co., Ltd.	11.76
10	Terasen Inc	18.97	25	Empire Co Ltd	11.39
11	IGM Financial Inc.	18.73	26	Metro Inc	11.26
12	Weston (George) Limited	15.86	27	Atco Ltd.	11.22
13	Leon's Furniture Ltd.	15.67	28	Melcor Developments Ltd.	8.11
14	Bank of Montreal	15.09	29	Quebecor World Inc.	N.M.
15	Bank of Nova Scotia	14.99	30	Toronto Dominion Bank	N.M.

Ranking the the 2004 Canadian Dividend Achievers by Total Return

Based on the 1 year period ending April 30, 2004

Rank	Name	1-Year Tot. Ret	Rank	Name	1-Year Tot. Ret
1	AGF Management Ltd	54.382%	16	Melcor Developments Ltd.	27.225%
2	BMTC Group Inc.	54.345%	17	Canadian Utilities Ltd.	23.971%
3	Imperial Oil Ltd.	40.299%	18	Buhler Industries, Inc.	21.014%
4	West Fraser Timber Co., Ltd.	39.873%	19	Atco Ltd.	20.457%
5	Power Financial Corp	38.303%	20	Enbridge Inc	18.786%
6	Power Corp. of Canada	37.217%	21	Leon's Furniture Ltd.	17.219%
7	Toronto Dominion Bank	34.767%	22	Empire Co Ltd	13.417%
8	Bank of Montreal	32.818%	23	Thomson Corp.	10.455%
9	IGM Financial Inc.	32.663%	24	Quebecor World Inc.	6.160"
10	Great-West Lifeco Inc.	32.528%	25	Loblaw Cos. Ltd.	6.054
11	National Bank of Canada	30.946%	26	Royal Bank of Canada	5.050'
12	Bank of Nova Scotia	29.378%	27	Weston (George) Limited	-0.075".
13	Emera Inc.	28.799%	28	Metro Inc	-0.364%
14	Terasen Inc	28.727%	29	Toromont Industries Ltd.	-17.748%
15	Jean Coutu Group (PJC) Inc.	28.278%	30	Canadian National Railway Co.	-24.767%

Based on the 3 year period ending April 30, 2004

Rank	Name	3-Year Ann. Ret.	Rank	Name	3-Year Ann. Ret.
1	BMTC Group Inc.	57.826%	16	Imperial Oil Ltd.	14.296%
2	Melcor Developments Ltd.	27.265%	17	Royal Bank of Canada	14.063%
3	Buhler Industries, Inc.	25.450%	18	Enbridge Inc	13.005%
4	Bank of Nova Scotia	23.873%	19	Great-West Lifeco Inc.	12.518%
5	IGM Financial Inc.	21.557%	20	West Fraser Timber Co., Ltd.	10.056%
6	Power Financial Corp	21.100%	21	Emera Inc.	8.801%
7	National Bank of Canada	20.928%	22	Toronto Dominion Bank	7.060%
8	Toromont Industries Ltd.	19.946%	23	Canadian Utilities Ltd.	6.732%
9	Terasen Inc	18.742%	24	Loblaw Cos. Ltd.	4.611%
10	Metro Inc	18.356%	25	Atco Ltd.	2.069%
11	Empire Co Ltd	17.522%	26	Weston (George) Limited	1.074%
12	Power Corp. of Canada	16.490%	27	Thomson Corp.	1.047%
13	Bank of Montreal	16.152%	28	Canadian National Railway Co.	-4.264%
14	Jean Coutu Group (PJC) Inc.	15.742%	29	AGF Management Ltd	-8.169%
15	Leon's Furniture Ltd.	14.377%	30	Quebecor World Inc.	-8.761%

Based on the 5 year period ending April 30, 2004

Rank	Name	5-Year Ann. Ret.	Rank	Name	5-Year Ann. Ret.
1	BMTC Group Inc.	35.065%	16	Terasen Inc	13.238%
2	Melcor Developments Ltd.	24.911%	17	IGM Financial Inc.	11.802%
3	Buhler Industries, Inc.	22.728%	18	AGF Management Ltd	11.389%
4	Jean Coutu Group (PJC) Inc.	20.134%	19	Enbridge Inc	11.077%
5	Bank of Nova Scotia	17.353%	20	Canadian Utilities Ltd.	10.948%
6	Power Financial Corp	17.057%	21	Loblaw Cos. Ltd.	10.614%
7	Imperial Oil Ltd.	16.260%	22	Weston (George) Limited	10.610%
8	Power Corp. of Canada	16.206%	23	Great-West Lifeco Inc.	7.827%
9	Empire Co Ltd	16.062%	24	Atco Ltd.	6.817%
10	Toromont Industries Ltd.	15.960%	25	Emera Inc.	6.497%
11	National Bank of Canada	15.869%	26	Toronto Dominion Bank	5.055%
12	Leon's Furniture Ltd.	14.371%	27	West Fraser Timber Co., Ltd.	5.011%
13	Royal Bank of Canada	13.907%	28	Thomson Corp.	4.394%
14	Bank of Montreal	13.640%	29	Canadian National Railway Co.	3.420%
15	Metro Inc	13.638%	30	Quebecor World Inc.	-3.792%

NAICS Classification Of Canadian Companies By Industry

Company	Description
AGF Management Ltd	Investment Advice
Atco Ltd.	Electric Power Distribution
Bank of Montreal	Commercial Banking
Bank of Nova Scotia	Commercial Banking
BMTC Group Inc.	Furniture Stores
Buhler Industries, Inc.	Farm and Garden Machinery and Equipment Merchant Wholesalers
Canadian National Railway Co.	Line-Haul Railroads
Canadian Utilities Ltd.	Electric Bulk Power Transmission and Control
Emera Inc.	Electric Power Distribution
Empire Co Ltd	Other Grocery and Related Products Merchant Wholesalers
Enbridge Inc	All Other Pipeline Transportation
Great-West Lifeco Inc.	Direct Life Insurance Carriers
IGM Financial Inc.	Investment Advice
Imperial Oil Ltd.	Crude Petroleum and Natural Gas Extraction
Jean Coutu Group (PJC) Inc.	Pharmacies and Drug Stores
Leon's Furniture Ltd.	Institutional Furniture Manufacturing
Loblaw Cos. Ltd.	Warehouse Clubs and Supercenters
Melcor Developments Ltd.	Land Subdivision
Metro Inc	General Line Grocery Merchant Wholesalers
National Bank of Canada	Commercial Banking
Power Corp. of Canada	Offices of Other Holding Companies
Power Financial Corp	Direct Life Insurance Carriers
Quebecor World Inc.	Commercial Screen Printing
Royal Bank of Canada	Commercial Banking
Terasen Inc	Pipeline Transportation of Refined Petroleum Products
Thomson Corp.	Data Processing, Hosting, and Related Services
Toromont Industries Ltd.	Air-Conditioning and Warm Air Heating Equipment
Toronto Dominion Bank	Commercial Banking
West Fraser Timber Co., Ltd.	Logging
Weston (George) Limited	Commercial Bakeries

Web Site & Dividend Reinvestment Plan Information

Company	Web Site	DRIP
AGF Management Ltd	www.agf.com	No
Atco Ltd.	www.atco.com	No
Bank of Montreal	www.bmo.com	Yes
Bank of Nova Scotia	www.scotiabank.com	Yes
BMTC Group Inc.	www.braultetmartineau.com	No
Buhler Industries, Inc.	www.buhler.com	No
Canadian National Railway Co.	www.cn.ca	No
Canadian Utilities Ltd.	www.canadian-utilities.com	No
Emera Inc.	www.emera.com	No
Empire Co Ltd	www.empireco.ca	No
Enbridge Inc	www.enbridge.com	Yes
Great-West Lifeco Inc.	www.greatwestlifeco.com	No
IGM Financial Inc.	www.investorsgroup.com	No
Imperial Oil Ltd.	www.imperialoil.ca	Yes
Jean Coutu Group (PJC) Inc.	www.jeancoutu.com	No
Leon's Furniture Ltd.	www.leons.ca	No
Loblaw Cos. Ltd.	www.loblaw.com	No
Melcor Developments Ltd.	www.melcor.ca	No
Metro Inc	www.metro.ca	No
National Bank of Canada	www.nbc.ca	No
Power Corp. of Canada	www.powercorp.com	No
Power Financial Corp	www.powerfinancial.com	No
Quebecor World Inc.	www.quebecorworld.com	No
Royal Bank of Canada	www.rbc.com	No
Terasen Inc	www.bcgas.com	No
Thomson Corp.	www.thomcorp.com	No
Toromont Industries Ltd.	www.toromont.com	No
Toronto Dominion Bank	www.td.com	Yes
West Fraser Timber Co., Ltd.	www.westfraser.com	No
Weston (George) Limited	www.weston.ca	No

Frequently Asked Questions

Topics Questions:

- How does a dividend-paying company become a Dividend Achiever?
- What percentage of dividend-paying companies classified as Dividend Achievers?
- How many economic sectors and industries are represented by Dividend Achievers?
- What distinguishes Dividend Achievers from other U.S. listed companies?
- How often is the Dividend Achievers Index reconstituted?
- How are corporate actions handled?
- What type of information is available on the Dividend Achievers constituents?

Q: How does a dividend-paying company become a Dividend Achiever?

A: A publicly-traded company that has increased its dividends for the last ten or more consecutive years will be classified as a Dividend Achiever. Depending on the industry, companies must also meet certain capitalization requirements in order to be considered a Dividend Achiever.

Q: What percentage of dividend-paying companies classified as Dividend Achievers?

A: Just 3.0.% of 10,000-plus North American-listed, dividend-paying common stocks are classified as Dividend Achievers.

Q: How many economic sectors and industries are represented by Dividend Achievers?

A: Dividend Achievers represent five economic sectors and more than 50 industries.

Q: What distinguishes Dividend Achievers from other U.S. listed companies?

A: Dividend Achievers have demonstrated the ability to consistently increase dividend payments over a substantial period of time, through volatile markets and challenging political climates.

Q: Does Mergent Inc. offer a Dividend Achiever Index?

A: Mergent currently offers an Index that tracks the daily performance of Dividend Achiever constituents. The inception date was January 17, 2003. The real time price appreciation values are published by the American Stock Exchange under the Symbol ^DAA.

Q: How often is the Index reconstituted?

A: The Dividend Achievers Index is reconstituted annually.

Q: How are corporate actions handled?

A: If an Index constituent is acquired and is no longer actively traded, the company will cease classification as a Dividend Achiever. If an Index constituent spins off a portion of its business or merges with another company, it will be handled on a case by case basis.

HOW TO USE THIS BOOK

MERGENT'S Dividend Achievers is a compact, easy-to-use reference that provides basic financial and business information on 303 companies that have increased their cash dividend payments for at least ten consecutive years, adjusting for splits. The presentation of background information plus current and historical data provides the answers to four basic questions for each company:

1. What does the company do?
   (See G.)
2. How has it done in the past?
   (See B, J.)
3. How is it doing now?
   (See C, D, H.)
4. How will it fare in the future?
   (See I.)

A. CAPSULE STOCK INFORMATION shows where the stock is traded and its symbol, a recent price and price/earnings ratio, plus the yield afforded by the indicated dividend based on a recent price. The indicated dividend is the current annualized dividend based on the most recent regular cash payment. Also shown is the 52-week range of the Company's stock price.

B. LONG-TERM PRICE CHART illustrates the pattern of monthly stock price movements, fully adjusted for stock dividends and splits. The chart points out the degree of volatility in the price movement of the company's stock and what its long-term trend has been, and shows how it has performed versus the S&P 500 Index. It indicates areas of price support and resistance, plus other technical points to be considered by the investor. The bars at the base of the long-term price chart indicate the monthly trading volume. Monthly trading volume offers the individual an opportunity to recognize at what periods stock accumulation occurs and what percent of a company's outstanding shares are traded.

PRICE SCORES – Above each company's price/volume chart are its *Mergent's Price Scores*. These are basic measures of the stock's performance. Each stock is measured against the New York Stock Exchange Composite Index.

A score of 100 indicates that the stock did as well as the New York Stock Exchange Composite Index during the time period. A score of less than 100 means that the stock did not do as well; a score of more than 100 means that the stock outperformed the NYSE Composite Index. All stock prices are adjusted for splits and stock dividends. The time periods measured for each company conclude with the date of the recent price shown in the top line of each company's profile.

The *7 YEAR PRICE SCORE* mirrors the common stock's price growth over the previous seven years. The higher the price score, the better the relative performance. It is based on the ratio of the latest 12-month average price to the current seven year average. This ratio is then indexed against the same ratio for the market as a whole (the New York Stock Exchange Composite Index), which is taken as 100.

The *12 MONTH PRICE SCORE* is a similar measurement but for a shorter period of time. It is based on the ratio of the latest two-month average price to the current 12-month average price. As was done for the Long-Term Price Score, this ratio is also indexed to the same ratio for the market as a whole.

C. INTERIM EARNINGS (Per Share) – Figures are reported before effect of extraordinary items, discontinued operations and cumulative effects of accounting changes. Each figure is for the quarterly period indicated. These figures are essentially as reported by the company, although all figures are adjusted for all stock dividends and splits.

D. INTERIM DIVIDENDS (Per Share) – The cash dividends are the actual dollar amounts declared by the company. No adjustments have been made for stock dividends and splits. **Ex-Dividend Date**: a stockholder must purchase the stock prior to this date in order to be entitled to the dividend. The **Record Date** indicates the date on which the

A ILLUSTRATIVE, INC.

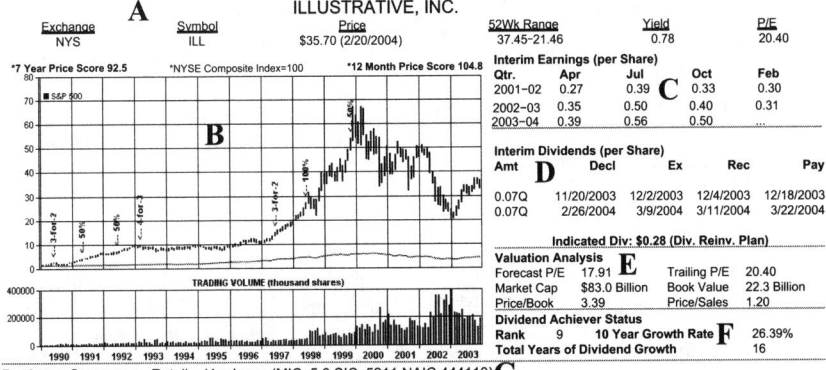

Exchange	Symbol	Price	52Wk Range	Yield	P/E
NYS	ILL	$35.70 (2/20/2004)	37.45-21.46	0.78	20.40

*7 Year Price Score 92.5   ***NYSE Composite Index=100**   ***12 Month Price Score 104.8**

B

Interim Earnings (per Share)

Qtr.	Apr	Jul	Oct	Feb
2001-02	0.27	0.39	0.33	0.30
2002-03	0.35	0.50	0.40	0.31
2003-04	0.39	0.56	0.50	...

C

Interim Dividends (per Share)

Amt	Decl	Ex	Rec	Pay
0.07Q	11/20/2003	12/2/2003	12/4/2003	12/18/2003
0.07Q	2/26/2004	3/9/2004	3/11/2004	3/22/2004

D

Indicated Div: $0.28 (Div. Reinv. Plan)

Valuation Analysis E

Forecast P/E	17.91	Trailing P/E	20.40
Market Cap	$83.0 Billion	Book Value	22.3 Billion
Price/Book	3.39	Price/Sales	1.20

Dividend Achiever Status

Rank	9	10 Year Dividend Growth Rate F	26.39%
Total Years of Dividend Growth	16		

TRADING VOLUME (thousand shares)

400000

200000

0

1990 1991 1992 1993 1994 1995 1996 1997 1998 1999 2000 2001 2002 2003

Business Summary – Retail – Hardware (MIC: 5.6 SIC: 5211 NAIC:444110) G

Illustrative, Inc. operated 1,607 retail warehouse stores as of Aug 3 2003 in the United States, Canada and Mexico that offer a wide assortment of building materials and home improvement products. The average Illustrative store has about 108,000 square feet of interior floor space and is stocked with approximately 40,000 to 50,000 separate items. Most stores have about 22,000 square feet of additional outdoor selling area for landscaping supplies. Co. operates 53 Illustrative Design Center stores that sell products and services primarily for home decorating and remodeling projects, five Illustrative Supply stores, nine Illustrative Landscape Supply stores and one Illustrative, Inc. Floor Store outlet.

Recent Developments H

For the three months ended Nov 2 2003, net earnings advanced 22.0% to $1.15 billion from $940.0 million in the corresponding prior-year period. Net sales increased 14.7% to $16.60 billion from $14.48 billion a year earlier. Comparable-store sales were up 7.8% year over year, while average sale per customer transaction rose to $52.10 from $49.66 in the third quarter of 2002. Gross profit totaled $5.19 billion, or 31.3% of net sales, compared with $4.58 billion, or 31.6% of net sales, the year before. Operating income climbed 21.9% to $1.82 billion from $1.50 billion the previous year. During the quarter, Co. opened 36 new stores.

Prospects I

Co. is projecting sales growth of between 9.0% and 12.0% and earnings growth of 15.0% to 17.0% during the current fiscal year. Results are being positively affected by Co.'s efforts to remodel many of its older stores and improve customer service through the installation of self–checkout stations, which have been installed in 760 stores as of Nov 2 2003. Separately, Co. is taking steps to expand its services business through acquisitions. On Nov 10 2003, Co. signed a definitive agreement to acquire RMA Home Services, Inc., an Atlanta, GA–based contract installer of replacement windows and siding. In September 2003, Co. acquired IPUSA, a Tampa, FL–based contract installer of roofing.

Financial Data J

(US$ in Thousands)	11/02/2003	08/03/2003	05/04/2003	02/02/2003	02/03/2002	01/28/2001	01/30/2000	01/31/1999	02/01/1998	02/02/1997
Earnings Per Share	1.46	0.95	0.39	1.56	1.29	1.10	1.00	0.70	0.51	0.43
Cash Flow Per Share	2.67	2.00	1.20	2.04	2.53	1.18	1.04	0.82	0.45	0.50
Tang. Book Val. Per Share	...	...	8.75	8.38	7.52	6.32	5.22	3.82	3.16	2.71
Dividends Per Share	0.25	0.23	0.22	0.21	0.17	0.16	0.11	0.08	0.06	0.05
Dividend Payout %	17.12	24.21	56.41	13.46	13.18	14.55	11.00	11.43	11.76	11.63
Income Statement										
Total Revenues	49,691,000	33,093,000	15,104,000	58,247,000	53,553,000	45,738,000	38,434,000	30,219,000	24,156,000	19,535,503
Total Indirect Exp.	10,290,000	6,920,000	3,381,000	12,278,000	11,215,000	9,490,000	7,616,000	5,944,000	4,869,000	3,900,430
Depreciation & Amort.	786,000	505,000	248,000	903,000	764,000	601,000	463,000	373,000	283,000	232,340
Operating Income	5,337,000	3,514,000	1,448,000	5,830,000	4,932,000	4,191,000	3,795,000	2,661,000	1,912,000	1,533,650
Net Interest Inc./(Exp.)	(7,000)	(7,000)	(6,000)	42,000	25,000	26,000	9,000	(7,000)	2,000	9,490
Income Before Income Taxes	5,330,000	3,507,000	1,442,000	5,872,000	4,957,000	4,217,000	3,804,000	2,654,000	1,898,000	1,534,769
Income Taxes	1,977,000	1,301,000	535,000	2,208,000	1,913,000	1,636,000	1,484,000	1,040,000	738,000	597,030
Net Income	3,353,000	2,206,000	907,000	3,664,000	3,044,000	2,581,000	2,320,000	1,614,000	1,160,000	937,739
Average Shs. Outstg.	2,295,000	2,300,000	2,297,000	2,344,000	2,353,000	2,352,000	2,342,000	2,320,000	2,286,000	2,194,884
Balance Sheet										
Cash & Cash Equivalents	4,944,000	5,209,000	4,264,000	2,253,000	2,546,000	177,000	170,000	62,000	174,000	558,436
Total Current Assets	15,697,000	15,567,000	15,309,000	11,917,000	10,361,000	7,777,000	6,390,000	4,933,000	4,460,000	3,709,373
Net Property	18,876,000	18,263,000	17,654,000	17,168,000	15,375,000	13,068,000	10,227,000	8,160,000	6,509,000	5,437,046
Total Assets	35,374,000	34,612,000	33,747,000	30,011,000	26,394,000	21,385,000	17,081,000	13,465,000	11,229,000	9,341,710
Total Current Liabilities	10,972,000	10,389,000	10,925,000	8,035,000	6,501,000	4,385,000	3,656,000	2,857,000	2,456,000	1,842,126
Long–Term Obligations	847,000	1,327,000	1,321,000	1,321,000	1,250,000	1,545,000	750,000	1,566,000	1,303,000	1,246,593
Net Stockholders' Equity	22,261,000	21,933,000	20,678,000	19,802,000	18,082,000	15,004,000	12,341,000	8,740,000	7,098,000	5,955,186
Net Working Capital	4,725,000	5,178,000	4,384,000	3,882,000	3,860,000	3,392,000	2,734,000	2,076,000	2,004,000	1,867,247
Year-end Shs. Outstg.	2,273,000	2,365,000	2,294,000	2,293,000	2,345,888	2,323,747	2,304,317	2,213,178	2,196,324	2,162,317
Statistical Record										
Operating Profit Margin %	10.74	10.61	9.58	10.00	9.20	9.16	9.87	8.80	7.91	7.85
Return on Equity %	15.06	10.05	4.38	18.50	16.83	17.20	18.79	18.46	16.34	15.74
Return on Assets %	9.47	6.37	2.68	12.20	11.53	12.06	13.58	11.98	10.33	10.03
Debt/Total Assets %	2.39	3.83	3.91	4.40	4.73	7.22	4.39	11.63	11.60	13.34
Price Range	37.43-20.52	34.41-20.52	28.34-20.52	51.31-20.35	52.52-32.28	67.06-34.68	68.31-32.28	40.00-19.50	19.60-10.59	12.43-8.98
P/E Ratio	25.64-14.05	36.22-21.60	72.67-52.62	32.89-13.04	40.71-25.02	60.96-31.10	67.26-35.25	57.14-28.50	38.43-20.76	28.91-20.88
Average Yield %	0.84	0.82	0.91	0.60	N/A	0.32	0.24	N/A	0.39	N/A

Address: 2455 Paces Ferry Road N.W., Atlanta, GA 30339–4024, United States
Telephone: (770) 433–8211 K
Fax: (770) 431–2707
Web Site: www.illusinc.com

Officers:
Robert L. Nardelli – Chmn. Pres., C.E.O.
Francis L. Blake – Exec. V.P., Bus. Devel., Strategy, Corp. Oper.
Transfer Agents: EquiServe Trust Company, N.A., Providence,
Auditors: KPMG LLP

Investor Contact: Investor Relations,
770–384–4388
Legal Counsel: Smith, Cohen, Ringel, Kohler &Martin
Institutional Holdings L
No of Institutions: 10   **Shares:** 5,387,488

HOW TO USE THIS BOOK (Continued)

shareholder had to have been a holder of record in order to have qualified for the dividend. The **Payable Date** indicates the date the company paid or intends to pay the dividend. The cash amount shown in the first column is followed by a letter (example ''Q'' for quarterly) to indicate the frequency of the dividend. A notation of 'Dividend payment suspended' indicates that dividend payments have been suspended within the most recent ten years.

Indicated Dividend – This is the annualized amount (fully adjusted for splits) of the latest regular cash dividend. Companies with Dividend Reinvestment Plans are indicated here.

E. VALUATION ANALYSIS is a tool for evaluating a company's stock. Included are: Forecast Price/Earnings, Trailing Price/Earnings, Market Capitalization, Book Value, Price/Book and Price/Sales.

F. DIVIDEND ACHIEVER STATUS – The company's rank among the Dividend Achievers for dividend growth is indicated. Each company is ranked by its ten-year compound annual average cash dividend growth rate, which is also shown here, along with the total consecutive years of increases.

G. BUSINESS SUMMARY explains what a company does in terms of the products or services it sells, its markets, and the position the company occupies in its industry. For a quick reference, included are the Company's Standard Industrial Classification (SIC), North American Industry Classification (NAIC) and Mergent's Industry Classification (MIC).

H. RECENT DEVELOPMENTS – This section captures what has happened in which results are available. It provides analysis of recently released sales and earnings figures, including special charges and credits, and may also include results by sector, expense trends and ratios, and other current information.

I. PROSPECTS – This section focuses on what is anticipated for the immediate future,

as well as the outlook for the next few years, based on analysis by Mergent.

J. FINANCIAL DATA (fully adjusted for stock dividends and splits) is provided for at least the past seven fiscal years, preceded by the most recent three-, six- and nine-month results if available.

Fiscal Years are the annual financial reporting periods as determined by each company. Annual prices and dividends are displayed based on the Company's fiscal year.

Per Share Data:

The Earnings Per Share figure essentially is what has been reported by the company. Earnings per share, and all per share figures, are adjusted for subsequent stock dividends and splits. Earnings per share reported after 12/15/97 are presented on a diluted basis, as described by Financial Accounting Standards Board Statement 128. Prior to that date, earnings per share are presented on a primary basis.

Cash Flow Per Share is computed by dividing the cash flow from operating activities by average shares outstanding.

Tangible Book Value Per Share is calculated as stockholders equity (the value of common shares, paid-in capital and retained earnings) minus preferred stock and intangibles such as goodwill, patents and excess acquisition costs, divided by year-end shares outstanding. It demonstrates the underlying cash value of each common share if the company were to be liquidated as of that date.

Dividends Per Share is the total of cash payments made per share to shareholders for the trailing 12-month period.

Dividend Payout % is the proportion of earnings available for common stock that is paid to common shareholders in the form of cash dividends. It is significant because it indicates what percentage of earnings is being reinvested in the business for internal growth.

INCOME STATEMENT, BALANCE SHEET AND STATISTICAL RECORD – Includes pertinent earnings and balance sheet information essential to analyzing a corporation's performance. The comparisons are shown as originally reported, provide the necessary historical perspective to intelligently review the various operating and financial trends. Generic definitions follow.

Income Statement:

Total Revenues figure is the total of gross revenues, gross sales, or equivalent items of income from operations.

Total Indirect Expenses consists of development costs than material and labor costs which are directly related to the construction of improvements, including administrative and office expenses, commissions, architectural, engineering and financing costs.

Depreciation and Amortization includes all non-cash charges such as depletion and amortization as well as depreciation.

Operating Income is the profit remaining after deducting depreciation as well as all operating costs and expenses from the company's net sales and revenues. This figure is *before* interest expenses, extraordinary gains and charges, and income and expense items of a non-operating nature.

Net Interest Income/(Expense) is the net amount of interest paid and received by a company during the fiscal year.

Income Before Income Taxes is the remaining income *after* deducting all costs, expenses, property charges, interest, etc. but *before* deducting income taxes.

Equity Earnings/Minority Interest is the net amount of profits allocated to minority owners or affiliates.

Income Taxes are shown as reported by the company and include both the amount of current taxes actually paid out and the amount deferred to future years.

Income From Continuing Operations is the amount remaining from total revenues after provisions for all operating and non-operating costs and expenses, including interest and taxes, have been deducted. Generally, extraordinary gains and losses and discontinued operations are excluded. Non-extraordinary charges such as restructuring or asset-

impairment charges are included in net income figures, as is income from minority interests in other companies.

Net Income is the amount remaining from total revenues after provisions for all operating and non-operating costs and expenses, including interest and taxes, have been deducted. Net income includes gains and losses from extraordinary items, accounting changes and discontinued operations. Non-extraordinary items such as restructuring or asset impairments are also included, as is income from minority interests in other companies. Net income is usually shown before preferred dividends have been deducted.

Average Shares Outstanding is the weighted average number of shares including common equivalent shares outstanding during the year, as reported by the corporation and fully adjusted for all stock dividends and splits. The use of *average shares* minimizes the distortion in *earnings per share* which could result from issuance of a large amount of stock or the company's purchase of a large amount of its own stock during the year.

Balance Sheet:

All balance sheet items are shown as reported by the corporation in its annual report. Because of the limited amount of space available and in an effort to simplify and standardize accounts, some items have been combined.

Cash & Cash Equivalents comprise unrestricted cash and temporary investments in marketable securities, such as U.S. Government securities, certificates of deposit and short-term investments.

Total Current Assets are all of the company's short-term assets, including cash, marketable securities, inventories, certain receivables, etc., as reported.

Net Property is total fixed assets, including all property, land, plants, buildings, equipment, fixtures, etc., less accumulated depreciation.

Total Assets represent the sum of the company's tangible and intangible property, as stated on its annual audited balance sheet.

HOW TO USE THIS BOOK (Continued)

Total Current Liabilities are all of the obligations the company due within one year, as reported.

Long-term Obligations are total long-term debts (due beyond one year) reported by the company, including bonds, capital lease obligations, notes, mortgages, debentures, etc.

Net Stockholders' Equity is the sum of all capital stock accounts – stated values of preferred and common stock, paid-in capital, earned surplus (retained earnings), etc., net of all treasury stock.

Net Working Capital is derived by subtracting Current Liabilities from Current Assets.

Year-end Shares Outstanding are the number of shares outstanding as of the date of the company's quarterly/annual report, exclusive of treasury stock and adjusted for subsequent stock dividends and splits.

Statistical Record:

Operating Profit Margin indicates operating profit as a percentage of net sales or revenues.

Net Profit % is the ratio of income from continuing operations to total revenues, expressed as a percentage.

Return on Equity % is the ratio of income from continuing operations to stockholders' equity, expressed as a percentage. This ratio illustrates how effectively the investment of the stockholders is being utilized to earn a profit.

Return on Assets % represents the ratio of income from continuing operations to total assets. This ratio indicates how effectively assets are being used to produce profit.

Debt/Total Assets represents the ratio of long-term obligations to total assets as a percentage.

Price Ranges are based on each Company's fiscal year. Where actual stock sales did not take place, a range of lowest bid and highest asked prices is shown.

Price/Earnings Ratio is shown as a range. The figures are calculated by dividing the

stock's highest price for the year and its lowest price by the year's earnings per share. Growth stocks tend to command higher P/Es than cyclical stocks.

Average Yield % is the ratio of annual dividends to the real average of the prices over the fiscal year.

EDITOR'S NOTE: In order to preserve the historical relationships between prices, earnings and dividends, figures are not restated to reflect subsequent events. Figures are presented in U.S. dollars unless otherwise indicated.

K. ADDITIONAL INFORMATION on each stock includes the officers of the company, investor relations contact, address, telephone and fax numbers, website, transfer agents, auditors, legal counsel and institutional holdings.

L. INSTITUTIONAL HOLDINGS indicates the number of investment companies, insurance companies, mutual funds, bank trust and college endowment funds holding the stock and the total number of shares held as last reported.

OTHER DEFINITIONS

FACTORS PERTAINING ESPECIALLY TO UTILITIES

Net Income/Net Property % is the ratio of income from continuing operations to net plant (including construction work in figure indicates the realized rate of return on book value of properties.

Net Income/Total Capitalization % is the ratio between net income and capitalization, which includes all long-term debt obligations and shareholders' equity.

Accumulated Depreciation/Gross Property % reflects the percentage of properties that have been depreciated. A lower percentage indicates a higher book value of properties.

HOW TO USE THIS BOOK (Continued)

FACTORS PERTAINING ESPECIALLY TO BANKS

Net Interest Income is interest income less interest expenses. It represents the amount of income generated by a bank's primary interest-related business. This figure is presented before any credit loss provisions.

Non-interest Income is any income that is not interest-related. Such income could include, among other things, credit card in income, advisory and other bank fees and gains on securities sales.

Total Deposits are total time and demand deposits entrusted to a bank.

Net Loans are all promissory notes held, including agricultural, commercial, personal, real estate and other loans outstanding, after deducting unearned discount and allowance for possible loan losses.

Equity/Assets % represents the amount of assets that are retained in the Company, or the amount of assets that are not obligated to outside parties.

Non Interest Expense/Total Income % is a measure of how effectively a bank is operating. It is the ratio of non-interest expense to total income.

FACTORS PERTAINING ESPECIALLY TO INSURANCE COMPANIES

Premium Income is the amount of insurance premiums received. This is the primary revenue source for insurance companies.

Net Investment Income is the amount received from investments during a reporting period.

Total Investments represents the invested assets of an insurance company. Certain invested assets may include, among other things, fixed maturities (such as bonds), common equity securities, mortgage loans and short-term investments.

Return on Revenues % (similar to Net Profit %) is the percentage of total revenues remaining after the deduction of all non-extraordinary costs, including interest and taxes.

FACTORS PERTAINING ESPECIALLY TO REAL ESTATE INVESTMENT TRUSTS

Total Income (similar to Total Revenues) is all income from operations. Total Income could include, among other things, rental income, mortgage income and certain interest income.

Net Income + Depreciation/Assets % represents the ratio of income from continuing operations and non-cash depreciation to total assets. This measures how effectively assets are being used to produce cash profits.

HOW TO USE THIS BOOK (Continued)

**ABBREVIATIONS
AND
SYMBOLS**

(Div. Reinv. Plan)....Dividend Reinvestment Plan Offered

A...................................... Annual

ASE .... American Stock Exchange

( )...Deficit

E... Extra

M ....Monthly

N/A............................ Not Applicable

N.M............................ Not Meaningful

NYS .... New York Stock Exchange

OTC ....Over-The-Counter Market

p .... Preliminary

Q....................................Quarterly

S .... Semi-annual

Sp............................ Special Dividend

U........................Frequency Unknown

1ST SOURCE CORP.

Exchange	Symbol	Price	52Wk Range	Yield	P/E
NMS	SRCE	$22.70 (5/28/2004)	25.45–17.25	1.76	24.15

*7 Year Price Score 96.0   *NYSE Composite Index=100   *12 Month Price Score 50.1

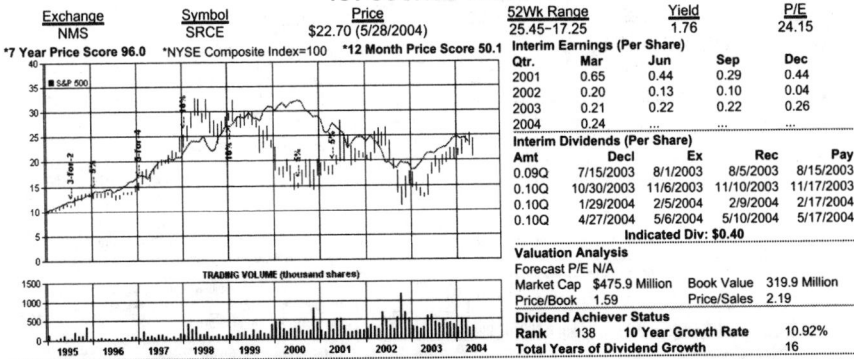

Interim Earnings (Per Share)

Qtr.	Mar	Jun	Sep	Dec
2001	0.65	0.44	0.29	0.44
2002	0.20	0.13	0.10	0.04
2003	0.21	0.22	0.22	0.26
2004	0.24	...	...	...

Interim Dividends (Per Share)

Amt	Decl	Ex	Rec	Pay
0.09Q	7/15/2003	8/1/2003	8/5/2003	8/15/2003
0.10Q	10/30/2003	11/6/2003	11/10/2003	11/17/2003
0.10Q	1/29/2004	2/5/2004	2/9/2004	2/17/2004
0.10Q	4/27/2004	5/6/2004	5/10/2004	5/17/2004

Indicated Div: $0.40

Valuation Analysis

Forecast P/E N/A

Market Cap $475.9 Million	Book Value 319.9 Million
Price/Book 1.59	Price/Sales 2.19

Dividend Achiever Status

Rank 138	10 Year Growth Rate 10.92%
Total Years of Dividend Growth 16	

Business Summary: Commercial Banking (MIC: 8.1 SIC: 6022 NAIC:522110)

1st Source is a registered bank holding company, with $3.33 billion in assets as of Dec 31 2003. Through its subsidiary, 1st Source Bank, Co. provides consumer and commercial banking services to individual and business customers through 60 banking locations in 15 counties in the northern Indiana–southwestern Michigan market area. Co. also competes for business nationwide by offering specialized financing services for used private and cargo aircraft, automobiles for leasing and rental agencies, medium and heavy duty trucks, construction and environmental equipment.

Recent Developments: For the first quarter ended Mar 31 2004, net income climbed 13.9% to $5.1 million compared with $4.5 million in the equivalent 2003 quarter. Total interest income fell 10.8% to $38.1 million from $42.7 million the year before. Total interest expense dropped 23.6% to $12.4 million versus $16.2 million a year earlier. Provision for loan losses plunged 98.1% to $101,000 from $5.6 million in 2002. Total non–interest income fell 30.0% to $14.0 million, reflecting a reduction of loan servicing and sale income. Total non–interest expense decreased 7.1% to $32.3 million due to decreased salaries and employee benefits, and decreased loan collection and repossession expense.

Prospects: Looking ahead, Co. will likely continue to benefit from the improvement in its nonperforming assets. Co. has spent the last year and a half working through the collection and sale of both aircraft and automobiles from troubled customers. Although Co. has not finished all reconditioning and sale of its nonperforming assets, the markets have stabilized. In addition, Co. is seeing some improvement among its customers in the air cargo and aircraft sales businesses as well as with its rental car customers. However, margins remain tight and Co. continues to expect significant volatility in the valuation of its mortgage servicing rights.

Financial Data

(US$ in Thousands)	3 Mos	12/31/2003	12/31/2002	12/31/2001	12/31/2000	12/31/1999	12/31/1998	12/31/1997
Earnings Per Share	0.94	0.91	0.47	1.82	1.79	1.68	1.45	1.23
Tang. Book Val. Per Share	13.18	15.01	14.60	16.71	15.99	15.00	13.67	12.46
Dividends Per Share	0.380	0.370	0.360	0.350	0.330	0.280	0.250	0.220
Dividend Payout %	40.43	40.65	76.59	19.30	18.69	16.81	17.37	18.35
Income Statement								
Total Interest Income	38,125	162,322	199,503	242,183	235,392	200,429	196,148	173,316
Total Interest Expense	12,363	59,070	80,817	123,397	130,425	100,726	102,227	87,324
Net Interest Income	25,762	103,252	118,686	118,786	104,967	99,703	93,921	85,992
Provision for Loan Losses	101	17,361	39,657	28,623	14,877	7,442	9,156	6,052
Non–Interest Income	14,019	80,196	73,117	92,836	73,914	63,260	51,521	35,656
Non–Interest Expense	32,342	138,904	137,735	121,232	104,003	99,023	85,500	72,977
Income Before Taxes	7,338	27,183	11,445	61,767	60,001	56,498	50,786	42,619
Income from Cont Ops	...	...	13,045	40,708	39,971	38,027	33,241	28,227
Net Income	5,079	19,154	10,039	38,498	37,513	35,768	31,020	26,489
Average Shs. Outstg.	21,035	21,150	21,310	21,170	20,982	21,210	21,356	21,546
Balance Sheet								
Cash & Due from Banks	78,134	109,787	120,894	129,431	118,123	101,911	132,514	90,864
Securities Avail. for Sale	729,924	1,527,526	1,308,581	1,280,956	1,067,032	1,017,270	983,390	714,841
Net Loans & Leases	2,106,068	2,160,955	2,266,874	2,477,740	2,264,418	2,022,979	1,840,767	1,761,357
Total Assets	3,222,713	3,330,153	3,407,468	3,562,691	3,182,181	2,872,945	2,732,021	2,418,154
Total Deposits	2,403,990	2,487,215	2,712,905	2,882,806	2,462,724	2,127,452	2,177,107	1,891,791
Long–Term Obligations	79,625	79,246	16,878	11,939	12,060	12,174	13,189	16,656
Total Liabilities	2,902,853	3,015,462	3,098,039	3,211,751	2,866,859	2,589,375	2,471,412	2,178,451
Net Stockholders' Equity	319,860	314,691	309,429	306,190	270,552	238,820	215,859	194,953
Shares Outstanding	20,737	20,962	21,188	20,994	19,714	18,901	19,063	19,231
Return on Equity %	1.58	6.08	4.21	11.59	12.67	13.41	12.75	11.77
Return on Assets %	0.15	0.57	0.38	1.14	1.25	1.32	1.21	1.16
Equity/Assets %	9.92	9.44	9.08	9.85	9.87	9.87	9.53	9.91
Non–Int. Exp./Tot. Inc. %	61.72	57.27	50.52	36.18	33.62	37.55	34.52	34.92
Price Range	24.75–21.01	22.40–12.70	26.68–10.95	28.00–17.08	22.68–14.23	32.43–21.77	32.78–22.86	24.92–14.39
P/E Ratio	26.33–22.35	24.62–13.96	56.77–23.30	15.38–9.39	12.67–7.95	19.30–12.96	22.60–15.77	20.26–11.70
Average Yield %	1.68	2.09	1.82	1.70	1.88	1.03	0.90	1.14

Address: 100 North Michigan Street, South Bend, IN 46601
Telephone: (574) 235–2000
Web Site: www.1stsource.com

Officers: Christopher J. Murphy III – Chmn., Pres., C.E.O., Wellington D. Jones III – Exec. V.P.
Transfer Agents: 1st Source Bank, South Bend, IN

Investor Contact: 574–235–2702
Institutional Holding
No of Institutions: 3
Shares: 5,238   **% Held:** –

1

3M CO

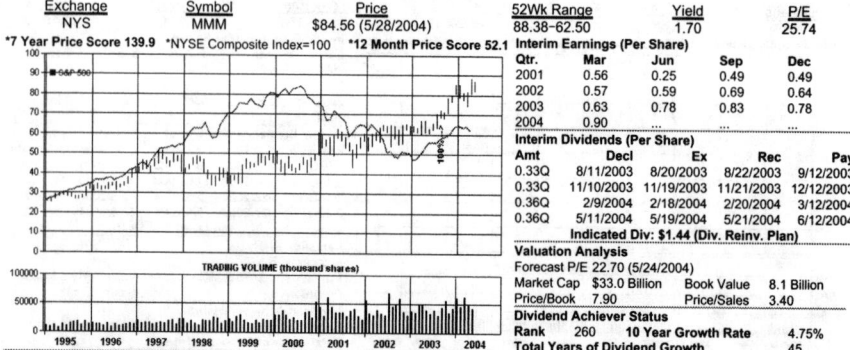

Exchange	Symbol	Price	52Wk Range	Yield	P/E
NYS	MMM	$84.56 (5/28/2004)	88.38-62.50	1.70	25.74

*7 Year Price Score 139.9   *NYSE Composite Index=100   *12 Month Price Score 52.1

Interim Earnings (Per Share)

Qtr.	Mar	Jun	Sep	Dec
2001	0.56	0.25	0.49	0.49
2002	0.57	0.59	0.69	0.64
2003	0.63	0.78	0.83	0.78
2004	0.90	...	...	...

Interim Dividends (Per Share)

Amt	Decl	Ex	Rec	Pay
0.33Q	8/11/2003	8/20/2003	8/22/2003	9/12/2003
0.33Q	11/10/2003	11/19/2003	11/21/2003	12/12/2003
0.36Q	2/9/2004	2/18/2004	2/20/2004	3/12/2004
0.36Q	5/11/2004	5/19/2004	5/21/2004	6/12/2004

Indicated Div: $1.44 (Div. Reinv. Plan)

Valuation Analysis

Forecast P/E 22.70 (5/24/2004)

Market Cap	$33.0 Billion	Book Value	8.1 Billion
Price/Book	7.90	Price/Sales	3.40

Dividend Achiever Status

Rank	260	10 Year Growth Rate	4.75%
Total Years of Dividend Growth			45

TRADING VOLUME (thousand shares)

Business Summary: Chemicals (MIC: 11.1 SIC: 2891 NAIC:325520)

3M is a diversified technology company with positions in health care, industrial, display and graphics, consumer and office, safety, security and protection services, electronics, telecommunications and electrical, and transportation. In the U.S., Co. has 12 sales offices in 10 states and operates 61 manufacturing facilities in 23 states. Internationally, Co. has 185 sales offices, and operates 75 manufacturing and converting facilities in 28 countries. Co.'s brands include icons such as *Scotch, Post-it, Scotchgard, Thinsulate, Scotch-Brite, Filtrete, Dyneon and O-Cel-O.*

Recent Developments: For the year ended Dec 31 2003, net income rose 21.7% to $2.40 billion from $1.97 billion the year before. Earnings for 2003 and 2002 included after-tax charges of $58.0 million and $108.0 million, respectively, related to restructuring and other one-time charges. Net sales grew 11.6% to $18.23 billion. Health care sales improved 12.2% to $4.00 billion, while industrial sales rose 6.6% to $3.35 billion. Display and graphics sales advanced 32.9% to $2.96 billion, and consumer and office sales increased 6.7% to $2.61 billion. Safety, security and protection services sales grew 14.4% to $1.93 billion, while transportation sales rose 10.8% to $1.54 billion.

Prospects: After weathering a difficult business environment through much of 2003, Co. believes that it is well positioned for solid business growth in the coming year as corporate initiatives are helping to drive improvements in productivity, cash flow and top-line growth. For 2004, Co. expects earnings per share to range from $0.80 to $0.82 in the first quarter and between $3.46 and $3.52 for the full year. Sales volumes are expected to grow between 5.0% and 8.0% in 2004. Separately, on Jan 12 2003, Co. entered into an agreement to acquire Hornell International, a global supplier of protective equipment for welding applications based in Sweden, in a cash transaction valued at about $100.0 million.

Financial Data

(US$ in Millions)	3 Mos	12/31/2003	12/31/2002	12/31/2001	12/31/2000	12/31/1999	12/31/1998	12/31/1997
Earnings Per Share	3.29	3.02	2.49	1.79	2.32	2.17	1.48	2.53
Cash Flow Per Share	1.17	4.74	3.78	3.84	2.90	3.73	2.90	2.03
Tang. Book Val. Per Share	6.75	6.62	4.90	6.17	7.16	7.06	7.40	7.31
Dividends Per Share	1.350	1.320	1.240	1.200	1.160	1.120	1.100	1.060
Dividend Payout %	41.16	43.70	49.69	67.03	50.00	51.61	74.07	41.89
Income Statement								
Total Revenues	4,939	18,232	16,332	16,054	16,724	15,659	15,021	15,070
Total Indirect Exp.	1,386	5,234	4,790	5,032	4,879	3,851	4,238	3,815
Depreciation & Amort.	252	964	954	1,089	1,025	900	866	870
Operating Income	1,117	3,713	3,046	2,273	3,058	2,956	2,039	2,675
Net Interest Inc./(Exp.)	(9)	(56)	(41)	(87)	(111)	(109)	(139)	(94)
Income Taxes	366	1,202	966	702	1,025	1,032	685	1,241
Income from Cont Ops	...	...	...	...	1,857	...	1,213	...
Net Income	722	2,403	1,974	1,430	1,782	1,763	1,175	2,121
Average Shs. Outstg.	799	795	791	799	799	813	816	838
Balance Sheet								
Cash & Cash Equivalents	1,818	1,836	618	616	302	387	211	230
Total Current Assets	8,063	7,720	6,059	6,296	6,379	6,066	6,318	6,168
Total Assets	17,978	17,600	15,329	14,606	14,522	13,896	14,153	13,238
Total Current Liabilities	5,163	5,082	4,457	4,509	4,754	3,819	4,386	3,983
Long-Term Obligations	1,718	1,805	2,140	1,520	971	1,480	1,614	1,015
Net Stockholders' Equity	8,101	7,885	5,993	6,086	6,531	6,289	5,936	5,926
Net Working Capital	2,900	2,638	1,602	1,787	1,625	2,247	1,932	2,185
Shares Outstanding	782	784	780	782	792	797	802	810
Statistical Record								
Operating Profit Margin %	22.61	20.36	18.65	14.15	18.28	18.87	13.57	17.75
Return on Equity %	8.91	30.47	32.93	23.49	28.43	28.03	20.43	35.79
Return on Assets %	4.01	13.65	12.87	9.79	12.78	12.68	8.57	16.02
Debt/Total Assets %	9.55	10.25	13.96	10.40	6.68	10.65	11.40	7.66
Price Range	85.48-74.87	85.25-60.51	65.49-51.85	62.75-43.49	60.97-39.50	51.41-34.94	48.72-34.00	51.75-40.50
P/E Ratio	25.98-22.76	28.23-20.03	26.30-20.82	35.06-24.30	26.28-17.03	23.69-16.10	32.92-22.97	20.45-16.01
Average Yield %	1.68	1.92	2.04	2.26	2.52	2.56	2.64	2.32

Address: 3M Center, St. Paul, MN 55144-1000
Telephone: (651) 733-1110
Web Site: www.3m.com

Officers: W. James McNerney – Chmn., C.E.O., Joseph A. Giordano – Exec. V.P., Intl. Oper.
Transfer Agents: Wells Fargo Shareowner Services, St. Paul, MN

Investor Contact: 651-733-8206
Institutional Holding
No of Institutions: 5
Shares: 222,885   **% Held:** –

ABBOTT LABORATORIES

Exchange	Symbol	Price	52Wk Range	Yield	P/E
NYS	ABT	$41.21 (5/28/2004)	47.15–37.85	2.52	23.41

*7 Year Price Score 98.5 ***NYSE Composite Index=100** ***12 Month Price Score 45.1**

Interim Earnings (Per Share)

Qtr.	Mar	Jun	Sep	Dec
2001	(0.14)	0.34	0.40	0.39
2002	0.54	0.38	0.46	0.40
2003	0.51	0.16	0.48	0.60
2004	0.52	...	...	...

Interim Dividends (Per Share)

Amt	Decl	Ex	Rec	Pay
0.245Q	6/20/2003	7/11/2003	7/15/2003	8/15/2003
0.245Q	9/12/2003	10/10/2003	10/15/2003	11/15/2003
0.245Q	12/12/2003	1/13/2004	1/15/2004	2/15/2004
0.26Q	2/20/2004	4/13/2004	4/15/2004	5/15/2004

Indicated Div: $1.04 (Div. Reinv. Plan)

Valuation Analysis

Forecast P/E 17.32 (5/24/2004)

Market Cap $64.4 Billion	Book Value	13.5 Billion
Price/Book 4.74	Price/Sales	3.15

Dividend Achiever Status

Rank 133	10 Year Growth Rate	11.38%
Total Years of Dividend Growth		31

TRADING VOLUME (thousand shares)

Business Summary: Pharmaceuticals (MIC: 9.1 SIC: 2834 NAIC:325412)

Abbott Laboratories' principal business is the discovery, development, manufacture, and sale of health care products has five reportable revenue segments. The Pharmaceutical Products segment's products include a line of adult and pediatric pharmaceuticals. The Diagnostic Products segment's products include diagnostic systems and tests. The Hospital Products segment's products include acute care injectable drugs and systems. The Ross Products segment's products include a line of pediatric and adult nutritionals. The International segment's products include products marketed and primarily manufactured outside the U.S.

Recent Developments: For the three months ended Mar 31 2004, net earnings increased 2.7% to $822.9 million from $801.0 million in the corresponding quarter of the previous year. Results for 2004 included pre–tax acquired in–process research and development charges of $59.9 million. Net sales advanced 13.9% to $5.22 billion from $4.58 billion in the year–earlier period. The improvement in sales was largely due to unit growth and the positive effect of the relatively weaker U.S. dollar. Operating income climbed 5.3% to $1.03 billion versus $980.5 million in the prior–year quarter.

Prospects: Results continue to benefit from strong growth in Co.'s Medical Products Group due to strength in U.S. sales of nutritionals and vascular devices. Co.'s diagnostics division is benefiting from the award of new contracts and the launch of 17 diagnostic products, including the cardiac marker, BNP. Meanwhile, Co.'s Pharmaceutical Products Group continues to benefit from the international launch of *Humira*. Looking ahead, Co. remains on track for a second–quarter spin–off of Hospira. Moreover, Co. continues to expect earnings to range from $2.40 to $2.48 per share for 2004. Co. is projecting worldwide sales of more than $1.20 billion for 2005.

Financial Data
(US$ in Thousands)

	3 Mos	12/31/2003	12/31/2002	12/31/2001	12/31/2000	12/31/1999	12/31/1998	12/31/1997
Earnings Per Share	1.76	1.75	1.78	0.99	1.78	1.57	1.51	1.34
Cash Flow Per Share	0.86	2.38	2.65	2.27	1.97	1.88	1.76	1.68
Tang. Book Val. Per Share	2.82	2.89	1.92	1.13	4.53	3.78	2.87	2.54
Dividends Per Share	0.980	0.970	0.910	0.820	0.740	0.660	0.580	0.520
Dividend Payout %	55.68	55.42	51.40	82.82	41.57	42.03	38.74	39.17
Income Statement								
Total Revenues	5,216,053	19,680,561	17,684,663	16,285,246	13,745,916	13,177,625	12,477,845	11,883,462
Total Indirect Exp.	1,703,606	6,884,613	5,648,268	6,642,832	3,968,188	4,051,067	3,965,481	3,987,338
Depreciation & Amort.	327,421	1,273,991	1,177,345	1,168,018	827,431	828,006	784,243	727,754
Operating Income	1,032,166	3,322,532	3,530,141	1,894,032	3,400,575	3,149,375	3,117,923	2,850,426
Net Interest Inc./(Exp.)	(35,345)	(146,123)	(205,220)	(234,759)	(23,221)	(81,765)	(104,118)	(86,802)
Income Taxes	286,475	981,184	879,710	332,758	1,030,430	951,129	907,368	855,484
Net Income	822,900	2,753,233	2,793,703	1,550,390	2,785,977	2,445,759	2,333,231	2,094,462
Average Shs. Outstg.	1,572,119	1,571,869	1,573,293	1,565,963	1,565,579	1,557,655	1,545,658	1,561,462
Balance Sheet								
Cash & Cash Equivalents	1,123,984	995,124	704,450	657,378	914,218	608,097	308,230	230,024
Total Current Assets	10,942,822	10,290,415	9,121,772	8,419,189	7,376,241	6,419,754	5,553,136	5,038,208
Total Assets	28,053,333	26,715,342	24,259,102	23,296,423	15,283,254	14,471,044	13,216,213	12,061,068
Total Current Liabilities	6,953,971	7,639,535	7,002,202	7,926,817	4,297,540	4,516,711	4,962,126	5,034,468
Long–Term Obligations	4,957,253	3,452,329	4,273,973	4,335,493	1,076,368	1,336,789	1,339,694	937,983
Net Stockholders' Equity	13,512,042	13,072,258	10,664,553	9,059,432	8,570,906	7,427,595	5,713,661	4,998,677
Net Working Capital	3,988,851	2,650,880	2,119,570	492,372	3,078,701	1,903,043	591,010	3,740
Shares Outstanding	1,559,676	1,564,511	1,563,068	1,554,530	1,545,934	1,547,019	1,516,063	1,528,188
Statistical Record								
Operating Profit Margin %	19.78	16.88	19.96	11.63	25.74	23.89	24.98	23.98
Return on Equity %	6.09	21.06	26.19	17.11	34.12	32.92	40.83	41.90
Return on Assets %	2.93	10.30	11.51	6.65	19.13	16.90	17.65	17.36
Debt/Total Assets %	17.67	12.92	17.61	18.61	7.04	9.23	10.13	7.77
Price Range	46.90–39.35	47.15–34.38	57.70–31.00	56.77–42.06	55.75–29.63	52.94–33.38	49.75–32.78	34.31–25.19
P/E Ratio	26.65–22.36	26.94–19.65	32.42–17.42	57.34–42.49	31.32–16.64	33.72–21.26	32.95–21.71	25.61–18.80
Average Yield %	2.27	2.35	1.98	1.64	1.78	1.51	1.42	1.69

Address: 100 Abbott Park Road, Abbott Park, IL 60064–6400 **Telephone:** (847) 937 6100 **Web Site:** www.abbott.com	**Officers:** Miles D. White – Chmn., C.E.O., Richard A. Gonzalez – Pres., C.O.O., Medical Products **Transfer Agents:** EquiServe, Providence, RI	**Investor Contact:** 847–937–3923 **Institutional Holding No of Institutions:** 1,079 **Shares:** 979,957,364 **% Held:** 62.80%

ABM INDUSTRIES, INC.

Exchange	Symbol	Price	52Wk Range	Yield	P/E
NYS	ABM	$19.02 (5/28/2004)	19.15-14.10	2.10	24.38

*7 Year Price Score 111.8   *NYSE Composite Index=100   ***12 Month Price Score 52.0**

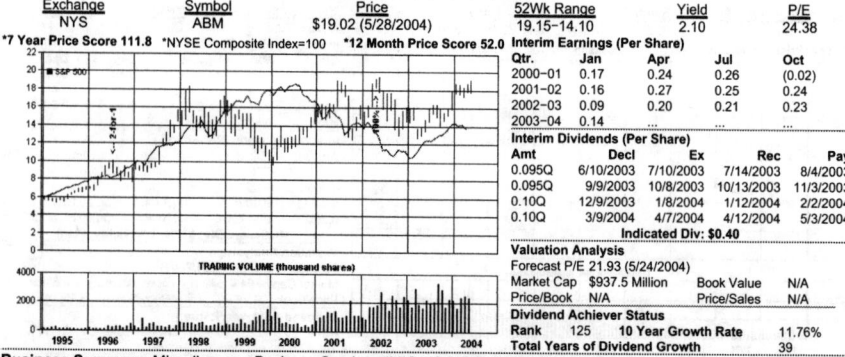

Interim Earnings (Per Share)

Qtr.	Jan	Apr	Jul	Oct
2000-01	0.17	0.24	0.26	(0.02)
2001-02	0.16	0.27	0.25	0.24
2002-03	0.09	0.20	0.21	0.23
2003-04	0.14	...	...	...

Interim Dividends (Per Share)

Amt	Decl	Ex	Rec	Pay
0.095Q	6/10/2003	7/10/2003	7/14/2003	8/4/2003
0.095Q	9/9/2003	10/8/2003	10/13/2003	11/3/2003
0.10Q	12/9/2003	1/8/2004	1/12/2004	2/2/2004
0.10Q	3/9/2004	4/7/2004	4/12/2004	5/3/2004

Indicated Div: $0.40

Valuation Analysis

Forecast P/E 21.93 (5/24/2004)

Market Cap	$937.5 Million	Book Value	N/A
Price/Book	N/A	Price/Sales	N/A

Dividend Achiever Status

Rank   125   10 Year Growth Rate   11.76%

Total Years of Dividend Growth   39

Business Summary: Miscellaneous Business Services (MIC: 12.8 SIC: 7349 NAIC:238210)

ABM Industries and its subsidiaries provide janitorial, parking, engineering, security, lighting and mechanical services for thousands of commercial, industrial, institutional and retail facilities in hundreds of cities in the United States and British Columbia, Canada. Co. conducts business through a number of subsidiaries, which are grouped into seven segments based on the nature of the business operations. Co.'s "ABM Family of Services" is comprised of seven segments: Janitorial, Parking, Engineering, Security, Lighting, Mechanical and Facility Services.

Recent Developments: For the quarter ended Jan 31 2004, net income surged 90.8% to $7.2 million compared with income of $3.8 million, before income from discontinued operations of $588,000, in the equivalent 2003 quarter. The improvement in earnings was primarily attributed to higher operating results from Co.'s Janitorial, Engineering, Parking and Security segment, and, to a lesser extent, the positive impact of Janitorial and Parking acquisitions completed in the last nine months of fiscal year 2003. This was partially offset by lack of growth in capital project sales from the Lighting segment. Sales and other income grew 3.3% to $570.8 million from $552.4 million a year earlier.

Prospects: On Apr 5 2004, Co. announced the acquisition of substantially all of the commercial janitorial assets of the Northeast United States Division of Initial Contract Services, Inc. The acquisition represents approximately $30.0 million in annual contract revenue. On Apr 16, 2004, Co. announced that it has been awarded a multi-year, multi-million dollar contract renewal for Gateway Village to provide comprehensive cleaning services and maintenance for all of the commercial office areas and restaurants at Gateway Village, a development comprising over one million square feet of business, residential and retail properties in Charlotte, NC.

Financial Data

(US$ in Thousands)	3 Mos	10/31/2003	10/31/2002	10/31/2001	10/31/2000	10/31/1999	10/31/1998	10/31/1997
Earnings Per Share	0.78	0.73	0.92	0.65	0.92	0.82	0.72	0.61
Cash Flow Per Share	(0.33)	1.20	2.17	1.31	0.39	0.74	0.69	0.63
Tang. Book Val. Per Share	5.08	5.00	4.46	5.08	4.48	3.82	3.11	2.38
Dividends Per Share	0.380	0.370	0.350	0.320	0.300	0.270	0.230	0.190
Dividend Payout %	20.43	51.36	38.31	50.00	32.70	32.72	31.94	31.76
Income Statement								
Total Revenues	570,823	2,262,476	2,191,957	1,950,038	1,807,557	1,629,716	1,501,827	1,252,472
Total Indirect Exp.	42,557	172,651	176,931	177,361	164,186	150,902	149,361	132,105
Depreciation & Amort.	3,475	14,829	15,182	26,328	23,524	20,698	19,593	16,118
Operating Income	11,431	54,852	69,328	52,945	72,693	67,232	57,508	46,964
Net Interest Inc./(Exp.)	(250)	(758)	(1,052)	(2,602)	(3,320)	(1,959)	(3,465)	(2,675)
Income Taxes	4,025	18,454	22,600	20,119	28,350	27,565	23,578	19,725
Income from Cont Ops	...	36,398	...	...	...	...	...	...
Net Income	7,156	90,458	46,728	32,826	44,343	39,667	33,930	27,239
Average Shs. Outstg.	49,785	50,004	51,015	50,020	47,418	47,496	46,322	43,744
Balance Sheet								
Cash & Cash Equivalents	90,705	110,947	19,427	3,052	2,000	2,139	1,844	1,783
Total Current Assets	492,766	500,648	437,785	465,541	436,819	367,589	324,308	294,417
Total Assets	789,325	795,983	704,939	683,100	641,985	563,384	501,363	467,152
Total Current Liabilities	243,178	256,691	227,090	235,999	212,620	183,310	157,824	156,660
Long-Term Obligations	...	...	...	942	36,811	28,903	33,720	38,402
Net Stockholders' Equity	449,071	444,036	386,670	361,177	309,909	270,551	231,134	191,413
Net Working Capital	249,588	243,957	210,695	229,542	224,199	184,279	166,484	137,757
Shares Outstanding	48,583	48,367	48,997	48,778	45,998	44,814	43,202	40,928
Statistical Record								
Operating Profit Margin %	2.00	2.39	3.11	2.58	3.83	4.00	3.59	3.53
Return on Equity %	1.59	8.02	11.81	8.36	12.96	13.61	12.82	12.41
Return on Assets %	0.90	4.47	6.47	4.42	6.39	6.69	6.07	5.25
Debt/Total Assets %	...	...	...	0.13	5.43	5.13	6.72	8.22
Price Range	18.80-15.25	16.44-12.72	19.43-13.05	19.10-12.50	13.97-9.69	17.31-11.00	18.41-12.63	14.53-7.75
P/E Ratio	24.10-19.55	22.52-17.42	21.12-14.18	29.38-19.23	15.18-10.53	21.11-13.41	25.56-17.53	23.82-12.70
Average Yield %	2.26	2.49	2.16	2.02	2.49	1.87	1.56	1.85

Address: 160 Pacific Avenue, San Francisco, CA 94111

Telephone: (415) 733-4000

Web Site: www.abm.com

Officers: Martin H. Mandles - Chmn., Chief Admin. Officer, Henrik C. Slipsager - Pres., C.E.O.

Transfer Agents: Mellon Investor Services LLC San Francisco, CA

Institutional Holding

No of Institutions: 18

Shares: 1,114,212   % Held: -

AFLAC INC.

Exchange	Symbol	Price	52Wk Range	Yield	P/E
NYS	AFL	$40.60 (5/28/2004)	42.23-30.10	0.94	24.17

*7 Year Price Score 136.6   *NYSE Composite Index=100   *12 Month Price Score 53.3

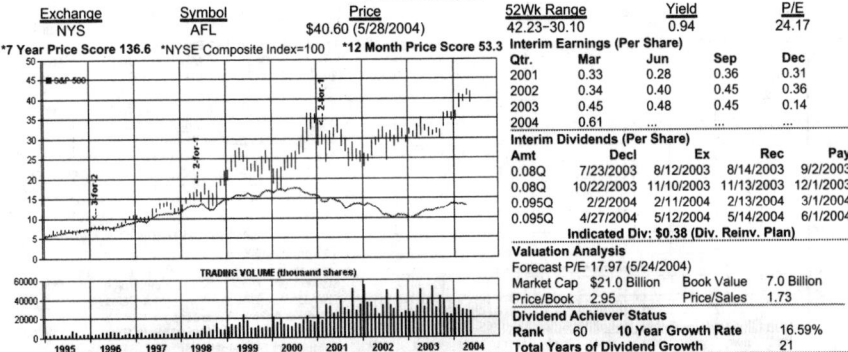

Interim Earnings (Per Share)

Qtr.	Mar	Jun	Sep	Dec
2001	0.33	0.28	0.36	0.31
2002	0.34	0.40	0.45	0.36
2003	0.45	0.48	0.45	0.14
2004	0.61	...	...	...

Interim Dividends (Per Share)

Amt	Decl	Ex	Rec	Pay
0.08Q	7/23/2003	8/12/2003	8/14/2003	9/2/2003
0.08Q	10/22/2003	11/10/2003	11/13/2003	12/1/2003
0.095Q	2/2/2004	2/11/2004	2/13/2004	3/1/2004
0.095Q	4/27/2004	5/12/2004	5/14/2004	6/1/2004
Indicated Div: $0.38 (Div. Reinv. Plan)				

Valuation Analysis

Forecast P/E 17.97 (5/24/2004)

Market Cap $21.0 Billion		Book Value	7.0 Billion
Price/Book 2.95		Price/Sales	1.73

Dividend Achiever Status

Rank	60	10 Year Growth Rate	16.59%
Total Years of Dividend Growth		21	

TRADING VOLUME (thousand shares)

Business Summary: Insurance (MIC: 8.2 SIC: 6321 NAIC:524114)

AFLAC is an international insurance organization whose principal subsidiary is American Family Life Assurance Company of Columbus. In addition to life, and health & accident insurance, Co. has pioneered cancer–expense and intensive–care insurance coverage. Co.'s subsidiary Communicorp specializes in printing, advertising, audio–visuals, sales incentives, business meetings and mailings. As of Feb 2 2004, Co. insured more than 40.0 million people worldwide, and offered policies to employees through 288,100 payroll accounts. Also, Co. insures one out of four Japanese households and is the second largest life insurer in Japan in terms of individual policies in force.

Recent Developments: For the quarter ended Mar 31 2004, net income advanced 32.9% to $315.0 million compared with $237.0 million in the corresponding period of the prior year. Net income included realized investment gains of $6.0 million in 2004 versus realized investment losses of $7.0 million in 2003. Results for the first quarter of 2004 also included non–recurring gains totaling $14.0 million. Total revenues advanced 16.8% to $3.28 billion from $2.81 billion a year earlier, primarily due to favorable foreign currency translation. Operating earnings were $295.0 million, up 21.2% from the year before.

Prospects: Looking ahead, Co. remains optimistic regarding opportunities in the U.S. Co. plans to tap into that potential by continuing to expand its distribution system and by broadening its product line. For the full year, Co.'s objective is a 10.0% to 12.0% increase in U.S. sales. Moreover, Co. expects Japanese sales in the second half of the year to benefit from new promotional campaigns and product enhancements. Meanwhile, Co.'s goal for 2004 is to increase operating earnings per diluted share 17.0%, excluding the impact of the yen. For 2005, Co.'s objective is to increase operations earnings per diluted share by 15.0%, excluding the impact of foreign currency translation.

Financial Data

(US$ in Thousands)	3 Mos	12/31/2003	12/31/2002	12/31/2001	12/31/2000	12/31/1999	12/31/1998	12/31/1997
Earnings Per Share	1.68	1.52	1.55	1.28	1.26	1.03	0.88	1.04
Tang. Book Val. Per Share	10.72	13.03	12.42	10.40	8.86	7.27	7.09	6.43
Dividends Per Share	0.320	0.300	0.230	0.190	0.160	0.140	0.120	0.110
Dividend Payout %	19.35	19.73	14.83	15.03	13.09	14.00	14.34	10.69
Income Statement								
Total Premium Income	2,773,000	9,921,000	8,595,000	8,061,000	8,239,000	7,264,000	5,943,000	5,873,661
Other Income	507,000	1,526,000	1,662,000	1,537,000	1,481,000	1,376,000	1,161,000	1,109,818
Total Revenues	3,280,000	11,447,000	10,257,000	9,598,000	9,720,000	8,640,000	7,104,000	6,983,479
Total Indirect Exp.	162,000	543,000	510,000	396,000	273,000	387,000	386,000	286,591
Inc. Before Inc. Taxes	478,000	1,225,000	1,259,000	1,081,000	1,012,000	778,000	551,000	864,820
Income Taxes	163,000	430,000	438,000	394,000	325,000	207,000	64,000	279,797
Net Income	315,000	795,000	821,000	687,000	687,000	571,000	487,000	585,023
Average Shs. Outstg.	519,355	522,138	528,326	537,380	544,906	550,846	551,744	563,192
Balance Sheet								
Cash & Cash Equivalents	1,169,000	1,052,000	1,379,000	852,000	609,000	616,000	374,000	235,675
Premiums Due	442,000	1,003,000	849,000	728,000	681,000	639,000	588,000	480,609
Invst. Assets: Total	45,610,000	42,999,000	37,768,000	31,941,000	31,558,000	31,408,000	26,610,000	22,600,891
Total Assets	53,289,000	50,964,000	45,058,000	37,860,000	37,232,000	37,041,000	31,183,000	29,454,005
Long–Term Obligations	1,423,000	1,409,000	1,312,000	1,207,000	1,079,000	1,111,000	596,000	523,209
Net Stockholders' Equity	6,993,000	6,646,000	6,394,000	5,425,000	4,694,000	3,868,000	3,770,000	3,430,472
Shares Outstanding	652,059	509,892	514,439	521,615	529,209	531,482	531,368	532,872
Statistical Record								
Return on Revenues %	9.42	6.94	8.00	7.15	7.06	6.60	6.85	4.55
Return on Equity %	4.41	11.96	12.84	12.66	14.63	14.76	12.91	9.26
Return on Assets %	0.57	1.55	1.82	1.81	1.84	1.54	1.56	1.07
Price Range	41.17–34.95	36.67–30.08	33.17–23.12	34.83–23.01	36.53–17.19	27.81–19.88	22.00–11.73	14.19–9.38
P/E Ratio	24.51–20.80	24.13–19.79	21.40–14.92	27.21–17.98	28.99–13.64	27.00–19.30	25.00–13.33	13.64–9.01
Average Yield %	0.83	0.92	0.78	0.66	0.60	0.59	0.74	0.92

Address: 1932 Wynnton Road, Columbus, GA 31999 Telephone: (706) 323–3431 Web Site: www.aflac.com	Officers: Daniel P. Amos – Chmn., C.E.O., Kriss Cloninger III – Pres., C.F.O., Treas. Transfer Agents:AFLAC Incorporated, Columbus, GA	Investor Contact:706–596–3264 Institutional Holding No of Institutions: 41 Shares: 5,225,868 % Held: –

AIR PRODUCTS & CHEMICALS, INC.

Exchange	Symbol	Price	52Wk Range	Yield	P/E
NYS	APD	$49.97 (5/28/2004)	55.00–41.07	2.32	26.30

*7 Year Price Score 116.0   *NYSE Composite Index=100   *12 Month Price Score 48.5

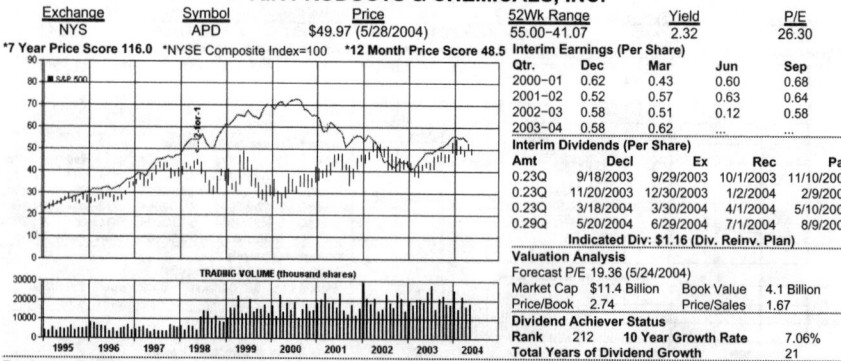

Interim Earnings (Per Share)

Qtr.	Dec	Mar	Jun	Sep
2000–01	0.62	0.43	0.60	0.68
2001–02	0.52	0.57	0.63	0.64
2002–03	0.58	0.51	0.12	0.58
2003–04	0.58	0.62	...	...

Interim Dividends (Per Share)

Amt	Decl	Ex	Rec	Pay
0.23Q	9/18/2003	9/29/2003	10/1/2003	11/10/2003
0.23Q	11/20/2003	12/30/2003	1/2/2004	2/9/2004
0.23Q	3/18/2004	3/30/2004	4/1/2004	5/10/2004
0.29Q	5/20/2004	6/29/2004	7/1/2004	8/9/2004

Indicated Div: $1.16 (Div. Reinv. Plan)

Valuation Analysis

Forecast P/E 19.36 (5/24/2004)

Market Cap	$11.4 Billion	Book Value	4.1 Billion
Price/Book	2.74	Price/Sales	1.67

Dividend Achiever Status

Rank	212	10 Year Growth Rate	7.06%
Total Years of Dividend Growth			21

Business Summary: Chemicals (MIC: 11.1 SIC: 2813 NAIC:325120)

Air Products & Chemicals is engaged in the business of industrial gas and related industrial process equipment and is a producer of certain chemicals. The gases business segment recovers and distributes industrial gases such as oxygen, nitrogen, argon, hydrogen, carbon monoxide, carbon dioxide, synthesis gas and helium. The chemicals business segment produces and markets performance materials and chemical intermediates. The equipment business segment designs and manufactures equipment for cryogenic air separation, gas processing, natural gas liquefaction, and hydrogen purification.

Recent Developments: For the three months ended Mar 31 2004, net income rose 24.3% to $141.2 million compared with $113.6 million in the equivalent quarter of 2003. Results for 2003 included global cost reduction plans of $200,000. Sales amounted to $1.86 billion, up 17.6% from $1.58 billion in the prior–year period. Revenues benefited from stronger volumes across Co.'s gases and chemicals segments, acquisitions, and favorable currency effects. Operating income increased 19.2% to $210.1 million compared with $176.3 million the year before. Operating income reflected improved asset loadings and volume growth, partially offset by higher costs.

Prospects: Co. expects earnings in the second half of fiscal 2004 to improve due to solid volume gains during the first half and improved manufacturing in North America and Asia. As a result, Co. is projecting earnings per share in the range of $2.45 to $2.65 for fiscal 2004 and between $0.63 and $0.68 for the third quarter of fiscal 2004. Separately, on Apr 22 2004, Co. sold certain assets related to its European methylamines and derivatives business to Taminco for an undisclosed amount. The transaction excludes Co.'s North American methylamines business and the global higher amines business. The sale is strategically in line with Co.'s plans to focus on high value growth platforms.

Financial Data

(US$ in Thousands)	6 Mos	3 Mos	09/30/2003	09/30/2002	09/30/2001	09/30/2000	09/30/1999	09/30/1998
Earnings Per Share	1.90	1.79	1.79	2.36	2.33	0.57	2.09	2.48
Cash Flow Per Share	1.63	0.90	4.63	4.77	4.94	5.43	5.04	4.42
Tang. Book Val. Per Share	14.46	13.64	12.99	13.33	13.67	12.30	11.38	11.07
Dividends Per Share	0.900	0.880	0.860	0.810	0.770	0.730	0.690	0.620
Dividend Payout %	47.36	49.16	48.04	34.32	33.04	128.07	33.01	25.00
Income Statement								
Total Revenues	3,541,400	1,684,900	6,297,300	5,401,200	5,742,000	5,493,100	5,065,600	4,942,100
Total Indirect Exp.	532,700	255,900	1,042,900	757,700	894,000	857,000	832,800	1,250,900
Depreciation & Amort.	347,200	170,400	10,300	3,800	19,400	17,900	19,100	18,600
Operating Income	408,900	198,800	604,500	774,900	745,400	830,800	724,700	845,000
Net Interest Inc./(Exp.)	(63,200)	(30,900)	(119,700)	(117,400)	(191,200)	(196,700)	(159,100)	(162,800)
Income Taxes	106,200	51,300	147,200	240,800	219,000	(13,700)	203,400	276,900
Eqty Earns/Minority Int.	33,500	15,200	66,400	57,900	76,100	80,000	46,400	38,000
Income from Cont Ops	...	...	400,200	...	512,900	...	...	...
Net Income	273,000	131,800	397,300	525,400	465,600	124,200	450,500	546,800
Average Shs. Outstg.	227,900	227,000	223,600	222,700	219,300	216,200	216,000	220,100
Balance Sheet								
Cash & Cash Equivalents	142,300	92,900	76,200	253,700	66,200	94,100	61,600	61,500
Total Current Assets	2,325,500	2,214,700	2,067,900	1,909,300	1,684,800	1,805,000	1,782,400	1,641,700
Total Assets	9,962,500	9,786,600	9,431,900	8,495,000	8,084,100	8,270,500	8,235,500	7,489,600
Total Current Liabilities	1,899,600	1,441,400	1,581,200	1,256,200	1,352,400	1,374,800	1,857,800	1,265,600
Long–Term Obligations	2,008,500	2,373,700	2,168,600	2,041,000	2,027,500	2,615,800	1,961,600	2,274,300
Net Stockholders' Equity	4,141,000	3,982,500	3,782,500	3,460,400	3,105,800	2,821,300	2,961,600	2,667,300
Net Working Capital	425,900	773,300	486,700	653,100	332,400	430,200	(75,400)	376,100
Shares Outstanding	224,081	227,265	227,265	227,219	227,186	229,305	229,304	211,500
Statistical Record								
Operating Profit Margin %	11.54	11.79	10.18	15.10	13.31	15.08	14.81	17.26
Return on Equity %	...	3.30	11.55	16.36	17.13	4.31	16.08	20.81
Return on Assets %	...	1.34	4.63	6.66	6.58	1.47	5.78	7.41
Debt/Total Assets %	...	24.25	22.99	24.02	25.08	31.62	23.81	30.36
Price Range	55.00–44.50	53.07–44.50	48.64–37.49	53.05–36.82	48.00–32.94	39.00–24.19	49.00–27.94	45.13–29.75
P/E Ratio	28.95–23.42	29.65–24.86	27.17–20.94	22.48–15.60	20.60–14.14	68.42–42.43	23.44–13.37	18.20–12.00
Average Yield %	1.84	1.83	1.99	1.74	1.90	2.32	1.85	1.58

Address: 7201 Hamilton Boulevard, Allentown, PA 18195–1501 Telephone: (610) 481-4911 Web Site: www.airproducts.com	Officers: John P. Jones III – Chmn., Pres., C.E.O., Mark L. Bye – Exec. V.P., Gases & Equipment Transfer Agents: American Stock Transfer &Trust Company, New York, NY	Investor Contact:610-481-5775 Institutional Holding No of Institutions: 4 Shares: 107,686 % Held: –

ALBERTO–CULVER CO.

Exchange	Symbol	Price	52Wk Range	Yield	P/E
NYS	ACV	$47.02 (5/28/2004)	48.00–33.10	0.85	33.11

*7 Year Price Score 155.0 ***NYSE Composite Index=100** ***12 Month Price Score 54.1**

Interim Earnings (Per Share)

Qtr.	Dec	Mar	Jun	Sep
2000–01	0.27	0.30	0.33	0.37
2001–02	0.33	0.36	0.40	0.45
2002–03	0.40	0.42	0.47	0.51
2003–04	0.02	0.44	...	...

Interim Dividends (Per Share)

Amt	Decl	Ex	Rec	Pay
0.09Q	10/24/2002	10/31/2002	11/4/2002	11/20/2002
0.105Q	1/23/2003	1/30/2003	2/3/2003	2/20/2003
0.105Q	4/24/2003	5/1/2003	5/5/2003	5/20/2003
0.105Q	7/24/2003	7/31/2003	8/4/2003	8/20/2003

Indicated Div: $0.40

Valuation Analysis

Forecast P/E 22.00 (5/24/2004)

Market Cap	$1.5 Billion	Book Value	1.2 Billion
Price/Book	3.26	Price/Sales	1.28

Dividend Achiever Status

Rank	113	10 Year Growth Rate	12.44%
Total Years of Dividend Growth			19

Business Summary: Chemicals (MIC: 11.1 SIC: 2844 NAIC:325620)

Alberto–Culver operates under two business segments. The Global Consumer Products segment develops, manufactures, and markets beauty, health care, food and household products to the U.S., Canada and internationally. Major products include *Alberto V05, St. Ives, TRESemme, Motions, Just for Me, Mrs. Dash* and *Molly McButter*. Co.'s second business, Sally Beauty Company, is comprised of two operations: Sally Beauty Supply, a chain of cash–and–carry outlets offering professional beauty supplies to both salon professionals and retail consumers, and Beauty Systems Group, a full–service beauty products distributor offering professional brands to salons and through professional–only stores.

Recent Developments: For the quarter ended Mar 31 2004, net income rose 7.2% to $40.6 million from $37.9 million in the prior-year quarter. Results for 2004 included a non-cash charge of $8.1 million related to the conversion to one class of common stock. Net sales advanced 15.9% to $819.3 million from $707.0 million the previous year, driven by strength in Co.'s consumer products and professional beauty supply distribution businesses. Gross profit grew 16.7% to $417.5 million. Advertising, marketing, selling and administrative expenses climbed 16.4% to $341.1 million. Operating income was $68.3 million, up 5.2% from $64.9 million the year before.

Prospects: Looking ahead, Co. has indicated that it will continue to focus on growing its Sally Beauty Supply business domestically and internationally. During the first quarter, Sally expanded to 2,087 stores in North America, including its first Canadian store in the Toronto area, and to 227 international stores in the U.K., Germany, and Japan. Meanwhile, the Beauty Systems Group grew its number of stores and increased its professional distributor sales consultants to 675 stores and 1,221 consultants, respectively. Meanwhile, Co. is on track to exceed $3.00 billion in sales in fiscal 2004, and expects to post higher profits, margins and cash flow.

Financial Data

(US$ in Thousands)	6 Mos	3 Mos	09/30/2003	09/30/2002	09/30/2001	09/30/2000	09/30/1999	09/30/1998
Earnings Per Share	1.44	1.42	1.80	1.54	1.27	1.22	1.00	0.91
Cash Flow Per Share	1.29	0.30	2.42	2.60	1.90	1.49	1.04	1.17
Tang. Book Val. Per Share	7.07	6.79	7.03	5.03	4.60	3.44	3.87	3.83
Dividends Per Share	0.310	0.420	0.400	0.350	0.320	0.290	0.250	0.230
Dividend Payout %	21.53	29.50	22.50	22.79	25.32	23.77	25.33	25.18
Income Statement								
Total Revenues	1,584,072	764,751	2,891,417	2,650,976	2,494,180	2,247,163	1,975,928	1,834,711
Total Indirect Exp.	723,219	373,975	1,168,376	1,060,018	1,087,685	967,923	855,724	791,631
Depreciation & Amort.	25,467	12,553	48,827	47,214	51,405	49,638	42,174	38,105
Operating Income	76,325	8,058	273,791	234,428	189,066	173,490	146,502	140,985
Net Interest Inc./(Exp.)	(11,209)	(5,380)	(22,391)	(22,636)	(21,830)	(19,209)	(12,719)	(8,607)
Income Taxes	22,790	937	89,247	74,127	56,860	51,097	47,493	49,311
Net Income	42,326	1,741	162,153	137,665	110,376	103,184	86,290	83,067
Average Shs. Outstg.	91,433	91,199	89,956	88,821	86,757	84,615	85,743	93,630
Balance Sheet								
Cash & Cash Equivalents	279,039	252,213	370,148	217,485	201,970	114,637	55,931	72,395
Total Current Assets	1,189,425	1,126,887	1,165,489	984,217	876,949	740,537	645,554	591,565
Total Assets	2,115,068	2,025,617	1,945,609	1,729,491	1,516,501	1,389,819	1,184,534	1,068,184
Total Current Liabilities	497,373	453,597	465,509	460,447	390,303	340,789	336,401	313,625
Long–Term Obligations	320,690	320,564	320,587	320,181	321,183	340,948	225,173	171,760
Net Stockholders' Equity	1,204,379	1,158,640	1,062,129	862,459	736,009	636,481	568,820	533,991
Net Working Capital	692,052	673,290	699,980	523,770	486,646	399,748	309,153	277,940
Shares Outstanding	90,477	90,032	88,460	87,268	85,242	83,909	83,588	85,815
Operating Profit Margin %	4.81	1.05	9.46	8.84	7.58	7.72	7.41	7.68
Net Profit Margin %	5.54	0.47	11.78	10.78	8.98	9.13	9.17	9.90
Return on Equity %	3.51	0.15	15.26	15.96	14.99	16.21	15.17	15.55
Return on Assets %	2.00	0.08	8.33	7.95	7.27	7.42	7.28	7.77
Debt/Total Assets %	15.16	15.82	16.47	18.51	21.17	24.53	19.00	16.07
Price Range	45.82–39.21	42.64–39.21	39.39–31.45	38.19–25.61	30.28–19.12	21.08–13.04	18.46–14.71	21.71–13.33
P/E Ratio	31.82–27.23	30.03–27.61	21.88–17.47	24.80–16.63	23.84–15.06	17.28–10.69	18.46–14.71	23.86–14.65
Average Yield %	0.74	1.02	1.16	1.09	1.22	1.68	1.49	1.19

Address: 2525 Armitage Avenue, Melrose Park, IL 60160	Officers: Leonard H. Lavin – Chmn., Bernice E. Lavin – Vice–Chmn., Treas., Sec.	Investor Contact:708–450–3000
Telephone: (708) 450–3000	**Transfer Agents:**EquiServe L.P., Providence, RI	**Institutional Holding**
Web Site: www.alberto.com		**No of Institutions:** 13
		Shares: 710,299 **% Held:** –

ALFA CORP

Exchange	Symbol	Price	52Wk Range	Yield	P/E
NMS	ALFA	$13.65 (5/28/2004)	14.00-12.40	2.56	12.75

*7 Year Price Score 123.2   *NYSE Composite Index=100   *12 Month Price Score 48.1

Interim Earnings (Per Share)

Qtr.	Mar	Jun	Sep	Dec
2001	0.18	0.22	0.23	0.25
2002	0.23	0.20	0.22	0.25
2003	0.23	0.24	0.23	0.28
2004	0.32	...	...	...

Interim Dividends (Per Share)

Amt	Decl	Ex	Rec	Pay
0.08Q	7/23/2003	8/13/2003	8/15/2003	8/29/2003
0.08Q	10/27/2003	11/12/2003	11/14/2003	12/1/2003
0.08Q	1/26/2004	2/11/2004	2/13/2004	3/1/2004
0.088Q	4/22/2004	5/12/2004	5/14/2004	6/1/2004

Indicated Div: $0.35 (Div. Reinv. Plan)

Valuation Analysis

Forecast P/E 12.99 (5/24/2004)

Market Cap $1.1 Billion	Book Value 638.5 Million
Price/Book 1.67	Price/Sales 1.73

Dividend Achiever Status

Rank 188	10 Year Growth Rate	8.45%
Total Years of Dividend Growth		18

Business Summary: Insurance (MIC: 8.2 SIC: 6331 NAIC:524126)

Alfa is a financial services holding company that operates predominantly in the insurance industry through its wholly owned subsidiaries Alfa Life Insurance Corporation, Alfa Insurance Corporation, Alfa General Insurance Corporation, Alfa Agency Mississippi, Inc. and Alfa Agency Georgia, Inc. Co.'s insurance subsidiaries write life insurance in Alabama, Georgia and Mississippi, and property and casualty insurance in Georgia and Mississippi. Co. has five non-insurance subsidiaries that are engaged in consumer financing, commercial leasing, residential and commercial construction and real estate sales.

Recent Developments: For the quarter ended Mar 31 2004, net income grew 36.0% to $25.5 million from $18.7 million in the prior-year quarter. Results included realized investment gains of $947,000 in 2004 versus realized investment losses of $1.2 million in 2003. Total revenues increased 6.8% to $161.7 million from $151.4 million the previous year. Property and casualty premiums improved 7.6% to $119.9 million. Life insurance premiums advanced 12.8% to $10.1 million, while revenues from life insurance policy charges rose 3.2% to $9.0 million. Net investment income grew 1.7% to $22.0 million. Benefits and settlement expenses were $90.5 million, up 2.9% from $88.0 million a year earlier.

Prospects: Going forward, Co. should continue to benefit from top-line growth, increasing property and casualty earned premium and life premium. In addition, Co.'s underwriting and expense control initiatives are expected to enhance near term results. As a result, Co. is well positioned to capitalize on opportunities throughout the remainder of 2004. Separately, Co. announced a preliminary estimate of losses from a series of storms that struck Alabama in early April 2004. The impact of these claims on Co.'s second quarter earnings, after reinsurance and taxes, is estimated to be between $0.05 and $0.07 per diluted share.

Financial Data

(US$ in Thousands)	12/31/2003	12/31/2002	12/31/2001	12/31/2000	12/31/1999	12/31/1998	12/31/1997	12/31/1996
Earnings Per Share	0.98	0.90	0.88	0.85	0.80	0.69	0.64	0.39
Tang. Book Val. Per Share	7.95	7.09	6.49	6.04	5.16	5.31	4.82	3.96
Dividends Per Share	0.310	0.290	0.280	0.250	0.230	0.210	0.199	0.190
Dividend Payout %	32.14	33.05	31.92	30.00	29.53	31.70	30.81	48.97
Income Statement								
Total Premium Income	525,229	491,105	452,869	429,197	405,330	391,838	370,965	337,186
Net Investment Income	83,509	88,519	84,714	72,891	67,807	62,512	57,529	54,194
Other Income	9,309	7,925	8,713	8,225	9,124	6,636	5,516	4,955
Total Revenues	618,047	587,548	546,296	510,313	482,261	460,986	434,010	396,336
Total Indirect Exp.	143,155	138,085	131,843	116,229	105,274	96,584	87,967	80,115
Inc. Before Inc. Taxes	106,597	99,345	98,094	94,746	92,077	83,265	76,800	45,854
Income Taxes	28,128	27,637	28,133	27,925	27,520	26,549	24,006	13,665
Income from Cont Ops	...	...	69,962	...	...	...	...	...
Net Income	78,469	71,708	69,506	66,821	64,557	56,716	52,794	32,189
Average Shs. Outstg.	80,390	79,546	78,963	78,814	80,471	82,296	81,861	81,573
Balance Sheet								
Cash & Cash Equivalents	10,893	9,762	10,225	4,476	6,650	5,948	5,821	4,424
Premiums Due	40,278	34,044	39,821	36,596	30,158	37,573	26,224	23,930
Invst. Assets: Total	1,421,077	1,308,867	1,202,289	1,182,519	1,058,712	990,378	967,141	813,304
Total Assets	2,045,075	1,884,055	1,697,604	1,546,303	1,335,347	1,246,659	1,170,066	1,019,330
Net Stockholders' Equity	638,512	566,098	509,112	473,561	408,667	423,622	382,931	323,312
Shares Outstanding	80,217	79,278	78,359	78,297	79,084	79,736	79,375	81,573
Statistical Record								
Return on Equity %	12.28	12.66	13.74	14.11	15.79	13.38	13.78	9.95
Return on Assets %	3.83	3.80	4.12	4.32	4.83	4.54	4.51	3.15
Price Range	13.50-10.92	16.05-10.75	12.35-9.06	9.69-7.31	12.13-7.50	12.13-8.13	9.00-5.63	7.25-5.31
P/E Ratio	13.78-11.14	17.83-11.94	14.03-10.30	11.40-8.60	15.16-9.38	17.57-11.78	14.06-8.79	18.59-13.62
Average Yield %	2.46	2.25	2.66	2.87	2.57	2.15	2.70	3.09

Address: 2108 East South Boulevard, Montgomery, AL 36116-2015	**Officers:** Jerry A. Newby - Chmn., Pres., C. Lee Ellis - Exec. V.P., Oper., Treas.	**Investor Contact:** 34—288-3900 **Institutional Holding**
Telephone: (334) 288-3900	**Transfer Agents:** American Stock Transfer and Trust Co., New York, NY	**No of Institutions:** 18
Web Site: www.alfains.com		**Shares:** 245,737,144 **% Held:** -

ALLTEL CORP.

Exchange	Symbol	Price	52Wk Range	Yield	P/E
NYS	AT	$50.63 (5/28/2004)	53.25–43.99	2.92	17.28

*7 Year Price Score 89.0   *NYSE Composite Index=100   ***12 Month Price Score 48.8**

TRADING VOLUME (thousand shares)

Interim Earnings (Per Share)

Qtr.	Mar	Jun	Sep	Dec
2001	1.19	0.70	0.71	0.74
2002	0.68	0.69	0.76	0.83
2003	0.73	0.72	0.78	0.82
2004	0.61	...	...	...

Interim Dividends (Per Share)

Amt	Decl	Ex	Rec	Pay
0.35Q	7/24/2003	9/4/2003	9/8/2003	10/3/2003
0.37Q	10/23/2003	12/4/2003	12/8/2003	1/3/2004
0.37Q	1/22/2004	2/20/2004	2/24/2004	4/3/2004
0.37Q	4/22/2004	6/9/2004	6/11/2004	7/3/2004

Indicated Div: $2.25 (Div. Reinv. Plan)

Valuation Analysis

Forecast P/E 15.90 (5/24/2004)

Market Cap	$15.7 Billion	Book Value	N/A
Price/Book	N/A	Price/Sales	N/A

Dividend Achiever Status

Rank	238	10 Year Growth Rate 5.76%
Total Years of Dividend Growth		43

Business Summary: Communications (MIC: 10.1 SIC: 4813 NAIC:517310)

ALLTEL is a provider of wireless and wireline local, long–distance, network access and Internet services. Telecommunications products are warehoused and sold by Co.'s distribution subsidiary. A subsidiary also publishes telephone directories for affiliates and other independent telephone companies. In addition, a subsidiary provides billing, customer care and other data processing and outsourcing services to telecommunications companies. As of Dec 31 2003, Co. provided wireless communications service to more than 8.0 million customers in 23 states, and local wireline telephone service to nearly 3.1 million customers primarily located in rural areas in 15 states.

Recent Developments: For the quarter ended Mar 31 2004, net income was $189.8 million versus income from continuing operations of $227.6 million in the corresponding year–earlier period. Results for 2004 included restructuring and other charges of $51.8 million. Results for 2003 excluded income from discontinued operations of $37.1 million and a gain of $15.6 million on the cumulative effect of an accounting change. Total revenues and sales increased 2.9% to $1.96 billion. Wireless revenue rose 6.9% to $1.18 billion; however, wireless operating income declined 10.6% to $210.9 million due to growth initiatives. Wireline revenue decreased 1.5% to $599.5 million, while operating income grew 2.4% to $228.2 million.

Prospects: Co.'s near–term prospects are strengthened by the recent healthy additions of wireless and digital subscriber line (DSL) customers. For instance, for the quarter ended Mar 31 2004, gross wireless customer additions totaled 737,385, while average post–pay churn, or the average monthly rate of customer disconnects, improved to 1.93% versus 2.16% the previous year. Separately, Co. noted that it has completed its Touch2Talk walkie–talkie service launch in all markets. Meanwhile, although total wireline customers slipped 2.3% to 3.1 million for the quarter ended Mar 31 2004, Co. added 21,000 DSL customers and ended the quarter with 174,489 DSL customers versus 87,732 DSL customers a year earlier.

Financial Data

(US$ in Thousands)	3 Mos	12/31/2003	12/31/2002	12/31/2001	12/31/2000	12/31/1999	12/31/1998	12/31/1997
Earnings Per Share	2.93	3.05	2.96	3.34	6.20	2.47	1.89	2.70
Cash Flow Per Share	1.77	7.91	8.30	6.60	4.72	4.73	4.49	4.25
Tang. Book Val. Per Share	2.34	2.65	N.M	6.86	5.91	7.02	5.81	8.67
Dividends Per Share	1.420	1.400	1.360	1.320	1.280	1.220	1.160	1.100
Dividend Payout %	35.86	45.90	45.94	39.52	20.64	49.39	61.37	40.74
Income Statement								
Total Revenues	1,961,200	7,979,900	7,983,400	7,598,900	7,067,000	6,302,271	5,194,008	3,263,563
Total Indirect Exp.	748,300	2,764,800	2,804,900	1,259,900	1,013,800	952,692	1,014,129	467,636
Depreciation & Amort.	321,300	1,247,700	1,178,600	1,167,700	988,400	862,172	707,129	450,762
Operating Income	394,800	1,898,000	1,815,600	1,664,700	1,667,500	1,525,107	889,026	747,024
Net Interest Inc./(Exp.)	(91,700)	(378,600)	(349,400)	(288,900)	(310,800)	(280,175)	(263,669)	(130,181)
Income Taxes	115,600	580,600	541,200	704,300	1,385,300	547,218	446,864	320,815
Income from Cont Ops	...	953,500	...	1,047,500	1,965,400	...	...	...
Net Income	189,800	1,330,100	924,300	1,067,000	1,928,800	783,634	525,475	507,886
Average Shs. Outstg.	311,500	312,800	312,300	313,500	317,200	316,814	277,276	187,689
Balance Sheet								
Cash & Cash Equivalents	637,400	657,800	155,500	85,300	67,200	17,595	55,472	16,212
Total Current Assets	1,666,000	1,729,100	1,646,000	1,767,800	1,780,700	1,167,179	980,831	665,844
Total Assets	16,539,600	16,661,100	16,389,100	12,609,000	12,182,000	10,774,203	9,374,226	5,633,445
Total Current Liabilities	1,402,500	1,492,700	1,819,200	1,285,100	1,515,900	1,193,967	1,206,508	637,281
Long–Term Obligations	5,608,100	5,581,200	6,145,500	3,861,500	4,611,700	3,750,413	3,491,755	1,874,172
Net Stockholders' Equity	6,898,500	7,022,200	5,998,100	5,565,800	5,095,400	4,205,737	3,270,872	2,208,506
Net Working Capital	263,500	236,400	(173,200)	482,700	264,800	(26,788)	(225,677)	28,563
Shares Outstanding	308,171	312,643	311,182	310,529	312,983	314,257	281,198	183,673
Statistical Record								
Operating Profit Margin %	20.13	23.78	22.74	21.90	23.59	24.19	17.11	22.88
Return on Equity %	2.75	13.57	15.40	18.82	38.57	18.63	16.06	22.99
Return on Assets %	1.14	5.72	5.63	8.30	16.13	7.27	5.60	9.01
Debt/Total Assets %	33.90	33.49	37.49	30.62	37.85	34.80	37.24	33.26
Price Range	53.25–46.58	56.05–41.15	62.58–36.93	68.25–50.49	82.69–47.94	91.38–57.06	61.13–39.38	41.38–30.00
P/E Ratio	18.17–15.90	18.38–13.49	21.14–12.48	20.43–15.12	13.34–7.73	36.99–23.10	32.34–20.83	15.32–11.11
Average Yield %	2.83	2.99	2.74	2.25	2.05	1.72	2.58	3.24

Address: One Allied Drive, Little Rock, AR 72202	**Officers:** Joe T. Ford – Chmn., Scott T. Ford – Pres., C.E.O.	**Investor Contact:**501–905–8991
Telephone: (501) 905–8000	**Transfer Agents:**Wachovia Bank, Charlotte, NC	**Institutional Holding**
Web Site: www.alltel.com		**No of Institutions:** 20
		Shares: 61,697,073 **% Held:** –

ALTRIA GROUP INC

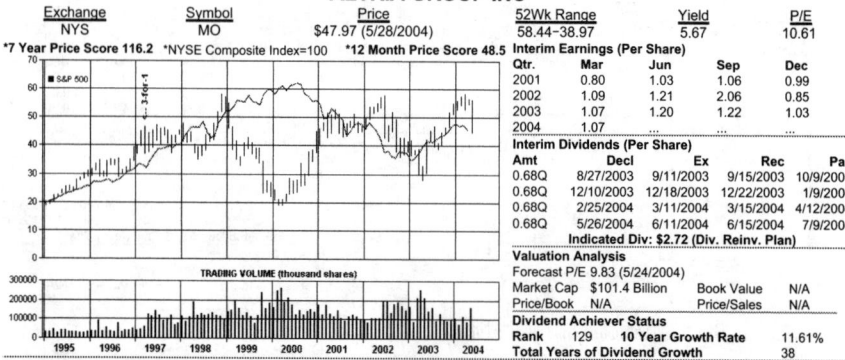

Exchange	Symbol	Price	52Wk Range	Yield	P/E
NYS	MO	$47.97 (5/28/2004)	58.44-38.97	5.67	10.61

*7 Year Price Score 116.2 *NYSE Composite Index=100 *12 Month Price Score 48.5

Interim Earnings (Per Share)

Qtr.	Mar	Jun	Sep	Dec
2001	0.80	1.03	1.06	0.99
2002	1.09	1.21	2.06	0.85
2003	1.07	1.20	1.22	1.03
2004	1.07	...	...	...

Interim Dividends (Per Share)

Amt	Decl	Ex	Rec	Pay
0.68Q	8/27/2003	9/11/2003	9/15/2003	10/9/2003
0.68Q	12/10/2003	12/18/2003	12/22/2003	1/9/2004
0.68Q	2/25/2004	3/11/2004	3/15/2004	4/12/2004
0.68Q	5/26/2004	6/11/2004	6/15/2004	7/9/2004

Indicated Div: $2.72 (Div. Reinv. Plan)

Valuation Analysis

Forecast P/E 9.83 (5/24/2004)
Market Cap $101.4 Billion Book Value N/A
Price/Book N/A Price/Sales N/A

Dividend Achiever Status

Rank 129 10 Year Growth Rate 11.61%
Total Years of Dividend Growth 38

Business Summary: Tobacco Products (MIC: 4.2 SIC: 2111 NAIC:312221)

Altria Group, through its wholly-owned subsidiaries, Philip Morris USA Inc., Philip Morris International Inc. and its 84.6% majority-owned subsidiary, Kraft Foods Inc., is engaged in the manufacture and sale of various consumer products, including cigarettes, packaged grocery products, snacks, beverages, cheese and convenient meals. Philip Morris USA's major premium brands are *Marlboro*, *Virginia Slims* and *Parliament*. Its principal discount brand is *Basic*. Philip Morris Capital Corporation, another wholly-owned subsidiary, is primarily engaged in leasing activities.

Recent Developments: For the quarter ended Mar 31 2004, net earnings were $2.19 billion, essentially unchanged from the corresponding year-earlier period. Results for 2004 included total asset impairment and exit costs of $325.0 million and domestic tobacco headquarters relocation charges of $10.0 million. Net revenues increased 12.7% to $21.84 billion from $19.37 billion the previous year. Co. attributed the higher revenues primarily to increases from its domestic and international tobacco businesses, favorable currency of $1.30 billion and an increase from North American food. Operating income declined 3.5% to $3.73 billion compared with $3.86 billion the year before.

Prospects: On Apr 3, 2004, Philip Morris International (PMI), Co.'s international tobacco business, announced that it is in discussions to reach an agreement with the European Commission that provides for cooperation with European law enforcement agencies on anti-contraband and anti-counterfeit efforts. Under the draft agreement, PMI would make 13 payments over 12 years and would record a pre-tax charge of $250.0 million for the initial payment when the agreement is signed. The draft agreement calls for base payments of $150.0 million on the first anniversary of the agreement, $100.0 million on the second anniversary and $75.0 million each year thereafter for 10 years.

Financial Data

(US$ in Thousands)	3 Mos	12/31/2003	12/31/2002	12/31/2001	12/31/2000	12/31/1999	12/31/1998	12/31/1997
Earnings Per Share	4.52	4.52	5.21	3.88	3.75	3.19	2.20	2.58
Cash Flow Per Share	0.14	5.30	4.98	4.02	4.86	4.73	3.31	3.41
Dividends Per Share	2.640	2.600	2.380	2.170	1.970	1.800	1.640	1.600
Dividend Payout %	58.41	57.52	45.68	55.92	52.53	56.42	74.54	62.01
Income Statement								
Total Revenues	21,839,000	81,832,000	80,408,000	89,924,000	80,356,000	78,596,000	74,391,000	72,055,000
Total Indirect Exp.	3,385,000	12,893,000	12,753,000	23,975,000	19,449,000	18,700,000	21,016,000	17,762,000
Depreciation & Amort.	4,000	9,000	7,000	1,014,000	591,000	582,000	584,000	585,000
Operating Income	3,728,000	15,910,000	16,601,000	15,702,000	14,679,000	13,490,000	9,777,000	11,663,000
Net Interest Inc./(Exp.)	(300,000)	(1,150,000)	(1,134,000)	(1,418,000)	(719,000)	(795,000)	(890,000)	(1,052,000)
Income Taxes	1,186,000	5,151,000	6,424,000	5,407,000	5,450,000	5,020,000	3,715,000	4,301,000
Income from Cont Ops	...	...	...	8,566,000	...	...	...	...
Net Income	2,194,000	9,204,000	11,102,000	8,560,000	8,510,000	7,675,000	5,372,000	6,310,000
Average Shs. Outstg.	2,059,000	2,038,000	2,129,000	2,210,000	2,272,000	2,403,000	2,446,000	2,442,000
Balance Sheet								
Cash & Cash Equivalents	3,204,000	3,777,000	565,000	453,000	937,000	5,100,000	4,081,000	2,282,000
Total Current Assets	28,507,000	21,382,000	17,441,000	17,275,000	17,238,000	20,895,000	20,230,000	17,440,000
Total Assets	95,565,000	96,175,000	87,540,000	84,968,000	79,067,000	61,381,000	59,920,000	55,947,000
Total Current Liabilities	18,823,000	21,393,000	19,082,000	20,141,000	25,949,000	18,017,000	16,379,000	15,071,000
Long-Term Obligations	21,371,000	21,163,000	21,355,000	19,163,000	20,181,000	12,226,000	12,615,000	12,430,000
Net Stockholders' Equity	26,840,000	25,077,000	19,478,000	19,620,000	15,005,000	15,305,000	16,197,000	14,920,000
Net Working Capital	9,684,000	(11,000)	(1,641,000)	(2,866,000)	(8,711,000)	2,878,000	3,851,000	2,369,000
Shares Outstanding	2,049,856	2,037,263	2,039,259	2,152,503	2,208,896	2,338,519	2,430,535	2,425,487
Statistical Record								
Operating Profit Margin %	17.07	19.44	20.64	17.46	18.26	17.16	13.41	16.18
Net Profit Margin %	20.90	23.83	29.78	21.55	24.15	22.53	17.20	20.69
Return on Equity %	8.17	36.70	56.99	43.65	56.71	50.14	33.16	42.29
Return on Assets %	2.30	9.57	12.68	10.08	10.76	12.50	8.96	11.27
Debt/Total Assets %	22.36	22.00	24.39	22.55	25.52	19.91	21.05	22.21
Price Range	58.44-52.80	54.92-28.10	57.72-36.17	52.96-40.13	45.25-18.88	55.13-22.06	58.31-35.19	47.38-37.12
P/E Ratio	12.93-11.68	12.15-6.22	11.08-6.94	13.65-10.34	12.07-5.03	17.28-6.92	26.51-15.99	18.36-14.39
Average Yield %	4.80	6.29	4.99	4.59	7.14	4.94	3.70	3.78

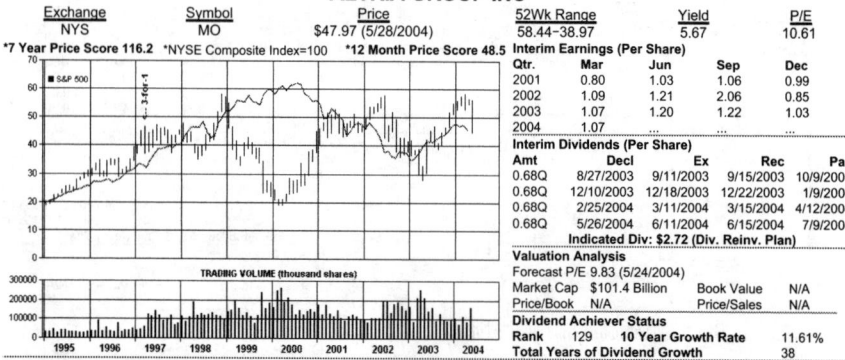

Address: 120 Park Avenue, New York, NY 10017	Officers: Louis C. Camilleri – Chmn., C.E.O., Nancy J. De Lisi – Sr. V.P., Mergers & Acquisitions	Investor Contact:917-663-3460
Telephone: (917) 663-5000	Transfer Agents:First Chicago Trust Company, Jersey City, NJ	Institutional Holding No of Institutions: 21
Web Site: www.philipmorris.com		Shares: 1,428,928 % Held: –

AMBAC FINANCIAL GROUP, INC.

Exchange	Symbol	Price	52Wk Range	Yield	P/E
NYS	ABK	$69.15 (5/28/2004)	79.25–63.02	0.64	11.49

*7 Year Price Score 142.6   *NYSE Composite Index=100   ***12 Month Price Score 45.3**

Interim Earnings (Per Share)

Qtr.	Mar	Jun	Sep	Dec
2001	0.90	0.99	1.02	1.06
2002	1.07	1.09	1.21	0.60
2003	1.27	1.48	1.45	1.54
2004	1.55	...	...	...

Interim Dividends (Per Share)

Amt	Decl	Ex	Rec	Pay
0.11Q	7/17/2003	8/7/2003	8/11/2003	9/3/2003
0.11Q	10/16/2003	11/6/2003	11/10/2003	12/3/2003
0.11Q	1/28/2004	2/6/2004	2/10/2004	3/3/2004
0.11Q	5/5/2004	5/13/2004	5/17/2004	6/2/2004

Indicated Div: $0.44

Valuation Analysis

Forecast P/E 11.13 (5/24/2004)

Market Cap $7.3 Billion		Book Value	4.5 Billion
Price/Book 1.75		Price/Sales	6.03

Dividend Achiever Status

Rank	140	10 Year Growth Rate		10.84%
Total Years of Dividend Growth				12

Business Summary: Insurance (MIC: 8.2 SIC: 6351 NAIC:524130)

Ambac Financial Group is a holding company whose subsidiaries provide financial guarantee products and other financial services to clients in both the public and private sectors. Co. provides financial guarantees for public finance and structured finance obligations through its principal operating subsidiary, Ambac Assurance. Through its financial services subsidiaries, Co. provides financial and investment products including investment agreements, interest rate and total return swaps and funding conduits, principally to its clients which include municipalities and their authorities, school districts, health care organizations and asset–backed issuers.

Recent Developments: For the quarter ended Mar 31 2004, income was $171.8 million versus income of $138.1 million in the prior–year quarter. Results for 2004 and 2003 excluded losses from discontinued operations of $144,000 and $139,000, respectively. Total revenues increased 16.0% to $337.4 million from $290.8 million in 2004. Revenues for 2004 and 2003 included net realized investment gains of $24.8 million and $2.8 million, respectively. Net premiums written grew 16.0% to $192.5 million. Net premiums earned and other credit enhancement fees advanced 21.9% to $176.9 million. Net investment income rose 13.2% to $86.7 million. Financial service interest and payment agreement revenue fell 11.3% to $52.4 million.

Prospects: Business activity remains upbeat despite the scarcity of large, high–premium deals in the market. For example, in public finance, Co. continues to see strong writings in the health care, general obligation, municipal lease and education sectors of the market. However, the strong growth in earned premium in the structured finance and international segments that has been exhibited over the past several years has moderated as those lines of business have grown significantly in the past few years. Nevertheless, transaction flow and average size has picked up recently. Given the continued expansion of the worldwide capital debt markets, Co. remains encouraged about future opportunities.

Financial Data

(US$ in Thousands)	3 Mos	12/31/2003	12/31/2002	12/31/2001	12/31/2000	12/31/1999	12/31/1998	12/31/1997
Earnings Per Share	6.02	5.74	3.97	3.97	3.41	2.87	2.37	2.08
Tang. Book Val. Per Share	41.78	39.70	34.20	28.25	24.59	19.23	19.97	17.84
Dividends Per Share	0.430	0.420	0.380	0.340	0.300	0.280	0.250	0.230
Dividend Payout %	7.14	7.31	9.57	8.56	8.99	9.74	10.67	11.02
Income Statement								
Total Premium Income	165,435	620,317	471,534	378,734	311,276	264,426	113,920	54,289
Net Investment Income	1,061	321,089	297,297	267,847	241,047	209,284	186,190	159,709
Other Income	170,884	330,802	202,987	78,339	68,987	59,607	58,162	68,053
Total Revenues	337,380	1,272,208	971,818	724,920	621,310	533,317	358,272	282,051
Total Indirect Exp.	48,576	14,562	7,170	...	...	...	...	...
Inc. Before Inc. Taxes	231,121	849,589	564,190	568,727	482,124	404,658	328,912	285,996
Income Taxes	59,366	221,490	131,596	135,821	115,952	96,741	74,918	62,966
Income from Cont Ops	171,755	628,099	...	...	...	...	155,230	123,319
Net Income	171,611	618,915	432,594	432,906	366,172	307,917	253,994	223,030
Average Shs. Outstg.	110,397	109,400	109,066	108,948	107,415	107,049	106,995	106,840
Balance Sheet								
Cash & Cash Equivalents	167,046	78,464	286,634	87,780	301,214	116,588	260,534	94,722
Premiums Due	21,089	7,455	11,947	15,282	9,680	778,787	843,013	293,506
Invst. Assets: Total	15,562,490	13,776,289	12,539,310	10,287,850	8,323,872	8,962,535	8,748,377	6,915,122
Total Assets	17,457,448	16,747,314	15,355,538	12,267,695	10,120,300	11,345,096	11,212,311	8,249,722
Long–Term Obligations	791,791	791,775	616,715	619,315	424,061	423,995	423,929	223,864
Net Stockholders' Equity	4,529,528	4,254,558	3,625,179	2,983,688	2,596,114	2,018,450	2,096,090	1,872,482
Shares Outstanding	108,402	107,144	105,990	105,584	105,550	104,936	104,913	104,920
Return on Revenues %	50.90	49.37	44.51	59.71	58.93	57.73	43.32	43.72
Return on Equity %	3.79	14.76	11.93	14.50	14.10	15.25	7.40	6.58
Return on Assets %	0.98	3.75	2.81	3.52	3.61	2.71	1.38	1.49
Price Range	79.25–69.14	72.19–44.51	69.69–49.90	63.43–45.50	58.31–26.13	40.92–30.08	43.79–27.54	31.54–21.00
P/E Ratio	13.16–11.49	12.58–7.75	17.55–12.57	15.98–11.46	17.10–7.66	14.26–10.48	18.48–11.62	15.16–10.10
Average Yield %	0.58	0.68	0.63	0.61	0.75	0.76	0.69	0.90

Address: One State Street Plaza, New York, NY 10004	Officers: Phillip B. Lassiter – Chmn., Howard C. Pfeffer – Vice–Chmn., Sr. Managing Dir., Public	Investor Contact:800–221–1854
Telephone: (212) 668–0340	Fin., Investment & Fin. Serv.	**Institutional Holding**
Web Site: www.ambac.com	**Transfer Agents:**Citibank, N.A., New York, NY	**No of Institutions:** 6
		Shares: 2,334,020 **% Held:** –

AMERICAN INTERNATIONAL GROUP INC

Exchange	Symbol	Price	52Wk Range	Yield	P/E
NYS	AIG	$73.30 (5/28/2004)	76.77–55.18	0.41	18.94

*7 Year Price Score 100.5 *NYSE Composite Index=100 *12 Month Price Score 51.8

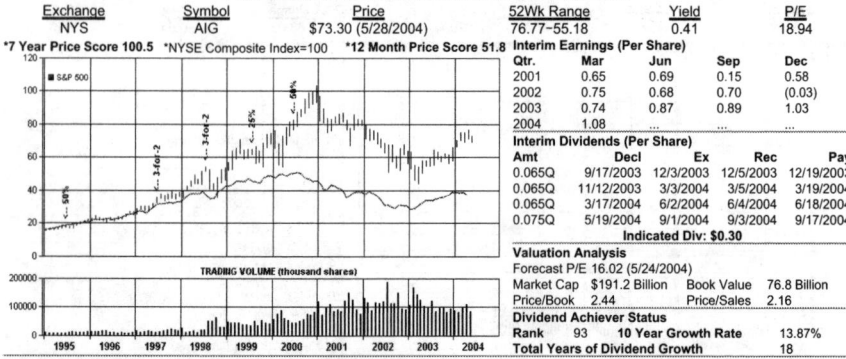

TRADING VOLUME (thousand shares)

Interim Earnings (Per Share)

Qtr.	Mar	Jun	Sep	Dec
2001	0.65	0.69	0.15	0.58
2002	0.75	0.68	0.70	(0.03)
2003	0.74	0.87	0.89	1.03
2004	1.08	...	...	...

Interim Dividends (Per Share)

Amt	Decl	Ex	Rec	Pay
0.065Q	9/17/2003	12/3/2003	12/5/2003	12/19/2003
0.065Q	11/12/2003	3/3/2004	3/5/2004	3/19/2004
0.065Q	3/17/2004	6/2/2004	6/4/2004	6/18/2004
0.075Q	5/19/2004	9/1/2004	9/3/2004	9/17/2004

Indicated Div: $0.30

Valuation Analysis

Forecast P/E 16.02 (5/24/2004)

Market Cap	$191.2 Billion	Book Value	76.8 Billion
Price/Book	2.44	Price/Sales	2.16

Dividend Achiever Status

Rank	93	10 Year Growth Rate	13.87%
Total Years of Dividend Growth		18	

Business Summary: Insurance (MIC: 8.2 SIC: 6331 NAIC:524126)

American International Group is a holding company. Through its subsidiaries, Co. is engaged in a broad range of insurance and insurance–related activities in the United States and abroad. AIG's primary activities include both General and Life Insurance operations. Other activities include Financial Services, and Retirement Services & Asset Management. General Insurance Operations: AIG's General Insurance subsidiaries are multiple line companies writing substantially all lines of property and casualty insurance. Premiums are earned primarily on a pro rata basis over the term of the related coverage.

Recent Developments: For the quarter ended Mar 31 2004, Co. reported income of $2.84 billion, before an accounting change charge of $181.4 million, versus net income of $1.95 billion in the prior–year quarter. Earnings were led by healthy general insurance results and strong gains in life insurance and retirement services. General insurance premiums increased 26.8% to $9.24 billion. Life insurance premiums advanced 19.3% to $6.90 billion. Financial services operating income slipped 1.4% to $523.0 million, while asset management operating income climbed 37.1% to $239.2 million. Realized capital gains were $1.2 million in 2004 versus realized capital losses of $633.6 million in 2003.

Prospects: Going forward, Co.'s general insurance business should benefit from solid market conditions as price increases continue to take hold. Co. noted that although some smaller insurers are selling insurance at cheaper prices in an effort to increase their market share, Co. will maintain a disciplined approach to underwriting and pricing. Co.'s life insurance operations should continue to enjoy strong operating results, supported by the introduction of new products, system enhancements that support product roll–outs and profitability initiatives. Meanwhile, Co.'s retirement business should benefit from Co.'s strategy of focusing on attractive international retirement services opportunities.

Financial Data
(US$ in Millions)

	3 Mos	12/31/2003	12/31/2002	12/31/2001	12/31/2000	12/31/1999	12/31/1998	12/31/1997
Earnings Per Share	3.87	3.53	2.10	2.07	2.41	2.15	1.90	1.68
Tang. Book Val. Per Share	26.49	24.38	20.31	19.93	16.98	14.33	13.78	12.19
Dividends Per Share	0.240	0.220	0.170	0.150	0.140	0.120	0.110	0.100
Dividend Payout %	6.37	6.34	8.47	7.63	5.83	5.87	5.93	5.99
Income Statement								
Total Premium Income	16,139	54,613	44,589	38,608	31,017	27,486	24,345	22,347
Other Income	7,415	28,123	25,334	16,851	11,423	10,265	6,507	5,601
Total Revenues	23,554	82,736	69,923	55,459	42,440	37,751	30,852	27,947
Total Indirect Exp.	19,346	67,395	59,340	...	...	...	...	...
Inc. Before Inc. Taxes	4,291	13,908	8,142	8,139	8,349	7,512	5,529	4,699
Income Taxes	1,356	4,264	2,328	2,339	2,458	2,219	1,594	1,367
Eqty Earns/Minority Int.	(98)	(379)	(295)	(301)	(255)	(238)	(112)	82
Income from Cont Ops	2,837	9,265	...	5,499	...	...	...	...
Net Income	2,656	9,274	5,519	5,363	5,636	5,055	3,766	3,332
Average Shs. Outstg.	2,633	2,628	2,634	2,650	2,343	2,350	1,978	1,982
Balance Sheet								
Cash & Cash Equivalents	43,578	78,869	70,517	65,150	53,692	43,995	36,784	28,972
Premiums Due	62,496	62,285	63,613	60,594	42,012	37,898	35,652	33,109
Invst. Assets: Total	457,910	386,830	308,378	279,763	161,281	140,070	106,279	87,051
Total Assets	724,154	678,346	561,229	492,982	306,577	268,238	194,398	163,971
Long–Term Obligations	5,813	56,003	47,923	37,447	20,672	2,344	1,620	13,885
Net Stockholders' Equity	76,586	71,061	56,950	49,948	38,272	32,411	26,731	23,601
Shares Outstanding	2,608	2,608	2,609	2,615	2,332	2,323	1,968	1,967
Return on Revenues %	11.69	12.93	11.38	9.91	13.27	13.39	12.20	11.92
Return on Equity %	3.58	15.01	13.46	10.54	14.22	15.17	13.88	13.88
Return on Assets %	0.38	1.57	1.41	1.11	1.83	1.88	1.93	2.03
Price Range	75.12–66.28	66.28–44.47	79.61–51.10	96.88–67.05	103.7–54.29	74.46–51.53	54.44–35.50	39.80–25.51
P/E Ratio	19.41–17.13	18.78–12.60	37.91–24.33	46.80–32.39	43.02–22.53	34.63–23.97	28.65–18.68	23.69–15.19
Average Yield %	0.34	0.38	0.26	0.18	0.17	0.19	0.24	0.30

Address: 70 Pine Street, New York, NY 10270 Telephone: (212) 770 7000 Web Site: www.aig.com	Officers: Maurice R. Greenberg – Chmn., C.E.O., Thomas R. Tizzio – Sr. Vice–Chmn., Gen. Insurance Transfer Agents:EquiServe Trust Company, N.A. Providence, RI	Investor Contact:212–770–6293 Institutional Holding No of Institutions: 9 Shares: 2,522,843 % Held: –

AMERICAN STATES WATER CO.

Exchange	Symbol	Price	52Wk Range	Yield	P/E
NYS	AWR	$23.40 (5/28/2004)	28.71-21.37	3.78	35.45

*7 Year Price Score 116.6 *NYSE Composite Index=100 ***12 Month Price Score 42.4**

Interim Earnings (Per Share)

Qtr.	Mar	Jun	Sep	Dec
2001	0.20	0.32	0.62	0.19
2002	0.24	0.36	0.50	0.24
2003	0.20	0.19	0.51	(0.12)
2004	0.08	...	...	...

Interim Dividends (Per Share)

Amt	Decl	Ex	Rec	Pay
0.221Q	7/28/2003	8/6/2003	8/8/2003	9/1/2003
0.221Q	10/28/2003	11/5/2003	11/8/2003	12/1/2003
0.221Q	2/3/2004	2/5/2004	2/9/2004	3/1/2004
0.221Q	4/30/2004	5/6/2004	5/10/2004	6/1/2004
	Indicated Div: $0.884 (Div. Reinv. Plan)			

Valuation Analysis

Forecast P/E 17.31 (5/24/2004)

Market Cap	$354.6 Million	Book Value	210.9 Million
Price/Book	1.79	Price/Sales	1.78

Dividend Achiever Status

Rank	301	10 Year Growth Rate	1.11%
Total Years of Dividend Growth			50

Business Summary: Water Utilities (MIC: 7.2 SIC: 4941 NAIC:221310)

American States Water is a public utility that purchases, produces, distributes, and sells water, and distributes electricity through its primary subsidiary Southern California Water Company (SCW). SCW is organized into one electric customer service area and three water service regions operating within 75 communities in 10 counties in California and provides water service in 21 customer service areas. Through its American States Utility Services subsidiary, Co. performs non-regulated, water related services and operations on a contract basis. Co.'s subsidiary, Chaparral City Water Company, is an Arizona public utility company serving Fountain Hills, AZ and and a portion of Scottsdale, AZ.

Recent Developments: For the first quarter ended Mar 31 2004, net income decreased 61.7% to $1.1 million compared with $3.0 million in the equivalent 2003 quarter. The decline in earnings was due to a delay in the implementation of a rate increase for the Region III customer service area of Co.'s Southern California Water Company (SCW) unit, coupled with the impact of higher supply cost due to more purchased water in SCW's resource mix. Operating revenues slid 0.1% to $46.7 million. Total operating expenses grew 5.1% to $41.1 million versus $39.1 million in 2003. Net operating income fell 26.5% to $5.6 million from $7.6 million the year before.

Prospects: Co. is incurring higher purchased water costs caused by the need to replace ground water supply, due to wells being removed from service for water quality and mechanical reasons. Also, operating expenses are higher, reflecting an increase in administrative and general expenses due to higher outside legal and consulting services, labor and pension costs, and depreciation and maintenance expenses. However, the impact of these higher costs should be mitigated in the future as additional revenues from the Mar 22 2004 rate increase are accounted. Also, Co. should benefit from another rate increase in the latter half of 2004, pending its approval by the California Public Utilities Commission.

Financial Data

(US$ in Thousands)	3 Mos	12/31/2003	12/31/2002	12/31/2001	12/31/2000	12/31/1999	12/31/1998	12/31/1997
Earnings Per Share	0.66	0.78	1.34	1.33	1.27	1.19	1.08	1.04
Cash Flow Per Share	1.25	3.07	1.70	2.59	2.18	2.90	2.34	2.14
Tang. Book Val. Per Share	13.83	13.96	14.04	13.22	12.75	11.82	11.48	11.24
Dividends Per Share	0.880	0.880	0.870	0.860	0.850	0.850	0.840	0.830
Dividend Payout %	133.94	113.33	65.02	65.00	67.27	71.43	77.78	79.81
Income Statement								
Total Revenues	46,651	212,669	209,205	197,514	183,960	173,421	148,060	153,755
Total Indirect Exp.	16,310	68,374	55,993	60,612	48,615	48,816	40,649	39,372
Costs & Expenses	41,101	179,064	171,557	160,822	151,653	144,907	123,049	130,297
Depreciation & Amort.	5,177	19,792	18,302	17,951	15,339	13,650	12,538	10,952
Operating Income	5,550	33,605	37,648	36,692	32,307	28,514	25,011	23,458
Net Interest Inc./(Exp.)	(4,321)	(18,070)	(17,699)	(15,735)	(14,122)	(12,945)	(11,207)	(10,157)
Income Taxes	...	3,285	12,949	15,379	15,127	13,345	10,130	9,830
Income from Cont Ops	...	...	...	...	...	...	14,573	...
Net Income	1,146	11,892	20,339	20,447	18,086	16,101	14,623	14,059
Average Shs. Outstg.	15,255	15,227	15,157	15,256	14,116	13,437	13,437	13,435
Balance Sheet								
Net Property	610,206	602,298	563,311	539,842	509,096	449,595	414,753	383,623
Total Assets	746,965	757,475	701,650	683,764	616,646	533,181	484,671	457,074
Long-Term Obligations	229,590	229,799	231,089	245,692	176,452	167,363	120,809	115,286
Net Stockholders' Equity	210,880	212,487	213,279	201,582	194,323	160,446	155,899	152,653
Shares Outstanding	15,244	15,212	15,180	15,119	15,113	13,436	13,437	13,437
Operating Profit Margin %	13.09	18.95	24.18	26.36	25.78	24.13	23.73	21.65
Net Inc./Net Property %	0.18	1.97	3.61	3.78	3.55	3.58	3.52	3.66
Net Inc./Tot. Capital %	0.23	2.35	4.06	4.06	4.26	4.25	4.48	4.48
Return on Equity %	0.80	8.75	15.60	17.77	17.09	18.35	15.84	15.64
Accum. Depr./Gross Prop. %	27.21	26.98	26.86	26.09	25.40	25.23	25.02	24.57
Price Range	26.78-24.16	28.71-21.80	28.85-21.01	25.32-19.35	24.75-17.00	26.50-14.87	19.42-14.50	16.92-13.67
P/E Ratio	40.58-36.61	36.81-27.95	21.53-15.68	19.04-14.55	19.49-13.39	22.27-12.50	17.98-13.43	16.27-13.14
Average Yield %	3.48	3.54	3.54	3.83	4.17	4.18	5.03	5.52

Address: 630 East Foothill Blvd., San Dimas, CA 91773-1212 Telephone: (909) 394-3600 Web Site: www.aswater.com	Officers: Lloyd E. Ross - Chmn., Floyd E. Wicks - Pres., C.E.O. Transfer Agents:ChaseMellon Shareholder Services, L.L.C., Ridgefield Park, NJ	Investor Contact:909-394-3633 Institutional Holding No of Institutions: 3 Shares: 11,514 % Held: -

AMSOUTH BANCORPORATION

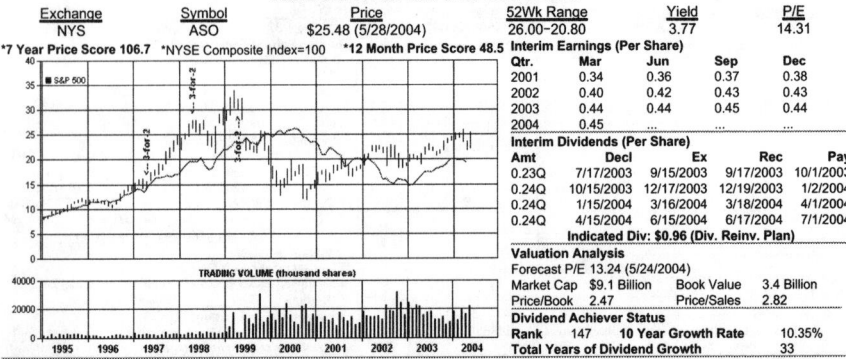

Exchange	Symbol	Price	52Wk Range	Yield	P/E
NYS	ASO	$25.48 (5/28/2004)	26.00-20.80	3.77	14.31

*7 Year Price Score 106.7   ***NYSE Composite Index=100**   ***12 Month Price Score 48.5**

Interim Earnings (Per Share)

Qtr.	Mar	Jun	Sep	Dec
2001	0.34	0.36	0.37	0.38
2002	0.40	0.42	0.43	0.43
2003	0.44	0.44	0.45	0.44
2004	0.45	...	...	...

Interim Dividends (Per Share)

Amt	Decl	Ex	Rec	Pay
0.23Q	7/17/2003	9/15/2003	9/17/2003	10/1/2003
0.24Q	10/15/2003	12/17/2003	12/19/2003	1/2/2004
0.24Q	1/15/2004	3/16/2004	3/18/2004	4/1/2004
0.24Q	4/15/2004	6/15/2004	6/17/2004	7/1/2004

Indicated Div: $0.96 (Div. Reinv. Plan)

Valuation Analysis
Forecast P/E 13.24 (5/24/2004)

Market Cap	$9.1 Billion	Book Value	3.4 Billion
Price/Book	2.47	Price/Sales	2.82

Dividend Achiever Status

Rank	147	10 Year Growth Rate	10.35%
Total Years of Dividend Growth			33

TRADING VOLUME (thousand shares)

Business Summary: Commercial Banking (MIC: 8.1 SIC: 6022 NAIC:522110)

AmSouth Bancorporation is a regional bank holding company headquartered in Birmingham, AL. As of Dec 31 2003, Co. had assets of $45.60 billion and operated more than 650 branch banking offices and over 1,200 ATMs in the following southeastern states: Alabama, Florida, Tennessee, Mississippi, Georgia, and Louisiana. Co., through its affiliates, provides a full line of traditional and nontraditional financial services including consumer and commercial banking, small business banking, mortgage lending, equipment leasing, annuity and mutual fund sales, and trust and investment management services.

Recent Developments: For the three months ended Mar 31 2004, net income totaled $160.1 million, up 3.1% compared with $155.4 million in the prior year. Net interest income slipped 1.0% to $359.5 million from $363.0 million a year earlier. Provision for loan losses fell 37.1% to $28.1 million from $44.7 million the year before. Non-interest revenues climbed 14.3% to $220.4 million from $192.9 million the previous year, stemming from continuing investments in branch expansion and other revenue producing initiatives. Non-interest expenses were $322.3 million, up 11.3% versus $289.6 million in 2003. Income before income taxes grew 3.6% to $229.6 million from $221.6 million in the prior year.

Prospects: Earnings are benefiting from growth in non-interest revenues, driven by increases in deposit service fees, income from trust and investment services, along with securities gains and other sources of fee income. Meanwhile, results are being positively affected by strong deposit growth and increased demand for residential mortgage loans, as well as improving trends in credit quality. Separately, results should benefit from Co.'s ongoing efforts to expand its operations and improving economic conditions. Looking ahead, Co. is targeting full-year 2004 earnings of between $1.87 and $1.92 per share.

Financial Data

(US$ in Thousands)	3 Mos	12/31/2003	12/31/2002	12/31/2001	12/31/2000	12/31/1999	12/31/1998	12/31/1997
Earnings Per Share	1.78	1.77	1.68	1.45	0.86	0.86	1.44	1.21
Tang. Book Val. Per Share	9.55	9.17	8.81	8.13	7.52	7.56	8.04	7.64
Dividends Per Share	0.930	0.920	0.880	0.840	0.800	0.670	0.530	0.490
Dividend Payout %	51.96	51.97	52.38	57.93	93.02	78.29	36.86	41.02
Income Statement								
Total Interest Income	524,636	2,086,451	2,254,116	2,634,540	3,070,426	2,932,750	1,462,541	1,377,788
Total Interest Expense	165,139	671,816	781,476	1,239,656	1,691,323	1,424,804	763,571	701,511
Net Interest Income	359,497	1,414,635	1,472,640	1,394,884	1,379,103	1,507,946	698,970	676,277
Provision for Loan Losses	28,100	173,700	213,550	187,100	227,600	165,626	58,134	67,399
Non-Interest Income	220,430	855,778	739,361	748,222	669,494	847,557	346,626	266,004
Non-Interest Expense	322,274	1,205,577	1,126,622	1,185,394	1,366,435	1,648,506	582,117	526,192
Income Before Taxes	229,553	891,136	871,829	770,612	454,562	541,371	405,345	348,690
Net Income	160,099	626,121	609,147	536,346	329,127	340,468	262,712	226,167
Average Shs. Outstg.	356,908	354,308	362,329	370,948	384,677	396,515	181,921	186,178
Balance Sheet								
Cash & Due from Banks	1,074,116	1,163,986	1,221,985	1,441,561	1,278,691	1,563,335	619,599	658,500
Securities Avail. for Sale	6,371,806	7,125,971	4,744,866	4,829,512	1,908,917	5,964,703	3,029,372	2,507,690
Net Loans & Leases	29,511,273	28,205,790	26,969,329	24,760,886	23,764,250	25,903,283	12,586,184	12,058,471
Total Assets	47,414,968	44,866,066	40,571,272	38,600,414	38,464,227	43,406,554	19,794,075	18,622,256
Total Deposits	31,544,692	30,440,353	27,315,624	26,167,017	26,623,304	27,912,443	13,283,804	12,945,197
Long-Term Obligations	8,069,691	7,852,434	6,889,283	6,102,255	5,883,405	5,603,486	3,239,759	1,633,224
Total Liabilities	44,042,619	42,385,847	37,455,275	35,645,315	36,122,571	40,447,349	18,474,050	17,237,011
Net Stockholders' Equity	3,372,349	3,229,669	3,115,997	2,955,099	2,813,407	2,959,205	1,427,629	1,385,245
Shares Outstanding	352,904	351,891	353,424	363,035	373,806	391,374	177,376	181,208
Statistical Record								
Return on Equity %	4.74	19.38	19.54	18.14	11.69	11.50	18.40	16.32
Return on Assets %	0.33	1.39	1.50	1.38	0.85	0.78	1.32	1.21
Equity/Assets %	7.11	7.19	7.68	7.65	7.31	6.81	7.21	7.43
Non-Int. Exp./Tot. Inc. %	43.25	40.97	37.63	35.04	36.53	43.60	32.17	32.01
Price Range	26.00-23.43	24.58-19.09	22.88-18.28	20.15-15.13	19.88-11.88	34.00-19.00	30.42-21.42	25.11-14.07
P/E Ratio	14.61-13.16	13.89-10.79	13.62-10.88	13.90-10.43	23.11-13.81	39.53-22.09	21.12-14.87	20.75-11.63
Average Yield %	3.78	4.23	4.19	4.70	5.02	2.58	2.05	2.67

Address: AMSOUTH CENTER, Birmingham, AL 35203	Officers: C. Dowd Ritter – Chmn., Pres., C.E.O., Candice W. Bagby – Sr. Exec. V.P., Consumer Banking, Mktg.	Investor Contact:205-801-0265
Telephone: (205) 320 7151		Institutional Holding
Web Site: www.amsouth.com	Transfer Agents:The Bank of New York, New York, NY	No of Institutions: 26
		Shares: 2,232,489 % Held: –

ANCHOR BANCORP WISCONSIN, INC

Exchange	Symbol	Price	52Wk Range	Yield	P/E
NMS	ABCW	$26.40 (5/28/2004)	27.10-23.03	1.67	12.82

*7 Year Price Score 130.7   *NYSE Composite Index=100   *12 Month Price Score 48.3

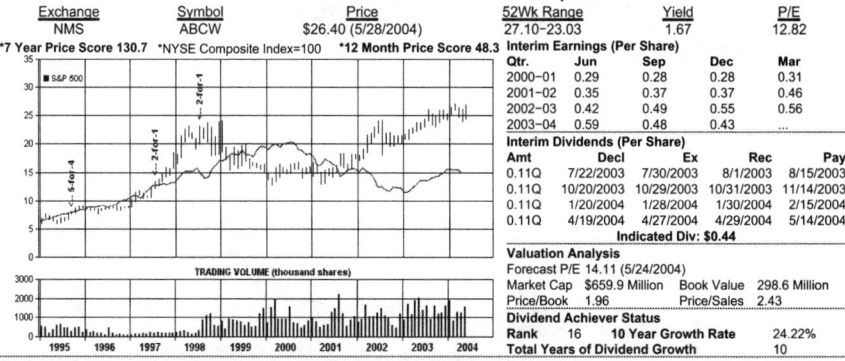

Interim Earnings (Per Share)

Qtr.	Jun	Sep	Dec	Mar
2000-01	0.29	0.28	0.28	0.31
2001-02	0.35	0.37	0.37	0.46
2002-03	0.42	0.49	0.55	0.56
2003-04	0.59	0.48	0.43	...

Interim Dividends (Per Share)

Amt	Decl	Ex	Rec	Pay
0.11Q	7/22/2003	7/30/2003	8/1/2003	8/15/2003
0.11Q	10/20/2003	10/29/2003	10/31/2003	11/14/2003
0.11Q	1/20/2004	1/28/2004	1/30/2004	2/15/2004
0.11Q	4/19/2004	4/27/2004	4/29/2004	5/14/2004

Indicated Div: $0.44

Valuation Analysis

Forecast P/E 14.11 (5/24/2004)

Market Cap	$659.9 Million	Book Value	298.6 Million
Price/Book	1.96	Price/Sales	2.43

Dividend Achiever Status

Rank	16	10 Year Growth Rate	24.22%
Total Years of Dividend Growth		10	

TRADING VOLUME (thousand shares)

Business Summary: Other Depository Banking (MIC: 8.5 SIC: 6036 NAIC:522120)

Anchor BanCorp Wisconsin is engaged in the savings and loan business through its wholly-owned banking subsidiary, AnchorBank, fsb. Co. also has a non-banking subsidiary, Investment Directions, Inc., which invests in real estate partnerships. Through AnchorBank, Co. offers checking, savings, money market accounts, mortgages, home equity and other consumer loans, student loans, credit cards, annuities and related consumer financial services. AnchorBank also offers banking services to businesses, including checking accounts, lines of credit, secured loans and commercial real estate loans. As of Mar 31 2004, total assets were $3.83 billion and total deposits amounted to $2.60 billion.

Recent Developments: For the year ended Mar 31 2004, net income slipped 4.4% to $47.4 million versus $49.6 million the year before. This decrease was due to lower interest income, partially offset by an increase in non-interest income and a decrease in income tax expense. Results for 2004 and 2003 included net gains on the sale of loans of $15.3 million and $20.7 million, respectively. Net interest income slid 5.5% to $110.4 million. Provision for loan losses was $2.0 million versus $1.8 million the year before. Non-interest income soared to $82.1 million from $32.8 million a year earlier. Non-interest expense grew 67.1% to $113.6 million.

Prospects: Co. remains cautiously optimistic about its prospects for fiscal 2004, although several factors, such as potential increases in interest rates and general business and economic conditions, could negatively affect its operations. Additionally, Co., like many Wisconsin financial institutions, is the subject of efforts by the Wisconsin Department of Revenue to retroactively and prospectively tax income from out-of-state subsidiaries which previously had not been subject to tax. If successful, these efforts would have a substantial negative impact on Co.'s results of operations.

Financial Data

(US$ in Thousands)	9 Mos	6 Mos	3 Mos	03/31/2003	03/31/2002	03/31/2001	03/31/2000	03/31/1999
Earnings Per Share	1.50	1.07	0.59	2.02	1.55	1.16	0.78	1.28
Tang. Book Val. Per Share	12.16	11.80	11.70	11.40	11.12	9.62	9.01	5.68
Dividends Per Share	0.420	0.400	0.380	0.360	0.320	0.290	0.250	0.190
Dividend Payout %	28.00	37.38	64.40	17.94	20.80	25.43	32.05	15.23
Income Statement								
Total Interest Income	144,169	96,928	49,042	209,605	225,701	228,647	202,065	155,966
Total Interest Expense	60,637	40,886	20,582	92,856	128,454	148,096	119,393	93,548
Net Interest Income	83,532	56,042	28,460	116,749	97,247	80,551	82,672	62,418
Provision for Loan Losses	1,350	900	450	1,800	2,485	945	1,306	815
Non-Interest Income	56,530	20,965	13,066	31,018	20,469	15,215	11,946	9,260
Non-Interest Expense	81,533	35,005	18,150	68,004	59,531	51,450	59,985	41,405
Income Before Taxes	57,179	41,102	22,926	79,698	56,846	41,659	35,098	38,214
Eqty Earns/Minority Int.	3,301	...	...	...	...	...	...	...
Net Income	35,231	25,293	14,093	49,563	36,367	26,977	19,502	23,544
Average Shs. Outstg.	23,507	23,669	23,771	24,592	23,462	23,207	25,159	18,379
Balance Sheet								
Securities Avail. for Sale	282,486	513,690	335,766	282,943	211,286	196,184	92,212	79,073
Net Loans & Leases	14,448	49,211	61,666	2,770,988	2,627,248	2,414,976	2,302,721	1,724,242
Total Assets	3,665,544	3,661,558	3,622,614	3,538,621	3,507,076	3,127,474	2,911,152	2,141,688
Total Deposits	2,552,279	2,579,353	2,633,503	2,574,188	2,553,987	2,119,320	1,897,369	1,505,990
Long-Term Obligations	750,729	721,994	607,614	595,816	621,590	712,650	664,446	428,395
Total Liabilities	3,366,904	3,368,541	3,322,915	3,245,617	3,229,564	2,907,862	2,693,937	1,999,449
Net Stockholders' Equity	298,640	293,017	299,699	293,004	277,512	219,612	217,215	142,239
Shares Outstanding	22,910	23,137	23,907	23,942	24,950	22,814	24,088	24,999
Statistical Record								
Return on Equity %	11.79	8.63	4.70	16.91	13.10	12.28	8.97	16.55
Return on Assets %	0.96	0.69	0.38	1.40	1.03	0.86	0.66	1.09
Equity/Assets %	8.14	8.00	8.27	8.28	7.91	7.02	7.46	6.64
Non-Int. Exp./Tot. Inc. %	40.62	29.69	29.22	28.26	24.18	21.09	28.02	25.05
Price Range	26.12-21.95	26.12-21.95	24.46-21.95	24.25-17.99	21.64-13.13	16.75-12.88	20.00-12.75	24.13-15.38
P/E Ratio	17.41-14.63	24.41-20.51	41.46-37.20	12.00-8.91	13.96-8.47	14.44-11.10	25.64-16.35	18.85-12.01
Average Yield %	1.73	1.67	1.63	1.68	1.92	1.89	1.54	0.93

Address: 25 West Main Street,	**Officers:** Douglas J. Timmerman – Chmn., Pres.,	**Investor Contact:**608-252-1810
Madison, WI 53703	C.E.O., Michael W. Helser – C.F.O., Treas.	**Institutional Holding**
Telephone: (608) 252-8700	**Transfer Agents:**US Bank, N.A., Milwaukee, WI	**No of Institutions:** 42
Web Site: www.anchorbank.com		**Shares:** 2,705,026 **% Held:** –

ANHEUSER-BUSCH COS., INC.

Exchange	Symbol	Price	52Wk Range	Yield	P/E
NYS	BUD	$53.27 (5/28/2004)	54.01–48.69	1.65	20.65

*7 Year Price Score 127.7   *NYSE Composite Index=100   *12 Month Price Score 47.7

Interim Earnings (Per Share)

Qtr.	Mar	Jun	Sep	Dec
2001	0.43	0.58	0.62	0.26
2002	0.51	0.66	0.71	0.32
2003	0.57	0.75	0.80	0.36
2004	0.67	...	...	...

Interim Dividends (Per Share)

Amt	Decl	Ex	Rec	Pay
0.22Q	7/23/2003	8/7/2003	8/11/2003	9/9/2003
0.22Q	10/22/2003	11/6/2003	11/10/2003	12/9/2003
0.22Q	1/14/2004	2/5/2004	2/9/2004	3/9/2004
0.22Q	4/28/2004	5/6/2004	5/10/2004	6/9/2004

Indicated Div: $0.88 (Div. Reinv. Plan)

Valuation Analysis

Forecast P/E 19.13 (5/24/2004)

Market Cap	$45.6 Billion	Book Value	2.7 Billion
Price/Book	15.25	Price/Sales	2.89

Dividend Achiever Status

Rank	173	10 Year Growth Rate	9.34%
Total Years of Dividend Growth		29	

Business Summary: Food (MIC: 4.1 SIC: 2082 NAIC:312120)

Anheuser–Busch Companies is the parent holding company of Anheuser–Busch, Inc., the world's largest brewer of beer. Co.'s beer is sold under brand names including *Budweiser*, *Michelob*, *Busch*, and *Natural Light*. Worldwide sales of Co.'s beer brands aggregated 111.0 million barrels in 2003. Additionally, theme park operations are conducted through Co.'s subsidiary, Busch Entertainment Corporation, which owned nine theme parks as of Dec 31 2003. Co. also engages in packaging, malt and rice production, international beer, non–beer beverages, real estate development, marketing communications, and transportation services.

Recent Developments: For the three months ended Mar 31 2004, net income increased 13.4% to $549.9 million compared with $484.8 million in the corresponding quarter of the previous year. Net sales climbed 6.0% to $3.48 billion from $3.28 billion in the year–earlier period. Domestic beer net sales grew 4.4% to $2.77 billion, reflecting higher revenue per barrel and increased beer volume. International beer net sales jumped 13.4% to $158.8 million, largely due to volume and profit growth. Packaging net sales advanced 10.2% to $311.3 million, reflecting higher soft drink can volume and improved plant operations. Entertainment net sales improved 22.5% to $154.1 million, due to increased attendance and pricing.

Prospects: Co. is enjoying strong growth in domestic revenue per barrel, which is driving profit margin growth. The growth reflects Co.'s successful implementation of pricing actions on approximately two–thirds of its domestic volume in two phases in Oct 2003 and Feb 2004, and consumers trading up to the premium *Michelob* family. Meanwhile, Co. will continue to place emphasis on its international growth strategy, which includes growing volume and profits in China and Canada. Looking ahead, Co. continues to expect double–digit earnings per share growth over the long term and 12.0% earnings per share growth for 2004.

Financial Data

(US$ in Thousands)	3 Mos	12/31/2003	12/31/2002	12/31/2001	12/31/2000	12/31/1999	12/31/1998	12/31/1997
Earnings Per Share	2.58	2.48	2.20	1.89	1.69	1.47	1.26	1.18
Cash Flow Per Share	0.72	3.54	3.14	2.61	2.45	2.18	2.23	1.81
Tang. Book Val. Per Share	2.76	2.73	3.19	4.15	4.11	3.79	3.95	3.61
Dividends Per Share	0.850	0.830	0.750	0.690	0.630	0.580	0.540	0.500
Dividend Payout %	33.14	33.46	34.09	36.50	37.27	39.45	42.68	42.37
Income Statement								
Total Revenues	3,477,000	14,146,700	13,566,400	12,911,500	12,261,800	11,703,700	11,245,800	11,066,200
Total Indirect Exp.	582,300	2,498,300	2,455,400	2,220,300	2,174,800	2,147,000	1,958,000	1,916,300
Depreciation & Amort.	224,000	877,200	847,300	834,500	803,500	777,000	738,400	683,700
Operating Income	821,400	3,199,300	2,979,700	2,723,000	2,494,700	2,302,300	2,125,300	2,053,000
Net Interest Inc./(Exp.)	(95,400)	(375,400)	(349,700)	(333,200)	(313,800)	(285,300)	(259,700)	(211,200)
Income Taxes	292,600	1,093,300	1,041,500	913,200	828,300	762,900	704,300	703,600
Eqty Earns/Minority Int.	88,900	344,900	351,700	240,100	200,000	157,500	85,000	50,300
Income from Cont Ops	...	...	...	...	...	...	...	1,179,200
Net Income	549,900	2,075,900	1,933,800	1,704,500	1,551,600	1,402,200	1,233,300	1,169,200
Average Shs. Outstg.	820,600	837,000	878,900	901,600	919,700	953,600	975,000	999,400
Balance Sheet								
Cash & Cash Equivalents	138,400	191,100	188,900	162,600	159,900	152,100	224,800	147,300
Total Current Assets	1,919,200	1,630,300	1,504,700	1,550,400	1,547,900	1,600,600	1,640,400	1,583,900
Total Assets	15,111,700	14,689,500	14,119,500	13,862,000	13,084,500	12,640,400	12,484,300	11,727,100
Total Current Liabilities	1,998,800	1,857,200	1,787,700	1,732,300	1,675,700	1,987,200	1,730,300	1,500,700
Long–Term Obligations	7,532,300	7,285,400	6,603,200	5,983,900	5,374,500	4,880,600	4,718,600	4,365,600
Net Stockholders' Equity	2,719,800	2,711,700	3,052,300	4,061,500	4,128,900	3,921,500	4,216,600	4,041,800
Net Working Capital	(79,600)	(226,900)	(283,000)	(181,900)	(127,800)	(386,600)	(89,900)	83,200
Shares Outstanding	804,216	813,100	846,600	879,100	903,600	922,200	953,200	974,040
Operating Profit Margin %	23.62	22.61	21.96	21.08	20.34	19.67	18.89	18.55
Net Profit Margin %	32.64	30.13	29.60	27.34	26.16	25.01	23.49	23.37
Return on Equity %	20.22	76.55	63.35	41.96	37.57	35.75	29.25	29.17
Return on Assets %	3.64	14.13	13.69	12.29	11.85	11.09	9.87	10.05
Debt/Total Assets %	49.84	49.59	46.76	43.16	41.07	38.61	37.79	37.22
Price Range	54.01–49.94	53.69–45.92	54.97–44.00	46.51–38.50	49.81–27.53	40.94–32.56	34.13–21.69	23.94–19.75
P/E Ratio	20.93–19.36	21.65–18.52	24.99–20.00	24.61–20.37	29.47–16.29	27.85–22.15	27.08–17.21	20.29–16.74
Average Yield %	1.64	1.65	1.49	1.62	1.62	1.59	2.11	2.32

Address: One Busch Place, St. Louis, MO 63118	Officers: August A. Busch III – Chmn., Patrick T. Stokes – Pres., C.E.O.	Investor Contact:314–577–9629
Telephone: (314) 577 2000	Transfer Agents:Mellon Investor Services, LLC,	Institutional Holding
Web Site: www.anheuser-busch.com	Ridgefield Park, NJ	No of Institutions: 14
		Shares: 1,107,435 % Held: –

APPLEBEE'S INTERNATIONAL, INC.

Exchange	Symbol	Price	52Wk Range	Yield	P/E
NMS	APPB	$37.90 (5/28/2004)	42.59–29.88	0.18	21.91

*7 Year Price Score 190.9 *NYSE Composite Index=100 ***12 Month Price Score 49.6**

TRADING VOLUME (thousand shares)

Interim Earnings (Per Share)

Qtr.	Mar	Jun	Sep	Dec
2001	0.29	0.31	0.29	0.26
2002	0.35	0.37	0.37	0.37
2003	0.43	0.35	0.45	0.41
2004	0.52	...	...	...

Interim Dividends (Per Share)

Amt	Decl	Ex	Rec	Pay
3-for-2	5/9/2002	6/12/2002	5/24/2002	6/11/2002
0.06A	12/12/2002	12/24/2002	12/27/2002	1/30/2003
0.07A	12/12/2003	12/23/2003	12/26/2003	1/23/2004
50%	5/13/2004	6/16/2004	5/28/2004	6/15/2004

Indicated Div: $0.07

Valuation Analysis

Forecast P/E 18.33 (5/24/2004)

Market Cap $2.1 Billion	Book Value	468.5 Million	
Price/Book 4.79	Price/Sales	2.18	

Dividend Achiever Status

Rank	62	10 Year Growth Rate	16.23%
Total Years of Dividend Growth			12

Business Summary: Hospitality &Tourism (MIC: 5.1 SIC: 5812 NAIC:722110)

Applebee's International develops, franchises and operates a national chain of casual dining restaurants under the trademark of "Applebee's Neighborhood Grill & Bar." Each of the restaurants is designed as a neighborhood establishment featuring a selection of moderately-priced food and beverage items with full-service luncheon and evening dining. The restaurants feature a selection of entrees, including beef, chicken, seafood and pasta items prepared in a variety of cuisines, as well as appetizers, salads, sandwiches, specialty drinks and desserts. As of Dec 28 2003, there were 1,585 Applebee's restaurants in 49 states and nine countries.

Recent Developments: For the first quarter ended Mar 28 2004, net earnings advanced 19.9% to $29.5 million compared with $24.6 million in the corresponding prior–year quarter. Results for 2004 and 2003 included losses on disposition of restaurants and equipment of $495,000 and $467,000, respectively. Total revenues climbed 16.5% to $277.4 million from $238.2 million a year earlier. Company restaurant sales grew 16.9% to $243.6 million, while franchise royalties and fees rose 13.3% to $30.8 million. System–wide same–store sales were up 8.2% year over year. Other franchise income increased 17.9% to $3.1 million. Operating earnings jumped 18.4% to $45.6 million from $38.5 million the year before.

Prospects: Co. is experiencing the highest levels of comparable sales and traffic growth it has seen in over ten years. Although this level of growth is not expected to be sustainable on an ongoing basis, Co. does expect system–wide comparable sales to rise by at least 5.0% in 2004. Meanwhile, more than 100 restaurants are expected to open in 2004, including at least 32 company restaurants and 70 to 80 franchise restaurants. On Apr 26 2004, Co. completed the acquisition of 10 franchise restaurants in southern California for $13.4 million in cash. Looking ahead to full–year 2004, Co. expects earnings to range from $2.02 to $2.06 per diluted share.

Financial Data

(US$ in Thousands)	3 Mos	12/28/2003	12/29/2002	12/30/2001	12/31/2000	12/26/1999	12/27/1998	12/28/1997
Earnings Per Share	1.73	1.64	1.46	1.15	1.06	0.84	0.74	0.63
Cash Flow Per Share	0.58	3.08	2.37	1.84	1.86	1.56	1.35	1.22
Tang. Book Val. Per Share	6.60	6.40	5.45	4.38	3.44	2.70	2.89	3.35
Dividends Per Share	0.070	0.060	0.050	0.048	0.044	0.036	0.031	0.027
Dividend Payout %	4.07	3.65	3.65	4.23	4.16	4.76	4.79	4.89
Income Statement								
Total Revenues	277,447	990,138	826,796	744,344	690,152	669,584	647,562	515,820
Total Indirect Exp.	26,593	109,472	83,795	81,770	73,524	80,549	65,486	58,255
Depreciation & Amort.	86	364	381	5,851	5,934	5,997	5,538	3,258
Operating Income	45,619	153,647	129,708	112,427	107,207	94,910	88,562	71,283
Net Interest Inc./(Exp.)	(344)	(1,733)	(2,168)	(7,456)	(9,304)	(10,814)	(9,922)	(1,705)
Income Taxes	15,886	52,627	47,109	38,227	36,777	31,537	29,753	26,710
Income from Cont Ops	...	...	...	65,650	...	...	50,656	...
Net Income	29,503	93,558	83,027	64,401	63,161	54,198	50,015	45,091
Average Shs. Outstg.	56,419	56,939	56,922	56,877	59,170	64,352	68,366	71,190
Balance Sheet								
Cash & Cash Equivalents	9,488	17,867	15,169	22,048	10,763	1,427	1,767	8,908
Total Current Assets	98,417	86,622	69,579	67,999	53,181	34,211	34,909	43,954
Total Assets	664,226	644,001	566,114	500,411	471,707	442,216	510,904	377,474
Total Current Liabilities	153,534	149,332	115,186	97,746	93,835	77,662	65,951	62,488
Long–Term Obligations	25,623	20,670	52,186	74,525	90,461	106,293	145,522	22,579
Net Stockholders' Equity	468,529	459,732	392,581	325,183	281,718	253,873	296,053	290,443
Net Working Capital	(55,117)	(62,710)	(45,607)	(29,747)	(40,654)	(43,451)	(31,042)	(18,534)
Shares Outstanding	54,821	55,192	55,388	55,814	56,744	59,843	66,465	70,834
Operating Profit Margin %	16.26	15.44	15.55	14.90	15.35	13.33	13.52	13.58
Return on Equity %	6.19	20.19	20.85	19.72	21.97	19.13	16.78	15.10
Return on Assets %	4.36	14.41	14.46	12.82	13.12	10.98	9.72	11.62
Debt/Total Assets %	3.85	3.20	9.21	14.89	19.17	24.03	28.48	5.98
Price Range	42.03–36.35	39.89–23.09	27.27–19.63	24.36–12.75	16.61–9.83	15.33–9.00	11.47–7.22	13.50–8.33
P/E Ratio	24.29–21.01	24.32–14.08	18.68–13.45	21.18–11.09	15.67–9.28	18.25–10.71	15.50–9.76	21.43–13.23
Average Yield %	0.18	0.20	0.21	0.22	0.32	0.32	0.32	0.27

Address: 4551 W. 107th Street, Overland Park, KS 66207	**Officers:** Lloyd L. Hill – Chmn., Pres., C.E.O., Steven K. Lumpkin – Exec. V.P., C.F.O., Treas.	**Investor Contact:**913–967–4109
Telephone: (913) 967–4000	**Transfer Agents:**American Stock Transfer &Trust	**Institutional Holding**
Web Site: www.applebees.com	Co, New York, NY	**No of Institutions:** 24
		Shares: 7,829,537 **% Held:** –

APTARGROUP INC.

Exchange	Symbol	Price	52Wk Range	Yield	P/E
NYS	ATR	$40.65 (5/28/2004)	41.47–34.40	0.69	18.48

*7 Year Price Score 124.3 *NYSE Composite Index=100 *12 Month Price Score 48.7

Interim Earnings (Per Share)

Qtr.	Mar	Jun	Sep	Dec
2001	0.50	0.41	0.43	0.27
2002	0.36	0.48	0.49	0.49
2003	0.53	0.58	0.51	0.54
2004	0.57	...	...	...

Interim Dividends (Per Share)

Amt	Decl	Ex	Rec	Pay
0.07Q	7/17/2003	7/25/2003	7/29/2003	8/19/2003
0.07Q	10/15/2003	10/27/2003	10/29/2003	11/19/2003
0.07Q	1/20/2004	2/2/2004	2/4/2004	2/26/2004
0.07Q	4/15/2004	4/28/2004	4/30/2004	5/21/2004

Indicated Div: $0.28

Valuation Analysis
Forecast P/E 16.84 (5/24/2004)
Market Cap $1.5 Billion   Book Value   791.1 Million
Price/Book 1.78   Price/Sales 1.21

Dividend Achiever Status
Rank 43   10 Year Growth Rate   17.92%
Total Years of Dividend Growth   10

TRADING VOLUME (thousand shares)

Business Summary: Plastics (MIC: 11.7 SIC: 3089 NAIC:326199)

AptarGroup is an international company that designs, manufactures and sells consumer product dispensing systems for the personal care, fragrance/cosmetic, pharmaceutical, household and food/beverage markets. Operations are divided into two segments, Dispensing Systems and SeaquistPerfect. The dispensing segment focuses on providing value–added dispensing systems (pumps, closures and aerosol valves), while SeaquistPerfect sells primarily aerosol valves and certain pumps to the personal care, household, and to a lesser degree, the food/beverage markets. Co. has manufacturing facilities located throughout the world, including North America, Europe, Asia and South America.

Recent Developments: For the quarter ended Mar 31 2004, net income advanced 10.6% to $21.2 million compared with $19.2 million in the equivalent 2003 quarter. Net sales climbed 19.0% to $315.6 million, reflecting favorable foreign currency exchange rates, custom tooling sales, and volume growth in all markets except for the pharmaceutical market. Operating income increased 4.5% to $31.7 million, but declined as a percentage of net sales to 10.0%, versus 11.4% in 2003. The decrease in operating margin was due to price competition, weakness in pharmaceutical product sales, increased cost of imports to the U.S. due to the weaker dollar and increased cost of raw materials.

Prospects: The positive momentum in the first quarter is anticipated to continue into the second quarter. In addition, Co. expects that its pharmaceutical volumes will trend upward in the second quarter and continue to improve throughout the year. Also, Co. has filed for income tax refunds totaling about $1.5 million in the U.S. relating to research and development expenditures incurred from 2000 through 2002. These funds will be recognized as a reduction of tax provision when they are received. Excluding the potential effect of these tax refunds net of related contingent consulting fees, Co. expects diluted earnings per share for the second quarter of 2004 to range from $0.58 to $0.63 per share.

Financial Data

(US$ in Thousands)	3 Mos	12/31/2003	12/31/2002	12/31/2001	12/31/2000	12/31/1999	12/31/1998	12/31/1997
Earnings Per Share	2.20	2.16	1.82	1.61	1.78	1.59	1.65	1.27
Cash Flow Per Share	0.95	3.78	4.21	3.52	3.58	3.20	2.30	2.36
Tang. Book Val. Per Share	17.53	16.75	12.11	9.00	8.54	8.02	10.13	8.37
Dividends Per Share	0.270	0.260	0.240	0.220	0.200	0.180	0.160	0.150
Dividend Payout %	12.27	12.03	13.18	13.66	11.23	11.32	9.69	11.76
Income Statement								
Total Revenues	315,603	1,114,689	926,691	891,986	883,481	834,317	713,506	655,390
Total Indirect Exp.	72,319	258,705	225,895	227,304	215,949	206,177	173,733	158,289
Depreciation & Amort.	24,050	85,851	72,141	73,584	70,949	68,670	54,446	49,917
Operating Income	31,703	123,946	107,073	101,868	113,890	108,436	95,158	78,991
Income Taxes	9,993	37,591	31,711	29,447	33,256	33,066	38,368	32,067
Income from Cont Ops	...	...	...	58,908	...	...	...	...
Net Income	21,235	79,679	66,647	58,844	64,666	58,712	60,821	46,529
Average Shs. Outstg.	37,355	36,901	36,623	36,529	36,369	36,913	36,799	36,518
Balance Sheet								
Cash & Cash Equivalents	181,590	164,982	90,205	48,013	55,559	32,416	25,159	17,717
Total Current Assets	631,324	602,454	447,196	374,915	407,549	351,234	316,649	256,161
Total Assets	1,280,104	1,264,343	1,047,671	915,327	952,239	863,298	714,673	585,433
Total Current Liabilities	290,264	283,220	162,688	154,151	203,102	159,905	167,433	125,397
Long–Term Obligations	124,761	125,196	219,182	239,387	252,752	235,649	80,875	70,740
Net Stockholders' Equity	791,142	783,051	594,467	469,204	440,540	420,269	415,508	342,055
Shares Outstanding	36,548	37,700	37,200	37,000	36,600	36,500	36,100	36,000
Operating Profit Margin %	10.04	11.11	11.55	11.42	12.89	12.99	13.33	12.05
Net Profit Margin %	13.06	13.89	14.03	13.20	14.84	14.96	19.27	16.88
Return on Equity %	2.68	10.17	11.21	12.55	14.67	13.97	14.63	13.60
Return on Assets %	1.66	6.30	6.36	6.43	6.79	6.80	8.51	7.94
Debt/Total Assets %	9.74	9.90	20.92	26.15	26.54	27.29	11.31	12.08
Price Range	41.40–37.38	39.48–26.51	38.70–25.12	36.90–27.38	30.00–19.88	30.81–22.75	32.94–20.25	29.38–16.44
P/E Ratio	18.82–16.99	18.28–12.27	21.26–13.80	22.92–17.00	16.85–11.17	19.38–14.31	19.96–12.27	23.13–12.94
Average Yield %	0.68	0.75	0.75	0.69	0.80	0.66	0.56	0.64

Address: 475 West Terra Cotta Avenue, Crystal Lake, IL 60014
Telephone: (815) 477–0424
Web Site: www.aptargroup.com

Officers: King Harris – Chmn., Peter Pfeiffer – Vice–Chmn.
Transfer Agents: National City Bank Corporate Trust Operations., Cleveland, OH

Institutional Holding
No of Institutions: 31
Shares: 997,090 **% Held:** –

AQUA AMERICA INC

Exchange	Symbol	Price	52Wk Range	Yield	P/E
NYS	WTR	$19.86 (5/28/2004)	22.55-18.43	2.42	24.58

*7 Year Price Score 139.4 *NYSE Composite Index=100 ***12 Month Price Score 46.1**

TRADING VOLUME (thousand shares)

Interim Earnings (Per Share)

Qtr.	Mar	Jun	Sep	Dec
2001	0.15	0.17	0.22	0.15
2002	0.13	0.16	0.24	0.24
2003	0.15	0.17	0.26	0.21
2004	0.17	...	...	...

Interim Dividends (Per Share)

Amt	Decl	Ex	Rec	Pay
0.112Q	8/5/2003	8/13/2003	8/15/2003	9/1/2003
25%	8/5/2003	12/2/2003	11/14/2003	12/1/2003
0.12Q	2/3/2004	2/11/2004	2/16/2004	3/1/2004
0.12Q	4/27/2004	5/12/2004	5/14/2004	6/1/2004

Indicated Div: $0.48 (Div. Reinv. Plan)

Valuation Analysis

Forecast P/E N/A

Market Cap	$1.4 Billion	Book Value	667.3 Million
Price/Book	2.95	Price/Sales	5.10

Dividend Achiever Status

Rank	235	10 Year Growth Rate	5.90%
Total Years of Dividend Growth			12

Business Summary: Water Utilities (MIC: 7.2 SIC: 4941 NAIC:221310)

Aqua America is a holding company. Through its subsidiaries, Co. is engaged in operating regulated utilities that provide water or wastewater services to approximately 2.5 million people in 14 states. Co.'s largest subsidiary, Aqua Pennsylvania, Inc. provides water or wastewater services to about 1.3 million residents in the suburban areas north and west of the city of Philadelphia and 19 other counties in PA. Co. also provides water and wastewater services through operating and maintenance contracts with municipal authorities and other parties close to its operating companies' service territories. Co. is the largest U.S.–based publicly–traded water utility based on number of people served.

Recent Developments: For the first quarter ended Mar 31 2004, net income grew 16.9% to $15.6 million compared with $13.3 million in the equivalent 2003 quarter. Results for 2004 and 2003 included gains on the sale of other assets of $450,000 and $55,000, respectively. Operating revenues climbed 24.0% to $99.8 million from $80.5 million a year earlier. The improvement in revenues was primarily attributed to contributions from the acquisition of the AquaSource utility operations, which was completed in July 2003. Operating income advanced 12.3% to $36.4 million versus $32.4 million the year before.

Prospects: Co.'s growth–through–acquisition continues to be the core of its strategy. On Apr 23 2004, Co. announced that its Florida subsidiary reached an agreement with Florida Water Services Corporation, a wholly–owned subsidiary of ALLETE, Inc., to acquire 63 water and wastewater systems for $13.8 million. A second agreement would allow Florida Water Services to acquire an additional nine water and wastewater systems for $4.2 million subject to the outcome of a previously negotiated right of first refusal with a nearby municipality. These transactions, which are expected to add more than 16,000 new customers Co.'s Florida operations, are expected to close by mid 2004

Financial Data

(US$ in Thousands)	3 Mos	12/31/2003	12/31/2002	12/31/2001	12/31/2000	12/31/1999	12/31/1998	12/31/1997
Earnings Per Share	0.81	0.79	0.77	0.69	0.64	0.45	0.52	0.45
Cash Flow Per Share	0.35	1.60	1.40	1.18	1.06	0.91	1.01	0.81
Tang. Book Val. Per Share	7.18	7.11	5.80	5.52	5.13	4.58	4.27	3.56
Dividends Per Share	0.490	0.480	0.430	0.400	0.370	0.350	0.340	0.310
Dividend Payout %	61.14	61.51	55.41	57.98	58.11	79.53	64.55	70.73
Income Statement								
Total Revenues	99,768	367,233	322,028	307,280	275,538	257,326	150,977	136,171
Total Indirect Exp.	21,493	73,070	63,789	61,055	55,484	57,523	26,124	23,473
Costs & Expenses	63,324	213,672	181,524	172,940	157,225	156,281	84,298	79,372
Depreciation & Amort.	14,344	51,463	44,322	40,168	34,100	31,903	16,089	14,580
Operating Income	36,444	153,561	140,504	134,340	118,313	101,045	66,679	56,799
Net Interest Inc./(Exp.)	(11,802)	(44,662)	(40,396)	(39,859)	(40,360)	(33,698)	(18,976)	(17,890)
Income Taxes	10,126	45,923	42,046	38,976	34,105	26,531	19,605	15,873
Net Income	15,575	70,795	67,206	60,111	52,890	36,384	28,819	23,188
Average Shs. Outstg.	93,806	89,244	86,538	85,943	81,767	80,673	54,445	51,314
Balance Sheet								
Net Property	1,841,725	1,824,291	1,486,703	1,368,115	1,251,427	1,135,364	609,808	534,483
Total Assets	2,080,738	2,069,736	1,717,069	1,560,339	1,414,010	1,280,805	701,450	618,472
Long–Term Obligations	686,312	696,666	582,910	516,520	468,769	413,752	261,826	232,471
Net Stockholders' Equity	667,282	659,030	493,097	473,833	432,347	368,901	234,759	194,745
Shares Outstanding	92,833	92,589	84,895	85,483	83,868	80,102	54,154	53,712
Statistical Record								
Operating Profit Margin %	36.52	80.10	80.19	80.13	79.86	77.64	82.69	82.76
Net Inc./Net Property %	0.84	3.88	4.52	4.39	4.22	3.20	4.72	4.33
Net Inc./Tot. Capital %	1.15	5.22	6.24	6.06	5.86	4.64	5.80	5.42
Return on Equity %	2.33	32.07	37.50	36.29	35.76	36.63	37.05	40.61
Accum. Depr./Gross Prop. %	21.00	20.76	19.06	18.42	18.53	18.49	18.20	18.52
Price Range	22.55-20.00	22.25-15.77	19.98-13.02	19.39-12.80	15.88-8.64	15.14-10.30	15.23-9.76	11.30-6.00
P/E Ratio	27.84-24.69	28.16-19.96	25.95-16.91	28.10-18.55	24.81-13.50	33.64-22.90	29.29-18.77	25.12-13.33
Average Yield %	2.27	2.58	2.54	2.49	3.28	2.95	2.87	3.85

Address: 762 W. Lancaster Avenue, Bryn Mawr, PA 19010–3489 **Telephone:** (610) 524–8000 Web Site: www.suburbanwater.com	**Officers:** Nicholas DeBenedictis – Chmn., Pres., Roy H. Stahl – Exec. V.P., Sec., Gen. Couns. **Transfer Agents:**BankBoston, N.A., Boston, MA	**Investor Contact:**610–525–1400 **Institutional Holding** No of Institutions: 11 Shares: 333,830 % Held: –

19

ARCHER DANIELS MIDLAND CO.

Exchange	Symbol	Price	52Wk Range	Yield	P/E
NYS	ADM	$16.63 (5/28/2004)	17.59–12.08	1.80	15.54

*7 Year Price Score 107.7 ***NYSE Composite Index=100** ***12 Month Price Score 53.8**

Interim Earnings (Per Share)

Qtr.	Sep	Dec	Mar	Jun
2000–01	0.16	0.19	0.14	0.09
2001–02	0.20	0.23	0.18	0.17
2002–03	0.17	0.20	0.18	0.15
2003–04	0.23	0.34	0.35	...

Interim Dividends (Per Share)

Amt	Decl	Ex	Rec	Pay
0.06Q	8/7/2003	8/20/2003	8/22/2003	9/10/2003
0.06Q	11/6/2003	11/14/2003	11/18/2003	12/11/2003
0.075Q	2/5/2004	2/11/2004	2/13/2004	3/9/2004
0.075Q	5/7/2004	5/14/2004	5/18/2004	6/10/2004

Indicated Div: $0.30 (Div. Reinv. Plan)

Valuation Analysis

Forecast P/E 13.80 (5/24/2004)

Market Cap	$10.8 Billion	Book Value	7.9 Billion
Price/Book	1.39	Price/Sales	0.32

Dividend Achiever Status

Rank	40	10 Year Growth Rate	18.62%
Total Years of Dividend Growth			29

Business Summary: Food (MIC: 4.1 SIC: 2075 NAIC:311225)

Archer Daniels Midland is engaged in procuring, transporting, storing, processing and merchandising agricultural commodities and products. Co. processes soybeans, cottonseed, sunflower seeds, canola, peanuts, flaxseed and corn germ into vegetable oils and meals primarily for the food and feed industries. In addition, Co.'s corn milling operations produce products for the food and beverage industry, along with ethyl alcohol, or ethanol, which is used as a gasoline additive. Co. also processes wheat, corn and milo into flour.

Recent Developments: For the three months ended Mar 31 2004, net earnings totaled $226.8 million, up 94.1% compared with $116.8 million in the corresponding prior-year period. Net sales and other operating income climbed 17.7% to $9.31 billion from $7.91 billion the year before. Gross profit was $587.0 million, or 6.3% of net sales and other operating income, versus $414.3 million, or 5.2% of net sales and other operating income, a year earlier. Operating profit more than doubled to $501.7 million compared with $242.4 million the year before stemming from increased demand for ethanol, a corn-based gasoline additive and expansion of Co.'s grain handling capabilities.

Prospects: Results are benefiting from improved market conditions across many of Co.'s business segments. Earnings in Co.'s corn processing segment are being bolstered by higher prices and increased demand for ethanol following the prohibited use of methyl tertiary butyl ether as a gasoline additive in New York and Connecticut effective Jan 1 2004. Meanwhile, results are being positively affected by sharply higher prices for corn and soybeans stemming from depleted U.S. crops due to drought conditions in 2003. Separately, earnings are benefiting from Co.'s efforts to expand its processing capacity in emerging markets such as South America and Asia.

Financial Data

(US$ in Thousands)	9 Mos	6 Mos	3 Mos	06/30/2003	06/30/2002	06/30/2001	06/30/2000	06/30/1999
Earnings Per Share	1.07	0.90	0.76	0.70	0.78	0.58	0.44	0.40
Cash Flow Per Share	(1.38)	(0.73)	0.26	1.67	2.30	1.30	1.21	1.77
Tang. Book Val. Per Share	12.13	11.20	10.63	10.42	10.39	9.55	9.39	9.13
Dividends Per Share	0.250	0.240	0.240	0.240	0.190	0.180	0.175	0.170
Dividend Payout %	23.36	26.67	31.58	34.28	25.33	32.44	40.04	41.82
Income Statement								
Total Revenues	26,465,425	17,156,406	7,967,902	30,708,033	23,453,561	20,051,421	12,876,817	14,283,335
Total Indirect Exp.	749,138	497,437	231,796	947,694	826,922	731,029	729,358	701,075
Depreciation & Amort.	513,293	340,878	167,114	648,726	614,070	621,974	647,639	622,181
Operating Income	895,929	560,611	221,958	779,444	856,534	700,769	490,217	530,954
Net Interest Inc./(Exp.)	...	...	...	(359,971)	(355,956)	(398,131)	(377,404)	(326,207)
Income Taxes	278,373	166,681	67,473	179,829	207,844	138,615	52,334	138,545
Eqty Earns/Minority Int.	...	...	...	65,991	61,532	104,909	88,206	(4,273)
Income from Cont Ops	...	...	...	451,144	...	...	...	281,288
Net Income	597,510	371,002	150,181	451,145	511,093	383,284	300,903	265,964
Average Shs. Outstg.	646,844	645,992	645,132	646,086	656,955	664,507	669,279	685,328
Balance Sheet								
Cash & Cash Equivalents	805,015	537,125	765,982	1,309,628	978,661	817,758	931,449	903,569
Total Current Assets	12,147,725	11,027,823	9,095,264	8,421,857	7,363,231	6,150,301	6,162,367	5,789,588
Total Assets	21,112,047	19,938,630	17,686,389	17,182,879	15,416,273	14,339,931	14,423,100	14,029,881
Total Current Liabilities	8,035,564	7,242,308	5,481,256	5,147,472	4,719,297	3,866,981	4,332,945	3,840,265
Long–Term Obligations	3,858,460	3,865,124	3,855,306	3,872,287	3,111,294	3,351,067	3,277,218	3,191,883
Net Stockholders' Equity	7,883,574	7,605,882	7,217,029	7,069,197	6,754,821	6,331,683	6,110,243	6,240,640
Net Working Capital	4,112,161	3,785,515	3,614,008	3,274,385	2,643,934	2,283,320	1,829,422	1,949,323
Shares Outstanding	649,977	647,992	646,664	644,855	649,993	662,378	650,682	683,340
Statistical Record								
Operating Profit Margin %	3.38	3.26	2.78	2.53	3.65	3.49	3.80	3.71
Return on Equity %	7.58	4.87	2.08	6.38	7.56	6.05	4.92	4.50
Return on Assets %	2.83	1.86	0.84	2.62	3.31	2.67	2.08	2.00
Debt/Total Assets %	18.28	19.38	21.79	22.53	20.18	23.36	22.72	22.75
Price Range	17.59–12.08	15.22–12.08	14.06–12.08	14.28–10.54	15.60–12.00	15.20–7.92	13.34–8.22	16.25–11.99
P/E Ratio	16.44–11.29	10.91–13.42	18.50–15.89	20.40–15.06	20.00–15.38	26.21–13.65	30.31–18.68	40.62–29.96
Average Yield %	1.72	1.75	1.83	1.98	1.39	1.58	1.57	1.23

Address: 4666 Faries Parkway, Decatur, IL 62525
Telephone: (217) 424–5200
Web Site: www.admworld.com

Officers: G. Allen Andreas – Chmn., C.E.O., Paul B. Mulhollem – Pres., C.O.O.
Transfer Agents: Hickory Point Bank &Trust, fsb, Decatur, IL

Investor Contact: 217-424-4586
Institutional Holding
No of Institutions: 14
Shares: 3,927,928 **% Held:** –

ARROW INTERNATIONAL,INC.

Exchange	Symbol	Price	52Wk Range	Yield	P/E
NMS	ARRO	$30.17 (5/28/2004)	31.28-21.41	1.19	25.35

*7 Year Price Score 139.3   *NYSE Composite Index=100   *12 Month Price Score 54.4

Interim Earnings (Per Share)

Qtr.	Nov	Feb	May	Aug
2000–01	0.25	0.26	0.27	0.27
2001–02	0.27	0.29	0.25	0.08
2002–03	0.26	0.27	0.33	0.18
2003–04	0.33	0.35	...	...

Interim Dividends (Per Share)

Amt	Decl	Ex	Rec	Pay
2-for-1	7/16/2003	8/18/2003	8/1/2003	8/15/2003
0.08Q	11/14/2003	11/25/2003	11/28/2003	12/12/2003
0.09Q	2/13/2004	2/25/2004	2/27/2004	3/12/2004
0.09Q	5/14/2004	5/26/2004	5/28/2004	6/11/2004

Indicated Div: $0.36

Valuation Analysis

Forecast P/E N/A

Market Cap $662.8 Million	Book Value 423.9 Million
Price/Book 2.62	Price/Sales 2.71

Dividend Achiever Status

Rank 52	10 Year Growth Rate	16.98%

Total Years of Dividend Growth   11

Business Summary: Medical Instruments &Equipment (MIC: 9.6 SIC: 3841 NAIC:339112)

Arrow International, Inc. develops, manufactures and markets a broad range of clinically advanced, disposable catheters and related products for critical and cardiac care. Co.'s critical care products are used principally for central vascular access in the administration of fluids, drugs, and blood products, patient monitoring and diagnostic purposes. Co.'s cardiac care products include cardiac assist products, such as intra–aortic balloon pumps and catheters, which are used primarily to augment temporarily the pumping capability of the heart following cardiac surgery, serious heart attack or balloon angioplasty.

Recent Developments: For the three months ended Feb 29 2004, net income improved 29.6% to $15.4 million compared with $11.9 million in the corresponding quarter of the previous year. Net sales increased 16.8% to $108.3 million from $92.8 million in the year–earlier period. The increase in sales was primarily due to favorable currency exchange rates and recent acquisitions. Sales of critical care products climbed 17.2% to $92.0 million from $78.5 million, while sales of cardiac care products advanced 14.0% to $16.3 million from $14.3 million in the prior–year quarter. Operating income jumped 30.6% to $23.0 million versus $17.6 million the year before.

Prospects: Co. will continue to focus on its strategy to grow its core business. Co.'s core growth rate for the first six months of fiscal 2004 was 9.7%, which is slightly below its goal of double–digit growth. The growth reflects continued growth of sharps protection kits for Central Venous Catheters, continued growth of the StimuCath®regional anesthesia catheter, new leadership and stronger sales and marketing in Europe. In 2004, Co. expects sales to range from $424.0 million to $428.0 million and diluted earnings from $1.35 to $1.40 per share. Co.'s sales and earnings targets reflect additional spending on the introduction of the AutoCAT®2 WAVE™and support of the LionHeart™program.

Financial Data

(US$ in Thousands)	6 Mos	3 Mos	08/31/2003	08/31/2002	08/31/2001	08/31/2000	08/31/1999	08/31/1998
Earnings Per Share	1.19	1.11	1.04	0.89	1.05	1.02	0.77	0.18
Cash Flow Per Share	0.98	0.54	1.79	1.76	0.96	1.26	1.22	0.86
Tang. Book Val. Per Share	8.75	8.41	6.90	6.69	5.48	4.66	4.53	4.16
Dividends Per Share	0.240	0.190	0.150	0.130	0.120	0.110	0.100	0.090
Dividend Payout %	20.16	17.11	14.42	15.16	11.90	11.21	13.63	51.35
Income Statement								
Total Revenues	211,395	103,101	380,376	340,759	334,042	320,340	295,946	260,890
Total Indirect Exp.	67,413	32,582	125,524	112,576	103,708	98,322	104,585	117,598
Depreciation & Amort.	11,468	5,676	23,226	21,693	22,696	20,931	18,606	15,623
Operating Income	44,587	21,616	64,606	58,558	71,761	71,595	52,120	29,220
Net Interest Inc./(Exp.)	(304)	(109)	1,203	(392)	(1,897)	(1,945)	(975)	(328)
Income Taxes	14,387	6,944	21,248	18,777	22,925	23,266	19,646	19,010
Net Income	29,882	14,424	45,670	39,000	46,545	46,184	35,695	8,572
Average Shs. Outstg.	44,092	43,982	43,773	44,211	44,240	45,037	46,390	46,451
Balance Sheet								
Cash & Cash Equivalents	75,563	62,948	46,975	33,103	2,968	3,959	3,939	4,652
Total Current Assets	280,192	266,824	241,880	224,873	203,985	179,651	166,627	154,617
Total Assets	532,748	519,746	493,897	425,680	417,710	385,814	357,484	322,881
Total Current Liabilities	84,444	87,322	77,966	50,425	78,429	89,601	58,726	54,361
Long–Term Obligations	2,000	2,000	3,735	9	300	600	11,105	11,686
Net Stockholders' Equity	423,911	408,261	390,646	360,356	326,089	285,204	278,167	247,868
Net Working Capital	195,748	179,502	163,914	174,448	125,556	90,050	107,901	100,256
Shares Outstanding	43,587	43,429	43,285	43,941	44,002	44,001	46,115	46,448
Statistical Record								
Operating Profit Margin %	21.09	20.96	16.98	17.18	21.48	22.34	17.61	11.20
Return on Equity %	7.05	3.53	11.69	10.82	14.27	16.19	12.83	3.45
Return on Assets %	5.61	2.75	9.24	9.16	11.14	11.97	9.98	2.65
Debt/Total Assets %	0.38	0.38	0.75	0.07	0.14	0.23	3.10	3.61
Price Range	29.37–22.43	27.10–22.43	25.80–15.75	24.20–16.93	20.16–17.06	19.81–11.88	15.69–9.44	20.38–13.00
P/E Ratio	24.68–18.85	24.41–20.21	24.81–15.14	27.19–19.02	19.20–16.25	19.42–11.64	20.37–12.26	113.2–72.22
Average Yield %	0.92	0.75	0.73	0.64	0.64	0.69	0.76	0.53

Address: 2400 Bernville Road, Reading, PA 19605 **Telephone:** (610) 378–0131 **Web Site:** www.arrowintl.com	**Officers:** Carl G. Anderson – Chmn, C.E.O., Philip B. Fleck – Pres., C.O.O. **Transfer Agents:** First Chicago Trust Division of EquiServe, Jersey City, NJ	**Investor Contact:** 610–478–3116 **Institutional Holding** **No of Institutions:** 24 **Shares:** 42,645,770 **% Held:** –

ARTESIAN RESOURCES CORP.

Exchange	Symbol	Price	52Wk Range	Yield	P/E
OTC	ARTN B	$27.28 (5/28/2004)	29.50–22.80	2.99	28.42

*7 Year Price Score 145.4   *NYSE Composite Index=100   *12 Month Price Score 47.9

Interim Earnings (Per Share)

Qtr.	Mar	Jun	Sep	Dec
2001	0.08	0.28	0.46	0.23
2002	0.16	0.26	0.39	0.33
2003	0.18	0.31	0.26	0.21
2004	0.18	...	...	...

Interim Dividends (Per Share)

Amt	Decl	Ex	Rec	Pay
0.1984Q	7/30/2003	8/7/2003	8/11/2003	8/22/2003
0.2025Q	10/29/2003	11/6/2003	11/10/2003	11/21/2003
0.2025Q	1/6/2004	2/5/2004	2/9/2004	2/20/2004
0.2075Q	4/28/2004	5/6/2004	5/10/2004	5/21/2004

Indicated Div: $8.16

Valuation Analysis

Forecast P/E N/A

Market Cap $59.3 Million	Book Value	N/A
Price/Book N/A	Price/Sales	N/A

Dividend Achiever Status

Rank	104	10 Year Growth Rate	13.08%
Total Years of Dividend Growth			11

Business Summary: Water Utilities (MIC: 7.2 SIC: 4941 NAIC:221310)

Artesian Resources distributes and sells water to residential, commercial, industrial, governmental, municipal and utility customers throughout Delaware. As of Dec 31 2003, Co. had approximately 70,000 metered customers and served a population of approximately 230,000 (including contract services), representing about 29.0% of Delaware's total population. Co. also provides water for public and private fire protection to customers in its service territories. Co.'s gross water sales revenue by major customer classifications for 2003 were 62.0% for residential, 32.0% for commercial, industrial, governmental, municipal and utility, and 6.0% for fire protection and other.

Recent Developments: For the three months ended Mar 31 2004, net income declined 7.0% to $718,000 compared with $772,000 million in the corresponding quarter of the previous year. Operating revenue grew 2.9% to $8.8 million from $8.5 million in the prior–year period. Revenue growth was primarily due to an increase in the number of water utility customers served versus the prior year. Total operating expenses climbed 4.6% to $7.0 million from $6.7 million in the year–earlier quarter, reflecting the replacement of the filter media used in a new water treatment process at one of Co.'s facilities. Operating income slipped 3.2% to $1.8 million versus $1.9 million the year before.

Prospects: Co. should continue to benefit from the number of water utility customers it serves as the warmer season approaches and the demand for water increases. Meanwhile, Co. will continue to invest in utility plant. Furthermore, Co. will continue to place emphasis on keeping controllable expense increases to a minimum. As a results of cost increases, Co. has filed a rate increase request with the Delaware Public Service Commission. Co. placed a temporary increase in water rates into effect during the second quarter, which represents approximately $2.5 million in additional annual revenue.

Financial Data

(US$ in Thousands)	3 Mos	12/31/2003	12/31/2002	12/31/2001	12/31/2000	12/31/1999	12/31/1998	12/31/1997
Earnings Per Share	0.96	0.96	1.14	1.05	0.78	0.97	0.96	0.71
Cash Flow Per Share	1.03	3.53	0.76	2.86	1.28	2.48	2.71	1.54
Tang. Book Val. Per Share	15.86	13.50	13.25	11.16	10.78	10.70	10.22	9.85
Dividends Per Share	0.800	0.790	0.770	0.740	0.720	0.700	0.640	0.610
Dividend Payout %	83.33	83.07	67.83	70.25	93.58	72.60	66.89	85.98
Income Statement								
Total Revenues	8,787	36,295	34,597	31,987	27,551	26,777	25,466	22,340
Total Indirect Exp.	1,998	8,276	8,263	7,145	6,120	6,224	5,754	5,405
Costs & Expenses	6,981	27,766	26,422	24,586	21,340	20,687	19,799	17,933
Depreciation & Amort.	924	3,635	3,392	3,001	2,706	2,417	2,183	2,441
Operating Income	1,806	8,529	8,175	7,401	6,211	6,090	5,667	4,407
Net Interest Inc./(Exp.)	(1,457)	(4,889)	(4,388)	(4,537)	(4,055)	(3,298)	(3,162)	(2,580)
Net Income	718	3,917	4,167	3,321	2,451	2,980	2,720	1,985
Average Shs. Outstg.	4,053	3,993	3,612	3,108	3,066	2,994	2,724	2,662
Balance Sheet								
Net Property	196,361	187,893	167,338	152,356	134,038	122,481	109,780	97,694
Total Assets	220,506	216,324	183,072	163,534	144,407	132,482	119,376	107,867
Long–Term Obligations	81,328	80,558	63,970	49,370	50,717	34,529	32,053	32,103
Net Stockholders' Equity	52,881	52,691	51,176	34,445	32,829	32,356	27,933	26,587
Shares Outstanding	3,332	3,900	3,861	3,059	3,019	2,997	2,705	2,670
Statistical Record								
Operating Profit Margin %	20.55	23.49	23.62	23.13	22.54	22.74	22.25	19.72
Net Profit Margin %	8.17	10.79	12.04	10.38	8.89	11.12	10.68	8.88
Net Inc./Net Property %	0.36	2.08	2.49	2.17	1.82	2.43	2.47	2.03
Net Inc./Tot. Capital %	0.48	2.70	3.38	3.70	2.78	4.25	4.39	3.33
Return on Equity %	1.35	7.43	8.14	9.64	7.46	9.21	9.73	7.46
Accum. Depr./Gross Prop. %	0.04	...	...	...	...	...	...	...
Price Range		29.50–27.30	29.33–19.71	22.67–16.76	20.63–15.50	21.00–14.00	21.17–14.00	18.25–12.17	12.67–10.83
P/E Ratio		30.73–28.44	30.55–20.53	19.88–14.70	19.64–14.76	26.92–17.95	21.82–14.43	19.01–12.67	17.84–15.26
Average Yield %		2.83	3.34	3.90	4.22	4.46	4.26	4.71	5.11

Address: 664 Churchmans Road, Newark, DE 19702	Officers: Dian C. Taylor – Chmn., Pres., C.E.O., Joseph A. DiNunzio – Sr. V.P., Sec.	Investor Contact:800–332–5114
Telephone: (302) 453 6900	Transfer Agents: ChaseMellon Shareholder Services, L.L.C.	Institutional Holding No of Institutions: 6
Web Site: www.artesianwater.com		Shares: 908,604 % Held: –

ASSOCIATED BANC-CORP.

Exchange	Symbol	Price	52Wk Range	Yield	P/E
NMS	ASBC	$29.25 (5/28/2004)	30.37–24.07	3.42	14.18

*7 Year Price Score 128.0 ***NYSE Composite Index=100** ***12 Month Price Score 49.1**

Interim Earnings (Per Share)

Qtr.	Mar	Jun	Sep	Dec
2001	0.38	0.41	0.41	0.43
2002	0.46	0.45	0.46	0.49
2003	0.51	0.50	0.52	0.51
2004	0.53	...	...	...

Interim Dividends (Per Share)

Amt	Decl	Ex	Rec	Pay
0.227Q	10/22/2003	10/30/2003	11/3/2003	11/17/2003
0.227Q	1/28/2004	1/30/2004	2/2/2004	2/16/2004
3-for-2	4/28/2004	5/13/2004	5/7/2004	5/12/2004
0.25Q	4/28/2004	5/14/2004	5/18/2004	5/21/2004
Indicated Div: $1.00 (Div. Reinv. Plan)				

Valuation Analysis

Forecast P/E 13.18 (5/24/2004)

Market Cap	$2.2 Billion	Book Value	1.4 Billion
Price/Book	2.34	Price/Sales	3.42

Dividend Achiever Status

Rank	111	10 Year Growth Rate	12.47%
Total Years of Dividend Growth			33

Business Summary: Commercial Banking (MIC: 8.1 SIC: 6022 NAIC:522110)

Associated Banc–Corp. is a multi-bank holding company headquartered in Green Bay, WI. Co. provides advice and specialized services to its affiliates in banking policy and operations, including auditing, data processing, marketing/advertising, investing, legal/compliance, personnel services, trust services, risk management, facilities management, and other financial services functionally related to banking. Through its affiliates, Co. provides a wide range of banking services to individuals and small– to medium–sized businesses. As of Dec 31 2003, Co. had total assets of $15.25 billion and 217 banking offices serving over 151 communities in Wisconsin, Illinois and Minnesota.

Recent Developments: For the quarter ended Mar 31 2004, net income rose 2.7% to $59.6 million from $58.0 million in the corresponding period the year before. Results for 2004 and 2003 included net asset sale gains of $222,000 and $122,000, respectively. Net interest income grew 1.3% to $129.1 million. Provision for loan losses dropped 60.1% to $5.2 million. Total non–interest income declined 16.7% to $53.0 million due to lower mortgage fee revenue. Total non–interest expense decreased 3.0% to $93.7 million. Total loans inched up 2.1% to $10.49 billion, reflecting growth in commercial loans and home equity loans. Total deposits rose 7.1% to $9.70 billion.

Prospects: Co. is experiencing positive momentum in its wealth management and consumer businesses, as well as improved volume in its commercial banking business. Based on significant improvement in its asset quality as well as its continued focus on expense management, Co. is optimistic that it can achieve or exceed its estimate of earnings per share of $3.25 for 2004. Separately, on Apr 1 2004, Co.'s subsidiary, Associated Financial Group, acquired Jabas Group, an employee benefits firm that serves over 1,000 business clients through seven offices throughout Wisconsin.

Financial Data

(US$ in Thousands)	3 Mos	12/31/2003	12/31/2002	12/31/2001	12/31/2000	12/31/1999	12/31/1998	12/31/1997
Earnings Per Share	2.06	2.04	1.86	1.63	1.49	1.41	1.35	0.44
Tang. Book Val. Per Share	10.08	9.63	9.14	10.92	8.87	7.93	7.69	7.11
Dividends Per Share	0.900	0.880	0.800	0.730	0.670	0.630	0.570	0.480
Dividend Payout %	43.94	43.32	43.43	45.18	45.01	45.13	42.43	108.98
Income Statement								
Total Interest Income	176,546	727,364	792,106	880,622	931,157	814,520	785,765	787,244
Total Interest Expense	47,471	216,602	290,840	458,637	547,590	418,775	411,028	411,637
Net Interest Income	129,075	510,762	501,266	421,985	383,567	395,745	374,737	375,607
Provision for Loan Losses	5,176	46,813	50,699	28,210	20,206	19,243	14,740	31,668
Non–Interest Income	52,959	246,435	220,308	195,603	184,196	165,906	167,951	95,976
Non–Interest Expense	93,656	388,668	374,549	338,369	317,736	305,092	294,985	323,647
Income Before Taxes	83,202	321,716	296,326	251,009	229,821	237,316	232,963	116,268
Net Income	59,560	228,657	210,719	179,522	167,983	164,943	157,020	52,359
Average Shs. Outstg.	111,830	111,760	113,239	109,751	112,876	116,270	115,777	116,042
Balance Sheet								
Cash & Due from Banks	323,686	389,140	430,691	587,994	368,186	284,652	331,532	288,021
Securities Avail. for Sale	3,883,470	3,773,784	3,362,669	3,197,021	2,891,647	2,841,498	2,356,960	2,167,694
Net Loans & Leases	10,308,893	10,114,188	10,140,684	8,891,660	8,793,147	8,244,752	7,173,020	6,983,845
Total Assets	15,510,868	15,247,894	15,043,275	13,604,374	13,128,394	12,519,902	11,250,667	10,691,439
Total Deposits	9,702,758	9,792,843	9,124,852	8,612,611	9,291,646	8,691,829	8,557,819	8,364,137
Long–Term Obligations	1,749,418	1,852,219	1,906,845	1,103,395	122,420	24,283	26,004	15,270
Total Liabilities	14,115,575	13,899,467	13,771,092	12,533,958	12,159,698	11,610,113	10,371,946	9,877,746
Net Stockholders' Equity	1,395,293	1,348,427	1,272,183	1,070,416	968,696	909,789	878,721	813,693
Shares Outstanding	110,168	110,040	111,420	98,003	109,091	114,708	114,139	114,290
Statistical Record								
Return on Equity %	4.26	16.95	16.56	16.77	17.34	18.12	17.86	6.43
Return on Assets %	0.38	1.49	1.40	1.31	1.27	1.31	1.39	0.48
Equity/Assets %	8.99	8.84	8.45	7.86	7.37	7.26	7.81	7.61
Non–Int. Exp./Tot. Inc. %	40.80	39.94	36.98	31.46	28.29	31.21	31.15	35.33
Price Range	30.37–28.08	28.75–21.43	25.50–18.13	22.37–18.03	18.87–12.29	23.73–16.70	24.30–14.74	25.90–15.24
P/E Ratio	14.74–13.63	14.09–10.51	13.71–9.75	13.72–11.06	12.66–8.25	16.83–11.84	18.00–10.92	58.85–34.64
Average Yield %	3.08	3.54	3.53	3.53	4.44	3.21	2.71	2.61

Address: 1200 Hansen Road, Green Bay, WI 54304 **Telephone:** (920) 491 7000 **Web Site:** www.associatedbank.com	**Officers:** Robert C. Gallagher – Chmn., John C. Seramur – Vice–Chmn. **Transfer Agents:** National City Bank, Cleveland, OH	**Investor Contact:** 920–491–7120 **Institutional Holding** **No of Institutions:** 16 **Shares:** 2,293,825 **% Held:** –

23

ATMOS ENERGY CORP.

Exchange	Symbol	Price	52Wk Range	Yield	P/E
NYS	ATO	$24.79 (5/28/2004)	26.86-23.20	4.92	15.89

*7 Year Price Score 102.4 *NYSE Composite Index=100 ***12 Month Price Score 46.3**

Interim Earnings (Per Share)

Qtr.	Dec	Mar	Jun	Sep
2000–01	0.70	1.13	(0.08)	(0.28)
2001–02	0.50	1.01	0.08	(0.14)
2002–03	0.60	1.24	0.00	(0.13)
2003–04	0.57	1.12	...	

Interim Dividends (Per Share)

Amt	Decl	Ex	Rec	Pay
0.30Q	8/13/2003	8/21/2003	8/25/2003	9/10/2003
0.305Q	11/11/2003	11/21/2003	11/25/2003	12/10/2003
0.305Q	2/10/2004	2/23/2004	2/25/2004	3/10/2004
0.305Q	5/11/2004	5/21/2004	5/25/2004	6/10/2004

Indicated Div: **$1.22** (Div. Reinv. Plan)

Valuation Analysis

Forecast P/E 15.78 (5/24/2004)

Market Cap $1.0 Billion	Book Value 932.8 Million		
Price/Book 1.42	Price/Sales 0.37		

Dividend Achiever Status

Rank 275	10 Year Growth Rate	3.43%
Total Years of Dividend Growth		16

TRADING VOLUME (thousand shares)

Business Summary: Gas Utilities (MIC: 7.4 SIC: 4922 NAIC:486210)

Atmos Energy is engaged in the natural gas utility business as well as certain non–regulated natural gas businesses. Co. distributes natural gas through sales and transportation arrangements to about 1.7 million residential, commercial public authority and industrial customers through its regulated utility operations in twelve states. Co. also transports natural gas through its distribution system. Co.'s non–regulated businesses provide natural gas storage services and own an interest in storage fields in Kansas, Kentucky, Louisiana and Mississippi. Co. also provides energy management and gas marketing services and electrical power generation to wholesale customers in Texas and Louisiana.

Recent Developments: For the second quarter ended Mar 31 2004, net income increased 3.6% to $58.3 million versus income of $56.3 million, before an accounting change charge of $7.8 million, in the equivalent 2003 quarter. Net revenues decreased 6.4% to $1.12 billion from $1.19 billion a year earlier. Natural Gas Marketing segment revenue fell 16.6% to $517.2 million, reflecting lower sales volumes, primarily due to weather that was warmer than the 2003 period. Utility segment revenue rose 1.7% to $708.3 million. Other Non–utility segment revenue climbed 10.3% to $10.7 million. Gross profit grew 1.6% to $206.1 million, or 18.4% of net revenues, from $203.0 million, or 17.0% of net revenues, the year before.

Prospects: On Apr 12 2004, Co. announced that a steering committee representing 66 cities in west Texas has recommended the approval of an overall increase of $3.2 million in the annual revenues of Co.'s natural gas utility operations. As part of its recommendation, the steering committee also recommended the approval of a weather–normalization adjustment rider for residential, commercial, public–authority and state–institution customers. Meanwhile, Co.'s non–utility operations are benefiting from improved optimization of managed proprietary and third–party storage assets. Looking ahead to fiscal–year 2004, Co. expects earnings to be in the range of $1.55 to $1.60 per diluted share.

Financial Data

(US$ in Thousands)	6 Mos	3 Mos	09/30/2003	09/30/2002	09/30/2001	09/30/2000	09/30/1999	09/30/1998
Earnings Per Share	1.56	1.68	1.71	1.45	1.47	1.14	0.58	1.84
Cash Flow Per Share	5.58	0.22	1.06	7.18	2.16	1.71	2.74	3.05
Tang. Book Val. Per Share	12.58	11.67	11.34	9.18	12.42	12.28	12.08	12.20
Dividends Per Share	1.210	1.200	1.200	1.180	1.160	1.140	1.100	1.060
Dividend Payout %	77.56	71.42	70.17	81.37	78.91	100.00	189.65	57.60
Income Statement								
Total Revenues	1,881,101	763,616	2,799,916	950,849	1,442,275	850,152	690,196	848,208
Total Indirect Exp.	80,215	38,596	142,046	40,614	104,343	92,493	91,599	77,343
Costs & Expenses	1,712,146	700,075	2,612,076	795,518	1,311,994	764,836	635,957	735,329
Depreciation & Amort.	46,611	23,473	87,001	81,469	67,664	63,855	56,874	47,555
Operating Income	168,955	63,541	187,840	155,331	130,281	85,316	54,239	112,879
Net Interest Inc./(Exp.)	(33,495)	(17,335)	(63,660)	(59,174)	(47,011)	(43,823)	(36,298)	(30,149)
Income from Cont Ops	...	...	79,461	...	...	...	...	...
Net Income	87,846	29,541	71,688	59,656	56,000	35,918	17,744	55,265
Average Shs. Outstg.	52,057	51,861	46,496	41,250	38,247	31,594	30,819	30,031
Balance Sheet								
Net Property	1,661,336	1,538,224	1,515,989	1,300,320	1,335,398	982,346	965,782	917,860
Total Assets	2,821,192	2,812,946	2,518,508	1,980,221	2,036,180	1,348,758	1,230,537	1,141,390
Long–Term Obligations	864,624	860,705	863,918	670,463	692,399	363,198	377,483	398,548
Net Stockholders' Equity	932,489	879,352	857,517	573,235	583,864	392,466	377,663	371,158
Shares Outstanding	52,235	51,797	51,475	41,675	40,791	31,952	31,247	30,398
Statistical Record								
Operating Profit Margin %	15.14	15.77	6.70	20.38	9.06	10.03	7.85	13.30
Net Inc./Net Property %	5.29	1.92	4.72	4.58	4.20	3.65	1.83	6.02
Net Inc./Tot. Capital %	1.42	1.48	3.68	4.32	3.96	4.04	2.04	6.50
Return on Equity %	9.42	9.83	9.26	17.12	9.69	9.15	4.69	14.88
Accum. Depr./Gross Prop. %	34.91	39.03	38.87	38.88	36.70	37.81	37.66	36.54
Price Range	26.86-23.94	24.99-23.94	25.45-20.70	24.46-18.37	26.25-19.31	25.00-14.75	32.69-23.06	31.06-24.63
P/E Ratio	17.22-15.35	14.88-14.28	14.88-12.11	16.87-12.67	17.86-13.14	21.93-12.94	56.36-39.76	16.88-13.39
Average Yield %	4.82	4.89	5.21	5.37	5.08	5.85	4.11	3.74

Address: Three Lincoln Centre, Dallas, TX 75240
Telephone: (972) 934 9227
Web Site: www.atmosenergy.com

Officers: Robert W. Best – Chmn., Pres., C.E.O., John P. Reddy – Sr. V.P., C.F.O.
Transfer Agents: EquiServe Trust Company, Providence, RI

Investor Contact: 972–855–3729
Institutional Holding
No of Institutions: 2
Shares: 58,796 **% Held:** –

AUTOMATIC DATA PROCESSING INC.

Exchange	Symbol	Price	52Wk Range	Yield	P/E
NYS	ADP	$44.43 (5/28/2004)	46.84-33.66	1.26	28.30

*7 Year Price Score 91.3 *NYSE Composite Index=100 ***12 Month Price Score 53.8**

Interim Earnings (Per Share)

Qtr.	Sep	Dec	Mar	Jun
2000-01	0.27	0.32	0.45	0.40
2001-02	0.31	0.42	0.56	0.46
2002-03	0.34	0.43	0.54	0.37
2003-04	0.32	0.38	0.50	...

Interim Dividends (Per Share)

Amt	Decl	Ex	Rec	Pay
0.12Q	8/11/2003	9/10/2003	9/12/2003	10/1/2003
0.14Q	11/11/2003	12/10/2003	12/12/2003	1/1/2004
0.14Q	1/29/2004	3/11/2004	3/15/2004	4/1/2004
0.14Q	5/11/2004	6/9/2004	6/11/2004	7/1/2004

Indicated Div: $0.56

Valuation Analysis

Forecast P/E 25.77 (5/24/2004)

Market Cap	$27.6 Billion	Book Value	N/A
Price/Book	N/A	Price/Sales	N/A

Dividend Achiever Status

Rank	85	10 Year Growth Rate	14.63%
Total Years of Dividend Growth			28

Business Summary: IT &Technology (MIC: 10.2 SIC: 7374 NAIC:518210)

Automatic Data Processing provides computerized transaction processing, data communication, and information services. Co.'s Employer Services group offers payroll processing, human resource and benefits administration products and services. Co.'s Brokerage Services group provides transaction processing systems, desktop productivity applications and investor communications services to the financial services industry. Co.'s Dealer Services group provides dealer management computer systems to automotive retailers and their manufacturers. Co.'s Claims Services group offers business solutions for clients in the property and casualty insurance, auto collision repair and auto recycling industries.

Recent Developments: For the three months ended Mar 31 2004, net earnings slipped 8.8% to $300.3 million compared with $329.4 million in the third quarter of 2003. Results were hampered by lower interest rates, incremental investment activity and by dilution from last year's acquisitions. Total revenues climbed 11.3% to $2.12 billion versus $1.91 billion in the prior year. Brokerage Services' revenues improved 12.7% to $452.0 million, primarily due to an increase in investor communications activity, higher trade volume and higher retail versus institutional mix. Revenue in the Dealer Services segment rose 8.1%, while Employer Services' revenues rose 10.2%.

Prospects: Co. will continue to invest in its businesses, particularly in Employer Services. As a result, Co. has increased its incremental spending level to $165.0 million to $180.0 million for fiscal 2004, which includes about $30.0 million to $35.0 million of non-recurring charges anticipated in the fourth quarter of fiscal 2004. Meanwhile, Co. expects stronger sales growth in Employer Services in the fourth quarter due to increases in Co.'s sales force and easier comparisons with 2003. Based on stronger revenues in Brokerage Services, Co. increased its revenue guidance to high-single digit growth and confirmed its earnings per share guidance for fiscal 2004 of $1.53 to $1.58.

Financial Data

(US$ in Thousands)	9 Mos	6 Mos	3 Mos	06/30/2003	06/30/2002	06/30/2001	06/30/2000	06/30/1999
Earnings Per Share	1.57	1.61	1.66	1.68	1.75	1.44	1.31	1.10
Cash Flow Per Share	1.88	0.92	0.27	2.58	2.42	2.30	1.65	1.34
Tang. Book Val. Per Share	4.63	4.64	4.64	4.57	5.25	4.96	4.70	3.96
Dividends Per Share	0.500	0.480	0.470	0.470	0.430	0.380	0.320	0.280
Dividend Payout %	31.84	29.81	28.31	27.97	24.85	26.38	25.00	25.90
Income Statement								
Total Revenues	5,669,112	3,547,677	1,720,277	7,147,017	7,004,263	7,017,570	6,287,512	5,540,141
Total Indirect Exp.	4,557,718	2,903,926	1,427,599	2,532,227	2,360,610	2,500,582	2,387,917	2,060,379
Depreciation & Amort.	225,520	148,335	74,726	274,682	279,077	320,856	284,282	272,807
Operating Income	1,111,394	643,751	292,678	1,518,071	1,673,008	1,616,864	1,335,099	1,103,590
Net Interest Inc./(Exp.)	47,297	35,741	17,449	97,575	97,508	(14,260)	(13,140)	(19,090)
Income Taxes	432,370	252,980	116,420	627,050	686,200	600,290	448,800	387,660
Net Income	723,680	423,430	194,850	1,018,150	1,100,770	924,720	840,800	696,840
Average Shs. Outstg.	599,127	599,242	600,849	605,917	630,579	645,989	646,098	636,892
Balance Sheet								
Cash & Cash Equivalents	855,928	835,630	1,351,711	1,410,218	798,810	1,275,356	1,227,637	861,280
Total Current Assets	2,836,571	2,946,252	3,325,867	3,675,501	2,817,257	3,083,460	3,064,452	2,194,257
Total Assets	25,425,481	24,700,123	18,714,386	19,833,671	18,276,522	17,889,090	16,850,816	5,824,820
Total Current Liabilities	1,827,081	1,665,296	1,707,534	1,998,783	1,411,102	1,336,273	1,296,668	1,286,393
Long-Term Obligations	82,049	84,585	84,713	84,674	90,648	110,227	132,017	145,765
Net Stockholders' Equity	5,624,698	5,374,413	5,349,633	5,371,473	5,114,205	4,700,997	4,582,818	4,007,941
Net Working Capital	1,009,490	1,280,956	1,618,333	1,676,718	1,406,155	1,747,187	1,767,784	907,864
Shares Outstanding	590,467	589,910	594,438	594,839	616,317	623,936	628,746	623,627
Statistical Record								
Operating Profit Margin %	19.60	18.14	17.01	21.24	23.88	23.04	21.23	19.91
Return on Equity %	12.87	7.87	3.64	18.95	21.52	19.67	18.34	17.38
Return on Assets %	2.85	1.71	1.04	5.13	6.02	5.16	4.98	11.96
Debt/Total Assets %	0.32	0.34	0.45	0.42	0.49	0.61	0.78	2.50
Price Range	44.54-33.86	40.49-33.86	40.49-33.86	44.70-27.25	60.27-43.10	68.49-49.56	57.69-38.00	46.19-31.88
P/E Ratio	28.37-21.57	25.15-21.03	24.39-20.40	26.61-16.22	34.44-24.63	47.83-34.42	44.04-29.01	41.99-28.98
Average Yield %	1.27	1.27	1.25	1.29	0.81	0.65	0.67	0.71

Address: One ADP Boulevard, Roseland, NJ 07068-1728 **Telephone:** (973) 974-5000 **Web Site:** www.adp.com	**Officers:** Arthur F. Weinbach – Chmn., C.E.O., Gary C. Butler – Pres., C.O.O. **Transfer Agents:** Mellon Investor Services, Ridgefield Park, NJ	**Investor Contact:** 973-974-5858 **Institutional Holding** **No of Institutions:** 4 **Shares:** 11,920,277 **% Held:** –

AVERY DENNISON CORP.

Exchange	Symbol	Price	52Wk Range	Yield	P/E
NYS	AVY	$59.04 (5/28/2004)	64.94-47.75	2.51	26.36

*7 Year Price Score 101.5   *NYSE Composite Index=100   *12 Month Price Score 51.0

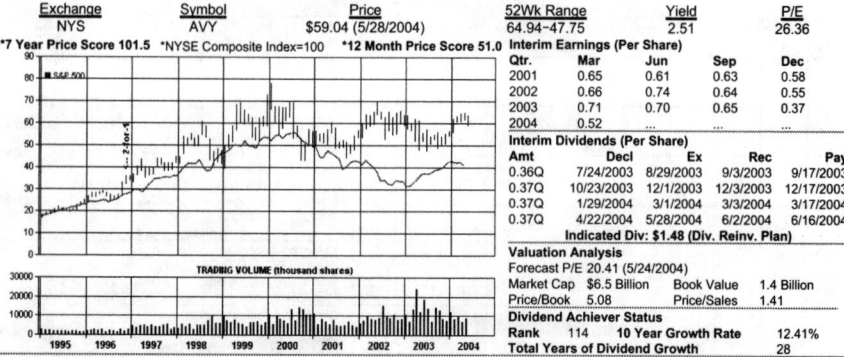

Interim Earnings (Per Share)

Qtr.	Mar	Jun	Sep	Dec
2001	0.65	0.61	0.63	0.58
2002	0.66	0.74	0.64	0.55
2003	0.71	0.70	0.65	0.37
2004	0.52	...	...	...

Interim Dividends (Per Share)

Amt	Decl	Ex	Rec	Pay
0.36Q	7/24/2003	8/29/2003	9/3/2003	9/17/2003
0.37Q	10/23/2003	12/1/2003	12/3/2003	12/17/2003
0.37Q	1/29/2004	3/1/2004	3/3/2004	3/17/2004
0.37Q	4/22/2004	5/28/2004	6/2/2004	6/16/2004

Indicated Div: $1.48 (Div. Reinv. Plan)

Valuation Analysis

Forecast P/E 20.41 (5/24/2004)

Market Cap	$6.5 Billion	Book Value	1.4 Billion
Price/Book	5.08	Price/Sales	1.41

Dividend Achiever Status

Rank	114	10 Year Growth Rate 12.41%
Total Years of Dividend Growth		28

Business Summary: Paper Products (MIC: 11.11 SIC: 2672 NAIC:322222)

Avery Dennison is a worldwide manufacturer of pressure-sensitive adhesives and materials, office products and converted products. A portion of self-adhesive material is converted into labels and other products through embossing, printing, stamping and die-cutting, and some are sold in unconverted form as base materials, tapes and reflective sheeting. Co. also manufactures and sells a variety of office products and other items not involving pressure-sensitive components, such as notebooks, three-ring binders, organization systems, felt-tip markers, glues, fasteners, business forms, tickets, tags, and imprinting equipment.

Recent Developments: For the three months ended Mar 27 2004, net income declined 23.1% to $52.6 million compared with income from continuing operations of $68.4 million in the corresponding quarter of 2003. Results for 2004 included expenses of $21.4 million for restructuring costs and asset impairments charges. Results for 2003 excluded gains of $2.4 million from discontinued operations. Net sales were $1.25 billion, up 9.8% from $1.14 billion in the prior-year period. Sales benefited from the favorable effect of currency translation, primarily the euro. In addition, the North American pressure-sensitive roll materials business posted strong results with mid single-digit sales growth.

Prospects: Co. expects earnings per share for the second quarter of 2004 in the range of $0.70 to $0.75, which excludes a restructuring charge related to the completion of the integration activities for the Jackstadt acquisition. Based on results for the first quarter of 2004, Co. updated its earnings per share guidance for full-year 2004 to be between $2.80 and $3.10, excluding restructuring charges, which is up from its previous expectation of $2.75 to $3.10,excluding restructuring charges. Meanwhile, Co. anticipates stronger sales for its office products business in the second half of 2004 due to share gains at several key accounts and new product introductions.

Financial Data
(US$ in Thousands)

	3 Mos	12/27/2003	12/28/2002	12/29/2001	12/30/2000	01/01/2000	01/02/1999	12/27/1997
Earnings Per Share	2.24	2.43	2.59	2.47	2.84	2.13	2.15	1.93
Cash Flow Per Share	0.65	3.34	5.25	3.80	4.10	4.29	4.06	3.47
Tang. Book Val. Per Share	4.88	4.52	2.53	4.69	3.93	4.17	6.88	6.87
Dividends Per Share	1.460	1.450	1.350	1.230	1.110	0.990	0.870	0.720
Dividend Payout %	58.40	59.67	52.12	49.79	39.08	46.47	40.46	37.30
Income Statement								
Total Revenues	1,246,700	4,762,600	4,206,900	3,803,300	3,893,500	3,768,200	3,459,900	3,345,700
Total Indirect Exp.	257,900	1,034,900	913,100	830,500	851,300	907,600	773,200	739,800
Depreciation & Amort.	46,200	179,300	152,800	156,000	156,900	150,400	127,200	116,800
Operating Income	108,600	423,100	440,600	409,700	480,900	373,800	371,300	342,900
Net Interest Inc./(Exp.)	(14,700)	(57,700)	(43,700)	(50,200)	(54,600)	(43,400)	(34,600)	(31,700)
Income Taxes	19,900	92,100	107,600	116,400	142,800	115,000	113,400	106,400
Income from Cont Ops	...	242,800	...	243,400	...	...	...	...
Net Income	52,600	267,900	257,200	243,200	283,500	215,400	223,300	204,800
Average Shs. Outstg.	100,300	100,000	99,400	98,600	99,800	101,300	104,100	106,100
Balance Sheet								
Cash & Cash Equivalents	31,300	29,500	22,800	19,100	11,400	6,900	18,500	3,300
Total Current Assets	1,416,500	1,440,900	1,215,500	982,500	982,400	956,000	802,000	793,500
Total Assets	4,077,200	4,105,300	3,652,400	2,819,200	2,699,100	2,592,500	2,142,600	2,046,500
Total Current Liabilities	1,433,000	1,496,000	1,296,100	951,300	800,700	850,400	664,300	629,900
Long-Term Obligations	887,100	887,700	837,200	626,700	772,900	617,500	465,900	404,100
Net Stockholders' Equity	1,351,200	1,318,700	1,056,400	929,400	828,100	809,900	833,300	837,200
Net Working Capital	(16,500)	(55,100)	(80,600)	31,200	181,700	105,600	137,700	163,600
Shares Outstanding	99,792	99,569	110,467	109,890	110,245	98,800	100,000	102,400
Statistical Record								
Operating Profit Margin %	8.71	8.88	10.47	10.77	12.35	9.91	10.73	10.24
Return on Equity %	3.89	18.41	24.34	26.18	34.23	26.59	26.79	24.46
Return on Assets %	1.29	5.91	7.04	8.63	10.50	8.30	10.42	10.00
Debt/Total Assets %	21.75	21.62	22.92	22.22	28.63	23.81	21.74	19.74
Price Range	64.50-55.49	63.51-47.75	69.49-52.86	60.24-44.39	78.00-43.31	72.88-39.75	60.75-40.88	44.13-33.38
P/E Ratio	28.79-24.77	26.14-19.65	26.83-20.41	24.39-17.97	27.46-15.25	34.21-18.66	28.26-19.01	22.86-17.29
Average Yield %	2.42	2.64	2.19	2.34	1.88	1.71	1.74	1.81

Address: 150 North Orange Grove Boulevard, Pasadena, CA 91103	Officers: Philip M. Neal – Chmn., C.E.O., Dean A. Scarborough – Pres., C.O.O.	Investor Contact:626-304-2204
Telephone: (626) 304-2000	Transfer Agents:EquiServe Trust Company, N.A., Jersey City, NJ	Institutional Holding
Web Site: www.averydennison.com		No of Institutions: 5
		Shares: 122,175 % Held: –

26

AVON PRODUCTS, INC.

Exchange	Symbol	Price	52Wk Range	Yield	P/E
NYS	AVP	$88.66 (5/28/2004)	89.53-60.14	0.63	29.75

*7 Year Price Score 146.6   *NYSE Composite Index=100   *12 Month Price Score 59.2

Interim Earnings (Per Share)

Qtr.	Mar	Jun	Sep	Dec
2001	0.34	0.57	0.42	0.46
2002	0.40	0.64	0.38	0.80
2003	0.42	0.71	0.56	1.09
2004	0.62	...	...	...

Interim Dividends (Per Share)

Amt	Decl	Ex	Rec	Pay
0.21Q	11/6/2003	11/19/2003	11/21/2003	12/1/2003
0.28Q	2/3/2004	2/11/2004	2/13/2004	3/1/2004
100%	2/3/2004	6/1/2004	5/17/2004	5/28/2004
0.14Q	5/6/2004	5/13/2004	5/17/2004	6/1/2004

Indicated Div: $0.56 (Div. Reinv. Plan)

Valuation Analysis

Forecast P/E 26.83 (5/24/2004)

Market Cap	$20.9 Billion	Book Value	419.5 Million
Price/Book	42.29	Price/Sales	2.47

Dividend Achiever Status

Rank	213	10 Year Growth Rate	7.05%
Total Years of Dividend Growth		13	

Business Summary: Chemicals (MIC: 11.1 SIC: 2844 NAIC:325620)

Avon Products is a global manufacturer and marketer of beauty and related products. Co.'s products fall into three product categories: Beauty, which consists of cosmetics, fragrances and toiletries; Beauty Plus, which consists of fashion jewelry, watches, apparel and accessories; and Beyond Beauty, which consists of home products, gift and decorative products and candles. Sales are made to the consumer principally through approximately 4.4 million independent representatives. As of Apr 3, 2004, Co. had operations in 60 countries and its products were distributed in 72 more for coverage in 132 countries.

Recent Developments: For the quarter ended Mar 31 2004, net income climbed 49.7% to $148.1 million from $98.9 million in the prior-year quarter. Results for 2003 included charges of $18.2 million related to Co.'s decision to reposition its *beComing* brand from retail to direct selling distribution. Total revenue grew 19.8% to $1.77 billion from $1.48 billion the previous year, driven by double-digit volume growth and 23.0% growth in sales of beauty products. Total units rose 12.0% and active representatives rose 9.0%, with particular strength coming from Latin America and Europe. Cost of sales rose 15.3% to $662.2 million. Operating profit increased 40.2% to $229.4 million from $163.6 million a year earlier.

Prospects: For the second quarter of 2004, Co. expects continued healthy double-digit growth in local-currency sales with one-to-two points of positive foreign exchange impact. Volume growth is expected to be similar to that of the first quarter, with solid gains projected in all regions. Operating profit is forecast to increase in the mid-teens range, and earnings are projected to be about $0.85 per share. Meanwhile, given the ongoing strength of Co.'s business transformation initiatives, Co. raised its full-year 2004 earnings forecast to $3.30 per share, up from its previous guidance of $3.18 to $3.20 per share.

Financial Data

(US$ in Thousands)	3 Mos	12/31/2003	12/31/2002	12/31/2001	12/31/2000	12/31/1999	12/31/1998	12/31/1997
Earnings Per Share	2.98	2.78	2.22	1.79	2.02	1.17	1.02	1.27
Cash Flow Per Share	(0.04)	3.08	2.30	3.06	1.33	1.79	1.21	1.18
Tang. Book Val. Per Share	1.77	1.57	N.M	N.M	N.M	N.M	1.08	1.08
Dividends Per Share	0.910	0.840	0.800	0.760	0.740	0.720	0.680	0.630
Dividend Payout %	30.54	30.21	36.03	42.45	36.63	61.53	66.66	49.60
Income Statement								
Total Revenues	1,774,600	6,876,000	6,228,300	5,994,500	5,714,600	5,289,100	5,212,700	5,079,400
Total Indirect Exp.	883,000	3,224,000	2,979,600	2,906,200	2,803,200	2,603,000	2,570,000	2,490,600
Depreciation & Amort.	33,200	133,200	142,900	124,000	97,100	83,000	72,000	72,100
Operating Income	229,400	1,042,800	870,000	749,400	788,700	549,400	473,200	537,800
Net Interest Inc./(Exp.)	(1,600)	(34,800)	(43,500)	(56,700)	(76,200)	(32,100)	(18,800)	(18,800)
Income Taxes	73,900	318,900	292,300	230,900	201,700	204,200	190,800	197,900
Eqty Earns/Minority Int.	(2,600)	(9,800)	(8,700)	(4,500)	(4,200)	...	4,900	1,800
Income from Cont Ops	...	...	...	430,300	485,100	...	...	...
Net Income	148,100	664,800	534,600	430,000	478,400	302,400	270,000	338,800
Average Shs. Outstg.	238,300	241,570	245,470	246,050	242,950	259,370	265,950	267,000
Balance Sheet								
Cash & Cash Equivalents	562,000	694,000	606,800	508,500	122,700	117,400	105,600	141,900
Total Current Assets	2,148,500	2,226,100	2,048,200	1,889,100	1,545,700	1,337,800	1,341,400	1,344,000
Total Assets	3,503,000	3,562,300	3,327,500	3,193,100	2,826,400	2,528,600	2,433,500	2,272,900
Total Current Liabilities	1,492,000	1,587,600	1,975,500	1,461,000	1,359,300	1,712,800	1,329,500	1,355,900
Long-Term Obligations	898,000	877,700	767,000	1,236,300	1,108,200	701,400	201,000	102,200
Net Stockholders' Equity	419,500	371,300	(127,700)	(74,600)	(215,800)	(406,100)	285,100	285,000
Net Working Capital	656,500	638,400	72,700	428,100	186,400	(375,000)	11,900	(11,900)
Shares Outstanding	235,932	235,298	235,257	236,681	238,162	237,895	262,520	263,628
Statistical Record								
Operating Profit Margin %	12.92	15.16	13.96	12.50	13.80	10.38	9.07	10.58
Return on Equity %	35.30	179.04	N.M	N.M	N.M	N.M	94.70	118.87
Return on Assets %	4.22	18.66	16.06	13.47	17.16	11.95	11.09	14.90
Debt/Total Assets %	25.63	24.63	23.05	38.71	39.20	27.73	8.25	4.49
Price Range	75.87-61.73	69.35-49.16	56.96-43.72	49.59-36.77	49.56-25.38	56.19-23.81	46.19-25.38	38.34-25.50
P/E Ratio	25.46-20.71	24.95-17.68	25.66-19.69	27.70-20.54	24.54-12.56	48.02-20.35	45.28-24.88	30.19-20.08
Average Yield %	1.32	1.38	1.58	1.71	1.94	1.69	1.82	1.99

Address: 1345 Avenue of the Americas, New York, NY 10105-0196	Officers: Andrea Jung – Chmn., C.E.O., Susan J. Kropf – Pres., C.O.O.	Investor Contact:212-282-5320
Telephone: (212) 282-5000	Transfer Agents:EquiServe Trust Company, N.A.	Institutional Holding
Web Site: www.avon.com	Providence, RI	No of Institutions: 14
		Shares: 430,086 % Held: –

BADGER METER, INC.

Exchange	Symbol	Price	52Wk Range	Yield	P/E
ASE	BMI	$42.02 (5/28/2004)	44.90-25.75	2.57	14.90

*7 Year Price Score 108.4 *NYSE Composite Index=100 *12 Month Price Score 56.7

Interim Earnings (Per Share)

Qtr.	Mar	Jun	Sep	Dec
2001	0.28	0.16	0.29	0.30
2002	0.49	0.70	0.70	0.31
2003	0.21	0.78	0.80	0.51
2004	0.73	...	...	...

Interim Dividends (Per Share)

Amt	Decl	Ex	Rec	Pay
0.27Q	8/15/2003	8/27/2003	8/29/2003	9/15/2003
0.27Q	11/14/2003	11/26/2003	12/1/2003	12/15/2003
0.27Q	2/13/2004	2/25/2004	2/27/2004	3/15/2004
0.27Q	5/14/2004	5/27/2004	6/1/2004	6/15/2004

Indicated Div: $1.08 (Div. Reinv. Plan)

Valuation Analysis

Forecast P/E 14.63 (5/24/2004)

Market Cap	$134.2 Million	Book Value	56.9 Million
Price/Book	2.19	Price/Sales	0.64

Dividend Achiever Status

Rank	110	10 Year Growth Rate 12.61%
Total Years of Dividend Growth		11

Business Summary: Instruments and Related Products (MIC: 11.15 SIC: 3824 NAIC:334514)

Badger Meter is a global marketer and manufacturer of products, and a provider of services, using flow measurement and control technologies. Co.'s products are used to measure and control the flow of liquids in a range of applications. Residential and commercial water meters are generally sold to water utilities. Industrial sales comprise the remainder of the sales and include automotive fluid meters and systems, small precision valves, electromagnetic meters, impeller flow meters and industrial process meters. Co.'s products are primarily manufactured and assembled in Wisconsin, Oklahoma, Arizona, Mexico and Czech Republic facilities.

Recent Developments: For the three months ended Mar 31 2004, net earnings more than tripled to $2.5 million compared with $706,000 in the corresponding quarter of 2003. Earnings benefited from increased sales of higher-margin automatic meter reading products, greater overhead absorption from the higher product volumes, and ongoing cost controls. Net sales rose 25.3% to $49.6 million from $39.6 million in the prior-year period. Gross margin increased 28.7% to $16.7 million compared with $12.9 million in the previous year. Sales increased in both the utility and industrial markets, primarily driven by stronger sales of automatic meter reading systems for the residential water utility market.

Prospects: As of Mar 31 2004, Co.'s inventories increased nearly $1.6 million, or 5.4%. This increase was primarily due to a build up of certain longer lead-time electronic materials and stock for new product offerings as well as the production of certain goods in the first quarter that are expected to be shipped early in the second quarter of 2004. Meanwhile, Co.'s financial condition remains strong. Co. believes that its operating cash flows and its ability to raise additional capital provide adequate resources to fund ongoing operating requirements, future capital requirements and the development of new products.

Financial Data

(US$ in Thousands)	3 Mos	12/31/2003	12/31/2002	12/31/2001	12/31/2000	12/31/1999	12/31/1998	12/31/1997
Earnings Per Share	2.82	2.30	2.20	1.03	2.00	2.60	2.12	1.65
Cash Flow Per Share	(0.86)	4.26	3.70	2.62	3.81	4.12	3.76	1.30
Tang. Book Val. Per Share	14.73	14.19	12.81	13.28	13.16	12.54	12.72	11.43
Dividends Per Share	1.070	1.060	1.020	1.000	0.860	0.720	0.600	0.480
Dividend Payout %	38.21	46.08	46.36	97.08	43.00	27.69	28.30	29.16
Income Statement								
Total Revenues	49,602	183,989	167,317	138,537	146,389	150,877	143,813	130,771
Total Indirect Exp.	12,063	46,419	42,805	38,430	41,995	42,495	43,317	37,769
Depreciation & Amort.	1,817	7,832	7,980	6,801	6,073	5,633	4,675	3,953
Operating Income	4,598	14,100	13,195	6,065	11,019	16,660	13,994	10,968
Net Interest Inc./(Exp.)	(428)	(1,737)	(1,849)	(1,381)	(2,206)	(1,256)	(630)	(455)
Income Taxes	1,593	5,774	4,166	1,646	3,786	5,959	5,117	3,683
Net Income	2,450	7,577	7,271	3,364	6,941	9,700	8,247	6,522
Average Shs. Outstg.	3,361	3,299	3,304	3,275	3,470	3,728	3,896	3,961
Balance Sheet								
Cash & Cash Equivalents	775	2,089	3,779	3,410	4,237	3,752	2,371	1,055
Total Current Assets	65,844	62,998	55,380	44,364	44,517	47,979	45,652	42,539
Total Assets	135,716	133,851	126,463	98,836	98,710	103,086	96,945	82,297
Total Current Liabilities	39,337	37,052	48,555	23,782	37,695	36,829	34,876	28,669
Long-Term Obligations	22,482	24,450	13,046	20,498	5,944	11,493	2,600	928
Net Stockholders' Equity	56,919	55,171	48,095	43,002	43,319	43,009	47,848	41,467
Net Working Capital	26,507	25,946	6,825	20,582	6,822	11,150	10,776	13,870
Shares Outstanding	3,300	3,292	3,220	3,179	3,207	3,339	3,645	3,571
Statistical Record								
Operating Profit Margin %	9.26	7.66	7.88	4.37	7.52	11.04	9.73	8.38
Return on Equity %	4.30	13.73	15.11	7.82	16.02	22.55	17.23	15.72
Return on Assets %	1.80	5.66	5.74	3.40	7.03	9.40	8.50	7.92
Debt/Total Assets %	16.56	18.26	10.31	20.73	6.02	11.14	2.68	1.12
Price Range	38.45-34.34	39.75-25.75	34.00-22.30	32.00-20.00	36.75-23.00	40.31-29.69	40.75-25.00	55.50-18.25
P/E Ratio	13.63-12.18	17.28-11.20	15.45-10.14	31.07-19.42	18.38-11.50	15.50-11.42	19.22-11.79	33.64-11.06
Average Yield %	2.92	3.30	3.49	3.85	2.96	2.12	1.73	1.44

Address: 4545 W. Brown Deer Road, Milwaukee, WI 53223
Telephone: (414) 355 0400
Web Site: www.badgermeter.com

Officers: James L. Forbes – Chmn., Richard A. Meeusen – Pres., C.E.O.
Transfer Agents: American Stock Transfer, New York, NY

Investor Contact: 414-371-5702
Institutional Holding
No of Institutions: 12
Shares: 609,646 **% Held:** –

BANCFIRST CORP. (OKLAHOMA CITY, OKLA)

Exchange	Symbol	Price	52Wk Range	Yield	P/E
NMS	BANF	$56.99 (5/28/2004)	59.80–50.83	1.75	14.39

*7 Year Price Score 136.9 *NYSE Composite Index=100 *12 Month Price Score 47.3

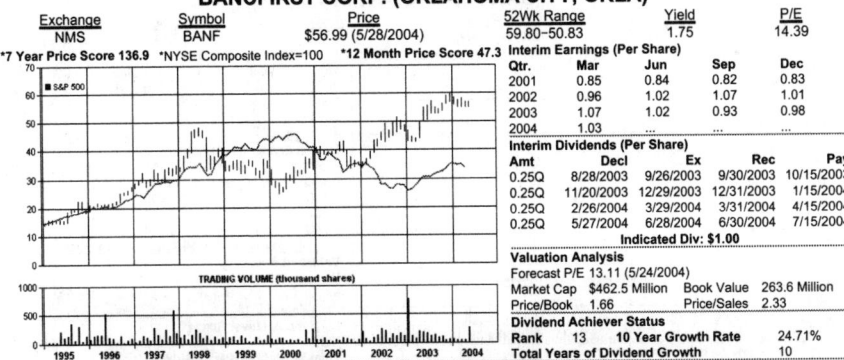

Interim Earnings (Per Share)

Qtr.	Mar	Jun	Sep	Dec
2001	0.85	0.84	0.82	0.83
2002	0.96	1.02	1.07	1.01
2003	1.07	1.02	0.93	0.98
2004	1.03	...	...	...

Interim Dividends (Per Share)

Amt	Decl	Ex	Rec	Pay
0.25Q	8/28/2003	9/26/2003	9/30/2003	10/15/2003
0.25Q	11/20/2003	12/29/2003	12/31/2003	1/15/2004
0.25Q	2/26/2004	3/29/2004	3/31/2004	4/15/2004
0.25Q	5/27/2004	6/28/2004	6/30/2004	7/15/2004

Indicated Div: $1.00

Valuation Analysis

Forecast P/E 13.11 (5/24/2004)
Market Cap $462.5 Million   Book Value 263.6 Million
Price/Book 1.66   Price/Sales 2.33

Dividend Achiever Status

Rank 13   10 Year Growth Rate 24.71%
Total Years of Dividend Growth 10

TRADING VOLUME (thousand shares)

Business Summary: Commercial Banking (MIC: 8.1 SIC: 6021 NAIC:522110)

BancFirst is a bank holding company that provides a range of commercial banking services to retail customers and small to medium-sized businesses both in the non-metropolitan trade centers of Oklahoma and the metropolitan markets of Oklahoma City, Tulsa, Lawton, Muskogee, Norman and Shawnee. Retail and commercial banking services include commercial, real estate, agricultural and consumer lending; depository and funds transfer services; collections; safe deposit boxes; cash management services; retail brokerage services; and other services tailored for both individual and corporate customers. As of Dec 31 2003, total assets were $2.92 billion and deposits amounted to $2.59 billion.

Recent Developments: For the quarter ended Mar 31 2004, net income slipped 4.7% to $8.2 million from $8.6 million in the corresponding period the year before. The decline in earnings was primarily due to margin compression from low interest rates coupled with higher operating costs. Net interest income improved 4.4% to $27.9 million. Provision for loan losses declined 8.0% to $720,000 from $783,000 the prior year. Total noninterest income slid 0.7% to $11.7 million from $11.8 million the previous year. Total noninterest expense climbed 6.5% to $26.2 million, mainly due to higher personnel costs partly related to the recent acquisitions of Gold Bank and Lincoln Bank.

Prospects: Co. continues to benefit from the acquisition of the Hobart and Lone Wolf, Oklahoma branches of Gold Bank, which at the time of purchase included approximately $16.3 million of loans and other assets and approximately $40.5 million of deposits. Looking ahead, continued low interest rates could further negatively impact Co.'s net interest margin, while slow economic growth could have an adverse effect on loan growth and asset quality. Additionally, complying with changes in corporate governance, reporting and other regulatory requirements will result in higher costs.

Financial Data

(US$ in Thousands)	3 Mos	12/31/2003	12/31/2002	12/31/2001	12/31/2000	12/31/1999	12/31/1998	12/31/1997
Earnings Per Share	3.96	4.00	4.06	3.34	3.19	2.75	2.27	2.41
Tang. Book Val. Per Share	29.51	28.51	28.24	24.33	21.17	17.33	19.13	17.40
Dividends Per Share	0.940	0.910	0.760	0.720	0.640	0.560	0.480	0.400
Dividend Payout %	23.73	22.75	18.71	21.55	20.06	20.36	21.14	16.59
Income Statement								
Total Interest Income	34,529	141,032	157,139	182,643	182,389	159,384	161,042	97,990
Total Interest Expense	6,609	31,915	47,809	77,711	80,054	66,149	68,290	40,291
Net Interest Income	27,920	109,117	109,330	104,932	102,335	93,235	92,752	57,699
Provision for Loan Losses	720	3,722	5,276	1,780	4,045	2,521	2,211	982
Non–Interest Income	11,702	48,820	45,212	36,908	29,902	28,707	24,019	15,821
Non–Interest Expense	26,192	105,382	98,380	96,620	87,724	81,453	80,482	48,537
Income Before Taxes	12,710	48,833	50,886	43,440	40,468	37,968	34,078	24,001
Net Income	8,191	31,882	33,562	27,961	26,217	23,949	21,550	15,749
Average Shs. Outstg.	7,977	7,972	8,260	8,371	8,224	8,699	9,510	6,533
Balance Sheet								
Cash & Due from Banks	129,806	155,367	152,239	152,577	162,455	126,691	132,286	69,652
Securities Avail. for Sale	...	564,735	565,225	544,291	560,551	596,715	582,649	310,343
Net Loans & Leases	1,914,480	1,921,075	1,790,495	1,692,902	1,640,958	1,432,933	1,319,220	845,612
Total Assets	3,051,815	2,921,369	2,796,862	2,757,045	2,570,255	2,335,807	2,335,883	1,345,789
Total Deposits	2,673,020	2,585,690	2,428,648	2,401,328	2,267,397	2,082,696	2,024,800	1,175,110
Long–Term Obligations	61,389	36,063	34,087	24,090	26,613	26,392	12,966	7,051
Total Liabilities	2,788,252	2,665,997	2,545,354	2,533,877	2,373,297	2,171,093	2,133,966	1,222,855
Net Stockholders' Equity	263,563	255,372	251,508	223,168	196,958	164,714	201,917	122,934
Shares Outstanding	7,830	7,822	8,136	8,260	8,112	8,112	9,291	6,345
Statistical Record								
Return on Equity %	3.10	12.48	13.34	12.52	13.31	14.53	10.67	12.81
Return on Assets %	0.26	1.09	1.19	1.01	1.02	1.02	0.92	1.17
Equity/Assets %	8.63	8.74	8.99	8.09	7.66	7.05	8.64	9.13
Non–Int. Exp./Tot. Inc. %	56.65	55.50	48.61	44.00	41.32	43.30	43.48	42.64
Price Range	58.50–55.00	59.80–42.85	51.74–34.45	43.25–33.75	40.25–24.88	37.13–30.50	48.25–32.88	34.75–27.06
P/E Ratio	14.77–13.89	14.95–10.71	12.74–8.49	12.95–10.10	12.62–7.80	13.50–11.09	21.26–14.48	14.42–11.23
Average Yield %	1.66	1.77	1.73	1.86	2.04	1.67	1.19	1.30

Address: 101 North Broadway, Oklahoma City, OK 73102-8401
Telephone: (405) 270-1086
Web Site: www.bancfirst.com

Officers: H. E. Rainbolt – Chmn., James R. Daniel – Vice–Chmn.
Transfer Agents: BancTrust Corporation, Oklahoma City, OK

Investor Contact: 405–270–1044
Institutional Holding
No of Institutions: 16
Shares: 42,480   **% Held:** –

BANCORPSOUTH INC.

Exchange	Symbol	Price	52Wk Range	Yield	P/E
NYS	BXS	$20.92 (5/28/2004)	24.45-19.90	3.44	13.67

*7 Year Price Score 120.3 *NYSE Composite Index=100 *12 Month Price Score 43.5

Interim Earnings (Per Share)

Qtr.	Mar	Jun	Sep	Dec
2001	0.27	0.28	0.26	0.38
2002	0.36	0.38	0.33	0.32
2003	0.50	0.37	0.43	0.38
2000	0.35	...	...	...

Interim Dividends (Per Share)

Amt	Decl	Ex	Rec	Pay
0.16Q	7/16/2003	9/11/2003	9/15/2003	10/1/2003
0.18Q	10/22/2003	12/11/2003	12/15/2003	1/2/2004
0.18Q	1/28/2004	3/11/2004	3/15/2004	4/1/2004
0.18Q	4/28/2004	6/11/2004	6/15/2004	7/1/2004

Indicated Div: $0.72 (Div. Reinv. Plan)

Valuation Analysis

Forecast P/E 13.44 (5/24/2004)

Market Cap $1.7 Billion		Book Value 868.9 Million	
Price/Book 2.15		Price/Sales 2.60	

Dividend Achiever Status

Rank 144	10 Year Growth Rate	10.55%
Total Years of Dividend Growth		17

TRADING VOLUME (thousand shares)

1995 1996 1997 1998 1999 2000 2001 2002 2003 2004

Business Summary: Commercial Banking (MIC: 8.1 SIC: 6022 NAIC:522110)

BancorpSouth is a bank holding company headquartered in Tupelo, MS with assets of $10.31 billion and total deposits of $8.60 billion as of Dec 31 2003. Co. operates 246 commercial banking, insurance, trust, broker/dealer and consumer finance locations in Mississippi, Tennessee, Alabama, Arkansas, Texas and Louisiana. Co. and its subsidiaries provide a range of financial services to individuals and small-to-medium size businesses. Co. operates investment services, consumer finance, credit insurance and insurance agency subsidiaries. Co.'s trust department offers a variety of services including personal trust and estate services, and certain employee benefit accounts and plans.

Recent Developments: For the three months ended Mar 31 2004, net income slid 30.6% to $27.2 million from $39.1 million in the corresponding period a year earlier. Results for 2003 included an $8.4 million after-tax gain from sales of securities. Net interest revenue slipped 7.4% to $83.5 million from $90.1 million the prior year. Provision for credit losses declined 38.4% to $4.0 million from $6.5 million the year before. Total non-interest revenue dipped 12.0% to $46.0 million from $52.3 million the previous year. Total non-interest expense rose 11.8% to $86.0 million from $76.9 million in 2003. As of Mar 31 2004, total assets was $10.58 billion, up 2.4% versus $10.34 billion on Mar 31 2003.

Prospects: Earnings are being negatively affected by a decline in net interest revenue stemming from low interest rate levels and weaker demand for loans due to uncertain economic conditions. Meanwhile, Co. is taking steps to boost non-interest revenues through growth of existing products and services within existing markets in an effort to reduce exposure to interest rate fluctuations. Separately, mortgage loan originations are expected to slow in 2004 following significant growth in 2003. However, results may benefit from Co.'s focus on expanding it's market share through acquisitions and geographic expansion.

Financial Data

(US$ in Thousands)	12/31/2003	12/31/2002	12/31/2001	12/31/2000	12/31/1999	12/31/1998	12/31/1997	12/31/1996
Earnings Per Share	1.68	1.39	1.19	0.88	1.20	1.01	1.01	1.01
Tang. Book Val. Per Share	10.38	10.39	9.91	9.39	8.68	8.47	8.09	7.50
Dividends Per Share	0.640	0.600	0.560	0.520	0.480	0.440	0.380	0.340
Dividend Payout %	38.09	43.16	47.05	59.09	40.00	43.56	37.43	33.66
Income Statement								
Total Interest Income	526,911	590,418	665,835	738,791	414,187	383,519	307,094	277,919
Total Interest Expense	175,805	218,892	331,093	346,883	196,686	187,412	144,055	126,505
Net Interest Income	351,106	371,526	334,742	391,908	217,501	196,107	163,039	151,414
Provision for Loan Losses	25,130	29,411	22,259	26,166	14,689	15,014	9,008	8,804
Non-Interest Income	190,086	132,239	128,633	85,578	79,331	53,018	43,667	40,745
Non-Interest Expense	322,594	312,398	295,313	274,227	183,000	152,084	131,988	118,472
Income Before Taxes	193,468	161,956	145,803	112,337	99,143	82,027	65,710	64,883
Income from Cont Ops	...	...	...	139,152				
Net Income	131,134	112,018	98,463	74,396	68,953	54,477	45,350	42,883
Average Shs. Outstg.	78,164	80,481	82,979	84,811	57,524	53,871	44,788	42,426
Balance Sheet								
Cash & Due from Banks	369,699	356,976	341,513	314,888	217,270	175,354	286,307	153,148
Securities Avail. for Sale	1,989,690	1,642,172	1,083,191	857,400	345,284	549,767	406,212	230,739
Net Loans & Leases	6,140,955	6,301,510	5,990,050	6,013,585	3,997,975	3,419,083	2,719,150	2,432,062
Total Assets	10,305,035	10,189,247	9,395,429	9,044,034	5,776,926	5,203,741	4,180,143	3,617,239
Total Deposits	8,599,128	8,548,918	7,856,840	7,480,920	4,815,415	4,441,923	3,540,255	3,161,379
Long-Term Obligations	267,364	139,757	140,939	152,049	138,560	178,318	47,539	55,778
Total Liabilities	9,436,129	9,256,424	8,590,026	8,254,458	5,279,526	4,747,384	3,819,721	3,301,915
Net Stockholders' Equity	868,906	807,823	805,403	789,576	497,400	456,357	360,422	315,324
Shares Outstanding	77,926	77,680	81,225	84,043	57,304	53,833	44,542	42,026
Statistical Record								
Return on Equity %	15.09	13.86	12.22	17.62	13.86	11.93	12.58	13.59
Return on Assets %	1.27	1.09	1.04	1.53	1.19	1.04	1.08	1.18
Equity/Assets %	8.43	7.92	8.57	8.73	8.61	8.78	8.62	8.71
Non-Int. Exp./Tot. Inc. %	44.99	43.22	37.17	33.26	37.08	34.83	37.62	37.17
Price Range	24.45-17.50	21.99-16.35	16.91-12.06	17.25-11.88	19.19-15.50	23.88-16.87	23.82-13.25	14.25-10.06
P/E Ratio	14.55-10.42	15.82-11.76	14.21-10.13	19.60-13.50	15.99-12.92	23.64-16.70	23.58-13.12	14.11-9.96
Average Yield %	3.03	3.07	3.71	3.54	2.84	2.14	2.38	2.85

Address: One Mississippi Plaza, Tupelo, MS 38804	**Officers:** Aubrey B. Patterson – Chmn., C.E.O., James V. Kelley – Pres., C.O.O.	**Institutional Holding** No of Institutions: 11
Telephone: (662) 680 2000	**Transfer Agents:** SunTrust Bank, Atlanta, GA	Shares: 167,669 % Held: –
Web Site: www.bancorpsouth.com		

BANDAG, INC.

Exchange	Symbol	Price	52Wk Range	Yield	P/E
NYS	BDG	$42.37 (5/28/2004)	51.05-33.12	3.07	13.28

*7 Year Price Score 108.4 ***NYSE Composite Index=100** ***12 Month Price Score 48.1**

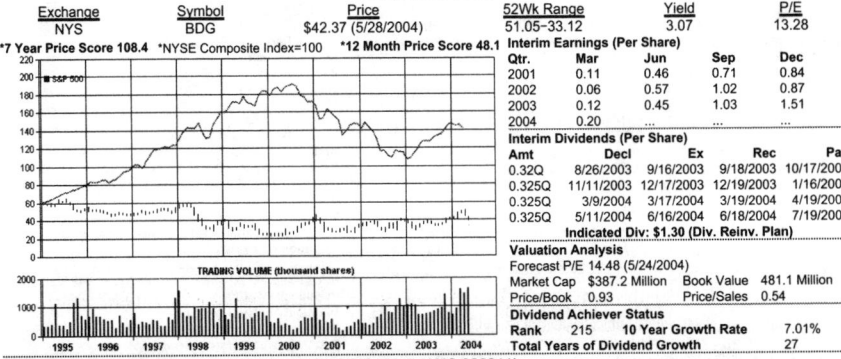

Interim Earnings (Per Share)

Qtr.	Mar	Jun	Sep	Dec
2001	0.11	0.46	0.71	0.84
2002	0.06	0.57	1.02	0.87
2003	0.12	0.45	1.03	1.51
2004	0.20	...	...	...

Interim Dividends (Per Share)

Amt	Decl	Ex	Rec	Pay
0.32Q	8/26/2003	9/16/2003	9/18/2003	10/17/2003
0.325Q	11/11/2003	12/17/2003	12/19/2003	1/16/2004
0.325Q	3/9/2004	3/17/2004	3/19/2004	4/19/2004
0.325Q	5/11/2004	6/16/2004	6/18/2004	7/19/2004

Indicated Div: $1.30 (Div. Reinv. Plan)

Valuation Analysis

Forecast P/E 14.48 (5/24/2004)

Market Cap $387.2 Million   Book Value 481.1 Million

Price/Book 0.93   Price/Sales 0.54

Dividend Achiever Status

Rank 215   10 Year Growth Rate   7.01%

Total Years of Dividend Growth   27

Business Summary: Rubber Products (MIC: 11.6 SIC: 3011 NAIC:326211)

Bandag is engaged in the manufacture of pre–cured tread rubber, equipment, and supplies primarily for the re–treading of truck and bus tires by a patented cold–bonding reaction process. Co. also does some custom processing of rubber compounds. As of Dec 31 2003, revenues were generated by more than 1,000 franchised dealers in the U.S. and abroad who are licensed to produce and market cold process retreads utilizing the Bandag process. Co.'s wholly–owned subsidiary, Tire Management Solutions, Inc., provides tire management systems outsourcing for commercial truck fleets. Tire Distribution Systems, Inc., also a wholly–owned subsidiary, sells and services new and retread tires.

Recent Developments: For the first quarter ended Mar 31 2004, net earnings advanced 67.9% to $4.0 million compared with $2.4 million in the corresponding prior–year quarter. Total revenues decreased 1.0% on $175.3 million from $177.1 million a year earlier. Net sales declined 1.0% to $173.5 million, while other revenues fell 4.0% to $1.8 million. Notably, sales for Tire Distribution Systems, Inc. dropped 35.6% to $40.9 million, reflecting divestitures and closures. From the date of its acquisition on Feb 13 2004, Speedco, Inc. contributed sales of $6.7 million. Currency translation favorably impacted net sales by $7.1 million. Cost of products sold decreased 2.2% to $112.8 million from $115.3 million in 2003.

Prospects: Both Co.'s U.S. tread sales and the results of Tire Distribution System, Inc. indicate continuing gradual improvement in the North American markets. Trucking activity is trending stronger than 2003 and Co.'s strategic alliance dealers have responded favorably to the acquisition of Speedco, Inc. Speedco provides quick–service truck lubrication nationwide through 26 company–owned and six licensed on–highway locations. Going forward, Speedco's nationwide presence should provide a solid platform for expanded delivery of en–route maintenance services. Together, Co. and Speedco expect to improve the efficiency and costs of delivering vehicle services to the commercial trucking industry.

Financial Data

(US$ in Thousands)	3 Mos	12/31/2003	12/31/2002	12/31/2001	12/31/2000	12/31/1999	12/31/1998	12/31/1997
Earnings Per Share	3.19	3.11	2.52	2.12	2.90	2.40	2.63	5.33
Cash Flow Per Share	1.58	4.03	6.60	5.63	4.77	5.16	3.83	3.11
Tang. Book Val. Per Share	23.58	24.60	21.96	21.21	20.02	18.61	17.84	16.99
Dividends Per Share	1.280	1.280	1.260	1.220	1.180	1.140	1.100	1.000
Dividend Payout %	40.40	41.15	50.00	57.54	40.68	47.50	41.82	18.76
Income Statement								
Total Revenues	175,291	828,186	911,953	982,209	1,013,426	1,027,878	1,079,498	836,615
Total Indirect Exp.	56,556	233,744	269,889	301,434	283,964	292,635	316,642	226,560
Depreciation & Amort.	5,845	27,179	32,333	46,155	50,465	53,764	51,410	36,857
Operating Income	5,932	86,303	78,375	73,881	108,107	101,817	110,285	206,255
Income Taxes	2,343	23,700	21,465	22,673	39,042	39,760	40,194	80,922
Income from Cont Ops	...	...	50,053	...	...	...	...	...
Net Income	4,019	60,200	2,793	43,832	60,333	52,330	59,319	121,994
Average Shs. Outstg.	19,655	19,369	19,888	20,686	20,778	21,764	22,559	22,908
Balance Sheet								
Cash & Cash Equivalents	166,573	189,976	129,412	145,625	86,008	50,633	37,912	196,400
Total Current Assets	411,153	466,286	416,082	450,174	427,179	428,118	439,124	598,994
Total Assets	667,357	660,529	617,827	718,572	714,549	722,421	755,729	899,904
Total Current Liabilities	145,185	148,193	147,861	186,075	132,735	154,053	174,909	306,542
Long–Term Obligations	38,929	22,857	28,571	94,286	100,000	100,000	100,000	100,000
Net Stockholders' Equity	481,122	477,077	424,593	488,996	474,157	454,075	467,297	463,414
Shares Outstanding	19,404	19,268	19,151	20,641	20,561	20,770	21,955	22,813
Statistical Record								
Operating Profit Margin %	3.38	10.42	8.59	7.52	10.66	9.90	10.21	13.28
Return on Equity %	0.83	12.61	11.78	8.96	12.72	11.52	12.69	5.80
Return on Assets %	0.60	9.11	8.10	6.09	8.44	7.24	7.84	2.98
Debt/Total Assets %	5.83	3.46	4.62	13.12	13.99	13.84	13.23	11.11
Price Range	49.77–40.40	42.30–28.67	41.16–26.40	46.19–25.34	42.63–22.38	41.31–23.63	59.50–28.38	55.00–45.75
P/E Ratio	15.60–12.66	13.60–9.22	16.33–10.50	21.79–11.95	14.70–7.72	17.21–9.84	22.62–10.79	10.32–8.58
Average Yield %	2.83	3.56	3.62	3.95	4.07	3.59	2.50	1.99

Address: 2905 North Highway 61, Muscatine, IA 52761–5886

Telephone: (563) 262–1400

Web Site: www.bandag.com

Officers: Martin G. Carver – Chmn., Pres., C.E.O., Warren W. Heidbreder – V.P., C.F.O., Sec.

Transfer Agents: Bank Boston, NA, Boston, MA

Investor Contact: 319–262–1260

Institutional Holding

No of Institutions: 12

Shares: 6,030   **% Held:** –

BANK OF AMERICA CORP.

Exchange	Symbol	Price	52Wk Range	Yield	P/E
NYS	BAC	$83.13 (5/28/2004)	83.53-72.85	3.85	11.28

*7 Year Price Score 121.7 *NYSE Composite Index=100 *12 Month Price Score 47.9

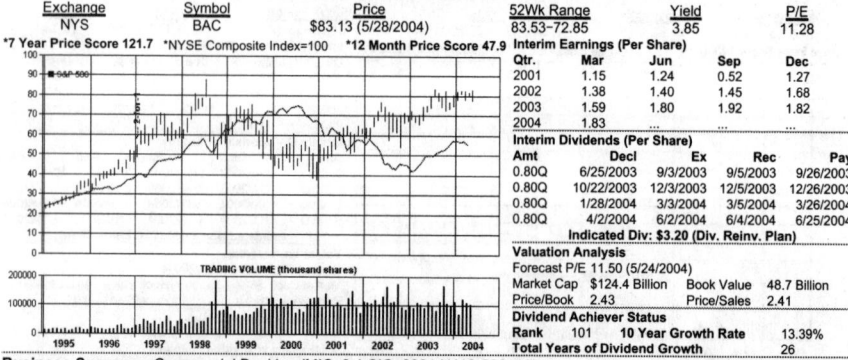

Interim Earnings (Per Share)

Qtr.	Mar	Jun	Sep	Dec
2001	1.15	1.24	0.52	1.27
2002	1.38	1.40	1.45	1.68
2003	1.59	1.80	1.92	1.82
2004	1.83	...	...	...

Interim Dividends (Per Share)

Amt	Decl	Ex	Rec	Pay
0.80Q	6/25/2003	9/3/2003	9/5/2003	9/26/2003
0.80Q	10/22/2003	12/3/2003	12/5/2003	12/26/2003
0.80Q	1/28/2004	3/3/2004	3/5/2004	3/26/2004
0.80Q	4/2/2004	6/2/2004	6/4/2004	6/25/2004

Indicated Div: $3.20 (Div. Reinv. Plan)

Valuation Analysis

Forecast P/E 11.50 (5/24/2004)

Market Cap	$124.4 Billion	Book Value	48.7 Billion
Price/Book	2.43	Price/Sales	2.41

Dividend Achiever Status

Rank	101	10 Year Growth Rate	13.39%
Total Years of Dividend Growth	26		

TRADING VOLUME (thousand shares)

Business Summary: Commercial Banking (MIC: 8.1 SIC: 6021 NAIC:522110)

Bank of America, with $736.45 billion in total assets as of Dec 31 2003, is a bank holding and financial holding company. Co.'s Consumer and Commercial Banking segment provides banking products and services. Co.'s Asset Management segment offers investment, fiduciary and banking and credit expertise; asset management services; and investment, securities and financial planning services. Co.'s Global Corporate and Investment Banking segment provides capital raising, advisory services, derivatives capabilities, equity and debt sales and trading. Equity Investments includes Principal Investing, which is comprised of investments in privately-held and publicly-traded companies.

Recent Developments: For the quarter ended Mar 31 2004, net income increased 10.6% to $2.68 billion from $2.42 billion in the prior-year quarter. Results for 2003 included a $285.0 million mutual fund settlement charge. Net interest income advanced 11.4% to $5.80 billion, reflecting higher asset/liability management portfolio levels and interest rate movements as well as consumer and middle market commercial loan growth and domestic deposit growth. Total non-interest income rose 0.6% to $3.72 billion driven by improvements in equity investments, card income investment and brokerage services, service charges and investment banking income. Co. opened over 1.0 million new credit card accounts during the quarter.

Prospects: On Apr 1 2004, Co. completed its acquisition of FleetBoston Financial Corp. In a tax-free, stock-for-stock exchange, Fleet shareholders received 0.5553 of a Co. share for each Fleet share owned. As a result of the acquisition, Co. announced related job reductions of 12,500, approximately 30.0% of which should be accomplished through attrition. These reductions are expected to occur over the next two years. Corporate-wide reductions will be primarily in overlapping processes and corporate staff functions. The integration of the two organizations is ahead of schedule, and Co. is optimistic about the combined business. The combined bank will be the third largest in the U.S. based on assets.

Financial Data

(US$ in Millions)	3 Mos	12/31/2003	12/31/2002	12/31/2001	12/31/2000	12/31/1999	12/31/1998	12/31/1997
Earnings Per Share	7.37	7.13	5.91	4.18	4.52	4.48	2.90	4.17
Tang. Book Val. Per Share	25.18	22.76	23.76	20.79	18.99	15.66	16.68	14.85
Dividends Per Share	3.040	2.880	2.440	2.280	2.060	1.850	1.590	1.370
Dividend Payout %	41.25	40.39	41.28	54.54	45.57	41.29	54.82	32.85
Income Statement								
Total Interest Income	8,572	31,643	32,161	38,293	43,258	37,323	38,588	16,579
Total Interest Expense	2,771	10,179	11,238	18,003	24,816	19,086	20,290	8,681
Net Interest Income	5,801	21,464	20,923	20,290	18,442	18,237	18,298	7,898
Provision for Loan Losses	624	...	...	...	2,535	1,820	2,920	800
Non-Interest Income	4,212	16,422	13,571	14,348	14,514	14,309	13,206	5,155
Non-Interest Expense	5,417	22,025	21,503	24,521	18,633	18,511	20,536	7,457
Income Before Taxes	3,972	15,861	12,991	10,117	11,788	12,215	8,048	4,796
Net Income	2,681	10,810	9,249	6,792	7,517	7,882	5,165	3,077
Average Shs. Outstg.	1,466	1,515	1,565	1,625	1,664	1,760	1,775	737
Balance Sheet								
Securities Avail. for Sale	214,550	67,993	68,122	84,450	64,651	81,647	78,590	46,047
Net Loans & Leases	369,888	365,300	335,904	322,278	385,355	363,834	350,206	141,010
Total Assets	816,012	736,445	660,458	621,764	642,191	632,574	617,679	264,562
Total Deposits	435,592	414,113	386,458	373,495	364,244	347,273	357,260	138,194
Long-Term Obligations	81,231	75,343	61,145	62,496	67,547	55,486	45,888	27,204
Total Liabilities	767,236	688,465	610,139	573,244	594,563	588,142	571,741	243,225
Net Stockholders' Equity	48,776	47,980	50,319	48,520	47,628	44,432	45,938	21,337
Shares Outstanding	1,445	1,441	1,500	1,559	1,613	1,677	1,724	712
Statistical Record								
Return on Equity %	5.49	24.49	19.63	14.97	15.78	17.73	11.24	14.42
Return on Assets %	0.32	1.59	1.49	1.16	1.17	1.24	0.83	1.16
Equity/Assets %	5.97	6.51	7.61	7.80	7.41	7.02	7.43	8.06
Non-Int. Exp./Tot. Inc. %	42.37	43.86	45.64	45.67	32.25	35.85	39.64	34.31
Price Range	82.76-78.30	83.53-65.63	76.90-54.15	65.00-46.75	60.81-38.00	75.75-48.06	87.88-47.81	71.19-48.69
P/E Ratio	11.23-10.62	11.72-9.20	13.01-9.16	15.55-11.18	13.45-8.41	16.91-10.73	30.30-16.49	17.07-11.68
Average Yield %	3.76	3.82	3.61	3.98	4.23	2.88	2.35	2.25

Address: Bank of America Corporate Center, Charlotte, NC 28255 **Telephone:** (704) 386-8486 **Web Site:** www.bankofamerica.com	**Officers:** Charles K. Gifford – Chmn., James H. Hance – Vice-Chmn. **Transfer Agents:** The Bank of New York, New York, NY	**Investor Contact:** 704-386-5681 **Institutional Holding** **No of Institutions:** 46 **Shares:** 4,388,253 **% Held:** –

BANK OF HAWAII CORP (DE)

Exchange	Symbol	Price	52Wk Range	Yield	P/E
NYS	BOH	$43.45 (5/28/2004)	47.15-33.04	2.76	17.88

*7 Year Price Score 154.5   *NYSE Composite Index=100   ***12 Month Price Score 51.2**

Interim Earnings (Per Share)

Qtr.	Mar	Jun	Sep	Dec
2001	0.42	0.32	0.37	0.35
2002	0.41	0.42	0.43	0.44
2003	0.47	0.48	0.61	0.65
2004	0.69	...	...	...

Interim Dividends (Per Share)

Amt	Decl	Ex	Rec	Pay
0.19Q	7/28/2003	8/20/2003	8/22/2003	9/15/2003
0.30Q	10/27/2003	11/19/2003	11/21/2003	12/12/2003
0.30Q	1/23/2004	2/26/2004	3/1/2004	3/12/2004
0.30Q	...	5/20/2004	5/24/2004	6/14/2004

Indicated Div: $1.20 (Div. Reinv. Plan)

Valuation Analysis

Forecast P/E 15.18 (5/24/2004)

Market Cap $2.8 Billion	Book Value 785.8 Million
Price/Book 3.21	Price/Sales 3.92

Dividend Achiever Status

Rank 219	10 Year Growth Rate	6.76%
Total Years of Dividend Growth		26

Business Summary: Commercial Banking (MIC: 8.1 SIC: 6022 NAIC:522110)

Bank of Hawaii, with assets of $9.46 billion as of Dec 31 2003, is a bank holding company. Co. operates in Hawaii, the West Pacific, and American Samoa. The Retail banking segment offers loan, lease and deposit products to consumers and small businesses. The Commercial banking segment provides corporate banking and commercial real estate loans, lease financing, auto dealer financing, deposit and cash management products to mid-to-large sized companies. The Investment Services group includes private banking, trust services, asset management, institutional investment advice and retail brokerage. The Treasury and Other Corporate segment provides corporate asset and liability management.

Recent Developments: For the first quarter ended Mar 31 2004, net income advanced 33.5% to $39.8 million compared with $29.8 million in the corresponding prior-year quarter. Results for 2003 included an information technology replacement charge of $7.4 million. Net interest income increased 5.5% to $96.0 million from $91.0 million a year earlier. Total interest income slipped 1.8% to $111.8 million, while total interest expense dropped 31.0% to $15.7 million. Total non-interest income climbed 9.1% to $48.8 million, while total non-interest expense declined 8.0% to $83.0 million. Return on average equity for the quarter was 19.98%, up from 12.42% in the 2003 quarter.

Prospects: First quarter 2004 visitor growth increased 6.0% in Hawaii. In addition, construction is expected to remain strong in 2004, based on 20.0% growth in the 2003 value of residential building permits, and a doubling in non-residential building permits, combined with military housing construction. These factors along with the lower levels of unemployment foreshadow higher interest rates in Hawaii, and should benefit Co.'s earnings. Separately, Co. is implementing plans to accelerate revenue growth in its island markets, better integrate its business segments, develop new management teams and improve its efficiency. Looking ahead to 2004, Co. expects net income of approximately $157.0 million.

Financial Data

(US$ in Thousands)	3 Mos	12/31/2003	12/31/2002	12/31/2001	12/31/2000	12/31/1999	12/31/1998	12/31/1997
Earnings Per Share	2.43	2.21	1.70	1.46	1.42	1.64	1.32	1.72
Tang. Book Val. Per Share	13.43	13.37	15.08	16.16	13.93	12.57	12.06	11.46
Dividends Per Share	0.980	0.870	0.730	0.720	0.710	0.680	0.650	0.620
Dividend Payout %	40.33	39.36	42.94	49.31	50.00	41.46	49.81	36.33
Income Statement								
Total Interest Income	111,756	442,521	516,538	828,262	1,057,493	1,026,519	1,099,786	1,062,576
Total Interest Expense	15,725	76,579	146,307	368,584	501,262	451,776	523,185	526,278
Net Interest Income	96,031	365,942	370,231	459,678	556,231	574,743	576,601	536,298
Provision for Loan Losses	...	...	11,616	74,339	142,853	60,915	84,014	30,338
Non-Interest Income	48,842	198,720	199,921	452,619	263,429	265,581	211,751	187,789
Non-Interest Expense	83,022	357,875	370,835	597,616	496,430	553,238	540,279	474,261
Net Income	39,799	135,195	121,180	117,795	113,661	132,957	106,964	139,488
Average Shs. Outstg.	57,746	61,085	71,447	80,577	79,813	80,044	81,142	80,946
Balance Sheet								
Cash & Due from Banks	313,090	363,495	374,352	405,981	523,969	639,895	564,243	795,332
Securities Avail. for Sale	1,995,713	1,991,116	2,287,201	2,001,420	2,507,076	2,542,232	3,018,403	2,651,270
Net Loans & Leases	5,587,811	5,637,331	5,256,265	5,966,530	9,168,140	9,280,848	9,416,809	9,114,325
Total Assets	10,013,442	9,461,602	9,515,797	10,644,079	14,013,816	14,440,315	15,016,563	14,995,464
Total Deposits	7,363,922	7,332,779	6,920,161	6,673,596	9,080,581	9,394,218	9,576,342	9,621,275
Long-Term Obligations	217,581	227,563	275,004	469,735	997,152	727,657	585,616	705,789
Total Liabilities	9,227,674	8,668,515	8,500,659	9,380,785	12,712,460	13,227,985	13,830,969	13,878,257
Net Stockholders' Equity	785,768	793,132	1,015,759	1,247,012	1,301,356	1,212,330	1,185,594	1,117,207
Shares Outstanding	54,216	54,928	63,015	73,218	79,612	80,036	80,326	79,685
Statistical Record								
Return on Equity %	5.06	17.04	11.92	9.44	8.73	10.96	9.02	12.48
Return on Assets %	0.39	1.42	1.27	1.10	0.81	0.92	0.71	0.93
Non-Int. Exp./Tot. Inc. %	51.69	55.80	51.75	46.65	37.58	42.81	41.19	37.92
Price Range	47.15-42.20	42.72-29.43	30.75-23.88	27.88-16.94	22.94-11.25	24.69-17.38	25.44-14.75	28.00-20.38
P/E Ratio	19.40-17.37	19.33-13.32	18.09-14.05	19.10-11.60	16.15-7.92	15.05-10.59	19.27-11.17	16.28-11.85
Average Yield %	2.20	2.54	2.62	3.13	4.26	3.25	3.00	2.61

Address: 130 Merchant Street, Honolulu, HI 96813 **Telephone:** (808) 538-4727 **Web Site:** www.boh.com	**Officers:** Michael E. ONeill – Chmn., C.E.O., Alton T. Kuioka – Vice–Chair, Commercial Banking **Transfer Agents:** Continental Stock Transfer &Trust Company, New York, NY; or Pacific Century Trust, a division of Bank of Hawaii, Honolulu, HI	**Investor Contact:** 808-537-8037 **Institutional Holding** **No of Institutions:** 4 **Shares:** 34,080 **% Held:** –

BANTA CORPORATION

Exchange	Symbol	Price	52Wk Range	Yield	P/E
NYS	BN	$43.64 (5/28/2004)	47.05-32.47	1.56	22.85

*7 Year Price Score 138.0 ***NYSE Composite Index=100** ***12 Month Price Score 52.3**

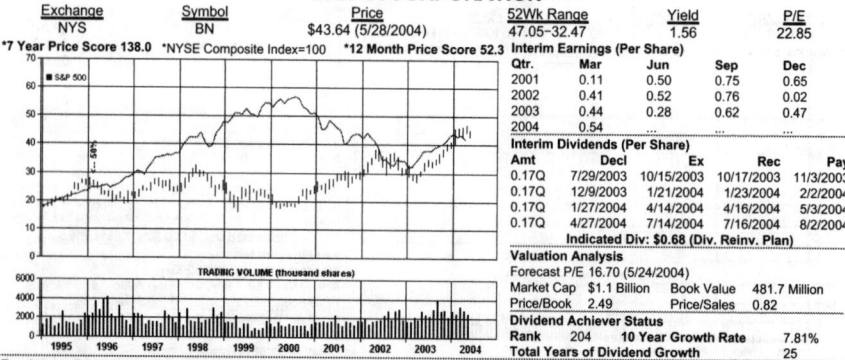

Interim Earnings (Per Share)

Qtr.	Mar	Jun	Sep	Dec
2001	0.11	0.50	0.75	0.65
2002	0.41	0.52	0.76	0.02
2003	0.44	0.28	0.62	0.47
2004	0.54	...	...	...

Interim Dividends (Per Share)

Amt	Decl	Ex	Rec	Pay
0.17Q	7/29/2003	10/15/2003	10/17/2003	11/3/2003
0.17Q	12/9/2003	1/21/2004	1/23/2004	2/2/2004
0.17Q	1/27/2004	4/14/2004	4/16/2004	5/3/2004
0.17Q	4/27/2004	7/14/2004	7/16/2004	8/2/2004

Indicated Div: $0.68 (Div. Reinv. Plan)

Valuation Analysis

Forecast P/E 16.70 (5/24/2004)

Market Cap $1.1 Billion	Book Value 481.7 Million
Price/Book 2.49	Price/Sales 0.82

Dividend Achiever Status

Rank 204	10 Year Growth Rate	7.81%
Total Years of Dividend Growth	25	

Business Summary: Printing (MIC: 13.4 SIC: 2759 NAIC:323119)

Banta provides a broad range of printing and digital imaging services. Co. operates in three business segments: print, turnkey services, and healthcare. The print segment provides products and services to publishers of educational and general books and special interest magazines. The print segment also supplies direct marketing materials and consumer and business catalogs. The turnkey services segment provides supply-chain management, product assembly, fulfillment and product localization services to technology companies. The healthcare products are primarily engaged in the production of disposable products used in outpatient clinics, dental offices and hospitals.

Recent Developments: For the three months ended Apr 3 2004, net income rose 25.1% to $14.1 million compared with $11.2 million in the corresponding quarter of 2003. Earnings benefited from productivity improvements from Co.'s restructuring activities in 2003, capital investments, and improved economic conditions, particularly in the commercial print and supply-chain management businesses. Results for 2003 included an after-tax restructuring charge of $600,000. Net sales were $373.1 million, up 10.9% from $336.4 million in the prior-year period. Earnings from operations increased 15.8% to $23.3 million compared with $20.1 million the year before.

Prospects: Co.'s investments in productivity initiatives, efforts to maximize facility utilization, and pursuit of new business opportunities, as well as a strengthening economy, supports its ability to deliver strong 2004 results. Pricing seems to have stabilized for some of Co.'s print businesses; however Co. has not seen an improvement in the industry. As a result, Co. is cautiously optimistic that a growing economy will create more demand for print and positively impact pricing. Meanwhile, Co. reaffirmed its guidance for full-year 2004 revenue growth in the low- to mid-single-digit range and diluted earnings per share growth in the high-single to low-double-digit range, before special charges.

Financial Data

(US$ in Thousands)	3 Mos	01/03/2004	12/28/2002	12/29/2001	12/30/2000	01/01/2000	01/02/1999	01/03/1998
Earnings Per Share	1.91	1.81	1.71	2.01	2.35	0.59	1.80	1.44
Cash Flow Per Share	0.95	4.29	5.79	7.18	5.04	4.62	4.60	3.84
Tang. Book Val. Per Share	16.71	17.35	15.46	13.88	12.41	12.31	11.82	11.79
Dividends Per Share	0.670	0.660	0.640	0.610	0.600	0.560	0.510	0.470
Dividend Payout %	35.08	36.46	37.42	30.34	25.53	94.91	28.33	32.63
Income Statement								
Total Revenues	373,072	1,418,497	1,366,457	1,457,935	1,537,729	1,278,278	1,335,796	1,202,483
Total Indirect Exp.	52,886	223,770	221,846	189,704	195,682	217,992	167,932	159,019
Depreciation & Amort.	15,127	63,848	78,430	75,378	75,744	68,212	66,862	62,107
Operating Income	23,256	81,614	81,643	108,409	114,793	48,370	97,545	79,544
Net Interest Inc./(Exp.)	(1,890)	(8,420)	(11,343)	(13,720)	(16,754)	(12,362)	(10,825)	(11,062)
Income Taxes	7,910	27,800	28,002	32,200	37,900	18,600	33,150	27,500
Net Income	14,074	46,614	43,799	49,997	58,743	16,010	52,940	43,323
Average Shs. Outstg.	26,100	25,742	25,565	24,857	24,980	27,177	29,474	30,113
Balance Sheet								
Cash & Cash Equivalents	139,710	181,112	154,836	65,976	27,660	27,651	26,584	16,432
Total Current Assets	482,413	523,166	460,150	373,616	406,675	355,861	354,620	365,676
Total Assets	845,261	886,023	805,264	788,046	854,524	773,344	769,966	781,216
Total Current Liabilities	219,667	223,851	185,782	184,750	240,319	245,353	196,491	200,368
Long-Term Obligations	86,487	87,712	111,489	130,981	179,202	113,520	120,628	130,065
Net Stockholders' Equity	481,676	513,429	453,113	407,278	370,912	353,775	409,931	414,103
Net Working Capital	262,746	299,315	274,368	188,866	166,356	110,508	158,129	165,308
Shares Outstanding	24,889	25,791	25,247	24,729	24,566	23,942	28,260	29,793
Statistical Record								
Operating Profit Margin %	6.23	5.75	5.97	7.43	7.46	3.78	7.30	6.61
Return on Equity %	2.92	9.07	9.66	12.27	15.83	4.52	12.91	10.46
Return on Assets %	1.66	5.26	5.43	6.34	6.87	2.07	6.87	5.54
Debt/Total Assets %	10.23	9.89	13.84	16.62	20.97	14.67	15.66	16.64
Price Range	46.70-40.93	40.95-27.10	38.81-29.38	30.90-22.98	25.37-17.44	26.51-16.31	32.59-21.79	28.03-20.69
P/E Ratio	24.45-21.43	22.62-14.97	22.70-17.18	15.37-11.43	10.80-7.42	44.93-27.64	18.11-12.11	19.47-14.37
Average Yield %	1.52	1.96	1.90	2.23	2.92	2.50	1.86	1.88

Address: 225 Main Street, Menasha, WI 54952-8003 **Telephone:** (920) 751-7777 **Web Site:** www.banta.com	Officers: Stephanie A. Streeter – Chmn., Pres., C.E.O., Ronald D. Kneezel – V.P., Sec., Gen. Couns. **Transfer Agents:**American Stock Transfer &Trust Company, New York, NY	Investor Contact:920-751-7777 **Institutional Holding** No of Institutions: 23 Shares: 420,071 % Held: –

BARD (C.R.), INC.

Exchange	Symbol	Price	52Wk Range	Yield	P/E
NYS	BCR	$112.17 (5/28/2004)	112.2–67.00	0.82	30.65

*7 Year Price Score 156.3   *NYSE Composite Index=100   *12 Month Price Score 61.6

Interim Earnings (Per Share)

Qtr.	Mar	Jun	Sep	Dec
2001	0.65	0.68	0.68	0.74
2002	0.65	0.83	0.57	0.89
2003	0.89	0.94	0.98	0.39
2004	1.35	...	...	...

Interim Dividends (Per Share)

Amt	Decl	Ex	Rec	Pay
0.23Q	10/8/2003	10/16/2003	10/20/2003	10/31/2003
0.23Q	12/10/2003	1/14/2004	1/19/2004	1/30/2004
0.23Q	4/21/2004	4/29/2004	5/3/2004	5/14/2004
100%	4/21/2004	6/1/2004	5/17/2004	5/28/2004

Indicated Div: $0.92 (Div. Reinv. Plan)

Valuation Analysis

Forecast P/E 24.25 (5/24/2004)

Market Cap	$5.8 Billion	Book Value	1.1 Billion
Price/Book	4.37	Price/Sales	3.36

Dividend Achiever Status

Rank	245	10 Year Growth Rate	5.24%
Total Years of Dividend Growth		32	

Business Summary: Medical Instruments &Equipment (MIC: 9.6 SIC: 3841 NAIC:339112)

Bard (C.R.) is a major multinational developer, manufacturer and marketer of health care products. Co. engages in the design, manufacture, packaging, distribution and sale of medical, surgical, diagnostic and patient–care devices. Co. holds strong positions in the fields of vascular, urology, oncology and surgical specialty products. Co.'s products are marketed worldwide to hospitals, individual health care professionals, extended care facilities, alternate site facilities and the home, employing a combination of direct delivery and medical specialty distributors.

Recent Developments: For the year ended Mar 31 2004, net income advanced 53.3% to $71.9 million compared with $46.9 million in the corresponding quarter of the previous year. Net sales improved 17.2% to $393.8 million from $335.9 million in the year–earlier period. Vascular net sales jumped 36.2% to $92.1 million from $67.6 million, while urology net sales climbed 6.6% to $116.5 million from $109.3 million in the prior–year quarter. Oncology net sales increased 21.4% to $94.3 million from $77.7 million, while surgery net sales jumped 16.8% to $75.2 million from $64.4 million the year before.

Prospects: Co.'s near–term outlook appears promising. Results continue to benefit from new products, which are becoming a more significant driver of Co.'s sales growth. This growth is indicative of Co.'s strategy to expand its research and development investment. Moreover, Co.believes that its gross margin remains strong and should continue to provide the necessary resources for this investment plan. During the first quarter, Co.'s research and development (R&D) spending was up 19.0%, and Co. projects its R&D investment will accelerate in the coming months.

Financial Data

(US$ in Thousands)	3 Mos	12/31/2003	12/31/2002	12/31/2001	12/31/2000	12/31/1999	12/31/1998	12/31/1997
Earnings Per Share	3.66	3.20	2.94	2.75	2.09	2.28	4.51	1.26
Cash Flow Per Share	1.47	4.99	5.15	4.77	4.03	1.74	3.71	1.71
Tang. Book Val. Per Share	12.04	10.70	9.67	2.05	N.M	N.M	N.M	N.M
Dividends Per Share	0.910	0.900	0.860	0.840	0.820	0.780	0.740	0.700
Dividend Payout %	24.86	28.12	29.25	30.54	39.23	34.21	16.40	55.55
Income Statement								
Total Revenues	393,800	1,433,100	1,273,800	1,181,300	1,098,800	1,036,500	1,164,700	1,213,500
Total Indirect Exp.	150,700	560,500	464,100	446,000	413,000	404,500	(153,700)	542,100
Depreciation & Amort.	13,800	44,700	42,300	53,200	49,600	49,100	58,700	57,300
Operating Income	84,900	275,700	239,600	199,000	190,400	179,800	461,500	131,500
Net Interest Inc./(Exp.)	(1,800)	(5,900)	(6,100)	(8,000)	(15,600)	(17,200)	(20,400)	(29,400)
Income Taxes	26,400	54,700	56,000	61,700	47,100	55,200	212,100	32,600
Net Income	71,900	168,500	155,000	143,200	106,900	118,100	252,300	72,300
Average Shs. Outstg.	53,300	52,600	52,800	52,000	51,221	51,881	55,970	57,273
Balance Sheet								
Cash & Cash Equivalents	458,400	417,400	23,100	30,800	21,300	17,300	25,600	8,000
Total Current Assets	934,700	875,100	758,000	647,400	526,600	529,100	488,500	563,500
Total Assets	1,786,400	1,692,000	1,416,700	1,539,400	1,469,100	1,476,700	1,435,700	1,670,100
Total Current Liabilities	387,700	421,900	316,900	234,500	224,500	352,500	302,800	310,600
Long–Term Obligations	151,400	151,500	152,200	156,400	204,300	158,400	160,000	340,700
Net Stockholders' Equity	1,146,200	1,045,700	880,400	788,700	613,900	574,300	567,600	573,100
Net Working Capital	547,000	453,200	441,100	412,900	302,100	176,600	185,700	252,900
Shares Outstanding	52,169	51,754	51,602	52,383	50,908	50,781	51,497	56,785
Statistical Record								
Operating Profit Margin %	20.69	18.36	17.82	15.64	16.97	16.37	65.62	8.12
Return on Equity %	5.97	14.91	16.17	16.35	16.35	16.77	18.80	97.79	6.87
Return on Assets %	3.83	9.21	10.05	8.37	7.01	7.31	38.66	2.35
Debt/Total Assets %	8.47	8.95	10.74	10.15	13.90	10.72	11.14	20.39
Price Range	97.64–80.40	81.25–54.82	64.50–46.25	64.51–41.99	54.69–35.25	59.13–42.25	49.50–28.69	38.00–26.50
P/E Ratio	26.68–21.97	25.39–17.13	21.94–15.73	23.46–15.27	26.17–16.87	25.93–18.53	10.98–6.36	30.16–21.03
Average Yield %	0.99	1.33	1.57	1.62	1.82	1.55	1.95	2.22

Address: 730 Central Avenue, Murray Hill, NJ 07974

Telephone: (908) 277-8000

Web Site: www.crbard.com

Officers: Timothy M. Ring – Chmn., C.E.O., John H. Weiland – Pres., C.O.O.

Transfer Agents: EquiServe Trust Company, N.A., Providence, RI

Investor Contact: 908–277–8139

Institutional Holding

No of Institutions: 11

Shares: 365,188   **% Held:** –

BB&T CORP.

Exchange	Symbol	Price	52Wk Range	Yield	P/E
NYS	BBT	$37.68 (5/28/2004)	39.66-33.33	3.40	19.03

*7 Year Price Score 107.3 *NYSE Composite Index=100 ***12 Month Price Score 46.1**

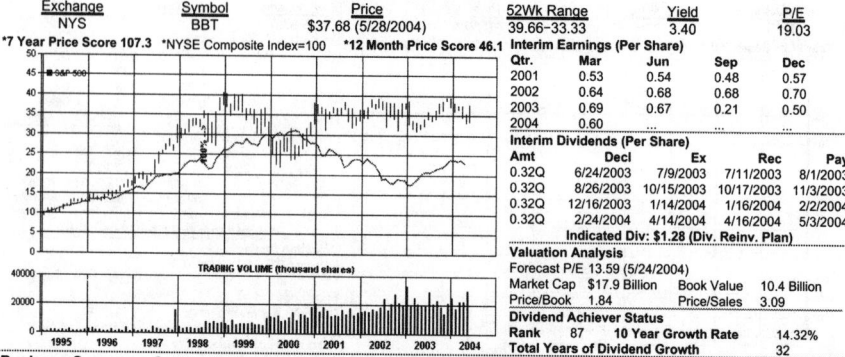

Interim Earnings (Per Share)

Qtr.	Mar	Jun	Sep	Dec
2001	0.53	0.54	0.48	0.57
2002	0.64	0.68	0.68	0.70
2003	0.69	0.67	0.21	0.50
2004	0.60	...	...	...

Interim Dividends (Per Share)

Amt	Decl	Ex	Rec	Pay
0.32Q	6/24/2003	7/9/2003	7/11/2003	8/1/2003
0.32Q	8/26/2003	10/15/2003	10/17/2003	11/3/2003
0.32Q	12/16/2003	1/14/2004	1/16/2004	2/2/2004
0.32Q	2/24/2004	4/14/2004	4/16/2004	5/3/2004

Indicated Div: $1.28 (Div. Reinv. Plan)

Valuation Analysis

Forecast P/E 13.59 (5/24/2004)

Market Cap	$17.9 Billion	Book Value	10.4 Billion
Price/Book	1.84	Price/Sales	3.09

Dividend Achiever Status

Rank	87	10 Year Growth Rate	14.32%
Total Years of Dividend Growth	32		

Business Summary: Commercial Banking (MIC: 8.1 SIC: 6021 NAIC:522110)

BB&T, a multi-bank holding company with assets of $80.44 billion as of June 30 2003, operates more than 1,100 banking offices in the Carolinas, Virginia, West Virginia, Tennessee, Kentucky, Georgia, Maryland, Florida, Alabama, Indiana and Washington, D.C. Co.'s largest subsidiary is Branch Banking and Trust Company (BB&T-NC). BB&T-NC's subsidiaries include BB&T Leasing Corp., BB&T Investment Services, and BB&T Insurance Services. Co.'s other subsidiaries include Branch Banking and Trust Co. of South Carolina, Branch Banking and Trust Co. of Virginia, and Fidelity Service Corporation.

Recent Developments: For the three months ended Mar 31 2004, net income totaled $328.5 million, up 0.2% compared with $327.7 million in the corresponding prior-year quarter. Results for 2004 and 2003 included after-tax merger-related charges of $6.1 million and $3.1 million, respectively. Net interest income climbed 16.6% to $806.8 million from $692.2 million the year before. Provision for loan and lease losses slipped 0.8% to $62.5 million from $63.0 million the previous year. Non-interest income increased 7.5% to $478.2 million from $444.9 million, while non-interest expense jumped 22.2% to $738.0 million from $604.1 million a year earlier.

Prospects: Earnings are being negatively affected by sharply lower mortgage banking income stemming primarily from a decline in mortgage originations due to higher interest rates. However, results are benefiting from increased loan demand and higher non-interest revenues, driven by growth in income from investment banking and brokerage fees and commissions, as well as service charges on deposit accounts. Separately, on Apr 15 2004, Co. announced that it has completed its acquisition of Republic Bancshares Inc., an operator of 71 banking offices in Florida with assets of $2.80 billion, for about $392.0 million. Looking ahead, Co. is targeting earnings of between $2.71 and $2.86 per share in 2004.

Financial Data

(US$ in Thousands)	3 Mos	12/31/2003	12/31/2002	12/31/2001	12/31/2000	12/31/1999	12/31/1998	12/31/1997
Earnings Per Share	1.98	2.07	2.70	2.12	1.55	1.83	1.71	1.30
Tang. Book Val. Per Share	11.01	10.91	12.04	13.49	11.91	9.66	9.50	8.22
Dividends Per Share	1.250	1.220	1.100	0.980	0.860	0.750	0.660	0.580
Dividend Payout %	352.78	58.93	40.74	46.22	55.48	40.98	38.59	44.61
Income Statement								
Total Interest Income	1,080,449	4,354,792	4,434,044	4,849,538	4,339,674	3,115,780	2,481,182	2,122,940
Total Interest Expense	273,626	1,272,787	1,686,584	2,415,053	2,322,046	1,534,065	1,233,778	1,023,415
Net Interest Income	806,823	3,082,005	2,747,460	2,434,485	2,017,628	1,581,715	1,247,404	1,099,525
Provision for Loan Losses	62,500	248,000	263,700	224,318	127,431	92,097	80,310	89,850
Non-Interest Income	478,178	1,782,057	1,522,375	1,256,478	995,553	766,487	520,250	472,638
Non-Interest Expense	737,986	3,106,110	2,385,538	2,228,430	1,761,539	1,346,904	961,374	937,150
Income Before Taxes	484,515	1,617,030	1,790,697	1,360,428	905,680	904,070	733,722	547,439
Income from Cont Ops	...	...	1,293,229	...	...	...	...	...
Net Income	328,500	1,064,903	1,303,009	973,638	626,442	612,847	501,825	359,942
Average Shs. Outstg.	550,547	514,082	478,792	459,269	398,915	335,298	293,571	276,440
Balance Sheet								
Cash & Due from Banks	1,867,913	2,217,961	1,929,650	1,871,437	1,471,035	1,138,820	938,797	839,579
Securities Avail. for Sale	17,949,168	16,256,773	17,747,965	16,719,359	13,878,582	10,575,265	8,031,796	6,549,393
Net Loans & Leases	62,359,880	60,794,990	50,416,621	44,891,339	38,932,351	28,524,467	22,350,692	19,516,871
Total Assets	94,281,503	90,466,613	80,216,816	70,869,945	59,340,228	43,480,996	34,427,227	29,177,600
Total Deposits	64,124,892	59,349,785	51,280,016	44,733,275	38,014,501	27,251,142	23,046,907	20,210,116
Long-Term Obligations	10,625,382	10,807,700	13,587,841	11,721,076	8,354,672	5,491,734	4,736,934	3,282,958
Total Liabilities	83,854,675	80,531,882	72,828,902	64,719,736	54,554,303	40,281,837	31,668,679	26,939,963
Net Stockholders' Equity	10,426,828	9,934,731	7,387,914	6,150,209	4,785,925	3,199,159	2,758,548	2,237,637
Shares Outstanding	548,022	541,942	470,452	455,682	401,678	331,170	290,211	272,104
Statistical Record								
Return on Equity %	3.15	5.76	15.20	13.84	17.65	19.31	17.91	15.98
Return on Assets %	0.34	0.63	1.40	1.20	1.42	1.42	1.43	1.22
Equity/Assets %	11.05	10.98	9.20	8.67	8.06	7.35	8.01	7.66
Non-Int. Exp./Tot. Inc. %	47.34	56.88	40.04	36.49	33.01	34.69	32.03	36.10
Price Range	38.64-34.65	39.66-31.15	39.23-31.26	38.48-31.42	38.25-22.00	40.44-27.31	40.63-27.31	32.50-17.63
P/E Ratio	19.52-14.50	19.16-15.05	14.53-11.58	18.15-14.82	24.68-14.19	22.10-14.92	23.76-15.97	25.00-13.56
Average Yield %	3.39	3.46	2.99	2.75	3.06	2.11	1.98	2.47

Address: 200 West Second Street, Winston-Salem, NC 27102	**Officers:** John A. Allison IV – Chmn., C.E.O., Kelly S. King – Pres.	**Investor Contact:**336-733-3058
Telephone: (336) 733-2000	**Transfer Agents:**Branch Banking &Trust Company, Wilson, NC	**Institutional Holding** **No of Institutions:** 25
Web Site: www.bbandt.com		**Shares:** 1,025,218 **% Held:** –

BECKMAN COULTER, INC.

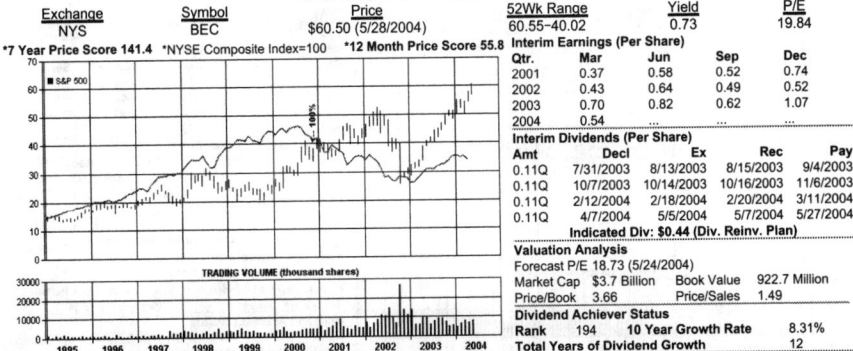

Business Summary: Instruments and Related Products (MIC: 11.15 SIC: 3826 NAIC:334516)

Beckman Coulter designs, manufactures, and markets systems, which consist of instruments, chemistries, software and supplies that are designed to meet a variety of biomedical laboratory needs. Co.'s products are used in a range of applications from instruments used for medical research, clinical research and drug discovery to diagnostic systems. Co. operates in two segments: clinical diagnostics and biomedical research. Clinical diagnostics offers products that aid in the detection and monitoring of disease by means of laboratory evaluation and analysis of substances from patients. Biomedical research provides products for a wide range of applications based on the study of life processes.

Recent Developments: For the quarter ended Mar 31 2004, net earnings decreased 20.2% to $35.6 million compared with $44.6 million in the corresponding period of the previous year. Results for 2003 included a pre-tax restructuring charge of $18.5 million and a pre-tax litigation credit of $26.9 million. Sales increased 14.9% to $536.8 million from $467.3 million in the year-earlier quarter. The improvement in sales growth was largely due to higher hardware shipments and installations as well as contributions from new products. Gross profit advanced 17.4% to $254.3 million from $216.6 million the year before. Operating income climbed 13.8% to $67.7 million versus $59.5 million in the prior-year period.

Prospects: In the second quarter of 2004, Co. expects sales to grow 8.0% to 10.0%, fueled by continued strength in Clinical Diagnostics and a recovering Biomedical Research market. Co. expects to gain market share in the high-volume immunoassay market with the *UniCel®Dxl 800 Access®*immunoassay system, increasing demand for laboratory automation systems and the ramp up of the recently launched *Coulter®LH 500* mid-range hematology systems. Co. should also benefit from new products taking hold in the Biomedical Research division. Furthermore, Co. expects net earnings to grow 11.0% to 14.0%, with earnings per share ranging from $0.87 to $0.91 for the second quarter of 2004.

Financial Data
(US$ in Thousands)

	3 Mos	12/31/2003	12/31/2002	12/31/2001	12/31/2000	12/31/1999	12/31/1998	12/31/1997
Earnings Per Share	3.05	3.21	2.08	2.21	2.03	1.78	0.57	(4.79)
Cash Flow Per Share	0.73	3.49	4.86	4.32	3.38	3.57	(0.03)	2.49
Tang. Book Val. Per Share	3.40	2.99	N.M	N.M	N.M	N.M	N.M	N.M
Dividends Per Share	0.420	0.400	0.350	0.340	0.325	0.320	0.305	0.300
Dividend Payout %	13.77	12.46	16.82	15.38	16.00	17.92	53.50	N.M.
Income Statement								
Total Revenues	536,800	2,192,500	2,059,400	1,984,000	1,886,900	1,808,700	1,718,200	1,198,000
Total Indirect Exp.	186,600	718,200	711,000	686,000	658,700	650,100	682,800	825,300
Depreciation & Amort.	...	106,800	109,800	126,400	136,100	143,700	152,400	109,100
Operating Income	67,700	329,500	223,500	239,600	232,600	216,500	114,800	(237,000)
Income Taxes	13,800	65,600	43,400	63,500	56,400	48,700	13,100	12,500
Income from Cont Ops	...	...	...	141,500	...	...	...	...
Net Income	35,600	207,200	135,500	138,400	125,500	106,000	33,500	(264,400)
Average Shs. Outstg.	66,063	64,493	65,060	64,011	61,800	59,400	58,600	55,200
Balance Sheet								
Cash & Cash Equivalents	49,000	74,600	91,400	36,000	29,600	34,400	24,700	33,100
Total Current Assets	1,104,700	1,161,200	1,056,200	1,035,600	927,800	966,400	956,600	976,700
Total Assets	2,535,000	2,558,200	2,263,600	2,178,000	2,018,200	2,110,800	2,133,300	2,331,000
Total Current Liabilities	524,200	578,200	611,600	509,900	501,100	575,900	719,300	894,900
Long-Term Obligations	633,200	625,600	626,600	760,300	862,800	980,700	982,200	1,181,300
Net Stockholders' Equity	922,700	897,700	592,100	518,200	343,900	227,900	126,900	81,800
Shares Outstanding	61,500	62,000	61,000	61,200	59,700	58,000	56,800	55,200
Operating Profit Margin %	12.61	15.02	10.85	12.07	12.32	11.96	6.68	N.M.
Return on Equity %	3.86	23.08	22.88	27.30	36.49	46.51	26.39	N.M.
Return on Assets %	1.40	8.09	5.98	6.49	6.21	5.02	1.57	N.M.
Debt/Total Assets %	24.97	24.45	27.68	34.90	42.75	46.46	46.04	50.67
Price Range	55.18-49.99	51.31-28.50	52.47-25.78	47.01-34.50	41.94-23.66	27.56-20.00	31.81-20.00	26.06-18.78
P/E Ratio	18.09-16.39	15.98-8.88	25.23-12.39	21.27-15.61	20.66-11.65	15.48-11.24	55.81-35.09	N/A
Average Yield %	0.80	0.98	0.84	0.83	0.99	1.34	1.13	1.39

Address: 4300 N. Harbor Boulevard, Fullerton, CA 92834-3100	Officers: John P. Wareham - Chmn., C.E.O., Scott Garrett - Pres., C.O.O.	Investor Contact:714-773-7620
Telephone: (714) 871-4848	Transfer Agents:EquiServe Trust Company, N.A.	Institutional Holding
Web Site: www.beckmancoulter.com	Providence, RI	No of Institutions: 20
		Shares: 394,969 % Held: –

BECTON, DICKINSON AND CO.

Exchange	Symbol	Price	52Wk Range	Yield	P/E
NYS	BDX	$50.32 (5/28/2004)	53.25-35.49	1.19	22.87

*7 Year Price Score 123.1   *NYSE Composite Index=100   *12 Month Price Score 55.5

Interim Earnings (Per Share)

Qtr.	Dec	Mar	Jun	Sep
2000-01	0.23	0.44	0.46	0.50
2001-02	0.37	0.48	0.44	0.50
2002-03	0.43	0.54	0.49	0.61
2003-04	0.48	0.62	...	...

Interim Dividends (Per Share)

Amt	Decl	Ex	Rec	Pay
0.10Q	7/22/2003	9/5/2003	9/9/2003	9/30/2003
0.15Q	11/24/2003	12/10/2003	12/12/2003	1/2/2004
0.15Q	1/27/2004	3/8/2004	3/10/2004	3/31/2004
0.15Q	5/25/2004	6/7/2004	6/9/2004	6/30/2004

Indicated Div: $0.60 (Div. Reinv. Plan)

Valuation Analysis

Forecast P/E 19.50 (5/24/2004)

Market Cap	$12.9 Billion	Book Value	3.1 Billion
Price/Book	3.94	Price/Sales	2.56

Dividend Achiever Status

Rank	174	10 Year Growth Rate	9.26%
Total Years of Dividend Growth			31

Business Summary: Medical Instruments &Equipment (MIC: 9.6 SIC: 3841 NAIC:339112)

Becton, Dickinson and Co. is engaged principally in the manufacture and sale of a broad range of medical supplies, devices, laboratory equipment and diagnostic products used by healthcare institutions, life science researchers, clinical laboratories, industry and the general public. Co.'s operations consist of three worldwide business segments: BD Medical, BD Diagnostics and BD Biosciences. BD Medical include products such as hypodermic syringes and needles for injection. BD Diagnostics include products such as clinical and industrial microbiology, and sample collection products. BD Biosciences include products and services for a variety of applications in life sciences.

Recent Developments: For the quarter ended Mar 31 2004, net income increased 16.3% to $165.2 million compared with $142.0 million in the equivalent period of the previous year. Revenues improved 12.0% to $1.27 billion from $1.13 billion in the prior-year quarter. Revenues for BD Medical jumped 13.4% to $682.6 million from $601.8 million, while revenues for BD Diagnostics climbed 7.3% to $382.9 million from $356.8 million in the year-earlier period. Revenues for BD Biosciences jumped 16.9% to $205.0 million from $175.4 million the year before. Operating income rose 17.5% to $231.3 million versus $196.8 million in 2003.

Prospects: Going forward, Co. estimates that diluted earnings per share for fiscal 2004, which includes a charge of $0.11 per share relating to its blood glucose monitoring products, will increase in the range of 10.0% to 12.0% over the prior period. Meanwhile, Co. is pleased with the strong performance in its BD Medical and BD Biosciences segments, reflecting contributions from prefillable drug delivery devices, diabetes related products and its BD *FACSAria*™cell sorter. Also, Co. is benefiting from strong revenue growth in nearly all of its international regions.

Financial Data

(US$ in Thousands)	6 Mos	3 Mos	09/30/2003	09/30/2002	09/30/2001	09/30/2000	09/30/1999	09/30/1998
Earnings Per Share	2.20	2.12	2.07	1.79	1.63	1.49	1.04	0.90
Cash Flow Per Share	2.00	0.81	3.43	3.11	2.89	2.33	1.63	1.91
Tang. Book Val. Per Share	7.80	7.15	6.63	4.94	5.35	3.80	2.74	3.30
Dividends Per Share	0.450	0.400	0.40	0.39	0.380	0.35	0.320	0.280
Dividend Payout %	20.45	18.86	19.32	21.78	23.31	23.48	31.49	31.38
Income Statement								
Total Revenues	2,470,054	1,199,531	4,527,940	4,033,069	3,754,302	3,618,334	3,418,412	3,116,873
Total Indirect Exp.	791,455	390,273	1,442,524	1,252,229	1,195,130	1,197,684	1,185,945	1,079,464
Depreciation & Amort.	186,009	90,316	344,456	304,865	305,700	288,255	258,863	228,749
Operating Income	399,666	168,374	749,126	675,663	645,880	514,804	445,248	405,432
Net Interest Inc./(Exp.)	(16,890)	(8,929)	(36,560)	(33,304)	(55,414)	(74,197)	(72,052)	(56,340)
Income Taxes	89,050	33,997	162,650	148,607	138,348	127,037	96,936	104,298
Income from Cont Ops	...	...	...	...	438,402	...	...	...
Net Income	290,562	125,402	547,056	479,982	401,652	392,897	275,719	236,568
Average Shs. Outstg.	263,763	261,872	263,635	268,183	268,833	263,239	264,580	262,128
Balance Sheet								
Cash & Cash Equivalents	660,469	534,640	519,886	243,115	82,129	49,196	59,932	83,251
Total Current Assets	2,484,331	2,367,343	2,338,569	1,928,707	1,762,942	1,660,677	1,683,725	1,542,762
Total Assets	5,714,972	5,608,919	5,572,253	5,040,460	4,802,287	4,505,096	4,436,958	3,846,038
Total Current Liabilities	819,456	940,815	1,043,374	1,252,453	1,264,676	1,353,538	1,329,322	1,091,913
Long-Term Obligations	1,183,113	1,164,923	1,184,031	802,967	782,996	779,569	954,169	765,176
Net Stockholders' Equity	3,160,453	3,045,015	2,896,954	2,487,974	2,328,767	1,955,998	1,768,688	1,613,820
Net Working Capital	1,592,875	1,426,528	1,295,195	676,254	498,266	307,139	354,403	450,849
Shares Outstanding	253,277	252,705	251,133	255,529	259,236	253,496	250,797	247,843
Statistical Record								
Operating Profit Margin %	16.18	14.03	16.54	16.75	17.20	14.22	13.02	13.00
Net Profit Margin %	18.97	16.12	19.26	19.27	19.04	17.88	13.73	14.28
Return on Equity %	9.19	4.11	18.88	19.29	18.82	20.08	15.58	14.65
Return on Assets %	5.08	2.23	9.81	9.52	9.12	8.72	6.21	6.15
Debt/Total Assets %	20.70	20.76	21.24	15.93	16.30	17.30	21.50	19.89
Price Range	49.89-35.71	41.45-35.71	40.43-28.40	38.47-25.01	39.00-26.56	34.13-23.88	46.88-25.44	43.75-21.81
P/E Ratio	22.68-16.23	19.55-16.84	19.53-13.72	21.49-13.97	23.93-16.30	22.90-16.02	45.07-24.46	48.61-24.24
Average Yield %	1.06	1.05	1.14	0.85	1.12	1.64	0.90	0.84

Address: 1 Becton Drive, Franklin Lakes, NJ 07417-1880	**Officers:** Edward J. Ludwig - Chmn., Pres., C.E.O., John R. Considine - Exec. V.P., C.F.O.	**Investor Contact:**800-284-6845 **Institutional Holding**
Telephone: (201) 847-6800 **Web Site:** www.bd.com	**Transfer Agents:**EquiServe Trust Company, N.A., Jersey City, NJ	**No of Institutions:** 4 **Shares:** 285,650 **% Held:** -

BEMIS, INC.

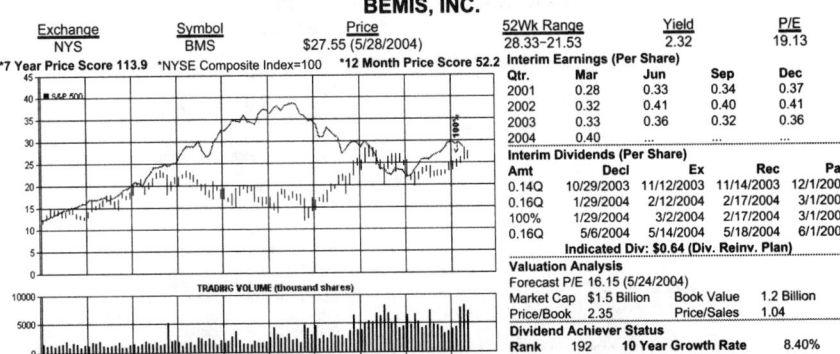

Exchange	Symbol	Price	52Wk Range	Yield	P/E
NYS	BMS	$27.55 (5/28/2004)	28.33-21.53	2.32	19.13

*7 Year Price Score 113.9   *NYSE Composite Index=100   *12 Month Price Score 52.2

Interim Earnings (Per Share)

Qtr.	Mar	Jun	Sep	Dec
2001	0.28	0.33	0.34	0.37
2002	0.32	0.41	0.40	0.41
2003	0.33	0.36	0.32	0.36
2004	0.40	...	...	...

Interim Dividends (Per Share)

Amt	Decl	Ex	Rec	Pay
0.14Q	10/29/2003	11/12/2003	11/14/2003	12/1/2003
0.16Q	1/29/2004	2/12/2004	2/17/2004	3/1/2004
100%	1/29/2004	3/2/2004	2/17/2004	3/1/2004
0.16Q	5/6/2004	5/14/2004	5/18/2004	6/1/2004

Indicated Div: $0.64 (Div. Reinv. Plan)

Valuation Analysis

Forecast P/E 16.15 (5/24/2004)

Market Cap	$1.5 Billion	Book Value	1.2 Billion
Price/Book	2.35	Price/Sales	1.04

Dividend Achiever Status

Rank	192	10 Year Growth Rate	8.40%
Total Years of Dividend Growth		20	

Business Summary: Paper Products (MIC: 11.11 SIC: 2671 NAIC:322221)

Bemis Company is a manufacturer of flexible packaging products and pressure−sensitive materials used by food, consumer products, manufacturing, and other companies worldwide. Flexible packaging products include a broad range of consumer andindustrial packaging consisting of high−barrier products that include advanced multi−layer coextruded, coated and laminated film structures; polyethylene products; and paper products. Pressure−Sensitive Materials include roll label products, graphics and distribution products, and technical and industrial products. As of Jul 23 2003, Co. manufactured from 56 facilities in ten countries.

Recent Developments: For the quarter ended Mar 31 2004, net income climbed 21.3% to $43.0 million compared with $35.5 million in the corresponding period of the prior year. The improvement in earnings was primarily attributed to higher sales, coupled with benefits from Co.'s 2003 restructuring activities. Net sales advanced 7.1% to $684.0 million. Segment operating profit for Flexible Packaging increased 10.9% to $73.6 million, reflecting better cost management and sales mix. Pressure−Sensitive Materials segment operating income was $5.6 million versus $2.5 million a year earlier, led by improved cost controls and operating efficiencies.

Prospects: Co. is executing a strategy to position itself in niche markets, and with the closure of its Las Vegas, NV plant in March 2004, Co. expects improved performances in future quarters. Accordingly, Co. expects second quarter 2004 earnings per share to be up modestly from the fourth quarter of 2004. For full−year 2004, Co. is revising its guidance upward to a range of $1.62 to $1.70 per share, from its previous guidance of $1.58 to $1.65 per share. Also, Co. anticipates making additional capital investments in 2004 to support growing demand for particular products. Capital expenditures for 2004 are expected to be in the range of $140.0 million to $145.0 million.

Financial Data

(US$ in Thousands)	3 Mos	12/31/2003	12/31/2002	12/31/2001	12/31/2000	12/31/1999	12/31/1998	12/31/1997
Earnings Per Share	1.44	1.37	1.54	1.32	1.22	1.09	1.04	1.00
Cash Flow Per Share	0.57	2.88	2.66	2.99	1.96	1.75	2.07	1.33
Tang. Book Val. Per Share	5.85	5.80	4.10	4.39	4.76	5.51	4.87	4.61
Dividends Per Share	0.580	0.560	0.520	0.500	0.480	0.460	0.440	0.400
Dividend Payout %	40.28	40.87	33.76	37.87	39.34	42.20	42.10	40.00
Income Statement								
Total Revenues	684,037	2,635,018	2,369,038	2,293,104	2,164,583	1,918,025	1,848,004	1,877,237
Total Indirect Exp.	75,041	278,143	246,771	217,471	202,355	205,477	198,065	201,602
Depreciation & Amort.	34,495	128,189	119,231	124,147	108,130	97,717	88,910	78,856
Operating Income	68,917	255,338	282,152	260,191	244,969	218,194	208,548	195,270
Net Interest Inc./(Exp.)	(2,600)	(12,564)	(15,445)	(30,343)	(31,609)	(21,218)	(21,866)	(18,893)
Income Taxes	27,000	92,100	101,500	87,100	80,900	71,100	70,500	67,400
Net Income	43,027	147,145	165,515	140,325	130,602	114,775	111,432	107,584
Average Shs. Outstg.	107,531	107,733	107,492	106,243	107,106	105,314	106,648	107,760
Balance Sheet								
Cash & Cash Equivalents	70,117	76,476	56,401	35,101	28,910	18,187	23,738	13,827
Total Current Assets	763,244	751,906	721,655	586,897	639,959	583,581	517,939	516,393
Total Assets	2,324,267	2,292,932	2,256,650	1,922,974	1,888,643	1,532,143	1,453,054	1,362,567
Total Current Liabilities	306,883	315,586	325,853	238,182	495,097	253,268	242,788	251,187
Long−Term Obligations	574,459	583,399	718,277	595,249	437,952	372,267	371,363	316,791
Net Stockholders' Equity	1,185,353	1,138,733	958,974	886,148	798,757	725,895	670,807	639,885
Net Working Capital	456,361	436,320	395,802	348,715	144,862	330,313	275,151	265,206
Shares Outstanding	115,620	106,242	105,887	105,739	105,204	104,378	104,538	105,936
Statistical Record								
Operating Profit Margin %	10.07	9.69	11.90	11.34	11.31	11.37	11.28	10.40
Return on Equity %	3.62	12.92	17.25	15.83	16.35	15.81	16.61	16.81
Return on Assets %	1.85	6.41	7.33	7.29	6.91	7.49	7.66	7.89
Debt/Total Assets %	24.71	25.44	31.82	30.95	23.18	24.29	25.55	23.24
Price Range	26.12−23.48	25.53−19.89	29.04−19.94	26.08−14.41	19.25−12.03	19.97−15.22	23.47−16.97	23.59−17.91
P/E Ratio	18.14−16.31	18.64−14.52	18.85−12.95	19.76−10.91	15.78−9.86	18.32−13.96	22.57−16.32	23.59−17.91
Average Yield %	2.33	2.47	2.03	2.50	2.93	2.57	2.16	1.91

Address: 222 South 9th Street, Minneapolis, MN 55402-4099 Telephone: (612) 376-3000 Web Site: www.bemis.com	Officers: John H. Roe − Chmn., Jeffrey H. Curler − Pres., C.E.O. Transfer Agents:Wells Fargo Bank Minnesota, South St. Paul, MN	Investor Contact:612−376−3000 Institutional Holding No of Institutions: 2 Shares: 18,146 % Held: −

BLACK HILLS CORPORATION

Exchange	Symbol	Price	52Wk Range	Yield	P/E
NYS	BKH	$29.30 (5/28/2004)	33.35-27.97	4.23	19.28

*7 Year Price Score 109.5   *NYSE Composite Index=100   *12 Month Price Score 45.1

Interim Earnings (Per Share)

Qtr.	Mar	Jun	Sep	Dec
2001	...	1.34	0.61	1.47
2002	0.52	0.54	0.64	0.63
2003	0.62	0.54	0.54	0.14
2004	0.30	...	...	...

Interim Dividends (Per Share)

Amt	Decl	Ex	Rec	Pay
0.30Q	8/4/2003	8/13/2003	8/15/2003	9/1/2003
0.30Q	10/21/2003	11/12/2003	11/14/2003	12/1/2003
0.31Q	2/4/2004	2/12/2004	2/17/2004	3/1/2004
0.31Q	4/27/2004	5/13/2004	5/17/2004	6/1/2004

Indicated Div: $1.24 (Div. Reinv. Plan)

Valuation Analysis
Forecast P/E 14.21 (5/24/2004)
Market Cap $686.1 Million   Book Value 703.3 Million
Price/Book 1.47   Price/Sales 0.84

Dividend Achiever Status
Rank 274   10 Year Growth Rate 3.47%
Total Years of Dividend Growth 32

TRADING VOLUME (thousand shares)

Business Summary: Electricity (MIC: 7.1 SIC: 4911 NAIC:221121)

Black Hills is an energy and communications company with three segments. Co.'s Wholesale Energy group generates and sells electricity, produces coal, natural gas and crude oil primarily in the Rocky Mountain region, and markets and transports fuel products. Co.'s Electric Utility group engages in the generation, transmission and distribution of electricity to about 61,000 customers in South Dakota, Wyoming and Montana. Co.'s Communications group offers broadband telecommunications services, including local and long distance telephone, expanded cable television, cable modem Internet access and high–speed data and video services to residential and business customers in part of South Dakota.

Recent Developments: For the quarter ended Mar 31 2004, income from continuing operations declined 36.4% to $10.0 million versus $15.7 million, before and accounting change charge of $2.7 million, in the 2003 quarter. Earnings excluded a loss of $178,000 in 2004 and income of $1.2 million in 2003 from discontinued operations. Total revenues decreased 5.8% to $274.3 million. Wholesale Energy group revenue fell 6.3% to $223.9 million, primarily due to the limited operation of Co.'s Las Vegas Cogeneration II power plant, partially offset by increased oil and gas production and prices. Electric Utility group revenue was down 4.9% to $41.6 million, while Communications group revenue slipped 2.7% to $8.5 million.

Prospects: Co.'s acquisition of Cheyenne Light, Fuel & Power is progressing through regulatory review. Co. remains confident that this transaction will close during 2004. Meanwhile, Effective Apr 1 2004, Co.'s Las Vegas Cogeneration II power plant plant began operating under its new long–term tolling contract with Nevada Power Company. Going forward, Co. expects strong results this year from its oil and gas operations due to higher production and a favorable pricing environment, and from its energy marketing business due to expected increases in daily volumes marketed. For full–year 2004, Co. expects income from continuing operations to range from $2.00 to $2.15 per share.

Financial Data

(US$ in Thousands)	3 Mos	12/31/2003	12/31/2002	12/31/2001	12/31/2000	12/31/1999	12/31/1998	12/31/1997
Earnings Per Share	1.52	1.84	2.33	3.42	2.37	1.73	1.19	1.49
Cash Flow Per Share	2.62	5.49	8.05	6.88	3.34	3.52	2.52	2.58
Tang. Book Val. Per Share	19.55	19.72	15.58	14.67	10.44	10.13	9.51	9.46
Dividends Per Share	1.210	1.200	1.160	1.120	1.080	1.040	1.000	0.940
Dividend Payout %	69.14	65.21	49.78	32.74	45.56	60.11	84.03	63.53
Income Statement								
Total Revenues	274,328	1,250,052	423,919	1,558,558	1,623,836	791,875	679,254	313,662
Total Indirect Exp.	49,211	289,759	148,207	157,679	92,191	56,219	65,802	45,938
Costs & Expenses	246,323	1,113,295	291,318	1,388,379	1,509,086	729,984	630,021	254,752
Depreciation & Amort.	22,272	80,791	69,738	54,051	32,864	25,067	24,037	22,311
Operating Income	28,005	136,757	132,601	170,179	114,750	61,891	49,233	58,910
Net Interest Inc./(Exp.)	(13,959)	(51,503)	(40,605)	(37,248)	(23,267)	(11,846)	(11,846)	(11,799)
Income from Cont Ops	9,964	56,995	63,193	...	...	...	...	...
Net Income	9,786	61,222	61,452	88,077	52,848	37,067	25,808	32,359
Average Shs. Outstg.	32,811	31,015	27,167	25,771	22,281	21,482	21,665	21,706
Balance Sheet								
Net Property	1,434,508	628,036	932,516	539,234	794,281	464,189	389,607	401,127
Total Assets	2,055,370	2,063,225	2,236,783	1,658,767	1,320,320	674,806	559,417	508,741
Long–Term Obligations	822,289	868,459	618,862	415,798	307,092	160,700	162,030	163,360
Net Stockholders' Equity	710,669	709,747	535,163	515,164	282,346	216,606	206,666	205,403
Shares Outstanding	32,408	32,297	27,102	26,890	22,921	21,371	21,719	21,705
Statistical Record								
Operating Profit Margin %	10.11	11.39	32.36	10.91	7.06	7.81	7.24	18.78
Net Inc./Net Property %	0.68	9.74	6.58	16.33	6.65	7.98	6.62	8.06
Net Inc./Tot. Capital %	0.58	3.58	4.75	8.58	7.65	8.49	6.08	7.67
Return on Equity %	1.36	8.84	12.66	17.09	18.71	17.11	12.48	15.75
Accum. Depr./Gross Prop. %	24.42	48.44	21.37	44.50	28.89	37.32	37.11	32.95
Price Range	32.00-29.36	33.35-22.26	36.84-19.15	58.05-26.35	45.13-20.56	26.38-20.50	27.38-20.75	24.21-17.50
P/E Ratio	21.05-19.32	18.13-12.10	15.81-8.22	16.97-7.70	19.04-8.68	15.25-11.85	23.00-17.44	16.25-11.74
Average Yield %	3.97	4.08	3.99	2.86	4.17	4.51	4.21	4.85

Address: 625 Ninth Street, Rapid City, SD 57701	**Officers:** Daniel P. Landguth – Chmn., David R. Emery – Pres., C.E.O.	**Investor Contact:** 605–721–1700 **Institutional Holding**
Telephone: (605) 721–1700	**Transfer Agents:** Wells Fargo Shareowner Services, St. Paul, MN	**No of Institutions:** 146
Web Site: www.blackhillscorp.com		**Shares:** 11,707,176 **% Held:** 43.60%

BOWL AMERICA INC.

Exchange	Symbol	Price	52Wk Range	Yield	P/E
ASE	BWL A	$14.15 (5/26/2004)	15.15–11.30	3.82	14.89

*7 Year Price Score 142.6 *NYSE Composite Index=100 *12 Month Price Score 49.4

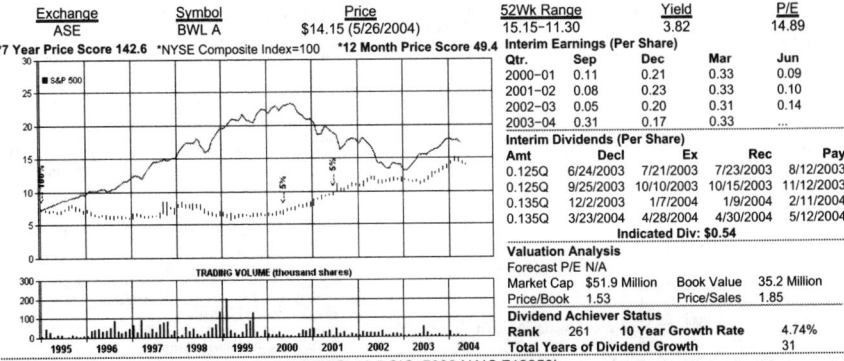

Interim Earnings (Per Share)

Qtr.	Sep	Dec	Mar	Jun
2000–01	0.11	0.21	0.33	0.09
2001–02	0.08	0.23	0.33	0.10
2002–03	0.05	0.20	0.31	0.14
2003–04	0.31	0.17	0.33	...

Interim Dividends (Per Share)

Amt	Decl	Ex	Rec	Pay
0.125Q	6/24/2003	7/21/2003	7/23/2003	8/12/2003
0.125Q	9/25/2003	10/10/2003	10/15/2003	11/12/2003
0.135Q	12/2/2003	1/7/2004	1/9/2004	2/11/2004
0.135Q	3/23/2004	4/28/2004	4/30/2004	5/12/2004

Indicated Div: $0.54

Valuation Analysis

Forecast P/E N/A
Market Cap $51.9 Million	Book Value 35.2 Million
Price/Book 1.53	Price/Sales 1.85

Dividend Achiever Status

Rank 261	10 Year Growth Rate	4.74%

Total Years of Dividend Growth 31

Business Summary: Sporting &Recreational (MIC: 13.5 SIC: 7933 NAIC:713950)

Bowl America, through its wholly-owned subsidiaries, operates bowling centers. Co. operates in the greater metropolitan area of Washington, D.C., the greater metropolitan area of Baltimore, MD, Orlando, FL, the greater metropolitan area of Jacksonville, FL, and the greater metropolitan area of Richmond, VA. These establishments are fully air-conditioned with facilities for service of food and beverages, game rooms, rental lockers, and playroom facilities. All centers provide shoes for rental, and bowling balls are provided free. In addition, each center retails bowling accessories. Most locations are equipped for glow-in-the-dark bowling, popular for parties and non-league bowling.

Recent Developments: For the thirteen weeks ended Mar 28 2004, net income rose 3.9% to $1.7 million compared with $1.6 million in the equivalent 2003 quarter. Operating revenues were essentially flat at $8.8 million. Bowling and other revenues grew 0.9% to $6.3 million from $6.2 million a year earlier, reflecting higher prices per average game, partially offset by fewer games bowled. Food, beverage and merchandise sales slid 4.5% to $2.5 million from $2.6 million the year before due to the closure of the Silver Spring location and the change in the food services operations at the Gaithersburg, VA location to emphasize service for the bowlers.

Prospects: Co. continues to actively seek property for the development of additional bowling centers. For instance, on Feb 20 2004, Co. completed the purchase of land in Henrico County, VA for $1.9 million. Co. is pursuing permits to build a new bowling center on the land. Additionally, Co. continues to upgrade existing locations through purchases of bowling and restaurant equipment and some amusement games. Separately, in late March 2004, Co. instituted an Internet site in order to encourage higher merchandise sales by making the merchandise available directly to consumers at more competitive prices.

Financial Data

(US$ in Thousands)	9 Mos	6 Mos	3 Mos	06/29/2003	06/30/2002	07/01/2001	07/02/2000	06/27/1999
Earnings Per Share	0.95	0.93	0.96	0.70	0.74	0.74	0.75	0.55
Cash Flow Per Share	1.69	0.62	0.20	1.05	1.16	0.91	1.18	0.88
Tang. Book Val. Per Share	6.85	6.63	6.54	6.41	6.34	6.66	6.78	6.12
Dividends Per Share	0.500	0.490	0.480	0.480	0.460	0.420	0.390	0.370
Dividend Payout %	52.63	52.69	50.00	68.57	62.16	57.91	51.83	67.21
Income Statement								
Total Revenues	22,236	13,453	6,145	29,376	29,810	29,401	28,902	27,547
Total Indirect Exp.	7,028	3,139	(579)	2,532	2,662	3,551	2,919	3,105
Depreciation & Amort.	1,178	787	395	1,613	1,764	1,940	2,100	2,268
Operating Income	6,297	3,713	2,401	5,113	5,394	4,893	5,751	4,552
Net Interest Inc./(Exp.)	...	...	...	476	599	1,036	823	685
Income Taxes	2,412	1,427	923	2,005	2,174	2,060	2,361	1,902
Net Income	4,190	2,486	1,574	3,583	3,819	3,868	4,213	3,335
Average Shs. Outstg.	5,138	5,138	5,138	5,145	5,132	5,222	5,587	6,026
Balance Sheet								
Cash & Cash Equivalents	2.312	2,294	2,750	1,503	1,634	1,338	1,523	1,557
Total Current Assets	16,057	15,232	14,643	12,608	11,538	9,613	11,495	10,453
Total Assets	42,722	39,973	38,842	37,537	36,563	37,598	40,711	41,748
Total Current Liabilities	4,833	4,051	3,454	2,711	1,820	2,407	2,165	2,064
Net Stockholders' Equity	35,215	34,069	33,652	32,953	32,682	32,703	34,868	35,477
Net Working Capital	11,224	11,181	11,189	9,897	9,718	7,206	9,330	8,389
Shares Outstanding	5,138	5,138	5,138	5,138	5,149	4,908	5,139	5,793
Statistical Record								
Operating Profit Margin %	28.32	27.60	39.07	17.40	18.09	16.64	19.89	16.52
Net Profit Margin %	18.84	18.48	25.61	25.84	27.39	27.17	30.91	25.91
Return on Equity %	11.90	7.29	4.67	10.87	11.68	11.82	12.08	9.40
Return on Assets %	9.81	6.21	4.05	9.54	10.44	10.28	10.34	7.98
Price Range	15.15–11.75	14.00–11.75	13.00–11.75	12.15–11.12	12.25–10.01	9.90–7.26	7.50–6.24	8.16–5.78
P/E Ratio	15.95–12.37	15.05–12.63	13.54–12.24	17.36–15.89	16.55–13.53	13.38–9.81	10.00–8.31	14.84–10.51
Average Yield %	3.72	3.79	3.83	4.12	4.16	4.93	5.94	5.56

Address: 6446 Edsall Road, Alexandria, VA 22312 Telephone: (703) 941 6300 Web Site: N/A	Officers: Leslie H. Goldberg – Pres., C.E.O., C.O.O., Ruth E. Macklin – Sr. V.P., Treas. Transfer Agents:American Stock Transfer &Trust Co., New York, NY	Institutional Holding No of Institutions: 11 Shares: 476,509 % Held: 9.30%

BRADY CORP.

Exchange	Symbol	Price	52Wk Range	Yield	P/E
NYS	BRC	$41.28 (5/28/2004)	42.50-31.55	2.03	17.13

*7 Year Price Score 115.3   *NYSE Composite Index=100   *12 Month Price Score 51.0

Interim Earnings (Per Share)

Qtr.	Oct	Jan	Apr	Jul
2000-01	0.49	0.37	0.44	1.03
2001-02	0.34	0.26	0.36	1.41
2002-03	0.35	0.12	0.37	0.95
2003-04	0.44	0.34	0.68	...

Interim Dividends (Per Share)

Amt	Decl	Ex	Rec	Pay
0.21Q	9/9/2003	10/8/2003	10/10/2003	10/31/2003
0.21Q	11/20/2003	1/7/2004	1/9/2004	1/30/2004
0.21Q	2/6/2004	4/6/2004	4/9/2004	4/30/2004
0.21Q	5/18/2004	7/7/2004	7/9/2004	7/30/2004

Indicated Div: $0.84 (Div. Reinv. Plan)

Valuation Analysis

Forecast P/E 20.34 (5/24/2004)

Market Cap $879.5 Million	Book Value 366.1 Million	
Price/Book 2.52	Price/Sales 1.56	

Dividend Achiever Status

Rank 84   10 Year Growth Rate 14.64%

Total Years of Dividend Growth 19

Business Summary: Consumer Accessories (MIC: 4.6 SIC: 3993 NAIC:339950)

Brady is an international manufacturer and marketer of identification products and specialty materials. Co.'s products include labels and signs, printing systems and software, label-application and data-collection systems, safety devices and precision die-cut materials. Co.'s major products include identification applications and specialty tape products, including wire and cable markers, high-performance labels, laboratory identification products, stand-alone printing systems, bar-code and other software, graphics and workplace applications. Co. serves more than 300,000 customers in electronics, telecommunications, manufacturing, electrical, construction, education and other industries.

Recent Developments: For the three months ended Apr 30 2004, net income totaled $16.4 million, up 90.8% compared with $8.6 million in the corresponding prior-year period. Results for the recent period included a pre-tax restructuring charge of $455,000. Net sales climbed 27.4% to $180.9 million from $142.0 million a year earlier, driven by acquisitions and favorable foreign currency exchange rates. Gross margin increased 29.7% to $94.9 million, or 52.5% of net sales, from $73.1 million, or 51.5% of net sales, the year before. Operating income jumped 96.4% to $23.7 million from $12.1 million the previous year.

Prospects: On Apr 5 2004, Co. announced that it has signed a definitive agreement to acquire EMED Co., Inc., a direct marketer and manufacturer of identification products, from Summit Partners for $190.0 million in cash. The acquisition is expected to be slightly accretive to earnings in fiscal 2004 and $0.15 to $0.20 accretive in fiscal 2005. Meanwhile, Co. is targeting sales of between $645.0 million and $655.0 million for fiscal 2004, along with net income in the range of $47.0 million to $49.0 million, or $1.96 to $2.04 per share. Looking ahead, Co. is projecting fiscal 2005 sales of between $670.0 million and $690.0 million and net income in the range of $50.0 million to $52.0 million.

Financial Data

(US$ in Thousands)	6 Mos	3 Mos	07/31/2003	07/31/2002	07/31/2001	07/31/2000	07/31/1999	07/31/1998
Earnings Per Share	2.10	1.88	1.79	2.37	2.33	4.07	3.43	2.43
Cash Flow Per Share	0.92	0.43	1.18	1.16	1.15	1.05	1.35	1.04
Tang. Book Val. Per Share	8.61	8.63	8.93	9.22	8.88	8.25	8.17	7.86
Dividends Per Share	1.020	0.800	0.790	0.750	0.710	0.510	0.790	0.580
Dividend Payout %	48.57	42.55	44.69	32.06	30.90	16.70	18.65	24.69
Income Statement								
Total Revenues	304,854	151,906	554,866	516,962	545,944	541,077	470,862	455,150
Total Indirect Exp.	129,172	63,005	248,124	219,273	244,109	242,179	204,887	204,325
Depreciation & Amort.	10,162	4,783	17,771	16,630	22,646	17,833	15,149	13,288
Operating Income	27,821	15,758	32,149	41,503	44,522	69,291	63,772	45,930
Net Interest Inc./(Exp.)	(31)	(30)	(121)	(82)	(418)	(578)	(445)	(403)
Income Taxes	9,263	5,216	11,035	14,982	17,244	28,930	25,198	18,129
Net Income	18,386	10,353	21,420	28,253	27,546	47,201	39,584	28,036
Average Shs. Outstg.	23,787	23,334	46,754	46,679	46,214	45,866	45,365	45,203
Balance Sheet								
Cash & Cash Equivalents	58,211	60,105	76,088	75,969	62,811	60,784	75,466	65,609
Total Current Assets	218,375	215,932	215,157	210,026	194,993	203,183	203,169	184,053
Total Assets	485,990	469,057	449,519	420,525	392,476	398,134	351,120	311,824
Total Current Liabilities	99,926	95,248	91,279	74,262	71,163	87,099	73,285	58,667
Long-Term Obligations	48	581	568	3,751	4,144	4,157	1,402	3,716
Net Stockholders' Equity	366,099	353,069	338,961	324,242	302,579	291,224	260,564	233,373
Net Working Capital	118,449	120,684	123,878	135,764	123,830	116,084	129,884	125,386
Shares Outstanding	23,643	23,470	23,309	23,121	22,914	22,731	22,604	22,496
Statistical Record								
Operating Profit Margin %	9.12	10.37	5.79	8.02	8.15	12.80	13.54	10.09
Return on Equity %	5.02	2.93	6.31	8.71	9.10	16.20	15.19	12.01
Return on Assets %	3.78	2.20	4.76	6.71	7.01	11.85	11.27	8.99
Debt/Total Assets %	0.01	0.12	0.12	0.89	1.05	1.04	0.39	1.19
Price Range	42.50-31.81	36.20-31.81	35.40-25.78	40.60-27.30	38.94-27.75	35.81-24.75	35.00-16.38	35.50-20.00
P/E Ratio	20.24-15.15	19.26-16.92	19.78-14.40	17.13-11.52	16.71-11.91	8.80-6.08	10.20-4.77	14.61-8.23
Average Yield %	2.77	2.31	2.50	2.20	2.20	1.68	3.23	1.91

| Address: 6555 West Good Hope Road, Milwaukee, WI 53223-0571 **Telephone:** (414) 358-6600 **Web Site:** www.bradycorp.com | **Officers:** Katherine M. Hudson - Chmn., Frank M. Jaehnert - Pres., C.E.O. **Transfer Agents:** Wells Fargo Shareowner Services, St. Paul, MN | **Investor Contact:** 414-438-6940 **Institutional Holding** **No of Institutions:** 90 **Shares:** 16,562,950   **% Held:** 72% |

BRIGGS & STRATTON CORP.

Exchange	Symbol	Price	52Wk Range	Yield	P/E
NYS	BGG	$75.88 (5/28/2004)	75.88–47.10	1.74	14.05

*7 Year Price Score 132.2 *NYSE Composite Index=100 *12 Month Price Score 54.4

Interim Earnings (Per Share)

Qtr.	Sep	Dec	Mar	Jun
2000–01	(0.29)	0.92	1.38	0.20
2001–02	(0.81)	0.11	1.58	1.48
2002–03	(0.32)	0.53	1.81	1.47
2003–04	0.18	0.87	2.88	...

Interim Dividends (Per Share)

Amt	Decl	Ex	Rec	Pay
0.33Q	8/6/2003	8/19/2003	8/21/2003	10/1/2003
0.33Q	10/15/2003	11/26/2003	12/1/2003	1/2/2004
0.33Q	1/21/2004	2/26/2004	3/1/2004	4/1/2004
0.33Q	4/21/2004	5/27/2004	6/1/2004	6/25/2004

Indicated Div: $1.32 (Div. Reinv. Plan)

Valuation Analysis

Forecast P/E 12.96 (5/24/2004)

Market Cap $1.6 Billion	Book Value 625.9 Million
Price/Book 2.44	Price/Sales 0.80

Dividend Achiever Status

Rank	266	10 Year Growth Rate	4.14%

Total Years of Dividend Growth 12

Business Summary: Industrial Machinery and Equipment (MIC: 11.5 SIC: 3519 NAIC:333618)

Briggs & Stratton is a producer of air cooled gasoline engines for outdoor power equipment. Co. designs, manufactures, markets and services these products for original equipment manufacturers (OEMs) worldwide. These engines are primarily aluminum alloy gasoline engines ranging from 3 to 31 horsepower. Co.'s engines are marketed under various brand names including Classic™, Sprint™, Quattro™, Quantum®, INTEK™, I/C®, Industrial Plus™and Vanguard™. Additionally, through its wholly owned subsidiary, Briggs & Stratton Power Products Group, LLC, Co. designs, manufactures and markets portable generators, pressure washers and related accessories.

Recent Developments: For the quarter ended Mar 31 2004, net income increased 65.8% to $71.3 million compared with $43.0 million in the same period a year earlier. Net sales advanced 16.8% to $654.7 million. Gross profit on sales was $167.8 million, or 25.6% of net sales, versus $116.2 million, or 20.7% of net sales, the year before. Net engines sales rose 17.1% to $581.9 million, primarily due to a 13.0% increase in engine unit shipments, and segment operating profit climbed 68.2% to $110.0 million. Net power products sales climbed 32.4% to $125.6 million, reflecting pressure washer shipment volume gains of 40.0% and a generator volume increase of 34.0%, while segment operating income grew 27.0% to $7.3 million.

Prospects: Co.'s near−term prospects remain solid, reflecting a number of positive trends that are contributing to strong top and bottom line growth. Factors that are fueling Co.'s results include increased sales volume, lower manufacturing expenses due to cost reduction initiatives, a favorable mix of engine shipments, greater production volume that is leading to lower unit costs, and favorable currency translation. Looking ahead, Co. expects that the spring retail selling season of 2004 will be strong for both its engine and power products business segments, further strengthening its immediate outlook.

Financial Data

(US$ in Thousands)	9 Mos	6 Mos	3 Mos	06/29/2003	06/30/2002	07/01/2001	07/02/2000	06/27/1999
Earnings Per Share	5.40	4.33	3.99	3.49	2.36	2.21	5.97	4.52
Cash Flow Per Share	(5.18)	(8.40)	(4.39)	6.83	8.17	3.09	3.39	4.85
Tang. Book Val. Per Share	21.02	17.66	16.96	16.30	13.33	11.53	18.51	15.44
Dividends Per Share	1.300	1.290	1.280	1.280	1.260	1.240	1.200	1.160
Dividend Payout %	24.07	29.79	32.08	36.67	53.38	56.10	20.10	25.66
Income Statement								
Total Revenues	1,402,060	747,379	331,395	1,657,633	1,529,372	1,312,446	1,590,557	1,501,726
Total Indirect Exp.	151,333	98,070	45,900	178,078	153,731	141,009	134,225	125,219
Depreciation & Amort.	48,167	32,290	15,846	56	56	1,052	51,370	49,604
Operating Income	167,475	52,971	14,295	152,404	118,358	99,106	205,229	180,136
Net Interest Inc./(Exp.)	(29,031)	(19,428)	(9,832)	(37,889)	(42,244)	(28,596)	(19,678)	(15,031)
Income Taxes	47,700	11,600	1,890	37,940	27,390	23,860	80,150	63,670
Income from Cont Ops	...	...	...	...	116,120	...	...	...
Net Income	95,919	24,651	4,016	80,638	53,120	48,013	136,473	106,101
Average Shs. Outstg.	25,191	25,096	22,105	24,480	24,452	21,966	22,842	23,459
Balance Sheet								
Cash & Cash Equivalents	184,800	119,323	238,556	324,815	215,945	88,743	16,989	60,806
Total Current Assets	1,005,375	871,817	795,484	807,147	669,944	613,430	471,952	459,146
Total Assets	1,657,424	1,523,601	1,454,036	1,475,193	1,349,039	1,296,195	930,245	875,885
Total Current Liabilities	367,857	314,521	266,119	301,395	266,023	242,182	312,778	282,502
Long−Term Obligations	502,378	501,356	501,063	503,397	499,022	508,134	98,512	113,307
Net Stockholders' Equity	625,923	549,090	530,393	514,987	449,646	422,752	409,465	365,910
Net Working Capital	637,518	557,296	529,365	505,752	403,921	371,248	159,219	176,644
Shares Outstanding	22,447	22,365	22,113	21,785	21,639	21,599	21,746	23,200
Statistical Record								
Operating Profit Margin %	11.94	7.08	4.31	9.19	7.73	7.55	12.90	11.99
Return on Equity %	15.32	4.48	0.75	15.65	25.82	11.35	33.32	28.99
Return on Assets %	5.79	1.61	0.27	5.46	8.60	3.70	14.67	12.11
Debt/Total Assets %	30.31	32.90	34.46	34.12	36.99	39.20	10.58	12.93
Price Range	70.35−50.50	68.50−50.50	60.76−50.50	50.80−31.18	48.12−30.24	48.00−30.88	63.00−31.31	68.25−33.69
P/E Ratio	13.03−9.35	15.82−11.66	15.23−12.66	14.56−8.93	20.39−12.81	21.72−13.97	10.55−5.24	15.10−7.45
Average Yield %	2.08	2.14	2.30	3.16	3.12	3.14	2.44	2.35

Address: 12301 West Wirth Street, Wauwatosa, WI 53222 Telephone: (414) 259−5333 Web Site: www.briggsandstratton.com	Officers: Frederick P. Stratton − Chmn. Emeritus, John S. Shiely − Chmn., Pres., C.E.O. Transfer Agents:National City Bank, Cleveland, OH	Investor Contact:414−259−5333 Institutional Holding No of Institutions: 76 Shares: 721,582 % Held: −

43

BROWN & BROWN, INC.

Exchange	Symbol	Price	52Wk Range	Yield	P/E
NYS	BRO	$39.98 (5/28/2004)	41.03-29.71	0.70	23.66

*7 Year Price Score 174.4 *NYSE Composite Index=100 *12 Month Price Score 54.1

Interim Earnings (Per Share)

Qtr.	Mar	Jun	Sep	Dec
2001	0.20	0.20	0.21	0.24
2002	0.31	0.31	0.29	0.31
2003	0.44	0.41	0.38	0.37
2004	0.53	...	...	...

Interim Dividends (Per Share)

Amt	Decl	Ex	Rec	Pay
0.058Q	7/23/2003	8/4/2003	8/6/2003	8/20/2003
0.07Q	10/22/2003	11/3/2003	11/5/2003	11/19/2003
0.07Q	1/21/2004	2/2/2004	2/4/2004	2/18/2004
0.07Q	4/22/2004	5/4/2004	5/6/2004	5/20/2004

Indicated Div: $0.28

Valuation Analysis

Forecast P/E 21.56 (5/24/2004)

Market Cap $2.7 Billion		Book Value	536.1 Million
Price/Book 5.01		Price/Sales	4.70

Dividend Achiever Status

Rank	97	10 Year Growth Rate	13.78%
Total Years of Dividend Growth			10

Business Summary: Insurance (MIC: 8.2 SIC: 6411 NAIC:524210)

Brown & Brown is primarily engaged in the property and casualty business. Co.'s business is divided into four divisions. The Retail Division sells insurance products to commercial, professional and individual clients. The National Programs Division is comprised of two units: Professional Programs, which provides professional liability and related package products; and Special Programs, which markets targeted products and services for specific industries, trade groups and market niches. The Service Division provides third–party administration for workers' compensation and employee benefit markets. The Brokerage Division sells commercial insurance through independent agents and brokers.

Recent Developments: For the quarter ended Mar 31 2004, net income increased 19.0% to $36.3 million from $30.5 million in the prior–year quarter. Total revenues advanced 14.4% to $165.6 million from $144.7 million the previous year. Revenues from commissions and fees grew 13.9% to $164.3 million. On a segment basis, Retail revenues advanced 12.4% to $101.3 million, while Program revenue rose 12.6% to $22.1 million. Brokerage revenues climbed 25.2% to $8.6 million, while Services revenue improved 13.3% to $6.5 million. Contingent commissions jumped 41.8% to $25.8 million. Total expenses were $106.2 million, up 10.9% from $95.7 million the year before.

Prospects: Going forward, Co. should benefit from its success in locating solid acquisition candidates that show sustainable earnings growth potential. For instance, as of Apr 14 2004, Co. has completed twelve acquisitions, representing sixteen entities with estimated annualized revenues of $52.0 million, which exceeds the amount of annualized revenues that Co. acquired in the full year of 2003. Moreover, these acquisitions will operate at a sustainable margin level generally expected from Co.'s more established offices. Co. remains encouraged with the activity in the acquisition pipeline and the increase in the number of agencies that have expressed an interest in joining Co.'s group of insurers.

Financial Data

(US$ in Thousands)	3 Mos	12/31/2003	12/31/2002	12/31/2001	12/31/2000	12/31/1999	12/31/1998	12/31/1997
Earnings Per Share	1.69	1.60	1.22	0.85	0.58	0.49	0.43	0.37
Tang. Book Val. Per Share	N.M	0.39	0.16	N.M	0.34	0.20	0.08	0.52
Dividends Per Share	0.250	0.240	0.200	0.160	0.130	0.110	0.100	0.080
Dividend Payout %	15.09	15.15	16.39	18.82	23.27	23.23	23.83	23.87
Income Statement								
Net Investment Income	...	1,428	2,945	3,686	3,890	2,560	3,308	4,085
Other Income	165,565	549,612	452,797	361,343	205,816	173,853	150,483	125,106
Total Revenues	165,565	551,040	455,742	365,029	209,706	176,413	153,791	129,191
Total Indirect Exp.	106,916	368,662	312,596	266,864	155,138	131,521	115,746	91,576
Inc. Before Inc. Taxes	59,360	176,482	134,664	90,478	53,978	44,208	37,485	31,638
Income Taxes	23,012	66,160	49,271	34,834	20,792	17,036	14,432	12,251
Eqty Earns/Minority Int.	...	...	(2,271)	(1,731)	...	...	...	...
Net Income	36,348	110,322	83,122	53,913	33,186	27,172	23,053	19,387
Average Shs. Outstg.	69,207	68,897	68,043	63,222	57,326	54,944	53,724	52,350
Balance Sheet								
Cash & Cash Equivalents	138,988	56,926	91,247	16,048	31,313	37,459	42,174	47,726
Premiums Due	146,435	146,672	144,244	101,449	83,199	67,783	69,186	62,148
Invst. Assets: Total	8,949	11,227	9,031	9,434	6,125	9,930	11,229	12,779
Total Assets	920,620	865,854	754,349	488,737	276,719	235,163	230,513	194,129
Long–Term Obligations	37,526	41,107	57,585	78,195	2,736	3,909	17,207	4,093
Net Stockholders' Equity	536,105	498,035	391,590	175,285	121,911	103,026	84,208	77,142
Shares Outstanding	68,788	68,561	68,178	63,194	57,398	54,880	53,992	52,428
Statistical Record								
Return on Revenues %	21.52	20.02	18.23	14.76	15.82	15.40	14.98	15.00
Return on Equity %	6.64	22.15	21.22	30.75	27.22	26.37	27.37	25.13
Return on Assets %	3.87	12.74	11.01	11.03	11.99	11.55	10.00	9.98
Price Range	39.30-32.08	37.44-27.29	36.13-24.74	30.81-15.45	17.72-7.81	10.03-7.42	10.42-7.24	7.82-4.25
P/E Ratio	23.25-18.98	23.40-17.06	29.61-20.28	36.25-18.18	30.55-13.47	20.47-15.15	24.24-16.84	21.14-11.49
Average Yield %	0.70	0.75	0.63	0.71	1.05	1.25	1.12	1.42

Address: 220 South Ridgewood Ave., Daytona Beach, FL 32114	**Officers:** J. Hyatt Brown – Chmn., C.E.O., Jim W. Henderson – Pres., C.O.O., Asst. Treas.	**Investor Contact:**904–239–7250	
Telephone: (368) 252–9601	**Transfer Agents:**Wachovia Bank N.A., Charlotte, NC	**Institutional Holding** **No of Institutions:** 193	
Web Site: www.bbinsurance.com		**Shares:** 41,567,275 **% Held:** 61.10%	

BROWN-FORMAN CORP.

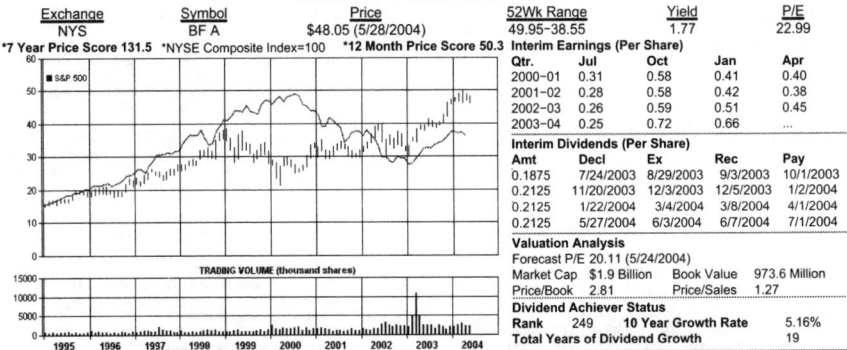

Exchange	Symbol	Price	52Wk Range	Yield	P/E
NYS	BF A	$48.05 (5/28/2004)	49.95-38.55	1.77	22.99

*7 Year Price Score 131.5 *NYSE Composite Index=100   *12 Month Price Score 50.3

Interim Earnings (Per Share)

Qtr.	Jul	Oct	Jan	Apr
2000-01	0.31	0.58	0.41	0.40
2001-02	0.28	0.58	0.42	0.38
2002-03	0.26	0.59	0.51	0.45
2003-04	0.25	0.72	0.66	...

Interim Dividends (Per Share)

Amt	Decl	Ex	Rec	Pay
0.1875	7/24/2003	8/29/2003	9/3/2003	10/1/2003
0.2125	11/20/2003	12/3/2003	12/5/2003	1/2/2004
0.2125	1/22/2004	3/4/2004	3/8/2004	4/1/2004
0.2125	5/27/2004	6/3/2004	6/7/2004	7/1/2004

Valuation Analysis

Forecast P/E 20.11 (5/24/2004)

Market Cap $1.9 Billion	Book Value 973.6 Million
Price/Book 2.81	Price/Sales 1.27

Dividend Achiever Status

Rank	249	10 Year Growth Rate	5.16%
Total Years of Dividend Growth		19	

Business Summary: Food (MIC: 4.1 SIC: 2084 NAIC:312130)

Brown-Forman, with assets of $2.28 billion as of Jul 31 2003, operates in two business segments: wines and spirits and consumer durables. The wines and spirits segment includes the production, importing and marketing of wines and distilled spirits under brand names of *Jack Daniel's, Southern Comfort, Finlandia* Vodka, *Canadian Mist, Korbel California* champagnes, and *Fetzer, Bolla* and *Bel Arbor California* wines. The consumer durables segment includes tableware and flatware sold under the *Lenox, Gorham* and *Dansk* brand names, as well as *Hartmann* luggage.

Recent Developments: For the quarter ended Jan 31 2004, net income improved 15.0% to $80.5 million compared with $70.0 million in the corresponding period of the year before. Net sales grew 9.7% to $697.0 million from $635.6 million the year before. Sales for the beverages segment rose 12.3% to $531.0 million, driven by the benefits of a weaker U.S. dollar, the addition of new markets to Co.'s distribution arrangement for Finlandia Vodka Worldwide, and continued volume and pricing growth for Co.'s spirits brands. Sales for the consumer durables segment inched up 2.0% to $166.0 million, reflecting slight improvements in the direct-to-consumer channel and Co.'s retail outlet stores.

Prospects: Co. expects the environment to remain challenging for its wine and consumer durables businesses. However, Co. is encouraged by the opportunities and trends for its spirits brands. As a result, Co. will be significantly increasing its advertising investments behind its spirits brands in the fourth quarter. This increased level of advertising investment, coupled with higher pension expenses and Co.'s ongoing focus on lowering wholesale and retail inventories on a global basis, is expected to temper earnings growth in the near term. Earnings per share is anticipated to range from $2.09 to $2.13 for fiscal 2004.

Financial Data

(US$ in Thousands)	9 Mos	6 Mos	3 Mos	04/30/2003	04/30/2002	04/30/2001	04/30/2000	04/30/1999
Earnings Per Share	2.08	1.93	1.80	1.81	1.66	1.70	1.59	1.46
Cash Flow Per Share	2.03	0.45	0.31	1.79	1.82	1.68	1.75	1.55
Tang. Book Val. Per Share	3.38	3.09	2.34	2.42	7.79	6.74	5.67	4.76
Dividends Per Share	0.770	0.750	0.730	0.720	0.680	0.640	0.600	0.570
Dividend Payout %	37.02	38.86	40.56	39.94	40.84	37.64	38.05	39.24
Income Statement								
Total Revenues	1,681,900	1,087,900	460,800	2,060,000	1,958,000	1,924,000	1,877,000	1,776,000
Total Indirect Exp.	664,300	446,200	220,200	800,000	780,000	779,000	755,000	723,000
Depreciation & Amort.	41,700	27,400	13,100	55,000	55,000	64,000	62,000	55,000
Operating Income	317,800	190,900	52,100	378,000	353,000	374,000	348,000	322,000
Net Interest Inc./(Exp.)	(15,000)	(10,000)	(5,000)	(5,000)	(5,000)	(8,000)	(5,000)	(4,000)
Income Taxes	102,900	61,500	16,000	128,000	120,000	133,000	125,000	116,000
Net Income	199,900	119,400	31,100	245,000	228,000	233,000	218,000	202,000
Average Shs. Outstg.	121,886	121,774	121,710	135,126	137,000	137,200	137,200	137,400
Balance Sheet								
Cash & Cash Equivalents	110,100	74,500	71,900	72,000	116,000	86,000	180,000	171,000
Total Current Assets	1,107,900	1,217,000	1,077,000	1,068,000	1,029,000	994,000	1,020,000	999,000
Total Assets	2,331,900	2,429,700	2,280,600	2,264,000	2,016,000	1,939,000	1,802,000	1,735,000
Total Current Liabilities	485,600	621,700	574,500	548,000	495,000	538,000	522,000	517,000
Long-Term Obligations	629,800	629,200	629,000	629,000	40,000	40,000	41,000	53,000
Net Stockholders' Equity	973,600	928,900	834,200	840,000	1,311,000	1,187,000	1,048,000	917,000
Net Working Capital	622,300	595,300	502,500	520,000	534,000	456,000	498,000	482,000
Shares Outstanding	121,431	121,356	121,287	121,134	136,696	136,918	137,024	137,012
Statistical Record								
Operating Profit Margin %	18.89	17.54	11.30	18.54	18.02	19.43	18.54	18.13
Return on Equity %	20.53	12.85	3.72	29.64	17.39	19.62	20.80	22.02
Return on Assets %	8.57	4.91	1.36	10.99	11.30	12.01	12.09	11.64
Debt/Total Assets %	27.00	25.89	27.58	27.78	1.98	2.06	2.27	3.05
Price Range	47.81-37.77	42.75-37.77	41.21-37.77	40.03-29.66	39.31-29.72	35.09-25.00	37.75-21.22	38.63-27.59
P/E Ratio	22.99-18.16	22.15-19.57	22.89-20.98	22.11-16.38	23.68-17.90	20.64-14.71	23.74-13.35	26.46-18.90
Average Yield %	1.85	1.88	1.86	2.03	2.07	2.17	2.00	1.75

Address: 850 Dixie Highway, Louisville, KY 40210 **Telephone:** (502) 585-1100 **Web Site:** www.brown-forman.com	**Officers:** Owsley Brown II - Chmn., C.E.O., Phoebe A. Wood - Exec. V.P., C.F.O. **Transfer Agents:** First Chicago Trust Company of New York, Jersey City, NJ	**Institutional Holding** **No of Institutions:** 2 **Shares:** 10,000 **% Held:** -

CALIFORNIA WATER SERVICE GROUP (DE)

Exchange	Symbol	Price	52Wk Range	Yield	P/E
NYS	CWT	$28.45 (5/28/2004)	30.97-25.20	3.97	21.23

*7 Year Price Score 105.5   ***NYSE Composite Index=100**   ***12 Month Price Score 46.8**

Interim Earnings (Per Share)

Qtr.	Mar	Jun	Sep	Dec
2001	0.01	0.37	0.39	0.20
2002	0.12	0.43	0.50	0.20
2003	(0.05)	0.30	0.53	0.43
2004	0.08	...	...	...

Interim Dividends (Per Share)

Amt	Decl	Ex	Rec	Pay
0.281Q	7/23/2003	7/30/2003	8/1/2003	8/15/2003
0.281Q	10/22/2003	10/29/2003	10/31/2003	11/14/2003
0.283Q	1/29/2004	2/4/2004	2/7/2004	2/21/2004
0.2825Q		5/6/2004	5/10/2004	5/21/2004

Indicated Div: **$1.13** (Div. Reinv. Plan)

Valuation Analysis

Forecast P/E 18.19 (5/24/2004)
Market Cap $431.9 Million   Book Value 241.1 Million
Price/Book 1.97   Price/Sales 1.66

Dividend Achiever Status

Rank	296	10 Year Growth Rate	1.60%
Total Years of Dividend Growth			36

TRADING VOLUME (thousand shares)

Business Summary: Water Utilities (MIC: 7.2 SIC: 4941 NAIC:221310)

California Water Service Group is a utility water company that provides regulated and non–regulated water utility services to over 2.0 million customers in 99 communities in California, Washington, New Mexico and Hawaii as of Dec 31 2003. Co. is the parent company of California Water Service Company, Washington Water Service Company, New Mexico Water Service Company, Hawaii Water Service Company and CWS Utility Services. The sole business of Co. consists of the production, purchase, storage, purification, distribution and sale of water for domestic, industrial, public, and irrigation uses, and for fire protection. Annual water production totaled nearly 132.00 billion gallons for 2003.

Recent Developments: For the quarter ended Mar 31 2004, net income advanced to $1.4 million compared with a net loss of $768,000 in the corresponding period of the previous year. Operating revenue grew 17.4% to $60.2 million from $51.3 million a year earlier. The improvement in revenue reflects rate increases that added $7.0 million, $1.6 million from sales to new customers, and, to a lesser extent, a $300,000 increase in sales from existing customers. Net operating income leapt 105.4% to $5.4 million versus $2.6 million the year before. Net non–regulated income fell 10.1% to $550,000 from $612,000 in 2002.

Prospects: Co. is planning capital expenditures in the range of $60.0 million to $75.0 million per year over the next five years. These funds will be used to upgrade infrastructure and comply with water quality regulations. Co. plans to fund these expenditures through a combination of funds from operations, debt and equity. Co. anticipates that these capital expenditures will be recovered through further rate increases. Although Co. has experienced delays by the the California Public Utilities Commission in granting rate relief to cover increased costs and higher capital expenditures. Co. remains persistent in securing timely decisions.

Financial Data

(US$ in Thousands)	3 Mos	12/31/2003	12/31/2002	12/31/2001	12/31/2000	12/31/1999	12/31/1998	12/31/1997
Earnings Per Share	1.34	1.21	1.25	0.97	1.31	1.53	1.45	1.83
Cash Flow Per Share	0.56	2.79	2.20	2.52	2.28	...	2.97	3.12
Tang. Book Val. Per Share	14.24	14.44	13.12	12.95	13.12	13.69	13.37	13.00
Dividends Per Share	1.120	1.120	1.120	1.110	1.100	1.080	1.070	1.050
Dividend Payout %	83.58	92.97	89.60	114.94	83.96	70.59	73.79	57.65
Income Statement								
Total Revenues	60,240	277,128	263,151	246,820	244,806	206,440	186,273	195,324
Total Indirect Exp.	9,212	122,919	112,901	115,234	111,114	95,482	85,647	87,039
Costs & Expenses	54,849	246,894	232,854	221,669	211,610	175,830	156,199	160,975
Depreciation & Amort.	6,518	23,256	21,238	19,226	18,368	15,802	14,563	13,670
Operating Income	5,391	30,234	30,297	25,151	33,196	30,610	30,074	34,349
Net Interest Inc./(Exp.)	(4,496)	(17,517)	(16,841)	(16,029)	(14,646)	(13,201)	(12,446)	(11,902)
Income Taxes	958	8,506	8,797	...	...	...	...	...
Net Income	1,446	19,417	19,073	14,965	19,963	19,919	18,395	23,305
Average Shs. Outstg.	16,953	15,893	15,185	15,285	15,173	12,936	12,619	12,619
Balance Sheet								
Net Property	763,533	759,498	696,988	624,342	582,008	515,354	478,305	460,407
Total Assets	873,902	873,035	800,582	710,214	666,605	587,618	548,499	531,297
Long–Term Obligations	272,042	272,226	250,365	202,600	187,098	156,572	136,345	139,205
Net Stockholders' Equity	244,624	247,999	202,692	200,094	202,309	180,657	172,279	167,540
Shares Outstanding	16,932	16,932	15,182	15,182	15,146	12,936	12,619	12,619
Statistical Record								
Operating Profit Margin %	10.53	15.56	16.28	10.19	13.56	14.82	16.14	17.58
Net Profit Margin %	3.99	11.66	12.02	6.06	8.15	9.64	9.87	11.93
Net Inc./Net Property %	0.18	2.55	2.73	2.39	3.43	3.86	3.84	5.06
Net Inc./Tot. Capital %	0.26	3.47	3.93	3.46	4.81	5.55	5.46	7.00
Return on Equity %	0.98	13.03	15.61	7.47	9.86	11.02	10.67	13.91
Accum. Depr./Gross Prop. %	29.94	29.60	30.39	31.36	31.63	30.10	29.73	28.91
Price Range	29.99-27.25	30.97-23.65	26.69-21.60	28.60-23.38	30.94-21.69	31.88-22.94	32.75-21.00	29.53-18.81
P/E Ratio	22.38-20.34	25.60-19.55	21.35-17.28	29.48-24.10	23.62-16.56	20.83-14.99	22.59-14.48	16.14-10.28
Average Yield %	3.90	4.20	4.53	4.35	4.28	3.97	4.16	4.58

Address: 1720 North First Street, San Jose, CA 95112 **Telephone:** (408) 367 8200 **Web Site:** www.calwater.com	**Officers:** Robert W. Foy – Chmn., Peter C. Nelson – Pres., C.E.O. **Transfer Agents:**The First National Bank of Boston, Boston, MA	**Investor Contact:**408–367–8200 **Institutional Holding No of Institutions:** 63 **Shares:** 2,548,306 **% Held:** 16.80%

CAMDEN PROPERTY TRUST

Exchange	Symbol	Price	52Wk Range	Yield	P/E
NYS	CPT	$46.71 (5/28/2004)	46.71–34.50	5.44	63.99

*7 Year Price Score 124.2 *NYSE Composite Index=100 *12 Month Price Score 51.5

Interim Earnings (Per Share)

Qtr.	Mar	Jun	Sep	Dec
2001	0.41	0.40	0.43	0.18
2002	0.32	0.28	0.24	0.16
2003	0.20	0.14	0.14	0.23
2004	0.22	...	...	...

Interim Dividends (Per Share)

Amt	Decl	Ex	Rec	Pay
0.635Q	6/13/2003	6/26/2003	6/30/2003	7/17/2003
0.635Q	9/17/2003	9/26/2003	9/30/2003	10/17/2003
0.635Q	12/8/2003	12/17/2003	12/19/2003	1/16/2004
0.635Q	3/15/2004	3/29/2004	3/31/2004	4/16/2004

Indicated Div: $2.54

Valuation Analysis
Forecast P/E 14.05 (5/24/2004)
Market Cap $1.8 Billion   Book Value 784.9 Million
Price/Book 2.22   Price/Sales 4.18

Dividend Achiever Status
Rank 14   10 Year Growth Rate 24.67%
Total Years of Dividend Growth 10

Business Summary: Property, Real Estate &Development (MIC: 8.3 SIC: 6798 NAIC:525930)

Camden Property Trust is a self–administered and self–managed real estate investment trust. Co. is engaged in the ownership, development, construction, and management of multifamily apartment communities in ten states. As of Dec 31 2003, Co. owned interests in, operated or was developing 146 properties containing 52,346 apartment homes geographically dispersed in the Sunbelt and Midwestern markets, from Florida to California. At Dec 31 2003, Co. had two recently completed multifamily properties containing 786 apartment homes in lease–up. Two of Co.'s multifamily properties containing 1,002 apartment homes were under development at Dec 31 2003.

Recent Developments: For the first quarter ended Mar 31 2004, net income grew 12.6% to $9.4 million compared with $8.3 million in the equivalent 2003 quarter. Results for 2004 and 2003 included gains on the sale of land of $1.2 million and $1.4 million, respectively. Results for 2004 also included an impairment loss of $1.1 million on land held for sale. Total property revenues rose 7.2% to $104.8 million from $97.7 million a year earlier. Total revenues climbed 10.1% to $111.2 million versus $101.1 million the year before. Physical occupancy levels averaged 94.3% versus 91.4% in the first quarter of 2003. Funds from operations amounted to $36.8 million, up 9.3% from $33.6 million in the year–earlier quarter.

Prospects: During the quarter, Co. began construction on two new development projects: Camden Lee Vista II in Orlando, FL and Camden Farmers Market II in Dallas, TX. Camden Lee Vista II is a suburban garden–style community featuring 366 one– and two–bedroom apartment homes. Camden Farmers Market II is a 284–home urban–infill apartment and loft community, featuring 132 traditional class "A" apartment layouts, and 152 "loft–style" units with amenities including concrete flooring, exposed heating, ventilation, and air–conditioning duct work, upgraded lighting features and open floorplans. Initial occupancy is scheduled for first quarter 2005 and second quarter 2005, respectively.

Financial Data

(US$ in Thousands)	12/31/2003	12/31/2002	12/31/2001	12/31/2000	12/31/1999	12/31/1998	12/31/1997	12/31/1996
Earnings Per Share	0.71	1.00	1.42	1.63	1.23	1.12	1.41	0.58
Tang. Book Val. Per Share	15.67	17.05	18.88	25.54	26.00	26.40	22.23	17.88
Dividends Per Share	2.540	2.510	2.390	2.200	2.060	2.000	1.940	1.880
Dividend Payout %	357.74	251.50	168.48	135.42	167.88	179.01	137.94	324.13
Income Statement								
Rental Income	371,019	365,883	374,187	364,111	341,168	300,632	187,928	105,785
Total Income	416,540	410,983	428,215	403,539	371,296	323,839	199,789	111,606
Total Indirect Exp.	453,330	426,015	422,749	401,168	360,216	315,651	198,006	114,993
Depreciation	108,076	103,342	101,660	96,966	89,516	78,113	44,836	23,894
Interest Expense	75,414	71,499	69,841	69,036	57,856	50,467	28,537	17,336
Eqty Earns/Minority Int.	(11,784)	(14,313)	(15,995)	(15,306)	(10,292)	(1,322)	(1,655)	...
Income from Cont Ops	...	42,513	61,680	...	...	...	39,232	...
Net Income	29,430	74,612	61,292	74,424	61,623	57,333	38,438	8,713
Average Shs. Outstg.	41,354	44,216	41,603	41,388	44,291	44,183	28,356	14,940
Balance Sheet								
Cash & Cash Equivalents	10,012	4,621	8,782	9,411	10,229	9,933	10,516	4,789
Total Assets	2,625,561	2,609,899	2,449,665	2,430,881	2,487,932	2,347,982	1,323,620	603,510
Long–Term Obligations	1,509,700	1,427,000	1,207,047	1,140,067	1,168,496	1,006,144	486,779	271,884
Total Liabilities	1,840,699	1,770,430	1,531,414	1,456,698	1,471,257	1,177,594	613,056	308,082
Net Stockholders' Equity	784,885	839,453	918,251	974,183	1,016,675	1,170,388	710,564	295,428
Shares Outstanding	50,060	49,233	48,627	38,129	39,093	44,322	31,954	16,521
Statistical Record								
Net Inc.+Depr./Assets %	5.23	6.82	6.65	7.05	6.07	5.77	6.29	5.40
Return on Equity %	3.74	5.06	6.71	7.63	6.06	4.89	5.52	2.94
Return on Assets %	1.12	1.62	2.51	3.06	2.47	2.44	2.96	1.44
Price Range	44.30–30.70	41.54–29.74	39.32–31.07	33.81–25.88	28.19–24.13	31.00–24.88	33.00–26.63	28.63–21.75
P/E Ratio	62.39–43.24	41.54–29.74	27.69–21.88	20.74–15.87	22.92–19.61	27.68–22.21	23.40–18.88	49.35–37.50
Average Yield %	6.97	7.06	6.83	7.57	7.76	7.01	6.58	7.56

Address: 3 Greenway Plaza, Houston, TX 77046	Officers: Richard J. Campo – Chmn., C.E.O., D. Keith Oden – Pres., C.O.O.	Investor Contact:713–354–2500
Telephone: (713) 354–2500	Transfer Agents:American Stock Transfer and Trust	Institutional Holding
Web Site: www.camdenliving.com	Company, New York, NY	No of Institutions: 24
		Shares: 42,950,874 % Held: –

CARLISLE COMPANIES INC.

Exchange	Symbol	Price	52Wk Range	Yield	P/E
NYS	CSL	$58.69 (5/28/2004)	63.99-42.16	1.50	19.06

*7 Year Price Score 123.6 ***NYSE Composite Index=100** ***12 Month Price Score 51.0**

Interim Earnings (Per Share)

Qtr.	Mar	Jun	Sep	Dec
2001	(0.33)	0.54	0.36	0.25
2002	0.42	0.81	0.65	0.49
2003	0.56	0.93	0.80	0.59
2004	0.76	...	...	...

Interim Dividends (Per Share)

Amt	Decl	Ex	Rec	Pay
0.215Q	5/1/2003	5/14/2003	5/16/2003	6/1/2003
0.22Q	8/6/2003	8/15/2003	8/19/2003	9/1/2003
0.22Q	2/4/2004	2/13/2004	2/18/2004	3/1/2004
0.22Q	5/5/2004	5/13/2004	5/17/2004	6/1/2004

Indicated Div: $0.88 (Div. Reinv. Plan)

Valuation Analysis

Forecast P/E 16.33 (5/24/2004)

Market Cap $1.8 Billion	Book Value 651.3 Million
Price/Book 2.74	Price/Sales 0.81

Dividend Achiever Status

Rank 168	10 Year Growth Rate	9.53%
Total Years of Dividend Growth		27

Business Summary: Rubber Products (MIC: 11.6 SIC: 3011 NAIC:326211)

Carlisle is a manufacturing company. The Industrial Components segment manufactures non–automotive tires, wheels, transmission belts and accessories. Co. produces rubber and plastic automotive components and roofing membranes and FleeceBACK™sheeting for flat roofs in its Automotive Components and Construction Materials segments. The Specialty Products segment manufactures heavy–duty friction and braking systems for trucks and heavy equipment. The General Industry produces aerospace wire, electronic cable and cable assemblies and interconnects, plastic foodservice permanentware and refrigerated truck bodies. The Transportation Products segment produces high–payload trailers and dump bodies.

Recent Developments: For the quarter ended Mar 31 2004, net income advanced 38.8% to $23.7 million versus $17.1 million in the 2003 quarter. Earnings for 2004 and 2003 included plant closure and severance costs of $0.05 per share and $0.01 per share, respectively. Net sales increased 18.2% to $562.3 million from $475.7 million a year earlier. Notably Industrial Components segment sales grew 18.5% to $195.8 million, while Construction Materials segment sales climbed 24.8% to $122.8 million. Transportation Products segment sales rose 16.0% to $32.6 million, and General Industry segment sales jumped 29.4% to $124.2 million. Cost of goods sold increased 18.8% to $458.0 million from $385.5 million the year before.

Prospects: Co is encouraged by its strong organic sales growth and its earnings performance in the first quarter of 2004. The introduction of new products, improved manufacturing efficiencies and cost containment efforts is enabling Co. to improve operating results despite significant raw material increases. However, Co. is taking actions to obtain selling price increases to offset the steep rise in raw material costs. Co. is optimistic about obtaining selling price increases; but, due to the volatility of raw material costs, it is maintaining its 2004 earnings expectations in the range of $3.25 to $3.40 per share, including plant closure and severance costs of between $0.10 and $0.20 per share.

Financial Data

(US$ in Thousands)	3 Mos	12/31/2003	12/31/2002	12/31/2001	12/31/2000	12/31/1999	12/31/1998	12/31/1997
Earnings Per Share	3.08	2.88	2.37	0.82	3.14	3.13	2.77	2.28
Cash Flow Per Share	0.25	3.78	7.39	7.32	4.08	4.44	3.15	2.67
Tang. Book Val. Per Share	10.92	10.37	8.08	6.72	9.79	10.62	8.85	7.48
Dividends Per Share	0.870	0.870	0.850	0.820	0.760	0.680	0.600	0.520
Dividend Payout %	28.32	30.20	35.86	100.00	24.20	21.72	21.66	23.02
Income Statement								
Total Revenues	562,314	2,108,164	1,971,280	1,849,477	1,771,067	1,611,256	1,517,494	1,260,550
Total Indirect Exp.	62,075	224,603	231,917	252,385	186,055	175,568	176,544	159,070
Depreciation & Amort.	15,556	60,366	56,994	63,960	59,549	47,414	45,221	38,755
Operating Income	42,277	146,194	127,651	67,045	178,883	174,637	151,571	127,391
Income Taxes	11,424	42,813	26,050	13,084	54,685	59,689	55,403	46,118
Income from Cont Ops	...	...	72,378	...	...	...	...	...
Net Income	23,727	88,920	28,625	24,841	96,180	95,794	84,866	70,666
Average Shs. Outstg.	31,268	30,863	30,583	30,450	30,599	30,635	30,674	31,025
Balance Sheet								
Cash & Cash Equivalents	30,056	26,848	23,041	15,606	8,967	10,417	3,883	1,732
Total Current Assets	633,702	584,381	481,508	553,272	576,477	541,038	478,525	417,533
Total Assets	1,478,765	1,436,909	1,315,900	1,397,987	1,305,679	1,080,662	1,022,832	861,216
Total Current Liabilities	362,337	339,343	324,262	273,779	399,948	240,378	255,337	226,083
Long–Term Obligations	293,374	294,581	293,124	461,744	281,864	281,744	273,521	209,642
Net Stockholders' Equity	651,251	631,930	553,077	540,284	547,879	478,133	406,905	348,836
Shares Outstanding	30,997	30,991	30,597	30,263	30,251	30,127	30,178	30,351
Operating Profit Margin %	7.51	6.93	6.47	3.62	10.10	10.83	9.98	10.10
Net Profit Margin %	9.56	8.27	7.53	2.75	11.60	13.35	12.89	12.92
Return on Equity %	3.64	14.07	13.08	4.59	17.55	20.03	20.85	20.25
Return on Assets %	1.60	6.18	5.50	1.77	7.36	8.86	8.29	8.20
Debt/Total Assets %	19.83	20.50	22.27	33.02	21.58	26.07	26.74	24.34
Price Range	63.40-54.71	61.49-39.24	46.91-32.65	43.69-26.40	49.75-31.19	52.94-31.06	51.75-32.88	47.63-27.13
P/E Ratio	20.58-17.76	21.35-13.63	19.79-13.78	53.28-32.20	15.84-9.93	16.91-9.92	18.68-11.87	20.89-11.90
Average Yield %	1.48	1.87	2.12	2.33	1.86	1.60	1.34	1.41

Address: 13925 Ballantyne Corporate Place, Charlotte, NC 28277 Telephone: (704) 501–1100 Web Site: www.carlisle.com	Officers: Stephen P. Munn – Chmn., Richmond D. McKinnish – Pres., C.E.O. Transfer Agents:Computershare Investor Services, LLC., Chicago, IL	Investor Contact:704–501–1100 Institutional Holding No of Institutions: 18 Shares: 1,176,098 % Held: –

CATERPILLAR INC.

Exchange	Symbol	Price	52Wk Range	Yield	P/E
NYS	CAT	$75.35 (5/28/2004)	85.01–52.18	1.96	19.22

*7 Year Price Score 138.5 *NYSE Composite Index=100 ***12 Month Price Score 48.9**

Interim Earnings (Per Share)

Qtr.	Mar	Jun	Sep	Dec
2001	0.47	0.78	0.59	0.48
2002	0.23	0.58	0.61	0.88
2003	0.37	1.15	0.62	0.99
2004	1.16	...	...	...

Interim Dividends (Per Share)

Amt	Decl	Ex	Rec	Pay
0.35Q	6/11/2003	7/17/2003	7/21/2003	8/20/2003
0.37Q	10/8/2003	10/16/2003	10/20/2003	11/20/2003
0.37Q	12/10/2003	1/15/2004	1/20/2004	2/20/2004
0.37Q	4/14/2004	4/22/2004	4/26/2004	5/20/2004

Indicated Div: $1.48 (Div. Reinv. Plan)

Valuation Analysis

Forecast P/E 14.04 (5/24/2004)

Market Cap $25.9 Billion   Book Value 6.3 Billion

Price/Book 4.34   Price/Sales 1.13

Dividend Achiever Status

Rank 12   10 Year Growth Rate 25.20%

Total Years of Dividend Growth 10

Business Summary: Industrial Machinery and Equipment (MIC: 11.5 SIC: 3531 NAIC:333120)

Caterpillar operates in three principal lines of business. The machinery division designs, manufactures and markets construction, mining, agricultural and forestry machinery. The engines division designs, manufactures and markets engines for Caterpillar machinery; electric power generation systems; on–highway trucks and locomotives; marine, petroleum, construction, industrial, agricultural, and other applications; and related parts. Engines range from 5 to over 22,000 horsepower, and turbines range from 1,600 to 19,500 horsepower. The financial products division consists primarily of Caterpillar Financial Services Corporation, Caterpillar Insurance Holdings, Inc. and their subsidiaries.

Recent Developments: For the three months ended Mar 31 2004, net income climbed to $412.0 million compared with $129.0 million in the same period a year earlier. Total sales and revenues advanced 34.1% to $6.47 billion from $4.82 billion the previous year. Co. attributed the jump in sales and revenues primarily to higher Machinery and Engines volume of $1.33 billion, a favorable currency effect on sales of $176.0 million, favorable price realization of $74.0 million and higher Financial Products revenues of $68.0 million. Operating income improved to $574.0 million versus $222.0 million the year before.

Prospects: Co.'s near-term outlook is strengthened by the recent acceleration in global economic growth. Accordingly, Co. is now projecting full-year 2004 sales and revenue growth of about 20.0% from 2003, up from its previous forecast of 12.0% growth. Co. expects Machinery and Engines volume to rise about 16.0%, the favorable effect of currency to add about 2.0%, and the remainder to come from improved price realization and Financial Products revenues. Co. noted that included in this outlook are worldwide machine price increases of 2.0% to 3.0% that have been communicated to dealers with an effective date of Jul 1 2004. Full-year 2004 profit is now expected to rise between 65.0% and 70.0% from 2003.

Financial Data

(US$ in Thousands)	3 Mos	12/31/2003	12/31/2002	12/31/2001	12/31/2000	12/31/1999	12/31/1998	12/31/1997
Earnings Per Share	3.92	3.13	2.30	2.32	3.02	2.63	4.11	4.37
Cash Flow Per Share	0.27	5.87	6.82	5.72	5.90	7.15	4.82	5.50
Tang. Book Val. Per Share	13.74	12.91	11.00	11.47	11.91	11.08	10.89	12.09
Dividends Per Share	1.440	1.420	1.400	1.380	1.330	1.250	1.100	0.900
Dividend Payout %	36.83	45.36	60.86	59.48	44.03	47.52	26.76	20.59
Income Statement								
Total Revenues	6,467,000	22,763,000	20,152,000	20,450,000	20,175,000	19,702,000	20,977,000	18,925,000
Total Indirect Exp.	1,312,000	4,600,000	4,645,000	5,044,000	4,629,000	4,287,000	4,182,000	3,482,000
Depreciation & Amort.	350,000	1,347,000	1,220,000	1,169,000	1,022,000	945,000	865,000	738,000
Operating Income	574,000	1,688,000	1,319,000	1,311,000	1,737,000	1,494,000	2,253,000	2,430,000
Net Interest Inc./(Exp.)	(175,000)	(716,000)	(800,000)	(942,000)	(980,000)	(829,000)	(753,000)	(580,000)
Income Taxes	158,000	398,000	312,000	367,000	447,000	455,000	665,000	796,000
Eqty Earns/Minority Int.	6,000	20,000	(4,000)	3,000	(28,000)	(20,000)	4,000	48,000
Net Income	412,000	1,099,000	798,000	805,000	1,053,000	946,000	1,513,000	1,665,000
Average Shs. Outstg.	355,736	351,400	346,900	347,100	348,897	359,367	368,130	381,000
Balance Sheet								
Cash & Cash Equivalents	368,000	342,000	309,000	400,000	334,000	548,000	360,000	292,000
Total Current Assets	17,866,000	16,791,000	14,628,000	13,400,000	12,521,000	11,734,000	11,459,000	9,814,000
Total Assets	37,858,000	36,465,000	32,851,000	30,657,000	28,464,000	26,635,000	25,128,000	20,756,000
Total Current Liabilities	13,200,000	12,621,000	11,344,000	10,276,000	8,568,000	8,178,000	7,565,000	6,379,000
Long–Term Obligations	14,570,000	14,078,000	11,596,000	11,291,000	11,334,000	9,928,000	9,404,000	6,942,000
Net Stockholders' Equity	6,334,000	6,078,000	5,472,000	5,611,000	5,600,000	5,465,000	5,131,000	4,679,000
Net Working Capital	4,666,000	4,170,000	3,284,000	3,124,000	3,953,000	3,556,000	3,894,000	3,435,000
Shares Outstanding	341,902	343,762	344,255	343,376	343,396	353,748	357,198	368,000
Operating Profit Margin %	7.05	5.35	3.95	3.19	5.19	4.74	8.40	10.93
Net Profit Margin %	9.43	6.26	4.47	4.31	6.24	6.57	11.22	15.30
Return on Equity %	4.64	10.34	5.06	2.63	6.51	7.06	19.95	27.86
Return on Assets %	0.77	1.72	0.84	0.48	1.28	1.44	4.07	6.28
Debt/Total Assets %	38.48	38.60	35.29	36.83	39.81	37.27	37.42	33.44
Price Range	85.01–73.15	84.75–42.04	59.79–33.86	56.20–40.09	53.31–29.81	65.50–42.94	60.69–40.31	60.94–36.50
P/E Ratio	21.69–18.66	27.08–13.43	26.00–14.72	24.22–17.28	17.65–9.87	24.90–16.33	14.77–9.81	13.94–8.35
Average Yield %	1.83	2.34	2.91	2.84	3.44	2.31	2.18	1.84

Address: 100 NE Adams Street, Peoria, IL 61629–7310	**Officers:** James W. Owens – Chmn., C.E.O., Ali M. Bahaj – V.P.	**Investor Contact:**309–675–4549	
Telephone: (309) 675 1000	**Transfer Agents:**Mellon Investor Services of South Hackensack, NJ	**Institutional Holding**	
Web Site: www.CAT.com		**No of Institutions:** 583	
		Shares: 249,420,375 **% Held:** 72.50%	

CEDAR FAIR, L.P.

Exchange	Symbol	Price	52Wk Range	Yield	P/E
NYS	FUN	$32.66 (5/28/2004)	35.71-24.65	5.51	19.21

*7 Year Price Score 124.6 **NYSE Composite Index=100* ***12 Month Price Score 50.0**

TRADING VOLUME (thousand shares)

Interim Earnings (Per Share)

Qtr.	Mar	Jun	Sep	Dec
2001	(0.60)	0.13	2.10	(0.50)
2002	(0.63)	0.40	2.01	(0.39)
2003	(0.62)	0.33	2.16	(0.20)
2004	(0.59)	...	...	...

Interim Dividends (Per Share)

Amt	Decl	Ex	Rec	Pay
0.44Q	6/23/2003	7/1/2003	7/3/2003	8/15/2003
0.44Q	9/26/2003	10/1/2003	10/3/2003	11/17/2003
0.44Q	12/12/2003	1/2/2004	1/6/2004	2/17/2004
0.45Q	3/8/2004	4/1/2004	4/5/2004	5/17/2004

Indicated Div: $1.80 (Div. Reinv. Plan)

Valuation Analysis

Forecast P/E 17.04 (5/24/2004)

Market Cap $1.6 Billion	Book Value 257.5 Million
Price/Book 6.81	Price/Sales 3.43

Dividend Achiever Status

Rank	228	10 Year Growth Rate	6.31%

Total Years of Dividend Growth 16

Business Summary: Sporting &Recreational (MIC: 13.5 SIC: 7996 NAIC:713110)

Cedar Fair is a limited partnership managed by Cedar Fair Management Company. Co. owns and operates six amusement parks: Cedar Point on Lake Erie in Sandusky, OH; Knott's Berry Farm, located in Buena Park, CA; Dorney Park & Wildwater Kingdom, near Allentown, PA; Valleyfair, near Minneapolis, MN; Worlds of Fun in Kansas City, MO; and Michigan's Adventure, located near Muskegon, MI. Co.'s five water parks are located near San Diego and Palm Springs, CA, and adjacent to Cedar Point, Knott's Berry Farm and Worlds of Fun. Co. owns and operates four hotel facilities. Co. also operates Knott's Camp Snoopy at the Mall of America in Bloomington, MN under a management contract.

Recent Developments: For the first quarter ended Mar 28 2004, Co. reported a net loss of $29.9 million compared with a net loss of $31.5 million in the corresponding period of the prior year. Net revenues grew 8.0% to $23.2 million from $21.5 million a year earlier. The first quarter revenues of Co. have been historically minimal as Co. typically realizes the majority of its revenues during a 130-day operating period beginning in early May. Meanwhile, the improvement in revenues was primarily attributed to higher early-season attendance at Knott's Berry Farm. Operating income amounted to $24.1 million versus an operating loss of $24.3 million the year before.

Prospects: On Apr 8 2004, Co. announced that it completed the acquisition of Six Flags Worlds of Adventure, located near Cleveland, OH, from Six Flags, Inc. for approximately $145.0 million in cash. Co. acquired substantially all of the assets of the park, including the adjacent hotel and campground. Co. has renamed the park Geauga Lake. Meanwhile, construction is progressing well on Cedar Point's new $22.0 million indoor water park, *Castaway Bay*, and Knott's Berry Farm's new $16.0 million inverted roller coaster, *Silver Bullet*. Both projects are on budget and are on schedule to open late in 2004.

Financial Data

(US$ in Thousands)	3 Mos	12/31/2003	12/31/2002	12/31/2001	12/31/2000	12/31/1999	12/31/1998	12/31/1997
Earnings Per Share	1.70	1.67	1.39	1.13	1.50	1.63	1.58	1.47
Cash Flow Per Share	(0.46)	2.62	2.85	2.44	2.20	2.36	2.45	2.08
Tang. Book Val. Per Share	5.07	6.09	N.M	N.M	N.M	N.M	N.M	N.M
Dividends Per Share	1.760	1.740	1.650	1.580	1.500	1.380	1.280	1.250
Dividend Payout %	104.14	104.19	118.70	139.82	100.16	85.12	81.32	85.54
Income Statement								
Total Revenues	23,210	509,976	502,851	477,256	472,920	438,001	419,500	264,137
Total Indirect Exp.	43,815	115,216	112,142	114,441	101,966	85,935	80,004	53,028
Depreciation & Amort.	3,443	44,693	41,682	42,486	39,572	35,082	32,065	21,528
Operating Income	(24,085)	125,149	121,192	98,557	115,516	116,725	112,608	76,303
Net Interest Inc./(Exp.)	(5,792)	(24,070)	(24,967)	(24,143)	(21,357)	(15,371)	(14,660)	(7,845)
Income Taxes	871	17,918	17,159	16,520	16,353	15,580	14,507	...
Income from Cont Ops	...	...	...	...	...	85,774	...	...
Net Income	(29,885)	85,888	71,417	57,894	77,806	85,804	83,441	68,458
Average Shs. Outstg.	50,679	51,334	51,263	51,113	51,679	52,390	52,414	46,265
Balance Sheet								
Cash & Cash Equivalents	3,218	2,194	2,171	2,280	2,392	638	1,137	2,520
Total Current Assets	34,318	29,777	29,237	26,868	25,378	24,184	20,967	21,954
Total Assets	840,657	819,341	822,257	810,231	764,143	708,961	631,325	599,619
Total Current Liabilities	110,239	111,694	106,338	96,700	114,024	86,559	77,231	62,426
Long-Term Obligations	415,632	348,647	365,150	373,000	300,000	261,200	200,350	189,750
Net Stockholders' Equity	257,516	308,891	305,320	308,250	330,589	349,986	341,991	285,381
Net Working Capital	(75,921)	(81,917)	(77,101)	(69,832)	(88,646)	(62,375)	(56,264)	(40,472)
Shares Outstanding	50,713	50,673	50,549	50,514	50,813	51,798	51,980	52,403
Operating Profit Margin %	N.M.	24.54	24.10	20.65	24.42	26.64	26.84	28.88
Return on Equity %	N.M.	27.80	23.39	18.78	23.53	24.50	24.39	23.98
Return on Assets %	N.M.	10.48	8.68	7.14	10.18	12.09	13.21	11.41
Debt/Total Assets %	49.44	42.55	44.40	46.03	39.25	36.84	31.73	31.64
Price Range	35.71-30.27	31.03-22.74	24.79-20.30	24.98-18.03	20.75-17.56	26.00-18.50	29.50-22.00	28.19-17.88
P/E Ratio	21.01-17.81	18.58-13.62	17.83-14.60	22.11-15.96	13.83-11.71	15.95-11.35	18.67-13.92	19.18-12.16
Average Yield %	5.37	6.51	7.10	7.50	8.04	6.04	4.86	5.78

Address: One Cedar Point Drive, Sandusky, OH 44870-5259	Officers: Richard L. Kinzel – Pres., C.E.O., Bruce A. Jackson – V.P., Fin., C.F.O.	Investor Contact:419-627-2233
Telephone: (419) 626-0830	**Transfer Agents:**American Stock Transfer &Trust Company, New York, NY	**Institutional Holding** No of Institutions: 3
Web Site: www.cedarfair.com		**Shares:** 218,576 **% Held:** –

CENTURYTEL, INC.

Exchange	Symbol	Price	52Wk Range	Yield	P/E
NYS	CTL	$29.89 (5/28/2004)	36.63-26.33	0.77	12.56

*7 Year Price Score 99.4 *NYSE Composite Index=100 ***12 Month Price Score 44.0**

Interim Earnings (Per Share)

Qtr.	Mar	Jun	Sep	Dec
2001	0.33	1.09	0.65	0.34
2002	0.30	0.28	0.45	0.30
2003	0.58	0.60	0.63	0.57
2004	0.58	...	...	...

Interim Dividends (Per Share)

Amt	Decl	Ex	Rec	Pay
0.055Q	8/26/2003	9/4/2003	9/8/2003	9/19/2003
0.055Q	11/20/2003	11/26/2003	12/1/2003	12/12/2003
0.058Q	2/25/2004	3/4/2004	3/8/2004	3/19/2004
0.0575Q	5/27/2004	6/3/2004	6/7/2004	6/18/2004

Indicated Div: $0.23 (Div. Reinv. Plan)

Valuation Analysis

Forecast P/E 12.91 (5/24/2004)

Market Cap $4.2 Billion	Book Value N/A
Price/Book N/A	Price/Sales N/A

Dividend Achiever Status

Rank 258	10 Year Growth Rate	4.79%
Total Years of Dividend Growth	30	

Business Summary: Communications (MIC: 10.1 SIC: 4813 NAIC:517110)

CenturyTel is a regional telecommunications company that is primarily engaged in providing local exchange telephone services. Co. also provides long distance, Internet access, fiber transport, competitive local exchange carrier, security monitoring, and other communications and business information services in certain local and regional markets. As of Dec 31 2003, Co.'s local exchange telephone subsidiaries operated approximately 2.4 million telephone access lines, primarily in rural, suburban and small urban areas in 22 states, with over 70.0% of these lines located in Wisconsin, Missouri, Alabama, Arkansas and Washington.

Recent Developments: For the quarter ended Mar 31 2004, net income fell slightly to $83.3 million compared with $83.9 million in the corresponding year-earlier period. Operating revenues rose 2.7% to $593.7 million from $578.0 million the previous year. Co. attributed the increased revenue primarily to the fiber assets acquired during 2003, data revenue growth from digital subscriber line and data circuit additions and increased enhanced calling feature penetration. Co. noted that these increases more than offset revenue declines attributable to lower intrastate toll revenues and universal service funding, along with access line losses. Operating income was $183.6 million versus $184.8 million the year before.

Prospects: Co.'s near-term prospects now appear moderately positive. Co.'s results going forward should benefit from continued long distance and digital subscriber line growth (DSL), the latter aided in part by the recent launch of tiered DSL service. Consequently, Co. now expects full-year 2004 diluted earnings of between $2.20 and $2.35 per share, an increase of $0.15 over its previously provided guidance. Co. attributed the increase in full-year 2004 earnings per share guidance to stronger than expected first quarter revenues, lower 2004 expenses than originally forecast and fewer fully diluted shares as a result of share repurchases during the three months ended Mar 31 2004.

Financial Data
(US$ in Thousands)

	3 Mos	12/31/2003	12/31/2002	12/31/2001	12/31/2000	12/31/1999	12/31/1998	12/31/1997
Earnings Per Share	2.38	2.38	1.33	2.41	1.63	1.70	1.64	1.86
Cash Flow Per Share	1.97	7.38	5.56	4.67	3.96	2.88	3.33	2.16
Tang. Book Val. Per Share	N.M	N.M	N.M	N.M	N.M	1.39	N.M	N.M
Dividends Per Share	0.220	0.220	0.210	0.200	0.190	0.180	0.170	0.160
Dividend Payout %	9.24	9.24	15.78	8.29	11.65	10.58	10.36	8.80
Income Statement								
Total Revenues	593,704	2,380,745	1,971,996	2,117,469	1,845,926	1,676,669	1,577,085	901,521
Total Indirect Exp.	228,598	1,630,349	1,396,590	1,559,550	1,320,513	1,168,600	1,097,274	633,751
Depreciation & Amort.	126,992	470,641	411,626	473,384	388,016	348,816	328,554	159,495
Operating Income	183,557	750,396	575,406	557,919	525,413	508,069	479,811	267,770
Net Interest Inc./(Exp.)	(52,543)	(226,751)	(221,845)	(225,523)	(183,302)	(150,557)	(167,552)	(56,474)
Income Taxes	52,098	187,252	103,537	210,025	154,711	189,503	158,701	152,363
Income from Cont Ops	...	...	189,919	...	...	...	...	...
Net Income	83,279	344,707	801,624	343,031	231,474	239,769	228,757	255,978
Average Shs. Outstg.	143,347	144,700	142,879	142,307	141,864	141,432	140,105	137,412
Balance Sheet								
Cash & Cash Equivalents	273,293	203,181	3,661	13,362	19,039	56,640	5,742	26,017
Total Current Assets	513,100	462,939	295,902	300,273	376,504	286,073	226,238	283,480
Total Assets	7,896,505	7,895,852	7,770,408	6,318,684	6,393,290	4,705,407	4,935,455	4,709,201
Total Current Liabilities	610,437	471,383	388,104	1,293,956	743,370	309,177	304,844	322,078
Long-Term Obligations	3,016,992	3,109,302	3,578,132	2,087,500	3,050,292	2,078,311	2,558,000	2,609,541
Net Stockholders' Equity	3,414,644	3,478,516	3,088,004	2,337,380	2,032,079	1,847,992	1,531,482	1,300,272
Net Working Capital	(97,337)	(8,444)	(92,202)	(993,683)	(366,866)	(23,104)	(78,606)	(38,598)
Shares Outstanding	139,493	144,364	142,955	141,232	140,667	139,945	138,083	136,656
Statistical Record								
Operating Profit Margin %	30.91	31.51	29.17	26.34	28.46	30.30	30.42	29.70
Net Profit Margin %	31.57	30.20	20.13	36.03	29.30	36.90	34.63	62.19
Return on Equity %	2.43	9.90	6.15	14.67	11.39	12.97	14.93	19.68
Return on Assets %	1.05	4.36	2.44	5.42	3.62	5.09	4.63	5.43
Debt/Total Assets %	38.20	39.37	46.04	33.03	47.71	44.16	51.82	55.41
Price Range	33.30-26.33	36.63-25.51	35.20-22.18	39.00-26.18	47.38-24.50	48.88-36.44	45.00-21.75	22.36-12.78
P/E Ratio	13.99-11.06	15.39-10.72	26.47-16.68	16.18-10.86	29.06-15.03	28.75-21.43	27.44-13.26	12.02-6.87
Average Yield %	0.75	0.69	0.71	0.64	0.57	0.43	0.54	1.00

Address: 100 CenturyTel Drive, Monroe, LA 71203	**Officers:** Glen F. Post III – Chmn., C.E.O., Karen A. Puckett – Pres., C.O.O.	**Investor Contact:**800 833-1188 **Institutional Holding**
Telephone: (318) 388-9000	**Transfer Agents:**Computershare Investor Services, LLC, Chicago, IL	**No of Institutions:** 12
Web Site: www.centurytel.com		**Shares:** 772,818 **% Held:** –

CHARTER ONE FINANCIAL, INC.

Exchange	Symbol	Price	52Wk Range	Yield	P/E
NYS	CF	$43.96 (5/28/2004)	44.00–30.31	2.64	18.95

*7 Year Price Score 133.2 *NYSE Composite Index=100 *12 Month Price Score 54.2

Interim Earnings (Per Share)

Qtr.	Mar	Jun	Sep	Dec
2001	0.48	0.51	0.54	0.57
2002	0.59	0.60	0.61	0.65
2003	0.64	0.72	0.69	0.69
2004	0.22	...	...	...

Interim Dividends (Per Share)

Amt	Decl	Ex	Rec	Pay
0.26Q	7/17/2003	8/4/2003	8/6/2003	8/20/2003
0.26Q	10/22/2003	11/4/2003	11/6/2003	11/20/2003
0.26Q	1/20/2004	2/4/2004	2/6/2004	2/20/2004
0.29Q	4/21/2004	5/4/2004	5/6/2004	5/20/2004

Indicated Div: $1.16 (Div. Reinv. Plan)

Valuation Analysis

Forecast P/E 15.14 (5/24/2004)

Market Cap $10.2 Billion	Book Value 3.3 Billion
Price/Book 2.42	Price/Sales 3.03

Dividend Achiever Status

Rank 28	10 Year Growth Rate	20.90%
Total Years of Dividend Growth	15	

TRADING VOLUME (thousand shares)

Business Summary: Other Depository Banking (MIC: 8.5 SIC: 6035 NAIC:522120)

Charter One is a financial holding company. Co. owns all of the outstanding capital stock of Charter One Bank, N.A. ("the Bank"). The Bank's primary business is providing consumer banking services to certain major markets in Ohio, Michigan, Illinois, New York, Vermont and in some markets of Massachusetts, Indiana, Connecticut and Pennsylvania. As of March 31, 2004, the Bank and its subsidiaries were doing business through 456 traditional banking centers, 160 in-store banking centers, 30 loan production offices and 988 ATMs. At March 31, 2004, total assets were $41.3 billion.

Recent Developments: For the quarter ended Mar 31 2004, net income declined 65.9% to $50.3 million compared with $147.5 million in the corresponding period the year before. Earnings included pre-tax net losses of $91.0 million in 2004 and net gains of $76.7 million in 2003. Net interest income rose 1.8% to $304.6 million from $299.0 million a year earlier. Provision for loan and lease losses fell 69.7% to $18.6 million. Total other income plunged 96.8% to $5.2 million, while total administrative expenses increased 19.0% to $218.0 million. Net loans and leases grew 20.1% to $29.65 billion, and total deposits slid 1.6% to $26.94 billion.

Prospects: Co. continues to expand its market presence, increasing its banking centers by 29.0% during the 12 months ended Mar 31 2004. Moreover, in Mar 2004, Co. entered into an agreement with Wal-Mart Stores to open 67 in-store banking centers across Ohio, Illinois, Indiana, Michigan, Pennsylvania, and New York, which will allow Co. to grow in existing markets as well as enter new markets. Meanwhile, Co. remains focused on reducing single-family loan exposure and growing noninterest-bearing deposits. During the first quarter, Co. reduced single-family loans and securities by $1.90 billion. Looking ahead, Co. expects earnings per share ranging from $2.41 to $2.51, including a debt prepayment penalty.

Financial Data

(US$ in Thousands)	3 Mos	12/31/2003	12/31/2002	12/31/2001	12/31/2000	12/31/1999	12/31/1998	12/31/1997
Earnings Per Share	2.32	2.74	2.45	2.10	1.81	1.32	1.33	0.91
Tang. Book Val. Per Share	12.70	12.81	11.99	10.94	9.94	9.11	8.53	7.75
Dividends Per Share	1.020	0.980	0.820	0.710	0.610	0.510	0.430	0.370
Dividend Payout %	43.97	35.76	33.85	34.04	33.76	39.09	32.45	40.55
Income Statement								
Total Interest Income	489,827	2,112,029	2,286,461	2,378,246	2,247,088	2,128,455	1,760,371	1,377,687
Total Interest Expense	185,273	943,142	1,116,631	1,387,830	1,344,053	1,194,351	1,031,299	850,724
Net Interest Income	304,554	1,168,887	1,169,830	990,416	903,035	934,104	729,072	526,963
Provision for Loan Losses	18,616	152,272	192,003	100,766	54,205	35,237	29,465	40,861
Non-Interest Income	5,197	698,470	547,546	473,624	392,871	199,282	203,685	110,927
Non-Interest Expense	218,035	790,721	678,972	629,662	603,955	633,327	492,513	373,930
Income Before Taxes	73,100	924,364	846,401	733,612	637,746	496,137	418,739	222,983
Income from Cont Ops	...	...	...	...	...	335,530	277,019	151,136
Net Income	50,256	630,891	577,668	500,714	433,962	333,976	215,361	148,409
Average Shs. Outstg.	230,219	230,257	236,115	238,383	239,894	252,183	207,533	165,291
Balance Sheet								
Cash & Due from Banks	535,273				530,771	689,082	334,054	214,716
Securities Avail. for Sale	7,707,107	273,260	210,095	129,312	426,701	496,075	253,317	582,589
Net Loans & Leases	29,785,432	28,130,017	25,852,846	25,396,071	23,950,172	22,276,862	17,502,729	12,360,134
Total Assets	41,278,929	42,628,066	41,896,072	38,174,516	32,971,427	31,819,063	24,467,255	19,760,265
Total Deposits	26,939,001	27,203,319	27,527,843	25,123,309	19,605,671	19,073,975	15,165,064	10,219,200
Long-Term Obligations	8,661,607	10,545,046	9,746,778	8,961,648	9,921,085	9,424,527	6,316,454	5,600,301
Total Liabilities	38,021,897	39,352,197	38,812,247	35,246,016	30,515,223	29,421,363	22,592,143	18,383,376
Net Stockholders' Equity	3,257,032	3,275,869	3,083,825	2,928,500	2,456,204	2,397,700	1,875,112	1,376,889
Shares Outstanding	223,651	223,173	224,790	235,556	229,571	242,241	201,043	165,809
Return on Equity %	1.54	19.25	18.73	17.09	17.66	13.99	14.77	10.97
Return on Assets %	0.12	1.48	1.37	1.31	1.31	1.05	1.13	0.76
Equity/Assets %	7.89	7.68	7.36	7.67	7.44	7.53	7.66	6.96
Non-Int. Exp./Tot. Inc. %	44.04	28.13	23.95	22.07	22.87	26.84	24.97	25.12
Price Range	37.30-33.30	34.73-27.22	34.43-25.41	28.44-22.46	25.54-12.96	24.97-14.96	27.33-14.89	23.88-14.66
P/E Ratio	16.08-14.35	12.68-9.93	14.05-10.37	13.54-10.70	14.11-7.16	18.92-11.34	20.55-11.19	26.24-16.11
Average Yield %	2.86	3.20	2.70	2.78	3.38	2.46	1.88	1.98

Address: 1215 Superior Avenue, Cleveland, OH 44114 Telephone: (216) 566-5300 Web Site: www.charterone.com	Officers: Charles John Koch – Chmn., Pres., C.E.O., Herbert G. Chorbajian – Vice-Chmn. Transfer Agents: EquiServe, Providence, RI	Investor Contact: 800-262-6301 Institutional Holding No of Institutions: 16 Shares: 2,694,312 % Held: –

CHEMICAL FINANCIAL CORP.

Exchange	Symbol	Price	52Wk Range	Yield	P/E
NMS	CHFC	$35.05 (5/28/2004)	37.91–29.12	3.02	14.91

*7 Year Price Score 122.5 *NYSE Composite Index=100 *12 Month Price Score 47.8

TRADING VOLUME (thousand shares)

Interim Earnings (Per Share)

Qtr.	Mar	Jun	Sep	Dec
2001	0.15	0.48	0.55	0.62
2002	0.55	0.54	0.56	0.66
2003	0.59	0.58	0.61	0.57
2004	0.59	...	...	...

Interim Dividends (Per Share)

Amt	Decl	Ex	Rec	Pay
0.25Q	7/21/2003	9/3/2003	9/5/2003	9/19/2003
0.25Q	10/20/2003	12/3/2003	12/5/2003	12/19/2003
0.265Q	12/8/2003	3/3/2004	3/5/2004	3/19/2004
0.265Q	4/19/2004	6/2/2004	6/4/2004	6/18/2004

Indicated Div: $1.06 (Div. Reinv. Plan)

Valuation Analysis

Forecast P/E 14.78 (5/24/2004)

Market Cap $790.4 Million	Book Value	469.8 Million
Price/Book 1.78	Price/Sales	3.74

Dividend Achiever Status

Rank	117	10 Year Growth Rate	12.13%
Total Years of Dividend Growth			28

Business Summary: Commercial Banking (MIC: 8.1 SIC: 6022 NAIC:522110)

Chemical Financial is a bank holding company headquartered in Midland, MI, with total assets of $3.71 billion as of Dec 31 2003. Co.'s four subsidiary banks, CB&T, Chemical Bank Shoreline, Chemical Bank West and State Bank of Caledonia, operate 133 branch offices and two loan production offices throughout 33 counties in the lower peninsula of Michigan. Non–bank subsidiaries include CFC Financial Services, an insurance company operating under the assumed names Chemical Financial Insurance Agency and CFC Investment Centers, and CFC Title Services, an issuer of title insurance to buyers and sellers of residential and commercial mortgage properties.

Recent Developments: For the quarter ended Mar 31 2004, net income rose 0.7% to $14.1 million from $14.0 million in the corresponding period of the year before. Net interest income grew 4.8% to $36.8 million due to the acquisition of Caledonia Financial, as well as increases in investment securities gains, service charge income and trust services revenue. Provision for loan losses more than doubled to $746,000 from $295,000 a year earlier. Total non–interest income improved 7.0% to $10.0 million. Total operating expenses increased 9.3% to $25.2 million. As of Mar 31 2004, total deposits were $3.02 billion versus $2.90 billion the year before. Total loans advanced 19.6% to $2.55 billion.

Prospects: Co. continues to benefit from its acquisition of Caledonia Financial, which was completed on Dec 1 2003. During the second quarter of 2004, Co. expects to restructure the State Bank of Caledonia into two of its three existing bank subsidiaries. The branches in Caledonia, Middleville and Dutton, MI are expected to become part of Chemical Bank West, and the Kalamazoo, MI branch is expected to become a part of Chemical Bank Shoreline. These locations should strengthen Co's branch system in the Grand Rapids and Kalamazoo marketplaces. Co. will also continue to operate Caledonia's bank subsidiary, State Bank of Caledonia, as a separate subsidiary until mid–2004.

Financial Data

(US$ in Thousands)	3 Mos	12/31/2003	12/31/2002	12/31/2001	12/31/2000	12/31/1999	12/31/1998	12/31/1997
Earnings Per Share	2.35	2.35	2.31	1.80	1.86	1.75	1.65	1.52
Tang. Book Val. Per Share	16.44	16.01	16.46	14.67	18.27	16.86	16.25	14.39
Dividends Per Share	1.010	1.000	0.910	0.870	0.790	0.720	0.660	0.570
Dividend Payout %	43.19	42.55	39.57	48.37	42.71	41.23	40.18	38.09
Income Statement								
Total Interest Income	47,197	185,037	211,044	219,250	131,085	121,917	121,633	117,319
Total Interest Expense	10,375	45,265	65,352	89,182	54,035	47,071	49,146	48,279
Net Interest Income	36,822	139,772	145,692	130,068	77,050	74,846	72,487	69,040
Provision for Loan Losses	746	2,834	3,765	2,004	487	483	964	1,002
Non–Interest Income	8,979	39,094	34,534	31,873	17,364	16,003	15,610	13,122
Non–Interest Expense	24,177	91,923	93,526	94,597	50,860	48,986	48,307	45,718
Net Income	14,119	55,716	54,945	42,723	29,006	27,709	26,046	23,889
Average Shs. Outstg.	23,986	23,756	23,741	23,691	15,526	15,722	15,785	15,727
Balance Sheet								
Cash & Due from Banks	106,610	131,184	148,112	150,546	95,047	98,827	98,483	95,794
Securities Avail. for Sale	840,957	1,650,361	1,986,726	1,663,658	1,079,743	1,099,493	1,218,799	1,239,366
Net Loans & Leases	2,515,625	2,448,096	2,044,514	2,151,547	1,067,636	990,827	880,222	828,241
Total Assets	3,910,572	3,708,888	3,568,893	3,488,306	1,973,424	1,890,376	1,872,626	1,765,100
Total Deposits	3,017,623	2,967,236	2,847,272	2,789,524	1,606,217	1,561,702	1,554,271	1,475,841
Long–Term Obligations	292,210	155,373	157,393	167,893	185	200	8,000	9,000
Total Liabilities	3,440,775	3,250,839	3,138,554	3,098,850	1,704,695	1,640,795	1,630,787	1,541,175
Net Stockholders' Equity	469,797	458,049	430,339	389,456	268,729	249,581	241,839	223,925
Shares Outstanding	23,931	23,801	23,684	23,639	14,704	14,799	14,879	15,559
Statistical Record								
Return on Equity %	3.21	12.16	12.76	10.96	10.79	11.10	10.76	10.66
Return on Assets %	0.38	1.50	1.53	1.22	1.46	1.46	1.39	1.35
Equity/Assets %	12.01	12.35	12.05	11.16	13.61	13.20	12.91	12.68
Non–Int. Exp./Tot. Inc. %	41.28	41.01	38.08	37.66	34.26	35.51	35.19	35.04
Price Range	37.37–33.83	37.91–26.53	36.15–25.43	30.23–17.52	27.53–17.80	30.23–25.05	31.44–24.01	31.40–20.73
P/E Ratio	15.90–14.40	16.13–11.29	15.65–11.01	16.79–9.73	14.80–9.57	17.28–14.32	19.06–14.55	20.66–13.64
Average Yield %	2.85	3.19	3.13	3.64	3.55	2.61	2.31	2.33

Address: 333 East Main Street, Midland, MI 48640–0569	Officers: Frank P. Popoff – Chmn., David B. Ramaker – Pres., C.E.O.	Investor Contact:989–839–5350
Telephone: (989) 839–5350	Transfer Agents:Computershare Investor Services, LLC, Chicago, IL	Institutional Holding
Web Site: www.chemicalbankmi.com		No of Institutions: 12
		Shares: 174,928 % Held: –

CHEVRONTEXACO CORP.

Exchange	Symbol	Price	52Wk Range	Yield	P/E
NYS	CVX	$90.40 (5/28/2004)	94.39-70.67	3.23	11.74

*7 Year Price Score 96.0   *NYSE Composite Index=100   ***12 Month Price Score 53.9**

Interim Earnings (Per Share)

Qtr.	Mar	Jun	Sep	Dec
2001	2.49	2.06	1.82	(2.67)
2002	0.68	0.39	(0.85)	0.85
2003	1.81	1.50	2.02	1.81
2004	2.37	...	...	...

Interim Dividends (Per Share)

Amt	Decl	Ex	Rec	Pay
0.73Q	7/30/2003	8/15/2003	8/19/2003	9/10/2003
0.73Q	10/29/2003	11/14/2003	11/18/2003	12/10/2003
0.73Q	1/28/2004	2/13/2004	2/18/2004	3/10/2004
0.73Q	4/28/2004	5/17/2004	5/19/2004	6/10/2004
Indicated Div: $2.92 (Div. Reinv. Plan)				

Valuation Analysis

Forecast P/E 12.14 (5/24/2004)

Market Cap	$96.5 Billion	Book Value	38.2 Billion
Price/Book	2.44	Price/Sales	0.76

Dividend Achiever Status

Rank	254	10 Year Growth Rate	5.03%
Total Years of Dividend Growth			16

Business Summary: Oil and Gas (MIC: 14.2 SIC: 2911 NAIC:324110)

ChevronTexaco is a global energy company engaged in fully integrated petroleum operations, chemicals operations and coal mining activities. Co. also holds investments in power generation and gasification businesses. Petroleum operations consist of exploring for, developing and producing crude oil and natural gas; refining crude oil into finished petroleum products; marketing crude oil, natural gas and the many products derived from petroleum; and transporting crude oil, natural gas and petroleum products. As of Dec 31 2003, net proved reserves of natural gas were 20,191 billion cubic feet and net proved reserves of crude oil, condensate and natural gas liquids totaled 8,599 million barrels.

Recent Developments: For the three months ended Mar 31 2004, income from continuing operations was $2.53 billion compared with $2.08 billion in the corresponding year-earlier period. Results for 2004 and 2003 included special charges of $55.0 million and $39.0 million, respectively. Total revenues and other income advanced 9.1% to $33.57 billion the previous year. Exploration and production income improved to $1.95 billion versus $1.94 billion last year. Refining, marketing and transportation income climbed to $640.0 million from $315.0 million the year before, reflecting increased demand for refined products.

Prospects: Co. continues to actively invest in its future. For instance, capital and exploratory expenditures for the quarter ended Mar 31 2004 were $1.70 billion versus $1.50 billion in the prior-year period. The increase from 2003 included about $150.0 million related to its share of expenditures by the 50.0%-owned Tengizchevroil affiliate for the expansion of production operations for the Tengiz and Korolev fields in Kazakhstan. Co. noted that expenditures for international exploration and production projects in 2004 were nearly $900.0 million, or slightly more than 50.0% of the total expenditures, reflecting its continued emphasis on international crude oil and natural gas production activities.

Financial Data
(US$ in Millions)

	3 Mos	12/31/2003	12/31/2002	12/31/2001	12/31/2000	12/31/1999	12/31/1998	12/31/1997
Earnings Per Share	7.70	7.14	1.07	3.70	7.97	3.14	2.04	4.95
Cash Flow Per Share	3.26	11.57	9.34	10.77	13.30	6.79	5.67	6.96
Tang. Book Val. Per Share	35.66	33.94	29.58	31.81	31.08	27.04	25.80	26.63
Dividends Per Share	2.890	2.860	2.800	2.650	2.600	2.480	2.440	2.280
Dividend Payout %	38.28	40.05	261.68	71.62	32.62	78.98	119.60	46.06
Income Statement								
Total Revenues	33,122	120,732	98,938	105,101	51,379	36,060	30,329	41,262
Total Indirect Exp.	7,063	28,301	29,174	28,801	9,930	9,394	9,448	10,633
Depreciation & Amort.	1,192	5,384	5,231	7,059	2,848	2,866	2,320	2,300
Operating Income	4,353	13,324	4,778	9,245	9,730	4,120	2,239	5,814
Net Interest Inc./(Exp.)	(93)	(474)	(565)	(833)	(460)	(472)	(405)	(312)
Income Taxes	1,710	5,344	3,024	4,360	4,085	1,578	495	2,246
Income from Cont Ops	2,528	7,426	...	3,931	...	...	...	...
Net Income	2,562	7,230	1,132	3,288	5,185	2,070	1,339	3,256
Average Shs. Outstg.	1,066	1,064	1,063	1,062	651	659	657	658
Balance Sheet								
Cash & Cash Equivalents	6,881	5,267	3,781	3,150	2,630	2,032	1,413	1,670
Total Current Assets	22,845	19,426	17,776	18,327	8,213	8,297	6,297	7,006
Total Assets	85,107	81,470	77,359	77,572	41,264	40,668	36,540	35,473
Total Current Liabilities	17,847	16,111	19,876	20,654	7,674	8,889	7,166	6,946
Long-Term Obligations	10,880	10,894	10,911	8,989	5,153	5,485	4,393	4,431
Net Stockholders' Equity	38,166	36,295	31,604	33,958	19,925	17,749	17,034	17,472
Net Working Capital	4,998	3,315	(2,100)	(2,327)	539	(592)	(869)	60
Shares Outstanding	1,070	1,069	1,068	1,067	641	656	660	655
Operating Profit Margin %	11.80	10.18	4.71	7.70	17.47	9.96	6.63	12.42
Net Profit Margin %	16.61	14.15	7.14	10.94	24.53	13.03	6.92	17.11
Return on Equity %	5.46	17.62	3.23	8.20	22.25	8.69	6.52	14.69
Return on Assets %	2.44	7.85	1.31	3.59	10.74	3.79	3.04	7.23
Debt/Total Assets %	12.78	13.37	14.10	11.58	12.48	13.48	12.02	12.49
Price Range	90.70-84.43	86.39-61.85	90.86-65.90	98.03-78.77	94.31-71.06	103.5-73.69	88.94-71.13	88.69-62.25
P/E Ratio	11.78-10.96	12.10-8.66	84.92-61.59	26.49-21.29	11.83-8.92	32.96-23.47	43.60-34.87	17.92-12.58
Average Yield %	3.32	4.04	3.51	2.98	3.07	2.76	3.00	3.06

Address: 6001 Bollinger Canyon Road, San Ramon, CA 94583-2324	Officers: David J. OReilly - Chmn., C.E.O., Peter J. Robertson - Vice-Chmn.	Investor Contact:415-894-5690
Telephone: (925) 842-1000	Transfer Agents:Mellon Investor Services, Ridgefield Park, NJ	**Institutional Holding** No of Institutions: 30
Web Site: www.chevrontexaco.com		Shares: 278,790 % Held: –

CHITTENDEN CORP. (BURLINGTON, VT.)

Exchange	Symbol	Price	52Wk Range	Yield	P/E
NYS	CHZ	$32.41 (5/28/2004)	34.45-27.30	2.72	15.81

*7 Year Price Score 118.2 *NYSE Composite Index=100 ***12 Month Price Score 46.2**

Interim Earnings (Per Share)

Qtr.	Mar	Jun	Sep	Dec
2001	0.44	0.44	0.46	0.46
2002	0.46	0.47	0.48	0.55
2003	0.49	0.51	0.54	0.53
2004	0.47	...	...	...

Interim Dividends (Per Share)

Amt	Decl	Ex	Rec	Pay
0.20Q	7/17/2003	7/30/2003	8/1/2003	8/15/2003
0.20Q	10/16/2003	10/29/2003	10/31/2003	11/14/2003
0.20Q	1/22/2004	1/28/2004	1/30/2004	2/13/2004
0.22Q	4/21/2004	4/28/2004	4/30/2004	5/14/2004

Indicated Div: $0.88 (Div. Reinv. Plan)

Valuation Analysis

Forecast P/E 14.37 (5/24/2004)

Market Cap $1.0 Billion	Book Value 599.5 Million
Price/Book 2.01	Price/Sales 3.29

Dividend Achiever Status

Rank 11	10 Year Growth Rate	25.35%

Total Years of Dividend Growth 11

Business Summary: Commercial Banking (MIC: 8.1 SIC: 6022 NAIC:522110)

Chittenden is a bank holding company with assets totaling $5.90 billion as of Dec 31 2003. Through its subsidiaries, Co. is engaged in providing financial services. Co. offers a variety of lending services, including commercial loans and residential real estate loans. In addition, Co. offers acceptance of demand, savings, money market, cash management and time deposits. Co. also provides personal trust services, including services as executor, trustee, administrator, custodian and guardian. Corporate trust services are also provided, including services as trustee for pension and profit sharing plans. Asset management services are provided for personal and corporate trust clients.

Recent Developments: For the quarter ended Mar 31 2004, net income grew 5.3% to $17.5 million versus $16.6 million in the equivalent 2003 quarter. Results for 2004 included a loss on prepayments of borrowings of $1.2 million and charges of $152,000 from conversion and restructuring items. Total interest income declined 1.5% to $64.9 million, while total interest expense fell 31.9% to $10.1 million. Provision for loan losses dropped 79.2% to $427,000 versus $2.1 million a year earlier, reflecting significantly lower net charge-offs, strong asset quality, and minimal growth in the total loan portfolio. Total noninterest income decreased 6.5% to $18.0 million. Total noninterest expense rose 5.8% to $44.6 million.

Prospects: Going forward, Co. should continue to report solid growth in most of its core businesses. Co.'s banks continue their strong growth in commercial lending by increasing their commercial and commercial real estate portfolios. However, the volatility of market interest rates and the timing of their movements have adversely impacted the mortgage banking business. Nevertheless, the interest rate dip in March 2004 led to significant mortgage application activity late in the first quarter, which should bode well for the better mortgage gains in the near future.

Financial Data

(US$ in Thousands)	3 Mos	12/31/2003	12/31/2002	12/31/2001	12/31/2000	12/31/1999	12/31/1998	12/31/1997
Earnings Per Share	2.05	2.07	1.96	1.80	1.72	(0.07)	1.67	1.55
Tang. Book Val. Per Share	9.52	8.96	10.81	9.43	9.13	9.69	9.17	8.23
Dividends Per Share	0.800	0.800	0.790	0.760	0.750	0.680	0.620	1.030
Dividend Payout %	39.02	38.64	40.30	42.55	43.72	N.M.	37.32	66.39
Income Statement								
Total Interest Income	64,858	271,442	259,019	266,497	288,102	288,216	151,511	150,189
Total Interest Expense	10,145	53,379	66,404	96,192	121,030	113,235	60,508	59,545
Net Interest Income	54,713	218,063	192,615	170,305	167,072	174,981	91,003	90,644
Provision for Loan Losses	427	7,175	8,331	8,041	8,700	8,700	5,100	4,050
Non-Interest Income	18,007	95,480	65,060	63,733	54,810	64,226	32,402	28,210
Non-Interest Expense	44,608	191,371	151,544	135,760	126,462	203,929	71,767	70,072
Income Before Taxes	27,685	116,548	97,800	90,237	86,720	26,578	46,538	44,732
Net Income	17,467	74,799	63,645	58,501	58,687	(2,496)	30,665	29,406
Average Shs. Outstg.	37,218	36,120	32,495	32,547	34,100	35,795	18,353	18,958
Balance Sheet								
Securities Avail. for Sale	1,473,497	3,176,302	2,994,222	1,652,990	1,170,562	1,298,942	1,007,398	726,558
Net Loans & Leases	3,722,667	3,667,220	2,925,666	2,792,909	2,815,843	2,854,651	1,375,593	1,372,417
Total Assets	5,807,632	5,900,644	4,920,544	4,153,714	3,769,861	3,827,297	2,122,019	1,977,150
Total Deposits	4,834,342	4,969,891	4,126,092	3,669,846	3,292,407	3,204,098	1,890,754	1,757,545
Long-Term Obligations	...	162,434	173,654	44,409	93,757	197,072	23,369	2,239
Total Liabilities	5,208,147	5,320,693	4,501,752	3,783,060	3,427,795	3,464,837	1,946,872	1,791,627
Net Stockholders' Equity	599,485	579,951	418,792	370,654	342,066	362,460	175,147	162,273
Shares Outstanding	36,763	36,636	31,939	35,743	35,736	35,472	17,727	18,026
Statistical Record								
Return on Equity %	2.91	12.89	15.19	15.78	17.15	N.M.	17.50	18.12
Return on Assets %	0.30	1.26	1.29	1.40	1.55	N.M.	1.44	1.48
Equity/Assets %	10.32	9.82	8.51	8.92	9.07	9.47	8.25	8.20
Non-Int. Exp./Tot. Inc. %	53.83	51.93	46.76	41.11	36.87	57.86	39.02	39.27
Price Range	34.35-32.10	34.45-24.96	34.05-23.57	28.75-21.90	25.00-18.40	26.70-21.10	31.60-20.80	28.80-14.88
P/E Ratio	16.76-15.66	16.64-12.06	17.37-12.03	15.97-12.17	14.53-10.70	N/A	18.92-12.46	18.58-9.60
Average Yield %	2.42	2.78	2.76	3.01	3.50	2.92	2.27	4.85

Address: Two Burlington Square, Burlington, VT 05401

Telephone: (802) 658-4000

Web Site: www.chittendencorp.com

Officers: Paul A. Perrault - Chmn., Pres., C.E.O., Kirk W. Walters - Exec. V.P., C.F.O., Treas.

Transfer Agents: BankBoston, N.A., Boston, MA

Investor Contact: 802 660 1412

Institutional Holding

No of Institutions: 2

Shares: 124,562   **% Held:** -

CHUBB CORP.

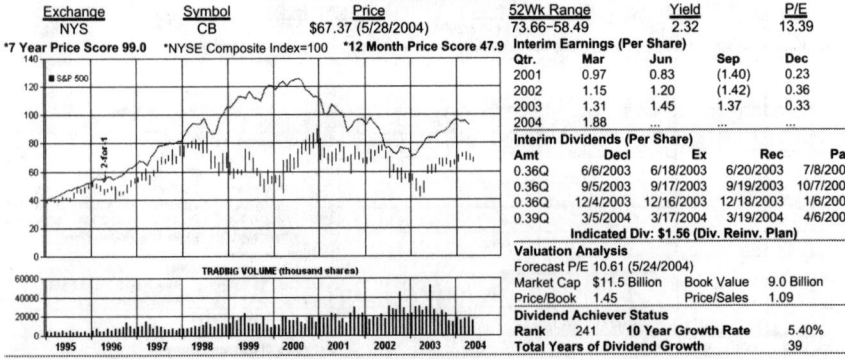

Interim Earnings (Per Share)

Qtr.	Mar	Jun	Sep	Dec
2001	0.97	0.83	(1.40)	0.23
2002	1.15	1.20	(1.42)	0.36
2003	1.31	1.45	1.37	0.33
2004	1.88	...	...	...

Interim Dividends (Per Share)

Amt	Decl	Ex	Rec	Pay
0.36Q	6/6/2003	6/18/2003	6/20/2003	7/8/2003
0.36Q	9/5/2003	9/17/2003	9/19/2003	10/7/2003
0.36Q	12/4/2003	12/16/2003	12/18/2003	1/6/2004
0.39Q	3/5/2004	3/17/2004	3/19/2004	4/6/2004

Indicated Div: $1.56 (Div. Reinv. Plan)

Valuation Analysis
Forecast P/E 10.61 (5/24/2004)
Market Cap $11.5 Billion   Book Value 9.0 Billion
Price/Book 1.45   Price/Sales 1.09

Dividend Achiever Status
Rank 241   10 Year Growth Rate 5.40%
Total Years of Dividend Growth 39

Business Summary: Insurance (MIC: 8.2 SIC: 6331 NAIC:524126)

Chubb is engaged in the property and casualty insurance business. Operations are divided into three strategic business units. Chubb Commercial Insurance specializes in commercial customer insurance products, including coverage for multiple peril, casualty, workers' compensation and property and marine. Chubb Specialty Insurance provides executive protection and professional liability products for privately and publicly owned companies. Chubb Specialty Insurance also includes Co.'s surety and accident businesses, as well as its reinsurance business. Chubb Personal Insurance offers products for individuals who require more coverage choices and higher limits than standard insurance policies.

Recent Developments: For the quarter ended Mar 31 2004, net income jumped 60.6% to $360.7 million from $224.6 million in the prior-year quarter. Results included realized after-tax investment gains of $52.6 million and $2.9 million, respectively. Also, results for 2004 and 2003 included after-tax losses of $9.3 million and $9.1 million, respectively, from Co.'s non-insurance business, Chubb Financial Solutions. Net premiums written advanced 12.8% to $3.02 billion. Premiums earned climbed 20.2% to $2.79 billion from $2.33 billion the previous year. Underwriting income surged 154.5% to $178.4 million. Investment income rose 12.7% to $277.7 million. Co.'s combined ratio improved to 92.6% from 95.3% a year earlier.

Prospects: Results are benefiting from the earn-through of higher premiums and favorable loss experience, including unusually low commercial property losses. Meanwhile, Co. continues to enjoy strong premium growth by attracting new customers, securing rate increases when needed and retaining a high percentage of its existing customers, all while maintaining underwriting discipline. Going forward, Co. expects to continue to benefit from higher earned premiums and favorable terms and conditions. Accordingly, Co. is well on its way to achieve or exceed its operating earnings guidance of $5.90 to $6.30 per share for 2004.

Financial Data

(US$ in Thousands)	3 Mos	12/31/2003	12/31/2002	12/31/2001	12/31/2000	12/31/1999	12/31/1998	12/31/1997
Earnings Per Share	5.03	4.46	1.29	0.63	4.01	3.66	4.19	4.39
Tang. Book Val. Per Share	45.22	42.85	37.33	35.61	37.12	32.84	34.78	32.10
Dividends Per Share	1.440	1.430	1.390	1.350	1.310	1.270	1.220	1.140
Dividend Payout %	28.63	32.06	107.75	214.28	32.66	34.76	29.11	25.96
Income Statement								
Total Premium Income	2,794,000	10,182,500	8,085,300	6,656,400	6,145,900	5,652,000	5,303,800	5,157,400
Other Income	384,300	1,211,500	1,055,000	1,097,600	1,105,600	1,077,600	1,046,000	1,506,600
Total Revenues	3,178,300	11,394,000	9,140,300	7,754,000	7,251,500	6,729,600	6,349,800	6,664,000
Total Indirect Exp.	2,689,300	2,709,100	2,187,100	1,855,000	1,722,600	1,588,400	1,537,700	1,415,400
Inc. Before Inc. Taxes	489,000	933,600	168,400	(66,000)	851,000	710,100	849,700	974,100
Income Taxes	128,300	124,800	(54,500)	(177,500)	136,400	89,000	142,700	204,600
Net Income	360,700	808,800	222,900	111,500	714,600	621,100	707,000	769,500
Average Shs. Outstg.	191,700	181,300	172,900	175,800	178,300	169,800	168,600	176,200
Balance Sheet								
Cash & Cash Equivalents	1,482,400	3,452,900	3,153,400	1,400,100	1,079,100	1,223,300	352,500	736,600
Premiums Due	5,755,100	2,474,800	2,287,500	1,940,500	1,656,600	1,477,600	1,420,300	1,348,200
Invst. Assets: Total	28,463,800	28,157,900	23,236,800	19,234,200	18,128,800	17,188,300	15,501,300	14,839,600
Total Assets	40,631,500	38,360,600	34,114,400	29,449,000	25,026,700	23,537,000	20,746,000	19,615,600
Long-Term Obligations	2,814,900	2,813,900	1,959,100	1,351,000	753,800	759,200	607,500	398,600
Net Stockholders' Equity	9,046,400	8,522,000	6,859,200	6,525,300	6,981,700	6,271,800	5,644,100	5,657,100
Shares Outstanding	189,715	187,963	171,201	170,071	174,919	175,489	162,267	176,200
Return on Revenues %	11.34	7.09	2.43	1.43	9.85	9.22	11.13	11.54
Return on Equity %	3.98	9.49	3.24	1.70	10.23	9.90	12.52	13.60
Return on Assets %	0.88	2.10	0.65	0.37	2.85	2.63	3.40	3.92
Price Range	73.66-66.59	69.24-42.45	78.20-52.20	83.44-58.59	90.00-44.75	75.94-45.50	88.25-57.00	78.13-51.25
P/E Ratio	14.64-13.24	15.52-9.52	60.62-40.47	132.4-93.00	22.44-11.16	20.75-12.43	21.06-13.60	17.80-11.67
Average Yield %	2.05	2.41	2.11	1.90	1.91	2.11	1.66	1.78

Address: 15 Mountain View Road, Warren, NJ 07061-1615
Telephone: (908) 903 2000
Web Site: www.chubb.com

Officers: John D. Finnegan – Chmn., Pres., C.E.O., Michael OReilly – Vice-Chmn., C.F.O., Chief Invest. Officer
Transfer Agents: EquiServe Trust Company, N.A., Jersey City, NJ

Investor Contact: 908-903-3579
Institutional Holding
No of Institutions: 23
Shares: 498,213   **% Held:** –

CINCINNATI FINANCIAL CORP.

Exchange	Symbol	Price	52Wk Range	Yield	P/E
NMS	CINF	$42.75 (5/28/2004)	43.32–35.20	2.57	15.45

*7 Year Price Score 107.8 *NYSE Composite Index=100 *12 Month Price Score 49.6

Interim Earnings (Per Share)

Qtr.	Mar	Jun	Sep	Dec
2001	0.41	0.28	0.20	0.24
2002	0.43	0.20	0.41	0.35
2003	0.33	0.49	0.60	0.78
2004	0.90	...	...	...

Interim Dividends (Per Share)

Amt	Decl	Ex	Rec	Pay
0.238Q	11/14/2003	12/19/2003	12/23/2003	1/15/2004
0.262Q	1/31/2004	3/22/2004	3/24/2004	4/15/2004
5%	1/31/2004	4/28/2004	4/30/2004	6/15/2004
0.275Q	5/21/2004	6/23/2004	6/25/2004	7/15/2004
Indicated Div: $1.10 (Div. Reinv. Plan)				

Valuation Analysis

Forecast P/E 15.31 (5/24/2004)

Market Cap	$6.9 Billion	Book Value	6.2 Billion
Price/Book	1.10	Price/Sales	2.05

Dividend Achiever Status

Rank	135	10 Year Growth Rate	11.33%
Total Years of Dividend Growth			43

Business Summary: Insurance (MIC: 8.2 SIC: 6331 NAIC:524126)

Cincinnati Financial offers property and casualty insurance, its main business, through The Cincinnati Insurance Company, The Cincinnati Indemnity Company and The Cincinnati Casualty Company. The Cincinnati Life Insurance Company markets life and disability income insurance and annuities. CFC Investment Company supports the insurance subsidiaries and their independent agent representatives through commercial leasing and financing activities. CinFin Capital Management Company provides asset management services to institutions, corporations and high net worth individuals.

Recent Developments: For the quarter ended Mar 31 2004, net income jumped to $146.0 million from $57.0 million in the prior–year quarter. Total revenues increased 23.1% to $870.0 million from $707.0 million the previous year. Revenues included realized investment gains of $7.0 million in 2004 and realized investment losses of $62.0 million in 2003. Earned property casualty premiums grew 13.8% to $716.0 million versus $629.0 million a year earlier. Life insurance premiums earned increased 14.3% to $24.0 million. Net investment income improved 3.4% to $120.0 million. Insurance losses and policyholder benefit expenses declined 1.4% to $434.0 million.

Prospects: Going forward, Co.'s personal lines should continue to benefit from by higher rates. However, Co. has not reached an overall performance level that it considers satisfactory. To address this shortfall, Co. will continue with a number of actions designed to improve underwriting and pricing deficiencies. While there is more competition for the high–quality accounts, Co. believes it will be able to obtain renewal price increases that average in the single digits. For full–year 2004, Co. expects written premium growth in the high single digits and a combined ratio of about 94.0%. Co. is also confident in its ability to achieve investment income growth of 3.5% to 4.5% for the year.

Financial Data

(US$ in Thousands)	3 Mos	12/31/2003	12/31/2002	12/31/2001	12/31/2000	12/31/1999	12/31/1998	12/31/1997
Earnings Per Share	2.77	2.20	1.39	1.13	0.69	1.44	1.34	1.68
Tang. Book Val. Per Share	38.74	36.92	32.91	35.26	35.48	31.86	32.11	27.00
Dividends Per Share	0.950	0.920	0.830	0.780	0.700	0.630	0.560	0.500
Dividend Payout %	34.42	42.09	60.10	68.90	101.37	43.63	42.31	30.13
Income Statement								
Total Premium Income	740,000	2,748,000	2,478,000	2,152,000	1,906,922	1,731,950	1,612,735	1,516,378
Net Investment Income	120,000	...	...	...	...	...	...	...
Other Income	10,000	433,000	365,000	409,000	424,072	396,273	441,554	426,006
Total Revenues	870,000	3,181,000	2,843,000	2,561,000	2,330,994	2,128,223	2,054,289	1,942,384
Total Indirect Exp.	183,000	686,000	628,000	559,000	539,104	445,649	416,810	382,417
Inc. Before Inc. Taxes	201,000	480,000	279,000	221,000	108,664	321,573	307,107	394,559
Income Taxes	55,000	106,000	41,000	28,000	(9,701)	66,851	65,540	95,184
Net Income	146,000	374,000	238,000	193,000	118,365	254,722	241,567	299,375
Average Shs. Outstg.	162,059	169,802	171,352	170,100	172,117	177,045	180,681	179,334
Balance Sheet								
Cash & Cash Equivalents	162,000	91,000	112,000	93,000	60,254	339,554	58,611	80,168
Premiums Due	1,858,000	1,716,000	1,516,000	1,274,000	897,634	358,745	332,510	299,364
Invst. Assets: Total	12,509,000	12,527,000	11,257,000	11,571,000	11,315,836	10,194,239	10,324,950	8,797,050
Total Assets	15,738,000	15,509,000	14,059,000	13,959,000	13,287,091	11,380,214	11,086,503	9,493,425
Long–Term Obligations	420,000	420,000	420,000	426,000	449,234	456,373	471,520	58,430
Net Stockholders' Equity	6,199,000	6,204,000	5,598,000	5,998,000	5,994,995	5,421,284	5,620,936	4,716,965
Shares Outstanding	160,000	168,000	170,100	170,100	168,935	170,122	175,015	174,673
Return on Revenues %	16.78	10.68	7.14	6.01	3.49	10.41	10.39	14.34
Return on Equity %	2.35	5.48	3.62	2.56	1.36	4.08	3.79	5.90
Return on Assets %	0.92	2.19	1.44	1.10	0.61	1.94	1.92	2.93
Price Range	43.32–39.44	39.81–32.05	44.80–31.13	40.67–33.63	40.83–25.48	40.24–28.69	44.68–29.29	44.68–19.68
P/E Ratio	15.64–14.24	18.10–14.57	32.23–22.40	35.99–29.76	59.18–36.92	27.94–19.92	33.35–21.86	26.60–11.72
Average Yield %	2.30	2.51	2.16	2.11	2.06	1.80	1.49	1.93

Address: 6200 S. Gilmore Road, Fairfield, OH 45014–5141
Telephone: (513) 870–2000
Web Site: www.cinfin.com

Officers: John J. Schiff – Chmn., Pres., C.E.O., James E. Benoski – Vice–Chmn., Chief Insurance Officer
Transfer Agents: Cincinnati Financial Corporation, Fairfield, OH

Investor Contact: 513–870–2639
Institutional Holding
No of Institutions: 4
Shares: 26,364 **% Held:** –

CINTAS CORPORATION

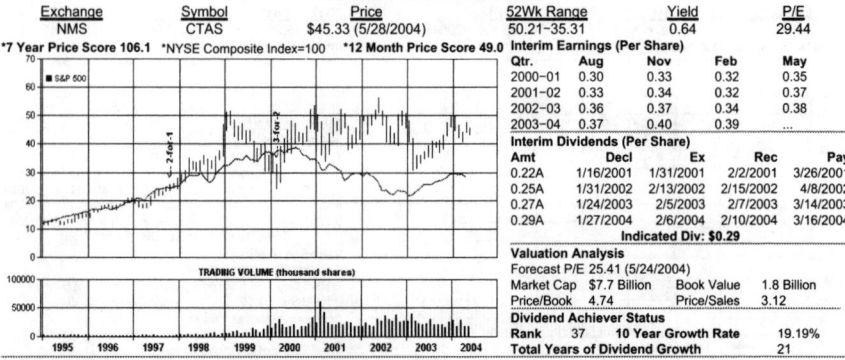

Exchange	Symbol	Price	52Wk Range	Yield	P/E
NMS	CTAS	$45.33 (5/28/2004)	50.21–35.31	0.64	29.44

*7 Year Price Score 106.1 ***NYSE Composite Index=100** ***12 Month Price Score 49.0**

Interim Earnings (Per Share)

Qtr.	Aug	Nov	Feb	May
2000–01	0.30	0.33	0.32	0.35
2001–02	0.33	0.34	0.32	0.37
2002–03	0.36	0.37	0.34	0.38
2003–04	0.37	0.40	0.39	...

Interim Dividends (Per Share)

Amt	Decl	Ex	Rec	Pay
0.22A	1/16/2001	1/31/2001	2/2/2001	3/26/2001
0.25A	1/31/2002	2/13/2002	2/15/2002	4/8/2002
0.27A	1/24/2003	2/5/2003	2/7/2003	3/14/2003
0.29A	1/27/2004	2/6/2004	2/10/2004	3/16/2004

Indicated Div: $0.29

Valuation Analysis
Forecast P/E 25.41 (5/24/2004)

Market Cap	$7.7 Billion	Book Value	1.8 Billion
Price/Book	4.74	Price/Sales	3.12

Dividend Achiever Status

Rank	37	10 Year Growth Rate	19.19%
Total Years of Dividend Growth		21

Business Summary: Apparel (MIC: 4.4 SIC: 2326 NAIC:315225)

Cintas designs, manufactures, and implements corporate identity uniform programs, provides entrance mats, restroom supplies, promotional products, and first aid and safety products for over 500,000 businesses. Co. classifies its businesses into two operating segments: Rentals and Other Services. The Rentals operating segment designs and manufactures corporate identity uniforms which it rents, along with other items, to its customers. The Other Services operating segment involves the design, manufacture and direct sale of uniforms to its customers as well as the sale of ancillary services including sanitation supplies, first aid and safety products and services and cleanroom supplies.

Recent Developments: For the quarter ended Feb 29 2004, net income increased 12.6% to $66.5 million from $59.1 million in the prior–year quarter. Earnings benefited from higher organic revenue growth, cost containment initiatives and lower outstanding debt levels. Total revenue increased 5.0% to $696.9 million from $663.8 million the previous year. Rental revenue rose 4.6% to $547.5 million, while other services revenue grew 6.3% to $149.5 million. Cost of rentals increased 3.2% to $303.5 million. Cost of other services rose 2.5% to $97.8 million. Gross margins improved to 42.4% from 41.3% a year earlier. Interest expense dropped 19.9% to $6.0 million.

Prospects: Going forward, although Co. should begin to benefit from the job recovery in several service–providing industries, some customers will likely continue to experience pressures in their business and, as a result, Co.'s revenue base may not experience significant growth for the next several quarters. Nevertheless, Co. will continue to focus on growing organically in this environment, mainly through the continued sale of new rental programs and the cross–selling of rental services such as entrance mats and hygiene services to its existing customers. For the full year, Co. expects revenue of about $2.78 billion to $2.82 billion and earnings per share of about $1.55 to $1.59.

Financial Data

(US$ in Thousands)	9 Mos	6 Mos	3 Mos	05/31/2003	05/31/2002	05/31/2001	05/31/2000	05/31/1999
Earnings Per Share	1.54	1.49	1.46	1.45	1.36	1.30	1.14	0.82
Cash Flow Per Share	2.09	1.45	0.41	1.92	2.19	1.43	1.51	1.19
Tang. Book Val. Per Share	6.16	5.07	4.63	5.41	4.38	7.26	6.19	5.23
Dividends Per Share	0.270	0.270	0.270	0.270	0.250	0.220	0.180	0.140
Dividend Payout %	17.53	18.12	18.49	18.62	18.38	16.92	16.37	17.88
Income Statement								
Total Revenues	2,075,905	1,378,965	677,656	2,686,585	2,271,052	2,160,700	1,901,991	1,751,568
Total Indirect Exp.	542,446	357,427	180,473	695,437	580,469	528,354	455,794	403,580
Depreciation & Amort.	107,195	71,334	35,435	143,061	120,025	112,089	99,513	90,228
Operating Income	334,150	223,458	106,975	423,771	376,901	367,913	323,758	281,282
Net Interest Inc./(Exp.)	(17,527)	(12,375)	(6,467)	(28,012)	(5,316)	(10,750)	(11,165)	(11,771)
Income Taxes	117,146	78,099	37,181	146,506	137,334	134,003	118,372	85,055
Net Income	199,477	132,984	63,327	249,253	234,251	222,451	193,387	138,939
Average Shs. Outstg.	172,215	172,021	171,922	172,037	172,244	171,629	169,987	169,341
Balance Sheet								
Cash & Cash Equivalents	113,752	98,596	54,914	57,659	85,086	110,229	109,822	88,118
Total Current Assets	1,033,032	997,457	897,381	877,544	853,250	819,670	721,470	634,485
Total Assets	2,755,004	2,694,943	2,596,126	2,582,946	2,519,234	1,752,224	1,581,342	1,407,818
Total Current Liabilities	345,045	322,251	259,295	304,839	312,634	250,903	235,392	212,097
Long–Term Obligations	482,576	482,850	527,714	534,763	703,250	220,940	254,378	283,581
Net Stockholders' Equity	1,810,732	1,788,418	1,709,978	1,646,332	1,423,759	1,231,315	1,042,876	871,423
Shares Outstanding	171,174	170,890	170,731	170,599	169,930	169,370	168,281	166,423
Statistical Record								
Operating Profit Margin %	16.09	16.20	15.78	15.77	16.59	17.02	17.02	16.05
Return on Equity %	11.02	7.43	3.70	15.13	16.45	18.06	18.54	15.94
Return on Assets %	7.24	4.93	2.43	9.65	9.29	12.69	12.22	9.86
Debt/Total Assets %	17.52	17.91	20.32	20.70	27.91	12.60	16.08	20.14
Price Range	50.21–35.31	47.47–35.31	41.21–35.31	52.21–30.90	56.28–37.92	53.56–34.00	45.19–24.25	51.67–27.17
P/E Ratio	32.60–22.93	31.86–23.70	28.22–24.18	36.01–21.31	41.38–27.88	41.20–26.15	39.64–21.27	63.01–33.13
Average Yield %	0.64	0.67	0.71	0.64	0.53	0.50	0.49	0.36

Address: 6800 Cintas Boulevard, Cincinnati, OH 45262–5737 **Telephone:** (513) 459–1200 **Web Site:** www.cintas.com	**Officers:** Richard T. Farmer – Chmn., Robert J. Kohlhepp – Vice–Chmn. **Transfer Agents:** Computershare Investor Services LLC, Chicago, IL	**Investor Contact:** 513–459–1200 **Institutional Holding** **No of Institutions:** 17 **Shares:** 11,895,379 **% Held:** –

CITIGROUP INC

Exchange	Symbol	Price	52Wk Range	Yield	P/E
NYS	C	$46.43 (5/28/2004)	52.29–41.37	3.45	12.76

*7 Year Price Score 119.5   *NYSE Composite Index=100   *12 Month Price Score 46.7

Interim Earnings (Per Share)

Qtr.	Mar	Jun	Sep	Dec
2001	0.70	0.71	0.61	0.73
2002	0.94	0.78	0.72	0.15
2003	0.79	0.83	0.90	0.90
2004	1.01	...	...	...

Interim Dividends (Per Share)

Amt	Decl	Ex	Rec	Pay
0.35Q	7/14/2003	7/31/2003	8/4/2003	8/22/2003
0.35Q	10/21/2003	10/30/2003	11/3/2003	11/26/2003
0.40Q	1/20/2004	1/29/2004	2/2/2004	2/27/2004
0.40Q	4/20/2004	4/29/2004	5/3/2004	5/28/2004

Indicated Div: $1.60 (Div. Reinv. Plan)

Valuation Analysis

Forecast P/E 11.78 (5/24/2004)

Market Cap	$235.0 Billion	Book Value	100.8 Billion
Price/Book	2.66	Price/Sales	2.75

Dividend Achiever Status

Rank	6	10 Year Growth Rate	29.70%
Total Years of Dividend Growth	17	

TRADING VOLUME (thousand shares)

Business Summary: Commercial Banking (MIC: 8.1 SIC: 6021 NAIC:523930)

Citigroup is a bank holding company that provides financial services to consumers and corporations. Co.'s Global Consumer segment delivers banking, lending, insurance and investment services. Co.'s Global Corporate and Investment Bank segment provides corporations, governments, institutions and investors with financial products and services. Co.'s Private Client Services segment provides investment advice, financial planning and brokerage services. Co.'s Global Investment Management segment offers life insurance, annuity, asset management and personalized wealth management products and services. Proprietary Investment Activities include private equity investments and other investments.

Recent Developments: For the first quarter ended Mar 31 2004, net income grew 28.5% to $5.27 billion compared with $4.10 billion in the equivalent 2003 quarter. Earnings in the 2004 quarter included the results of the acquisition of the Sears Credit Card and Financial Products business, The Home Depot private label card portfolios, and the consumer finance business of Washington Mutual. In addition, results for 2004 included a $180.0 million after-tax gain from the sale of a portion of Co.'s electronic funds services business. Co. achieved double-digit income growth in each of its nine products as well as in every one of the regions in which it operates. Total revenues climbed 12.0% to $25.98 billion.

Prospects: During the 2004 first quarter, Co. announced its intended acquisition of KorAm Bank, the sixth-largest commercial bank in Korea with over 200 branches across Korea for $2.73 billion. KorAm Bank shareholders accepted Co.'s bid on Apr 30 2004. Co. will likely close the deal in May 2004. Meanwhile, Co. executed a risk capital allocation model, which should give it a more refined set of tools to make investment decisions across the businesses and geographies in which Co. operates. Also, as global economies continue to strengthen around the world, interest rates are expected to rise. Consequently, Co. has positioned itself to benefit modestly over the medium-term from a higher rate environment.

Financial Data

(US$ in Millions)	3 Mos	12/31/2003	12/31/2002	12/31/2001	12/31/2000	12/31/1999	12/31/1998	12/31/1997
Earnings Per Share	3.64	3.42	2.59	2.75	2.62	2.14	1.21	1.27
Tang. Book Val. Per Share	11.26	10.74	9.69	15.57	12.83	10.63	8.94	6.98
Dividends Per Share	1.300	1.100	0.700	0.600	0.520	0.400	0.270	0.200
Dividend Payout %	35.62	32.16	27.02	21.81	19.84	18.88	22.83	15.74
Income Statement								
Total Premium Income	879	3,749	3,410	13,460	12,429	10,441	9,850	8,995
Net Investment Income	15,822	57,047	58,939	66,565	64,939	44,900	46,239	17,618
Other Income	9,275	33,917	30,207	31,997	34,458	26,664	20,342	10,996
Total Revenues	25,976	94,713	92,556	112,022	111,826	82,005	76,431	37,609
Total Indirect Exp.	10,346	39,168	37,298	39,601	38,559	29,781	28,551	36,049
Inc. Before Inc. Taxes	7,740	26,333	20,537	21,897	21,143	15,948	9,269	5,012
Income Taxes	2,398	8,195	6,998	7,526	7,525	5,703	3,234	1,696
Eqty Earns/Minority Int.	(69)	(285)	(91)	(87)	(99)	(251)	(228)	(212)
Income from Cont Ops	...	...	13,448	14,284	...	9,994	...	...
Net Income	5,273	17,853	15,276	14,126	13,519	9,867	5,807	3,104
Average Shs. Outstg.	5,203	5,193	5,166	5,147	5,122	4,591	4,630	2,359
Balance Sheet								
Cash & Cash Equivalents	462,524	40,926	33,708	37,731	30,785	27,587	25,480	4,033
Premiums Due	39,757	31,053	29,714	47,528	36,237	32,677	30,905	30,939
Invst. Assets: Total	435,538	418,211	324,721	305,741	252,635	222,281	223,517	201,566
Total Assets	1,317,591	1,264,032	1,097,190	1,051,450	902,210	716,937	668,641	386,555
Long-Term Obligations	178,588	162,702	126,927	121,631	111,778	47,092	48,671	28,352
Net Stockholders' Equity	101,884	98,014	86,718	81,200	66,206	49,686	42,568	18,368
Shares Outstanding	5,171	5,156	5,140	5,118	5,022	4,490	4,515	2,289
Return on Revenues %	20.30	18.84	14.52	12.75	12.08	12.18	7.59	8.25
Return on Equity %	5.18	18.21	15.50	17.59	20.41	20.11	13.59	14.85
Return on Assets %	0.40	1.41	1.22	1.35	1.49	1.39	0.86	0.80
Price Range	51.94–48.11	49.00–31.42	52.00–26.73	56.30–36.36	58.38–36.05	43.59–24.75	36.50–15.88	28.28–14.83
P/E Ratio	14.27–13.22	14.33–9.19	20.08–10.32	20.47–13.22	22.28–13.76	20.37–11.57	30.17–13.12	22.27–11.68
Average Yield %	2.61	2.63	1.75	1.23	1.08	1.17	0.99	0.95

Address: 399 Park Avenue, New York, NY 10043	**Officers:** Sanford I. Weill – Chmn., William R. Rhodes – Sr. Vice-Chmn.	**Investor Contact:**212–559–9446
Telephone: (212) 559–1000	**Transfer Agents:**Citibank Shareholder Services, Providence, RI	**Institutional Holding** **No of Institutions:** 8
Web Site: www.citigroup.com		**Shares:** 5,710,204 **% Held:** –

CITIZENS BANKING CORP

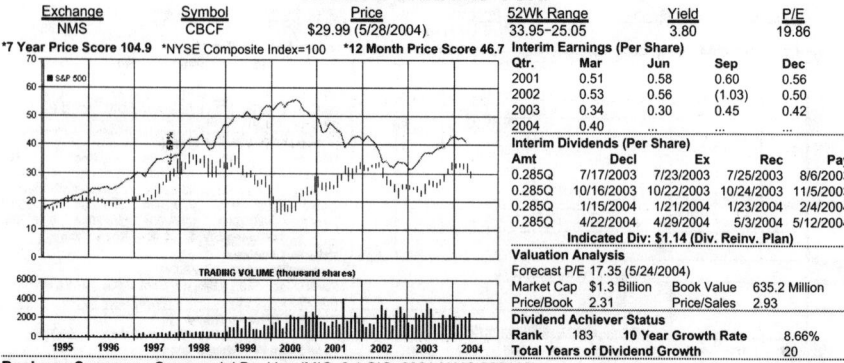

Exchange	Symbol	Price	52Wk Range	Yield	P/E
NMS	CBCF	$29.99 (5/28/2004)	33.95-25.05	3.80	19.86

*7 Year Price Score 104.9 *NYSE Composite Index=100 ***12 Month Price Score 46.7**

Interim Earnings (Per Share)

Qtr.	Mar	Jun	Sep	Dec
2001	0.51	0.58	0.60	0.56
2002	0.53	0.56	(1.03)	0.50
2003	0.34	0.30	0.45	0.42
2004	0.40	...	...	...

Interim Dividends (Per Share)

Amt	Decl	Ex	Rec	Pay
0.285Q	7/17/2003	7/23/2003	7/25/2003	8/6/2003
0.285Q	10/16/2003	10/22/2003	10/24/2003	11/5/2003
0.285Q	1/15/2004	1/21/2004	1/23/2004	2/4/2004
0.285Q	4/22/2004	4/29/2004	5/3/2004	5/12/2004

Indicated Div: $1.14 (Div. Reinv. Plan)

Valuation Analysis
Forecast P/E 17.35 (5/24/2004)
Market Cap $1.3 Billion   Book Value 635.2 Million
Price/Book 2.31   Price/Sales 2.93

Dividend Achiever Status
Rank 183   10 Year Growth Rate   8.66%
Total Years of Dividend Growth   20

Business Summary: Commercial Banking (MIC: 8.1 SIC: 6021 NAIC:522110)

Citizens Banking is a multibank holding company, which directly or indirectly owns four banking subsidiaries and four nonbanking subsidiaries, with total assets of $7.71 billion as of Dec 31 2003. Co.'s subsidiary banks are full−service commercial banks offering a variety of financial services to corporate, commercial, correspondent and individual bank customers. These services include commercial, mortgage and consumer lending, demand and time deposits, trust services, investment banking, retirement, and other financial products and services. Citizens operated 176 branch, private banking, and financial center locations throughout Michigan, Wisconsin, Iowa, and Illinois as of Dec 31 2003.

Recent Developments: For the quarter ended Mar 31 2004, net income advanced 15.8% to $17.4 million from $15.1 million in the comparable prior−year period. The increase in earnings resulted from continued improvement in Co.'s credit quality. Net interest income slid 4.4% to $68.3 million, reflecting decreases in commercial loans and mortgage loans held for sale. Provision for loan losses dropped 63.1% to $7.0 million, primarily reflecting lower net charge−offs and a reduction in non−performing assets. Total non−interest income slid 3.3% to $22.5 million due to a decline in mortgage income from a lower volume of mortgage loan originations and sales. Total non−interest expense increased 7.0% to $60.5 million.

Prospects: On Apr 2 2004, Co. signed a definitive agreement to sell its subsidiary, Citizens Bank−Illinois, to Metropolitan Bank Group in a cash transaction valued at $26.3 million. The sale, which is expected to close in the third quarter of 2004, is anticipated to have a neutral to slightly positive impact on future earnings per share. Looking ahead, Co. expects net interest income to grow during the second half of 2004 due to a higher volume of earning assets, while non−interest expense is expected to increase slightly. Moreover, Co. expects both net charge−offs and provision expense to continue to decline in the second quarter, which should further strengthen credit quality.

Financial Data

(US$ in Thousands)	3 Mos	12/31/2003	12/31/2002	12/31/2001	12/31/2000	12/31/1999	12/31/1998	12/31/1997
Earnings Per Share	1.57	1.51	0.56	2.25	1.91	1.28	1.98	1.11
Tang. Book Val. Per Share	13.45	13.03	13.17	13.70	12.66	11.28	13.75	12.47
Dividends Per Share	1.140	1.140	1.130	1.080	1.010	0.910	0.820	0.740
Dividend Payout %	77.54	75.49	201.78	48.22	53.14	71.48	41.41	66.96
Income Statement								
Total Interest Income	94,394	405,977	463,384	573,559	622,008	542,407	339,880	335,863
Total Interest Expense	26,066	119,719	161,602	265,578	307,134	231,917	142,034	144,015
Net Interest Income	68,328	286,258	301,782	307,981	314,874	310,490	197,846	191,848
Provision for Loan Losses	7,000	62,962	120,200	26,407	20,983	24,675	14,090	15,332
Non−Interest Income	22,512	94,819	96,376	117,481	90,344	79,796	56,252	46,694
Non−Interest Expense	60,534	233,679	245,981	251,183	242,221	236,778	158,291	153,427
Income Before Taxes	23,306	85,127	23,975	147,872	126,473	89,983	81,717	46,049
Net Income	17,443	65,951	25,038	104,657	90,660	61,994	56,785	31,508
Average Shs. Outstg.	43,860	43,609	45,076	46,589	47,542	48,617	28,743	28,420
Balance Sheet								
Cash & Due from Banks	156,220	182,545	171,864	224,416	318,115	250,745	140,543	168,351
Securities Avail. for Sale	2,009,310	1,965,201	1,457,281	1,297,696	1,384,108	1,397,347	613,529	575,382
Net Loans & Leases	5,076,208	5,122,157	5,323,094	5,842,107	6,342,736	5,841,086	3,538,062	3,495,708
Total Assets	7,692,421	7,711,070	7,522,034	7,678,875	8,405,091	7,899,357	4,501,409	4,439,271
Total Deposits	5,460,932	5,442,267	5,936,913	5,965,126	6,244,141	6,128,998	3,764,356	3,694,346
Long−Term Obligations	941,089	936,859	599,313	629,099	471,117	127,104	130,937	108,165
Total Liabilities	7,038,239	7,075,908	6,871,565	6,981,411	7,725,112	7,265,688	4,060,327	4,029,429
Net Stockholders' Equity	654,182	635,162	650,469	697,464	679,979	633,669	441,082	409,842
Shares Outstanding	43,338	43,241	43,702	45,097	46,510	47,567	28,100	28,048
Return on Equity %	2.66	10.38	3.84	15.00	13.33	9.78	12.87	7.68
Return on Assets %	0.22	0.85	0.33	1.36	1.07	0.78	1.26	0.70
Equity/Assets %	8.50	8.23	8.64	9.08	8.09	8.02	9.79	9.23
Non−Int. Exp./Tot. Inc. %	51.78	46.66	43.52	36.34	34.00	37.97	39.95	40.10
Price Range	33.70−31.67	33.95−22.08	33.78−21.61	33.92−23.94	29.06−15.50	39.75−21.38	37.13−28.56	34.75−20.00
P/E Ratio	21.46−20.17	22.48−14.62	60.32−38.59	15.08−10.64	15.22−8.12	31.05−16.70	18.75−14.43	31.31−18.02
Average Yield %	3.45	4.26	3.92	3.83	4.94	3.07	2.46	2.97

Address: 328 S. Saginaw Street, Flint, MI 48502−2401
Telephone: (810) 766−7500
Web Site: www.citizensonline.com

Officers: Willaim R. Hartman − Chmn., Pres., C.E.O., Charles D. Christy − Exec. V.P., C.F.O.
Transfer Agents:Computershare Investor Services, Chicago, IL

Investor Contact:810−257−2489
Institutional Holding
No of Institutions: 4
Shares: 11,044   % Held: −

CLARCOR INC.

Exchange	Symbol	Price	52Wk Range	Yield	P/E
NYS	CLC	$42.41 (5/28/2004)	45.90-36.11	1.18	19.10

*7 Year Price Score 161.8 *NYSE Composite Index=100 *12 Month Price Score 47.8

Interim Earnings (Per Share)

Qtr.	Feb	May	Aug	Nov
2000-01	0.40	0.36	0.41	0.51
2001-02	0.32	0.42	0.48	0.63
2002-03	0.38	0.51	0.56	0.70
2003-04	0.45	...	...	...

Interim Dividends (Per Share)

Amt	Decl	Ex	Rec	Pay
0.123Q	6/23/2003	7/9/2003	7/11/2003	7/25/2003
0.125Q	9/22/2003	10/15/2003	10/17/2003	10/31/2003
0.125Q	12/15/2003	1/14/2004	1/16/2004	1/30/2004
0.125Q	3/22/2004	4/14/2004	4/16/2004	4/30/2004

Indicated Div: $0.50 (Div. Reinv. Plan)

Valuation Analysis
Forecast P/E 18.19 (5/24/2004)
Market Cap $1.1 Billion   Book Value 381.9 Million
Price/Book 3.01   Price/Sales 1.54

Dividend Achiever Status
Rank 292   10 Year Growth Rate 1.93%
Total Years of Dividend Growth 23

Business Summary: Automotive (MIC: 15.1 SIC: 3714 NAIC:336399)

Clarcor manufactures filtration products and consumer and industrial packaging products. The Engine/Mobile Filtration segment includes filters for oil, air, fuel, coolants and hydraulic fluids for trucks, automobiles, construction, mining and industrial equipment, locomotives, marine and agricultural equipment. The Industrial/Environmental Filtration segment produces air and antimicrobial treated filters and high efficiency electronic air cleaners, specialty filters, industrial process liquid filters, pharmaceutical process and beverage filters, filtration systems, bilge separators and sand control filters. The Packaging segment includes a variety of containers and packaging items.

Recent Developments: For the first quarter ended Feb 28 2004, net earnings advanced 21.5% to $11.7 million compared with $9.6 million in the corresponding prior-year quarter. Net sales increased 2.2% to $175.3 million from $171.5 million a year earlier. On a segment basis, Engine/Mobile Filtration sales rose 6.0% to $70.8 million, due to additional sales through aftermarket distribution and to national accounts, and new business from railroads and railroad equipment maintenance companies. Packaging sales climbed 8.1% to $15.5 million, while Industrial/Environmental Filtration sales decreased 1.6% to $89.0 million. Gross profit grew 6.5% to $51.5 million from $48.3 million the year before.

Prospects: In 2004, Co. plans to expand its production facilities at several of its filtration companies. Co. will also expand technical and research facilities in its Industrial/Environmental segment at its environmental and air filtration and process liquid filtration companies. Co. is investing in areas it expects to grow strongly in the future, such as process liquid filter applications. Co. also plans to complete various restructuring programs in an effort to improve profitability. Meanwhile, based on strong first quarter results and an improving economy, Co. is raising its 2004 earnings guidance to a range of $2.25 to $2.40 per share from its previous forecast of $2.25 to $2.35 per share.

Financial Data

(US$ in Thousands)	3 Mos	11/30/2003	11/30/2002	11/30/2001	11/30/2000	11/27/1999	11/28/1998	11/29/1997
Earnings Per Share	2.22	2.15	1.85	1.68	1.64	1.46	1.30	1.09
Cash Flow Per Share	0.57	3.46	3.37	2.54	2.20	1.58	1.71	1.72
Tang. Book Val. Per Share	10.22	9.80	7.74	6.39	5.75	4.97	6.89	6.40
Dividends Per Share	0.490	0.490	0.480	0.470	0.460	0.450	0.440	0.430
Dividend Payout %	22.40	22.90	26.08	28.12	28.20	30.99	34.03	39.78
Income Statement								
Total Revenues	175,272	741,358	715,563	666,964	652,148	477,869	426,773	394,264
Total Indirect Exp.	33,671	134,629	129,515	119,677	122,358	92,510	83,573	76,138
Depreciation & Amort.	4,792	18,985	19,760	21,850	21,079	15,372	12,380	11,600
Operating Income	17,813	87,062	77,775	75,810	75,987	56,077	51,663	44,424
Net Interest Inc./(Exp.)	(67)	(1,532)	(5,612)	(9,616)	(10,836)	(2,282)	(1,053)	(2,759)
Income Taxes	6,703	31,371	24,773	23,804	23,201	20,137	19,262	17,164
Eqty Earns/Minority Int.	(34)	(136)	(76)	(37)	(49)	(66)	(6)	(110)
Net Income	11,661	54,552	46,601	41,893	40,323	35,412	32,079	26,918
Average Shs. Outstg.	25,813	25,372	25,171	24,892	24,506	24,313	24,648	24,603
Balance Sheet								
Cash & Cash Equivalents	18,150	8,348	13,747	7,418	10,864	14,745	33,321	30,324
Total Current Assets	266,484	257,402	259,746	244,350	230,479	227,670	168,173	160,527
Total Assets	548,365	538,237	546,119	530,617	501,930	472,991	305,766	282,519
Total Current Liabilities	106,422	111,373	174,255	94,931	97,826	97,475	61,183	54,237
Long-Term Obligations	18,414	16,913	22,648	135,203	141,486	145,981	36,419	37,656
Net Stockholders' Equity	381,859	370,392	315,461	274,261	242,093	210,718	186,807	171,162
Net Working Capital	159,506	146,029	85,491	149,419	132,653	130,195	106,990	106,290
Shares Outstanding	25,372	25,309	24,918	24,626	24,381	24,019	23,949	24,243
Operating Profit Margin %	10.16	11.74	10.86	11.36	11.65	11.73	12.10	11.26
Net Profit Margin %	14.30	15.82	13.43	13.41	13.28	15.83	16.54	15.53
Return on Equity %	3.05	14.72	14.77	15.27	16.62	16.80	17.17	15.72
Return on Assets %	2.12	10.13	8.53	7.89	8.01	7.48	10.49	9.52
Debt/Total Assets %	3.35	3.14	4.14	25.48	28.18	30.86	11.91	13.32
Price Range	45.59-41.75	45.90-31.05	34.00-25.64	27.60-17.13	21.38-16.69	21.25-15.31	24.35-14.50	20.14-13.92
P/E Ratio	20.54-18.81	21.35-14.44	18.38-13.86	16.43-10.19	13.03-10.18	14.55-10.49	18.73-11.15	18.47-12.77
Average Yield %	1.12	1.30	1.60	1.93	2.46	2.43	2.28	2.57

Address: 2323 Sixth St, Rockford, IL 61125	**Officers:** Norman E. Johnson – Chmn., Pres., C.E.O., William B. Walker – Vice-Chmn.	**Institutional Holding**
Telephone: (815) 962-8867	**Transfer Agents:** First Chicago Trust Company of New York, Jersey City, NJ	**No of Institutions:** 166
Web Site: www.clarcor.com		**Shares:** 18,754,210 **% Held:** 75%

CLECO CORP. (NEW)

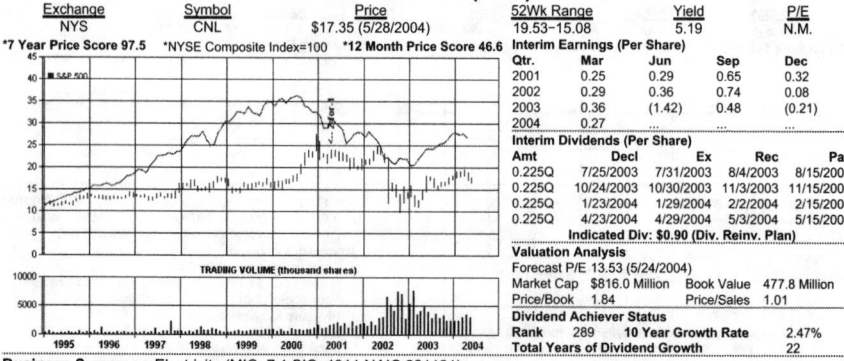

Exchange	Symbol	Price	52Wk Range	Yield	P/E
NYS	CNL	$17.35 (5/28/2004)	19.53–15.08	5.19	N.M.

*7 Year Price Score 97.5   *NYSE Composite Index=100   *12 Month Price Score 46.6

Interim Earnings (Per Share)

Qtr.	Mar	Jun	Sep	Dec
2001	0.25	0.29	0.65	0.32
2002	0.29	0.36	0.74	0.08
2003	0.36	(1.42)	0.48	(0.21)
2004	0.27	...	...	...

Interim Dividends (Per Share)

Amt	Decl	Ex	Rec	Pay
0.225Q	7/25/2003	7/31/2003	8/4/2003	8/15/2003
0.225Q	10/24/2003	10/30/2003	11/3/2003	11/15/2003
0.225Q	1/23/2004	1/29/2004	2/2/2004	2/15/2004
0.225Q	4/23/2004	4/29/2004	5/3/2004	5/15/2004

Indicated Div: $0.90 (Div. Reinv. Plan)

Valuation Analysis

Forecast P/E 13.53 (5/24/2004)
Market Cap $816.0 Million   Book Value 477.8 Million
Price/Book 1.84   Price/Sales 1.01

Dividend Achiever Status

Rank 289   10 Year Growth Rate   2.47%
Total Years of Dividend Growth   22

Business Summary: Electricity (MIC: 7.1 SIC: 4911 NAIC:221121)

Cleco, under an energy services holding structure, is the parent company of Cleco Power and Cleco Midstream Resources. Cleco Power is a regulated electric utility company that served approximately 264,000 customers in 104 communities in central and southeastern Louisiana as of Dec 31 2003. Cleco Midstream Resources is a nonregulated regional energy services group that develops and operates electric power generation facilities, invests in and develops natural gas pipelines and other gas–related assets, and provides energy services to organizations that operate electric utility systems. Co.'s other operations consist of a shared services subsidiary and an investment subsidiary.

Recent Developments: For the first quarter ended Mar 31 2004, net income declined 24.9% to $13.4 million from $17.8 million in the corresponding prior–year quarter. Total revenue decreased 2.0% to $183.7 million from $187.4 million a year earlier. Tolling operations revenue dropped 56.9% to $10.2 million, while Energy operations revenue fell 8.3% to $17.1 million. Electric operations revenue advanced 7.6% to $149.4 million, benefiting from customer growth, warmer than normal March 2004 weather, new energy management services that began in May 2003, and a renegotiated contract for additional ancillary services with a municipal customer. Operating income decreased 22.6% to $27.2 million.

Prospects: The Perryville bankruptcy process continues on schedule. On Apr 23 2004, the U.S. Bankruptcy Court for the Western District of Louisiana approved Perryville's previously announced asset sales agreement with Entergy. Certain regulatory and customary approvals must be obtained to complete the sale. In the meantime, the unit continues to perform well and is providing power to Entergy under an interim power purchase agreement. Separately, Co. recently received a twelve–month extension of its Louisiana rate stabilization plan through September 2005. Looking ahead, Co. expects full-year 2004 earnings to range from $1.25 to $1.35 per share.

Financial Data

(US$ in Thousands)	3 Mos	12/31/2003	12/31/2002	12/31/2001	12/31/2000	12/31/1999	12/31/1998	12/31/1997
Earnings Per Share	(0.88)	(0.79)	1.47	1.51	1.45	1.18	1.12	1.09
Cash Flow Per Share	0.43	4.21	3.39	2.61	1.71	2.40	2.37	2.46
Tang. Book Val. Per Share	10.06	10.23	11.95	10.94	10.33	9.77	9.44	9.09
Dividends Per Share	0.900	0.900	0.890	0.870	0.840	0.830	0.810	0.790
Dividend Payout %	64.29	N.M.	60.88	57.61	58.07	70.33	72.32	72.48
Income Statement								
Total Revenues	182,868	874,637	721,224	1,058,619	820,015	768,200	515,175	456,245
Total Indirect Exp.	26,467	272,328	121,720	98,006	93,269	86,091	83,789	81,203
Costs & Expenses	156,501	893,277	564,228	909,079	672,820	655,659	408,210	349,706
Depreciation & Amort.	16,363	77,550	69,157	60,246	55,840	50,019	48,369	45,890
Operating Income	27,209	(18,640)	156,996	149,540	147,195	112,541	106,965	106,539
Net Interest Inc./(Exp.)	(17,276)	(69,063)	(59,033)	(40,002)	(42,677)	(27,915)	(26,988)	(28,159)
Income Taxes	5,653	(23,974)	42,243	38,356	34,961	27,224	26,666	27,729
Eqty Earns/Minority Int.	9,480	31,631	16,204	...	...	...	...	...
Income from Cont Ops	...	...	...	72,273	69,335	...	...	...
Net Income	13,378	(34,929)	71,875	70,238	64,982	56,766	53,801	52,519
Average Shs. Outstg.	49,266	46,820	48,771	47,763	47,654	47,697	47,734	47,728
Balance Sheet								
Net Property	1,052,702	1,417,066	1,566,155	1,224,659	1,232,758	1,211,617	1,089,798	1,025,562
Total Assets	1,741,281	2,159,426	2,344,606	1,768,125	1,845,704	1,704,650	1,429,000	1,361,044
Long–Term Obligations	550,590	907,058	868,684	626,777	659,135	579,595	343,042	365,897
Net Stockholders' Equity	502,005	501,468	579,978	507,954	480,015	452,545	431,806	413,967
Shares Outstanding	47,476	47,183	47,035	44,961	44,990	44,883	44,962	44,926
Statistical Record								
Operating Profit Margin %	14.41	N.M.	21.76	14.12	17.95	14.64	20.76	23.35
Net Inc./Net Property %	1.27	N.M.	4.58	5.73	5.27	4.68	4.93	5.12
Net Inc./Tot. Capital %	0.96	N.M.	4.11	5.22	4.48	3.91	4.66	4.56
Return on Equity %	2.49	N.M.	12.39	14.22	14.44	12.54	12.29	12.50
Accum. Depr./Gross Prop. %	41.76	35.47	31.31	34.87	32.88	31.44	33.60	33.58
Price Range	19.53–17.87	18.29–11.10	24.78–9.79	26.03–19.60	27.69–15.22	17.53–14.13	18.00–14.41	16.44–12.44
P/E Ratio	N/A	N/A	16.86–6.66	17.24–12.98	19.09–10.50	14.86–11.97	16.07–12.86	15.08–11.41
Average Yield %	4.83	5.79	4.79	3.94	4.35	2.58	5.00	5.47

Address: 2030 Donahue Ferry Road, Pineville, LA 71360–5226 Telephone: (318) 484 7400 Web Site: www.cleco.com	Officers: David M. Eppler – Pres., C.E.O., R. ONeal Chadwick – Sr. V.P., Sec., Gen. Couns. Transfer Agents:EquiServe Trust Company, N.A., Providence, RI	Investor Contact:318–484–7400 Institutional Holding No of Institutions: 1 Shares: 97 % Held: –

CLOROX CO.

Exchange	Symbol	Price	52Wk Range	Yield	P/E
NYS	CLX	$52.36 (5/28/2004)	52.84–42.00	2.06	21.55

*7 Year Price Score 107.3 ***NYSE Composite Index=100** ***12 Month Price Score 51.5**

Interim Earnings (Per Share)

Qtr.	Sep	Dec	Mar	Jun
2000–01	0.42	0.27	0.33	0.34
2001–02	0.33	0.22	0.20	0.62
2002–03	0.71	0.39	0.51	0.72
2003–04	0.60	0.52	0.59	...

Interim Dividends (Per Share)

Amt	Decl	Ex	Rec	Pay
0.27Q	9/17/2003	10/28/2003	10/30/2003	11/14/2003
0.27Q	11/19/2003	1/27/2004	1/29/2004	2/13/2004
0.27Q	3/17/2004	4/26/2004	4/28/2004	5/14/2004
0.27Q	5/19/2004	7/26/2004	7/28/2004	8/13/2004

Indicated Div: $1.08 (Div. Reinv. Plan)

Valuation Analysis

Forecast P/E 19.51 (5/24/2004)

Market Cap	$12.1 Billion	Book Value	1.3 Billion
Price/Book	7.66	Price/Sales	2.41

Dividend Achiever Status

Rank	196	10 Year Growth Rate	8.28%
Total Years of Dividend Growth		27	

Business Summary: Chemicals (MIC: 11.1 SIC: 2842 NAIC:325612)

Clorox is a manufacturer of household products and products for institutional markets. The Household Products North America segment includes products such as *Soft Scrub, Clorox, Tuffy, Formula 409, Liquid−Plumr, Pine− Sol, Tilex, and SOS.* The Specialty Products segment includes brand names such as *Armor All, STP, and Kingsford Charcoal, Hidden Valley and K C Masterpiece* dressings and sauces, *Glad, and GladWare* businesses and *Scoop Away, and Fresh Step* cat litters. The Household Products Latin America/Other segment includes Co.'s overseas operations, excluding the European automotive care business, which focuses on the laundry, household cleaning and insecticide categories.

Recent Developments: For the quarter ended Mar 31 2004, income was $127.0 million versus income of $112.0 million in the prior−year quarter. Results for 2004 and 2003 excluded losses from discontinued operations of $1.0 million and $2.0 million, respectively. Net sales increased 6.6% to $1.09 billion, aided by new product introductions, higher prices and favorable foreign currency. North American Household Product sales grew 6.2% to $583.0 million. Specialty Products sales increased 4.9% to $361.0 million, while Latin America and Other Household Product sales rose 12.7% to $142.0 million. Gross margin slipped to 45.1% from 45.5% in 2003 due to higher raw material, warehousing and transportation costs.

Prospects: For the fourth quarter, Co. expects mid−single−digit volume growth, with sales growing faster than volume. Co. expects earnings per share of about $0.82 to $0.85. For full−year 2004, Co. expects volume and sales growth in the range of 3.0% to 5.0%. Meanwhile, Co. raised its earnings per share guidance to a range of $2.52 to $2.55. For the first quarter of fiscal 2005, Co. expects sales and volume growth of 3.0% to 5.0% and earnings per share in the range of $0.53 to $0.55. First quarter earnings are expected to be constrained by significant new product spending and include a $0.09 charge for possible restructuring charges related to Co.'s U.S. Glad®manufacturing operations.

Financial Data

(US$ in Thousands)	9 Mos	6 Mos	3 Mos	06/30/2003	06/30/2002	06/30/2001	06/30/2000	06/30/1999
Earnings Per Share	2.43	2.35	2.22	2.33	1.37	1.36	1.64	1.03
Cash Flow Per Share	2.48	1.53	0.65	3.63	3.73	3.11	2.74	2.44
Tang. Book Val. Per Share	N.M	N.M	N.M	N.M	0.23	1.37	1.09	0.31
Dividends Per Share	1.030	0.980	0.930	0.880	0.840	0.840	0.800	0.720
Dividend Payout %	42.39	41.70	41.89	37.76	61.31	61.76	48.78	69.90
Income Statement								
Total Revenues	3,081,000	1,995,000	1,048,000	4,144,000	4,061,000	3,903,000	4,083,000	4,003,000
Total Indirect Exp.	809,000	512,000	265,000	1,108,000	1,254,000	1,033,000	1,144,000	1,581,000
Depreciation & Amort.	144,000	95,000	47,000	11,000	12,000	60,000	55,000	61,000
Operating Income	566,000	371,000	201,000	822,000	511,000	611,000	744,000	551,000
Income Taxes	198,000	130,000	71,000	288,000	176,000	161,000	228,000	184,000
Income from Cont Ops	368,000	241,000	130,000	514,000	...	326,000	...	...
Net Income	364,000	238,000	129,000	493,000	322,000	323,000	394,000	246,000
Average Shs. Outstg.	214,052	213,924	214,807	220,692	234,704	239,483	239,614	240,002
Balance Sheet								
Cash & Cash Equivalents	199,000	201,000	187,000	172,000	177,000	251,000	245,000	132,000
Total Current Assets	1,033,000	903,000	891,000	951,000	1,002,000	1,103,000	1,454,000	1,116,000
Total Assets	3,710,000	3,597,000	3,558,000	3,652,000	3,630,000	3,995,000	4,353,000	4,132,000
Total Current Liabilities	1,421,000	1,446,000	1,443,000	1,451,000	1,225,000	1,069,000	1,541,000	1,368,000
Long−Term Obligations	473,000	475,000	479,000	495,000	678,000	685,000	590,000	702,000
Net Stockholders' Equity	1,333,000	1,185,000	1,157,000	1,215,000	1,354,000	1,900,000	1,794,000	1,570,000
Shares Outstanding	212,141	210,151	211,027	213,676	223,009	236,691	235,361	235,311
Statistical Record								
Operating Profit Margin %	17.85	17.89	18.32	19.83	12.58	15.65	18.22	13.76
Net Profit Margin %	24.27	24.41	25.09	26.30	16.59	16.60	20.81	15.33
Return on Equity %	27.61	20.33	10.45	42.30	23.78	17.15	21.96	15.66
Return on Assets %	9.92	6.70	3.40	14.07	8.87	8.16	9.05	5.95
Debt/Total Assets %	12.75	13.20	13.46	13.46	18.67	17.14	13.55	16.98
Price Range	50.15-42.00	49.10-42.00	46.25-42.00	48.24-32.18	47.62-34.64	47.94-30.06	56.97-29.88	66.16-39.75
P/E Ratio	20.64-17.28	20.89-17.87	20.83-18.92	20.70-13.81	34.76-25.28	35.25-22.10	34.74-18.22	64.23-38.59
Average Yield %	2.22	2.16	2.11	2.07	2.07	2.28	1.83	1.33

Address: 1221 Broadway, Oakland, CA 94612–1888	Officers: G. Craig Sullivan − Chmn., C.E.O., Gerald E. Johnston − Pres., C.E.O.	Institutional Holding
Telephone: (510) 271 7000	Transfer Agents:EquiServe Trust Company, N.A., Providence, RI	No of Institutions: 7
Web Site: www.clorox.com		Shares: 61,600,469 % Held: –

COCA-COLA CO (THE)

Exchange	Symbol	Price	52Wk Range	Yield	P/E
NYS	KO	$51.35 (5/28/2004)	53.00-42.91	1.95	27.17

*7 Year Price Score 84.4   *NYSE Composite Index=100   *12 Month Price Score 49.8

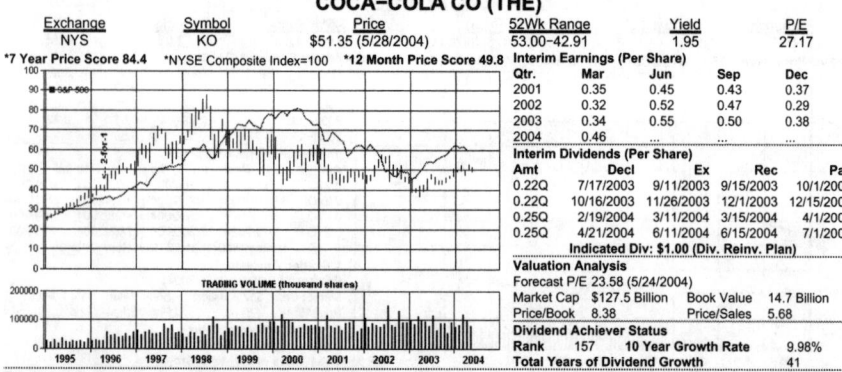

Interim Earnings (Per Share)

Qtr.	Mar	Jun	Sep	Dec
2001	0.35	0.45	0.43	0.37
2002	0.32	0.52	0.47	0.29
2003	0.34	0.55	0.50	0.38
2004	0.46	...	...	...

Interim Dividends (Per Share)

Amt	Decl	Ex	Rec	Pay
0.22Q	7/17/2003	9/11/2003	9/15/2003	10/1/2003
0.22Q	10/16/2003	11/26/2003	12/1/2003	12/15/2003
0.25Q	2/19/2004	3/11/2004	3/15/2004	4/1/2004
0.25Q	4/21/2004	6/11/2004	6/15/2004	7/1/2004

Indicated Div: $1.00 (Div. Reinv. Plan)

Valuation Analysis

Forecast P/E 23.58 (5/24/2004)

Market Cap $127.5 Billion	Book Value 14.7 Billion
Price/Book 8.38	Price/Sales 5.68

Dividend Achiever Status

Rank	157	10 Year Growth Rate	9.98%

Total Years of Dividend Growth   41

Business Summary: Food (MIC: 4.1 SIC: 2086 NAIC:312111)

The Coca-Cola Company is engaged in the manufacturing, distributing and marketing of nonalcoholic beverage concentrates and syrups. Principal beverage products include: *Coca-Cola, Coca-Cola Classic, Diet Coke, Vanilla Coke, Cherry Coke, Fanta, Sprite, Mr. Pibb, Mello Yellow, Barq's, Powerade, Fresca, Dasani* plus other assorted diet and caffeine-free versions. Co. also produces, distributes and markets juice and juice-drink products. Brands include *Minute Maid, Simply Orange* orange juice, *Odwalla* super premium juices and drinks, *Five Alive, Bacardi* tropical fruit mixers (manufactured and marketed under a license from Bacardi & Company Limited) and *Hi-C* ready to serve fruit drinks.

Recent Developments: For the three months ended Mar 31 2004, net income was $1.13 billion compared with $835.0 million in the corresponding year-earlier period. Results for 2003 included streamlining initiative charges of $159.0 million and a gain of $52.0 million related to a litigation settlement. Net operating revenues increased 12.8% to $5.08 billion from $4.50 billion the previous year. Co. attributed the higher revenues to an increase in gallon shipments of 6.0%, improved pricing for concentrate, and positive currency trends, partially offset by the effect of creating a supply chain management company in Japan. Operating income was $1.45 billion, 34.9% higher than the year before.

Prospects: Co.'s near-term outlook appears favorable, reflecting recent solid unit case volume gains. For instance, for the quarter ended Mar 31 2004, unit case volume growth, on an average daily sales basis, increased 2.0% driven by strong growth in markets such as China, Argentina, Spain, South Africa and North America. Separately, Co. announced that it intends to launch *Coca-Cola C2*, a soft drink with half the sugar, carbohydrates and calories of regular colas, first in Japan and then the United States during the summer of 2004. Co. indicated that an integrated marketing campaign will support the summer roll-outs, including television, radio, out-of-home and Internet advertising.

Financial Data

(US$ in Millions)	3 Mos	12/31/2003	12/31/2002	12/31/2001	12/31/2000	12/31/1999	12/31/1998	12/31/1997
Earnings Per Share	1.89	1.77	1.60	1.60	0.88	0.98	1.42	1.64
Cash Flow Per Share	0.47	2.21	1.90	1.65	1.44	1.56	1.37	1.60
Tang. Book Val. Per Share	4.32	4.13	3.33	3.53	2.97	3.05	3.18	2.66
Dividends Per Share	0.880	0.880	0.800	0.720	0.680	0.640	0.600	0.560
Dividend Payout %	46.56	49.71	50.00	45.00	77.27	65.30	42.25	34.14
Income Statement								
Total Revenues	5,078	21,044	19,564	20,092	20,458	19,805	18,813	18,868
Total Indirect Exp.	1,874	8,061	7,001	8,696	10,563	9,814	8,284	7,852
Depreciation & Amort.	213	850	806	803	773	792	645	626
Operating Income	1,451	5,221	5,458	5,352	3,691	3,982	4,967	5,001
Income Taxes	385	1,148	1,523	1,691	1,222	1,388	1,665	1,926
Income from Cont Ops	...	...	3,976	3,979	...	...	...	...
Net Income	1,127	4,347	3,050	3,969	2,177	2,431	3,533	4,129
Average Shs. Outstg.	2,444	2,462	2,483	2,487	2,487	2,487	2,496	2,515
Balance Sheet								
Cash & Cash Equivalents	4,432	3,362	2,126	1,866	1,819	1,611	1,648	1,737
Total Current Assets	9,627	8,396	7,352	7,171	6,620	6,480	6,380	5,969
Total Assets	29,167	27,342	24,501	22,417	20,834	21,623	19,145	16,940
Total Current Liabilities	8,968	7,886	7,341	8,429	9,321	9,856	8,640	7,379
Long-Term Obligations	2,614	2,517	2,701	1,219	835	854	687	801
Net Stockholders' Equity	14,662	14,090	11,800	11,366	9,316	9,513	8,403	7,311
Shares Outstanding	2,433	2,441	2,470	2,486	2,484	2,471	2,466	2,471
Operating Profit Margin %	28.57	24.80	27.89	26.63	18.04	20.10	26.40	26.50
Net Profit Margin %	37.35	31.56	35.89	36.63	22.58	26.29	36.48	42.29
Return on Equity %	7.68	30.85	33.69	35.00	23.36	25.55	42.04	56.47
Return on Assets %	3.86	15.89	16.22	17.74	10.44	11.24	18.45	24.37
Debt/Total Assets %	8.96	9.20	11.02	5.43	4.00	3.94	3.58	4.72
Price Range	52.40-47.71	50.75-37.07	57.64-43.47	60.82-42.85	66.88-43.13	70.63-47.56	87.94-56.19	72.00-51.88
P/E Ratio	27.72-25.24	28.67-20.94	36.03-27.17	38.01-26.78	75.99-49.01	72.07-48.53	61.93-39.57	43.90-31.63
Average Yield %	1.77	2.00	1.61	1.48	1.23	1.03	0.83	0.90

Address: One Coca-Cola Plaza, Atlanta, GA 30313 Telephone: (404) 676-2121 Web Site: www.coca-cola.com	Officers: Douglas N. Daft – Chmn., C.E.O., Steven J. Heyer – Pres., C.O.O. Transfer Agents:EquiServe Trust Company, N.A., Providence, RI	Investor Contact:404-676-5766 Institutional Holding No of Institutions: 9 Shares: 42,025 % Held: –

COLGATE-PALMOLIVE CO.

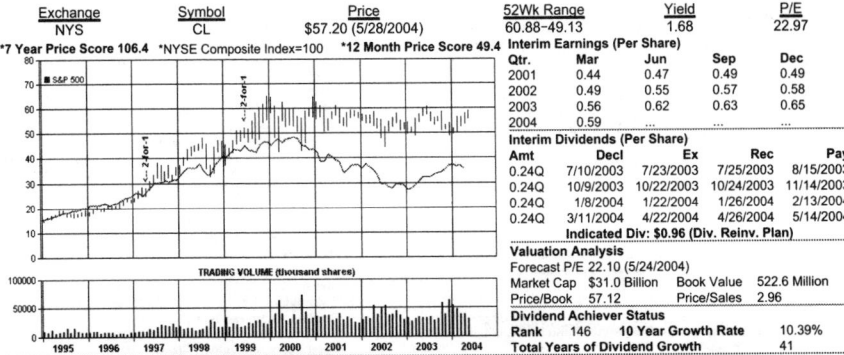

Exchange	Symbol	Price	52Wk Range	Yield	P/E
NYS	CL	$57.20 (5/28/2004)	60.88-49.13	1.68	22.97

*7 Year Price Score 106.4   ***NYSE Composite Index=100**   ***12 Month Price Score 49.4**

Interim Earnings (Per Share)

Qtr.	Mar	Jun	Sep	Dec
2001	0.44	0.47	0.49	0.49
2002	0.49	0.55	0.57	0.58
2003	0.56	0.62	0.63	0.65
2004	0.59	...	...	...

Interim Dividends (Per Share)

Amt	Decl	Ex	Rec	Pay
0.24Q	7/10/2003	7/23/2003	7/25/2003	8/15/2003
0.24Q	10/9/2003	10/22/2003	10/24/2003	11/14/2003
0.24Q	1/8/2004	1/22/2004	1/26/2004	2/13/2004
0.24Q	3/11/2004	4/22/2004	4/26/2004	5/14/2004

Indicated Div: $0.96 (Div. Reinv. Plan)

Valuation Analysis
Forecast P/E 22.10 (5/24/2004)
Market Cap $31.0 Billion   Book Value 522.6 Million
Price/Book 57.12   Price/Sales 2.96

Dividend Achiever Status
Rank 146   10 Year Growth Rate 10.39%
Total Years of Dividend Growth 41

Business Summary: Chemicals (MIC: 11.1 SIC: 2844 NAIC:325620)

Colgate–Palmolive is a consumer products company whose products are marketed in over 200 countries worldwide. Co. operates in two business segments. Co.'s oral, personal, household surface and fabric care segment include toothpaste, oral rinses and toothbrushes, hand soaps, shower gels, shampoos, deodorants, shave products, laundry and dishwashing detergents, cleansers and other similar items. Co.'s pet nutrition segment includes pet food products manufactured and marketed by Hill's Pet Nutrition. Principal global trademarks include *Colgate, Palmolive, Kolynos, Sorriso, Mennen, Protex, Ajax, Soupline, Suavitel, Fab, Science Diet* and *Prescription Diet* in addition to other regional trademarks.

Recent Developments: For the quarter ended Mar 31 2004, net income rose 4.5% to $338.5 million from $324.0 million in the prior-year quarter. Net sales increased 7.0% to $2.51 billion. By geography, North American sales and unit volume declined 3.5% and 3.0%, respectively, while operating profit fell 8.0%. In Europe, sales climbed 13.5%, unit volume grew 4.0% and operating profit climbed 14.0%. Latin America sales and unit volume increased 7.0% and 5.5%, while operating profit increased 6.0%. Asia/Africa sales increased 11.0%, unit volume rose 6.0% and operating profit climbed 28.0%. In the Hills Pet Nutrition business, sales grew 8.5%, unit volume rose 4.0% and operating profit improved 9.0%.

Prospects: Looking ahead, prospects appear bright as market share gains and new product launches are generating strong top-line growth. Growth opportunities are especially evident in Latin America where Co. has increased its commercial investment in brand-building activities. In the U.S., New products such as *Colgate Simply White* and *Colgate Total Advanced Fresh* toothpastes, *Colgate Whitening* and *Colgate Massager* manual toothbrushes should continue to drive momentum. Meanwhile, the recent roll-out of *Colgate Total Advanced Fresh* toothpaste and the continued success of *Colgate Sensitive* toothpaste should bolster Co.'s market share gains in Western Europe.

Financial Data (US$ in Thousands)	3 Mos	12/31/2003	12/31/2002	12/31/2001	12/31/2000	12/31/1999	12/31/1998	12/31/1997
Earnings Per Share	2.49	2.46	2.19	1.89	1.70	1.47	1.30	1.13
Cash Flow Per Share	0.64	3.05	2.73	2.63	2.44	2.02	1.81	1.68
Tang. Book Val. Per Share	N.M	N.M	N.M	N.M	N.M	N.M	N.M	N.M
Dividends Per Share	0.960	0.900	0.720	0.670	0.630	0.590	0.550	0.530
Dividend Payout %	38.55	36.58	32.87	35.71	37.05	40.13	42.14	46.69
Income Statement								
Total Revenues	2,513,500	9,903,400	9,294,300	9,427,800	9,357,900	9,118,200	8,971,600	9,056,700
Total Indirect Exp.	868,300	3,149,500	3,026,200	3,342,500	3,299,500	3,295,600	3,209,700	3,266,200
Depreciation & Amort.	79,900	12,300	12,500	68,000	72,100	75,600	81,700	86,500
Operating Income	531,300	2,166,000	2,013,100	1,834,800	1,740,500	1,566,200	1,423,000	1,285,800
Net Interest Inc./(Exp.)	(28,300)	(124,100)	(142,800)	(166,100)	(173,300)	(171,600)	(172,900)	(183,500)
Income Taxes	164,500	620,600	582,000	522,100	503,400	457,300	401,500	361,900
Net Income	338,500	1,421,300	1,288,300	1,146,600	1,063,800	937,300	848,600	740,400
Average Shs. Outstg.	572,500	578,800	589,100	607,700	627,300	638,800	648,400	650,200
Balance Sheet								
Cash & Cash Equivalents	271,500	265,300	167,900	172,700	212,500	235,200	194,500	205,300
Total Current Assets	2,565,000	2,496,500	2,228,100	2,203,400	2,347,200	2,354,800	2,244,900	2,196,500
Total Assets	7,501,100	7,478,800	7,087,200	6,984,800	7,252,300	7,423,100	7,685,200	7,538,700
Total Current Liabilities	2,542,800	2,445,400	2,148,700	2,123,500	2,244,100	2,273,500	2,114,400	1,959,500
Long-Term Obligations	2,687,300	2,684,900	3,210,800	2,812,000	2,536,900	2,243,300	2,300,600	2,340,300
Net Stockholders' Equity	807,400	887,100	350,300	846,400	1,468,100	1,833,700	2,085,600	2,178,600
Shares Outstanding	532,087	533,697	536,001	550,722	566,655	578,863	585,420	591,280
Operating Profit Margin %	21.13	23.65	22.43	20.03	19.50	17.86	16.71	14.99
Net Profit Margin %	26.55	28.67	27.16	23.80	23.03	20.99	19.26	16.96
Return on Equity %	41.92	180.17	388.35	141.81	78.25	54.54	44.36	37.30
Return on Assets %	4.51	21.37	19.19	17.18	15.84	13.47	12.04	10.78
Debt/Total Assets %	35.82	35.90	45.30	40.25	34.98	30.22	29.93	31.04
Price Range	56.55-49.62	60.88-49.10	58.73-44.36	62.50-51.00	65.00-42.75	65.00-37.47	48.47-32.78	38.56-22.72
P/E Ratio	22.71-19.93	24.75-19.96	26.82-20.26	33.07-26.98	38.24-25.15	44.22-25.49	37.28-25.22	34.13-20.11
Average Yield %	1.79	1.64	1.33	1.18	1.13	1.18	1.31	1.72

Address: 300 Park Avenue, New York, NY 10022-7499	**Officers:** Reuben Mark – Chmn., C.E.O., William S. Shanahan – Pres.	**Investor Contact:** 212-310-3072
Telephone: (212) 310 2000	**Transfer Agents:** Equiserve Trust Company, N.A.,	**Institutional Holding** No of Institutions: 9
Web Site: www.colgate.com	Providence, RI	**Shares:** 260,874 **% Held:** –

COMERICA, INC.

Exchange	Symbol	Price	52Wk Range	Yield	P/E
NYS	CMA	$56.61 (5/28/2004)	58.25-45.48	3.67	15.43

*7 Year Price Score 93.7   ***NYSE Composite Index=100**   ***12 Month Price Score 48.9**

Interim Earnings (Per Share)

Qtr.	Mar	Jun	Sep	Dec
2001	0.50	1.13	1.14	1.11
2002	1.20	1.03	0.14	1.03
2003	1.00	0.97	0.89	0.89
2004	0.92	...	...	...

Interim Dividends (Per Share)

Amt	Decl	Ex	Rec	Pay
0.50Q	7/22/2003	9/11/2003	9/15/2003	10/1/2003
0.50Q	11/25/2003	12/11/2003	12/15/2003	1/1/2004
0.52Q	1/27/2004	3/11/2004	3/15/2004	4/1/2004
0.52Q	5/18/2004	6/11/2004	6/15/2004	7/1/2004

Indicated Div: **$2.08** (Div. Reinv. Plan)

Valuation Analysis

Forecast P/E 14.68 (5/24/2004)
Market Cap $9.9 Billion   Book Value 5.1 Billion
Price/Book 1.86   Price/Sales 2.97

Dividend Achiever Status

Rank 137   **10 Year Growth Rate**   11.01%
Total Years of Dividend Growth 20

Business Summary: Commercial Banking (MIC: 8.1 SIC: 6021 NAIC:522110)

Comerica is a bank holding company with assets of $52.59 billion and total deposits of $41.46 billion as of Dec 31 2003. Co. operates banking subsidiaries in Michigan, Texas and California, banking operations in Florida, and businesses in several other states. Co. is a diversified financial services provider, offering a broad range of financial products and services for businesses and individuals. Through its subsidiaries, the Company has aligned its operations into three major lines of business: the Business Bank, the Individual Bank and the Investment Bank. Co. also has an investment services affiliate, Munder Capital Management, and operates banking subsidiaries in Canada and Mexico.

Recent Developments: For the quarter ended Mar 31 2004, net income climbed 8.0% to $162.0 million from $176.0 million in the comparable prior-year period. Earnings for 2004 included warrant income of $1.0 million. Net interest income declined 12.9% to $445.0 million from $511.0 million a year earlier. Net interest margin fell to 3.83% from 4.30% in 2003. Provision for loan losses fell 38.7% to $65.0 million. Total non-interest income remained the same at $220.0 million, while total non-interest expense rose 0.5% to $369.0 million. Total loans declined 6.0% to $40.01 billion, while total deposits slid 1.9% to $43.52 billion.

Prospects: Earnings continue to benefit from ongoing improvement in credit quality and expense control. However, in the current economic environment, Co.'s commercial customers are still cautious about investing and as a result, loan demand remains soft. Going forward, Co. will focus on increasing contributions from its Small Business & Personal Financial Services and Wealth & Institutional Management segments, building enhanced tools to more effectively manage risk throughout the company, and adding new branches in Texas, California and Michigan in order to grow market share.

Financial Data

(US$ in Thousands)	3 Mos	12/31/2003	12/31/2002	12/31/2001	12/31/2000	12/31/1999	12/31/1998	12/31/1997
Earnings Per Share	3.67	3.75	3.40	3.88	4.63	4.14	3.72	3.19
Tang. Book Val. Per Share	29.41	29.19	28.30	27.14	23.94	20.60	17.94	16.01
Dividends Per Share	2	1.980	1.880	1.720	1.560	1.400	1.240	1.120
Dividend Payout %	54.50	52.80	55.29	44.32	33.69	33.81	33.51	35.10
Income Statement								
Total Interest Income	543,000	2,412,000	2,797,000	3,393,547	3,261,636	2,672,710	2,616,774	2,647,403
Total Interest Expense	98,000	486,000	665,000	1,291,209	1,602,785	1,125,569	1,155,503	1,204,627
Net Interest Income	445,000	1,926,000	2,132,000	2,102,338	1,658,851	1,547,141	1,461,271	1,442,776
Provision for Loan Losses	65,000	377,000	635,000	236,000	145,000	114,000	113,000	146,000
Non-Interest Income	220,000	875,000	872,000	858,213	778,306	716,888	603,148	527,952
Non-Interest Expense	369,000	1,483,000	1,515,000	1,559,033	1,188,370	1,116,957	1,020,044	1,007,986
Income Before Taxes	231,000	953,000	882,000	1,110,637	1,151,371	1,033,072	931,375	816,742
Eqty Earns/Minority Int.	...	6,000	8,000	(43,057)	...	...	...	...
Net Income	162,000	661,000	601,000	709,578	749,326	672,589	607,076	530,476
Average Shs. Outstg.	176,000	176,000	177,000	177,665	156,398	158,397	158,757	161,040
Balance Sheet								
Cash & Due from Banks	1,661,000	1,527,000	1,902,000	1,925,262	1,496,705	1,201,990	1,773,100	1,927,087
Securities Avail. for Sale	4,639,000	4,489,000	3,053,000	4,290,724	2,677,762	2,739,464	2,712,165	4,005,962
Net Loans & Leases	39,214,000	39,499,000	41,490,000	40,541,248	35,522,235	32,216,808	30,152,454	28,470,897
Total Assets	54,468,000	52,592,000	53,301,000	50,731,973	41,985,185	38,653,332	36,600,831	36,292,398
Total Deposits	43,523,000	41,463,000	41,775,000	37,570,379	27,168,012	23,291,403	24,313,133	22,586,317
Long-Term Obligations	4,597,000	4,801,000	5,216,000	5,502,511	8,088,661	8,579,857	5,282,259	7,286,387
Total Liabilities	49,375,000	47,482,000	48,354,000	45,924,509	37,977,919	33,743,054	33,083,050	30,930,581
Net Stockholders' Equity	5,093,000	5,110,000	4,947,000	4,807,464	4,007,266	3,474,644	3,046,613	2,761,776
Shares Outstanding	173,158	175,000	174,775	177,074	156,943	156,517	155,881	156,815
Return on Equity %	3.18	12.81	11.74	15.00	17.51	19.35	19.92	19.20
Return on Assets %	0.29	1.24	1.09	1.42	1.67	1.74	1.65	1.46
Equity/Assets %	9.35	9.71	9.28	9.47	9.54	8.98	8.32	7.60
Non-Int. Exp./Tot. Inc. %	48.36	45.03	41.20	37.04	29.41	32.95	31.67	31.74
Price Range	58.25-52.62	56.31-37.61	65.30-35.53	64.95-44.66	60.31-33.81	69.75-44.94	71.54-50.13	61.88-34.58
P/E Ratio	15.87-14.34	15.02-10.03	19.21-10.45	16.74-11.51	13.03-7.30	16.85-10.85	19.23-13.47	19.40-10.84
Average Yield %	3.57	4.29	3.40	3.04	3.21	2.38	1.93	2.42

Address: Comerica Tower at Detroit Center, Detroit, MI 48226-3509
Telephone: (313) 222 9743
Web Site: www.comerica.com

Officers: Ralph W. Babb – Chmn., Pres., C.E.O., Elizabeth S. Acton – Exec. V.P., C.F.O.
Transfer Agents: Wells Fargo Shareowner Services, South St. Paul, MN

Investor Contact:313-222-2840
Institutional Holding
No of Institutions: 23
Shares: 811,583   **% Held:** –

COMMERCE BANCORP, INC.

Exchange	Symbol	Price	52Wk Range	Yield	P/E
NYS	CBH	$61.50 (5/28/2004)	67.05–37.11	1.24	22.28

*7 Year Price Score 163.1 ***NYSE Composite Index=100** ***12 Month Price Score 54.2**

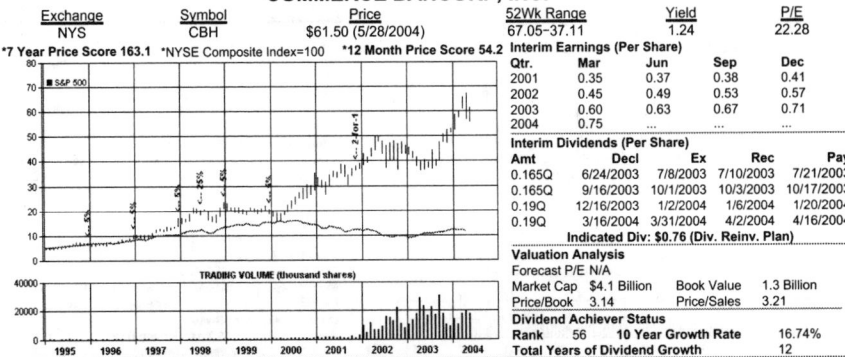

Interim Earnings (Per Share)

Qtr.	Mar	Jun	Sep	Dec
2001	0.35	0.37	0.38	0.41
2002	0.45	0.49	0.53	0.57
2003	0.60	0.63	0.67	0.71
2004	0.75	...	...	...

Interim Dividends (Per Share)

Amt	Decl	Ex	Rec	Pay
0.165Q	6/24/2003	7/8/2003	7/10/2003	7/21/2003
0.165Q	9/16/2003	10/1/2003	10/3/2003	10/17/2003
0.19Q	12/16/2003	1/2/2004	1/6/2004	1/20/2004
0.19Q	3/16/2004	3/31/2004	4/2/2004	4/16/2004

Indicated Div: $0.76 (Div. Reinv. Plan)

Valuation Analysis

Forecast P/E N/A

Market Cap	$4.1 Billion	Book Value	1.3 Billion
Price/Book	3.14	Price/Sales	3.21

Dividend Achiever Status

Rank	56	10 Year Growth Rate	16.74%
Total Years of Dividend Growth			12

TRADING VOLUME (thousand shares)

Business Summary: Commercial Banking (MIC: 8.1 SIC: 6021 NAIC:522110)

Commerce Bancorp, with assets of $22.71 billion as of Dec 31 2003, is a bank holding company primarily serving the Metropolitan Philadelphia, New Jersey, Delaware and New York markets. Co. operates five bank subsidiaries, including Commerce Bank, Commerce Bank/Pennsylvania, Commerce Bank/Shore, Commerce Bank/Delaware, and Commerce Bank/North. As of Dec 31 2003, these banks provided a full range of retail and commercial banking services through 270 retail branch offices. Co. also operates Commerce Capital Markets, which is engaged in securities, investment banking and brokerage activities, and Commerce National Insurance Services, which operates an insurance brokerage agency.

Recent Developments: For the quarter ended Mar 31 2004, net income increased 44.5% to $62.0 million from $42.9 million in the corresponding period the year before. Earnings included net investment securities gains of $424,000 and losses of $136,000 in 2003. Net interest income advanced 37.6% to $230.2 million, reflecting growth in deposits and interest earning assets. Net interest margin was 4.39% versus 4.27% in the previous year. Provision for loan losses grew 37.7% to $9.5 million. Total non-interest income improved 13.4% to $86.2 million, primarily as a result of increased deposit charges and service fees. Total non-interest expense increased 23.3% to $212.3 million.

Prospects: Co. opened eight new branch offices during the first quarter of 2004, increasing the total offices opened to 278. During the remainder of 2004, Co. plans to open an additional 42 branches, including approximately 34 in Metro New York and 8 in Metro Philadelphia. This expansion is expected to create more than 1,800 positions in 2004. By 2009, Co. intends to nearly double its size to create a network of 700 stores along the eastern seaboard and hire approximately 10,000 new employees. Looking ahead, Co. expects earnings per share in 2004 to total $0.76 in the second quarter, $0.80 in the third quarter, $0.83 in the fourth quarter and $3.12 for the full year.

Financial Data

(US$ in Thousands)	12/31/2003	12/31/2002	12/31/2001	12/31/2000	12/31/1999	12/31/1998	12/31/1997	12/31/1996
Earnings Per Share	2.61	2.04	1.51	1.24	1.08	0.94	0.80	0.71
Tang. Book Val. Per Share	16.69	13.53	9.66	7.74	5.97	5.96	5.28	4.93
Dividends Per Share	0.660	0.600	0.550	0.480	0.410	0.430	0.270	0.220
Dividend Payout %	25.28	29.41	36.42	38.88	38.16	46.26	34.34	31.68
Income Statement								
Total Interest Income	915,631	755,371	604,367	505,300	386,448	289,280	244,177	179,364
Total Interest Expense	159,765	182,616	203,041	208,370	142,081	115,553	97,037	70,858
Net Interest Income	755,866	572,755	401,326	296,930	244,367	173,727	147,140	108,506
Provision for Loan Losses	31,850	33,150	26,384	13,931	9,175	5,867	4,668	2,997
Non-Interest Income	332,478	257,466	196,805	150,760	114,596	88,947	57,374	30,014
Non-Interest Expense	763,392	579,168	420,036	315,357	252,523	181,967	137,929	94,071
Net Income	194,287	144,815	103,022	80,047	65,960	49,318	40,325	26,625
Average Shs. Outstg.	74,462	70,903	68,102	64,222	60,930	52,397	49,950	35,109
Balance Sheet								
Cash & Due from Banks	910,092	811,434	557,738	443,918	317,624	245,352	167,900	159,577
Securities Avail. for Sale	10,821,113	8,133,258	4,435,515	2,130,632	1,782,094	1,368,863	1,323,031	741,244
Net Loans & Leases	7,328,519	5,731,856	4,516,431	3,638,580	2,922,706	1,904,954	1,390,028	1,081,830
Total Assets	22,712,180	16,403,981	11,363,703	8,296,516	6,635,993	4,894,065	3,938,967	2,861,952
Total Deposits	20,701,400	14,548,841	10,185,594	7,387,594	5,608,920	4,435,115	3,369,404	2,573,405
Long-Term Obligations	200,000	200,000	80,500	80,500	80,500	80,500	80,500	23,000
Total Liabilities	21,434,892	15,485,971	10,727,133	7,804,292	6,279,037	4,593,349	3,688,207	2,680,599
Net Stockholders' Equity	1,277,288	918,010	636,570	492,224	356,756	300,716	250,760	181,353
Shares Outstanding	76,506	67,833	65,832	63,522	59,688	50,410	46,029	35,260
Return on Equity %	15.21	15.77	16.18	16.26	18.48	16.40	16.08	14.68
Return on Assets %	0.85	0.88	0.90	0.96	0.99	1.00	1.02	0.93
Non-Int. Exp./Tot. Inc. %	61.16	57.18	52.42	48.06	50.39	48.11	45.73	44.92
Price Range	53.15-36.37	50.20-36.60	39.28-26.75	35.13-15.75	23.18-18.60	23.35-14.98	17.04-8.84	10.17-6.05
P/E Ratio	20.36-13.93	24.61-17.94	26.01-17.72	28.33-12.70	21.46-17.23	24.84-15.94	21.30-11.05	14.33-8.52
Average Yield %	1.53	1.35	1.60	2.04	2.02	2.31	2.30	3.01

Address: Commerce Atrium, Cherry Hill, NJ 08034-5400	Officers: Vernon W. Hill II – Chmn., Pres., C.E.O., Peter M. Musumeci – Exec. V.P., Sr. Credit Officer, Treas., Asst. Sec.	Investor Contact:888-751-9000
Telephone: (856) 751-9000		Institutional Holding
Web Site: www.commerceonline.com	Transfer Agents:Mellon Investor Services, LLP, New York, NY	No of Institutions: 49 Shares: 5,842,619 % Held: –

COMMERCE BANCSHARES, INC.

Exchange	Symbol	Price	52Wk Range	Yield	P/E
NMS	CBSH	$46.55 (5/28/2004)	49.99-36.83	1.98	15.31

*7 Year Price Score 129.4   *NYSE Composite Index=100   *12 Month Price Score 48.1

Interim Earnings (Per Share)

Qtr.	Mar	Jun	Sep	Dec
2001	0.59	0.62	0.61	0.65
2002	0.64	0.68	0.70	0.73
2003	0.66	0.71	0.79	0.79
2004	0.75	...	...	...

Interim Dividends (Per Share)

Amt	Decl	Ex	Rec	Pay
0.214Q	10/24/2003	11/25/2003	11/28/2003	12/12/2003
5%	10/24/2003	11/25/2003	11/28/2003	12/12/2003
0.23Q	1/30/2004	3/4/2004	3/8/2004	3/26/2004
0.23Q	4/21/2004	6/3/2004	6/7/2004	6/28/2004

Indicated Div: $0.92 (Div. Reinv. Plan)

Valuation Analysis

Forecast P/E 18.65 (5/24/2004)

Market Cap	$3.0 Billion	Book Value	1.5 Billion
Price/Book	2.18	Price/Sales	3.50

Dividend Achiever Status

Rank	118	10 Year Growth Rate	12.02%

Total Years of Dividend Growth   35

Business Summary: Commercial Banking (MIC: 8.1 SIC: 6022 NAIC:522110)

Commerce Bancshares, with assets of $14.29 billion as of Dec 31 2003, is a bank holding company that operates in approximately 330 banking locations. Co. presently owns all of the outstanding capital stock of four national banking associations, which are headquartered in Missouri, Illinois, Kansas, and Nebraska. The Nebraska bank is limited in its activities to the issuance of credit cards. The remaining three banking subsidiaries engage in general banking business, providing a broad range of retail, corporate, investment and private banking products and services to individuals and businesses. Co. also owns, directly or through its banking subsidiaries, various non-banking subsidiaries.

Recent Developments: For the quarter ended Mar 31 2004, net income rose 8.7% to $51.3 million from $47.2 million in the comparable prior-year period. Results for 2004 and 2003 included net gains of $9.0 million and $2.3 million, respectively, on securities transactions. Net interest income slipped 1.0% to $123.0 million from $124.2 million a year earlier, due to re-pricing in earning assets as a result of a low interest rate environment. Provision for loan losses grew 2.3% to $10.3 million. Total non-interest income rose 15.2% to $86.0 million, primarily due to growth in trust fees, deposit account fees and bank card fee income. Total non-interest expense declined 1.5% to $118.9 million.

Prospects: Co. continues to experience solid growth in net income, primarily due to increases in deposit account charges and other fees, bank card transaction fees, and trust fees, as well as continued good expense control. Also, Co.'s asset quality remains strong with allowance for loan losses totaling more than $133.1 million, or 400.0% of non-performing loans as of Mar 31 2004. Moreover, net charge-offs for the first quarter of 2004 were 0.61% of average loans compared with 0.46% the year before. The increase in net loan charge-offs was the result of a single business loan, which was charged down during the first quarter.

Financial Data

(US$ in Thousands)	3 Mos	12/31/2003	12/31/2002	12/31/2001	12/31/2000	12/31/1999	12/31/1998	12/31/1997
Earnings Per Share	3.04	2.95	2.75	2.47	2.38	2.13	1.89	1.67
Tang. Book Val. Per Share	21.27	20.60	19.43	16.93	14.98	13.34	12.85	11.52
Dividends Per Share	0.810	0.740	0.580	0.550	0.510	0.470	0.430	0.380
Dividend Payout %	26.89	25.18	21.42	22.32	21.39	22.06	22.82	23.24
Income Statement								
Total Interest Income	148,787	617,410	652,553	750,962	812,168	750,626	728,471	682,876
Total Interest Expense	25,803	115,018	152,588	283,052	331,515	284,625	300,726	285,102
Net Interest Income	122,984	502,392	499,965	467,910	480,653	466,001	427,745	397,774
Provision for Loan Losses	10,250	40,676	34,108	36,423	35,159	35,335	36,874	31,354
Non-Interest Income	85,969	286,922	264,618	262,180	244,214	225,899	205,304	172,672
Non-Interest Expense	118,912	472,144	452,927	439,638	430,381	419,015	379,344	344,450
Income Before Taxes	79,791	291,239	293,502	269,361	267,921	247,860	225,564	202,062
Net Income	51,324	206,524	199,498	181,974	178,574	166,213	150,091	132,702
Average Shs. Outstg.	68,778	70,112	72,489	73,561	74,846	77,120	79,262	79,446
Balance Sheet								
Cash & Due from Banks	409,924	567,123	710,406	824,218	616,724	685,157	738,672	978,239
Securities Avail. for Sale	5,336,250	4,966,024	4,213,112	3,667,184	1,885,665	2,475,424	3,002,440	2,620,517
Net Loans & Leases	8,016,049	8,007,458	7,745,326	7,508,509	7,778,220	7,453,850	6,929,760	6,118,463
Total Assets	14,485,217	14,287,164	13,308,415	12,902,806	11,115,117	11,400,936	11,402,023	10,306,941
Total Deposits	10,252,635	10,206,208	9,913,311	10,031,966	9,081,738	9,164,123	9,530,197	8,700,578
Long-Term Obligations	499,465	400,977	338,457	392,586	224,684	25,735	27,130	7,207
Total Liabilities	13,001,421	12,836,210	11,892,078	11,630,323	9,971,362	10,321,104	10,321,238	9,326,157
Net Stockholders' Equity	1,483,796	1,450,954	1,416,337	1,272,483	1,143,755	1,079,832	1,080,785	980,784
Shares Outstanding	67,392	67,968	70,457	72,144	72,441	75,816	78,056	77,686
Return on Equity %	3.45	14.23	14.08	14.30	15.61	15.39	13.88	13.53
Return on Assets %	0.35	1.44	1.49	1.41	1.60	1.45	1.31	1.28
Equity/Assets %	10.24	10.15	10.64	9.86	10.29	9.47	9.47	9.51
Non-Int. Exp./Tot. Inc. %	50.65	51.37	48.53	42.74	40.41	42.46	40.24	39.91
Price Range	49.99-45.48	49.28-33.74	42.17-31.52	37.31-28.71	36.71-22.11	33.79-26.84	37.50-26.58	34.51-20.20
P/E Ratio	16.44-14.96	16.71-11.44	15.33-11.46	15.10-11.63	15.43-9.29	15.86-12.60	19.84-14.07	20.67-12.09
Average Yield %	1.67	1.84	1.53	1.68	1.83	1.53	1.25	1.54

Address: 1000 Walnut, Kansas City, MO 64106	Officers: David W. Kemper - Chmn., Pres., C.E.O. Johnathan M. Kemper - Vice-Chmn.	Investor Contact:800-892-7100
Telephone: (816) 234-2000	Transfer Agents:EquiServe Trust Company, N.A., Jersey City, NJ	Institutional Holding No of Institutions: 12
Web Site: www.commercebank.com		Shares: 479,772 % Held: -

68

COMMERCIAL NET LEASE REALTY, INC.

Exchange	Symbol	Price	52Wk Range	Yield	P/E
NYS	NNN	$17.07 (5/28/2004)	19.95-15.49	7.50	14.84

*7 Year Price Score 123.6 *NYSE Composite Index=100 *12 Month Price Score 43.5

Interim Earnings (Per Share)

Qtr.	Mar	Jun	Sep	Dec
2001	0.38	0.34	0.00	0.19
2002	0.29	0.27	0.23	0.25
2003	0.21	0.28	0.30	0.29
2004	0.28	...	...	...

Interim Dividends (Per Share)

Amt	Decl	Ex	Rec	Pay
0.32Q	7/15/2003	7/29/2003	7/31/2003	8/15/2003
0.32Q	10/15/2003	10/29/2003	10/31/2003	11/15/2003
0.32Q	1/16/2004	1/28/2004	1/30/2004	2/13/2004
0.32Q	4/14/2004	4/28/2004	4/30/2004	5/14/2004

Indicated Div: $1.28 (Div. Reinv. Plan)

Valuation Analysis

Forecast P/E 11.54 (5/24/2004)

Market Cap $688.9 Million   Book Value 661.2 Million

Price/Book 1.25   Price/Sales 8.05

Dividend Achiever Status

Rank 297   10 Year Growth Rate 1.53%

Total Years of Dividend Growth 14

Business Summary: Property, Real Estate &Development (MIC: 8.3 SIC: 6798 NAIC:525930)

Commercial Net Lease Realty is a fully integrated, self–administered real estate investment trust. Co. and its wholly–owned subsidiaries acquire, own, manage and indirectly, through investment interests, develop primarily single–tenant retail, office and industrial properties that are generally leased under long–term commercial net leases. As of Dec 31 2003, Co. owned 339 properties in 39 states that are generally leased to major retail businesses under long–term commercial net leases. These businesses include Academy, Barnes & Noble, Bennigan's, Best Buy, Borders, Eckerd, Jared Jewelers, OfficeMax, The Sports Authority and the United States of America.

Recent Developments: For the three months ended Mar 31 2004, income was $15.8 million, before a gain of $486,000 from discontinued operations, compared with income of $9.2 million, before a gain of $916,000 from discontinued operations, in the corresponding quarter of the previous year. Results for 2003 included a pre–tax settlement charge of $2.4 million. Total revenues advanced 41.0% to $35.9 million from $25.5 million in the year–earlier period. Rental and earned income increased 22.6% to $27.5 million from $22.4 million the year before. Revenues for 2003 and 2002 also included gains of $3.4 million and $984,000, respectively, from the disposition of real estate held for sale.

Prospects: Co. continues to maintain an active acquisition and investment strategy in an effort to strengthen its portfolio of properties. For instance, during the first quarter, Co. invested $37.6 million in additional properties and construction in progress. Co. also disposed of five properties generating net proceeds of $14.1 million. Meanwhile, Co. continued to enjoy strong occupancy growth as well as solid revenues and funds from operations during the first quarter of 2004. However, despite this recent favorable performance, Co. announced that it is undertaking a review of all areas of its operations in an effort to further improve results.

Financial Data

(US$ in Thousands)	12/31/2003	12/31/2002	12/31/2001	12/31/2000	12/31/1999	12/31/1998	12/31/1997	12/31/1996
Earnings Per Share	1.08	1.04	0.91	1.27	1.16	1.10	1.25	1.18
Tang. Book Val. Per Share	13.22	12.48	12.67	12.93	12.93	13.00	12.95	15.03
Dividends Per Share	1.280	1.270	1.260	1.245	1.245	1.230	1.200	1.180
Dividend Payout %	118.51	122.11	138.46	98.03	106.89	111.81	96.00	100.00
Income Statement								
Rental Income	84,851	73,874	58,092	60,591	58,417	48,935	38,143	25,140
Interest Income	15,805	18,397	20,550	19,147	16,243	13,476	11,992	8,229
Total Income	102,658	93,827	80,526	80,891	76,543	64,773	50,135	33,369
Total Indirect Exp.	85,234	77,703	79,688	68,912	68,910	47,514	31,981	20,809
Depreciation	13,467	11,425	9,211	9,088	8,634	6,759	5,302	3,553
Interest Expense	55,462	53,440	49,904	53,056	43,840	26,920	22,956	14,412
Eqty Earns/Minority Int.	6,154	3,216	(1,475)	(3,980)	(966)	367	29,734	19,766
Income from Cont Ops	51,309	46,060	...	38,618	...	...	60,017	39,605
Net Income	53,473	48,058	28,963	38,251	35,311	32,441	30,385	19,839
Average Shs. Outstg.	43,896	40,588	31,717	30,407	30,408	29,337	24,220	16,798
Balance Sheet								
Cash & Cash Equivalents	4,364	1,737	6,974	2,190	3,329	1,442	2,160	1,410
Ttl Real Estate Inv.	887,124	703,465	706,280	514,962	546,193	519,948	400,977	269,031
Total Assets	1,208,310	954,108	1,006,628	761,611	749,789	685,595	537,014	370,953
Long–Term Obligations	437,338	345,689	327,933	258,681	242,271	154,807	56,736	116,956
Total Liabilities	477,556	404,967	441,988	367,710	358,427	301,705	174,870	118,379
Net Stockholders' Equity	730,754	549,141	564,640	393,901	391,362	383,890	362,144	252,574
Shares Outstanding	50,001	40,403	40,599	30,456	30,255	29,521	27,953	16,798
Net Inc.+Depr./Assets %	5.54	6.00	3.80	6.30	5.90	5.70	6.60	6.30
Return on Equity %	7.02	8.38	5.12	9.80	9.02	8.45	16.57	15.68
Return on Assets %	4.24	4.82	2.87	5.07	4.70	4.73	11.17	10.67
Price Range	18.30-14.37	16.34-13.00	14.25-10.25	11.31-9.69	13.88-9.50	18.00-12.63	18.06-14.13	16.00-12.88
P/E Ratio	16.94-13.31	15.71-12.50	15.66-11.26	8.91-7.63	11.96-8.19	16.36-11.48	14.45-11.30	13.56-10.91
Average Yield %	7.70	8.50	9.97	11.90	10.38	7.92	7.66	8.67

Address: 450 South Orange Avenue, Orlando, FL 32801 **Telephone:** (407) 265–7348 **Web Site:** www.cnlreit.com	**Officers:** James M. Seneff – Chmn., Robert A. Bourne – Vice–Chmn. **Transfer Agents:** First Union National Bank, Charlotte, NC	**Investor Contact:** 407–265–7348 **Institutional Holding** **No of Institutions:** 98 **Shares:** 12,042,896 **% Held:** 30.10%

COMMUNITY BANK SYSTEM, INC.

Exchange	Symbol	Price	52Wk Range	Yield	P/E
NYS	CBU	$22.02 (5/28/2004)	25.28-18.50	2.91	14.68

*7 Year Price Score 144.7 *NYSE Composite Index=100 *12 Month Price Score 43.3

Interim Earnings (Per Share)

Qtr.	Mar	Jun	Sep	Dec
2001	0.28	0.09	0.27	0.17
2002	0.28	0.31	0.42	0.45
2003	0.37	0.37	0.43	0.32
2004	0.38	...	...	...

Interim Dividends (Per Share)

Amt	Decl	Ex	Rec	Pay
0.16Q	11/21/2003	12/11/2003	12/15/2003	1/9/2004
100%	1/21/2004	4/13/2004	3/17/2004	4/12/2004
0.16Q	2/19/2004	3/11/2004	3/15/2004	4/9/2004
0.16Q	5/21/2004	6/11/2004	6/15/2004	7/9/2004

Indicated Div: $0.64 (Div. Reinv. Plan)

Valuation Analysis

Forecast P/E 13.35 (5/24/2004)

Market Cap	$285.4 Million	Book Value	404.8 Million
Price/Book	1.59	Price/Sales	2.84

Dividend Achiever Status

Rank	180	10 Year Growth Rate	8.84%

Total Years of Dividend Growth 12

Business Summary: Commercial Banking (MIC: 8.1 SIC: 6021 NAIC:522110)

Community Bank System is a bank holding company with $3.86 billion in assets and total deposits of $2.73 billion as of Dec 31 2003. As of Dec 31 2003, Co.'s wholly-owned community banking subsidiary, Community Bank, N.A., operated 126 customer facilities throughout 22 counties of Upstate New York and five counties of Northeastern Pennsylvania offering a range of commercial and retail banking services. Another Co. subsidiary, Benefit Plans Adminstrative Services, Inc., provides administration, consulting and actuarial services to sponsors of employee benefit plans.

Recent Developments: For the quarter ended Mar 31 2004, net income advanced 12.1% to $11.2 million compared with $9.9 million in the same period a year earlier. Net interest income rose 10.7% to $36.0 million from $32.5 million the previous year, primarily due to a $381.0 million increase in average earning assets. Co. attributed the growth in average earning assets to organic loan growth, its 2003 Grange acquisition that added 12 branches, and securities purchases. Loan loss provision was $2.1 million versus $3.4 million last year. Total noninterest income climbed 19.6% to $10.5 million, due principally to the 2003 acquisitions of Harbridge Consulting Group and Grange.

Prospects: Co.'s near-term outlook appears promising, supported by contributions from recent acquisitions, the pending acquisition of First Heritage Bank, a $270.0 million asset bank with three branches, and improving asset quality indicators. For instance, for the quarter ended Mar 31 2004, total delinquent loans, or loans in excess of 30 days past due, declined to 1.65% from 1.85% in the year-ago period. Also, non-performing loans decreased 11.9% to $14.0 million compared with $15.8 million the year before. Co. noted that this improvement, combined with loan growth, resulted in an improvement in the ratio of non-performing loans to total loans, to 0.66% at Mar 31 2004 from 0.87% last year.

Financial Data

(US$ in Thousands)	12/31/2003	12/31/2002	12/31/2001	12/31/2000	12/31/1999	12/31/1998	12/31/1997	12/31/1996
Earnings Per Share	1.49	1.46	0.81	1.42	1.21	1.02	1.01	0.91
Tang. Book Val. Per Share	7.36	7.32	4.86	6.32	4.04	4.50	3.91	4.92
Dividends Per Share	0.590	0.550	0.540	0.510	0.470	0.410	0.370	0.330
Dividend Payout %	39.79	37.54	66.66	35.78	38.84	40.48	36.63	63.73
Income Statement								
Total Interest Income	191,129	204,870	197,850	145,221	123,888	122,938	117,628	97,688
Total Interest Expense	59,301	77,020	101,195	74,012	55,947	58,543	54,752	42,422
Net Interest Income	131,828	127,850	96,655	71,208	67,941	64,395	62,876	55,266
Provision for Loan Losses	11,195	12,222	7,097	7,182	5,136	5,123	4,480	2,897
Non-Interest Income	34,981	32,600	29,083	20,989	15,487	17,040	11,808	8,874
Non-Interest Expense	102,461	95,824	89,039	55,989	52,733	51,876	45,799	37,450
Income from Cont Ops	...	...	20,711	...	...	15,534	...	...
Net Income	40,380	38,517	19,129	20,319	17,635	15,728	15,562	14,133
Average Shs. Outstg.	27,034	26,334	23,650	14,271	14,590	15,341	15,352	13,885
Balance Sheet								
Cash & Due from Banks	103,923	113,531	106,554	59,304	76,527	...	82,106	52,535
Securities Avail. for Sale	1,190,882	...	...	...	...	...	...	...
Net Loans & Leases	2,099,414	1,780,574	1,708,969	1,084,112	995,802	904,779	830,778	644,346
Total Assets	3,855,397	3,434,204	3,210,833	2,022,635	1,840,702	1,680,689	1,633,742	1,343,865
Total Deposits	2,725,488	2,505,356	2,545,970	1,457,730	1,360,306	1,378,066	1,345,686	1,027,213
Long-Term Obligations	631,486	430,000	263,100	331,100	324,000	...	...	...
Total Liabilities	3,450,569	3,109,166	2,942,853	1,883,260	1,732,214	1,560,523	1,515,730	1,234,512
Net Stockholders' Equity	404,828	325,038	267,980	139,376	108,487	120,165	118,012	109,352
Shares Outstanding	28,330	25,957	25,805	13,986	14,592	14,592	15,173	14,948
Statistical Record								
Return on Equity %	9.97	11.84	7.72	14.57	16.25	12.92	13.18	12.92
Return on Assets %	1.04	1.12	0.64	1.00	0.95	0.92	0.95	1.05
Non-Int. Exp./Tot. Inc. %	45.31	40.35	39.23	33.68	37.83	37.06	35.38	35.14
Price Range	25.23-15.50	17.10-13.04	14.84-12.45	13.13-10.13	16.28-11.35	19.13-12.53	23.75-10.25	20.00-15.13
P/E Ratio	16.93-10.40	11.71-8.93	18.32-15.36	9.24-7.13	13.45-9.38	18.75-12.28	23.51-10.15	21.98-16.62
Average Yield %	2.97	3.60	3.96	4.46	3.65	2.60	2.47	1.98

Address: 5790 Widewaters Parkway, DeWitt, NY 13214-1883	**Officers:** James A. Gabriel – Chmn., Sanford A. Belden – Pres., C.E.O.	**Investor Contact:** 315-445-2282 **Institutional Holding**
Telephone: (315) 445-2282	**Transfer Agents:** ChaseMellon Shareholder	**No of Institutions:** 87
Web Site: www.communitybankna.com	Services, L.L.C., Ridgefield Park, NJ	**Shares:** 4,562,995 **% Held:** 35.10%

COMMUNITY FIRST BANKSHARES, INC.

Exchange	Symbol	Price	52Wk Range	Yield	P/E
NMS	CFBX	$32.10 (5/28/2004)	32.40-26.04	2.99	16.89

*7 Year Price Score 124.6 ***NYSE Composite Index=100** ***12 Month Price Score 52.8**

Interim Earnings (Per Share)

Qtr.	Mar	Jun	Sep	Dec
2001	0.24	0.43	0.45	0.45
2002	0.47	0.49	0.51	0.50
2003	0.50	0.49	0.48	0.48
2004	0.45	...	...	...

Interim Dividends (Per Share)

Amt	Decl	Ex	Rec	Pay
0.23Q	8/7/2003	8/27/2003	9/1/2003	9/15/2003
0.23Q	10/30/2003	11/26/2003	12/1/2003	12/15/2003
0.24Q	2/4/2004	2/26/2004	3/1/2004	3/15/2004
0.24Q	4/21/2004	5/27/2004	6/1/2004	6/15/2004
Indicated Div: $0.96 (Div. Reinv. Plan)				

Valuation Analysis

Forecast P/E 15.64 (5/24/2004)

Market Cap $1.3 Billion	Book Value 361.8 Million
Price/Book 2.97	Price/Sales 2.67

Dividend Achiever Status

Rank 63	10 Year Growth Rate	16.23%
Total Years of Dividend Growth		12

Business Summary: Commercial Banking (MIC: 8.1 SIC: 6022 NAIC:522110)

Community First Bankshares is a bank holding company that, as of Dec 31 2003 operated through one bank subsidiary with banking offices in 136 communities in Arizona, California, Colorado, Iowa, Minnesota, Nebraska, New Mexico, North Dakota, South Dakota, Utah, Wisconsin and Wyoming. The banks are community banks that offer a range of commercial and consumer banking services primarily to individuals and businesses in small and medium-sized communities and surrounding market areas. Co. provides its banking offices with the advantages of affiliation with a bank holding company, such as access to its lines of financial services. As of Dec 31 2003, Co. had total assets of $5.47 billion.

Recent Developments: For the three months ended Mar 31 2004, net income fell 12.9% to $16.9 million compared with $19.4 million in the same period a year earlier. Net interest income slid 7.9% to $56.3 million from $61.2 million, reflecting declines in interest rates and decreases in loans outstanding. Provision for loan losses was $2.4 million versus $3.5 million the year before. Total non-interest income increased 4.8% to $22.9 million, due in part to higher insurance commissions and increased security sales commissions. Total non-interest income for 2004 and 2003 included net gains on the sales of securities of $1.5 million and $464,000, respectively.

Prospects: On Mar 16 2004, Co. and BancWest Corporation announced the signing of a definitive agreement wherein BancWest will acquire Co. for $32.25 per share in a cash transaction valued at $1.20 billion. BancWest is a bank holding company whose principal subsidiaries are Bank of the West and First Hawaiian Bank. The boards of directors of Co. and BancWest have approved the transaction. The transaction also has been approved by the board of BancWest's parent, BNP Paribas. The merger requires approval from Co. shareholders and federal and state banking regulators. Upon all regulatory approvals, it is expected that the transaction will close during the third quarter of 2004.

Financial Data

(US$ in Thousands)	3 Mos	12/31/2003	12/31/2002	12/31/2001	12/31/2000	12/31/1999	12/31/1998	12/31/1997
Earnings Per Share	1.90	1.95	1.97	1.57	1.54	1.48	0.98	1.20
Tang. Book Val. Per Share	7.27	7.17	10.41	9.42	8.37	8.50	8.31	8.90
Dividends Per Share	0.920	0.900	0.800	0.680	0.600	0.560	0.440	0.350
Dividend Payout %	48.17	46.15	40.60	43.31	38.96	37.83	44.89	29.16
Income Statement								
Total Interest Income	70,552	309,242	358,183	434,016	477,558	465,206	449,244	278,597
Total Interest Expense	14,214	70,538	89,928	162,220	210,281	185,818	188,484	117,253
Net Interest Income	56,338	238,704	268,255	271,796	267,277	279,388	260,760	161,344
Provision for Loan Losses	2,365	12,602	13,262	17,520	15,781	20,184	22,509	5,352
Non-Interest Income	22,919	92,693	81,319	76,682	75,205	72,509	60,260	36,564
Non-Interest Expense	51,752	206,859	217,555	232,423	219,319	218,227	230,092	125,190
Income Before Taxes	25,140	111,936	118,757	98,535	107,382	113,486	68,419	67,366
Income from Cont Ops	...	...	...	...	...	...	46,971	45,850
Net Income	16,904	75,021	79,208	65,059	71,634	74,913	43,063	46,552
Average Shs. Outstg.	37,514	38,553	40,243	41,471	46,578	50,670	47,882	38,138
Balance Sheet								
Cash & Due from Banks	212,583	234,076	242,887	248,260	256,136	247,051	250,963	222,088
Securities Avail. for Sale	3,192,726	1,563,419	1,672,445	1,437,066	1,714,510	1,937,517	1,980,530	1,498,877
Net Loans & Leases	3,255,652	3,271,341	3,521,737	3,681,701	3,686,034	3,641,475	3,335,969	2,600,863
Total Assets	5,461,570	5,465,107	5,827,170	5,772,326	6,089,729	6,302,235	6,002,972	4,855,526
Total Deposits	4,391,257	4,389,210	4,669,746	4,750,813	5,019,891	4,909,863	4,884,672	3,619,334
Long-Term Obligations	178,211	222,211	127,500	136,841	123,957	75,622	93,472	116,476
Total Liabilities	5,100,297	5,103,307	5,328,721	5,295,621	5,624,298	5,774,966	5,477,726	4,396,232
Net Stockholders' Equity	361,273	361,800	378,449	356,705	345,431	407,269	405,246	339,294
Shares Outstanding	36,862	37,357	38,678	40,246	41,866	47,118	47,119	40,646
Return on Equity %	4.67	20.73	15.89	13.64	15.39	14.20	8.94	9.98
Return on Assets %	0.30	1.37	1.35	1.12	1.17	1.18	0.78	0.94
Equity/Assets %	6.61	6.62	8.55	8.25	7.64	8.36	8.74	9.45
Non-Int. Exp./Tot. Inc. %	55.36	51.46	49.50	45.51	39.67	40.58	45.15	39.72
Price Range	32.16-27.13	29.26-24.35	28.45-22.36	26.97-18.06	19.13-12.41	24.00-13.94	27.00-14.13	27.56-13.69
P/E Ratio	16.93-14.28	15.01-12.49	14.44-11.35	17.18-11.50	12.42-8.06	16.22-9.42	27.55-14.41	22.97-11.41
Average Yield %	3.17	3.32	3.04	3.03	3.75	2.85	1.92	1.83

Address: 520 Main Avenue, Fargo, ND 58124-0001	Officers: Mark A. Anderson – Pres., C.E.O., Ronald K. Strand – Vice-Chmn., C.O.O.	Investor Contact:888-292-2378
Telephone: (701) 298-5600	Transfer Agents:Wells Fargo Bank Minnesota, NA, South St. Paul, MN	Institutional Holding
Web Site: www.communityfirst.com		No of Institutions: 9
		Shares: 3,687,355 % Held: –

COMMUNITY TRUST BANCORP, INC.

Exchange	Symbol	Price	52Wk Range	Yield	P/E
NMS	CTBI	$31.17 (5/28/2004)	34.25-23.78	2.95	N/A

*7 Year Price Score 145.2 ***NYSE Composite Index=100** ***12 Month Price Score 49.5**

Interim Earnings (Per Share)

Qtr.	Mar	Jun	Sep	Dec
2001	0.37	0.42	0.38	0.42
2002	0.45	0.45	0.57	0.52
2003	0.50	0.51	0.53	0.57
2004	0.53	...	...	...

Interim Dividends (Per Share)

Amt	Decl	Ex	Rec	Pay
10%	10/29/2003	11/26/2003	12/1/2003	12/15/2003
0.23Q	10/29/2003	12/11/2003	12/15/2003	1/1/2004
0.23Q	1/27/2004	3/11/2004	3/15/2004	4/1/2004
0.23Q	4/27/2004	6/11/2004	6/15/2004	7/1/2004

Indicated Div: $0.92

Valuation Analysis
Forecast P/E 14.21 (5/24/2004)

Market Cap $353.5 Million	Book Value	N/A
Price/Book N/A	Price/Sales	N/A

Dividend Achiever Status

Rank 177	10 Year Growth Rate	8.97%
Total Years of Dividend Growth	15	

Business Summary: Commercial Banking (MIC: 8.1 SIC: 6021 NAIC:522110)

Community Trust Bancorp is a bank holding company with assets of $2.47 billion as of Dec 31 2003 that owns all the capital stock of one commercial bank and one trust company, serving small and mid–sized communities in eastern, northeast central, south central Kentucky, and southern West Virginia. The commercial bank is Community Trust Bank, Pikeville, KY. The trust company, Community Trust and Investment, Lexington, KY, has offices in Lexington, Pikeville, Ashland, Middlesboro and Versailles, KY. Co. operates 69 banking locations across Kentucky, and five banking locations in West Virginia.

Recent Developments: For the three months ended Mar 31 2004, net income climbed 4.1% to $7.3 million versus $7.0 million in the same quarter of 2003. Results for 2004 and 2003 included securities gains of $1,000 and $979,000, and gains on sales of loans of $459,000 and $1.5 million, respectively. Net interest income rose 10.5% to $22.7 million from $20.5 million the year before. Provision for loan losses jumped 37.9% to $2.1 million. Non-interest income declined 6.2% to $8.0 million, reflecting lower trust revenue, insurance commissions and a decline in gains from securities. Non-interest expense grew 3.3% to $18.2 million due to increased personnel and occupancy and equipment expenses.

Prospects: Co. is seeing a slowdown in refinancing activity, most likely due to increased interest rates, which have slowly ticked upward during the first few months of 2004. Nevertheless, Co. continues to experience solid growth in its loan portfolio, which is up at an annualized rate of 8.9% from the prior year and 7.9% from the fourth quarter of 2003. Also, Co.'s asset quality is much improved from the prior year with non-performing loans decreasing to $17.9 million as of Mar 31 2004, down 29.9% from the prior-year quarter. This improvement in asset quality should help further strengthen Co.'s balance sheet position.

Financial Data

(US$ in Thousands)	3 Mos	12/31/2003	12/31/2002	12/31/2001	12/31/2000	12/31/1999	12/31/1998	12/31/1997
Earnings Per Share	2.14	2.11	1.99	1.59	1.54	1.62	1.03	1.18
Tang. Book Val. Per Share	12.06	11.69	15.04	11.68	8.87	8.45	7.63	9.52
Dividends Per Share	0.820	0.780	0.690	0.660	0.610	0.580	0.540	0.490
Dividend Payout %	38.32	37.05	34.86	41.45	39.76	36.07	52.89	41.63
Income Statement								
Total Interest Income	31,297	128,514	146,550	176,835	175,749	163,516	160,570	150,588
Total Interest Expense	8,616	43,895	57,293	93,717	91,515	79,740	83,986	74,076
Net Interest Income	22,681	84,619	89,257	83,118	84,234	83,776	76,584	76,512
Provision for Loan Losses	2,133	9,332	10,086	9,185	9,217	9,105	16,008	11,154
Non–Interest Income	8,015	36,372	27,928	23,774	19,526	21,026	19,466	18,442
Non–Interest Expense	18,194	70,735	67,341	64,938	61,927	64,388	62,166	59,892
Income Before Taxes	10,369	40,924	39,758	32,769	32,616	31,309	17,876	23,908
Income from Cont Ops	...	...	...	...	...	...	...	15,984
Net Income	7,280	28,891	27,600	22,272	22,346	21,845	13,969	19,069
Average Shs. Outstg.	13,467	13,677	13,868	13,997	14,464	13,417	13,393	13,469
Balance Sheet								
Cash & Due from Banks	83,229	79,907	92,955	96,173	72,725	99,773	98,133	61,404
Securities Avail. for Sale	366,869	421,855	527,339	367,233	236,620	270,281	301,052	165,611
Net Loans & Leases	1,745,181	1,711,607	1,611,336	1,687,424	1,668,639	1,594,378	1,476,297	1,407,964
Total Assets	2,460,433	2,474,039	2,487,911	2,503,905	2,261,975	2,176,090	2,248,039	1,852,667
Total Deposits	2,055,603	2,067,615	2,127,716	2,155,772	1,943,916	1,877,334	1,921,141	1,465,003
Long–Term Obligations	62,298	62,692	6,721	22,969	61,386	70,598	105,207	155,290
Total Liabilities	2,234,525	2,252,646	2,218,992	2,277,799	2,080,071	2,003,671	2,083,244	1,694,648
Net Stockholders' Equity	225,908	221,393	209,419	191,606	181,904	172,419	164,795	158,019
Shares Outstanding	13,438	13,461	13,582	13,825	14,158	13,362	13,396	14,732
Return on Equity %	3.22	13.04	10.26	9.85	12.28	12.66	8.47	10.11
Return on Assets %	0.29	1.16	1.10	0.88	0.98	1.00	0.62	0.86
Equity/Assets %	9.18	8.94	10.80	9.03	8.04	7.92	7.33	8.52
Non–Int. Exp./Tot. Inc. %	46.28	42.89	38.59	32.37	31.71	34.89	34.52	35.43
Price Range	33.00-27.77	33.30-22.80	26.73-18.11	20.25-12.71	15.87-11.42	18.06-15.03	22.88-15.20	21.43-15.21
P/E Ratio	15.42-12.98	15.78-10.81	13.43-9.10	12.73-7.99	10.31-7.41	11.15-9.28	14.24-14.75	18.16-12.89
Average Yield %	2.76	2.99	3.18	3.90	4.62	3.51	2.79	2.76

Address: 346 North Mayo Trail, Pikeville, KY 41501–2947 Telephone: (606) 432–1414 Web Site: www.ctbi.com	Officers: Burlin Coleman – Chmn., Jean R. Hale – Vice–Chmn., Pres., C.E.O. Transfer Agents:Community Trust Bancorp, Inc., Pikeville, KY	Investor Contact:606–432–1414 Institutional Holding No of Institutions: 14 Shares: 472,891 % Held: –

COMPASS BANCSHARES INC.

Exchange	Symbol	Price	52Wk Range	Yield	P/E
NMS	CBSS	$42.05 (5/28/2004)	42.86-33.19	2.97	15.35

*7 Year Price Score 134.3   *NYSE Composite Index=100   *12 Month Price Score 50.0

Interim Earnings (Per Share)

Qtr.	Mar	Jun	Sep	Dec
2001	0.50	0.52	0.53	0.56
2002	0.59	0.60	0.61	0.62
2003	0.64	0.68	0.68	0.69
2004	0.69	...	...	...

Interim Dividends (Per Share)

Amt	Decl	Ex	Rec	Pay
0.28Q	8/19/2003	9/11/2003	9/15/2003	10/1/2003
0.28Q	11/17/2003	12/11/2003	12/15/2003	1/2/2004
0.313Q	2/17/2004	3/11/2004	3/15/2004	4/1/2004
0.313Q	5/14/2004	6/11/2004	6/15/2004	7/1/2004

Indicated Div: $1.25 (Div. Reinv. Plan)

Valuation Analysis
Forecast P/E 14.63 (5/24/2004)

Market Cap $5.4 Billion	Book Value	1.9 Billion
Price/Book 2.60	Price/Sales	2.77

Dividend Achiever Status

Rank	108	10 Year Growth Rate	12.78%
Total Years of Dividend Growth			22

Business Summary: Commercial Banking (MIC: 8.1 SIC: 6021 NAIC:522110)

Compass Bancshares is a bank holding company headquartered in Birmingham, AL, with total assets of $26.96 billion as of Dec 31 2003. Co.'s principal subsidiary is Compass Bank, which operates 376 full–service bank offices, including 136 in Texas, 89 in Alabama, 71 in Arizona, 42 in Florida, 28 in Colorado, and 10 in New Mexico. In addition, Compass Bank operates loan production offices in Georgia and Maryland. Compass Bank provides general commercial banking and trust services such as receiving demand and time deposits, making personal and commercial loans and furnishing personal and commercial checking accounts.

Recent Developments: For the three months ended Mar 31 2004, net income climbed 5.1% to $86.2 million from $82.1 million in the corresponding prior-year period. Results for 2004 and 2003 included merger and integration expenses of $245,000 and $466,000, respectively. Results for 2004 also included an investment securities gain of $2.2 million. Net interest income slipped 1.9% to $222.9 million from $227.2 million a year earlier. Provision for loan losses declined 18.2% to $24.3 million from $29.8 million in 2003. Total non-interest income advanced 13.5% to $139.7 million from $123.1 million the year before, while total non-interest expense rose 7.1% to $210.1 million from $196.1 million in the prior year.

Prospects: Earnings are being positively affected by strong growth in Co.'s fee-based businesses, including service charges on deposit accounts and credit card service charges and fees, partially offset by continued pressure on net interest margin stemming from low interest rates and the corresponding negative effect on investment opportunities. Meanwhile, earnings are benefiting from Co.'s efforts to contain non-interest expense growth following the opening of new banking offices in 2003, as well as several insurance agency acquisitions during the past year. In addition, Co. is enjoying solid loan and deposit growth, as well as stable credit quality.

Financial Data
(US$ in Thousands)

	3 Mos	12/31/2003	12/31/2002	12/31/2001	12/31/2000	12/31/1999	12/31/1998	12/31/1997
Earnings Per Share	2.74	2.69	2.42	2.11	2.00	1.88	1.56	1.56
Tang. Book Val. Per Share	13.32	12.92	13.06	13.53	12.23	10.51	10.29	9.69
Dividends Per Share	1.120	1.090	0.980	0.910	0.860	0.770	0.680	0.610
Dividend Payout %	40.88	40.52	40.49	43.12	43.00	41.22	43.58	39.46
Income Statement								
Total Interest Income	310,679	1,277,287	1,386,923	1,517,721	1,432,844	1,247,571	1,134,544	949,034
Total Interest Expense	87,818	367,757	462,068	691,862	752,044	608,403	555,157	473,869
Net Interest Income	222,861	909,530	924,855	825,859	680,800	639,168	579,387	475,165
Provision for Loan Losses	24,345	119,681	136,331	106,241	53,539	31,122	38,445	22,412
Non–Interest Income	134,353	498,744	414,958	352,981	280,364	220,033	203,370	164,910
Non–Interest Expense	210,147	797,883	752,429	685,770	569,589	517,916	491,017	395,727
Income Before Taxes	130,280	518,150	477,158	410,226	356,576	331,239	272,425	238,493
Net Income	86,247	341,868	314,399	270,397	240,591	217,045	180,880	155,563
Average Shs. Outstg.	125,146	127,186	129,850	129,138	120,454	114,441	113,745	99,771
Balance Sheet								
Cash & Due from Banks	684,290	726,492	734,540	715,991	719,487	684,540	831,614	693,687
Securities Avail. for Sale	4,617,082	4,434,232	4,806,406	6,585,036	5,049,473	4,243,813	3,773,432	2,422,170
Net Loans & Leases	17,107,488	17,120,920	16,248,490	13,515,893	11,340,877	10,645,849	9,964,608	8,549,545
Total Assets	27,480,584	26,963,113	23,884,709	23,015,000	19,992,242	18,150,752	17,288,908	13,459,555
Total Deposits	16,524,445	15,687,823	15,135,387	13,735,245	14,033,244	12,808,918	12,013,446	9,632,545
Long–Term Obligations	4,812,828	4,827,814	4,900,132	3,837,450	2,529,264	2,564,328	2,045,980	1,387,121
Total Liabilities	25,553,394	25,091,230	21,953,207	21,299,359	18,511,780	16,954,548	16,092,767	12,499,547
Net Stockholders' Equity	1,927,190	1,871,883	1,931,502	1,715,641	1,480,462	1,196,204	1,196,141	960,008
Shares Outstanding	122,195	122,086	126,116	126,800	120,972	113,708	113,350	98,986
Statistical Record								
Return on Equity %	4.47	18.26	16.27	15.76	16.25	18.14	15.12	16.20
Return on Assets %	0.31	1.26	1.31	1.17	1.20	1.19	1.04	1.15
Equity/Assets %	7.01	6.94	8.08	7.45	7.40	6.59	6.91	7.13
Non–Int. Exp./Tot. Inc. %	46.43	44.24	41.16	36.20	32.89	34.79	36.18	35.00
Price Range	42.86-37.77	39.59-29.99	35.87-26.18	29.08-19.13	24.28-15.75	30.50-20.69	35.46-19.25	31.08-17.31
P/E Ratio	15.64-13.78	14.72-11.15	14.82-10.82	13.78-9.06	12.14-7.88	16.22-11.00	22.73-12.34	19.93-11.09
Average Yield %	2.78	3.14	3.10	3.69	4.54	2.95	2.41	2.65

Address: 15 South 20th Street, Birmingham, AL 35233
Telephone: (205) 297–3000
Web Site: www.compassweb.com

Officers: D. Paul Jones – Chmn., C.E.O., George M. Boltwood – Sr. Exec. V.P., Corp. Banking

Investor Contact:205–297–3331
Institutional Holding
No of Institutions: 9
Shares: 228,769   % Held: –

CONAGRA FOODS, INC.

Exchange	Symbol	Price	52Wk Range	Yield	P/E
NYS	CAG	$28.12 (5/28/2004)	29.34–21.15	3.70	17.58

*7 Year Price Score 97.7 *NYSE Composite Index=100 ***12 Month Price Score 53.7**

Interim Earnings (Per Share)

Qtr.	Aug	Nov	Feb	May
2000–01	0.30	0.58	0.19	0.26
2001–02	0.36	0.44	0.31	0.36
2002–03	0.42	0.45	0.30	0.41
2003–04	0.38	0.45	0.36	...

Interim Dividends (Per Share)

Amt	Decl	Ex	Rec	Pay
0.248Q	7/11/2003	7/30/2003	8/1/2003	9/1/2003
0.26Q	9/25/2003	10/29/2003	10/31/2003	12/1/2003
0.26Q	12/4/2003	1/28/2004	1/30/2004	3/1/2004
0.26Q	4/9/2004	4/29/2004	5/3/2004	6/1/2004

Indicated Div: $1.04 (Div. Reinv. Plan)

Valuation Analysis

Forecast P/E 16.89 (5/24/2004)

Market Cap	$15.1 Billion	Book Value	4.9 Billion
Price/Book	2.89	Price/Sales	0.99

Dividend Achiever Status

Rank	119	10 Year Growth Rate	12.01%
Total Years of Dividend Growth		26	

Business Summary: Food (MIC: 4.1 SIC: 2011 NAIC:311611)

ConAgra Foods operates through three business segments: Packaged Foods includes Co.'s shelf–stable, frozen and refrigerated foods, which are processed and packaged. Food Ingredients includes Co.'s basic ingredients, milled ingredients and specialty ingredients operations. Agricultural Products includes operations involved in the distribution of agricultural crop inputs. Co.'s major brands include: *Healthy Choice, Banquet, Chef Boyardee, Wesson, Hunt's, Orville Redenbacher's, Slim Jim, Peter Pan, Parkay, Van Camp's, PAM, Swiss Miss, Louis Kemp, Reddi–wip, Act II, La Choy, Butterball* and *Armour*, among numerous others.

Recent Developments: For the 13 weeks ended Feb 22 2004, income from continuing operations totaled $191.8 million, before a $1.4 million accounting change charge, compared with income from continuing operations of $200.3 million in the corresponding prior–year period. Net sales slipped 0.5% to $3.60 billion from $3.61 billion the year before. Packaged Foods segment sales slid 1.4% to $2.97 billion from $3.01 billion a year earlier, while Food Ingredients segment sales climbed 4.2% to $630.2 million from $605.0 million the previous year. Operating profit grew 1.0% to $450.5 million from $446.0 million the prior year.

Prospects: Results are being positively affected by Co.'s efforts to boost sales and increase profitability. In January 2004, Co. launched *Life Choice*, a new line of frozen meals that have fewer carbohydrates. Co. is pleased with the initial customer response to Life Choice and has expanded its availability throughout the U.S. Meanwhile, on Feb 17 2004, Co. introduced *Golden Cuisine*, a line of affordable and nutritional frozen meals targeting the growing market of Americans ages 55 and older. Co. has partnered with senior caregivers, including Meals On Wheels Association of America™ and Coordinated Care Solutions–CareGuide™, to deliver the *Golden Cuisine* meals to seniors at home.

Financial Data

(US$ in Thousands)	9 Mos	6 Mos	3 Mos	05/25/2003	05/26/2002	05/27/2001	05/28/2000	05/30/1999
Earnings Per Share	1.60	1.60	1.60	1.58	1.47	1.33	0.86	0.75
Cash Flow Per Share	1.45	0.58	0.42	1.34	4.44	0.24	1.44	2.47
Tang. Book Val. Per Share	0.05	0.05	0.16	N.M	N.M	N.M	1.21	1.02
Dividends Per Share	1.000	0.990	0.970	0.960	0.920	0.850	0.760	0.660
Dividend Payout %	62.50	61.87	60.62	61.07	62.58	64.43	88.83	89.26
Income Statement								
Total Revenues	10,766,100	7,168,400	4,393,700	19,839,200	27,629,600	27,194,200	25,385,800	24,594,300
Total Indirect Exp.	1,330,500	903,500	550,800	2,308,400	2,423,400	2,355,100	3,210,400	3,039,200
Depreciation & Amort.	263,200	173,900	91,200	396,700	623,200	592,900	536,500	499,800
Operating Income	1,047,900	671,800	290,300	1,514,500	1,669,700	1,527,400	969,500	998,900
Net Interest Inc./(Exp.)	(195,900)	(133,900)	(65,700)	(276,300)	(401,500)	(423,300)	(303,400)	(316,600)
Income Taxes	251,700	129,400	20,900	436,000	483,200	421,600	253,100	323,900
Income from Cont Ops	600,300	408,500	203,700	840,100	785,000	682,500	...	...
Net Income	668,300	465,000	194,900	774,800	783,000	638,600	413,000	358,400
Average Shs. Outstg.	532,200	531,700	531,500	530,700	528,000	514,300	478,600	476,700
Balance Sheet								
Cash & Cash Equivalents	533,700	26,700	680,700	628,600	157,900	198,100	157,600	62,800
Total Current Assets	5,482,900	5,772,400	6,573,700	6,059,600	6,433,900	7,362,600	5,966,500	5,656,100
Total Assets	14,475,700	14,532,700	15,539,200	15,071,400	15,496,200	16,480,800	12,295,800	12,146,100
Total Current Liabilities	3,183,600	3,532,200	4,368,900	3,803,400	4,313,400	6,935,600	5,489,200	5,386,400
Long–Term Obligations	5,312,200	4,965,900	5,284,300	5,395,200	5,743,700	4,109,500	2,566,800	2,543,100
Net Stockholders' Equity	4,876,200	4,898,300	4,743,600	4,621,700	4,308,200	3,983,200	2,964,100	2,908,800
Net Working Capital	2,299,300	2,240,200	2,204,800	2,256,200	2,120,500	427,000	477,300	269,700
Shares Outstanding	528,207	536,614	536,657	536,765	537,040	537,067	492,212	488,173
Statistical Record								
Operating Profit Margin %	10.00	9.75	6.82	7.63	6.04	5.61	3.81	4.06
Return on Equity %	13.7	8.33	4.49	18.17	18.22	17.13	13.93	12.32
Return on Assets %	4.62	2.81	1.37	5.57	5.06	4.14	3.35	2.95
Debt/Total Assets %	36.70	34.17	34.00	35.79	37.06	24.93	20.87	20.93
Price Range	26.54–21.15	25.41–21.15	25.41–21.71	27.65–19.65	25.64–19.02	26.13–17.99	28.06–15.50	34.19–23.31
P/E Ratio	16.59–13.22	15.88–13.22	15.88–13.47	17.50–12.44	17.44–12.94	19.64–13.53	32.63–18.02	45.58–31.08
Average Yield %	4.16	4.27	4.12	3.99	4.01	3.99	3.36	2.29

Address: One ConAgra Drive, Omaha, NE 68102–5001 **Telephone:** (402) 595–4000 **Web Site:** www.conagra.com	**Officers:** Bruce C. Rohde – Chmn., Pres., C.E.O., Dwight J. Goslee – Exec. V.P., Oper. Control & Devel. **Transfer Agents:** Wells Fargo Sharehowner Services, St. Paul, MN	**Investor Contact:** 800–214–0349 **Institutional Holding** **No of Institutions:** 495 **Shares:** 328,005,141 **% Held:** 61.10%

CONNECTICUT WATER SERVICE, INC.

Exchange	Symbol	Price	52Wk Range	Yield	P/E
NMS	CTWS	$25.06 (5/28/2004)	30.40-24.70	3.31	21.79

*7 Year Price Score 126.8   *NYSE Composite Index=100   *12 Month Price Score 44.2

Interim Earnings (Per Share)

Qtr.	Mar	Jun	Sep	Dec
2001	0.30	0.24	0.38	0.18
2002	0.20	0.24	0.50	0.18
2003	0.26	0.15	0.48	0.26
2004	0.25	...	...	...

Interim Dividends (Per Share)

Amt	Decl	Ex	Rec	Pay
0.208Q	8/13/2003	8/28/2003	9/2/2003	9/16/2003
0.208Q	11/12/2003	11/26/2003	12/1/2003	12/15/2003
0.208Q	1/7/2004	2/26/2004	3/1/2004	3/15/2004
0.208Q	5/13/2004	5/27/2004	6/1/2004	6/15/2004
Indicated Div: $0.90 (Div. Reinv. Plan)				

Valuation Analysis

Forecast P/E 21.36 (5/24/2004)

Market Cap $192.6 Million	Book Value 84.2 Million
Price/Book N/A	Price/Sales N/A

Dividend Achiever Status

Rank 300	10 Year Growth Rate 1.25%
Total Years of Dividend Growth 28	

TRADING VOLUME (thousand shares)

Business Summary: Water Utilities (MIC: 7.2 SIC: 4941 NAIC:221310)

Connecticut Water Service is the parent company of five regulated water companies that supplied water to 85,536 customers for residential, commercial, industrial and municipal purposes in 42 towns in Connecticut and Massachusetts as of Dec 31 2002. Co. represents the largest domestic investor-owned water system in the state of Connecticut in terms of operating revenues and utility plant investment. The area served has an estimated population of approximately 300,000 as of Aug 13 2003. In addition, Co. had six unregulated water companies as of Dec 31 2002.

Recent Developments: For the first quarter ended Mar 31 2004, net income declined 6.4% to $2.0 million compared with $2.1 million in the corresponding period of the previous year. The decline in operating results was mainly attributed to lower earnings from Co.'s real estate operations, which more than offset improved results from Co.'s water activities and services and rentals business segments. Operating revenues were essentially the same at $10.9 million versus 2003. Utility operating income fell 5.5% to $1.9 million versus $2.0 million the year before. Net gain on property transactions amounted to $706,000 versus $943,000 in 2003.

Prospects: Despite lower overall earnings in the first quarter, Co. is pleased with the operating performance of its water utility and services and rentals business segments, which produced earnings increases of $79,000 and $23,000, respectively. Meanwhile, the lower first quarter earnings for Co.'s real estate segment reflects the relative size of the land donated year-to-date in 2004 versus the prior year. Meanwhile, on March 4 2004, Co.'s main subsidiary, The Connecticut Water Company, refinanced a portion of its long-term debt, which is expected to result in a reduction in annual interest payments of approximately $400,000.

Financial Data

(US$ in Thousands)	3 Mos	12/31/2003	12/31/2002	12/31/2001	12/31/2000	12/31/1999	12/31/1998	12/31/1997
Earnings Per Share	1.14	1.15	1.12	1.10	1.08	1.02	1.02	0.99
Cash Flow Per Share	(0.01)	1.68	1.77	1.93	2.04	1.93	1.71	2.06
Tang. Book Val. Per Share	10.05	10.11	9.72	9.36	9.02	8.71	8.62	8.37
Dividends Per Share	0.820	0.820	0.810	0.800	0.790	0.780	0.770	0.760
Dividend Payout %	73.23	71.73	72.71	73.13	73.20	76.61	76.25	77.23
Income Statement								
Total Revenues	10,919	47,115	45,830	45,392	41,512	42,624	37,924	38,501
Total Indirect Exp.	2,860	10,817	9,983	9,225	8,908	8,577	8,403	9,456
Costs & Expenses	9,013	35,584	33,996	34,078	30,353	31,397	27,620	28,167
Depreciation & Amort.	1,511	5,684	5,187	4,837	4,500	4,390	3,854	3,505
Operating Income	1,906	11,531	11,834	11,314	11,159	11,227	10,304	10,334
Net Interest Inc./(Exp.)	(911)	(4,635)	(4,534)	(4,632)	(4,541)	(4,391)	(4,177)	(4,182)
Income Taxes	529	2,008	4,482	4,777	4,417	5,065	3,641	3,876
Net Income	1,984	9,210	8,780	8,439	7,963	7,494	6,965	6,804
Average Shs. Outstg.	8,023	8,002	7,771	7,662	7,308	7,272	6,802	6,786
Balance Sheet								
Net Property	233,540	235,098	229,097	202,330	186,971	181,342	167,326	163,757
Total Assets	278,054	277,546	264,799	231,714	215,399	210,885	194,586	189,277
Long-Term Obligations	65,072	64,754	64,734	63,953	64,658	65,399	62,501	54,532
Net Stockholders' Equity	84,702	83,315	79,975	70,783	64,906	62,495	57,945	56,069
Shares Outstanding	7,986	7,967	7,939	7,649	7,279	7,258	6,804	6,790
Operating Profit Margin %	22.30	28.73	35.60	35.44	37.52	38.08	36.08	36.34
Net Inc./Net Property %	0.84	3.91	3.83	4.17	4.25	4.13	4.16	4.15
Net Inc./Tot. Capital %	1.06	4.98	4.98	5.18	5.07	4.87	4.81	5.10
Return on Equity %	2.96	13.32	16.40	18.45	18.84	19.76	17.61	18.41
Accum. Depr./Gross Prop. %	28.72	28.24	27.66	27.48	26.56	25.87	25.18	24.22
Price Range	29.21-27.65	30.40-24.15	31.00-23.79	31.25-19.50	22.58-17.37	24.50-14.50	19.00-13.67	14.44-12.22
P/E Ratio	25.62-24.25	26.43-21.00	27.68-21.24	28.41-17.73	20.91-16.09	24.02-14.22	18.63-13.40	14.59-12.35
Average Yield %	2.90	3.04	2.98	3.29	3.98	4.19	4.89	5.93

Address: 93 West Main Street, Clinton, CT 06413-1600
Telephone: (860) 669-8636
Web Site: www.ctwater.com

Officers: Marshall T. Chiaraluce - Chmn., Pres., C.E.O., David C. Benoit - V.P., Fin., C.F.O. Treas.
Transfer Agents: Registrar and Transfer Company, Cranford, NJ

Investor Contact: 3985 ex 3015
Institutional Holding
No of Institutions: -
Shares: -   **% Held:** -

CONSOLIDATED EDISON, INC.

Exchange	Symbol	Price	52Wk Range	Yield	P/E
NYS	ED	$39.26 (5/28/2004)	44.94-37.26	5.76	16.92

*7 Year Price Score 102.6   *NYSE Composite Index=100   *12 Month Price Score 44.5

TRADING VOLUME (thousand shares)

Interim Earnings (Per Share)

Qtr.	Mar	Jun	Sep	Dec
2001	0.84	0.48	1.30	0.59
2002	0.78	0.46	1.33	0.56
2003	0.72	0.29	1.16	0.19
2004	0.68	...	...	...

Interim Dividends (Per Share)

Amt	Decl	Ex	Rec	Pay
0.56Q	7/17/2003	8/11/2003	8/13/2003	9/15/2003
0.56Q	10/16/2003	11/7/2003	11/12/2003	12/15/2003
0.565Q	1/22/2004	2/9/2004	2/11/2004	3/15/2004
0.565Q	4/22/2004	5/10/2004	5/12/2004	6/15/2004

Indicated Div: $2.26 (Div. Reinv. Plan)

Valuation Analysis

Forecast P/E 14.63 (5/24/2004)

Market Cap $8.4 Billion		Book Value 6.5 Billion	
Price/Book 1.54		Price/Sales 1.01	

Dividend Achiever Status

Rank 299	10 Year Growth Rate	1.45%
Total Years of Dividend Growth		29

Business Summary: Electricity (MIC: 7.1 SIC: 4931 NAIC:221121)

Consolidated Edison provides a range of energy–related products and services through six subsidiaries. Consolidated Edison Company of New York is a regulated utility providing electric, gas and steam service to New York City and Westchester County, New York. Orange and Rockland Utilities is a regulated utility serving customers in southeastern New York state and adjacent sections of New Jersey and northeastern Pennsylvania. Con Edison Solutions is a retail energy services company and Con Edison Energy is a wholesale energy supply company. Con Edison Development is an infrastructure development company and Con Edison Communications is a telecommunications infrastructure company.

Recent Developments: For the three months ended Mar 31 2004, income climbed 0.6% to $158.0 million compared with $157.0 million in the corresponding quarter of 2003. Results benefited from the continuing economic recovery and anticipated new rates for Con Edison of New York's electric, gas and steam businesses. Total operating revenues rose 4.5% to $2.69 billion from $2.57 billion in the prior–year period. Net revenues for Con Edison of New York reflected 6.0% fewer heating degree days in the electric, gas and steam billing cycles in the first quarter of 2004. Operating income decreased 0.8% to $255.0 million compared with $257.0 million the year before.

Prospects: Co. confirmed its previous forecast of earnings per share for full–year 2004 in the range of $2.60 to $2.80. This forecast reflects increased pension and other post–retirement benefit costs, insurance premiums and depreciation expense, partially offset by sales growth. Separately, regulated utility construction expenditures for 2004 are estimated at $1.20 billion. Several large construction projects are scheduled for completion in 2004, which include three major substations that will be on–line this summer. Co. expects Con Edison of New York's construction program to be fully reflected in rates to be set through its current gas and steam rate proceedings and its upcoming electric proceeding.

Financial Data

(US$ in Thousands)	3 Mos	12/31/2003	12/31/2002	12/31/2001	12/31/2000	12/31/1999	12/31/1998	12/31/1997
Earnings Per Share	2.32	2.36	3.13	3.21	2.74	3.13	3.04	2.95
Cash Flow Per Share	0.66	5.94	7.03	6.34	4.52	5.39	5.82	5.26
Tang. Book Val. Per Share	26.35	30.19	26.39	25.21	27.52	27.00	26.79	26.17
Dividends Per Share	2.240	2.240	2.220	2.200	2.180	2.140	2.120	2.10
Dividend Payout %	95.94	94.91	70.92	68.53	79.56	68.37	69.73	71.20
Income Statement								
Total Revenues	2,685,000	9,827,000	8,481,860	9,633,962	9,431,391	7,491,323	7,093,048	7,121,254
Total Indirect Exp.	524,000	2,236,000	1,913,362	2,129,915	2,026,040	2,105,694	2,134,255	2,066,770
Costs & Expenses	2,430,000	8,893,000	7,421,724	8,506,489	8,415,255	6,471,524	6,039,723	6,075,866
Depreciation & Amort.	137,000	529,000	494,553	526,235	586,407	526,182	518,514	502,779
Operating Income	255,000	934,000	1,060,136	1,127,473	1,016,136	1,019,799	1,053,325	1,045,388
Net Interest Inc./(Exp.)	(114,000)	(434,000)	(441,582)	(430,880)	(407,445)	(337,563)	(325,825)	(333,061)
Income from Cont Ops	...	536,000	680,554	695,835	596,428	714,208	729,749	712,823
Net Income	155,000	528,000	646,036	682,242	582,835	700,615	712,742	694,479
Average Shs. Outstg.	227,500	221,800	214,049	212,919	212,186	223,442	234,308	235,082
Balance Sheet								
Net Property	14,488,000	15,225,000	13,329,175	12,248,375	11,893,419	11,353,845	11,406,543	11,267,102
Total Assets	21,513,000	20,966,000	18,820,310	16,996,111	16,767,245	15,531,476	14,381,403	14,722,518
Long–Term Obligations	7,022,000	6,769,000	6,206,917	5,542,305	5,446,913	4,559,148	4,087,403	4,228,785
Net Stockholders' Equity	6,705,000	6,423,000	5,921,079	5,629,218	5,435,339	5,374,957	5,988,555	5,845,529
Shares Outstanding	226,795	202,629	213,932	212,146	188,816	192,452	232,833	235,940
Operating Profit Margin %	9.49	12.87	17.26	11.70	10.77	13.61	14.85	14.67
Net Inc./Net Property %	1.06	3.46	4.84	5.57	4.90	6.17	6.24	6.16
Net Inc./Tot. Capital %	0.90	3.19	4.32	4.97	4.32	5.61	5.58	5.43
Return on Equity %	2.31	13.06	17.68	11.83	10.49	12.69	11.69	11.56
Accum. Depr./Gross Prop. %	22.18	21.08	25.94	26.75	30.75	29.57	29.47	28.23
Price Range	44.94-42.28	45.99-37.00	45.10-33.58	42.18-32.38	39.25-26.19	52.88-33.75	55.94-39.63	41.31-27.13
P/E Ratio	19.37-18.22	19.49-15.68	14.41-10.73	13.14-10.09	14.32-9.56	16.89-10.78	18.40-13.03	14.00-9.19
Average Yield %	5.13	5.53	5.35	5.72	6.65	4.89	4.57	N/A

Address: 4 Irving Place, New York, NY 10003	**Officers:** Eugene R. McGrath – Chmn., Pres., C.E.O., Joan S. Freilich – Exec. V.P., C.F.O.	**Investor Contact:**212–460–6611 **Institutional Holding**
Telephone: (212) 460–4600	**Transfer Agents:**The Bank of New York, New York, NY	**No of Institutions:** 50
Web Site: www.conedison.com		**Shares:** 2,057,774 **% Held:** –

CORUS BANKSHARES, INC.

Exchange	Symbol	Price	52Wk Range	Yield	P/E
NMS	CORS	$39.08 (5/28/2004)	40.86-23.50	3.20	19.16

*7 Year Price Score 148.2   *NYSE Composite Index=100   *12 Month Price Score 56.7

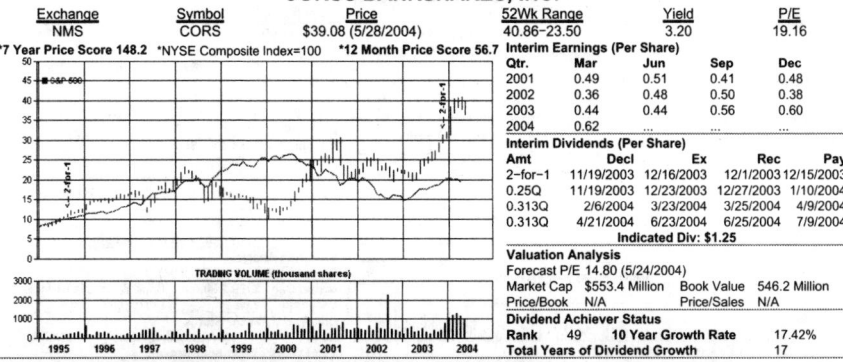

Interim Earnings (Per Share)

Qtr.	Mar	Jun	Sep	Dec
2001	0.49	0.51	0.41	0.48
2002	0.36	0.48	0.50	0.38
2003	0.44	0.44	0.56	0.60
2004	0.62	...	...	...

Interim Dividends (Per Share)

Amt	Decl	Ex	Rec	Pay
2-for-1	11/19/2003	12/16/2003	12/1/2003	12/15/2003
0.25Q	11/19/2003	12/23/2003	12/27/2003	1/10/2004
0.313Q	2/6/2004	3/23/2004	3/25/2004	4/9/2004
0.313Q	4/21/2004	6/23/2004	6/25/2004	7/9/2004
	Indicated Div: $1.25			

Valuation Analysis

Forecast P/E 14.80 (5/24/2004)

Market Cap	$553.4 Million	Book Value	546.2 Million
Price/Book	N/A	Price/Sales	N/A

Dividend Achiever Status

Rank	49	10 Year Growth Rate	17.42%
Total Years of Dividend Growth			17

Business Summary: Commercial Banking (MIC: 8.1 SIC: 6022 NAIC:522110)

Corus Bankshares is a bank holding company with total assets of $3.64 billion as of Dec 31 2003. Co. provides consumer and corporate banking products and services through its wholly-owned banking subsidiary, Corus Bank, N.A. The two main business activities for Co. are commercial real estate lending and deposit gathering. The third, and smaller, business is servicing the check cashing industry. The bank has eleven retail branches in the Chicago metropolitan area and offers general banking services such as checking, savings, money market and time deposit accounts, as well as safe deposit boxes and a variety of additional services.

Recent Developments: For the three months ended Mar 31 2004, net income advanced 52.1% to $17.9 million compared with $12.0 million in the same period a year earlier. Net interest income increased 37.4% to $36.8 million from $26.8 million the previous year, driven by strong loan growth. Provision for loan losses amounted to nil in 2004 and 2003. Total noninterest income climbed 30.8% to $4.7 million, reflecting net securities gains of $1.3 million for 2004 versus net securities losses of $101,000 the year before. Noninterest expense rose 12.1% to $14.2 million, mainly due to an increase of $1.4 million in salaries and benefits expense.

Prospects: Co.'s near-term outlook is enhanced by the recent growth of its commercial real estate loans. For example, for the quarter ended Mar 31 2004, Co. originated 19 loans with commitments aggregating $529.0 million, 50.3% higher than the 15 loans aggregating $352.0 million in the prior-year period. As a result, Co.'s total assets have grown to $3.69 billion as of Mar 31 2004 from $2.60 billion the previous year. Moreover, Co. expects continued growth in its loan portfolio going forward. Co. noted that this expectation is supported by its loan pipeline of $3.80 billion at the close of its first quarter ended Mar 31 2004.

Financial Data

(US$ in Thousands)	3 Mos	12/31/2003	12/31/2002	12/31/2001	12/31/2000	12/31/1999	12/31/1998	12/31/1997
Earnings Per Share	2.22	2.04	1.72	1.89	2.61	1.41	1.37	1.31
Tang. Book Val. Per Share	19.64	19.31	16.91	15.76	14.03	11.09	10.57	9.62
Dividends Per Share	0.830	0.660	0.310	0.300	0.290	0.280	0.270	0.260
Dividend Payout %	37.30	32.35	18.26	16.09	11.28	20.21	20.00	19.77
Income Statement								
Total Interest Income	50,732	170,239	152,878	188,630	223,676	196,580	187,525	183,932
Total Interest Expense	13,951	46,812	54,591	80,921	102,625	90,449	89,305	82,661
Net Interest Income	36,781	123,427	98,287	107,709	121,051	106,131	98,220	101,271
Provision for Loan Losses	...	...	...	...	...	...	10,000	16,000
Non-Interest Income	4,737	16,920	23,079	25,716	45,514	18,948	25,666	26,913
Non-Interest Expense	14,235	52,533	47,472	51,100	52,908	63,096	51,889	51,677
Income Before Taxes	27,283	87,814	73,894	82,325	113,657	61,983	61,997	60,507
Net Income	17,935	58,410	49,314	54,183	74,754	40,726	40,628	39,371
Average Shs. Outstg.	28,888	28,703	28,590	28,618	28,604	28,928	29,546	29,932
Balance Sheet								
Cash & Due from Banks	66,144	63,524	61,560	58,514	111,115	72,316	72,050	62,217
Securities Avail. for Sale	...	244,062	272,799	...	...	...	...	...
Net Loans & Leases	2,336,033	2,397,323	1,705,340	1,434,788	1,512,279	1,695,267	1,515,814	1,515,315
Total Assets	3,691,906	3,643,830	2,617,050	2,659,322	2,598,467	2,388,198	2,589,415	2,251,927
Total Deposits	2,869,321	2,846,402	2,059,773	2,121,456	2,107,630	1,964,420	2,154,676	1,863,066
Long-Term Obligations	211,942	208,903	48,110	55,816	41,085	46,866	64,933	49,264
Total Liabilities	3,139,204	3,097,650	2,135,009	2,208,436	2,196,114	2,060,373	2,271,285	1,960,294
Net Stockholders' Equity	552,702	546,180	482,041	450,886	402,353	327,825	318,130	291,633
Shares Outstanding	27,900	28,036	28,238	28,319	28,286	28,738	29,102	29,362
Return on Equity %	3.24	10.69	10.23	12.01	18.57	12.42	12.77	13.50
Return on Assets %	0.48	1.60	1.88	2.03	2.87	1.70	1.56	1.74
Equity/Assets %	14.97	14.98	18.41	16.95	15.48	13.72	12.28	12.95
Non-Int. Exp./Tot. Inc. %	25.66	28.42	28.14	24.74	20.34	29.10	24.93	25.11
Price Range	40.59-31.02	32.09-19.73	26.69-19.49	30.58-20.26	24.94-10.22	17.94-11.50	23.44-14.31	19.88-11.75
P/E Ratio	18.28-13.97	15.73-9.67	15.52-11.33	16.18-10.72	9.55-3.92	12.72-8.16	17.11-10.45	15.17-8.97
Average Yield %	2.23	2.64	1.33	1.22	1.92	1.84	1.38	1.58

Address: 3959 N. Lincoln Avenue, Chicago, IL 60613-2431	**Officers:** Joseph C. Glickman - Chmn., Robert J. Glickman - Pres., C.E.O.	**Investor Contact:**773-832-3088
Telephone: (773) 832 3088	**Transfer Agents:**Mellon Investor Services, LLC, Ridgefield Park, NJ	**Institutional Holding**
Web Site: www.corusbank.com		**No of Institutions:** 2
		Shares: 600 **% Held:** -

COURIER CORP.

Exchange	Symbol	Price	52Wk Range	Yield	P/E
NMS	CRRC	$38.47 (5/28/2004)	45.61-31.99	0.91	16.14

*7 Year Price Score 204.5 *NYSE Composite Index=100 *12 Month Price Score 48.8

TRADING VOLUME (thousand shares)

1995 1996 1997 1998 1999 2000 2001 2002 2003 2004

Interim Earnings (Per Share)

Qtr.	Dec	Mar	Jun	Sep
2000-01	0.38	0.27	0.37	0.67
2001-02	0.33	0.36	0.50	0.83
2002-03	0.46	0.47	0.58	0.86
2003-04	0.48	0.47	...	...

Interim Dividends (Per Share)

Amt	Decl	Ex	Rec	Pay
0.088Q	11/6/2003	11/13/2003	11/17/2003	12/5/2003
50%	11/6/2003	12/8/2003	11/17/2003	12/5/2003
0.088Q	1/15/2004	2/11/2004	2/13/2004	2/27/2004
0.088Q	4/15/2004	5/5/2004	5/7/2004	5/28/2004

Indicated Div: $0.35

Valuation Analysis

Forecast P/E 14.81 (5/24/2004)

Market Cap	$199.2 Million	Book Value	119.1 Million
Price/Book	2.66	Price/Sales	1.58

Dividend Achiever Status

Rank	4	10 Year Growth Rate	35.65%
Total Years of Dividend Growth		10	

Business Summary: Printing (MIC: 13 4 SIC: 2732 NAIC:323117)

Courier and its subsidiaries are engaged in book manufacturing and specialty publishing. Co. has two business segments. Co.'s book manufacturing segment produces hard and softcover books, as well as related services involved in managing the process of creating and distributing these products. Co.'s specialty publishing segment publishes over 30 specialty categories, including fine and commercial arts, children's books, crafts, musical scores, graphic design, mathematics, physics and other areas of science, puzzles, games, social science, stationery items, and classics of literature for both juvenile and adult markets, including the Dover Thrift Editions.

Recent Developments: For the three months ended Mar 27 2004, net income totaled $3.9 million, up 1.7% compared with income of $3.8 million, before a $33,000 gain from discontinued operations, in the corresponding prior-year period. Net sales grew 2.2% to $49.7 million from $48.6 million the previous year. Gross profit slipped 0.4% to $15.5 million, or 31.3% of net sales, versus $15.6 million, or 32.1% of net sales, a year earlier. Selling and administrative expenses declined 1.6% to $9.6 million from $9.8 million the year before. Income before taxes was $5.9 million, up 2.5% compared with $5.8 million in 2003.

Prospects: Sales in Co.'s specialty publishing segment are being positively affected by the Jan 6 2004 acquisition of Research & Education Association, a publisher of study guide books for users ranging from high school students to professionals in a variety of fields. Meanwhile, increased book manufacturing sales to the education and religious markets are being more than offset by lower sales to the specialty trade publishing markets. Separately, a new four-color press at Co.'s Kendallville, IN plant is expected to increase operating efficiencies. Looking ahead, Co. is targeting full fiscal-2004 sales of between $214.0 million and $219.0 million, and earnings per share in the range of $2.57 to $2.67.

Financial Data

(US$ in Thousands)	6 Mos	3 Mos	09/27/2003	09/28/2002	09/29/2001	09/30/2000	09/25/1999	09/26/1998
Earnings Per Share	2.39	2.39	2.37	2.02	1.69	1.40	1.12	1.05
Cash Flow Per Share	0.73	0.57	3.83	3.62	3.60	2.96	1.92	1.72
Tang. Book Val. Per Share	11.21	11.87	11.42	9.00	7.15	5.54	6.43	5.37
Dividends Per Share	0.320	0.310	0.300	0.260	0.240	0.210	0.180	0.170
Dividend Payout %	13.38	12.97	12.65	13.15	14.17	15.23	16.66	16.24
Income Statement								
Total Revenues	96,482	46,819	202,002	202,184	211,943	188,320	163,991	151,591
Total Indirect Exp.	19,274	9,638	37,898	40,562	42,006	32,414	28,774	25,173
Depreciation & Amort.	5,329	2,590	9,798	10,687	1,466	8,062	8,282	8,541
Operating Income	11,882	5,991	29,526	24,111	20,034	15,886	12,557	11,755
Net Interest Inc./(Exp.)	54	27	(52)	(480)	(1,899)	(325)	(524)	(1,303)
Income Taxes	4,173	2,106	10,254	7,936	6,817	5,249	4,181	4,030
Income from Cont Ops	...	...	19,272	...	...	...	...	...
Net Income	7,763	3,912	20,120	16,175	13,217	10,637	8,376	7,725
Average Shs. Outstg.	8,210	8,189	8,120	7,992	7,797	7,589	7,467	7,321
Balance Sheet								
Cash & Cash Equivalents	8,164	22,838	23,824	5,630	173	562	3,460	722
Total Current Assets	66,978	76,196	77,673	61,722	59,709	71,353	49,266	42,096
Total Assets	153,639	152,091	151,101	131,658	133,615	142,241	91,512	87,630
Total Current Liabilities	21,043	23,424	26,813	27,755	31,029	38,006	27,351	25,569
Long-Term Obligations	553	573	593	674	16,501	31,327	1,193	6,781
Net Stockholders' Equity	122,707	119,102	115,420	95,919	80,325	67,771	57,559	49,790
Net Working Capital	45,935	52,772	50,860	33,967	28,680	33,347	21,915	16,527
Shares Outstanding	7,955	7,934	7,931	7,822	7,668	7,524	7,274	7,137
Statistical Record								
Operating Profit Margin %	12.31	12.79	14.59	11.68	9.13	8.32	7.33	8.24
Return on Equity %	6.33	3.28	16.65	16.36	15.62	15.39	13.64	17.00
Return on Assets %	5.05	2.57	12.71	11.92	9.39	7.33	8.58	9.65
Debt/Total Assets %	0.36	0.37	0.39	0.51	12.34	22.02	1.30	7.73
Price Range	45.61-33.94	39.51-33.94	37.33-23.61	29.67-14.00	19.10-12.00	13.67-9.50	13.78-8.00	13.33-6.15
P/E Ratio	19.08-14.20	16.53-14.20	15.75-9.96	14.69-6.93	11.30-7.10	9.76-6.79	12.30-7.14	12.70-5.86
Average Yield %	0.80	0.83	0.95	1.08	1.62	1.87	1.77	1.76

Address: 15 Wellman Avenue, North Chelmsford, MA 01863	Officers: James F. Conway III – Chmn., Pres., C.E.O., George Q. Nichols – Corp. Sr. V.P.	Investor Contact:978-251-6000
Telephone: (978) 251-6000	Transfer Agents:EquiServe Trust Company, N.A.	Institutional Holding No of Institutions: –
Web Site: www.courier.com		Shares: – % Held: –

CULLEN/FROST BANKERS, INC.

Exchange	Symbol	Price	52Wk Range	Yield	P/E
NYS	CFR	$43.82 (5/28/2004)	44.11–31.95	2.42	17.46

*7 Year Price Score 127.0 *NYSE Composite Index=100 *12 Month Price Score 51.5

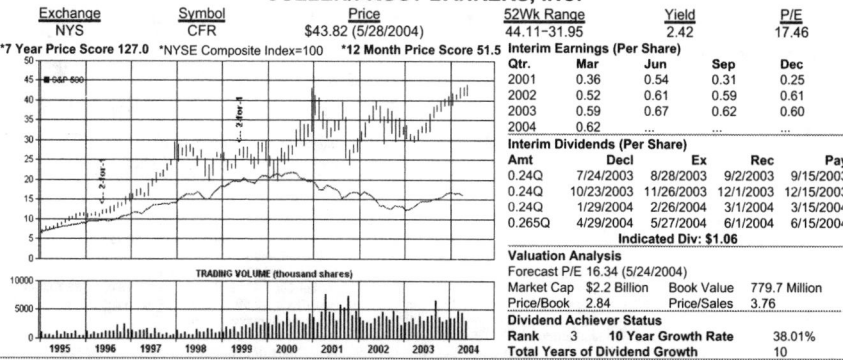

Interim Earnings (Per Share)

Qtr.	Mar	Jun	Sep	Dec
2001	0.36	0.54	0.31	0.25
2002	0.52	0.61	0.59	0.61
2003	0.59	0.67	0.62	0.60
2004	0.62	...	...	...

Interim Dividends (Per Share)

Amt	Decl	Ex	Rec	Pay
0.24Q	7/24/2003	8/28/2003	9/2/2003	9/15/2003
0.24Q	10/23/2003	11/26/2003	12/1/2003	12/15/2003
0.24Q	1/29/2004	2/26/2004	3/1/2004	3/15/2004
0.265Q	4/29/2004	5/27/2004	6/1/2004	6/15/2004

Indicated Div: $1.06

Valuation Analysis

Forecast P/E 16.34 (5/24/2004)

Market Cap $2.2 Billion	Book Value 779.7 Million
Price/Book 2.84	Price/Sales 3.76

Dividend Achiever Status

Rank 3	10 Year Growth Rate	38.01%
Total Years of Dividend Growth		10

Business Summary: Commercial Banking (MIC: 8.1 SIC: 6029 NAIC:522110)

Cullen/Frost Bankers is a financial holding company offering a broad range of banking and financial services to retail and commercial customers throughout Texas. As of Dec 31 2003, Co. operated 79 financial centers in Texas through its wholly–owned subsidiary, The Frost National Bank. In addition to general commercial banking, Co.'s other product and services include trust and investment management, investment banking, insurance brokerage, leasing, asset–based lending, treasury management and item processing. As of Dec 31 2003, Co. had consolidated total assets of $9.67 billion and total deposits of $8.07 billion.

Recent Developments: For the three months ended Mar 31 2004, net income totaled $32.9 million, up 6.8% compared with $30.9 million in the corresponding period a year earlier. Results for 2004 included a $1.7 million loss from securities transactions. Net interest income rose 0.3% to $78.3 million from $78.1 million the previous year. Provision for possible loan losses was $500,000 versus $3.6 million in 2003. Total non–interest income grew 10.3% to $57.4 million from $52.0 million the year before. Total non–interest expense increased 6.8% to $86.6 million from $81.1 million the prior year. Income before income taxes climbed 6.9% to $48.6 million from $45.5 million a year earlier.

Prospects: Net interest income is being hampered by continued pressure from low interest rates, partially offset by strong deposit growth and an increase in average earning assets. Meanwhile, earnings are being positively affected by continued growth of non–interest income. This growth is being driven primarily by higher trust fees stemming from increased investment levels due to improved market conditions, along with higher insurance commissions and fees due to Co.'s increased sales efforts and higher premiums. Separately, higher non–interest expenses are resulting from increases in salaries and employee benefits.

Financial Data

(US$ in Thousands)	3 Mos	12/31/2003	12/31/2002	12/31/2001	12/31/2000	12/31/1999	12/31/1998	12/31/1997
Earnings Per Share	2.51	2.48	2.33	1.46	2.03	1.78	1.38	1.37
Tang. Book Val. Per Share	12.97	12.65	11.39	11.58	11.14	9.64	9.60	9.17
Dividends Per Share	0.960	0.940	0.870	0.840	0.760	0.670	0.570	0.480
Dividend Payout %	38.71	37.90	37.55	57.53	37.43	37.92	41.51	34.90
Income Statement								
Total Interest Income	91,331	368,946	389,898	460,976	512,331	447,580	428,091	324,715
Total Interest Expense	12,999	55,188	75,865	144,759	189,568	150,602	160,118	127,471
Net Interest Income	78,332	313,758	314,033	316,217	322,763	296,978	267,973	197,244
Provision for Loan Losses	500	10,544	22,546	40,031	14,103	12,427	10,393	7,900
Non–Interest Income	57,389	215,361	200,709	192,891	170,865	157,085	138,666	109,332
Non–Interest Expense	86,597	326,035	312,142	352,606	313,280	293,015	278,506	199,956
Income Before Taxes	48,624	192,540	180,054	116,471	166,245	148,621	117,740	98,720
Income from Cont Ops	...	...	122,233	77,906	...	...	...	...
Net Income	32,905	130,501	116,986	80,916	108,817	97,642	75,645	63,485
Average Shs. Outstg.	53,191	52,658	52,423	53,348	53,657	54,746	54,678	46,130
Balance Sheet								
Cash & Due from Banks	895,710	1,067,888	1,331,136	994,622	820,459	760,612	684,941	604,227
Securities Avail. for Sale	3,230,176	2,946,327	2,422,121	2,105,365	1,597,331	1,544,866	1,980,264	1,342,759
Net Loans & Leases	4,643,676	4,507,245	4,436,329	4,445,727	4,471,380	4,108,383	3,592,987	2,601,676
Total Assets	9,989,821	9,672,114	9,552,318	8,369,584	7,660,372	6,996,680	6,869,605	5,230,588
Total Deposits	7,773,306	8,068,857	7,628,143	7,098,007	6,499,690	5,953,832	5,845,487	4,483,911
Long–Term Obligations	377,889	255,845	149,445	152,152	...	...	...	...
Total Liabilities	9,210,144	8,902,110	8,848,528	7,774,665	7,087,346	6,487,369	6,356,686	4,822,183
Net Stockholders' Equity	779,677	770,004	703,790	594,919	573,026	509,311	512,919	408,405
Shares Outstanding	51,329	51,776	51,295	51,355	51,430	52,823	53,426	44,530
Return on Equity %	4.22	16.94	17.36	13.09	18.98	19.17	14.74	15.54
Return on Assets %	0.32	1.34	1.27	0.93	1.42	1.39	1.10	1.21
Equity/Assets %	7.80	7.96	7.36	7.10	7.48	7.27	7.46	7.80
Non–Int. Exp./Tot. Inc. %	58.22	55.79	52.85	53.92	45.85	48.45	49.14	46.06
Price Range	43.25–38.97	41.05–29.65	40.09–29.15	41.38–23.81	43.12–19.81	29.69–22.48	29.58–19.71	29.58–15.14
P/E Ratio	17.23–15.53	16.55–11.96	17.21–12.51	28.34–16.31	21.24–9.76	16.68–12.63	21.43–14.28	21.59–11.05
Average Yield %	2.33	2.69	2.52	2.54	2.69	2.61	2.22	2.39

Address: 100 W. Houston Street, San Antonio, TX 78205
Telephone: (210) 220–4011
Web Site: www.frostbank.com

Officers: Tom C. Frost – Sr. Chmn., Richard W. Evans – Chmn., C.E.O.
Transfer Agents: Bank of New York, New York, NY

Institutional Holding
No of Institutions: 13
Shares: 794,060 **% Held:** –

CVB FINANCIAL CORP.

Exchange	Symbol	Price	52Wk Range	Yield	P/E
NMS	CVBF	$20.78 (5/28/2004)	21.95–16.69	2.31	20.37

*7 Year Price Score 156.6 *NYSE Composite Index=100 *12 Month Price Score 49.8

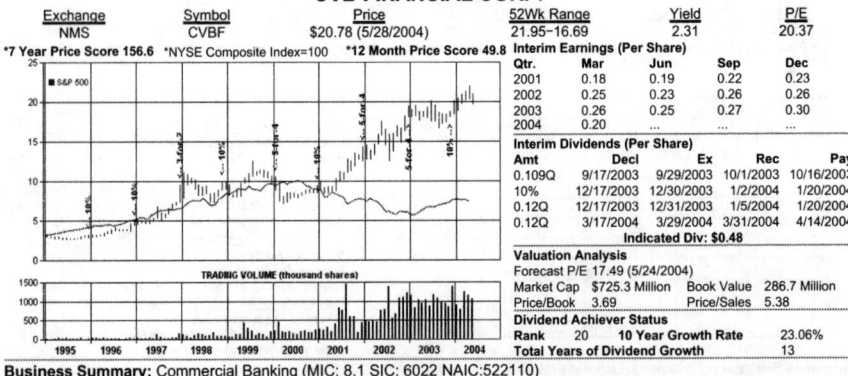

Interim Earnings (Per Share)

Qtr.	Mar	Jun	Sep	Dec
2001	0.18	0.19	0.22	0.23
2002	0.25	0.23	0.26	0.26
2003	0.26	0.25	0.27	0.30
2004	0.20	...	...	...

Interim Dividends (Per Share)

Amt	Decl	Ex	Rec	Pay
0.109Q	9/17/2003	9/29/2003	10/1/2003	10/16/2003
10%	12/17/2003	12/30/2003	1/2/2004	1/20/2004
0.12Q	12/17/2003	12/31/2003	1/5/2004	1/20/2004
0.12Q	3/17/2004	3/29/2004	3/31/2004	4/14/2004

Indicated Div: $0.48

Valuation Analysis
Forecast P/E 17.49 (5/24/2004)

Market Cap $725.3 Million	Book Value 286.7 Million
Price/Book 3.69	Price/Sales 5.38

Dividend Achiever Status

Rank 20	10 Year Growth Rate	23.06%
Total Years of Dividend Growth	13	

Business Summary: Commercial Banking (MIC: 8.1 SIC: 6022 NAIC:522110)

CVB Financial is a bank holding company, with assets of $3.40 billion as of June 30 2003. Co.'s Citizens Business Bank, operates 33 business financial centers located in the Inland Empire, Los Angeles County, Orange County, and the Central Valley areas of California. Co. provides a full complement of all business banking products and services, including asset management services. Co.'s Community Trust Deed Services prepares and files notices of default and reconveyances and acts as a trustee under deeds of trust. Co.'s CVB Ventures Inc. charges fees and collects commissions for acting as an intermediary for emerging growth companies in obtaining capital, loans, leases and other financing.

Recent Developments: For the first quarter ended Mar 31 2004, net earnings declined 20.7% to $10.1 million compared with $12.7 million in the corresponding prior–year quarter. Results included an other–than–temporary write–down on the carrying amount of certain equity investments of $6.3 million in 2004 and a gain on the sale of investment securities of $794,000 in 2003. Net interest income increased 13.8% to $35.6 million from $31.2 million a year earlier. Total interest income climbed 13.9% to $46.0 million, while total interest expense grew 14.1% to $10.4 million. Non–interest income dropped 88.7% to $781,000, while non–interest expense advanced 21.2% to $21.5 million.

Prospects: Co.'s acquisition of Kaweah National Bank is seen as an excellent complement to its existing business financial centers in Bakersfield and Fresno, CA. Going forward, Co. will continue to focus on growing its business both internally and through strategic acquisitions. Co. anticipates that assets will grow to $5.00 billion by the end of 2005 and $10.00 billion by the end of 2010. Separately, Co. and its principal subsidiary, Citizens Business Bank, expect to benefit from solid growth in the near term due to the recent stability of interest rates.

Financial Data

(US$ in Thousands)	12/31/2003	12/31/2002	12/31/2001	12/31/2000	12/31/1999	12/31/1998	12/31/1997	12/31/1996
Earnings Per Share	1.08	1.00	0.82	0.71	0.53	0.51	0.42	0.50
Tang. Book Val. Per Share	5.38	5.09	4.48	3.81	2.83	2.71	2.57	2.98
Dividends Per Share	0.430	0.400	0.320	0.250	0.200	0.150	0.100	0.070
Dividend Payout %	40.40	39.63	38.93	35.47	37.64	30.05	23.46	14.00
Income Statement								
Total Interest Income	166,346	154,323	155,877	150,867	128,478	96,840	84,656	74,894
Total Interest Expense	37,053	40,439	52,806	56,760	38,466	31,248	24,976	21,466
Net Interest Income	129,293	113,884	103,071	94,107	90,012	65,592	59,680	53,428
Provision for Loan Losses	...	...	1,750	2,800	2,700	2,500	2,670	2,888
Non–Interest Income	29,989	29,018	22,192	19,023	18,630	14,976	13,823	14,279
Non–Interest Expense	77,794	66,056	60,155	56,345	64,737	45,024	42,890	41,909
Income Before Taxes	81,488	76,846	63,358	53,985	41,205	33,043	27,943	22,910
Net Income	52,832	49,745	40,058	34,683	25,960	20,787	17,370	13,333
Average Shs. Outstg.	49,110	49,035	48,695	48,410	48,146	40,697	40,525	26,722
Balance Sheet								
Cash & Due from Banks	112,008	124,973	82,651	130,315	118,360	100,033	107,725	142,502
Securities Avail. for Sale	1,865,782	1,452,499	1,181,503	1,070,074	877,332	676,162	434,106	333,348
Net Loans & Leases	1,738,659	1,424,343	1,167,071	1,032,341	935,791	675,668	605,484	576,687
Total Assets	3,854,349	3,123,411	2,514,102	2,307,996	2,010,757	1,555,201	1,258,769	1,160,421
Total Deposits	2,660,510	2,309,964	1,876,959	1,595,030	1,501,073	1,215,305	1,075,695	990,597
Long–Term Obligations	467,310	286,888	334,999	11,234	16,951	95	7,922	12,610
Total Liabilities	3,567,628	2,863,590	2,293,354	2,119,366	1,869,987	1,439,500	1,156,684	1,071,334
Net Stockholders' Equity	286,721	259,821	220,748	188,630	140,770	115,707	102,085	89,087
Shares Outstanding	48,289	47,886	47,825	47,539	46,730	39,070	35,389	25,925
Return on Equity %	18.42	19.14	18.14	18.38	18.44	17.96	17.01	14.96
Return on Assets %	1.37	1.59	1.59	1.50	1.29	1.33	1.37	1.14
Equity/Assets %	7.43	8.31	8.78	8.17	7.00	7.43	8.10	7.67
Non–Int. Exp./Tot. Inc. %	39.62	36.02	33.78	33.16	44.00	40.26	43.55	46.99
Price Range	20.12–16.69	19.43–12.51	14.28–8.44	10.53–7.14	12.54–7.96	11.08–7.21	9.55–4.58	4.87–3.00
P/E Ratio	18.63–15.45	19.43–12.51	17.42–10.29	14.82–10.06	23.65–15.02	21.73–14.14	22.74–10.91	9.73–6.00
Average Yield %	2.33	2.57	2.97	2.94	2.00	1.65	1.69	1.90

Address: 701 North Haven Avenue, ON, CA 91764 Telephone: (909) 980–4030 Web Site: www.cvbcorp.com	Officers: George A. Borba – Chmn., D. Linn Wiley – Pres., C.E.O. Transfer Agents:U.S. Stock Transfer Corporation, Glendale, CA	Investor Contact:909–980–4030 Institutional Holding No of Institutions: 13 Shares: 3,582,555 % Held: –

DANAHER CORP.

Exchange	Symbol	Price	52Wk Range	Yield	P/E
NYS	DHR	$47.03 (5/28/2004)	48.03-33.06	0.11	12.99

*7 Year Price Score 146.2 *NYSE Composite Index=100 *12 Month Price Score 52.0

Interim Earnings (Per Share)

Qtr.	Mar	Jun	Sep	Dec
2001	0.56	0.63	0.59	0.23
2002	0.55	0.66	0.74	0.84
2003	0.65	0.79	0.87	1.06
2004	0.90	...	...	...

Interim Dividends (Per Share)

Amt	Decl	Ex	Rec	Pay
0.013Q	9/18/2003	9/24/2003	9/26/2003	10/31/2003
0.013Q	12/19/2003	12/23/2003	12/26/2003	1/30/2004
0.013Q	3/17/2004	3/24/2004	3/26/2004	4/30/2004
100%	4/22/2004	5/21/2004	5/6/2004	5/20/2004

Indicated Div: $0.05

Valuation Analysis

Forecast P/E 21.60 (5/24/2004)

Market Cap $7.1 Billion	Book Value 3.8 Billion
Price/Book 3.78	Price/Sales 2.54

Dividend Achiever Status

Rank 66	10 Year Growth Rate	16.09%
Total Years of Dividend Growth		10

Business Summary: Metal Products (MIC: 11.4 SIC: 3429 NAIC:332510)

Danaher conducts its operations through two business segments: Process/Environmental Controls and Tools & Components. The Process/Environmental Controls segment encompasses five strategic platforms (Motion, Environmental, Electronic Test, Medical Technologies and Product Identification) and three focused niche businesses (Power Quality, Aerospace and Defense, and Industrial Controls). The Tools & Components segment encompasses one strategic platform, Mechanics'Hand Tools, and five focused niche businesses. Products are distributed by Co.'s sales personnel and independent representatives to distributors, end-users, and original equipment manufacturers.

Recent Developments: For the three months ended Apr 2 2004, net income advanced 40.8% to $145.2 million compared with $103.1 million in the corresponding quarter of the previous year. Earnings growth was largely due to increased sales volume and cost improvements in existing business units. Results for 2004 and 2003 included pre-tax gains of $686,000 and $775,000, respectively, from the sale of real estate. Net sales improved 29.0% to $1.54 billion from $1.20 billion in the year-earlier period. The increase in sales was primarily attributed to solid revenue growth from both of Co.'s operating segments. Operating income jumped 34.7% to $225.0 million versus $167.0 million in the prior-year quarter

Prospects: Co. continues to generate strong growth across most of its businesses as well as in many of its end markets. On a segment basis, Co.'s Process/Environment Controls segment is benefiting from sales increases in the motion, electronic test, environmental and product identification businesses. The Tools and Components segment is experiencing higher sales of hand tools, which grew 16.5% for the first three months of 2004. Co. is also benefiting from higher demand from its engine retarder and wheel service equipment businesses. Going forward, Co. will continue to place emphasis on cost improvements and growing sales across all business lines.

Financial Data
(US$ in Thousands)

	3 Mos	12/31/2003	12/31/2002	12/31/2001	12/31/2000	12/31/1999	12/31/1998	12/31/1997
Earnings Per Share	3.62	3.37	2.79	2.01	2.23	1.79	1.32	1.28
Cash Flow Per Share	1.54	5.33	4.48	4.00	3.52	2.86	2.38	2.30
Tang. Book Val. Per Share	N.M	1.98	0.01	N.M	0.55	2.92	0.49	0.60
Dividends Per Share	0.050	0.050	0.043	0.040	0.033	0.030	0.026	0.025
Dividend Payout %	2.76	1.48	1.52	1.99	1.45	1.67	1.98	1.94
Income Statement								
Total Revenues	1,543,191	5,293,876	4,577,232	3,782,444	3,777,777	3,197,238	2,910,038	2,050,968
Total Indirect Exp.	405,609	1,270,572	1,084,935	942,406	909,897	778,409	722,116	401,608
Depreciation & Amort.	37,909	133,436	129,565	178,390	149,721	126,419	108,651	76,116
Operating Income	224,966	845,995	701,122	502,011	552,149	458,007	366,838	266,885
Net Interest Inc./(Exp.)	(12,931)	(48,960)	(43,654)	(25,747)	(29,225)	(16,667)	(24,931)	(13,104)
Income Taxes	66,791	260,201	223,327	178,599	198,711	167,938	118,165	200,053
Income from Cont Ops	...	...	434,141	...	...	...	...	53,728
Net Income	145,244	536,834	290,391	297,665	324,213	261,624	182,946	154,806
Average Shs. Outstg.	163,242	161,570	158,482	151,848	145,499	146,089	138,885	120,512
Balance Sheet								
Cash & Cash Equivalents	642,486	1,230,156	810,463	706,559	176,924	260,281	41,923	33,317
Total Current Assets	2,516,165	2,942,151	2,387,266	1,874,615	1,474,306	1,202,117	886,904	618,339
Total Assets	7,285,127	6,890,050	6,029,145	4,820,483	4,031,679	3,047,071	2,738,715	1,879,717
Total Current Liabilities	1,607,105	1,380,003	1,265,312	1,017,294	1,018,540	708,786	688,705	524,235
Long-Term Obligations	1,274,393	1,284,498	1,197,422	1,119,333	713,557	341,037	412,918	162,720
Net Stockholders' Equity	3,782,234	3,646,709	3,009,599	2,228,586	1,942,333	1,708,754	1,351,831	916,881
Net Working Capital	909,060	1,562,148	1,121,954	857,321	455,766	493,331	198,199	94,104
Shares Outstanding	153,984	153,681	152,532	143,314	142,013	142,440	135,107	105,440
Operating Profit Margin %	14.57	15.98	15.31	13.27	14.61	14.32	12.60	13.01
Net Profit Margin %	18.06	19.97	19.24	17.31	19.10	18.68	14.40	22.12
Return on Equity %	3.84	14.72	14.42	13.35	16.69	15.31	13.53	5.85
Return on Assets %	1.99	7.79	7.20	6.17	8.04	8.58	6.68	2.85
Debt/Total Assets %	17.49	18.64	19.86	23.22	17.69	11.19	15.07	8.65
Price Range	47.68-44.00	45.98-30.23	37.67-26.62	33.84-22.77	34.34-18.56	34.28-21.56	27.16-14.69	15.94-9.91
P/E Ratio	13.17-12.15	13.64-8.97	13.50-9.54	16.84-11.33	15.40-8.32	19.15-12.05	20.57-11.13	12.45-7.74
Average Yield %	0.11	0.14	0.13	0.14	0.12	0.11	0.10	0.16

Address: 2099 Pennsylvania Ave. NW, Washington, DC 20006-1813
Telephone: (202) 828 0850
Web Site: www.danaher.com

Officers: Steven M. Rales - Chmn., H. Lawrence Culp - Pres., C.E.O.
Transfer Agents: SunTrust Bank, Atlanta, GA

Investor Contact: 202-828-0850
Institutional Holding
No of Institutions: 440
Shares: 111,017,252 **% Held:** 72.60%

DIEBOLD, INC.

Exchange	Symbol	Price	52Wk Range	Yield	P/E
NYS	DBD	$49.13 (5/28/2004)	57.43-40.70	1.51	20.14

*7 Year Price Score 135.5 *NYSE Composite Index=100   *12 Month Price Score 44.8

Interim Earnings (Per Share)

Qtr.	Mar	Jun	Sep	Dec
2001	0.11	0.39	0.20	0.23
2002	0.37	0.55	0.61	0.30
2003	0.36	0.57	0.66	0.81
2004	0.40	...	...	...

Interim Dividends (Per Share)

Amt	Decl	Ex	Rec	Pay
0.17Q	8/7/2003	8/13/2003	8/15/2003	9/5/2003
0.17Q	10/9/2003	11/12/2003	11/14/2003	12/5/2003
0.185Q	2/11/2004	2/17/2004	2/19/2004	3/11/2004
0.185Q	4/22/2004	5/12/2004	5/14/2004	6/4/2004

Indicated Div: $0.74 (Div. Reinv. Plan)

Valuation Analysis

Forecast P/E 18.57 (5/24/2004)

Market Cap $3.5 Billion	Book Value 1.2 Billion
Price/Book 3.04	Price/Sales 1.59

Dividend Achiever Status

Rank 220	10 Year Growth Rate	6.70%
Total Years of Dividend Growth		50

Business Summary: Office Equipment Supplies (MIC: 11.12 SIC: 3578 NAIC:333313)

Diebold develops, manufactures, sells and services self-service transaction systems, electronic and physical security systems, software and various products used to equip bank facilities to global financial and commercial markets and electronic voting terminals and solutions to the government. Co.'s primary customers include banks and financial institutions, as well as hospitals, colleges and universities, public libraries, government agencies, utilities and various retail outlets. Sales of systems and equipment are made directly to customers by Co.' sales personnel and by manufacturer's representatives and distributors.

Recent Developments: For the three months ended Mar 31 2004, net income totaled $29.3 million, up 12.6% compared with $25.9 million in the prior year. Total net sales rose 21.5% to $498.3 million from $410.2 million a year earlier. Product net sales advanced 33.4% to $219.6 million from $164.7 million the year before, while service net sales grew 13.5% to $278.7 million from $245.5 million the previous year. Gross profit was $140.0 million, or 28.1% of net sales, versus $123.8 million, or 30.2% of net sales, in 2003. Operating profit climbed 6.8% to $43.8 million from $41.0 million the prior year.

Prospects: Looking ahead, Co. anticipates second-quarter 2004 earnings of between $0.58 and $0.62 per share, and full-year 2004 earnings in the range of $2.58 to $2.66 per share. In addition, Co. is targeting second-quarter 2004 revenue growth of between 13.0% and 16.0%, driven by strong revenue increases for Co.'s financial self-service and security products and services, and full-year 2004 revenue growth of between 8.0% and 12.0%. Co. is lowering its election systems revenue projection to between $80.0 million and $95.0 million for 2004 due to the public debate over voter confidentiality in electronic voting.

Financial Data

(US$ in Thousands)	3 Mos	12/31/2003	12/31/2002	12/31/2001	12/31/2000	12/31/1999	12/31/1998	12/31/1997
Earnings Per Share	2.44	2.40	1.83	0.93	1.92	1.85	1.10	1.76
Cash Flow Per Share	0.12	2.87	2.26	2.15	2.04	2.71	2.55	1.60
Tang. Book Val. Per Share	11.30	11.24	9.32	8.79	8.94	9.62	9.86	9.68
Dividends Per Share	0.690	0.680	0.660	0.640	0.620	0.600	0.560	0.500
Dividend Payout %	28.48	28.33	36.06	68.81	32.29	32.43	50.90	28.40
Income Statement								
Total Revenues	498,255	2,109,673	1,940,163	1,760,297	1,743,608	1,259,177	1,185,707	1,226,936
Total Indirect Exp.	96,197	364,293	353,469	385,156	330,200	270,689	300,003	246,239
Depreciation & Amort.	18,903	64,301	61,296	45,453	35,901	34,709	25,649	18,701
Operating Income	43,830	262,848	241,169	138,909	228,955	186,123	106,247	183,861
Net Interest Inc./(Exp.)	(2,001)	(9,285)	(26,679)	(12,668)	(17,681)	...	...	...
Income Taxes	13,727	82,247	86,250	32,946	67,438	72,482	43,659	63,143
Income from Cont Ops	...	...	132,301	...	...	...	...	...
Net Income	29,116	174,776	99,154	66,893	136,919	128,856	76,148	122,516
Average Shs. Outstg.	73,371	72,924	72,297	71,783	71,479	69,562	69,310	69,490
Balance Sheet								
Cash & Cash Equivalents	146,614	176,101	163,355	125,669	126,512	84,647	79,973	56,769
Total Current Assets	1,121,847	1,105,159	924,888	952,426	804,363	647,936	543,548	549,837
Total Assets	1,924,579	1,900,502	1,625,081	1,651,913	1,585,427	1,298,831	1,004,188	991,050
Total Current Liabilities	641,658	618,653	564,962	658,018	566,792	382,407	235,533	242,080
Long-Term Obligations	...	...	...	20,800	20,800	20,800	20,800	20,800
Net Stockholders' Equity	1,152,685	1,148,238	940,823	903,110	936,066	844,395	699,123	668,581
Net Working Capital	480,189	486,506	359,926	294,408	237,571	265,529	308,015	307,757
Shares Outstanding	72,582	72,649	72,111	71,356	71,547	71,096	68,880	69,005
Operating Profit Margin %	8.79	12.45	12.43	7.89	13.13	14.78	8.96	14.98
Return on Equity %	2.53	15.22	14.06	7.40	14.62	15.26	10.89	18.32
Return on Assets %	1.51	9.19	8.14	4.04	8.63	9.92	7.58	12.36
Debt/Total Assets %	...	...	...	1.25	1.31	1.60	2.07	2.09
Price Range	54.63-46.96	57.43-33.94	42.41-31.00	41.00-25.96	34.56-21.63	39.88-20.50	54.63-20.13	50.63-31.38
P/E Ratio	22.39-19.25	23.93-14.14	23.17-16.94	44.09-27.91	18.00-11.26	21.55-11.08	49.66-18.30	28.76-17.83
Average Yield %	1.34	1.52	1.76	1.93	2.24	2.22	1.59	1.16

Address: 5995 Mayfair Road, North Canton, OH 44720-8077	Officers: Walden W. ODell - Chmn., C.E.O., Eric C. Evans - Pres., C.O.O.	Investor Contact:800-766-5859
Telephone: (330) 490-4000	Transfer Agents:The Bank of New York, New York, NY	Institutional Holding No of Institutions: 18
Web Site: www.diebold.com		Shares: 449,066 % Held: -

DONNELLEY (R.R.) & SONS CO.

Exchange	Symbol	Price	52Wk Range	Yield	P/E
NYS	RRD	$30.26 (5/28/2004)	32.21–23.30	3.44	27.76

*7 Year Price Score 91.7 *NYSE Composite Index=100 *12 Month Price Score 49.8

Interim Earnings (Per Share)

Qtr.	Mar	Jun	Sep	Dec
2001	0.12	0.05	0.36	(0.32)
2002	0.20	0.22	0.42	0.40
2003	0.05	0.17	0.47	0.85
2004	(0.35)	...	...	...

Interim Dividends (Per Share)

Amt	Decl	Ex	Rec	Pay
0.26Q	7/24/2003	8/6/2003	8/8/2003	8/30/2003
0.26Q	9/25/2003	11/5/2003	11/7/2003	11/29/2003
0.26Q	1/22/2004	2/2/2004	2/4/2004	2/28/2004
0.26Q	3/26/2004	5/6/2004	5/10/2004	6/2/2004

Indicated Div: $1.04 (Div. Reinv. Plan)

Valuation Analysis

Forecast P/E N/A

Market Cap $3.4 Billion Book Value 890.4 Million

Price/Book 3.17 Price/Sales 0.59

Dividend Achiever Status

Rank 303 10 Year Growth Rate 0.82%

Total Years of Dividend Growth 34

Business Summary: Printing (MIC: 13.4 SIC: 2752 NAIC:323110)

R. R. Donnelley & Sons is engaged in preparing, producing and delivering integrated communications services designed to produce, manage and deliver its customers'content, regardless of the communications medium. Co.'s services include content creation, digital content management, production and distribution. Co. operates primarily in three business segments: print, logistics and financial. Co. serves the following end–markets: magazines, catalogs and retail, telecommunications, book publishing premedia, financial services, direct mail, international, and logistics.

Recent Developments: For the three months ended Mar 31 2004, loss was $52.3 million, before an accounting change charge of $6.6 million, compared with net earnings of $5.7 million in the equivalent quarter of 2003. Results for 2004 and 2003 included after–tax restructuring charges of $22.3 million and $2.6 million, respectively. Results for 2004 also included asset impairments of $27.8 million. Sales jumped 34.7% to $1.45 billion from $1.07 billion in the prior–year period. Sales were up primarily due to the acquisition of Moore Wallace. In addition, Co. experienced strong growth in the financial segment, the directories business within the print segment and certain international markets.

Prospects: Even though customer retention remained stable, the Co.'s forms and labels segment continues to be challenged by industry factors, including volume declines due to electronic substitution for multi–part forms and aggressive pricing competition. The outsourcing segment should continue to benefit from Moore Wallace's acquisition of Payment Processing Solutions in December 2003 and volume increases with a new customer. Separately, Co. is targeting non–GAAP diluted earnings per share for full–year 2004 of about $1.50. In addition, Co. has no plans to change its quarterly dividend rate of $0.26 per share in 2004. This guidance excludes any acquisition–related and restructuring charges.

Financial Data

(US$ in Thousands)	3 Mos	12/31/2003	12/31/2002	12/31/2001	12/31/2000	12/31/1999	12/31/1998	12/31/1997
Earnings Per Share	1.14	1.54	1.24	0.21	2.17	2.40	2.08	1.40
Cash Flow Per Share	0.94	3.09	3.57	4.62	6.01	4.90	5.16	5.03
Tang. Book Val. Per Share	1.94	5.13	4.50	3.91	5.05	6.00	6.84	8.31
Dividends Per Share	1.030	1.020	0.980	0.940	0.900	0.860	0.820	0.780
Dividend Payout %	93.64	66.23	79.03	447.61	41.47	35.83	39.42	55.71
Income Statement								
Total Revenues	1,446,195	4,787,162	4,754,937	5,297,760	5,764,335	5,183,408	5,018,436	4,850,033
Total Indirect Exp.	340,003	564,893	622,632	763,180	597,823	628,580	729,913	581,817
Depreciation & Amort.	80,905	329,359	352,372	378,723	390,402	374,382	367,803	370,445
Operating Income	(67,507)	270,793	244,937	147,271	501,040	530,427	408,351	368,788
Net Interest Inc./(Exp.)	(16,964)	(50,359)	(62,818)	(71,183)	(89,639)	(88,164)	(78,166)	(90,765)
Income Taxes	(22,001)	31,768	33,496	49,906	167,084	195,014	214,725	97,240
Income from Cont Ops	(52,268)	...	...	...	...	311,515	...	206,525
Net Income	(58,846)	176,509	142,237	24,988	266,900	308,314	294,580	130,631
Average Shs. Outstg.	151,278	114,302	114,372	118,498	123,093	129,566	141,865	147,508
Balance Sheet								
Cash & Cash Equivalents	174,258	60,837	60,543	48,615	60,873	41,873	66,226	47,814
Total Current Assets	2,142,940	999,510	866,439	940,194	1,206,449	1,229,850	1,144,993	1,146,571
Total Assets	8,224,468	3,188,950	3,151,772	3,400,017	3,914,202	3,853,464	3,787,819	4,134,166
Total Current Liabilities	1,364,658	883,582	954,730	984,290	1,190,561	1,203,463	898,300	812,622
Long–Term Obligations	1,756,750	752,497	752,870	881,318	739,190	748,498	998,978	1,153,226
Net Stockholders' Equity	3,687,571	983,152	914,594	888,407	1,232,548	1,138,258	1,300,878	1,591,497
Net Working Capital	778,282	115,928	(88,291)	(44,096)	15,888	26,387	246,693	333,949
Shares Outstanding	217,242	113,674	113,124	113,121	140,889	123,237	134,322	145,118
Operating Profit Margin %	N.M.	5.65	5.15	2.77	8.69	10.23	6.54	7.60
Return on Equity %	N.M	17.95	15.55	2.81	21.65	27.36	16.48	12.97
Return on Assets %	N.M.	5.53	4.51	0.73	6.81	8.08	5.66	4.99
Debt/Total Assets %	21.36	23.59	23.88	25.92	18.88	19.42	26.37	27.89
Price Range	32.21–27.95	30.15–17.05	31.96–19.06	31.62–24.83	27.00–19.13	43.81–22.81	47.75–34.00	41.06–29.63
P/E Ratio	28.25–24.52	19.58–11.07	25.77–15.37	150.6–118.2	12.44–8.81	18.26–9.51	22.96–16.35	29.33–21.16
Average Yield %	3.39	4.29	3.70	3.33	3.88	2.65	1.98	2.22

Address: 77 West Wacker Drive, Chicago, IL 60601 **Telephone:** (312) 326 8000 **Web Site:** www.rrdonnelley.com	**Officers:** William L. Davis – Pres., C.E.O., Gregory A. Stoklosa – Exec. V.P., C.F.O. **Transfer Agents:**EquiServe Trust Company, N.A., Jersey City, NJ	**Investor Contact:**312–326–8313 **Institutional Holding No of Institutions:** 292 **Shares:** 86,984,304 **% Held:** 76.80%

DORAL FINANCIAL CORP.

Exchange	Symbol	Price	52Wk Range	Yield	P/E
NYS	DRL	$32.41 (5/28/2004)	35.63-26.66	1.85	10.88

*7 Year Price Score 233.1   *NYSE Composite Index=100   *12 Month Price Score 47.0

TRADING VOLUME (thousand shares)

Interim Earnings (Per Share)

Qtr.	Mar	Jun	Sep	Dec
2001	0.26	0.28	0.32	0.39
2002	0.40	0.44	0.49	0.56
2003	0.60	0.64	0.70	0.78
2004	0.86	...	...	...

Interim Dividends (Per Share)

Amt	Decl	Ex	Rec	Pay
0.12Q	10/15/2003	11/12/2003	11/14/2003	12/4/2003
50%	10/15/2003	12/12/2003	11/21/2003	12/11/2003
0.12Q	1/23/2004	2/11/2004	2/13/2004	3/5/2004
0.15Q	4/21/2004	5/11/2004	5/13/2004	6/4/2004

Indicated Div: $0.60

Valuation Analysis

Forecast P/E 8.81 (5/24/2004)

Market Cap $2.3 Billion	Book Value 1.1 Billion
Price/Book 3.34	Price/Sales 4.00

Dividend Achiever Status

Rank   8   10 Year Growth Rate   28.21%

Total Years of Dividend Growth   14

Business Summary: Finance Intermediaries &Services (MIC: 8.7 SIC: 6162 NAIC:522292)

Doral Financial is a diversified financial services company engaged in mortgage banking, commercial banking, institutional broker-dealer activities and insurance agency activities. Co.'s activities are principally conducted in Puerto Rico and in the New York City metropolitan area. As of Dec 31 2003, Doral Bank, Co.'s Puerto Rico banking subsidiary, operated 37 branches in Puerto Rico, concentrated in the greater San Juan metropolitan area and the Island's northeast region. As of Dec 31 2003, Co. had consolidated assets of $10.39 billion and deposits of $2.97 billion.

Recent Developments: For the quarter ended Mar 31 2004, net income increased 48.0% to $103.6 million compared with $70.0 million in the same period a year earlier. Net interest income advanced 43.1% to $59.1 million from $41.3 million the previous year. Co. attributed the rise in net interest income to higher average net interest earning assets. Provision for loan losses was $1.6 million versus $4.8 million last year. Total non-interest income climbed 25.5% to $114.8 million, due in large part to a 77.0% jump associated with net gains on mortgage loan sales and fees to $136.9 million. Mortgage banking net income rose 5.8% to $37.7 million, while banking net income grew 79.7% to $60.4 million.

Prospects: The continued high demand for new housing in Puerto Rico enhances Co.'s near-term outlook. Consequently, Co. now anticipates that loan production for the remainder of 2004 will be stronger than the first quarter and is projecting in excess of $7.50 billion for full-year 2004 versus $6.50 billion for 2003. Meanwhile, Co. expects continued strong growth from its Doral Bank, Puerto Rico banking segment. Co. indicated that it intends to open at least eight additional branches during 2004, bringing its total branches to 45. Also, Co. expects to increase its lending activities, particularly secured commercial lending which it anticipates will grow by at least 75.0% during 2004.

Financial Data

(US$ in Thousands)	3 Mos	12/31/2003	12/31/2002	12/31/2001	12/31/2000	12/31/1999	12/31/1998	12/31/1997
Earnings Per Share	2.98	2.72	1.89	1.25	0.82	0.66	0.56	0.37
Tang. Book Val. Per Share	10.60	9.44	7.57	5.92	3.89	4.10	2.90	2.18
Dividends Per Share	0.420	0.400	0.280	0.210	0.160	0.130	0.100	0.080
Dividend Payout %	14.32	14.70	14.78	16.84	20.54	19.99	18.25	22.64
Income Statement								
Total Interest Income	126,099	452,570	415,600	356,095	325,545	211,679	148,051	90,131
Total Interest Expense	67,046	271,090	263,178	271,668	283,241	161,795	114,786	61,438
Net Interest Income	59,053	181,480	152,422	84,427	42,304	49,884	33,265	28,693
Provision for Loan Losses	1,561	14,085	7,429	4,445	4,078	2,626	883	600
Non-Interest Income	114,762	462,216	255,393	191,132	164,585	126,911	88,340	45,286
Non-Interest Expense	45,940	185,802	139,410	112,854	106,659	97,556	60,883	35,582
Income from Cont Ops	...	...	...	137,022	...	...	...	32,548
Net Income	103,577	321,299	220,968	143,851	84,656	67,926	52,832	20,231
Average Shs. Outstg.	110,758	110,434	109,438	102,381	94,710	95,448	94,338	87,139
Balance Sheet								
Cash & Due from Banks	139,278	84,713	156,137	45,970	28,999	25,793	31,945	17,390
Securities Avail. for Sale	8,146,759	2,850,598	862,090	928,179	182,374	66,325	408,888	240,876
Net Loans & Leases	1,497,008	1,410,849	1,022,342	644,113	398,191	231,184	166,987	133,055
Total Assets	12,012,587	10,393,996	8,421,689	6,694,283	5,463,386	4,537,343	2,918,113	1,857,789
Total Deposits	3,203,810	2,971,272	2,217,211	1,669,969	1,303,525	1,010,424	533,113	300,494
Long-Term Obligations	1,894,260	1,206,500	1,311,500	687,500	389,000	134,000	32,000	32,000
Total Liabilities	10,294,554	8,801,556	7,376,718	5,932,163	4,957,676	4,152,361	2,648,554	1,670,834
Net Stockholders' Equity	1,718,033	1,592,440	1,044,971	762,120	505,710	384,982	269,559	186,955
Shares Outstanding	107,907	107,903	107,761	107,573	95,384	90,965	90,965	82,788
Return on Equity %	6.02	23.34	21.14	18.09	16.74	17.64	19.59	17.40
Return on Assets %	0.86	3.57	2.62	2.06	1.54	1.49	1.81	1.75
Non-Int. Exp./Tot. Inc. %	19.07	20.31	20.77	20.62	21.76	28.81	25.75	26.27
Price Range	35.42-29.87	34.67-18.73	19.94-13.68	17.50-9.97	11.36-3.89	9.83-4.72	10.08-4.67	5.67-2.72
P/E Ratio	11.89-10.02	12.75-6.89	10.55-7.24	14.00-7.98	13.85-4.74	14.90-7.15	18.01-8.33	15.32-7.36
Average Yield %	1.27	1.45	1.69	1.52	2.65	1.82	1.40	2.13

Address: 1451 Franklin D. Roosevelt Avenue, San Juan, PR 00920-2717, Puerto Rico
Telephone: (787) 474-6700
Web Site: www.doralfinancial.com

Officers: Salomon Levis - Chmn., C.E.O., Zoila Lewis - Pres., C.O.O.
Transfer Agents: Mellon Investor Services, LLC, Ridgefield Park, NJ

Investor Contact: 212-329-3729
Institutional Holding
No of Institutions: 6
Shares: 1,623,032   **% Held:** -

DOVER CORP.

Exchange	Symbol	Price	52Wk Range	Yield	P/E
NYS	DOV	$38.96 (5/28/2004)	44.02-29.96	1.54	25.63

*7 Year Price Score 101.9 *NYSE Composite Index=100 *12 Month Price Score 47.5

Interim Earnings (Per Share)

Qtr.	Mar	Jun	Sep	Dec
2001	0.39	0.70	0.01	(0.28)
2002	0.22	0.31	0.28	0.23
2003	0.29	0.36	0.37	0.38
2004	0.41	...	...	...

Interim Dividends (Per Share)

Amt	Decl	Ex	Rec	Pay
0.15Q	8/7/2003	8/27/2003	8/29/2003	9/12/2003
0.15Q	11/6/2003	11/25/2003	11/28/2003	12/12/2003
0.15Q	2/12/2004	2/25/2004	2/27/2004	3/15/2004
0.15Q	5/6/2004	5/25/2004	5/28/2004	6/15/2004

Indicated Div: $0.60 (Div. Reinv. Plan)

Valuation Analysis

Forecast P/E 20.26 (5/24/2004)

Market Cap	$7.9 Billion	Book Value	2.8 Billion
Price/Book	2.85	Price/Sales	1.71

Dividend Achiever Status

Rank	161	10 Year Growth Rate	9.74%
Total Years of Dividend Growth		48

Business Summary: Industrial Machinery and Equipment (MIC: 11.5 SIC: 3531 NAIC:333120)

Dover is a diversified industrial manufacturing corporation made up of 52 operating companies. Dover Diversified's products include packaging and printing machinery, heat transfer equipment, food refrigeration and display cases as well as products for use in the defense, aerospace and automotive industries. Dover Industries makes products for use in the waste handling, bulk transport, automotive service, commercial food service and packaging, welding, cash dispenser and construction industries. Dover Technologies' products include automated assembly and testing equipment, specialized electronic components and industrial printers. Dover Resources manufactures products for various industries.

Recent Developments: For the quarter ended Mar 31 2004, earnings from continuing operations were $83.8 million versus earnings of $57.7 million in the corresponding year–earlier period. Net sales increased 24.4% to $1.24 billion. Co.'s results were fueled by higher sales and increased earnings from across its four business segments with the exception of Diversified, which posted a 1.2% decline in earnings to $30.9 million. Co. noted that favorable year–over–year earnings from 7 of 11 operating companies within Diversified were offset by a sizable unfavorable comparison at Belvac, which shipped two large can lines in the first quarter of 2003 that produced nearly half of its annual earnings.

Prospects: Co.'s near–term prospects appear positive, reflecting favorable operating trends from across its business segments. For instance, Co. noted that 36 of its 48 operating companies posted favorable year–over–year earnings growth for the quarter ended Mar 31 2004, and 34 of those companies achieved favorable earnings comparisons over last year's fourth quarter. Notably, Co.'s Circuit Board Assembly and Test equipment business is experiencing very strong bookings, enhancing its outlook for the remainder of 2004. Meanwhile, previous restructuring efforts and Co.'s focus on new product development should allow it to capitalize on the pick up in demand across the markets it serves.

Financial Data

(US$ in Thousands)	3 Mos	12/31/2003	12/31/2002	12/31/2001	12/31/2000	12/31/1999	12/31/1998	12/31/1997
Earnings Per Share	1.52	1.40	1.04	0.82	2.61	1.92	1.45	1.79
Cash Flow Per Share	0.66	2.91	1.94	3.32	2.70	2.18	2.17	2.03
Tang. Book Val. Per Share	2.96	2.70	2.65	1.97	1.78	1.06	2.10	2.66
Dividends Per Share	0.580	0.570	0.540	0.520	0.480	0.440	0.400	0.360
Dividend Payout %	37.74	40.71	51.92	63.41	18.39	22.91	27.58	20.11
Income Statement								
Total Revenues	1,242,380	4,413,296	4,183,664	4,459,695	5,400,717	4,446,420	3,977,666	4,547,656
Total Indirect Exp.	303,177	1,076,664	1,018,696	1,096,346	1,124,012	973,049	894,325	959,067
Depreciation & Amort.	38,201	151,309	161,003	219,963	203,384	183,244	167,687	170,663
Operating Income	132,688	443,758	341,620	299,023	843,210	635,411	531,960	612,669
Income Taxes	33,886	86,676	58,542	71,595	239,108	209,950	162,249	211,405
Income from Cont Ops	83,809	285,216	211,149	166,839	533,207	405,054	326,397	...
Net Income	83,112	292,927	(121,261)	248,537	519,612	928,992	378,845	405,431
Average Shs. Outstg.	204,763	203,614	203,346	204,013	204,677	210,679	224,386	226,815
Balance Sheet								
Cash & Cash Equivalents	422,533	370,379	294,448	175,865	181,399	138,038	96,774	124,780
Total Current Assets	1,993,702	1,849,640	1,658,001	1,654,928	1,974,849	1,611,562	1,304,524	1,591,345
Total Assets	5,257,806	5,133,752	4,437,385	4,602,202	4,892,116	4,131,940	3,627,276	3,277,524
Total Current Liabilities	971,531	910,801	696,938	819,171	1,604,640	1,334,865	989,747	1,196,573
Long–Term Obligations	1,006,051	1,003,915	1,030,299	1,033,243	631,846	608,025	610,090	262,630
Net Stockholders' Equity	2,779,799	2,742,671	2,394,623	2,519,539	2,441,575	2,038,756	1,910,884	1,703,584
Shares Outstanding	203,253	202,912	202,402	202,579	203,183	204,628	220,407	234,507
Operating Profit Margin %	10.68	10.05	8.16	6.70	15.61	14.29	13.37	13.47
Return on Equity %	3.01	10.39	8.81	6.62	21.83	19.86	17.08	23.79
Return on Assets %	1.59	5.55	4.75	3.62	10.89	9.80	8.99	12.37
Debt/Total Assets %	19.13	19.55	23.21	22.45	12.91	14.71	16.81	8.01
Price Range	44.02-36.74	40.08-23.35	43.31-23.91	43.32-28.77	53.81-36.00	47.25-29.50	39.81-25.94	36.31-24.38
P/E Ratio	28.96-24.17	28.63-16.68	41.64-22.99	52.83-35.09	20.62-13.79	24.61-15.36	27.46-17.89	20.29-13.62
Average Yield %	1.44	1.76	1.63	1.39	1.07	1.14	1.17	1.18

Address: 280 Park Avenue, New York, NY 10017

Telephone: (212) 922–1640

Web Site: www.dovercorporation.com

Officers: Thomas L. Reece – Chmn., C.E.O., Ronald L. Hoffman – Pres., C.O.O.

Transfer Agents: Mellon Investor Services, Ridgefield Park, NJ

Investor Contact: 212–922–1640

Institutional Holding

No of Institutions: 11

Shares: 1,880,755 **% Held:** –

EASTGROUP PROPERTIES, INC.

Exchange	Symbol	Price	52Wk Range	Yield	P/E
NYS	EGP	$31.75 (5/28/2004)	35.95−25.45	6.05	42.91

*7 Year Price Score 132.5   *NYSE Composite Index=100   ***12 Month Price Score 46.6**

TRADING VOLUME (thousand shares)

Interim Earnings (Per Share)

Qtr.	Mar	Jun	Sep	Dec
2001	0.27	0.53	0.38	0.33
2002	0.22	0.27	0.16	0.19
2003	0.16	0.21	0.13	0.19
2004	0.21	...	...	...

Interim Dividends (Per Share)

Amt	Decl	Ex	Rec	Pay
0.475Q	9/4/2003	9/17/2003	9/19/2003	9/30/2003
0.475Q	12/5/2003	12/17/2003	12/19/2003	12/30/2003
0.48Q	3/11/2004	3/18/2004	3/22/2004	3/31/2004
0.48Q	5/27/2004	6/16/2004	6/18/2004	6/30/2004

Indicated Div: $1.92 (Div. Reinv. Plan)

Valuation Analysis

Forecast P/E 12.59 (5/24/2004)

Market Cap $510.8 Million	Book Value 297.8 Million
Price/Book 2.45	Price/Sales 6.68

Dividend Achiever Status

Rank 229	10 Year Growth Rate 6.28%
Total Years of Dividend Growth	11

Business Summary: Property, Real Estate &Development (MIC: 8.3 SIC: 6798 NAIC:525930)

Eastgroup Properties is a self−administered, equity real estate investment trust focused on the acquisition, operation and development of industrial properties in the major Sunbelt markets throughout the U.S. with an emphasis in the states of Arizona, California, Florida and Texas. Co.'s strategy for growth is based on ownership of premier distribution facilities generally clustered near major transportation features in supply constrained submarkets. As of Dec 31 2003, Co.'s portfolio includes 19.4 million square feet with an additional 746,000 square feet under development.

Recent Developments: For the three months ended Mar 31 2004, net income was $5.0 million compared with income of $5.2 million before a gain of $104,000 from discontinued operations, in the corresponding quarter of the previous year. Revenues rose 3.1% to $27.7 million from $26.8 million in the year-earlier period. The improvement in revenues was primarily due to growth from real estate operations of 4.3%. Property net operating income climbed 7.7% to $20.0 million versus $18.5 million in the prior-year quarter. Funds from operations increased 6.3% to $12.6 million from $11.8 million the year before.

Prospects: Co. is benefiting from higher occupancy, which is more than offsetting lower rents resulting from lease renewals and new leasing at lower rates. Meanwhile, Co. believes that its development program is well−positioned to take advantage of the opportunities offered by an improving economy. For 2004, Co. expects earnings to range from $0.86 to $0.98 per share, and funds from operations to range from $2.42 to $2.54 per share. Separately, Co. plans to begin construction of site improvements and the first two buildings at its South Ridge development in Orlando and hopes to start additional buildings in the third quarter in Houston and Fort Lauderdale.

Financial Data

(US$ in Thousands)	3 Mos	12/31/2003	12/31/2002	12/31/2001	12/31/2000	12/31/1999	12/31/1998	12/31/1997
Earnings Per Share	0.74	0.69	0.84	1.51	1.68	1.99	1.66	1.56
Tang. Book Val. Per Share	15.75	16.04	17.96	19.07	19.44	19.42	18.78	15.87
Dividends Per Share	1.900	1.900	1.880	1.800	1.580	1.480	1.400	1.330
Dividend Payout %	256.75	275.36	223.80	119.20	94.04	74.37	84.33	85.68
Income Statement								
Interest Income	...	22	45	560	136	244	164	558
Total Income	27,663	108,441	105,810	105,295	98,103	86,236	76,728	53,622
Total Indirect Exp.	9,939	75,462	69,661	67,610	66,196	60,134	54,292	13,844
Depreciation	8,263	32,050	30,333	27,041	23,449	20,178	16,574	10,409
Interest Expense	...	19,015	17,387	17,823	18,570	17,688	16,948	...
Eqty Earns/Minority Int.	(121)	416	375	350	...	...	...	512
Income from Cont Ops	...	20,335	23,705	...	...	38,773	...	...
Net Income	5,012	20,445	23,626	34,182	36,512	38,355	29,336	20,779
Average Shs. Outstg.	21,114	18,194	16,237	16,046	15,798	17,362	16,432	13,338
Balance Sheet								
Cash & Cash Equivalents	2,118	1,786	1,383	1,767	2,861	2,657	2,784	1,298
Ttl Real Estate Inv.	701,509	695,643	672,694	644,039	624,535	589,469	531,415	376,693
Total Assets	737,009	729,267	702,341	683,782	666,205	632,151	567,548	413,127
Long−Term Obligations	282,826	338,272	322,300	291,072	270,709	243,665	236,816	147,150
Total Liabilities	406,918	362,322	387,213	354,429	332,170	304,196	292,881	155,812
Net Stockholders' Equity	362,417	366,945	356,485	370,710	375,392	369,312	316,024	257,315
Shares Outstanding	20,950	20,853	16,104	15,912	15,849	15,555	16,307	16,205
Statistical Record								
Net Inc.+Depr./Assets %	1.80	7.70	7.70	9.00	9.00	9.30	8.10	7.50
Return on Equity %	1.38	0.47	1.87	4.50	4.77	5.70	3.91	8.27
Return on Assets %	0.68	0.23	0.95	2.44	2.69	3.33	2.18	5.15
Price Range	35.95−32.38	32.90−23.88	26.35−22.40	23.90−20.19	23.88−17.56	21.00−15.75	22.06−16.69	22.88−17.75
P/E Ratio	48.58−43.76	47.68−34.61	31.37−26.67	15.83−13.37	14.21−10.45	10.55−7.91	13.29−10.05	14.66−11.38
Average Yield %	5.55	6.93	7.61	8.10	7.55	8.09	7.14	6.68

Address: 300 One Jackson Place, Jackson, MS 39201−2195	Officers: Leland R. Speed − Chmn., David H. Hoster II − Pres., C.E.O.	Institutional Holding
Telephone: (601) 354 3555	Transfer Agents:First Chicago Trust Company of New York, Jersey City, NJ	No of Institutions: 7
Web Site: www.eastgroup.net		Shares: 1,448,160 % Held: −

EATON VANCE CORP

Exchange	Symbol	Price	52Wk Range	Yield	P/E
NYS	EV	$36.90 (5/28/2004)	39.60-30.30	1.30	23.35

*7 Year Price Score 148.6 *NYSE Composite Index=100 *12 Month Price Score 46.6

TRADING VOLUME (thousand shares)

Interim Earnings (Per Share)

Qtr.	Jan	Apr	Jul	Oct
2000-01	0.44	0.29	0.44	0.43
2001-02	0.46	0.46	0.44	0.34
2002-03	0.37	0.36	0.38	0.40
2003-04	0.44	...	...	...

Interim Dividends (Per Share)

Amt	Decl	Ex	Rec	Pay
0.12Q	7/9/2003	7/29/2003	7/31/2003	8/11/2003
0.12Q	10/22/2003	10/29/2003	10/31/2003	11/10/2003
0.12Q	1/14/2004	1/28/2004	1/30/2004	2/9/2004
0.12Q	4/14/2004	4/28/2004	4/30/2004	5/10/2004
		Indicated Div: $0.48		

Valuation Analysis

Forecast P/E 18.25 (5/24/2004)

Market Cap $2.6 Billion	Book Value 423.7 Million
Price/Book 6.00	Price/Sales 4.58

Dividend Achiever Status

Rank	30	10 Year Growth Rate	20.64%
Total Years of Dividend Growth			22

Business Summary: Wealth Management (MIC: 8.8 SIC: 6282 NAIC:523930)

Eaton Vance is engaged in the provision of investment advisory and distribution services to mutual funds and other investment funds, and investment management services to individual high-net-worth investors, family offices and institutional clients. As of Oct 31 2003, Co. managed $75.0 billion in assets with investment objectives ranging from high current income to maximum long-term capital gain. Co. conducts its investment management business through its two wholly owned subsidiaries, Eaton Vance Management and Boston Management and Research, and its three majority-owned subsidiaries, Atlanta Capital, Fox Asset Management and Parametric.

Recent Developments: For the quarter ended Apr 30 2004, net income surged 40.6% to $35.2 million compared with $25.0 million in the corresponding period of 2003. Total revenues jumped 36.7% to $165.3 million. Investment adviser and administration fees increased 48.9% to $101.2 million. Operating income soared 45.5% to $56.2 million versus $38.6 million a year earlier. For the six months ended Apr 30 2004, net income climbed 29.6% to $66.0 million. Average assets under management increased 44.8% to $81.50 billion in the first half of fiscal 2004 from $56.30 billion in the first half last year. As a result of higher average assets under management, fiscal 2004 first half revenue increased 31.0% to $322.3 million.

Prospects: Prospects appear promising as results continue to be driven by increases in assets under management, the acquisitions of Atlanta Capital Management Company, LLC and Fox Asset Management LLC in September of 2001 and Parametric Portfolio Associates in September 2003, and five successful closed-end fund offerings. Also, Co. is benefiting from strong open-end fund, private fund, institutional and retail managed account flows. Meanwhile, cash, cash equivalents and short-term investments were $308.3 million as of Apr 30 2004, up 29.4% versus $238.3 million on Apr 30 2003.

Financial Data

(US$ in Thousands)	3 Mos	10/31/2003	10/31/2002	10/31/2001	10/31/2000	10/31/1999	10/31/1998	10/31/1997
Earnings Per Share	1.58	1.51	1.70	1.60	1.58	0.70	0.40	0.52
Cash Flow Per Share	0.04	0.62	1.87	1.94	1.00	0.29	0.13	0.57
Tang. Book Val. Per Share	4.24	4.11	3.83	2.80	3.64	2.73	2.94	3.02
Dividends Per Share	0.400	0.360	0.290	0.240	0.190	0.150	0.120	0.100
Dividend Payout %	25.16	23.84	17.05	15.00	12.02	21.27	29.62	...
Income Statement								
Total Revenues	156,973	523,133	522,985	486,372	429,566	348,950	249,987	200,910
Total Indirect Exp.	106,870	359,989	339,062	295,479	246,902	271,046	201,335	137,005
Depreciation & Amort.	20,763	85,192	83,690	74,344	82,809	63,991	64,570	54,464
Operating Income	50,103	163,144	183,923	190,893	182,664	77,904	48,652	63,905
Net Interest Inc./(Exp.)	(863)	(913)	1,921	4,556	3,652	671	1,791	(380)
Income Taxes	19,131	57,700	65,184	62,469	71,128	33,505	19,515	27,236
Income from Cont Ops	...	...	...	...	...	52,405	...	...
Net Income	30,813	106,123	121,057	116,020	116,051	15,798	30,523	40,234
Average Shs. Outstg.	70,336	70,375	71,412	72,300	73,222	74,494	75,514	78,392
Balance Sheet								
Cash & Cash Equivalents	132,105	138,328	144,078	115,681	60,479	77,395	54,386	61,928
Total Current Assets	316,492	272,317	213,567	237,480	120,242	90,488	130,433	164,168
Total Assets	695,205	658,702	616,619	675,301	432,989	358,229	380,260	387,375
Total Current Liabilities	58,769	82,795	68,270	83,844	61,793	48,890	48,957	39,968
Long-Term Obligations	119,180	118,736	124,118	215,488	21,429	28,571	35,714	50,964
Net Stockholders' Equity	423,690	416,277	372,302	301,126	254,950	194,268	211,809	226,280
Net Working Capital	257,723	189,522	145,297	153,636	58,449	41,598	81,476	124,200
Shares Outstanding	68,148	68,405	69,257	68,616	69,543	70,519	71,331	73,876
Operating Profit Margin %	31.91	31.18	35.16	39.24	42.52	22.32	19.46	31.80
Net Profit Margin %	43.10	42.34	48.07	49.54	60.13	34.22	27.82	47.13
Return on Equity %	7.27	25.49	32.51	38.52	45.51	26.97	14.41	17.78
Return on Assets %	4.43	16.11	19.63	17.18	26.80	14.62	8.02	10.38
Debt/Total Assets %	17.14	18.02	20.12	31.90	4.94	7.97	9.39	13.15
Price Range	38.53-34.25	35.80-23.55	40.75-22.76	38.31-22.56	27.38-16.94	19.32-9.50	12.38-8.06	9.31-5.24
P/E Ratio	24.39-21.68	23.71-15.60	23.97-13.39	23.94-14.10	17.33-10.72	27.59-13.57	30.94-20.16	17.91-10.07
Average Yield %	1.10	1.17	0.88	0.77	0.88	1.13	1.14	1.54

Address: 255 State Street, Boston, MA 02109
Telephone: (617) 482-8260
Web Site: www.eatonvance.com

Officers: James B. Hawkes - Chmn., Pres., C.E.O., Thomas E. Faust - Exec. V.P., Chief Investment Officer
Transfer Agents: EquiServe Trust Company, N.A., Providence, RI

Investor Contact:617-482-8260
Institutional Holding
No of Institutions: 5
Shares: 36,197,532 **% Held:** -

ECOLAB, INC.

Exchange	Symbol	Price	52Wk Range	Yield	P/E
NYS	ECL	$30.51 (5/28/2004)	30.81–24.00	1.05	27.74

*7 Year Price Score 133.4   *NYSE Composite Index=100   *12 Month Price Score 51.7

Interim Earnings (Per Share)

Qtr.	Mar	Jun	Sep	Dec
2001	0.17	0.18	0.22	0.15
2002	0.14	0.20	0.28	0.19
2003	0.21	0.25	0.33	0.27
2004	0.25	...	...	...

Interim Dividends (Per Share)

Amt	Decl	Ex	Rec	Pay
0.073Q	8/15/2003	9/12/2003	9/16/2003	10/15/2003
0.08Q	12/11/2003	12/19/2003	12/23/2003	1/15/2004
0.08Q	3/1/2004	3/12/2004	3/16/2004	4/15/2004
0.08Q	5/7/2004	6/11/2004	6/15/2004	7/15/2004

Indicated Div: $0.32 (Div. Reinv. Plan)

Valuation Analysis

Forecast P/E 25.71 (5/24/2004)

Market Cap $3.9 Billion	Book Value 1.3 Billion
Price/Book 5.42	Price/Sales 1.89

Dividend Achiever Status

Rank 124	10 Year Growth Rate	11.81%
Total Years of Dividend Growth		11

Business Summary: Chemicals (MIC: 11.1 SIC: 2842 NAIC:325612)

Ecolab develops and markets products and services for the hospitality, foodservice, institutional and industrial markets. Co. operates in three business segments. The Cleaning and Sanitizing segment consists of seven business units and offers cleaners, sanitizers, detergents, lubricants, chemical cleaning, animal health, water treatment, infection control and janitorial products. Other U.S. Services consists of two business units focused on the elimination and prevention of pests, and the manufacturing of dishwashing and customized machines for the foodservice industry. The International segment serves customers in Europe, Asia Pacific, Canada, Latin America, the Middle East and Africa.

Recent Developments: For the quarter ended Mar 31 2004, net income grew 19.3% to $66.0 million from $55.3 million in the prior–year quarter. Results for 2004 included a charge of $3.8 million related to the disposition of a business. Results for 2003 included a special gain of $197,000. Net sales increased 11.8% to $979.4 million from $875.9 million in 2003. Sales benefited from increased sales volume from Co.'s core markets, successful new product launches and favorable foreign currency translation. U.S. cleaning and sanitizing net sales increased 3.2% to $430.7 million. Other U.S. Services net sales rose 6.1% to $77.8 million. International cleaning and sanitizing net sales advanced 5.6% to $439.2 million.

Prospects: For the second quarter of 2004, Co. expects sales for both domestic and international operations to increase, supported by improving business trends, particularly in Co.'s core hospitality and foodservice markets. Gross margins are expected to approach 52.0%. Co. expects diluted earnings per share to be in the range of $0.28 to $0.30. For the second half of 2004, Co. should continue to benefit from improving fixed currency sales trends, though the benefit to earnings per share from currency and lower tax rates will not be as great as in 2003. Nevertheless, Co. increased its full–year 2004 earnings per share forecast to a range of $1.17 to $1.19.

Financial Data

(US$ in Thousands)	3 Mos	12/31/2003	12/31/2002	12/31/2001	12/31/2000	12/31/1999	12/31/1998	12/31/1997
Earnings Per Share	1.10	1.06	0.81	0.72	0.79	0.65	0.57	0.50
Cash Flow Per Share	0.34	2.01	1.61	1.40	1.19	1.09	0.87	0.87
Tang. Book Val. Per Share	0.80	1.14	0.82	0.40	1.76	1.97	1.75	1.29
Dividends Per Share	0.290	0.290	0.270	0.260	0.240	0.210	0.190	0.160
Dividend Payout %	27.29	27.35	33.33	35.86	30.37	32.06	33.04	32.00
Income Statement								
Total Revenues	979,371	3,761,819	3,403,585	2,354,723	2,264,313	2,080,012	1,888,226	1,640,352
Total Indirect Exp.	385,333	1,433,551	1,283,091	946,089	869,343	852,449	775,073	699,764
Depreciation & Amort.	61,286	229,656	223,428	162,990	148,436	134,530	121,971	100,879
Operating Income	116,139	482,658	395,866	318,179	343,139	289,951	261,980	218,504
Net Interest Inc./(Exp.)	(11,173)	(45,345)	(43,895)	(28,434)	(24,605)	(22,713)	(21,742)	(12,637)
Income Taxes	38,960	171,070	140,081	117,408	129,495	109,769	101,782	85,345
Income from Cont Ops	...	...	211,890	...	208,555	...	154,506	...
Net Income	66,006	277,348	209,770	188,170	206,127	175,786	192,506	133,955
Average Shs. Outstg.	260,227	262,737	261,574	259,856	263,892	268,838	268,094	267,644
Balance Sheet								
Cash & Cash Equivalents	46,322	85,626	49,205	41,793	43,965	47,748	28,425	61,169
Total Current Assets	1,185,278	1,150,340	1,015,937	929,583	600,568	577,321	503,514	509,501
Total Assets	3,451,174	3,228,918	2,878,429	2,525,000	1,714,011	1,585,946	1,470,995	1,416,299
Total Current Liabilities	975,093	851,942	866,531	827,952	532,034	470,674	399,791	404,464
Long–Term Obligations	620,642	604,441	539,743	512,280	234,377	169,014	227,041	259,384
Net Stockholders' Equity	1,345,656	1,295,426	1,099,751	880,352	757,007	762,016	690,541	551,701
Net Working Capital	210,185	298,398	149,587	101,631	68,534	106,647	103,723	105,037
Shares Outstanding	256,922	257,416	259,880	255,800	254,322	258,832	258,958	258,254
Operating Profit Margin %	11.85	12.83	11.63	13.51	16.29	13.93	13.87	13.32
Return on Equity %	4.90	21.40	19.26	21.37	30.97	23.06	22.37	24.28
Return on Assets %	1.91	8.58	7.36	7.45	13.68	11.08	10.50	9.45
Debt/Total Assets %	17.98	18.71	18.75	20.28	13.67	10.65	15.43	18.31
Price Range	28.53–26.22	27.92–23.36	25.08–18.36	21.97–15.49	22.34–14.13	22.09–16.06	18.84–13.42	13.91–9.13
P/E Ratio	25.94–23.84	26.33–22.04	30.96–22.67	30.51–21.51	28.28–17.88	33.99–24.71	33.06–23.55	27.81–18.25
Average Yield %	1.06	1.13	1.20	1.32	1.29	1.09	1.26	1.44

Address: 370 Wabasha Street North, St. Paul, MN 55102–1390	Officers: Allan L. Schuman – Chmn., C.E.O., Douglas M. Baker – Pres., C.O.O.	Investor Contact:612–293–2809
Telephone: (651) 293–2233	Transfer Agents:EquiServe Trust Company, N.A., Providence, RI	Institutional Holding No of Institutions: 8
Web Site: www.ecolab.com		Shares: 352,379 % Held: –

EMERSON ELECTRIC CO.

Exchange	Symbol	Price	52Wk Range	Yield	P/E
NYS	EMR	$59.70 (5/28/2004)	68.46–50.47	2.68	22.44

*7 Year Price Score 98.8   *NYSE Composite Index=100   *12 Month Price Score 47.2

Interim Earnings (Per Share)

Qtr.	Dec	Mar	Jun	Sep
2000–01	0.83	0.83	0.77	(0.03)
2001–02	0.61	0.65	0.68	0.58
2002–03	0.52	0.56	0.66	0.67
2003–04	0.58	0.75	...	...

Interim Dividends (Per Share)

Amt	Decl	Ex	Rec	Pay
0.393Q	8/5/2003	8/13/2003	8/15/2003	9/10/2003
0.40Q	11/4/2003	11/12/2003	11/14/2003	12/10/2003
0.40Q	2/3/2004	2/11/2004	2/13/2004	3/10/2004
0.40Q	5/4/2004	5/12/2004	5/14/2004	6/10/2004
	Indicated Div: $1.60 (Div. Reinv. Plan)			

Valuation Analysis

Forecast P/E 20.85 (5/24/2004)

Market Cap	$25.1 Billion	Book Value	7.0 Billion
Price/Book	3.64	Price/Sales	1.74

Dividend Achiever Status

Rank	202	10 Year Growth Rate	7.94%
Total Years of Dividend Growth			47

Business Summary: Instruments and Related Products (MIC: 11.15 SIC: 3621 NAIC:335312)

Emerson Electric designs and manufactures electrical, electromechanical and electronic products, systems and services. The Process Control segment makes process management products. The Industrial automation (IA) segment provides industrial motors, drives, controls and equipment for IA markets. The Electronics and Telecommunications segment designs, manufactures, installs and maintains power products for network–dependent clients. The Heating, Ventilation and Air Conditioning segment engineers and manufactures climate control components and systems. The Appliance and Tools segment provides motors, controls and components for appliance, industrial and comfort control applications.

Recent Developments: For the second quarter ended Mar 31 2004, net earnings advanced 32.0% to $318.0 million compared with earnings of $241.0 million, before a loss from discontinued operations of $5.0 million, in the equivalent 2003 quarter. Net sales increased 11.4% to $3.86 billion from $3.47 billion a year earlier. On a segment basis, Process Control sales rose 10.5% to $905.0 million, while Industrial Automation sales grew 11.9% to $723.0 million. Electronics and Telecommunications sales jumped 13.4% to $628.0 million, and Heating, Ventilation, and Air Conditioning sales climbed 11.1% to $770.0 million. Appliance and Tools sales ascended 9.2% to $950.0 million.

Prospects: Solid global demand continues across all of Co.'s segments, particularly in emerging markets where it is well–positioned to win new business. Co.'s emerging market growth is being led by strength in China, Eastern Europe, the Middle East, and Russia. Meanwhile, sales are also accelerating in the U.S. with the continuation of consumer spending and strengthening in the professional tools, storage and motors businesses. These businesses are seeing higher end–market demand, which is driving higher sales and orders. Looking ahead to fiscal year 2004, Co. expects earnings to range from $2.75 to $2.85 per share.

Financial Data

(US$ in Thousands)	6 Mos	3 Mos	09/30/2003	09/30/2002	09/30/2001	09/30/2000	09/30/1999	09/30/1998
Earnings Per Share	2.66	2.66	2.41	2.52	2.40	3.30	3.00	2.77
Cash Flow Per Share	1.73	0.67	4.11	4.31	3.97	4.26	4.12	3.71
Tang. Book Val. Per Share	4.70	4.06	3.60	1.97	2.22	2.53	4.42	4.79
Dividends Per Share	1.580	1.570	1.570	1.550	1.530	1.430	1.300	1.180
Dividend Payout %	59.39	59.02	65.14	61.50	63.75	43.33	43.33	42.59
Income Statement								
Total Revenues	7,459,000	3,600,000	13,958,000	13,824,000	15,479,600	15,544,800	14,269,500	13,447,200
Total Indirect Exp.	1,607,000	796,000	3,229,000	2,795,000	3,468,200	3,062,900	2,865,100	2,776,400
Depreciation & Amort.	10,000	6,000	17,000	28,000	708,500	678,500	637,500	562,500
Operating Income	1,041,000	492,000	1,645,000	1,798,000	1,892,900	2,465,900	2,210,600	2,075,200
Net Interest Inc./(Exp.)	(110,000)	(57,000)	(231,000)	(233,000)	(304,300)	(287,600)	(189,700)	(151,700)
Income Taxes	261,000	113,000	401,000	505,000	556,800	755,900	707,300	694,900
Income from Cont Ops	...	...	1,013,000	1,060,000	...	...	...	...
Net Income	562,000	244,000	1,089,000	122,000	1,031,800	1,422,400	1,313,600	1,228,600
Average Shs. Outstg.	422,600	422,200	420,900	420,900	429,500	431,400	438,400	444,100
Balance Sheet								
Cash & Cash Equivalents	1,165,000	1,009,000	696,000	381,000	355,700	280,800	266,100	209,700
Total Current Assets	6,308,000	5,980,000	5,500,000	4,961,000	5,320,100	5,482,700	5,124,400	5,001,300
Total Assets	16,021,000	15,707,000	15,194,000	14,545,000	15,046,400	15,164,300	13,623,500	12,659,800
Total Current Liabilities	3,612,000	3,643,000	3,417,000	4,400,000	5,379,100	5,218,800	4,590,400	4,021,700
Long–Term Obligations	3,756,000	3,733,000	3,733,000	2,990,000	2,255,600	2,247,700	1,317,100	1,056,600
Net Stockholders' Equity	7,005,000	6,726,000	6,460,000	5,741,000	6,114,000	6,402,800	6,180,500	5,803,300
Net Working Capital	2,696,000	2,337,000	2,083,000	561,000	(59,000)	263,900	534,000	979,600
Shares Outstanding	421,821	421,567	421,154	420,709	419,625	427,476	433,044	438,224
Statistical Record								
Operating Profit Margin %	13.95	13.66	11.95	14.67	12.22	15.86	15.49	15.43
Return on Equity %	8.02	3.62	16.05	22.48	16.87	22.21	21.25	21.17
Return on Assets %	3.51	1.55	6.82	8.87	6.85	9.37	9.64	9.70
Debt/Total Assets %	23.44	23.76	24.56	20.55	14.99	14.82	9.66	8.34
Price Range	68.46–52.65	64.95–52.65	56.79–42.42	65.51–43.20	78.81–45.80	70.19–41.13	70.94–51.81	67.13–51.56
P/E Ratio	25.74–19.79	112.0–90.78	23.56–17.60	26.00–17.14	32.84–19.08	21.27–12.46	23.65–17.27	24.23–18.61
Average Yield %	2.58	2.65	3.11	2.88	2.34	2.47	2.09	1.96

Address: 8000 West Florissant Avenue, St. Louis, MO 63136	Officers: Charles F. Knight – Chmn., J. G. Berges – Pres.	Institutional Holding
Telephone: (314) 553–2000	Transfer Agents:Mellon Investor Services, LLC, South Hackensack, NJ	No of Institutions: 2
Web Site: www.gotoemerson.com		Shares: 140,486 % Held: –

ENERGEN CORP.

Exchange	Symbol	Price	52Wk Range	Yield	P/E
NYS	EGN	$44.80 (5/28/2004)	44.86-31.70	1.65	13.91

*7 Year Price Score 151.4 *NYSE Composite Index=100 *12 Month Price Score 52.0

Interim Earnings (Per Share)

Qtr.	Dec	Jun	Sep	Dec
2001	0.12	...	...	...

Qtr.	Mar	Jun	Sep	Dec
2002	1.24	0.01	0.01	0.83
2003	1.52	0.69	0.32	0.56
2004	1.65	...	...	...

Interim Dividends (Per Share)

Amt	Decl	Ex	Rec	Pay
0.185Q	7/23/2003	8/13/2003	8/15/2003	9/2/2003
0.185Q	10/29/2003	11/12/2003	11/14/2003	12/1/2003
0.185Q	1/28/2004	2/11/2004	2/13/2004	3/1/2004
0.185Q	4/28/2004	5/12/2004	5/14/2004	6/1/2004

Indicated Div: $0.74 (Div. Reinv. Plan)

Valuation Analysis

Forecast P/E 13.59 (5/24/2004)

Market Cap	$1.5 Billion	Book Value	742.4 Million
Price/Book	2.02	Price/Sales	1.70

Dividend Achiever Status

Rank	280	10 Year Growth Rate	3.25%
Total Years of Dividend Growth			21

TRADING VOLUME (thousand shares)

1995 1996 1997 1998 1999 2000 2001 2002 2003 2004

Business Summary: Gas Utilities (MIC: 7.4 SIC: 4924 NAIC:221210)

Energen is a diversified energy holding company engaged in the business of natural gas distribution and oil and gas exploration and production. Co. provides natural gas to residential, commercial and industrial customers located in Alabama. Alagasco, Co.'s principal subsidiary, is the largest natural gas distribution utility in the State of Alabama. Co.'s utility operations are subject to regulation by the Alabama Public Service Commission. The oil and gas exploration and production arm of Co. is Energen Resources, which conducts its activities in the Gulf of Mexico.

Recent Developments: For the three months ended Mar 31 2004, income was $60.2 million, before a loss of $12,000 from discontinued operations, compared with income of $53.3 million, before a gain of $1.3 million from discontinued operations, in the corresponding quarter of the previous year. Total operating revenues increased 13.5% to $351.4 million from $309.7 million in the year-earlier period. Operating income climbed 10.3% to $106.0 million versus $96.1 million in the prior-year quarter. Overall results benefited from higher prices for the natural gas and oil production at Energen Resources Corporation.

Prospects: Results continue to benefit from rising natural gas and oil prices, which facilitated Co.'s ability to hedge a significant portion of its flowing production at prices greater than those in the previous year. The higher price environment is also having a positive impact on the prices applicable to its unhedged volumes. Meanwhile, Co. expects diluted earnings to range from $3.20 to $3.30 per share for full-year 2004, including about $0.06 per diluted share from a fourth quarter, $200.0 million property acquisition. Going forward, Co. will focus on the continued implementation of its acquire-and-exploit strategy to invest $1.00 billion in property acquisitions throughout 2008.

Financial Data

(US$ in Thousands)	3 Mos	12/31/2003	12/31/2002	12/31/2001	09/30/2001	09/30/2000	09/30/1999	09/30/1998
Earnings Per Share	3.22	3.09	2.09	1.12	2.18	1.75	1.38	1.23
Cash Flow Per Share	3.70	6.80	6.30	0.68	5.03	3.45	4.36	4.19
Tang. Book Val. Per Share	20.42	19.29	16.77	15.17	15.60	13.20	12.08	11.22
Dividends Per Share	0.730	0.730	0.710	0.690	0.680	0.660	0.640	0.620
Dividend Payout %	22.90	23.62	33.97	61.60	31.42	38.00	46.73	50.81
Income Statement								
Total Revenues	351,429	842,221	677,175	146,164	784,973	555,595	497,517	502,627
Total Indirect Exp.	53,504	182,291	155,325	35,383	149,183	133,957	125,881	118,715
Costs & Expenses	245,389	624,333	541,089	135,304	660,964	459,794	420,134	441,142
Depreciation & Amort.	28,736	116,858	105,087	24,502	86,975	87,073	88,615	80,999
Operating Income	106,040	217,888	136,086	10,860	124,009	95,801	77,383	61,485
Net Interest Inc./(Exp.)	(10,318)	(42,262)	(43,713)	(10,634)	(42,070)	(37,769)	(37,173)	(30,001)
Income Taxes	35,362	64,128	20,509	(3,384)	15,976	6,789	135	(2,221)
Income from Cont Ops	60,197	110,265	70,586	3,579	...	...	...	...
Net Income	60,185	110,654	68,639	3,658	67,896	53,018	41,410	36,249
Average Shs. Outstg.	36,566	35,716	33,838	31,277	31,083	30,359	29,920	29,437
Balance Sheet								
Net Property	1,441,887	1,433,451	1,256,803	1,005,679	998,334	907,829	861,107	756,344
Total Assets	1,840,010	1,781,432	1,530,891	1,240,356	1,223,879	1,203,041	1,184,895	993,455
Long-Term Obligations	552,874	552,842	512,954	544,133	544,110	353,932	371,824	372,782
Net Stockholders' Equity	742,356	699,032	582,810	474,205	480,767	400,860	361,504	329,249
Shares Outstanding	36,344	36,223	34,745	31,248	30,799	30,350	29,903	29,326
Operating Profit Margin %	30.17	25.87	20.09	7.43	15.79	17.24	15.55	12.23
Net Profit Margin %	37.25	28.32	16.48	N.M.	12.71	11.98	8.37	6.32
Net Inc./Net Property %	4.17	7.71	5.46	0.36	6.80	5.84	4.80	4.79
Net Inc./Tot. Capital %	4.48	8.61	6.26	0.35	6.62	7.02	5.64	5.16
Return on Equity %	8.10	15.77	12.11	0.75	14.12	13.22	11.45	11.00
Accum. Depr./Gross Prop. %	75.31	31.34	35.13	37.99	37.16	36.50	34.86	34.47
Price Range	44.70-39.99	41.96-28.23	29.80-21.86	25.20-22.00	39.71-22.21	30.06-14.75	20.25-13.63	22.31-15.56
P/E Ratio	13.88-12.42	13.58-9.14	14.26-10.46	22.50-19.64	18.22-10.19	17.18-8.43	14.67-9.87	18.14-12.65
Average Yield %	1.73	2.14	2.76	2.91	2.25	3.33	3.59	3.22

Address: 605 Richard Arrington Jr. Blvd. N., Birmingham, AL 35203-2707	**Officers:** William Michael Warren - Chmn., Pres., C.E.O., Geoffrey C. Ketcham - Exec. V.P., C.F.O., Treas.	**Investor Contact:**800-654-3206 **Institutional Holding** **No of Institutions:** 12
Telephone: (205) 326-2700 **Web Site:** www.energen.com	**Transfer Agents:**EquiServe Trust Company, N.A., Providence, RI	**Shares:** 191,272 **% Held:** -

ENERGYSOUTH, INC.

Exchange	Symbol	Price	52Wk Range	Yield	P/E
NMS	ENSI	$36.36 (5/28/2004)	38.60–28.16	3.30	15.02

*7 Year Price Score 133.4 *NYSE Composite Index=100 *12 Month Price Score 50.4

Interim Earnings (Per Share)

Qtr.	Dec	Mar	Jun	Sep
2000–01	0.55	0.73	0.10	0.14
2001–02	0.75	0.93	0.18	0.17
2002–03	0.66	1.09	0.19	0.23
2003–04	0.78	1.22	...	...

Interim Dividends (Per Share)

Amt	Decl	Ex	Rec	Pay
0.285Q	7/25/2003	9/11/2003	9/15/2003	10/1/2003
0.285Q	10/25/2003	12/8/2003	12/10/2003	1/1/2004
0.285Q	1/30/2004	3/11/2004	3/15/2004	4/1/2004
0.30Q	4/30/2004	6/11/2004	6/15/2004	7/1/2004

Indicated Div: $1.20 (Div. Reinv. Plan)

Valuation Analysis

Forecast P/E N/A

Market Cap $182.4 Million	Book Value 92.9 Million
Price/Book 1.92	Price/Sales 1.56

Dividend Achiever Status

Rank 298	10 Year Growth Rate	1.46%

Total Years of Dividend Growth 26

Business Summary: Gas Utilities (MIC: 7.4 SIC: 4924 NAIC:221210)

EnergySouth is a holding company for a family of energy businesses. Co.'s operations are classified into three business segments. The Natural Gas Distribution segment is engaged in the distribution and transportation of natural gas to about 100,000 residential, commercial and industrial customers in Southwest Alabama, including the City of Mobile, through Mobile Gas and Southern Gas Transmission Company. The Natural Gas Storage segment provides for the underground storage of natural gas and transportation services through the operations of Bay Gas and Storage. Co.'s Other business segment includes marketing, merchandising, and other energy–related services.

Recent Developments: For the quarter ended Mar 31 2004, net income increased 14.6% to $6.4 million from $5.6 million in the prior–year quarter. Results were primarily fueled by strong earnings growth from the gas distribution business of Co.'s Mobile Gas subsidiary. Additionally, Co. also benefited from higher earnings from Bay Gas' storage operations. Total operating revenues advanced 20.3% to $42.8 million from $35.6 million the previous year. On a segment basis, Earnings from Mobile Gas' distribution business increased about $0.13 per diluted share from the year–earlier quarter. Bay Gas' earnings rose by $0.03 per diluted share, or 20.0%. Earnings from other businesses declined by $0.03 per diluted share.

Prospects: Earnings for Co.'s Mobile Gas subsidiary are benefiting from higher margins, primarily due to the impact of rate adjustments. Margins are also being positively affected by increases in temperature–sensitive customers' gas consumption. These increases are being partially offset by higher operating and maintenance expenses and increased depreciation expense due to an additional plant placed in service. Meanwhile, Bay Gas' earnings are being supported by additional storage revenues associated with the commencement of operations of a second storage cavern in April 2003 and a new storage agreement, which was entered into during the first quarter of fiscal 2004.

Financial Data

(US$ in Thousands)	6 Mos	3 Mos	09/30/2003	09/30/2002	09/30/2001	09/30/2000	09/30/1999	09/30/1998
Earnings Per Share	2.42	2.29	2.17	2.03	1.52	1.78	1.75	1.71
Cash Flow Per Share	3.36	1.27	3.35	4.38	3.36	2.75	3.74	2.95
Tang. Book Val. Per Share	18.00	16.99	16.49	15.30	14.20	13.95	13.10	12.29
Dividends Per Share	1.120	1.110	1.090	1.050	1.010	0.950	0.890	0.420
Dividend Payout %	46.28	48.47	50.46	51.72	66.44	53.65	51.14	24.56
Income Statement								
Total Revenues	75,562	32,716	99,615	86,419	107,759	74,097	68,060	74,022
Total Indirect Exp.	9,918	4,687	16,200	14,720	14,861	12,357	11,829	11,870
Costs & Expenses	54,376	23,979	73,957	63,675	90,160	54,843	49,072	55,872
Depreciation & Amort.	4,868	2,434	8,923	8,172	7,312	6,735	6,467	6,278
Operating Income	21,186	8,737	25,658	22,744	17,599	19,254	18,988	18,150
Net Interest Inc./(Exp.)	(3,996)	(2,015)	(7,067)	(5,791)	(4,783)	(4,424)	(4,850)	(4,240)
Income Taxes	6,355	2,458	6,702	5,983	4,604	5,270	5,003	4,967
Income from Cont Ops	...	...	...	...	7,561	...	8,624	...
Net Income	10,440	4,068	11,135	10,231	6,138	8,792	8,275	8,417
Average Shs. Outstg.	5,206	5,200	5,124	5,046	4,987	4,944	4,933	4,926
Balance Sheet								
Net Property	204,681	194,434	194,367	187,823	170,592	134,351	129,676	127,128
Total Assets	245,563	233,367	225,686	221,474	218,852	167,380	173,635	166,541
Long–Term Obligations	87,703	88,488	92,640	98,645	90,592	55,222	58,017	58,979
Net Stockholders' Equity	92,854	87,458	84,655	77,283	70,124	68,544	64,154	59,895
Shares Outstanding	5,158	5,145	5,133	5,133	5,048	4,937	4,912	4,894	4,872
Statistical Record								
Operating Profit Margin %	28.03	26.70	25.75	26.31	16.33	25.98	27.89	24.51
Net Inc./Net Property %	5.10	2.09	5.72	5.44	3.59	6.54	6.38	6.62
Net Inc./Tot. Capital %	5.64	2.03	5.56	5.25	3.45	6.27	6.02	6.31
Return on Equity %	11.24	4.65	13.15	13.23	10.78	12.82	13.44	14.05
Accum. Depr./Gross Prop. %	24.66	28.12	27.54	26.26	26.29	28.97	27.76	26.08
Price Range	37.14–31.34	37.14–31.34	33.96–24.28	32.04–21.10	23.30–19.75	22.00–17.00	23.00–18.94	40.25–18.94
P/E Ratio	15.35–12.95	16.22–13.69	15.65–11.19	15.78–10.39	15.33–12.99	12.36–9.55	13.14–10.82	23.54–11.07
Average Yield %	3.22	3.25	3.83	4.00	4.72	4.96	4.32	1.54

Address: 2828 Dauphin Street, Mobile, AL 36606 Telephone: (251) 450 4774 Web Site: www.energysouth.com	Officers: John C. Hope III – Chmn., Walter L. Hovell – Vice–Chmn.	Institutional Holding No of Institutions: 23 Shares: 331,614 % Held: –

EXXON MOBIL CORP.

Exchange	Symbol	Price	52Wk Range	Yield	P/E
NYS	XOM	$43.25 (5/28/2004)	43.99–34.92	2.50	14.37

*7 Year Price Score 101.9   *NYSE Composite Index=100   ***12 Month Price Score 51.9**

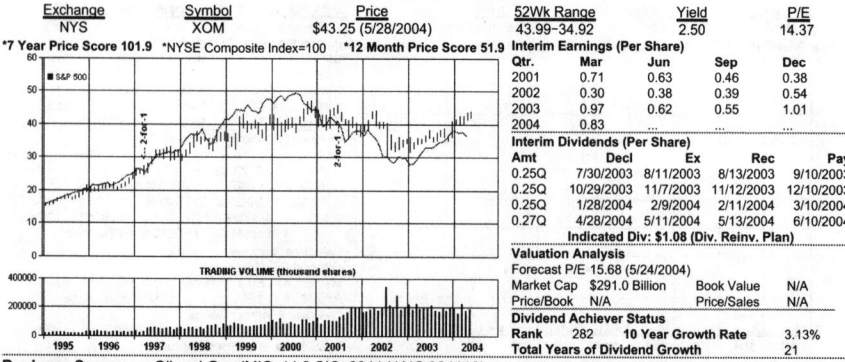

Interim Earnings (Per Share)

Qtr.	Mar	Jun	Sep	Dec
2001	0.71	0.63	0.46	0.38
2002	0.30	0.38	0.39	0.54
2003	0.97	0.62	0.55	1.01
2004	0.83	...	...	...

Interim Dividends (Per Share)

Amt	Decl	Ex	Rec	Pay
0.25Q	7/30/2003	8/11/2003	8/13/2003	9/10/2003
0.25Q	10/29/2003	11/7/2003	11/12/2003	12/10/2003
0.25Q	1/28/2004	2/9/2004	2/11/2004	3/10/2004
0.27Q	4/28/2004	5/11/2004	5/13/2004	6/10/2004

Indicated Div: $1.08 (Div. Reinv. Plan)

Valuation Analysis

Forecast P/E 15.68 (5/24/2004)
Market Cap	$291.0 Billion	Book Value	N/A
Price/Book	N/A	Price/Sales	N/A

Dividend Achiever Status

Rank	282	10 Year Growth Rate	3.13%
Total Years of Dividend Growth	21		

Business Summary: Oil and Gas (MIC: 14.2 SIC: 2911 NAIC:324110)

Exxon Mobil's principal business is energy, involving exploration for, and production of, crude oil and natural gas, manufacturing of petroleum products and transportation and sale of crude oil, natural gas and petroleum products. Co. is a major manufacturer and marketer of basic petrochemicals, including olefins, aromatics, polyethylene and polypropylene plastics and a wide variety of specialty products. Co. also has interests in electric power generation facilities. As of Dec 31 2003, worldwide proved developed and undeveloped reserves were: crude oil and natural gas liquids, 12,075 million barrels; and natural gas, 54,769 billion cubic feet.

Recent Developments: For the three months ended Mar 31 2004, net income was $5.44 billion compared with income of $6.49 billion a year earlier. Results for 2003 excluded a one-time gain of $1.70 billion from the transfer of shares in Ruhrgas AG and an accounting change gain of $550.0 million. Total revenues and other income rose 6.0% to $67.60 billion. Upstream earnings, excluding special items, rose to $4.01 billion from $3.99 billion last year. Downstream earnings advanced 38.9% to $1.00 billion, reflecting improved worldwide refining margins, partly offset by weaker marketing conditions. Chemical earnings jumped 96.5% to $564.0 million, due to stronger worldwide margins and favorable foreign exchange effects.

Prospects: Favorable crude oil and natural gas prices, coupled with improving chemical results, bode well for Co.'s near-term outlook. In addition, rising liquids production, due to primarily to higher production from new fields in West Africa and Norway, further strengthen Co.'s intermediate prospects. Separately, Co. noted that it continued with its active investment program, spending $3.40 billion on capital and exploration projects during the three months ended Mar 31 2004, compared with $3.50 billion last year, reflecting continued strong levels of upstream spending that could lead to future production increases.

Financial Data

(US$ in Millions)	3 Mos	12/31/2003	12/31/2002	12/31/2001	12/31/2000	12/31/1999	12/31/1998	12/31/1997
Earnings Per Share	3.01	3.15	1.61	2.18	2.27	1.12	1.30	1.68
Cash Flow Per Share	1.54	4.27	3.12	3.29	3.26	2.17	2.27	2.92
Tang. Book Val. Per Share	14.01	13.68	11.13	10.74	10.21	9.11	8.98	8.84
Dividends Per Share	1.000	0.980	0.920	0.910	0.880	0.830	0.820	0.810
Dividend Payout %	33.22	31.11	57.14	41.74	38.68	74.22	62.83	48.21
Income Statement								
Total Revenues	66,346	242,365	204,506	213,488	232,748	185,527	117,772	137,242
Total Indirect Exp.	22,466	106,213	95,439	96,221	95,715	96,526	63,411	65,652
Costs & Expenses	58,486	213,871	186,389	188,507	204,666	173,537	108,431	123,623
Depreciation & Amort.	2,373	9,047	8,310	7,944	8,130	8,304	5,340	5,474
Operating Income	9,116	32,867	18,117	24,981	28,082	11,990	9,341	13,619
Net Interest Inc./(Exp.)	(48)	(207)	(398)	(293)	(589)	(695)	(100)	(415)
Income Taxes	3,522	11,006	6,499	9,014	11,091	3,240	2,616	4,338
Eqty Earns/Minority Int.	1,256	4,373	...	...	...	...	...	...
Income from Cont Ops	...	20,960	11,011	15,105	15,990	...	6,440	...
Net Income	5,440	21,510	11,460	15,320	17,720	7,910	6,370	8,460
Average Shs. Outstg.	6,582	6,662	6,803	6,941	7,034	6,906	4,856	5,010
Balance Sheet								
Net Property	104,784	104,965	94,940	89,602	89,829	94,043	65,199	66,414
Total Assets	180,202	174,278	152,644	143,174	149,000	144,521	92,630	96,064
Long–Term Obligations	5,135	4,756	6,655	7,099	7,280	8,402	4,530	7,050
Net Stockholders' Equity	91,681	89,915	74,597	73,161	70,757	63,466	43,750	43,660
Shares Outstanding	6,540	6,568	6,700	6,809	6,930	6,959	4,856	4,914
Operating Profit Margin %	11.77	11.75	8.85	11.70	12.06	6.46	7.93	9.92
Net Inc./Net Property %	5.19	20.49	12.07	17.09	19.72	8.41	9.77	12.73
Net Inc./Tot. Capital %	4.65	18.20	11.40	15.40	18.13	8.61	10.07	12.71
Return on Equity %	4.51	18.44	14.76	20.64	22.59	12.46	14.72	19.37
Accum. Depr./Gross Prop. %	...	54.22	53.67	52.96	52.15	50.29	49.16	48.02
Price Range	42.78–40.10	41.00–31.82	44.38–30.27	45.78–35.83	47.16–35.50	43.22–32.41	38.34–29.06	33.41–24.50
P/E Ratio	14.21–13.32	13.02–10.10	27.57–18.80	21.00–16.44	20.77–15.64	38.59–28.93	29.50–22.36	19.88–14.58
Average Yield %	2.41	2.71	2.44	2.20	2.13	2.16	2.37	2.76

Address: 5959 Las Colinas Boulevard, Irving, TX 75039-2298	Officers: Lee R. Raymond – Chmn., C.E.O., Harry J. Longwell – Exec. V.P.	Investor Contact:212-444-1900
Telephone: (972) 444 1000	Transfer Agents:ExxonMobil Shareholder Services	Institutional Holding
Web Site: www.exxonmobil.com	c/o EquiServe Trust Company, NA, Boston, MA	No of Institutions: 74
		Shares: 30,807,999 % Held: –

F.N.B. CORP (PA)

Exchange	Symbol	Price	52Wk Range	Yield	P/E
NYS	FNB	$19.96 (5/28/2004)	35.45-18.98	4.61	18.31

*7 Year Price Score 115.8   *NYSE Composite Index=100   *12 Month Price Score 33.1

Interim Earnings (Per Share)

Qtr.	Mar	Jun	Sep	Dec
2001	0.21	0.37	0.46	0.48
2002	(0.19)	0.50	0.51	0.52
2003	0.50	0.53	0.01	0.21
2004	0.34	...	...	...

Interim Dividends (Per Share)

Amt	Decl	Ex	Rec	Pay
0.24Q	11/18/2003	11/26/2003	12/1/2003	12/15/2003
Q	12/18/2003	1/2/2004	12/26/2003	1/1/2004
0.23Q	2/19/2004	2/26/2004	3/1/2004	3/15/2004
0.23Q	5/12/2004	5/27/2004	6/1/2004	6/15/2004

Indicated Div: $0.92 (Div. Reinv. Plan)

Valuation Analysis

Forecast P/E N/A

Market Cap	$874.0 Million	Book Value	250.0 Million
Price/Book	4.06	Price/Sales	2.03

Dividend Achiever Status

Rank	50	10 Year Growth Rate	17.38%
Total Years of Dividend Growth		19	

Business Summary: Commercial Banking (MIC: 8.1 SIC: 6021 NAIC:522110)

F.N.B., with assets of $8.31 billion as of Dec 31 2003, is a financial holding company that provides a full range of financial services to consumers and small– to medium–size businesses in its market areas. Co.'s bank subsidiaries offer traditional full–service commercial banking services, including commercial and individual demand and time deposit accounts and commercial, mortgage and individual installment loans. In addition, Co.'s bank subsidiaries offer various alternative investment products, including mutual funds and annuities. The consumer finance subsidiary offers personal installment loans to individuals and purchase installment sales finance contracts from retail merchants.

Recent Developments: For the quarter ended Mar 31 2004, net income rose 11.0% to $16.2 million versus income from continuing operations of $14.6 million in the same period of 2003. Results for 2004 and 2003 included gains on the sale of securities of $445,000 and $382,000, and gains on the sale of loans of $267,000 and $782,000, respectively. Results for 2004 also included gains on the sale of branches of $4.1 million. Net interest income slipped 6.5% to $42.2 million. Provision for loan losses grew 12.0% to $4.6 million from $4.1 million the year before. Total non–interest income increased 22.7% to $20.8 million, while total non–interest expense decreased 7.2% to $34.6 million.

Prospects: In March of 2004, Regency Finance, Co. 's consumer finance subsidiary, entered into a definitive agreement to purchase eight consumer finance offices in the greater Columbus, Ohio region. This purchase will bring the total number of Regency offices to 56. The value of the loans purchased is approximately $10.0 million and the transaction was expected to close by the end of April 2004. Separately, Co. expects to achieve its financial goals in 2004. Based on a stable net interest margin and an efficiency ratio of 55.0%, Co. projects diluted earnings per share for full–year 2004 in the range of $1.26 to $1.32.

Financial Data

(US$ in Thousands)	3 Mos	12/31/2003	12/31/2002	12/31/2001	12/31/2000	12/31/1999	12/31/1998	12/31/1997
Earnings Per Share	1.09	1.25	1.34	1.52	1.62	1.48	1.31	1.62
Tang. Book Val. Per Share	4.77	8.73	11.07	13.02	12.51	11.35	11.76	11.61
Dividends Per Share	0.950	0.920	0.800	0.690	0.650	0.620	0.580	0.500
Dividend Payout %	86.36	74.36	60.31	45.30	40.10	41.90	43.90	30.70
Income Statement								
Total Interest Income	61,976	423,313	426,784	296,693	290,936	254,916	235,985	195,508
Total Interest Expense	19,771	129,836	145,671	125,667	135,308	106,467	103,385	84,478
Net Interest Income	42,205	293,477	281,113	171,026	155,628	148,449	132,600	111,030
Provision for Loan Losses	4,622	24,339	19,094	12,915	10,877	9,240	7,255	10,585
Non–Interest Income	20,769	130,571	120,873	82,799	55,645	46,928	31,745	23,113
Non–Interest Expense	34,611	315,323	289,444	174,830	137,501	129,679	109,174	88,208
Income Before Taxes	23,741	84,386	93,448	66,080	62,895	56,458	47,916	35,350
Income from Cont Ops	...	...	...	...	...	...	...	24,314
Net Income	16,222	58,789	63,335	44,572	42,776	39,295	31,872	33,123
Average Shs. Outstg.	47,067	46,972	47,073	29,311	25,484	26,468	24,265	20,322
Balance Sheet								
Cash & Due from Banks	90,889	204,824	246,802	155,946	141,844	171,183	128,868	87,869
Securities Avail. for Sale	983,941	1,641,972	1,026,191	413,793	436,441	408,731	447,005	432,327
Net Loans & Leases	3,193,838	5,634,336	5,152,098	3,161,659	2,923,336	2,767,463	2,298,834	1,858,214
Total Assets	4,635,436	8,308,310	7,090,232	4,129,087	3,886,548	3,706,184	3,250,695	2,649,494
Total Deposits	3,313,381	6,159,499	5,426,157	3,292,392	3,102,937	2,909,434	2,708,572	2,192,713
Long–Term Obligations	602,511	855,808	450,647	103,013	116,140	117,634	69,492	67,246
Total Liabilities	4,385,392	7,701,401	6,491,636	3,759,890	3,565,304	3,415,869	2,978,537	2,418,858
Net Stockholders' Equity	250,044	606,909	598,596	369,197	321,244	290,315	272,158	230,636
Shares Outstanding	46,284	46,313	46,055	28,346	25,541	25,385	22,928	19,612
Return on Equity %	6.48	9.68	10.58	12.07	13.31	13.53	11.71	10.54
Return on Assets %	0.34	0.70	0.89	1.07	1.10	1.06	0.98	0.91
Equity/Assets %	5.39	7.30	8.44	8.94	8.26	7.83	8.37	8.70
Non–Int. Exp./Tot. Inc. %	41.82	56.92	52.85	46.06	39.67	42.96	40.77	40.34
Price Range	35.45-19.30	35.45-25.61	30.23-23.36	25.49-18.57	19.65-15.01	23.04-17.24	29.97-19.20	28.92-16.35
P/E Ratio	33.52-17.71	28.36-20.49	22.56-17.43	16.77-12.22	12.13-9.27	15.56-11.65	22.88-14.65	17.85-10.09
Average Yield %	4.42	3.02	2.94	2.34	N/A	N/A	N/A	N/A

Address: 2150 Goodlette Road North, Naples, FL 34102
Telephone: (239) 262–7600
Web Site: www.fnbcorporation.com

Officers: Peter Mortensen – Chmn., Stephen J. Gurgovits – Pres., C.E.O.
Transfer Agents: F.N.B. Shareholder Services, Naples, FL

Investor Contact: 239–659–9894
Institutional Holding
No of Institutions: 20
Shares: 1,023,816   **% Held:** –

FAMILY DOLLAR STORES, INC.

Exchange	Symbol	Price	52Wk Range	Yield	P/E
NYS	FDO	$31.36 (5/28/2004)	43.61-27.50	1.08	20.63

*7 Year Price Score 148.3   *NYSE Composite Index=100   *12 Month Price Score 37.9

Interim Earnings (Per Share)

Qtr.	Nov	Feb	May	Aug
2000-01	0.24	0.35	0.31	0.20
2001-02	0.29	0.37	0.35	0.24
2002-03	0.33	0.42	0.40	0.28
2003-04	0.37	0.47	...	...

Interim Dividends (Per Share)

Amt	Decl	Ex	Rec	Pay
0.075Q	8/21/2003	9/11/2003	9/15/2003	10/15/2003
0.075Q	11/5/2003	12/11/2003	12/15/2003	1/15/2004
0.085Q	1/15/2004	3/11/2004	3/15/2004	4/15/2004
0.085Q	5/14/2004	6/11/2004	6/15/2004	7/15/2004

Indicated Div: $0.34

Valuation Analysis

Forecast P/E 19.78 (5/24/2004)

Market Cap	$5.4 Billion	Book Value	1.4 Billion
Price/Book	4.36	Price/Sales	1.22

Dividend Achiever Status

Rank	131	10 Year Growth Rate	11.61%
Total Years of Dividend Growth		27	

TRADING VOLUME (thousand shares)

1995 1996 1997 1998 1999 2000 2001 2002 2003 2004

Business Summary: Retail – General (MIC: 5.2 SIC: 5331 NAIC:452990)

Family Dollar Stores is engaged in the operation of a chain of self–service retail discount stores. The stores offer a variety of hardlines and softlines merchandise. Hardlines merchandise includes primarily household chemical and paper products, candy, snack and other food, health and beauty aids, electronics, housewares and giftware, pet food and supplies, toys, stationery and school supplies, seasonal goods, hardware and automotive supplies. Softlines merchandise includes men's, women's, boys', girls' and infants' clothing, shoes, and domestic items such as blankets, sheets and towels. As of Nov 1 2003, Co. operated 5,066 stores in 43 states and the District of Columbia.

Recent Developments: For the quarter ended Feb 28 2004, net income climbed 12.0% to $81.4 million from $72.7 million in the corresponding prior–year period. Net sales totaled $1.40 billion, up 11.7% compared with $1.26 billion the previous year. Results for the recent period benefited from a 2.2% increase in existing–store sales and sales from new stores opened as part of Co.'s store expansion program. During the quarter, Co. opened 95 new stores and closed 22 existing locations. Gross margin advanced 13.5% to $473.8 million, or 33.8% of net sales, from $417.5 million, or 33.2% of net sales, the year before.

Prospects: Results are benefiting from higher initial margins on merchandise reflecting improved sourcing, lower levels of markdowns, and improved inventory management. Looking ahead, Co. anticipates earnings per share growth of between 14.0% and 16.0% during the second half of fiscal 2004. This guidance is based on the expectation that sales in existing stores will increase by 3.0% to 5.0% in the second half of the current fiscal year. Separately, Co. plans to open between 525 and 565 new stores during the current fiscal year. Co. is focusing on opening stores in urban locations, however, Co. is targeting certain small and mid–sized towns, where new stores can typically be opened more quickly.

Financial Data

(US$ in Thousands)	6 Mos	3 Mos	08/30/2003	08/31/2002	09/01/2001	08/26/2000	08/28/1999	08/29/1998
Earnings Per Share	1.52	1.52	1.43	1.25	1.10	1.00	0.81	0.60
Cash Flow Per Share	1.50	0.42	1.70	2.31	0.96	1.06	0.64	1.22
Tang. Book Val. Per Share	8.21	7.93	7.61	6.66	5.57	4.66	3.99	3.35
Dividends Per Share	0.300	0.290	0.280	0.250	0.230	0.210	0.190	0.170
Dividend Payout %	19.73	19.07	19.58	20.00	20.90	21.00	23.45	28.33
Income Statement								
Total Revenues	2,647,481	1,244,683	4,750,171	4,162,652	3,665,362	3,132,639	2,751,181	2,361,930
Total Indirect Exp.	675,386	329,826	1,214,658	1,054,298	927,679	784,812	695,060	607,287
Depreciation & Amort.	48,444	24,009	88,315	77,015	67,685	54,509	43,788	34,843
Operating Income	229,753	101,499	389,725	341,621	298,422	270,911	222,679	165,988
Income Taxes	83,860	37,047	142,250	124,692	108,917	98,894	82,600	62,700
Net Income	145,893	64,452	247,475	216,929	189,505	172,017	140,079	103,288
Average Shs. Outstg.	173,319	173,641	173,354	174,049	172,774	172,648	172,511	173,223
Balance Sheet								
Cash & Cash Equivalents	354,787	247,809	206,731	220,265	21,753	43,558	95,301	134,221
Total Current Assets	1,280,988	1,203,433	1,156,492	1,055,859	807,265	750,673	719,955	646,630
Total Assets	2,129,009	2,035,940	1,985,695	1,754,619	1,399,745	1,243,714	1,095,252	942,180
Total Current Liabilities	631,886	582,527	595,331	530,780	390,294	412,017	378,546	343,275
Net Stockholders' Equity	1,409,758	1,369,187	1,310,969	1,154,948	959,015	797,964	690,651	578,151
Net Working Capital	649,102	620,906	561,161	525,079	416,971	338,656	341,408	303,354
Shares Outstanding	171,771	172,446	172,208	173,329	172,035	171,131	172,750	172,203
Statistical Record								
Operating Profit Margin %	8.67	8.15	8.20	8.20	8.14	8.64	8.09	7.03
Return on Equity %	10.35	4.70	18.87	18.78	19.76	21.55	20.28	17.86
Return on Assets %	6.85	3.16	12.46	12.36	13.53	13.83	12.78	10.96
Price Range	43.61-32.65	43.61-38.41	40.25-24.16	36.86-24.56	30.09-16.88	23.25-14.38	25.56-12.69	21.50-10.63
P/E Ratio	28.69-21.48	28.69-25.27	28.15-16.90	29.49-19.65	27.35-15.34	23.25-14.38	31.56-15.66	35.83-17.71
Average Yield %	0.78	0.71	0.87	0.80	0.96	1.13	0.92	1.07

Address: 10401 Old Monroe Road, Charlotte, NC 28205
Telephone: (704) 847–6961
Web Site: www.familydollar.com

Officers: Howard R. Levine – Chmn., C.E.O., R. James Kelly – Vice–Chmn., C.F.O., Admin. Officer
Transfer Agents: Mellon Investor Services LLC, Ridgefield Park, NJ

Investor Contact: 704–847–6961
Institutional Holding
No of Institutions: 70
Shares: 46,633,515   **% Held:** –

FANNIE MAE

Exchange	Symbol	Price	52Wk Range	Yield	P/E
NYS	FNM	$67.70 (5/28/2004)	79.88-60.40	3.07	8.80

*7 Year Price Score 103.5 *NYSE Composite Index=100 *12 Month Price Score 45.4

Interim Earnings (Per Share)

Qtr.	Mar	Jun	Sep	Dec
2001	1.25	1.36	1.33	1.95
2002	1.17	1.44	0.98	0.94
2003	1.93	1.09	2.50	2.20
2004	1.90	...	...	...

Interim Dividends (Per Share)

Amt	Decl	Ex	Rec	Pay
0.45Q	7/14/2003	7/29/2003	7/31/2003	8/25/2003
0.45Q	10/21/2003	10/29/2003	10/31/2003	11/25/2003
0.52Q	1/23/2004	1/28/2004	1/31/2004	2/25/2004
0.52Q	4/20/2004	4/28/2004	4/30/2004	5/25/2004

Indicated Div: $2.08 (Div. Reinv. Plan)

Valuation Analysis

Forecast P/E 13.20 (5/24/2004)

Market Cap	$67.8 Billion	Book Value	16.7 Billion
Price/Book	4.39	Price/Sales	1.37

Dividend Achiever Status

Rank	96	10 Year Growth Rate	13.83%
Total Years of Dividend Growth			18

Business Summary: Credit &Lending (MIC: 8.6 SIC: 6111 NAIC:522292)

Fannie Mae facilitates the flow of low–cost mortgage capital in order to increase the availability and affordability of homeownership for low–, moderate– and middle–income Americans. Co. is the nation's largest source of funds for mortgage lenders and investors, providing resources for customers to make additional mortgage loans or investments in mortgage–related securities. Co. operates exclusively in the secondary mortgage market by purchasing mortgages and mortgage–related securities from primary market institutions, such as commercial banks, savings and loan associations, mortgage companies, securities dealers and other investors.

Recent Developments: For the quarter ended Mar 31 2004, net income declined 2.1% to $1.90 billion from $1.94 billion in the prior-year quarter. Results for 2004 and 2003 included losses of $26.7 million and $392.2 million, respectively, from the retirement of debt, and purchased options expenses of $959.3 million and $624.6 million. Net interest income fell 5.1% to $3.20 billion, while net interest margin dropped 18 basis points to 1.07%. Guaranty fee income climbed 34.8% to $736.9 million, driven by a 23.9% rise in average outstanding mortgage-backed security growth and a 1.8 basis point increase in the effective guaranty fee rate on that business. Co.'s portfolio of mortgages declined 7.7% to $880.91 billion.

Prospects: Co. cautioned that its financial results could be more variable in the coming quarters as the volume of refinancing eases due to the uptick in interest rates. However, the impact of lower portfolio balances on core net interest income may be diminished by higher than anticipated net interest margin. These improvements in mortgage spreads and resulting increases in portfolio commitments in March 2004 suggest a return to positive portfolio growth at some point during the second quarter. However, for the quarter as a whole, portfolio growth is likely to be negative. Accordingly, Co. expects its mortgage portfolio growth for the full year to fall short of the double–digit threshold.

Financial Data

(US$ in Thousands)	3 Mos	12/31/2003	12/31/2002	12/31/2001	12/31/2000	12/31/1999	12/31/1998	12/31/1997
Earnings Per Share	7.69	7.72	4.53	5.89	4.26	3.73	3.26	2.84
Tang. Book Val. Per Share	17.21	18.82	13.76	15.86	18.57	16.02	13.95	12.33
Dividends Per Share	1.810	1.680	1.320	1.200	1.120	1.080	0.960	0.840
Dividend Payout %	22.94	21.76	29.13	20.37	26.29	28.95	29.44	29.57
Income Statement								
Total Interest Income	12,344,000	50,920,000	50,853,000	49,170,000	42,781,000	35,495,000	29,995,000	26,378,000
Total Interest Expense	9,148,000	37,351,000	40,287,000	41,080,000	37,107,000	30,601,000	25,885,000	22,429,000
Net Interest Income	3,196,000	13,569,000	10,566,000	8,090,000	5,674,000	4,894,000	4,110,000	3,949,000
Provision for Loan Losses	32,000	100,000	128,000	(115,000)	(120,000)	(120,000)	(50,000)	100,000
Non–Interest Income	739,000	575,000	1,374,000	1,440,000	1,093,000	1,226,000	1,193,000	1,124,000
Non–Interest Expense	1,345,000	3,631,000	5,764,000	1,354,000	905,000	800,000	708,000	636,000
Income Before Taxes	2,558,000	10,413,000	6,048,000	8,291,000	5,982,000	5,440,000	4,645,000	4,337,000
Income from Cont Ops	...	7,720,000	...	6,067,000	4,416,000	3,921,000	3,444,000	3,068,000
Net Income	1,899,000	7,905,000	4,619,000	5,894,000	4,448,000	3,912,000	3,418,000	3,056,000
Average Shs. Outstg.	975,000	981,000	997,000	1,006,000	1,009,000	1,031,000	1,037,000	1,056,000
Balance Sheet								
Securities Avail. for Sale	45,105,000	243,466,000	210,500,000	35,883,000	21,136,000	18,091,000	16,216,000	5,906,000
Net Loans & Leases	886,316,000	240,582,000	186,055,000	705,167,000	607,399,000	522,780,000	415,223,000	316,016,000
Total Assets	995,268,000	1,009,569,000	887,515,000	799,791,000	675,072,000	575,167,000	485,014,000	391,373,000
Long–Term Obligations	474,091,000	478,539,000	468,570,000	419,975,000	362,360,000	321,037,000	254,878,000	194,374,000
Total Liabilities	974,463,000	987,196,000	871,227,000	781,673,000	654,234,000	557,538,000	469,561,000	377,880,000
Net Stockholders' Equity	20,805,000	22,373,000	16,288,000	18,118,000	20,838,000	17,629,000	15,453,000	13,793,000
Shares Outstanding	970,000	970,000	989,000	997,000	999,000	1,019,000	1,025,000	1,037,000
Return on Equity %	4.63	34.50	28.35	33.48	21.19	22.24	22.28	22.24
Return on Assets %	0.09	0.76	0.52	0.75	0.65	0.68	0.71	0.78
Equity/Assets %	2.09	2.21	1.83	2.26	3.08	3.06	3.18	3.52
Non–Int. Exp./Tot. Inc. %	17.42	6.75	10.89	2.66	2.05	2.16	2.24	2.28
Price Range	79.88–71.33	75.37–58.93	83.15–59.54	87.49–72.95	87.81–48.19	75.31–58.88	75.94–56.31	57.06–36.13
P/E Ratio	10.39–9.28	9.76–7.63	18.36–13.14	14.85–12.39	20.61–11.31	20.19–15.78	23.29–17.27	20.09–12.72
Average Yield %	2.38	2.45	1.78	1.50	1.78	1.60	1.51	1.88

Address: 3900 Wisconsin Avenue, NW, Washington, DC 20016–2892	Officers: Franklin D. Raines – Chmn., C.E.O., J. Timothy Howard – Vice–Chmn., Exec. V.P., C.F.O.	Investor Contact:202–752–7119
Telephone: (202) 752–7000	Transfer Agents:First Chicago Trust Company of New York, a division of EquiServe, Jersey City, NJ	Institutional Holding No of Institutions: 12
Web Site: www.fanniemae.com		Shares: 688,038 % Held: –

FARMER BROS. CO.

Exchange	Symbol	Price	52Wk Range	Yield	P/E
NMS	FARM	$28.83 (5/28/2004)	38.71-26.13	1.32	28.10

*7 Year Price Score 137.9 *NYSE Composite Index=100 *12 Month Price Score 44.4

TRADING VOLUME (thousand shares)

Interim Earnings (Per Share)

Qtr.	Sep	Dec	Mar	Jun
2000-01	0.43	0.64	0.53	0.37
2001-02	0.42	0.52	0.34	0.37
2002-03	0.30	0.32	0.35	0.33
2003-04	0.14	0.14	0.41	...

Interim Dividends (Per Share)

Amt	Decl	Ex	Rec	Pay
0.095Q	8/19/2003	10/22/2003	10/24/2003	11/10/2003
0.095Q	1/7/2004	1/21/2004	1/23/2004	2/9/2004
0.095Q	3/5/2004	4/21/2004	4/23/2004	5/10/2004
900%	3/5/2004	5/11/2004	4/23/2004	5/10/2004

Indicated Div: $0.38

Valuation Analysis

Forecast P/E N/A

Market Cap	$55.5 Million	Book Value	267.0 Million
Price/Book	1.99	Price/Sales	2.74

Dividend Achiever Status

Rank	211	10 Year Growth Rate	7.33%
Total Years of Dividend Growth			15

Business Summary: Food (MIC: 4.1 SIC: 2095 NAIC:311920)

Farmer Bros. manufactures and distributes a product line that includes roasted coffee, coffee related products (coffee filters, stir sticks, sugar and creamers), teas, cocoa, spices, and soup and beverage bases to restaurants and other institutional establishments that prepare food, including hotels, hospitals, convenience stores and fast food outlets. As of June 30 2003, Co.'s product line included over 300 items. Co.'s products are sold directly from its delivery trucks by sales representatives who solicit, sell, and otherwise maintain its customer's accounts.

Recent Developments: For the three months ended Mar 31 2004, net income declined 11.6% to $5.6 million compared with $6.3 million in the corresponding quarter of 2003. Results were negatively affected by costs related to legal and other services associated with litigation and proxy matters, higher employee related costs, and costs related to the implementation of a new information system. Net sales slipped 0.4% to $49.1 million from $49.3 million a year earlier, primarily due to weak economic conditions. Gross profit decreased 4.5% to $30.6 million versus $32.0 million in 2003. Income from operations plunged 85.1% to $743,000 compared with $5.0 million the year before.

Prospects: Co.'s multi-year information systems project, possibly the largest undertaking of its type Co. has ever attempted, has two major milestones left. The project began in the fall of 2002, and the initial milestone was on Jul 1 2003 when certain of the financial systems went live. The manufacturing systems are expected to go live on Sep 1 2004, and the sales system is expected to be phased into Co.'s branches beginning in February of 2005 and be completed by June 30 2005. The additional cost of the information systems portion of the project, through fiscal 2005, is expected to exceed $7.0 million.

Financial Data

(US$ in Thousands)	9 Mos	6 Mos	3 Mos	06/30/2003	06/30/2002	06/30/2001	06/30/2000	06/30/1999
Earnings Per Share	1.02	1.02	0.14	1.30	1.65	1.97	2.02	1.51
Tang. Book Val. Per Share	16.61	17.61	19.26	19.16	19.36	18.01	16.25	15.37
Dividends Per Share	0.370	0.360	0.360	0.350	0.330	0.310	0.290	0.270
Dividend Payout %	N.M.	N.M.	N.M.	273.08	203.30	159.90	146.04	182.12
Income Statement								
Total Revenues	146,245	97,176	45,665	201,558	205,857	215,431	218,688	221,571
Total Indirect Exp.	87,862	58,024	28,575	107,008	99,883	99,285	92,754	94,967
Depreciation & Amort.	5,302	3,508	1,745	5,776	5,493	5,527	5,628	5,202
Operating Income	4,924	4,181	1,057	23,888	38,210	42,115	48,965	36,770
Net Interest Inc./(Exp.)	2,156	1,221	651	3,974	7,261	12,308	10,080	8,870
Income Taxes	5,077	3,178	1,571	13,942	18,791	23,028	23,643	19,650
Income from Cont Ops	...	...	...	...	...	36,488	...	...
Net Income	10,679	5,076	2,511	23,629	30,569	36,178	37,576	28,865
Average Shs. Outstg.	16,266	17,670	17,829	18,145	18,483	18,433	18,580	19,030
Balance Sheet								
Cash & Cash Equivalents	192,425	187,060	32,029	294,405	292,587	263,180	129,850	126,606
Total Current Assets	247,996	239,656	348,703	346,617	348,434	318,879	188,560	181,549
Total Assets	316,109	308,490	417,997	416,415	417,524	390,395	353,467	324,836
Total Current Liabilities	22,416	15,574	15,665	16,659	16,259	17,655	16,966	15,918
Net Stockholders' Equity	266,968	261,138	371,174	369,145	373,053	347,048	313,113	287,711
Net Working Capital	225,580	224,082	333,038	329,958	332,175	301,224	171,594	165,631
Shares Outstanding	16,075	14,825	19,264	19,264	19,264	19,264	19,264	18,710
Statistical Record								
Operating Profit Margin %	3.36	4.30	2.31	11.85	18.56	19.54	22.39	16.59
Return on Equity %	4.00	1.94	0.67	6.40	8.19	10.51	12.00	10.03
Return on Assets %	3.38	1.64	0.60	5.67	7.32	9.34	10.63	8.88
Price Range	36.00-30.20	35.20-31.23	35.20-32.00	34.80-30.40	36.28-20.20	24.90-16.53	20.70-15.10	23.90-17.43
P/E Ratio	35.29-29.61	34.51-30.62	251.4-228.6	26.77-23.38	21.99-12.24	12.64-8.39	10.25-7.48	15.83-11.54
Average Yield %	1.12	1.09	1.06	1.10	1.21	1.55	1.68	1.32

Address: 20333 South Normandie Avenue, Torrance, CA 90502 **Telephone:** (310) 787-5200 **Web Site:** N/A	**Officers:** Roy E. Farmer – Pres., Guenter W. Berger – V.P., Prodn.

Institutional Holding
No of Institutions: 6
Shares: 451,406 % Held: –

FEDERAL REALTY INVESTMENT TRUST (MD)

Exchange	Symbol	Price	52Wk Range	Yield	P/E
NYS	FRT	$39.90 (5/28/2004)	46.73-31.47	4.91	34.10

*7 Year Price Score 147.9 ***NYSE Composite Index=100** ***12 Month Price Score 46.0**

Interim Earnings (Per Share)

Qtr.	Mar	Jun	Sep	Dec
2001	0.32	0.31	0.33	0.33
2002	0.08	0.27	0.31	(0.06)
2003	0.26	0.28	0.30	0.31
2004	0.28	...	...	...

Interim Dividends (Per Share)

Amt	Decl	Ex	Rec	Pay
0.485Q	6/3/2003	6/23/2003	6/25/2003	7/15/2003
0.49Q	8/11/2003	9/23/2003	9/25/2003	10/15/2003
0.49Q	12/2/2003	12/30/2003	1/2/2004	1/15/2004
0.49Q	3/3/2004	3/22/2004	3/24/2004	4/15/2004

Indicated Div: $1.96 (Div. Reinv. Plan)

Valuation Analysis

Forecast P/E 13.83 (5/24/2004)

Market Cap $1.7 Billion	Book Value 548.6 Million
Price/Book 4.13	Price/Sales 6.15

Dividend Achiever Status

Rank 290	10 Year Growth Rate	2.33%
Total Years of Dividend Growth		36

Business Summary: Property, Real Estate &Development (MIC: 8.3 SIC: 6798 NAIC:525930)

Federal Realty Investment Trust specializes in the ownership, management, development and redevelopment of high quality retail and mixed–use properties. As of Dec 31 2003, Co. owned or had an interest in 62 community and neighborhood shopping centers comprising about 13.5 million square feet, primarily located in densely populated and affluent communities throughout the Northeast and Mid–Atlantic U.S. In addition, Co. owned 49 urban and retail mixed–use properties comprising over 2.7 million square feet and one apartment complex, primarily located in strategic metropolitan markets in the Northeast and Mid–Atlantic regions and California. As of Dec 31 2003, Co.'s properties were 93.1% leased.

Recent Developments: For the quarter ended Mar 31 2004, income was $17.2 million versus income of $16.4 million in the prior–year quarter. Results for 2004 and 2003 excluded income from discontinued operations of $9,000 and $350,000, respectively. Total revenue increased 13.8% to $96.2 million from $84.5 million the previous year. The increase in revenue was due to the impact of properties acquired, as well as a 2.8% increase in same–center revenues and the recognition of $1.1 million of rental income from an insurance claim. Funds from operations improved 20.4% to $34.8 million from $28.9 million a year earlier. Co.'s overall portfolio was 93.3% leased as of Mar 31 2004 compared with 94.3% on Mar 31 2003.

Prospects: Going forward, prospects remain solid as Co. continues to successfully execute all aspects of its business plan. For instance, Co. has improved the value of its existing portfolio through the re–leasing and redevelopment of properties. In addition, Co. acquired Westgate Mall, a 637,000 square foot shopping center in San Jose, CA. Although Westgate is currently accretive to earnings, Co. expects its performance will improve through the recapture of spaces that have under–market rents. For full–year 2004, Co. expects funds from operations in the range of $2.81 to $2.84 per share.

Financial Data

(US$ in Thousands)	3 Mos	12/31/2003	12/31/2002	12/31/2001	12/31/2000	12/31/1999	12/31/1998	12/31/1997
Earnings Per Share	1.17	1.15	0.60	1.29	1.26	1.19	0.94	0.98
Tang. Book Val. Per Share	11.12	11.30	9.40	8.91	9.31	9.99	10.72	11.59
Dividends Per Share	1.950	1.940	1.920	1.890	1.820	1.770	1.750	1.690
Dividend Payout %	116.07	169.13	320.83	146.51	144.44	...	...	...
Income Statement								
Rental Income	...	334,697	298,085	279,935	260,684	245,833	222,186	188,529
Total Income	96,173	357,876	318,834	300,502	279,281	264,713	238,478	204,271
Total Indirect Exp.	67,442	86,909	100,310	74,195	66,577	65,131	62,508	53,143
Depreciation	20,622	75,089	64,251	59,914	53,259	50,011	46,047	41,399
Interest Expense	21,319	75,232	65,054	69,313	66,418	61,492	55,125	47,288
Eqty Earns/Minority Int.	...	(4,670)	(4,112)	(5,170)	(6,554)	(3,899)	(3,124)	(1,342)
Income from Cont Ops	17,237	73,022	44,581	59,571	56,842	55,493	...	40,129
Net Income	17,246	94,497	55,287	68,756	60,523	48,443	44,960	46,504
Average Shs. Outstg.	50,613	48,619	42,882	40,266	39,910	40,638	40,080	38,988
Balance Sheet								
Cash & Cash Equivalents	27,940	34,968	23,123	17,563	11,357	11,738	17,230	17,043
Ttl Real Estate Inv.	2,064,668	1,955,972	1,856,129	1,708,537	1,503,655	1,403,538	1,356,083	1,206,142
Total Assets	2,249,055	2,143,435	1,999,378	1,837,978	1,621,079	1,534,048	1,484,317	1,316,573
Long–Term Obligations	984,028	949,357	1,003,212	935,625	809,200	757,862	583,769	551,862
Total Liabilities	1,565,416	1,452,061	1,355,091	1,245,590	1,153,425	1,032,221	954,370	762,763
Net Stockholders' Equity	683,639	691,374	644,287	592,388	467,654	501,827	529,947	553,810
Shares Outstanding	49,320	49,200	43,535	40,071	39,469	40,201	40,080	39,148
Net Inc.+Depr./Assets %	1.68	6.91	5.44	6.50	6.79	6.88	6.13	6.19
Return on Equity %	N.M.	10.56	6.91	10.05	12.15	11.05	8.48	7.24
Return on Assets %	N.M.	3.40	2.22	3.24	3.50	3.61	3.02	3.04
Price Range	46.20-38.39	39.80-26.75	28.75-22.93	23.71-18.98	22.31-17.88	24.50-16.63	25.94-19.56	28.75-24.63
P/E Ratio	39.49-32.81	34.61-23.26	47.92-38.22	18.38-14.71	17.71-14.19	20.59-13.97	27.59-20.81	29.34-25.13
Average Yield %	4.62	5.78	7.28	8.98	9.03	2.10	N/A	N/A

Address: 1626 East Jefferson Street, Rockville, MD 20852–4041 **Telephone:** (301) 998–8100 **Web Site:** www.federalrealty.com	**Officers:** Mark Ordan – Chmn., Donald C. Wood – Pres., C.E.O., C.O.O. **Transfer Agents:** American Stock Transfer &Trust Company, New York, NY	**Institutional Holding** **No of Institutions:** 4 **Shares:** 74,400 **% Held:** –	

FEDERAL SIGNAL CORP.

Exchange	Symbol	Price	52Wk Range	Yield	P/E
NYS	FSS	$17.81 (5/28/2004)	20.70-13.90	2.25	25.44

*7 Year Price Score 84.7   *NYSE Composite Index=100   *12 Month Price Score 47.0

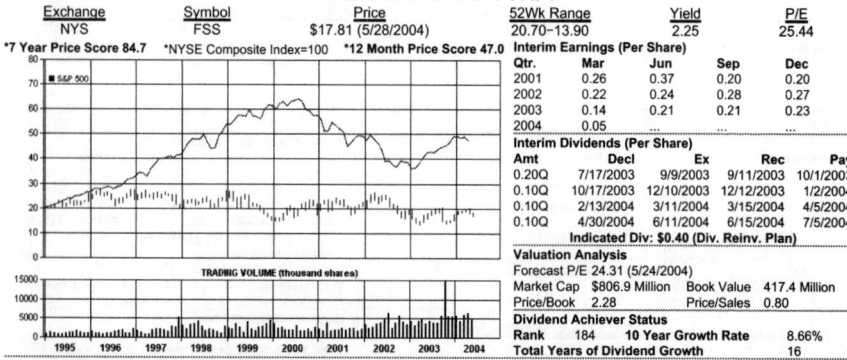

Interim Earnings (Per Share)

Qtr.	Mar	Jun	Sep	Dec
2001	0.26	0.37	0.20	0.20
2002	0.22	0.24	0.28	0.27
2003	0.14	0.21	0.21	0.23
2004	0.05	...	...	...

Interim Dividends (Per Share)

Amt	Decl	Ex	Rec	Pay
0.20Q	7/17/2003	9/9/2003	9/11/2003	10/1/2003
0.10Q	10/17/2003	12/10/2003	12/12/2003	1/2/2004
0.10Q	2/13/2004	3/11/2004	3/15/2004	4/5/2004
0.10Q	4/30/2004	6/11/2004	6/15/2004	7/5/2004

Indicated Div: $0.40 (Div. Reinv. Plan)

Valuation Analysis

Forecast P/E 24.31 (5/24/2004)

Market Cap $806.9 Million		Book Value 417.4 Million
Price/Book 2.28		Price/Sales 0.80

Dividend Achiever Status

Rank	184	10 Year Growth Rate	8.66%
Total Years of Dividend Growth		16

Business Summary: Automotive (MIC: 15.1 SIC: 3711 NAIC:336120)

Federal Signal is a worldwide manufacturer and supplier of street cleaning, vacuum loader and refuse collection vehicles; fire rescue vehicles; safety, signaling and communication equipment and tooling products. Co. operates manufacturing facilities in 52 plants around the world in 12 countries serving customers in North America, South America, Europe and Asia. Co. also provides customer and dealer financing to support the sale of its vehicles.

Recent Developments: For the quarter ended Mar 31 2004, net income plummeted 66.0% to $2.2 million compared with $6.5 million in the corresponding period of the previous year. The decrease in earnings was largely due to lower operating margins for Fire Rescue, increased corporate expense and one-time costs associated with legal settlements. Net sales fell 5.3% to $276.5 million from $292.0 million in the year-earlier quarter. Environmental Products Group sales climbed 7.5% to $91.1 million, while Fire Rescue Group sales dropped 27.5% to $71.6 million. Safety Products Group sales grew 3.1% to $69.3 million, and Tool Group sales jumped 7.8% to $44.6 million.

Prospects: Co. continues to face operational issues within its fire rescue and refuse truck businesses, which are negatively affecting margins. Consequently, Co. is looking to improve its production flow to help boost the performance of its fire rescue business, while strengthening demand and growing market share through its dealer network should benefit its refuse truck unit. Also, Co. is planning restructuring operations for both businesses in the coming months. Although the results of Co.'s other businesses are improving as planned, the volatility of the fire rescue business and upcoming restructuring actions make it difficult for Co. to forecast 2004 operating earnings.

Financial Data

(US$ in Thousands)	3 Mos	12/31/2003	12/31/2002	12/31/2001	12/31/2000	12/31/1999	12/31/1998	12/31/1997
Earnings Per Share	0.70	0.79	1.01	1.03	1.27	1.25	1.30	1.29
Cash Flow Per Share	0.04	1.57	1.92	2.09	1.41	1.25	1.64	1.40
Tang. Book Val. Per Share	1.07	1.17	1.04	1.74	1.82	1.66	1.97	2.45
Dividends Per Share	0.700	0.800	0.790	0.770	0.750	0.730	0.700	0.640
Dividend Payout %	1.00	101.26	78.71	75.24	59.44	58.60	53.84	50.19
Income Statement								
Total Revenues	276,518	1,206,798	1,057,201	1,072,175	1,106,127	1,061,896	1,002,787	924,912
Total Indirect Exp.	58,590	249,097	217,053	220,257	220,690	214,856	206,378	191,170
Depreciation & Amort.	5,997	24,435	23,995	30,258	29,057	27,237	23,586	20,545
Operating Income	8,868	65,978	81,943	92,004	116,654	106,505	101,750	99,674
Net Interest Inc./(Exp.)	(4,865)	(19,750)	(20,075)	(26,368)	(31,401)	(23,339)	(19,336)	(17,163)
Income Taxes	777	8,345	14,923	17,864	26,759	26,859	26,838	25,878
Income from Cont Ops	...	37,672	46,179	46,590	57,655	...	...	...
Net Income	2,199	37,303	38,195	47,573	57,537	57,537	59,396	58,969
Average Shs. Outstg.	48,117	47,984	45,939	45,443	45,521	45,958	45,846	45,840
Balance Sheet								
Cash & Cash Equivalents	2,038	10,119	9,782	16,882	13,556	8,764	15,316	10,686
Total Current Assets	399,155	403,552	394,817	342,325	348,936	346,137	311,207	268,622
Total Assets	1,174,228	1,186,409	1,168,410	1,015,614	991,118	960,961	835,999	727,905
Total Current Liabilities	283,891	284,370	221,884	179,430	288,920	269,463	195,193	227,029
Long-Term Obligations	396,550	395,477	481,566	446,595	316,932	307,020	288,812	177,523
Net Stockholders' Equity	417,404	422,509	398,065	359,436	357,431	354,033	321,782	299,772
Net Working Capital	115,264	119,182	172,933	162,895	60,016	76,674	116,014	41,593
Shares Outstanding	48,115	47,918	47,660	45,129	45,304	46,114	45,329	45,606
Operating Profit Margin %	3.20	5.46	7.75	8.58	10.54	10.02	10.14	10.77
Return on Equity %	0.52	8.91	11.60	12.96	16.13	16.25	18.45	19.67
Return on Assets %	0.18	3.17	3.95	4.58	5.81	5.98	7.10	8.10
Debt/Total Assets %	33.77	33.33	41.21	43.97	31.97	31.94	34.54	24.38
Price Range	20.00-17.52	20.70-13.67	26.75-16.16	24.50-17.25	23.88-14.88	27.38-15.13	27.38-20.25	27.25-20.19
P/E Ratio	28.57-25.03	26.20-17.30	26.49-16.00	23.79-16.75	18.80-11.71	21.90-12.10	21.06-15.58	21.12-15.65
Average Yield %	3.71	4.73	3.64	3.59	3.89	3.41	3.06	2.57

Address: 1415 West 22nd Street, Oak Brook, IL 60523-2004	Officers: Robert D. Welding - Pres., C.E.O., Stephanie K. Kushner - V.P., C.F.O.	Investor Contact:630-954-2000
Telephone: (630) 954-2000	Transfer Agents:National City Bank, Cleveland, OH	Institutional Holding No of Institutions: 5
Web Site: www.federalsignal.com		Shares: 21,819 % Held: -

FIDELITY NATIONAL FINANCIAL, INC.

Exchange	Symbol	Price	52Wk Range	Yield	P/E
NYS	FNF	$37.59 (5/28/2004)	41.06-25.59	1.92	6.88

*7 Year Price Score 177.5   ***NYSE Composite Index=100**   ***12 Month Price Score 52.0**

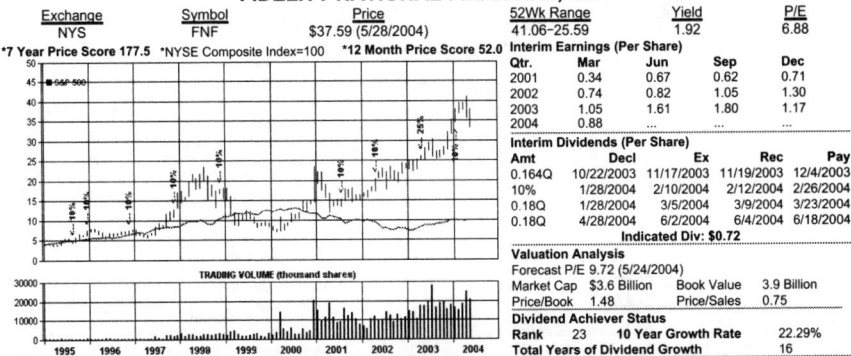

Interim Earnings (Per Share)

Qtr.	Mar	Jun	Sep	Dec
2001	0.34	0.67	0.62	0.71
2002	0.74	0.82	1.05	1.30
2003	1.05	1.61	1.80	1.17
2004	0.88	...	...	...

Interim Dividends (Per Share)

Amt	Decl	Ex	Rec	Pay
0.164Q	10/22/2003	11/17/2003	11/19/2003	12/4/2003
10%	1/28/2004	2/10/2004	2/12/2004	2/26/2004
0.18Q	1/28/2004	3/5/2004	3/9/2004	3/23/2004
0.18Q	4/28/2004	6/2/2004	6/4/2004	6/18/2004

Indicated Div: $0.72

Valuation Analysis

Forecast P/E 9.72 (5/24/2004)

Market Cap	$3.6 Billion	Book Value	3.9 Billion
Price/Book	1.48	Price/Sales	0.75

Dividend Achiever Status

Rank	23	10 Year Growth Rate	22.29%
Total Years of Dividend Growth		16	

Business Summary: Insurance (MIC: 8.2 SIC: 6361 NAIC:524127)

Fidelity National Financial, through its principal subsidiaries, is a major U.S. title insurance and diversified real estate–related services company. As of Dec 31 2003, Co. provided title insurance in 49 states, the District of Columbia, Guam, Puerto Rico, the U.S. Virgin Islands and in Canada and Mexico. Co. also provides information–based technology applications and processing services to financial institutions and the mortgage and financial services industries. Co.'s reporting segments include title insurance; financial institution processing and outsourcing; real estate information services; specialty insurance; and corporate and other.

Recent Developments: For the three months ended Mar 31 2004, net earnings increased 4.6% to $150.2 million compared with $143.6 million in the corresponding year–earlier period. Total revenues climbed 27.8% to $1.84 billion from $1.44 billion the previous year. Total revenues benefited from an increase in financial institution processing and outsourcing revenues to $288.4 million from $41.1 million in the prior–year period, primarily due to Co.'s acquisition of Fidelity Information Services on Apr 1 2003. Also, total title and escrow revenue rose 8.3% to $1.33 billion, real estate information services revenue grew 25.4% to $143.0 million, and specialty insurance increased 75.5% to $48.7 million.

Prospects: On Apr 27 2004, Co. announced that it has signed stock purchase agreements with Covansys Corporation, a U.S. based provider of application management and development and offshore outsourcing, and its Co–Chairman of the Board Rajendra Vattikuti. Co. will purchase 8.7 million common shares of Covansys and 2.3 million shares from Mr. Vattikuti, for a total purchase price of $131.0 million. Also, Co. and Covansys have entered into a five–year Master Service Agreement, under which Covansys will become Co.'s primary vendor of outsourced information technology services. Following the closing of the transaction, which is expected by June 30 2004, Co. will own about 29.0% of Covansys' common stock.

Financial Data

(US$ in Thousands)	12/31/2003	12/31/2002	12/31/2001	12/31/2000	12/31/1999	12/31/1998	12/31/1997	12/31/1996
Earnings Per Share	5.63	3.91	2.34	1.07	1.36	1.94	1.13	0.73
Tang. Book Val. Per Share	6.92	10.55	13.01	10.58	9.66	8.28	6.06	3.97
Dividends Per Share	0.630	0.290	0.246	0.240	0.160	0.150	0.130	0.120
Dividend Payout %	11.23	7.46	10.52	22.44	12.33	7.88	12.23	17.31
Income Statement								
Total Premium Income	4,873,482	3,547,729	2,694,479	1,946,159	939,452	910,278	533,220	475,961
Other Income	2,735,348	1,522,892	1,179,628	795,835	412,752	378,187	213,492	160,952
Total Revenues	7,608,830	5,070,621	3,874,107	2,741,994	1,352,204	1,288,465	746,712	636,913
Total Indirect Exp.	4,172,538	2,498,323	2,075,845	1,506,660	742,362	651,364	401,423	365,711
Inc. Before Inc. Taxes	1,420,639	851,300	572,796	229,143	117,828	175,134	73,430	40,553
Income Taxes	539,843	306,468	207,456	85,825	46,975	69,442	31,959	16,216
Eqty Earns/Minority Int.	(18,976)	(13,115)	...	...	...	...	...	...
Income from Cont Ops	...	...	311,185	...	...	...	41,471	...
Net Income	861,820	531,717	305,476	108,315	70,853	105,692	39,771	24,337
Average Shs. Outstg.	153,171	135,870	133,189	101,382	52,135	55,692	39,316	37,609
Balance Sheet								
Cash & Cash Equivalents	491,819	482,600	542,620	262,955	38,569	51,309	54,005	63,971
Premiums Due	446,102	233,205	992,694	936,417	79,088	86,701	61,548	65,672
Invst. Assets: Total	2,689,817	2,565,608	1,803,821	1,685,331	506,916	510,515	326,277	227,674
Total Assets	7,295,339	5,245,744	4,415,998	3,833,985	1,029,173	969,470	600,559	509,296
Long–Term Obligations	659,186	493,458	565,690	791,430	226,359	214,624	123,023	148,922
Net Stockholders' Equity	3,873,359	2,253,936	1,638,870	1,106,737	432,494	396,740	196,319	110,251
Shares Outstanding	164,840	131,594	129,592	105,117	45,234	48,074	32,967	28,024
Return on Revenues %	9.92	10.24	8.03	3.95	5.23	8.20	5.55	3.82
Return on Equity %	19.42	21.78	18.45	9.73	16.20	26.53	20.74	21.81
Return on Assets %	10.35	9.90	7.04	2.82	6.88	10.90	6.90	4.77
Price Range	35.25–22.36	24.44–15.78	22.20–12.08	23.67–7.10	18.33–8.26	23.53–13.28	17.08–5.71	8.02–5.64
P/E Ratio	6.26–3.97	6.25–4.04	9.49–5.16	22.12–6.64	13.48–6.08	12.13–6.85	15.11–5.06	10.98–7.73
Average Yield %	2.33	1.42	1.46	2.11	1.49	0.82	1.47	1.74

Address: 17911 Von Karman Avenue, Irvine, CA 92614 Telephone: (949) 622–4333 Web Site: www.fnf.com	Officers: William P. Foley II – Chmn., C.E.O., Frank P. Willey – Vice–Chmn. Transfer Agents: Continental Stock Transfer and Trust Co., New York, NY	Investor Contact:949–622–4333 Institutional Holding No of Institutions: 19 Shares: 228,483 % Held: –

99

FIFTH THIRD BANCORP (CINCINNATI, OH)

Exchange	Symbol	Price	52Wk Range	Yield	P/E
NMS	FITB	$54.29 (5/28/2004)	60.18–51.50	2.36	18.10

*7 Year Price Score 113.4   *NYSE Composite Index=100   *12 Month Price Score 44.1

Interim Earnings (Per Share)

Qtr.	Mar	Jun	Sep	Dec
2001	0.51	0.22	0.47	0.66
2002	0.66	0.68	0.70	0.72
2003	0.72	0.75	0.76	0.74
2004	0.75	...	...	...

Interim Dividends (Per Share)

Amt	Decl	Ex	Rec	Pay
0.29Q	6/17/2003	6/26/2003	6/30/2003	7/15/2003
0.29Q	9/16/2003	9/26/2003	9/30/2003	10/14/2003
0.29Q	12/16/2003	12/29/2003	12/31/2003	1/15/2004
0.32Q	3/16/2004	3/29/2004	3/31/2004	4/15/2004

Indicated Div: $1.28 (Div. Reinv. Plan)

Valuation Analysis

Forecast P/E 17.06 (5/24/2004)

Market Cap	$31.5 Billion	Book Value	8.9 Billion
Price/Book	3.52	Price/Sales	4.80

Dividend Achiever Status

Rank	38	10 Year Growth Rate	18.85%

Total Years of Dividend Growth   31

Business Summary: Commercial Banking (MIC: 8.1 SIC: 6022 NAIC:522110)

Fifth Third Bancorp is a bank holding company headquartered in Cincinnati, OH. As of Dec 31 2002, Co. had $80.89 billion in assets and operated 17 affiliates with 943 full–service banking centers, including 132 Bank Mart®locations open seven days a week inside select grocery stores and 1,883 Jeanie®ATMs in Ohio, Kentucky, Indiana, Florida, Michigan, Illinois, Tennessee and West Virginia. Co. operates four main businesses: Retail, Commercial, Investment Advisors and Fifth Third Processing Solutions. Through its subsidiaries, Co. engages primarily in commercial, retail and trust banking, investment services and leasing activities.

Recent Developments: For the quarter ended Mar 31 2004, Co. reported net income of $430.3 million compared with income from continuing operations of $389.1 million in the comparable prior–year period. Earnings for 2004 and 2003 included net securities gains of $25.6 million and $25.9 million, respectively. Earnings for 2004 also included operating lease revenue of $51.7 million. Earnings for 2003 excluded a gain of $813,000 from discontinued operations. Net interest income rose 6.2% to $749.7 million. Provision for credit losses slid 1.9% to $83.2 million. Total other operating income climbed 7.0% to $626.4 million. Total other operating expenses grew 6.2% to $652.1 million.

Prospects: Although the interest rate environment continues to be volatile, Co. is optimistic about the remainder of 2004 due to its strong balance sheet, improving trends in service income and credit quality, consistent growth in spread–based revenues, and disciplined expense control. Meanwhile, Co. continues to focus on new customer acquisition and cross–sell initiatives within its core middle–market commercial banking franchise. For instance, Fifth Third Processing Solutions continues to realize strong sales momentum from the addition of new customer relationships in both its Merchant Services and Electronic Funds Transfer businesses.

Financial Data

(US$ in Thousands)	3 Mos	12/31/2003	12/31/2002	12/31/2001	12/31/2000	12/31/1999	12/31/1998	12/31/1997
Earnings Per Share	3.00	2.97	2.76	1.86	1.83	1.43	1.17	1.12
Tang. Book Val. Per Share	13.65	12.92	12.64	13.09	10.50	8.79	7.93	6.52
Dividends Per Share	1.130	1.100	0.950	0.780	0.680	0.550	0.430	0.360
Dividend Payout %	36.93	37.03	34.42	41.93	37.15	39.07	37.31	32.54
Income Statement								
Total Interest Income	990,125	3,991,000	4,129,000	4,709,000	3,263,000	2,738,000	2,018,677	1,478,388
Total Interest Expense	240,382	1,086,000	1,429,000	2,276,000	1,793,000	1,333,000	1,015,853	733,426
Net Interest Income	749,743	2,905,000	2,700,000	2,433,000	1,470,000	1,405,000	1,002,824	744,962
Provision for Loan Losses	83,240	399,000	246,000	236,000	89,000	134,000	109,171	80,342
Non–Interest Income	626,405	2,483,000	2,194,000	1,797,000	1,013,000	877,000	636,194	445,461
Non–Interest Expense	652,068	2,442,000	2,216,000	2,341,000	1,119,000	1,122,000	803,577	506,158
Income Before Taxes	640,842	2,547,000	2,432,000	1,653,000	1,275,000	1,026,000	726,270	603,923
Eqty Earns/Minority Int.	...	(20,000)	(38,000)	(2,000)	...	...	...	...
Income from Cont Ops	...	1,722,000	1,634,700	1,101,000	...	...	...	...
Net Income	430,316	1,755,000	1,635,000	1,094,000	863,000	668,000	476,128	401,237
Average Shs. Outstg.	571,612	580,000	592,020	591,316	475,978	471,855	398,007	354,789
Balance Sheet								
Cash & Due from Banks	2,012,466	2,359,000	1,891,000	2,301,000	985,000	1,213,000	819,862	720,133
Securities Avail. for Sale	30,767,679	29,054,000	25,464,000	20,507,000	15,602,000	12,688,000	8,334,625	6,397,077
Net Loans & Leases	53,129,468	51,538,000	45,245,000	40,924,000	25,569,000	24,597,000	17,512,163	13,237,786
Total Assets	93,732,210	91,143,000	80,894,000	71,296,000	45,857,000	41,589,000	28,921,782	21,375,054
Total Deposits	55,250,265	57,095,000	52,208,000	45,854,000	30,948,000	26,083,000	18,780,355	14,914,132
Long–Term Obligations	10,990,799	9,063,000	8,178,700	7,029,000	4,034,000	1,977,000	2,288,151	457,878
Total Liabilities	84,868,453	82,618,000	72,418,700	63,386,900	40,966,000	37,512,000	25,743,260	19,097,643
Net Stockholders' Equity	8,863,757	8,525,000	8,475,000	7,639,000	4,891,000	4,077,000	3,178,522	2,277,411
Shares Outstanding	562,131	566,685	574,355	582,674	465,651	463,329	400,377	349,256
Return on Equity %	4.85	20.19	19.28	14.41	17.64	16.38	14.97	17.61
Return on Assets %	0.45	1.88	2.02	1.54	1.88	1.60	1.64	1.87
Equity/Assets %	9.45	9.35	10.47	10.71	10.66	9.80	10.99	10.65
Non–Int. Exp./Tot. Inc. %	40.33	37.72	35.04	35.98	26.16	31.03	30.26	26.30
Price Range	59.90–54.26	61.81–47.73	69.40–55.86	64.43–47.19	60.50–30.00	50.29–39.42	48.92–32.33	36.72–18.37
P/E Ratio	19.97–18.09	20.81–16.07	25.14–20.24	34.64–25.37	33.06–16.39	35.17–27.56	41.81–27.64	32.79–16.40
Average Yield %	1.97	1.98	1.49	1.35	1.35	1.50	1.12	1.37

Address: 38 Fountain Square Plaza, Cincinnati, OH 45263	Officers: George A. Schaefer – Pres., C.E.O., Neal E. Arnold – Exec. V.P., C.F.O.	Investor Contact:513–579–4356
Telephone: (513) 534–5300	Transfer Agents:Fifth Third Bank, Cincinnati, OH	Institutional Holding No of Institutions: 4
Web Site: www.53.com		Shares: 294,606 % Held: –

FIRST CHARTER CORP.

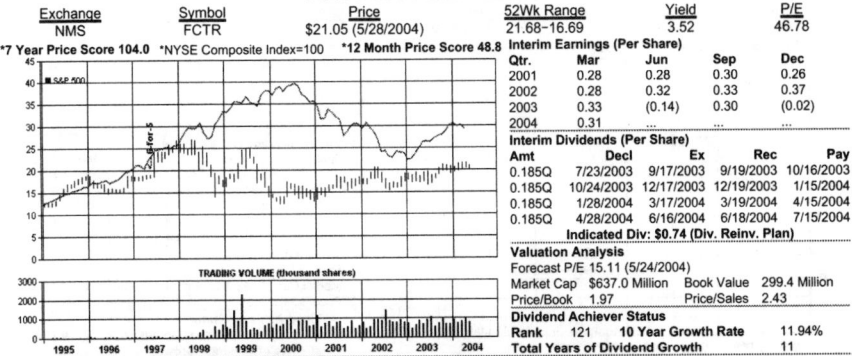

Exchange	Symbol	Price	52Wk Range	Yield	P/E
NMS	FCTR	$21.05 (5/28/2004)	21.68-16.69	3.52	46.78

*7 Year Price Score 104.0 *NYSE Composite Index=100 ***12 Month Price Score 48.8**

Interim Earnings (Per Share)

Qtr.	Mar	Jun	Sep	Dec
2001	0.28	0.28	0.30	0.26
2002	0.28	0.32	0.33	0.37
2003	0.33	(0.14)	0.30	(0.02)
2004	0.31	...	...	...

Interim Dividends (Per Share)

Amt	Decl	Ex	Rec	Pay
0.185Q	7/23/2003	9/17/2003	9/19/2003	10/16/2003
0.185Q	10/24/2003	12/17/2003	12/19/2003	1/15/2004
0.185Q	1/28/2004	3/17/2004	3/19/2004	4/15/2004
0.185Q	4/28/2004	6/16/2004	6/18/2004	7/15/2004

Indicated Div: $0.74 (Div. Reinv. Plan)

Valuation Analysis

Forecast P/E 15.11 (5/24/2004)

Market Cap $637.0 Million	Book Value 299.4 Million
Price/Book 1.97	Price/Sales 2.43

Dividend Achiever Status

Rank	121	10 Year Growth Rate	11.94%
Total Years of Dividend Growth		11	

Business Summary: Commercial Banking (MIC: 8.1 SIC: 6021 NAIC:522110)

First Charter is a regional financial services company with assets of $4.21 billion as of Dec 31 2003. Co. is the holding company for First Charter Bank, which operates 54 financial centers, five insurance offices and 93 ATMs located in 17 counties throughout the piedmont and western half of North Carolina. Co. also operates one mortgage origination office in Virginia. Co. provides businesses and individuals with a broad range of financial services, including banking, financial planning, funds management, investments, insurance, mortgages and employee benefit programs.

Recent Developments: For the three months ended Mar 31 2004, net income totaled $9.2 million, down 7.1% compared with $9.9 million in the corresponding prior-year period. Results for 2003 included a $1.6 million after-tax gain from the sale of Co.'s credit card portfolio. Total interest income was down 0.3% to $45.2 million, while interest expense declined 20.9% to $14.9 million. Net interest income climbed 14.3% to $30.4 million from $26.6 million the previous year. Provision for loan losses was $3.0 million versus $2.1 million a year earlier. Non-interest income slipped 5.6% to $14.7 million from $15.5 million the year before. Non-interest expense increased 8.7% to $28.3 million from $26.0 million in 2003.

Prospects: Net interest income is being positively affected by a decline in interest expense, partially offset by lower yields on earning assets due to lower interest rates. Co. is beginning to realize the benefits from the refinancing of fixed-term advances during 2003 and certain asset-liability management transactions entered into during the first quarter of 2004. Meanwhile, results are benefiting from continued growth in financial management income, brokerage services income, and service charges. In addition, higher insurance services income is being driven by the acquisitions of a third-party benefits administrator and two insurance agencies during 2003.

Financial Data

(US$ in Thousands)	3 Mos	12/31/2003	12/31/2002	12/31/2001	12/31/2000	12/31/1999	12/31/1998	12/31/1997
Earnings Per Share	0.45	0.47	1.30	1.12	0.79	1.45	0.50	0.90
Tang. Book Val. Per Share	10.37	10.07	10.79	10.06	9.78	12.95	13.33	8.39
Dividends Per Share	0.740	0.740	0.725	0.720	0.690	0.680	0.580	0.510
Dividend Payout %	164.44	157.44	55.76	64.28	87.34	46.89	116.00	57.22
Income Statement								
Total Interest Income	45,230	178,292	196,388	215,276	216,244	136,717	136,509	55,954
Total Interest Expense	14,857	70,490	83,227	109,912	108,314	67,269	70,623	24,751
Net Interest Income	30,373	107,802	113,161	105,364	107,930	69,448	65,886	31,203
Provision for Loan Losses	3,000	27,518	8,270	4,465	7,615	3,350	2,376	2,702
Non-Interest Income	13,377	64,180	47,631	38,773	30,565	18,213	13,650	9,452
Non-Interest Expense	28,308	127,032	97,772	87,579	92,727	45,869	59,166	25,642
Income Before Taxes	14,665	17,432	54,750	52,093	38,153	38,442	17,994	12,311
Eqty Earns/Minority Int.	(224)	...	...	...	...	...	...	...
Net Income	9,240	14,146	39,803	35,325	24,841	26,092	9,236	8,401
Average Shs. Outstg.	30,029	30,007	30,702	31,660	31,580	18,053	18,572	9,339
Balance Sheet								
Cash & Due from Banks	75,040	88,564	162,087	134,084	71,196	59,967	41,884	33,077
Securities Avail. for Sale	3,245,934	1,601,900	1,129,212	1,077,365	441,031	342,136	331,799	...
Net Loans & Leases	2,254,130	2,227,030	2,045,266	1,929,052	2,128,960	1,408,953	1,406,967	515,799
Total Assets	4,247,861	4,206,693	3,745,949	3,332,737	2,932,199	1,894,317	2,196,156	938,725
Total Deposits	2,507,442	2,427,897	2,322,647	2,162,945	1,998,234	1,149,512	1,123,035	621,354
Long-Term Obligations	...	1,432,200	1,042,440	808,512	570,024	491,976	469,944	53,279
Total Liabilities	3,939,124	3,907,254	3,421,263	3,023,396	2,622,912	1,666,605	1,618,385	683,890
Net Stockholders' Equity	308,737	299,439	324,686	309,341	309,287	227,712	245,972	77,804
Shares Outstanding	29,748	29,720	30,069	30,742	31,601	17,571	18,442	9,268
Return on Equity %	2.81	4.72	12.25	11.41	8.03	11.45	3.75	10.79
Return on Assets %	0.20	0.33	1.06	1.05	0.84	1.37	0.42	0.89
Equity/Assets %	7.26	7.11	8.66	9.28	10.54	12.02	11.20	8.28
Non-Int. Exp./Tot. Inc. %	47.70	52.39	40.06	34.47	37.57	29.60	39.40	39.20
Price Range	21.68-19.52	21.20-16.69	20.57-15.33	18.75-13.44	17.50-12.50	24.88-14.00	27.00-14.00	26.75-17.71
P/E Ratio	48.18-43.38	45.11-35.51	15.82-11.79	16.74-12.00	22.15-15.82	17.16-9.66	54.00-28.00	29.72-19.68
Average Yield %	3.61	3.92	4.06	4.37	4.71	3.46	2.64	2.34

Address: 10200 David Taylor Drive, Charlotte, NC 28262-2373

Telephone: (704) 688-4300

Web Site: www.firstcharter.com

Officers: J. Roy Davis – Chmn., Michael R. Coltrane – Vice-Chmn.

Transfer Agents: Registrar &Transfer Company, Cranford, NJ

Investor Contact: 800-422-4650

Institutional Holding

No of Institutions: –

Shares: – **% Held:** –

FIRST COMMONWEALTH FINANCIAL CORP.

Exchange	Symbol	Price	52Wk Range	Yield	P/E
NYS	FCF	$13.31 (5/28/2004)	14.98-12.01	4.81	14.96

*7 Year Price Score 112.3   *NYSE Composite Index=100   *12 Month Price Score 44.6

Interim Earnings (Per Share)

Qtr.	Mar	Jun	Sep	Dec
2001	0.21	0.21	0.22	0.22
2002	0.13	0.19	0.21	0.21
2003	0.23	0.23	0.23	0.21
2004	0.22	...	...	...

Interim Dividends (Per Share)

Amt	Decl	Ex	Rec	Pay
0.155Q	6/10/2003	6/26/2003	6/30/2003	7/15/2003
0.155Q	9/16/2003	9/26/2003	9/30/2003	10/15/2003
0.16Q	12/16/2003	12/29/2003	12/31/2003	1/16/2004
0.16Q	3/16/2004	3/29/2004	3/31/2004	4/15/2004
Indicated Div: $0.64 (Div. Reinv. Plan)				

Valuation Analysis
Forecast P/E N/A
Market Cap $783.1 Million   Book Value 430.9 Million
Price/Book 2.01   Price/Sales 3.03

Dividend Achiever Status
Rank 169   10 Year Growth Rate 9.51%
Total Years of Dividend Growth 16

Business Summary: Commercial Banking (MIC: 8.1 SIC: 6021 NAIC:522110)

First Commonwealth Financial is a financial services holding company with $5.19 billion in assets, as of Dec 31 2003. Co. operates 91 community banking offices in Pennsylvania through First Commonwealth Bank, a Pennsylvania chartered bank. Financial services and insurance products are also provided by First Commonwealth Trust, First Commonwealth Financial Advisors, and First Commonwealth Insurance Agency. Co. also operates First Commonwealth Systems, a data processing subsidiary, First Commonwealth Professional Resources, a support services subsidiary, and jointly owns Commonwealth Trust Credit Life Insurance, a credit life reinsurance company.

Recent Developments: For the quarter ended Mar 31 2004, net income was unchanged at $13.3 million compared with the corresponding quarter of 2003. Results for 2004 and 2003 included securities gains of $3.9 million and $2.2 million, respectively. Results for 2004 included merger and related charges of $1.3 million, while results for 2003 included a litigation settlement credit of $610,000. Net interest income was unchanged at $36.8 million versus the year before. Provision for credit losses dropped 39.3% to $2.1 million from $3.5 million a year earlier. Total other income rose 22.7% to $13.6 million from $11.1 million, while total other expenses grew 14.2% to $31.7 million from $27.8 million.

Prospects: On Apr 1 2004, Co. announced that it had received all required regulatory approvals for the acquisition of GA Financial. A special shareholders meeting to vote on the acquisition is scheduled for May 24 2004. GA Financial and Co. will file a definitive proxy statement/prospectus and other documents concerning the acquisition with the Securities and Exchange Commission. Under the terms of the agreement, shareholders of GA Financial can elect to receive $35.00 in cash or an equivalent value of Co.'s common stock for each share held. The transaction is expected to be completed in the second quarter of 2004.

Financial Data

(US$ in Thousands)	3 Mos	12/31/2003	12/31/2002	12/31/2001	12/31/2000	12/31/1999	12/31/1998	12/31/1997
Earnings Per Share	0.89	0.90	0.74	0.86	0.82	0.88	0.55	0.69
Tang. Book Val. Per Share	6.72	6.55	6.66	6.33	5.74	4.93	5.74	6.16
Dividends Per Share	0.620	0.620	0.600	0.580	0.560	0.490	0.440	0.400
Dividend Payout %	70.22	68.88	81.08	67.44	68.29	55.68	80.00	57.55
Income Statement								
Total Interest Income	61,972	243,773	275,568	308,891	311,882	297,507	283,421	199,811
Total Interest Expense	25,165	100,241	122,673	167,170	174,539	152,653	148,282	102,753
Net Interest Income	36,807	143,532	152,895	141,721	137,343	144,854	135,139	97,058
Provision for Loan Losses	2,100	12,770	12,223	11,495	10,030	9,450	15,049	6,929
Non-Interest Income	13,583	42,593	36,564	36,895	31,938	30,288	24,881	13,157
Non-Interest Expense	31,717	112,655	125,441	105,007	99,461	93,615	100,201	65,909
Income Before Taxes	16,573	66,551	52,437	65,443	61,535	72,642	46,227	44,063
Income from Cont Ops	...	...	...	...	...	...	33,998	...
Net Income	13,323	53,300	43,526	50,189	47,246	53,030	33,374	30,534
Average Shs. Outstg.	61,289	59,387	58,742	58,118	57,618	60,569	61,666	43,932
Balance Sheet								
Cash & Due from Banks	71,448	82,510	81,114	98,130	90,723	92,673	96,615	60,109
Securities Avail. for Sale	1,959,877	1,969,176	1,482,771	1,469,118	1,238,230	1,144,042	1,042,636	396,631
Net Loans & Leases	2,850,832	2,787,497	2,574,138	2,533,777	2,457,226	2,466,520	2,342,546	1,901,137
Total Assets	5,225,461	5,189,195	4,524,743	4,583,504	4,372,312	4,340,846	4,096,789	2,929,315
Total Deposits	3,305,393	3,288,275	3,044,124	3,093,150	3,064,146	2,948,829	2,931,131	2,242,478
Long-Term Obligations	824,915	793,972	579,934	664,220	656,855	638,355	630,850	193,054
Total Liabilities	4,781,073	4,758,249	4,123,353	4,213,464	4,038,156	4,054,163	3,741,384	2,657,481
Net Stockholders' Equity	444,388	430,946	401,390	370,066	334,156	286,683	355,405	271,834
Shares Outstanding	61,120	60,712	58,962	58,451	58,195	58,142	61,876	44,092
Return on Equity %	2.99	11.01	10.68	12.66	13.61	18.30	9.15	8.77
Return on Assets %	0.25	0.91	0.94	1.02	1.04	1.20	0.79	0.81
Equity/Assets %	8.50	8.30	8.87	8.07	7.64	6.60	8.67	9.27
Non-Int. Exp./Tot. Inc. %	41.97	39.33	40.18	30.36	28.92	28.55	32.50	30.94
Price Range	14.91-14.05	14.98-11.50	14.12-10.84	15.00-9.50	12.00-8.63	14.31-10.16	17.53-11.50	17.53-8.63
P/E Ratio	16.75-15.79	16.64-12.78	19.08-14.65	17.44-11.05	14.63-10.52	16.26-11.54	31.87-20.91	25.41-12.50
Average Yield %	4.26	4.78	4.83	4.99	5.67	4.13	3.26	3.78

Address: Old Courthouse Square, Indiana, PA 15701	**Officers:** E. James Trimarchi – Chmn., Johnston A. Glass – Vice-Chmn.	**Investor Contact:**800-331-4107
Telephone: (724) 349-7220	**Transfer Agents:**The Bank of New York, New York, NY	**Institutional Holding** **No of Institutions:** –
Web Site: www.fcbanking.com		**Shares:** 905,058 **% Held:** –

FIRST FEDERAL CAPITAL CORP. (LA CROSSE, WI)

Exchange	Symbol	Price	52Wk Range	Yield	P/E
NMS	FTFC	$27.18 (5/28/2004)	27.18-19.54	2.21	16.47

*7 Year Price Score 133.5   ***NYSE Composite Index=100**   ***12 Month Price Score 57.0**

Interim Earnings (Per Share)

Qtr.	Mar	Jun	Sep	Dec
2001	0.32	0.34	0.36	0.49
2002	0.38	0.40	0.45	0.50
2003	0.40	0.44	0.51	0.34
2004	0.36	...	...	...

Interim Dividends (Per Share)

Amt	Decl	Ex	Rec	Pay
0.14Q	7/24/2003	8/12/2003	8/14/2003	9/4/2003
0.14Q	10/30/2003	11/18/2003	11/20/2003	12/11/2003
0.14Q	1/29/2004	2/17/2004	2/19/2004	3/11/2004
0.15Q	4/21/2004	5/11/2004	5/13/2004	6/3/2004

Indicated Div: $0.60 (Div. Reinv. Plan)

Valuation Analysis

Forecast P/E N/A

Market Cap	$536.2 Million	Book Value	284.1 Million
Price/Book	1.65	Price/Sales	1.99

Dividend Achiever Status

Rank	44	10 Year Growth Rate	17.72%
Total Years of Dividend Growth			12

Business Summary: Other Depository Banking (MIC: 8.5 SIC: 6035 NAIC:522120)

First Federal Capital, through its First Federal Capital Bank subsidiary, is a savings bank with assets of $3.18 billion, as of June 30 2003. Co.'s primary business is community banking, which includes attracting deposits from and making loans to the general public, businesses, government, and professional customers. Co.'s primary market areas include communities located in the western, south-central, and eastern portions of Wisconsin and the northern portion of Illinois, as well as contiguous counties in Iowa and Minnesota. As of Jul 24 2003, Co. maintained 92 retail and mortgage loan production offices, which included 48 in-store supermarket banking locations.

Recent Developments: For the three months ended Mar 31 2004, net income of $8.0 million was essentially unchanged from the same period a year earlier. Net interest income climbed 51.8% to $27.8 million from $18.3 million the previous year. Co. attributed the higher net interest income to, in part, a significant increase in earning assets as a result of loan growth, security purchases, and the acquisition of Liberty Bancshares, Inc., in the fourth quarter of 2003. Provision for loan losses amounted to $1.6 million versus $379,000 last year. Total non-interest income fell 12.9% to $15.6 million, reflecting a 45.1% drop in mortgage banking revenue to $4.7 million from $8.5 million the year before.

Prospects: On Apr 28 2004, Co. and Associated Banc-Corp announced a definitive agreement under which Associated will acquire Co. The stock and cash transaction is valued at $613.0 million, including stock options, based on the closing Associated share price on Apr 27 2004. Under terms of the agreement, Co. shareholders will receive 0.635 shares of Associated Banc-Corp stock for each share of First Federal stock they hold, an equivalent amount of cash, or a combination thereof. Associated will allocate, in aggregate, 10.0% cash and 90.0% stock.The transaction is expected to be completed during the fall of 2004, subject to regulatory approvals.

Financial Data

(US$ in Thousands)	3 Mos	12/31/2003	12/31/2002	12/31/2001	12/31/2000	12/31/1999	12/31/1998	12/31/1997
Earnings Per Share	1.65	1.69	1.73	1.51	1.25	1.17	0.98	0.88
Tang. Book Val. Per Share	6.92	6.64	6.67	6.80	6.09	5.05	4.79	4.74
Dividends Per Share	0.560	0.550	0.510	0.470	0.420	0.340	0.270	0.230
Dividend Payout %	34.15	32.54	29.47	31.12	33.60	29.05	27.55	26.36
Income Statement								
Total Interest Income	41,461	147,918	161,250	171,533	161,436	130,071	118,668	114,976
Total Interest Expense	13,709	66,125	79,726	108,330	101,896	75,953	71,457	70,265
Net Interest Income	27,752	81,793	81,525	63,202	59,540	54,117	47,211	44,711
Provision for Loan Losses	1,606	1,456	3,468	1,763	1,009	387	293	539
Non-Interest Income	15,626	86,546	63,655	49,527	35,633	35,178	31,360	24,294
Non-Interest Expense	29,279	111,717	87,378	67,119	58,250	54,299	47,597	40,197
Income Before Taxes	12,492	55,166	54,313	43,847	35,914	34,609	30,681	28,269
Income from Cont Ops	...	34,727	34,916	...	23,144	...	19,424	...
Net Income	8,041	34,727	34,916	28,448	23,144	22,441	19,424	17,390
Average Shs. Outstg.	22,627	20,597	20,163	18,870	18,472	19,137	19,864	19,690
Balance Sheet								
Cash & Due from Banks	85,783	94,536	84,483	70,757	25,446	65,566	43,643	29,939
Securities Avail. for Sale	...	...	...	35,462	817	873	...	21,377
Net Loans & Leases	2,572,865	2,518,683	2,100,642	1,851,316	1,772,477	1,538,595	1,177,526	1,193,893
Total Assets	3,743,097	3,308,324	3,025,624	2,717,710	2,352,726	2,084,554	1,786,504	1,544,294
Total Deposits	2,672,072	2,552,837	2,355,148	2,029,254	1,699,252	1,471,259	1,460,136	381,994
Long-Term Obligations	650,200	416,699	417,613	467,447	370,846	469,580	189,778	275,779
Total Liabilities	3,459,000	3,031,735	2,820,172	2,525,312	2,206,176	1,957,279	1,663,819	670,393
Net Stockholders' Equity	284,097	276,589	205,452	192,398	146,549	127,275	122,685	109,361
Shares Outstanding	22,435	22,394	19,704	20,200	18,345	18,403	18,360	18,381
Return on Equity %	2.83	12.55	16.99	14.78	15.79	17.63	15.83	15.90
Return on Assets %	0.21	1.04	1.15	1.04	0.98	1.07	1.08	1.12
Equity/Assets %	7.58	8.36	6.79	7.07	6.22	6.10	6.86	7.08
Non-Int. Exp./Tot. Inc. %	51.28	47.64	38.85	30.36	29.55	32.85	31.72	28.86
Price Range	23.48-20.48	24.00-18.50	22.47-14.68	16.63-12.75	14.88-10.13	18.00-11.75	18.38-12.00	17.00-7.83
P/E Ratio	14.23-12.41	14.20-10.95	12.99-8.49	11.01-8.44	11.90-8.10	15.38-10.04	18.75-12.24	19.32-8.90
Average Yield %	2.59	2.66	2.71	3.17	3.62	2.29	1.70	2.03

Address: 605 State Street, La Crosse, WI 54601-1868 **Telephone:** (608) 784-8000 **Web Site:** www.firstfed.com	**Officers:** Thomas W. Schini - Chmn., Jack C. Rusch - Pres., C.E.O., C.O.O.	**Investor Contact:**608-784-8000 **Institutional Holding** **No of Institutions:** 13 **Shares:** 2,288,882 **% Held:** -

103

FIRST FINANCIAL CORP. (IN)

Exchange	Symbol	Price	52Wk Range	Yield	P/E
NMS	THFF	$28.93 (5/28/2004)	32.25-26.16	2.70	13.03

*7 Year Price Score 131.3 *NYSE Composite Index=100 ***12 Month Price Score 45.8**

TRADING VOLUME (thousand shares)

1995 1996 1997 1998 1999 2000 2001 2002 2003 2004

Interim Earnings (Per Share)

Qtr.	Mar	Jun	Sep	Dec
2001	0.44	0.42	0.46	0.46
2002	0.49	0.48	0.45	0.68
2003	0.52	0.45	0.47	0.51
2004	0.79	...	...	...

Interim Dividends (Per Share)

Amt	Decl	Ex	Rec	Pay
0.34S	5/22/2003	6/9/2003	6/11/2003	7/1/2003
2-for-1	9/10/2003	10/16/2003	9/30/2003	10/15/2003
0.36S	11/19/2003	12/3/2003	12/5/2003	1/2/2004
0.39S	5/19/2004	6/14/2004	6/16/2004	7/1/2004

Indicated Div: $0.78

Valuation Analysis

Forecast P/E N/A

Market Cap $197.5 Million   Book Value 255.3 Million

Price/Book 1.68   Price/Sales 2.79

Dividend Achiever Status

Rank 127   10 Year Growth Rate 11.65%

Total Years of Dividend Growth 11

Business Summary: Commercial Banking (MIC: 8.1 SIC: 6022 NAIC:522110)

First Financial is a multi-bank holding company with $2.22 billion in assets as of Dec 31 2003. Co. offers a wide variety of financial services, including commercial, mortgage and consumer lending, lease financing, trust account services, and depositor services through 46 branch offices of its ten wholly-owned subsidiaries located in Indiana and Illinois. First Financial Bank, N.A. of Vigo County, IN, a wholly-owned subsidiary, operates 14 full-service banking branches and two investment subsidiaries, which hold and manage $230.9 million of securities.

Recent Developments: For the three months ended Mar 31 2004, net income advanced 51.9% to $10.7 million from $7.0 million in the corresponding period a year earlier. Net interest income declined 5.3% to $17.9 million from $18.9 million the previous year. Provision for loan losses totaled $1.9 million, down 13.7% compared with $2.2 million the prior year. Non-interest expense jumped 55.7% to $12.6 million from $8.1 million the year before. Non-interest income increased 0.7% to $15.5 million from $15.4 million in 2003. Net interest margin declined to 3.8% compared with 4.0% a year earlier.

Prospects: Results are benefiting from increased loan and deposit fees, insurance commissions, and trust and financial services fees. Results are also being positively affected by increased income from capitalized mortgage servicing rights, higher loan servicing and origination fees, and net cash gains on sales of low fixed-rate mortgage loans in the secondary market. Meanwhile, Co. is focusing on implementing initiatives to help boost non-interest income growth in an effort to offset the decline in net interest income, which is being hampered by lower long-term interest rates.

Financial Data

(US$ in Thousands)	3 Mos	12/31/2003	12/31/2002	12/31/2001	12/31/2000	12/31/1999	12/31/1998	12/31/1997
Earnings Per Share	2.22	1.95	2.10	1.78	1.72	1.55	1.29	1.29
Tang. Book Val. Per Share	18.88	18.00	16.93	15.09	14.28	12.32	12.76	11.79
Dividends Per Share	0.700	0.650	0.600	0.560	0.510	0.440	0.390	0.330
Dividend Payout %	31.53	33.33	28.57	31.46	29.56	28.38	30.23	25.58
Income Statement								
Total Interest Income	29,276	122,661	136,262	144,673	146,417	133,576	129,137	122,737
Total Interest Expense	11,343	48,225	58,086	74,125	80,583	66,815	66,430	62,072
Net Interest Income	17,933	74,436	78,176	70,548	65,834	66,761	62,707	60,300
Provision for Loan Losses	1,923	7,455	9,478	6,615	4,392	4,725	5,396	5,382
Non-Interest Income	12,577	30,819	30,468	21,468	13,610	12,012	10,611	8,957
Non-Interest Expense	15,532	62,461	63,317	53,329	42,703	43,543	42,567	39,629
Income Before Taxes	13,055	35,339	35,849	32,072	32,349	30,505	25,355	24,246
Net Income	10,685	26,493	28,640	24,116	23,213	21,622	18,558	18,100
Average Shs. Outstg.	13,557	13,588	13,652	13,600	13,460	13,928	14,412	14,032
Balance Sheet								
Cash & Due from Banks	62,952	94,198	96,043	68,205	68,755	58,075	54,877	53,815
Securities Avail. for Sale	1,121,964	567,733	511,548	463,509	568,405	594,319	633,365	527,993
Net Loans & Leases	1,411,419	1,408,286	1,411,315	1,330,148	1,278,934	1,173,949	1,095,336	992,296
Total Assets	2,198,863	2,223,057	2,169,748	2,041,905	2,043,267	1,905,201	1,849,752	1,634,936
Total Deposits	1,432,495	1,479,347	1,434,654	1,313,656	1,322,559	1,256,115	1,260,365	1,194,524
Long-Term Obligations	380,663	383,233	423,290	426,078	489,063	382,322	89,519	30,596
Total Liabilities	1,932,730	1,967,778	1,927,777	1,824,394	1,852,044	1,736,519	1,660,950	1,462,815
Net Stockholders' Equity	266,133	255,279	241,971	217,511	191,223	168,682	182,183	165,480
Shares Outstanding	13,532	13,578	13,618	13,688	13,388	13,690	14,268	14,032
Statistical Record								
Return on Equity %	2.46	10.37	11.83	11.12	12.13	12.81	10.18	10.93
Return on Assets %	0.29	1.19	1.31	1.18	1.13	1.13	1.00	1.10
Equity/Assets %	12.10	11.48	11.15	10.65	9.35	8.85	9.84	10.12
Non-Int. Exp./Tot. Inc. %	41.15	40.69	37.97	32.09	26.68	29.90	30.45	30.17
Price Range		31.49-28.50	32.25-23.36	26.84-21.35	24.07-15.25	20.75-13.75	25.75-17.25	28.81-19.44	28.81-15.71
P/E Ratio		14.18-12.84	16.54-11.98	12.78-10.17	13.52-8.57	12.06-7.99	16.61-11.13	22.33-15.07	22.33-12.18
Average Yield %		2.33	2.38	2.52	2.88	3.18	2.19	1.61	1.77

Address: One First Financial Plaza, Terre Haute, IN 47807 **Telephone:** (812) 238-6000 **Web Site:** www.first-online.com	**Officers:** Donald E. Smith - Pres., C.E.O., Michael A. Carty - C.F.O., Treas., Principal Acctg. Officer	**Investor Contact:** 812-238-6264 **Institutional Holding** **No of Institutions:** 8 **Shares:** 240,100 % Held: -

FIRST FINANCIAL HOLDINGS, INC.

Exchange	Symbol	Price	52Wk Range	Yield	P/E
NMS	FFCH	$29.50 (5/28/2004)	33.10-27.07	2.98	15.21

*7 Year Price Score 131.4 *NYSE Composite Index=100 *12 Month Price Score 46.3

Interim Earnings (Per Share)

Qtr.	Dec	Mar	Jun	Sep
2000-01	0.36	0.42	0.43	0.43
2001-02	0.49	0.54	0.51	0.50
2002-03	0.50	0.54	0.50	0.53
2003-04	0.41	0.50	...	...

Interim Dividends (Per Share)

Amt	Decl	Ex	Rec	Pay
0.19Q	7/25/2003	8/6/2003	8/8/2003	8/22/2003
0.22Q	10/24/2003	11/5/2003	11/7/2003	11/21/2003
0.22Q	2/2/2004	2/11/2004	2/13/2004	2/27/2004
0.22Q	4/23/2004	5/5/2004	5/7/2004	5/21/2004
	Indicated Div: $0.88 (Div. Reinv. Plan)			

Valuation Analysis

Forecast P/E 16.79 (5/24/2004)

Market Cap	$394.3 Million	Book Value	169.8 Million
Price/Book	N/A	Price/Sales	N/A

Dividend Achiever Status

Rank	77	10 Year Growth Rate	15.02%
Total Years of Dividend Growth			11

Business Summary: Other Depository Banking (MIC: 8.5 SIC: 6035 NAIC:522120)

First Financial Holdings, with assets of $2.30 billion as of Sep 30 2003, is a savings and loan holding company. Through its subsidiary, First Federal Savings and Loan Association of Charleston, Co. offers a complete line of banking and related financial services to consumer and commercial customers through its 45 branch sales offices. Co. also engages in full-service brokerage activities, property, casualty, life and health insurance, third-party administrative services, trust and fiduciary services, reinsurance of private mortgage insurance and certain passive investment activities.

Recent Developments: For the three months ended Mar 31 2004, net income declined 10.9% to $6.4 million compared with $7.2 million in the equivalent quarter of 2003. Results for 2004 and 2003 included net gains on the sale of loans of $744,000 and $2.6 million, and net gains on the sale of investments and mortgage-backed securities of $958,000 and $860,000, respectively. Net interest income declined 0.4% to $19.6 million from $19.7 million the year before. Provision for loan losses grew 10.6% to $1.8 million versus $1.7 million a year earlier. Non-interest income slipped 0.6% to $10.4 million from $10.5 million, while non-interest expense climbed 5.6% to $18.3 million from $17.3 million.

Prospects: Market interest rates continue to be well below historical rates, and Co. is optimistic that residential loan demand will grow during 2004, although growth may be slower versus the prior year. Accordingly, Co.'s forecast for total single-family mortgage lending in 2004 is $410 million, or approximately 43.0% of fiscal 2003 volumes. Meanwhile, Co. will continue to strive towards maintaining a diversified loan portfolio to spread its risk and reduce exposure to downturns that may occur in different segments of the economy, geographic locations or industries. One of Co. 's goals continues to be expansion of non-interest revenues by acquiring additional insurance operations.

Financial Data

(US$ in Thousands)	6 Mos	3 Mos	09/30/2003	09/30/2002	09/30/2001	09/30/2000	09/30/1999	09/30/1998
Earnings Per Share	1.94	1.98	2.07	2.04	1.64	1.47	1.40	1.20
Tang. Book Val. Per Share	13.53	11.81	13.01	12.55	11.71	10.35	9.42	9.16
Dividends Per Share	0.820	0.790	0.760	0.680	0.620	0.560	0.480	0.420
Dividend Payout %	42.26	39.89	36.71	33.33	37.80	38.09	34.28	35.00
Income Statement								
Total Interest Income	63,797	31,760	134,381	154,026	173,277	161,642	140,832	136,345
Total Interest Expense	25,049	12,621	55,921	71,342	102,908	98,888	80,394	81,689
Net Interest Income	38,748	19,139	78,460	82,684	70,369	62,754	60,438	54,656
Provision for Loan Losses	3,250	1,425	6,235	5,888	4,975	2,745	2,765	2,405
Non-Interest Income	18,890	8,465	39,256	30,330	24,346	18,166	15,277	13,051
Non-Interest Expense	36,310	18,005	70,781	63,944	55,143	47,884	43,280	40,158
Income from Cont Ops	...	...	...	...	...	...	...	16,879
Net Income	11,644	5,254	27,211	28,152	22,559	19,928	19,307	16,539
Average Shs. Outstg.	12,926	12,949	13,173	13,832	13,733	13,559	13,786	14,101
Balance Sheet								
Securities Avail. for Sale	36,857	24,626	13,787	7,285	6,259	5,918	7,569	11,264
Net Loans & Leases	1,800,658	1,789,990	1,781,881	1,924,828	1,905,333	1,838,497	1,742,150	1,565,040
Total Assets	2,455,616	2,434,081	2,322,882	2,264,674	2,325,664	2,256,511	2,070,752	1,839,708
Total Deposits	1,470,305	1,428,440	1,481,651	1,440,271	1,395,785	1,241,295	1,219,848	1,164,440
Long-Term Obligations	46,392	664,000	598,000	577,000	625,000	766,500	594,500	471,500
Total Liabilities	2,285,784	2,269,271	2,159,876	2,099,026	2,168,771	2,118,660	1,944,871	1,714,545
Net Stockholders' Equity	169,832	164,810	163,006	165,648	156,893	137,851	125,881	125,163
Shares Outstanding	12,550	12,574	12,522	13,195	13,395	13,317	13,353	13,659
Statistical Record								
Return on Equity %	6.86	3.18	16.69	16.99	14.37	14.45	15.33	13.48
Return on Assets %	0.47	0.21	1.17	1.24	0.97	0.88	0.93	0.91
Equity/Assets %	6.92	6.77	7.01	7.31	6.74	6.10	6.07	6.80
Non-Int. Exp./Tot. Inc. %	43.91	44.76	40.36	34.56	27.82	26.60	27.71	26.82
Price Range	33.10-27.07	33.10-29.41	30.96-23.70	32.74-22.04	26.00-15.13	19.06-12.75	20.88-14.50	27.00-17.00
P/E Ratio	17.06-13.95	16.72-14.85	14.96-11.45	16.05-10.80	15.85-9.22	12.97-8.67	14.91-10.36	22.50-14.17
Average Yield %	2.70	2.54	2.84	2.51	3.07	3.75	2.58	1.85

Address: 34 Broad Street, Charleston, SC 29401	**Officers:** A. Thomas Hood – Pres., C.E.O., John L. Ott – Sr. V.P.	**Investor Contact:**843-529-5933
Telephone: (843) 529 5933	**Transfer Agents:**Register &Transfer Company, Cranford, NJ	**Institutional Holding** **No of Institutions:** 2
Web Site: www.firstfinancialholdings.com		**Shares:** 28,656 **% Held:** –

FIRST INDIANA CORP.

Exchange	Symbol	Price	52Wk Range	Yield	P/E
NMS	FINB	$19.58 (5/28/2004)	21.88-16.93	3.37	97.90

*7 Year Price Score 105.4   *NYSE Composite Index=100   *12 Month Price Score 46.3

Interim Earnings (Per Share)

Qtr.	Mar	Jun	Sep	Dec
2001	0.41	0.42	0.43	(0.01)
2002	0.41	0.43	0.43	0.07
2003	0.30	(0.11)	(0.16)	0.13
2004	0.34	...	...	...

Interim Dividends (Per Share)

Amt	Decl	Ex	Rec	Pay
0.165Q	7/18/2003	9/3/2003	9/5/2003	9/16/2003
0.165Q	10/29/2003	12/3/2003	12/5/2003	12/16/2003
0.165Q	1/21/2004	3/2/2004	3/4/2004	3/16/2004
0.165Q	4/21/2004	6/2/2004	6/4/2004	6/15/2004

Indicated Div: $0.66 (Div. Reinv. Plan)

Valuation Analysis

Forecast P/E 14.99 (5/24/2004)
Market Cap $304.9 Million   Book Value 212.9 Million
Price/Book 1.49   Price/Sales 1.98

Dividend Achiever Status

Rank 75   10 Year Growth Rate   15.22%
Total Years of Dividend Growth   12

Business Summary: Other Depository Banking (MIC: 8.5 SIC: 6035 NAIC:522120)

First Indiana is a full-service financial services company offering comprehensive financial solutions to businesses and individuals. Co. is the holding company for First Indiana Bank, N.A., a national bank headquartered in Indianapolis, and Somerset Financial Services, an accounting and consulting firm. As of Dec 31 2003, First Indiana Bank has $2.19 billion in assets and owned 33 offices in Central Indiana, plus construction and consumer loan offices in Indiana, Arizona, Florida, Illinois, North Carolina, and Ohio. Co. also originates consumer loans in 47 states through a national independent agent network.

Recent Developments: For the quarter ended Mar 31 2004, net income increased 14.3% to $5.4 million compared with $4.7 million in the corresponding period of the previous year. Total interest income declined 13.4% to $26.1 million from $30.1 million in the prior-year quarter. Total interest expense jumped 20.0% to $8.5 million from $10.6 million in 2002. Net interest income decreased 9.8% to $17.6 million from $19.5 million the year before. Provision for loan losses fell 51.9% to $3.0 million from $6.2 million in the year-earlier period. Total non-interest income climbed 6.3% to $14.8 million from $13.9 million, while total non-interest expense rose 5.8% to $20.9 million from $19.8 million the year before.

Prospects: Co. is benefiting from an increase in demand and savings deposits despite the sluggish economy. As a result, Co. will continue to place emphasis on relationship building with its business and consumer clients. Co. is also benefiting from lower provision for loan losses due to a decline in net loan charge-offs. However, Co. continues to experience a decrease in net interest income due to lower loans outstanding and narrowed interest rate spreads. Going forward, Co. should begin to realize the benefits of its shift toward businesses that are less sensitive to economic trends. Meanwhile, Co. will continue to focus its efforts on reducing its controllable expenses.

Financial Data

(US$ in Thousands)	3 Mos	12/31/2003	12/31/2002	12/31/2001	12/31/2000	12/31/1999	12/31/1998	12/31/1997
Earnings Per Share	0.20	0.16	1.34	1.25	1.55	1.41	1.15	1.08
Tang. Book Val. Per Share	10.58	10.37	13.39	12.69	11.87	11.31	10.45	9.66
Dividends Per Share	0.660	0.660	0.640	0.510	0.440	0.410	0.380	0.320
Dividend Payout %	347.37	412.50	47.76	40.96	28.86	29.37	33.33	29.41
Income Statement								
Total Interest Income	26,115	114,330	125,923	157,128	172,810	146,015	135,834	127,330
Total Interest Expense	8,489	37,430	52,143	83,079	95,042	75,575	73,080	64,351
Net Interest Income	17,626	76,900	73,780	74,049	77,768	70,440	62,754	62,979
Provision for Loan Losses	3,000	38,974	20,756	15,228	9,756	9,410	9,780	10,700
Non-Interest Income	14,798	49,563	46,765	43,963	25,638	19,368	22,676	16,950
Non-Interest Expense	20,905	83,637	66,502	70,501	53,728	52,346	45,756	41,104
Income Before Taxes	8,519	3,852	33,287	32,283	39,922	36,053	30,991	29,180
Income from Cont Ops	...	...	...	...	...	22,322	...	...
Net Income	5,406	2,529	21,180	20,009	24,817	22,733	19,147	17,744
Average Shs. Outstg.	15,837	15,720	15,809	15,998	15,997	16,049	16,571	16,313
Balance Sheet								
Securities Avail. for Sale	212,220	430,906	276,914	295,726	317,568	206,338	226,582	212,190
Net Loans & Leases	1,706,772	1,761,794	1,793,164	1,719,351	1,750,848	1,673,422	1,518,543	1,348,529
Total Assets	2,160,875	2,193,137	2,125,214	2,046,657	2,085,948	2,012,341	1,908,388	1,670,923
Total Deposits	1,486,053	1,489,972	1,339,204	1,379,478	1,399,983	1,312,115	1,227,918	1,107,555
Long-Term Obligations	296,991	312,022	346,532	296,647	336,754	366,854	327,247	257,458
Total Liabilities	1,948,002	1,984,243	1,904,003	1,837,626	1,887,136	1,802,671	1,626,230	1,460,369
Net Stockholders' Equity	212,873	208,894	221,211	209,031	198,812	177,103	165,970	153,036
Shares Outstanding	15,653	15,546	15,540	15,443	15,574	15,653	15,878	15,835
Return on Equity %	2.53	1.21	9.57	9.57	12.48	12.60	11.53	11.59
Return on Assets %	0.25	0.11	0.99	0.97	1.18	1.10	1.00	1.06
Equity/Assets %	9.85	9.52	10.40	10.21	9.53	8.80	8.69	9.15
Non-Int. Exp./Tot. Inc. %	51.09	51.03	38.50	35.05	27.07	30.26	28.66	28.28
Price Range	21.88-18.74	20.39-15.30	22.46-16.25	21.48-16.12	20.85-13.45	20.90-14.40	22.67-13.90	21.17-11.58
P/E Ratio	109.40-93.70	127.4-95.63	16.76-12.13	17.18-12.90	13.45-8.68	14.82-10.21	19.71-12.09	19.60-10.73
Average Yield %	3.24	3.67	3.39	2.63	2.73	2.44	2.02	2.11

Address: 135 North Pennsylvania Street, Indianapolis, IN 46204 **Telephone:** (317) 269 1200 **Web Site:** www.firstindiana.com	**Officers:** Robert H. McKinney – Chmn., Marni M. McKinney – Vice–Chmn., C.E.O. **Transfer Agents:** National City, Corporate Trust Operations, Cleveland, OH	**Investor Contact:** 317–472–2184 **Institutional Holding** **No of Institutions:** 8 **Shares:** 338,909 **% Held:** –

FIRST MERCHANTS CORP.

Exchange	Symbol	Price	52Wk Range	Yield	P/E
NMS	FRME	$24.00 (5/28/2004)	27.25-22.51	3.83	15.48

*7 Year Price Score 113.9   *NYSE Composite Index=100   ***12 Month Price Score 43.8**

Interim Earnings (Per Share)

Qtr.	Mar	Jun	Sep	Dec
2001	0.38	0.41	0.44	0.38
2002	0.39	0.45	0.45	0.39
2003	0.32	0.47	0.39	0.32
2004	0.37	...	...	...

Interim Dividends (Per Share)

Amt	Decl	Ex	Rec	Pay
5%	8/15/2003	8/27/2003	8/29/2003	9/12/2003
0.23Q	10/14/2003	12/3/2003	12/5/2003	12/19/2003
0.23Q	2/10/2004	3/3/2004	3/5/2004	3/19/2004
0.23Q	4/14/2004	6/2/2004	6/4/2004	6/18/2004

Indicated Div: $0.92 (Div. Reinv. Plan)

Valuation Analysis

Forecast P/E 15.39 (5/24/2004)

Market Cap	$392.4 Million	Book Value	309.1 Million
Price/Book	1.44	Price/Sales	2.34

Dividend Achiever Status

Rank	167	10 Year Growth Rate	9.55%
Total Years of Dividend Growth			19

TRADING VOLUME (thousand shares)

Business Summary: Commercial Banking (MIC: 8.1 SIC: 6021 NAIC:522110)

First Merchants is a bank holding company. Through its bank subsidiaries, Co. offers a range of financial services, including accepting time, savings and demand deposits; making consumer, commercial, agri-business and real estate mortgage loans; renting safe deposit facilities; providing personal and corporate trust services; providing full service brokerage; and providing other corporate services. Through various nonbank subsidiaries, Co. also offers personal and commercial lines of insurance and engages in the title agency business and the reinsurance of credit life, accident, and health insurance. As of Dec 31 2003, Co. had total assets of $3.08 billion and deposits of $2.36 billion.

Recent Developments: For the three months ended Mar 31 2004, net income totaled $6.9 million, up 22.6% compared with $5.7 million in the corresponding period a year earlier. Net interest income slipped 1.5% to $25.6 million from $26.0 million in 2003. Provision for loan losses dropped 70.2% to $1.4 million from $4.6 million the year before. Total other income declined 0.8% to $8.2 million from $8.3 million the prior year. Total other expenses increased 4.7% to $22.6 million from $21.5 million the previous year. As of Mar 31 2004, total assets were $3.03 billion versus $3.00 billion on Mar 31 2003.

Prospects: Results are benefiting from an increase in earning assets, including loans, investments and bank-owned life insurance, along with a reduction in the provision for loan losses, partially offset by lower net interest margins due primarily to lower interest rates. Meanwhile, Co. is focused on driving non-interest income growth through a range of fee-based services, increased mortgage refinancing and higher service charge income on deposit accounts. Separately, results are expected to be positively affected by increased efficiencies and consistency to the regulatory process stemming from the conversion of all of Co.'s state chartered banks to national charters effective Jan 1 2004.

Financial Data

(US$ in Thousands)	3 Mos	12/31/2003	12/31/2002	12/31/2001	12/31/2000	12/31/1999	12/31/1998	12/31/1997
Earnings Per Share	1.55	1.50	1.68	1.61	1.51	1.36	1.30	1.23
Tang. Book Val. Per Share	9.02	8.70	8.98	10.51	10.52	9.74	10.99	10.39
Dividends Per Share	0.900	0.890	0.850	0.810	0.770	0.720	0.660	0.590
Dividend Payout %	58.79	59.87	50.74	50.45	51.42	53.16	51.21	48.59
Income Statement								
Total Interest Income	38,224	155,530	146,682	120,435	116,528	100,463	79,728	75,475
Total Interest Expense	12,592	52,388	53,759	56,074	60,546	46,898	38,050	35,725
Net Interest Income	25,632	103,142	92,923	64,361	55,982	53,565	41,678	39,750
Provision for Loan Losses	1,372	9,477	7,174	3,576	2,625	2,241	1,984	1,297
Non-Interest Income	8,216	35,902	27,077	18,543	16,634	14,573	11,725	9,229
Non-Interest Expense	22,564	91,279	71,009	45,195	40,083	36,710	27,895	25,748
Income Before Taxes	9,912	38,288	41,817	34,133	29,908	29,187	23,524	21,934
Net Income	6,935	27,571	27,836	22,209	19,940	19,088	15,399	14,373
Average Shs. Outstg.	18,645	18,371	16,502	13,769	13,442	14,026	11,808	11,675
Balance Sheet								
Cash & Due from Banks	60,366	77,112	87,638	68,743	52,563	58,893	33,908	33,127
Securities Avail. for Sale	370,469	348,860	332,925	231,668	295,730	329,668	308,507	212,040
Net Loans & Leases	2,293,644	2,328,010	1,981,960	1,344,445	1,163,132	988,767	735,560	696,535
Total Assets	3,025,141	3,076,812	2,678,687	1,787,035	1,621,063	1,474,048	1,177,172	1,020,136
Total Deposits	2,313,420	2,362,101	2,036,688	1,421,251	1,288,299	1,147,203	926,844	843,812
Long-Term Obligations	...	383,170	356,927	174,404	163,581	189,862	111,400	47,529
Total Liabilities	2,715,994	2,772,847	2,417,558	1,607,907	1,465,000	1,347,752	1,045,675	898,167
Net Stockholders' Equity	309,147	303,965	261,129	179,128	156,063	126,296	131,497	121,969
Shares Outstanding	18,532	18,512	17,138	13,969	12,823	12,660	11,675	11,572
Return on Equity %	2.24	9.07	10.65	12.39	12.77	15.11	11.71	11.78
Return on Assets %	0.22	0.89	1.03	1.24	1.23	1.29	1.30	1.40
Equity/Assets %	10.21	9.87	9.74	10.02	9.62	8.56	11.17	11.95
Non-Int. Exp./Tot. Inc. %	48.62	47.68	40.86	32.51	30.10	31.91	30.50	30.39
Price Range	26.25-23.50	27.25-21.29	27.21-19.95	22.66-18.09	23.00-16.20	25.05-18.57	26.92-18.72	21.45-14.54
P/E Ratio	16.94-15.16	18.17-14.19	16.20-11.88	14.07-11.23	15.23-10.73	18.42-13.66	20.71-14.40	17.44-11.82
Average Yield %	3.58	3.69	3.68	3.99	4.00	3.52	2.87	3.31

Address: 200 East Jackson Street, Muncie, IN 47305-2814	**Officers:** Michael L. Cox – Pres., C.E.O., Roger M. Arwood – Exec. V.P., C.O.O.	**Institutional Holding**
Telephone: (765) 747-1500	**Transfer Agents:** First Merchants Bank, N.A.,	**No of Institutions:** 20
Web Site: www.firstmerchants.com	Muncie, IN	**Shares:** 899,990 **% Held:** –

FIRST MIDWEST BANCORP, INC.

Exchange	Symbol	Price	52Wk Range	Yield	P/E
NMS	FMBI	$34.25 (5/28/2004)	34.65-28.50	2.57	17.13

*7 Year Price Score 128.6   ***NYSE Composite Index=100**   ***12 Month Price Score 49.9**

Interim Earnings (Per Share)

Qtr.	Mar	Jun	Sep	Dec
2001	0.37	0.40	0.42	0.44
2002	0.45	0.47	0.47	0.47
2003	0.48	0.53	0.45	0.51
2004	0.51	...	...	...

Interim Dividends (Per Share)

Amt	Decl	Ex	Rec	Pay
0.19Q	8/21/2003	9/24/2003	9/26/2003	10/21/2003
0.22Q	11/20/2003	12/23/2003	12/26/2003	1/20/2004
0.22Q	2/24/2004	3/24/2004	3/26/2004	4/20/2004
0.22Q	5/21/2004	6/23/2004	6/25/2004	7/20/2004
	Indicated Div: $0.88 (Div. Reinv. Plan)			

Valuation Analysis
Forecast P/E 15.77 (5/24/2004)

Market Cap	$1.5 Billion	Book Value	522.5 Million
Price/Book	2.89	Price/Sales	4.14

Dividend Achiever Status

Rank	123	10 Year Growth Rate	11.87%
Total Years of Dividend Growth		11	

Business Summary: Commercial Banking (MIC: 8.1 SIC: 6021 NAIC:522110)

First Midwest Bancorp is a bank holding company with assets of approximately $6.91 billion as of Dec 31 2003. Co. operates two wholly-owned subsidiaries, First Midwest Bank and First Midwest Insurance Company. First Midwest Bank is engaged in commercial and retail banking and offers a range of lending, depository, and related financial services. As of Dec 31 2003, First Midwest Bank operated 66 banking offices that are located in various communities throughout Northern Illinois. First Midwest Insurance Company operates as a reinsurer of credit life, accident, and health insurance sold through First Midwest Bank, primarily in conjunction with the consumer lending operations.

Recent Developments: For the quarter ended Mar 31 2004, net income increased 5.7% to $24.0 million compared with $22.7 million in the same period a year earlier. Net interest income advanced 9.1% to $56.9 million from $52.1 million the previous year, reflecting earning asset growth due primarily to the acquisition of CoVest Bancshares on Dec 31 2003. Provision for loan losses amounted to $1.9 million versus $2.5 million last year. Total noninterest income slipped 2.1% to $17.4 million from $17.8 million in 2003, and included net security gains of $1.9 million for 2004 and $66,000 for 2003. Total noninterest income for 2004 also included losses of $1.2 million on the early retirement of debt.

Prospects: Co.'s near-term outlook appears reasonably positive, due in part to recent indications of a pick up in the U.S. economy. For instance, Co. remains optimistic regarding its prospects for commercial and real estate commercial loan growth over the balance of 2004. Co. noted that the pipeline of loan proposals currently under review is significantly compared with the corresponding year-earlier period. In addition, Co. expects to benefit from cost savings associated with its Dec 31 2003 acquisition of CoVest Bancshares, Inc. Accordingly, Co. has reaffirmed its earlier full-year 2004 earnings guidance of between $2.15 and $2.20 per share.

Financial Data

(US$ in Thousands)	12/31/2003	12/31/2002	12/31/2001	12/31/2000	12/31/1999	12/31/1998	12/31/1997	12/31/1996
Earnings Per Share	1.97	1.86	1.63	1.46	1.33	0.98	1.02	1.05
Tang. Book Val. Per Share	9.08	10.07	9.17	8.74	7.18	8.31	8.96	8.26
Dividends Per Share	0.760	0.680	0.640	0.570	0.510	0.480	0.420	0.340
Dividend Payout %	38.57	36.55	39.26	39.34	38.32	48.90	41.66	32.38
Income Statement								
Total Interest Income	291,067	329,664	385,218	421,517	361,279	364,597	270,506	237,171
Total Interest Expense	81,313	110,910	180,838	231,906	168,615	177,016	125,782	114,422
Net Interest Income	209,754	218,754	204,380	189,611	192,664	187,581	144,724	122,749
Provision for Loan Losses	10,805	15,410	19,084	9,094	5,760	5,542	8,765	7,469
Non-Interest Income	74,170	66,991	68,866	63,198	58,334	55,462	37,222	31,433
Non-Interest Expense	149,452	148,052	145,356	144,416	149,809	158,802	113,810	94,327
Income Before Taxes	123,667	122,283	108,806	99,299	95,429	78,699	59,371	52,386
Net Income	92,778	90,150	82,138	75,540	70,909	54,704	38,815	33,716
Average Shs. Outstg.	46,982	48,415	50,401	51,603	53,071	55,880	37,946	32,030
Balance Sheet								
Cash & Due from Banks	186,900	195,153	155,822	166,423	155,407	156,524	117,974	107,595
Securities Avail. for Sale	2,229,650	1,986,186	1,771,667	2,130,148	2,033,247	1,979,115	974,467	770,256
Net Loans & Leases	4,003,378	3,358,917	3,324,561	3,188,103	2,919,842	2,621,127	2,295,908	2,055,129
Total Assets	6,906,658	5,980,533	5,667,919	5,906,484	5,511,588	5,192,887	3,614,173	3,119,238
Total Deposits	4,815,108	4,172,954	4,193,921	4,252,205	4,001,183	4,050,451	2,795,975	2,260,667
Long-Term Obligations	1,500,388	1,237,408	971,851	1,145,872	1,077,732	623,899	438,037	493,142
Total Liabilities	6,384,118	5,488,580	5,220,652	5,459,761	5,142,327	4,739,989	3,276,661	2,857,098
Net Stockholders' Equity	522,540	491,953	447,267	446,723	369,261	452,898	337,512	262,140
Shares Outstanding	46,581	47,206	48,725	51,082	51,391	54,435	37,635	31,700
Return on Equity %	17.75	18.32	18.36	16.90	19.20	12.07	11.50	12.86
Return on Assets %	1.34	1.50	1.44	1.27	1.28	1.05	1.07	1.08
Equity/Assets %	7.56	8.22	7.89	7.56	6.69	8.72	9.33	8.40
Non-Int. Exp./Tot. Inc. %	40.91	37.32	32.01	29.79	35.70	37.80	36.98	35.11
Price Range	32.57-25.08	31.85-24.02	29.19-20.95	23.20-17.00	23.37-18.43	27.67-18.90	23.47-15.67	17.40-11.41
P/E Ratio	16.53-12.73	17.12-12.91	17.91-12.85	15.89-11.64	17.57-13.86	28.23-19.29	23.01-15.36	16.57-10.87
Average Yield %	2.63	2.41	2.60	2.91	2.44	2.15	2.31	2.66

Address: 300 Park Blvd., Itasca, IL 60143-9768	**Officers:** Robert P. OMeara – Chmn., John M. OMeara – Pres., C.E.O.	**Investor Contact:**630-875-7345
Telephone: (630) 875-7450	**Transfer Agents:**Mellon Investor Services,	**Institutional Holding**
Web Site: www.firstmidwest.com	Ridgefield Park, NJ	**No of Institutions:** 4
		Shares: 593,189 **% Held:** –

FIRSTMERIT CORP

Exchange	Symbol	Price	52Wk Range	Yield	P/E
NMS	FMER	$24.70 (5/28/2004)	27.81-22.67	4.21	17.27

*7 Year Price Score 100.7 ***NYSE Composite Index=100** ***12 Month Price Score 45.5**

Interim Earnings (Per Share)

Qtr.	Mar	Jun	Sep	Dec
2001	0.45	0.46	0.49	0.02
2002	0.51	0.49	0.38	0.43
2003	0.45	0.44	0.46	0.08
2004	0.15	...	...	...

Interim Dividends (Per Share)

Amt	Decl	Ex	Rec	Pay
0.26Q	8/21/2003	8/28/2003	9/2/2003	9/15/2003
0.26Q	11/20/2003	11/26/2003	12/1/2003	12/15/2003
0.26Q	2/19/2004	2/26/2004	3/1/2004	3/15/2004
0.26Q	5/20/2004	5/27/2004	6/1/2004	6/21/2004
	Indicated Div: $1.04 (Div. Reinv. Plan)			

Valuation Analysis

Forecast P/E 18.54 (5/24/2004)

Market Cap $2.1 Billion	Book Value 987.2 Million
Price/Book 2.32	Price/Sales 2.95

Dividend Achiever Status

Rank 185	10 Year Growth Rate	8.53%
Total Years of Dividend Growth		21

Business Summary: Commercial Banking (MIC: 8.1 SIC: 6022 NAIC:522110)

FirstMerit is a multi-bank holding company with $10.47 billion in assets as of Dec 31 2003. Co., through its affiliates, operates principally as a regional banking organization, providing banking, fiduciary, financial, insurance and investment services to corporate, institutional and individual customers throughout northeastern and Central Ohio and Western Pennsylvania counties. FirstMerit Bank, Co.'s largest subsidiary, is the parent company of 16 wholly-owned subsidiaries. At Dec 31 2003, FirstMerit Bank operated 158 full-service banking offices in 24 Ohio and western Pennsylvania counties.

Recent Developments: For the quarter ended Mar 31 2004, net income dropped 66.8% to $12.7 million from $38.3 million in the comparable prior-year period. Net interest income slipped 12.4% to $89.7 million, reflecting the sale of Co.'s manufactured housing loan portfolio, as well as reduced mortgage banking activity. Net interest margin was 3.74% versus 4.21% in 2003. Provision for loan losses grew 74.4% to $41.0 million. Non-interest income slipped 11.5% to $45.9 million due to reduced loan sales and servicing income from a lower level of mortgage banking activity. Non-interest expenses increased 4.3% to $77.1 million, reflecting an increase in salary and benefits expenses.

Prospects: Co. continues to focus on improving credit and generating more revenues, as well as strengthening its reserves. Additionally, Co.'s retail loan portfolio continues to reflect the solid progress it has made in improving its underwriting methodologies and collection experience. Retail delinquencies, especially in Co.'s indirect portfolio, have been declining consistently, and Co. is seeing lower retail charge-offs. Although this level of improvement is not yet evident in Co.'s commercial portfolio, Co. is optimistic that actions taken will result in improved performance. Moreover, Co. has expanded its presence in new markets, such as Toledo and Columbus, OH.

Financial Data

(US$ in Thousands)	12/31/2003	12/31/2002	12/31/2001	12/31/2000	12/31/1999	12/31/1998	12/31/1997	12/31/1996
Earnings Per Share	1.43	1.81	1.42	1.80	1.31	1.34	1.36	1.09
Tang. Book Val. Per Share	9.94	9.67	9.06	10.48	9.38	10.38	8.55	8.19
Dividends Per Share	1.020	0.980	0.930	0.860	0.760	0.660	0.610	0.550
Dividend Payout %	71.32	54.14	65.49	47.77	58.01	49.25	44.85	50.46
Income Statement								
Total Interest Income	567,269	648,013	726,899	791,495	684,851	503,097	407,825	411,745
Total Interest Expense	173,656	226,417	335,443	415,251	300,865	197,651	152,369	160,773
Net Interest Income	393,613	421,596	391,456	376,244	383,986	305,446	255,456	250,972
Provision for Loan Losses	102,211	98,628	61,807	32,708	37,430	28,383	21,593	17,751
Non-Interest Income	210,146	186,402	176,780	163,891	154,710	110,480	83,578	82,496
Non-Interest Expense	326,952	287,030	328,597	275,192	316,506	242,723	191,080	209,702
Income Before Taxes	174,596	222,340	183,471	232,235	184,760	144,820	126,361	106,015
Income from Cont Ops	121,657	...	122,604	...	125,717	...	...	...
Net Income	120,969	154,366	116,305	159,787	119,870	97,478	86,363	70,940
Average Shs. Outstg.	84,929	85,317	86,288	88,861	91,523	72,703	63,537	65,216
Balance Sheet								
Cash & Due from Banks	199,049	233,568	190,020	235,918	215,071	245,950	166,742	222,164
Securities Avail. for Sale	3,061,497							
Net Loans & Leases	6,454,046	7,091,515	7,262,085	7,128,800	6,909,284	4,918,447	3,781,101	3,606,662
Total Assets	10,473,635	10,688,206	10,193,374	10,215,203	10,115,477	7,127,365	5,307,461	5,227,980
Total Deposits	7,502,784	7,711,259	7,539,400	7,614,932	6,860,147	5,461,563	4,255,211	4,204,875
Long-Term Obligations	311,038	1,821,120	1,588,279	1,563,404	2,281,243	807,433	441,755	423,701
Total Liabilities	9,486,460	9,723,549	9,282,567	9,300,314	9,260,452	6,358,729	4,777,125	4,704,273
Net Stockholders' Equity	987,175	964,657	910,807	914,889	812,125	768,636	530,336	523,707
Shares Outstanding	84,724	84,505	84,991	87,032	88,375	74,009	61,967	63,912
Return on Equity %	12.32	16.00	13.46	17.46	15.48	12.68	16.28	13.54
Return on Assets %	1.16	1.44	1.20	1.56	1.24	1.36	1.62	1.35
Equity/Assets %	9.42	9.02	8.93	8.95	8.24	10.78	9.99	10.01
Non-Int. Exp./Tot. Inc. %	42.05	34.39	36.13	28.80	37.69	39.55	38.88	42.42
Price Range	27.81-18.16	29.49-18.89	27.94-21.10	27.63-13.50	28.78-22.94	34.00-21.50	30.38-17.50	17.81-14.00
P/E Ratio	19.45-12.70	16.29-10.44	19.68-14.86	15.35-7.50	21.97-17.51	25.37-15.67	22.33-12.87	16.34-12.84
Average Yield %	4.42	3.87	3.71	4.24	2.87	2.37	2.62	3.56

Address: III Cascade Plaza, Akron, OH 44308-1103	Officers: John R. Cochran - Chmn., C.E.O., Sid A. Bostic - Pres., C.O.O.	Investor Contact:330-996-6300
Telephone: (330) 996-6300	Transfer Agents:American Stock Transfer &Trust Co., New York, NY	Institutional Holding
Web Site: www.firstmerit.com		No of Institutions: 2
		Shares: 30,358 % Held: -

FLORIDA PUBLIC UTILITIES CO.

Exchange	Symbol	Price	52Wk Range	Yield	P/E
ASE	FPU	$19.00 (5/28/2004)	22.20-15.07	3.11	35.19

*7 Year Price Score 132.2   *NYSE Composite Index=100   *12 Month Price Score 52.9

Interim Earnings (Per Share)

Qtr.	Mar	Jun	Sep	Dec
2001	0.39	0.12	0.14	0.14
2002	0.40	0.18	0.12	(0.00)
2003	0.46	0.13	(0.02)	0.07
2004	0.36	...	...	...

Interim Dividends (Per Share)

Amt	Decl	Ex	Rec	Pay
0.148Q	8/26/2003	9/10/2003	9/12/2003	10/1/2003
0.148Q	12/2/2003	12/10/2003	12/12/2003	1/2/2004
0.148Q	3/2/2004	3/10/2004	3/12/2004	4/1/2004
0.15Q	6/2/2004	6/9/2004	6/11/2004	7/1/2004

Indicated Div: $4.75 (Div. Reinv. Plan)

Valuation Analysis

Forecast P/E N/A

Market Cap $73.8 Million		Book Value 42.5 Million	
Price/Book 1.82		Price/Sales 0.76	

Dividend Achiever Status

Rank	278	10 Year Growth Rate	3.37%
Total Years of Dividend Growth			35

Business Summary: Electricity (MIC: 7.1 SIC: 4931 NAIC:221121)

Florida Public Utilities is regulated by the Florida Public Service Commission (except for propane gas service) and provides natural gas, electricity and propane gas services to retail and commercial customers in Florida. As of Dec 31 2003, Co.'s regulated segment sold natural gas and electricity to 74,582 customers in Central, Northeast, Northwest and Southern Florida. Co.'s unregulated segment operates through its wholly owned subsidiary, Flo-Gas Corporation, and sells propane gas to 12,413 customers throughout the State of Florida.

Recent Developments: For the quarter ended Mar 31 2004, net income was $1.4 million versus income of $1.8 million, before income from discontinued operations of $9.9 million, in the prior-year quarter. Earnings were hampered by higher medical expenses, increased premiums for workers' compensation, and higher general liability insurance expenses. Total revenues declined 1.4% to $30.7 million due to lower natural gas revenues. However, both electric and propane revenues rose by $510,000 and $388,000, respectively. Electric revenues benefited from increased fuel revenue and higher units sold. Propane revenues benefited from higher gas prices and the addition of a large wholesale customer.

Prospects: On Mar 17 2004, Co. was granted rate relief of $1.8 million for the electric segment by the Florida Public Service Commission (FPSC). Meanwhile, Co. is preparing to file for rate relief for the natural gas segment in the second quarter of 2004. Co. is requesting about $8.2 million in annual rate relief. The request includes recovery for $9.1 million for environmental liabilities, as well as recovery for recent increases to certain operating expenses. If an increase is granted, it is anticipated the rate relief will take effect in the fourth quarter of 2004. Co. is also requesting interim relief in the amount of $1.5 million annually which, if granted, will take effect this summer.

Financial Data

(US$ in Thousands)	3 Mos	12/31/2003	12/31/2002	12/31/2001	12/31/2000	12/31/1999	12/31/1998	12/31/1997
Earnings Per Share	0.54	0.64	0.70	0.79	0.87	0.87	0.76	0.79
Cash Flow Per Share	1.14	1.78	1.88	2.00	1.81	1.88	...	...
Tang. Book Val. Per Share	9.22	9.00	6.36	6.08	7.29	6.92	6.90	6.59
Dividends Per Share	0.580	0.580	0.560	0.540	0.520	0.490	0.460	0.450
Dividend Payout %	107.40	90.62	80.35	68.86	60.34	56.41	60.53	56.96
Income Statement								
Total Revenues	30,725	102,723	88,461	92,143	84,759	74,098	76,192	78,134
Total Indirect Exp.	2,210	8,144	7,338	8,626	8,463	8,396	8,033	7,366
Costs & Expenses	27,606	95,030	80,692	85,876	78,231	67,928	70,296	72,616
Depreciation & Amort.	1,504	5,492	5,026	4,839	4,698	4,557	4,269	4,029
Operating Income	3,119	7,693	7,769	6,267	6,528	6,170	5,896	5,518
Net Interest Inc./(Exp.)	(1,107)	(4,488)	(4,513)	(3,591)	(3,487)	(2,968)	(2,840)	(2,895)
Income Taxes	782	1,167	1,402	...	...	...	...	...
Income from Cont Ops	...	2,522	2,761	...	...	...	...	...
Net Income	1,413	12,423	3,363	3,052	3,288	3,529	3,068	3,191
Average Shs. Outstg.	3,928	3,905	3,871	3,801	3,759	3,994	3,990	3,957
Balance Sheet								
Net Property	109,801	108,342	97,955	97,329	84,200	78,272	75,227	72,724
Total Assets	162,781	162,990	144,823	139,989	108,588	96,807	92,406	88,622
Long-Term Obligations	52,500	52,500	52,500	52,500	23,500	23,500	23,500	23,500
Net Stockholders' Equity	43,070	41,463	30,883	29,329	27,510	25,866	27,622	26,189
Shares Outstanding	3,931	3,916	3,881	3,848	3,770	3,736	3,999	3,970
Statistical Record								
Operating Profit Margin %	10.15	7.48	8.78	6.80	7.70	8.32	7.73	7.06
Net Inc./Net Property %	1.28	11.46	3.43	3.13	3.90	4.50	4.07	4.38
Net Inc./Tot. Capital %	1.47	11.22	3.68	3.40	5.56	6.20	5.30	5.68
Return on Equity %	3.28	5.99	8.76	10.19	11.69	13.33	10.87	11.91
Accum. Depr./Gross Prop. %	32.79	32.55	35.93	35.82	35.64	36.82	36.06	35.27
Price Range	20.50-15.60	17.90-13.90	15.82-11.85	13.02-10.69	14.25-9.84	15.00-10.97	13.13-8.67	9.23-7.36
P/E Ratio	37.96-28.89	27.97-21.72	22.60-16.93	16.48-13.53	16.38-11.31	17.24-12.61	17.27-11.41	11.69-9.32
Average Yield %	3.27	3.75	4.01	4.55	4.45	3.77	4.27	5.66

Address: 401 South Dixie Highway, West Palm Beach, FL 33401 **Telephone:** (561) 832-0872 **Web Site:** www.fpuc.com	**Officers:** John T. English – Pres., C.E.O., Charles L. Stein – Sr. V.P., C.O.O. **Transfer Agents:** American Stock Transfer and Trust Company, New York, NY	**Investor Contact:** 561-838-1729 **Institutional Holding** **No of Institutions:** – **Shares:** – **% Held:** –

FRANKLIN ELECTRIC CO., INC.

Exchange	Symbol	Price	52Wk Range	Yield	P/E
NMS	FELE	$63.60 (5/28/2004)	66.91-52.73	1.01	20.85

*7 Year Price Score 149.2   *NYSE Composite Index=100   ***12 Month Price Score 48.8**

Interim Earnings (Per Share)

Qtr.	Mar	Jun	Sep	Dec
2001	0.26	0.58	0.72	0.83
2002	0.32	0.79	0.85	0.87
2003	0.36	0.83	0.93	0.93
2004	0.45	...	...	...

Interim Dividends (Per Share)

Amt	Decl	Ex	Rec	Pay
0.14Q	7/18/2003	8/5/2003	8/7/2003	8/21/2003
0.14Q	10/24/2003	11/4/2003	11/6/2003	11/20/2003
0.14Q	2/6/2004	2/10/2004	2/12/2004	2/26/2004
0.16Q	5/5/2004	5/13/2004	5/17/2004	5/27/2004

Indicated Div: $0.64

Valuation Analysis

Forecast P/E 18.99 (5/24/2004)

Market Cap $688.7 Million	Book Value 192.9 Million
Price/Book 3.44	Price/Sales 1.85

Dividend Achiever Status

Rank 25	10 Year Growth Rate	22.05%
Total Years of Dividend Growth		10

Business Summary: Electrical (MIC: 11.14 SIC: 3621 NAIC:335312)

Franklin Electric's business consists of two operating segments: the motor segment and the electronic controls segment. The motor segment designs, manufactures and sells motors and related parts and equipment for use in submersible water and fueling systems, and in a wide variety of industrial motor products. These products consist of over 500 items, including submersible pumping systems, nozzles, fittings, flexible piping, electronic tank monitoring equipment and vapor recovery systems. The electronic controls segment designs and manufactures electronic controls for the principal purpose of being a supplier to the motor segment.

Recent Developments: For the three months ended Apr 3 2004, net income advanced 27.1% to $5.1 million compared with $4.0 million in the corresponding quarter of the previous year. Results for 2004 included a pre-tax restructuring charge of $565,000. Net sales increased 14.9% to $80.2 million from $69.8 million in the year-earlier period, attributed in part to favorable foreign currency exchange, particularly the Euro. Net sales also benefited from increased sales of small and large submersible motor products to North American customers. Gross profit jumped 20.1% to $23.6 million from $19.7 million in the prior-year quarter. Operating income soared 39.3% to $8.1 million versus $5.8 million the year before.

Prospects: Co. is pleased with the broad based strengthening of its operations, led by increased sales in essentially all of its end use and geographic markets. Moreover, Co.'s manufacturing realignment program is on schedule and budget, and its new product initiatives are progressing as anticipated. Looking ahead, Co. should continue to benefit from strong sales of submersible motors in the North America residential and agricultural end markets. In addition, Co. should benefit from strong demand for the *SubDrive*™ family of electronic drive systems for water wells as the product line has been extended.

Financial Data

(US$ in Thousands)	01/03/2004	12/28/2002	12/29/2001	12/30/2000	01/01/2000	01/02/1999	01/03/1998	12/28/1996
Earnings Per Share	3.05	2.83	2.39	1.95	2.30	2.01	2.00	1.61
Cash Flow Per Share	4.15	5.09	3.51	1.64	3.09	2.51	1.72	2.31
Tang. Book Val. Per Share	12.52	10.56	10.19	9.12	8.89	8.21	7.93	7.83
Dividends Per Share	0.550	0.510	0.470	0.430	0.380	0.330	0.280	0.230
Dividend Payout %	18.03	18.02	19.66	21.99	16.73	16.41	14.21	...
Income Statement								
Total Revenues	359,502	354,872	322,908	325,731	293,236	272,533	303,298	300,689
Total Indirect Exp.	59,106	54,637	47,522	44,967	41,898	42,027	49,194	45,854
Depreciation & Amort.	13,748	12,878	12,660	10,839	7,460	6,687	7,628	8,389
Operating Income	51,890	50,298	45,349	40,219	42,273	37,928	36,339	33,199
Net Interest Inc./(Exp.)	(1,107)	(1,317)	(1,193)	(1,111)	(1,317)	(1,364)	(1,435)	(1,308)
Income Taxes	16,847	18,273	16,235	13,683	15,591	15,237	15,004	11,827
Net Income	34,480	32,204	27,150	22,226	26,805	24,784	25,505	21,510
Average Shs. Outstg.	11,313	11,366	11,370	11,368	11,646	12,340	12,732	13,352
Balance Sheet								
Cash & Cash Equivalents	29,962	20,133	23,749	9,631	36,812	44,955	71,688	54,592
Total Current Assets	128,041	113,009	109,583	101,961	104,243	106,283	128,500	131,516
Total Assets	281,971	258,583	195,843	197,119	176,101	167,590	163,110	173,459
Total Current Liabilities	45,401	50,247	40,425	47,064	47,357	44,405	40,527	43,292
Long-Term Obligations	14,960	25,946	14,465	15,874	17,057	18,089	19,163	20,276
Net Stockholders' Equity	192,938	153,138	123,269	115,998	96,293	91,597	92,841	99,823
Net Working Capital	82,640	62,762	69,158	54,897	56,886	61,878	87,973	88,224
Shares Outstanding	10,914	10,824	10,668	11,008	10,826	11,148	11,694	12,742
Operating Profit Margin %	14.43	14.17	14.04	12.34	14.41	13.91	11.98	11.04
Return on Equity %	17.87	21.02	22.02	19.16	27.83	27.05	27.47	21.54
Return on Assets %	12.22	12.45	13.87	11.27	15.22	14.78	15.63	12.40
Debt/Total Assets %	5.30	10.03	7.39	8.05	9.68	10.79	11.74	11.68
Price Range	65.00-46.27	59.00-39.96	42.05-32.00	36.38-28.72	37.44-29.50	36.25-26.75	32.13-20.63	22.63-15.38
P/E Ratio	21.31-15.17	20.85-14.12	17.59-13.39	18.65-14.73	16.28-12.83	18.03-13.31	16.06-10.31	14.05-9.55
Average Yield %	0.98	1.08	1.30	1.28	1.13	1.02	1.10	1.28

Address: 400 East Spring Street, Bluffton, IN 46714-3798 **Telephone:** (260) 824-2900 **Web Site:** www.franklin-electric.com	**Officers:** R. Scott Trumbull - Chmn., C.E.O., Gregg C. Sengstack - Sr. V.P., C.F.O., Sec.	**Investor Contact:** 219-824-2900 **Institutional Holding** **No of Institutions:** 6 **Shares:** 72,000 **% Held:** -

FRANKLIN RESOURCES, INC.

Exchange	Symbol	Price	52Wk Range	Yield	P/E
NYS	BEN	$50.28 (5/28/2004)	60.05–37.80	0.68	20.44

*7 Year Price Score 121.2 *NYSE Composite Index=100 *12 Month Price Score 49.8

Interim Earnings (Per Share)

Qtr.	Dec	Mar	Jun	Sep
2000–01	0.61	0.54	0.46	0.30
2001–02	0.45	0.46	0.48	0.26
2002–03	0.43	0.43	0.52	0.59
2003–04	0.67	0.68	...	...

Interim Dividends (Per Share)

Amt	Decl	Ex	Rec	Pay
0.075Q	6/18/2003	6/26/2003	6/30/2003	7/15/2003
0.075Q	9/26/2003	10/2/2003	10/6/2003	10/15/2003
0.085Q	12/11/2003	12/29/2003	12/31/2003	1/15/2004
0.085Q	3/17/2004	3/29/2004	3/31/2004	4/14/2004

Indicated Div: $0.34 (Div. Reinv. Plan)

Valuation Analysis

Forecast P/E 16.61 (5/24/2004)

Market Cap	$13.1 Billion	Book Value	4.8 Billion
Price/Book	2.90	Price/Sales	4.51

Dividend Achiever Status

Rank	115	10 Year Growth Rate	12.39%
Total Years of Dividend Growth		14

Business Summary: Wealth Management (MIC: 8.8 SIC: 6282 NAIC:523930)

Franklin Resources, operating as Franklin Templeton Investments, is engaged in providing investment management, marketing, distribution, transfer agency and other administrative services to the open–end investment companies of the Franklin Templeton Group and to U.S. and international managed and institutional accounts. Co. also provides investment management and related services to a number of closed–end investment companies. In addition, Co. provides investment management, marketing and distribution services to certain sponsored investment companies organized in the Grand Duchy of Luxembourg. As of Sep 30 2003, Co.'s subsidiaries had $301.90 billion in assets under management.

Recent Developments: For the quarter ended Mar 31 2004, net income advanced 57.7% to $172.8 million compared with $109.6 million in the corresponding period the year before. Results for 2004 included a one–time net loss of $23.9 million related to various items. Total operating revenues grew 42.7% to $874.6 million from $613.1 million a year earlier. Investment management fees increased 43.6% to $499.6 million from $347.9 million in the prior year. Underwriting and distribution fees advanced 51.4% to $294.0 million, while shareholder servicing fees increased 11.6% to $61.7 million. Operating income climbed 61.2% to $225.2 million.

Prospects: Revenues continue to be solid, primarily resulting from robust growth in underwriting and distribution fees and investment management fees. Additionally, Co. continues to benefit from significant growth in assets under management, both domestically and globally. For instance, during the second quarter of 2004, Franklin Templeton's assets under management in Switzerland and Japan totaled more than $1.00 billion and $3.00 billion, respectively. Meanwhile, as of Mar 31 2004, equity assets comprised 55.0% of total assets under management, fixed–income assets comprised 28.0%, and hybrid/balanced assets comprised 15.0%.

Financial Data

(US$ in Thousands)	6 Mos	3 Mos	09/30/2003	09/30/2002	09/30/2001	09/30/2000	09/30/1999	09/30/1998
Earnings Per Share	2.46	2.21	1.97	1.65	1.91	2.28	1.69	1.98
Cash Flow Per Share	0.87	0.41	2.15	2.81	2.18	2.84	2.31	2.74
Tang. Book Val. Per Share	...	10.20	9.31	8.69	7.62	7.36	5.79	4.07
Dividends Per Share	0.310	0.300	0.290	0.270	0.250	0.230	0.210	0.190
Dividend Payout %	12.60	13.57	14.97	16.66	13.35	10.30	12.72	9.84
Income Statement								
Total Revenues	1,680,810	806,169	2,624,448	2,518,532	2,354,843	2,340,140	2,262,497	2,577,272
Total Indirect Exp.	1,232,740	583,309	1,976,372	1,933,030	1,842,848	1,676,697	1,723,389	1,935,176
Depreciation & Amort.	56,248	26,850	90,462	84,715	125,567	120,790	133,168	142,262
Operating Income	448,070	222,860	648,076	585,502	511,995	663,443	539,108	642,096
Net Interest Inc./(Exp.)	(14,910)	(7,111)	(19,910)	(12,300)	(10,556)	(13,960)	(20,958)	(22,535)
Income Taxes	147,808	68,423	197,373	145,552	153,069	177,502	147,373	175,834
Income from Cont Ops	340,308	167,517	...	...	...	...	...	...
Net Income	345,087	172,296	502,803	432,723	484,721	562,099	426,711	500,450
Average Shs. Outstg.	251,588	250,234	254,681	262,054	253,663	246,624	252,757	252,941
Balance Sheet								
Cash & Cash Equivalents	2,549,580	1,352,776	2,934,015	2,533,696	2,081,232	1,408,675	1,231,750	1,047,955
Total Current Assets	3,504,995	3,729,237	3,887,252	3,414,031	3,159,520	1,955,856	1,703,667	1,470,756
Total Assets	7,850,480	7,417,402	6,970,749	6,422,738	6,265,650	4,042,443	3,666,790	3,480,049
Total Current Liabilities	729,386	649,846	1,290,506	1,338,955	1,528,094	728,513	662,896	655,474
Long–Term Obligations	1,157,828	1,158,846	1,108,881	595,148	566,013	294,090	294,260	494,459
Net Stockholders' Equity	4,800,853	4,598,629	4,310,108	4,266,946	3,977,896	2,965,493	2,656,994	2,280,767
Net Working Capital	2,775,609	3,079,391	2,596,746	2,075,076	1,631,426	1,227,343	1,040,771	815,282
Shares Outstanding	249,934	248,761	245,931	258,555	260,797	243,730	251,006	251,742
Statistical Record								
Operating Profit Margin %	26.65	27.64	24.69	23.24	21.74	28.35	23.82	24.91
Return on Equity %	7.09	3.64	11.66	10.14	12.18	18.95	16.05	21.94
Return on Assets %	4.33	2.25	7.21	6.73	7.73	13.90	11.63	14.38
Debt/Total Assets %	14.75	15.62	15.90	9.26	9.03	7.27	8.02	14.20
Price Range	60.05–43.56	52.06–43.56	46.80–28.18	44.13–30.97	47.83–31.90	44.75–25.19	45.00–27.25	57.31–26.38
P/E Ratio	44.48–32.27	77.70–65.01	23.76–14.30	26.75–18.77	25.04–16.70	19.63–11.05	26.63–16.12	28.95–13.32
Average Yield %	0.59	0.63	0.79	0.72	0.60	0.70	0.58	0.41

Address: One Franklin Parkway, San Mateo, CA 94403	Officers: Charles B. Johnson – Chmn., Co–C.E.O., Harmon E. Burns – Vice–Chmn.	Investor Contact: 650–525–8900
Telephone: (650) 312–2000	Transfer Agents: Bank of New York, New York, NY	Institutional Holding
Web Site: www.frk.com		No of Institutions: 68
		Shares: 167,571,600 % Held: –

FREDDIE MAC

Exchange	Symbol	Price	52Wk Range	Yield	P/E
NYS	FRE	$58.39 (5/28/2004)	65.00-47.35	2.06	4.12

*7 Year Price Score 102.5 *NYSE Composite Index=100 ***12 Month Price Score 48.2**

Interim Earnings (Per Share)

Qtr.	Mar	Jun	Sep	Dec
1999	0.69	0.74	0.74	0.79
2000	0.81	0.83	0.86	0.89
2001	1.12	1.24	1.49	2.11
2002	2.07	1.50	2.13	8.48

Interim Dividends (Per Share)

Amt	Decl	Ex	Rec	Pay
0.26Q	6/6/2003	6/12/2003	6/16/2003	6/30/2003
0.26Q	9/5/2003	9/11/2003	9/15/2003	9/30/2003
0.26Q	12/5/2003	12/11/2003	12/15/2003	12/31/2003
0.30Q	3/5/2004	3/11/2004	3/15/2004	3/31/2004

Indicated Div: $1.20 (Div. Reinv. Plan)

Valuation Analysis

Forecast P/E 10.10 (5/24/2004)

Market Cap	$40.6 Billion	Book Value	26.7 Billion
Price/Book	1.54	Price/Sales	1.07

Dividend Achiever Status

Rank	54	10 Year Growth Rate	16.80%
Total Years of Dividend Growth		13	

Business Summary: Credit &Lending (MIC: 8.6 SIC: 6111 NAIC:522292)

Freddie Mac purchases conventional residential mortgages from mortgage lending institutions and finances most of its purchases with sales of guaranteed mortgage securities called Mortgage Participation Certificates for which Co. ultimately assumes the risk of borrower default. Co. also maintains an investment portfolio that consists principally of federal funds sold, reverse repurchase agreements and tax–advantaged and other short–term investments. Co.'s financial performance is driven primarily by the growth of its total servicing portfolio, the mix of sold versus retained portfolios, the spreads earned on the sold and retained portfolios and mortgage default costs.

Recent Developments: Spurred by low interest rates and record home sales, home prices took off in the fourth quarter of 2003, jumping at an annualized rate of 17.8% nationwide. This represents a marked increase from the third quarter of 2003, when the annualized growth rate was revised upward to 5.9%. The largest annual home price gains were in the Pacific states, where prices rose 13.1%, followed by Middle Atlantic states, with an 11.9% growth rate. In the West South Central states, values rose 3.9%. Co. noted that these figures are subject to revision as Co. does not yet have all of the data on originations in the fourth quarter.

Prospects: Looking ahead to 2004, housing construction and home sales are expected to slow from the strong fourth quarter pace. Likewise, house–price appreciation is anticipated to moderate, but remain at a healthy 6.5%. Co. expects the refinance share to gradually decline from about 55.0% of applications during the first quarter of 2004 to 35.0% in the fourth quarter, and average 42% for the year. In addition, because of lesser refinance volume, single–family originations are expected to drop by about one–third to $2.40 trillion. Separately, Co. expects to provide its 2002 annual report in the first quarter 2004 and release quarterly and full–year 2003 results by June 30 2004.

Financial Data

(US$ in Millions)	12/31/2002	12/31/2001	12/31/2000	12/31/1999	12/31/1998	12/31/1997	12/31/1996	12/31/1995
Earnings Per Share	14.18	5.96	3.39	2.96	2.31	1.88	1.67	1.42
Tang. Book Val. Per Share	38.87	15.49	16.80	11.98	11.54	8.73	9.61	8.13
Dividends Per Share	0.880	0.800	0.680	0.600	0.480	0.400	0.350	0.300
Dividend Payout %	6.20	13.42	20.05	20.27	20.77	21.27	20.95	21.13
Income Statement								
Total Interest Income	38,476	34,288	28,350	22,753	16,638	13,001	10,783	8,393
Total Interest Expense	26,564	28,808	25,512	20,213	14,711	11,370	9,241	6,997
Net Interest Income	11,912	5,480	2,838	2,540	1,927	1,631	1,542	1,396
Provision for Loan Losses	128	45	40	60	190	310	320	255
Non–Interest Income	(68)	1,639	1,489	1,405	1,307	1,298	1,249	1,087
Non–Interest Expense	1,737	1,020	883	834	791	755	758	681
Income Before Taxes	14,803	6,300	3,534	3,161	2,356	1,964	1,797	1,586
Eqty Earns/Minority Int.	184	...	...	...	...	...	...	...
Income from Cont Ops	...	4,373	2,539	2,218	...	...	1,258	...
Net Income	10,090	4,147	2,547	2,223	1,700	1,395	1,243	1,091
Average Shs. Outstg.	695	696	696	700	684	692	710	720
Balance Sheet								
Net Loans & Leases	589,722	494,259	385,117	322,569	255,348	164,250	137,520	107,411
Total Assets	752,249	617,340	459,297	386,684	321,421	194,597	173,866	137,181
Long–Term Obligations	456,347	314,733	243,323	185,186	93,525	87,714	76,876	57,820
Total Liabilities	720,919	601,967	444,460	375,159	310,586	187,076	167,135	131,318
Net Stockholders' Equity	31,330	15,373	14,837	11,525	10,835	7,521	6,731	5,863
Shares Outstanding	687	695	692	695	695	679	695	716
Statistical Record								
Return on Equity %	32.20	28.44	17.11	19.24	15.68	18.54	18.68	18.60
Return on Assets %	1.34	0.70	0.55	0.57	0.52	0.71	0.72	0.79
Equity/Assets %	4.16	2.49	3.23	2.98	3.37	3.86	3.87	4.27
Non–Int. Exp./Tot. Inc. %	4.52	2.83	2.95	3.45	4.40	5.28	6.29	7.18
Price Range	68.60–53.98	70.79–60.00	69.00–37.69	64.63–45.75	65.13–39.50	43.38–27.00	28.66–19.47	20.88–12.59
P/E Ratio	4.84–3.81	11.88–10.07	20.35–11.12	21.83–15.46	28.19–17.10	23.07–14.36	17.16–11.66	14.70–8.87
Average Yield %	1.38	0.92	1.72	1.03	0.94	1.12	1.14	1.82

Address: 8200 Jones Branch Drive, McLean, VA 22102–3110 **Telephone:** (703) 903–2000 **Web Site:** www.freddiemac.com	**Officers:** Richard F. Syron – Chmn., C.E.O., Paul T. Peterson – Exec. V.P., C.O.O. **Transfer Agents:**Equiserve Trust Company, N.A., Jersey City, NJ	**Institutional Holding** **No of Institutions:** 1 **Shares:** 20,000 **% Held:** –

FRISCH'S RESTAURANTS, INC.

Exchange	Symbol	Price	52Wk Range	Yield	P/E
ASE	FRS	$28.55 (5/28/2004)	32.12–18.00	1.54	13.93

*7 Year Price Score 166.7   *NYSE Composite Index=100   *12 Month Price Score 51.4

Interim Earnings (Per Share)

Qtr.	Sep	Dec	Feb	May
2000–01	0.38	0.24	0.26	0.39
2001–02	0.39	0.42	0.37	0.41
2002–03	0.58	0.44	0.32	0.61
2003–04	0.65	0.47	0.43	...

Interim Dividends (Per Share)

Amt	Decl	Ex	Rec	Pay
0.09Q	6/10/2003	6/24/2003	6/26/2003	7/10/2003
0.11Q	9/3/2003	9/24/2003	9/26/2003	10/10/2003
0.11Q	11/25/2003	12/23/2003	12/26/2003	1/9/2004
0.11Q	3/16/2004	3/24/2004	3/26/2004	4/9/2004

Indicated Div: $0.44

Valuation Analysis

Forecast P/E N/A

Market Cap $140.6 Million	Book Value 74.9 Million
Price/Book 1.91	Price/Sales 0.58

Dividend Achiever Status

Rank 227	10 Year Growth Rate	6.36%
Total Years of Dividend Growth		20

TRADING VOLUME (thousand shares)

Business Summary: Hospitality &Tourism (MIC: 5.1 SIC: 5812 NAIC:722310)

Frisch's Restaurants is a regional company that operates and licenses others to operate full service family–style restaurants under the name "Frisch's Big Boy", and operates grill buffet style restaurants under the name "Golden Corral" under certain licensing agreements. As of June 1 2003, Co. operated 88 family–style restaurants using the "Big Boy" trade name and 20 "Golden Corral" grill–buffet style family restaurants. Additionally, Co. had licensed 32 "Big Boy" restaurants to other operators. All of these restaurants are located in various markets of Ohio, Kentucky and Indiana.

Recent Developments: For the twelve weeks ended Mar 7 2004, net earnings jumped 39.6% to $2.2 million compared with $1.6 million in the corresponding quarter of 2003. Results for 2003 included an impairment of long–lived assets of $145,000. Total revenue climbed 14.8% to $59.6 million from $51.9 million a year earlier. Sales grew 14.9% to $59.4 million from $51.7 million, while other revenues were unchanged at $271,000 versus the same period of 2003. Same–store sales at Co.'s Big Boy restaurants increased 7.3% year over year, while same–store sales at Co.'s Golden Corral restaurants decreased 0.8% year over year, but were up year to date by 1.5%.

Prospects: Co.'s development agreements with Golden Corral Franchising Systems calls for the opening of 41 Golden Corral restaurants by Dec 31 2007. As of Mar 7 2004, 25 restaurants were in operation, which included one that opened in the third quarter of fiscal 2004, and two restaurants are under construction. Costs remaining to complete construction of these two restaurants were estimated at $3.6 million and construction of three more Golden Corrals is scheduled to be completed over the next twelve months. Separately, current plans call for two more Big Boy Restaurants to be under construction before fiscal 2004 ends on May 30 2004.

Financial Data

(US$ in Thousands)	9 Mos	6 Mos	3 Mos	06/01/2003	06/02/2002	06/03/2001	05/28/2000	05/30/1999
Earnings Per Share	2.16	2.16	2.16	1.95	1.59	1.27	1.08	1.36
Cash Flow Per Share	4.10	2.76	1.41	4.48	4.00	3.13	2.74	2.16
Tang. Book Val. Per Share	15.01	14.55	14.18	13.72	12.11	11.11	9.99	9.24
Dividends Per Share	0.400	0.380	0.360	0.360	0.350	0.320	0.310	0.280
Dividend Payout %	18.52	17.59	16.67	18.46	22.01	25.19	28.70	20.58
Income Statement								
Total Revenues	197,420	137,787	77,403	234,911	211,758	190,030	167,200	159,551
Total Indirect Exp.	13,525	9,547	5,426	11,311	11,061	11,834	9,225	10,421
Depreciation & Amort.	8,333	5,736	3,328	10,973	9,551	8,599	9,621	9,937
Operating Income	12,271	8,836	5,059	17,501	14,654	12,599	11,837	9,394
Net Interest Inc./(Exp.)	(1,875)	(1,316)	(734)	(2,800)	(2,420)	(2,607)	(2,410)	(2,437)
Income Taxes	4,356	3,137	1,771	4,924	4,262	3,435	3,351	2,539
Income from Cont Ops	...	...	...	...	...	6,557	6,075	4,418
Net Income	7,915	5,699	3,288	9,778	7,971	7,686	6,146	8,130
Average Shs. Outstg.	5,123	5,096	5,067	5,023	5,012	5,144	5,658	5,966
Balance Sheet								
Cash & Cash Equivalents	3,324	1,424	2,691	1,133	671	280	565	200
Total Current Assets	11,883	9,293	12,269	9,809	7,487	6,965	20,778	6,924
Total Assets	153,984	147,235	142,980	138,636	129,335	108,310	107,779	103,426
Total Current Liabilities	29,983	28,013	26,010	23,746	22,351	17,932	17,722	16,534
Long–Term Obligations	39,869	37,700	37,875	37,990	40,151	28,183	30,842	26,395
Net Stockholders' Equity	77,445	74,907	72,597	69,766	61,230	56,446	54,167	55,288
Net Working Capital	(18,100)	(18,720)	(13,741)	(13,937)	(14,864)	(10,967)	3,056	(9,610)
Shares Outstanding	5,032	5,015	4,986	4,951	4,910	5,011	5,345	5,901
Statistical Record								
Operating Profit Margin %	5.26	5.45	5.58	7.45	6.92	6.62	7.07	5.88
Net Profit Margin %	7.47	7.73	7.87	8.35	7.79	7.06	7.64	5.95
Return on Equity %	2.86	7.60	3.51	14.01	13.01	11.61	11.21	7.99
Return on Assets %	1.44	3.87	1.78	7.05	6.16	6.05	5.63	4.27
Debt/Total Assets %	25.89	25.60	26.48	27.40	31.04	26.02	28.61	25.52
Price Range	32.12–18.00	27.90–18.00	24.48–18.00	21.35–15.51	24.75–12.90	15.13–9.63	10.75–8.50	12.00–8.25
P/E Ratio	14.87–8.33	12.92–8.33	37.66–27.69	10.95–7.95	15.57–8.11	11.91–7.58	9.95–7.87	8.82–6.07
Average Yield %	1.60	1.66	1.72	1.92	2.14	2.61	3.19	2.71

Address: 2800 Gilbert Avenue, Cincinnati, OH 45206–1206	Officers: Jack C. Maier – Chmn., Craig F. Maier – Pres., C.E.O.	Investor Contact:513–961–2660
Telephone: (513) 961–2660	Transfer Agents:Continental Stock Transfer &Trust Company, New York, NY	Institutional Holding
Web Site: www.frischs.com		No of Institutions: 19
		Shares: 73,132 % Held: –

FULLER (H.B.) COMPANY

Exchange	Symbol	Price	52Wk Range	Yield	P/E
NYS	FUL	$26.79 (5/28/2004)	30.19-22.02	1.72	19.14

*7 Year Price Score 100.9 *NYSE Composite Index=100 *12 Month Price Score 48.0

Interim Earnings (Per Share)

Qtr.	Feb	May	Aug	Nov
2000-01	0.19	0.42	0.51	0.47
2001-02	0.02	0.28	0.32	0.36
2002-03	0.11	0.34	0.43	0.47
2003-04	0.16	...	...	...

Interim Dividends (Per Share)

Amt	Decl	Ex	Rec	Pay
0.113Q	7/11/2003	8/1/2003	8/5/2003	8/15/2003
0.113Q	10/3/2003	10/15/2003	10/17/2003	10/31/2003
0.113Q	1/29/2004	2/10/2004	2/12/2004	2/26/2004
0.115Q	4/15/2004	4/27/2004	4/29/2004	5/13/2004

Indicated Div: $0.46 (Div. Reinv. Plan)

Valuation Analysis

Forecast P/E 15.86 (5/24/2004)

Market Cap $759.6 Million	Book Value 517.5 Million	
Price/Book 1.64	Price/Sales 0.65	

Dividend Achiever Status

Rank 247	10 Year Growth Rate	5.18%
Total Years of Dividend Growth		36

Business Summary: Chemicals (MIC: 11.1 SIC: 2891 NAIC:325520)

H.B. Fuller and its subsidiaries manufacture and market adhesives and specialty chemical products globally, with sales operations in 33 countries in North America, Europe, Latin America and the Asia/Pacific region. Co.'s products, in thousands of formulations, are sold to customers in a wide range of industries. Also, Co. is a producer and supplier of specialty chemical products for a variety of applications such as ceramic tile installation, HVAC insulation installation, powder coatings applied to metal surfaces such as office furniture, appliances and lawn and garden equipment, specialty hot melt adhesives for packaging applications, and liquid paint sold through retail outlets.

Recent Developments: For the 13 weeks ended Feb 28 2004, net income advanced 42.1% to $4.6 million compared with $3.2 million the year before. Earnings for 2003 included net charges related to Co.'s restructuring initiative of $3.1 million. Net revenue grew 8.1% to $318.6 million from $294.6 million a year earlier, reflecting improved volumes and positive currency effects. Gross profit improved 4.4% to $85.8 million from $82.1 million, while gross profit as a percentage of sales slid to 26.9% from 27.9% the year before. Interest expense decreased 5.3% to $3.6 million.

Prospects: Co. is experiencing volume improvement in all regions, driven by new products, improved processes, and an upswing in the economy. Separately, on Mar 4 2004, Co. announced that it has acquired the adhesives and resins businesses of Probos, based in Oporto, Portugal. The businesses serve primarily the Portuguese and Spanish markets and have combined annual sales of about $30.0 million. The acquired product lines include water-based, hot melt, reactive and solvent-based adhesives for the assembly, woodworking, footwear and converting industries, and emulsions for the paints, textiles and food product industries. Probos' businesses will be incorporated into H.B. Fuller's European operations.

Financial Data

(US$ in Thousands)	3 Mos	11/29/2003	11/30/2002	12/01/2001	12/02/2000	11/27/1999	11/28/1998	11/29/1997
Earnings Per Share	1.40	1.35	0.98	1.59	1.74	1.57	0.57	1.43
Cash Flow Per Share	(0.17)	2.07	2.87	3.16	2.76	4.06	1.87	2.43
Tang. Book Val. Per Share	14.70	14.52	12.59	12.37	11.07	9.87	8.50	10.51
Dividends Per Share	0.450	0.440	0.430	0.420	0.410	0.400	0.390	0.360
Dividend Payout %	32.14	33.14	44.64	26.88	23.99	25.87	68.26	...
Income Statement								
Total Revenues	318,573	1,287,331	1,256,210	1,274,059	1,352,562	1,364,458	1,347,241	1,306,789
Total Indirect Exp.	75,409	286,324	283,978	257,446	311,010	322,171	333,912	325,702
Depreciation & Amort.	13,545	2,082	2,418	54,401	52,165	50,776	49,541	46,773
Operating Income	10,368	67,954	56,422	88,107	102,501	103,747	61,212	87,252
Net Interest Inc./(Exp.)	(3,564)	(13,741)	(16,613)	(21,247)	(23,814)	(26,823)	(26,989)	(19,836)
Income Taxes	1,879	14,307	12,973	19,833	28,455	31,807	18,826	26,651
Income from Cont Ops	...	...	...	44,940	...	44,111	...	40,308
Net Income	4,613	38,619	28,176	44,439	49,163	43,370	15,990	36,940
Average Shs. Outstg.	28,888	28,694	28,601	28,330	28,206	27,956	27,688	28,200
Balance Sheet								
Cash & Cash Equivalents	996	3,260	3,666	11,454	10,489	5,821	4,605	2,710
Total Current Assets	454,241	448,492	408,874	403,873	435,064	440,143	457,900	409,156
Total Assets	1,015,741	1,007,588	961,439	966,173	1,010,361	1,025,615	1,046,169	917,646
Total Current Liabilities	195,680	200,026	214,846	204,163	226,725	265,920	285,160	237,549
Long-Term Obligations	160,406	161,047	161,763	203,001	250,464	263,715	300,074	229,996
Net Stockholders' Equity	517,523	509,338	448,330	434,026	404,710	376,380	341,404	339,114
Net Working Capital	258,561	248,466	194,028	199,710	208,339	174,223	172,740	171,607
Shares Outstanding	28,495	28,435	28,362	28,280	28,240	28,800	27,965	27,682
Operating Profit Margin %	3.25	5.27	4.49	6.91	7.57	7.60	4.54	6.67
Return on Equity %	0.89	7.58	6.28	10.35	12.14	11.71	4.68	11.88
Return on Assets %	0.45	3.83	2.93	4.65	4.86	4.30	1.52	4.39
Debt/Total Assets %	15.79	15.98	16.82	21.01	24.78	25.71	28.68	25.06
Price Range	30.19-26.48	29.50-20.00	32.50-24.54	30.95-16.59	34.25-14.34	36.09-19.19	32.41-17.25	30.00-22.88
P/E Ratio	21.56-18.91	21.85-14.81	33.16-25.04	19.47-10.44	19.68-8.24	22.99-12.22	56.85-30.26	20.98-16.00
Average Yield %	1.59	1.80	1.51	1.82	1.88	1.40	1.50	1.41

Address: 1200 Willow Lake Boulevard, Vadnais Heights, MN 55110-5101	**Officers:** Albert P. L. Stroucken - Chmn., Pres., C.E.O., John A. Feenan - Sr. V.P., C.F.O.	**Investor Contact:**651-236-5150
Telephone: (651) 236-5900	**Transfer Agents:**Wells Fargo Shareowner Services, Minnesota, MN	**Institutional Holding** **No of Institutions:** 2
Web Site: www.hbfuller.com		**Shares:** 10,000 **% Held:** -

FULTON FINANCIAL CORP. (PA)

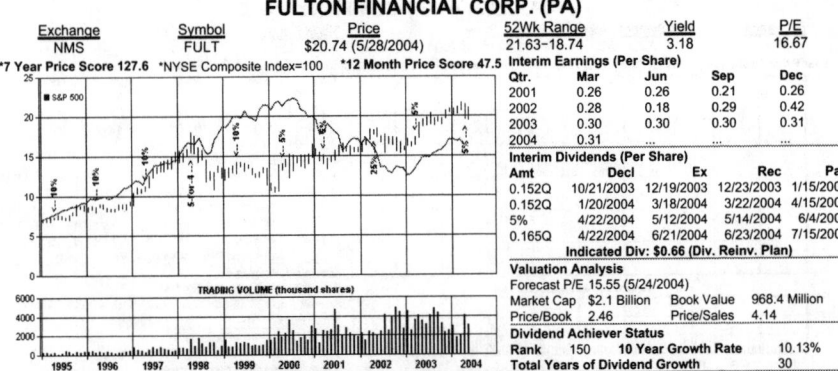

Exchange	Symbol	Price	52Wk Range	Yield	P/E
NMS	FULT	$20.74 (5/28/2004)	21.63-18.74	3.18	16.67

*7 Year Price Score 127.6 *NYSE Composite Index=100 ***12 Month Price Score 47.5**

Interim Earnings (Per Share)

Qtr.	Mar	Jun	Sep	Dec
2001	0.26	0.26	0.21	0.26
2002	0.28	0.18	0.29	0.42
2003	0.30	0.30	0.30	0.31
2004	0.31	...	...	...

Interim Dividends (Per Share)

Amt	Decl	Ex	Rec	Pay
0.152Q	10/21/2003	12/19/2003	12/23/2003	1/15/2004
0.152Q	1/20/2004	3/18/2004	3/22/2004	4/15/2004
5%	4/22/2004	5/12/2004	5/14/2004	6/4/2004
0.165Q	4/22/2004	6/21/2004	6/23/2004	7/15/2004

Indicated Div: $0.66 (Div. Reinv. Plan)

Valuation Analysis

Forecast P/E 15.55 (5/24/2004)

Market Cap $2.1 Billion	Book Value 968.4 Million
Price/Book 2.46	Price/Sales 4.14

Dividend Achiever Status

Rank 150	10 Year Growth Rate	10.13%
Total Years of Dividend Growth		30

TRADING VOLUME (thousand shares)

Business Summary: Commercial Banking (MIC: 8.1 SIC: 6021 NAIC:522110)

Fulton Financial, with $9.77 billion in assets at Dec 31 2003, is a financial holding company. As of Dec 31 2003, Co. operated 200 banking offices in Delaware, Maryland, New Jersey and Pennsylvania through the following affiliates: Fulton Bank, Lebanon Valley Farmers Bank, Swineford National Bank, Lafayette Ambassador Bank, FNB Bank, Hagerstown Trust, Delaware National Bank, The Bank, The Peoples Bank of Elkton, Skylands Community Bank and Premier Bank. Co.'s financial services affiliates include Fulton Financial Advisors, Fulton Insurance Services Group, and Dearden, Maguire, Weaver and Barrett. Residential mortgage lending is offered by all banks through Fulton Mortgage.

Recent Developments: For the quarter ended Mar 31 2004, net income climbed 5.3% to $35.8 million compared with $34.0 million in the corresponding quarter of 2003. Results for 2004 and 2003 included investment securities gains of $5.8 million and $2.2 million, respectively. Net interest income rose 9.7% to $83.0 million from $75.6 million in the prior-year period. Net interest income benefited from increases in average earnings assets, primarily due to the acquisition of Premier Bank. Provision for loan losses declined 38.6% to $1.7 million. Non-interest income rose 1.8% to $32.2 million from $31.7 million a year earlier. Non-interest expense grew 11.8% to $62.5 million from $55.9 million the year before.

Prospects: On Apr 1 2004, Co. completed the acquisition of Virginia-based Resource Bankshares in a transaction valued at $213.5 million, or $22.27 per share based on the closing price for Co.'s common stock on Mar 31 2004. With approximately $870.0 million in assets, Resource Bankshares operates six community banking offices in Virginia and 14 loan production and residential mortgage offices in Virginia, North Carolina, Maryland and Florida. Resource Bankshares' sole banking subsidiary, Resource Bank, will now operate as a separate subsidiary of Co. Upon completion, Co. now has assets of about $10.60 billion and operates 206 banking offices in Pennsylvania, Maryland, Delaware, New Jersey and Virginia.

Financial Data

(US$ in Thousands)	3 Mos	12/31/2003	12/31/2002	12/31/2001	12/31/2000	12/31/1999	12/31/1998	12/31/1997
Earnings Per Share	1.22	1.21	1.17	0.99	1.00	0.92	0.83	0.69
Tang. Book Val. Per Share	7.37	7.20	7.10	6.48	6.52	5.90	5.77	5.09
Dividends Per Share	0.590	0.570	0.510	0.460	0.410	0.370	0.340	0.310
Dividend Payout %	48.28	47.32	44.33	47.06	41.77	40.91	40.86	44.63
Income Statement								
Total Interest Income	113,936	435,531	469,288	518,178	462,581	418,914	409,292	319,628
Total Interest Expense	30,969	131,094	158,219	227,962	210,481	174,827	177,805	137,018
Net Interest Income	82,967	304,437	311,069	290,216	252,100	244,087	231,487	182,610
Provision for Loan Losses	1,740	9,705	11,900	14,585	8,645	8,216	5,582	7,742
Non-Interest Income	32,243	136,987	115,783	100,994	69,611	62,822	60,641	41,055
Non-Interest Expense	62,477	234,176	225,536	216,669	165,022	160,988	158,203	122,293
Net Income	35,846	138,180	132,948	113,589	103,804	97,226	88,511	65,199
Average Shs. Outstg.	114,681	113,135	113,898	114,592	103,685	105,385	105,574	93,921
Balance Sheet								
Cash & Due from Banks	308,269	300,966	314,857	356,539	267,178	245,572	247,558	172,392
Securities Avail. for Sale	2,691,836	2,904,157	2,383,607	1,687,787	1,140,646	1,137,846	1,206,121	597,448
Net Loans & Leases	6,138,806	6,082,294	5,245,148	5,301,148	4,806,498	4,364,776	3,972,976	3,260,606
Total Assets	9,620,191	9,767,288	8,387,778	7,770,711	6,571,155	6,070,019	5,838,663	4,460,823
Total Deposits	6,784,175	6,751,783	6,245,528	5,986,804	4,934,405	4,546,813	4,592,969	3,621,569
Long-Term Obligations	571,964	568,730	535,555	456,802	441,973	328,250	296,018	47,695
Total Liabilities	8,651,742	8,820,352	7,524,036	6,959,257	5,891,819	5,455,725	5,230,329	3,985,529
Net Stockholders' Equity	968,449	946,936	863,742	811,454	679,336	614,294	608,334	475,294
Shares Outstanding	113,715	113,820	111,462	113,833	104,041	104,000	105,269	93,306
Return on Equity %	3.70	14.59	15.39	13.99	15.28	15.82	14.54	13.71
Return on Assets %	0.37	1.41	1.58	1.46	1.57	1.60	1.51	1.46
Equity/Assets %	10.06	9.69	10.29	10.44	10.33	10.12	10.41	10.65
Non-Int. Exp./Tot. Inc. %	42.74	40.90	38.54	34.99	31.00	33.41	33.66	33.90
Price Range	21.63-19.97	20.86-16.02	18.40-15.25	16.54-13.30	16.50-10.49	14.23-11.31	17.99-10.77	15.56-8.92
P/E Ratio	17.73-16.37	17.24-13.24	15.73-13.06	16.71-13.44	16.50-10.49	15.47-12.30	21.67-12.98	22.55-12.93
Average Yield %	2.83	3.04	3.02	3.00	3.03	2.82	2.35	2.48

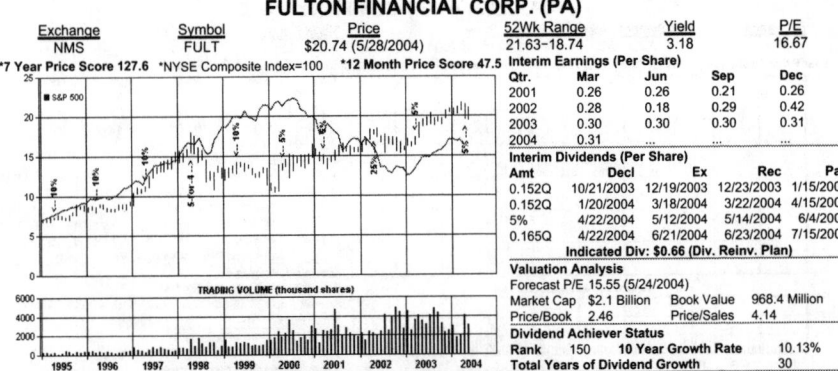

Address: One Penn Square, Lancaster, PA 17604 Telephone: (717) 291 2411 Web Site: www.fult.com	Officers: Rufus A. Fulton - Chmn., C.E.O., R. Scott Smith - Pres., C.O.O. Transfer Agents:Stock Transfer Department, Lancaster, PA	Investor Contact:717-291-2739 Institutional Holding No of Institutions: 20 Shares: 9,356,088 % Held: -

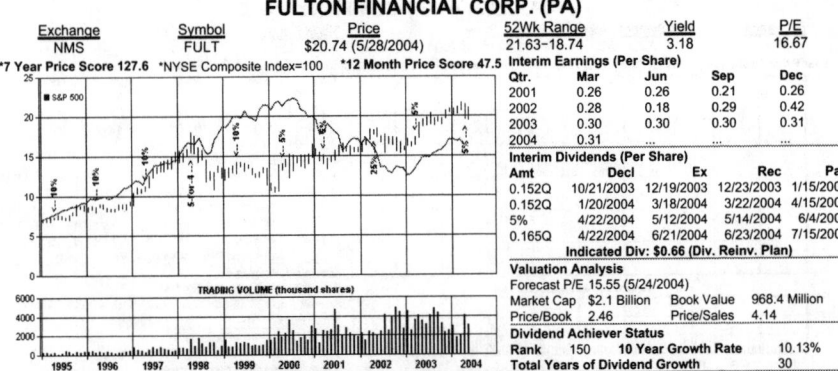

GALLAGHER (ARTHUR J.) & CO.

Exchange	Symbol	Price	52Wk Range	Yield	P/E
NYS	AJG	$31.85 (5/28/2004)	33.86-24.78	3.14	17.22

*7 Year Price Score 137.5 *NYSE Composite Index=100 *12 Month Price Score 49.2

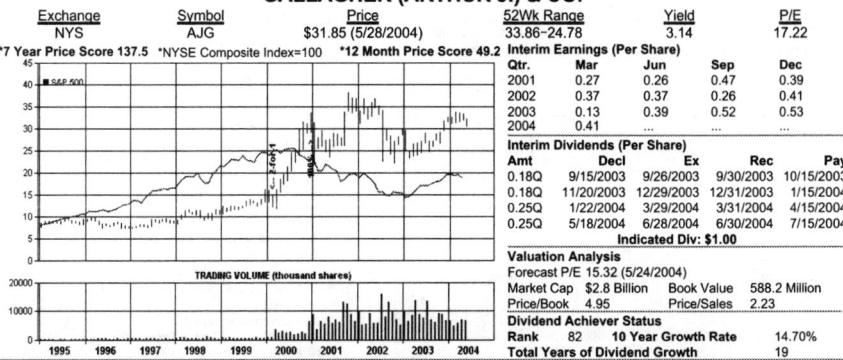

Interim Earnings (Per Share)

Qtr.	Mar	Jun	Sep	Dec
2001	0.27	0.26	0.47	0.39
2002	0.37	0.37	0.26	0.41
2003	0.13	0.39	0.52	0.53
2004	0.41	...	...	...

Interim Dividends (Per Share)

Amt	Decl	Ex	Rec	Pay
0.18Q	9/15/2003	9/26/2003	9/30/2003	10/15/2003
0.18Q	11/20/2003	12/29/2003	12/31/2003	1/15/2004
0.25Q	1/22/2004	3/29/2004	3/31/2004	4/15/2004
0.25Q	5/18/2004	6/28/2004	6/30/2004	7/15/2004

Indicated Div: $1.00

Valuation Analysis

Forecast P/E 15.32 (5/24/2004)

Market Cap $2.8 Billion	Book Value 588.2 Million
Price/Book 4.95	Price/Sales 2.23

Dividend Achiever Status

Rank	82	10 Year Growth Rate	14.70%
Total Years of Dividend Growth			19

Business Summary: Insurance (MIC: 8.2 SIC: 6411 NAIC:524210)

Arthur J. Gallagher & Co. is engaged in providing insurance brokerage, risk management and related services to clients in the U.S. and abroad. Co.'s principal activity is the negotiation and placement of insurance for its clients. Co. also specializes in furnishing risk management services. Risk management involves assisting clients in analyzing risks and determining whether proper protection is best obtained through the purchase of insurance or through retention of all or a portion of those risks and the adoption of corporate risk management policies and cost–effective loss control and prevention programs. Co. also has a financial services group that manages its investment portfolio.

Recent Developments: For the quarter ended Mar 31 2004, net earnings jumped to $38.9 million from $11.9 million in the prior year. Results for 2003 included an after–tax charge of $19.3 million from the exit of investments in venture capital, development stage enterprises and turn–arounds. Total revenues climbed 34.3% to $341.5 million. By segment, brokerage revenue increased 8.6% to $204.1 million, while earnings improved 31.8% to $26.5 million. Risk management revenue rose 15.3% to $88.4 million, while earnings grew 28.4% to $10.4 million. Financial services revenue was $49.0 million versus a revenue loss of $10.4 million, while earnings were $2.0 million compared with a loss of $16.3 million a year earlier.

Prospects: Going forward, Co.'s risk management business should continue to benefit from strong new business sales and the impact of recovering economic conditions on existing clients. Meanwhile, while the favorable market continues for Co.'s brokerage business, first quarter 2004 renewals indicate that the rate of increase in premiums is moderating for some lines. Separately, on Apr 1 2004, Co. acquired B&P International Insurance Brokerage, a full–service marine insurance broker. On Apr 22 2004, Co. acquired Edwin M. Rollins, Inc., which specializes in the placement of transportation–related lines of insurance.

Financial Data

(US$ in Thousands)	12/31/2003	12/31/2002	12/31/2001	12/31/2000	12/31/1999	12/31/1998	12/31/1997	12/31/1996
Earnings Per Share	1.57	1.41	1.39	1.05	0.88	0.77	0.78	0.65
Tang. Book Val. Per Share	4.40	4.43	3.59	3.75	3.14	2.69	2.31	1.89
Dividends Per Share	0.690	0.580	0.500	0.440	0.380	0.340	0.300	0.280
Dividend Payout %	43.94	41.13	36.33	42.38	44.03	43.87	38.97	43.08
Income Statement								
Net Investment Income	126,600	9,289	21,335	...	...	...	...	...
Other Income	1,296,600	1,097,784	910,043	740,596	605,836	540,655	488,028	456,679
Total Revenues	1,304,500	1,101,222	910,043	740,596	605,836	540,655	488,028	456,679
Total Indirect Exp.	964,700	915,880	747,111	615,202	501,601	456,126	407,246	387,280
Inc. Before Inc. Taxes	193,200	185,342	141,853	125,394	104,235	84,529	80,782	69,399
Income Taxes	47,100	55,603	16,597	37,618	36,482	28,028	27,466	23,596
Eqty Earns/Minority Int.	(41,100)	(44,278)	...	...	...	...	...	...
Net Income	146,200	129,739	125,256	87,776	67,753	56,501	53,316	45,803
Average Shs. Outstg.	93,300	91,861	90,127	83,924	77,132	72,824	68,152	71,100
Balance Sheet								
Cash & Cash Equivalents	631,200	464,796	359,431	318,077	233,812	205,508	211,019	197,623
Premiums Due	1,286,400	1,183,737	555,276	405,164	364,854	288,276	217,555	237,640
Invst. Assets: Total	152,900	70,556	70,878	83,251	84,131	77,457	101,884	90,290
Total Assets	2,901,600	2,463,574	1,471,823	1,062,298	884,146	746,010	641,752	590,424
Long–Term Obligations	153,000	128,349	...	...	...	...	...	...
Net Stockholders' Equity	619,100	528,155	371,614	314,372	242,467	202,468	163,907	134,530
Shares Outstanding	90,000	88,548	85,111	79,497	73,680	70,580	66,364	65,172
Return on Equity %	23.61	24.56	33.70	27.92	27.94	27.90	32.52	34.04
Return on Assets %	5.03	5.26	8.51	8.26	7.66	7.57	8.30	7.75
Price Range	32.65–23.45	36.86–22.10	38.30–22.00	33.66–11.75	16.19–10.59	11.59–8.44	9.56–7.47	9.81–7.31
P/E Ratio	20.80–14.94	26.14–15.67	27.55–15.83	32.05–11.19	18.39–12.04	15.06–10.96	12.26–9.58	15.10–11.25
Average Yield %	2.52	1.87	1.71	2.04	3.01	3.26	3.54	3.34

Address: Two Pierce Place, Itasca, IL 60143–3141 **Telephone:** (630) 773–3800 **Web Site:** www.ajg.com	**Officers:** Robert E. Gallagher – Chmn., J. Patrick Gallagher – Pres., C.E.O. **Transfer Agents:** Computershare Investor Services, Chicago, IL	**Institutional Holding** **No of Institutions:** 17 **Shares:** 1,338,088 **% Held:** –

117

GANNETT CO., INC.

Exchange	Symbol	Price	52Wk Range	Yield	P/E
NYS	GCI	$87.80 (5/28/2004)	91.00-75.86	1.14	19.38

*7 Year Price Score 120.7   *NYSE Composite Index=100   *12 Month Price Score 49.1

Interim Earnings (Per Share)

Qtr.	Mar	Jun	Sep	Dec
2001	0.66	0.88	0.66	0.92
2002	0.91	1.13	0.99	1.28
2003	0.93	1.20	1.03	1.30
2004	1.00	...	...	...

Interim Dividends (Per Share)

Amt	Decl	Ex	Rec	Pay
0.25Q	8/5/2003	9/10/2003	9/13/2003	10/1/2003
0.25Q	10/21/2003	12/10/2003	12/12/2003	1/2/2004
0.25Q	2/24/2004	3/3/2004	3/5/2004	4/1/2004
0.25Q	5/4/2004	6/2/2004	6/4/2004	7/1/2004

Indicated Div: $1.00 (Div. Reinv. Plan)

Valuation Analysis

Forecast P/E 17.61 (5/24/2004)

Market Cap	$23.4 Billion	Book Value	8.6 Billion
Price/Book	2.80	Price/Sales	3.51

Dividend Achiever Status

Rank	265	10 Year Growth Rate	4.16%
Total Years of Dividend Growth			32

Business Summary: Media (MIC: 13.1 SIC: 2711 NAIC:511110)

Gannett is a news and information company that publishes newspapers and operates broadcasting stations. Co. is also engaged in marketing, commercial printing, a newswire service, data services, and news programming. Co. has operations in 43 states, the District of Columbia, Guam, the U.K., and in certain European and Asian markets. Co. is the largest U.S. newspaper group in terms of circulation, with 100 daily newspapers, including *USA Today*, more than 500 non-daily publications and *USA Weekend*, a weekly newspaper magazine. In the U.K., Co.'s subsidiary Newsquest publishes nearly 300 titles, including 17 daily newspapers. Co. owns and operates 22 television stations in major markets.

Recent Developments: For the thirteen weeks ended Mar 28 2004, net income climbed 9.8% to $274.4 million compared with $249.8 million in the equivalent quarter of 2003. Newspaper segment results reflected stronger advertising revenue growth and the benefit of acquisitions, tempered by higher newsprint and benefit costs. The television group benefited from politically-related advertising demand. Total operating revenues were $1.73 billion, up 11.4% from $1.55 billion in the previous year. Operating income increased 8.5% to $445.8 million compared with $411.0 million the year before.

Prospects: On Apr 2 2004, Co. acquired the assets of Captivate Network, a national news and entertainment network that delivers programming and advertising on television screens in elevators in office towers in North America. Captivate Network has an estimated 1.4 million viewers of screens in about 400 buildings in North America, with more than 1,000 buildings in 35 markets under contract. The acquisition should enhance Co.'s advertising platform. Terms of the transaction were undisclosed. Separately, Co. anticipates modest advertising revenue and volume growth in 2004 in most categories and in most newspaper markets.

Financial Data

(US$ in Thousands)

	3 Mos	12/28/2003	12/29/2002	12/30/2001	12/31/2000	12/26/1999	12/27/1998	12/28/1997
Earnings Per Share	4.53	4.46	4.31	3.12	3.63	3.26	3.50	2.50
Cash Flow Per Share	1.42	5.44	3.83	4.94	1.87	4.07	3.39	3.08
Tang. Book Val. Per Share	N.M	N.M	N.M	N.M	N.M	N.M	0.66	N.M
Dividends Per Share	0.980	0.970	0.930	0.890	0.850	0.810	0.770	0.730
Dividend Payout %	21.58	21.74	21.57	28.52	23.41	24.84	22.00	29.20
Income Statement								
Total Revenues	1,729,684	6,711,115	6,422,249	6,344,245	6,222,318	5,260,190	5,121,291	4,729,491
Total Indirect Exp.	1,283,835	1,276,328	1,241,937	1,434,249	1,347,810	1,088,620	1,083,807	1,044,651
Depreciation & Amort.	61,357	231,532	222,444	443,777	375,915	280,091	310,206	301,073
Operating Income	445,849	1,981,018	1,926,309	1,589,835	1,817,256	1,563,101	1,443,502	1,316,268
Net Interest Inc./(Exp.)	(31,791)	(134,064)	(142,911)	(217,178)	(192,019)	(88,880)	(60,094)	(91,725)
Income Taxes	142,500	629,100	604,400	539,400	636,900	607,800	669,500	496,300
Income from Cont Ops	...	...	...	...	971,940	919,387	...	...
Net Income	274,408	1,211,213	1,160,128	831,197	1,719,077	957,928	999,913	712,679
Average Shs. Outstg.	275,507	271,872	269,286	266,833	268,118	281,608	285,711	285,610
Balance Sheet								
Cash & Cash Equivalents	75,738	67,188	90,374	140,629	193,196	46,160	66,187	52,778
Total Current Assets	1,203,996	1,223,261	1,133,079	1,178,198	1,302,336	1,075,222	906,385	884,634
Total Assets	14,929,279	14,706,239	13,733,014	13,096,101	12,980,411	9,006,446	6,979,480	6,890,351
Total Current Liabilities	1,032,180	961,837	958,625	1,127,737	1,174,001	883,778	727,967	767,501
Long-Term Obligations	3,718,997	3,834,511	4,547,265	5,080,025	5,747,856	2,463,250	1,306,859	1,740,534
Net Stockholders' Equity	8,627,892	8,422,981	6,911,795	5,735,922	5,103,410	4,629,646	3,979,824	3,479,736
Net Working Capital	171,816	261,424	174,454	50,461	128,335	191,444	178,418	117,133
Shares Outstanding	272,232	272,417	267,909	265,797	264,271	277,926	279,001	283,874
Operating Profit Margin %	25.77	29.51	29.99	25.05	29.20	29.71	28.18	27.83
Return on Equity %	3.18	14.37	16.78	14.49	19.04	19.85	25.12	20.48
Return on Assets %	1.83	8.23	8.44	6.34	7.48	10.20	14.32	10.34
Debt/Total Assets %	24.91	26.07	33.11	38.79	44.28	27.34	18.72	25.26
Price Range	90.01-84.50	88.93-67.68	79.87-63.39	71.10-55.55	83.25-48.69	79.31-61.81	74.69-48.94	61.00-35.81
P/E Ratio	19.87-18.65	19.94-15.17	18.53-14.71	22.79-17.80	22.93-13.41	24.33-18.96	21.34-13.98	24.40-14.33
Average Yield %	1.12	1.25	1.27	1.38	1.39	1.15	1.21	1.53

Address: 7950 Jones Branch Drive, McLean, VA 22107-0910 **Telephone:** (703) 854-6000 **Web Site:** www.gannett.com	**Officers:** Douglas H. McCorkindale - Chmn., Pres., C.E.O., Larry F. Miller - Exec. V.P., Oper. **Transfer Agents:** Wells Fargo Bank Minnesota, N.A., St. Paul, MN	**Investor Contact:** 703-854-6918 **Institutional Holding** **No of Institutions:** 42 **Shares:** 1,733,994 **% Held:** -

GENERAL DYNAMICS CORP.

Exchange	Symbol	Price	52Wk Range	Yield	P/E
NYS	GD	$95.63 (5/28/2004)	96.88-67.19	1.51	18.28

*7 Year Price Score 125.6 *NYSE Composite Index=100 ***12 Month Price Score 51.8**

Interim Earnings (Per Share)

Qtr.	Mar	Jun	Sep	Dec
2001	1.19	1.12	1.13	1.21
2002	1.13	1.29	1.32	1.44
2003	1.11	1.22	1.28	1.39
2004	1.34	...	...	...

Interim Dividends (Per Share)

Amt	Decl	Ex	Rec	Pay
0.32Q	8/6/2003	10/8/2003	10/10/2003	11/14/2003
0.32Q	12/3/2003	1/14/2004	1/16/2004	2/6/2004
0.36Q	3/3/2004	4/6/2004	4/8/2004	5/7/2004
0.36Q	6/2/2004	6/30/2004	7/2/2004	8/6/2004
		Indicated Div: $1.44		

Valuation Analysis

Forecast P/E 16.18 (5/24/2004)

Market Cap	$19.3 Billion	Book Value	6.2 Billion
Price/Book	2.80	Price/Sales	0.97

Dividend Achiever Status

Rank	140	10 Year Growth Rate	10.84%
Total Years of Dividend Growth			12

Business Summary: Shipping (MIC: 15.3 SIC: 3731 NAIC:336611)

General Dynamics is a major defense contractor operating in four business segments. Information Systems and Technology provides defense and commercial customers with infrastructure and systems integration skills required to process, communicate and manage information. Marine Systems provides the U.S. Navy with combat vessels. Aerospace designs and develops technologically advanced business jet aircraft. Combat Systems provides systems integration, design, and production for armored vehicles, armaments, munitions and components. Other businesses consist of a coal mining operation, an aggregates operation and a leasing operation for liquefied natural gas tankers.

Recent Developments: For the quarter ended Mar 31 2004, net earnings advanced 21.7% to $269.0 million compared with $221.0 million in the corresponding period of the previous year. Net sales rose 39.1% to $4.76 billion from $3.42 billion the year before. Information Systems and Technology segment sales soared 72.5% to $1.72 billion, while Combat Systems segment sales advanced 36.3% to $1.11 billion. Marine Systems segment sales increased 31.1% to $1.28 billion, and Aerospace segment sales inched up 2.0% to $606.0 million. Co. ended the quarter with a total backlog of $41.62 billion.

Prospects: Co. continues to focus on program performance, resulting in improved margins in it business aviation and marine groups. In addition, Information Systems and Technology and Combat Systems are providing healthy margins on increased volume, reflecting the successful integration of the General Motors Defense and Veridian acquisitions. Separately, Co.'s recent new contract wins include a $580.0 million U.S. Navy contract to build the fifth and sixth T−AKE dry−cargo ships. Co. was also awarded a $165.0 million contract to provide a full range of services for the Canadian Forces Wheeled Light Armoured Vehicles. Looking ahead, Co. expects earnings per share to range from $5.70 to $5.75 in 2004.

Financial Data

(US$ in Millions)	3 Mos	12/31/2003	12/31/2002	12/31/2001	12/31/2000	12/31/1999	12/31/1998	12/31/1997
Earnings Per Share	5.23	5.00	5.18	4.65	4.48	4.36	2.86	2.50
Cash Flow Per Share	1.64	8.65	5.54	5.43	5.32	5.02	2.91	4.38
Tang. Book Val. Per Share	N.M	N.M	5.61	3.83	6.42	3.27	5.46	5.64
Dividends Per Share	1.280	1.260	1.180	1.100	1.020	0.940	0.860	0.820
Dividend Payout %	24.47	25.20	22.77	23.65	22.76	21.55	30.24	32.80
Income Statement								
Total Revenues	4,760	16,617	13,829	12,163	10,356	8,959	4,970	4,062
Total Indirect Exp.	4,318	15,150	12,247	10,678	9,027	7,756	4,428	3,616
Depreciation & Amort.	77	277	213	271	226	200	126	91
Operating Income	442	1,467	1,582	1,485	1,329	1,203	542	446
Income Taxes	134	375	533	481	361	246	185	163
Income from Cont Ops	...	997	1,051	...	...	...	...	...
Net Income	269	1,004	917	943	901	880	364	316
Average Shs. Outstg.	200	199	202	202	201	202	127	127
Balance Sheet								
Cash & Cash Equivalents	869	860	328	442	177	270	220	441
Total Current Assets	6,772	6,394	5,098	4,893	3,551	3,491	1,873	1,689
Total Assets	16,668	16,183	11,731	11,069	7,987	7,774	4,572	4,091
Total Current Liabilities	5,723	5,616	4,582	4,579	2,901	3,453	1,461	1,291
Long−Term Obligations	3,297	3,296	718	724	162	169	249	257
Net Stockholders' Equity	6,217	5,921	5,199	4,528	3,820	3,171	2,219	1,915
Shares Outstanding	199	197	200	200	200	201	127	126
Statistical Record								
Operating Profit Margin %	9.28	8.82	11.43	12.20	12.83	13.42	10.90	10.97
Return on Equity %	4.32	16.83	20.21	20.82	23.58	27.75	16.40	16.50
Return on Assets %	1.61	6.16	8.95	8.51	11.28	11.31	7.96	7.72
Debt/Total Assets %	19.78	20.36	6.12	6.54	2.02	2.17	5.44	6.28
Price Range	96.88-86.10	90.39-52.37	110.6-74.57	94.99-61.00	78.00-37.00	74.81-46.94	61.25-40.38	44.97-31.63
P/E Ratio	18.52-16.46	18.08-10.47	21.35-14.40	20.43-13.12	17.41-8.26	17.16-10.77	21.42-14.12	17.99-12.65
Average Yield %	1.40	1.72	1.34	1.43	1.76	1.53	1.79	2.12

Address: 3190 Fairview Park Drive, Falls Church, VA 22042−4523 **Telephone:** (703) 876−3000 **Web Site:** www.generaldynamics.com	**Officers:** Nicholas D. Chabraja − Chmn., C.E.O., Michael W. Toner − Exec. V.P., Group Exec., Marine Systems **Transfer Agents:** EquiServe Trust Company, N.A., Jersey City, NJ	**Investor Contact:** 703−876−3195 **Institutional Holding** **No of Institutions:** 4 **Shares:** 272,865 **% Held:** −

GENERAL ELECTRIC CO.

Exchange	Symbol	Price	52Wk Range	Yield	P/E
NYS	GE	$31.12 (5/28/2004)	34.19-27.10	2.57	20.08

*7 Year Price Score 84.9   *NYSE Composite Index=100   *12 Month Price Score 47.5

Interim Earnings (Per Share)

Qtr.	Mar	Jun	Sep	Dec
2001	0.30	0.39	0.33	0.39
2002	0.35	0.44	0.41	0.31
2003	0.32	0.38	0.40	0.45
2004	0.32	...	...	...

Interim Dividends (Per Share)

Amt	Decl	Ex	Rec	Pay
0.19Q	6/13/2003	6/26/2003	6/30/2003	7/25/2003
0.19Q	9/12/2003	9/25/2003	9/29/2003	10/27/2003
0.20Q	12/12/2003	12/29/2003	12/31/2003	1/26/2004
0.20Q	2/13/2004	2/26/2004	3/1/2004	4/26/2004
	Indicated Div: $0.80 (Div. Reinv. Plan)			

Valuation Analysis

Forecast P/E 19.93 (5/24/2004)

Market Cap	$309.7 Billion	Book Value	86.5 Billion
Price/Book	3.58	Price/Sales	2.27

Dividend Achiever Status

Rank	98	10 Year Growth Rate	13.73%
Total Years of Dividend Growth			28

Business Summary: Electrical (MIC: 11.14 SIC: 3641 NAIC:335110)

General Electric is engaged in developing, manufacturing and marketing a wide variety of products for the generation, transmission, distribution, control and utilization of electricity. Co.'s operating segments include: Commercial Finance, Consumer Finance, Energy, Healthcare, Infrastructure, Transportation, NBC, Advanced Materials, Consumer and Industrial, Equipment Services and Insurance. Co. products include major appliances; lighting products; industrial automation products; medical diagnostic imaging equipment; motors; electrical distribution and control equipment; locomotives; power generation and delivery products; nuclear power support services and fuel assemblies.

Recent Developments: For the three months ended Mar 31 2004, net income was $3.24 billion compared with income of $3.21 billion, before an accounting change charge of $215.0 million, in the corresponding quarter of the previous year. Nine of Co.'s eleven businesses contributed double-digit improvements to earnings. Total revenues climbed 9.5% to $33.35 billion from $30.46 billion in the year-earlier period. The improvement in revenues was primarily attributed to growth in equipment and other services, consumer finance and healthcare sales, partially offset by lower energy and insurance segment sales. Total costs and expenses rose 11.1% to $29.13 billion from $26.21 billion in 2003.

Prospects: On Apr 8 2004, Co. completed the acquisition of all of the outstanding shares of Amersham plc. Amersham will be combined with Co.'s medical business, creating a $14.00 billion company to be known as GE Healthcare. The new company is expected to generate $16.00 billion in revenues in 2005. Co. expects the acquisition to accelerate the development of molecular imaging and personalized medicine by more rapidly developing and bringing to market new targeted imaging agents and diagnostics that will enable its customers to diagnose, treat and monitor disease at an earlier stage.

Financial Data

(US$ in Millions)	3 Mos	12/31/2003	12/31/2002	12/31/2001	12/31/2000	12/31/1999	12/31/1998	12/31/1997
Earnings Per Share	1.55	1.55	1.51	1.41	1.27	1.07	0.93	0.82
Cash Flow Per Share	0.78	3.00	2.94	3.20	2.25	2.46	1.93	1.41
Tang. Book Val. Per Share	2.87	2.40	1.75	2.33	2.32	1.67	1.55	1.56
Dividends Per Share	0.770	0.760	0.720	0.640	0.540	0.460	0.400	0.340
Dividend Payout %	50.99	49.03	47.68	45.39	43.04	43.49	42.85	42.27
Income Statement								
Total Revenues	33,350	133,492	131,698	125,913	129,853	111,630	100,469	90,840
Total Indirect Exp.	9,252	...	...	...	...	...	...	...
Depreciation & Amort.	1,997	6,956	5,998	7,089	7,736	6,691	5,860	5,269
Operating Income	4,291	82,981	78,842	76,816	78,030	65,672	58,189	50,752
Net Interest Inc./(Exp.)	...	(10,432)	(10,216)	(11,062)	(11,720)	(10,013)	(9,753)	(8,384)
Income Taxes	982	4,315	3,758	5,573	5,711	4,860	4,181	2,976
Income from Cont Ops	...	15,589	15,133	14,128	...	...	...	...
Net Income	3,240	15,002	14,118	13,684	12,735	10,717	9,296	8,203
Average Shs. Outstg.	10,186	10,075	10,028	10,052	10,057	9,996	9,990	10,035
Balance Sheet								
Cash & Cash Equivalents	13,371	12,664	8,910	9,082	8,195	8,554	4,317	5,861
Total Current Assets	157,235	32,148	28,838	27,237	25,509	24,092	18,590	20,680
Total Assets	662,106	647,483	575,244	495,023	437,006	405,200	355,935	304,012
Total Current Liabilities	183,924	176,530	181,827	198,904	156,112	161,216	141,579	120,668
Long-Term Obligations	169,472	170,004	140,632	79,806	82,132	71,427	59,663	46,603
Net Stockholders' Equity	86,486	79,180	63,706	54,824	50,492	42,557	38,880	34,438
Net Working Capital	(26,689)	(144,382)	(152,989)	(171,667)	(130,603)	(137,124)	(122,989)	(99,988)
Shares Outstanding	10,212	10,063	9,969	9,925	9,932	9,854	9,813	9,795
Operating Profit Margin %	12.86	61.64	59.86	61.00	60.09	58.83	57.91	55.86
Return on Equity %	3.74	18.81	23.75	25.76	25.22	25.18	23.90	23.81
Return on Assets %	0.48	2.30	2.63	2.85	2.91	2.64	2.61	2.69
Debt/Total Assets %	25.59	26.25	24.44	16.12	18.79	17.62	16.76	15.32
Price Range	34.19-29.18	32.11-22.17	41.55-22.00	53.40-30.37	60.00-41.71	53.17-31.98	34.35-23.85	25.15-16.25
P/E Ratio	22.06-18.83	20.72-14.30	27.52-14.57	37.87-21.54	47.24-32.84	49.69-29.89	36.94-25.65	30.67-19.82
Average Yield %	2.40	2.71	2.31	1.47	1.04	1.20	1.42	1.64

Address: 3135 Easton Turnpike, Fairfield, CT 06828-0001
Telephone: (203) 373-2211
Web Site: www.ge.com

Officers: Jeffrey R. Immelt – Chmn., C.E.O., Dennis D. Dammerman – Vice-Chmn.
Transfer Agents: GE Share Owner Services, c/o The Bank of New York, New York, NY

Investor Contact: 203 373 2816
Institutional Holding
No of Institutions: 41
Shares: 7,407,325   **% Held:** –

GENERAL GROWTH PROPERTIES, INC.

Exchange	Symbol	Price	52Wk Range	Yield	P/E
NYS	GGP	$29.38 (5/28/2004)	35.30-19.87	4.08	23.89

*7 Year Price Score 179.2 *NYSE Composite Index=100 *12 Month Price Score 48.8

Interim Earnings (Per Share)

Qtr.	Mar	Jun	Sep	Dec
2001	0.13	(0.15)	0.18	0.37
2002	0.17	0.18	0.23	0.41
2003	0.24	0.23	0.28	0.45
2004	0.27	...	...	...

Interim Dividends (Per Share)

Amt	Decl	Ex	Rec	Pay
0.30Q	10/1/2003	10/10/2003	10/15/2003	10/31/2003
3-for-1	10/1/2003	12/8/2003	11/20/2003	12/5/2003
0.30Q	1/5/2004	1/13/2004	1/15/2004	1/30/2004
0.30Q	4/5/2004	4/13/2004	4/15/2004	4/30/2004

Indicated Div: $1.20 (Div. Reinv. Plan)

Valuation Analysis

Forecast P/E N/A

Market Cap	$1.8 Billion	Book Value	1.7 Billion
Price/Book	3.59	Price/Sales	4.72

Dividend Achiever Status

Rank	63	10 Year Growth Rate	16.23%
Total Years of Dividend Growth			10

TRADING VOLUME (thousand shares)

Business Summary: Property, Real Estate &Development (MIC: 8.3 SIC: 6798 NAIC:525930)

General Growth Properties is primarily engaged in the ownership, operation, management, leasing, acquisition, development and expansion of regional mall and community shopping centers in the United States. As of December 31, 2003 Co. Portfolio is comprised primarily of 162 operating retail properties (regional malls or community centers). Co. also has certain office space associated with Co.'s retail properties and approximately 1.4 million square feet of commercial/industrial space at 6 former JP Realty properties. The 162 operating retail properties are shopping centers with a variety of smaller Mall Stores.

Recent Developments: For the quarter ended Mar 31 2004, net income was $59.1 million compared with income of $48.3 million, before income from discontinued operations of $3.3 million, in the prior-year quarter. Total revenues increased 32.0% to $361.6 million from $273.9 million the previous year. Revenue from minimum rents grew 31.2% to $222.7 million, while tenant recoveries advanced 44.4% to $102.6 million. Total tenant sales increased 9.3% for the quarter, and comparable tenant sales increased 6.9%. Mall shop occupancy was flat versus the year-earlier quarter at 90.4%. Funds from operations were $163.7 million, up 28.6% from $127.3 million the year before.

Prospects: On Apr 12 2004, Co. agreed to acquire a 100.0% interest in The Grand Canal Shoppes at The Venetian Casino Resort in Las Vegas, NV. Upon completion, Co. will also acquire the adjacent multi-level retail space under development at The Palazzo. The aggregate price for The Grand Canal Shoppes will be about $766.0 million. On Apr 20 2004, Co. agreed to acquire a 100.0% interest in the Mall of Louisiana in Baton Rouge, LA, and a 50.0% interest in Riverchase Galleria in Birmingham, AL. Co.'s total purchase price for both acquisitions is $430.8 million. For fiscal year 2004, Co. raised its guidance for funds from operations to a range of $2.62 to $2.70 per diluted share.

Financial Data

(US$ in Thousands)	12/31/2003	12/31/2002	12/31/2001	12/31/2000	12/31/1999	12/31/1998	12/31/1997	12/31/1996
Earnings Per Share	1.20	0.99	0.53	0.72	0.65	0.53	0.92	0.73
Tang. Book Val. Per Share	7.68	6.39	6.37	5.98	5.98	5.00	5.39	3.57
Dividends Per Share	1.020	0.890	0.740	0.680	0.640	0.620	0.590	0.570
Dividend Payout %	85.00	89.89	139.12	93.57	98.98	116.98	64.49	78.08
Income Statement								
Rental Income	816,603	615,307	491,466	468,607	414,558	285,202	183,806	145,880
Total Income	1,270,728	980,466	803,709	698,767	612,342	426,576	291,147	217,405
Total Indirect Exp.	563,610	254,821	272,960	188,951	175,340	120,025	79,011	64,297
Depreciation	231,172	180,028	145,352	126,689	112,874	75,227	48,509	39,809
Interest Expense	278,543	218,935	214,277	218,075	185,984	125,851	78,775	70,272
Eqty Earns/Minority Int.	(17,631)	(4,885)	22,774	(2,273)	(8,957)	(18,531)	27,994	26,830
Income from Cont Ops	259,466	210,576	109,666	...	114,921	71,194	90,703	62,033
Net Income	263,411	209,258	92,310	137,948	101,125	66,445	89,551	59,742
Average Shs. Outstg.	215,079	212,553	158,721	156,288	138,093	109,146	98,520	84,435
Balance Sheet								
Cash & Cash Equivalents	10,677	54,116	315,858	27,229	25,593	19,630	25,898	15,947
Ttl Real Estate Inv.	8,573,613	6,159,565	4,460,905	4,203,070	3,949,878	3,375,007	1,630,190	1,366,324
Total Assets	9,582,897	7,280,822	5,646,807	5,284,104	4,954,895	4,027,474	2,097,719	1,757,717
Long-Term Obligations	6,649,490	4,592,311	3,398,207	3,244,126	3,119,534	2,648,776	1,275,785	1,168,522
Total Liabilities	7,912,488	5,746,797	4,125,921	4,008,186	3,689,637	3,104,267	1,599,214	1,427,450
Net Stockholders' Equity	1,670,409	1,196,525	1,183,386	938,418	927,758	585,707	498,505	330,267
Shares Outstanding	217,293	187,191	185,771	156,843	155,092	117,003	92,367	92,367
Net Inc.+Depr./Assets %	5.16	5.40	4.50	5.00	4.60	3.60	6.60	5.80
Return on Equity %	15.53	13.72	7.21	10.81	9.08	7.71	18.19	18.78
Return on Assets %	2.70	2.89	1.94	2.61	2.31	1.76	4.32	3.52
Price Range	27.89-16.09	17.33-12.91	13.39-11.00	12.06-8.94	12.85-8.35	12.90-10.96	12.67-10.17	10.87-7.00
P/E Ratio	23.24-13.41	17.51-13.04	25.27-20.75	16.75-12.41	19.78-12.85	24.33-20.68	13.77-11.05	14.90-9.59
Average Yield %	4.78	5.71	6.04	6.47	5.79	5.14	5.29	6.97

Address: 110 North Wacker Drive, Chicago, IL 60606 Telephone: (312) 960-5000 Web Site: www.generalgrowth.com	Officers: Matthew Bucksbaum – Chmn., Robert Michaels – Pres., C.O.O. Transfer Agents:Mellon Investor Services, LLC, South Hackensack, NJ	Institutional Holding No of Institutions: 5 Shares: 7,721,143 % Held: –

GENUINE PARTS CO.

Exchange	Symbol	Price	52Wk Range	Yield	P/E
NYS	GPC	$37.64 (5/28/2004)	37.64-30.03	3.19	18.01

*7 Year Price Score 106.6   *NYSE Composite Index=100   *12 Month Price Score 52.2

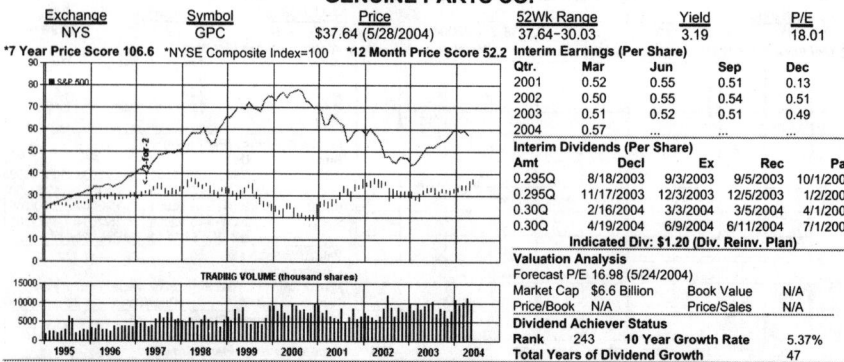

Interim Earnings (Per Share)

Qtr.	Mar	Jun	Sep	Dec
2001	0.52	0.55	0.51	0.13
2002	0.50	0.55	0.54	0.51
2003	0.51	0.52	0.51	0.49
2004	0.57	...	...	...

Interim Dividends (Per Share)

Amt	Decl	Ex	Rec	Pay
0.295Q	8/18/2003	9/3/2003	9/5/2003	10/1/2003
0.295Q	11/17/2003	12/3/2003	12/5/2003	1/2/2004
0.30Q	2/16/2004	3/3/2004	3/5/2004	4/1/2004
0.30Q	4/19/2004	6/9/2004	6/11/2004	7/1/2004

Indicated Div: $1.20 (Div. Reinv. Plan)

Valuation Analysis

Forecast P/E 16.98 (5/24/2004)

Market Cap	$6.6 Billion	Book Value	N/A
Price/Book	N/A	Price/Sales	N/A

Dividend Achiever Status

Rank	243	10 Year Growth Rate	5.37%
Total Years of Dividend Growth			47

Business Summary: Retail – Automotive (MIC: 5.7 SIC: 5013 NAIC:423120)

Genuine Parts is a service distribution and sales organization. Co.'s Automotive Parts group distributes automotive replacement parts and accessory items to independent and company–owned NAPA auto parts stores. The Industrial Parts group's Motion Industries distributes industrial bearings and power transmission replacement parts, including hydraulic and pneumatic products, material handling equipment and agricultural and irrigation equipment. The Office Products group's S. P. Richards Company distributes a line of office and business–related products. The Electrical and Electronic Materials Group's EIS distributes a range of materials and products for electrical and electronic apparatus.

Recent Developments: For the first quarter ended Mar 31 2004, net income increased 13.3% to $100.2 million compared with income of $88.4 million, before an accounting change charge of $19.5 million, in the corresponding prior–year quarter. Net sales advanced 8.7% to $2.20 billion from $2.02 billion a year earlier. On a segment basis, Automotive sales grew 10.2% to $1.13 billion, while Industrial sales rose 6.8% to $608.5 million. Office Products sales increased 6.3% to $386.8 million, and Electrical/Electronic sales jumped 10.2% to $83.1 million. Gross profit advanced 7.6% to $686.9 million from $638.3 million the year before.

Prospects: Co. believes that its sales improvement is being driven by growth initiatives that have been implemented across all of its businesses. In addition, sales are benefiting from the overall pickup being experienced in the manufacturing sectors. Co.'s operating margins and net earnings are benefiting from the stronger sales, and also provided for an improved balance sheet position. As a result of the better–than–expected results, Co. anticipates earnings for 2004 to range from $2.15 to $2.25 per share, up from its previously expected range of $2.10 to $2.20 per share. For the second quarter of 2004, Co. expects earnings in the range of $0.55 to $0.56 per share.

Financial Data

(US$ in Thousands)	3 Mos	12/31/2003	12/31/2002	12/31/2001	12/31/2000	12/31/1999	12/31/1998	12/31/1997
Earnings Per Share	2.09	2.03	2.10	1.71	2.20	2.11	1.98	1.90
Cash Flow Per Share	0.46	2.30	1.55	1.91	1.79	2.04	1.57	1.39
Tang. Book Val. Per Share	13.23	12.95	11.87	10.97	10.49	9.79	9.51	10.39
Dividends Per Share	1.180	1.170	1.150	1.130	1.080	1.030	0.990	0.940
Dividend Payout %	56.46	57.88	55.00	66.08	49.31	48.81	50.00	49.64
Income Statement								
Total Revenues	2,196,991	8,449,300	8,258,927	8,220,668	8,369,857	7,981,687	6,614,032	6,005,245
Total Indirect Exp.	524,514	2,050,873	1,948,442	1,951,559	1,958,747	1,766,063	1,413,390	1,261,003
Depreciation & Amort.	16,193	69,013	70,151	85,793	92,303	89,967	69,305	58,867
Operating Income	162,397	571,743	605,736	496,013	646,750	628,067	589,117	565,600
Income Taxes	62,198	218,101	238,236	198,866	261,427	250,445	233,323	223,203
Income from Cont Ops	...	353,642	367,500	...	...	...	...	...
Net Income	100,199	334,101	(27,590)	297,147	385,323	377,622	355,794	342,397
Average Shs. Outstg.	174,900	174,480	175,104	173,633	175,327	179,238	180,081	180,165
Balance Sheet								
Cash & Cash Equivalents	28,088	15,393	19,995	85,770	27,738	45,735	84,972	72,823
Total Current Assets	3,446,988	3,417,626	3,335,775	3,146,212	3,019,481	2,895,203	2,683,357	2,093,551
Total Assets	4,167,171	4,116,497	4,019,843	4,206,646	4,142,114	3,929,672	3,600,380	2,754,363
Total Current Liabilities	1,010,603	1,016,931	1,069,718	919,181	988,313	916,012	818,409	556,938
Long–Term Obligations	625,000	625,108	674,796	835,580	770,581	702,417	588,640	209,490
Net Stockholders' Equity	2,366,030	2,312,283	2,130,009	2,345,123	2,260,806	2,177,517	2,053,332	1,859,468
Net Working Capital	2,436,385	2,400,695	2,266,057	2,227,031	2,031,168	1,979,191	1,864,948	1,536,613
Shares Outstanding	174,441	174,045	174,380	173,473	172,389	177,275	179,505	178,948
Operating Profit Margin %	7.39	6.76	7.33	6.03	7.72	7.86	8.90	9.41
Return on Equity %	4.23	15.29	17.25	12.67	17.04	17.34	17.32	18.41
Return on Assets %	2.40	8.59	9.14	7.06	9.30	9.60	9.88	12.43
Debt/Total Assets %	14.99	15.18	16.78	19.86	18.60	17.87	16.34	7.60
Price Range	34.95-32.13	33.66-27.43	38.08-27.64	37.44-24.26	26.44-18.63	35.75-23.13	38.13-29.38	35.63-28.92
P/E Ratio	16.72-15.37	16.58-13.51	18.13-13.16	21.89-14.19	12.02-8.47	16.94-10.96	19.26-14.84	18.75-15.22
Average Yield %	3.52	3.70	3.45	3.74	4.89	3.46	2.92	2.93

Address: 2999 Circle 75 Parkway, Atlanta, GA 30339	**Officers:** Larry L. Prince – Chmn., C.E.O., Thomas C. Gallagher – Pres., C.O.O.	**Investor Contact:** 770–953–1700
Telephone: (770) 953–1700	**Transfer Agents:** Sun Trust Bank, Atlanta, GA	**Institutional Holding**
Web Site: www.genpt.com		**No of Institutions:** 8
		Shares: 45,035 **% Held:** –

GLACIER BANCORP, INC. (NEW)

Exchange	Symbol	Price	52Wk Range	Yield	P/E
NMS	GBCI	$26.42 (5/28/2004)	26.95-19.70	2.54	12.73

*7 Year Price Score 161.1   *NYSE Composite Index=100   *12 Month Price Score 51.0

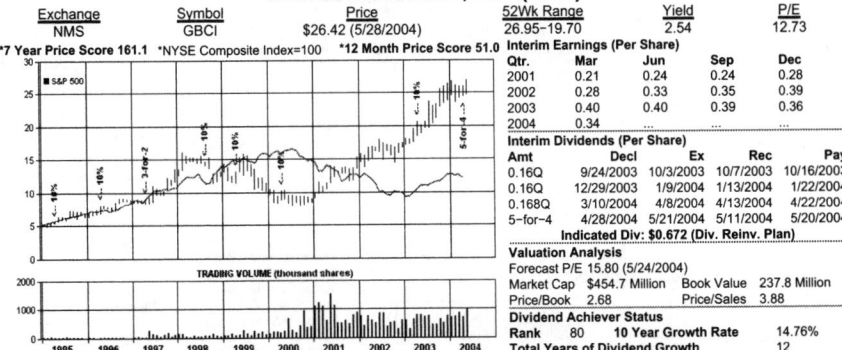

Interim Earnings (Per Share)

Qtr.	Mar	Jun	Sep	Dec
2001	0.21	0.24	0.24	0.28
2002	0.28	0.33	0.35	0.39
2003	0.40	0.40	0.39	0.36
2004	0.34	...	...	...

Interim Dividends (Per Share)

Amt	Decl	Ex	Rec	Pay
0.16Q	9/24/2003	10/3/2003	10/7/2003	10/16/2003
0.16Q	12/29/2003	1/9/2004	1/13/2004	1/22/2004
0.168Q	3/10/2004	4/8/2004	4/13/2004	4/22/2004
5-for-4	4/28/2004	5/21/2004	5/11/2004	5/20/2004

Indicated Div: $0.672 (Div. Reinv. Plan)

Valuation Analysis

Forecast P/E 15.80 (5/24/2004)

Market Cap $454.7 Million	Book Value 237.8 Million
Price/Book 2.68	Price/Sales 3.88

Dividend Achiever Status

Rank 80	10 Year Growth Rate	14.76%
Years of Dividend Growth	12	

TRADING VOLUME (thousand shares)

Business Summary: Other Depository Banking (MIC: 8.5 SIC: 6035 NAIC:522120)

Glacier Bancorp is the parent holding company of its eight wholly-owned subsidiaries, Glacier Bank, First Security Bank of Missoula, Western Security Bank, Mountain West Bank in Idaho, Big Sky Western Bank, Valley Bank of Helena, Glacier Bank of Whitefish and Glacier Capital Trust I. Co. provides commercial banking services from 54 banking offices throughout Montana, Idaho and Utah. Co. offers a range of banking products and services, including transaction and savings deposits, commercial, consumer and real estate loans, mortgage origination services, and retail brokerage services. As of Dec 31 2003, Co. had total assets of $2.74 billion and total deposits of $1.60 billion.

Recent Developments: For the first quarter ended Mar 31 2004, net earnings advanced 19.9% to $10.6 million versus $8.8 million in the corresponding 2003 quarter. Results for 2003 included a net gain on the sale of investments of $437,000. Net interest income climbed 20.9% to $26.4 million from $21.8 million a year earlier. Total interest income increased 10.6% to $35.5 million, while total interest expense declined 11.3% to $9.1 million. Provision for loan losses slipped 1.3% to $830,000. Total non-interest income rose 5.6% to $7.4 million. Total non-interest expense grew 17.1% to $17.4 million, which included expenses of the three branches from the Pend Oreille Bancorp acquisition and other additional branches.

Prospects: All of Co.'s bank subsidiaries now utilize the same data systems across all channels of the organization allowing for greater efficiency and productivity. In addition, this makes Co.'s locations, products, people and account information more accessible to customers. This should drive results and customer satisfaction going forward. Separately, Co. continues to search externally for sound acquisitions that strategically provide a good fit. On Apr 1 2004, Co.'s Mountain West Bank subsidiary agreed to acquire the Ione, WA branch of American West Bank. This branch is in the vicinity of the Mountain West branch in Newport, WA which was acquired in 2003.

Financial Data

(US$ in Thousands)	3 Mos	12/31/2003	12/31/2002	12/31/2001	12/31/2000	12/31/1999	12/31/1998	12/31/1997
Earnings Per Share	1.49	1.55	1.35	0.97	0.88	0.83	0.76	0.72
Tang. Book Val. Per Share	6.88	8.05	7.24	5.82	5.82	4.96	5.19	4.64
Dividends Per Share	0.600	0.570	0.460	0.430	0.440	0.410	0.300	0.240
Dividend Payout %	39.46	36.97	34.42	44.77	51.08	49.38	39.98	34.34
Income Statement								
Total Interest Income	35,465	130,830	133,989	137,920	78,837	58,921	51,081	44,004
Total Interest Expense	9,076	38,478	47,522	65,546	37,357	25,592	22,204	19,878
Net Interest Income	26,389	92,352	86,467	72,374	41,480	33,329	28,877	24,126
Provision for Loan Losses	830	3,809	5,745	4,525	1,864	1,506	1,490	747
Non-Interest Income	7,411	33,562	25,917	23,251	13,294	11,064	11,259	8,339
Non-Interest Expense	17,426	65,944	57,813	57,385	31,327	24,077	21,606	17,219
Income Before Taxes	15,544	56,161	48,826	33,715	21,583	18,810	17,040	14,499
Eqty Earns/Minority Int.	...	...	...	35	61	51	145	68
Net Income	10,610	38,008	32,402	21,689	14,003	12,179	10,744	9,180
Average Shs. Outstg.	30,960	24,525	23,986	22,193	15,873	14,538	13,958	12,421
Balance Sheet								
Cash & Due from Banks	53,213	77,093	74,624	73,456	41,456	46,277	31,509	26,463
Securities Avail. for Sale	1,109,585	1,050,311	739,961	508,578	211,888	191,385	90,735	93,254
Net Loans & Leases	1,449,535	1,413,392	1,248,666	1,294,924	726,503	586,952	494,249	421,048
Total Assets	2,829,041	2,739,633	2,281,344	2,085,747	1,056,712	884,117	666,651	580,398
Total Deposits	1,591,446	1,597,625	1,459,923	1,446,064	720,570	576,282	444,459	346,784
Long-Term Obligations	886,801	812,294	483,660	367,295	196,791	194,650	120,586	139,257
Total Liabilities	2,576,140	2,501,794	2,069,095	1,908,764	958,599	805,304	591,714	520,789
Net Stockholders' Equity	252,901	237,839	212,249	176,983	98,113	78,813	74,937	59,609
Shares Outstanding	30,563	24,203	23,767	23,202	15,739	14,445	13,930	12,530
Return on Equity %	4.19	15.98	15.26	12.27	14.33	15.51	14.53	15.51
Return on Assets %	0.37	1.38	1.42	1.04	1.33	1.38	1.63	1.59
Equity/Assets %	8.93	8.68	9.30	8.48	9.28	8.91	11.24	10.27
Non-Int. Exp./Tot. Inc. %	40.64	40.11	36.15	35.58	33.93	34.33	34.42	32.76
Price Range	26.74-23.61	26.38-17.13	18.00-13.91	15.27-9.14	10.66-8.00	15.87-10.21	16.12-11.42	13.66-8.38
P/E Ratio	17.95-15.85	17.02-11.05	13.33-10.30	15.75-9.42	12.11-9.09	19.12-12.30	21.21-15.03	18.97-11.64
Average Yield %	2.36	2.71	2.84	3.50	4.82	3.24	2.13	2.41

Address: 49 Commons Loop, Kalispell, MT 59901
Telephone: (406) 756-4200
Web Site: www.glacierbancorp.com

Officers: John S. MacMillan – Chmn., Michael J. Blodnick – Pres., C.E.O.

Institutional Holding
No of Institutions: 17
Shares: 1,694,935   % Held: –

GOLDEN WEST FINANCIAL CORP.

Exchange	Symbol	Price	52Wk Range	Yield	P/E
NYS	GDW	$108.77 (5/28/2004)	116.8-78.14	0.37	14.70

*7 Year Price Score 179.1 *NYSE Composite Index=100 ***12 Month Price Score 50.5**

TRADING VOLUME (thousand shares)

Interim Earnings (Per Share)

Qtr.	Mar	Jun	Sep	Dec
2001	1.10	1.30	1.28	1.43
2002	1.51	1.44	1.56	1.61
2003	1.67	1.76	1.83	1.88
2004	1.93	...	...	...

Interim Dividends (Per Share)

Amt	Decl	Ex	Rec	Pay
0.085Q	7/31/2003	8/13/2003	8/15/2003	9/10/2003
0.10Q	10/28/2003	11/12/2003	11/15/2003	12/10/2003
0.10Q	1/28/2004	2/11/2004	2/15/2004	3/10/2004
0.10Q	4/27/2004	5/12/2004	5/15/2004	6/10/2004

Indicated Div: $0.40

Valuation Analysis

Forecast P/E 13.62 (5/24/2004)

Market Cap	$16.8 Billion	Book Value	6.2 Billion
Price/Book	2.70	Price/Sales	4.32

Dividend Achiever Status

Rank	81	10 Year Growth Rate	14.71%
Total Years of Dividend Growth		20	

Business Summary: Other Depository Banking (MIC: 8.5 SIC: 6035 NAIC:522120)

Golden West Financial, with assets of $82.55 billion as of Dec 31 2003, is the holding company of World Savings Bank, FSB, a federally chartered savings and lending institution. As of Dec 31 2003, Co. operated 479 savings and lending offices in 38 states under the World name. Also, Co. has two other subsidiaries, Atlas Advisers and Atlas Securities, which provide services to Atlas Assets, a registered open-end management investment company sponsored by Co. Atlas Advisers is a registered investment adviser and the investment manager of Atlas Assets's portfolios. Atlas Securities is a registered broker-dealer and the sole distributor of Atlas Fund shares.

Recent Developments: For the quarter ended Mar 31 2004, net income increased 15.2% to $299.7 million from $260.1 million in the corresponding period of the year before. Results for 2004 and 2003 included gains on the sale of securities, mortgage-backed securities and loans of $3.0 million and $15.3 million, and pre-tax gains from changes in the fair value of derivatives of $1.1 million and $2.9 million, respectively. Net interest income advanced 17.1% to $619.3 million. Provision for loan losses dropped 94.6% to $241,000. Total non-interest income declined 10.8% to $59.8 million, while total non-interest expense rose 17.6% to $199.5 million.

Prospects: Earnings continue to benefit from the expansion of Co.'s mortgage portfolio. During the first quarter of 2004, Co.'s mortgage originations amounted to a record $9.40 billion of loans, driven by low interest rates on new home loans. Meanwhile, with regard to lending activity, Co.'s primary product is an adjustable rate mortgage (ARM). During the first quarter of 2004, ARMs comprised 98.0% of Co.'s new originations, which should help limit Co.'s earnings exposure once market interest rates rise. Separately, at Mar 31 2004, Co.'s ratio of nonperforming assets and troubled debt restructured to total assets was 48%.

Financial Data

(US$ in Thousands)	3 Mos	12/31/2003	12/31/2002	12/31/2001	12/31/2000	12/31/1999	12/31/1998	12/31/1997
Earnings Per Share	7.40	7.14	6.12	5.11	3.41	2.87	2.58	2.04
Tang. Book Val. Per Share	40.90	39.09	32.73	27.54	23.27	19.79	18.31	15.75
Dividends Per Share	0.370	0.350	0.300	0.260	0.220	0.190	0.170	0.150
Dividend Payout %	4.99	4.97	4.94	5.08	6.45	6.70	6.65	7.42
Income Statement								
Total Interest Income	939,757	3,528,344	3,497,034	4,209,612	3,796,540	2,825,845	2,962,553	2,832,497
Total Interest Expense	320,503	1,319,960	1,566,740	2,578,280	2,645,372	1,822,360	1,995,231	1,942,002
Net Interest Income	619,254	2,208,384	1,930,294	1,631,332	1,151,168	1,003,485	967,322	890,495
Provision for Loan Losses	241	11,864	21,170	22,265	9,456	(2,089)	11,260	57,609
Non-Interest Income	59,807	313,330	247,000	236,739	160,820	143,302	137,613	81,268
Non-Interest Expense	199,514	720,515	601,494	513,802	424,847	386,147	354,507	326,959
Income Before Taxes	479,306	1,789,335	1,554,630	1,332,004	877,946	762,729	739,168	587,195
Income from Cont Ops	...	...	...	818,823	...	...	447,091	...
Net Income	299,724	1,106,099	958,279	812,805	545,791	479,979	434,580	354,138
Average Shs. Outstg.	155,040	154,987	156,682	160,358	160,277	166,951	173,461	173,319
Balance Sheet								
Securities Avail. for Sale	1,123,463	3,803,028	1,913,440	1,712,146	925,602	796,906	981,180	1,531,742
Net Loans & Leases	80,279,352	74,205,578	58,268,899	41,065,375	33,762,643	27,919,817	25,721,288	33,260,709
Total Assets	86,604,771	82,549,890	68,405,828	58,586,271	55,703,969	42,142,205	38,468,729	39,421,342
Total Deposits	47,384,000	46,726,965	41,038,797	34,472,585	30,047,919	27,714,910	26,219,095	24,109,717
Long–Term Obligations	26,795,874	22,991,491	19,824,656	18,835,235	20,330,588	9,728,168	7,075,225	9,737,085
Total Liabilities	80,361,289	76,602,622	63,380,578	54,302,081	52,016,682	38,947,351	35,344,411	36,892,240
Net Stockholders' Equity	6,243,859	5,947,268	5,025,250	4,284,190	3,687,287	3,194,854	3,124,318	2,698,031
Shares Outstanding	152,635	152,119	153,521	155,531	158,410	161,357	170,583	171,207
Return on Equity %	4.80	18.59	19.06	19.11	14.80	15.02	14.31	13.12
Return on Assets %	0.34	1.33	1.40	1.39	0.97	1.13	1.16	0.89
Equity/Assets %	7.20	7.20	7.34	7.31	6.61	7.58	8.12	6.84
Non–Int. Exp./Tot. Inc. %	19.96	18.75	16.06	11.55	10.73	13.00	11.43	11.22
Price Range	116.8-98.65	103.5-69.67	72.98-57.91	70.00-47.15	69.44-27.19	38.02-29.27	38.08-24.12	32.60-19.96
P/E Ratio	15.78-13.33	14.49-9.76	11.92-9.46	13.70-9.23	20.36-7.97	13.25-10.20	14.76-9.35	15.98-9.78
Average Yield %	0.34	0.42	0.45	0.45	0.52	0.58	0.55	0.59

Address: 1901 Harrison Street, Oakland, CA 94612
Telephone: (510) 446–3420
Web Site: www.gdw.com

Officers: Herbert M. Sandler – Co–Chmn., Co–C.E.O., Marion O. Sandler – Co–Chmn., Co–C.E.O.
Transfer Agents: Mellon Investor Services, LLC, San Francisco, CA

Investor Contact: 510–446–3614
Institutional Holding
No of Institutions: 20
Shares: 28,991,892 **% Held:** –

GORMAN-RUPP CO.

Exchange	Symbol	Price	52Wk Range	Yield	P/E
ASE	GRC	$26.50 (5/28/2004)	28.50-21.95	2.57	23.04

*7 Year Price Score 119.5 ***NYSE Composite Index=100** ***12 Month Price Score 48.6**

Interim Earnings (Per Share)

Qtr.	Mar	Jun	Sep	Dec
2001	0.42	0.47	0.42	0.39
2002	0.25	0.38	0.23	0.19
2003	0.14	0.30	0.30	0.41
2004	0.26	...	...	...

Interim Dividends (Per Share)

Amt	Decl	Ex	Rec	Pay
0.17Q	7/24/2003	8/13/2003	8/15/2003	9/10/2003
0.17Q	10/23/2003	11/12/2003	11/14/2003	12/10/2003
0.17Q	1/26/2004	2/11/2004	2/13/2004	3/10/2004
0.17Q	4/22/2004	5/12/2004	5/14/2004	6/10/2004

Indicated Div: $0.68 (Div. Reinv. Plan)

Valuation Analysis

Forecast P/E 19.05 (5/24/2004)

Market Cap	$226.2 Million	Book Value	116.5 Million
Price/Book	1.98	Price/Sales	1.18

Dividend Achiever Status

Rank	273	10 Year Growth Rate	3.54%
Total Years of Dividend Growth			31

Business Summary: Industrial Machinery and Equipment (MIC: 11.5 SIC: 3561 NAIC:333911)

Gorman-Rupp designs, manufactures and sells pumps and related equipment for use in water, wastewater, construction, industrial, petroleum, original equipment, agricultural, fire protection, heating, ventilating and air conditioning, military and other liquid-handling applications. The types of pumps Co. produces include self-priming, standard and magnetic drive centrifugal, axial and mixed flow, rotary gear, diaphragm, bellows and oscillating. Co.'s larger pumps are sold for use in the construction, industrial, sewage and waste handling fields; for boosting low residential water pressure; for pumping refined petroleum products, for agricultural applications; and for fire fighting.

Recent Developments: For the three months ended Mar 31 2004, net income soared 83.6% to $2.2 million compared with $1.2 million in the corresponding period of 2003. Net income benefited from higher product sales in the industrial, construction and international markets and increased manufacturing utilization. Net sales were $49.4 million, up 12.6% from $43.9 million in the prior-year period. Gross profit rose 20.1% to $10.1 million, or 20.5% of net sales, from $8.4 million, or 19.2% of net sales, the previous year. Operating profit leapt 95.3% to $3.3 million compared with $1.7 million the year before.

Prospects: Although some markets are showing signs of recovery, overall sluggish spending in the capital sector, including the municipal market, continues to pressure companies selling products into this sector. Co.'s shipments during the first quarter of 2004 of fabricated components for the power generation market appeared to level after two years of decline. As of Mar 31 2004, Co.'s order backlog was $56.4 million compared to $58.4 million at Dec 31 2003. Looking ahead, Co. expects to continue to be well-positioned for the long term due to its positive cash flow from operations, no debt and improved profitability.

Financial Data

(US$ in Thousands)	3 Mos	12/31/2003	12/31/2002	12/31/2001	12/31/2000	12/31/1999	12/31/1998	12/31/1997
Earnings Per Share	1.27	1.15	1.05	1.70	1.61	1.52	1.37	1.23
Cash Flow Per Share	0.53	1.64	2.50	3.07	1.90	2.03	2.54	1.37
Tang. Book Val. Per Share	13.69	12.79	12.21	12.63	11.67	10.74	9.75	9.06
Dividends Per Share	0.680	0.680	0.650	0.640	0.620	0.600	0.580	0.560
Dividend Payout %	53.54	59.13	61.90	37.64	38.50	39.47	42.33	45.52
Income Statement								
Total Revenues	49,431	195,826	194,075	203,813	191,484	180,165	172,246	165,568
Total Indirect Exp.	6,859	27,974	27,921	25,959	27,574	25,687	25,562	24,718
Depreciation & Amort.	1,790	7,117	7,035	7,128	6,863	6,489	6,330	5,959
Operating Income	3,271	14,020	13,530	23,035	22,196	21,541	19,152	16,952
Income Taxes	1,296	4,613	5,267	8,450	8,400	8,460	7,400	6,340
Net Income	2,207	9,787	8,936	14,585	13,796	13,081	11,752	10,612
Average Shs. Outstg.	8,543	8,542	8,539	8,555	8,583	8,585	8,600	8,609
Balance Sheet								
Cash & Cash Equivalents	18,033	16,272	13,086	20,583	7,630	4,114	2,359	836
Total Current Assets	97,422	94,262	83,859	89,119	82,289	78,185	78,556	81,695
Total Assets	163,105	160,939	152,846	148,113	145,881	136,875	127,477	127,865
Total Current Liabilities	23,417	21,908	19,282	18,103	19,079	17,439	17,431	17,036
Long-Term Obligations	...	...	291	...	3,413	3,107	783	6,689
Net Stockholders' Equity	116,971	116,462	111,456	107,910	99,999	92,295	83,706	78,060
Net Working Capital	74,005	72,354	64,577	71,016	63,210	60,746	61,125	64,659
Shares Outstanding	8,543	8,543	8,540	8,537	8,565	8,592	8,581	8,609
Operating Profit Margin %	6.61	7.15	6.97	11.30	11.59	11.95	11.11	10.23
Return on Equity %	1.88	8.40	8.01	13.51	13.79	14.17	14.03	13.59
Return on Assets %	1.35	6.08	5.84	9.84	9.45	9.55	9.21	8.29
Debt/Total Assets %	...	...	0.19	...	2.33	2.26	0.61	5.23
Price Range	27.17-23.44	26.98-18.50	31.50-20.51	27.15-17.50	19.00-14.50	18.00-14.44	21.13-13.75	22.00-13.38
P/E Ratio	21.39-18.46	23.46-16.09	30.00-19.53	15.97-10.29	11.80-9.01	11.84-9.50	15.42-10.04	17.89-10.87
Average Yield %	2.68	2.97	2.53	2.91	3.71	3.73	3.19	3.17

Address: 305 Bowman St., Mansfield, OH 44903	Officers: James C. Gorman – Chmn., Jeffrey S. Gorman – Pres., C.E.O., Gen. Man., Mansfield Div.	Investor Contact:419-755-1294
Telephone: (419) 755-1011	Transfer Agents:National City Bank, Cleveland, OH	Institutional Holding
Web Site: www.gormanrupp.com		No of Institutions: 43
		Shares: 3,813,871 % Held: 44.70%

GRAINGER (W.W.) INC.

Exchange	Symbol	Price	52Wk Range	Yield	P/E
NYS	GWW	$54.45 (5/28/2004)	56.09-44.17	1.47	21.10

*7 Year Price Score 105.3 *NYSE Composite Index=100 *12 Month Price Score 51.1

Interim Earnings (Per Share)

Qtr.	Mar	Jun	Sep	Dec
2001	0.45	0.15	0.59	0.65
2002	0.61	0.57	0.64	0.68
2003	0.57	0.60	0.62	0.67
2004	0.69	...	...	...

Interim Dividends (Per Share)

Amt	Decl	Ex	Rec	Pay
0.185Q	7/30/2003	8/7/2003	8/11/2003	9/1/2003
0.185Q	10/29/2003	11/6/2003	11/10/2003	12/1/2003
0.185Q	1/29/2004	2/5/2004	2/9/2004	3/1/2004
0.20Q	4/28/2004	5/6/2004	5/10/2004	6/1/2004

Indicated Div: $0.80

Valuation Analysis

Forecast P/E 19.43 (5/24/2004)

Market Cap	$5.1 Billion	Book Value	N/A
Price/Book	N/A	Price/Sales	N/A

Dividend Achiever Status

Rank	209	10 Year Growth Rate	7.62%
Total Years of Dividend Growth		32	

Business Summary: Engineering Services (MIC: 12.1 SIC: 5063 NAIC:423610)

W.W. Grainger is primarily a supplier of facilities maintenance products in North America through its Branch-based Distribution segment, which includes a network of 575 branches in the U.S., Canada, and Mexico, 17 distribution facilities, and multiple Web sites. Co.'s Lab Safety segment is a direct marketer of safety and other industrial products to U.S. and Canadian businesses. Co.'s Integrated Supply segment offers customers on-site outsourcing services, including business process reengineering, inventory and tool crib management, purchasing management and information management.

Recent Developments: For the three months ended Mar 31 2004, net earnings totaled $62.6 million, up 19.4% compared with $52.4 million in the corresponding period the year before. Results for 2004 included a pre-tax gain of $750,000 from sales of unconsolidated entities. Net sales increased 7.8% to $1.23 billion from $1.14 billion a year earlier. Gross profit climbed 9.1% to $447.5 billion, or 36.4% of net sales, from $410.1 million, or 36.0% of net sales, the previous year. Operating earnings were $100.7 million, up 10.2% compared with $91.4 million in the prior year.

Prospects: Results are being positively affected by increased sales to government accounts, favorable foreign currency exchange rates, and increased Internet sales. Going forward, sales and earnings growth are expected to be driven by Co.'s aggressive branch expansion program, as well as from the addition of new sales representatives, and increased product availability. During 2004, Co. plans to open branches in three new markets including, Houston, TX, St. Louis, MO, and Tampa, FL. Looking ahead, Co. anticipates full-year 2004 earnings of between $2.60 and $2.80 per share, as well as capital expenditures of up to $200.0 million.

Financial Data

(US$ in Thousands)	3 Mos	12/31/2003	12/31/2002	12/31/2001	12/31/2000	12/31/1999	12/31/1998	12/31/1997
Earnings Per Share	2.58	2.46	2.50	1.84	2.05	1.92	2.44	2.27
Cash Flow Per Share	1.01	4.26	3.21	5.39	2.94	0.31	3.41	4.16
Tang. Book Val. Per Share	18.85	18.20	16.58	15.08	14.07	13.46	11.38	11.13
Dividends Per Share	0.740	0.730	0.710	0.690	0.670	0.630	0.580	0.530
Dividend Payout %	28.68	29.87	28.60	37.77	32.68	32.81	23.97	23.34
Income Statement								
Total Revenues	1,227,799	4,667,014	4,643,898	4,754,317	4,977,044	4,533,853	4,341,269	4,136,560
Total Indirect Exp.	346,721	1,250,816	1,205,057	1,250,714	1,250,217	1,335,406	1,189,689	1,101,193
Depreciation & Amort.	26,353	90,253	93,488	103,209	106,893	98,227	78,865	79,651
Operating Income	100,748	387,261	393,155	338,573	335,120	317,228	407,982	393,159
Net Interest Inc./(Exp.)	(181)	(2,668)	(1,590)	(7,847)	(22,512)	(13,990)	(5,092)	(2,565)
Income Taxes	38,554	154,119	162,349	122,750	138,692	123,019	162,343	157,803
Eqty Earns/Minority Int.	(345)	(2,288)	(3,025)	(27,328)	(10,855)	...	...	...
Income from Cont Ops	...	...	235,488	...	...	...	...	...
Net Income	62,559	226,971	211,567	174,530	192,903	180,731	238,504	231,833
Average Shs. Outstg.	91,273	92,394	94,303	94,727	94,223	94,315	97,846	102,178
Balance Sheet								
Cash & Cash Equivalents	434,732	402,824	208,528	168,846	63,384	62,683	43,107	46,929
Total Current Assets	1,715,695	1,633,413	1,484,947	1,392,611	1,483,002	1,471,145	1,206,365	1,182,988
Total Assets	2,685,578	2,624,678	2,437,448	2,331,246	2,459,601	2,564,826	2,103,902	1,997,821
Total Current Liabilities	751,013	706,640	586,266	553,811	747,324	870,534	664,493	533,881
Long-Term Obligations	4,895	4,895	119,693	118,219	125,258	124,928	122,883	131,201
Net Stockholders' Equity	1,858,114	1,845,135	1,667,698	1,603,189	1,537,386	1,480,529	1,278,741	1,294,661
Net Working Capital	964,682	926,773	898,681	838,800	735,678	600,611	541,872	649,107
Shares Outstanding	90,341	91,020	91,568	93,344	93,932	93,381	93,505	97,722
Operating Profit Margin %	8.20	8.29	8.46	7.12	6.73	6.99	9.39	9.50
Return on Equity %	3.36	12.30	14.12	10.88	12.54	12.20	18.65	17.90
Return on Assets %	2.32	8.64	9.66	7.48	7.84	7.04	11.33	11.60
Debt/Total Assets %	0.18	0.18	4.91	5.07	5.09	4.87	5.84	6.56
Price Range	48.65-45.17	53.11-41.93	59.27-39.82	48.52-30.23	56.00-24.63	58.06-37.13	54.47-37.63	49.00-36.06
P/E Ratio	188.86-17.51	21.59-17.04	23.71-15.93	26.37-16.43	27.32-12.01	30.24-19.34	22.32-15.42	21.59-15.89
Average Yield %	1.58	1.55	1.41	1.71	1.75	1.34	1.23	1.25

Address: 100 Grainger Parkway, Lake Forest, IL 60045-5201	**Officers:** Richard L. Keyser - Chmn., C.E.O., Wesley M. Clark - Pres., C.O.O.	**Investor Contact:**847-535-0881 **Institutional Holding**
Telephone: (847) 535-1000	**Transfer Agents:**BankBoston, N.A. c/o EquiServe, Boston, MA	**No of Institutions:** 354
Web Site: www.grainger.com		**Shares:** 61,231,668 **% Held:** 66.60%

HARLEY-DAVIDSON, INC.

Exchange	Symbol	Price	52Wk Range	Yield	P/E
NYS	HDI	$57.49 (5/28/2004)	59.50-38.50	0.70	22.37

*7 Year Price Score 131.5 *NYSE Composite Index=100 *12 Month Price Score 53.4

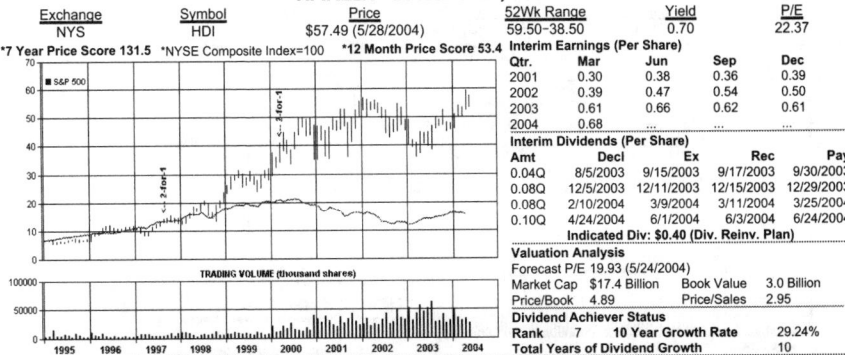

Interim Earnings (Per Share)

Qtr.	Mar	Jun	Sep	Dec
2001	0.30	0.38	0.36	0.39
2002	0.39	0.47	0.54	0.50
2003	0.61	0.66	0.62	0.61
2004	0.68	...	...	...

Interim Dividends (Per Share)

Amt	Decl	Ex	Rec	Pay
0.04Q	8/5/2003	9/15/2003	9/17/2003	9/30/2003
0.08Q	12/5/2003	12/11/2003	12/15/2003	12/29/2003
0.08Q	2/10/2004	3/9/2004	3/11/2004	3/25/2004
0.10Q	4/24/2004	6/1/2004	6/3/2004	6/24/2004

Indicated Div: $0.40 (Div. Reinv. Plan)

Valuation Analysis

Forecast P/E 19.93 (5/24/2004)

Market Cap	$17.4 Billion	Book Value	3.0 Billion
Price/Book	4.89	Price/Sales	2.95

Dividend Achiever Status

Rank	7	10 Year Growth Rate	29.24%
Total Years of Dividend Growth		10	

Business Summary: Automotive (MIC: 15.1 SIC: 3751 NAIC:336991)

Harley-Davidson is a motorcycle manufacturer. Co.'s Motorcycles and Related Products segment designs, manufactures and sells primarily heavyweight touring, custom and performance motorcycles as well as a full line of motorcycle parts, accessories, clothing and collectibles. Co.'s motorcycle brands include Harley-Davidson®and Buell®. The Financial Services segment, consisting of Co.'s subsidiary Harley-Davidson Financial Services, Inc. and its subsidiaries, provides financing and servicing of wholesale inventory receivables and retail loans, primarily for the purchase of motorcycles, as well as property/casualty insurance and extended service contracts through certain unaffiliated carriers.

Recent Developments: For the first quarter ended Mar 28 2004, net income advanced 9.9% to $204.6 million compared with $186.2 million in the corresponding prior-year quarter. Net product revenue increased 4.7% to $1.17 billion from $1.11 billion a year earlier. Harley-Davidson®motorcycle sales grew 4.8% to $918.8 million, while Buell®motorcycle sales rose 7.7% to $22.1 million. Sales of parts and accessories climbed 5.8% to $169.2 million, while general merchandise and other product sales decreased 2.1% to $55.6 million. Financial services revenue jumped 13.7% to $80.5 million from $70.8 million in 2003. Total Harley-Davidson motorcycle shipments climbed 4.9% to 74,090 units.

Prospects: Co. began 2004 with continuing momentum from its 100th Anniversary as its U.S. dealer network continues to post higher sales. In addition, Co. achieved its first quarter motorcycle production target, setting the pace to reach its goal of 317,000 Harley-Davidson®motorcycles for the full year. The strong manufacturing performance supports Co.'s long-range objective to satisfy demand for 400,000 Harley-Davidson motorcycles in 2007 and to deliver an annual earnings growth rate in the mid-teens. On Apr 26 2004, Co. increased its quarterly dividend by 25.0% to $0.10 share and authorized an additional purchase of up to 20.0 million of its shares.

Financial Data
(US$ in Thousands)

	3 Mos	12/31/2003	12/31/2002	12/31/2001	12/31/2000	12/31/1999	12/31/1998	12/31/1997
Earnings Per Share	2.57	2.50	1.90	1.43	1.13	0.86	0.69	0.56
Cash Flow Per Share	1.16	3.07	2.55	2.47	1.83	1.34	1.02	1.17
Tang. Book Val. Per Share	9.19	9.63	7.21	5.63	4.47	3.65	3.19	2.58
Dividends Per Share	0.240	0.195	0.135	0.110	0.090	0.080	0.070	0.060
Dividend Payout %	9.33	7.80	7.10	8.04	8.62	10.11	10.14	10.71
Income Statement								
Total Revenues	1,246,195	4,903,733	4,302,470	3,544,959	2,943,543	2,480,624	2,084,167	1,774,924
Total Indirect Exp.	177,520	684,175	639,366	578,777	513,024	447,512	377,265	328,569
Depreciation & Amort.	50,947	196,918	175,778	153,061	133,348	113,822	87,422	70,178
Operating Income	312,922	1,149,264	882,702	662,501	514,972	415,859	333,616	270,003
Net Interest Inc./(Exp.)	4,970	23,088	16,541	17,478	17,583	8,014	3,828	7,871
Income Taxes	112,599	405,107	305,610	235,709	200,843	153,592	122,729	102,232
Net Income	204,580	760,928	580,217	437,746	347,713	267,201	213,500	174,070
Average Shs. Outstg.	299,932	304,470	305,158	306,248	307,470	309,714	309,406	307,896
Balance Sheet								
Cash & Cash Equivalents	1,102,687	812,449	280,928	439,438	419,736	183,415	165,170	147,462
Total Current Assets	2,707,275	2,729,127	2,066,586	1,665,264	1,297,264	948,994	844,963	704,021
Total Assets	4,689,970	4,923,088	3,861,217	3,118,495	2,436,404	2,112,077	1,920,209	1,598,901
Total Current Liabilities	895,661	955,773	990,052	716,110	497,743	518,154	468,515	361,688
Long-Term Obligations	670,000	670,000	380,000	380,000	355,000	280,000	280,000	280,000
Net Stockholders' Equity	2,767,200	2,957,692	2,232,915	1,756,283	1,405,655	1,161,080	1,029,911	826,668
Shares Outstanding	295,145	301,510	302,662	302,789	302,070	302,722	305,862	304,650
Statistical Record								
Operating Profit Margin %	25.11	23.43	20.51	18.68	17.49	16.76	16.00	15.21
Return on Equity %	7.39	25.72	25.98	24.92	24.73	23.01	20.72	21.05
Return on Assets %	4.36	15.45	15.02	14.03	14.27	12.65	11.11	10.88
Debt/Total Assets %	14.28	13.60	9.84	12.18	14.57	13.25	14.58	17.51
Price Range	54.09-46.00	52.45-35.95	57.00-42.83	55.66-35.19	50.00-29.63	32.03-23.22	23.69-12.56	15.41-8.47
P/E Ratio	21.05-17.90	20.98-14.38	30.00-22.54	38.92-24.61	44.25-26.22	37.25-27.00	34.33-18.21	27.51-15.12
Average Yield %	0.47	0.52	0.20	0.24	0.22	0.28	0.52	0.42

Address: 3700 West Juneau Avenue, Milwaukee, WI 53208	Officers: Jeffrey L. Bleustein – Chmn., C.E.O., James M. Brostowitz – V.P., Treas., Contr.	Investor Contact:877-437-8625
Telephone: (414) 342-4680	Transfer Agents:Computershare Investor Services, LLC, Chicago, IL	Institutional Holding No of Institutions: 3
Web Site: www.harley-davidson.com		Shares: 837,804 % Held: –

HARLEYSVILLE GROUP, INC. (PA)

Exchange	Symbol	Price	52Wk Range	Yield	P/E
NMS	HGIC	$18.95 (5/28/2004)	25.86–17.84	3.59	N.M.

*7 Year Price Score 94.8   *NYSE Composite Index=100   ***12 Month Price Score 42.0**

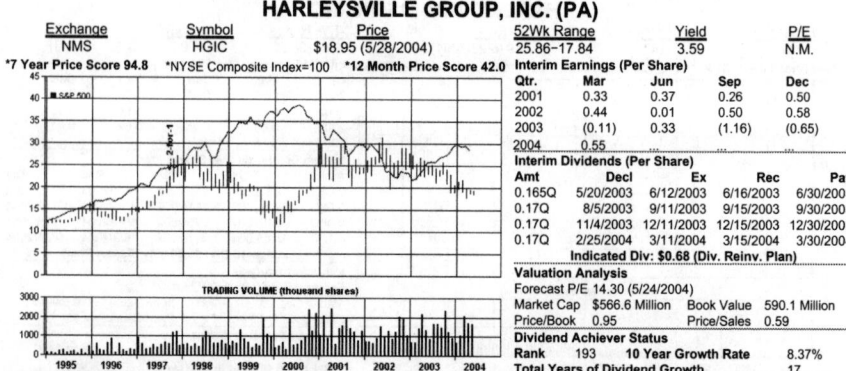

Interim Earnings (Per Share)

Qtr.	Mar	Jun	Sep	Dec
2001	0.33	0.37	0.26	0.50
2002	0.44	0.01	0.50	0.58
2003	(0.11)	0.33	(1.16)	(0.65)
2004	0.55			

Interim Dividends (Per Share)

Amt	Decl	Ex	Rec	Pay
0.165Q	5/20/2003	6/12/2003	6/16/2003	6/30/2003
0.17Q	8/5/2003	9/11/2003	9/15/2003	9/30/2003
0.17Q	11/4/2003	12/11/2003	12/15/2003	12/30/2003
0.17Q	2/25/2004	3/11/2004	3/15/2004	3/30/2004

Indicated Div: $0.68 (Div. Reinv. Plan)

Valuation Analysis

Forecast P/E 14.30 (5/24/2004)

Market Cap $566.6 Million	Book Value 590.1 Million
Price/Book 0.95	Price/Sales 0.59

Dividend Achiever Status

Rank 193	10 Year Growth Rate	8.37%
Total Years of Dividend Growth		17

Business Summary: Insurance (MIC: 8.2 SIC: 6331 NAIC:524126)

Harleysville Group Inc. is an insurance holding company that engages, through its subsidiaries, in the property and casualty insurance business on a regional basis. Harleysville Group and Harleysville Mutual Insurance Company, which owned 57.0% of Co.'s outstanding shares as of Dec 31 2003, operate together as a network of regional insurance companies that underwrite a broad line of personal and commercial coverages, including automobile, homeowners, commercial multi-peril and workers compensation. These insurance coverages are marketed primarily in the Eastern and Midwestern U.S. through approximately 1,700 insurance agencies.

Recent Developments: For the quarter ended Mar 31 2004, net income was $16.5 million versus a net loss of $3.2 million in the prior–year quarter. Results for 2003 included an after–tax charge of about $12.9 million related to a workers compensation reserve adjustment. Total revenues increased 9.5% to $245.6 million from $224.4 million the previous year. Revenues included realized investment gains of $12.5 million in 2004 and realized investment losses of $433,000 in 2003. Premiums earned grew 4.1% to $206.9 million. Net investment income rose 0.9% to $21.6 million. Losses and loss settlement expenses declined 7.7% to $151.1 million. Co.'s combined ratio improved to $107.2% from $115.4% a year earlier.

Prospects: Going forward, results should continue to benefit from solid premium growth, controlled loss experience, and the benefits of Co.'s sales distribution network. However, these improvements may be hampered by a small overall decline in renewed business, especially in the workers compensation and personal lines, as Co.'s disciplined approach to program selection will result in a rise in the number of risks it declines. Nevertheless, Co. remains encouraged with the recent profitability trends of its current book of business, and is confident that this strategy will contribute to improving results in the future.

Financial Data

(US$ in Thousands)	12/31/2003	12/31/2002	12/31/2001	12/31/2000	12/31/1999	12/31/1998	12/31/1997	12/31/1996
Earnings Per Share	(1.59)	1.53	1.46	1.67	1.45	2.15	1.86	1.03
Tang. Book Val. Per Share	19.15	21.12	20.04	19.53	18.28	18.16	15.49	13.09
Dividends Per Share	0.670	0.630	0.580	0.550	0.520	0.480	0.440	0.400
Dividend Payout %	N.M.	41.17	39.72	32.93	35.86	22.32	23.65	38.83
Income Statement								
Total Premium Income	823,407	764,636	729,889	688,330	707,200	664,604	624,905	615,197
Net Investment Income	86,597	86,265	85,518	86,791	85,894	86,025	81,783	78,008
Other Income	14,961	(3,165)	12,344	27,450	31,662	28,682	17,491	14,220
Total Revenues	924,965	847,736	827,751	802,571	824,756	779,311	724,179	707,425
Total Indirect Exp.	207,762	189,834	185,655	184,537	187,386	173,766	160,705	157,047
Inc. Before Inc. Taxes	(89,450)	56,482	51,800	57,705	47,752	80,441	67,281	31,375
Income Taxes	(41,821)	10,227	8,307	9,013	4,935	17,028	13,209	2,695
Income from Cont Ops	...	...	...	...	42,817	...	...	...
Net Income	(47,629)	46,255	43,493	48,692	39,913	63,413	54,072	28,680
Average Shs. Outstg.	29,985	30,295	29,818	29,136	29,565	29,519	29,032	27,844
Balance Sheet								
Cash & Cash Equivalents	13,430	2,944	1,839	28,395	20,273	3,799	1,460	2,120
Premiums Due	328,601	235,945	226,010	201,668	196,293	197,569	183,951	173,653
Invst. Assets: Total	1,823,222	1,617,208	1,574,449	1,575,244	1,544,799	1,564,544	1,423,240	1,256,104
Total Assets	2,680,389	2,311,524	2,045,290	2,021,862	2,020,056	1,934,497	1,801,195	1,622,612
Long–Term Obligations	120,145	95,620	96,055	96,450	96,810	97,140	97,440	97,715
Net Stockholders' Equity	572,747	632,112	590,298	566,581	526,894	529,658	446,515	370,245
Shares Outstanding	29,900	29,917	29,444	29,001	28,812	29,150	28,821	28,278
Statistical Record								
Return on Equity %	N.M.	7.31	7.36	8.59	8.12	11.97	12.10	7.74
Return on Assets %	N.M.	2.00	2.12	2.40	2.11	3.27	3.00	1.76
Price Range	27.50-18.99	31.44-19.90	30.00-20.40	29.81-11.81	25.81-13.13	28.22-18.88	27.13-14.50	16.38-12.38
P/E Ratio	N/A	20.55-13.01	20.55-13.97	17.85-7.07	17.80-9.05	13.13-8.78	14.58-7.80	15.90-12.01
Average Yield %	2.86	3.01	1.69	3.09	2.79	2.06	2.30	2.90

Address: 355 Maple Avenue,	Officers: William W. Scranton III – Chmn., M. Lee	Investor Contact:215–256–5020
Harleysville, PA 19438-2297	Patkus – Pres., C.O.O.	Institutional Holding
Telephone: (215) 256-5000	Transfer Agents:Mellon Investor Services,	No of Institutions: 11
Web Site: www.harleysvillegroup.com	Ridgefield Park, NJ	Shares: 185,306,015 % Held: –

HARLEYSVILLE NATIONAL CORP.

Exchange	Symbol	Price	52Wk Range	Yield	P/E
NMS	HNBC	$24.95 (5/28/2004)	32.47-20.98	2.73	17.09

*7 Year Price Score 161.2 ***NYSE Composite Index=100** ***12 Month Price Score 44.2**

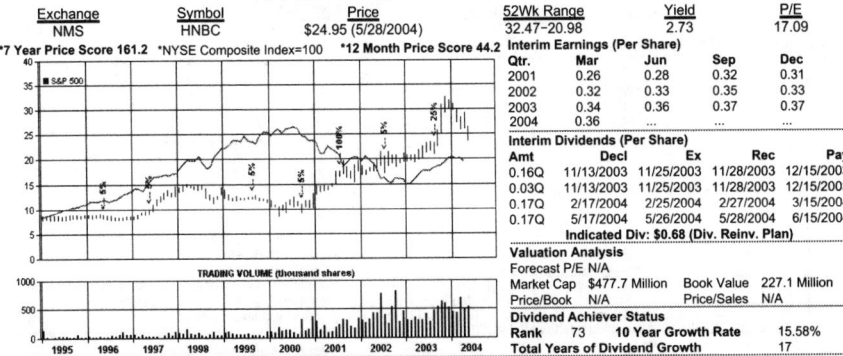

Interim Earnings (Per Share)

Qtr.	Mar	Jun	Sep	Dec
2001	0.26	0.28	0.32	0.31
2002	0.32	0.33	0.35	0.33
2003	0.34	0.36	0.37	0.37
2004	0.36	...	...	...

Interim Dividends (Per Share)

Amt	Decl	Ex	Rec	Pay
0.16Q	11/13/2003	11/25/2003	11/28/2003	12/15/2003
0.03Q	11/13/2003	11/25/2003	11/28/2003	12/15/2003
0.17Q	2/17/2004	2/25/2004	2/27/2004	3/15/2004
0.17Q	5/17/2004	5/26/2004	5/28/2004	6/15/2004

Indicated Div: $0.68 (Div. Reinv. Plan)

Valuation Analysis

Forecast P/E N/A

Market Cap	$477.7 Million	Book Value	227.1 Million
Price/Book	N/A	Price/Sales	N/A

Dividend Achiever Status

Rank	73	10 Year Growth Rate	15.58%

10 Year Years of Dividend Growth 17

Business Summary: Commercial Banking (MIC: 8.1 SIC: 6021 NAIC:522110)

Harleysville National Corporation, is the parent bank holding company of Harleysville National Bank and Trust Company, Citizen's National Bank and Security National Bank. Through its banking subsidiaries, Co. is engaged in the full–service commercial banking and trust business, including accepting time and demand deposits, making secured and unsecured commercial and consumer loans, financing commercial transactions, making construction and mortgage loans and performing corporate pension and personal investment and trust services. Co. operates 40 branch offices located in ten counties throughout Eastern Pennsylvania. As of Dec 31 2003, Co. had total assets of $2.51 billion.

Recent Developments: For the three months ended Mar 31 2004, net income rose 5.2% to $8.9 million compared with $8.5 million in the corresponding quarter of the previous year. Interest income fell 4.6% to $29.2 million from $30.6 million in the year–earlier period. Interest expense dropped 21.5% to $8.9 million from $11.4 million in 2003. Net interest income climbed 5.4% to $20.2 million from $19.2 million in the prior–year quarter. Total non–interest income decreased 19.8% to $5.8 million from $7.2 million the year before. Total non–interest expense declined 10.9% to $13.8 million from $15.5 million in the previous year.

Prospects: On May 4 2004, Co. announced that it has completed the acquisition of Millennium Bank, a $200.0 million bank, which specializes in commercial lending and client relationship banking, and its wholly–owned subsidiary, Cumberland Advisors, Inc., a registered investment advisor that specializes in fixed income and money management, for approximately $46.0 million The transaction brings Co.'s assets to $2.70 billion and doubles the size of its trust and wealth management group to $1.40 billion in assets. Co. expects the transaction to be accretive to earnings per share within the first year after consummation.

Financial Data

(US$ in Thousands)	12/31/2003	12/31/2002	12/31/2001	12/31/2000	12/31/1999	12/31/1998	12/31/1997	12/31/1996
Earnings Per Share	1.44	1.33	1.17	1.05	1.02	0.92	0.82	0.71
Tang. Book Val. Per Share	9.52	8.66	7.83	7.06	5.85	5.93	5.31	4.74
Dividends Per Share	0.650	0.560	0.490	0.540	0.360	0.340	0.300	0.190
Dividend Payout %	45.41	42.22	42.20	51.96	35.79	37.07	37.27	27.35
Income Statement								
Total Interest Income	119,200	132,630	138,679	131,811	106,117	87,597	80,202	73,718
Total Interest Expense	40,079	52,610	64,937	65,774	46,873	37,809	33,851	30,876
Net Interest Income	79,121	80,020	73,742	66,037	59,244	49,788	46,351	42,842
Provision for Loan Losses	3,200	4,370	3,930	2,312	1,907	2,140	2,500	2,082
Non–Interest Income	27,638	22,523	22,225	12,206	10,092	9,810	7,391	5,115
Non–Interest Expense	59,629	56,297	55,043	44,677	38,438	32,573	28,529	25,874
Income Before Taxes	43,930	41,876	36,994	31,254	28,991	24,885	22,713	20,001
Net Income	35,333	32,927	28,820	25,604	22,347	18,776	16,662	14,408
Average Shs. Outstg.	24,624	24,625	24,623	24,358	21,844	20,353	20,293	20,241
Balance Sheet								
Cash & Due from Banks	56,306	62,177	62,974	52,018	42,154	37,763	38,471	39,407
Securities Avail. for Sale	904,870	949,056	706,371	570,619	450,959	389,344	257,068	209,795
Net Loans & Leases	1,391,638	1,316,102	1,301,051	1,196,845	1,047,768	829,937	727,528	670,700
Total Assets	2,510,939	2,490,864	2,208,971	1,935,213	1,635,679	1,332,389	1,116,254	1,026,128
Total Deposits	1,979,081	1,979,822	1,746,862	1,489,050	1,231,265	1,033,968	919,071	847,699
Long–Term Obligations	177,750	167,750	132,750	110,750	130,250	93,500	17,000	35,000
Total Liabilities	2,283,886	2,284,658	2,019,622	1,761,677	1,506,019	1,209,578	1,006,462	928,497
Net Stockholders' Equity	227,053	206,206	189,349	173,536	129,660	122,811	109,792	97,631
Shares Outstanding	23,845	23,785	23,997	24,305	21,816	20,368	20,316	20,229
Statistical Record								
Return on Equity %	15.56	15.96	15.22	14.75	17.23	15.28	15.17	14.75
Return on Assets %	1.40	1.32	1.30	1.32	1.36	1.40	1.49	1.40
Equity/Assets %	9.04	8.27	8.57	8.96	7.92	9.21	9.83	9.51
Non–Int. Exp./Tot. Inc. %	40.60	36.28	34.20	31.02	33.07	33.44	32.56	32.82
Price Range	32.47-19.46	21.52-16.82	19.76-13.05	13.21-8.62	13.82-11.43	15.03-11.23	14.51-7.98	9.01-7.73
P/E Ratio	22.55-13.52	16.18-12.65	16.89-11.15	12.59-8.21	13.55-11.20	16.34-12.21	17.70-9.73	12.69-10.89
Average Yield %	2.76	2.93	3.07	5.00	2.96	2.48	2.76	2.28

Address: 483 Main Street, Harleysville, PA 19438	Officers: Walter E. Daller – Chmn., Pres., C.E.O., Gregg J. Wagner – Exec. V.P., C.O.O., Treas.	Investor Contact: 800–423–3955
Telephone: (215) 256–8851	Transfer Agents: American Stock Transfer &Trust Company, New York, NY	Institutional Holding No of Institutions: –
Web Site: www.hncbank.com		Shares: – % Held: –

HAVERTY FURNITURE COS., INC.

Exchange	Symbol	Price	52Wk Range	Yield	P/E
NYS	HVT	$17.55 (5/28/2004)	24.15-15.30	1.42	15.53

*7 Year Price Score 147.6   *NYSE Composite Index=100   *12 Month Price Score 42.7

Interim Earnings (Per Share)

Qtr.	Mar	Jun	Sep	Dec
2001	0.20	0.12	0.26	0.48
2002	0.30	0.17	0.27	0.36
2003	0.22	0.10	0.33	0.43
2004	0.27	...	...	...

Interim Dividends (Per Share)

Amt	Decl	Ex	Rec	Pay
0.058Q	7/21/2003	8/6/2003	8/8/2003	8/22/2003
0.063Q	10/30/2003	11/7/2003	11/12/2003	11/26/2003
0.063Q	2/6/2004	2/11/2004	2/16/2004	2/27/2004
0.063Q	5/4/2004	5/12/2004	5/14/2004	5/31/2004
		Indicated Div: $0.23		

Valuation Analysis

Forecast P/E 14.06 (5/24/2004)
Market Cap $300.8 Million   Book Value 259.0 Million
Price/Book 1.53   Price/Sales 0.52

Dividend Achiever Status

Rank 236   10 Year Growth Rate   5.90%
Total Years of Dividend Growth   33

Business Summary: Retail – Furniture &Home Furnishings (MIC: 5.9 SIC: 5712 NAIC:442110)

Haverty Furniture Companies is a full−service home furnishings retailer with 113 stores in 14 southern and central states as of Jul 31 2003. Co.'s stores, primarily targeted at middle and upper−middle income families, offer a wide selection of well−known brand names of furniture, such as *Broyhill, Thomasville, Lane/Action, La−Z−Boy, Bernhardt,* and *Clayton Marcus.* Co. has regional warehouses located in Charlotte, NC, Jackson, MS and Ocala, FL serving all of Co.'s local markets except for Dallas, TX, and Atlanta, GA, which each have a metropolitan area warehouse.

Recent Developments: For the first quarter ended Mar 31 2004, net income jumped 25.6% to $6.2 million compared with $4.9 million in the equivalent 2003 quarter. The improvement in earnings was primarily attributed to sales, pricing discipline, merchandising strategy and efforts to leverage all aspects of Co.'s business. Net sales advanced 8.5% to $190.3 million from $175.4 million a year earlier, reflecting increased demand for Co.'s merchandise offerings stimulated by an improving economy and strong housing activity. Gross profit climbed 14.0% to $98.0 million from $85.9 million the year before. Credit service charges dropped 31.1% to $1.3 million. Comparable−store sales increased 4.0% year over year.

Prospects: Co. announced its expansion plans into Cincinnati, OH and the additional stores to be opened in the Washington, DC and San Antonio, TX markets. Meanwhile, Co.'s Florida distribution center is currently under construction and is scheduled to open in the fall of 2004. Co. is optimistic about its expansion programs that will extend its reach and continue to strengthen its presence in key markets by investing in distinguished locations and the distribution network needed to efficiently support that growth. Overall prospects for the near term appear favorable.

Financial Data

(US$ in Thousands)	3 Mos	12/31/2003	12/31/2002	12/31/2001	12/31/2000	12/31/1999	12/31/1998	12/31/1997
Earnings Per Share	1.13	1.08	1.10	1.06	1.31	1.19	0.72	0.57
Cash Flow Per Share	0.49	3.65	3.84	1.39	0.78	3.04	2.36	1.06
Tang. Book Val. Per Share	11.48	11.02	10.30	9.45	8.63	7.81	7.07	6.79
Dividends Per Share	0.240	0.230	0.220	0.210	0.200	0.190	0.160	0.160
Dividend Payout %	20.34	21.75	20.00	19.81	15.45	15.96	22.91	28.07
Income Statement								
Total Revenues	191,605	751,027	713,010	689,178	693,575	633,721	557,258	506,118
Total Indirect Exp.	89,994	331,600	307,196	288,088	280,753	253,921	231,407	211,887
Depreciation & Amort.	4,774	17,199	15,903	16,239	15,738	14,844	14,272	13,792
Operating Income	9,808	40,442	41,287	46,602	55,324	54,008	40,102	35,028
Net Interest Inc./(Exp.)	(1,125)	(3,872)	(6,561)	(10,581)	(11,707)	(11,402)	(13,183)	(14,330)
Income Taxes	3,658	14,444	14,588	13,630	16,010	15,470	9,460	7,400
Income from Cont Ops	...	24,281	...	...	27,851	...	...	...
Net Income	6,150	25,331	24,315	22,710	24,495	27,400	16,835	13,387
Average Shs. Outstg.	23,185	22,437	22,145	21,502	21,203	22,982	23,404	23,340
Balance Sheet								
Cash & Cash Equivalents	39,535	31,591	3,764	727	3,256	1,762	1,874	390
Total Current Assets	249,390	256,485	263,825	305,755	295,992	271,678	278,177	289,629
Total Assets	429,258	433,202	404,839	460,905	448,163	404,648	392,901	406,514
Total Current Liabilities	92,420	104,196	101,520	123,903	95,520	98,434	70,467	132,908
Long−Term Obligations	63,547	65,402	69,821	131,599	170,369	134,687	161,778	111,489
Net Stockholders' Equity	259,031	252,736	224,881	201,398	179,375	168,793	158,058	159,554
Net Working Capital	156,970	152,289	162,305	181,852	200,472	173,244	207,710	156,721
Shares Outstanding	22,549	22,931	21,832	21,302	20,773	21,610	22,330	23,482
Operating Profit Margin %	4.83	5.38	5.79	6.76	7.97	8.52	7.19	6.92
Return on Equity %	2.16	9.60	10.81	11.27	15.52	16.23	10.65	8.39
Return on Assets %	1.30	5.60	6.00	4.92	6.21	6.77	4.28	3.29
Debt/Total Assets %	14.80	15.09	17.24	28.55	38.01	33.28	41.17	27.42
Price Range	23.30−19.35	24.15−9.48	20.86−9.77	16.55−9.25	13.37−8.25	18.72−9.01	11.45−6.27	7.07−5.15
P/E Ratio	20.62−17.12	22.36−8.78	18.96−8.88	15.61−8.73	10.21−6.30	15.73−7.57	15.90−8.71	12.40−9.03
Average Yield %	1.12	1.44	1.41	1.58	1.83	1.40	1.69	2.66

Address: 780 Johnson Ferry Road, Atlanta, GA 30342
Telephone: (404) 443−2900
Web Site: www.havertys.com

Officers: Clarence H. Ridley − Chmn., Clarence H. Smith − Pres., C.E.O.
Transfer Agents: SunTrust Bank, Atlanta, GA

Investor Contact: 404−443−2900
Institutional Holding
No of Institutions: 22
Shares: 2,576,185   **% Held:** −

HEALTH CARE PROPERTY INVESTORS, INC.

Exchange	Symbol	Price	52Wk Range	Yield	P/E
NYS	HCP	$24.03 (5/28/2004)	29.09-19.83	6.95	24.27

*7 Year Price Score 132.6 *NYSE Composite Index=100 *12 Month Price Score 44.8

Interim Earnings (Per Share)

Qtr.	Mar	Jun	Sep	Dec
2001	0.19	0.27	0.16	0.27
2002	0.21	0.29	0.26	0.20
2003	0.18	0.18	0.26	0.32
2004	0.23	...	...	...

Interim Dividends (Per Share)

Amt	Decl	Ex	Rec	Pay
0.415Q	10/23/2003	10/31/2003	11/4/2003	11/20/2003
0.418Q	1/22/2004	2/2/2004	2/4/2004	2/19/2004
100%	1/22/2004	3/2/2004	2/4/2004	3/1/2004
0.418Q	4/26/2004	5/4/2004	5/6/2004	5/21/2004

Indicated Div: $1.67 (Div. Reinv. Plan)

Valuation Analysis

Forecast P/E 13.12 (5/24/2004)

Market Cap $1.4 Billion	Book Value 1.2 Billion
Price/Book 2.87	Price/Sales 8.36

Dividend Achiever Status

Rank 233	10 Year Growth Rate	6.05%
Total Years of Dividend Growth		18

Business Summary: Property, Real Estate &Development (MIC: 8.3 SIC: 6798 NAIC:525930)

Health Care Property Investors is a real estate investment trust that invests in healthcare–related facilities throughout the United States, including long–term care facilities, congregate care and assisted living facilities, acute care and rehabilitation hospitals, medical office buildings and physician group practice clinics. Co.'s investment portfolio as of Dec 31 2003 included 554 facilities in 44 states. Co.'s investments included 173 long–term care facilities, 124 retirement and assisted living facilities, 196 medical office buildings, 31 hospitals and 30 other health care facilities.

Recent Developments: For the first quarter ended Mar 31 2004, income from continuing operations increased 15.2% to $36.3 million from $31.5 million in the corresponding prior–year quarter. Earnings excluded income of $10.6 million in 2004 and a loss of $3.8 million in 2003 from discontinued operations. Total revenue advanced 14.2% to $98.1 million from $85.9 million a year earlier. Notably, rental income grew 13.9% to $63.1 million, while medical office building rental income climbed 20.8% to $24.6 million. Income from operations rose 16.9% to $39.1 million from $33.5 million the year before. Funds from operations increased 38.9% to $54.0 million from $38.9 million in 2003.

Prospects: Co. recently acquired a healthcare laboratory and biotech research facility located in San Diego, CA for approximately $40.0 million. On Feb 27 2004, Co. sold a portfolio of seven medical office buildings and ten other healthcare facilities for a sales price of $127.6 million and used a portion of the proceeds to retire $31.3 million of related mortgage debt. Separately, on Apr 30 2004, Co. acquired seven long–term care facilities with a total of 700 beds for approximately $47.0 million. Looking ahead, Co. expects full–year 2004 earnings to be approximately $1.19 per share. Funds from operations for 2004 are expected to range from $1.76 to $1.81 per share.

Financial Data

(US$ in Thousands)	12/31/2003	12/31/2002	12/31/2001	12/31/2000	12/31/1999	12/31/1998	12/31/1997	12/31/1996
Earnings Per Share	0.94	0.96	0.89	1.06	1.12	1.27	1.09	1.05
Tang. Book Val. Per Share	8.81	8.46	8.62	8.55	8.99	6.57	6.36	5.87
Dividends Per Share	1.660	1.630	1.550	1.470	1.390	1.310	1.230	1.150
Dividend Payout %	176.59	168.91	174.15	138.02	123.55	103.14	112.32	109.52
Income Statement								
Rental Income	248,773	331,737	310,602	306,830	199,570	138,439	113,920	104,627
Total Income	394,405	359,576	332,460	329,807	224,793	161,549	128,503	120,393
Total Indirect Exp.	105,916	103,330	97,337	87,856	75,694	46,142	33,232	29,975
Depreciation	79,095	75,722	84,098	72,590	47,860	32,523	25,656	23,149
Eqty Earns/Minority Int.	2,889	...	...	...	...	...	...	...
Income from Cont Ops	152,184	137,178	...	133,493	...	...	...	...
Net Income	158,585	137,380	121,166	133,767	96,225	87,167	64,789	60,641
Average Shs. Outstg.	126,130	116,294	107,950	102,200	69,722	67,328	57,988	57,652
Balance Sheet								
Cash & Cash Equivalents	17,768	8,495	8,408	58,623	7,696	4,504	4,084	2,811
Ttl Real Estate Inv.	2,505,845	2,371,411	2,194,556	2,100,509	2,192,988	1,131,119	786,502	623,734
Total Assets	3,035,957	2,748,417	2,431,153	2,398,703	2,469,390	1,356,612	940,964	753,653
Long–Term Obligations	1,407,284	1,333,848	1,057,752	1,158,928	1,179,507	709,045	452,858	379,504
Total Liabilities	1,595,340	1,467,528	1,184,429	1,254,148	1,269,133	761,193	498,695	416,847
Net Stockholders' Equity	1,440,617	1,280,889	1,246,724	1,144,555	1,200,257	595,419	442,269	336,806
Shares Outstanding	131,039	118,939	112,773	101,747	102,842	61,974	60,432	57,356
Net Inc.+Depr./Assets %	7.82	7.70	8.40	8.60	5.80	8.80	9.60	11.10
Return on Equity %	10.56	10.70	9.71	11.66	8.01	14.63	14.64	18.00
Return on Assets %	5.01	4.99	4.98	5.56	3.89	6.42	6.88	8.04
Price Range	25.63-16.68	22.43-18.11	19.51-14.78	14.97-11.84	16.47-10.97	19.63-14.44	20.16-16.00	18.75-15.50
P/E Ratio	27.27-17.74	23.36-18.86	21.92-16.61	14.12-11.17	14.70-9.79	15.45-11.37	18.49-14.68	17.86-14.76
Average Yield %	8.01	8.00	8.87	10.77	10.09	7.57	6.83	6.81

Address: 4675 MacArthur Court, Newport Beach, CA 92660	Officers: Kenneth B. Roath – Chmn., James F. Flaherty III – Pres., C.E.O.	Investor Contact:949–221–0600
Telephone: (949) 221–0600	Transfer Agents:The Bank of New York, New York, NY	Institutional Holding
Web Site: www.hcpi.com		No of Institutions: 20
		Shares: 1,759,046 % Held: –

HEALTHCARE REALTY TRUST, INC.

Exchange	Symbol	Price	52Wk Range	Yield	P/E
NYS	HR	$36.55 (5/28/2004)	43.66-29.09	6.95	22.42

*7 Year Price Score 132.7   *NYSE Composite Index=100   ***12 Month Price Score 46.6**

Interim Earnings (Per Share)

Qtr.	Mar	Jun	Sep	Dec
2001	0.47	0.44	0.45	0.45
2002	0.44	0.50	0.44	0.17
2003	0.45	0.42	0.42	0.37
2004	0.42	...	...	...

Interim Dividends (Per Share)

Amt	Decl	Ex	Rec	Pay
0.62Q	7/22/2003	8/13/2003	8/15/2003	9/4/2003
0.625Q	10/28/2003	11/12/2003	11/14/2003	12/4/2003
0.63Q	1/27/2004	2/11/2004	2/13/2004	3/4/2004
0.635Q	4/27/2004	5/12/2004	5/14/2004	6/3/2004

Indicated Div: $2.54 (Div. Reinv. Plan)

Valuation Analysis

Forecast P/E 12.78 (5/24/2004)

Market Cap	$1.5 Billion	Book Value	902.3 Million
Price/Book	1.73	Price/Sales	8.13

Dividend Achiever Status

Rank	65	10 Year Growth Rate	16.19%
Total Years of Dividend Growth		10	

Business Summary: Property, Real Estate &Development (MIC: 8.3 SIC: 6798 NAIC:525930)

Healthcare Realty Trust is a self–managed and self–administered real estate investment trust (REIT) that integrates owning, acquiring, managing and developing real estate properties and mortgages associated with the delivery of healthcare services throughout the U.S. Co. focuses predominantly on outpatient healthcare facilities, which are designed to provide medical services outside of traditional inpatient hospital or nursing home settings. As of Dec 31 2003, Co. had investments of $1.70 billion in 218 properties and mortgages located in 30 states, and affiliated with 61 healthcare–related entities.

Recent Developments: For the quarter ended Mar 31 2004, Co. reported net income of $17.8 million compared with income from continuing operations of $18.1 million in the corresponding period of the year before. Results for 2003 excluded a gain of $464,000 from discontinued operations. Revenues rose 9.9% to $51.7 million from $47.0 million a year earlier. Property operating income grew 25.1% to $24.8 million from $19.8 million the prior year. Master lease rental income improved 3.0% to $23.0 million from $22.3 million the year before. Mortgage interest income fee increased 5.0% to $2.8 million from $2.7 million the previous year.

Prospects: Co. is required to recognize income from leases with fixed rate increases over the lease term, rather than when the rental increases are contractually due. Co. anticipates that its straight line rental income will decline, negatively impacting net income for 2004 and beyond. As leases requiring straight line rent reach the midpoint of the lease term, the straight line rental receivable recognized during the first half of the lease term begins to reverse, resulting in a reversal of previously recognized income. Separately, Co.'s agreement to acquire 18 medical office facilities from various healthcare companies is anticipated to close in 2004.

Financial Data

(US$ in Thousands)	12/31/2003	12/31/2002	12/31/2001	12/31/2000	12/31/1999	12/31/1998	12/31/1997	12/31/1996
Earnings Per Share	1.66	1.55	1.81	1.82	1.99	1.63	1.68	1.49
Tang. Book Val. Per Share	21.06	21.71	24.40	25.00	25.44	25.57	19.52	17.69
Dividends Per Share	2.470	2.390	2.310	2.230	2.150	2.070	1.990	1.910
Dividend Payout %	148.79	154.19	127.62	122.52	108.04	126.99	118.45	128.19
Income Statement								
Rental Income	91,516	101,210	105,711	105,065	98,955	48,777	40,298	35,329
Interest Income	10,441	13,308	17,254	22,755	26,254	...	...	...
Total Income	191,997	194,527	194,538	195,338	187,257	93,104	59,796	38,574
Total Indirect Exp.	88,193	93,629	77,751	72,874	67,403	39,568	20,615	11,498
Depreciation	42,195	41,598	41,126	39,507	39,039	16,464	11,800	8,996
Interest Expense	34,601	34,195	38,110	42,995	38,603	13,057	7,969	7,344
Income from Cont Ops	69,203	...	...	...	...	...	...	...
Net Income	70,507	70,091	79,887	79,801	86,027	40,479	31,212	19,732
Average Shs. Outstg.	41,780	41,606	40,463	40,301	39,810	24,524	18,572	13,254
Balance Sheet								
Cash & Cash Equivalents	3,840	402	2,930	2,365	4,386	14,411	5,325	1,354
Ttl Real Estate Inv.	1,340,009	1,292,646	1,349,664	1,358,826	1,315,150	1,337,439	470,981	416,034
Total Assets	1,525,710	1,489,546	1,555,910	1,587,076	1,607,964	1,615,423	488,514	427,505
Long–Term Obligations	590,281	545,063	505,222	536,781	563,884	559,924	101,300	168,618
Total Liabilities	623,432	581,347	543,823	579,039	590,061	597,719	112,042	181,541
Net Stockholders' Equity	902,278	908,199	1,012,087	1,008,037	1,017,903	1,017,704	376,472	245,964
Shares Outstanding	42,823	41,823	41,465	40,314	40,004	39,792	19,485	13,898
Net Inc.+Depr./Assets %	7.38	7.50	7.78	7.52	7.78	3.52	8.80	6.33
Return on Equity %	7.66	7.34	7.77	7.98	7.98	3.97	8.29	8.02
Return on Assets %	4.53	4.47	5.05	5.07	5.05	2.50	6.38	4.61
Price Range	36.45-24.42	32.15-27.28	28.25-21.38	21.44-15.63	22.81-14.69	29.94-21.25	29.88-25.50	26.88-20.88
P/E Ratio	21.96-14.71	20.74-17.60	15.61-11.81	11.78-8.59	11.46-7.38	18.37-13.04	17.78-15.18	18.04-14.01
Average Yield %	8.06	7.94	9.14	12.25	10.90	7.86	7.17	8.33

Address: 3310 West End Avenue, Nashville, TN 37203

Telephone: (615) 269–8175

Web Site: www.healthcarerealty.com

Officers: David R. Emery – Chmn., C.E.O., Scott W. Holmes – Sr. V.P., C.F.O.

Transfer Agents: BankBoston, Boston, MA

Investor Contact:781–575–3400

Institutional Holding

No of Institutions: 4

Shares: 268,149   **% Held:** –

HEINZ (H.J.) CO.

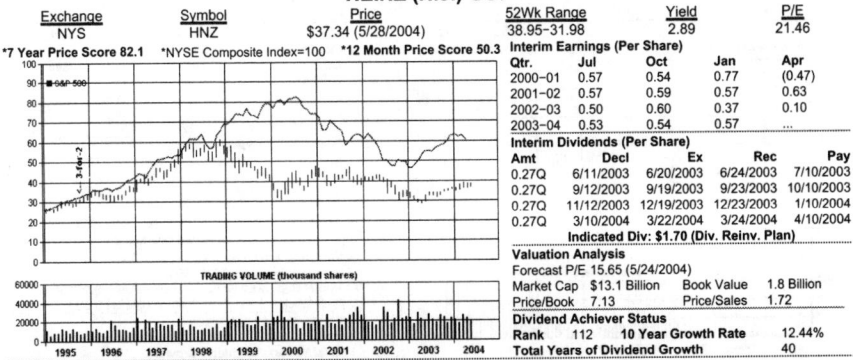

Exchange	Symbol	Price	52Wk Range	Yield	P/E
NYS	HNZ	$37.34 (5/28/2004)	38.95-31.98	2.89	21.46

*7 Year Price Score 82.1   *NYSE Composite Index=100   *12 Month Price Score 50.3

Interim Earnings (Per Share)

Qtr.	Jul	Oct	Jan	Apr
2000-01	0.57	0.54	0.77	(0.47)
2001-02	0.57	0.59	0.57	0.63
2002-03	0.50	0.60	0.37	0.10
2003-04	0.53	0.54	0.57	...

Interim Dividends (Per Share)

Amt	Decl	Ex	Rec	Pay
0.27Q	6/11/2003	6/20/2003	6/24/2003	7/10/2003
0.27Q	9/12/2003	9/19/2003	9/23/2003	10/10/2003
0.27Q	11/12/2003	12/19/2003	12/23/2003	1/10/2004
0.27Q	3/10/2004	3/22/2004	3/24/2004	4/10/2004

Indicated Div: $1.70 (Div. Reinv. Plan)

Valuation Analysis

Forecast P/E 15.65 (5/24/2004)

Market Cap	$13.1 Billion	Book Value	1.8 Billion
Price/Book	7.13	Price/Sales	1.72

Dividend Achiever Status

Rank	112	10 Year Growth Rate	12.44%
Total Years of Dividend Growth		40

Business Summary: Food (MIC: 4.1 SIC: 2099 NAIC:311941)

H.J. Heinz manufactures and markets an extensive line of processed food products throughout the world, including ketchup and other sauces/condiments, frozen dinners, pet food, baby food, frozen potato products and canned soups, vegetables and fruits. Major U.S. brands include *Heinz*, *Ore-Ida*, *Boston Market* and *Smart Ones*. Overseas, well-known brands include *Plasmon*, *Pudliszki*, *Orlando*, *Wattie's*, *Olivine*, *Farley's*, *ABC*, and *Juran*.

Recent Developments: For the three months ended Jan 28 2004, net income totaled $202.2 million, up 55.7% versus income from continuing operations of $129.8 million in the corresponding period the year before. Results for the prior year included one-time pre-tax charges of $61.6 million. Sales slipped 0.4% to $2.10 billion from $2.11 billion a year earlier. Sales gains from favorable foreign currency exchange rates were more than offset by the reduction in sales stemming from divestitures. Gross profit was $779.2 million, or 37.2% of sales, compared with $762.0 million, or 36.2% of sales, the previous year. Operating income climbed 10.5% to $355.4 million from $321.6 million in 2002.

Prospects: Co. anticipates full fiscal-2004 earnings per share in the range of $2.19 to $2.21 per share, along with net sales growth of between 1.0% and 2.0%. Results are being positively affected by improved marketing and new product introductions. Co. is enjoying strong customer response to its new *Ore-Ida®* Extra Crispy frozen french fries, which were launched in January 2004, and its new *Smart Ones®* "Truth About Carbs" line of frozen entrees. Meanwhile, Co. is taking aggressive steps to reduce costs in an effort to improve profitability. Co. is targeting capital expenditures of about 2.5% of net sales in fiscal 2004, and between 2.5% and 3.0% of net sales in fiscal 2005.

Financial Data
(US$ in Thousands)

	9 Mos	6 Mos	3 Mos	04/30/2003	05/01/2002	05/02/2001	05/03/2000	04/28/1999
Earnings Per Share	1.74	1.74	1.74	1.57	2.36	1.41	2.47	1.29
Cash Flow Per Share	2.30	1.39	0.75	2.55	2.52	1.44	1.50	2.47
Dividends Per Share	1.080	1.210	1.350	1.480	1.600	1.540	1.440	1.340
Dividend Payout %	62.07	69.54	77.59	94.58	68.11	109.57	58.50	104.06
Income Statement								
Total Revenues	6,083,166	3,985,985	1,895,524	8,236,836	9,431,000	9,430,422	9,407,949	9,299,610
Total Indirect Exp.	1,214,063	790,183	358,000	1,758,658	1,746,702	2,564,450	1,421,708	2,245,431
Depreciation & Amort.	169,780	112,061	56,232	214,762	301,697	299,166	306,483	302,212
Operating Income	1,053,478	698,111	349,076	1,173,816	1,590,471	982,354	1,733,099	1,109,312
Net Interest Inc./(Exp.)	(144,353)	(96,216)	(46,472)	(192,449)	(266,824)	(310,265)	(244,418)	(233,731)
Income Taxes	293,557	193,659	98,800	313,372	444,701	178,140	573,123	360,790
Income from Cont Ops	580,549	378,312	186,825	555,359	...	494,918	...	...
Net Income	607,749	405,512	214,025	566,285	833,889	478,012	890,553	474,341
Average Shs. Outstg.	354,254	354,258	354,522	354,144	352,871	351,041	360,095	367,830
Balance Sheet								
Cash & Cash Equivalents	1,016,166	848,696	804,734	801,732	206,921	138,849	137,617	115,982
Total Current Assets	3,609,028	3,456,619	3,224,421	3,284,320	3,373,566	3,116,814	3,169,949	2,886,778
Total Assets	9,909,977	9,410,200	9,060,814	9,224,751	10,278,354	9,035,150	8,850,667	8,053,634
Total Current Liabilities	2,340,734	1,871,450	1,760,988	1,926,134	2,509,169	3,655,097	2,126,070	2,786,322
Long-Term Obligations	4,717,385	4,971,816	4,608,272	4,776,143	4,642,968	3,014,853	3,935,826	2,472,206
Net Stockholders' Equity	1,797,671	1,541,908	1,358,297	1,199,157	1,718,616	1,373,727	1,595,856	1,803,004
Net Working Capital	1,268,294	1,585,169	1,463,433	1,358,186	864,397	(538,283)	1,043,879	100,456
Shares Outstanding	352,096	351,868	351,675	351,448	350,904	348,948	347,443	359,127
Statistical Record								
Operating Profit Margin %	17.31	17.51	18.41	14.25	16.86	10.41	23.36	11.92
Return on Equity %	32.29	24.53	13.75	46.31	48.52	36.02	84.91	26.30
Return on Assets %	5.85	4.02	2.06	6.02	8.11	5.47	15.31	5.88
Debt/Total Assets %	47.60	52.83	50.85	51.77	45.17	33.36	44.46	30.69
Price Range	36.62-29.71	35.67-29.71	34.40-29.71	43.19-29.05	46.96-38.12	47.63-35.44	53.88-31.06	61.25-44.56
P/E Ratio	21.05-17.07	20.50-17.07	19.77-17.07	27.51-18.50	19.90-16.15	33.78-25.13	21.81-12.58	47.48-34.54
Average Yield %	3.16	3.62	4.13	4.24	3.83	3.76	3.39	2.46

Address: 600 Grant Street, Pittsburgh, PA 15219 **Telephone:** (412) 456-5700 **Web Site:** www.heinz.com	**Officers:** William R. Johnson - Chmn., Pres., C.E.O., Arthur Winkleback - Exec. V.P., C.F.O. **Transfer Agents:** ChaseMellon Shareholder Services, L.L.C., Ridgefield Park, NJ	**Investor Contact:** 412-456-6034 **Institutional Holding** **No of Institutions:** 548 **Shares:** 221,630,503 **% Held:** 63.10%

133

HELMERICH & PAYNE, INC.

Exchange	Symbol	Price	52Wk Range	Yield	P/E
NYS	HP	$24.95 (5/28/2004)	32.34-23.77	1.28	55.44

*7 Year Price Score 91.2   *NYSE Composite Index=100   *12 Month Price Score 43.9

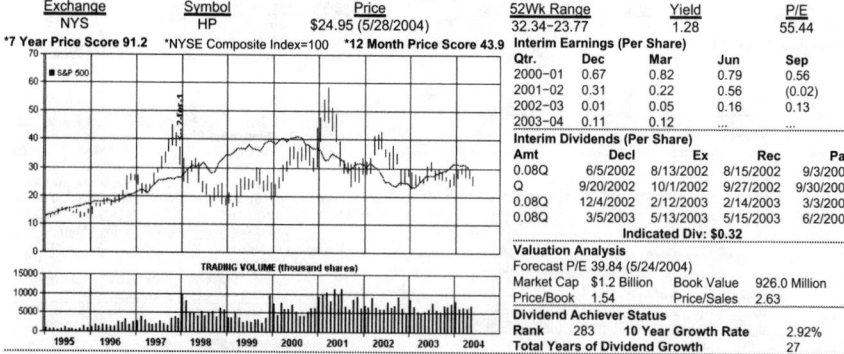

Interim Earnings (Per Share)

Qtr.	Dec	Mar	Jun	Sep
2000-01	0.67	0.82	0.79	0.56
2001-02	0.31	0.22	0.56	(0.02)
2002-03	0.01	0.05	0.16	0.13
2003-04	0.11	0.12	...	...

Interim Dividends (Per Share)

Amt	Decl	Ex	Rec	Pay
0.08Q	6/5/2002	8/13/2002	8/15/2002	9/3/2002
Q	9/20/2002	10/1/2002	9/27/2002	9/30/2002
0.08Q	12/4/2002	2/12/2003	2/14/2003	3/3/2003
0.08Q	3/5/2003	5/13/2003	5/15/2003	6/2/2003

Indicated Div: $0.32

Valuation Analysis

Forecast P/E 39.84 (5/24/2004)

Market Cap $1.2 Billion	Book Value 926.0 Million
Price/Book 1.54	Price/Sales 2.63

Dividend Achiever Status

Rank 283	10 Year Growth Rate	2.92%
Total Years of Dividend Growth		27

Business Summary: Oil and Gas (MIC: 14.2 SIC: 1381 NAIC:213111)

Helmerich & Payne is engaged in contract drilling of oil and gas wells for others. Co. is also engaged in the ownership, development, and operation of commercial real estate. Co.'s contract drilling business is composed of three business segments: domestic land drilling, domestic offshore platform drilling and international drilling. Co.'s domestic contract drilling is conducted primarily in Oklahoma, Texas, Wyoming, and Louisiana, and offshore from platforms in the Gulf of Mexico and California. Co. also operates in Venezuela, Ecuador, Colombia, Argentina, Bolivia, Equatorial Guinea, and Hungary. As of Dec 31 2003, Co.'s total rig fleet was comprised of 127 drilling rigs.

Recent Developments: For the three months ended Mar 31 2004, net income was $6.0 million compared with $2.6 million in the same period a year earlier. Total revenues climbed to $151.2 million from $126.3 million the previous year and included income from investments of $7.7 million and $861,000, respectively. Operating profit fell 12.7% to $13.0 million versus $14.9 million the year before. Co. attributed the decline in operating profit primarily to a $1.4 million currency devaluation loss in Venezuela, reduced profitability from its offshore platform rig segment, and higher depreciation expenses due to four additional FlexRigs®brought into service during its first two fiscal quarters.

Prospects: Lackluster utilization levels from Co.'s U.S. offshore and international operations temper its near-term outlook. For instance, U.S. offshore utilization for the quarter ended Mar 31 2004 amounted to 42.0%, flat versus the prior quarter and down from 50.0% a year earlier. Meanwhile, international operations' utilization was 51.0%, lower than 53.0% in the prior quarter but up from 41.0% the previous year. Co. noted that together these two segments comprise a third of its rig fleet. Looking ahead, Co. remains hopeful that the continued strength in commodity prices will lead to improvement in activity; however, the timing and duration of such a pick up remains uncertain.

Financial Data

(US$ in Thousands)	6 Mos	3 Mos	09/30/2003	09/30/2002	09/30/2001	09/30/2000	09/30/1999	09/30/1998
Earnings Per Share	0.52	0.52	0.35	1.07	2.84	1.64	0.86	2.00
Cash Flow Per Share	0.73	0.50	1.90	3.01	5.49	4.03	3.18	2.24
Tang. Book Val. Per Share	18.60	18.44	18.29	17.89	20.59	19.12	17.09	16.06
Dividends Per Share	0.320	0.320	0.320	0.300	0.300	0.280	0.280	0.270
Dividend Payout %	61.53	61.53	91.42	28.50	10.56	17.37	32.55	13.75
Income Statement								
Total Revenues	290,080	138,894	515,284	510,928	826,854	631,095	564,319	636,640
Total Indirect Exp.	77,229	37,814	123,516	81,838	178,406	174,323	160,570	137,412
Depreciation & Amort.	45,670	22,268	82,513	61,447	87,309	110,851	109,167	88,350
Operating Income	20,998	10,775	46,231	92,200	235,070	139,839	71,419	153,162
Income Taxes	9,010	4,526	14,649	40,573	93,027	57,684	25,706	56,677
Income from Cont Ops	...	...	...	53,706	...	...	...	...
Net Income	11,677	5,629	17,873	63,517	144,254	82,300	42,788	101,154
Average Shs. Outstg.	50,784	50,667	50,596	50,345	50,772	50,035	49,817	50,565
Balance Sheet								
Cash & Cash Equivalents	30,558	35,497	38,189	46,883	122,962	108,087	21,758	24,476
Total Current Assets	212,861	205,335	197,531	178,751	331,412	265,144	160,624	184,345
Total Assets	1,451,000	1,440,075	1,415,835	1,227,313	1,364,507	1,259,492	1,109,699	1,090,430
Total Current Liabilities	76,033	88,471	88,618	72,899	121,221	78,894	71,904	125,484
Long-Term Obligations	200,000	200,000	200,000	100,000	50,000	50,000	50,000	50,000
Net Stockholders' Equity	936,992	926,047	917,251	895,170	1,026,477	955,703	848,109	793,148
Shares Outstanding	50,387	50,204	50,140	50,010	49,852	49,980	49,625	49,383
Statistical Record								
Operating Profit Margin %	5.05	5.43	8.97	18.04	28.42	22.15	12.65	24.05
Return on Equity %	1.25	0.25	1.94	5.99	14.05	8.61	5.04	12.75
Return on Assets %	0.80	0.16	1.26	4.37	10.57	6.53	3.85	9.27
Debt/Total Assets %	13.78	13.88	14.12	8.14	3.66	3.96	4.50	4.58
Price Range	30.61-23.77	28.37-23.77	34.23-23.57	42.91-25.13	58.51-23.74	38.31-19.13	30.19-16.06	44.97-16.25
P/E Ratio	58.87-45.71	54.56-45.71	97.80-67.34	40.10-23.49	20.60-8.36	23.36-11.66	35.10-18.68	22.48-8.13
Average Yield %	1.16	1.22	1.17	0.89	0.77	0.96	1.24	0.93

Address: Utica at Twenty-First Street, Tulsa, OK 74114	**Officers:** W. H. Helmerich III – Chmn., Hans C. Helmerich – Pres., C.E.O.	**Investor Contact:**918-742-5531
Telephone: (918) 742-5531		**Institutional Holding**
Web Site: www.hpinc.com	**Transfer Agents:**UMB Bank, Kansas City, MO	**No of Institutions:** 5
		Shares: 3,726,949 **% Held:** –

HERSHEY FOODS CORP.

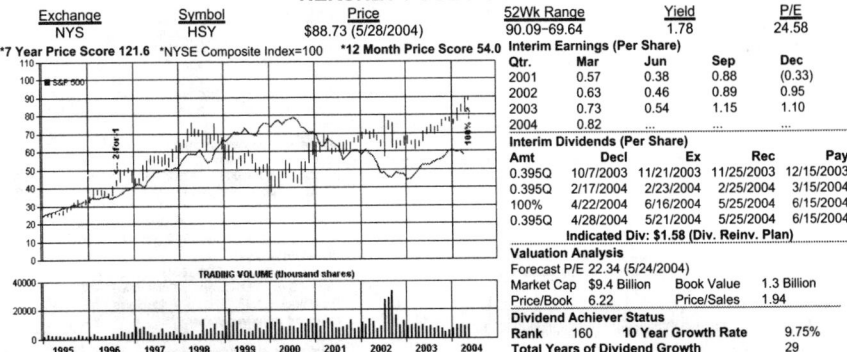

Exchange	Symbol	Price	52Wk Range	Yield	P/E
NYS	HSY	$88.73 (5/28/2004)	90.09-69.64	1.78	24.58

*7 Year Price Score 121.6 *NYSE Composite Index=100 *12 Month Price Score 54.0

Interim Earnings (Per Share)

Qtr.	Mar	Jun	Sep	Dec
2001	0.57	0.38	0.88	(0.33)
2002	0.63	0.46	0.89	0.95
2003	0.73	0.54	1.15	1.10
2004	0.82	...	...	...

Interim Dividends (Per Share)

Amt	Decl	Ex	Rec	Pay
0.395Q	10/7/2003	11/21/2003	11/25/2003	12/15/2003
0.395Q	2/17/2004	2/23/2004	2/25/2004	3/15/2004
100%	4/22/2004	6/16/2004	5/25/2004	6/15/2004
0.395Q	4/28/2004	5/21/2004	5/25/2004	6/15/2004

Indicated Div: $1.58 (Div. Reinv. Plan)

Valuation Analysis

Forecast P/E 22.34 (5/24/2004)

Market Cap	$9.4 Billion	Book Value	1.3 Billion
Price/Book	6.22	Price/Sales	1.94

Dividend Achiever Status

Rank	160	10 Year Growth Rate	9.75%
Total Years of Dividend Growth			29

TRADING VOLUME (thousand shares)

Business Summary: Food (MIC: 4.1 SIC: 2066 NAIC:311320)

Hershey Foods is engaged in the manufacture, distribution and sale of consumer food products including: chocolate and non-chocolate confectionery products sold in the form of bar goods, bagged items and boxed items; and grocery products sold in the form of baking ingredients, chocolate drink mixes, peanut butter, dessert toppings and beverages. Co.'s products are marketed in over 90 countries worldwide under more than 50 brands. Principal confectionery brands include: *Hershey's®, Reese's®, Mr. Goodbar®, Jolly Rancher®, Kit Kat®, Milk Duds®, Whoppers®, York®, Twizzlers®, Super Bubble®, Ice Breakers®, Breath Savers®and Care*free®.*

Recent Developments: For the first quarter ended Apr 4 2004, net income increased 9.8% to $107.1 million compared with $97.6 million in the corresponding prior-year quarter. The combination of higher-margin, on-trend new items and continued cost control, yielded strong sales growth, market share expansion and improved profitability. Net sales advanced 6.3% to $1.01 billion from $953.2 million a year earlier. Gross profit improved to 38.2% of net sales from 37.4% of net sales the year before. Income from operations climbed 8.6% to $183.3 million from $168.7 million in 2003.

Prospects: On Apr 12 2004, Co. announced a multi-year partnership with Thalia Sodi, a Latin singer and actress popular with Hispanics around the world. The partnership includes the sponsorship of an upcoming U.S. tour, a Spanish-language advertising campaign and consumer and retail promotions. Separately, in 2004, Co. plans to invest in new growth platforms both within its core confectionery market, as well as in the broader snack market. For full-year 2004, Co. expects net sales to grow from 3.0% to 4.0% and diluted earnings per share to grow between 9.0% and 11.0%.

Financial Data

(US$ in Thousands)	3 Mos	12/31/2003	12/31/2002	12/31/2001	12/31/2000	12/31/1999	12/31/1998	12/31/1997
Earnings Per Share	3.61	3.52	2.93	1.50	2.42	3.26	2.34	2.23
Cash Flow Per Share	1.81	4.48	4.54	5.13	2.97	2.31	2.67	3.15
Tang. Book Val. Per Share	6.88	6.58	7.10	4.32	5.14	4.68	3.57	2.10
Dividends Per Share	1.510	1.440	1.260	1.160	1.080	1.000	0.920	0.840
Dividend Payout %	42.61	41.05	43.00	77.66	44.62	30.67	39.31	37.66
Income Statement								
Total Revenues	1,013,089	4,172,551	4,120,317	4,557,241	4,220,976	3,970,924	4,435,615	4,302,236
Total Indirect Exp.	204,133	823,139	860,978	1,459,804	1,127,175	570,270	1,167,895	1,183,130
Depreciation & Amort.	47,020	180,567	177,908	190,494	175,964	163,308	158,161	152,750
Operating Income	183,324	796,356	698,287	412,634	622,650	802,145	642,663	630,210
Net Interest Inc./(Exp.)	(14,854)	(63,529)	(60,722)	(69,093)	(76,011)	(74,271)	(85,657)	(76,255)
Income Taxes	61,323	267,875	233,987	136,385	212,096	267,564	216,118	217,704
Income from Cont Ops	...	464,952	...	...	...	...	...	...
Net Income	107,147	457,584	403,578	207,156	334,543	460,310	340,888	336,251
Average Shs. Outstg.	131,027	132,266	137,714	137,696	138,365	141,300	145,563	151,016
Balance Sheet								
Cash & Cash Equivalents	235,372	114,793	297,743	134,147	31,969	118,078	39,024	54,237
Total Current Assets	1,184,440	1,131,569	1,263,618	1,167,541	1,295,348	1,279,980	1,133,966	1,034,814
Total Assets	3,640,963	3,582,540	3,480,551	3,247,430	3,447,764	3,346,652	3,404,098	3,291,236
Total Current Liabilities	594,312	585,810	546,846	606,444	766,901	712,829	814,824	795,715
Long-Term Obligations	971,418	968,499	851,800	876,972	877,654	878,213	879,103	1,029,136
Net Stockholders' Equity	1,319,863	1,279,866	1,371,703	1,147,204	1,175,036	1,098,627	1,042,301	852,806
Net Working Capital	590,128	545,759	716,772	561,097	528,447	567,151	319,142	239,099
Shares Outstanding	129,662	129,529	134,220	166,072	136,281	138,459	143,147	142,932
Operating Profit Margin %	18.09	19.28	16.94	9.47	14.75	26.33	14.48	14.64
Return on Equity %	8.11	36.97	29.42	19.73	28.47	64.08	32.70	39.42
Return on Assets %	2.94	13.21	11.59	6.97	9.70	21.03	10.01	10.21
Debt/Total Assets %	26.68	27.03	24.47	27.00	25.45	26.24	25.82	31.26
Price Range	85.45-74.85	78.51-61.30	79.49-57.36	69.32-57.00	65.63-37.75	64.00-46.31	76.06-59.81	63.31-42.25
P/E Ratio	23.67-20.73	22.30-17.41	27.13-19.58	46.21-38.00	27.12-15.60	19.63-14.21	32.51-25.56	28.39-18.95
Average Yield %	1.89	2.05	1.86	1.84	2.20	1.82	1.36	1.57

Address: 100 Crystal A Drive, Hershey, PA 17033
Telephone: (717) 534 6799
Web Site: www.hersheys.com

Officers: Richard H. Lenny – Chmn., Pres., C.E.O., Frank Cerminara – Sr. V.P., C.F.O.
Transfer Agents: Mellon Investor Services, LLC, Ridgefield Park, NJ

Investor Contact:00 539-0291)
Institutional Holding
No of Institutions: 8
Shares: 2,809 **% Held:** –

HIBERNIA CORP.

*7 Year Price Score 128.4 ***NYSE Composite Index=100** ***12 Month Price Score 49.4**

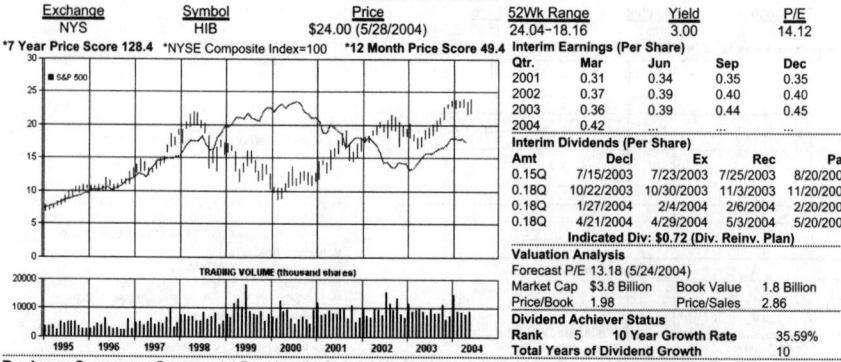

Interim Earnings (Per Share)

Qtr.	Mar	Jun	Sep	Dec
2001	0.31	0.34	0.35	0.35
2002	0.37	0.39	0.40	0.40
2003	0.36	0.39	0.44	0.45
2004	0.42	...	...	...

Interim Dividends (Per Share)

Amt	Decl	Ex	Rec	Pay
0.15Q	7/15/2003	7/23/2003	7/25/2003	8/20/2003
0.18Q	10/22/2003	10/30/2003	11/3/2003	11/20/2003
0.18Q	1/27/2004	2/4/2004	2/6/2004	2/20/2004
0.18Q	4/21/2004	4/29/2004	5/3/2004	5/20/2004

Indicated Div: $0.72 (Div. Reinv. Plan)

Valuation Analysis

Forecast P/E 13.18 (5/24/2004)

Market Cap	$3 Billion	Book Value	1.8 Billion
Price/Book	1.98	Price/Sales	2.86

Dividend Achiever Status

Rank	5	10 Year Growth Rate	35.59%
Total Years of Dividend Growth		10	

Business Summary: Commercial Banking (MIC: 8.1 SIC: 6021 NAIC:522110)

Hibernia is a bank holding company headquartered in Louisiana. As of June 30 2003, Co. had assets of $17.92 billion and 263 locations in 34 Louisiana parishes, 17 Texas counties and two Mississippi counties. Co. conducts its business through its sole depository institution subsidiary, Hibernia National Bank. In addition, Co. also owns Hibernia Capital, which is licensed as a small business investment company and provides private equity investments to small businesses. Co. offers financial products and services, including retail, small business, commercial, international, mortgage and private banking; leasing; investment banking; corporate finance; treasury management; and insurance.

Recent Developments: For the quarter ended Mar 31 2004, net income grew 17.5% to $66.0 million from $56.2 million in the comparable prior-year period. Results for 2004 and 2003 included net foreclosed property expenses of $35,000 and $86,000, and net securities gains of $1.9 million and $9,000, respectively. Net interest income improved 3.9% to $178.4 million from $171.7 million a year earlier. Provision for loan losses decreased 32.4% to $12.0 million. Non-interest income advanced 10.5% to $80.1 million due to service charges on deposits and fee income from card products and Co.'s brokerage, investment banking, trust and insurance businesses. Non-interest expense rose 3.5% to $145.1 million.

Prospects: Co.'s consumer, small-business and commercial businesses continue to perform well, reflecting Co.'s diverse business mix and strong sales culture. Additionally, Co. continues to make progress in its Texas expansion program. In the second quarter of 2004, Co. plans to open two offices in North Dallas and one in Houston. Meanwhile, Co. remains on schedule with the acquisition of Coastal Bancorp, the parent company of a $2.70-billion-asset Texas savings bank. Once the transaction is completed in May 2004, conversion of Coastal's operational systems to Co.'s and availability of Co.'s product line for Coastal's customers are scheduled for June 2004.

Financial Data

(US$ in Thousands)	3 Mos	12/31/2003	12/31/2002	12/31/2001	12/31/2000	12/31/1999	12/31/1998	12/31/1997
Earnings Per Share	1.70	1.64	1.56	1.35	1.04	1.06	1.10	0.98
Tang. Book Val. Per Share	9.71	9.25	8.51	9.80	8.82	7.95	7.78	7.14
Dividends Per Share	0.660	0.630	0.570	0.530	0.490	0.430	0.370	0.330
Dividend Payout %	36.70	38.41	36.53	39.25	47.11	41.03	34.09	33.67
Income Statement								
Total Interest Income	227,879	910,305	987,094	1,159,400	1,217,319	1,055,325	953,722	750,082
Total Interest Expense	49,436	239,552	282,857	494,729	606,760	470,520	423,188	322,325
Net Interest Income	178,443	670,753	704,237	664,671	610,559	584,805	530,534	427,757
Provision for Loan Losses	12,000	60,050	80,625	97,250	120,650	87,800	26,000	620
Non-Interest Income	80,056	350,083	324,918	297,051	248,685	214,703	184,935	145,431
Non-Interest Expense	145,059	564,383	593,697	548,295	476,078	440,921	416,584	361,944
Income Before Taxes	101,440	396,403	382,820	337,250	262,516	270,787	272,885	210,624
Net Income	66,021	258,336	249,857	218,798	170,633	175,103	178,629	137,389
Average Shs. Outstg.	156,959	157,600	160,057	159,236	158,020	158,902	156,165	133,325
Balance Sheet								
Cash & Due from Banks	...	699,060	...	...	...	...	555,756	529,724
Securities Avail. for Sale	3,869,465	3,866,470	3,519,714	3,259,355	2,686,988	2,660,322	3,026,443	2,541,320
Net Loans & Leases	12,878,397	12,669,711	11,279,447	11,045,216	11,946,425	10,700,604	9,878,206	7,472,711
Total Assets	18,716,814	18,560,442	17,392,661	16,618,176	16,698,046	15,314,179	14,011,531	11,023,038
Total Deposits	14,882,232	14,159,519	13,481,022	12,953,112	12,692,732	11,855,903	10,603,006	8,633,329
Long-Term Obligations	1,101,720	1,101,812	1,102,241	1,042,983	1,043,996	844,849	805,689	506,548
Total Liabilities	16,884,988	16,782,957	15,711,799	15,058,397	15,218,395	13,938,664	12,693,430	9,972,724
Net Stockholders' Equity	1,831,571	1,777,485	1,680,862	1,559,779	1,479,651	1,375,515	1,318,101	1,050,314
Shares Outstanding	155,285	155,261	157,412	159,066	157,729	160,324	156,400	133,001
Return on Equity %	3.60	15.44	14.86	14.02	11.53	12.72	13.55	13.08
Return on Assets %	0.35	1.47	1.43	1.31	1.02	1.14	1.27	1.24
Equity/Assets %	9.78	9.57	9.66	9.38	8.86	8.98	9.40	9.52
Non-Int. Exp./Tot. Inc. %	47.10	43.49	44.30	37.10	32.47	34.71	36.58	40.41
Price Range	24.04-22.68	23.69-16.47	21.60-16.80	19.23-11.88	13.75-8.75	17.38-10.38	21.94-13.06	19.38-12.38
P/E Ratio	14.14-13.34	14.45-10.04	13.85-10.77	14.24-8.80	13.22-8.41	16.39-9.79	19.94-11.87	19.77-12.63
Average Yield %	2.84	3.18	2.95	3.34	4.33	3.09	2.02	2.18

Address: 313 Carondelet Street, New Orleans, LA 70130	Officers: E. R. "Bo" Campbell – Vice-Chmn., Paul J. Bonitatibus – Pres., Consumer & Buss. Banking	Investor Contact:504-533-2180
Telephone: (504) 533-2831	Transfer Agents:Mellon Investor Services, Ridgefield Park, NJ	Institutional Holding
Web Site: www.hibernia.com		No of Institutions: 12
		Shares: 424,049 % Held: –

HILB, ROGAL AND HAMILTON CO.

Exchange	Symbol	Price	52Wk Range	Yield	P/E
NYS	HRH	$35.57 (5/28/2004)	38.75-28.34	1.18	16.02

*7 Year Price Score 152.3 *NYSE Composite Index=100 *12 Month Price Score 50.4

Interim Earnings (Per Share)

Qtr.	Mar	Jun	Sep	Dec
2001	0.26	0.26	0.31	0.24
2002	0.48	0.40	0.53	0.48
2003	0.51	0.52	0.50	0.53
2004	0.67	...	...	...

Interim Dividends (Per Share)

Amt	Decl	Ex	Rec	Pay
0.093Q	7/15/2003	9/11/2003	9/15/2003	9/30/2003
0.093Q	11/18/2003	12/11/2003	12/15/2003	12/31/2003
0.093Q	2/10/2004	3/11/2004	3/15/2004	3/31/2004
0.105Q	5/4/2004	6/11/2004	6/15/2004	6/30/2004

Indicated Div: $0.42

Valuation Analysis

Forecast P/E N/A
Market Cap	$1.0 Billion	Book Value	434.3 Million
Price/Book	2.71	Price/Sales	2.09

Dividend Achiever Status

Rank	255	10 Year Growth Rate	5.03%
Total Years of Dividend Growth			17

TRADING VOLUME (thousand shares)

Business Summary: Insurance (MIC: 8.2 SIC: 6411 NAIC:524210)

Hilb, Rogal & Hamilton serves as an intermediary between its clients and insurance companies that underwrite client risks. Co. assists clients in managing their risks in areas such as property and casualty, executive and employee benefits and other areas of specialized exposure. Co. has offices located throughout the U.S. and London, England. Co.'s client base ranges from personal to large national accounts and is primarily comprised of middle–market and top–tier commercial and industrial accounts. Co. also advises clients on risk management and employee benefits and provides claims administration and loss control consulting services to clients.

Recent Developments: For the three months ended Mar 31 2004, net income rose 33.9% to $24.2 million compared with $18.1 million in the corresponding quarter of 2003. Results for 2004 included integration costs of $991,000, while results for 2003 included a retirement benefit charge of $5.2 million. Total revenues were $158.2 million, up 11.4% from $142.0 million the previous year. Commissions and fees increased 11.3% to $156.4 million from $140.5 million the year before, reflecting acquisitions, higher contingent commissions, new business and a moderating rate environment. Operating margin improved to 29.3% from 28.7% a year earlier.

Prospects: On Apr 13 2004, Co. announced the acquisition of the Vero Beach, FL and Melbourne, Australia offices of Sid Banak Insurance, a multi-line property and casualty agency serving the middle market commercial and select personal clients. Separately, Co. is on track to achieve its long-term financial goal of 15.0% to 20.0% annual growth in operating net income per share. Co.'s three primary sources for driving earnings is organic growth, margin improvement and acquisitions. As for acquisitions, Co. believes its pipeline of potential deals is sufficient for it to achieve its stated 2004 objective of acquiring firms with aggregate annualized revenues of between $30.0 million and $60.0 million.

Financial Data

(US$ in Thousands)	12/31/2003	12/31/2002	12/31/2001	12/31/2000	12/31/1999	12/31/1998	12/31/1997	12/31/1996
Earnings Per Share	2.06	1.89	1.07	0.78	0.72	0.59	0.48	0.42
Tang. Book Val. Per Share	N.M	N.M	N.M	N.M	N.M	N.M	1.73	1.94
Dividends Per Share	0.368	0.358	0.348	0.338	0.328	0.318	0.310	0.303
Dividend Payout %	17.86	18.94	32.52	43.33	45.56	53.90	63.91	72.14
Income Statement								
Net Investment Income	3,151	2,439	2,585	2,626	2,046	1,579	...	...
Other Income	560,496	450,287	327,683	259,493	225,180	173,785	173,709	158,243
Total Revenues	563,647	452,726	330,267	262,119	227,226	175,364	173,709	158,243
Total Indirect Exp.	418,765	338,804	264,476	214,202	185,768	147,683	149,827	137,954
Inc. Before Inc. Taxes	124,901	103,257	56,730	39,737	33,069	25,364	21,845	19,045
Income Taxes	49,947	42,082	24,381	17,610	13,583	10,418	9,055	7,638
Income from Cont Ops	...	61,175	...	22,127	...	...	...	...
Net Income	74,954	65,119	32,349	21,802	19,486	14,945	12,790	11,406
Average Shs. Outstg.	36,304	29,240	27,411	29,783	28,014	25,417	26,430	26,986
Balance Sheet								
Cash & Cash Equivalents	126,464	134,692	51,580	28,881	22,337	19,395	22,315	19,774
Premiums Due	255,251	201,364	133,892	94,001	75,271	51,571	47,013	47,576
Invst. Assets: Total	...	1,260	1,336	1,654	1,761	3,068	5,030	6,186
Total Assets	1,049,227	833,024	499,301	353,371	317,981	188,066	106,413	105,073
Long–Term Obligations	174,012	177,151	114,443	103,113	111,826	43,658	32,458	27,196
Net Stockholders' Equity	434,267	310,648	142,801	88,222	71,176	45,710	51,339	55,298
Shares Outstanding	35,446	33,484	28,310	26,560	26,117	24,234	25,626	26,641
Statistical Record								
Return on Equity %	17.25	19.69	22.65	25.08	27.37	32.69	24.91	20.62
Return on Assets %	7.14	7.34	6.47	6.26	6.12	7.94	12.01	10.85
Price Range	43.85-28.34	45.40-27.75	31.08-16.97	20.97-12.91	14.56-7.78	9.94-7.75	9.69-6.31	7.00-5.81
P/E Ratio	21.29-13.76	24.02-14.68	29.05-15.86	26.88-16.55	20.23-10.81	16.84-13.14	20.18-13.15	16.67-13.84
Average Yield %	1.09	0.67	1.53	2.46	2.95	3.43	3.92	3.31

Address: 4951 Lake Brook Drive, Glen Allen, VA 23060 Telephone: (804) 747–6500 Web Site: www.hrh.com	Officers: Martin L. Vaughan III – Chmn., C.E.O., Robert B. Lockhart – Pres., C.O.O. Transfer Agents:Mellon Investor Services, LLC, Ridgefield Park, NJ	Investor Contact:804–747–6500 Institutional Holding No of Institutions: 18 Shares: 781,645 % Held: –

HILLENBRAND INDUSTRIES, INC.

Exchange	Symbol	Price	52Wk Range	Yield	P/E
NYS	HB	$58.90 (5/28/2004)	70.22-49.65	1.83	16.59

*7 Year Price Score 117.8 *NYSE Composite Index=100 ***12 Month Price Score 48.4**

Interim Earnings (Per Share)

Qtr.	Feb	May	Aug	Nov
2000–01	0.40	0.65	0.65	1.01
Qtr.	Dec	Mar	Jun	Sep
2001–02	1.00	0.85	0.52	(2.53)
2002–03	0.12	1.00	1.00	0.81
2003–04	0.89	0.85	...	...

Interim Dividends (Per Share)

Amt	Decl	Ex	Rec	Pay
0.25Q	9/10/2003	9/12/2003	9/16/2003	9/30/2003
0.27Q	12/4/2003	12/15/2003	12/17/2003	12/31/2003
0.27Q	2/12/2004	3/1/2004	3/3/2004	3/31/2004
0.27Q	5/12/2004	5/28/2004	6/2/2004	6/30/2004

Indicated Div: $1.08 (Div. Reinv. Plan)

Valuation Analysis

Forecast P/E 17.52 (5/24/2004)

Market Cap	$3.6 Billion	Book Value	1.0 Billion
Price/Book	4.03	Price/Sales	2.08

Dividend Achiever Status

Rank	185	10 Year Growth Rate	8.53%
Total Years of Dividend Growth			33

Business Summary: Chemicals (MIC: 11.1 SIC: 2599 NAIC:339995)

Hillenbrand is a diversified holding company and the owner of 100% of the capital stock of its three major operating companies serving the health care and funeral services industries in the United States and abroad. Hill–Rom Company is a manufacturer of equipment for the health care industry and a provider of associated systems for wound, pulmonary and circulatory care. Batesville Casket Company, Inc. and Forethought Financial Services both serve the funeral services industry. Batesville Casket is a manufacturer of caskets and cremation–related products, while Forethought is a provider of financial products and services designed to help people prefund anticipated funeral and cemetery costs.

Recent Developments: For the second quarter ended Mar 31 2004, income from continuing operations increased 1.9% to $53.0 million compared with $52.0 million in the equivalent 2003 quarter. Earnings excluded a loss of $101.0 million in 2004 and a gain of $10.0 million in 2003 from discontinued operations. Net revenues advanced 12.4% to $482.0 million. Health care therapy rentals revenue jumped 48.8% to $119.0 million, due to the acquisitions of Advanced Respiratory, Inc. and Mediq. Funeral Services sales rose 7.3% to $176.0 million, reflecting higher volumes and favorable pricing. Health care sales decreased 4.3% to $177.0 million, due to volume declines in bedframe and non–bedframe products.

Prospects: Co. recently launched the CareAssist^{TM} hospital bed targeted for the low– to medium–acuity medical–surgical environment and designed to help improve caregiver efficiency and reduce the risk of injury. In addition, on May 5 2004, Hil–Rom expanded its patient care furniture offering to include a premium line of healthcare furniture, which features visitor chairs, high back chairs, multiple seating, large capacity chairs, large capacity seating, bedside cabinets and tables. Looking ahead, Batesville Caskets expects rising costs due to higher commodity prices. For fiscal 2004, Co. expects revenues to range from $1.90 to $1.92 billion, and earnings to range from $3.25 to $3.30 per diluted share.

Financial Data

(US$ in Thousands)	6 Mos	3 Mos	09/30/2003	09/30/2002	12/01/2001	12/02/2000	11/27/1999	11/28/1998
Earnings Per Share	3.55	3.55	2.93	(0.16)	2.71	2.44	1.87	2.73
Cash Flow Per Share	2.07	(0.20)	6.04	5.21	7.08	4.70	2.26	2.56
Tang. Book Val. Per Share	8.03	14.94	15.78	12.72	13.23	10.41	10.16	11.29
Dividends Per Share	1.040	1.020	1.000	0.767	0.840	0.800	0.780	0.720
Dividend Payout %	29.29	28.73	34.12	N.M.	30.99	32.78	41.71	26.37
Income Statement								
Total Revenues	916,000	528,000	2,042,000	1,757,000	2,107,000	2,096,000	2,047,000	2,001,000
Total Indirect Exp.	286,000	153,000	582,000	780,000	618,000	582,000	565,000	606,000
Operating Income	178,000	90,000	319,000	(32,000)	236,000	244,000	211,000	228,000
Income Taxes	67,000	30,000	100,000	(25,000)	53,000	86,000	71,000	109,000
Income from Cont Ops	98,000	56,000	182,000	...	...	...	...	...
Net Income	9,000	57,000	138,000	(10,000)	170,000	154,000	124,000	184,000
Average Shs. Outstg.	62,588	62,432	62,184	62,921	62,814	62,913	66,295	67,577
Balance Sheet								
Cash & Cash Equivalents	80,000	70,000	180,000	296,000	284,000	132,000	170,000	297,000
Total Current Assets	65,800	627,000	708,000	958,000	868,000	724,000	782,000	858,000
Total Assets	5,915,000	5,401,000	5,412,000	5,442,000	5,049,000	4,597,000	4,433,000	4,280,000
Total Current Liabilities	454,000	266,000	367,000	551,000	320,000	282,000	371,000	375,000
Long–Term Obligations	439,000	154,000	155,000	322,000	305,000	302,000	302,000	303,000
Net Stockholders' Equity	1,045,000	1,190,000	1,159,000	999,000	1,026,000	831,000	838,000	952,000
Shares Outstanding	62,259	61,903	61,814	61,702	62,466	62,404	63,546	66,759
Statistical Record								
Operating Profit Margin %	19.43	17.04	15.62	N.M.	11.20	11.64	10.30	11.39
Return on Equity %	9.38	4.70	15.70	N.M.	16.56	18.53	14.79	19.32
Return on Assets %	1.03	1.03	3.36	N.M.	3.36	3.36	2.79	4.29
Price Range	19.72- 15.89	62.06-56.42	57.64-46.91	65.99-48.75	58.10-43.88	51.00-29.06	56.88-26.38	64.38-44.56
P/E Ratio	44.88-36.17	17.48-15.89	19.67-16.01	N/A	21.44-16.19	20.90-11.91	30.41-14.10	23.58-16.32
Average Yield %	1.66	1.72	1.91	1.28	1.62	2.28	2.33	1.54

Address: 700 State Route 46 East, Batesville, IN 47006–8835 **Telephone:** (812) 934–7000 **Web Site:** www.hillenbrand.com	**Officers:** Ray J. Hillenbrand – Chmn., Rolf A. Classon – Vice–Chmn. **Transfer Agents:** Computershare Investor Services, Chicago, IL	**Investor Contact:** 812–934–8400 **Institutional Holding** **No of Institutions:** 215 **Shares:** 29,055,573 **% Held:** 46.90%

HOLLY CORP.

Exchange	Symbol	Price	52Wk Range	Yield	P/E
NYS	HOC	$31.86 (3/31/2004)	31.86-24.30	1.63	10.80

*7 Year Price Score N/A   *NYSE Composite Index=100   *12 Month Price Score N/A

Interim Earnings (Per Share)

Qtr.	Mar	Jun	Sep	Dec
2003	----------------2.88----------------			
Qtr.	Mar			
2004	0.87	...	...	...

Interim Dividends (Per Share)

Amt	Decl	Ex	Rec	Pay
0.11Q	6/12/2003	6/19/2003	6/23/2003	7/1/2003
0.11Q	9/17/2003	9/25/2003	9/29/2003	10/6/2003
0.11Q	12/18/2003	12/31/2003	1/5/2004	1/12/2004
0.13Q	3/11/2004	3/18/2004	3/22/2004	4/2/2004

Indicated Div: $0.52

Valuation Analysis

Forecast P/E 13.92 (5/24/2004)

Market Cap	$496.3 Million	Book Value	283.3 Million
Price/Book	1.73	Price/Sales	0.31

Dividend Achiever Status

Rank	134	10 Year Growth Rate	11.36%
Total Years of Dividend Growth			10

Business Summary: Oil and Gas (MIC: 14.2 SIC: 2911 NAIC:324110)

Holly operates through two business segments: Refining and Pipeline Transportation. The Refining segment involves the refining of crude oil and wholesale marketing of refined products, such as gasoline, diesel fuel and jet fuel, and includes Co.'s Navajo refinery and Montana refinery. Certain pipelines and terminals operate in conjunction with the Refining segment as part of the supply and distribution networks of the refineries. The Refining segment also includes the equity earnings from Co.'s 49.0% interest in NK Asphalt Partners. The Pipeline Transportation segment includes about 1,000 miles of Co.'s pipeline assets in Texas and New Mexico.

Recent Developments: For the first quarter ended Mar 31 2004, net income increased 3.2% to $14.0 million compared with $13.5 million in the corresponding prior-year quarter. Results for 2003 included a gain on the sale of assets of $16.2 million. Total sales and other revenue advanced 47.0% to $463.1 million from $314.9 million a year earlier. Refining segment sales jumped 47.1% to $456.0 million, primarily due to higher volumes from the Woods Cross refinery, acquired in June 2003, and the Navajo refinery, and to a lesser degree, higher refined product sales. Pipeline Transportation segment sales climbed 46.8% to $6.7 million. Income from operations rose 8.6% to $25.1 million.

Prospects: Refining margins are continuing to improve at all three of Co.'s refineries. Industry-wide refinery gross margin improvements, increased high-value boutique fuel capabilities with the Navajo refinery's new hydrotreater start-up, the expansion of the Navajo refinery and the acquisition of the Woods Cross refinery are combining to drive significant growth in refinery production and income. Capital employed for the Navajo upgrade and expansion, as well as the Woods Cross acquisition, has Co. well-positioned to prosper in the improving refinery market. Looking ahead, Co. will continue to pursue prudent acquisition and organic growth opportunities.

Financial Data

(US$ in Thousands)	3 Mos	12/31/2003	07/31/2002	07/31/2001	07/31/2000	07/31/1999	07/31/1998	07/31/1997
Earnings Per Share	2.83	2.88	2.01	4.77	0.71	1.21	0.92	0.79
Cash Flow Per Share	2.32	4.41	2.64	6.86	2.90	2.88	2.31	0.33
Tang. Book Val. Per Share	17.99	16.63	14.68	13.03	8.58	7.80	6.92	6.36
Dividends Per Share	0.440	0.440	0.410	0.370	0.340	0.320	0.300	0.250
Dividend Payout %	15.55	15.27	20.39	7.75	47.88	26.44	32.60	32.07
Income Statement								
Total Revenues	463,057	1,403,244	888,906	1,142,130	965,946	597,986	590,299	721,346
Total Indirect Exp.	24,424	187,319	147,615	152,902	145,282	130,541	117,492	37,233
Depreciation & Amort.	9,924	36,275	27,699	27,327	27,496	26,358	24,379	20,153
Operating Income	25,066	60,067	43,046	117,907	20,001	38,973	32,765	27,500
Net Interest Inc./(Exp.)	(878)	(1,678)	(1,425)	(2,467)	(5,153)	(7,779)	(7,725)	(6,095)
Income Taxes	8,882	28,306	18,867	48,445	7,189	13,222	9,699	8,732
Eqty Earns/Minority Int.	(655)	1,398	7,753	5,302	1,586	1,965	1,766	414
Net Income	13,962	46,053	32,029	73,450	11,445	19,937	15,167	13,087
Average Shs. Outstg.	16,090	16,016	15,971	15,387	16,130	16,508	16,508	16,508
Balance Sheet								
Cash & Cash Equivalents	22,262	11,690	71,630	65,840	3,628	4,194	2,602	20,042
Total Current Assets	334,364	336,406	278,844	284,130	267,104	194,778	154,387	194,728
Total Assets	703,931	708,892	502,306	490,429	464,362	390,982	349,857	349,803
Total Current Liabilities	345,116	364,667	218,971	226,399	266,741	180,927	139,594	149,487
Long-Term Obligations	8,571	8,571	25,714	34,286	42,857	56,595	70,341	75,516
Net Stockholders' Equity	283,256	268,609	228,556	201,734	129,581	128,880	114,349	105,121
Net Working Capital	(10,752)	(28,261)	59,873	57,731	363	13,851	14,793	45,241
Shares Outstanding	15,743	15,514	15,561	15,480	15,101	16,508	16,508	16,508
Statistical Record								
Operating Profit Margin %	13.76	4.28	4.84	10.32	2.07	6.51	5.55	3.81
Return on Equity %	18.58	17.14	14.01	36.40	8.83	15.46	13.26	12.44
Return on Assets %	7.47	6.49	6.37	14.97	2.46	5.09	4.33	3.74
Debt/Total Assets %	1.21	1.20	5.11	6.99	9.22	14.47	20.10	21.58
Price Range	31.86-27.20	29.98-15.00	21.15-14.66	24.98-6.00	7.63-4.69	13.00-6.22	16.44-12.06	14.81-11.63
P/E Ratio	11.26-9.61	10.41-5.21	10.52-7.29	5.24-1.26	10.74-6.60	10.74-5.14	17.87-13.11	18.75-14.72
Average Yield %	1.54	1.88	2.27	3.29	5.24	4.18	2.20	1.91

Address: 100 Crescent Court, Dallas, TX 75201-6927	Officers: Lamar Norsworthy – Chmn., C.E.O., Matthew P. Clifton – Pres.	Institutional Holding
Telephone: (214) 871-3555	Transfer Agents:American Stock Transfer &Trust Company, New York, NY	No of Institutions: –
Web Site: www.hollycorp.com		Shares: – % Held: –

HOME DEPOT, INC.

Exchange	Symbol	Price	52Wk Range	Yield	P/E
NYS	HD	$35.92 (5/28/2004)	37.52-30.36	0.78	18.14

*7 Year Price Score 91.7   *NYSE Composite Index=100   *12 Month Price Score 46.9

Interim Earnings (Per Share)

Qtr.	Apr	Jul	Oct	Jan
2001	0.27	0.39	0.33	0.30
2002	0.36	0.50	0.40	0.30
2003	0.39	0.56	0.50	0.43
2004	0.49	...	...	...

Interim Dividends (Per Share)

Amt	Decl	Ex	Rec	Pay
0.07Q	8/29/2003	9/2/2003	9/4/2003	9/18/2003
0.07Q	11/20/2003	12/2/2003	12/4/2003	12/18/2003
0.07Q	2/26/2004	3/9/2004	3/11/2004	3/22/2004
0.085Q	5/26/2004	6/8/2004	6/10/2004	6/24/2004

Indicated Div: $0.28 (Div. Reinv. Plan)

Valuation Analysis

Forecast P/E 14.47 (5/24/2004)

Market Cap	$83.5 Billion	Book Value	22.4 Billion
Price/Book	3.58	Price/Sales	1.24

Dividend Achiever Status

Rank	9	10 Year Growth Rate	26.39%
Total Years of Dividend Growth	16		

Business Summary: Retail – Hardware (MIC: 5.6 SIC: 5211 NAIC:444110)

The Home Depot operated 1,707 retail warehouse stores as of Feb 1 2004 in the United States, Canada and Mexico that offer a wide assortment of building materials and home improvement products. The average Home Depot store has about 107,000 square feet of interior floor space and about 22,000 square feet of additional outdoor selling area for landscaping supplies. Co. also operates 54 EXPO Design Center stores that sell products and services primarily for home decorating and remodeling projects, 11 Home Depot Landscape Supply stores, five Home Depot Supply stores, and two Home Depot Floor Store outlets.

Recent Developments: For the quarter ended May 2 2004, net earnings advanced 21.1% to $1.10 billion from $907.0 million in the prior year. Net sales increased 16.2% to $17.55 billion from $15.10 billion a year earlier. Comparable–store sales were up 7.7% year over year, while the average sale per customer transaction rose to $55.11 from $51.29 in fiscal 2003. Gross profit totaled $5.77 billion, or 32.9% of net sales, compared with $4.83 billion, or 32.0% of net sales, the year before. Operating income climbed 20.6% to $1.75 billion from $1.45 billion the previous year. During the first quarter of fiscal 2004, Co. opened 33 new stores.

Prospects: Co. is taking steps to expand its operations through acquisitions. On May 13 2004, Co. announced it has entered into a definitive agreement to acquire Home Mart, a home improvement retailer operating 20 stores in Mexico. Separately, on May 6 2004, Co. announced that it has entered into an agreement to acquire White Cap Construction Supply, Inc., a distributor of specialty hardware and tools with annual sales of about $500.0 million. Terms of the transactions were not disclosed. Looking ahead, Co. anticipates sales growth of between 10.0% and 12.0% and earnings per share growth of 10.0% to 14.0% during the current fiscal year.

Financial Data

(US$ in Thousands)	02/01/2004	02/02/2003	02/03/2002	01/28/2001	01/30/2000	01/31/1999	02/01/1998	02/02/1997
Earnings Per Share	1.88	1.56	1.29	1.10	1.00	0.71	0.51	0.43
Cash Flow Per Share	2.85	2.04	2.53	1.18	1.04	0.82	0.45	0.50
Tang. Book Val. Per Share	9.55	8.38	7.52	6.32	5.22	3.82	3.16	2.71
Dividends Per Share	0.260	0.210	0.170	0.160	0.110	0.070	0.060	0.050
Dividend Payout %	13.82	13.46	13.17	14.54	11.33	10.79	12.25	11.63
Income Statement								
Total Revenues	64,816,000	58,247,000	53,553,000	45,738,000	38,434,000	30,219,000	24,156,000	19,535,503
Total Indirect Exp.	13,734,000	12,278,000	11,215,000	9,490,000	7,616,000	5,944,000	4,765,000	3,900,430
Depreciation & Amort.	1,076,000	903,000	764,000	601,000	463,000	373,000	283,000	232,340
Operating Income	6,846,000	5,830,000	4,932,000	4,191,000	3,795,000	2,661,000	1,912,000	1,533,650
Net Interest Inc./(Exp.)	(3,000)	42,000	25,000	26,000	9,000	(7,000)	2,000	9,490
Income Taxes	2,539,000	2,208,000	1,913,000	1,636,000	1,484,000	1,040,000	738,000	597,030
Net Income	4,304,000	3,664,000	3,044,000	2,581,000	2,320,000	1,614,000	1,160,000	937,739
Average Shs. Outstg.	2,289,000	2,344,000	2,353,000	2,352,000	2,342,000	2,320,000	2,286,000	2,194,884
Balance Sheet								
Cash & Cash Equivalents	2,826,000	2,188,000	2,477,000	167,000	168,000	62,000	172,000	146,006
Total Current Assets	13,328,000	11,917,000	10,361,000	7,777,000	6,390,000	4,933,000	4,460,000	3,709,373
Total Assets	34,437,000	30,011,000	26,394,000	21,385,000	17,081,000	13,465,000	11,229,000	9,341,710
Total Current Liabilities	9,554,000	8,035,000	6,501,000	4,385,000	3,656,000	2,857,000	2,456,000	1,842,126
Long–Term Obligations	856,000	1,321,000	1,250,000	1,545,000	750,000	1,566,000	1,303,000	1,246,593
Net Stockholders' Equity	22,407,000	19,802,000	18,082,000	15,004,000	12,341,000	8,740,000	7,098,000	5,955,186
Net Working Capital	3,774,000	3,882,000	3,860,000	3,392,000	2,734,000	2,076,000	2,004,000	1,867,247
Shares Outstanding	2,257,000	2,293,000	2,345,888	2,323,747	2,304,317	2,213,178	2,196,324	2,162,317
Operating Profit Margin %	10.56	10.00	9.20	9.16	9.87	8.80	7.91	7.85
Return on Equity %	19.20	18.50	16.83	17.20	18.79	18.46	16.34	15.74
Return on Assets %	12.49	12.20	11.53	12.06	13.58	11.98	10.33	10.03
Debt/Total Assets %	2.48	4.40	4.73	7.22	4.39	11.63	11.60	13.34
Price Range	37.52-20.70	52.07-20.53	53.45-32.80	68.00-34.88	68.56-36.29	41.04-20.60	20.23-11.11	13.14-9.61
P/E Ratio	19.96-11.01	33.38-13.16	41.43-25.43	61.82-31.70	68.56-36.29	57.81-29.02	39.67-21.79	30.56-22.35
Average Yield %	0.83	0.60	0.37	0.31	0.24	0.25	0.38	0.44

Address: 2455 Paces Ferry Road N.W., Atlanta, GA 30339–4024 **Telephone:** (770) 433–8211 **Web Site:** www.homedepot.com	**Officers:** Robert L. Nardelli – Chmn. Pres., C.E.O., Francis S. Blake – Exec. V.P., Bus. Devel., Corp. Oper. **Transfer Agents:** EquiServe Trust Company, N.A., Providence, RI	**Investor Contact:** 770–384–4388 **Institutional Holding** **No of Institutions:** 10 **Shares:** 5,387,488 **% Held:** –

HNI Corp

Exchange	Symbol	Price	52Wk Range	Yield	P/E
NYS	HNI	$39.87 (5/28/2004)	45.58-29.12	1.40	23.73

*7 Year Price Score 137.3   *NYSE Composite Index=100   *12 Month Price Score 47.8

Interim Earnings (Per Share)

Qtr.	Mar	Jun	Sep	Dec
2001	0.31	0.07	0.48	0.40
2002	0.27	0.34	0.46	0.48
2003	0.27	0.35	0.59	0.47
2004	0.38	...	...	...

Interim Dividends (Per Share)

Amt	Decl	Ex	Rec	Pay
0.13Q	8/4/2003	8/12/2003	8/14/2003	8/29/2003
0.13Q	11/7/2003	11/13/2003	11/17/2003	12/1/2003
0.14Q	2/11/2004	2/18/2004	2/20/2004	3/1/2004
0.14Q	5/4/2004	5/12/2004	5/14/2004	6/1/2004

Indicated Div: $0.56

Valuation Analysis

Forecast P/E N/A

Market Cap	$2.3 Billion	Book Value	709.9 Million
Price/Book	3.54	Price/Sales	1.43

Dividend Achiever Status

Rank	155	10 Year Growth Rate	10.03%
Total Years of Dividend Growth			15

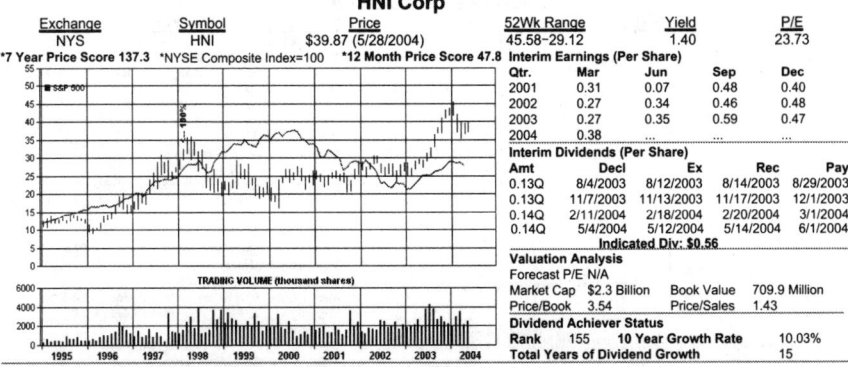

Business Summary: Chemicals (MIC: 11.1 SIC: 2522 NAIC:337214)

Hon Industries manufactures and markets office furniture and hearth products. Co.'s office furniture products are in four categories: storage, seating, office systems, and desks and related products. The office products are sold to dealers, wholesalers, warehouse clubs, retail superstores, end–user customers, and federal and state governments. Co.'s hearth products include wood–burning, pellet–burning, gas–burning and electric factory–built fireplaces, fireplace inserts, stoves, gas logs, and accessories. The hearth products are sold through a national system of dealers, wholesalers, large regional contractors and Co.–owned retail outlets. Co. has locations in the U.S., Canada and Mexico.

Recent Developments: For the quarter ended Apr 3 2004, net income advanced 41.1% to $22.4 million compared with $15.9 million in the equivalent 2003 quarter. The improvement in earnings was primarily attributed to Co.'s restructuring initiatives, volume leverage and new products. Results for 2004 included restructuring and impairment charges of $520,000. Net sales climbed 18.4% to $464.0 million from $392.0 million a year earlier. Sales benefited from strong growth in both Co.'s office furniture and hearth products segments. Gross profit advanced 22.0% to $169.8 million versus $139.1 million in 2003. Operating income grew 40.3% to $34.7 million from $24.7 million the year before.

Prospects: Going forward, Co. believes that its volumes will remain strong, although, it will be faced with cost pressures on material and freight. Steel and freight costs began to increase during the end of the first quarter and Co. is expecting to see a more significant impact in the second quarter. As a result, Co. announced selective price increases to offset a portion of these costs; however, they will not be effective until the third quarter. Meanwhile, Co. will look to continue growing its business through aggressive investments in building brands and rapid continuous improvement programs to build best total cost.

Financial Data

(US$ in Thousands)	3 Mos	01/03/2004	12/28/2002	12/29/2001	12/30/2000	01/01/2000	01/02/1999	01/03/1998
Earnings Per Share	1.79	1.68	1.55	1.26	1.77	1.44	1.72	1.45
Cash Flow Per Share	0.31	2.41	3.42	3.85	3.40	...	...	...
Tang. Book Val. Per Share	8.88	8.89	7.78	6.44	5.96	6.45	5.76	4.58
Dividends Per Share	0.530	0.520	0.500	0.480	0.440	0.380	0.320	0.280
Dividend Payout %	29.61	30.95	32.25	38.09	24.85	26.39	18.60	19.31
Income Statement								
Total Revenues	464,037	1,755,728	1,692,622	1,792,438	2,046,286	1,789,281	1,696,433	1,362,713
Total Indirect Exp.	135,100	489,254	457,189	488,206	487,848	406,226	344,259	284,397
Depreciation & Amort.	17,312	4,625	4,317	12,646	10,679	5,362	4,789	2,943
Operating Income	34,662	149,961	142,690	123,092	178,034	146,443	179,177	145,159
Net Interest Inc./(Exp.)	355	970	(2,136)	(6,831)	(12,070)	(8,868)	(9,068)	(6,031)
Income Taxes	12,606	52,826	49,194	41,854	59,747	50,215	63,796	52,173
Net Income	22,411	98,105	91,360	74,407	106,217	87,360	106,313	86,955
Average Shs. Outstg.	58,690	58,545	59,040	59,087	60,140	60,855	61,650	59,780
Balance Sheet								
Cash & Cash Equivalents	80,889	138,982	139,165	78,838	3,181	22,168	17,500	46,080
Total Current Assets	362,676	462,122	405,054	319,657	330,141	316,556	290,329	295,150
Total Assets	976,436	1,021,826	1,020,552	961,891	1,022,470	906,723	864,469	754,673
Total Current Liabilities	189,937	245,816	298,680	230,443	264,868	225,123	217,438	200,759
Long–Term Obligations	3,935	4,126	9,837	80,830	128,285	124,173	135,563	134,511
Net Stockholders' Equity	718,849	709,889	646,893	592,680	573,342	501,271	462,022	381,662
Net Working Capital	172,739	216,306	106,374	89,214	65,273	91,433	72,891	94,391
Shares Outstanding	58,132	58,239	58,373	58,672	59,796	60,171	61,290	61,659
Statistical Record								
Operating Profit Margin %	7.46	8.54	8.43	6.86	8.70	8.18	10.56	10.65
Return on Equity %	3.11	13.81	14.12	12.55	18.52	17.42	23.01	22.78
Return on Assets %	2.29	9.60	8.95	7.73	10.38	9.63	12.29	11.52
Debt/Total Assets %	0.40	0.40	0.96	8.40	12.54	13.69	15.68	17.82
Price Range	45.58–35.50	43.82–24.82	30.65–23.40	28.85–20.60	27.56–16.12	29.29–18.74	36.00–19.57	30.80–15.78
P/E Ratio	25.46–19.83	26.08–14.77	19.77–15.10	22.90–16.35	15.57–9.11	20.34–13.01	20.93–11.38	21.24–10.88
Average Yield %	1.33	1.57	1.83	1.96	1.88	1.65	1.15	1.20

Address: 414 East Third Street, Muscatine, IA 52761–0071 **Telephone:** (563) 264–7400 **Web Site:** www.honi.com	**Officers:** Jack D. Michaels – Chmn., Pres., C.E.O., Stanley A. Askren – Pres.,, Chief, Oper. Officer **Transfer Agents:** Computershare Investor Services, LLC, Chicago, IL	**Investor Contact:** 563–264–7400 **Institutional Holding** **No of Institutions:** 24 **Shares:** 951,268 **% Held:** –

HORMEL FOODS CORP.

Exchange	Symbol	Price	52Wk Range	Yield	P/E
NYS	HRL	$31.25 (5/28/2004)	31.30–21.25	1.44	22.98

*7 Year Price Score 124.7   *NYSE Composite Index=100   *12 Month Price Score 55.4

Interim Earnings (Per Share)

Qtr.	Jan	Apr	Jul	Oct
2000–01	0.30	0.28	0.24	0.48
2001–02	0.36	0.23	0.27	0.49
2002–03	0.34	0.24	0.25	0.50
2003–04	0.37	...	...	...

Interim Dividends (Per Share)

Amt	Decl	Ex	Rec	Pay
0.105Q	9/22/2003	10/15/2003	10/18/2003	11/15/2003
0.113Q	11/26/2003	1/21/2004	1/24/2004	2/15/2004
0.113Q	3/26/2004	4/14/2004	4/17/2004	5/15/2004
0.1125Q	5/24/2004	7/21/2004	7/24/2004	8/15/2004

Indicated Div: $0.45 (Div. Reinv. Plan)

Valuation Analysis

Forecast P/E 19.54 (5/24/2004)

Market Cap $4.3 Billion		Book Value	1.3 Billion
Price/Book 2.78		Price/Sales	0.84

Dividend Achiever Status

Rank	221	10 Year Growth Rate	6.68%
Total Years of Dividend Growth			36

Business Summary: Food (MIC: 4.1 SIC: 2011 NAIC:311611)

Hormel Foods is primarily engaged in the production of a variety of meat and food products and the marketing of those products throughout the United States. Although pork and turkey remain the major raw materials for Co. products, Co. has emphasized for several years the manufacture and distribution of branded, consumer packaged items rather than the commodity fresh meat business. Co.'s business is reported in five segments: Grocery Products, Refrigerated Foods, Jennie–O Turkey Store, Specialty Foods, and All Other. Co.'s products primarily consist of meat and other food products. The meat products are sold fresh, frozen, cured, smoked, cooked and canned.

Recent Developments: For the 13 weeks ended Apr 24 2004, net earnings were $53.7 million, up 58.7% compared with $33.8 million in the corresponding prior–year period. Net sales climbed 14.0% to $1.14 billion from $1.00 billion the year before, driven in part by a 55.9% increase to $123.1 million in Specialty Foods sales, which benefited from the acquisition of Century Foods International. Gross profit totaled $273.4 million, or 23.9% of net sales, versus $238.4 million, or 23.8% of net sales, the year before. Operating income advanced 36.5% to $81.5 million from $59.7 million a year earlier.

Prospects: Earnings are benefiting from strong demand for Co.'s pork and turkey products, partially offset by increased cost pressures from the grain markets. Co. is enjoying sharply higher sales of *Hormel* bacon, pepperoni and Canadian bacon and *Jennie–O Turkey Store* bacon, marinated tenderloins and homestyle deli breasts. Meanwhile, Grocery Products segment sales and volume are being hampered by increased pork and beef raw material costs. In an effort to boost margins, Co. will implement price increases of between 4.5% and 6.5% for all of its Grocery Products items effective June 14 2004. Looking ahead, Co. is targeting full fiscal–2004 earnings of between $1.50 and $1.62 per share.

Financial Data

(US$ in Thousands)	3 Mos	10/25/2003	10/26/2002	10/27/2001	10/28/2000	10/30/1999	10/31/1998	10/25/1997
Earnings Per Share	1.36	1.33	1.35	1.30	1.20	1.11	0.92	0.71
Cash Flow Per Share	0.22	1.81	2.32	2.28	1.06	1.62	1.52	1.06
Tang. Book Val. Per Share	5.68	5.40	5.46	4.45	5.63	5.20	4.81	4.55
Dividends Per Share	0.420	0.410	0.380	0.360	0.340	0.320	0.310	0.300
Dividend Payout %	30.88	31.01	28.51	28.07	28.75	29.50	34.32	43.00
Income Statement								
Total Revenues	1,135,533	4,200,328	3,910,314	4,124,112	3,675,132	3,357,757	3,261,045	3,256,551
Total Indirect Exp.	184,846	696,857	636,862	834,469	737,651	737,125	620,449	585,543
Depreciation & Amort.	23,025	88,020	83,238	90,193	65,886	64,656	60,273	52,925
Operating Income	85,224	310,410	318,250	300,306	262,607	240,907	211,884	173,346
Net Interest Inc./(Exp.)	(6,810)	(31,864)	(31,425)	(27,953)	(14,906)	(13,746)	(13,692)	(15,043)
Income Taxes	29,790	103,552	104,648	102,573	94,164	88,035	78,045	61,369
Eqty Earns/Minority Int.	1,706	5,886	7,741	2,866	476	6,995	4,323	3,402
Net Income	51,826	185,779	189,322	182,441	170,217	163,438	139,291	109,492
Average Shs. Outstg.	140,102	139,710	140,292	140,125	141,523	147,010	150,406	153,458
Balance Sheet								
Cash & Cash Equivalents	81,938	97,976	309,563	186,276	100,646	188,310	203,934	146,853
Total Current Assets	827,212	823,974	962,170	883,281	711,109	800,143	717,365	671,352
Total Assets	2,416,384	2,393,121	2,220,196	2,162,698	1,641,940	1,685,585	1,555,892	1,528,535
Total Current Liabilities	419,654	441,990	410,111	420,203	342,625	385,407	267,651	260,578
Long–Term Obligations	395,256	395,273	409,648	462,407	145,928	184,723	204,874	198,232
Net Stockholders' Equity	1,299,171	1,252,735	1,115,255	995,881	873,877	841,142	813,315	802,202
Net Working Capital	407,558	381,984	552,059	463,078	368,484	414,736	449,714	410,774
Shares Outstanding	138,421	138,596	138,411	138,663	138,569	142,724	146,992	151,552
Statistical Record								
Operating Profit Margin %	7.65	7.53	8.33	7.28	7.14	7.17	7.36	5.32
Return on Equity %	4.12	15.29	17.66	18.31	19.47	19.43	20.61	13.64
Return on Assets %	2.21	8.00	8.87	8.43	10.36	9.69	10.77	7.16
Debt/Total Assets %	16.35	16.51	18.45	21.38	8.88	10.95	13.16	12.96
Price Range	27.45–23.80	24.98–20.18	28.03–20.50	26.39–16.75	22.28–14.13	22.63–14.78	19.44–13.09	16.25–11.75
P/E Ratio	20.18–17.50	18.78–15.17	20.76–15.19	20.30–12.88	18.57–11.77	20.38–13.32	21.13–14.23	22.89–16.55
Average Yield %	1.62	1.81	1.54	1.68	1.94	1.72	1.91	2.23

Address: 1 Hormel Place, Austin, MN 55912–3680	Officers: Joel W. Johnson – Chmn., Pres., C.E.O., Michael J. McCoy – Exec. V.P., C.F.O.	Investor Contact:507–437–5007
Telephone: (507) 437–5611	Transfer Agents:Wells Fargo Bank Minnesota, N.A., South St. Paul, MN	Institutional Holding No of Institutions: 11
Web Site: www.hormel.com		Shares: 16,330 % Held: –

HUDSON UNITED BANCORP

Exchange	Symbol	Price	52Wk Range	Yield	P/E
NYS	HU	$36.64 (5/28/2004)	40.20–33.75	3.60	14.31

*7 Year Price Score 127.4 *NYSE Composite Index=100 *12 Month Price Score 46.3

Interim Earnings (Per Share)

Qtr.	Mar	Jun	Sep	Dec
2001	0.46	0.49	0.51	0.54
2002	0.93	0.56	0.60	0.63
2003	0.63	0.65	0.68	0.54
2004	0.69	...	...	...

Interim Dividends (Per Share)

Amt	Decl	Ex	Rec	Pay
0.30Q	6/18/2003	8/13/2003	8/15/2003	9/2/2003
0.30Q	10/23/2003	11/12/2003	11/14/2003	12/1/2003
0.33Q	1/27/2004	2/11/2004	2/13/2004	3/1/2004
0.33Q	4/22/2004	5/12/2004	5/14/2004	6/1/2004

Indicated Div: $1.32 (Div. Reinv. Plan)

Valuation Analysis

Forecast P/E 12.88 (5/24/2004)

Market Cap $1.7 Billion	Book Value 458.2 Million
Price/Book 3.67	Price/Sales 3.19

Dividend Achiever Status

Rank	59	10 Year Growth Rate	16.64%
Total Years of Dividend Growth		13	

Business Summary: Commercial Banking (MIC: 8.1 SIC: 6022 NAIC:522110)

Hudson United Bancorp is a bank holding company. Co. directly owns Hudson United Bank, a full–service commercial bank that operated 205 offices, as of Dec 31 2003, throughout the state of New Jersey; in the Hudson Valley area of New York State; in New York City; in southern Connecticut; and in Philadelphia and surrounding areas in Pennsylvania. Co. also directly owns six additional subsidiaries, which are HUBCO Capital Trust I, HUBCO Capital Trust II, JBI Capital Trust I, Hudson United Capital Trust I, Hudson United Capital Trust II and Jefferson Delaware Inc. As of Dec 31 2003, Co., through its subsidiaries, had total deposits of $6.24 billion and total assets of $8.10 billion.

Recent Developments: For the quarter ended Mar 31 2004, net income rose 9.5% to $31.0 million compared with $28.3 million in the corresponding year–earlier period. Net interest income grew 3.6% to $77.9 million from $75.2 million the previous year. Co. attributed the higher net interest income primarily to lower interest expense on deposits. This was offset in part by lower interest income on loans mainly due to prepayments on existing loans and subsequent new loans being originated at lower interest rates. Provision for loan losses was $5.6 million versus $7.0 million last year. Non–interest income climbed 32.3% to $35.6 million, reflecting gains on sales of securities and income from landfill gas companies.

Prospects: Co.'s primary strategies for 2004 include increasing its share of business with its existing customers by targeting market areas with the greatest potential for growth. Co. also indicated that it will consider acquisitions to supplement internal growth provided they add customer relationships and product capabilities, and can be accretive to earnings per share. In addition, Co. is seeking to add new individuals and businesses that are being affected by market disruptions due to mergers and acquisitions. Lastly, during 2004 Co. intends to launch initiatives to strengthen the image and awareness of Hudson United Bank.

Financial Data

(US$ in Thousands)	3 Mos	12/31/2003	12/31/2002	12/31/2001	12/31/2000	12/31/1999	12/31/1998	12/31/1997
Earnings Per Share	2.56	2.50	2.72	2.00	0.92	1.18	0.49	1.79
Tang. Book Val. Per Share	8.74	7.91	7.38	6.49	5.58	7.06	8.25	6.32
Dividends Per Share	1.230	1.180	1.100	1.010	0.930	0.880	0.770	0.640
Dividend Payout %	48.05	47.20	40.44	50.50	101.28	74.68	157.32	35.87
Income Statement								
Total Interest Income	98,145	394,129	430,003	470,363	608,309	644,576	468,547	218,041
Total Interest Expense	20,254	94,871	129,246	184,997	288,583	301,510	214,353	77,797
Net Interest Income	77,891	299,258	300,757	285,366	319,726	343,066	254,194	140,244
Provision for Loan Losses	5,600	26,000	51,333	34,147	24,000	52,200	14,374	7,327
Non–Interest Income	35,563	121,876	185,122	109,425	31,095	88,698	33,299	41,107
Non–Interest Expense	66,569	256,295	247,126	227,240	250,031	271,287	232,096	93,593
Net Income	30,982	112,321	123,206	94,461	49,821	69,338	23,151	49,314
Average Shs. Outstg.	45,003	44,892	45,349	47,160	54,186	58,566	47,241	27,357
Balance Sheet								
Cash & Due from Banks	194,126	272,636	275,580	231,641	276,784	277,558	217,954	167,096
Securities Avail. for Sale	1,851,445	2,706,185	2,616,452	1,302,397	422,727	2,804,302	2,260,625	550,505
Net Loans & Leases	4,534,243	4,591,909	4,267,546	4,374,556	5,182,343	5,571,759	3,333,311	1,736,598
Total Assets	7,972,645	8,100,658	7,651,261	6,999,535	6,817,226	9,686,286	6,778,661	3,046,505
Total Deposits	6,242,598	6,243,359	6,199,701	5,983,545	5,813,267	6,455,345	5,051,390	2,314,399
Long–Term Obligations	541,732	1,160,992	751,939	123,000	123,000	132,000	100,000	461,319
Total Liabilities	7,479,894	7,642,468	7,218,735	6,615,631	6,448,753	9,167,120	6,321,846	2,860,365
Net Stockholders' Equity	492,751	458,190	432,526	383,904	368,473	519,166	456,815	186,140
Shares Outstanding	44,826	44,798	45,023	45,814	47,964	57,085	45,786	25,571
Statistical Record								
Return on Equity %	6.28	24.51	28.48	24.60	13.52	13.35	5.06	26.49
Return on Assets %	0.38	1.38	1.61	1.34	0.73	0.71	0.34	1.61
Equity/Assets %	6.18	5.65	5.65	5.48	5.40	5.35	6.73	6.10
Non–Int. Exp./Tot. Inc. %	49.78	48.61	40.17	39.19	39.10	36.99	46.24	36.11
Price Range	39.87–34.18	40.20–30.05	32.67–22.90	29.48–19.56	25.05–16.59	31.77–22.73	34.64–18.98	33.54–19.30
P/E Ratio	15.57–13.35	16.08–12.02	12.01–8.42	14.74–9.78	27.23–18.03	26.93–19.26	70.70–38.73	18.74–10.78
Average Yield %	3.28	3.43	3.71	4.07	4.54	3.13	2.68	2.49

Address: 1000 Macarthur Boulevard, Mahwah, NJ 07430	Officers: Kenneth T. Neilson – Chmn., Pres., C.E.O., James Mayo – Exec. V.P., Oper. & Technology	Investor Contact:201–236–2803
Telephone: (201) 236–2600		Institutional Holding
Web Site: www.hudsonunitedbank.com	Transfer Agents:American Stock Transfer Company, New York, NY	No of Institutions: 182
		Shares: 21,597,254 % Held: 48%

ILLINOIS TOOL WORKS, INC.

Exchange	Symbol	Price	52Wk Range	Yield	P/E
NYS	ITW	$89.88 (5/28/2004)	90.10–63.60	1.07	24.62

*7 Year Price Score 115.9   *NYSE Composite Index=100   *12 Month Price Score 54.1

Interim Earnings (Per Share)

Qtr.	Mar	Jun	Sep	Dec
2001	0.60	0.76	0.65	0.61
2002	0.63	0.86	0.79	0.74
2003	0.65	0.92	0.87	0.93
2004	0.93	...	...	...

Interim Dividends (Per Share)

Amt	Decl	Ex	Rec	Pay
0.24Q	8/8/2003	9/26/2003	9/30/2003	10/20/2003
0.24Q	10/31/2003	12/29/2003	12/31/2003	1/26/2004
0.24Q	2/11/2004	3/29/2004	3/31/2004	4/19/2004
0.24Q	5/7/2004	6/28/2004	6/30/2004	7/19/2004

Indicated Div: $0.96 (Div. Reinv. Plan)

Valuation Analysis

Forecast P/E 21.21 (5/24/2004)

Market Cap	$27.5 Billion	Book Value	8.2 Billion
Price/Book	2.96	Price/Sales	2.34

Dividend Achiever Status

Rank	88	10 Year Growth Rate	14.27%
Total Years of Dividend Growth		41	

Business Summary: Plastics (MIC: 11.7 SIC: 3089 NAIC:326199)

Illinois Tool Works is a global manufacturer of engineered products and specialty systems, and has 625 operations in 44 countries that are organized into five segments. Engineered Products – North America segment and Engineered Products – International segment manufacture short lead–time plastic and metal components and fasteners, and specialty products. Specialty Systems – North America segment and Specialty Systems – International segment design and manufacture longer lead–time machinery and related consumables, and specialty equipment. Leasing and Investments segment invests in mortgage entities, and leases telecommunications, aircraft, air traffic control and other equipment.

Recent Developments: For the three months ended Mar 31 2004, income from continuing operations jumped 45.4% to $290.0 million compared with $199.5 million in the equivalent quarter of 2003. Results benefited primarily from substantial improvement in Co.'s North American end markets in the last two months of the first quarter of 2004. Results for 2004 and 2003 excluded a gain of $171,000 and a loss of $4.1 million, respectively, from discontinued operations. Operating revenues rose 17.1% to $2.71 billion from $2.31 billion in the prior–year period. Operating income increased 39.5% to $447.6 million compared with $321.0 million the year before.

Prospects: During the first quarter of 2004, Co. completed 10 acquisitions, which represents $250.0 million of acquired annual revenues. The increase in acquisitions gives Co. increased confidence that pricing requirements by sellers are becoming more reasonable. Looking ahead, Co. is optimistic about its prospects for full–year 2004 due to the apparent strengthening in Co.'s end markets. As a result, Co. is forecasting earnings per share for the second quarter of 2004 in the range of $1.04 to $1.12. For full year 2004, Co. is forecasting earnings per share in the range of $4.06 to $4.26. The mid–points of the second quarter and full–year 2004 ranges represent growth of 17.0% and 23.0%, respectively.

Financial Data

(US$ in Thousands)	3 Mos	12/31/2003	12/31/2002	12/31/2001	12/31/2000	12/31/1999	12/31/1998	12/31/1997
Earnings Per Share	3.65	3.37	3.02	2.62	3.15	2.76	2.67	2.33
Cash Flow Per Share	1.02	4.43	4.18	4.41	3.68	3.40	2.85	2.62
Tang. Book Val. Per Share	17.23	16.44	13.12	10.82	9.55	9.26	8.59	8.14
Dividends Per Share	0.940	0.930	0.890	0.820	0.740	0.630	0.510	0.430
Dividend Payout %	29.97	27.59	29.47	31.29	23.49	22.82	19.10	18.45
Income Statement								
Total Revenues	2,710,349	10,035,623	9,467,740	9,292,791	9,983,577	9,333,185	5,647,889	5,220,433
Total Indirect Exp.	512,364	1,874,473	1,748,178	1,795,435	1,934,911	1,885,273	942,480	914,416
Depreciation & Amort.	29,023	24,276	27,933	104,585	121,456	74,222	51,899	44,148
Operating Income	447,642	1,633,458	1,505,771	1,306,103	1,563,437	1,405,364	1,079,286	927,223
Net Interest Inc./(Exp.)	(15,882)	(44,501)	(50,881)	(51,875)	(56,528)	(49,950)	(4,487)	(4,791)
Income Taxes	149,400	535,900	501,750	428,400	520,200	511,600	386,800	337,400
Income from Cont Ops	290,025	1,040,214	931,810	802,449	...	...	...	...
Net Income	290,196	1,023,680	712,592	805,659	957,980	841,112	672,784	586,951
Average Shs. Outstg.	310,400	308,750	308,045	306,306	304,414	304,649	252,443	251,760
Balance Sheet								
Cash & Cash Equivalents	1,729,058	1,684,483	1,057,687	282,224	151,295	232,953	93,485	185,856
Total Current Assets	5,095,393	4,783,202	3,878,809	3,163,244	3,329,061	3,272,931	1,834,473	1,858,642
Total Assets	11,766,114	11,193,321	10,623,101	9,822,349	9,603,456	9,060,259	5,997,379	5,291,830
Total Current Liabilities	1,698,772	1,488,903	1,567,162	1,518,158	1,817,610	2,045,361	1,222,009	1,157,880
Long–Term Obligations	920,849	920,360	1,460,381	1,267,141	1,549,038	1,360,746	947,008	854,328
Net Stockholders' Equity	8,234,116	7,874,286	6,649,071	6,040,738	5,400,987	4,815,423	3,338,035	2,806,454
Net Working Capital	3,396,621	3,294,299	2,311,647	1,645,086	1,511,451	1,227,570	612,464	700,762
Shares Outstanding	309,752	308,636	306,582	304,926	305,448	300,568	250,128	249,598
Operating Profit Margin %	16.51	16.27	15.90	14.05	15.66	15.05	19.10	17.76
Return on Equity %	3.52	13.21	14.01	13.28	17.73	17.46	20.15	20.91
Return on Assets %	2.46	9.29	8.77	8.16	9.97	9.28	11.21	11.09
Debt/Total Assets %	7.82	8.22	13.74	12.90	16.13	15.01	15.79	16.14
Price Range	84.78–73.42	84.15–55.15	77.38–55.73	71.20–49.15	68.31–51.06	82.00–58.00	71.81–45.44	60.13–38.38
P/E Ratio	23.23–20.12	24.97–16.36	25.62–18.45	27.18–18.76	21.69–16.21	29.71–21.01	26.90–17.02	25.80–16.47
Average Yield %	1.18	1.37	1.32	1.31	1.27	0.88	0.84	0.89

Address: 3600 West Lake Avenue, Glenview, IL 60025–5811
Telephone: (847) 724–7500
Web Site: www.itw.com

Officers: W. James Farrell – Chmn., C.E.O., Frank S. Ptak – Vice–Chmn.
Transfer Agents: Computershare Investor Service, L.L.C., Chicago, IL

Institutional Holding
No of Institutions: 25
Shares: 49,367,852   **% Held:** –

INDEPENDENT BANK CORPORATION

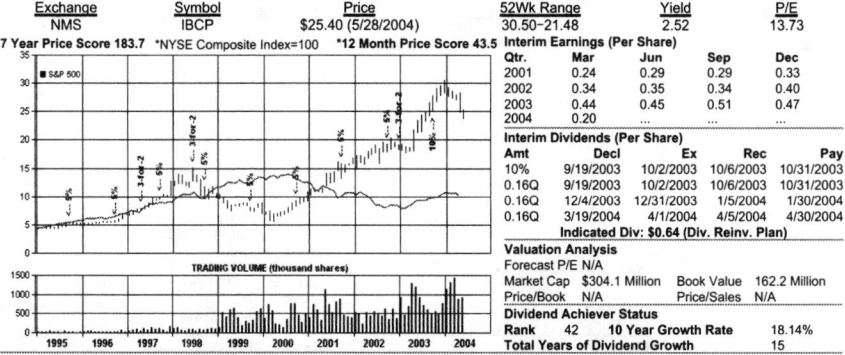

Exchange	Symbol	Price	52Wk Range	Yield	P/E
NMS	IBCP	$25.40 (5/28/2004)	30.50–21.48	2.52	13.73

*7 Year Price Score 183.7 *NYSE Composite Index=100 *12 Month Price Score 43.5

Interim Earnings (Per Share)

Qtr.	Mar	Jun	Sep	Dec
2001	0.24	0.29	0.29	0.33
2002	0.34	0.35	0.34	0.40
2003	0.44	0.45	0.51	0.47
2004	0.20	...	...	...

Interim Dividends (Per Share)

Amt	Decl	Ex	Rec	Pay
10%	9/19/2003	10/2/2003	10/6/2003	10/31/2003
0.16Q	9/19/2003	10/2/2003	10/6/2003	10/31/2003
0.16Q	12/4/2003	12/31/2003	1/5/2004	1/30/2004
0.16Q	3/19/2004	4/1/2004	4/5/2004	4/30/2004

Indicated Div: $0.64 (Div. Reinv. Plan)

Valuation Analysis

Forecast P/E N/A
Market Cap $304.1 Million   Book Value 162.2 Million
Price/Book N/A   Price/Sales N/A

Dividend Achiever Status

Rank 42   10 Year Growth Rate   18.14%
Total Years of Dividend Growth   15

Business Summary: Commercial Banking (MIC: 8.1 SIC: 6022 NAIC:522110)

Independent Bank is a bank holding company. Through its subsidiaries, Co. covers all phases of commercial banking, including checking and savings accounts, commercial lending, direct and indirect consumer financing, mortgage lending and safe deposit box services. Co. also offers title insurance services. Co.'s principal markets are the rural and suburban communities across lower Michigan, in which it serves through four main offices and a total of 77 branches, four drive–thru facilities and 12 loan production offices. As of Dec 31 2003, total assets were $2.36 billion and deposits amounted to $1.70 billion.

Recent Developments: For the quarter ended Mar 31 2004, net income slipped 4.2% to $8.4 million from $8.8 million in the comparable prior–year period. The decline was due to lower net gains on real estate mortgage loan sales, title insurance fees and real estate mortgage loan servicing fees, resulting from an increase in the impairment reserve on capitalized mortgage loan servicing rights. Results for 2004 and 2003 included a net gain of $1.6 million and $4.5 million, respectively, on asset sales. Net interest income grew 22.0% to $25.4 million. Provision for loan losses fell 20.0% to $801,000. Total non–interest income rose 28.6% to $7.4 million, while total non–interest expense climbed 14.4% to $20.7 million.

Prospects: On May 5 2004, Co. announced a definitive agreement to acquire North Bancorp, a $173.0 million bank that operates three branches in the Northern Lower Peninsula of Michigan. Upon completion of the transaction, Co. will have $2.50 billion in assets and $1.80 billion in loans and deposits, with approximately 100 offices across Michigan's Lower Peninsula. The transaction is scheduled to close by Jul 31 2004. Separately, Co. continues to benefit from the acquisition of Mepco Insurance Premium Financing, which was acquired in 2003. At Mar 31 2004, Mepco had total assets of $193.7 million, including finance receivables of $175.8 million.

Financial Data

(US$ in Thousands)	12/31/2003	12/31/2002	12/31/2001	12/31/2000	12/31/1999	12/31/1998	12/31/1997	12/31/1996
Earnings Per Share	1.87	1.43	1.15	0.92	0.39	0.68	0.60	0.57
Tang. Book Val. Per Share	7.05	7.04	6.41	6.38	5.30	4.70	4.10	3.82
Dividends Per Share	0.550	0.410	0.340	0.300	0.270	0.240	0.210	0.190
Dividend Payout %	29.94	28.93	30.00	33.24	69.83	35.42	36.09	34.01
Income Statement								
Total Interest Income	139,366	129,815	141,359	138,415	125,510	86,073	77,414	59,485
Total Interest Expense	44,113	48,008	62,460	67,865	58,730	36,840	34,775	24,813
Net Interest Income	95,253	81,807	78,899	70,550	66,780	49,233	42,639	34,672
Provision for Loan Losses	4,032	3,562	3,737	3,287	2,661	3,043	1,750	1,233
Non–Interest Income	42,604	30,911	27,085	18,961	17,323	13,845	8,515	5,552
Non–Interest Expense	82,506	68,293	68,526	58,949	69,480	45,688	36,845	27,861
Income Before Taxes	51,319	40,863	33,721	27,275	11,962	14,347	12,559	11,130
Income from Cont Ops	...	...	24,433	...	...	...	...	...
Net Income	37,592	29,467	24,398	20,009	8,669	10,221	8,924	7,852
Average Shs. Outstg.	20,059	20,516	21,174	21,525	21,985	14,893	14,615	13,560
Balance Sheet								
Cash & Due from Banks	61,741	60,731	50,525	58,149	58,646	42,846	30,371	40,631
Securities Avail. for Sale	453,996	371,246	290,303	217,447	195,300	99,515	110,769	136,852
Net Loans & Leases	1,649,665	1,364,737	1,368,517	1,365,682	1,277,656	812,890	736,508	602,744
Total Assets	2,358,557	2,057,562	1,888,457	1,783,791	1,725,205	1,085,258	983,817	888,597
Total Deposits	1,702,806	1,535,603	1,387,561	1,389,900	1,310,602	830,514	700,480	672,534
Long–Term Obligations	331,819	310,413	288,010	196,032	224,570	130,964	167,185	152,544
Total Liabilities	2,196,341	1,919,515	1,756,554	1,655,455	1,611,459	1,015,553	924,301	836,761
Net Stockholders' Equity	162,216	138,047	131,903	128,336	113,746	69,705	59,516	51,836
Shares Outstanding	19,568	19,604	20,555	20,113	21,459	14,806	14,488	13,558
Return on Equity %	23.17	21.34	18.52	15.59	7.62	14.66	14.99	15.14
Return on Assets %	1.59	1.43	1.29	1.12	0.50	0.94	0.90	0.88
Equity/Assets %	6.87	6.70	6.98	7.19	6.59	6.42	6.04	5.83
Non–Int. Exp./Tot. Inc. %	45.34	42.49	40.68	37.45	48.64	45.72	42.87	42.83
Price Range	30.50–17.74	20.32–15.02	16.74–10.24	10.86–5.66	10.47–6.94	15.04–9.47	12.82–6.73	7.04–4.98
P/E Ratio	16.31–9.48	14.21–10.51	14.56–8.90	11.80–6.15	26.85–17.79	22.11–13.93	21.37–11.22	12.34–8.73
Average Yield %	2.33	2.29	2.53	3.82	3.15	2.00	2.36	3.37

Address: 230 West Main Street, Ionia, MI 48846
Telephone: (616) 527–9450
Web Site: www.ibcp.com

Officers: Charles C. Van Loan – Pres., C.E.O., Robert N. Shuster – Exec. V.P., C.F.O.

Investor Contact: 616–527–9450
Institutional Holding
No of Institutions: 21
Shares: 723,878 **% Held:** –

IRWIN FINANCIAL CORP. (COLUMBUS, IN)

Exchange	Symbol	Price	52Wk Range	Yield	P/E
NYS	IFC	$25.45 (5/28/2004)	35.75-20.92	1.26	10.39

*7 Year Price Score 126.2 *NYSE Composite Index=100 *12 Month Price Score 42.8

Interim Earnings (Per Share)

Qtr.	Mar	Jun	Sep	Dec
2001	0.41	0.56	0.50	0.52
2002	0.37	0.28	0.29	0.93
2003	0.41	0.45	1.03	0.56
2004	0.67	...	...	...

Interim Dividends (Per Share)

Amt	Decl	Ex	Rec	Pay
0.07Q	8/7/2003	9/10/2003	9/12/2003	9/26/2003
0.07Q	12/1/2003	12/10/2003	12/12/2003	12/26/2003
0.08Q	2/20/2004	3/10/2004	3/12/2004	3/26/2004
0.08Q	5/3/2004	6/9/2004	6/11/2004	6/25/2004

Indicated Div: $0.32 (Div. Reinv. Plan)

Valuation Analysis
Forecast P/E 10.45 (5/24/2004)
Market Cap $705.9 Million   Book Value 432.3 Million
Price/Book 2.08   Price/Sales 1.13

Dividend Achiever Status
Rank 91   10 Year Growth Rate   14.08%
Total Years of Dividend Growth   14

Business Summary: Commercial Banking (MIC: 8.1 SIC: 6022 NAIC:522110)

Irwin Financial is a diversified financial services company with $4.99 billion in assets at Dec 31 2003. Co.'s major lines of business are: mortgage banking, commercial banking, home equity lending, commercial finance and venture capital. Direct and indirect major subsidiaries include Irwin Union Bank and Trust, a commercial bank, which together with Irwin Union Bank, F.S.B., a federal savings bank, conduct Co.'s commercial banking activities; Irwin Mortgage Corporation, a mortgage banking company; Irwin Home Equity Corporation, a consumer home equity lending company; Irwin Commercial Finance Corporation, a commercial finance subsidiary; and IrwinVentures LLC, a venture capital company.

Recent Developments: For the quarter ended Mar 31 2004, net income increased 72.7% to $20.3 million compared with $11.8 million in the corresponding year earlier period. Net interest income declined 8.1% to $59.2 million from $64.4 million the previous year. Provision for loan and lease losses amounted to $8.1 million versus $9.2 million last year. Noninterest income climbed 31.3% to $82.5 million. Mortgage banking net income slid 50.5% to $9.7 million, reflecting declines in production. Commercial banking net income rose 3.8% to $5.4 million. Home equity net income was $6.6 million versus a net loss of $9.5 million, due mainly to improvement in credit quality.

Prospects: Co.'s near-term prospects are mixed. On one hand, Co.'s results going forward will likely be affected by lower mortgage originations due to rising interest rates. However, Co. is hopeful that its credit portfolio, coupled with the investment it has made in its mortgaging servicing portfolio over the past few years, will help counterbalance the year-over-year decline in anticipated mortgage production. Moreover, Co. indicated that it is experiencing improving credit quality trends. Accordingly, Co. continues to expect 2004 earnings to exceed those of 2003.

Financial Data

(US$ in Thousands)	3 Mos	12/31/2003	12/31/2002	12/31/2001	12/31/2000	12/31/1999	12/31/1998	12/31/1997
Earnings Per Share	2.71	2.45	1.87	1.99	1.67	1.51	1.38	1.07
Tang. Book Val. Per Share	4.07	15.36	12.98	10.83	8.96	7.54	6.70	5.81
Dividends Per Share	0.290	0.280	0.270	0.260	0.240	0.200	0.160	0.140
Dividend Payout %	10.70	11.42	14.43	13.06	14.37	13.24	11.59	13.02
Income Statement								
Total Interest Income	79,803	370,984	311,442	268,233	184,530	126,613	122,386	99,441
Total Interest Expense	20,600	99,099	97,795	121,084	93,534	54,794	59,202	44,582
Net Interest Income	59,203	271,885	213,647	147,149	90,996	71,819	63,184	54,859
Provision for Loan Losses	8,146	47,583	43,996	17,505	5,403	4,443	5,995	6,238
Non-Interest Income	82,481	420,302	465,994	321,525	251,240	219,771	243,729	174,564
Non-Interest Expense	100,463	435,199	340,853	327,420	237,962	214,111	245,436	176,534
Eqty Earns/Minority Int.	...	...	...	350	...	...	...	...
Income from Cont Ops	...	...	52,833	45,341	...	...	...	...
Net Income	20,341	72,817	53,328	45,516	...	37,853	35,128	28,918
Average Shs. Outstg.	31,290	30,850	29,675	24,173	21,593	21,886	22,139	22,722
Balance Sheet								
Cash & Due from Banks	175,704							
Securities Avail. for Sale	67,411	67,569	62,599	...	...	...	...	...
Net Loans & Leases	3,158,615	3,096,769	2,764,340	2,115,464	1,221,793	724,869	547,103	602,281
Total Assets	5,146,170	4,988,359	4,884,722	3,439,795	2,422,429	1,680,847	1,946,179	1,496,794
Total Deposits	3,309,007	2,899,662	2,694,344	2,309,018	1,443,330	870,318	1,009,211	719,596
Long-Term Obligations	796,506	860,315	421,495	29,654	29,608	29,784	2,839	7,096
Total Liabilities	4,692,985	4,556,099	4,524,167	3,207,472	2,232,504	1,521,551	1,800,946	1,368,811
Net Stockholders' Equity	453,185	432,260	360,555	232,323	189,925	159,296	145,233	127,983
Shares Outstanding	29,612	28,134	27,771	21,305	21,025	21,104	21,672	22,000
Return on Equity %	4.48	37.89	72.49	41.09	39.59	33.61	24.18	22.59
Return on Assets %	0.39	3.28	5.35	2.77	3.10	3.18	1.80	1.93
Equity/Assets %	8.80	8.66	7.38	6.75	7.84	9.47	7.46	8.55
Non-Int. Exp./Tot. Inc. %	61.90	54.99	43.84	55.51	54.60	61.81	67.03	64.42
Price Range	35.75-26.95	31.99-16.02	20.45-14.00	27.56-14.51	21.00-13.75	28.29-17.76	36.46-19.65	21.43-11.81
P/E Ratio	13.19-9.94	13.06-6.54	10.94-7.49	13.85-7.29	12.57-8.23	18.74-11.76	26.42-14.24	20.02-11.03
Average Yield %	0.95	1.21	1.58	1.23	1.52	0.90	0.61	0.90

Address: 500 Washington Street, Columbus, IN 47201
Telephone: (812) 376 1909
Web Site: www.irwinfinancial.com

Officers: William I. Miller – Chmn., C.E.O., Thomas D. Washburn – Exec. V.P.
Transfer Agents: The Fifth Third Bank, Cincinnati, OH

Investor Contact: 812-376-1020
Institutional Holding
No of Institutions: 30
Shares: 104,437   **% Held:** –

JACK HENRY & ASSOCIATES, INC.

Exchange	Symbol	Price	52Wk Range	Yield	P/E
NMS	JKHY	$19.37 (5/28/2004)	21.97-15.13	0.83	30.26

*7 Year Price Score 117.3 *NYSE Composite Index=100 ***12 Month Price Score 46.7**

Interim Earnings (Per Share)

Qtr.	Sep	Dec	Mar	Jun
2000-01	0.13	0.14	0.17	0.17
2001-02	0.16	0.14	0.15	0.17
2002-03	0.13	0.13	0.14	0.15
2003-04	0.15	0.16	0.18	...

Interim Dividends (Per Share)

Amt	Decl	Ex	Rec	Pay
0.035Q	8/27/2003	9/3/2003	9/5/2003	9/19/2003
0.035Q	10/29/2003	11/14/2003	11/18/2003	12/2/2003
0.04Q	1/26/2004	2/9/2004	2/11/2004	2/26/2004
0.04Q	4/26/2004	5/4/2004	5/6/2004	5/21/2004

Indicated Div: $0.16 (Div. Reinv. Plan)

Valuation Analysis

Forecast P/E 23.85 (5/24/2004)
Market Cap $1.7 Billion Book Value 406.8 Million
Price/Book 4.57 Price/Sales 4.32

Dividend Achiever Status

Rank 46 10 Year Growth Rate 17.67%
Total Years of Dividend Growth 12

Business Summary: IT &Technology (MIC: 10.2 SIC: 7373 NAIC:541512)

Jack Henry & Associates offers a suite of integrated computer systems that provide data processing and management information to banks, credit unions and other financial institutions in the U.S. Co.'s core proprietary applications include: Silverlake System®, typically for banks with total assets up to $30,000,000,000; CIF 20/20®, used primarily by banks with total assets up to $300,000,000; and Core Director®, which is used by banks employing client–server technology. Also, Co. offers Episys™, used primarily by credit unions with total assets greater than $25,000,000 and Cruise™, which is mainly used by credit unions with total assets under $25,000,000.

Recent Developments: For the three months ended Mar 31 2004, net income rose 32.5% to $16.3 million compared with $12.3 million in the equivalent quarter of 2003. Total revenues increased 21.0% to $119.7 million from $98.9 million a year earlier, driven by a 47.0% increase in license revenue, an 18.0% improvement in support and service revenue and a 19.0% jump in hardware revenue. Gross profit grew to $47.3 million, or 39.5% of total revenues, from $38.4 million, or 38.8% of total revenues, in the previous year. The increase in gross margin was primarily due to an improved sales mix of hardware, and a decrease in rebates received on specific hardware sold. Operating income increased 32.2% to $25.5 million.

Prospects: On Apr 12 2004, Co. signed an agreement to purchase e–ClassicSystems, a provider of a suite of software products developed to enable institutions to manage the complete operations and accounting of their ATM networks. The acquisition should enhance Co.'s line of products. Terms of the transaction were not disclosed. Separately, Co. opened a new item processing center in Atlanta, GA and will open another one in St. Louis, MO by the end of fiscal 2004. In addition, Co. plans to open at least one more item processing center during the calendar year. Going forward, Co. should continue to benefit from the realignment of its sales force, and increases in revenue and backlog.

Financial Data

(US$ in Thousands)	6 Mos	3 Mos	06/30/2003	06/30/2002	06/30/2001	06/30/2000	06/30/1999	06/30/1998
Earnings Per Share	0.60	0.57	0.55	0.62	0.61	0.40	0.38	0.28
Cash Flow Per Share	1.00	0.93	1.10	0.97	0.79	0.57	0.44	0.32
Tang. Book Val. Per Share	3.22	2.99	2.78	2.54	2.19	0.47	1.07	0.73
Dividends Per Share	0.140	0.140	0.140	0.130	0.110	0.090	0.070	0.060
Dividend Payout %	22.65	24.56	25.45	20.96	18.03	22.22	18.83	21.23
Income Statement								
Total Revenues	221,670	108,940	404,627	396,657	345,468	225,300	184,497	113,423
Total Indirect Exp.	43,212	21,096	76,065	74,574	65,857	47,106	35,636	24,017
Depreciation & Amort.	16,526	7,958	30,194	27,470	21,888	15,473	7,858	5,105
Operating Income	44,154	21,561	77,271	86,646	85,740	51,010	49,406	33,776
Net Interest Inc./(Exp.)	539	261	520	1,827	466	(1,047)	1,571	1,221
Income Taxes	16,313	7,965	28,394	31,408	31,292	17,415	18,821	13,127
Income from Cont Ops	...	...	...	...	...	34,350	32,526	22,237
Net Income	28,380	13,857	49,397	57,065	55,631	34,018	31,768	21,569
Average Shs. Outstg.	91,534	91,069	89,270	92,367	91,344	85,278	84,448	79,044
Balance Sheet								
Cash & Cash Equivalents	108,536	103,032	32,014	17,765	18,589	5,186	3,185	23,306
Total Current Assets	210,592	201,898	217,262	179,977	172,050	104,000	79,842	69,138
Total Assets	548,375	543,352	548,575	486,142	433,121	321,082	174,721	115,286
Total Current Liabilities	102,419	120,290	146,780	112,656	107,018	151,140	57,666	39,260
Long–Term Obligations	...	...	...	...	...	228	320	...
Net Stockholders' Equity	406,802	385,479	365,223	340,739	302,504	154,545	114,469	73,500
Net Working Capital	108,173	81,608	70,482	67,321	65,032	(47,140)	22,176	29,878
Shares Outstanding	89,558	88,856	88,156	88,950	88,846	82,715	80,400	75,740
Statistical Record								
Operating Profit Margin %	19.91	19.79	19.09	21.84	24.81	22.64	26.77	29.77
Return on Equity %	6.97	3.59	13.52	16.74	18.39	22.22	28.41	30.25
Return on Assets %	5.17	2.55	9.00	11.73	12.84	10.69	18.61	19.28
Debt/Total Assets %	...	...	...	...	...	0.05	0.09	...
Price Range	21.97-16.53	19.31-16.53	17.79-8.31	31.51-16.09	31.47-18.88	25.97-8.13	13.50-6.63	9.50-5.75
P/E Ratio	36.62-27.55	33.88-29.00	32.35-15.11	50.82-25.95	51.59-30.94	64.92-20.31	35.53-17.43	33.93-20.54
Average Yield %	0.73	0.77	1.07	0.56	0.43	0.64	0.69	0.81

Address: 663 Highway 60, Monett, MO 65708
Telephone: (417) 235 6652
Web Site: www.jackhenry.com

Officers: Michael E. Henry – Chmn., C.E.O., John W. Henry – Vice–Chmn., Sr. V.P.
Transfer Agents:UMB Bank, N.A. Kansas City, MO

Investor Contact:417-235-6652
Institutional Holding
No of Institutions: 15
Shares: 49,826,088 **% Held:** –

JEFFERSON-PILOT CORP.

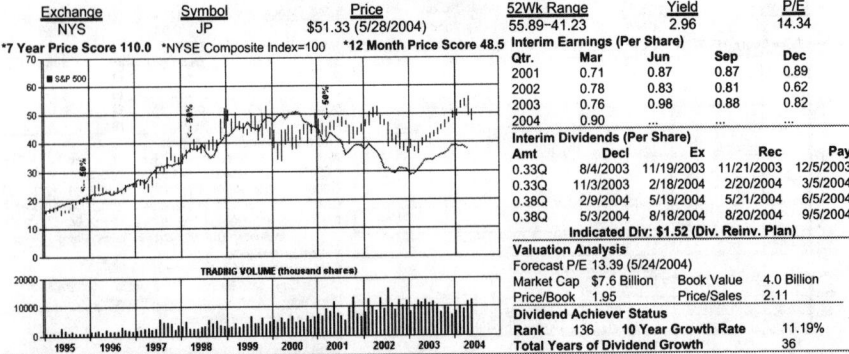

Exchange	Symbol	Price	52Wk Range	Yield	P/E
NYS	JP	$51.33 (5/28/2004)	55.89-41.23	2.96	14.34

*7 Year Price Score 110.0 *NYSE Composite Index=100 *12 Month Price Score 48.5

Interim Earnings (Per Share)

Qtr.	Mar	Jun	Sep	Dec
2001	0.71	0.87	0.87	0.89
2002	0.78	0.83	0.81	0.62
2003	0.76	0.98	0.88	0.82
2004	0.90	...	...	...

Interim Dividends (Per Share)

Amt	Decl	Ex	Rec	Pay
0.33Q	8/4/2003	11/19/2003	11/21/2003	12/5/2003
0.33Q	11/3/2003	2/18/2004	2/20/2004	3/5/2004
0.38Q	2/9/2004	5/19/2004	5/21/2004	6/5/2004
0.38Q	5/3/2004	8/18/2004	8/20/2004	9/5/2004

Indicated Div: $1.52 (Div. Reinv. Plan)

Valuation Analysis

Forecast P/E 13.39 (5/24/2004)

Market Cap	$7.6 Billion	Book Value	4.0 Billion
Price/Book	1.95	Price/Sales	2.11

Dividend Achiever Status

Rank	136	10 Year Growth Rate 11.19%
Total Years of Dividend Growth		36

Business Summary: Insurance (MIC: 8.2 SIC: 6311 NAIC:524113)

Jefferson-Pilot is a holding company that conducts insurance, investment, broadcasting and other business through its subsidiaries. Jefferson-Pilot Life Insurance Company, Jefferson Pilot Financial Insurance Company, and Jefferson Pilot LifeAmerica Insurance Company, together known as Jefferson Pilot Financial, offer full lines of individual and group life insurance products as well as annuity and investment products. As of Dec 31 2003, Jefferson-Pilot Communications Company owned and operated three network television stations and 17 radio stations, and produced and syndicated sports programming.

Recent Developments: For the quarter ended Mar 31 2004, income was $141.2 million, before an accounting charge of $12.9 million, versus net income of $109.1 million in the prior-year quarter. Total revenue advanced 13.5% to $984.8 million from $867.7 million in 2003. Revenue included realized investment gains of $23.5 million in 2004 and realized investment losses of $19.1 million in 2003. Premiums and other considerations increased 21.2% to $279.8 million. Revenue from universal life and investment product charges rose 5.4% to $181.6 million. Net investment income slipped 0.9% to $406.5 million. Communication sales grew 16.0% to $58.1 million, while broker-dealer concessions jumped 50.1% to $35.4 million.

Prospects: Co. is pleased with the overall health of its businesses. For example, in the Annuity and Investment Products segment, fixed annuity sales were $310.1 million, up sharply from $115.3 million in the prior-year period, reflecting good market acceptance of Co.'s equity-indexed products. In addition, Co.'s Individual Products business continues to perform well, with Premier Partners contributing over 71.0% of total life insurance production. Going forward, Co. will look to build its business platforms by investing in technology, distribution support, and product capability. Moreover, the addition of Canada Life should strengthen Co.'s group insurance distribution and platform.

Financial Data

(US$ in Millions)	3 Mos	12/31/2003	12/31/2002	12/31/2001	12/31/2000	12/31/1999	12/31/1998	12/31/1997
Earnings Per Share	3.58	3.44	3.04	3.34	3.28	2.94	2.60	2.31
Tang. Book Val. Per Share	26.16	24.84	22.60	20.52	18.37	15.80	17.77	15.72
Dividends Per Share	1.320	1.290	1.180	1.070	0.960	0.850	0.760	0.690
Dividend Payout %	36.87	37.57	38.89	32.08	29.20	29.07	29.45	30.00
Income Statement								
Total Premium Income	280	951	1,564	1,424	1,365	903	1,049	1,135
Net Investment Income	...	1,657	1,623	1,533	1,430	1,272	1,202	1,103
Other Income	705	965	293	373	443	386	359	340
Total Revenues	985	3,573	3,480	3,330	3,238	2,561	2,610	2,578
Total Indirect Exp.	240	523	485	497	503	402	745	697
Inc. Before Inc. Taxes	215	738	710	800	814	751	670	591
Income Taxes	74	246	235	263	277	256	226	195
Income from Cont Ops	141	...	...	...	...	...	...	...
Net Income	128	492	475	...	537	495	444	396
Average Shs. Outstg.	142	142	148	153	155	159	160	160
Balance Sheet								
Cash & Cash Equivalents	120	72	67	139	26	62	21	9
Premiums Due	1,659	1,340	1,375	1,433	1,450	1,576	1,342	1,526
Invst. Assets: Total	22,667	21,411	20,076	18,130	16,805	16,087	15,570	14,956
Total Assets	34,184	32,696	30,609	28,996	27,321	26,446	24,338	23,131
Long-Term Obligations	909	309	300	450	439	590	627	631
Net Stockholders' Equity	3,970	3,806	3,540	3,391	3,159	2,753	3,049	2,679
Shares Outstanding	139	140	142	150	154	155	158	159
Return on Revenues %	13.19	12.81	13.64	16.12	16.58	19.32	17.01	15.36
Return on Equity %	3.27	12.03	13.41	15.83	16.99	17.98	14.54	14.49
Return on Assets %	0.38	1.40	1.55	1.85	1.96	1.87	1.82	1.71
Price Range	55.01-49.13	50.65-36.20	52.60-36.53	48.95-39.60	50.29-33.63	52.92-41.21	52.21-32.89	38.47-23.11
P/E Ratio	15.37-13.72	14.72-10.52	17.30-12.02	14.66-11.86	15.33-10.25	18.00-14.02	20.08-12.65	16.65-10.00
Average Yield %	2.52	3.02	2.64	2.37	2.28	1.84	1.92	2.31

Address: 100 North Greene Street, Greensboro, NC 27401 **Telephone:** (336) 691 3000 **Web Site:** www.jpfinancial.com	**Officers:** David A. Stonecipher – Chmn., Dennis R. Glass – Pres., C.E.O. **Transfer Agents:** Wachovia Bank, Charlotte, NC	**Investor Contact:** 336–691–3379 **Institutional Holding** **No of Institutions:** 21 **Shares:** 1,730,156 **% Held:** –

JOHNSON & JOHNSON

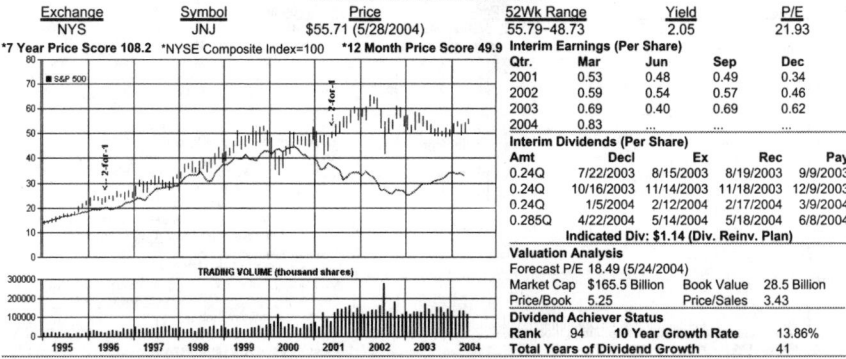

Exchange	Symbol	Price	52Wk Range	Yield	P/E
NYS	JNJ	$55.71 (5/28/2004)	55.79-48.73	2.05	21.93

*7 Year Price Score 108.2 *NYSE Composite Index=100 *12 Month Price Score 49.9

Interim Earnings (Per Share)

Qtr.	Mar	Jun	Sep	Dec
2001	0.53	0.48	0.49	0.34
2002	0.59	0.54	0.57	0.46
2003	0.69	0.40	0.69	0.62
2004	0.83	...	...	...

Interim Dividends (Per Share)

Amt	Decl	Ex	Rec	Pay
0.24Q	7/22/2003	8/15/2003	8/19/2003	9/9/2003
0.24Q	10/16/2003	11/14/2003	11/18/2003	12/9/2003
0.24Q	1/5/2004	2/12/2004	2/17/2004	3/9/2004
0.285Q	4/22/2004	5/14/2004	5/18/2004	6/8/2004

Indicated Div: $1.14 (Div. Reinv. Plan)

Valuation Analysis

Forecast P/E 18.49 (5/24/2004)

Market Cap $165.5 Billion	Book Value 28.5 Billion
Price/Book 5.25	Price/Sales 3.43

Dividend Achiever Status

Rank	94	10 Year Growth Rate	13.86%
Total Years of Dividend Growth			41

Business Summary: Pharmaceuticals (MIC: 9.1 SIC: 2834 NAIC:325412)

Johnson & Johnson is engaged in the manufacture and sale of a broad range of products in the health care field. The Pharmaceutical segment consists of prescription drugs in the antifungal, anti-infective, cardiovascular, dermatology, gastrointestinal, hematology, immunology, neurology, oncology, pain management, psychotropic and urology fields. The Medical Devices and Diagnostics segment includes products used by or under the direction of health care professionals. The Consumer segment manufactures and markets products used in the baby and child care, skin care, oral and wound care and women's health care fields, as well as nutritional and over-the-counter pharmaceutical products.

Recent Developments: For the quarter ended Mar 29 2004, net earnings advanced 20.4% to $2.49 billion compared with $2.07 billion in the corresponding period of the previous year. Results for 2003 included a pre-tax in-process research and development charge of $18.0 million. Sales improved 17.7% to $11.56 billion from $9.82 billion in the year-earlier quarter. Consumer segment sales increased 14.3% to $2.05 billion from $1.79 billion, while Pharmaceutical segment sales climbed 15.2% to $5.38 billion from $4.67 billion in the prior-year period. Sales in the Medical Device and Diagnostics segment jumped 22.9% to $4.14 billion from $3.36 billion the year before.

Prospects: Co. continues to benefit from strong sales growth in its Medical Devices and Diagnostics segment, which is being fueled by Cordis' circulatory disease management products, particularly the *Cypher* sirolimus-eluting coronary stent. Also contributing to the performance of the segment were strong results from DePuy's spinal products. Co.'s Pharmaceutical segment is expected to benefit from solid domestic and international growth for products such as *Risperdal, Levaquin, Topamax* and *Remicade*. The Consumer segment's results are being driven by McNeil Nutritional's *Splenda* sweetner, the skin care lines of *Neutrogena, RoC, Aveeno* and *Clean & Clear*, and wound care products.

Financial Data
(US$ in Millions)

	3 Mos	12/28/2003	12/29/2002	12/30/2001	12/31/2000	01/02/2000	01/03/1999	12/28/1997
Earnings Per Share	2.54	2.40	2.16	1.84	1.70	1.47	1.11	1.20
Cash Flow Per Share	0.88	3.52	2.67	2.86	2.31	2.00	1.78	1.58
Tang. Book Val. Per Share	5.74	5.16	4.53	4.97	4.15	3.10	2.37	3.38
Dividends Per Share	0.960	0.920	0.790	0.700	0.620	0.540	0.480	0.420
Dividend Payout %	37.80	38.54	36.80	38.04	36.47	37.07	43.49	35.26
Income Statement								
Total Revenues	11,559	41,862	36,298	33,004	29,139	27,471	23,657	22,629
Total Indirect Exp.	4,641	19,733	16,362	15,688	13,822	13,103	11,893	10,855
Depreciation & Amort.	502	1,869	1,662	1,605	1,515	1,444	1,246	1,067
Operating Income	3,504	9,953	9,489	7,780	6,456	5,926	4,268	4,622
Net Interest Inc./(Exp.)	(6)	(30)	96	303	233	49	152	83
Income Taxes	1,011	3,111	2,694	2,230	1,822	1,586	1,210	1,273
Net Income	2,493	7,197	6,597	5,668	4,800	4,167	3,059	3,303
Average Shs. Outstg.	3,004	3,008	3,054	3,099	2,834	2,836	2,743	2,739
Balance Sheet								
Cash & Cash Equivalents	10,361	5,377	2,894	3,758	3,411	2,363	1,927	2,753
Total Current Assets	24,364	22,995	19,266	18,473	15,450	13,200	11,132	10,563
Total Assets	48,868	48,263	40,556	38,488	31,321	29,163	26,211	21,453
Total Current Liabilities	12,449	13,448	11,449	8,044	7,161	7,448	8,115	5,283
Long-Term Obligations	2,961	2,955	2,022	2,217	2,037	2,450	1,269	1,126
Net Stockholders' Equity	28,494	26,869	22,697	24,233	18,808	16,213	13,590	12,359
Shares Outstanding	2,967	2,967	2,968	3,047	2,781	2,779	2,688	2,690
Operating Profit Margin %	30.72	23.77	26.14	23.57	22.15	21.57	18.04	20.42
Return on Equity %	8.91	26.78	29.06	23.38	25.52	25.70	22.50	26.72
Return on Assets %	5.19	14.91	16.26	14.72	15.32	14.28	11.67	15.39
Debt/Total Assets %	6.05	6.12	4.98	5.76	6.50	8.40	4.84	5.24
Price Range	54.65-49.50	58.67-48.73	65.49-41.85	60.97-41.63	52.53-33.50	53.06-39.03	44.44-32.00	33.47-24.81
P/E Ratio	21.52-19.49	24.45-20.30	30.32-19.38	33.14-22.62	30.90-19.71	36.10-26.55	40.03-28.83	27.89-20.68
Average Yield %	1.83	1.75	1.37	1.35	1.39	1.15	1.28	1.41

Address: One Johnson &Johnson Plaza, NB, NJ 08933
Telephone: (732) 524 0400
Web Site: www.jnj.com

Officers: William C. Weldon - Chmn., C.E.O., Robert J. Darretta - Vice-Chmn., C.F.O.
Transfer Agents: EquiServe Trust Company, N.A., Providence, RI

Investor Contact: 800-950-5089
Institutional Holding
No of Institutions: 18
Shares: 1,225,161 **% Held:** -

JOHNSON CONTROLS INC

Exchange	Symbol	Price	52Wk Range	Yield	P/E
NYS	JCI	$53.92 (5/28/2004)	60.90–42.20	1.67	14.04

*7 Year Price Score 148.2 *NYSE Composite Index=100 *12 Month Price Score 47.5

Interim Earnings (Per Share)

Qtr.	Dec	Mar	Jun	Sep
2000–01	0.55	0.44	0.72	0.84
2001–02	0.63	0.60	0.92	1.02
2002–03	0.74	0.70	1.00	1.16
2003–04	0.86	0.82	...	...

Interim Dividends (Per Share)

Amt	Decl	Ex	Rec	Pay
0.225Q	11/19/2003	12/10/2003	12/12/2003	1/2/2004
2–for–1	11/19/2003	1/5/2004	12/12/2003	1/2/2004
0.225Q	1/28/2004	3/10/2004	3/12/2004	3/31/2004
0.225Q	5/26/2004	6/9/2004	6/11/2004	6/30/2004

Indicated Div: $0.90 (Div. Reinv. Plan)

Valuation Analysis
Forecast P/E 13.13 (5/24/2004)
Market Cap $4.8 Billion   Book Value 4.8 Billion
Price/Book 2.25   Price/Sales 0.43

Dividend Achiever Status
Rank 205   10 Year Growth Rate 7.79%
Total Years of Dividend Growth 28

Business Summary: Chemicals (MIC: 11.1 SIC: 2531 NAIC:561790)

Johnson Controls conducts its business in two operating segments: the Controls Group and the Automotive Group. The Controls Group provides installed building control systems and technical and facility management services, including comfort, energy and security management for the non–residential buildings market. The Automotive Group designs and manufactures products and systems for passenger cars and light trucks, including vans and SUVs. The segment produces automotive interior systems for original equipment manufacturers and automotive batteries for the replacement and original equipment markets.

Recent Developments: For the three months ended Mar 31 2004, net income rose 19.3% to $157.7 million compared with $132.2 million in the corresponding quarter of 2003. Net income benefited from higher operating income, improved foreign currency results and a lower effective income tax rate. Net sales were $6.62 billion, up 20.3% from $5.50 billion in the prior–year period. Sales in the Automotive Group grew 23.5% to $5.10 billion due to new business to the supply of interior systems and higher battery sales. Sales in the Controls Group rose 10.8% to $1.52 billion due to increased activity in installed systems, technical services and facilities management. Operating income climbed 9.9% to $260.9 million.

Prospects: Co. confirmed its guidance for consolidated sales growth for fiscal 2004 of 13.0% to 15.0% and expects to achieve double–digit increases in operating income and net income. The Automotive Group guidance includes sales growth of 13.0% to 18.0%, North American light vehicle production of approximately 15.9 million units and European production of 19.8 million units, and a flat to slightly lower operating margin percentage. The Controls Group guidance includes sales growth of 10.0% to 12.0%, up from the high end of 5.0% to 10.0%, and a slightly lower operating margin percentage. Capital expenditures for fiscal 2004 are estimated to be $750.0 million.

Financial Data

(US$ in Thousands)	6 Mos	3 Mos	09/30/2003	09/30/2002	09/30/2001	09/30/2000	09/30/1999	09/30/1998
Earnings Per Share	3.84	3.84	3.60	3.17	2.55	2.54	2.24	1.81
Cash Flow Per Share	3.13	1.29	4.06	5.25	5.23	4.05	5.49	3.04
Tang. Book Val. Per Share	5.75	5.12	3.79	2.23	3.51	1.82	0.22	N.M
Dividends Per Share	0.760	0.720	0.702	0.660	0.620	0.560	0.490	0.450
Dividend Payout %	19.79	18.75	19.50	20.82	24.26	22.05	21.87	24.93
Income Statement								
Total Revenues	13,004,200	6,384,100	22,646,000	20,103,400	18,427,200	17,154,600	16,139,400	12,586,800
Total Indirect Exp.	1,188,400	599,500	2,058,600	1,724,900	1,642,900	1,629,500	1,469,000	1,146,600
Depreciation & Amort.	301,200	148,600	558,000	516,800	515,900	461,800	445,600	384,200
Operating Income	522,700	261,800	1,161,600	1,122,000	961,100	965,000	854,900	664,000
Net Interest Inc./(Exp.)	(47,800)	(25,300)	(103,500)	(110,400)	(110,000)	(111,500)	(136,000)	(118,700)
Income Taxes	121,900	49,700	327,800	347,600	335,500	338,900	311,700	256,000
Eqty Earns/Minority Int.	(800)	2,300	8,100	(20,000)	(21,500)	(44,400)	(38,600)	(23,100)
Net Income	322,200	164,500	682,900	600,500	478,300	472,400	419,600	337,700
Average Shs. Outstg.	192,300	191,800	189,200	188,200	186,000	183,800	184,200	183,200
Balance Sheet								
Cash & Cash Equivalents	226,400	302,600	136,100	262,000	374,600	275,600	276,200	134,000
Total Current Assets	6,002,400	5,750,100	5,620,300	4,946,200	4,544,000	4,277,200	3,848,500	3,404,200
Total Assets	14,118,300	13,670,900	13,127,300	11,165,300	9,911,500	9,428,000	8,614,200	7,942,100
Total Current Liabilities	5,986,100	5,731,500	5,584,100	4,806,200	4,579,700	4,510,000	4,266,600	4,288,400
Long–Term Obligations	1,888,900	1,830,600	1,776,600	1,826,600	1,394,800	1,315,300	1,283,300	997,500
Net Stockholders' Equity	4,769,300	4,581,600	4,261,300	3,499,700	2,985,400	2,576,100	2,270,000	1,941,400
Net Working Capital	16,300	18,600	36,200	140,000	(35,700)	(232,800)	(418,100)	(884,200)
Shares Outstanding	190,026	188,551	180,310	177,760	174,997	171,978	170,790	169,400
Statistical Record								
Operating Profit Margin %	4.01	4.10	5.12	5.58	5.21	5.62	5.29	5.27
Return on Equity %	6.76	3.59	16.02	17.15	16.02	18.33	18.48	17.39
Return on Assets %	2.28	1.20	5.20	5.37	4.82	5.01	4.87	4.25
Debt/Total Assets %	13.38	13.39	13.53	16.35	14.07	13.95	14.89	12.55
Price Range	60.90–47.30	58.06–47.30	50.35–35.26	46.53–32.75	40.78–23.84	35.19–23.50	37.56–20.97	30.50–21.38
P/E Ratio	15.86–12.32	67.51–55.00	13.98–9.79	14.68–10.33	15.99–9.35	13.85–9.25	16.77–9.36	16.85–11.81
Average Yield %	1.35	1.34	1.55	1.19	1.88	2.41	1.55	1.73

Address: 5757 North Green Bay Avenue, Milwaukee, WI 53201	Officers: John M. Barth – Chmn., Pres., C.E.O., Giovanni Fiori – Exec. V.P.	Investor Contact:414–524–2363
Telephone: (414) 524 1200	Transfer Agents:Firstar Trust Company,	Institutional Holding
Web Site: www.johnsoncontrols.com	Milwaukee, WI	No of Institutions: 9
		Shares: 124,664 % Held: –

KEYCORP (NEW)

Exchange	Symbol	Price	52Wk Range	Yield	P/E
NYS	KEY	$31.41 (5/28/2004)	32.94-25.20	3.95	14.28

*7 Year Price Score 102.7 ***NYSE Composite Index=100** ***12 Month Price Score 50.7**

Interim Earnings (Per Share)

Qtr.	Mar	Jun	Sep	Dec
2001	0.51	(0.38)	0.58	(0.34)
2002	0.56	0.57	0.57	0.57
2003	0.51	0.53	0.53	0.55
2004	0.59	...	...	...

Interim Dividends (Per Share)

Amt	Decl	Ex	Rec	Pay
0.305Q	7/17/2003	8/28/2003	9/2/2003	9/15/2003
0.305Q	11/21/2003	11/28/2003	12/2/2003	12/12/2003
0.31Q	1/16/2004	2/27/2004	3/2/2004	3/15/2004
0.31Q	5/14/2004	5/27/2004	6/1/2004	6/15/2004

Indicated Div: $1.24 (Div. Reinv. Plan)

Valuation Analysis

Forecast P/E 13.72 (5/24/2004)

Market Cap	$13.4 Billion	Book Value	7.0 Billion
Price/Book	1.78	Price/Sales	2.19

Dividend Achiever Status

Rank	199	10 Year Growth Rate	8.10%

Total Years of Dividend Growth 24

Business Summary: Commercial Banking (MIC: 8.1 SIC: 6021 NAIC:522110)

KeyCorp is a multi-line financial services company, with assets of $84.49 billion as of Dec 31 2003. Co. provides investment management, retail and commercial banking, consumer finance, and investment banking products and services to individuals and companies throughout the United States and, for certain businesses, internationally. As of Dec 31 2003, Co. operates nationwide through 906 KeyCenters and offices, a network of 2,167 ATMs, telephone banking centers, and a Web site named Key.com that provides account access and financial products 24 hours a day.

Recent Developments: For the quarter ended Mar 31 2004, net income climbed 15.2% to $250.0 million from $217.0 million in the corresponding period of the year before. Results for 2004 and 2003 included net gains from loan securitizations and sales of $25.0 million and $15.0 million, respectively. Net interest income slipped 2.9% to $661.0 million. Provision for loan losses decreased 37.7% to $81.0 million. Total non-interest income improved 8.6% to $431.0 million, reflecting a decrease in losses incurred on the residual values of leased vehicles and equipment and an increase in net gains from loan sales. Total non-interest expense grew 0.3% to $659.0 million.

Prospects: Co. continues to perform well, reflecting improved revenues, stable expenses and significantly improved asset quality. Co.'s market-sensitive businesses, including trust and investment services, and principal investing are benefiting from strengthening equity markets, as well as the integration of Co.'s banking, investments and trust businesses. Meanwhile, the improvement in Co.'s asset quality continues to be driven by declines in non-performing loans and net loan charge-offs. Looking ahead, Co. expects earnings per share in the range of $0.54 to $0.59 for the second quarter of 2004 and to be between $2.30 to $2.45 for the full year.

Financial Data

(US$ in Thousands)	3 Mos	12/31/2003	12/31/2002	12/31/2001	12/31/2000	12/31/1999	12/31/1998	12/31/1997
Earnings Per Share	2.20	2.12	2.27	0.37	2.30	2.45	2.23	2.07
Tang. Book Val. Per Share	14.10	13.88	13.34	11.84	12.41	11.14	10.29	9.14
Dividends Per Share	1.220	1.220	1.200	1.180	1.120	1.040	0.940	0.840
Dividend Payout %	55.68	57.54	52.86	318.91	48.69	42.44	42.15	40.57
Income Statement								
Total Interest Income	939,000	3,970,000	4,366,000	5,627,000	6,277,000	5,695,000	5,525,000	5,262,000
Total Interest Expense	278,000	1,245,000	1,617,000	2,802,000	3,547,000	2,908,000	2,841,000	2,468,000
Net Interest Income	661,000	2,725,000	2,749,000	2,825,000	2,730,000	2,787,000	2,684,000	2,794,000
Provision for Loan Losses	81,000	501,000	553,000	1,350,000	490,000	348,000	297,000	320,000
Non-Interest Income	431,000	1,760,000	1,769,000	1,725,000	2,194,000	2,294,000	1,575,000	1,306,000
Non-Interest Expense	659,000	2,742,000	2,653,000	2,941,000	2,917,000	3,049,000	2,483,000	2,435,000
Income Before Taxes	352,000	1,242,000	1,312,000	259,000	1,517,000	1,684,000	1,479,000	1,345,000
Income from Cont Ops	...	...	...	157,000	...	...	...	...
Net Income	250,000	903,000	976,000	132,000	1,002,000	1,107,000	996,000	919,000
Average Shs. Outstg.	421,572	426,157	430,703	429,573	435,573	452,363	447,437	444,544
Balance Sheet								
Cash & Due from Banks	2,113,000	2,712,000	3,364,000	2,891,000	3,189,000	2,816,000	3,296,000	3,651,000
Securities Avail. for Sale	7,463,000	7,638,000	8,507,000	5,346,000	7,329,000	6,665,000	5,278,000	7,708,000
Net Loans & Leases	61,207,000	61,305,000	61,005,000	61,632,000	65,904,000	56,894,000	54,103,000	52,480,000
Total Assets	84,448,000	84,487,000	85,202,000	80,938,000	87,270,000	76,997,000	73,011,000	73,699,000
Total Deposits	49,931,000	50,858,000	49,346,000	44,795,000	48,649,000	43,233,000	42,583,000	45,073,000
Long-Term Obligations	15,333,000	15,294,000	15,605,000	14,554,000	14,161,000	15,881,000	12,967,000	7,446,000
Total Liabilities	77,449,000	77,518,000	78,367,000	74,783,000	80,647,000	77,006,000	73,853,000	67,768,000
Net Stockholders' Equity	6,999,000	6,969,000	6,835,000	6,155,000	6,623,000	6,389,000	6,167,000	4,431,000
Shares Outstanding	412,153	416,494	423,943	424,005	423,254	443,427	452,452	438,064
Return on Equity %	3.57	12.95	14.27	2.55	15.12	17.32	16.15	17.73
Return on Assets %	0.29	1.06	1.14	0.19	1.14	1.43	1.36	1.24
Equity/Assets %	8.28	8.24	8.02	7.60	7.58	8.29	8.44	7.02
Non-Int. Exp./Tot. Inc. %	48.10	47.85	43.24	40.00	34.43	38.16	34.97	37.07
Price Range	32.94-28.80	29.32-22.52	29.00-21.30	28.44-20.75	28.25-15.69	36.94-21.19	42.94-24.94	36.44-24.19
P/E Ratio	14.97-13.09	13.83-10.62	12.78-9.38	76.86-56.08	12.28-6.82	15.08-8.65	19.25-11.18	17.60-11.68
Average Yield %	3.94	4.71	4.66	4.75	5.36	3.48	2.77	2.88

Address: 127 Public Square, Cleveland, OH 44114-1306

Telephone: (216) 689-6300

Web Site: www.key.com

Officers: Henry L. Meyer III - Chmn., Pres., C.E.O., Thomas C. Stevens - Vice-Chmn., Chief Admin. Officer, Sec.

Transfer Agents: Computershare Investor Services, Chicago, IL

Investor Contact:16 689-4520)

Institutional Holding

No of Institutions: 437

Shares: 222,276,452 **% Held:** 52.50%

KIMBERLY–CLARK CORP.

Exchange	Symbol	Price	52Wk Range	Yield	P/E
NYS	KMB	$65.90 (5/28/2004)	66.43–47.38	2.43	19.05

*7 Year Price Score 99.9   *NYSE Composite Index=100   *12 Month Price Score 53.8

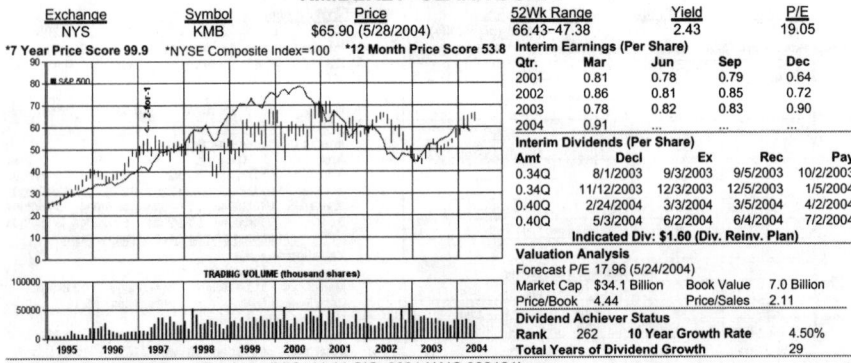

Interim Earnings (Per Share)

Qtr.	Mar	Jun	Sep	Dec
2001	0.81	0.78	0.79	0.64
2002	0.86	0.81	0.85	0.72
2003	0.78	0.82	0.83	0.90
2004	0.91	...	...	...

Interim Dividends (Per Share)

Amt	Decl	Ex	Rec	Pay
0.34Q	8/1/2003	9/3/2003	9/5/2003	10/2/2003
0.34Q	11/12/2003	12/3/2003	12/5/2003	1/5/2004
0.40Q	2/24/2004	3/3/2004	3/5/2004	4/2/2004
0.40Q	5/3/2004	6/2/2004	6/4/2004	7/2/2004

Indicated Div: $1.60 (Div. Reinv. Plan)

Valuation Analysis

Forecast P/E 17.96 (5/24/2004)

Market Cap $34.1 Billion	Book Value 7.0 Billion
Price/Book 4.44	Price/Sales 2.11

Dividend Achiever Status

Rank 262	10 Year Growth Rate	4.50%
Total Years of Dividend Growth		29

Business Summary: Paper Products (MIC: 11.11 SIC: 2621 NAIC:322121)

Kimberly–Clark is engaged in the manufacturing and marketing of health and hygiene products. The Personal Care segment manufactures disposable diapers, training and youth pants and swimpants and feminine and incontinence care products. The Consumer Tissue segment manufactures facial and bathroom tissue, paper towels and napkins for household use and wet wipes. The Business–to–Business segment manufactures facial and bathroom tissue, paper towels, wipers and napkins for away–from–home use, health care products; and printing papers. Brands include *Huggies, Pull–Ups, Little Swimmers, GoodNites, Kotex, Lightdays, Depend, Kleenex, Scott, Cottonelle, Viva, Scottex, Kimberly–Clark and Kimwipes.*

Recent Developments: For the quarter ended Mar 31 2004, net income grew 15.5% to $459.3 million compared with $397.7 million in the equivalent 2003 quarter. Results for 2003 included an unusual charge of $15.6 million. Net sales rose 9.8% to $3.80 billion from $3.46 billion a year earlier. The increase in sales was primarily attributed to a 6.0% improvement in sales volumes. Sales volume gains were boosted by double–digit growth for Co.'s child care products in North America, driven by record shipments of *Pull–Ups* training pants and mid single–digit growth for *Huggies* diapers in North America. Gross profit advanced 7.0% to $1.29 billion. Operating income grew 11.9% to $648.3 million from $579.3 million in 2003.

Prospects: In the second quarter 2004, Co. expects to overcome recent increases in fiber, polymer and oil costs to deliver earnings in a range of $0.87 to $0.89 per share, an improvement of 6.0% to 9.0% compared with earnings of $0.82 per share in 2003. This is consistent with Co.'s bottom–line growth targets both for 2004 and longer–term. For full–year 2004, Co. expects to achieve its targets of between 3.0% to 5.0% volume growth and $150.0 million of cost reductions. Co. also anticipates that earnings per share will be toward the high end of its targeted range of $3.55 to $3.65. Going forward, Co. plans to emphasize brand–building in an effort to drive growth.

Financial Data

(US$ in Thousands)	3 Mos	12/31/2003	12/31/2002	12/31/2001	12/31/2000	12/31/1999	12/31/1998	12/31/1997
Earnings Per Share	3.46	3.33	3.24	3.02	3.31	3.09	2.13	1.58
Cash Flow Per Share	1.21	5.13	4.66	4.22	3.92	3.95	3.60	2.51
Tang. Book Val. Per Share	8.66	9.34	7.73	8.12	7.04	7.11	6.12	6.34
Dividends Per Share	1.360	1.320	1.180	1.110	1.070	1.030	0.990	0.950
Dividend Payout %	39.19	39.63	36.41	36.75	32.32	33.33	46.47	60.12
Income Statement								
Total Revenues	3,799,100	14,348,000	13,566,300	14,524,400	13,982,000	13,006,800	12,297,800	12,546,600
Total Indirect Exp.	653,800	2,487,500	2,351,800	3,570,700	3,119,700	2,889,800	3,023,900	3,270,800
Depreciation & Amort.	200,400	745,800	706,600	89,400	81,700	41,800	33,300	16,800
Operating Income	648,300	2,412,400	2,463,800	2,338,200	2,633,800	2,435,400	1,676,100	1,303,200
Income Taxes	116,700	514,200	666,600	645,700	758,500	730,200	561,900	433,100
Income from Cont Ops	...	...	1,686,000	...	...	...	1,177,000	884,000
Net Income	459,300	1,694,200	1,674,600	1,609,900	1,800,600	1,668,100	1,165,800	901,500
Average Shs. Outstg.	505,300	508,600	520,000	533,200	543,800	540,100	553,100	559,300
Balance Sheet								
Cash & Cash Equivalents	329,000	290,600	494,500	405,200	206,500	322,800	144,000	90,800
Total Current Assets	4,480,900	4,438,100	4,273,900	3,922,200	3,789,900	3,561,800	3,366,900	3,489,000
Total Assets	16,888,100	16,779,900	15,585,800	15,007,600	14,479,800	12,815,500	11,510,300	11,266,000
Total Current Liabilities	3,707,500	3,918,700	4,038,300	4,168,300	4,573,900	3,845,800	3,790,700	3,706,300
Long–Term Obligations	2,811,700	2,733,700	2,844,000	2,424,000	2,000,600	1,926,600	2,068,200	1,803,900
Net Stockholders' Equity	6,992,900	6,766,300	5,650,300	5,646,900	5,767,300	5,093,100	3,887,200	4,125,300
Shares Outstanding	501,325	501,589	510,800	521,000	533,400	540,600	538,300	556,300
Operating Profit Margin %	16.68	16.81	18.16	16.09	18.83	18.72	13.62	10.38
Return on Equity %	6.36	23.09	27.17	26.02	31.22	32.75	30.27	21.42
Return on Assets %	2.63	10.09	10.81	10.72	12.43	13.01	10.22	7.84
Debt/Total Assets %	16.64	16.29	18.24	16.15	13.81	15.03	17.96	16.01
Price Range	65.03–56.47	59.09–43.39	66.50–46.05	71.79–52.24	71.80–45.19	68.06–45.75	58.94–37.38	56.25–44.75
P/E Ratio	18.79–16.32	17.74–13.03	20.52–14.21	23.77–17.30	21.69–13.65	22.03–14.81	27.67–17.55	35.60–28.32
Average Yield %	2.24	2.63	2.01	1.81	1.80	1.82	2.04	1.88

Address: P.O. Box 619100, Dallas, TX 75261–9100	Officers: Thomas J. Falk – Chmn., Pres., C.E.O., Mark A. Buthman – Sr. V.P., C.F.O.	Investor Contact:800–639–1352
Telephone: (972) 281 1200	Transfer Agents:EquiServe Trust Company, N.A.,	Institutional Holding No of Institutions: 834
Web Site: www.kimberly–clark.com	Providence, RI	Shares: 360,807,114 % Held: 70.90%

KIMCO REALTY CORP.

Exchange	Symbol	Price	52Wk Range	Yield	P/E
NYS	KIM	$45.95 (5/28/2004)	51.19-37.20	4.96	22.41

*7 Year Price Score 143.7 ***NYSE Composite Index=100** ***12 Month Price Score 47.0**

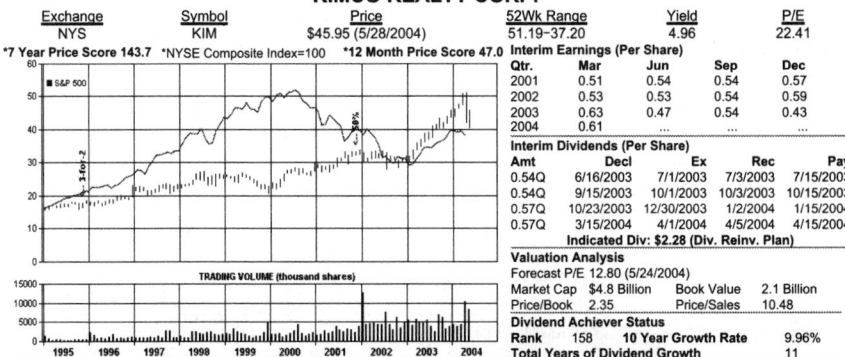

Interim Earnings (Per Share)

Qtr.	Mar	Jun	Sep	Dec
2001	0.51	0.54	0.54	0.57
2002	0.53	0.53	0.54	0.59
2003	0.63	0.47	0.54	0.43
2004	0.61	...	...	...

Interim Dividends (Per Share)

Amt	Decl	Ex	Rec	Pay
0.54Q	6/16/2003	7/1/2003	7/3/2003	7/15/2003
0.54Q	9/15/2003	10/1/2003	10/3/2003	10/15/2003
0.57Q	10/23/2003	12/30/2003	1/2/2004	1/15/2004
0.57Q	3/15/2004	4/1/2004	4/5/2004	4/15/2004
	Indicated Div: $2.28 (Div. Reinv. Plan)			

Valuation Analysis

Forecast P/E 12.80 (5/24/2004)

Market Cap $4.8 Billion	Book Value 2.1 Billion
Price/Book 2.35	Price/Sales 10.48

Dividend Achiever Status

Rank 158	10 Year Growth Rate 9.96%
Total Years of Dividend Growth	11

Business Summary: Property, Real Estate &Development (MIC: 8.3 SIC: 6798 NAIC:525930)

Kimco Realty is an owner and operator of neighborhood and community shopping centers. As of Feb 5 2004, Co. had interests in 699 properties totaling approximately 102.6 million square feet of leasable space located in 41 states, Canada and Mexico. Co.'s portfolio includes properties relating to the Kimco Income REIT, a joint venture arrangement with institutional investors established for the purpose of investing in retail properties financed primarily with individual non–recourse mortgages debt. Co.'s ownership interests also include the RioCan Venture and Kimco Retail Opportunity Portfolio and other properties or portfolios where Co. also retains management.

Recent Developments: For the three months ended Mar 31 2004, income from continuing operations rose 15.5% to $70.9 million compared with $61.4 million in the same period of 2003. Results for 2003 included a gain on the early extinguishment of debt of $2.9 million. Results for 2004 and 2003 excluded a loss of $3.4 million and a gain of $8.8 million from discontinued operations, and gains on the sale of development properties of $3.9 million and $824,000, respectively. Revenues from rental properties increased 17.1% to $139.9 million versus $119.5 million in the prior–year period. Funds from operations rose 13.6% to $101.3 million from $89.2 million in the previous year.

Prospects: During the quarter, Co. acquired interests in six shopping center properties and a parcel of land for development. The properties, which total 1.7 million square feet of gross leasable area, were acquired in separate transactions for an aggregate amount of $256.6 million. Four of these acquisitions were designated for Co.'s co–investment programs, which should further enhance Co.'s management business. Separately, Co. increased its guidance for funds from operations per share for 2004 to a range of $3.47 to $3.52, up from its previous range of $3.41 to $3.46. The increase is due to Co.'s strong operating performance and improved outlook for 2004.

Financial Data

(US$ in Thousands)	12/31/2003	12/31/2002	12/31/2001	12/31/2000	12/31/1999	12/31/1998	12/31/1997	12/31/1996
Earnings Per Share	2.07	2.19	2.16	1.90	1.64	1.34	1.18	1.07
Tang. Book Val. Per Share	19.30	18.22	18.27	17.98	17.59	17.55	12.25	11.12
Dividends Per Share	2.160	2.080	1.920	1.770	1.580	1.310	1.140	1.040
Dividend Payout %	104.34	94.97	88.88	93.00	96.34	97.52	96.62	97.20
Income Statement								
Rental Income	479,664	450,829	468,616	459,407	433,880	338,798	198,929	168,144
Total Income	479,664	450,829	468,616	459,407	433,880	338,798	198,929	168,144
Total Indirect Exp.	240,149	147,624	93,437	160,209	161,165	136,306	81,330	70,443
Depreciation	86,237	74,223	148,418	142,258	134,832	102,695	60,105	54,133
Interest Expense	102,709	86,896	...	...	...	...	...	...
Income Taxes	1,516	12,904	19,376	...	...	...	...	...
Eqty Earns/Minority Int.	34,408	37,999	56,451	16,624	12,000	4,382	1,581	1,291
Income from Cont Ops	233,781	248,570	...	...	...	127,166	...	...
Net Income	307,879	245,668	236,538	205,025	176,778	122,266	85,836	73,827
Average Shs. Outstg.	108,770	105,969	101,163	93,653	91,466	75,960	56,775	53,859
Balance Sheet								
Cash & Cash Equivalents	93,965	102,954	176,844	19,097	28,076	43,921	30,978	37,425
Ttl Real Estate Inv.	4,168,988	3,394,627	3,027,539	2,935,116	2,822,791	2,847,387	1,222,520	925,641
Total Assets	4,603,925	3,756,838	3,384,799	3,171,348	3,007,476	3,051,178	1,343,890	1,022,566
Long–Term Obligations	468,698	274,732	292,829	245,413	212,321	434,311	121,364	54,405
Total Liabilities	2,468,079	1,849,550	1,494,695	1,467,009	1,402,041	1,466,160	600,571	417,262
Net Stockholders' Equity	2,135,846	1,907,328	1,890,084	1,704,339	1,605,435	1,585,019	743,319	605,305
Shares Outstanding	110,623	104,601	103,352	94,717	91,193	90,200	60,592	54,322
Net Inc.+Depr./Assets %	8.56	8.60	7.00	6.50	5.90	4.20	6.40	7.20
Return on Equity %	10.94	13.03	12.51	12.02	11.01	8.02	11.54	12.19
Return on Assets %	5.07	6.61	6.98	6.46	5.87	4.16	6.38	7.21
Price Range	45.86-30.50	33.61-28.01	34.00-27.27	29.75-22.04	26.92-20.83	27.37-22.42	23.83-20.33	23.25-17.00
P/E Ratio	22.15-14.73	15.35-12.79	15.74-12.62	15.66-11.60	16.41-12.70	20.43-16.73	20.20-17.23	21.73-15.89
Average Yield %	5.62	6.62	6.29	6.73	6.41	5.28	5.16	5.55

Address: 3333 New Hyde Park Road, New Hyde Park, NY 11042–0020	Officers: Milton Cooper – Chmn., C.E.O., Michael J. Flynn – Vice–Chmn., Pres., C.O.O.	Investor Contact:516–869–9000
Telephone: (516) 869 9000	Transfer Agents:The Bank of New York, New York, NY	Institutional Holding
Web Site: www.kimcorealty.com		No of Institutions: 31
		Shares: 46,703,074 % Held: –

LANCASTER COLONY CORP.

*7 Year Price Score 118.8 *NYSE Composite Index=100   ***12 Month Price Score 45.5**

Interim Earnings (Per Share)

Qtr.	Sep	Dec	Mar	Jun
2000–01	0.57	0.78	0.52	0.53
2001–02	0.55	0.47	0.78	0.69
2002–03	0.56	1.43	0.50	0.62
2003–04	0.55	0.74	0.45	...

Interim Dividends (Per Share)

Amt	Decl	Ex	Rec	Pay
0.20Q	8/27/2003	9/8/2003	9/10/2003	9/30/2003
0.23Q	11/17/2003	12/8/2003	12/10/2003	12/31/2003
0.23Q	2/25/2004	3/8/2004	3/10/2004	3/31/2004
0.23Q	5/26/2004	6/8/2004	6/10/2004	6/30/2004

Indicated Div: $0.92 (Div. Reinv. Plan)

Valuation Analysis
Forecast P/E 16.58 (5/24/2004)
Market Cap $1.5 Billion   Book Value 583.3 Million
Price/Book 2.44   Price/Sales 1.30

Dividend Achiever Status
Rank 122   10 Year Growth Rate 11.94%
Total Years of Dividend Growth 34

Business Summary: Food (MIC: 4.1 SIC: 2038 NAIC:311412)

Lancaster Colony operates in three business segments. The Specialty Foods segment manufactures and sells salad dressings and sauces, frozen unbaked pies, frozen breads, refrigerated chip and produce dips, dairy snacks and desserts, premium dry egg noodles, frozen noodles, pastas and specialty items, croutons, and caviar. The Glassware and Candles segment produces machine–pressed and machine–blown consumer glassware, technical glass products, and candles and other home fragrances of all sizes, forms and fragrance. The Automotive segment manufactures and sells rubber, vinyl and carpeted car mats, pickup truck bed mats, running boards, bed liners, tool boxes, and other accessories.

Recent Developments: For the three months ended Mar 31 2004, net income totaled $16.0 million, down 11.1% versus $18.0 million in the previous year. Results for 2003 included an $84,000 pre–tax restructuring and impairment gain. Net sales grew 3.8% to $269.5 million from $259.5 million a year earlier. Specialty foods segment net sales climbed 11.2% to $156.7 million from $141.0 million in 2003. Net sales in the glassware and candles segment slipped 2.8% to $55.7 million, while net sales in the automotive segment slid 6.9% to $57.1 million. Gross profit was $49.8 million, or 18.5% of net sales, versus $53.6 million, or 20.6% of net sales, the year before. Operating income was down 12.5% to $25.4 million.

Prospects: Top–line growth is being fueled by increased sales in the Specialty Foods segment, resulting primarily from the December 2003 acquisition of Warren Frozen Foods, Inc. This growth is being partially offset by sluggish demand for Co.'s candles and glassware products, along with the loss of an OEM program for aluminum accessories in 2003. Meanwhile, operating profitability is being hampered by sharply higher costs for soybean oil and dairy–related ingredients, as well as for raw materials in the automotive segment. Going forward, sales may benefit from Co.'s efforts to expand the market presence of Warren products.

Financial Data

(US$ in Thousands)	9 Mos	6 Mos	3 Mos	06/30/2003	06/30/2002	06/30/2001	06/30/2000	06/30/1999
Earnings Per Share	1.74	1.29	0.55	3.11	2.49	2.40	2.51	2.28
Cash Flow Per Share	2.36	2.36	0.47	4.30	4.34	3.35	3.24	3.02
Tang. Book Val. Per Share	13.98	13.91	13.54	13.19	11.71	10.37	10.03	9.34
Dividends Per Share	0.860	0.830	0.800	0.780	0.710	0.670	0.630	0.590
Dividend Payout %	47.70	62.01	141.81	25.08	28.51	27.92	25.10	25.88
Income Statement								
Total Revenues	827,311	557,848	266,652	1,106,800	1,129,687	1,098,464	1,104,258	1,045,702
Total Indirect Exp.	73,473	49,072	24,169	103,967	119,196	113,858	173,449	166,228
Depreciation & Amort.	23,183	15,322	7,432	31,669	35,287	35,528	34,340	35,569
Operating Income	97,189	71,786	31,638	139,943	134,369	147,674	161,949	155,688
Net Interest Inc./(Exp.)	...	...	...	...	(54)	(1,239)	(1,588)	(2,718)
Income Taxes	38,077	28,262	12,284	68,255	57,402	55,649	60,925	58,333
Income from Cont Ops	...	...	...	...	...	90,236	...	...
Net Income	62,395	46,350	19,700	112,546	91,940	89,238	99,264	95,129
Average Shs. Outstg.	35,814	35,815	35,831	36,243	36,910	37,636	39,554	41,799
Balance Sheet								
Cash & Cash Equivalents	159,377	152,505	145,633	142,847	83,378	4,873	2,656	18,860
Total Current Assets	443,059	436,247	444,574	414,385	366,100	317,605	315,895	328,379
Total Assets	709,978	705,014	697,639	667,716	618,705	571,937	531,844	550,014
Total Current Liabilities	87,844	91,585	101,617	84,923	89,304	92,294	96,475	116,217
Long–Term Obligations	...	...	...	...	...	1,095	3,040	3,575
Net Stockholders' Equity	583,335	576,385	559,807	547,665	501,277	459,901	415,483	414,855
Net Working Capital	355,215	344,662	342,957	329,462	276,796	225,311	219,420	212,162
Shares Outstanding	35,697	35,364	35,757	35,770	36,598	37,253	37,962	40,547
Statistical Record								
Operating Profit Margin %	11.74	12.86	11.86	12.64	11.89	13.44	14.66	14.88
Net Profit Margin %	16.74	18.44	16.60	22.50	18.30	18.34	20.02	20.25
Return on Equity %	10.70	8.04	3.51	20.55	18.34	19.62	23.89	22.93
Return on Assets %	8.79	6.57	2.82	16.85	14.86	15.77	18.66	17.29
Debt/Total Assets %	...	...	...	...	...	0.19	0.57	0.64
Price Range	46.11-38.68	45.18-38.68	42.00-38.68	46.74-32.68	40.16-26.10	33.46-19.50	36.25-19.50	39.44-25.50
P/E Ratio	19.54-16.39	19.14-16.39	76.36-70.33	15.03-10.51	16.13-10.48	13.94-8.13	14.44-7.77	17.30-11.18
Average Yield %	2.00	1.96	1.94	1.49	2.06	3.05	2.03	1.88

Address: 37 West Broad Street, Columbus, OH 43215	**Officers:** John B. Gerlach – Chmn., Pres., C.E.O., John L. Boylan – V.P., C.F.O., Treas., Asst. Sec.	**Institutional Holding** No of Institutions: –
Telephone: (614) 224–7141	**Transfer Agents:** American Stock Transfer and Trust Company, New York, NY	**Shares:** – **% Held:** –
Web Site: www.lancastercolony.com		

LA-Z-BOY INC.

Exchange	Symbol	Price	52Wk Range	Yield	P/E
NYS	LZB	$18.45 (5/28/2004)	24.12–17.95	2.38	16.47

*7 Year Price Score 111.5 *NYSE Composite Index=100 *12 Month Price Score 42.7

Interim Earnings (Per Share)

Qtr.	Jul	Oct	Jan	Apr
2000–01	0.21	0.48	0.27	0.17
2001–02	0.05	0.20	0.35	0.41
2002–03	0.32	0.50	0.41	0.44
2003–04	0.11	0.28	0.29	...

Interim Dividends (Per Share)

Amt	Decl	Ex	Rec	Pay
0.10Q	8/12/2003	8/27/2003	8/29/2003	9/10/2003
0.10Q	11/10/2003	11/25/2003	11/28/2003	12/10/2003
0.10Q	2/10/2004	2/25/2004	2/27/2004	3/10/2004
0.11Q	5/4/2004	5/26/2004	5/28/2004	6/10/2004

Indicated Div: $0.44 (Div. Reinv. Plan)

Valuation Analysis

Forecast P/E 12.17 (5/24/2004)

Market Cap $1.1 Billion	Book Value 583.4 Million
Price/Book 1.91	Price/Sales 0.56

Dividend Achiever Status

Rank 217	10 Year Growth Rate	6.83%
Total Years of Dividend Growth		22

Business Summary: Chemicals (MIC: 11.1 SIC: 2511 NAIC:337121)

La–Z–Boy is a furniture manufacturer and import distributor. Co. is comprised of two business groups: upholstery and casegoods. The upholstery segment includes recliners, sofas, chairs, sleeper chairs, loveseats and ottomans. The casegoods segment includes tables, chairs, dressers, headboards and accent pieces. In addition to upholstery and wood, Co. markets contract furniture to the hospitality, healthcare and assisted living industries. Brand names include *La–Z–Boy, England, Sam Moore, Bauhaus, Pennsylvania House, Clayton Marcus, Kincaid, Hammary, Alexvale, American Drew, La–Z–Boy Contract Furniture, American of Martinsville, Drew* and *Lea*.

Recent Developments: For the third quarter ended Jan 24 2004, net income plunged 34.0% to $15.3 million compared with $23.2 million in the equivalent 2003 quarter. Earnings were hampered by a change in product mix and increased selling, general and administrative expenses and higher rent and advertising costs in the upholstery segment, as well as weakness in the lodging market initiated by 9–11, which is hurting Co.'s hospitality business in the casegoods segment. Sales dropped 3.6% to $492.2 million from $510.5 million a year earlier. Gross profit fell 8.7% to $108.1 million versus $118.3 million in 2003. Operating income decreased 34.2% to $26.0 million.

Prospects: Co. expects fourth quarter results to be lifted by the recent pickup in its incoming order rate. Accordingly, Co. anticipates April 2004 fourth quarter sales to be up in the low single–digit range, with earnings in the range of $0.40 to $0.45 per diluted share. Meanwhile, Co. is forecasting full–year fiscal 2004 earnings per diluted share to be between $1.07 and $1.12, including $0.11 of restructuring charges. Going forward, Co. plans to aggressively expand its furniture Galleries®stores. Co.'s plans include opening as many as 20 or more new stores per year and relocating or remodeling an equal number of stores annually for the next four to five years.

Financial Data

(US$ in Thousands)	9 Mos	6 Mos	3 Mos	04/26/2003	04/27/2002	04/28/2001	04/29/2000	04/24/1999
Earnings Per Share	1.12	1.24	1.46	1.67	1.01	1.13	1.60	1.24
Cash Flow Per Share	2.12	1.31	0.30	2.17	2.17	1.91	1.06	1.54
Tang. Book Val. Per Share	8.24	8.19	8.29	8.35	8.14	7.40	6.70	7.02
Dividends Per Share	0.400	0.400	0.400	0.400	0.360	0.350	0.320	0.310
Dividend Payout %	35.71	32.25	27.40	23.95	35.64	30.97	20.00	25.00
Income Statement								
Total Revenues	1,454,657	962,490	451,472	2,111,830	2,153,952	2,256,197	1,717,420	1,287,645
Total Indirect Exp.	251,164	169,146	81,419	331,695	421,607	382,403	288,962	234,075
Depreciation & Amort.	21,830	14,637	7,311	30,695	43,988	45,697	30,342	22,081
Operating Income	64,397	38,357	11,299	162,874	96,700	120,794	144,300	106,839
Net Interest Inc./(Exp.)	(8,936)	(6,239)	(3,213)	(10,510)	(8,701)	(16,181)	(7,679)	(2,259)
Income Taxes	22,223	12,858	3,555	58,899	27,185	43,708	52,699	41,096
Income from Cont Ops	...	...	...	96,098	...	...	...	...
Net Income	36,259	20,980	5,803	36,316	61,751	68,336	87,614	66,142
Average Shs. Outstg.	54,066	54,627	54,916	57,435	61,125	60,692	54,860	53,148
Balance Sheet								
Cash & Cash Equivalents	25,774	24,587	28,422	28,817	26,771	23,565	14,353	33,550
Total Current Assets	602,653	639,237	622,772	679,494	671,692	708,776	692,369	425,588
Total Assets	1,043,500	1,078,265	1,058,170	1,123,066	1,160,776	1,222,503	1,218,297	629,792
Total Current Liabilities	198,385	218,405	156,027	214,587	226,893	249,915	237,006	132,428
Long–Term Obligations	185,903	196,174	222,762	222,371	139,386	199,419	236,094	62,688
Net Stockholders' Equity	583,417	587,746	603,231	609,939	713,522	695,146	663,092	414,915
Net Working Capital	404,268	420,832	466,745	464,907	444,799	458,861	455,363	293,160
Shares Outstanding	52,584	53,408	54,645	55,027	59,953	60,501	61,328	52,340
Statistical Record								
Operating Profit Margin %	4.42	3.98	2.50	7.71	3.94	5.35	8.40	8.29
Return on Equity %	6.21	3.56	0.96	15.75	7.01	9.83	13.21	15.94
Return on Assets %	3.47	1.94	0.54	8.55	4.31	5.58	7.19	10.50
Debt/Total Assets %	17.81	18.19	21.05	19.80	12.00	16.31	19.37	9.95
Price Range	24.12–18.90	24.12–18.90	23.86–18.90	30.04–16.45	30.88–15.16	18.50–13.44	24.44–13.69	22.50–15.25
P/E Ratio	21.54–16.88	63.47–49.74	216.9–171.8	17.99–9.85	30.57–15.01	16.37–11.89	15.27–8.55	18.15–12.30
Average Yield %	1.88	1.85	1.85	1.74	1.71	2.21	1.67	1.71

Address: 1284 North Telegraph Road, Monroe, MI 48162	Officers: Patrick H. Norton – Chmn., Kurt L.	Investor Contact:734–241–4414
Telephone: (734) 241–1444	Darrow – Pres., C.E.O.	**Institutional Holding**
Web Site: www.la-z-boy.com	**Transfer Agents:**American Stock Transfer &Trust Company, New York, NY	**No of Institutions:** 157
		Shares: 34,290,439 % Held: 58.80%

LEGG MASON, INC.

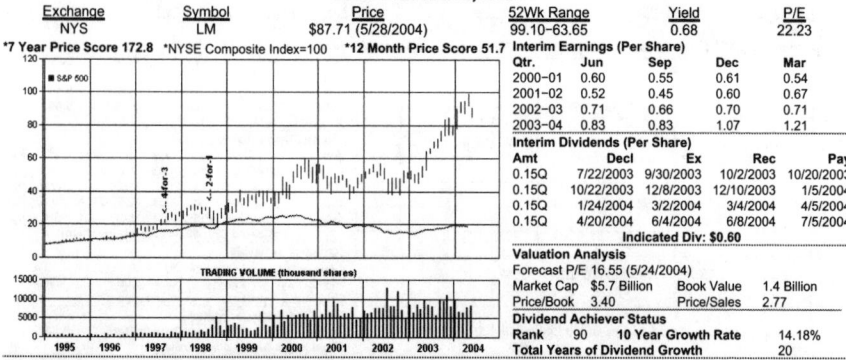

Exchange	Symbol	Price	52Wk Range	Yield	P/E
NYS	LM	$87.71 (5/28/2004)	99.10-63.65	0.68	22.23

*7 Year Price Score 172.8   *NYSE Composite Index=100   *12 Month Price Score 51.7

Interim Earnings (Per Share)

Qtr.	Jun	Sep	Dec	Mar
2000–01	0.60	0.55	0.61	0.54
2001–02	0.52	0.45	0.60	0.67
2002–03	0.71	0.66	0.70	0.71
2003–04	0.83	0.83	1.07	1.21

Interim Dividends (Per Share)

Amt	Decl	Ex	Rec	Pay
0.15Q	7/22/2003	9/30/2003	10/2/2003	10/20/2003
0.15Q	10/22/2003	12/8/2003	12/10/2003	1/5/2004
0.15Q	1/24/2004	3/2/2004	3/4/2004	4/5/2004
0.15Q	4/20/2004	6/4/2004	6/8/2004	7/5/2004
		Indicated Div: $0.60		

Valuation Analysis

Forecast P/E 16.55 (5/24/2004)

Market Cap $5.7 Billion	Book Value	1.4 Billion
Price/Book 3.40	Price/Sales	2.77

Dividend Achiever Status

Rank	90	10 Year Growth Rate	14.18%
Total Years of Dividend Growth			20

Business Summary: Finance Intermediaries &Services (MIC: 8.7 SIC: 6211 NAIC:523120)

Legg Mason, through its subsidiaries, is engaged in providing asset management, securities brokerage, investment advisory, corporate and public finance, and mortgage banking services to individuals, institutions, corporations, governments and government agencies. As an investment advisor, Co. managed about $286.40 billion in assets as of Mar 31 2004. Co.'s mortgage–banking subsidiaries have direct and master servicing responsibility for commercial mortgages. Co. provides financial services through four business segments: Asset Management, Private Client, Capital Markets and Other.

Recent Developments: For the year ended Mar 31 2004, Co. reported income from continuing operations of $290.6 million compared with income of $189.4 million the year before. Results for 2004 and 2003 excluded net gains of $675,000 and $1.5 million from discontinued operations. Total revenues rose 26.3% to $2.00 billion from $1.59 billion a year earlier. Investment advisory and related fees improved 41.5% to $1.22 billion due to an increase in assets under management primarily resulting from strong investment performance and positive cash flows. Commissions revenues rose 8.5% to $343.5 million, while principal transactions grew 4.6% to $165.5 million. Investment banking increased 37.7% to $150.1 million.

Prospects: Co. is enjoying stronger revenues from all sectors of its business. Also, Co.'s assets under management continue to be robust, supported by improved investment performance and positive cash flows from Co.'s larger equity managers. For instance, as of Mar 31 2004, equity assets amounted to 39.0% of the total managed assets versus 31.0% the previous year. Moreover, Co.'s institutional asset management division accounted for 65.0% of total assets under management, while Co.'s mutual funds management division accounted for 25.0%. Separately, Co. acquired the business of Singapore–based Rothschild Asset Management, which manages about $1.00 billion of fixed income and equity assets.

Financial Data

(US$ in Thousands)	6 Mos	3 Mos	03/31/2003	03/31/2002	03/31/2001	03/31/2000	03/31/1999	03/31/1998
Earnings Per Share	3.07	2.90	2.78	2.24	2.30	2.33	1.55	1.31
Cash Flow Per Share	(3.53)	(2.58)	4.44	1.26	3.29	2.70	(1.02)	1.69
Tang. Book Val. Per Share	...	6.07	4.98	2.28	12.38	10.60	8.83	7.97
Dividends Per Share	0.440	0.430	0.420	0.380	0.340	0.290	0.240	0.200
Dividend Payout %	14.33	14.82	15.10	16.96	14.78	12.44	15.48	15.77
Income Statement								
Total Revenues	906,618	440,150	1,615,382	1,578,612	1,536,253	1,370,804	1,046,006	889,060
Total Indirect Exp.	683,113	328,281	1,079,655	1,063,376	966,919	886,737	703,759	616,343
Depreciation & Amort.	10,858	5,992	24,915	18,808	36,495	29,320	21,566	21,986
Operating Income	191,958	95,058	448,591	387,965	393,945	349,745	342,247	272,717
Net Interest Inc./(Exp.)	...	...	...	...	...	...	(94,910)	(73,706)
Income Taxes	74,108	36,692	117,412	100,313	109,590	96,616	59,441	52,258
Income from Cont Ops	117,850	...	...	...	...	...	...	...
Net Income	125,000	58,366	190,909	152,936	156,230	142,525	89,334	76,121
Average Shs. Outstg.	70,914	70,125	68,760	68,262	67,916	60,787	57,657	58,000
Balance Sheet								
Cash & Cash Equivalents	3,686,587	3,198,569	3,351,708	3,094,990	2,627,534	2,058,106	1,740,643	1,334,327
Total Current Assets	4,983,642	4,742,257	4,669,691	4,458,426	4,087,802	3,813,436	2,805,908	2,129,175
Total Assets	6,511,202	6,209,081	6,067,450	5,939,614	4,687,626	4,785,053	3,473,687	2,832,329
Total Current Liabilities	4,092,777	3,874,179	3,866,288	3,808,048	3,397,852	3,532,642	2,718,386	2,147,235
Long–Term Obligations	790,471	788,603	786,753	877,122	218,970	338,991	99,676	99,628
Net Stockholders' Equity	1,395,361	1,324,802	1,247,957	1,084,548	927,720	751,929	554,177	500,095
Net Working Capital	890,865	868,078	803,403	650,378	689,950	280,794	87,522	(18,060)
Shares Outstanding	66,200	65,731	64,827	64,443	62,849	58,599	56,376	55,050
Statistical Record								
Operating Profit Margin %	21.17	21.59	27.76	24.57	25.64	25.51	32.71	30.67
Return on Equity %	8.44	4.40	15.29	14.10	16.84	18.95	16.12	15.22
Return on Assets %	1.80	0.94	3.14	2.57	3.33	2.97	2.57	2.68
Debt/Total Assets %	12.14	12.70	12.96	14.76	4.67	7.08	2.86	3.51
Price Range	76.70-48.74	66.38-48.74	56.97-38.16	56.80-35.75	59.94-35.94	49.00-31.25	35.69-18.50	31.72-15.84
P/E Ratio	15.05-15.88	22.89-16.81	20.49-13.73	25.36-15.96	26.06-15.63	21.03-13.41	23.02-11.94	24.21-12.09
Average Yield %	0.68	0.73	0.87	0.80	0.68	0.79	0.84	0.85

Address: 100 Light Street, Baltimore, MD 21202 Telephone: (410) 539–0000 Web Site: www.leggmason.com	Officers: Raymond A. Mason – Chmn., Pres., C.E.O., James W. Brinkley – Sr. Exec. V.P. Transfer Agents:Wachovia Bank, N.A., Charlotte, North Carolina	Investor Contact:410–539–0000 Institutional Holding No of Institutions: 42 Shares: 20,100,609 % Held: –

LEGGETT & PLATT, INC.

Exchange	Symbol	Price	52Wk Range	Yield	P/E
NYS	LEG	$25.28 (5/28/2004)	25.45-19.81	2.22	22.57

*7 Year Price Score 101.4 ***NYSE Composite Index=100** ***12 Month Price Score 49.7**

Interim Earnings (Per Share)

Qtr.	Mar	Jun	Sep	Dec
2001	0.23	0.25	0.28	0.18
2002	0.28	0.35	0.29	0.25
2003	0.25	0.24	0.26	0.30
2004	0.32	...	...	...

Interim Dividends (Per Share)

Amt	Decl	Ex	Rec	Pay
0.14Q	8/6/2003	9/11/2003	9/15/2003	10/15/2003
0.14Q	11/11/2003	12/11/2003	12/15/2003	1/15/2004
0.14Q	2/11/2004	3/11/2004	3/15/2004	4/15/2004
0.14Q	5/5/2004	6/11/2004	6/15/2004	7/15/2004

Indicated Div: $0.56

Valuation Analysis

Forecast P/E 18.28 (5/24/2004)

Market Cap	$4.9 Billion	Book Value	2.2 Billion
Price/Book	2.09	Price/Sales	1.00

Dividend Achiever Status

Rank	83	10 Year Growth Rate	14.66%
Total Years of Dividend Growth			32

Business Summary: Chemicals (MIC: 11.1 SIC: 2515 NAIC:337121)

Leggett & Platt is primarily engaged in the manufacture of engineered components and products that are used in homes, offices, retail stores, and automobiles. Products include: retail store fixtures and point of purchase displays; components for residential furniture and bedding; components for office furniture; non-automotive aluminum die castings; drawn steel wire; automotive seat support and lumbar systems; and bedding industry machinery for wire forming, sewing and quilting. Operations consists of 29 business units, which are organized into 11 groups that make up five business segments.

Recent Developments: For the quarter ended Mar 31 2004, net income climbed 27.1% to $62.8 million compared with $49.4 million in the corresponding period of the prior year. The improvement in earnings was primarily attributed to higher sales and improved overhead recovery. Net sales advanced 14.4% to $1.19 billion from $1.04 billion a year earlier. Same-location sales increased 8.5% year over year. Gross profit increased 18.6% to $215.0 million versus $181.3 million the year before. Cash from operating activities more than doubled to $81.3 million from $36.1 million the year before.

Prospects: For the second quarter of 2004, Co. expects earnings to be in the range of $0.31 to $0.36 per share. Also, Co. anticipates sequential sales growth of between zero and $50.0 million, yielding second quarter sales of between $1.19 billion and $1.24 billion. At this sales level, year over year organic sales growth should be approximately 9.0%. Moreover, organic sales growth is now anticipated in the range of 5.0% to 9.0% for 2004 versus the prior 3.0% to 8.0% forecast. Acquisitions are expected to contribute in the range of $150.0 million to $200.0 million of incremental revenue, resulting in full year trade sales of between $4.70 billion and $5.00 billion.

Financial Data
(US$ in Thousands)

	3 Mos	12/31/2003	12/31/2002	12/31/2001	12/31/2000	12/31/1999	12/31/1998	12/31/1997
Earnings Per Share	1.12	1.05	1.17	0.94	1.32	1.45	1.24	1.08
Cash Flow Per Share	0.41	2.00	2.28	2.66	2.19	1.84	1.76	1.49
Tang. Book Val. Per Share	5.74	5.62	5.35	4.80	4.58	4.50	4.59	3.88
Dividends Per Share	0.540	0.530	0.490	0.470	0.400	0.350	0.300	0.260
Dividend Payout %	48.21	50.47	41.88	50.00	30.30	24.13	24.59	24.07
Income Statement								
Total Revenues	1,187,200	4,388,200	4,271,800	4,113,800	4,276,300	3,779,000	3,370,400	2,909,200
Total Indirect Exp.	111,600	416,400	437,800	651,400	612,800	515,600	440,200	369,300
Depreciation & Amort.	43,300	8,400	10,200	39,900	34,100	28,800	21,800	17,300
Operating Income	103,300	355,300	400,600	351,200	480,800	502,500	429,100	365,100
Net Interest Inc./(Exp.)	(10,300)	(40,200)	(37,100)	(53,900)	(62,200)	(39,900)	(33,500)	(31,800)
Income Taxes	30,200	109,200	130,400	109,700	154,500	172,100	147,600	125,000
Net Income	62,800	205,900	233,100	187,600	264,100	290,500	248,000	208,300
Average Shs. Outstg.	197,100	196,953	199,795	200,434	200,388	200,938	200,669	193,190
Balance Sheet								
Cash & Cash Equivalents	428,700	443,900	225,000	187,200	37,300	20,600	83,500	7,700
Total Current Assets	1,909,300	1,819,400	1,488,000	1,421,900	1,405,300	1,256,200	1,137,100	944,600
Total Assets	4,004,000	3,889,700	3,501,100	3,412,900	3,373,200	2,977,500	2,535,300	2,106,300
Total Current Liabilities	1,062,800	625,900	598,000	457,000	476,600	431,500	401,400	372,500
Long-Term Obligations	640,900	1,012,200	808,600	977,600	988,400	787,400	574,100	466,200
Net Stockholders' Equity	2,164,800	2,114,000	1,976,900	1,866,600	1,793,800	1,646,200	1,436,800	1,174,000
Net Working Capital	846,500	1,193,500	890,000	964,900	928,700	824,700	735,700	572,100
Shares Outstanding	191,976	192,102	194,498	196,298	196,097	196,880	197,683	192,754
Operating Profit Margin %	8.71	8.09	8.98	8.27	11.10	13.35	12.79	12.66
Net Profit Margin %	10.39	9.66	11.17	9.63	13.26	16.85	16.18	15.87
Return on Equity %	2.91	9.73	10.94	9.48	14.39	17.78	17.41	18.03
Return on Assets %	1.57	5.29	6.18	5.18	7.65	9.83	9.86	10.05
Debt/Total Assets %	16.00	26.02	23.09	28.64	29.30	26.44	22.64	22.13
Price Range	25.45-21.35	23.57-17.40	27.16-18.90	24.23-17.00	22.38-14.44	27.88-18.81	28.44-17.13	23.53-15.81
P/E Ratio	22.72-19.06	22.45-16.57	23.21-16.15	25.78-18.09	16.95-10.94	19.22-12.97	22.93-13.81	21.79-14.64
Average Yield %	2.31	2.53	2.08	2.22	2.23	1.53	1.24	1.31

Address: No. 1 Leggett Road, Carthage, MO 64836 **Telephone:** (417) 358 8131 **Web Site:** www.leggett.com	**Officers:** Felix E. Wright – Chmn., C.E.O., David S. Haffner – Pres., C.O.O. **Transfer Agents:** U.M.B. Bank, Kansas City, MO	**Investor Contact:** 417-358-8131 **Institutional Holding** **No of Institutions:** 277 **Shares:** 117,648,191 **% Held:** 61%

LILLY (ELI) & CO.

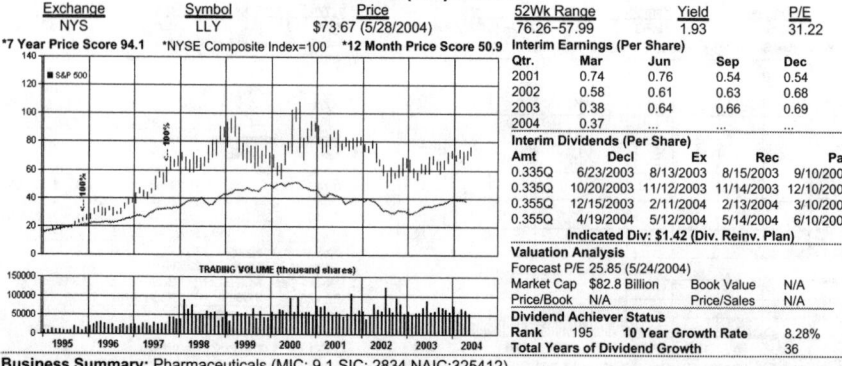

Exchange	Symbol	Price	52Wk Range	Yield	P/E
NYS	LLY	$73.67 (5/28/2004)	76.26–57.99	1.93	31.22

*7 Year Price Score 94.1 *NYSE Composite Index=100 *12 Month Price Score 50.9

Interim Earnings (Per Share)

Qtr.	Mar	Jun	Sep	Dec
2001	0.74	0.76	0.54	0.54
2002	0.58	0.61	0.63	0.68
2003	0.38	0.64	0.66	0.69
2004	0.37	...	...	...

Interim Dividends (Per Share)

Amt	Decl	Ex	Rec	Pay
0.335Q	6/23/2003	8/13/2003	8/15/2003	9/10/2003
0.335Q	10/20/2003	11/12/2003	11/14/2003	12/10/2003
0.355Q	12/15/2003	2/11/2004	2/13/2004	3/10/2004
0.355Q	4/19/2004	5/12/2004	5/14/2004	6/10/2004
Indicated Div: $1.42 (Div. Reinv. Plan)				

Valuation Analysis

Forecast P/E 25.85 (5/24/2004)

Market Cap	$82.8 Billion	Book Value	N/A
Price/Book	N/A	Price/Sales	N/A

Dividend Achiever Status

Rank	195	10 Year Growth Rate	8.28%
Total Years of Dividend Growth			36

Business Summary: Pharmaceuticals (MIC: 9.1 SIC: 2834 NAIC:325412)

Eli Lilly discovers, develops, manufactures, and sells pharmaceuticals and animal health products. Neuroscience products include *Prozac®, Zyprexa®, Strattera™Darvon®, Permax®, Symbyax®*and *Sarafem™*. Endocrine products include *Humulin®, Humalog®, Humalog Mix 75/25®, Actos®, Evista®, Forteo®*and *Humatrope®*. Oncology products include *Gemzar®*and *Alimta®*. Animal Health products include *Tylan®, Rumensin®, Coban®, Monteban®, Maxiban®, Apralan®, Micotil®, Pulmotil®, Surmax®, Optaflexx®*and *Paylean®*. Cardiovascular products, consist primarily of *ReoPro®, Dobutrex®, Xigris®*and *Cynt®*. Anti–infective products include *Ceclor®, Keflex®, Keftab®, Lorabid®,* and *Vancocin®,* and other products.

Recent Developments: For the three months ended Mar 31 2004, net income slipped 1.6% to $400.4 million compared with $407.0 million in the corresponding quarter of the previous year. Results for 2004 included a pre–tax acquired in–process research and development charge of $362.3 million, while results for 2003 included pre–tax asset impairments, restructuring and other special charges of $353.9 million. Net sales advanced 16.9% to $3.38 billion from $2.89 billion in the year–earlier period. The improvement was primarily due to higher sales of *Zyprexa®, Gemzar®*and *Evista®,* as well as growing sales from new products. Operating income climbed 17.5% to $552.4 million versus $470.1 million in 2003.

Prospects: For the full year 2004, Co. continues to expect low double–digit sales growth. U.S. sales are expected to benefit from the recent launches of *Symbyax* as well as the bipolar maintenance indication and injectable formulation of *Zyprexa*. Earnings per share for 2004 are forecasted to range between $2.47 and $2.52, excluding unusual items. Meanwhile, Co. plans to continue launching new products over the next year with the addition of *Cymbalta™*and *Yentreve*. Due to its multiple launches and strong pipeline, Co. appears well–positioned to deliver solid results going forward.

Financial Data
(US$ in Thousands)

	3 Mos	12/31/2003	12/31/2002	12/31/2001	12/31/2000	12/31/1999	12/31/1998	12/31/1997
Earnings Per Share	2.36	2.37	2.50	2.58	2.79	2.30	1.87	(0.35)
Cash Flow Per Share	0.53	3.36	1.90	3.35	3.39	2.36	2.34	2.18
Tang. Book Val. Per Share	9.34	8.68	7.37	6.32	5.37	4.48	2.85	2.78
Dividends Per Share	1.360	1.340	1.240	1.120	1.040	0.920	0.800	0.740
Dividend Payout %	57.63	56.54	49.60	43.41	37.27	40.00	42.78	N.M.
Income Statement								
Total Revenues	3,376,900	12,582,500	11,077,500	11,542,500	10,862,200	10,002,900	9,236,800	8,517,600
Total Indirect Exp.	1,946,600	6,405,600	5,657,300	5,843,000	5,246,800	4,541,200	4,524,700	3,696,400
Depreciation & Amort.	147,600	548,500	493,000	454,900	435,800	439,700	490,400	509,800
Operating Income	615,500	3,501,800	3,243,700	3,539,300	3,559,700	3,363,700	2,697,000	2,458,300
Net Interest Inc./(Exp.)	(9,300)	(61,000)	(79,700)	(146,500)	(182,300)	(183,800)	(181,300)	(234,100)
Income Taxes	215,100	700,900	749,800	742,700	800,900	698,700	568,700	895,300
Income from Cont Ops	...	...	...	2,809,400	...	2,546,700	2,096,300	...
Net Income	400,400	2,560,800	2,707,900	2,780,000	3,057,800	2,721,000	2,097,900	(385,100)
Average Shs. Outstg.	1,080,300	1,082,230	1,085,088	1,090,793	1,097,725	1,106,055	1,121,486	1,101,099
Balance Sheet								
Cash & Cash Equivalents	2,410,400	2,756,300	1,945,900	2,702,300	4,114,900	3,700,400	1,495,700	1,947,500
Total Current Assets	8,798,900	8,758,700	7,804,100	6,938,900	7,943,000	7,055,500	5,406,800	5,320,700
Total Assets	22,442,400	21,678,100	19,042,000	16,434,100	14,690,800	12,825,200	12,595,500	12,577,400
Total Current Liabilities	5,551,100	5,550,600	5,063,500	5,203,000	4,960,700	3,935,400	4,607,200	4,191,600
Long–Term Obligations	4,503,600	4,687,800	4,358,200	3,132,100	2,633,700	2,811,900	2,185,500	2,326,100
Net Stockholders' Equity	10,558,500	9,764,800	8,273,600	7,104,000	6,046,900	5,013,000	4,429,600	4,645,600
Net Working Capital	3,247,800	3,208,100	2,740,600	1,735,900	2,982,300	3,120,100	799,600	1,129,100
Shares Outstanding	1,129,485	1,123,725	1,122,443	1,123,348	1,125,560	1,090,238	1,019,090	1,110,522
Operating Profit Margin %	20.09	27.83	29.28	30.66	32.77	33.62	29.19	28.86
Return on Equity %	4.38	26.22	32.72	39.54	50.56	50.80	47.32	N.M.
Return on Assets %	2.06	11.81	14.22	17.09	20.81	19.85	16.64	N.M.
Debt/Total Assets %	20.10	21.62	22.88	19.05	17.92	21.92	17.35	18.49
Price Range	74.70–65.00	73.89–53.70	80.69–48.15	91.50–72.59	108.6–54.38	97.44–61.50	90.88–56.37	69.94–36.25
P/E Ratio	31.65–27.54	31.18–22.66	32.28–19.26	35.47–28.14	38.91–19.49	42.36–26.74	48.60–31.12	N/A
Average Yield %	1.93	2.11	1.91	1.40	1.32	1.21	1.12	1.41

Address: Lilly Corporate Center, Indianapolis, IN 46285
Telephone: (317) 276–2000
Web Site: www.lilly.com

Officers: Sidney Taurel – Chmn., Pres., C.E.O., Charles E. Golden – Exec. V.P., C.F.O.
Transfer Agents: Norwest Shareowner Services, South St. Paul, MN

Investor Contact:317–276–2506
Institutional Holding
No of Institutions: 31
Shares: 1,725,606,124 **% Held:** –

LINCOLN NATIONAL CORP. (ID)

Exchange	Symbol	Price	52Wk Range	Yield	P/E
NYS	LNC	$47.49 (5/28/2004)	49.95-34.64	2.95	9.69

*7 Year Price Score 97.0   ***NYSE Composite Index=100**   ***12 Month Price Score 52.5**

Interim Earnings (Per Share)

Qtr.	Mar	Jun	Sep	Dec
2001	0.83	0.74	0.61	0.87
2002	0.49	0.81	(0.68)	(0.13)
2003	0.23	0.80	0.74	2.50
2004	0.86	...	...	...

Interim Dividends (Per Share)

Amt	Decl	Ex	Rec	Pay
0.335Q	9/11/2003	10/8/2003	10/10/2003	11/1/2003
0.35Q	11/13/2003	1/7/2004	1/9/2004	2/1/2004
0.35Q	3/11/2004	4/6/2004	4/9/2004	5/1/2004
0.35Q	5/13/2004	7/7/2004	7/9/2004	8/1/2004

Indicated Div: $3.00 (Div. Reinv. Plan)

Valuation Analysis

Forecast P/E 11.91 (5/24/2004)

Market Cap $8.7 Billion	Book Value 6.1 Billion
Price/Book 1.38	Price/Sales 1.58

Dividend Achiever Status

Rank 237	10 Year Growth Rate	5.83%
Total Years of Dividend Growth	20	

TRADING VOLUME (thousand shares)

Business Summary: Insurance (MIC: 8.2 SIC: 6311 NAIC:524113)

Lincoln National operates multiple insurance and investment management businesses, divided into four business segments. The Lincoln Retirement segment provides fixed and variable annuities products to the individual annuities and employer–sponsored markets. The Life Insurance segment provides life insurance products designed specifically for the high net–worth and affluent markets. The Investment Management segment provides investment products and services to both individual and institutional investors. The Lincoln UK segment provides life insurance products in the United Kingdom.

Recent Developments: For the three months ended Mar 31 2004, income totaled $155.0 million, before a $24.5 million accounting change charge, compared with net income of $41.6 million in the corresponding prior–year quarter. Results included after–tax losses on investments and derivatives of $10.3 million and $59.4 million in 2004 and 2003, respectively. Total revenue climbed 14.5% to $1.26 billion from $1.10 billion the previous year. Net investment income grew 3.5% to $677.5 million from $654.6 million the year before. Income before taxes was $208.6 million versus $35.4 million a year earlier.

Prospects: Results are benefiting from strong inflows into Co.'s annuities, mutual funds, life insurance and other personal wealth accumulation products stemming from improved conditions in the equity markets. Separately, on May 5 2004, Co. announced that its asset management company, Delaware Investments, has entered into an agreement to sell its international unit for $172.0 million in cash to a newly–formed company associated with the unit's management and Hellman & Friedman LLC, a private equity company. Also, on Apr 16 2004, Co. announced that it has entered into a definitive agreement to sell Group One Source, an employee benefits marketing organization, to BenefitMall. Terms were not disclosed.

Financial Data

(US$ in Thousands)	3 Mos	12/31/2003	12/31/2002	12/31/2001	12/31/2000	12/31/1999	12/31/1998	12/31/1997
Earnings Per Share	4.90	4.27	0.49	3.05	3.19	2.30	2.51	0.10
Tang. Book Val. Per Share	20.70	18.77	15.62	14.11	11.06	5.59	10.16	19.38
Dividends Per Share	1.350	1.340	1.280	1.220	1.160	1.100	1.040	0.980
Dividend Payout %	40.57	31.38	261.22	40.00	36.36	47.82	41.43	933.33
Income Statement								
Total Premium Income	75,563	280,951	315,943	1,704,002	1,813,111	1,881,515	1,620,629	1,328,735
Other Income	1,165,260	4,927,088	4,245,785	4,670,964	5,038,775	4,916,388	4,463,098	3,569,744
Total Revenues	1,240,823	5,208,039	4,561,728	6,374,966	6,851,886	6,797,903	6,083,727	4,898,479
Total Indirect Exp.	(18,207)	(75,842)	(74,381)	...	...	...	...	...
Inc. Before Inc. Taxes	208,629	1,047,563	1,624	764,139	836,291	569,964	697,398	34,881
Income Taxes	53,670	280,400	(90,000)	158,362	214,898	109,610	187,623	12,651
Eqty Earns/Minority Int.	...	...	(647)	5,672	(379)	5,797	3,336	...
Income from Cont Ops	154,959	767,163	91,624	605,777	...	...	...	22,230
Net Income	130,457	511,936	91,590	590,211	621,393	460,354	509,775	933,988
Average Shs. Outstg.	181,214	179,441	185,596	193,303	194,920	200,417	203,262	207,992
Balance Sheet								
Cash & Cash Equivalents	2,255,519	1,711,196	1,690,534	3,095,480	1,927,393	1,895,883	2,433,350	3,794,706
Premiums Due	8,203,216	8,759,932	8,296,179	7,009,051	4,798,380	5,092,168	4,105,871	2,971,283
Invst. Assets: Total	37,636,471	36,658,220	33,848,755	29,645,979	28,751,167	28,976,420	31,715,232	25,788,561
Total Assets	109,869,913	106,744,868	93,133,422	98,001,304	99,844,059	103,095,733	93,836,260	77,174,708
Long–Term Obligations	1,317,730	1,458,835	1,511,858	1,336,410	1,457,231	711,963	712,171	511,037
Net Stockholders' Equity	6,143,537	5,811,625	5,296,267	5,263,484	4,954,084	4,263,868	5,387,941	4,982,915
Shares Outstanding	178,504	178,212	177,307	186,943	190,748	195,494	202,112	201,718
Return on Revenues %	11.02	13.27	0.39	9.41	9.07	6.68	8.32	0.45
Return on Equity %	2.22	11.89	0.33	11.40	12.55	10.66	9.39	0.44
Return on Assets %	0.12	0.64	0.01	0.61	0.62	0.44	0.53	0.02
Price Range	48.72-40.17	41.32-25.17	53.50-25.17	52.55-39.10	56.13-23.19	57.31-36.50	48.78-34.38	39.06-24.69
P/E Ratio	9.94- 8.20	9.68-5.89	109.2-51.37	17.23-12.82	17.59-7.27	24.92-15.87	19.43-13.70	390.6-246.9
Average Yield %	2.99	3.87	3.13	2.63	2.87	2.38	2.44	3.07

Address: 1500 Market Street, Philadelphia, PA 19102–2112 **Telephone:** (215) 448–1400 **Web Site:** www.lfg.com	Officers: Jon A. Boscia – Chmn., C.E.O., Richard C. Vaughan – Exec. V.P., C.F.O. **Transfer Agents:** First Chicago Trust Company of New York, Jersey City, NJ	Investor Contact:215–448–1422 **Institutional Holding** **No of Institutions:** 5 **Shares:** 69,197 **% Held:** –

LINEAR TECHNOLOGY CORP.

Exchange	Symbol	Price	52Wk Range	Yield	P/E
NMS	LLTC	$39.78 (5/28/2004)	44.95-31.58	0.80	43.24

*7 Year Price Score 111.3 *NYSE Composite Index=100 ***12 Month Price Score 45.5**

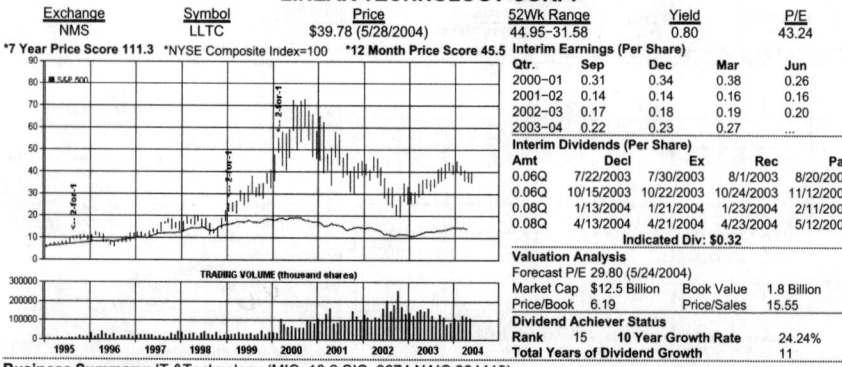

Interim Earnings (Per Share)

Qtr.	Sep	Dec	Mar	Jun
2000–01	0.31	0.34	0.38	0.26
2001–02	0.14	0.14	0.16	0.16
2002–03	0.17	0.18	0.19	0.20
2003–04	0.22	0.23	0.27	...

Interim Dividends (Per Share)

Amt	Decl	Ex	Rec	Pay
0.06Q	7/22/2003	7/30/2003	8/1/2003	8/20/2003
0.06Q	10/15/2003	10/22/2003	10/24/2003	11/12/2003
0.08Q	1/13/2004	1/21/2004	1/23/2004	2/11/2004
0.08Q	4/13/2004	4/21/2004	4/23/2004	5/12/2004

Indicated Div: $0.32

Valuation Analysis

Forecast P/E 29.80 (5/24/2004)

Market Cap $12.5 Billion	Book Value 1.8 Billion
Price/Book 6.19	Price/Sales 15.55

Dividend Achiever Status

Rank 15	10 Year Growth Rate	24.24%
Total Years of Dividend Growth	11	

Business Summary: IT &Technology (MIC: 10.2 SIC: 3674 NAIC:334413)

Linear Technology designs, manufactures and markets a broad line of standard high performance linear integrated circuits. Applications for Co.'s products include telecommunications, cellular telephones, networking products, notebook and desktop computers, computer peripherals, video/multimedia, industrial instrumentation, security monitoring devices, high–end consumer products such as digital cameras and MP3 players, complex medical devices, automotive electronics, factory automation, process control, and military and space systems. Co. focuses its product development and marketing efforts on high–performance applications where it can compete effectively.

Recent Developments: For the third quarter ended Mar 28 2004, net income advanced 41.1% to $85.5 million from $60.6 million in the corresponding prior–year quarter. Net sales increased 36.0% to $209.1 million from $153.8 million a year earlier, primarily due to continuing strong demand for Co.'s products across all of its end markets and in all geographic regions. Gross profit climbed 41.3% to $161.5 million, or 77.2% of net sales, from $114.4 million, or 74.4% of net sales, in the previous year. Operating income jumped 50.8% to $114.4 million from $75.8 million the year before.

Prospects: Demand for Co.'s products continues to be robust, increasing in each major end market, particularly the industrial and communications end markets. The demand is also broad–based increasing in every major geographical area. In each of the last three quarters, Co. has accelerated its year–over–year sales and profit growth. Looking ahead, should the recent trends of very broad based marketplace strength continue, Co. expects to grow sales by a roughly similar percentage in the fourth quarter of fiscal 2004 as in the third quarter. Meanwhile, growth in telecommunications and networking markets as well as a general strengthening in the overall economy may support improved results going forward.

Financial Data

(US$ in Thousands)	9 Mos	6 Mos	3 Mos	06/29/2003	06/30/2002	07/01/2001	07/02/2000	06/27/1999
Earnings Per Share	0.92	0.84	0.79	0.74	0.60	1.29	0.88	0.61
Cash Flow Per Share	0.90	0.58	0.23	0.88	0.78	1.68	1.34	0.88
Tang. Book Val. Per Share	5.74	6.03	6.03	5.80	5.63	5.58	4.19	2.94
Dividends Per Share	0.260	0.230	0.220	0.210	0.170	0.130	0.090	0.070
Dividend Payout %	27.96	27.38	27.85	28.37	28.33	10.07	10.22	11.88
Income Statement								
Total Revenues	569,231	360,098	174,077	606,573	512,282	972,625	705,917	506,669
Total Indirect Exp.	133,324	86,138	41,906	156,996	142,464	195,218	152,572	108,922
Depreciation & Amort.	36,725	24,512	12,234	45,903	46,261	35,788	24,958	21,972
Operating Income	303,125	188,774	90,762	294,511	225,099	546,285	374,396	257,926
Net Interest Inc./(Exp.)	19,909	13,769	7,085	38,715	53,251	64,366	42,858	27,801
Income Taxes	93,679	58,737	28,376	96,635	80,721	183,195	129,348	91,434
Net Income	229,355	143,806	69,471	236,591	197,629	427,456	287,906	194,293
Average Shs. Outstg.	322,614	323,167	322,894	321,375	328,538	332,527	328,002	317,888
Balance Sheet								
Cash & Cash Equivalents	214,184	221,251	145,974	136,276	211,706	321,106	230,455	154,220
Total Current Assets	1,847,242	1,881,009	1,865,573	1,776,000	1,727,581	1,727,848	1,310,103	905,112
Total Assets	2,101,328	2,142,493	2,135,390	2,056,879	1,988,433	2,017,074	1,507,256	1,046,914
Total Current Liabilities	177,652	176,641	160,793	162,029	168,997	202,224	168,677	125,275
Net Stockholders' Equity	1,846,474	1,889,907	1,896,639	1,814,929	1,781,454	1,781,957	1,322,197	906,794
Net Working Capital	1,669,590	1,704,368	1,704,780	1,613,971	1,558,584	1,525,624	1,141,426	779,837
Shares Outstanding	311,079	313,134	314,244	312,706	316,150	318,908	315,167	307,462
Operating Profit Margin %	53.25	52.42	52.13	48.55	43.94	56.16	53.03	50.90
Return on Equity %	12.42	7.60	3.66	13.03	11.09	23.98	21.77	21.42
Return on Assets %	10.91	6.71	3.25	11.50	9.93	21.19	19.10	18.55
Price Range	44.95-32.38	44.33-32.38	41.94-32.38	36.77-19.61	48.24-28.58	72.94-33.95	72.31-27.89	32.84-10.25
P/E Ratio	48.86-35.20	52.77-38.55	53.09-40.99	49.69-26.50	80.40-47.63	56.54-26.32	82.17-31.69	53.84-16.80
Average Yield %	0.66	0.59	0.59	0.71	0.42	0.24	0.21	0.33

Address: 1630 McCarthy Blvd., Milpitas, CA 95035-7417 Telephone: (408) 432-1900 Web Site: www.linear.com	Officers: Robert H. Swanson – Chmn., C.E.O., David B. Bell – Pres. Transfer Agents:EquiServe Trust Company, N.A., Providence, RI	Investor Contact:408-432-1900 Institutional Holding No of Institutions: 35 Shares: 2,667,159 % Held: –

LOWE'S COS., INC.

Exchange	Symbol	Price	52Wk Range	Yield	P/E
NYS	LOW	$53.57 (5/28/2004)	60.05–42.12	0.22	23.09

*7 Year Price Score 166.0 ***NYSE Composite Index=100** ***12 Month Price Score 46.0**

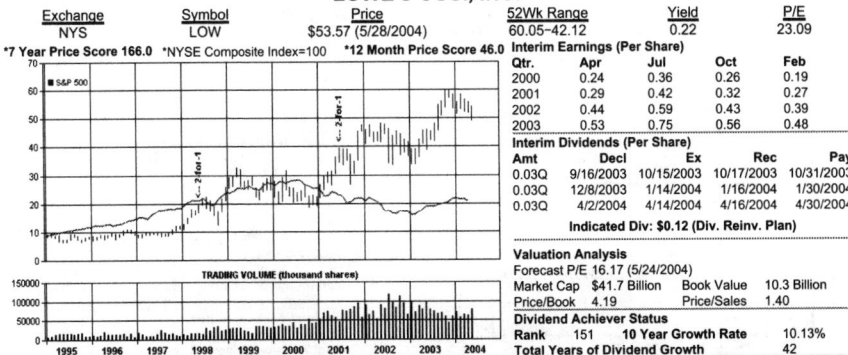

Interim Earnings (Per Share)

Qtr.	Apr	Jul	Oct	Feb
2000	0.24	0.36	0.26	0.19
2001	0.29	0.42	0.32	0.27
2002	0.44	0.59	0.43	0.39
2003	0.53	0.75	0.56	0.48

Interim Dividends (Per Share)

Amt	Decl	Ex	Rec	Pay
0.03Q	9/16/2003	10/15/2003	10/17/2003	10/31/2003
0.03Q	12/8/2003	1/14/2004	1/16/2004	1/30/2004
0.03Q	4/2/2004	4/14/2004	4/16/2004	4/30/2004

Indicated Div: $0.12 (Div. Reinv. Plan)

Valuation Analysis

Forecast P/E 16.17 (5/24/2004)

Market Cap	$41.7 Billion	Book Value	10.3 Billion
Price/Book	4.19	Price/Sales	1.40

Dividend Achiever Status

Rank	151	10 Year Growth Rate	10.13%
Total Years of Dividend Growth			42

Business Summary: Retail – Hardware (MIC: 5.6 SIC: 5211 NAIC:444110)

Lowe's Companies is a major worldwide retailer of home improvement products, with a specific emphasis on retail do–it–yourself and commercial business customers. Co. specializes in offering products and services for home improvement, home decor, home maintenance, home repair and remodeling and maintenance of commercial buildings. As of Jan 30 2004, Co. operated 952 stores in 45 states representing 108.8 million square feet of selling space. Each store is stocked with more than 40,000 separate items, while Co.'s special order program features more than 400,000 additional items.

Recent Developments: For the year ended Oct 31 2003, Co. reported earnings from continuing operations of $1.86 billion compared with income of $1.46 billion the year before. Earnings for 2003 and 2002 included store opening costs of $128.0 million and $129.0 million, and excluded net gains from discontinued operations of $15.0 million and $12.0 million, respectively. Net sales climbed 18.1% to $30.84 billion from $26.11 billion the previous year, reflecting Co.'s ongoing store expansion and relocation program. Comparable–store sales increased 6.7% year over year. Gross margin totaled $9.61 billion, or 31.2% of net sales, compared with $7.95 billion, or 30.4% of net sales, a year earlier.

Prospects: Looking ahead, Co. expects to open 140 stores in fiscal 2004, reflecting total square footage growth of approximately 14.0%, with store opening costs of about $137.0 million. Co. also anticipates total sales growth of approximately 17.0%, comparable store sales growth of 5.0% to 6.0%, and diluted earnings per share ranging from $2.63 to $2.66, including an accounting change charge of $0.13, in fiscal 2004. In fiscal 2005, Co. expects to open 150 stores, reflecting total square footage growth of approximately 13.0% to 14.0%. Additionally, total sales growth is anticipated to total 17.0%, while diluted earnings per share are expected to be between $3.29 and $3.34 in fiscal 2005.

Financial Data

(US$ in Thousands)	01/30/2004	01/31/2003	02/01/2002	02/02/2001	01/28/2000	01/29/1999	01/30/1998	01/31/1997
Earnings Per Share	2.32	1.85	1.30	1.05	0.87	0.68	0.51	0.42
Cash Flow Per Share	3.77	3.37	2.03	1.46	1.52	0.98	0.95	0.80
Tang. Book Val. Per Share	13.09	10.61	8.60	7.16	6.14	4.44	3.70	3.19
Dividends Per Share	0.100	0.085	0.078	0.070	0.063	0.059	0.050	0.045
Dividend Payout %	4.52	4.32	5.76	4.97	6.85	8.45	10.67	11.69
Income Statement								
Total Revenues	30,838,000	26,491,000	22,111,108	18,778,559	15,905,595	12,244,882	10,136,890	8,600,241
Total Indirect Exp.	6,429,000	5,485,000	4,570,053	3,888,503	3,232,613	2,461,569	2,065,659	1,721,086
Depreciation & Amort.	758,000	626,000	516,828	408,618	337,359	271,769	240,880	198,115
Operating Income	3,178,000	2,541,000	1,797,788	1,402,265	1,147,969	833,157	624,114	502,673
Net Interest Inc./(Exp.)	(180,000)	(182,000)	(173,537)	(120,825)	(84,852)	(74,735)	(65,567)	(49,067)
Income Taxes	1,136,000	888,000	600,989	471,569	390,322	276,000	201,063	161,456
Income from Cont Ops	1,862,000	...	...	...	...	...	...	...
Net Income	1,877,000	1,471,000	1,023,262	809,871	672,795	482,422	357,484	292,150
Average Shs. Outstg.	806,000	800,000	794,597	768,950	767,708	707,590	697,518	670,712
Balance Sheet								
Cash & Cash Equivalents	1,446,000	853,000	798,839	455,658	491,122	222,709	195,146	40,387
Total Current Assets	6,687,000	5,568,000	4,920,392	4,175,013	3,709,541	2,585,683	2,109,602	1,851,466
Total Assets	19,042,000	16,109,000	13,736,219	11,375,754	9,012,323	6,344,651	5,219,277	4,434,954
Total Current Liabilities	4,368,000	3,578,000	3,016,830	2,928,585	2,385,954	1,765,344	1,449,320	1,348,531
Long–Term Obligations	3,678,000	3,736,000	3,734,011	2,697,669	1,726,579	1,283,092	1,045,570	767,338
Net Stockholders' Equity	10,309,000	8,302,000	6,674,442	5,494,485	4,695,471	3,135,952	2,600,609	2,217,476
Net Working Capital	2,319,000	1,990,000	1,903,562	1,246,428	1,323,587	820,339	660,282	502,935
Shares Outstanding	787,300	781,900	775,714	766,484	764,718	705,286	701,264	693,616
Operating Profit Margin %	10.30	9.59	8.13	7.46	7.21	6.80	6.15	5.84
Net Profit Margin %	13.40	12.25	10.06	9.33	9.13	8.44	7.49	7.15
Return on Equity %	18.06	17.71	15.33	14.73	14.32	15.38	13.74	13.17
Return on Assets %	9.77	9.13	7.44	7.11	7.46	7.60	6.84	6.58
Debt/Total Assets %	19.31	23.19	27.18	23.71	19.15	20.22	20.03	17.30
Price Range	60.05–34.01	48.10–33.50	47.50–25.00	31.75–18.72	32.56–21.50	29.16–12.47	12.64–8.09	10.88–7.41
P/E Ratio	25.88–14.66	26.00–18.11	36.54–19.23	30.24–17.83	37.43–24.71	42.88–18.34	24.79–15.87	25.89–17.63
Average Yield %	0.21	0.19	0.20	0.22	0.22	0.26	0.50	0.55

Address: 1000 Lowe's Boulevard, Mooresville, NC 28117	Officers: Robert L. Tillman – Chmn., C.E.O., Robert A. Niblock – Pres.	Investor Contact:704–758–2033
Telephone: (704) 758–1000	**Transfer Agents:**EquiServe Trust Company, NA, Canton, MA	**Institutional Holding**
Web Site: www.lowes.com		**No of Institutions:** 2
		Shares: 14,180 **% Held:** –

M & T BANK CORP

Exchange	Symbol	Price	52Wk Range	Yield	P/E
NYS	MTB	$90.57 (5/28/2004)	98.55-83.37	1.77	18.04

*7 Year Price Score 140.5 *NYSE Composite Index=100 ***12 Month Price Score 45.7**

Interim Earnings (Per Share)

Qtr.	Mar	Jun	Sep	Dec
2001	0.85	0.94	0.98	1.05
2002	1.25	1.26	1.23	1.33
2003	1.23	1.10	1.28	1.34
2004	1.30	...	...	...

Interim Dividends (Per Share)

Amt	Decl	Ex	Rec	Pay
0.30Q	7/15/2003	8/28/2003	9/2/2003	9/30/2003
0.30Q	10/21/2003	11/26/2003	12/1/2003	12/31/2003
0.40Q	2/17/2004	2/25/2004	2/27/2004	3/31/2004
0.40Q	4/20/2004	5/27/2004	6/1/2004	6/30/2004

Indicated Div: $1.60 (Div. Reinv. Plan)

Valuation Analysis

Forecast P/E 15.32 (5/24/2004)

Market Cap $8.3 Billion	Book Value	5.7 Billion
Price/Book 1.89	Price/Sales	3.42

Dividend Achiever Status

Rank	33	10 Year Growth Rate	20.24%
Total Years of Dividend Growth			23

Business Summary: Commercial Banking (MIC: 8.1 SIC: 6022 NAIC:522110)

M&T Bank, with assets of $49.83 billion as of Dec 31 2003, is a bank holding company with two wholly-owned bank subsidiaries, Manufacturers and Traders Trust and M&T Bank, National Association. The banks collectively offer commercial banking, trust and investment services to their customers. Through its subsidiaries, Co. provides individuals, corporations and institutions with operations in the following six segments: Commercial Banking, Commercial Real Estate, Discretionary Portfolio, Residential Mortgage Banking, Retail Banking, and Other operations.

Recent Developments: For the quarter ended Mar 31 2004, net income increased 36.9% to $159.5 million from $116.5 million in the corresponding period of the year before. Earnings for 2004 included charges for impairment of capitalized residential mortgage servicing rights of $7.0 million, while earnings for 2003 included after-tax merger-related expenses of $4.0 million. Net interest income advanced 32.7% to $419.3 million. Provision for credit losses dropped 39.4% to $20.0 million. Total other income surged 71.7% to $228.2 million, primarily reflecting revenues related to operations in market areas associated with Allfirst Financial. Total other expense increased 61.0% to $390.0 million.

Prospects: Co. is encouraged by the resumption of growth in its commercial loan portfolios and the improvement of its overall credit quality, including lower levels of net charge-offs, as well as the positive impact of the acquisition of Allfirst. Additionally, higher service charges on deposit accounts and trust income are contributing to growth in non-interest income. However, Co.'s residential mortgage banking business continues to experience declines in revenue. Looking ahead, diluted earnings for full-year 2004 are expected to range from $5.90 to $6.10 per share.

Financial Data

(US$ in Thousands)	3 Mos	12/31/2003	12/31/2002	12/31/2001	12/31/2000	12/31/1999	12/31/1998	12/31/1997
Earnings Per Share	5.02	4.95	5.07	3.82	3.44	3.28	2.61	2.52
Tang. Book Val. Per Share	21.95	21.41	21.35	17.84	16.09	14.87	13.72	15.58
Dividends Per Share	1.200	1.200	1	0.750	0.620	0.450	0.460	0.310
Dividend Payout %	28.81	24.24	19.72	19.63	18.16	13.70	17.58	12.27
Income Statement								
Total Interest Income	546,132	2,126,565	1,842,099	2,101,885	1,772,784	1,478,631	1,351,794	1,064,961
Total Interest Expense	126,829	527,810	594,514	943,597	918,597	719,234	687,503	508,093
Net Interest Income	419,303	1,598,755	1,247,585	1,158,288	854,187	759,397	664,291	556,868
Provision for Loan Losses	20,000	131,000	122,000	103,500	38,000	44,500	43,200	46,000
Non-Interest Income	228,151	831,095	511,931	477,426	324,672	282,375	270,595	193,067
Non-Interest Expense	389,967	1,448,180	921,032	948,318	694,453	578,958	566,123	421,776
Income Before Taxes	237,487	850,670	716,484	583,896	446,406	418,314	325,563	282,159
Net Income	159,490	573,942	485,092	378,075	286,156	265,626	207,974	176,241
Average Shs. Outstg.	122,316	115,932	95,663	99,024	83,171	80,900	79,500	69,770
Balance Sheet								
Cash & Due from Banks	1,827,401	1,877,494	963,772	965,664	750,259	592,755	493,792	333,805
Securities Avail. for Sale	7,474,983	7,077,770	3,650,763	2,702,113	3,071,735	2,321,874	2,756,862	1,640,564
Net Loans & Leases	35,899,668	35,158,377	25,291,312	24,762,752	22,368,111	17,090,606	15,485,183	11,221,912
Total Assets	50,832,480	49,826,081	33,174,525	31,450,196	28,949,456	22,409,115	20,583,891	14,002,935
Total Deposits	33,340,880	33,114,944	21,664,923	21,580,400	20,232,673	15,373,620	14,737,152	11,163,158
Long-Term Obligations	5,747,951	5,535,425	4,497,374	3,461,769	3,414,516	1,775,133	1,567,543	427,819
Total Liabilities	45,098,339	44,108,871	29,992,702	28,510,745	26,248,971	20,612,069	18,981,525	12,972,669
Net Stockholders' Equity	5,734,141	5,717,210	3,181,823	2,939,451	2,700,485	1,797,046	1,602,366	1,030,266
Shares Outstanding	118,908	120,106	92,028	93,683	93,244	77,238	76,980	66,100
Return on Equity %	2.78	10.03	15.24	12.86	10.59	14.78	12.97	17.10
Return on Assets %	0.31	1.15	1.46	1.20	0.98	1.18	1.01	1.25
Equity/Assets %	11.28	11.47	9.59	9.34	9.32	8.01	7.78	7.35
Non-Int. Exp./Tot. Inc. %	50.36	48.96	39.12	36.76	33.10	32.87	34.89	33.52
Price Range	98.30-89.08	98.55-75.69	89.94-68.00	81.23-61.09	68.00-36.40	56.66-41.00	57.53-41.00	46.50-28.10
P/E Ratio	19.58-17.75	19.91-15.29	17.74-13.41	21.26-15.99	19.77-10.58	17.27-12.50	22.04-15.71	18.45-11.15
Average Yield %	1.29	1.39	1.24	1.05	1.33	0.91	0.94	0.87

Address: One MTPlaza, Buffalo, NY 14203	**Officers:** Robert G. Wilmers - Chmn., Pres., CEO, Carl L. Campbell - Vice-Chmn.	**Investor Contact:** 716 842-5445
Telephone: (716) 842-5445	**Transfer Agents:** BankBoston, N.A. c/o Equiserve, Boston, MA	**Institutional Holding**
Web Site: www.mandtbank.com		**No of Institutions:** 26
		Shares: 15,630,683 **% Held:** -

MARSH & McLENNAN COS., INC.

Exchange	Symbol	Price	52Wk Range	Yield	P/E
NYS	MMC	$44.12 (5/28/2004)	54.74-42.59	3.08	15.59

*7 Year Price Score 110.3   *NYSE Composite Index=100   *12 Month Price Score 43.2

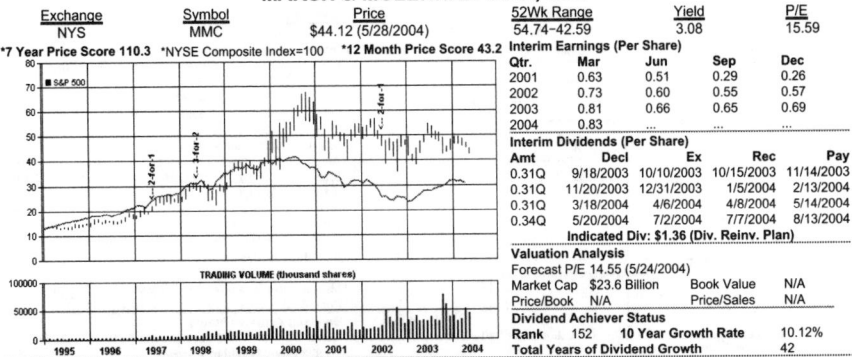

Interim Earnings (Per Share)

Qtr.	Mar	Jun	Sep	Dec
2001	0.63	0.51	0.29	0.26
2002	0.73	0.60	0.55	0.57
2003	0.81	0.66	0.65	0.69
2004	0.83	...	...	...

Interim Dividends (Per Share)

Amt	Decl	Ex	Rec	Pay
0.31Q	9/18/2003	10/10/2003	10/15/2003	11/14/2003
0.31Q	11/20/2003	12/31/2003	1/5/2004	2/13/2004
0.31Q	3/18/2004	4/6/2004	4/8/2004	5/14/2004
0.34Q	5/20/2004	7/2/2004	7/7/2004	8/13/2004

Indicated Div: $1.36 (Div. Reinv. Plan)

Valuation Analysis

Forecast P/E 14.55 (5/24/2004)

Market Cap	$23.6 Billion	Book Value	N/A
Price/Book	N/A	Price/Sales	N/A

Dividend Achiever Status

Rank	152	10 Year Growth Rate	10.12%
Total Years of Dividend Growth			42

Business Summary: Insurance (MIC: 8.2 SIC: 6411 NAIC:524210)

Marsh & McLennan Companies is engaged in the worldwide business of providing retail and wholesale insurance services, principally as a broker or consultant for insurers, insurance underwriters and other brokers. Co.'s subsidiaries include Marsh, a risk and insurance services firm; Putnam Investments, one of the largest investment management companies in the U.S.; and Mercer Consulting Group, a major global provider of consulting services. Other subsidiaries render advisory services in the area of employee benefits and compensation consulting, management consulting, economic consulting and environmental consulting.

Recent Developments: For the quarter ended Mar 31 2004, net income rose to $446.0 million from $443.0 million the prior year. Results for 2004 included a gain of $105.0 million related to an insurance settlement and a charge of $140.0 million related to an investment trading settlement. Total revenue grew 12.6% to $3.21 billion. By segment, risk and insurance service revenue increased 12.5% to $1.99 billion, and operating income grew 13.8% to $637.0 million. Investment management services revenue rose 3.6% to $461.0 million, while operating loss was $26.0 million versus operating profit of $103.0 million in 2003. Consulting revenue grew 19.1% to $755.0 million, and operating income rose 7.2% to $89.0 million.

Prospects: Going forward, the risk and insurance services business should remain solid, supported by Co.'s ability to deliver services across a wide spectrum of needs. Co.'s consulting business should be poised to expand revenues and profits, led by continued strength in its international operations. However, Co.'s investment management business will likely continue to suffer from lower management fees due to a significant reduction in assets under management. Total assets under management on Mar 31 2004 were $227.00 billion versus $241.00 billion on Mar 31 2003. Separately, on Apr 8 2004, Co. reached agreements with the SEC and the State of Massachusetts on market trading issues for $110.0 million.

Financial Data

(US$ in Thousands)	3 Mos	12/31/2003	12/31/2002	12/31/2001	12/31/2000	12/31/1999	12/31/1998	12/31/1997
Earnings Per Share	2.83	2.81	2.45	1.69	2.05	1.31	1.49	0.79
Tang. Book Val. Per Share	N.M	N.M	N.M	N.M	N.M	N.M	N.M	1.53
Dividends Per Share	1.210	1.180	1.090	1.030	0.950	0.850	0.730	0.630
Dividend Payout %	42.76	41.99	44.48	60.76	46.34	64.88	49.21	79.49
Income Statement								
Other Income	3,210,000	11,588,000	10,440,000	9,943,000	10,157,000	9,157,000	7,190,000	6,008,600
Total Revenues	3,210,000	11,588,000	10,440,000	9,943,000	10,157,000	9,157,000	7,190,000	6,008,600
Total Indirect Exp.	2,437,000	9,092,000	8,166,000	8,180,000	7,978,000	7,698,000	5,770,000	5,263,800
Inc. Before Inc. Taxes	728,000	2,335,000	2,133,000	1,590,000	1,955,000	1,247,000	1,305,000	662,400
Income Taxes	281,000	770,000	747,000	599,000	753,000	521,000	509,000	263,000
Eqty Earns/Minority Int.	(1,000)	(25,000)	(21,000)	(17,000)	(21,000)	...	...	...
Income from Cont Ops	...	1,565,000	1,386,000	991,000	1,202,000	...	...	...
Net Income	446,000	1,540,000	1,365,000	974,000	1,181,000	726,000	796,000	399,400
Average Shs. Outstg.	540,000	548,000	557,000	572,000	568,000	544,000	528,000	501,600
Balance Sheet								
Cash & Cash Equivalents	634,000	665,000	546,000	537,000	240,000	428,000	610,000	424,300
Premiums Due	3,012,000	2,703,000	2,478,000	2,692,000	2,812,000	2,323,000	1,909,000	1,498,200
Invst. Assets: Total	624,000	648,000	578,000	826,000	976,000	687,000	828,000	720,200
Total Assets	15,510,000	15,053,000	13,855,000	13,293,000	13,769,000	13,021,000	11,871,000	7,914,200
Long-Term Obligations	2,908,000	2,910,000	2,891,000	2,334,000	2,347,000	2,357,000	1,590,000	1,239,800
Net Stockholders' Equity	5,582,000	5,451,000	5,018,000	5,173,000	5,228,000	4,170,000	3,659,000	3,198,800
Shares Outstanding	523,539	526,736	538,199	548,654	552,052	534,051	514,000	509,850
Return on Revenues %	13.89	13.50	13.27	9.96	11.83	7.92	11.07	6.64
Return on Equity %	7.98	28.71	27.62	19.15	22.99	17.41	21.75	12.48
Return on Assets %	2.87	10.39	10.00	7.45	8.72	5.57	6.70	5.04
Price Range	49.30-45.89	54.74-38.52	56.85-35.53	58.56-40.25	67.44-36.50	48.16-28.72	32.00-22.25	26.58-17.23
P/E Ratio	17.42-16.22	19.48-13.71	23.20-14.50	34.65-23.82	32.90-17.80	36.76-21.92	21.48-14.93	33.65-21.81
Average Yield %	2.54	2.51	2.23	2.04	1.75	2.30	2.59	2.81

Address: 1166 Avenue Of The Americas, New York, NY 10036
Telephone: (212) 345-5000
Web Site: www.mmc.com

Officers: Jeffrey W. Greenberg - Chmn., C.E.O., Mathis Cabiallavetta - Vice-Chmn.
Transfer Agents: The Bank of New York, New York, NY

Investor Contact:212-345-5475
Institutional Holding
No of Institutions: 1
Shares: 22,000   **% Held:** -

MARSHALL & ILSLEY CORP.

Exchange	Symbol	Price	52Wk Range	Yield	P/E
NYS	MI	$41.15 (5/28/2004)	41.15-29.91	2.04	16.66

*7 Year Price Score 122.0 *NYSE Composite Index=100 ***12 Month Price Score 51.9**

Interim Earnings (Per Share)

Qtr.	Mar	Jun	Sep	Dec
2001	0.40	0.27	0.37	0.50
2002	0.52	0.54	0.54	0.56
2003	0.56	0.59	0.61	0.62
2004	0.65	...	...	...

Interim Dividends (Per Share)

Amt	Decl	Ex	Rec	Pay
0.18Q	8/21/2003	8/27/2003	9/1/2003	9/12/2003
0.18Q	10/16/2003	11/26/2003	12/1/2003	12/12/2003
0.18Q	2/19/2004	2/26/2004	3/1/2004	3/12/2004
0.21Q	4/27/2004	5/26/2004	5/28/2004	6/11/2004

Indicated Div: $0.84 (Div. Reinv. Plan)

Valuation Analysis

Forecast P/E 15.20 (5/24/2004)

Market Cap	$9.0 Billion	Book Value	3.4 Billion
Price/Book	2.48	Price/Sales	3.12

Dividend Achiever Status

Rank	159	10 Year Growth Rate	9.93%
Total Years of Dividend Growth			31

TRADING VOLUME (thousand shares)

Business Summary: Commercial Banking (MIC: 8.1 SIC: 6021 NAIC:522110)

Marshall & Ilsley, a multibank holding company with assets of $34.40 billion as of Dec 31 2003, is headquartered in Milwaukee, WI. Co. has 199 banking offices in Wisconsin, 28 locations throughout Arizona, 11 offices in Minnesota, six offices in Missouri, two offices in Florida, one office in Nevada and one office in Illinois, as well as on the Internet. Co. also provides trust services, residential mortgage banking, capital markets, brokerage and insurance, commercial leasing and commercial mortgage banking. Co.'s principal subsidiary is Metavante Corporation, a provider of integrated financial transaction processing, outsourcing services, software and consulting services.

Recent Developments: For the three months ended Mar 31 2004, net income rose 14.1% to $146.1 million compared with $128.0 million in the same period of 2003. Results for 2004 and 2003 included a net loss of $500,000 and a net gain of $1.6 million, respectively, from investment securities. Net interest income grew 5.1% to $286.5 million from $272.5 million the year before. Provision for loan and lease losses dropped 65.0% to $9.0 million versus $25.7 million a year earlier. Total non-interest revenues increased 7.9% to $313.4 million from $290.4 million in the previous year. Total non-interest expense rose 8.8% to $362.3 million versus $333.1 million the year before.

Prospects: On Apr 21 2004, Co. signed a definitive agreement to acquire The Kirchman Corporation, a provider of automation software and compliance services to the banking industry, for an undisclosed amount. The Kirchman Corporation will become a subsidiary of Metavante and operate within the Metavante Financial Services Group. The acquisition will enhance Metavante's core-processing software application that financial institutions can run in-house. Separately, Co. expects commercial loan growth in 2004 for the banking segment will be in the high single digit range.

Financial Data

(US$ in Thousands)	3 Mos	12/31/2003	12/31/2002	12/31/2001	12/31/2000	12/31/1999	12/31/1998	12/31/1997
Earnings Per Share	2.47	2.38	2.16	1.54	1.45	1.57	1.30	1.21
Tang. Book Val. Per Share	10.34	9.96	8.60	9.16	9.22	8.26	8.98	9.45
Dividends Per Share	0.720	0.700	0.620	0.560	0.510	0.470	0.430	0.390
Dividend Payout %	29.27	29.41	28.93	36.73	35.56	29.93	32.95	32.43
Income Statement								
Total Interest Income	389,073	1,529,920	1,567,336	1,709,107	1,747,982	1,496,584	1,434,044	1,143,670
Total Interest Expense	110,437	472,634	561,038	866,328	1,074,976	791,303	757,974	579,623
Net Interest Income	278,636	1,057,286	1,006,298	842,779	673,006	705,281	676,070	564,047
Provision for Loan Losses	9,027	62,993	74,416	54,115	30,352	25,419	27,000	17,253
Non-Interest Income	306,749	1,161,658	1,082,688	1,002,812	928,352	845,774	756,333	598,858
Non-Interest Expense	362,328	1,451,707	1,295,978	1,290,431	1,100,656	997,697	940,028	775,401
Income Before Taxes	220,710	758,387	718,592	501,045	470,350	527,939	465,285	370,251
Income from Cont Ops	...	...	...	337,921	317,402	...	...	...
Net Income	146,109	544,105	480,327	337,485	315,123	354,511	301,323	245,144
Average Shs. Outstg.	226,025	228,285	222,048	218,264	217,766	226,010	230,480	203,020
Balance Sheet								
Cash & Due from Banks	690,920	810,088	1,012,090	617,183	760,103	705,293	760,405	800,120
Securities Avail. for Sale	6,099,541	4,843,908	4,370,697	4,210,653	4,785,869	4,429,837	4,161,138	4,101,500
Net Loans & Leases	25,589,254	24,800,756	23,570,437	19,027,174	17,351,972	16,109,199	13,770,114	12,339,463
Total Assets	35,476,435	34,372,643	32,874,642	27,253,734	26,077,739	24,369,723	21,566,293	19,477,452
Total Deposits	23,151,011	22,270,105	20,393,706	16,493,047	19,248,621	16,435,182	15,919,919	14,355,998
Long-Term Obligations	3,221,121	2,734,623	2,283,781	1,560,177	921,276	665,024	794,482	791,176
Total Liabilities	32,074,077	31,043,950	29,837,974	24,760,766	23,835,550	22,252,797	19,322,514	17,557,381
Net Stockholders' Equity	3,402,358	3,328,693	3,036,668	2,492,968	2,242,189	2,116,926	2,243,779	1,920,071
Shares Outstanding	222,064	223,226	226,232	207,897	205,693	211,632	212,206	203,074
Return on Equity %	4.29	14.71	15.81	13.55	14.15	16.74	13.42	12.76
Return on Assets %	0.41	1.42	1.46	1.23	1.21	1.45	1.39	1.25
Equity/Assets %	9.59	9.68	9.23	9.14	8.59	8.68	10.40	9.85
Non-Int. Exp./Tot. Inc. %	51.57	53.93	48.90	47.58	41.12	42.59	42.91	44.49
Price Range	40.20-36.10	38.30-25.16	31.91-23.33	32.00-24.05	31.28-19.38	35.88-27.25	31.13-20.50	29.82-16.50
P/E Ratio	16.28-14.62	16.09-10.57	14.77-10.80	20.78-15.62	21.57-13.36	22.85-17.36	23.94-15.77	24.64-13.64
Average Yield %	1.87	2.26	2.09	2.04	2.12	1.50	1.61	1.77

Address: 770 North Water Street, Milwaukee, WI 53202	Officers: James B. Wigdale – Chmn., Dennis J. Kuester – Pres., C.E.O.	Investor Contact:414-765-7801
Telephone: (414) 765-7700	Transfer Agents:Continental Stock Transfer &Trust Company, New York, NY	Institutional Holding No of Institutions: 24
Web Site: www.micorp.com		Shares: 2,729,615 % Held: –

164

MASCO CORP.

*7 Year Price Score 106.7 *NYSE Composite Index=100 *12 Month Price Score 49.4

Interim Earnings (Per Share)

Qtr.	Mar	Jun	Sep	Dec
2001	0.25	0.30	(0.39)	0.26
2002	0.31	0.43	0.24	0.35
2003	0.32	0.46	0.53	0.20
2004	0.52	...	...	...

Interim Dividends (Per Share)

Amt	Decl	Ex	Rec	Pay
0.14Q	6/26/2003	7/9/2003	7/11/2003	8/11/2003
0.16Q	9/17/2003	10/8/2003	10/10/2003	11/10/2003
0.16Q	12/10/2003	1/7/2004	1/9/2004	2/9/2004
0.16Q	3/18/2004	4/6/2004	4/9/2004	5/10/2004

Indicated Div: $0.64 (Div. Reinv. Plan)

Valuation Analysis

Forecast P/E 14.05 (5/24/2004)

Market Cap	$14.0 Billion	Book Value	5.5 Billion
Price/Book	2.32	Price/Sales	1.16

Dividend Achiever Status

Rank	234	10 Year Growth Rate	5.96%
Total Years of Dividend Growth			45

Business Summary: Metal Products (MIC: 11.4 SIC: 3432 NAIC:337122)

Masco is engaged in the manufacture and sale of cabinets and related products, plumbing products, architectural coatings and other specialty home improvement and building products. These products are sold to the home improvement and home construction markets through mass merchandisers, hardware stores, home centers, builders, distributors and other outlets for consumers and builders. Co.'s brand names and tradenames include the following: *Kraftmaid®, Merillat®, Mill's Pride®, Quality Cabinets®, Delta®, Peerless®, Newport Brass®, Behr®, Premium Plus®, Masterchem®, Franklin Brass®, Ginger®, Bath Unlimited®, Milgard®, Griffin*TM, and *Cambrian*TM.

Recent Developments: For the quarter ended Mar 31 2004, income from continuing operations rose 52.5% to $241.0 million compared with $158.0 million in the equivalent 2003 quarter. The improvement in earnings was primarily due to market share gains, new products and better economic conditions impacting new home construction and home improvement markets. Results for 2004 and 2003 excluded discontinued operations losses of $73.0 million and gains of $8.0 million, respectively. Results included income of $21.0 million in 2004 and $13.0 million in 2003 regarding a litigation settlement. Net sales advanced 19.3% to $2.81 billion versus $2.35 billion a year earlier. Operating income grew 28.6% to $387.0 million.

Prospects: Based on current business trends, Co. expects second quarter 2004 earnings from continuing operations to be in the range of $0.50 to $0.53 per common share compared with second quarter 2003 earnings of $0.44 per share. Meanwhile, thus far in 2004, Co. is experiencing better-than-anticipated sales performance. Based on current business trends, Co. expects full-year 2004 sales to be higher year over year, and earnings from continuing operations to be between $2.00 and $2.10 per share. This includes the benefit of recent common share repurchases and reflects increases in certain operating expenses.

Financial Data

(US$ in Thousands)	3 Mos	12/31/2003	12/31/2002	12/31/2001	12/31/2000	12/31/1999	12/31/1998	12/31/1997
Earnings Per Share	1.71	1.51	1.33	0.42	1.31	1.28	1.39	1.15
Cash Flow Per Share	0.20	2.89	2.38	2.03	1.62	1.09	1.21	1.19
Tang. Book Val. Per Share	0.84	1.35	1.31	1.30	2.77	3.14	4.98	4.52
Dividends Per Share	0.600	0.580	0.540	0.520	0.490	0.450	0.430	0.400
Dividend Payout %	35.93	38.41	40.97	125.00	37.40	35.15	30.93	35.21
Income Statement								
Total Revenues	2,806,000	10,936,000	9,419,400	8,358,000	7,243,000	6,307,000	4,345,000	3,760,000
Total Indirect Exp.	464,000	1,926,000	1,653,340	1,511,400	1,288,140	1,400,070	870,510	794,650
Depreciation & Amort.	...	244,000	220,300	93,200	66,200	45,430	28,510	18,720
Operating Income	387,000	1,424,000	1,331,100	1,039,800	966,700	911,400	680,500	587,100
Net Interest Inc./(Exp.)	(51,000)	(254,000)	(230,840)	(203,660)	(130,930)	(67,890)	(38,920)	(32,300)
Income Taxes	140,000	463,000	348,900	102,200	301,700	334,500	279,000	248,500
Income from Cont Ops	241,000	740,000	682,100	...	...	...	...	...
Net Income	168,000	806,000	589,700	198,500	591,700	569,600	476,000	382,400
Average Shs. Outstg.	468,000	491,000	514,100	474,900	451,800	446,200	343,700	337,600
Balance Sheet								
Cash & Cash Equivalents	624,000	795,000	1,066,570	311,990	169,430	230,780	541,740	441,330
Total Current Assets	3,747,000	3,804,000	3,949,770	2,626,920	2,308,160	2,109,780	1,862,620	1,626,720
Total Assets	12,249,000	12,149,000	12,050,430	9,183,330	7,744,000	6,634,920	5,167,350	4,333,760
Total Current Liabilities	2,107,000	2,099,000	1,932,450	1,236,560	1,078,050	846,430	846,580	620,000
Long-Term Obligations	4,197,000	3,848,000	4,316,470	3,627,630	3,018,240	2,431,270	1,391,430	1,321,470
Net Stockholders' Equity	5,127,000	5,456,000	5,293,840	4,119,830	3,426,060	3,136,500	2,728,580	2,229,020
Net Working Capital	1,640,000	1,705,000	2,017,320	1,390,360	1,230,110	1,263,350	1,016,040	1,006,720
Shares Outstanding	442,730	458,380	488,890	459,050	444,750	443,510	339,330	331,140
Operating Profit Margin %	13.79	13.02	14.13	12.44	13.34	14.45	15.66	15.61
Return on Equity %	4.70	13.56	12.88	4.81	17.27	18.16	17.44	17.15
Return on Assets %	1.96	6.09	5.66	2.16	7.64	8.58	9.21	8.82
Debt/Total Assets %	34.26	31.67	35.82	39.50	38.97	36.64	26.92	30.49
Price Range	30.62-26.02	28.31-16.82	29.08-17.68	26.49-18.00	25.69-14.81	33.50-23.00	32.50-21.13	26.53-17.06
P/E Ratio	17.91-15.22	18.75-11.14	21.86-13.29	63.07-42.86	19.61-11.31	26.17-17.97	23.38-15.20	23.07-14.84
Average Yield %	2.16	2.50	2.22	2.22	2.46	1.55	1.55	1.92

Address: 21001 Van Born Road, Taylor, MI 48180	**Officers:** Richard A. Manoogian – Chmn., C.E.O., Alan Barry – Pres., C.O.O.	**Investor Contact:**313-274-7400 **Institutional Holding**
Telephone: (313) 274 7400	**Transfer Agents:**Bank of New York, New York, NY	**No of Institutions:** 4
Web Site: www.masco.com		**Shares:** 1,029,779 **% Held:** –

MAY DEPARTMENT STORES CO. (THE)

Exchange	Symbol	Price	52Wk Range	Yield	P/E
NYS	MAY	$28.66 (5/28/2004)	36.31–22.07	3.38	19.90

*7 Year Price Score 86.4   ***NYSE Composite Index=100**   ***12 Month Price Score 47.7**

Interim Earnings (Per Share)

Qtr.	Apr	Jul	Oct	Feb
2000	0.35	0.41	0.27	1.59
2001	0.34	0.35	0.17	1.36
2002	0.23	0.22	0.05	1.26
2003	0.23	(0.39)	0.15	1.42
2004	0.26	...	...	...

Interim Dividends (Per Share)

Amt	Decl	Ex	Rec	Pay
0.24Q	3/21/2003	5/28/2003	6/1/2003	6/15/2003
0.24Q	11/14/2003	11/26/2003	12/1/2003	12/15/2003
0.243Q	2/12/2004	2/26/2004	3/1/2004	3/15/2004
0.243Q	3/19/2004	5/27/2004	6/1/2004	6/15/2004

Indicated Div: $0.97 (Div. Reinv. Plan)

Valuation Analysis

Forecast P/E 11.30 (5/24/2004)

Market Cap	$8.3 Billion	Book Value	4.2 Billion
Price/Book	1.97	Price/Sales	0.62

Dividend Achiever Status

Rank	257	10 Year Growth Rate	4.84%
Total Years of Dividend Growth			28

Business Summary: Retail – General (MIC: 5.2 SIC: 5311 NAIC:452111)

The May Department Stores Company operated 444 department stores in 36 states and the District of Columbia as of Jan 31 2004 under the following names: Lord & Taylor, Filene's, Kaufmann's, Robinsons–May, Meier & Frank, Hecht's, Strawbridge's, Foley's, Famous–Barr, L.S. Ayers, and The Jones Store. Co. is also a major retailer of bridal gowns and bridal–related merchandise through David's Bridal, Inc. and Priscilla of Boston, Inc., and provides tuxedo rental services through After Hours Formalwear, Inc. At Jan 31 2004, Co. operated 210 David's Bridal stores in 44 states and Puerto Rico, 460 After Hours Formalwear stores in 30 states, and ten Priscilla of Boston stores in nine states.

Recent Developments: For the 13 weeks ended May 1 2004, net earnings totaled $76.0 million, up 5.6% compared with $72.0 million in the corresponding prior–year period. Results for 2004 included pre–tax restructuring charges of $7.0 million. Net sales increased 3.1% to $2.96 billion from $2.87 billion the year before. Comparable–store sales were up 1.7% year–over–year. Cost of sales, excluding one–time restructuring charges, totaled $2.12 billion, or 71.6% of net sales, versus $2.09 billion, or 72.7% of net sales, a year earlier. Earnings before income taxes jumped 86.2% to $121.0 million from $65.0 million the previous year.

Prospects: Top–line growth is being fueled by strong sales of handbags, small leather goods, costume jewelry, ladies' footwear, and apparel. Meanwhile, Co. continues to aggressively expand its store base. During the current fiscal year, Co. plans to open eight new department stores, including a new Hecht's that opened in Wilmington, NC during the first quarter. Co. also anticipates opening 30 David's Bridal stores, 20 After Hours stores, and two Priscilla of Boston stores during fiscal 2004. Separately, as of the end of the first quarter of fiscal 2004, Co. had completed the closure of 15 of the 34 department stores scheduled to be divested as part of a cost–reduction plan announced in July 2003.

Financial Data

(US$ in Millions)	01/31/2004	02/01/2003	02/02/2002	02/03/2001	01/29/2000	01/30/1999	01/31/1998	02/01/1997
Earnings Per Share	1.41	1.76	2.22	2.62	2.60	2.30	2.07	1.88
Cash Flow Per Share	5.45	4.74	5.17	4.10	4.30	4.09	4.08	3.43
Tang. Book Val. Per Share	8.72	8.38	7.76	8.52	9.51	8.67	8.82	8.08
Dividends Per Share	0.960	0.950	0.940	0.930	0.890	0.840	0.800	0.760
Dividend Payout %	68.08	53.97	42.34	35.49	34.23	36.81	38.64	40.95
Income Statement								
Total Revenues	13,343	13,491	14,175	14,511	13,866	13,413	12,685	12,000
Total Indirect Exp.	3,008	2,863	2,912	2,835	2,686	2,516	2,375	2,265
Depreciation & Amort.	564	557	559	511	469	439	412	373
Operating Income	957	1,165	1,493	1,747	1,810	1,673	1,578	1,509
Net Interest Inc./(Exp.)	(318)	(345)	(349)	(345)	(287)	(278)	(299)	(277)
Income Taxes	205	278	438	544	596	546	500	483
Income from Cont Ops	...	...	706	...	...	...	779	749
Net Income	434	542	703	858	927	849	775	755
Average Shs. Outstg.	307	307	317	327	355	367	373	396
Balance Sheet								
Cash & Cash Equivalents	564	55	52	156	41	112	199	102
Total Current Assets	5,143	4,722	4,925	5,270	5,115	4,987	4,878	5,035
Total Assets	12,097	11,936	11,920	11,574	10,935	10,533	9,913	10,059
Total Current Liabilities	2,685	2,666	2,538	2,214	2,415	2,059	1,828	1,923
Long–Term Obligations	3,797	4,035	4,403	4,534	3,560	3,825	3,512	3,849
Net Stockholders' Equity	4,191	4,035	3,841	3,855	4,077	3,836	3,809	3,650
Net Working Capital	2,458	2,056	2,387	3,056	2,700	2,928	3,050	3,112
Shares Outstanding	288	288	287	298	325	334	346	355
Operating Profit Margin %	7.17	8.63	10.53	12.03	13.05	12.47	12.43	12.57
Net Profit Margin %	6.32	8.13	11.16	13.41	15.28	14.47	14.02	14.29
Return on Equity %	10.35	13.43	18.38	22.25	22.73	22.13	20.45	20.52
Return on Assets %	3.58	4.54	5.92	7.41	8.47	8.06	7.85	7.44
Debt/Total Assets %	31.38	33.80	36.93	39.17	32.55	36.31	35.42	38.26
Price Range	33.61–18.01	37.60–20.43	41.25–27.98	38.95–19.63	45.00–29.56	47.08–33.50	37.96–29.33	34.17–27.42
P/E Ratio	23.84–12.77	21.36–11.61	18.58–12.60	14.87–7.49	17.31–11.37	20.47–14.57	18.34–14.17	18.17–14.58
Average Yield %	3.91	3.22	2.71	3.41	2.34	2.04	2.35	2.43

Address: 611 Olive Street, St. Louis, MO 63101–1799	**Officers:** Eugene S. Kahn – Chmn., C.E.O., William P. McNamara – Vice–Chmn.	**Investor Contact:**314–342–6413
Telephone: (314) 342–6300	**Transfer Agents:**The Bank of New York, New York, NY	**Institutional Holding** No of Institutions: 7
Web Site: www.maycompany.com		**Shares:** 756,476 **% Held:** –

MBIA INC.

Exchange	Symbol	Price	52Wk Range	Yield	P/E
NYS	MBI	$55.39 (5/28/2004)	67.13–48.75	1.73	10.09

*7 Year Price Score 124.4 *NYSE Composite Index=100 *12 Month Price Score 46.5

Interim Earnings (Per Share)

Qtr.	Mar	Jun	Sep	Dec
2001	0.78	0.96	1.03	1.05
2002	1.03	0.97	1.11	0.87
2003	1.54	1.51	1.31	1.25
2004	1.42	...	...	...

Interim Dividends (Per Share)

Amt	Decl	Ex	Rec	Pay
0.20Q	6/13/2003	6/23/2003	6/25/2003	7/15/2003
0.20Q	9/15/2003	9/23/2003	9/25/2003	10/15/2003
0.20Q	12/8/2003	12/17/2003	12/19/2003	1/15/2004
0.24Q	3/11/2004	3/24/2004	3/26/2004	4/15/2004

Indicated Div: $0.96

Valuation Analysis

Forecast P/E 10.66 (5/24/2004)

Market Cap	$8.1 Billion	Book Value	6.6 Billion
Price/Book	1.37	Price/Sales	5.09

Dividend Achiever Status

Rank	156	10 Year Growth Rate	10.01%
Total Years of Dividend Growth			16

Business Summary: Insurance (MIC: 8.2 SIC: 6351 NAIC:524130)

MBIA is engaged in providing financial guarantee insurance, investment management services and municipal and other services to public finance clients and structured finance clients on a global basis. Financial guarantee insurance provides an unconditional and irrevocable guarantee of the payment of the principal of, and interest or other amounts owing on, insured obligations when due. Co. conducts its financial guarantee business through its wholly-owned subsidiary, MBIA Insurance Corporation. Co. also owns MBIA Assurance S.A., a French insurance company, which writes financial guarantee insurance in the member countries of the European Union.

Recent Developments: For the quarter ended Mar 31 2004, income from continuing operations fell 7.0% to $207.6 million versus income of $223.2 million last year. Results included a loss of $10.7 million for 2004 and a gain of $60.2 million for 2003 on derivative instruments and foreign exchange. Total insurance, investment management services, and municipal services revenues rose 19.5% to $454.9 million. Adjusted direct premiums, which consists of both upfront premiums written and the present value of estimated installment premiums for new business writings and excludes premiums assumed or ceded, slid 43.3% to $138.0 million, due in part to lower insured penetration in the U.S. markets and tighter credit spreads.

Prospects: Despite a recent pick up in business, Co. believes that the lower new business production it experienced during the three months ended Mar 31 2004 will make it difficult to equal 2003's record new business production. Separately, on Mar 10 2004, Co. announced that it is opening a representative office of MBIA Assurance S.A. in Milan, Italy to meet growing market needs in Europe. Also, on Mar 29 2004, Co. announced that it has agreed to sell the assets of 1838 Investment Advisors, LLC, an asset management firm focusing primarily on equities, to the management of 1838 together with an investor group led by Orca Bay Partners. Co. expects the sale to result in a small gain.

Financial Data

(US$ in Thousands)	12/31/2003	12/31/2002	12/31/2001	12/31/2000	12/31/1999	12/31/1998	12/31/1997	12/31/1996
Earnings Per Share	5.61	3.98	3.82	3.55	2.12	2.88	2.81	2.47
Tang. Book Val. Per Share	42.87	37.32	31.56	27.86	22.78	24.58	21.81	18.28
Dividends Per Share	0.770	0.660	0.580	0.540	0.530	0.520	0.510	0.470
Dividend Payout %	13.72	16.58	15.35	15.38	25.07	18.17	18.12	...
Income Statement								
Total Premium Income	732,997	588,509	523,870	446,353	442,796	424,550	297,377	251,712
Net Investment Income	437,696	432,949	412,763	393,985	359,456	331,802	281,459	247,561
Other Income	518,188	195,900	199,152	184,232	162,169	164,695	75,146	46,264
Total Revenues	1,688,881	1,217,358	1,135,785	1,024,570	964,421	921,047	653,982	545,537
Total Indirect Exp.	14,874	17,259	20,874	19,494	126,075	85,904	40,470	17,297
Inc. Before Inc. Taxes	1,148,640	792,581	790,984	714,857	387,883	565,038	479,569	408,130
Income Taxes	335,055	205,763	207,826	186,220	67,353	132,310	105,393	85,967
Income from Cont Ops	...	586,818	583,158	...	...	...	...	...
Net Income	813,585	579,087	570,091	528,637	320,530	432,728	374,176	322,163
Average Shs. Outstg.	144,980	147,574	149,282	148,668	150,603	150,244	133,120	130,044
Balance Sheet								
Cash & Cash Equivalents	778,783	8,184,687	6,781,021	5,405,194	4,844,281	4,237,267	3,837,538	3,517,654
Premiums Due	81,461	135,595	192,954	45,186	55,741	49,497	13,435	980
Invst. Assets: Total	26,373,625	16,195,119	14,087,004	12,051,359	10,534,701	10,100,563	8,681,611	7,659,998
Total Assets	30,267,734	18,852,101	16,199,685	13,894,338	12,263,899	11,796,564	9,810,762	8,562,015
Long-Term Obligations	1,021,795	1,033,070	805,062	795,102	689,204	688,996	473,878	374,010
Net Stockholders' Equity	6,259,015	5,493,351	4,782,638	4,223,413	3,513,101	3,792,217	3,048,253	2,479,697
Shares Outstanding	143,875	144,773	148,434	147,845	149,328	149,322	134,191	129,882
Return on Equity %	12.99	10.68	12.19	12.51	9.12	11.41	12.27	12.99
Return on Assets %	2.68	3.11	3.59	3.80	2.61	3.66	3.81	3.76
Price Range	60.08–34.64	59.65–35.32	57.25–39.21	49.96–24.42	47.71–30.37	53.46–31.71	44.83–30.58	34.71–23.50
P/E Ratio	10.71–6.17	14.99–8.87	14.99–10.26	14.07–6.88	22.50–14.33	18.56–11.01	15.95–10.88	14.05–9.51
Average Yield %	1.55	1.33	1.14	1.42	1.36	1.15	1.37	1.74

Address: 113 King Street, Armonk, NY 10504	**Officers:** Joseph W. Brown – Chmn., C.E.O., Gary C. Dunton – Pres., C.O.O.	**Investor Contact:**914–765–3014
Telephone: (914) 273–4545	**Transfer Agents:**Wells Fargo Shareowner Services, St. Paul, MN	**Institutional Holding**
Web Site: www.mbia.com		**No of Institutions:** 6
		Shares: 877,908 **% Held:** –

MBNA CORP.

Exchange	Symbol	Price	52Wk Range	Yield	P/E
NYS	KRB	$25.40 (5/28/2004)	28.78-20.35	1.89	13.66

*7 Year Price Score 126.5 *NYSE Composite Index=100 *12 Month Price Score 46.9

Interim Earnings (Per Share)

Qtr.	Mar	Jun	Sep	Dec
2001	0.23	0.28	0.36	0.41
2002	0.28	0.35	0.30	0.41
2003	0.33	0.42	0.51	0.53
2004	0.40	...	...	...

Interim Dividends (Per Share)

Amt	Decl	Ex	Rec	Pay
0.10Q	7/24/2003	9/11/2003	9/15/2003	10/1/2003
0.10Q	10/16/2003	12/11/2003	12/15/2003	1/1/2004
0.12Q	1/22/2004	3/11/2004	3/15/2004	4/1/2004
0.12Q	4/22/2004	6/10/2004	6/14/2004	7/1/2004

Indicated Div: $0.48

Valuation Analysis

Forecast P/E 12.29 (5/24/2004)

Market Cap $32.5 Billion	Book Value 11.4 Billion
Price/Book 3.09	Price/Sales 2.97

Dividend Achiever Status

Rank 79	10 Year Growth Rate	14.87%
Total Years of Dividend Growth		12

TRADING VOLUME (thousand shares)

Business Summary: Commercial Banking (MIC: 8.1 SIC: 6021 NAIC:522110)

MBNA is a registered bank holding company, with assets of $59.13 billion as of Dec 31 2003. Co. is the parent of MBNA America Bank, N.A., which has two wholly-owned foreign bank subsidiaries, MBNA Europe Bank and MBNA Canada Bank. MBNA.com, provides credit card, consumer loan, retail deposit, travel and shopping services. Co. is an independent credit card lender and an issuer of affinity credit cards, marketed primarily to members of associations and customers of financial institutions. Co. offers credit cards in the U.S., the U.K., Ireland, Canada and Spain. In addition to its credit card lending, Co. also makes other consumer loans and offers insurance and deposit products.

Recent Developments: For the first quarter ended Mar 31 2004, net income advanced 20.2% to $519.7 million versus $432.5 million in the prior-year quarter. Net interest income grew 20.2% to $667.8 million from $555.6 million a year earlier. Provision for possible credit losses decreased 3.6% to $365.2 million from $378.9 million the year before. Non-interest expense jumped 12.0% to $1.44 billion. During the quarter Co. added 2.5 million new accounts and acquired credit card endorsements from new domestic and international partners. Losses on loan receivables decreased to 4.5% from 5.1%, and losses on managed loans declined to 5.0% from 5.5% in 2003.

Prospects: Co. recently announced that it plans to issue its own American Express-branded credit cards which will carry the American Express logo and will be accepted on the American Express global merchant network. Co. will own the loans and manage and service the accounts on its own systems. Separately, Co.'s Europe Bank Ltd. unit has acquire Premium Credit Ltd., an insurance premium financing company in the U.K. and Sky Financial Solutions, a medical practice financing company in the U.S. Looking ahead, Co. expects full-year 2004 earnings to range from $5.30 to $5.60 per share.

Financial Data

(US$ in Thousands)	3 Mos	12/31/2003	12/31/2002	12/31/2001	12/31/2000	12/31/1999	12/31/1998	12/31/1997
Earnings Per Share	1.86	1.79	1.34	1.28	1.02	0.80	0.64	0.51
Tang. Book Val. Per Share	6.19	6.20	4.62	4.08	3.03	3.49	2.12	1.74
Dividends Per Share	0.360	0.330	0.260	0.230	0.200	0.180	0.150	0.130
Dividend Payout %	19.25	18.43	19.65	18.22	20.26	22.31	24.05	27.05
Income Statement								
Total Interest Income	1,033,105	3,858,884	3,678,070	3,205,102	2,775,679	2,262,271	1,966,172	1,711,013
Total Interest Expense	365,300	1,508,511	1,603,495	1,814,065	1,691,727	1,328,506	1,223,833	1,018,623
Net Interest Income	667,805	2,350,373	2,074,575	1,391,037	1,083,952	933,765	742,339	692,390
Provision for Loan Losses	365,161	1,392,701	1,340,157	1,140,615	409,017	408,914	310,039	260,040
Non-Interest Income	373,990	7,825,480	6,752,923	6,939,619	5,093,174	4,207,821	3,228,969	2,812,879
Non-Interest Expense	1,441,914	5,124,147	4,701,925	4,474,831	3,647,702	3,077,708	2,407,204	2,223,121
Income Before Taxes	803,258	3,659,005	2,785,416	2,715,210	2,120,407	1,654,964	1,254,065	1,022,108
Net Income	519,708	2,338,104	1,765,954	1,694,291	1,312,532	1,024,423	776,266	622,500
Average Shs. Outstg.	1,301,071	1,295,142	1,277,787	1,314,229	1,269,796	1,255,557	1,184,131	1,184,701
Balance Sheet								
Cash & Due from Banks	783,911	660,022	721,972	962,118	971,469	488,386	382,882	263,064
Securities Avail. for Sale	4,739,593	4,363,087	3,655,808	3,106,884	2,666,196	2,752,663	1,663,704	2,162,464
Net Loans & Leases	28,823,092	19,323,656	16,585,582	13,870,193	11,296,336	7,615,134	11,559,188	8,099,490
Total Assets	61,123,832	59,113,355	52,856,746	45,447,945	38,678,096	30,859,132	25,806,260	21,305,513
Total Deposits	31,835,765	31,836,081	30,616,216	27,094,745	24,343,595	18,714,753	15,407,040	12,913,213
Long-Term Obligations	12,190,451	12,145,628	9,538,173	6,867,033	5,735,635	5,708,880	5,939,025	5,478,917
Total Liabilities	49,679,124	48,000,315	43,755,427	37,649,227	32,050,818	26,659,689	23,415,225	19,335,463
Net Stockholders' Equity	11,444,708	11,113,040	9,101,319	7,798,718	6,627,278	4,199,443	2,391,035	1,970,050
Shares Outstanding	1,277,667	1,277,597	1,277,671	1,277,671	1,277,705	1,202,671	1,127,693	1,127,673
Statistical Record								
Return on Equity %	4.54	21.03	19.40	21.72	19.80	24.39	32.46	31.59
Return on Assets %	0.85	3.95	3.34	3.72	3.39	3.31	3.00	2.92
Equity/Assets %	18.72	18.79	17.21	17.15	17.13	13.60	9.26	9.24
Non-Int. Exp./Tot. Inc. %	48.45	43.85	45.07	44.10	46.35	47.56	46.33	49.14
Price Range	28.78-24.62	25.45-12.15	25.97-13.80	26.04-16.70	26.54-13.07	21.67-13.96	16.92-9.30	13.39-8.07
P/E Ratio	15.47-13.24	14.22-6.79	19.38-10.30	20.34-13.05	26.02-13.07	27.08-17.45	26.43-14.78	26.25-15.83
Average Yield %	1.33	1.59	1.20	1.02	0.99	1.03	1.04	1.18

Address: 1100 North King Street, Wilmington, DE 19884-0141	Officers: Randolph D. Lerner Esq. - Chmn., Richard K. Struthers - Vice-Chmn., Chief Loan Officer	Investor Contact:800-362-6255
Telephone: (302) 456-8588	Transfer Agents:National City Bank, Cleveland, OH	Institutional Holding No of Institutions: 37
Web Site: www.mbna.com		Shares: 55,454,894 % Held: -

MCCORMICK & CO., INC.

Exchange	Symbol	Price	52Wk Range	Yield	P/E
NYS	MKC	$35.45 (5/28/2004)	35.54-25.30	1.58	24.96

*7 Year Price Score 146.9 *NYSE Composite Index=100* ***12 Month Price Score 55.8**

Interim Earnings (Per Share)

Qtr.	Feb	May	Aug	Nov
2000-01	0.19	0.19	0.24	0.42
2001-02	0.24	0.24	0.25	0.53
2002-03	0.25	0.28	0.28	0.59
2003-04	0.27	...	...	...

Interim Dividends (Per Share)

Amt	Decl	Ex	Rec	Pay
0.12Q	6/24/2003	7/2/2003	7/7/2003	7/18/2003
0.12Q	9/23/2003	10/1/2003	10/3/2003	10/17/2003
0.14Q	11/25/2003	12/29/2003	12/31/2003	1/21/2004
0.14Q	3/24/2004	4/1/2004	4/5/2004	4/16/2004

Indicated Div: $0.56

Valuation Analysis

Forecast P/E N/A

Market Cap	$4.3 Billion	Book Value	838.3 Million
Price/Book	0.54	Price/Sales	0.20

Dividend Achiever Status

Rank	208	10 Year Growth Rate	7.65%
Total Years of Dividend Growth			17

Business Summary: Food (MIC: 4.1 SIC: 2099 NAIC:311942)

McCormick & Co. is engaged in the manufacture, marketing and distribution of spices, herbs, seasonings and other flavors to the entire food industry. Co. operates in two business segments: consumer and industrial. The consumer segment sells spices, herbs, extracts, seasoning blends, sauces, marinades and specialty foods to the consumer food market under a variety of brands, including *McCormick*, *Zatarain's* in the US, *Ducros* in continental Europe, *Club House* in Canada and *Schwartz* in the U.K. The industrial segment sells spices, blended seasonings, condiments, coatings and compound flavors to food processors, restaurants, distributors, warehouse clubs and institutional operations.

Recent Developments: For the three months ended Feb 29 2004, net income totaled $38.1 million, up 14.0% compared with income of $33.4 million, before a $1.7 million gain from discontinued operations, in the corresponding quarter a year earlier. Results included one-time pre-tax special charges of $69,000 and $120,000 in 2004 and 2003, respectively. Net sales climbed 17.9% to $572.4 million from $485.4 million the year before, driven primarily by the 2003 acquisition of Zatarain's and favorable foreign currency exchange rates. Gross profit was $221.7 million, or 38.7% of net sales, versus $186.1 million, or 38.3% of net sales, the prior year.

Prospects: Results are being positively affected by Co.'s aggressive acquisition activity in 2003, increased distribution in the U.S. and new product introductions. Looking ahead, Co. is boosting its projected full-year 2004 sales growth to a low double-digit percentage increase, while earnings are expected to range between $1.51 and $1.54 per share for the year.In addition, Co. anticipates cash from operations after net capital expenditures and dividends of more than $100.0 million in the current fiscal year. Results are expected to benefit from Co.'s efforts to reduce costs, improve efficiencies and launch new consumer and industrial products.

Financial Data

(US$ in Thousands)	3 Mos	11/30/2003	11/30/2002	11/30/2001	11/30/2000	11/30/1999	11/30/1998	11/30/1997
Earnings Per Share	1.42	1.40	1.26	1.04	0.99	0.71	0.70	0.64
Cash Flow Per Share	0.02	1.37	1.57	1.45	1.45	1.59	0.97	1.19
Tang. Book Val. Per Share	0.70	0.27	0.61	N.M	N.M	1.70	1.56	1.58
Dividends Per Share	0.490	0.460	0.420	0.400	0.380	0.340	0.320	0.300
Dividend Payout %	32.67	32.85	33.33	38.27	38.38	47.55	45.39	46.51
Income Statement								
Total Revenues	572,362	2,269,600	2,320,000	2,218,500	2,123,500	2,006,900	1,881,100	1,800,966
Total Indirect Exp.	160,233	597,600	570,900	546,100	578,700	522,300	463,800	461,022
Depreciation & Amort.	16,238	65,300	66,800	73,000	61,300	57,400	54,800	49,344
Operating Income	61,384	295,500	277,700	240,600	225,000	176,900	182,800	170,843
Net Interest Inc./(Exp.)	(9,572)	(38,600)	(43,600)	(52,300)	(39,700)	(32,400)	(36,900)	(36,332)
Income Taxes	16,056	83,400	74,300	62,900	66,600	60,100	54,900	52,653
Income from Cont Ops	...	199,200	...	...	...	...	...	97,415
Net Income	38,106	210,800	179,800	146,600	137,500	103,300	103,800	98,428
Average Shs. Outstg.	141,817	142,600	142,300	140,200	139,200	144,000	147,600	151,800
Balance Sheet								
Cash & Cash Equivalents	17,735	25,100	47,300	31,300	23,900	12,000	17,700	13,500
Total Current Assets	739,552	762,100	724,600	635,800	620,000	490,600	503,800	506,518
Total Assets	2,164,405	2,148,200	1,930,800	1,772,000	1,659,900	1,188,800	1,259,100	1,256,232
Total Current Liabilities	632,938	712,700	673,400	713,700	1,027,200	470,600	518,000	498,249
Long-Term Obligations	450,024	448,600	453,900	454,100	160,200	241,400	250,400	276,489
Net Stockholders' Equity	838,278	755,200	592,300	463,100	359,300	382,400	388,100	393,110
Net Working Capital	106,614	49,400	51,200	(77,900)	(407,200)	20,000	(14,200)	8,269
Shares Outstanding	137,507	137,200	140,000	138,400	136,600	140,800	145,000	148,048
Operating Profit Margin %	10.72	13.01	11.96	10.84	10.59	8.81	9.71	9.48
Return on Equity %	4.54	26.37	30.35	31.65	38.26	27.01	26.74	24.78
Return on Assets %	1.76	9.27	9.31	8.27	8.28	8.68	8.24	7.75
Debt/Total Assets %	20.79	20.88	23.50	25.62	9.65	20.30	19.88	22.00
Price Range	31.00-28.71	30.15-22.10	26.90-20.35	23.03-17.00	18.25-12.13	17.32-13.38	18.00-13.00	13.63-11.31
P/E Ratio	21.83-20.22	21.54-15.79	21.35-16.15	22.14-16.35	18.43-12.25	24.39-18.84	25.71-18.57	21.29-17.67
Average Yield %	1.64	1.79	1.78	1.95	2.49	2.16	2.05	2.43

Address: 18 Loveton Circle, Sparks, MD 21152 **Telephone:** (410) 771-7301 **Web Site:** www.mccormick.com	**Officers:** Robert J. Lawless – Chmn., Pres., C.E.O., Francis A. Contino – Exec. V.P., Supply Chain, C.F.O. **Transfer Agents:** Wells Fargo Bank Minnesota, N.A., St. Paul, MN	**Investor Contact:** 410-771-7244 **Institutional Holding** **No of Institutions:** 7 **Shares:** 7,016 **% Held:** –

MCDONALD'S CORP

Exchange	Symbol	Price	52Wk Range	Yield	P/E
NYS	MCD	$26.40 (5/28/2004)	29.85-18.90	1.52	20.47

*7 Year Price Score 84.3 ***NYSE Composite Index=100** ***12 Month Price Score 50.2**

Interim Earnings (Per Share)

Qtr.	Mar	Jun	Sep	Dec
2001	0.29	0.34	0.42	0.20
2002	0.27	0.39	0.38	(0.27)
2003	0.29	0.37	0.43	0.09
2004	0.40	...	...	...

Interim Dividends (Per Share)

Amt	Decl	Ex	Rec	Pay
0.215A	9/12/2000	11/13/2000	11/15/2000	12/1/2000
0.225A	10/29/2001	11/13/2001	11/15/2001	12/3/2001
0.235A	10/22/2002	11/13/2002	11/15/2002	12/2/2002
0.40A	9/24/2003	11/12/2003	11/14/2003	12/1/2003

Indicated Div: $0.40 (Div. Reinv. Plan)

Valuation Analysis

Forecast P/E 15.33 (5/24/2004)

Market Cap	$33.5 Billion	Book Value	N/A
Price/Book	N/A	Price/Sales	N/A

Dividend Achiever Status

Rank	89	10 Year Growth Rate	14.24%
Total Years of Dividend Growth		27	

Business Summary: Hospitality & Tourism (MIC: 5.1 SIC: 5812 NAIC:722211)

McDonald's develops, licenses, leases and services a worldwide system of restaurants in more than 100 countries. Co.'s menu includes hamburgers, cheeseburgers, the Big Mac, Quarter Pounder with Cheese, Big N'Tasty, Filet–O–Fish, Chicken McNuggets, several chicken sandwiches, french fries, salads, milk shakes, McFlurry desserts, ice cream sundaes and cones, pies, cookies and beverages. As of Dec 31 2003, there were approximately 18,000 units operated by franchisees, more than 8,000 units operated by Co., and about 4,000 units operated by affiliates. The Company also operates Boston Market and Chipotle Mexican Grill in the U.S. and has a minority ownership interest in U.K.–based Pret A Manger.

Recent Developments: For the quarter ended Mar 31 2004, Co. reported net income of $511.5 million compared with income of $364.2 million in the corresponding period the year before. Results for 2003 excluded accounting change charges of $36.8 million. Systemwide sales improved 17.0%. Total revenues increased 15.8% to $4.40 billion from $3.80 billion a year earlier, primarily reflecting healthy sales in the United States. Sales by Company–operated restaurants climbed 14.9% to $3.28 billion, while revenues from franchised and affiliated restaurants rose 18.3% to $1.12 billion. Operating income advanced 27.2% to $858.4 million from $674.6 million the prior year.

Prospects: Co. continues to perform well, fueled by the overall performance of its U.S. business, improved comparable sales across all geographic segments, and increased margins. Moreover, Europe's sales trends are improving significantly, as a result of the successful launch of the Salads Plus menu in several key markets. Meanwhile, as of Mar 31 2004, Co. served 2.3 million more customers compared with Mar 31 2003. Looking ahead to 2005 and beyond, Co. anticipates annual Systemwide sales and revenue growth of 3.0% to 5.0% and annual operating income growth of 6.0% to 7.0%.

Financial Data

(US$ in Thousands)	3 Mos	12/31/2003	12/31/2002	12/31/2001	12/31/2000	12/31/1999	12/31/1998	12/31/1997
Earnings Per Share	1.29	1.18	0.77	1.25	1.46	1.39	1.10	1.14
Cash Flow Per Share	0.67	2.56	2.25	2.05	2.02	2.14	1.96	1.73
Tang. Book Val. Per Share	8.48	8.17	6.87	6.30	5.94	6.20	6.26	4.83
Dividends Per Share	0.400	0.400	0.230	0.220	0.210	0.190	0.170	0.160
Dividend Payout %	30.77	33.89	30.51	18.00	14.72	14.02	16.02	14.08
Income Statement								
Total Revenues	4,399,700	17,140,500	15,405,700	14,870,000	14,243,000	13,259,300	12,421,400	11,408,800
Total Indirect Exp.	687,100	9,902,100	9,237,700	8,093,100	7,160,600	6,611,200	6,441,900	5,714,400
Depreciation & Amort.	297,200	1,148,200	1,050,800	1,086,300	1,010,700	956,300	881,100	793,800
Operating Income	858,400	2,832,200	2,112,900	2,697,000	3,329,300	3,319,500	2,761,900	2,808,300
Net Interest Inc./(Exp.)	(91,700)	(388,000)	(374,100)	(452,400)	(429,900)	(396,300)	(413,800)	(364,400)
Income Taxes	246,300	838,200	670,000	693,100	905,000	936,200	757,300	764,800
Income from Cont Ops	...	1,508,200	992,100	...	1,976,900	1,947,800	...	...
Net Income	511,500	1,471,400	893,500	1,636,600	1,977,300	1,947,900	1,550,100	1,642,500
Average Shs. Outstg.	1,275,500	1,276,500	1,281,500	1,309,300	1,356,500	1,404,200	1,405,700	1,410,200
Balance Sheet								
Cash & Cash Equivalents	969,600	492,800	330,400	418,100	421,700	419,500	299,200	341,400
Total Current Assets	2,315,300	1,885,400	1,715,400	1,819,300	1,662,400	1,572,300	1,309,400	1,142,300
Total Assets	25,817,900	25,525,100	23,970,500	22,534,500	21,683,500	20,983,200	19,784,400	18,241,500
Total Current Liabilities	2,627,300	2,485,800	2,422,300	2,248,300	2,360,900	3,274,300	2,497,100	2,984,500
Long–Term Obligations	9,114,200	9,342,500	9,703,600	8,555,500	7,843,900	5,632,400	6,188,600	4,834,100
Net Stockholders' Equity	12,368,400	11,981,900	10,280,900	9,488,400	9,204,400	9,639,100	9,464,700	8,851,600
Net Working Capital	(312,000)	(600,400)	(706,900)	(429,000)	(698,500)	(1,702,000)	(1,187,700)	(1,842,200)
Shares Outstanding	1,259,400	1,261,900	1,268,200	1,280,700	1,304,900	1,350,800	1,356,200	1,660,600
Statistical Record								
Operating Profit Margin %	20.11	17.05	14.60	18.66	24.75	25.97	22.71	25.61
Return on Equity %	4.35	13.35	10.98	18.06	23.60	21.49	17.01	19.83
Return on Assets %	2.08	6.26	4.71	7.60	10.02	9.87	8.13	9.62
Debt/Total Assets %	35.30	36.60	40.48	37.96	36.17	26.84	31.28	26.50
Price Range	29.85–24.64	26.56–12.38	30.65–15.48	34.69–25.00	42.81–26.81	48.38–37.66	39.16–22.69	27.34–21.63
P/E Ratio	23.14–19.10	22.51–10.49	39.81–20.10	27.75–20.00	29.32–18.36	34.80–27.09	35.60–20.63	23.99–18.97
Average Yield %	1.48	1.98	0.95	0.77	0.63	0.45	0.55	0.67

Address: McDonald's Plaza, Oak Brook, IL 60523	**Officers:** Andrew J. McKenna – Chmn., James A. Skinner – Vice-Chmn.	**Investor Contact:**630–623–7428
Telephone: (630) 623-3000	**Transfer Agents:**First Chicago Trust Company, Jersey City, NJ	**Institutional Holding** **No of Institutions:** 36
Web Site: www.mcdonalds.com		**Shares:** 1,068,717 **% Held:** –

MCGRATH RENTCORP

Exchange	Symbol	Price	52Wk Range	Yield	P/E
NMS	MGRC	$31.15 (5/28/2004)	33.18-25.88	2.83	16.22

*7 Year Price Score 126.6   *NYSE Composite Index=100   *12 Month Price Score 50.9

Interim Earnings (Per Share)

Qtr.	Mar	Jun	Sep	Dec
2001	0.54	0.62	0.58	0.40
2002	(0.19)	(0.10)	0.68	0.61
2003	0.40	0.39	0.50	0.56
2004	0.47	...	...	...

Interim Dividends (Per Share)

Amt	Decl	Ex	Rec	Pay
0.20Q	8/28/2003	10/10/2003	10/15/2003	10/31/2003
0.20Q	11/21/2003	1/13/2004	1/15/2004	1/30/2004
0.22Q	3/9/2004	4/13/2004	4/15/2004	4/30/2004
0.22Q	6/2/2004	7/13/2004	7/15/2004	7/30/2004

Indicated Div: $0.88

Valuation Analysis

Forecast P/E N/A
Market Cap	$388.9 Million	Book Value	147.4 Million
Price/Book	2.51	Price/Sales	2.77

Dividend Achiever Status

Rank	78	10 Year Growth Rate	14.87%
Total Years of Dividend Growth		13	

TRADING VOLUME (thousand shares)

Business Summary: General Construction Supplies &Services (MIC: 3.3 SIC: 7359 NAIC:532490)

McGrath RentCorp is comprised of three business segments: Mobile Modular Management Corporation (MMMC), its modular building rental division; RenTelco, its electronic test equipment rental division; and Enviroplex, its 81.0%–owned portable classroom manufacturing business. MMMC rents and sells modular buildings and accessories to fulfill customers' temporary and permanent space needs in California and Texas. RenTelco rents and sells electronic test equipment nationally from its two locations in Plano, TX and Livermore, CA. Enviroplex sells its portable classrooms directly to the California public school districts.

Recent Developments: For the three months ended Mar 31 2004, net income rose 17.4% to $5.7 million compared with $4.9 million in the equivalent period of 2003. Total revenues increased 8.8% to $29.9 million from $27.5 million a year earlier. Mobile Modular revenues increased 11.0% due to continued strength in the educational market. Enviroplex revenues increased 56.3% to $1.3 million, with quarter ending backlog decreasing 45.1% to $6.7 million due to several large projects booked in the prior-year quarter. RenTelco's rental revenues increased 18.0% to $3.2 million. Income from operations was $10.1 million, up 15.4% from $8.7 million in the prior-year period.

Prospects: On May 3 2004, Co. agreed to acquire substantially all of the assets of Technology Rentals & Services (TRS), a rental provider of general purpose and communications test equipment in North America, for approximately $116.0 million in cash. Co. plans to finance the acquisition from a revolving line of credit facility with its banks and a fixed–rate senior note. The acquisition is strategically in line with Co.'s plans to expand RenTelco, its core test equipment rental business. Separately, Co. expects 2004 full–year earnings per share to be in a range of $2.00 to $2.10, excluding any potential accretive impact in 2004 of the TRS acquisition.

Financial Data

(US$ in Thousands)	3 Mos	12/31/2003	12/31/2002	12/31/2001	12/31/2000	12/31/1999	12/31/1998	12/31/1997
Earnings Per Share	1.92	1.85	1.00	2.14	2.19	1.78	1.67	1.58
Cash Flow Per Share	0.63	3.91	4.14	4.71	4.02	3.97	3.88	3.89
Tang. Book Val. Per Share	12.14	11.87	11.13	10.66	8.98	7.60	7.54	6.79
Dividends Per Share	0.800	0.780	0.680	0.620	0.540	0.460	0.380	0.310
Dividend Payout %	41.45	42.16	68.00	28.97	24.65	25.84	22.75	19.62
Income Statement								
Total Revenues	29,879	130,971	145,086	159,394	164,158	129,962	135,428	134,976
Total Indirect Exp.	9,318	35,371	37,891	52,225	43,832	36,883	33,082	30,315
Depreciation & Amort.	3,261	12,745	15,792	27,270	23,850	19,780	16,862	14,358
Operating Income	10,091	40,708	25,235	52,045	56,516	45,564	47,236	45,450
Net Interest Inc./(Exp.)	(540)	(2,668)	(3,982)	(7,078)	(8,840)	(6,606)	(6,326)	(4,070)
Income Taxes	3,811	15,178	8,459	17,807	19,762	14,874	16,010	16,323
Eqty Earns/Minority Int.	(2)	(170)	(161)	(482)	(670)	(251)	(1,005)	(1,011)
Income from Cont Ops	...	...	...	...	...	23,833		
Net Income	5,738	22,692	12,633	26,678	27,244	22,466	23,895	24,045
Average Shs. Outstg.	12,303	12,259	12,619	12,495	12,428	13,383	14,349	15,181
Balance Sheet								
Cash & Cash Equivalents	4	4	4	4	643	490	857	538
Total Current Assets	29,309	32,203	33,253	36,900	46,330	25,585	22,668	22,332
Total Assets	322,641	323,858	313,134	354,884	357,246	297,722	278,676	252,392
Total Current Liabilities	74,879	28,695	29,889	30,745	37,012	24,811	22,964	27,047
Long–Term Obligations	...	47,266	55,523	...	...	...	...	...
Net Stockholders' Equity	147,391	143,978	139,019	131,595	108,958	95,403	105,394	98,646
Net Working Capital	(45,570)	3,508	3,364	6,155	9,318	774	(296)	(4,715)
Shares Outstanding	12,140	12,122	12,490	12,335	12,125	12,546	13,970	14,521
Operating Profit Margin %	33.77	31.08	17.39	32.65	34.42	35.05	34.87	33.67
Return on Equity %	3.89	15.76	9.08	20.27	25.00	24.98	22.67	24.37
Return on Assets %	1.78	7.00	4.03	7.51	7.62	8.00	8.57	9.52
Debt/Total Assets %	...	14.59	17.73	...	...	...	...	...
Price Range	30.90–27.25	29.76–21.81	37.64–18.80	37.53–18.13	19.88–14.00	22.50–16.13	24.50–16.75	27.25–12.38
P/E Ratio	16.06–14.19	16.09–11.79	37.64–18.80	17.54–8.47	9.08–6.39	12.64–9.06	14.67–10.03	17.25–7.83
Average Yield %	2.71	3.01	2.65	2.60	3.24	2.47	1.86	1.63

Address: 5700 Las Positas Road, Livermore, CA 94550 **Telephone:** (925) 606–9200 **Web Site:** www.mgrc.com	**Officers:** Robert P. McGrath – Chmn., Dennis C. Kakures – Pres., C.E.O. **Transfer Agents:**U.S. Stock Transfer, Glendale, CA	**Investor Contact:**925–606–9200 **Institutional Holding** **No of Institutions:** 10 **Shares:** 10,108,508 **% Held:** –

MCGRAW-HILL COS., INC. (THE)

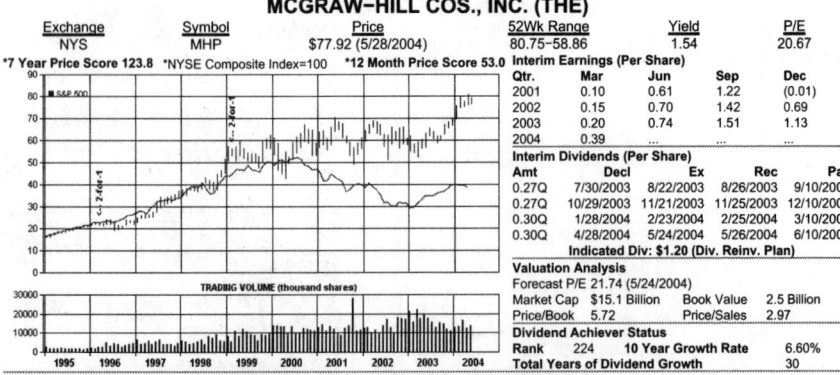

Exchange	Symbol	Price	52Wk Range	Yield	P/E
NYS	MHP	$77.92 (5/28/2004)	80.75-58.86	1.54	20.67

*7 Year Price Score 123.8 ***NYSE Composite Index=100** ***12 Month Price Score 53.0**

Interim Earnings (Per Share)

Qtr.	Mar	Jun	Sep	Dec
2001	0.10	0.61	1.22	(0.01)
2002	0.15	0.70	1.42	0.69
2003	0.20	0.74	1.51	1.13
2004	0.39	...	...	...

Interim Dividends (Per Share)

Amt	Decl	Ex	Rec	Pay
0.27Q	7/30/2003	8/22/2003	8/26/2003	9/10/2003
0.27Q	10/29/2003	11/21/2003	11/25/2003	12/10/2003
0.30Q	1/28/2004	2/23/2004	2/25/2004	3/10/2004
0.30Q	4/28/2004	5/24/2004	5/26/2004	6/10/2004

Indicated Div: $1.20 (Div. Reinv. Plan)

Valuation Analysis

Forecast P/E 21.74 (5/24/2004)

Market Cap	$15.1 Billion	Book Value	2.5 Billion
Price/Book	5.72	Price/Sales	2.97

Dividend Achiever Status

Rank	224	10 Year Growth Rate	6.60%
Total Years of Dividend Growth			30

Business Summary: Non-Media Publishing (MIC: 13.3 SIC: 2731 NAIC:511130)

McGraw-Hill, a multimedia publishing and information services company, serves worldwide markets in education, finance and business information. As of Dec 31 2003, Co. operated more than 322 offices in 33 countries. Co. provides information in print through books, newsletters, and magazines, including Business Week; on-line over electronic networks; over the air by television, satellite and FM sideband; and on software, videotape, facsimile and compact disks. Among Co.'s business units are Standard & Poor's Financial Information Services and Standard & Poor's Ratings Services divisions.

Recent Developments: For the quarter ended Mar 31 2004, Co. reported income from continuing operations of $76.3 million versus income of $39.9 million the year before. Earnings excluded a loss of $587,000 in 2004 and a gain of $55.5 million in 2003 from discontinued operations. Operating revenue rose 9.7% to $911.6 million from $830.8 million a year earlier. Revenue for 2004 included a gain of $6.1 million from favorable foreign exchange rates. On a segment basis, revenue from McGraw-Hill Education climbed 6.4% to $278.2 million, while revenue from Financial Services grew 15.6% to $456.6 million. Revenue from Information and Media Services improved 1.3% to $176.7 million.

Prospects: Co. continues to benefit from the increased emphasis on testing as states prepare to meet mandatory federal requirements to test annually every child in grades 3 through 8 in reading and math beginning in the 2005-2006 school year. Additionally, school products are contributing to improved international sales in Latin America, the U.K. and Canada. Meanwhile, Co.'s corporate and structured financing activity is improving, particularly in the residential mortgage-backed securities market. Looking ahead, Co. expects income from continuing operations to increase in the mid-to-high single digits in 2004, excluding an after-tax benefit from the sale of the equity interest in Rock-McGraw.

Financial Data

(US$ in Thousands)	3 Mos	12/31/2003	12/31/2002	12/31/2001	12/31/2000	12/31/1999	12/31/1998	12/31/1997
Earnings Per Share	3.77	3.58	2.96	1.92	2.41	2.14	1.71	1.45
Cash Flow Per Share	(0.79)	7.19	5.87	5.46	3.59	3.56	3.79	1.87
Tang. Book Val. Per Share	2.20	4.48	1.87	0.18	0.32	2.24	1.48	0.63
Dividends Per Share	1.110	1.080	1.020	0.980	0.940	0.860	0.780	0.720
Dividend Payout %	31.99	30.16	34.45	51.04	39.00	40.18	45.76	49.48
Income Statement								
Total Revenues	911,575	4,827,857	4,787,668	4,645,535	4,280,968	3,991,997	3,729,145	3,534,095
Total Indirect Exp.	442,459	1,512,493	1,781,775	1,850,753	1,643,541	1,449,936	1,402,368	1,332,087
Depreciation & Amort.	29,061	115,800	128,378	420,598	362,325	308,355	299,240	293,518
Operating Income	91,048	1,137,374	927,582	670,128	820,183	739,987	608,383	523,808
Net Interest Inc./(Exp.)	(1,737)	(7,097)	(22,517)	(55,070)	(52,841)	(42,013)	(47,961)	(52,542)
Income Taxes	13,045	442,500	328,300	238,100	295,400	272,200	218,600	180,600
Income from Cont Ops	76,266	687,777	576,765	376,958	471,942	425,774	341,822	290,666
Net Income	75,679	687,650	576,760	377,031	403,794	425,764	333,141	290,675
Average Shs. Outstg.	193,490	192,005	194,573	195,873	196,072	198,557	199,104	199,504
Balance Sheet								
Cash & Cash Equivalents	403,949	695,591	58,186	53,535	3,171	6,489	10,451	4,768
Total Current Assets	1,808,687	2,256,152	1,674,307	1,812,947	1,801,690	1,553,725	1,428,761	1,464,421
Total Assets	4,901,964	5,394,046	5,032,182	5,161,191	4,931,444	4,088,797	3,788,144	3,724,474
Total Current Liabilities	1,551,065	1,993,734	1,775,291	1,876,393	1,780,785	1,525,453	1,291,451	1,206,242
Long-Term Obligations	385	389	458,900	833,660	817,500	354,800	452,100	607,030
Net Stockholders' Equity	2,542,575	2,557,051	2,165,822	1,853,885	1,761,044	1,691,493	1,551,808	1,434,651
Net Working Capital	257,622	262,418	(100,984)	(63,446)	20,905	28,272	137,310	258,179
Shares Outstanding	190,500	190,396	191,832	193,218	194,285	195,708	197,111	198,204
Statistical Record								
Operating Profit Margin %	9.98	27.11	19.77	15.42	20.43	20.13	17.83	15.92
Return on Equity %	2.99	33.60	27.52	22.82	29.89	28.95	25.68	22.96
Return on Assets %	1.55	15.93	11.84	8.19	10.67	11.97	10.52	8.84
Debt/Total Assets %	0.01	0.01	9.11	16.15	16.57	8.67	11.93	16.29
Price Range	80.12-69.50	69.92-52.50	68.89-51.15	70.45-49.30	67.13-42.75	62.25-47.63	51.53-34.72	37.31-22.69
P/E Ratio	21.25-18.44	19.53-14.66	23.27-17.28	36.69-25.68	27.85-17.74	29.09-22.25	30.14-20.30	25.73-15.65
Average Yield %	1.48	1.76	1.63	1.62	1.69	1.58	1.93	2.42

Address: 1221 Avenue Of The Americas, New York, NY 10020	**Officers:** Harold McGraw III – Chmn., Pres., C.E.O., Robert J. Bahash – Exec. V.P., C.F.O.	**Investor Contact:**212-512-4321 **Institutional Holding**
Telephone: (212) 512-2000	**Transfer Agents:**Mellon Investor Services, South Hackensack, NJ	**No of Institutions:** 3
Web Site: www.mcgraw-hill.com		**Shares:** 399,735 **% Held:** –

MDU RESOURCES GROUP INC.

Exchange	Symbol	Price	52Wk Range	Yield	P/E
NYS	MDU	$23.45 (5/28/2004)	24.26-20.53	2.90	14.84

*7 Year Price Score 129.1   *NYSE Composite Index=100   ***12 Month Price Score 46.8**

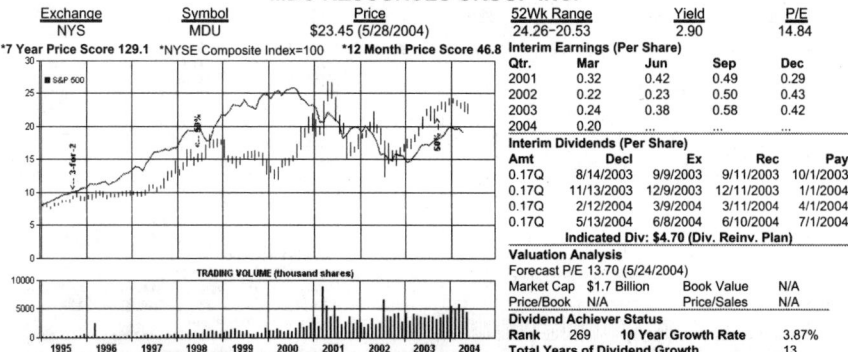

Interim Earnings (Per Share)

Qtr.	Mar	Jun	Sep	Dec
2001	0.32	0.42	0.49	0.29
2002	0.22	0.23	0.50	0.43
2003	0.24	0.38	0.58	0.42
2004	0.20			

Interim Dividends (Per Share)

Amt	Decl	Ex	Rec	Pay
0.17Q	8/14/2003	9/9/2003	9/11/2003	10/1/2003
0.17Q	11/13/2003	12/9/2003	12/11/2003	1/1/2004
0.17Q	2/12/2004	3/9/2004	3/11/2004	4/1/2004
0.17Q	5/13/2004	6/8/2004	6/10/2004	7/1/2004

Indicated Div: $4.70 (Div. Reinv. Plan)

Valuation Analysis

Forecast P/E 13.70 (5/24/2004)

Market Cap	$1.7 Billion	Book Value	N/A
Price/Book	N/A	Price/Sales	N/A

Dividend Achiever Status

Rank	269	10 Year Growth Rate	3.87%
Total Years of Dividend Growth			13

Business Summary: Construction – Public Infrastructure (MIC: 3.1 SIC: 1611 NAIC:237310)

MDU Resources Group is a diversified natural resource company operating through six reportable segments. Co.'s electric and natural gas distribution segments include the operations of Montana– Dakota and Great Plains Natural Gas Co. The utility services segment includes all the operations of Utility Services, Inc. The pipeline and energy services segment includes WBI Holdings' natural gas transportation, underground storage, gathering services, and energy–related management services. The natural gas and oil production segment includes the operations of WBI Holdings. The construction materials and mining segment includes the results of Knife River's operations.

Recent Developments: For the quarter ended Mar 31 2004, net income was $23.6 million compared with income of $27.7 million, before an accounting change charge of $7.6 million, in the prior–year quarter. Operating revenues increased 10.2% to $515.5 million. Notably, electric earnings fell 29.2% to $3.4 million, while natural gas distribution earnings dropped 45.2% to $2.3 million. Pipeline and energy earnings decreased 37.2% to $2.7 million. Natural gas and oil production earnings jumped 116.2% to $25.3 million. Construction materials and mining loss widened to $11.9 million from $7.4 million in 2002. Independent power production and other earnings surged 191.7% to $3.5 million.

Prospects: Co. is encouraged by the increase in earnings contributions from its natural gas and oil production and independent power production businesses. Although Co. experienced seasonal losses at its construction materials and mining segment, Co. is optimistic that this business will perform well in 2004 given its extensive backlog and the recent acquisition activity. Going forward, based on the continued strength of natural gas and oil prices as well as general optimism throughout its organization, Co. is increasing its earnings per share guidance. For the full year of 2004, earnings per share are now expected to be in the range of $1.60 to $1.75.

Financial Data
(US$ in Thousands)

	3 Mos	12/31/2003	12/31/2002	12/31/2001	12/31/2000	12/31/1999	12/31/1998	12/31/1997
Earnings Per Share	1.58	1.62	1.38	1.52	1.20	1.01	0.44	0.82
Cash Flow Per Share	0.89	3.72	3.05	3.42	2.24	1.88	1.81	2.12
Tang. Book Val. Per Share	9.56	9.19	8.25	10.60	9.03	7.82	6.92	5.89
Dividends Per Share	0.660	0.650	0.610	0.590	0.560	0.530	0.510	0.490
Dividend Payout %	42.13	40.12	44.92	38.86	47.22	53.29	117.42	60.21
Income Statement								
Total Revenues	515,459	2,352,189	2,031,537	2,223,632	1,873,671	1,279,809	896,627	607,674
Total Indirect Exp.	71,396	268,587	223,854	195,344	146,765	110,937	171,221	89,533
Depreciation & Amort.	49,511	188,337	157,961	139,917	110,888	81,818	77,786	65,767
Operating Income	44,023	312,072	266,117	273,268	216,987	159,751	70,943	111,561
Net Interest Inc./(Exp.)	(13,846)	(52,794)	(45,015)	(45,899)	(48,033)	(36,006)	(30,273)	(30,209)
Income Taxes	11,390	98,572	86,230	98,341	69,650	49,310	17,485	30,743
Eqty Earns/Minority Int.	...	5,968	...	...	...	...	...	...
Income from Cont Ops	...	182,913	...	...	...	...	...	...
Net Income	23,580	175,324	148,444	155,849	111,028	84,080	34,107	54,617
Average Shs. Outstg.	115,709	112,460	106,863	101,803	92,085	82,305	76,255	65,217
Balance Sheet								
Cash & Cash Equivalents	113,183	86,341	67,556	41,811	36,512	77,504	39,216	28,174
Total Current Assets	626,020	613,540	537,548	481,492	480,286	351,696	240,649	179,916
Total Assets	3,455,459	3,380,592	2,937,249	2,623,071	2,312,959	1,766,303	1,452,775	1,113,892
Total Current Liabilities	358,328	314,061	299,645	245,327	284,473	187,327	169,469	149,014
Long–Term Obligations	878,541	939,450	819,558	783,709	728,166	563,545	413,264	298,561
Net Stockholders' Equity	1,524,704	1,450,636	1,298,645	1,124,671	895,960	684,433	565,742	401,196
Net Working Capital	267,692	299,479	237,903	236,165	195,813	164,369	71,180	30,902
Shares Outstanding	116,760	113,357	111,063	104,665	97,542	85,557	79,549	65,572
Statistical Record								
Operating Profit Margin %	8.54	13.26	13.09	12.28	11.58	12.48	7.91	18.35
Return on Equity %	1.54	12.60	11.43	13.85	12.39	12.28	6.02	13.61
Return on Assets %	0.68	5.41	5.05	5.94	4.80	4.76	2.34	4.90
Debt/Total Assets %	25.42	27.78	27.90	29.87	31.48	31.90	28.44	26.80
Price Range	15.35-14.45	24.25-16.69	22.23-12.47	26.82-15.20	22.00-12.00	17.96-12.83	18.83-12.67	14.86-9.44
P/E Ratio	121.3-114.2	14.97-10.30	16.11-9.03	17.64-10.00	18.33-10.00	17.78-12.71	42.80-28.79	18.12-11.52
Average Yield %	2.80	3.10	3.45	2.92	3.52	3.46	3.20	4.43

Address: Schuchart Building, Bismarck, ND 58506–5650	**Officers:** Martin A. White – Chmn., Pres., C.E.O., Warren L. Robinson – Exec. V.P., Treas., C.F.O.	**Investor Contact:**7–8000 x7621
Telephone: (701) 222–7900	**Transfer Agents:**Wells Fargo Bank Minnesota,	**Institutional Holding** **No of Institutions:** 6
Web Site: www.mdu.com	N.A.Shareowner Services, St. Paul, MN	**Shares:** 9,708 **% Held:** –

MEDTRONIC, INC.

Exchange	Symbol	Price	52Wk Range	Yield	P/E
NYS	MDT	$47.90 (5/28/2004)	52.65-43.36	0.61	31.31

*7 Year Price Score 116.1 ***NYSE Composite Index=100** ***12 Month Price Score 47.5**

Interim Earnings (Per Share)

Qtr.	Jul	Oct	Jan	Apr
2000-01	0.24	0.26	0.25	0.10
2001-02	0.25	0.05	0.26	0.24
2002-03	0.31	0.25	0.35	0.39
2003-04	0.37	0.39	0.38	...

Interim Dividends (Per Share)

Amt	Decl	Ex	Rec	Pay
0.073Q	6/26/2003	7/1/2003	7/3/2003	7/25/2003
0.073Q	8/28/2003	10/1/2003	10/3/2003	10/24/2003
0.073Q	10/23/2003	12/30/2003	1/2/2004	1/23/2004
0.073Q	2/27/2004	3/31/2004	4/2/2004	4/30/2004

Indicated Div: $0.29 (Div. Reinv. Plan)

Valuation Analysis

Forecast P/E 24.55 (5/24/2004)

Market Cap	$58.2 Billion	Book Value	8.7 Billion
Price/Book	6.82	Price/Sales	6.92

Dividend Achiever Status

Rank	27	10 Year Growth Rate	21.43%
Total Years of Dividend Growth			26

TRADING VOLUME (thousand shares)

Business Summary: Medical Instruments &Equipment (MIC: 9.6 SIC: 3845 NAIC:334510)

Medtronic operates in five business segments that manufacture and sell device-based medical therapies. Cardiac Rhythm Management offers physicians and their patients a variety of products to treat heart rhythm disorders. Cardiac Surgery offers a broad range of products for use by cardiac surgeons in the operating room. The Vascular segment offers minimally invasive products for the treatment of coronary vascular disease. The Neurological and Diabetes segment offers products for the treatment of neurological disorders. The Spinal and Ear, Nose & Throat segment offers a range of products and therapies to treat a variety of disorders of the cranium, spine, ear, nose and throat.

Recent Developments: For the three months ended Jan 23 2004, net earnings climbed 8.6% to $464.4 million compared with $427.7 million in the corresponding quarter of the previous year. Results for 2003 included a pre-tax purchased in-process research and development charge of $22.0 million. Net sales advanced 14.8% to $2.19 billion from $1.91 billion in 2003. Revenues for the Cardiac Rhythm Management segment increased 11.0% to $1.00 billion, while revenues for the Spinal and Ear, Nose & Throat segment improved 26.0% to $433.9 million. Neurological and Diabetes segment revenues jumped 15.0% to $395.3 million, while revenues for the Vascular segment rose 16.0% to $211.7 million.

Prospects: Results continue to benefit from strong sales growth in Co.'s spinal, implantable defibrillators, diabetes and vascular product lines. Conversely, revenue growth for pacemakers, external defibrillators and several neurological devices are not meeting expectations. Nevertheless, Co. remains well-positioned in a number of attractive, under-penetrated markets. In order to expand patient access and to further improve market share, Co. will continue to invest in research and development, clinical trials, technical support and other market development activities.

Financial Data

(US$ in Thousands)	9 Mos	6 Mos	3 Mos	04/25/2003	04/26/2002	04/27/2001	04/30/2000	04/30/1999
Earnings Per Share	1.53	1.50	1.36	1.30	0.80	0.85	0.90	0.39
Cash Flow Per Share	1.52	0.89	0.47	1.69	1.29	1.49	0 85	0.38
Tang. Book Val. Per Share	2.81	2.50	2.43	2.20	1.09	3.53	2.61	1.98
Dividends Per Share	0.270	0.260	0.250	0.240	0.220	0.195	0.190	0.120
Dividend Payout %	17.65	17.33	18.38	18.84	27.81	22.38	21.38	31.64
Income Statement								
Total Revenues	6,421,800	4,228,000	2,064,200	7,665,200	6,410,800	5,551,800	5,014,600	4,134,100
Total Indirect Exp.	2,627,800	1,719,400	841,800	3,238,000	3,192,900	2,601,600	2,081,400	2,231,500
Depreciation & Amort.	332,600	216,800	99,700	408,100	329,800	297,300	243,300	213,100
Operating Income	2,210,400	1,463,400	708,400	2,536,900	1,565,200	1,539,600	1,613,600	799,800
Net Interest Inc./(Exp.)	1,100	(2,500)	(1,400)	(7,200)	(6,600)	74,200	15,400	22,200
Income Taxes	592,300	398,400	193,000	741,500	540,200	503,400	530,500	353,600
Net Income	1,390,400	926,500	450,400	1,599,800	984,000	1,046,000	1,098,500	468,400
Average Shs. Outstg.	1,226,400	1,228,700	1,229,900	1,227,900	1,224,400	1,226,000	1,220,800	1,185,800
Balance Sheet								
Cash & Cash Equivalents	1,443,900	1,190,300	1,173,200	1,470,100	410,700	1,030,300	448,400	222,100
Total Current Assets	4,636,200	4,393,000	4,367,600	4,605,500	3,488,000	3,756,800	3,013,400	2,395,200
Total Assets	13,437,700	12,901,100	12,626,900	12,320,800	10,904,500	7,038,900	5,669,400	4,870,300
Total Current Liabilities	4,074,400	3,947,000	1,813,200	1,813,300	3,984,900	1,359,300	991,500	990,300
Long-Term Obligations	2,100	2,100	1,979,600	1,980,300	9,500	13,300	14,100	17,600
Net Stockholders' Equity	8,687,500	8,301,900	8,176,700	7,906,400	6,431,100	5,509,500	4,491,500	3,654,600
Net Working Capital	561,800	446,000	2,554,400	2,792,200	(496,900)	2,397,500	2,021,900	1,404,900
Shares Outstanding	1,212,202	1,212,066	1,216,705	1,218,128	1,215,208	1,209,514	1,197,698	1,170,452
Statistical Record								
Operating Profit Margin %	34.42	34.61	34.31	33.09	24.41	27.73	32.17	19.34
Return on Equity %	16.00	11.16	5.50	20.23	15.30	18.98	24.45	12.81
Return on Assets %	10.34	7.18	3.56	12.98	9.02	14.86	19.37	9.61
Debt/Total Assets %	0.01	0.01	15.67	16.07	0.08	0.18	0.24	0.36
Price Range	52.65-43.36	52.65-44.27	50.64-46.45	48.95-33.74	51.24-38.99	61.00-40.71	57.19-31.19	44.06-24.44
P/E Ratio	34.41-28.34	35.10-29.51	37.24-34.15	37.65-25.95	64.05-48.74	71.76-47.89	63.54-34.65	113.0-62.66
Average Yield %	0.56	0.53	0.51	0.54	0.48	0.37	0.47	0.37

Address: 710 Medtronic Parkway, Minneapolis, MN 55432
Telephone: (763) 514-4000
Web Site: www.medtronic.com

Officers: Arthur D. Collins - Chmn., C.E.O., Robert L. Ryan - Sr. V.P., C.F.O.
Transfer Agents: Wells Fargo Bank Minnesota N.A., St. Paul, MN

Investor Contact: 612-514-3035
Institutional Holding
No of Institutions: 10
Shares: 2,060,498 **% Held:** -

MERCANTILE BANKSHARES CORP.

Exchange	Symbol	Price	52Wk Range	Yield	P/E
NMS	MRBK	$46.69 (5/28/2004)	46.73–39.05	2.83	17.55

*7 Year Price Score 113.7   *NYSE Composite Index=100   ***12 Month Price Score 49.2**

Interim Earnings (Per Share)

Qtr.	Mar	Jun	Sep	Dec
2001	0.65	0.62	0.65	0.63
2002	0.66	0.67	0.69	0.70
2003	0.71	0.72	0.63	0.62
2004	0.69	...	...	...

Interim Dividends (Per Share)

Amt	Decl	Ex	Rec	Pay
0.30Q	3/11/2003	3/20/2003	3/24/2003	3/31/2003
0.33Q	6/10/2003	6/19/2003	6/23/2003	6/30/2003
0.33Q	9/9/2003	9/19/2003	9/23/2003	9/30/2003
0.33Q	3/9/2004	3/22/2004	3/24/2004	3/31/2004

Indicated Div: $1.32 (Div. Reinv. Plan)

Valuation Analysis

Forecast P/E N/A

Market Cap $3.2 Billion	Book Value 1.9 Billion
Price/Book 1.81	Price/Sales 4.24

Dividend Achiever Status

Rank 126	10 Year Growth Rate	11.70%

Total Years of Dividend Growth   27

Business Summary: Commercial Banking (MIC: 8.1 SIC: 6022 NAIC:522110)

Mercantile Bankshares, with assets of $13.70 billion as of Dec 31 2003, is a bank holding company that owns substantially all of the outstanding shares of capital stock of Mercantile–Safe Deposit and Trust (MSD&T) and 19 community banks and a mortgage banking company. Sixteen banks are located in Maryland, three are in Virginia and one is in southern Delaware. MSD&T is Co.'s largest bank and operates 24 offices in Maryland, one office in Washington, D.C., and one commercial office in Pennsylvania. The banks are engaged in the general commercial and retail banking business, including acceptance of demand, savings and time deposits and the making of various types of loans.

Recent Developments: For the quarter ended Mar 31 2004, net income climbed 13.7% to $55.7 million compared with $49.0 million in the corresponding quarter of 2003. Results for 2004 and 2003 included after–tax charges of $248,000 related to the acquisition of F&M Bancorp, which took place on Aug 12 2003. Net interest income grew 20.3% to $133.7 million from $111.1 million the year before. The growth in net interest income was attributed to 27.0% growth in average loans and 20.0% growth in average securities. Provision for loan losses declined 19.6% to $2.4 million. Total non–interest income increased 31.8% to $49.9 million, while total non–interest expenses jumped 33.8% to $93.4 million.

Prospects: During the first quarter of 2004, Co. reported improvements in net interest margin and credit quality, and began to realize the benefits of the acquisition of F&M Bancorp. So far, the deposit flow pattern in 2004 has been more typical of what Bankshares have historically experienced in the first quarter versus previous first quarters over the past several years. As a result, Co. expects deposit inflows to improve in the second quarter of 2004. Going forward, Co. plans to focus on controlling costs, while continuing to invest for the future. In addition, Co. should benefit from an improving economy that generates stronger loan growth and higher interest rates.

Financial Data

(US$ in Thousands)	3 Mos	12/31/2003	12/31/2002	12/31/2001	12/31/2000	12/31/1999	12/31/1998	12/31/1997
Earnings Per Share	2.66	2.68	2.72	2.55	2.51	2.25	2.04	1.84
Tang. Book Val. Per Share	16.39	15.83	17.63	16.02	15.02	13.51	13.36	12.50
Dividends Per Share	1.290	1.290	1.180	1.100	1.020	0.940	0.860	0.730
Dividend Payout %	48.50	48.13	43.38	43.14	40.64	41.78	42.16	42.01
Income Statement								
Total Interest Income	157,774	596,575	586,386	649,766	646,495	559,168	555,392	533,970
Total Interest Expense	27,441	117,245	144,582	231,525	237,110	190,082	202,027	197,921
Net Interest Income	130,333	479,330	441,804	418,241	409,385	369,086	353,365	336,049
Provision for Loan Losses	2,426	12,105	16,378	13,434	17,231	12,056	11,489	13,703
Non–Interest Income	46,467	176,591	143,750	145,490	125,541	121,991	108,693	98,653
Non–Interest Expense	93,386	337,447	272,608	263,959	243,505	230,420	219,005	213,404
Income Before Taxes	87,747	306,369	296,568	286,338	274,190	248,601	231,564	207,595
Net Income	55,697	196,814	190,238	181,295	175,230	157,737	147,128	132,043
Average Shs. Outstg.	80,258	73,421	70,067	71,199	69,719	70,020	72,237	71,904
Balance Sheet								
Cash & Due from Banks	296,077	321,882	281,130	290,177	244,913	219,420	254,994	337,234
Securities Avail. for Sale	3,090,089	3,123,514	2,511,192	2,288,694	1,676,554	1,743,942	1,880,462	1,607,313
Net Loans & Leases	9,277,785	9,116,823	7,173,426	6,764,783	6,554,682	5,600,945	5,108,467	4,872,425
Total Assets	14,142,382	13,695,472	10,790,376	9,928,786	8,938,030	7,895,024	7,609,563	7,170,669
Total Deposits	10,543,587	10,262,553	8,260,940	7,447,372	6,796,541	5,925,083	5,958,346	5,693,911
Long–Term Obligations	657,411	647,722	287,214	269,437	92,547	82,683	40,934	50,016
Total Liabilities	12,254,377	11,854,031	9,466,018	8,698,580	7,764,729	6,920,984	6,610,204	6,235,665
Net Stockholders' Equity	1,888,005	1,841,441	1,324,358	1,230,206	1,173,301	974,040	999,359	935,004
Shares Outstanding	79,974	79,772	68,836	69,775	71,098	68,646	71,027	71,874
Statistical Record								
Return on Equity %	2.95	10.68	14.36	14.73	14.93	16.19	14.72	14.12
Return on Assets %	0.39	1.43	1.76	1.82	1.96	1.99	1.93	1.84
Equity/Assets %	13.34	13.44	12.27	12.39	13.12	12.33	13.13	13.03
Non–Int. Exp./Tot. Inc. %	44.25	43.64	37.33	33.19	31.54	33.82	32.97	33.73
Price Range	45.69–41.68	45.59–32.75	45.20–32.65	43.74–34.06	44.69–23.84	39.88–30.38	39.94–26.38	40.00–21.21
P/E Ratio	17.18–15.67	17.01–12.22	16.62–12.00	17.15–13.36	17.80–9.50	17.72–13.50	19.58–12.93	21.74–11.53
Average Yield %	2.92	3.16	2.86	2.07	3.88	2.63	2.44	1.99

Address: Two Hopkins Plaza, Baltimore, MD 21203	Officers: Edward J. Kelly III – Chmn., Pres., C.E.O., Alexander T. Mason – Vice–Chmn.	Investor Contact:410–347–8039
Telephone: (410) 237–5900	Transfer Agents:American Stock Transfer &Trust Company, New York, NY	Institutional Holding
Web Site: www.mercantile.com		No of Institutions: –
		Shares: – % Held: –

MERCK & CO., INC

Exchange	Symbol	Price	52Wk Range	Yield	P/E
NYS	MRK	$47.30 (5/28/2004)	63.24-40.60	3.13	16.37

*7 Year Price Score 77.9   *NYSE Composite Index=100   ***12 Month Price Score 45.0**

Interim Earnings (Per Share)

Qtr.	Mar	Jun	Sep	Dec
2001	0.71	0.78	0.84	0.81
2002	0.71	0.77	0.83	0.83
2003	0.76	0.83	0.83	0.50
2004	0.73	...	...	...

Interim Dividends (Per Share)

Amt	Decl	Ex	Rec	Pay
0.37Q	7/22/2003	9/3/2003	9/5/2003	10/1/2003
0.37Q	11/25/2003	12/3/2003	12/5/2003	1/2/2004
0.37Q	2/24/2004	3/3/2004	3/5/2004	4/1/2004
0.37Q	5/25/2004	6/2/2004	6/4/2004	7/1/2004

Indicated Div: $1.48 (Div. Reinv. Plan)

Valuation Analysis
Forecast P/E 14.94 (5/24/2004)
Market Cap $106.4 Billion   Book Value 16.3 Billion
Price/Book 6.03   Price/Sales 6.66

Dividend Achiever Status
Rank 139   10 Year Growth Rate 10.91%
Total Years of Dividend Growth 20

TRADING VOLUME (thousand shares)

Business Summary: Pharmaceuticals (MIC: 9.1 SIC: 2834 NAIC:325412)

Merck & Co. is a research–driven pharmaceutical company that discovers, develops, manufactures and markets human and animal health products, directly and through its joint ventures. Co.'s products include therapeutic and preventive agents, generally sold by prescription, for the treatment of human disorders. Among these products are *Zocor*, a cholesterol–lowering medicine, *Fosamax*, a treatment for osteoporosis, *Vioxx*, a prescription arthritis medicine, *Singulair*, for the treatment of chronic asthma, and *Cozaar* and *Hyzaar* for the treatment of high blood pressure.

Recent Developments: For the three months ended Mar 31 2004, net income was $1.62 billion compared with income of $1.55 billion, before a gain of $165.4 million from discontinued operations, in the corresponding quarter of the previous year. Sales inched up 1.1% to $5.63 billion from $5.57 billion in the year–earlier period. The increase in sales was primarily attributable to solid sales growth of Co.'s major products. Sales growth was partially offset by lower revenues from Co.'s relationship with AstraZeneca LP. Research and development expense jumped 22.9% to $996.3 million from $810.7 million in the prior–year quarter.

Prospects: Co. undertook several actions during the first quarter of 2004 designed to improve its long–term operating performance. These initiatives include the Mar 2004 acquisitions of Aton Pharma, a biotechnology company, and Banyu Pharmaceutical Co., and the securing of several licensing agreements to further bolster its product pipeline. Additionally, Co. completed the sale of its 50.0% equity stake in Johnson & Johnson MSD Europe, a non–prescription pharmaceuticals joint venture. Looking ahead, Co. continues to expect earnings to range from $3.11 to $3.17 per share for full–year 2004.

Financial Data

(US$ in Thousands)	3 Mos	12/31/2003	12/31/2002	12/31/2001	12/31/2000	12/31/1999	12/31/1998	12/31/1997
Earnings Per Share	2.89	2.92	3.14	3.14	2.90	2.45	2.15	1.87
Cash Flow Per Share	0.77	3.73	4.18	3.90	3.26	2.54	2.18	2.55
Tang. Book Val. Per Share	6.46	6.13	4.88	3.77	3.23	2.42	1.91	2.44
Dividends Per Share	1.460	1.450	1.410	1.370	1.210	1.100	0.940	0.840
Dividend Payout %	50.51	49.65	44.90	43.63	41.72	44.89	43.95	45.18
Income Statement								
Total Revenues	5,630,800	22,485,900	51,790,300	47,715,700	40,363,200	32,714,000	26,898,200	23,636,900
Total Indirect Exp.	2,255,600	8,867,200	7,779,500	7,639,100	7,300,800	6,112,700	1,572,300	4,297,500
Depreciation & Amort.	37,300	140,800	204,900	330,100	319,100	317,400	264,300	197,200
Operating Income	2,064,700	8,970,000	10,517,400	10,744,300	10,173,100	8,622,500	8,632,800	6,805,000
Net Interest Inc./(Exp.)	(7,100)	(42,200)	28,500	25,400	(13,800)	47,800	102,100	91,900
Income Taxes	724,300	2,462,000	3,064,100	3,120,800	3,002,400	2,729,000	2,884,900	1,848,200
Eqty Earns/Minority Int.	194,700	333,400	439,800	355,800	445,800	444,600	620,000	530,700
Income from Cont Ops	...	6,589,600	...	...	...	...	...	...
Net Income	1,618,600	6,830,900	7,149,500	7,281,800	6,821,700	5,890,500	5,248,200	4,614,100
Average Shs. Outstg.	2,332,500	2,253,100	2,277,000	2,322,300	2,353,200	2,404,600	2,441,100	2,469,400
Balance Sheet								
Cash & Cash Equivalents	1,762,100	1,201,000	2,243,000	2,144,000	2,536,800	2,021,900	2,606,200	1,125,100
Total Current Assets	12,961,300	11,527,200	14,833,900	12,961,600	13,353,400	11,259,200	10,228,500	8,213,000
Total Assets	41,665,200	40,587,500	47,561,200	44,006,700	39,910,400	35,634,900	31,853,400	25,811,900
Total Current Liabilities	10,114,200	9,569,600	12,375,200	11,544,200	9,709,600	8,758,800	6,068,800	5,568,600
Long–Term Obligations	4,931,700	5,096,000	4,879,000	4,798,600	3,600,700	3,143,900	3,220,800	1,346,500
Net Stockholders' Equity	16,271,200	15,576,400	18,200,500	16,050,100	14,832,400	13,241,600	12,801,800	12,613,500
Net Working Capital	2,847,100	1,957,600	2,458,700	1,417,400	3,643,800	2,500,400	4,159,700	2,644,400
Shares Outstanding	2,222,567	2,221,763	2,244,983	2,272,729	2,307,599	2,329,077	2,360,452	2,387,296
Statistical Record								
Operating Profit Margin %	40.12	42.00	21.55	23.95	27.09	28.68	43.36	32.77
Net Profit Margin %	57.92	53.31	26.88	29.77	33.67	37.01	52.23	39.14
Return on Equity %	11.14	45.34	42.82	49.64	51.14	50.23	64.67	44.04
Return on Assets %	4.35	17.40	16.38	18.10	19.00	18.66	25.99	21.52
Debt/Total Assets %	11.83	12.55	10.25	10.90	9.02	8.82	10.11	5.21
Price Range	49.08–43.01	63.24–40.60	64.37–39.05	93.00–57.17	94.88–53.94	86.38–60.94	79.41–51.56	53.66–39.63
P/E Ratio	16.98–14.88	21.66–13.90	20.50–12.44	29.62–18.21	32.72–18.60	35.26–24.87	36.93–23.98	28.69–21.19
Average Yield %	3.12	2.72	2.61	1.92	1.64	1.50	1.46	1.78

Address: One Merck Drive, Whitehouse Station, NJ 08889–0100 **Telephone:** (908) 423–1000 **Web Site:** www.merck.com	**Officers:** Raymond V. Gilmartin – Chmn., Pres., C.E.O., Judy C. Lewent – Exec. V.P., C.F.O. **Transfer Agents:**Wells Fargo Bank Minnesota, N.A., South St. Paul, MN	**Investor Contact:**908–423–5881 **Institutional Holding** **No of Institutions:** 17 **Shares:** 388,274 **% Held:** –

MERCURY GENERAL CORP.

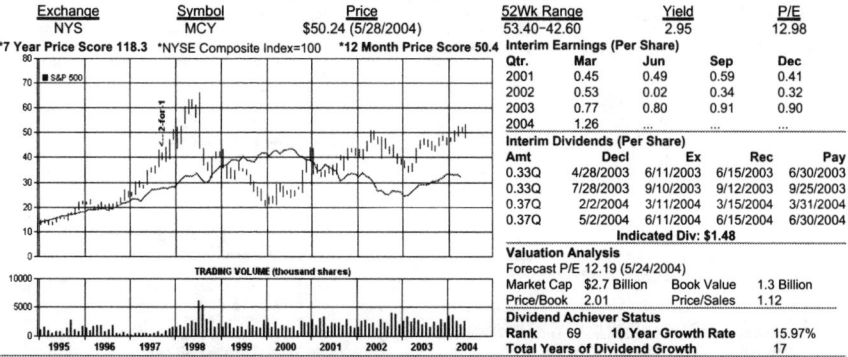

Exchange	Symbol	Price	52Wk Range	Yield	P/E
NYS	MCY	$50.24 (5/28/2004)	53.40-42.60	2.95	12.98

*7 Year Price Score 118.3   *NYSE Composite Index=100   *12 Month Price Score 50.4

Interim Earnings (Per Share)

Qtr.	Mar	Jun	Sep	Dec
2001	0.45	0.49	0.59	0.41
2002	0.53	0.02	0.34	0.32
2003	0.77	0.80	0.91	0.90
2004	1.26	...	...	...

Interim Dividends (Per Share)

Amt	Decl	Ex	Rec	Pay
0.33Q	4/28/2003	6/11/2003	6/15/2003	6/30/2003
0.33Q	7/28/2003	9/10/2003	9/12/2003	9/25/2003
0.37Q	2/2/2004	3/11/2004	3/15/2004	3/31/2004
0.37Q	5/2/2004	6/11/2004	6/15/2004	6/30/2004

Indicated Div: $1.48

Valuation Analysis

Forecast P/E 12.19 (5/24/2004)

Market Cap	$2.7 Billion	Book Value	1.3 Billion
Price/Book	2.01	Price/Sales	1.12

Dividend Achiever Status

Rank	69	10 Year Growth Rate	15.97%

Total Years of Dividend Growth   17

TRADING VOLUME (thousand shares)

Business Summary: Insurance (MIC: 8.2 SIC: 6331 NAIC:524126)

Mercury General, through its subsidiaries, engages primarily in writing all risk classifications of automobile insurance in a number of states, principally in California. Co. offers automobile policyholders the following types of coverage: bodily injury liability, underinsured and uninsured motorist, personal injury protection, property damage liability, comprehensive, collision and other hazards specified in the policy. Co. sells its policies through independent agents in California, Florida, Georgia, Illinois, New York, Texas, Oklahoma, New Jersey and Virginia. In addition, Co. writes other lines of insurance in various states, including mechanical breakdown and homeowners insurance.

Recent Developments: For the quarter ended Mar 31 2004, net income advanced 63.4% to $68.8 million from $42.1 million in the comparable prior-year quarter. Earnings included net realized investment gains of $3.7 million in 2004 and net realized investment losses of $493,000 in 2003. Net premiums written increased 17.0% to $630.3 million. Net premiums earned grew 18.2% to $591.9 million from $500.7 million the previous year. Net investment income rose 4.4% to $25.7 million. Incurred losses and loss adjustment expenses increased 8.9% to $372.0 million. Co.'s combined ratio improved to 89.1% from 94.4% the year before.

Prospects: Co.'s favorable performance is being led by ongoing improvements in its core California automobile lines operation, which generated a 9.7% increase in net premiums written and a combined ratio of 90.3% for the quarter. Additionally, Co. continues to make progress in its California homeowners line, which experienced a 20.7% increase in net written premiums in the first quarter. The overall outlook for Co.'s business remains favorable as premiums are expected to continue increasing in the near term. Separately, Co. announced that it began issuing private passenger automobile insurance policies in Arizona in April 2004, marking the 10th state where Co. sells automobile insurance.

Financial Data

(US$ in Thousands)	3 Mos	12/31/2003	12/31/2002	12/31/2001	12/31/2000	12/31/1999	12/31/1998	12/31/1997
Earnings Per Share	3.87	3.38	1.21	1.94	2.02	2.44	3.21	2.82
Tang. Book Val. Per Share	24.09	23.06	20.21	19.70	19.05	16.71	16.77	14.50
Dividends Per Share	1.400	1.320	1.200	1.060	0.960	0.840	0.700	0.580
Dividend Payout %	25.58	39.05	99.17	54.63	47.52	34.42	21.80	20.56
Income Statement								
Total Premium Income	591,937	2,145,047	1,741,527	1,380,561	1,249,259	1,188,307	1,121,584	1,031,280
Net Investment Income	...	104,520	113,083	114,511	106,466	99,374	96,169	86,812
Other Income	32,519	15,950	(68,339)	11,908	10,293	(7,005)	4,370	9,854
Total Revenues	624,456	2,265,517	1,786,271	1,506,980	1,366,018	1,280,676	1,222,123	1,127,946
Total Indirect Exp.	23,300	91,295	74,875	62,335	59,733	50,675	44,941	33,579
Inc. Before Inc. Taxes	96,285	245,801	60,668	124,809	128,555	168,539	235,280	209,779
Income Taxes	27,469	61,480	(5,437)	19,470	19,189	34,830	57,754	53,473
Net Income	68,816	184,321	66,105	105,339	109,366	133,709	177,526	156,306
Average Shs. Outstg.	54,606	54,547	54,502	54,382	54,258	54,815	55,354	55,383
Balance Sheet								
Cash & Cash Equivalents	51,220	36,964	13,191	3,851	5,935	8,052	1,887	3,011
Premiums Due	317,619	299,094	259,445	218,376	199,392	172,079	168,929	166,149
Invst. Assets: Total	2,631,800	2,209,702	1,863,852	1,864,220	1,761,984	1,531,897	1,544,653	1,388,508
Total Assets	3,258,639	3,119,766	2,645,296	2,316,540	2,142,263	1,906,367	1,877,025	1,725,532
Long-Term Obligations	...	124,714	128,859	129,513	107,889	92,000	78,000	75,000
Net Stockholders' Equity	1,312,098	1,255,503	1,098,786	1,069,711	1,032,905	909,591	917,375	799,592
Shares Outstanding	54,447	54,424	54,361	54,276	54,193	54,425	54,684	55,125
Return on Revenues %	11.02	8.13	3.70	6.99	8.00	10.44	14.52	13.85
Return on Equity %	5.24	14.68	6.01	9.84	10.58	14.69	19.35	19.54
Return on Assets %	2.11	5.90	2.49	4.54	5.10	7.01	9.45	9.05
Price Range	52.76-46.50	48.70-34.30	50.80-37.36	43.90-32.21	44.12-20.89	43.52-20.70	66.02-32.09	51.07-24.52
P/E Ratio	13.63-12.02	14.41-10.15	41.98-30.88	22.63-16.60	21.84-10.34	17.84-8.48	20.57-10.00	18.11-8.69
Average Yield %	2.02	3.07	2.74	2.83	3.45	2.66	1.42	1.62

Address: 4484 Wilshire Boulevard, Los Angeles, CA 90010
Telephone: (323) 937-1060
Web Site: www.mercuryinsurance.com

Officers: George Joseph - Chmn., C.E.O., Gabriel Tirador - Pres., C.O.O.
Transfer Agents: The Bank of New York, New York, NY

Investor Contact: 800-900-6729
Institutional Holding
No of Institutions: 7
Shares: 109,840   **% Held:** -

177

MEREDITH CORP.

Exchange	Symbol	Price	52Wk Range	Yield	P/E
NYS	MDP	$52.46 (5/28/2004)	53.22–41.81	0.91	28.20

*7 Year Price Score 126.6   ***NYSE Composite Index=100**   ***12 Month Price Score 50.6**

Interim Earnings (Per Share)

Qtr.	Sep	Dec	Mar	Jun
2000–01	0.32	0.47	0.37	0.23
2001–02	0.17	0.17	0.35	1.10
2002–03	0.32	0.38	0.50	0.58
2003–04	0.39	0.39	0.65	...

Interim Dividends (Per Share)

Amt	Decl	Ex	Rec	Pay
0.095Q	8/13/2003	8/27/2003	8/29/2003	9/15/2003
0.095Q	11/10/2003	11/24/2003	11/26/2003	12/15/2003
0.12Q	2/1/2004	2/25/2004	2/27/2004	3/15/2004
0.12Q	5/12/2004	5/26/2004	5/28/2004	6/15/2004

Indicated Div: $0.48

Valuation Analysis
Forecast P/E 20.56 (5/24/2004)
Market Cap $2.1 Billion   Book Value 525.8 Million
Price/Book 3.73   Price/Sales 1.73

Dividend Achiever Status
Rank 176   10 Year Growth Rate 9.04%
Total Years of Dividend Growth 10

Business Summary: Media (MIC: 13.1 SIC: 2721 NAIC:511120)

Meredith is engaged in magazine and book publishing, television broadcasting, integrated marketing, and interactive media. The publishing segment consists of 17 magazine brands, including *Better Homes and Gardens*, *Ladies' Home Journal*, and *American Baby*, as well as 170 special interest publications; book publishing with nearly 300 books in print; integrated marketing relationships; a consumer database; an Internet presence, including 24 web sites and strategic alliances with Internet destinations; brand licensing relationships; and other related operations. The broadcasting segment includes the operations of 11 network–affiliated television stations located across the continental U.S.

Recent Developments: For the quarter ended Mar 31 2004, net income improved 32.0% to $33.6 million compared with $25.5 million in the corresponding period of the previous year. Total revenues increased 7.7% to $299.6 million from $278.2 million the year before. Publishing segment revenues grew 4.4% to $230.4 million from $220.8 million a year earlier. Broadcasting segment revenues advanced 20.5% to $69.1 million compared with $57.4 million the prior year. Income from operations rose 26.1% to $60.5 million from $48.0 million the previous year. Total depreciation and amortization declined 20.7% to $7.5 million.

Prospects: Co.'s Broadcasting segment continues to report revenue and profit growth in all of its markets as it benefits from increased spot advertising at its television stations and more political advertising. Meanwhile, Co.'s Publishing segment continues to increase its advertising market share, as well as improve the circulation contribution of its magazines and grow its custom publishing business. Looking ahead, publishing advertising revenues are anticipated to grow in the low single–digits, and earnings per share are expected to total $0.71 for the fourth quarter of fiscal 2004.

Financial Data

(US$ in Thousands)	9 Mos	6 Mos	3 Mos	06/30/2003	06/30/2002	06/30/2001	06/30/2000	06/30/1999
Earnings Per Share	2.01	1.86	1.85	1.78	1.79	1.39	1.35	1.67
Cash Flow Per Share	1.96	1.20	0.38	3.37	2.75	2.66	2.80	2.50
Tang. Book Val. Per Share	N.M	N.M	N.M	N.M	N.M	N.M	N.M	N.M
Dividends Per Share	0.400	0.380	0.370	0.370	0.350	0.330	0.310	0.290
Dividend Payout %	19.90	20.43	20.00	20.78	19.55	23.74	22.96	17.36
Income Statement								
Total Revenues	852,602	553,049	272,670	1,080,104	987,829	1,053,213	1,097,165	1,036,122
Total Indirect Exp.	337,942	231,563	111,517	438,021	436,335	438,840	459,048	437,479
Depreciation & Amort.	22,609	15,104	7,479	31,443	53,640	51,572	52,349	44,083
Operating Income	137,190	76,116	38,102	177,319	117,849	126,624	161,337	171,087
Net Interest Inc./(Exp.)	(17,084)	(11,477)	(5,799)	(27,209)	(32,589)	(31,901)	(33,751)	(21,287)
Income Taxes	46,485	25,251	12,502	57,941	57,691	44,928	56,556	62,518
Income from Cont Ops	...	...	...	91,068	...	...	...	...
Net Income	73,621	39,988	19,801	5,319	91,381	71,272	71,030	89,657
Average Shs. Outstg.	51,630	51,583	51,557	51,093	50,921	51,354	52,774	53,761
Balance Sheet								
Cash & Cash Equivalents	10,075	9,693	9,403	22,294	28,225	36,254	22,861	11,029
Total Current Assets	286,443	275,199	290,208	268,429	272,211	291,082	288,799	256,175
Total Assets	1,449,761	1,443,118	1,456,821	1,436,721	1,460,264	1,437,747	1,439,773	1,423,396
Total Current Liabilities	385,463	306,799	311,774	297,199	307,406	371,406	358,701	344,115
Long–Term Obligations	247,256	349,232	380,135	375,000	385,000	400,000	455,000	485,000
Net Stockholders' Equity	555,830	525,798	515,743	500,765	507,717	447,908	379,844	360,158
Net Working Capital	(99,020)	(31,600)	(21,566)	(28,770)	(35,195)	(80,324)	(69,902)	(87,940)
Shares Outstanding	50,246	50,083	50,184	50,149	49,575	49,791	49,209	50,284
Statistical Record								
Operating Profit Margin %	16.09	13.87	13.97	16.41	11.93	12.02	14.70	16.51
Net Profit Margin %	19.53	16.36	16.43	19.07	20.93	15.29	16.78	20.72
Return on Equity %	13.25	7.60	3.83	18.18	17.99	15.91	16.81	21.69
Return on Assets %	5.08	2.77	1.35	6.33	6.25	4.95	4.93	6.29
Debt/Total Assets %	17.05	24.19	26.09	26.10	26.36	27.82	31.60	34.07
Price Range	52.90–44.00	50.28–44.00	48.12–44.00	47.58–34.09	44.75–27.20	38.52–27.19	41.94–22.44	48.25–27.19
P/E Ratio	36.99–30.77	64.46–56.41	26.01–23.78	26.73–19.15	25.00–15.20	27.71–19.56	31.06–16.62	28.89–16.28
Average Yield %	0.83	0.80	0.79	0.89	0.94	1.00	0.92	0.80

Address: 1716 Locust Street, Des Moines, IA 50309–3023	**Officers:** William T. Kerr – Chmn., C.E.O., Suku V. Radia – V.P., C.F.O.	**Investor Contact:**800–284–4236
Telephone: (515) 284–3000	**Transfer Agents:**Boston EquiServe, Boston, MA	**Institutional Holding** No of Institutions: 4
Web Site: www.meredith.com		Shares: 10,678 % Held: –

MERIDIAN BIOSCIENCE INC.

Exchange	Symbol	Price	52Wk Range	Yield	P/E
NMS	VIVO	$8.30 (5/31/2004)	12.58–8.29	4.82	16.27

*7 Year Price Score 134.8   *NYSE Composite Index=100   *12 Month Price Score 44.1

Interim Earnings (Per Share)

Qtr.	Dec	Mar	Jun	Sep
2000–01	(0.56)	(0.11)	(0.04)	0.01
2001–02	0.08	0.10	0.11	0.05
2002–03	0.10	0.13	0.12	0.12
2003–04	0.12	0.15	...	...

Interim Dividends (Per Share)

Amt	Decl	Ex	Rec	Pay
0.09Q	7/24/2003	7/30/2003	8/1/2003	8/8/2003
0.09Q	11/18/2003	11/25/2003	11/28/2003	12/5/2003
0.10Q	1/22/2004	1/29/2004	2/2/2004	2/9/2004
0.10Q	4/22/2004	4/29/2004	5/3/2004	5/10/2004

Indicated Div: $0.40 (Div. Reinv. Plan)

Valuation Analysis

Forecast P/E 19.55 (5/24/2004)

Market Cap $121.5 Million	Book Value 29.0 Million
Price/Book 5.49	Price/Sales 2.35

Dividend Achiever Status

Rank 36	10 Year Growth Rate	19.53%
Total Years of Dividend Growth		11

Business Summary: Biotechnology (MIC: 9.2 SIC: 2835 NAIC:325413)

Meridian Bioscience is an integrated life sciences company whose principal businesses include the development, manufacture, sale and distribution of diagnostic test kits, primarily for certain respiratory, gastrointestinal, viral and parasitic infectious diseases; the manufacture and distribution of bulk antigens and reagents used by researchers and other diagnostic manufacturers; and the contract manufacture of proteins and other biologicals for use by biopharmaceutical and biotechnology companies engaged in research for new drugs and vaccines.

Recent Developments: For the three months ended Mar 31 2004, net earnings advanced 19.0% to $2.3 million compared with $1.9 million in the same period a year earlier. Net sales climbed 23.8% to $20.9 million compared with $16.9 million the previous year. Co. noted that the higher sales were positively influenced by strong sales of its rapid tests for gastrointestinal infections as well as shipments of its highly purified biologicals to researchers and third party manufacturers. Gross profit was $12.0 million, or 57.5% of net sales, versus $10.1 million, or 59.5% of net sales, the year before. Operating income was $4.0 million, an increase of 5.2% from the prior–year period.

Prospects: Co.'s outlook appears positive, aided by its research and development pipeline that is expected to yield near–term new product introductions to support its second half goals. In addition, Co. anticipates further contributions from its Life Science business in the areas of vaccine manufacturing and in the production and sale of new purified proteins. Accordingly, Co. has increased its full–year fiscal 2004 guidance for net sales to between $73.0 million and $77.0 million versus its previous guidance of $71.0 million to $75.0 million. Also, Co. has raised its diluted earnings guidance to between $0.50 and $0.55 per share versus its previous guidance of $0.47 to $0.53 per diluted share.

Financial Data

(US$ in Thousands)	6 Mos	3 Mos	09/30/2003	09/30/2002	09/30/2001	09/30/2000	09/30/1999	09/30/1998
Earnings Per Share	0.51	0.49	0.47	0.34	(0.70)	0.49	0.16	0.34
Cash Flow Per Share	0.21	0.24	0.82	0.77	0.59	0.35	0.61	0.46
Tang. Book Val. Per Share	1.04	0.95	0.83	0.57	0.49	0.83	0.66	1.87
Dividends Per Share	0.370	0.360	0.340	0.270	0.250	0.230	0.200	0.178
Dividend Payout %	72.54	73.46	72.34	80.88	N.M.	46.93	125.00	51.47
Income Statement								
Total Revenues	39,106	18,166	65,864	59,104	56,527	57,096	54,351	33,169
Total Indirect Exp.	14,976	6,969	25,499	24,604	39,213	26,092	27,842	14,168
Depreciation & Amort.	2,122	984	3,780	3,719	4,746	4,811	5,673	2,884
Operating Income	7,174	3,148	12,789	9,994	(12,507)	9,354	7,036	8,351
Net Interest Inc./(Exp.)	(833)	(358)	(1,676)	(1,936)	(2,380)	(1,742)	(1,638)	(284)
Income Taxes	2,272	1,029	4,573	3,212	(4,631)	(173)	2,935	3,097
Net Income	4,084	1,795	7,018	5,031	(10,275)	7,111	2,386	4,958
Average Shs. Outstg.	15,225	15,170	14,950	14,760	14,589	14,652	14,580	14,703
Balance Sheet								
Cash & Cash Equivalents	1,566	3,714	2,683	3,060	4,673	4,766	6,229	19,400
Total Current Assets	3,683	33,690	33,161	30,375	32,502	40,166	31,972	39,763
Total Assets	66,256	66,931	66,420	65,095	65,982	84,769	72,389	59,147
Total Current Liabilities	17,643	14,980	15,330	15,249	16,368	17,303	13,517	3,869
Long–Term Obligations	16,624	20,879	21,505	23,626	24,349	27,105	21,366	20,595
Net Stockholders' Equity	30,038	29,018	27,484	24,381	22,944	36,611	33,904	34,683
Shares Outstanding	14,885	14,823	14,720	14,624	14,590	14,587	14,429	14,382
Statistical Record								
Operating Profit Margin %	18.34	17.32	19.41	16.90	N.M.	16.38	12.94	25.17
Return on Equity %	13.60	6.18	25.53	20.63	N.M.	19.42	7.03	14.29
Return on Assets %	6.16	2.68	10.56	7.72	N.M.	8.38	3.29	8.38
Debt/Total Assets %	25.09	31.19	32.37	36.29	36.90	31.97	29.51	34.82
Price Range	12.58–9.70	11.30–9.70	11.20–5.46	7.54–4.30	7.91–2.48	10.84–5.95	8.43–4.79	13.94–4.79
P/E Ratio	24.64–19.02	23.06–19.80	23.83–11.62	22.18–12.65	N/A	22.12–12.14	52.69–29.94	41.00–14.09
Average Yield %	3.44	3.49	4.08	4.36	5.04	3.07	2.95	...

Address: 3471 River Hills Drive, Cincinnati, OH 45244	Officers: William J. Motto – Chmn., C.E.O., John A. Kraeutler – Pres., C.O.O.	Investor Contact:513–271–3700
Telephone: (513) 271-3700	Transfer Agents:Computershare Investor Services LLC, OH	Institutional Holding
Web Site: www.meridianbioscience.com		No of Institutions: 3
		Shares: 7,166,604 % Held: –

MGE ENERGY INC

Exchange	Symbol	Price	52Wk Range	Yield	P/E
NMS	MGEE	$30.34 (5/28/2004)	34.45-28.57	4.46	15.80

*7 Year Price Score 128.3 *NYSE Composite Index=100 ***12 Month Price Score 44.7**

Interim Earnings (Per Share)

Qtr.	Mar	Jun	Sep	Dec
2001	0.58	0.32	0.36	0.37
2002	0.64	0.26	0.60	0.19
2003	0.53	0.33	0.56	0.29
2004	0.74	...	...	...

Interim Dividends (Per Share)

Amt	Decl	Ex	Rec	Pay
0.338Q	8/15/2003	8/27/2003	9/1/2003	9/15/2003
0.338Q	11/21/2003	11/26/2003	12/1/2003	12/15/2003
0.338Q	1/16/2004	2/26/2004	3/1/2004	3/15/2004
0.338Q	5/11/2004	5/27/2004	6/1/2004	6/15/2004

Indicated Div: $1.35332 (Div. Reinv. Plan)

Valuation Analysis

Forecast P/E N/A

Market Cap $526.3 Million	Book Value 277.3 Million
Price/Book 1.94	Price/Sales 1.32

Dividend Achiever Status

Rank	302	10 Year Growth Rate	0.95%
Total Years of Dividend Growth			28

TRADING VOLUME (thousand shares)

Graph years: 1995 1996 1997 1998 1999 2000 2001 2002 2003 2004

Business Summary: Electricity (MIC: 7.1 SIC: 4931 NAIC:221121)

MGE Energy is the holding company for Madison Gas & Electric, which is a public utility that generates and distributes electricity to nearly 132,000 customers in Dane County, WI as of Dec 31 2003. Co. also purchases, transports and distributes natural gas to more than 129,000 customers in the Wisconsin cities of Elroy, Fitchburg, Lodi, Madison, Middleton, Monona, Prairie du Chien, Verona, and Viroqua; 24 villages and 46 townships. Co. has a 22.0% ownership interest in two, 512-megawatt coal-burning units at the Columbia Energy Center in Columbia, WI. The units burn low-sulfur coal obtained from the Powder River Basin coal fields located in Wyoming and Montana.

Recent Developments: For the three months ended Mar 31 2004, net income jumped 45.5% to $13.6 million compared with $9.4 million in the equivalent period of 2003. Total operating revenues rose 5.3% to $135.3 million from $128.5 million a year earlier. Electric retail sales climbed 3.2% and electric revenues were up $3.8 million. Gas revenues were up $2.3 million, despite a 5.1% decrease in retail gas deliveries. Operating and maintenance expenses increased to $600,000, primarily due to higher uncollectible accounts and increased maintenance costs for electric distribution. Operating income increased 36.5% to $23.8 million compared with $17.5 million the year before.

Prospects: Co.'s liquidity and capital position remains strong even though its overall debt increased due to a cogeneration facility that MGE Power West Campus is constructing on the University of Wisconsin - Madison campus. Co. anticipates relying on short- and long-term borrowings to support that construction and the associated capital expenditures. In addition, Co. anticipates a need for additional equity capital during 2004 beyond the amounts it was able to raise through its dividend reinvestment and direct stock purchase plan. Co. estimates total capital expenditures for 2004 to be about $98.2 million.

Financial Data

(US$ in Thousands)	3 Mos	12/31/2003	12/31/2002	12/31/2001	12/31/2000	12/31/1999	12/31/1998	12/31/1997
Earnings Per Share	1.92	1.71	1.69	1.63	1.67	1.48	1.38	1.40
Cash Flow Per Share	1.97	3.83	3.27	4.44	2.91	3.74	4.38	2.53
Tang. Book Val. Per Share	14.89	14.34	12.93	12.66	12.05	11.48	11.33	11.25
Dividends Per Share	1.350	1.340	1.330	1.320	1.310	1.300	1.290	1.280
Dividend Payout %	70.36	78.84	79.18	81.48	78.93	88.37	94.07	91.90
Income Statement								
Total Revenues	135,281	401,547	347,096	333,711	324,108	274,034	249,752	264,648
Total Indirect Exp.	9,371	34,936	40,223	60,359	60,677	56,728	53,171	49,054
Costs & Expenses	111,456	341,716	288,966	299,040	284,007	241,484	219,940	233,658
Depreciation & Amort.	6,061	23,344	29,362	35,659	35,081	35,154	33,185	28,317
Operating Income	23,825	59,831	58,130	34,671	40,101	32,550	29,812	30,990
Net Interest Inc./(Exp.)	(2,851)	(11,776)	(12,545)	(13,572)	(14,129)	(12,039)	(10,855)	(10,724)
Income Taxes	8,909	19,901	18,727	2,105	...	...	...	...
Eqty Earns/Minority Int.	...	...	...	3,345	...	...	...	...
Income from Cont Ops	...	...	...	27,362	...	...	...	...
Net Income	13,644	30,640	29,193	27,245	27,355	23,746	22,230	22,523
Average Shs. Outstg.	18,426	17,894	17,311	16,819	16,382	16,084	16,080	16,080
Balance Sheet								
Net Property	546,464	537,511	460,328	401,249	441,654	394,825	367,302	363,093
Total Assets	716,750	721,687	628,895	541,451	571,604	495,510	466,265	471,790
Long-Term Obligations	202,217	200,204	192,149	157,600	183,437	148,599	159,761	129,923
Net Stockholders' Equity	277,285	263,070	227,370	216,292	200,312	185,686	182,275	180,923
Shares Outstanding	18,613	18,343	17,554	17,071	16,618	16,161	16,080	16,080
Operating Profit Margin %	17.61	14.90	16.74	10.38	12.37	11.87	11.93	11.70
Net Inc./Net Property %	2.49	5.70	6.34	6.79	6.19	6.01	6.05	6.20
Net Inc./Tot. Capital %	2.45	5.66	6.05	6.33	6.40	6.29	5.75	6.31
Return on Equity %	4.92	11.64	12.83	12.65	13.65	12.78	12.19	12.44
Accum. Depr./Gross Prop. %	...	44.24	45.91	53.60	55.09	54.89	52.88	
Price Range	32.20-30.00	34.45-25.20	29.84-25.01	27.80-21.06	22.75-17.00	23.38-17.25	23.56-20.88	23.00-19.25
P/E Ratio	16.77-15.63	20.15-14.74	17.66-14.80	17.06-12.92	13.62-10.18	15.79-11.66	17.07-15.13	16.43-13.75
Average Yield %	4.32	4.47	4.94	5.50	6.66	6.25	5.75	6.30

Address: 133 South Blair Street, Madison, WI 53701-1231	Officers: Gary J. Wolter – Chmn., Pres., C.E.O., David C. Mebane – Vice–Chmn.	Investor Contact:608-252-7907
Telephone: (608) 252-7000	Transfer Agents:Continental Stock Transfer &Trust Company, New York, NY	Institutional Holding No of Institutions:
Web Site: www.mge.com		Shares: % Held:

MIDDLESEX WATER CO.

Exchange	Symbol	Price	52Wk Range	Yield	P/E
NMS	MSEX	$19.66 (5/28/2004)	21.56-17.29	3.36	33.46

*7 Year Price Score 130.5   *NYSE Composite Index=100   ***12 Month Price Score 48.4**

Interim Earnings (Per Share)

Qtr.	Mar	Jun	Sep	Dec
2001	0.08	0.18	0.22	0.18
2002	0.12	0.18	0.24	0.18
2003	0.11	0.16	0.22	0.12
2004	0.09	...	...	...

Interim Dividends (Per Share)

Amt	Decl	Ex	Rec	Pay
4-for-3	8/28/2003	11/17/2003	11/1/2003	11/14/2003
0.165Q	10/30/2003	11/12/2003	11/14/2003	12/1/2003
0.165Q	1/29/2004	2/12/2004	2/17/2004	3/1/2004
0.165Q	4/26/2004	5/12/2004	5/14/2004	6/1/2004

Indicated Div: $7.00 (Div. Reinv. Plan)

Valuation Analysis

Forecast P/E 25.05 (5/24/2004)

Market Cap $151.9 Million	Book Value 79.2 Million
Price/Book 3.68	Price/Sales 4.57

Dividend Achiever Status

Rank	288	10 Year Growth Rate		2.51%
Total Years of Dividend Growth				31

Business Summary: Water Utilities (MIC: 7.2 SIC: 4941 NAIC:221310)

Middlesex Water is a water utility company that owns and operates water utility systems in central and southern New Jersey and in Delaware as well as a wastewater utility in southern New Jersey. Operations are divided into two segments. Co.'s regulated segment collects, treats and distributes water on a retail and wholesale basis to residential, commercial, industrial and fire protection customers in parts of New Jersey and Delaware. Co. also operates a regulated wastewater system in New Jersey. Co.'s non-regulated contract services segment operates and maintains municipal and private water and wastewater systems in New Jersey and Delaware.

Recent Developments: For the quarter ended Mar 31 2004, net income decreased 15.6% to $1.0 million compared with $1.2 million in the equivalent 2002 quarter. Operating revenues advanced 6.0% to $15.9 million from $15.0 million a year earlier. The improvement in revenues was primarily attributed to double-digit growth in base rates and customer growth for Co.'s Delaware subsidiary, Tidewater Utilities, which generated an additional $400,000 in revenues during the quarter, while its meter installation joint venture added $500,000 to revenues. Operating income fell 6.5% to $2.2 million versus $2.4 million the year before. Total other income dropped 29.2% to $66,131 versus $93,380 the year before.

Prospects: Looking ahead, Co. expects the level of revenue and earnings for 2004 to be contingent upon the outcome of the New Jersey base rate cases under review by the Board of Public Utilities and the anticipated base rate filing in Delaware for Co.'s Tidewater System. Meanwhile, Co. continues to explore viable plans to streamline operations and reduce costs, particularly in Delaware, where customer growth continues to exceed industry averages. Part of the challenge is that Co.'s Delaware operations are a combination of over 70 stand-alone production and distribution systems serving 240 communities.

Financial Data

(US$ in Thousands)	3 Mos	12/31/2003	12/31/2002	12/31/2001	12/31/2000	12/31/1999	12/31/1998	12/31/1997
Earnings Per Share	0.59	0.61	0.72	0.66	0.50	0.76	0.70	0.66
Cash Flow Per Share	0.26	1.31	1.04	1.17	0.96	0.97	1.13	1.44
Tang. Book Val. Per Share	7.47	7.53	7.38	7.10	6.99	7.04	6.81	5.99
Dividends Per Share	0.650	0.640	0.630	0.620	0.610	0.590	0.570	0.560
Dividend Payout %	111.54	106.35	87.11	94.31	121.28	78.28	81.56	84.58
Income Statement								
Total Revenues	15,876	64,111	61,933	59,638	54,477	53,497	43,058	40,294
Total Indirect Exp.	3,381	13,581	12,822	12,692	11,633	10,756	9,386	8,852
Costs & Expenses	13,655	52,611	49,466	48,145	44,538	42,832	33,909	31,501
Depreciation & Amort.	1,436	5,363	4,963	5,051	4,701	3,885	3,285	3,071
Operating Income	2,220	11,500	12,467	11,493	9,938	10,665	9,149	8,793
Net Interest Inc./(Exp.)	(1,203)	(5,227)	(5,143)	(5,042)	(4,997)	(4,695)	(4,424)	(3,337)
Income Taxes	507	2,835	3,878	3,714	2,637	3,189	2,999	3,135
Income from Cont Ops	...	6,631	...	...	...	...	...	...
Net Income	1,034	6,631	7,765	6,953	5,305	7,881	6,521	5,861
Average Shs. Outstg.	10,922	10,818	10,623	10,474	10,387	10,296	9,160	8,764
Balance Sheet								
Net Property	228,407	230,932	211,368	199,060	191,196	181,809	162,827	137,109
Total Assets	265,408	263,192	244,604	236,374	219,400	215,036	203,501	159,761
Long-Term Obligations	98,251	97,377	87,483	88,140	82,109	82,330	78,032	52,918
Net Stockholders' Equity	83,234	83,706	80,564	76,353	74,698	74,552	71,725	56,221
Shares Outstanding	10,588	10,566	10,356	10,168	10,097	10,001	9,794	8,538
Statistical Record								
Operating Profit Margin %	17.18	23.11	26.39	25.49	23.08	25.89	28.21	29.60
Net Inc./Net Property %	0.45	2.87	3.67	3.49	2.77	4.33	4.00	4.27
Net Inc./Tot. Capital %	0.52	3.39	4.28	3.92	3.13	4.66	4.02	4.83
Return on Equity %	1.85	11.88	14.45	13.97	10.63	14.84	13.27	16.00
Accum. Depr./Gross Prop. %	17.54	17.32	18.72	18.21	17.10	16.36	16.90	18.29
Price Range	21.01-19.50	20.82-15.73	20.04-14.92	17.92-14.94	16.87-12.87	19.75-10.69	12.81-9.69	11.25-8.19
P/E Ratio	35.61-33.05	34.13-25.78	27.83-20.72	27.16-22.63	33.75-25.75	25.99-14.06	18.30-13.84	17.05-12.41
Average Yield %	3.19	3.51	3.67	3.81	4.20	4.42	5.31	6.30

Address: 1500 Ronson Road, Iselin, NJ 08830-3020	**Officers:** J. Richard Tompkins – Chmn., Dennis G. Sullivan – Pres., C.E.O.	**Investor Contact:** 732-634-1500
Telephone: (732) 634-1500	**Transfer Agents:** Registrar and Transfer Company, Cranford, NJ	**Institutional Holding**
Web Site: www.middlesexwater.com		**No of Institutions:** 24
		Shares: 81,570 **% Held:** –

181

MIDLAND CO.

Exchange	Symbol	Price	52Wk Range	Yield	P/E
NMS	MLAN	$26.12 (5/28/2004)	26.98-20.31	0.78	16.02

*7 Year Price Score 142.4   *NYSE Composite Index=100   *12 Month Price Score 53.5

Interim Earnings (Per Share)

Qtr.	Mar	Jun	Sep	Dec
2001	0.53	0.34	0.10	0.54
2002	0.52	0.33	(0.15)	0.44
2003	0.56	(0.06)	0.23	0.57
2004	0.90	...	...	...

Interim Dividends (Per Share)

Amt	Decl	Ex	Rec	Pay
0.048Q	7/31/2003	9/17/2003	9/19/2003	10/2/2003
0.048Q	10/30/2003	12/19/2003	12/23/2003	1/6/2004
0.051Q	1/29/2004	3/17/2004	3/19/2004	4/1/2004
0.051Q	4/29/2004	6/16/2004	6/18/2004	7/1/2004

Indicated Div: $0.205 (Div. Reinv. Plan)

Valuation Analysis

Forecast P/E 12.53 (5/24/2004)

Market Cap $457.8 Million	Book Value 395.4 Million
Price/Book 1.18	Price/Sales 0.65

Dividend Achiever Status

Rank	206	10 Year Growth Rate	7.75%

Total Years of Dividend Growth   17

Business Summary: Insurance (MIC: 8.2 SIC: 6399 NAIC:524128)

Midland is a provider of specialty insurance products and services through two wholly owned subsidiaries. American Modern specializes in writing physical damage insurance and related coverages on manufactured housing, as well as other areas of insurance, including coverage for site–built homes, motorcycles, watercraft, snowmobiles, recreational vehicles, physical damage on long–haul trucks, extended service contracts, credit life and related products as well as collateral protection and mortgage fire products sold to financial institutions and their customers. Co.'s other subsidiary, M/G Transport, charters barges and brokers freight for the movement of commodities on the inland waterways.

Recent Developments: For the first quarter ended Mar 31 2003, net income climbed 67.7% to $16.8 million from $10.0 million in the prior–year quarter. Earnings benefited from the continued strength in the underwriting results of Co.'s core manufactured housing line of business, as well as significant underwriting improvement in Co.'s motorcycle, site–built dwelling, watercraft and recreational vehicle lines of business. Total revenue increased 12.6% to $190.6 million. Premiums earned grew 6.8% to $163.6 million. Net investment income rose 1.8% to $8.5 million. Transportation revenue climbed 59.1% to $9.3 million. Co.'s combined ratio improved to 94.3% from 96.2% a year earlier.

Prospects: Rate increases averaging more than 21.0% have already been approved for Co.'s motorcycle products and should be in place for the better part of the 2004 season. These increases, along with additional rate increases Co. is seeking, are expected to have a positive 19.0% impact on motorcycle earned premium and drive double–digit improvement in the combined ratio related to this business in 2004. Nevertheless, Co. does not expect this line to return to profitability in 2004. For full–year 2004, Co. expects net income, excluding capital gains or losses, in the range of $2.00 to $2.20 per share and near double–digit top–line growth.

Financial Data

(US$ in Thousands)	3 Mos	12/31/2003	12/31/2002	12/31/2001	12/31/2000	12/31/1999	12/31/1998	12/31/1997
Earnings Per Share	1.64	1.30	1.14	1.51	1.89	1.65	1.43	1.31
Tang. Book Val. Per Share	21.10	20.18	17.58	16.52	15.73	13.55	13.30	10.55
Dividends Per Share	0.190	0.180	0.170	0.150	0.140	0.130	0.120	0.110
Dividend Payout %	8.30	14.32	15.02	10.39	7.73	8.03	8.59	8.75
Income Statement								
Total Premium Income	181,133	652,128	584,342	515,408	464,904	407,784	377,986	314,378
Other Income	9,488	66,059	52,348	71,135	69,518	61,342	64,376	61,052
Total Revenues	190,621	718,187	636,690	586,543	534,422	469,126	442,362	375,430
Total Indirect Exp.	...	...	508	1,286	2,305	6,973	4,064	4,204
Inc. Before Inc. Taxes	24,441	30,232	25,741	36,704	50,669	43,713	37,527	34,703
Income Taxes	7,593	6,956	5,437	9,482	15,206	12,534	10,595	10,336
Income from Cont Ops	...	...	20,304	...	...	...	...	24,367
Net Income	16,848	23,276	18,841	27,222	35,463	31,179	26,932	17,550
Average Shs. Outstg.	18,644	17,937	17,789	17,990	18,758	18,926	18,824	18,582
Balance Sheet								
Cash & Cash Equivalents	878,386	2,386	5,975	11,286	8,391	10,098	3,687	5,277
Premiums Due	82,010	81,297	91,633	88,108	70,396	60,426	59,341	58,739
Invst. Assets: Total	873,723	846,322	739,758	704,009	692,657	610,859	598,870	513,608
Total Assets	1,212,033	1,179,505	1,090,674	1,053,942	993,850	888,057	837,220	760,463
Long–Term Obligations	61,831	62,217	47,163	48,619	40,025	44,288	54,563	62,518
Net Stockholders' Equity	395,449	356,058	308,908	291,876	283,177	258,002	248,832	197,026
Shares Outstanding	18,737	17,643	17,566	17,660	18,000	19,032	18,704	18,666
Statistical Record								
Return on Revenues %	8.83	3.24	3.18	4.64	6.63	6.64	6.08	6.49
Return on Equity %	4.26	6.53	6.57	9.32	12.52	12.08	10.82	12.36
Return on Assets %	1.39	1.97	1.86	2.58	3.56	3.51	3.21	3.20
Price Range	25.45-23.04	24.29-16.32	25.24-16.44	23.60-13.25	14.75-9.25	14.38-9.63	15.83-9.71	10.75-6.21
P/E Ratio	15.52-14.05	18.68-12.55	22.14-14.42	15.63-8.77	7.80-4.89	8.71-5.83	11.07-6.79	8.21-4.74
Average Yield %	0.78	0.87	0.82	0.81	1.13	1.07	0.94	1.32

Address: 7000 Midland Blvd., Amelia, OH 45102-2607	Officers: John P. Hayden III – Chmn., C.O.O., John W. Hayden – Pres., C.E.O.	Investor Contact:513–943–7100
Telephone: (513) 943–7100	Transfer Agents:National City Bank., Cleveland OH	Institutional Holding No of Institutions: 4
Web Site: www.midlandcompany.com		Shares: 4,474,168 % Held: –

MINE SAFETY APPLIANCES CO

Exchange	Symbol	Price	52Wk Range	Yield	P/E
ASE	MSA	$29.87 (5/28/2004)	32.85-13.12	1.34	20.46

*7 Year Price Score 199.9 *NYSE Composite Index=100 ***12 Month Price Score 59.0**

TRADING VOLUME (thousand shares)

Interim Earnings (Per Share)

Qtr.	Mar	Jun	Sep	Dec
2001	0.22	0.19	0.21	0.25
2002	0.21	0.25	0.15	0.23
2003	0.28	0.33	0.29	0.41
2004	0.43	...	...	...

Interim Dividends (Per Share)

Amt	Decl	Ex	Rec	Pay
1.46E	11/4/2003	11/12/2003	11/14/2003	11/24/2003
3-for-1	12/10/2003	1/29/2004	1/16/2004	1/28/2004
0.07Q	1/20/2004	2/18/2004	2/20/2004	3/10/2004
0.10Q	4/29/2004	5/19/2004	5/21/2004	6/10/2004

Indicated Div: $2.25

Valuation Analysis

Forecast P/E N/A

Market Cap $364.1 Million	Book Value	N/A
Price/Book N/A	Price/Sales	N/A

Dividend Achiever Status

Rank	165	10 Year Growth Rate	9.64%

Total Years of Dividend Growth 33

Business Summary: Apparel (MIC: 4.4 SIC: 2326 NAIC:423840)

Mine Safety Appliances manufactures and sells products designed to protect the safety and health of people throughout the world. Co.'s principal products include respiratory protective equipment; instruments that monitor and analyze workplace environments and control industrial processes; thermal imaging cameras; and personal protective products including head, eye and face, hearing protectors and fall protection equipment. Many of these products have wide applications, including manufacturing, municipal and volunteer fire departments, public utilities, mining, chemicals, petroleum, construction, transportation, the military and hazardous materials clean-up.

Recent Developments: For the quarter ended Mar 31 2004, net income was $16.1 million versus income of $10.5 million, before income from discontinued operations of $1.5 million, in the prior-year quarter. Net sales increased 21.3% to $194.5 million from $160.4 million the previous year. Sales were led by strong North American shipments of self-contained breathing apparatus (SCBA) and thermal imaging cameras to the fire service market. Sales also grew in the international segment, due mainly to growth in the Africa/Mideast and Latin America regions and, to a lesser extent, favorable foreign currency exchange. Local currency sales in Europe were flat during the quarter. Operating income grew 51.7% to $26.0 million.

Prospects: Going forward, demand should continue to be strong for Co.'s latest generation of SCBA which, in 2003, was the first to be certified for use by emergency responders in environments involving chemical, biological, radiological, and nuclear agents. Co. should also benefit from higher sales of advanced combat helmets for the military and related communication systems. Moreover, Co. is experiencing increasing demand for thermal imaging cameras, particularly its *Evolution®5000* TIC, which combines the functionality and durability required by the fire service with features and performance not found on other small format cameras.

Financial Data

(US$ in Thousands)	3 Mos	12/31/2003	12/31/2002	12/31/2001	12/31/2000	12/31/1999	12/31/1998	12/31/1997
Earnings Per Share	1.46	1.31	0.84	0.87	0.62	0.41	0.45	0.53
Cash Flow Per Share	0.27	1.08	1.33	0.85	1.41	1.01	0.53	0.75
Tang. Book Val. Per Share	7.40	7.02	6.62	5.95	6.28	6.18	6.07	5.93
Dividends Per Share	1.730	1.710	0.210	0.180	0.158	0.151	0.140	0.130
Dividend Payout %	93.35	131.04	25.58	20.68	25.17	36.26	32.43	25.83
Income Statement								
Total Revenues	195,276	698,197	566,697	545,666	502,833	498,051	497,207	499,409
Total Indirect Exp.	61,127	217,427	171,605	174,376	159,562	163,952	160,900	163,766
Depreciation & Amort.	5,820	23,208	21,525	26,471	24,557	23,356	22,398	21,516
Operating Income	25,999	73,759	48,083	52,886	34,050	23,185	28,208	36,239
Net Interest Inc./(Exp.)	(514)	(4,564)	(4,769)	(6,061)	(4,502)	(4,273)	(3,258)	(2,781)
Income Taxes	9,861	24,835	16,870	21,255	10,811	6,859	9,933	14,385
Income from Cont Ops	...	48,924	31,213	...	...	16,326	...	...
Net Income	16,138	65,267	35,077	31,631	23,239	15,134	18,275	21,854
Average Shs. Outstg.	37,949	37,264	36,885	36,237	37,068	39,015	40,023	40,941
Balance Sheet								
Cash & Cash Equivalents	73,917	73,244	36,477	26,992	26,541	17,108	24,020	19,921
Total Current Assets	341,188	323,242	282,944	217,686	201,153	203,090	229,209	219,613
Total Assets	663,428	643,885	579,765	520,698	489,683	451,741	456,716	406,404
Total Current Liabilities	119,667	114,715	99,700	82,500	86,978	80,005	110,006	103,240
Long-Term Obligations	59,717	59,915	64,350	67,381	71,806	36,550	11,919	12,270
Net Stockholders' Equity	321,878	307,858	289,062	253,504	226,465	242,457	242,846	241,449
Net Working Capital	221,521	208,527	183,244	135,186	114,175	123,085	119,203	116,373
Shares Outstanding	36,994	36,927	36,621	36,302	35,482	38,625	39,411	40,104
Statistical Record								
Operating Profit Margin %	12.70	10.39	7.67	8.36	5.96	3.93	4.95	6.69
Return on Equity %	4.64	15.49	9.21	9.61	8.46	5.25	6.05	7.88
Return on Assets %	2.25	7.41	4.59	4.68	3.91	2.82	3.21	4.68
Debt/Total Assets %	9.00	9.30	11.09	12.94	14.66	8.09	2.60	3.01
Price Range	31.67-23.00	28.33-10.18	16.80-9.22	17.07-7.58	8.67-6.28	8.32-5.61	9.67-6.44	8.17-5.92
P/E Ratio	21.69-15.75	21.63-7.77	20.00-10.97	19.62-8.72	13.98-10.13	20.29-13.69	21.48-14.32	15.41-11.16
Average Yield %	6.50	10.90	1.65	1.70	2.03	2.14	1.81	1.87

Address: 121 Gamma Drive, Pittsburgh, PA 15238 Telephone: (412) 967-3000 Web Site: www.msanet.com	Officers: John T. Ryan III - Chmn., C.E.O., J. H. Baillie - V.P., Pres., MSA Europe Transfer Agents:Wells Fargo Shareowner Services, South St.Paul, MN	Investor Contact:412-967-3000 Institutional Holding No of Institutions: 23 Shares: 264,664 % Held: -

MYERS INDUSTRIES INC.

Exchange	Symbol	Price	52Wk Range	Yield	P/E
NYS	MYE	$13.51 (5/28/2004)	14.11–9.40	1.48	22.90

*7 Year Price Score 102.9 *NYSE Composite Index=100 ***12 Month Price Score 53.3**

Interim Earnings (Per Share)

Qtr.	Mar	Jun	Sep	Dec
2001	0.27	0.10	0.05	0.09
2002	0.33	0.22	0.10	0.15
2003	0.24	0.11	0.05	0.14
2004	0.29	...	...	...

Interim Dividends (Per Share)

Amt	Decl	Ex	Rec	Pay
0.05Q	6/26/2003	9/3/2003	9/5/2003	10/1/2003
0.05Q	9/18/2003	12/10/2003	12/12/2003	1/2/2004
0.05Q	2/12/2004	3/3/2004	3/5/2004	4/1/2004
0.05Q	4/21/2004	6/9/2004	6/11/2004	7/1/2004

Indicated Div: $0.20 (Div. Reinv. Plan)

Valuation Analysis

Forecast P/E 15.39 (5/24/2004)
Market Cap $403.3 Million   Book Value 298.5 Million
Price/Book 1.24   Price/Sales 0.54

Dividend Achiever Status

Rank	128	10 Year Growth Rate	11.61%
Total Years of Dividend Growth			27

Business Summary: Plastics (MIC: 11.7 SIC: 3089 NAIC:326199)

Myers Industries designs, manufactures and markets plastic and rubber products, including plastic material handling containers and storage boxes to rubber OEM parts and tire repair materials. These products are made through a variety of molding processes in 25 facilities throughout North America and Europe. Co. also distributes tools, equipment, and supplies used for tire and wheel service and automotive underbody repair. Co.'s distribution operations are conducted through 40 branches located in major cities throughout the U.S. and in foreign countries through export and businesses in which Co. holds an equity interest.

Recent Developments: For the quarter ended Mar 31 2004, net income advanced 23.1% to $8.9 million compared with $7.2 million in the equivalent 2003 quarter. Net sales grew 13.7% to $185.5 million from $163.2 million a year earlier. The improvement in net sales was primarily attributed to favorable foreign currency translation and contributions from acquisitions. Gross profit increased to $61.1 million, or 32.9% as a percentage of net sales, versus $53.8 million, or 33.0% as a percentage of net sales, in 2003. Operating income advanced 23.3% to $17.2 million from $13.9 million in the corresponding period of the previous year.

Prospects: Co. is benefiting from an improving business climate as well as contributions from the recent acquisitions of Michigan Rubber Products and WEK Industries, which increased sales by approximately $4.4 million and net income by $267,000 for the quarter ended Mar 31 2004. Also, operating results reflect actions to advance internal growth and margin improvement and lower costs, which in turn is helping to offset the higher prices for plastic raw materials that continue to trend upward. Going forward, Co. plans to pursue new opportunities that are arising in the service niche of the automotive dealer market.

Financial Data
(US$ in Thousands)

	3 Mos	12/31/2003	12/31/2002	12/31/2001	12/31/2000	12/31/1999	12/31/1998	12/31/1997
Earnings Per Share	0.59	0.54	0.80	0.51	0.80	1.02	0.94	0.72
Cash Flow Per Share	0.46	1.69	2.18	2.58	2.25	1.88	1.38	1.17
Tang. Book Val. Per Share	1.17	2.24	1.62	0.89	0.56	0.27	5.34	5.05
Dividends Per Share	0.200	0.200	0.190	0.170	0.160	0.140	0.120	0.110
Dividend Payout %	33.90	37.03	24.25	34.94	20.14	14.42	13.37	15.40
Income Statement								
Total Revenues	185,519	661,092	607,991	607,950	652,660	580,761	392,020	339,626
Total Indirect Exp.	43,906	165,567	149,248	159,000	154,308	143,618	86,141	68,936
Depreciation & Amort.	9,819	36,555	35,714	43,905	42,828	37,542	17,518	13,214
Operating Income	17,152	34,721	52,171	45,939	63,270	69,507	49,373	38,313
Net Interest Inc./(Exp.)	(3,144)	(10,074)	(11,810)	(18,699)	(22,360)	(15,206)	(888)	(248)
Income Taxes	5,152	8,321	16,401	12,049	16,909	23,125	19,806	15,727
Net Income	8,856	16,326	23,960	15,191	24,001	31,176	28,679	22,339
Average Shs. Outstg.	30,205	30,125	29,971	29,752	29,828	30,502	30,454	30,731
Balance Sheet								
Cash & Cash Equivalents	9,442	5,667	1,702	7,075	2,178	1,094	34,832	6,298
Total Current Assets	237,557	207,933	201,140	196,619	219,307	206,991	153,650	107,427
Total Assets	700,381	621,627	602,482	582,166	624,797	600,410	306,708	224,078
Total Current Liabilities	108,367	94,175	117,936	104,899	115,583	102,244	51,234	39,644
Long–Term Obligations	268,705	211,003	212,223	247,145	284,273	280,104	48,832	4,261
Net Stockholders' Equity	298,482	294,524	255,690	217,526	213,903	207,747	202,689	176,677
Net Working Capital	129,190	113,758	83,771	91,719	103,724	104,747	102,417	67,783
Shares Outstanding	30,215	30,183	30,071	29,809	29,686	30,231	30,509	30,411
Statistical Record								
Operating Profit Margin %	9.24	5.25	8.58	7.55	9.69	11.96	12.59	11.28
Return on Equity %	2.96	5.54	9.37	6.98	11.22	15.00	14.14	12.64
Return on Assets %	1.26	2.62	3.97	2.60	3.84	5.19	9.35	9.96
Debt/Total Assets %	38.36	33.94	35.22	42.45	45.49	46.65	15.92	1.90
Price Range	12.85–11.07	13.26–8.80	14.48–9.36	11.45–8.36	10.55–7.09	18.03–8.60	17.24–9.99	11.27–8.47
P/E Ratio	21.78–18.76	24.56–16.30	18.10–11.70	22.46–16.40	13.18–8.86	17.68–8.43	18.34–10.63	15.65–11.76
Average Yield %	1.66	1.87	1.61	1.68	1.79	1.09	0.91	1.14

Address: 1293 South Main Street, Akron, OH 44301
Telephone: (330) 253–5592
Web Site: www.myersind.com

Officers: Stephen E. Myers – Chmn., C.E.O., Milton I. Wiskind – Vice-Chmn., Sec.
Transfer Agents: National City Bank, Cleveland, Ohio

Investor Contact: 330–253–5592
Institutional Holding
No of Institutions: 6
Shares: 1,255,496 **% Held:** –

NACCO INDUSTRIES INC.

Exchange	Symbol	Price	52Wk Range	Yield	P/E
NYS	NC	$88.74 (5/28/2004)	95.00-58.00	1.76	17.16

*7 Year Price Score 108.4 *NYSE Composite Index=100 ***12 Month Price Score 51.9**

Interim Earnings (Per Share)

Qtr.	Mar	Jun	Sep	Dec
2001	1.76	0.74	(3.36)	(3.38)
2002	0.77	0.34	0.98	3.96
2003	0.35	1.17	1.43	3.12
2004	(0.55)	...	...	...

Interim Dividends (Per Share)

Amt	Decl	Ex	Rec	Pay
0.38Q	8/13/2003	8/28/2003	9/2/2003	9/15/2003
0.38Q	11/12/2003	11/26/2003	12/1/2003	12/15/2003
0.38Q	2/11/2004	2/26/2004	3/1/2004	3/15/2004
0.39Q	5/12/2004	5/27/2004	6/1/2004	6/15/2004
		Indicated Div: $1.56		

Valuation Analysis

Forecast P/E N/A

Market Cap $583.5 Million	Book Value 638.4 Million
Price/Book 0.85	Price/Sales 0.22

Dividend Achiever Status

Rank	218	10 Year Growth Rate	6.76%
Total Years of Dividend Growth			20

Business Summary: Industrial Machinery and Equipment (MIC: 11.5 SIC: 3537 NAIC:333924)

NACCO Industries is a holding company with three principal businesses. NACCO Materials Handling Group (NMHG) designs, engineers, manufactures, sells, services and leases a full line of lift trucks and replacement parts marketed worldwide under the Hyster™ and Yale™ brand names. NACCO Housewares Group consists of Hamilton Beach/Procter–Silex, Inc., a manufacturer and marketer of small household appliances and commercial products for restaurants, bars and hotels, and The Kitchen Collection, Inc., a national specialty retailer of brand–name kitchenware and electrical appliances. The North American Coal Corporation mines and markets lignite coal primarily as fuel for power generators.

Recent Developments: For the first quarter ended Mar 31 2004, Co. reported a net loss of $4.5 million versus income of $2.9 million, before an accounting change gain of $1.2 million, in the corresponding prior–year quarter. Total revenues advanced 10.0% to $614.2 million. Material Handling group revenue jumped 12.4% to $470.8 million, primarily due to favorable currency translation, both sales of higher–priced lift trucks and increased parts sales in the Americas, and increased unit volumes in Europe. Housewares group revenues inched up 1.3% to $117.5 million, while North American Coal Corp. revenue increased 11.6% to $25.9 million. Comparisons were made with restated results for the previous year.

Prospects: In 2004, Co.'s Material Handling group continues to expect stronger lift truck markets in the Americas and Japan, strong growth in the China lift truck market and relatively flat lift truck markets in Europe and the rest of Asia–Pacific. Adverse currency movements and increasing materials costs are anticipated to continue to be a significant factor for the remainder of 2004. However, price increases implemented at the Material Handling group should help mitigate the effects of these items beginning in mid–2004. Longer–term, global lift truck markets are expected to gradually return to average pre–recession levels by 2007 to 2008.

Financial Data

(US$ in Thousands)	12/31/2003	12/31/2002	12/31/2001	12/31/2000	12/31/1999	12/31/1998	12/31/1997	12/31/1996
Earnings Per Share	6.07	6.05	(4.24)	4.63	6.66	12.53	7.55	5.66
Cash Flow Per Share	15.02	18.19	16.60	16.28	15.83	17.67	25.53	27.02
Tang. Book Val. Per Share	14.67	5.73	1.97	9.43	11.50	9.51	N.M	N.M
Dividends Per Share	1.260	0.970	0.930	0.890	0.850	0.810	0.770	0.740
Dividend Payout %	20.75	16.03	N.M.	19.22	12.76	6.46	10.23	13.11
Income Statement								
Total Revenues	2,472,600	2,285,000	2,637,900	2,871,300	2,602,800	2,536,200	2,246,900	2,273,200
Total Indirect Exp.	350,700	340,500	439,200	398,300	353,400	317,400	289,000	297,800
Depreciation & Amort.	68,400	70,200	15,900	15,700	15,200	14,700	15,800	15,400
Operating Income	117,200	115,500	5,700	117,900	131,300	198,100	132,000	131,200
Net Interest Inc./(Exp.)	(51,000)	(52,900)	(56,900)	(47,100)	(43,300)	(34,600)	(36,600)	(45,900)
Income Taxes	15,800	11,300	(9,900)	22,300	31,700	60,700	26,400	34,300
Income from Cont Ops	49,800	49,600	(34,700)	37,800	54,300	...	...	...
Net Income	52,800	42,400	(36,000)	67,700	53,100	102,300	61,800	50,600
Average Shs. Outstg.	8,204	8,198	8,190	8,167	8,154	8,166	8,189	8,931
Balance Sheet								
Cash & Cash Equivalents	68,900	57,800	71,900	33,700	36,200	34,700	24,100	47,800
Total Current Assets	812,900	739,500	770,000	815,700	772,200	703,200	599,600	591,800
Total Assets	1,839,800	1,780,800	2,161,900	2,193,900	2,013,000	1,898,300	1,729,100	1,708,100
Total Current Liabilities	589,800	545,500	874,300	650,200	583,100	548,600	506,500	416,000
Long–Term Obligations	363,200	416,100	519,400	732,700	615,500	569,600	558,200	674,800
Net Stockholders' Equity	637,000	559,400	529,300	606,400	562,200	518,300	425,100	379,300
Net Working Capital	223,100	194,000	(104,300)	165,500	189,100	154,600	93,100	175,800
Shares Outstanding	8,206	8,201	8,195	8,171	9,804	8,120	8,154	8,186
Operating Profit Margin %	4.73	5.05	0.21	4.10	5.04	7.81	5.87	5.77
Return on Equity %	7.81	8.86	N.M	6.23	9.65	19.73	14.53	13.34
Return on Assets %	2.70	2.78	N.M.	1.72	2.69	5.38	3.57	2.96
Debt/Total Assets %	19.74	23.36	24.02	33.39	30.57	30.00	32.28	39.50
Price Range	93.77-37.99	75.25-36.65	81.47-42.63	55.56-33.75	96.25-45.13	172.5-78.94	125.9-44.63	63.50-43.25
P/E Ratio	15.45-6.26	12.44-6.06	N/A	12.00-7.29	14.45-6.78	13.77-6.30	16.67-5.91	11.22-7.64
Average Yield %	2.01	1.79	1.47	2.09	1.17	0.69	1.05	1.39

Address: 5875 Landerbrook Drive, Mayfield Heights, OH 44124–4017 **Telephone:** (440) 449–9600 **Web Site:** www.naccoind.com	**Officers:** Alfred M. Rankin – Chmn., Pres., C.E.O., J. C. Butler – V.P., Corp. Devel., Treas. **Transfer Agents:**National City Bank, Cleveland, OH	**Investor Contact:** (440) 449–9676 **Institutional Holding** **No of Institutions:** 21 **Shares:** 1,819,161 **% Held:** –

NATIONAL CITY CORP

Exchange	Symbol	Price	52Wk Range	Yield	P/E
NYS	NCC	$35.49 (5/28/2004)	36.89-29.43	3.61	9.39

*7 Year Price Score 111.8 *NYSE Composite Index=100 *12 Month Price Score 49.0

Interim Earnings (Per Share)

Qtr.	Mar	Jun	Sep	Dec
2001	0.55	0.57	0.58	0.57
2002	0.73	0.63	0.61	0.62
2003	0.81	0.99	0.62	1.01
2004	1.16	...	...	...

Interim Dividends (Per Share)

Amt	Decl	Ex	Rec	Pay
0.32Q	7/1/2003	7/9/2003	7/11/2003	8/1/2003
0.32Q	10/1/2003	10/8/2003	10/13/2003	11/1/2003
0.32Q	1/2/2004	1/8/2004	1/12/2004	2/1/2004
0.32Q	4/1/2004	4/7/2004	4/12/2004	5/1/2004

Indicated Div: $1.28 (Div. Reinv. Plan)

Valuation Analysis

Forecast P/E N/A

Market Cap	$21.7 Billion	Book Value	9.9 Billion
Price/Book	2.19	Price/Sales	2.23

Dividend Achiever Status

Rank	178	10 Year Growth Rate	8.96%
Total Years of Dividend Growth		11	

TRADING VOLUME (thousand shares)

[Price chart 1995–2004]

Business Summary: Commercial Banking (MIC: 8.1 SIC: 6021 NAIC:522110)

National City is a financial holding company with total assets of $113.93 billion and total deposits of $63.93 billion as of Dec 31 2003. Co. operates through a distribution network in Ohio, Michigan, Pennsylvania, Indiana, Kentucky, and Illinois and conducts selected consumer lending businesses and other financial services nationwide. Co.'s businesses include commercial and retail banking, consumer finance, asset management, mortgage financing and servicing, and payment processing. Operations are primarily conducted through more than 1,100 branch banking offices located within Co.'s six-state footprint and over 330 retail mortgage offices located throughout the United States.

Recent Developments: For the quarter ended Mar 31 2004, net income increased 10.4% to $710.0 million from $643.0 million in the corresponding period the year before. Results for 2004 included a gain of $9.0 million on the securitization of automobile loans. Results for 2003 included severance and related charges of $72.0 million. Net interest income slid 6.9% to $1.03 billion from $1.10 billion a year earlier. Net interest margin slipped to 4.16% from 4.21% the prior year. Total fees and other income grew 1.4% to $1.12 billion from $1.10 billion the previous year. Total non-interest expense decreased 2.3% to $986.0 million from $1.01 billion a year earlier.

Prospects: Co. signed a definitive agreement to acquire Cincinnati, OH-based Provident Financial Group, a bank holding company that operates 65 branches in Southwestern Ohio and Northern Kentucky, 480 ATMs, on-line banking and TeleBank, a telephone customer service center. The transaction, which is expected to close in the second quarter of 2004, is valued at about $2.10 billion. Separately, on Apr 9 2004, Co. acquired Allegiant Bancorp in a transaction valued at about $500.0 million. As a result of the acquisition, Co. added 36 branch locations to its network of 1,100 retail offices located throughout the Midwest. Both acquisitions should position Co. well for further growth in 2004 and beyond.

Financial Data

(US$ in Thousands)	3 Mos	12/31/2003	12/31/2002	12/31/2001	12/31/2000	12/31/1999	12/31/1998	12/31/1997
Earnings Per Share	3.78	3.43	2.59	2.27	2.13	2.22	1.61	1.83
Tang. Book Val. Per Share	12.35	13.47	11.70	12.15	11.06	9.38	10.68	10.14
Dividends Per Share	1.260	1.250	1.200	1.160	1.140	1.060	0.940	0.830
Dividend Payout %	33.47	36.44	46.33	51.10	53.52	47.74	58.38	45.62
Income Statement								
Total Interest Income	1,343,938	5,997,822	5,915,920	6,414,752	6,566,583	5,912,609	5,756,677	3,776,140
Total Interest Expense	325,311	1,629,816	1,910,541	2,975,903	3,608,221	2,912,587	2,845,029	1,833,312
Net Interest Income	1,018,627	4,368,006	4,005,379	3,438,849	2,958,362	3,000,022	2,911,648	1,942,828
Provision for Loan Losses	82,507	638,418	681,918	605,295	286,795	249,674	201,400	139,660
Non-Interest Income	1,117,697	3,596,001	2,811,999	2,677,823	2,484,234	2,380,769	2,314,142	1,375,936
Non-Interest Expense	986,340	4,088,123	3,729,634	3,344,876	3,183,909	2,982,504	3,377,113	2,010,577
Income Before Taxes	1,067,477	3,237,466	2,405,826	2,166,501	1,971,892	2,148,613	1,647,277	1,168,527
Net Income	710,368	2,117,064	1,593,598	1,388,108	1,302,371	1,405,485	1,070,681	807,433
Average Shs. Outstg.	612,596	616,410	616,174	611,936	612,625	632,452	665,720	441,380
Balance Sheet								
Cash & Due from Banks	3,386,459	3,595,706	3,756,426	4,403,962	3,535,186	3,480,756	4,783,491	2,967,181
Securities Avail. for Sale	6,880,816	13,731,232	18,422,536	19,717,736	19,809,066	29,808,686	32,238,740	17,745,186
Net Loans & Leases	78,801,588	78,153,524	71,035,824	67,043,315	64,675,857	59,233,441	57,040,923	37,743,821
Total Assets	111,355,060	113,933,460	118,258,415	105,816,700	88,534,609	87,121,499	88,245,632	54,683,521
Total Deposits	67,213,234	63,930,020	65,118,768	63,129,932	55,256,422	50,066,310	58,246,909	36,861,136
Long-Term Obligations	19,372,323	23,666,292	22,550,295	17,136,232	17,964,800	14,858,014	9,009,448	4,810,417
Total Liabilities	101,500,949	104,604,789	109,950,403	98,435,477	81,764,788	81,393,766	81,232,724	50,402,170
Net Stockholders' Equity	9,854,111	9,328,671	8,308,012	7,381,223	6,769,821	5,727,733	7,012,908	4,281,351
Shares Outstanding	606,559	605,996	611,491	607,354	609,188	607,058	652,654	422,196
Statistical Record								
Return on Equity %	...	22.69	19.18	18.80	19.23	24.53	15.26	18.85
Return on Assets %	...	1.85	1.34	1.31	1.47	1.61	1.21	1.47
Equity/Assets %	8.84	8.18	7.02	6.97	7.64	6.57	7.94	7.82
Non-Int. Exp./Tot. Inc. %	40.06	42.61	42.73	36.78	35.17	35.96	41.84	39.02
Price Range	36.89-32.36	34.58-26.75	33.69-24.68	32.51-24.50	29.38-16.00	37.81-22.13	38.75-28.72	33.50-21.88
P/E Ratio	9.76-8.56	10.08-7.80	13.01-9.53	14.32-10.79	13.79-7.51	17.03-9.97	24.07-17.84	18.31-11.95
Average Yield %	3.61	4.03	4.06	4.06	5.53	3.40	2.79	3.03

Address: 1900 East Ninth Street, Cleveland, OH 44114-3484	Officers: David A. Daberko - Chmn., C.E.O., William E. MacDonald III - Vice-Chmn.	Investor Contact:800-622-4204
Telephone: (216) 222-2000	Transfer Agents:National City Bank, Corporate Trust Operations, Cleveland, OH	Institutional Holding No of Institutions: 38
Web Site: www.nationalcity.com		Shares: 1,107,727 % Held: -

NATIONAL COMMERCE FINANCIAL CORP.

Exchange	Symbol	Price	52Wk Range	Yield	P/E
NYS	NCF	$32.54 (5/28/2004)	32.54–21.80	2.46	21.41

*7 Year Price Score 117.7 ***NYSE Composite Index=100** ***12 Month Price Score 52.5**

TRADING VOLUME (thousand shares)

Interim Earnings (Per Share)

Qtr.	Mar	Jun	Sep	Dec
2001	0.25	0.27	0.28	0.29
2002	0.36	0.39	0.40	0.40
2003	0.31	0.35	0.42	0.31
2004	0.44	...	...	...

Interim Dividends (Per Share)

Amt	Decl	Ex	Rec	Pay
0.20Q	7/15/2003	9/10/2003	9/12/2003	10/1/2003
0.20Q	10/20/2003	12/3/2003	12/5/2003	1/2/2004
0.20Q	1/21/2004	3/3/2004	3/5/2004	4/1/2004
0.20Q	4/28/2004	6/2/2004	6/4/2004	7/1/2004

Indicated Div: $0.80 (Div. Reinv. Plan)

Valuation Analysis

Forecast P/E 17.59 (5/24/2004)

Market Cap	$6.7 Billion	Book Value	2.8 Billion
Price/Book	2.06	Price/Sales	3.83

Dividend Achiever Status

Rank	26	10 Year Growth Rate	21.65%
Total Years of Dividend Growth			29

Business Summary: Commercial Banking (MIC: 8.1 SIC: 6021 NAIC:522110)

National Commerce Financial is a bank holding company with assets of $23.02 billion as of Dec 31 2003. Co.'s primary banking subsidiary, National Bank of Commerce (NBC), provides commercial and retail banking, savings and trust services through 258 Central Carolina Bank offices located in North Carolina and South Carolina, 16 Wal–Mart Money Centers in Georgia and Tennessee, and 175 NBC offices located in Tennessee, Mississippi, Arkansas, Georgia, Virginia and West Virginia. Co. also owns a 49.0% interest in First Market Bank, FSB, which operates 30 offices in the Richmond, VA area. In addition to its banking subsidiaries, Co. operates several other non–banking financial businesses.

Recent Developments: For the three months ended Mar 31 2004, net income advanced 40.8% to $90.2 million from $64.1 million in the corresponding quarter a year earlier. Results for 2004 included a one–time gain of $45,000 from a branch sale, while results for 2003 included one–time charges of $19.8 million, primarily related to a litigation settlement. Net interest income rose 7.7% to $191.1 million from $177.4 million the previous year. Provision for loan losses was $12.1 million, down 57.3% versus $7.7 million in 2003. Total non–interest income climbed 14.7% to $119.9 million from $104.6 million the year before. Total non–interest expense increased 9.1% to $163.7 million from $180.1 million the prior year.

Prospects: Results should benefit from Co.'s aggressive branch expansion efforts. On Apr 23 2004, Co. announced that it has entered into an agreement with Wal–Mart Stores Inc. to add approximately 70 new National Bank of Commerce branches in Wal–Mart stores located in Florida and Georgia. The agreement will expand Co.'s operations in Florida with approximately 75.0% of the planned branches being located in Florida, primarily in Jacksonville, Orlando, and Tampa/St. Petersburg. The first branch under this agreement is expected to open in the third quarter of 2004, with the remainder to open throughout 2005.

Financial Data

(US$ in Thousands)	3 Mos	12/31/2003	12/31/2002	12/31/2001	12/31/2000	12/31/1999	12/31/1998	12/31/1997
Earnings Per Share	1.52	1.39	1.55	1.09	0.57	0.99	0.83	0.69
Tang. Book Val. Per Share	7.60	7.42	6.66	6.13	6.47	5.61	4.51	4.11
Dividends Per Share	0.740	0.710	0.620	0.540	0.440	0.360	0.290	0.220
Dividend Payout %	44.85	51.07	40.00	49.54	78.07	36.36	34.93	31.88
Income Statement								
Total Interest Income	260,527	1,054,136	1,130,497	1,222,865	1,250,478	468,028	383,587	336,993
Total Interest Expense	69,456	314,626	396,891	571,752	664,737	231,490	190,969	174,172
Net Interest Income	191,071	739,510	733,606	651,113	585,741	236,538	192,618	162,821
Provision for Loan Losses	12,088	48,414	32,344	29,199	20,892	15,206	9,599	17,013
Non–Interest Income	108,739	337,270	296,947	250,247	214,319	74,422	64,233	69,370
Non–Interest Expense	163,726	724,439	618,228	588,118	627,897	155,258	140,304	123,460
Eqty Earns/Minority Int.	1,285	4,530	3,447	...	...	...	...	...
Income from Cont Ops	...	286,765	...	...	...	...	...	...
Net Income	90,244	311,674	323,610	225,296	117,474	107,234	85,141	69,780
Average Shs. Outstg.	207,082	206,368	208,144	207,484	207,496	108,823	102,884	101,368
Balance Sheet								
Cash & Due from Banks	458,494	558,313	517,295	561,429	446,712	179,082	224,875	206,191
Securities Avail. for Sale	5,115,759	5,238,429	4,777,009	3,611,706	2,401,526	553,928	721,268	408,083
Net Loans & Leases	13,245,183	13,079,628	12,760,516	11,818,364	10,889,638	3,926,192	3,148,551	2,565,670
Total Assets	23,038,522	23,016,916	21,472,116	19,273,713	16,553,514	6,806,173	5,811,054	4,692,011
Total Deposits	15,790,968	15,549,587	14,494,734	12,619,479	11,982,283	4,495,900	3,947,275	3,251,242
Long–Term Obligations	2,155,866	2,579,187	2,403,181	2,588,572	1,696,472	720,707	737,982	546,136
Total Liabilities	20,239,583	20,235,730	18,789,684	16,818,382	15,225,038	6,198,886	5,352,609	4,289,979
Net Stockholders' Equity	2,798,939	2,781,186	2,682,432	2,455,331	1,278,554	557,378	408,549	352,148
Shares Outstanding	203,911	205,136	205,408	205,058	205,246	108,223	101,443	97,703
Return on Equity %	3.17	9.82	11.93	9.17	8.84	17.65	18.57	17.35
Return on Assets %	0.38	1.18	1.49	1.16	0.70	1.57	1.46	1.48
Equity/Assets %	12.14	12.08	12.49	12.73	8.02	8.92	7.88	8.56
Non–Int. Exp./Tot. Inc. %	43.18	48.45	40.72	37.99	41.91	27.69	29.95	29.43
Price Range	29.20–26.08	28.15–19.42	29.25–21.35	27.70–21.85	24.94–15.31	26.12–17.75	26.37–13.88	17.82–8.94
P/E Ratio	19.21–17.16	20.25–13.97	18.87–13.77	25.41–20.05	43.75–26.86	26.38–17.93	31.77–16.72	25.82–12.95
Average Yield %	2.64	2.93	2.39	2.19	2.30	1.59	1.48	1.79

Address: One Commerce Square, Memphis, TN 38150	Officers: Eugene J. nald – Chmn., William R. Reed – Pres., C.E.O.	Institutional Holding
Telephone: (901) 523–3434	Transfer Agents:Bank of New York, New York, NY	No of Institutions: 30
Web Site: www.ncbccorp.com		Shares: 1,665,555 % Held: –

NATIONAL FUEL GAS CO. (NJ)

Exchange	Symbol	Price	52Wk Range	Yield	P/E
NYS	NFG	$25.15 (5/28/2004)	27.17–21.86	4.29	10.79

*7 Year Price Score 102.7   *NYSE Composite Index=100   *12 Month Price Score 47.8

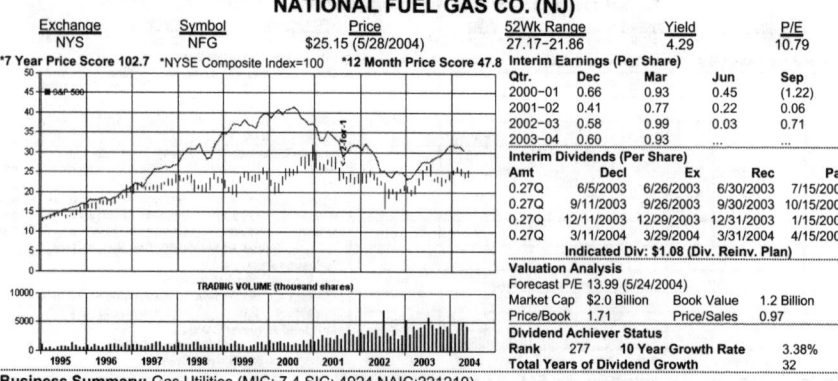

Interim Earnings (Per Share)

Qtr.	Dec	Mar	Jun	Sep
2000–01	0.66	0.93	0.45	(1.22)
2001–02	0.41	0.77	0.22	0.06
2002–03	0.58	0.99	0.03	0.71
2003–04	0.60	0.93	...	...

Interim Dividends (Per Share)

Amt	Decl	Ex	Rec	Pay
0.27Q	6/5/2003	6/26/2003	6/30/2003	7/15/2003
0.27Q	9/11/2003	9/26/2003	9/30/2003	10/15/2003
0.27Q	12/11/2003	12/29/2003	12/31/2003	1/15/2004
0.27Q	3/11/2004	3/29/2004	3/31/2004	4/15/2004

Indicated Div: $1.08 (Div. Reinv. Plan)

Valuation Analysis

Forecast P/E 13.99 (5/24/2004)

Market Cap $2.0 Billion	Book Value 1.2 Billion
Price/Book 1.71	Price/Sales 0.97

Dividend Achiever Status

Rank	277	10 Year Growth Rate	3.38%

Total Years of Dividend Growth 32

Business Summary: Gas Utilities (MIC: 7.4 SIC: 4924 NAIC:221210)

National Fuel Gas is a diversified energy holding company. Through its subsidiaries, Co. ioperates in six business segments. The Utility segment operations are carried out by National Fuel Gas Distribution Corporation, sells natural gas to approximately 733,000 customers in western New York and northwestern Pennsylvania. Other business segments include the Exploration and Production segment, the Energy Marketing segment, the International segment, the Pipeline and Storage segment, and the Timber segment. As of Sep 30, 2003, proved developed reserves for crude oil and natural gas were 45,142 thousand barrels and 223,345 million cubic feet, respectively.

Recent Developments: For the quarter ended Mar 31 2004, net income was $77.1 million compared with $80.5 million in the same period a year earlier. Results for 2004 included after–tax expenses of $6.4 million associated with the settlement of a pension obligation and a $4.6 million after–tax gain related to Co.'s September 2003 sale of Canadian oil properties. Operating revenues slipped to $801.7 million from $809.1 million in 2003. Co. attributed the lower results to several factors, including lower margins and higher operating costs from its Utility segment, lower throughput in the Energy Marketing segment, and lower harvesting activity in the Timber segment. Operating income fell 5.2% to $148.6 million.

Prospects: Co.'s Exploration and Production segment has increased its production hedge position. Currently, 8.8 billion cubic feet (Bcf) of its expected remaining 2004 gas production is hedged at an average price of $4.92 per million cubic feet (Mcf), and 1.3 million barrels of remaining 2004 oil production is hedged at an average price of $26.60 per barrel. For 2005, 12.9 Bcf of natural gas production is hedged at an average price of $5.72 per Mcf, while 2.2 million barrels of oil production is hedged at an average price of $28.68 per barrel. Meanwhile, due to higher oil and gas prices, Co. raised its full–year fiscal 2004 earnings guidance to $1.75 to $1.85 per share from $1.65 to $1.75 per share.

Financial Data

(US$ in Thousands)	6 Mos	3 Mos	09/30/2003	09/30/2002	09/30/2001	09/30/2000	09/30/1999	09/30/1998
Earnings Per Share	2.27	2.33	2.31	1.46	0.82	1.60	1.47	0.42
Cash Flow Per Share	3.47	1.22	4.01	4.29	5.15	3.00	3.48	3.26
Tang. Book Val. Per Share	14.29	13.76	13.28	12.44	12.62	12.55	12.09	11.38
Dividends Per Share	1.070	1.060	1.050	1.010	0.970	0.930	0.900	0.870
Dividend Payout %	47.13	45.49	45.45	69.69	118.59	58.41	61.52	208.92
Income Statement								
Total Revenues	1,334,191	532,513	2,035,471	1,464,496	2,100,352	1,425,277	1,263,274	1,248,000
Total Indirect Exp.	128,158	64,680	99,874	252,823	439,425	221,048	220,836	340,693
Costs & Expenses	1,089,818	436,696	1,621,055	1,232,506	1,941,622	1,207,009	1,071,266	1,164,069
Depreciation & Amort.	94,416	46,458	195,226	180,668	174,914	142,170	129,690	118,880
Operating Income	244,373	95,817	414,416	231,990	158,730	218,268	192,008	83,931
Net Interest Inc./(Exp.)	(48,007)	(25,333)	(104,521)	(120,595)	(107,145)	(100,085)	(87,698)	(85,284)
Income Taxes	69,540	21,567	128,161	72,034	37,106	77,068	64,829	24,024
Eqty Earns/Minority Int.	(3,575)	(1,734)	(785)	(730)	(1,342)	(1,384)	(1,616)	(2,213)
Income from Cont Ops	...	...	187,836	...	...	...	...	32,304
Net Income	126,269	49,214	178,944	117,682	65,499	127,207	115,037	23,188
Average Shs. Outstg.	82,612	82,307	81,357	80,534	80,361	79,166	78,084	77,406
Balance Sheet								
Net Property	3,011,367	3,020,513	2,999,087	2,844,745	2,780,713	2,683,391	2,353,894	2,248,137
Total Assets	3,846,621	3,840,027	3,727,915	3,401,309	3,445,566	3,236,888	2,842,586	2,684,459
Long–Term Obligations	1,140,218	1,144,094	1,147,779	1,145,341	1,046,694	953,622	822,743	692,669
Net Stockholders' Equity	1,224,514	1,178,564	1,137,390	1,006,858	1,002,655	987,437	939,293	875,555
Shares Outstanding	81,931	81,652	81,438	80,264	79,406	78,659	77,674	76,938
Statistical Record								
Operating Profit Margin %	18.31	17.99	25.77	20.75	9.32	20.72	20.33	8.65
Net Inc./Net Property %	4.19	1.62	5.96	4.13	2.35	4.74	4.88	1.03
Net Inc./Tot. Capital %	5.34	1.76	6.52	4.63	2.71	5.55	5.57	1.25
Return on Equity %	10.31	4.17	26.21	18.84	10.23	20.68	19.14	6.43
Accum. Depr./Gross Prop. %	36.80	36.27	35.60	36.96	34.93	29.93	30.43	29.45
Price Range	26.39–21.86	24.72–21.86	27.17–18.33	25.37–15.97	32.06–22.12	28.97–19.84	24.94–18.94	24.41–19.97
P/E Ratio	11.63– 9.63	10.61– 9.38	11.76–7.94	17.38–10.94	39.10–26.98	18.11–12.40	16.96–12.88	58.11–47.54
Average Yield %	4.41	4.55	4.68	4.48	3.62	3.86	3.94	3.87

Address: 6363 Main Street, Williamsville, NY 14221 Telephone: (716) 857–7000 Web Site: www.nationalfuelgas.com	Officers: Philip C. Ackerman – Chmn., Pres., C.E.O., Joseph P. Pawlowski – Treas. Transfer Agents:Computershare Investor Services, LLC Chicago, IL	Investor Contact:716–857–6987 Institutional Holding No of Institutions: 201 Shares: 36,489,525 % Held: 45%

188

NATIONAL PENN BANCSHARES, INC.

Exchange	Symbol	Price	52Wk Range	Yield	P/E
NMS	NPBC	$28.53 (5/28/2004)	34.28-25.76	3.36	15.68

*7 Year Price Score 136.6   *NYSE Composite Index=100   ***12 Month Price Score 45.1**

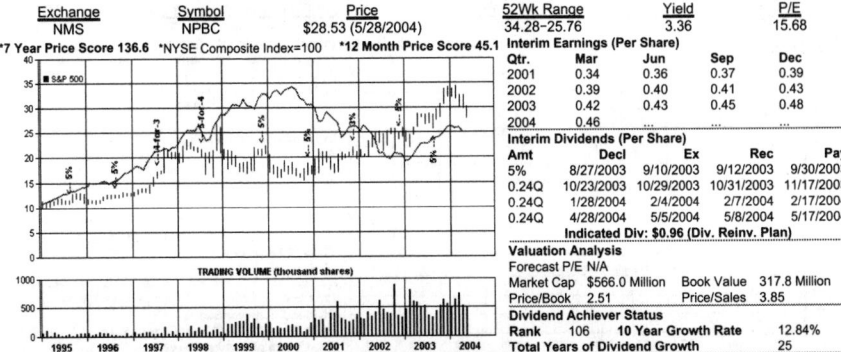

Interim Earnings (Per Share)

Qtr.	Mar	Jun	Sep	Dec
2001	0.34	0.36	0.37	0.39
2002	0.39	0.40	0.41	0.43
2003	0.42	0.43	0.45	0.48
2004	0.46	...	...	...

Interim Dividends (Per Share)

Amt	Decl	Ex	Rec	Pay
5%	8/27/2003	9/10/2003	9/12/2003	9/30/2003
0.24Q	10/23/2003	10/29/2003	10/31/2003	11/17/2003
0.24Q	1/28/2004	2/4/2004	2/7/2004	2/17/2004
0.24Q	4/28/2004	5/5/2004	5/8/2004	5/17/2004

Indicated Div: $0.96 (Div. Reinv. Plan)

Valuation Analysis

Forecast P/E N/A

Market Cap	$566.0 Million	Book Value	317.8 Million
Price/Book	2.51	Price/Sales	3.85

Dividend Achiever Status

Rank	106	10 Year Growth Rate	12.84%
Total Years of Dividend Growth			25

Business Summary: Commercial Banking (MIC: 8.1 SIC: 6021 NAIC:522110)

National Penn Bancshares, with total assets of $3.51 billion as of Dec 31 2003, is a bank holding company. As of Dec 31 2003, Co. operated 66 community offices throughout nine counties in southeastern Pennsylvania through National Penn Bank. Trust and investment management services are provided through Investors Trust Company; brokerage services are provided through Penn Securities, Inc.; mortgage banking activities are provided through Penn 1st Financial Services, Inc.; leasing products are offered through National Penn Leasing Company; and insurance products are provided through FirstService Insurance Agency, Inc.

Recent Developments: For the three months ended Mar 31 2004, net income was $11.4 million compared with income of $9.8 million in the corresponding year–earlier period. Results for 2003 excluded net income of $632,000 from discontinued operations. Net interest income increased 15.6% to $31.4 million from $27.2 million the previous year. Provision for loan losses amounted to $1.8 million versus $2.3 million in 2003. Total noninterest income advanced 17.6% to $10.8 million from $9.2 million the year before. Total noninterest income results reflect the addition of FirstService Insurance, which was acquired in February 2003, increased service charges on deposit accounts, and higher other service charges and fees.

Prospects: Co.'s near–term outlook appears promising. For instance, Co.'s results going forward should benefit from its December 2003 acquisition and subsequent swift systems conversion of HomeTowne Heritage Bank. Also, Co.'s pending acquisition of Peoples First, Inc., which is expected to be completed during the second quarter of 2004, will expand Co.'s presence in southern Chester County with eight additional offices. Meanwhile, Co. expects continued solid growth from its FirstService Insurance Agency, Inc. non–banking subsidiary. Moreover, Co. continues to actively pursue opportunities to acquire additional agencies within the nine–county National Penn market.

Financial Data

(US$ in Thousands)	12/31/2003	12/31/2002	12/31/2001	12/31/2000	12/31/1999	12/31/1998	12/31/1997	12/31/1996
Earnings Per Share	1.78	1.63	1.46	1.37	1.26	1.21	1.09	1.01
Tang. Book Val. Per Share	8.50	10.23	8.90	8.35	7.33	7.91	7.40	6.88
Dividends Per Share	0.890	0.800	0.740	0.670	0.630	0.570	0.490	0.420
Dividend Payout %	50.40	49.28	50.94	49.44	49.75	47.63	45.54	41.58
Income Statement								
Total Interest Income	165,648	173,010	188,497	184,652	164,270	131,910	119,027	106,558
Total Interest Expense	51,099	63,446	92,512	99,702	82,753	67,002	54,620	46,018
Net Interest Income	114,549	109,564	95,985	84,950	81,517	64,908	64,407	60,540
Provision for Loan Losses	9,371	14,000	9,000	5,600	5,960	5,100	4,575	3,900
Non–Interest Income	35,607	33,632	29,609	24,532	22,029	16,948	11,645	8,280
Non–Interest Expense	103,033	89,831	80,723	70,777	65,724	51,283	46,147	41,258
Income from Cont Ops	34,733	...	...	...	...	...	...	...
Net Income	43,354	36,234	32,734	29,237	27,409	20,483	18,616	16,922
Average Shs. Outstg.	24,411	22,102	22,295	21,334	21,551	16,895	17,061	16,638
Balance Sheet								
Cash & Due from Banks	96,164	83,831	101,796	80,859	62,953	46,574	40,009	40,194
Securities Avail. for Sale	934,375	733,774	658,581	593,316	516,027	421,738	321,760	236,814
Net Loans & Leases	2,192,092	1,842,987	1,814,162	1,683,198	1,536,404	1,220,673	1,097,662	1,028,334
Total Assets	3,512,576	2,858,262	2,727,482	2,512,508	2,242,432	1,811,594	1,534,378	1,358,013
Total Deposits	2,435,296	2,112,640	2,076,795	1,814,253	1,593,254	1,208,061	1,115,600	980,808
Long–Term Obligations	164,037	169,703	139,974	146,432	223,077	248,478	155,460	76,110
Total Liabilities	3,194,761	2,635,902	2,531,800	2,335,080	2,094,736	1,681,138	1,411,190	1,243,292
Net Stockholders' Equity	317,813	222,360	195,682	177,428	147,696	130,456	123,188	114,721
Shares Outstanding	24,284	21,734	21,969	21,224	20,141	16,485	16,631	16,657
Return on Equity %	10.92	16.29	16.72	16.47	18.55	15.70	15.11	14.75
Return on Assets %	0.98	1.26	1.20	1.16	1.22	1.13	1.21	1.24
Non–Int. Exp./Tot. Inc. %	49.79	42.20	36.19	33.41	35.03	34.43	35.19	35.67
Price Range	34.20-22.13	26.01-19.95	22.02-16.62	21.07-15.52	22.43-16.97	26.76-16.22	21.97-12.52	13.18-10.84
P/E Ratio	19.21-12.43	15.96-12.24	15.08-11.38	15.38-11.33	17.81-13.47	22.11-13.41	20.15-11.49	13.05-10.73
Average Yield %	3.19	3.43	3.78	3.84	3.23	2.69	3.00	3.52

Address: Philadelphia and Reading Avenues, Boyertown, PA 19512 **Telephone:** (610) 367–6001 **Web Site:** www.nationalpennbancshares.com	**Officers:** Wayne R. Weidner – Chmn., C.E.O., Glenn E. Moyer – Pres. **Transfer Agents:** Mellon Investor Services, L.L.C., Ridgefield Park, NJ	**Investor Contact:** 610–369–6291 **Institutional Holding** **No of Institutions:** 29 **Shares:** 1,603,181 **% Held:** –

NATIONAL SECURITY GROUP, INC

Exchange	Symbol	Price	52Wk Range	Yield	P/E
NMS	NSEC	$22.30 (5/28/2004)	26.00-13.49	3.77	12.53

*7 Year Price Score 137.5   *NYSE Composite Index=100   ***12 Month Price Score 55.6**

Interim Earnings (Per Share)

Qtr.	Mar	Jun	Sep	Dec
2001	0.27	0.41	0.37	0.62
2002	0.14	0.04	0.07	0.12
2003	0.31	0.54	0.37	0.44
2004	0.43	...	...	...

Interim Dividends (Per Share)

Amt	Decl	Ex	Rec	Pay
0.205Q	7/19/2003	7/30/2003	8/1/2003	8/29/2003
0.21Q	10/16/2003	10/30/2003	11/3/2003	11/28/2003
0.21Q	1/17/2004	1/29/2004	2/2/2004	2/27/2004
0.21Q	4/15/2004	4/29/2004	5/3/2004	5/31/2004

Indicated Div: $0.84

Valuation Analysis

Forecast P/E N/A

Market Cap	$55.0 Million	Book Value	47.0 Million
Price/Book	1.21	Price/Sales	0.96

Dividend Achiever Status

Rank	222	10 Year Growth Rate	6.65%
Total Years of Dividend Growth			13

Business Summary: Insurance (MIC: 8.2 SIC: 6311 NAIC:524113)

National Security Group is an insurance holding company that, through its subsidiaries, writes primarily dwelling fire and windstorm, homeowners, mobile homeowners, and personal non–standard automobile lines of insurance. Co., through its life insurance subsidiary, offers a basic line of life, and health and accident insurance products. Property–casualty insurance is Co.'s most significant segment. Co.'s property–casualty insurance is conducted through National Security Fire & Casualty Company, a wholly–owned subsidiary of Co., and Omega One Insurance Company, a wholly–owned subsidiary of National Security Fire & Casualty Company.

Recent Developments: For the three months ended Mar 31 2004, net income advanced 36.8% to $1.1 million compared with $770,000 in the corresponding year–earlier period. Total revenues climbed 36.6% to $16.0 million from $11.7 million the previous year. Net insurance premiums earned increased 39.0% to $13.8 million, due primarily to a 43.8% jump in property and casualty earned premium revenue to $12.2 million. Co.'s Property and Casualty business benefited from a number of developments, including increased marketing efforts, modernization of product lines including increases in policy limits, decreased competition in several markets, and rate increases implemented in several states.

Prospects: Co.'s results are being driven by strong growth from its property and casualty insurance operations. For instance, Co. stated that its property/casualty subsidiaries have sustained significant growth rates in excess of 40.0% over the prior two years. Going forward, Co. expects the rate of growth to moderate to more sustainable levels over the next year with total property and casualty premium revenue expecte to increase in the range of 25.0% to 30.0% for 2004. Also, Co. expects its core lines of business to settle into a sustainable growth rate of between 10.0% and 20.0%, subject to market conditions.

Financial Data

(US$ in Thousands)	3 Mos	12/31/2003	12/31/2002	12/31/2001	12/31/2000	12/31/1999	12/31/1998	12/31/1997
Earnings Per Share	1.78	1.66	0.37	1.67	1.53	1.52	0.35	1.06
Tang. Book Val. Per Share	19.05	18.59	17.09	18.19	17.74	16.97	17.05	16.69
Dividends Per Share	0.830	0.820	0.800	0.750	0.700	0.670	0.640	0.580
Dividend Payout %	46.63	49.39	217.57	44.91	45.75	44.08	182.86	54.72
Income Statement								
Total Premium Income	13,795	47,536	32,631	25,357	22,921	25,936	28,451	31,156
Other Income	2,157	6,948	6,454	7,426	6,754	6,690	8,853	7,619
Total Revenues	15,952	54,484	39,085	32,783	29,675	32,626	37,304	38,775
Total Indirect Exp.	713	12,444	8,939	7,331	5,282	5,752	6,814	7,080
Inc. Before Inc. Taxes	1,577	5,669	1,194	5,470	4,844	4,516	1,106	3,360
Income Taxes	475	1,550	422	1,392	1,068	760	176	362
Eqty Earns/Minority Int.	(49)	(29)	136	52	...	...	...	...
Income from Cont Ops	1,102	...	...	...	...	...	...	...
Net Income	1,053	4,090	908	4,130	3,776	3,756	930	2,998
Average Shs. Outstg.	2,466	2,466	2,466	2,466	2,466	2,466	2,674	2,780
Balance Sheet								
Cash & Cash Equivalents	765	21,514	62,499	59,243	52,602	50,995	52,018	53,183
Premiums Due	5,047	5,331	5,607	4,762	4,558	5,517	7,987	9,722
Invst. Assets: Total	98,057	96,827	83,569	82,399	82,092	82,080	83,671	84,459
Total Assets	128,242	114,802	101,602	99,484	97,563	98,105	103,973	106,958
Long–Term Obligations	10,838	3,059	3,380	2,108	2,401	2,672	3,004	...
Net Stockholders' Equity	46,997	45,872	42,159	44,884	43,780	41,888	41,968	46,352
Shares Outstanding	2,466	2,466	2,466	2,466	2,466	2,466	2,461	2,775
Statistical Record								
Return on Revenues %	6.90	7.50	2.32	12.59	12.72	11.51	2.49	7.73
Return on Equity %	2.34	8.91	2.15	9.20	8.62	8.96	2.21	6.46
Return on Assets %	0.85	3.56	0.89	4.15	3.87	3.82	0.89	2.80
Price Range	26.00-19.03	20.00-12.57	15.80-13.00	15.62-10.89	15.83-9.17	12.08-8.12	17.71-8.75	19.17-10.62
P/E Ratio	14.61-10.69	12.05-7.57	42.70-35.14	9.36-6.52	10.35-5.99	7.95-5.35	50.60-25.00	18.08-10.02
Average Yield %	3.62	5.23	5.51	6.03	5.95	6.49	4.70	4.35

Address: 661 East Davis Street, Elba, AL 36323	**Officers:** W. L. Brunson – Pres., C.E.O., Brian R. McLeod – C.F.O., Treas.	**Investor Contact:** 334–897–2273 **Institutional Holding**
Telephone: (334) 897–2273	**Transfer Agents:** The National Security Group, Inc., Elba, AL	**No of Institutions:** 4
Web Site: www.nationalsecuritygroup.com		**Shares:** 86,508 **% Held:**

NICOR INC.

Exchange	Symbol	Price
NYS	GAS	$33.28 (5/28/2004)

7 Year Price Score 93.0   **NYSE Composite Index=100**   **12 Month Price Score 45.1**

52Wk Range	Yield	P/E
39.10-32.21	5.59	18.70

Interim Earnings (Per Share)

Qtr.	Mar	Jun	Sep	Dec
2001	0.85	0.59	0.73	1.00
2002	0.90	0.46	0.68	0.84
2003	1.14	0.54	0.01	0.79
2004	0.44	...	...	...

Interim Dividends (Per Share)

Amt	Decl	Ex	Rec	Pay
0.465Q	7/17/2003	9/26/2003	9/30/2003	11/1/2003
0.465Q	11/20/2003	12/29/2003	12/31/2003	2/1/2004
0.465Q	3/18/2004	3/29/2004	3/31/2004	5/1/2004
0.465Q	6/18/2004	6/28/2004	6/30/2004	8/1/2004

Indicated Div: $2.24 (Div. Reinv. Plan)

Valuation Analysis

Forecast P/E 15.26 (5/24/2004)

Market Cap $1.5 Billion	Book Value 754.6 Million
Price/Book 2.04	Price/Sales 0.59

Dividend Achiever Status

Rank 264	10 Year Growth Rate	4.37%

Total Years of Dividend Growth 16

Business Summary: Gas Utilities (MIC: 7.4 SIC: 4924 NAIC:221210)

NICOR is engaged in the purchase, storage, distribution, transportation, sale, and gathering of natural gas. Co.'s natural gas unit, Northern Illinois Gas, is the largest gas distribution company in Illinois and one of the biggest in the nation. As of Dec 31 2003, Northern Illinois served more than 2.0 million customers in the northern third of the state, generally outside of Chicago. Co. also owns Tropical Shipping Co., a transporter of containerized freight in the Bahamas and Caribbean. Co.'s shipments consist primarily of southbound cargo such as food, building materials and other necessities for developers, manufacturers and residents, as well as tourist–related shipments.

Recent Developments: For the three months ended Mar 31 2004, net income was $19.6 million compared with income of $50.4 million, before an accounting change charge of $4.5 million, in the corresponding quarter of the previous year. Results for 2004 and 2003 included pre–tax mercury–related recoveries of $100,000 and $300,000, respectively. Results for 2004 included a pre–tax litigation charge of $38.5 million. Operating revenues decreased 4.7% to $1.12 billion from $1.17 billion in the year–earlier period. The decrease in revenues was primarily attributable to lower results in Co.'s gas distribution segment. Operating income fell 57.8% to $34.3 million versus $81.3 million in the prior–year quarter.

Prospects: Co.'s gas distribution segment results are being hampered by higher operating costs. Co. expect these unfavorable pressures to continue to negatively affect this segment for the remainder of 2004. Meanwhile, Co. expects both the shipping segment and its other energy–related businesses to benefit from increased volumes shipped and improved results in the wholesale natural gas marketing business. Going forward, Co. estimates diluted earning to range from $1.58 to $1.78 per share, excluding one–time adjustments and assuming normal weather throughout the remainder of the year.

Financial Data

(US$ in Thousands)	3 Mos	12/31/2003	12/31/2002	12/31/2001	12/31/2000	12/31/1999	12/31/1998	12/31/1997
Earnings Per Share	1.79	2.48	2.88	3.17	1.00	2.62	2.42	2.61
Cash Flow Per Share	9.92	(0.28)	6.05	10.86	4.97	4.33	7.65	4.29
Tang. Book Val. Per Share	17.12	17.13	16.55	16.38	15.55	16.79	15.97	15.43
Dividends Per Share	1.860	1.850	1.820	1.730	1.630	1.540	1.460	1.370
Dividend Payout %	104.49	74.79	63.19	54.73	163.50	58.77	60.33	52.49
Income Statement								
Total Revenues	1,115,700	2,662,700	1,897,400	2,544,100	2,298,100	1,615,200	1,465,100	1,992,600
Total Indirect Exp.	176,600	577,900	526,100	266,100	413,300	244,900	235,800	258,300
Costs & Expenses	1,081,400	2,473,300	1,670,900	2,300,600	2,204,000	1,403,200	1,256,500	1,762,800
Depreciation & Amort.	37,300	143,500	137,600	148,800	144,300	140,300	136,500	131,200
Operating Income	34,300	189,400	226,500	243,500	94,100	212,000	208,600	229,800
Net Interest Inc./(Exp.)	(10,800)	(35,400)	(38,500)	(44,900)	(48,600)	(45,100)	(46,600)	(46,200)
Income Taxes	5,100	59,600	57,600	73,400	14,400	65,700	61,100	69,000
Eqty Earns/Minority Int.	1,200	15,300	(5,800)	...	...	...	...	...
Income from Cont Ops	...	109,800	...	...	...	...	...	...
Net Income	19,600	105,300	128,000	143,700	46,700	124,400	116,400	127,900
Average Shs. Outstg.	44,200	44,200	44,300	45,200	46,300	47,400	48,100	48,900
Balance Sheet								
Net Property	2,486,700	2,484,200	1,796,800	1,768,600	1,729,600	1,735,200	1,731,800	1,735,800
Total Assets	3,608,500	3,797,200	2,899,400	2,574,800	2,885,400	2,451,800	2,364,600	2,394,600
Long–Term Obligations	494,900	495,100	396,200	446,400	347,100	436,100	557,300	550,200
Net Stockholders' Equity	752,800	754,600	728,400	727,600	707,800	787,700	759,000	744,100
Shares Outstanding	44,057	44,040	44,011	44,397	45,491	46,890	47,514	48,217
Statistical Record								
Operating Profit Margin %	7.43	7.12	12.15	9.57	4.09	13.12	14.23	11.53
Net Inc./Net Property %	0.78	4.23	7.12	8.12	2.70	7.16	6.72	7.36
Net Inc./Tot. Capital %	1.05	5.65	8.11	9.12	3.26	7.91	7.09	8.00
Return on Equity %	9.05	14.60	18.13	19.74	6.59	15.79	15.33	17.18
Accum. Depr./Gross Prop. %	38.20	37.88	53.60	52.62	51.64	50.18	48.76	46.88
Price Range	37.31-32.50	39.10-23.85	48.96-22.75	41.66-34.12	43.56-29.81	42.88-31.31	44.00-37.25	42.56-31.25
P/E Ratio	20.96-18.26	15.77-9.62	17.00-7.90	13.14-10.76	43.56-29.81	16.36-11.95	18.18-15.39	16.31-11.97
Average Yield %	5.36	5.55	4.84	4.51	4.66	4.11	3.59	3.79

Address: 1844 Ferry Road, Naperville, IL 60563–9600	Officers: Thomas L. Fisher – Chmn., C.E.O., Russ M. Strobel – Pres.	Institutional Holding
Telephone: (630) 305–9500	Transfer Agents:ComputerShare Investor Services., Chicago, IL	No of Institutions: 7
Web Site: www.nicor.com		Shares: 71,790 % Held: –

NORDSON CORP.

Exchange	Symbol	Price	52Wk Range	Yield	P/E
NMS	NDSN	$37.85 (5/28/2004)	38.25-22.69	1.64	27.43

*7 Year Price Score 114.6 *NYSE Composite Index=100 *12 Month Price Score 53.6

Interim Earnings (Per Share)

Qtr.	Jan	Apr	Jul	Oct
2000-01	0.23	0.27	0.17	0.07
2001-02	0.17	0.23	0.21	0.05
2002-03	0.15	0.24	0.26	0.39
2003-04	0.27	0.46	...	...

Interim Dividends (Per Share)

Amt	Decl	Ex	Rec	Pay
0.155Q	8/6/2003	8/27/2003	8/29/2003	9/16/2003
0.155Q	11/5/2003	12/11/2003	12/15/2003	1/6/2004
0.155Q	2/4/2004	2/18/2004	2/20/2004	3/9/2004
0.155Q	5/19/2004	6/2/2004	6/4/2004	6/22/2004

Indicated Div: $0.62 (Div. Reinv. Plan)

Valuation Analysis

Forecast P/E 22.49 (5/24/2004)
Market Cap $1.3 Billion   Book Value 339.8 Million
Price/Book N/A   Price/Sales N/A

Dividend Achiever Status

Rank	164	10 Year Growth Rate	9.69%
Total Years of Dividend Growth		23	

Business Summary: Industrial Machinery and Equipment (MIC: 11.5 SIC: 3569 NAIC:333999)

Nordson designs, manufactures and markets precision dispensing systems that apply adhesives, sealants and coatings to a range of consumer and industrial products during manufacturing operations, helping customers meet quality, productivity and environmental targets. Co. also manufactures technology–based systems for curing and surface treatment processes. Co. products are used in a diverse range of industries, including appliance, automotive, bookbinding, container, converting, electronics, food and beverage, furniture, medical, metal finishing, nonwovens, packaging, semiconductor and other diverse industries.

Recent Developments: For the quarter ended May 2 2004, net income surged to $16.7 million from $8.1 million in the corresponding period of the prior year. Results for 2003 included severance and restructuring costs of $1.4 million. Net sales rose 18.0% to $196.6 million, reflecting volume gains and favorable currency effects due to the weaker U.S. dollar. On a segment basis, adhesive dispensing and nonwoven fiber systems sales grew 11.1% to $121.8 million. Advanced technology systems sales advanced 48.7% to $45.7 million. Coating and finishing systems sales rose 10.6% to $29.1 million. On a geographic basis, North America sales improved 1.2% to $64.4 million, while sales in Europe climbed 21.4% to $73.9 million.

Prospects: Co. should continue to benefit from the high pace of business activity in its advanced technology segment, a favorable currency environment, efficient cost controls, strong market positions in Asia, and an increase in new orders. Backlog at the end of the second quarter of fiscal 2004 was $103.0 million, up $36.0 million from the beginning of the year. Separately, on Apr 1 2004, Co. acquired the assets of W. Puffe Technologie, a manufacturer of hot melt adhesive dispensing systems for the textile, aerospace, life science, and automotive industries. The acquisition will expand Co.'s existing technology base in adhesive dispensing systems while providing access to new European markets.

Financial Data

(US$ in Thousands)	3 Mos	11/02/2003	11/03/2002	10/28/2001	10/29/2000	10/31/1999	11/01/1998	11/02/1997
Earnings Per Share	1.16	1.04	0.66	0.74	1.67	1.42	0.62	1.42
Cash Flow Per Share	0.66	2.58	3.87	2.22	2.59	2.46	2.10	1.51
Tang. Book Val. Per Share	N.M	N.M	N.M	N.M	4.72	2.44	3.89	4.75
Dividends Per Share	0.610	0.600	0.570	0.560	0.520	0.480	0.440	0.400
Dividend Payout %	52.59	58.17	86.36	75.67	31.13	33.80	70.40	28.07
Income Statement								
Total Revenues	170,640	667,347	647,756	731,416	740,568	700,465	660,900	636,710
Total Indirect Exp.	74,733	297,185	284,195	334,750	316,519	305,250	312,158	286,226
Depreciation & Amort.	7,060	29,240	29,487	16,052	30,325	29,300	25,003	25,307
Operating Income	18,140	68,596	53,019	59,537	91,452	76,985	45,071	74,059
Net Interest Inc./(Exp.)	(3,989)	(18,063)	(21,713)	(29,489)	(11,665)	(10,244)	(9,647)	(7,763)
Income Taxes	4,760	17,317	10,872	13,106	28,776	23,932	18,102	21,778
Net Income	9,664	35,160	22,072	24,610	54,632	47,506	20,825	49,967
Average Shs. Outstg.	35,632	33,899	33,690	33,050	32,767	33,048	33,322	35,106
Balance Sheet								
Cash & Cash Equivalents	16,902	6,945	5,872	7,881	785	16,030	6,820	1,477
Total Current Assets	284,066	277,370	274,573	362,177	369,238	341,316	328,476	318,815
Total Assets	771,050	766,806	764,472	862,453	610,040	591,790	538,944	502,996
Total Current Liabilities	173,126	211,662	252,647	355,653	253,008	251,940	207,082	179,663
Long–Term Obligations	172,683	176,725	174,895	191,773	60,800	65,975	70,444	66,502
Net Stockholders' Equity	339,797	300,109	268,890	263,726	247,223	221,398	214,775	220,545
Net Working Capital	110,940	65,708	21,926	6,524	116,230	89,376	121,394	139,152
Shares Outstanding	35,231	34,035	33,613	33,137	32,449	49,012	33,480	33,678
Statistical Record								
Operating Profit Margin %	10.63	10.27	8.18	8.13	12.34	10.99	6.81	11.63
Return on Equity %	2.84	11.71	8.20	9.33	22.09	21.45	9.69	22.65
Return on Assets %	1.25	4.58	2.88	2.85	8.95	8.02	3.86	9.93
Debt/Total Assets %	22.39	23.04	22.87	22.23	9.96	11.14	13.07	13.22
Price Range	37.73-28.23	28.11-20.72	33.32-21.45	31.75-21.14	32.56-18.09	32.38-22.13	26.75-21.31	32.13-23.75
P/E Ratio	32.53-24.34	27.03-19.92	50.48-32.50	42.91-28.57	19.50-10.83	22.80-15.58	43.15-34.38	22.62-16.73
Average Yield %	1.80	2.40	2.17	2.10	2.10	1.77	1.83	1.41

Address: 28601 Clemens Road, Westlake, OH 44145–4551 Telephone: (440) 892–1580 Web Site: www.nordson.com	Officers: Edward P. Campbell – Chmn., C.E.O., Peter S. Hellman – Pres., C.F.O., Chief Admin. Officer Transfer Agents:National City Bank, Cleveland, OH	Investor Contact:440–414–5344 Institutional Holding No of Institutions: 12 Shares: 487,942 % Held: –

NORTHERN TRUST CORP.

Exchange	Symbol	Price	52Wk Range	Yield	P/E
NMS	NTRS	$42.95 (5/28/2004)	50.76-38.00	1.77	21.05

*7 Year Price Score 91.4   *NYSE Composite Index=100   *12 Month Price Score 44.1

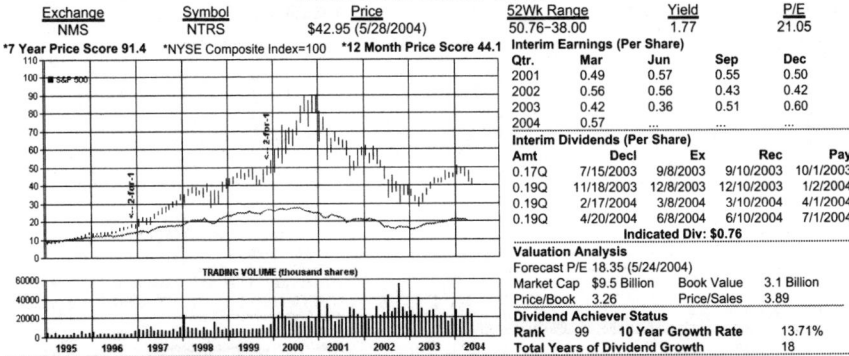

Interim Earnings (Per Share)

Qtr.	Mar	Jun	Sep	Dec
2001	0.49	0.57	0.55	0.50
2002	0.56	0.56	0.43	0.42
2003	0.42	0.36	0.51	0.60
2004	0.57	...	...	...

Interim Dividends (Per Share)

Amt	Decl	Ex	Rec	Pay
0.17Q	7/15/2003	9/8/2003	9/10/2003	10/1/2003
0.19Q	11/18/2003	12/8/2003	12/10/2003	1/2/2004
0.19Q	2/17/2004	3/8/2004	3/10/2004	4/1/2004
0.19Q	4/20/2004	6/8/2004	6/10/2004	7/1/2004

Indicated Div: $0.76

Valuation Analysis

Forecast P/E 18.35 (5/24/2004)

Market Cap	$9.5 Billion	Book Value	3.1 Billion
Price/Book	3.26	Price/Sales	3.89

Dividend Achiever Status

Rank	99	10 Year Growth Rate	13.71%
Total Years of Dividend Growth			18

Business Summary: Commercial Banking (MIC: 8.1 SIC: 6022 NAIC:522110)

Northern Trust is a multibank holding company. Co.'s principal subsidiary is The Northern Trust Company, an Illinois banking corporation. Co. also owns national bank subsidiaries in Arizona, California, Colorado, Florida and Texas; a federal savings bank with offices in ten states; trust companies in New York and Connecticut; and various other nonbank subsidiaries. Co. offers financial services including fiduciary, banking, investment and financial consulting services for individuals as well as credit operating, trust and investment management services for corporations. Total assets for Co. were $41.45 billion as of Dec 31 2003.

Recent Developments: For the quarter ended Mar 31 2004, income from continuing operations totaled $127.2 million versus income of $96.6 million in 2003. Results excluded a gain of $300,000 in 2004 and a loss of $1.9 million in 2003 from discontinued operations. Net interest income slipped 1.2% to $151.7 million. Net interest margin slid to 1.73% from 1.87%, primarily due to a decline in the yield of the residential mortgage loan portfolio attributed to the prior year refinancing activity. Provision for credit losses amounted to $5.0 million versus a recovery of credit losses of $5.0 million in 2003. Total non-interest income grew 19.9% to $426.5 million. Total non-interest expense rose 8.0% to $377.5 million.

Prospects: Co.'s strong performance continues to be driven by record trust fees, increased foreign exchange trading profits and continued improvement in credit quality. Additionally, assets under administration as of Mar 31 2004 rose 44.0% to $2.30 trillion, while assets under management increased 43.0% to $521.00 billion, both reaching record levels. Meanwhile, Co. continues to implement strategic initiatives aimed at reducing operating costs and positioning Co. for improved profitability. For instance, Co. continues to eliminate positions. As of Mar 31 2004, Co.'s staffing level was 7.9% lower compared with Mar 31 2003.

Financial Data (US$ in Thousands)	3 Mos	12/31/2003	12/31/2002	12/31/2001	12/31/2000	12/31/1999	12/31/1998	12/31/1997
Earnings Per Share	2.04	1.89	1.97	2.11	2.08	1.74	1.52	1.33
Tang. Book Val. Per Share	14.14	13.88	13.04	11.97	10.53	9.24	8.18	7.26
Dividends Per Share	0.700	0.700	0.685	0.635	0.560	0.495	0.435	0.375
Dividend Payout %	34.31	37.03	34.51	30.09	26.92	28.48	28.62	28.20
Income Statement								
Total Interest Income	254,400	1,055,700	1,238,300	1,681,500	2,011,100	1,568,600	1,503,100	1,332,800
Total Interest Expense	115,900	507,500	636,500	1,086,200	1,442,500	1,049,800	1,025,900	894,600
Net Interest Income	138,500	548,200	601,800	595,300	568,600	518,800	477,200	438,200
Provision for Loan Losses	(5,000)	2,500	37,500	66,500	24,000	12,500	9,000	9,000
Non-Interest Income	426,500	1,524,400	1,536,800	1,580,000	1,537,000	1,235,200	1,071,600	934,500
Non-Interest Expense	377,500	1,456,800	1,432,100	1,376,900	1,351,500	1,125,000	997,100	891,800
Income Before Taxes	192,500	631,100	669,000	731,900	730,100	616,500	542,700	471,900
Income from Cont Ops	127,200	423,300	...	...	...	...	...	...
Net Income	127,500	404,800	447,100	487,500	485,100	405,000	353,900	309,400
Average Shs. Outstg.	224,384	224,067	225,834	228,971	230,613	229,874	229,734	229,322
Balance Sheet								
Cash & Due from Banks	1,417,400	1,595,900	2,672,200	2,592,300	2,287,800	1,977,900	2,366,000	1,738,900
Securities Avail. for Sale	7,547,500	8,422,400	5,681,200	5,648,600	6,477,800	5,480,000	5,375,200	3,733,000
Net Loans & Leases	17,073,600	17,664,600	17,902,600	17,818,300	17,981,700	15,223,600	13,500,100	12,440,600
Total Assets	40,178,900	41,450,200	39,478,200	39,664,500	36,022,300	28,708,200	27,870,000	25,315,100
Total Deposits	28,447,600	26,270,000	26,062,100	25,019,300	22,827,900	21,371,000	18,202,700	16,360,000
Long-Term Obligations	1,490,700	1,490,900	1,483,600	1,484,500	1,405,700	1,426,900	1,425,600	1,491,900
Total Liabilities	37,060,500	38,394,900	36,478,400	36,891,000	33,560,100	26,533,500	25,929,700	23,576,400
Net Stockholders' Equity	3,118,400	3,055,300	2,999,800	2,773,500	2,462,200	2,174,700	1,940,300	1,739,000
Shares Outstanding	220,388	220,118	220,800	221,647	222,232	222,161	222,430	222,734
Statistical Record								
Return on Equity %	4.07	13.27	14.90	17.57	19.70	18.62	18.23	17.79
Return on Assets %	0.31	0.97	1.13	1.22	1.34	1.41	1.26	1.22
Equity/Assets %	7.76	7.37	7.59	6.99	6.83	7.57	6.96	6.86
Non-Int. Exp./Tot. Inc. %	55.44	56.46	51.60	42.21	38.09	40.12	38.72	39.33
Price Range	50.76-45.21	48.02-28.27	62.02-30.74	81.30-45.25	90.19-47.19	53.83-40.44	43.81-27.88	35.19-17.38
P/E Ratio	24.88-22.16	25.41-14.96	31.48-15.60	38.53-21.45	43.36-22.69	30.94-23.24	28.82-18.34	26.46-13.06
Average Yield %	1.46	1.72	1.47	0.99	0.76	1.06	1.15	1.41

Address: 50 South La Salle Street, Chicago, IL 60675	Officers: William A. Osborn - Chmn., C.E.O., Pres., Perry R. Pero - Vice-Chmn., Corp. Risk Management	Investor Contact:312-444-7811
Telephone: (312) 630-6000		**Institutional Holding** No of Institutions: 10
Web Site: www.northerntrust.com	**Transfer Agents:**Wells Fargo Shareowner Services, St. Paul, MN	Shares: 1,138,485 % Held: -

NUCOR CORP.

Exchange	Symbol	Price	52Wk Range	Yield	P/E
NYS	NUE	$65.85 (5/28/2004)	67.00–45.59	1.28	32.92

*7 Year Price Score 110.9   *NYSE Composite Index=100   *12 Month Price Score 53.5

Interim Earnings (Per Share)

Qtr.	Mar	Jun	Sep	Dec
2001	0.42	1.92	0.26	(1.15)
2002	0.26	0.76	0.50	0.55
2003	0.23	0.11	0.20	0.26
2004	1.43	...	...	...

Interim Dividends (Per Share)

Amt	Decl	Ex	Rec	Pay
0.20Q	9/3/2003	9/26/2003	9/30/2003	11/11/2003
0.20Q	12/3/2003	12/29/2003	12/31/2003	2/11/2004
0.21Q	2/25/2004	3/29/2004	3/31/2004	5/11/2004
0.20Q	6/2/2004	6/28/2004	6/30/2004	8/11/2004

Indicated Div: $0.84 (Div. Reinv. Plan)

Valuation Analysis

Forecast P/E 8.80 (5/24/2004)

Market Cap	$5.1 Billion	Book Value	2.5 Billion
Price/Book	2.01	Price/Sales	0.70

Dividend Achiever Status

Rank	45	10 Year Growth Rate	17.69%
Total Years of Dividend Growth			31

TRADING VOLUME (thousand shares)

1995 1996 1997 1998 1999 2000 2001 2002 2003 2004

Business Summary: Metal Works (MIC: 11.3 SIC: 3312 NAIC:331111)

Nucor is engaged in the manufacture and sale of steel and steel products. Co.'s principal products from the steel mills segment are hot–and cold–rolled steel, while the steel products segment produces steel joists and joist girders, steel deck, cold finished steel, steel fasteners, metal building systems and light gauge steel framing. Steel joists and hoist girders, and steel deck are sold to general contractors and fabricators domestically. Cold finished steel and steel fasteners are sold primarily to distributors and manufacturers, and hot–rolled steel and cold–rolled steel are sold primarily to steel services centers, fabricators and manufacturers in the U.S.

Recent Developments: For the thirteen weeks ended Apr 3 2004, net income grew to $113.2 million compared with $17.8 million in the corresponding period of the prior year. The improvement in earnings was primarily attributed to improved product demand, higher base prices, the implementation of a raw material surcharge to address higher scrap costs and the turnaround at Co.'s two newest mills, the sheet mill in Decatur, AL and the plate mill in Hertford County, NC. Net sales advanced 54.5% to $2.29 billion from $1.48 billion a year earlier. Average sales price per ton increased 33.0% year over year, while total tons shipped to outside customers increased 16.0% from the first quarter of 2003.

Prospects: The surcharges that were imposed on Co.'s customers to offset its rising raw material costs are decreasing on scrap steel in the second quarter as scrap prices decline. However, Co. plans to raise its base price for flat–rolled steel in June 2004 due to solid demand for its products. This increase should help offset the planned cut in surcharges. Meanwhile, Co. anticipates that improving economic conditions and strengthening steel demand will result in increased margins in the second quarter of 2004. Consequently, Co. expects second quarter of 2004 earnings in the range of $2.00 and $2.20 per share versus $0.11 per share in the second quarter of 2003.

Financial Data

(US$ in Thousands)	3 Mos	12/31/2003	12/31/2002	12/31/2001	12/31/2000	12/31/1999	12/31/1998	12/31/1997
Earnings Per Share	2.00	0.80	2.07	1.45	3.80	2.80	3.00	3.35
Cash Flow Per Share	2.54	6.30	6.35	6.36	10.01	6.92	7.30	6.56
Tang. Book Val. Per Share	31.09	29.80	29.71	28.32	27.46	25.92	23.72	21.32
Dividends Per Share	0.800	0.790	0.740	0.660	0.580	0.510	0.460	0.380
Dividend Payout %	40.00	98.75	35.74	45.51	15.26	18.21	15.33	11.34
Income Statement								
Total Revenues	2,286,416	6,265,823	4,801,777	4,139,249	4,586,146	4,009,346	4,151,232	4,184,498
Total Indirect Exp.	98,329	165,369	175,588	138,559	183,176	154,774	147,973	145,410
Depreciation & Amort.	96,298	364,112	307,101	289,063	259,365	256,637	253,119	218,764
Operating Income	176,784	103,907	293,911	180,386	477,492	374,094	411,476	460,147
Net Interest Inc./(Exp.)	(6,662)	(24,627)	(14,286)	(6,525)	816	5,095	3,832	35
Income Taxes	63,546	4,096	67,973	60,900	167,400	134,600	151,600	165,700
Eqty Earns/Minority Int.	10,798	...	...	...	...	...	...	...
Net Income	113,238	62,781	162,080	112,961	310,908	244,589	263,709	294,482
Average Shs. Outstg.	79,186	78,416	78,249	77,783	81,777	87,287	87,878	87,922
Balance Sheet								
Cash & Cash Equivalents	397,914	350,332	219,005	462,349	490,576	572,185	308,696	283,381
Total Current Assets	1,948,341	1,620,560	1,424,139	1,373,666	1,381,447	1,538,509	1,129,467	1,125,508
Total Assets	4,829,068	4,492,353	4,381,001	3,759,348	3,721,788	3,729,848	3,226,546	2,984,383
Total Current Liabilities	893,907	629,595	591,536	484,159	558,068	531,031	486,897	524,454
Long–Term Obligations	903,550	903,550	878,550	460,450	460,450	390,450	215,450	167,950
Net Stockholders' Equity	2,454,506	2,342,078	2,322,989	2,201,460	2,130,952	2,262,248	2,072,552	1,876,426
Net Working Capital	1,054,434	990,965	832,603	889,507	823,378	1,007,478	642,570	601,055
Shares Outstanding	78,931	78,590	78,180	77,707	77,582	87,247	87,352	87,996
Statistical Record								
Operating Profit Margin %	7.98	1.65	6.12	4.35	10.41	9.33	9.91	10.99
Net Profit Margin %	10.76	1.13	6.20	5.67	14.07	12.81	13.65	14.95
Return on Equity %	4.84	2.68	6.97	5.13	14.59	10.81	12.72	15.69
Return on Assets %	2.46	1.39	3.69	3.00	8.35	6.55	8.17	9.86
Debt/Total Assets %	18.71	20.11	20.05	12.24	12.37	10.46	6.67	5.62
Price Range	65.48–53.34	57.90–35.98	69.15–37.90	56.00–34.50	55.94–30.00	60.69–41.81	60.06–35.94	63.31–45.25
P/E Ratio	32.74–26.67	72.38–44.97	33.41–18.31	38.62–23.79	14.72–7.89	21.67–14.93	20.02–11.98	18.60–13.51
Average Yield %	1.36	1.68	1.37	1.43	1.43	1.04	0.98	0.71

Address: 2100 Rexford Road, Charlotte, NC 28211	Officers: Peter C. Browning – Chmn., Daniel R. DiMicco – Vice–Chmn., Pres., C.E.O.	Investor Contact:704–366–7000
Telephone: (704) 366 7000	Transfer Agents:American Stock Transfer &Trust Company, New York, NY	Institutional Holding
Web Site: www.nucor.com		No of Institutions: 27
		Shares: 216,632 % Held: –

NUVEEN INVESTMENTS INC

Exchange	Symbol	Price	52Wk Range	Yield	P/E
NYS	JNC	$26.24 (5/28/2004)	30.30–23.89	2.74	16.61

*7 Year Price Score 145.9 *NYSE Composite Index=100 *12 Month Price Score 43.8

Interim Earnings (Per Share)

Qtr.	Mar	Jun	Sep	Dec
2001	0.27	0.28	0.28	0.30
2002	0.30	0.31	0.33	0.35
2003	0.34	0.36	0.39	0.41
2004	0.42	...	...	...

Interim Dividends (Per Share)

Amt	Decl	Ex	Rec	Pay
0.15Q	8/7/2003	8/28/2003	9/2/2003	9/15/2003
0.15Q	11/7/2003	11/26/2003	12/1/2003	12/15/2003
0.15Q	2/5/2004	2/26/2004	3/1/2004	3/15/2004
0.18Q	5/14/2004	5/27/2004	6/1/2004	6/15/2004

Indicated Div: $0.72

Valuation Analysis

Forecast P/E 16.25 (5/24/2004)

Market Cap $2.4 Billion Book Value 464.0 Million

Price/Book 1.10 Price/Sales 1.13

Dividend Achiever Status

Rank	130	10 Year Growth Rate	11.61%
Total Years of Dividend Growth	11		

Business Summary: Finance Intermediaries &Services (MIC: 8.7 SIC: 6211 NAIC:523110)

Nuveen Investments is engaged in asset management and related research, as well as the development, marketing and distribution of investment products and services primarily targeted at affluent, high net–worth individuals and institutional markets. As of Dec 31 2003, total assets under management was approximately $95.36 billion. Co. distributes closed–end exchange–traded funds, mutual funds and defined portfolios through unaffiliated intermediary firms, including broker/dealers, commercial banks, affiliates of insurance providers, financial planners, accountants, consultants and investment advisors. The St. Paul Companies, Inc. owned about 79.0% of Co.'s common stock as of Mar 15 2004.

Recent Developments: For the three months ended Mar 31 2004, net income climbed 22.6% to $40.0 million from $32.6 million a year earlier. Total operating revenues advanced 17.9% to $119.7 million from $101.5 million the previous year. Investment advisory fees from assets under management rose 18.0% to $112.4 million, while performance fees/other revenue grew 4.1% to $4.9 million. Product distribution revenues jumped 53.2% to $2.4 million. Operating income increased 20.0% to $65.2 million from $54.3 million the year before. As of Mar 31 2004, total assets under management were $100.92 billion, up 24.0% versus $81.36 billion at Mar 31 2003.

Prospects: Results are being positively affected by Co.'s efforts to diversify its assets under management beyond its traditional municipal bond offerings and into growth and value stocks, as well as preferred securities, convertible bonds, REITs, senior loans and other investments. This asset base broadening should help boost long–term returns through improved portfolio diversification. Meanwhile, Co. is enjoying strong sales of both equity and fixed income products and positive net flows into its managed accounts, closed–end exchange–traded funds, and mutual funds due to the recent strength in the equity markets.

Financial Data

(US$ in Thousands)	12/31/2003	12/31/2002	12/31/2001	12/31/2000	12/31/1999	12/31/1998	12/31/1997	12/31/1996
Earnings Per Share	1.50	1.29	1.13	1.04	0.95	0.81	0.71	0.65
Cash Flow Per Share	2.18	2.24	2.04	1.16	1.27	1.25	1.55	1.58
Tang. Book Val. Per Share	N.M	N.M	0.0083	2.40	1.58	1.07	0.66	2.73
Dividends Per Share	0.560	0.500	0.460	0.400	0.370	0.320	0.290	0.260
Dividend Payout %	37.33	38.75	41.29	38.85	39.64	40.32	41.31	39.59
Income Statement								
Total Revenues	452,028	396,447	371,103	358,393	338,760	307,535	268,927	232,452
Total Indirect Exp.	211,569	184,602	182,348	190,275	188,689	172,395	150,443	117,275
Depreciation & Amort.	5,208	3,803	9,409	8,005	14,298	14,093	10,865	6,708
Operating Income	240,459	211,845	188,755	168,118	150,071	137,737	122,170	117,502
Net Interest Inc./(Exp.)	(7,435)	(4,892)	(3,798)	(3,025)	(2,994)	...	...	...
Income Taxes	91,292	80,675	74,856	70,700	63,701	54,092	47,990	44,973
Net Income	143,996	126,185	114,698	106,666	97,310	83,645	74,180	72,529
Average Shs. Outstg.	95,944	98,042	101,688	101,979	102,429	103,281	104,706	110,667
Balance Sheet								
Cash & Cash Equivalents	161,584	70,480	83,659	72,351	27,422	77,894	106,476	178,183
Total Current Assets	226,659	138,375	149,999	199,778	150,772	124,731	147,193	213,745
Total Assets	954,393	841,042	696,611	576,039	540,965	467,961	492,232	355,251
Total Current Liabilities	33,242	...	739	4,172	296	17,413	84,500	...
Long–Term Obligations	302,113	305,000	183,000	...	...	...	...	...
Net Stockholders' Equity	463,953	385,763	400,640	388,828	301,062	259,108	228,120	271,894
Net Working Capital	193,417	138,375	149,260	195,606	150,476	107,318	62,693	213,745
Shares Outstanding	92,506	92,726	95,142	93,941	93,189	94,068	95,347	99,357
Statistical Record								
Operating Profit Margin %	53.19	53.43	50.86	46.90	44.30	44.78	45.42	50.54
Net Profit Margin %	72.24	72.52	71.24	69.21	66.33	62.37	63.27	69.89
Return on Equity %	31.03	32.71	28.62	27.43	32.32	32.28	32.51	26.67
Return on Assets %	15.08	15.00	16.46	18.51	17.98	17.87	15.07	20.41
Debt/Total Assets %	31.65	36.26	26.27	...	...	...	...	...
Price Range	30.30–19.99	30.79–20.18	26.87–16.83	19.17–11.19	14.46–11.50	13.83–10.52	12.58–8.79	9.50–7.96
P/E Ratio	20.20–13.33	23.86–15.64	23.77–14.90	18.43–10.76	15.22–12.11	17.08–12.99	17.72–12.38	14.62–12.24
Average Yield %	2.18	1.93	2.23	2.82	2.83	2.65	2.76	3.04

Address: 333 West Wacker Drive, Chicago, IL 60606	Officers: Timothy R. Schwertfeger – Chmn., C.E.O., John P. Amboian – Pres.	Institutional Holding
Telephone: (312) 917–7700	Transfer Agents:The Bank of New York, New York, NY	No of Institutions: 97
Web Site: www.nuveen.com		Shares: 13,046,264 % Held: 14

OLD NATIONAL BANCORP

Exchange	Symbol	Price	52Wk Range	Yield	P/E
NYS	ONB	$24.53 (5/28/2004)	24.53-20.48	3.10	25.82

*7 Year Price Score 94.9   ***NYSE Composite Index=100**   ***12 Month Price Score 51.0**

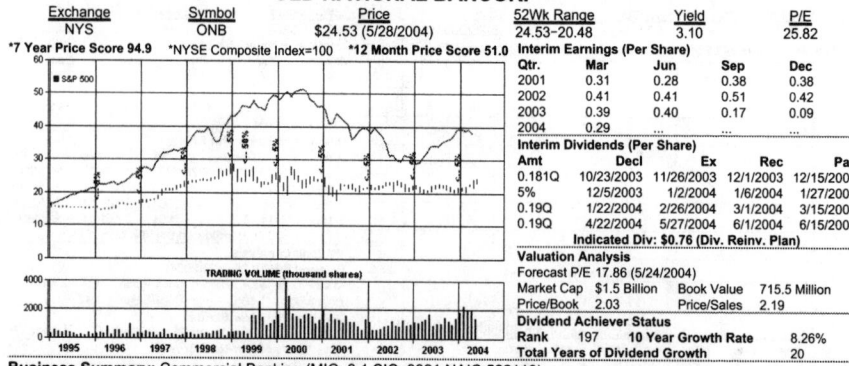

Interim Earnings (Per Share)

Qtr.	Mar	Jun	Sep	Dec
2001	0.31	0.28	0.38	0.38
2002	0.41	0.41	0.51	0.42
2003	0.39	0.40	0.17	0.09
2004	0.29	...	...	...

Interim Dividends (Per Share)

Amt	Decl	Ex	Rec	Pay
0.181Q	10/23/2003	11/26/2003	12/1/2003	12/15/2003
5%	12/5/2003	1/2/2004	1/6/2004	1/27/2004
0.19Q	1/22/2004	2/26/2004	3/1/2004	3/15/2004
0.19Q	4/22/2004	5/27/2004	6/1/2004	6/15/2004

Indicated Div: $0.76 (Div. Reinv. Plan)

Valuation Analysis

Forecast P/E 17.86 (5/24/2004)

Market Cap	$1.5 Billion	Book Value	715.5 Million
Price/Book	2.03	Price/Sales	2.19

Dividend Achiever Status

Rank	197	10 Year Growth Rate	8.26%
Total Years of Dividend Growth		20	

Business Summary: Commercial Banking (MIC: 8.1 SIC: 6021 NAIC:522110)

Old National Bancorp, with total assets of $9.35 billion as of Dec 31 2003, is a financial holding company headquartered in Evansville, IN with banking activity in Indiana, Illinois, Kentucky, Tennessee, and Ohio. As of Dec 31 2003, Co. operated over 120 banking offices serving customers in both urban and rural markets. Co.'s banking centers provide a wide range of financial services, such as commercial, real estate, and consumer loans; lease financing; checking, savings, time deposits; and letters of credit. Co.'s non–bank affiliates provide additional financial or support services incidental to its operations, including issuance and reinsurance of credit life services.

Recent Developments: For the quarter ended Mar 31 2004, net income declined 25.7% to $19.5 million from $26.3 million in the corresponding period of the year before. Results for 2004 and 2003 included net securities gains of $2.0 million and $2.7 million, respectively. Net interest income slipped 6.5% to $71.2 million. Net interest margin slid to 3.37% from 3.46% in 2003 due to a shift from loans into lower-yielding securities and lower levels of interest rates. Provision for loan losses fell 16.7% to $7.5 million from $9.0 million a year earlier. Total non-interest income climbed 8.6% to $43.6 million, while total non-interest expense rose 14.7% to $80.5 million.

Prospects: Income is being negatively affected by a reduced level of earning assets, resulting from weak commercial loan demand. However, Co. is optimistic as its credit quality is beginning to stabilize and its level of net charge-offs is decreasing. Meanwhile, Co.'s ASCEND project, a company-wide program aimed at improving operating efficiency and funding significant new business growth, is scheduled to be fully implemented over the next 18 months. Once fully implemented, Co. expects to realize about $55.0 million to $60.0 million in annualized pre-tax earnings from the project, excluding one-time implementation charges which will be incurred in the second quarter of 2004.

Financial Data

(US$ in Thousands)	3 Mos	12/31/2003	12/31/2002	12/31/2001	12/31/2000	12/31/1999	12/31/1998	12/31/1997
Earnings Per Share	0.95	1.05	1.75	1.35	0.88	1.37	1.25	1.05
Tang. Book Val. Per Share	8.40	7.95	8.82	9.47	8.97	8.57	9.00	9.07
Dividends Per Share	0.730	0.720	0.650	0.580	0.550	0.510	0.450	0.430
Dividend Payout %	77.18	68.93	37.26	43.46	62.87	37.82	36.35	41.32
Income Statement								
Total Interest Income	108,121	469,748	547,383	629,707	638,275	488,923	437,909	429,446
Total Interest Expense	43,010	197,741	257,954	338,408	368,404	250,536	223,059	210,208
Net Interest Income	65,111	272,007	289,429	291,299	269,871	238,387	214,850	219,238
Provision for Loan Losses	7,500	85,000	33,500	28,700	29,803	11,489	11,420	26,965
Non–Interest Income	45,628	192,149	154,497	112,967	101,713	67,508	54,557	47,090
Non–Interest Expense	80,453	299,716	257,845	254,812	265,537	185,564	158,125	154,364
Income Before Taxes	22,786	79,440	152,581	120,754	76,244	108,842	99,862	84,999
Income from Cont Ops	...	...	...	...	...	82,694	71,718	...
Net Income	19,509	70,413	117,932	93,044	61,696	86,795	61,864	60,660
Average Shs. Outstg.	66,460	66,832	67,308	68,607	69,689	60,623	57,838	58,879
Balance Sheet								
Cash & Due from Banks	176,022	222,385	223,007	224,663	202,600	169,184	150,884	147,337
Securities Avail. for Sale	1,385,921	2,720,844	3,091,017	2,320,088	1,825,112	1,678,651	1,596,882	1,566,976
Net Loans & Leases	5,451,054	5,465,546	5,681,893	6,058,613	6,274,480	4,780,888	4,112,804	3,683,969
Total Assets	9,259,334	9,353,896	9,612,556	9,080,473	8,767,748	6,982,932	6,165,968	5,688,215
Total Deposits	6,385,103	6,493,092	6,439,280	6,616,440	6,583,906	5,071,298	4,443,472	4,298,730
Long–Term Obligations	1,533,202	1,624,092	1,247,857	1,000,046	863,165	662,973	629,868	388,832
Total Liabilities	8,518,473	8,638,406	8,871,846	8,441,238	8,141,407	6,490,188	5,671,388	5,211,012
Net Stockholders' Equity	740,861	715,490	740,710	639,235	626,341	492,744	494,580	477,203
Shares Outstanding	66,449	66,575	67,048	67,444	69,817	57,480	54,917	52,564
Statistical Record								
Return on Equity %	2.63	9.84	15.92	14.55	9.85	16.78	14.50	12.71
Return on Assets %	0.21	0.75	1.22	1.02	0.70	1.18	1.16	1.06
Equity/Assets %	8.00	7.64	7.70	7.03	7.14	7.05	8.02	8.38
Non–Int. Exp./Tot. Inc. %	52.32	45.28	36.73	34.31	35.88	33.34	32.10	32.39
Price Range	22.95-20.50	22.82-20.00	24.04-20.68	24.72-17.94	28.08-19.43	28.76-21.94	28.85-22.64	23.33-17.17
P/E Ratio	24.16-21.58	21.73-19.05	13.74-11.82	18.31-13.29	31.91-22.08	20.99-16.01	23.08-18.11	22.22-16.36
Average Yield %	3.34	3.34	2.92	2.68	2.30	2.07	1.84	2.17

Address: 420 Main Street, Evansville, IN 47708	**Officers:** James A. Risinger – Chmn., C.E.O., Michael R. Hinton – Pres., C.O.O.	**Investor Contact:**812–464–1366
Telephone: (812) 464–1200	**Transfer Agents:**Old National Bancorp, Evansville, IN	**Institutional Holding**
Web Site: www.oldnational.com		**No of Institutions:** 32
		Shares: 1,181,632 **% Held:** –

OLD REPUBLIC INTERNATIONAL CORP.

Exchange	Symbol	Price	52Wk Range	Yield	P/E
NYS	ORI	$22.76 (5/28/2004)	27.19-21.37	2.28	9.07

*7 Year Price Score 135.8   ***NYSE Composite Index=100**   ***12 Month Price Score 44.1**

Interim Earnings (Per Share)
Qtr.	Mar	Jun	Sep	Dec
2001	0.46	0.50	0.46	0.50
2002	0.52	0.58	0.52	0.53
2003	0.57	0.66	0.65	0.63
2004	0.57	...	...	...

Interim Dividends (Per Share)
Amt	Decl	Ex	Rec	Pay
0.113Q	5/15/2003	6/4/2003	6/6/2003	6/16/2003
0.667E	12/4/2003	12/11/2003	12/15/2003	12/26/2003
50%	12/4/2003	12/31/2003	12/15/2003	12/30/2003
0.13Q	5/14/2004	6/2/2004	6/4/2004	6/15/2004

Indicated Div: $0.52 (Div. Reinv. Plan)

Valuation Analysis
Forecast P/E 9.08 (5/24/2004)

Market Cap $2.7 Billion	Book Value	3.6 Billion
Price/Book 1.92	Price/Sales	2.08

Dividend Achiever Status

Rank	103	10 Year Growth Rate 13.19%
Total Years of Dividend Growth		22

Business Summary: Insurance (MIC: 8.2 SIC: 6351 NAIC:524130)

Old Republic International is an insurance holding company. Through its general insurance group, Co. assumes risks and provides related risk management and marketing services pertaining to a large variety of property and liability commercial insurance coverages. Through its mortgage guaranty group, Co. protects mortgage lenders and investors from default related losses on residential mortgage loans. Through its title insurance group, Co. issues policies to real estate purchasers and investors. Co.'s life insurance group markets and writes consumer credit life and disability insurance primarily through automobile dealers.

Recent Developments: For the quarter ended Mar 31 2004, net income rose 1.9% to $106.4 million from $104.4 million in the prior–year quarter. Results for 2004 included stock option charges of $6.4 million. Total revenues increased 11.3% to $822.4 million. Revenues included realized investment gains of $15.6 million in 2004 and realized investment losses of $6.7 million in 2003. By segment, operating income for the general insurance group climbed 25.1% to $74.3 million. Operating income for the mortgage guaranty group dropped 24.3% to $57.4 million. Operating income for the title group slid 48.6% to $13.2 million, while operating income for the life and health group decreased 27.3% to $900,000.

Prospects: Co.'s prospects remain positive. Co.'s general insurance group should continue to benefit from the steadily improved pricing and risk selection standards that have been applied since 2001 and the well–controlled expense initiatives for substantially all of its general insurance coverages. Meanwhile, despite a 1.3% decrease in mortgage guaranty premiums, persistency for the traditional primary book of business improved for the second consecutive quarter, rising to 50.2%. Moreover, the loss ratio of 29.5%, while significantly higher than the 15.2% loss ratio posted in the first three months of 2003, was moderately lower than the 32.0% posted in the fourth quarter of 2003.

Financial Data
(US$ in Thousands)	3 Mos	12/31/2003	12/31/2002	12/31/2001	12/31/2000	12/31/1999	12/31/1998	12/31/1997
Earnings Per Share	2.51	2.51	2.15	1.92	1.64	1.16	1.55	1.40
Tang. Book Val. Per Share	19.84	19.26	16.99	15.18	13.38	9.35	11.51	10.39
Dividends Per Share	1.110	1.110	0.420	0.390	0.360	0.320	0.250	0.220
Dividend Payout %	44.22	44.35	19.50	20.48	22.26	27.99	16.59	15.87
Income Statement								
Total Premium Income	660,700	2,582,100	2,135,400	1,786,800	1,550,300	1,567,200	1,568,100	1,464,600
Net Investment Income		279,200	272,600	274,700	273,900	263,200	273,100	270,800
Other Income	145,900	424,400	348,200	311,700	246,100	271,500	330,300	227,200
Total Revenues	806,600	3,285,700	2,756,200	2,373,200	2,070,300	2,101,900	2,171,500	1,962,600
Inc. Before Inc. Taxes	158,200	680,000	560,900	503,900	426,400	317,000	466,700	426,700
Income Taxes	51,700	219,900	167,600	159,600	131,000	92,900	145,700	129,100
Eqty Earns/Minority Int.	...	(200)	(200)	2,700	2,200	2,700	2,700	600
Income from Cont Ops	...	460,100	393,000	...	297,400	...	323,800	297,600
Net Income	106,400	459,800	392,900	346,900	297,500	226,800	323,700	298,100
Average Shs. Outstg.	184,504	183,302	182,323	180,491	180,295	194,680	208,725	212,652
Balance Sheet								
Cash & Cash Equivalents	58,900	47,200	37,200	38,000	33,000	17,500	22,900	26,900
Premiums Due	2,386,300	2,330,600	2,084,200	1,910,700	1,732,400	1,697,600	1,643,300	1,706,800
Invst. Assets: Total	6,943,100	6,720,200	6,051,200	5,472,900	5,038,900	4,739,400	4,854,200	4,720,100
Total Assets	9,959,000	9,711,700	8,714,700	7,919,500	7,280,900	6,937,700	7,018,900	6,922,800
Long–Term Obligations	137,400	137,500	141,500	159,000	238,000	208,300	145,100	142,900
Net Stockholders' Equity	3,668,000	3,553,500	3,155,700	2,783,900	2,439,300	2,199,100	2,305,400	2,153,000
Shares Outstanding	184,835	184,471	185,687	183,253	182,167	235,018	200,104	207,105
Statistical Record								
Return on Revenues %	11.25	14.00	14.25	14.61	14.36	10.79	14.91	15.16
Return on Equity %	2.47	12.94	12.45	12.46	12.19	10.31	14.04	13.82
Return on Assets %	0.91	4.73	4.50	4.38	4.08	3.26	4.61	4.29
Price Range	27.19-23.47	25.79-16.53	23.15-16.85	20.04-15.10	21.33-7.17	15.04-8.25	21.25-12.00	17.75-10.94
P/E Ratio	10.83-9.35	10.27-6.58	10.77-7.84	10.44-7.86	13.01-4.37	12.97-7.11	13.71-7.74	12.68-7.82
Average Yield %	4.47	5.15	2.06	2.14	2.81	2.82	1.45	1.55

Address: 307 North Michigan Avenue, Chicago, IL 60601 **Telephone:** (312) 346–8100 **Web Site:** www.oldrepublic.com	**Officers:** Aldo C. Zucaro – Chmn., Pres., C.E.O., John S. Adams – Sr. V.P., C.F.O. **Transfer Agents:** EquiServe, First Chicago Trust Division, Jersey City, NJ	**Institutional Holding** **No of Institutions:** 10 **Shares:** 539,906 **% Held:** –

OTTER TAIL CORP.

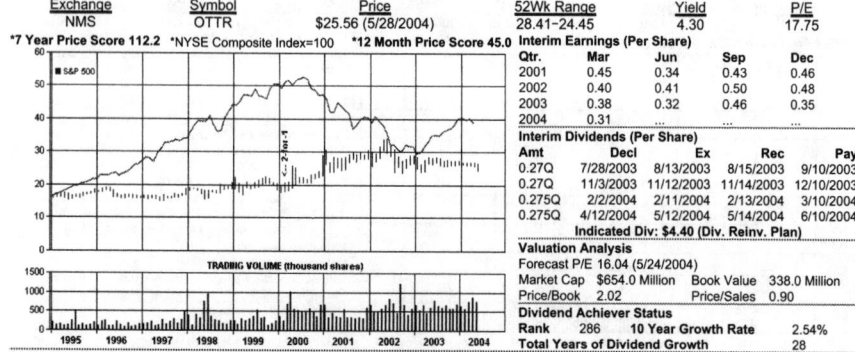

Exchange	Symbol	Price	52Wk Range	Yield	P/E
NMS	OTTR	$25.56 (5/28/2004)	28.41–24.45	4.30	17.75

*7 Year Price Score 112.2 *NYSE Composite Index=100 ***12 Month Price Score 45.0**

Interim Earnings (Per Share)

Qtr.	Mar	Jun	Sep	Dec
2001	0.45	0.34	0.43	0.46
2002	0.40	0.41	0.50	0.48
2003	0.38	0.32	0.46	0.35
2004	0.31	...	...	...

Interim Dividends (Per Share)

Amt	Decl	Ex	Rec	Pay
0.27Q	7/28/2003	8/13/2003	8/15/2003	9/10/2003
0.27Q	11/3/2003	11/12/2003	11/14/2003	12/10/2003
0.275Q	2/2/2004	2/11/2004	2/13/2004	3/10/2004
0.275Q	4/12/2004	5/12/2004	5/14/2004	6/10/2004

Indicated Div: $4.40 (Div. Reinv. Plan)

Valuation Analysis

Forecast P/E 16.04 (5/24/2004)
Market Cap $654.0 Million   Book Value 338.0 Million
Price/Book 2.02   Price/Sales 0.90

Dividend Achiever Status

Rank 286   10 Year Growth Rate   2.54%
Total Years of Dividend Growth   28

Business Summary: Electricity (MIC: 7.1 SIC: 4911 NAIC:221121)

Otter Tail is an operating electric utility engaged in the production, transmission and distribution and sale of electric energy in 48 states and 6 Canadian provinces. The Electric segment includes the production, transmission, distribution and sale of electric energy in Minnesota, North Dakota and South Dakota. The Manufacturing segment includes the production of waterfront equipment, wind towers, custom plastic pallets, and material and handling trays. The Health Services segment consists of the sale of diagnostic medical and patient monitoring equipment. The Plastics segment produces polyvinyl chloride pipe and polyethylene pipe.

Recent Developments: For the three months ended Mar 31 2004, net income declined 17.9% to $8.1 million compared with $9.9 million in the equivalent quarter of 2003. The decline in earnings was attributed to continued weakness in plastics, manufacturing and other business operations due to soft economic conditions and pricing pressures. Operating revenues rose 20.0% to $206.6 million from $172.2 million the year before. Electric revenues benefited from higher consumption by commercial and industrial customers, increased steam sales and revenue from transmission related services. Operating income decreased 12.2% to $16.1 million compared with $18.3 million a year earlier.

Prospects: Co. reaffirmed its diluted earnings per share guidance for full–year 2004 in the range of $1.55 to $1.70. Operating results are expected to show the strongest improvement in the second half of 2004. In the electric segment, Co. anticipates continued strong performance for the remainder of the year even though results are not expected to equal the levels of 2003. Co. also expects increased operating expenses in the electric segment due to higher employee benefit costs and less opportunity for outside construction work. Meanwhile, Co. expects the plastics segment to perform strongly throughout the remainder of the year due to increases in polyvinyl chloride resin prices.

Financial Data

(US$ in Thousands)	3 Mos	12/31/2003	12/31/2002	12/31/2001	12/31/2000	12/31/1999	12/31/1998	12/31/1997
Earnings Per Share	1.44	1.51	1.79	1.68	1.60	1.79	1.20	1.29
Cash Flow Per Share	0.03	2.97	3.02	3.12	2.51	3.28	2.71	2.98
Tang. Book Val. Per Share	9.99	9.88	9.50	9.30	9.05	9.32	8.58	8.06
Dividends Per Share	1.080	1.080	1.060	1.040	1.020	0.990	0.960	0.930
Dividend Payout %	44.67	71.52	59.21	61.90	63.75	55.30	79.66	72.09
Income Statement								
Total Revenues	206,585	753,239	710,116	654,132	559,445	464,577	431,078	394,279
Total Indirect Exp.	13,662	55,560	52,036	51,564	38,624	35,598	36,537	36,401
Costs & Expenses	190,524	682,079	628,134	576,648	486,955	397,211	373,848	335,246
Depreciation & Amort.	11,173	45,962	42,613	42,100	28,648	25,420	25,813	25,536
Operating Income	16,061	71,160	81,982	77,484	72,490	67,366	57,230	59,033
Net Interest Inc./(Exp.)	(4,429)	(17,865)	(17,850)	(15,991)	(16,583)	(14,771)	(15,566)	(18,519)
Income Taxes	3,574	14,930	20,061	20,083	17,515	23,915	15,140	14,308
Income from Cont Ops	...	...	...	...	...	...	30,701	...
Net Income	8,095	39,656	46,128	43,603	40,224	44,977	34,520	32,346
Average Shs. Outstg.	25,936	25,826	25,397	24,832	23,928	23,831	23,596	23,278
Balance Sheet								
Net Property	630,712	633,325	587,886	542,977	515,929	502,956	500,186	509,766
Total Assets	984,441	986,423	878,736	782,541	722,115	680,788	655,612	655,441
Long–Term Obligations	262,975	265,193	258,229	227,360	191,493	176,437	181,046	189,973
Net Stockholders' Equity	338,009	349,387	328,965	294,808	292,879	279,193	245,907	230,987
Shares Outstanding	25,847	25,723	25,592	24,653	23,852	23,849	23,760	23,462
Operating Profit Margin %	7.77	9.44	11.54	11.84	12.95	14.50	13.27	14.97
Net Profit Margin %	7.37	9.22	12.14	12.80	13.45	19.97	14.14	15.46
Net Inc./Net Property %	1.28	6.26	7.84	8.03	7.79	8.94	6.90	6.34
Net Inc./Tot. Capital %	1.12	5.53	6.77	7.17	7.05	8.27	6.44	6.02
Return on Equity %	...	11.35	14.02	14.79	13.73	16.10	12.48	14.00
Accum. Depr./Gross Prop. %	41.93	41.74	44.31	44.86	44.29	43.46	42.53	40.75
Price Range	27.00–26.02	28.50–24.00	34.12–23.80	30.69–23.88	29.00–17.81	22.63–17.00	20.78–15.63	18.94–15.13
P/E Ratio	18.75–18.07	18.87–15.89	19.06–13.30	18.27–14.21	18.13–11.13	12.64–9.50	17.32–13.02	14.68–11.72
Average Yield %	4.06	4.02	3.70	3.76	4.72	4.91	5.16	5.63

Address: 215 South Cascade Street, Fergus Falls, MN 56538–0496	**Officers:** John C. MacFarlane – Chmn., John D. Erickson – Pres., C.E.O.	**Investor Contact:** 800 664 1259
Telephone: (866) 410–8780	**Transfer Agents:** Wells Fargo Bank, Minnesota, N.A., St. Paul, MN	**Institutional Holding**
Web Site: www.ottertail.com		**No of Institutions:** –
		Shares: – **% Held:** –

PACIFIC CAPITAL BANCORP (NEW)

Exchange	Symbol	Price	52Wk Range	Yield	P/E
NMS	PCBC	$36.85 (5/28/2004)	40.55-30.49	2.39	16.83

*7 Year Price Score 149.2   *NYSE Composite Index=100   *12 Month Price Score 47.6

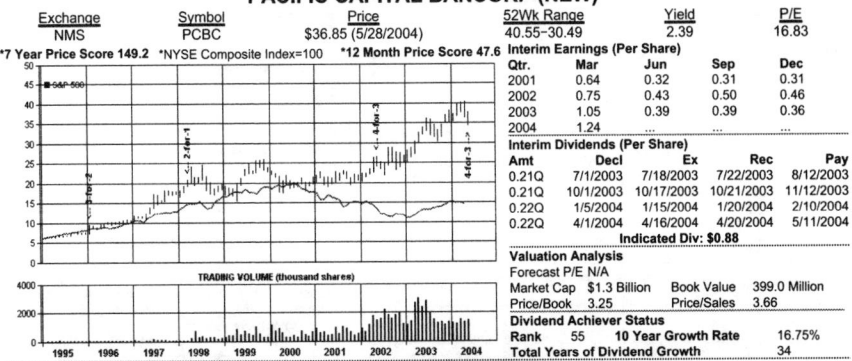

Interim Earnings (Per Share)

Qtr.	Mar	Jun	Sep	Dec
2001	0.64	0.32	0.31	0.31
2002	0.75	0.43	0.50	0.46
2003	1.05	0.39	0.39	0.36
2004	1.24	...	...	...

Interim Dividends (Per Share)

Amt	Decl	Ex	Rec	Pay
0.21Q	7/1/2003	7/18/2003	7/22/2003	8/12/2003
0.21Q	10/1/2003	10/17/2003	10/21/2003	11/12/2003
0.22Q	1/5/2004	1/15/2004	1/20/2004	2/10/2004
0.22Q	4/1/2004	4/16/2004	4/20/2004	5/11/2004

Indicated Div: $0.88

Valuation Analysis

Forecast P/E N/A

Market Cap	$1.3 Billion	Book Value	399.0 Million
Price/Book	3.25	Price/Sales	3.66

Dividend Achiever Status

Rank	55	10 Year Growth Rate	16.75%
Total Years of Dividend Growth			34

Business Summary: Commercial Banking (MIC: 8.1 SIC: 6022 NAIC:522110)

Pacific Capital Bancorp is the parent of Pacific Capital Bank, N.A., a nationally chartered bank with four brands: Santa Barbara Bank and Trust, First National Bank of Central California, South Valley National Bank and San Benito Bank. The banks provide commercial banking services to households, professionals, and small- to medium-sized businesses. Co. also offers products related to income tax returns filed electronically. As of Dec 31 2003, Co. had assets of $4.86 billion and deposits of $3.3 billion. Pacific Capital Bank, N.A. is a 41-branch community bank network serving the California central coast counties of Monterey, Santa Cruz, San Benito, Santa Barbara, Ventura and Santa Clara.

Recent Developments: For the first quarter ended Mar 31 2004, net income advanced 17.0% to $42.6 million compared with $36.4 million in the corresponding prior-year quarter. Net interest income climbed 14.5% to $85.9 million from $75.0 million a year earlier. Total interest income increased 12.9% to $100.8 million, while total interest expense rose 4.7% to $14.9 million. Provision for credit losses dropped 34.7% to $7.6 million, primarily due to a reversal of $1.4 million for non-refund anticipation loan-related credit, partially offset by higher provisions for refund anticipation loans. Total non-interest income decreased 5.7% to $36.6 million, while total non-interest expense grew 6.0% to $47.1 million.

Prospects: Economic conditions continue to improve in the markets served by Co., and the diversity of its lending and fee-generating businesses are providing numerous vehicles for capitalizing on this growth. A steady stream of lending opportunities, further improvement in credit quality, strong demand for new checking products, and solid performance from the Trust division, along with the accretive effect of the Pacific Crest Capital, Inc. acquisition is driving earnings. For full-year 2004, Co. expects earnings to range from $2.49 to $2.61 per diluted share. Looking ahead, Co.'s loan pipeline appears solid, and it expects to attract low-cost deposits to fund its lending opportunities.

Financial Data

(US$ in Thousands)	3 Mos	12/31/2003	12/31/2002	12/31/2001	12/31/2000	12/31/1999	12/31/1998	12/31/1997
Earnings Per Share	2.38	2.19	2.14	1.58	1.44	1.34	0.90	0.96
Tang. Book Val. Per Share	9.70	10.77	9.74	9.32	8.39	7.16	6.62	5.81
Dividends Per Share	0.840	0.800	0.690	0.660	0.600	0.540	0.450	0.340
Dividend Payout %	35.15	36.52	32.24	41.70	41.45	40.22	50.41	35.65
Income Statement								
Total Interest Income	100,765	272,189	266,746	291,108	290,916	211,643	193,516	114,935
Total Interest Expense	14,897	53,933	62,799	97,226	110,526	6,556	3,343	43,205
Net Interest Income	85,868	218,256	203,947	193,882	180,390	205,087	190,173	71,730
Provision for Loan Losses	7,584	18,286	19,727	26,671	14,440	6,375	9,123	6,980
Non-Interest Income	36,621	81,745	73,784	65,726	49,388	41,618	35,972	25,144
Non-Interest Expense	47,116	163,702	143,288	143,150	131,957	110,389	103,710	60,105
Income from Cont Ops	...	...	...	...	...	105,574	94,337	...
Net Income	42,591	75,671	74,851	56,111	51,456	44,274	29,567	20,136
Average Shs. Outstg.	34,363	34,562	34,990	35,518	35,478	33,053	32,595	20,778
Balance Sheet								
Cash & Due from Banks	151,701	150,010	151,540	136,457	176,274	121,500	114,206	67,799
Securities Avail. for Sale	1,483,736	1,317,962	803,429	699,076	669,631	528,426	596,996	286,998
Net Loans & Leases	3,640,921	3,131,329	2,965,999	2,750,220	2,481,979	1,953,193	1,553,485	860,400
Total Assets	5,629,675	4,859,630	4,219,213	3,960,929	3,677,625	2,879,282	2,649,418	1,592,386
Total Deposits	4,291,495	3,854,717	3,516,017	3,365,575	3,102,819	2,440,181	2,329,676	1,404,155
Long-Term Obligations	720,669	499,548	264,969	188,331	129,658	98,801	44,953	39,000
Total Liabilities	5,187,126	4,460,582	3,848,138	3,635,053	3,381,364	2,644,709	2,435,418	1,474,220
Net Stockholders' Equity	442,549	399,048	371,075	325,876	296,261	234,573	214,000	118,166
Shares Outstanding	34,075	33,963	34,550	34,942	35,307	32,738	32,278	20,322
Return on Equity %	9.62	18.96	20.17	17.21	17.36	45.00	44.08	17.04
Return on Assets %	0.75	1.55	1.77	1.41	1.39	3.66	3.56	1.26
Non-Int. Exp./Tot. Inc. %	34.29	46.25	42.07	40.11	38.77	43.58	45.19	42.90
Price Range	40.25-35.66	38.22-25.37	29.00-20.50	23.10-19.08	23.06-17.58	25.92-15.47	24.75-16.59	18.19-10.36
P/E Ratio	16.91-14.98	17.45-11.58	13.55-9.58	14.62-12.07	16.02-12.21	19.34-11.54	27.50-18.44	18.95-10.79
Average Yield %	2.20	2.47	2.81	3.11	2.96	2.52	2.29	2.32

Address: 1021 Anacapa Street, Santa Barbara, CA 93101	Officers: David W. Spainhour – Chmn., D. Vernon Horton – Vice-Chmn.	Institutional Holding
Telephone: (805) 564-6300	Transfer Agents: Norwest Shareowner Services, South St. Paul, MN	No of Institutions: 9
Web Site: www.pcbancorp.com		Shares: 336,050 % Held: –

PARK NATIONAL CORP.

Exchange	Symbol	Price	52Wk Range	Yield	P/E
ASE	PRK	$115.46 (5/28/2004)	120.0-106.0	3.05	18.47

*7 Year Price Score 119.1   *NYSE Composite Index=100   ***12 Month Price Score 47.7**

Interim Earnings (Per Share)

Qtr.	Mar	Jun	Sep	Dec
2001	1.34	1.45	1.45	1.34
2002	1.53	1.57	1.59	1.46
2003	1.68	1.81	1.46	1.32
2004	1.66	...	...	...

Interim Dividends (Per Share)

Amt	Decl	Ex	Rec	Pay
0.83Q	7/21/2003	8/21/2003	8/25/2003	9/10/2003
0.88Q	11/17/2003	12/17/2003	12/19/2003	1/2/2004
0.88Q	1/20/2004	2/19/2004	2/23/2004	3/10/2004
0.88Q	4/19/2004	5/20/2004	5/24/2004	6/10/2004

Indicated Div: $3.52 (Div. Reinv. Plan)

Valuation Analysis

Forecast P/E 16.40 (5/24/2004)

Market Cap	$1.6 Billion	Book Value	543.0 Million
Price/Book	2.85	Price/Sales	4.84

Dividend Achiever Status

Rank	92	10 Year Growth Rate	13.88%

Total Years of Dividend Growth   16

Business Summary: Commercial Banking (MIC: 8.1 SIC: 6021 NAIC:522110)

Park National is a bank holding company with $5.03 billion in total assets at Dec 31 2003. Through its subsidiaries, Co. engages in general commercial banking and trust business in small and medium population Ohio communities. Co.'s subsidiaries provide the following services: the acceptance and servicing of demand, savings and time deposit accounts; commercial, industrial, consumer and real estate lending, including installment loans, credit cards, home equity lines of credit and commercial and auto leasing; trust services; cash management; safe deposit operations; electronic funds transfers; and online Internet banking with bill pay service.

Recent Developments: For the three months ended Mar 31 2004, net income declined slightly to $23.0 million compared with $23.2 million in the same period a year earlier. Net interest income was $52.6 million versus $52.2 million the previous year. Provision for loan losses amounted to $1.5 million compared with $3.4 million the year before. Total non–interest income declined 16.7% to $12.9 million from $15.5 million last year, primarily due to decreased fee income earned from the origination and sale of fixed rate mortgage loans. Total other expenses rose 4.8% to $31.5 million, due in part to higher salaries and employee benefits.

Prospects: Co.'s near term outlook is tempered by the prospect of lower fee income earned from the origination and sale of fixed rate mortgage loans, primarily due to decreased demand associated with higher rates. For instance, during the quarter ended Mar 31 2004, Co. originated and sold fixed rate mortgage loans totaling $53.1 million compared with $211.6 million for the quarter ended Mar 31 2003. On the positive side, Co. noted that demand for commercial and commercial real estate loans improved during the quarter ended Mar 31 2004. Furthermore, Co. anticipates that total loans will continue to increase throughout the remainder of 2004.

Financial Data

(US$ in Thousands)	12/31/2003	12/31/2002	12/31/2001	12/31/2000	12/31/1999	12/31/1998	12/31/1997	12/31/1996
Earnings Per Share	6.27	6.15	5.58	5.10	4.67	4.21	3.80	3.42
Tang. Book Val. Per Share	39.44	36.92	33.59	29.66	24.59	23.49	22.52	19.89
Dividends Per Share	3.320	3.040	2.840	2.600	2.280	1.820	1.520	1.330
Dividend Payout %	52.95	49.43	50.89	50.98	48.94	43.34	40.00	...
Income Statement								
Total Interest Income	264,629	287,920	320,348	249,332	191,920	185,946	180,511	122,291
Total Interest Expense	61,992	82,588	127,404	110,437	76,063	78,295	77,033	49,332
Net Interest Income	202,637	205,332	192,944	138,895	115,857	107,651	103,478	72,959
Provision for Loan Losses	12,595	15,043	13,059	8,729	6,969	6,798	6,999	4,520
Non–Interest Income	55,523	50,850	45,238	29,691	23,088	23,969	20,479	13,142
Non–Interest Expense	122,376	119,964	114,207	82,919	67,540	64,309	62,408	43,239
Income Before Taxes	123,189	121,175	110,916	76,938	64,436	60,513	54,550	38,342
Net Income	86,878	85,579	78,362	55,405	45,747	41,572	37,693	25,664
Average Shs. Outstg.	13,858	13,909	14,051	10,876	9,810	9,855	9,907	7,493
Balance Sheet								
Cash & Due from Banks	169,782	157,088	169,143	109,870	104,222	100,291	93,585	61,454
Securities Avail. for Sale	1,928,697	1,030,264	1,436,661	740,924	619,009	646,403	532,922	386,187
Net Loans & Leases	2,667,661	2,630,159	2,735,849	2,229,259	1,792,682	1,603,523	1,556,332	1,084,801
Total Assets	5,034,956	4,446,625	4,569,515	3,211,068	2,634,337	2,460,779	2,288,383	1,614,767
Total Deposits	3,414,249	3,495,135	3,314,203	2,415,575	2,015,147	1,939,778	1,854,964	1,336,617
Long–Term Obligations	485,977	187,226	392,540	181,578	76	8,430	30,868	...
Total Liabilities	4,491,915	3,937,333	4,101,169	2,891,316	2,394,757	2,225,089	2,066,266	1,465,781
Net Stockholders' Equity	543,041	509,292	468,346	319,752	239,580	235,690	222,117	148,986
Shares Outstanding	13,766	13,791	13,940	10,778	9,739	10,030	9,861	7,489
Return on Equity %	15.99	16.80	16.73	17.32	19.09	17.63	16.96	17.22
Return on Assets %	1.72	1.92	1.71	1.72	1.73	1.68	1.64	1.58
Equity/Assets %	10.78	11.45	10.24	9.95	9.09	9.57	9.70	9.22
Non–Int. Exp./Tot. Inc. %	38.22	35.41	31.23	29.71	31.41	30.63	31.05	31.92
Price Range	120.0-93.30	102.1-84.01	102.5-75.10	103.9-78.50	116.0-87.32	102.1-80.95	93.33-48.69	50.48-44.17
P/E Ratio	19.14-14.88	16.60-13.66	18.37-13.46	20.37-15.39	24.84-18.70	24.26-19.23	24.56-12.81	14.76-12.91
Average Yield %	3.07	3.21	3.18	2.82	2.43	1.98	2.28	2.86

Address: 50 North Third Street, Newark, OH 43055

Telephone: (740) 349–8451

Web Site: www.parknationalcorp.com

Officers: William T. McConnell – Chmn., Harry O. Egger – Vice Chmn.

Transfer Agents: First-Knox National Bank, Mount Vernon, OH

Investor Contact: 740–349–3708

Institutional Holding

No of Institutions: 3

Shares: 21,589   % Held: –

PARKER HANNIFIN CORP.

Exchange	Symbol	Price	52Wk Range	Yield	P/E
NYS	PH	$55.56 (5/28/2004)	60.92–39.95	1.37	24.48

*7 Year Price Score 118.1   *NYSE Composite Index=100   *12 Month Price Score 49.2

Interim Earnings (Per Share)

Qtr.	Sep	Dec	Mar	Jun
2000–01	1.09	0.68	0.80	0.42
2001–02	0.52	0.25	0.45	(0.10)
2002–03	0.52	0.32	0.42	0.42
2003–04	0.48	0.47	0.90	...

Interim Dividends (Per Share)

Amt	Decl	Ex	Rec	Pay
0.19Q	7/17/2003	8/19/2003	8/21/2003	9/5/2003
0.19Q	10/22/2003	11/18/2003	11/20/2003	12/5/2003
0.19Q	1/29/2004	2/17/2004	2/19/2004	3/5/2004
0.19Q	4/22/2004	5/18/2004	5/20/2004	6/4/2004

Indicated Div: $0.76 (Div. Reinv. Plan)

Valuation Analysis

Forecast P/E 16.32 (5/24/2004)

Market Cap	$6.6 Billion	Book Value	2.8 Billion
Price/Book	2.42	Price/Sales	1.00

Dividend Achiever Status

Rank	239	10 Year Growth Rate	5.66%
Total Years of Dividend Growth			47

Business Summary: Metal Products (MIC: 11.4 SIC: 3491 NAIC:332911)

Parker–Hannifin is a manufacturer of motion–control products, including fluid power systems, electromechanical controls and related components. Co. operates in two main business segments: The Industrial segment includes several business units that manufacture motion–control and fluid power system components for builders and users of various types of manufacturing, packaging, processing, transportation, agricultural, construction, and military vehicles and equipment. The Aerospace segment produces hydraulic, fuel and pneumatic systems and components for domestic commercial, military and general aviation aircraft, and naval vessels, land–based weapons systems, satellites and space vehicles.

Recent Developments: For the three months ended Mar 31 2004, net income increased to $107.8 million compared with $48.7 million in the corresponding year–earlier period. Co. attributed the improved earnings to an upsurge in volume throughout the industrial segment. Net sales climbed 15.7% to $1.91 billion from $1.65 billion the previous year. Co. noted that organic growth contributed 9.0% of the approximately 16.0% increase in top–line growth, while currency translation added 5.0% and 2.0% came from acquisitions completed since last year. Gross profit was $361.9 million, or 19.0% of net sales, versus $278.4 million, or 16.9% of net sales, the year before.

Prospects: Co.'s near–term outlook has improved and now appears favorable. Led by its Industrial segment, Co. is benefiting from improved top–line and operating profit trends across its segments with the exception of the Aerospace segment, which posted a 2.8% decline in operating profit due to continued softness in the commercial aerospace aftermarket and additional costs associated with pensions and product liability insurance. Co.'s prospects are enhanced by its previous efforts to achieve sustainable margin improvements through lower fixed costs and realignment activities. Consequently, Co. expects continued growth and increased profitability going forward reflecting strong order momentum.

Financial Data

(US$ in Thousands)	9 Mos	6 Mos	3 Mos	06/30/2003	06/30/2002	06/30/2001	06/30/2000	06/30/1999
Earnings Per Share	2.27	1.79	1.64	1.68	1.12	2.99	3.31	2.83
Cash Flow Per Share	4.24	3.19	1.22	4.76	5.43	4.62	4.83	4.18
Tang. Book Val. Per Share	12.48	12.60	11.94	11.44	12.27	13.42	14.93	12.62
Dividends Per Share	0.760	0.760	0.750	0.740	0.720	0.700	0.680	0.640
Dividend Payout %	33.48	42.46	45.73	44.04	64.28	23.41	20.54	22.61
Income Statement								
Total Revenues	5,113,980	3,207,939	1,586,918	6,410,610	6,149,122	5,979,604	5,355,337	4,958,800
Total Indirect Exp.	571,758	370,294	180,204	721,065	726,001	679,963	575,906	550,681
Depreciation & Amort.	189,659	127,664	63,379	259,178	281,598	264,527	206,408	202,046
Operating Income	367,652	207,225	107,938	379,770	306,551	571,485	622,862	538,749
Income Taxes	88,149	53,522	27,922	101,110	87,886	189,426	193,955	167,193
Income from Cont Ops	...	...	...	...	...	344,170	...	...
Net Income	220,310	112,462	56,691	196,272	130,150	340,792	368,232	310,501
Average Shs. Outstg.	118,803	118,386	117,769	116,894	116,060	115,064	111,224	109,679
Balance Sheet								
Cash & Cash Equivalents	169,956	138,047	205,409	245,850	46,384	23,565	68,460	33,277
Total Current Assets	2,493,055	2,206,928	2,305,955	2,396,807	2,235,618	2,196,362	2,153,113	1,774,684
Total Assets	6,230,801	5,799,495	5,882,592	5,985,633	5,752,583	5,337,661	4,646,299	3,705,888
Total Current Liabilities	1,331,416	1,015,965	1,256,363	1,423,727	1,359,837	1,413,129	1,186,303	754,513
Long–Term Obligations	968,326	975,235	956,356	966,332	1,088,883	857,078	701,762	724,757
Net Stockholders' Equity	2,790,664	2,704,273	2,587,861	2,520,911	2,583,516	2,528,915	2,309,458	1,853,862
Shares Outstanding	119,556	119,239	118,572	118,165	118,024	117,309	116,387	111,901
Statistical Record								
Operating Profit Margin %	7.18	6.45	6.80	5.92	4.98	9.55	11.63	10.86
Return on Equity %	7.89	4.15	2.19	7.78	5.03	13.60	15.94	16.74
Return on Assets %	3.54	1.93	0.96	3.27	2.26	6.44	7.92	8.37
Debt/Total Assets %	15.54	16.81	16.25	16.14	18.92	16.05	15.10	19.55
Price Range	60.92–41.71	59.50–41.71	50.65–41.71	48.80–34.65	54.63–31.65	50.03–31.94	52.13–33.94	50.44–27.19
P/E Ratio	26.84–18.37	33.24–23.30	30.88–25.43	29.05–20.63	48.78–28.26	16.73–10.68	15.75–10.25	17.82–9.61
Average Yield %	1.46	1.53	1.63	1.77	1.59	1.72	1.55	1.77

Address: 6035 Parkland Blvd., Cleveland, OH 44124–4141 Telephone: (216) 896–3000 Web Site: www.parker.com	Officers: Duane E. Collins – Chmn., Donald E. Washkewicz – Pres., C.E.O. Transfer Agents:National City Bank, Cleveland, OH	Investor Contact:216–896–2240 Institutional Holding No of Institutions: 19 Shares: 343,242 % Held: –

PAYCHEX INC

Exchange	Symbol	Price	52Wk Range	Yield	P/E
NMS	PAYX	$37.51 (5/28/2004)	40.14-28.84	1.28	45.74

*7 Year Price Score 119.9   *NYSE Composite Index=100   ***12 Month Price Score 49.5**

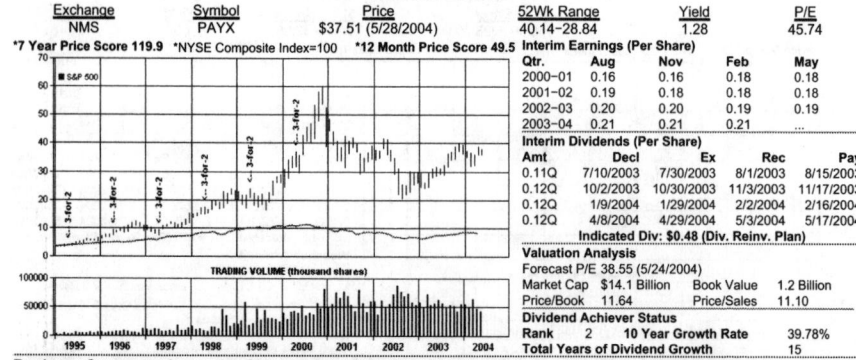

Interim Earnings (Per Share)

Qtr.	Aug	Nov	Feb	May
2000-01	0.16	0.16	0.18	0.18
2001-02	0.19	0.18	0.18	0.18
2002-03	0.20	0.20	0.19	0.19
2003-04	0.21	0.21	0.21	...

Interim Dividends (Per Share)

Amt	Decl	Ex	Rec	Pay
0.11Q	7/10/2003	7/30/2003	8/1/2003	8/15/2003
0.12Q	10/2/2003	10/30/2003	11/3/2003	11/17/2003
0.12Q	1/9/2004	1/29/2004	2/2/2004	2/16/2004
0.12Q	4/8/2004	4/29/2004	5/3/2004	5/17/2004
Indicated Div: $0.48 (Div. Reinv. Plan)				

Valuation Analysis

Forecast P/E 38.55 (5/24/2004)

Market Cap $14.1 Billion	Book Value 1.2 Billion
Price/Book 11.64	Price/Sales 11.10

Dividend Achiever Status

Rank 2	10 Year Growth Rate	39.78%
Total Years of Dividend Growth		15

Business Summary: Accounting &Management Consulting Services (MIC: 12.2 SIC: 8721 NAIC:541214)

Paychex operates in two business segments: Payroll and Human Resource Services–Professional Employer Organization (HRS–PEO). The Payroll segment is engaged in the preparation of payroll checks, internal accounting records, all federal, state and local payroll tax returns, and collection and remittance of payroll obligations for small– to medium–sized businesses. The HRS–PEO segment specializes in providing small– and medium–sized businesses with outsourcing services for their employee benefits. HRS–PEO products include 401(k) plan recordkeeping services, group benefits and workers' compensation insurance services, section 125 plans, employee handbooks and management services.

Recent Developments: For the third quarter ended Feb 29 2004, net income advanced 12.6% to $80.5 million compared with $71.5 million in the equivalent period of the previous year. Revenues improved 19.0% to $342.6 million from $287.8 million in the year–earlier quarter, largely due to recent acquisitions. Services revenues increased 19.6% to $328.1 million from $274.3 million in the prior–year period, primarily due to client base growth, increased utilization of ancillary services and price increases. Interest on funds held for clients rose 7.7% to $14.5 million from $13.5 million in 2002, due to increased net realized gains on the sale of securities.

Prospects: Co. is pleased with its operating results and remains optimistic that the signs of improving small business conditions will continue. Meanwhile, Co.'s payroll service should continue to benefit from the integration of the Advantage and InterPay acquisitions and strong growth in the client base. Co.'s human resource and benefits service should also benefit from client growth. However, operating income growth may continue to be hampered by lower average interest rates on earned funds held for clients. Nevertheless, for fiscal 2004, Co. expects total revenue growth to range from 16.0% to 18.0%, and net income growth to range from 8.0% to 10.0%.

Financial Data

(US$ in Thousands)	9 Mos	6 Mos	3 Mos	05/31/2003	05/31/2002	05/31/2001	05/31/2000	05/31/1999
Earnings Per Share	0.82	0.80	0.79	0.78	0.73	0.68	0.51	0.37
Cash Flow Per Share	0.85	0.48	0.29	0.98	0.80	0.80	0.66	0.46
Tang. Book Val. Per Share	1.88	1.76	1.64	1.55	2.43	2.00	1.50	1.16
Dividends Per Share	0.460	0.450	0.440	0.440	0.420	0.330	0.220	0.140
Dividend Payout %	56.09	56.25	55.69	56.41	57.53	48.52	43.13	39.28
Income Statement								
Total Revenues	963,958	621,352	309,253	1,099,079	954,910	869,857	728,119	597,296
Total Indirect Exp.	392,247	245,353	122,504	440,389	370,519	332,803	295,745	257,778
Depreciation & Amort.	61,116	40,154	19,796	64,555	47,392	39,139	36,484	32,911
Operating Income	346,366	229,893	115,078	401,041	363,694	336,702	258,893	187,562
Net Interest Inc./(Exp.)	...	...	...	30,503	31,315	27,279	16,479	12,581
Income Taxes	117,007	77,886	38,684	138,092	120,478	109,112	85,365	61,044
Net Income	241,545	161,027	80,343	293,452	274,531	254,869	190,007	139,099
Average Shs. Outstg.	379,410	379,234	378,815	378,083	378,002	377,510	375,081	373,182
Balance Sheet								
Cash & Cash Equivalents	208,621	134,238	131,819	2,577,912	2,005,984	2,086,829	1,824,104	1,414,215
Total Current Assets	3,616,734	2,998,451	2,956,641	3,032,642	2,814,574	2,791,273	2,362,575	1,793,120
Total Assets	4,275,062	3,660,508	3,612,336	3,690,783	2,953,075	2,907,196	2,455,577	1,873,101
Total Current Liabilities	3,052,708	2,477,506	2,476,089	2,587,525	2,023,406	2,143,842	1,886,945	1,432,336
Net Stockholders' Equity	1,195,512	1,154,600	1,109,227	1,077,371	923,981	757,842	563,432	435,800
Net Working Capital	1,195,512	520,945	480,552	445,117	791,168	647,431	475,630	360,784
Shares Outstanding	377,663	377,526	377,036	376,698	375,859	373,647	371,769	369,489
Statistical Record								
Operating Profit Margin %	35.93	36.99	37.21	36.48	38.08	38.70	35.55	31.40
Return on Equity %	20.20	13.94	7.24	27.23	29.71	33.63	33.72	31.91
Return on Assets %	5.65	4.39	2.22	7.95	9.29	8.76	7.73	7.42
Price Range	40.14-28.84	40.14-28.84	36.53-28.84	35.00-20.55	42.00-29.28	59.69-31.44	36.88-16.58	24.06-16.53
P/E Ratio	48.95-35.17	50.18-36.05	46.24-36.51	44.87-26.35	57.53-40.11	87.78-46.24	72.30-32.52	65.02-44.67
Average Yield %	1.32	1.31	1.39	1.61	1.14	0.75	0.84	0.69

Address: 911 Panorama Trail South, Rochester, NY 14625-2396	Officers: B. Thomas Golisano – Chmn., Pres., C.E.O., Martin Mucci – Sr. V.P., Oper.	Investor Contact:585-383-3406
Telephone: (585) 385-6666		Institutional Holding
Web Site: www.paychex.com		No of Institutions: 26
		Shares: 159,676,830 % Held: –

PENNICHUCK CORP.

Exchange	Symbol	Price	52Wk Range	Yield	P/E
NMS	PNNW	$26.40 (5/28/2004)	28.99-23.90	3.26	58.67

*7 Year Price Score 130.4 *NYSE Composite Index=100 *12 Month Price Score 47.5

Interim Earnings (Per Share)

Qtr.	Mar	Jun	Sep	Dec
2001	0.17	0.40	0.42	0.51
2002	0.26	(0.30)	0.57	0.44
2003	0.06	0.16	0.43	(0.13)
2004	(0.01)	...	...	...

Interim Dividends (Per Share)

Amt	Decl	Ex	Rec	Pay
0.215Q	8/5/2003	8/13/2003	8/15/2003	9/2/2003
0.215Q	10/3/2003	11/12/2003	11/14/2003	12/1/2003
0.215Q	1/26/2004	2/11/2004	2/13/2004	3/1/2004
0.215Q	4/26/2004	5/13/2004	5/17/2004	6/1/2004

Indicated Div: $0.86 (Div. Reinv. Plan)

Valuation Analysis

Forecast P/E N/A

Market Cap	$63.1 Million	Book Value	29.7 Million
Price/Book	2.26	Price/Sales	3.15

Dividend Achiever Status

Rank	153	10 Year Growth Rate	10.10%
Total Years of Dividend Growth		10

Business Summary: Water Utilities (MIC: 7.2 SIC: 4941 NAIC:221310)

Pennichuck is a holding company. Through its subsidiaries, Co. is engaged primarily in the collection, storage, treatment, distribution and sale of potable water throughout southern and central New Hampshire. Pennichuck Water Works, Pennichuck East Utility and Pittsfield Aquaduct Company each operate as regulated public utilities. As of Dec 31 2003, Co. served approximately 29,400 residential and commercial and industrial customers. Co. is also involved in the development of commercial and residential real estate through its Southwood real estate subsidiary, and additional non-regulated, water-related management services and contract operations through Pennichuck Water Service Corporation.

Recent Developments: For the first quarter ended Mar 31 2004, Co. reported a net loss of $21,000,000 versus net income of $147,000,000 in the corresponding prior-year quarter. Results for 2004 and 2003 included eminent domain taking and other non-recurring charges of $289.0 million and $479.0 million, respectively. Total revenues decreased 1.3% to $4.8 million from $4.9 million a year earlier. Real Estate operations revenue dropped 77.7% to $101,000, while water utility operations revenue increased 4.1% to $4.2 million. Contract operations revenue climbed 34.6% to $463,000, and other revenues rose 16.7% to $14,000. Operating income fell 37.5% to $742,000, due to higher maintenance costs and contract expense.

Prospects: On Apr 20 2004, Co. sued the City of Nashua for over $5.0 million for the deprivation of its civil rights and abuse of government powers in an attempt to illegally seize assets and disrupt normal operations. In Jan 2004, Co. agreed to acquire community water systems in Bow and Windham, NH. White Rock Senior Living Community in Bow serves about 400 people in a residential setting, while Lamplighter Village in Windham serves about 200 customers. Co. will assume ownership of the two water systems upon completion of the water system construction. Separately, Co. continues to secure new water service contracts in southern New Hampshire.

Financial Data

(US$ in Thousands)	3 Mos	12/31/2003	12/31/2002	12/31/2001	12/31/2000	12/31/1999	12/31/1998	12/31/1997
Earnings Per Share	0.45	0.52	0.97	1.50	1.55	1.12	1.19	0.85
Cash Flow Per Share	0.22	1.77	1.65	3.02	3.25	2.09	1.56	2.10
Tang. Book Val. Per Share	12.38	12.59	12.72	12.81	12.19	11.30	10.91	9.16
Dividends Per Share	0.860	0.840	0.810	0.750	0.720	0.690	0.590	0.530
Dividend Payout %	191.11	161.53	83.81	50.62	46.85	61.74	49.47	61.99
Income Statement								
Total Revenues	4,798	21,388	23,422	22,754	23,671	17,809	17,395	11,841
Total Indirect Exp.	393	...	...	...	...	...	...	...
Costs & Expenses	4,056	16,193	15,774	14,202	14,456	11,733	11,676	8,031
Operating Income	742	5,195	7,647	8,552	9,216	6,076	5,719	3,810
Net Interest Inc./(Exp.)	(495)	(1,969)	(1,978)	(1,981)	(1,991)	(2,025)	(2,264)	(1,774)
Income Taxes	(27)	888	1,450	2,657	2,870	1,625	1,342	791
Eqty Earns/Minority Int.	...	(33)	2	(523)	(855)	19	(41)	...
Net Income	(21)	1,247	2,341	3,612	3,683	2,616	2,106	1,290
Average Shs. Outstg.	2,396	2,398	2,411	2,400	2,363	2,335	1,765	1,506
Balance Sheet								
Net Property	85,955	85,727	79,672	73,960	68,438	63,005	58,389	47,094
Total Assets	97,696	97,210	90,982	87,841	82,880	75,581	70,838	55,090
Long-Term Obligations	26,936	26,879	26,860	27,072	26,918	27,223	28,002	25,436
Net Stockholders' Equity	29,667	30,172	30,434	30,595	28,596	26,257	24,811	13,833
Shares Outstanding	2,396	2,396	2,391	2,387	2,343	2,323	2,274	1,508
Statistical Record								
Operating Profit Margin %	15.46	24.28	32.65	37.58	38.93	34.11	32.87	32.17
Net Profit Margin %	N.M.	14.13	22.37	39.23	39.80	32.93	27.54	24.25
Net Inc./Net Property %	N.M.	1.45	2.93	4.88	5.38	4.15	3.60	2.73
Net Inc./Tot. Capital %	N.M.	1.90	3.66	5.65	5.94	4.49	3.72	3.07
Return on Equity %	N.M.	4.13	7.69	11.80	12.87	9.96	8.48	9.32
Accum. Depr./Gross Prop. %	26.17	25.76	25.50	25.22	24.70	24.15	23.82	25.56
Price Range	28.99-27.95	28.94-21.01	32.01-24.00	27.00-19.50	24.75-15.66	25.50-14.48	19.97-9.00	10.13-7.75
P/E Ratio	64.42-62.11	55.65-40.40	33.00-24.74	18.00-13.00	15.97-10.10	22.77-12.93	16.78-7.56	11.91-9.12
Average Yield %	3.02	3.36	2.94	3.39	3.66	3.95	4.37	5.81

Address: 25 Manchester Street, Merrimack, NH 03054	**Officers:** Donald L. Correll – Pres., C.E.O., Stephen J. Densberger – Exec. V.P.	**Investor Contact:**603-882-5191
Telephone: (603) 882 5191	**Transfer Agents:**EquiServe, LP, Canton, MA	**Institutional Holding**
Web Site: www.pennichuck.com		**No of Institutions:** –
		Shares: – **% Held:** –

PENTAIR, INC.

Exchange	Symbol	Price	52Wk Range	Yield	P/E
NYS	PNR	$61.28 (5/28/2004)	61.57–36.85	0.72	19.52

*7 Year Price Score 121.6 *NYSE Composite Index=100 *12 Month Price Score 60.0

Interim Earnings (Per Share)

Qtr.	Mar	Jun	Sep	Dec
2001	0.42	0.58	0.50	(0.33)
2002	0.43	0.86	0.75	0.57
2003	0.56	0.88	0.77	0.69
2004	0.80	...	...	...

Interim Dividends (Per Share)

Amt	Decl	Ex	Rec	Pay
0.21Q	1/15/2004	1/28/2004	1/30/2004	2/13/2004
0.21Q	4/15/2004	4/28/2004	4/30/2004	5/14/2004
100%	5/17/2004	6/9/2004	6/1/2004	6/8/2004
0.11Q	5/17/2004	7/28/2004	7/30/2004	8/13/2004

Indicated Div: $0.44 (Div. Reinv. Plan)

Valuation Analysis

Forecast P/E 16.87 (5/24/2004)

Market Cap $3.0 Billion	Book Value 1.3 Billion
Price/Book 2.25	Price/Sales 1.02

Dividend Achiever Status

Rank	175	10 Year Growth Rate	9.20%
Total Years of Dividend Growth			27

Business Summary: Industrial Machinery and Equipment (MIC: 11.5 SIC: 3553 NAIC:333210)

Pentair is a diversified industrial manufacturer operating in three segments. The Water segment manufactures and markets products and systems used in the movement, treatment, storage and use of water. The Enclosures segment designs, manufactures, and markets standard, modified and custom enclosures that protect sensitive controls and components. The Tools segment designs, manufactures and markets a range of power tools under such trade names as PorterCable™, Delta®, Delta Shopmaster™, Delta Industrial™, Biesemeyer®, FLEX™, Ex–Cell™, Air America®, Charge Air Pro®, 2 x 4™, Oldham®, Contractor SuperDuty™, Viper®, Hickory Woodworking®, and The Woodworker's Choice®.

Recent Developments: For the three months ended Apr 3 2004, net income advanced 44.4% to $40.2 million compared with $27.8 million in the corresponding year-earlier period. Net sales climbed 20.3% to $767.1 million from $637.5 million the previous year. Co. noted that excluding the effects of an acquisition, favorable currency translation, and four additional days in the first quarter of 2004, sales increased approximately 11.0%. Co.'s improved results were driven by higher revenues and improved operating profit from across its three operating segments. Operating income was $73.0 million, an increase of 39.9% from the year before.

Prospects: Co.'s outlook appears favorable, reflecting solid top-line growth from across its three operating segments as well as strengthening margins, due in part to on-going productivity improvements. Accordingly, Co. expects organic sales growth in the mid- to high-single digits for the remainder of 2004. Also, Co. anticipates full-year 2004 earnings of between $3.45 and $3.60 per share, excluding the effect of its acquisition of WICOR Industries. Co. noted that the FTC is reviewing its proposed acquisition of WICOR and that it expects to complete the acquisition in the second or third quarter of 2004. Lastly, Co.'s review of strategic alternatives for its Tools Group continues on schedule.

Financial Data

(US$ in Thousands)	3 Mos	12/31/2003	12/31/2002	12/31/2001	12/31/2000	12/31/1999	12/31/1998	12/31/1997
Earnings Per Share	3.14	2.90	2.61	1.17	1.68	2.33	2.46	2.11
Cash Flow Per Share	0.05	5.27	5.44	4.71	3.80	3.29	3.13	2.73
Tang. Book Val. Per Share	N.M	N.M	N.M	N.M	N.M	N.M	4.70	3.70
Dividends Per Share	0.840	0.820	0.740	0.700	0.660	0.640	0.600	0.540
Dividend Payout %	27.27	28.27	28.35	59.82	39.28	27.46	24.39	25.59
Income Statement								
Total Revenues	767,141	2,724,365	2,580,783	2,615,944	2,748,013	2,367,753	1,937,578	1,839,056
Total Indirect Exp.	128,622	419,484	379,715	490,238	494,468	520,699	414,076	378,456
Depreciation & Amort.	18,815	65,643	64,702	104,349	99,028	88,645	68,388	67,836
Operating Income	73,036	259,554	235,992	157,761	202,030	214,331	193,192	169,802
Net Interest Inc./(Exp.)	(11,174)	(40,936)	(43,545)	(61,488)	(74,899)	(47,802)	(22,248)	(21,733)
Income Taxes	21,652	74,330	62,545	35,772	45,263	63,220	64,104	66,782
Income from Cont Ops	...	144,288	...	57,516	81,886	...	...	...
Net Income	40,210	141,352	129,902	32,869	55,887	103,309	106,840	91,600
Average Shs. Outstg.	50,265	49,810	49,744	49,297	48,645	44,287	43,149	43,067
Balance Sheet								
Cash & Cash Equivalents	63,247	47,989	39,648	39,844	34,944	66,228	32,039	34,340
Total Current Assets	950,221	829,451	810,808	835,603	1,091,802	1,150,478	748,569	705,370
Total Assets	2,889,197	2,780,677	2,514,450	2,372,198	2,644,025	2,802,966	1,554,666	1,472,862
Total Current Liabilities	476,820	497,451	476,200	428,433	648,792	760,947	394,793	392,177
Long–Term Obligations	829,135	732,862	673,911	714,977	781,834	857,296	288,026	294,549
Net Stockholders' Equity	1,299,949	1,261,478	1,105,724	1,015,002	1,010,591	993,205	709,365	630,562
Net Working Capital	473,401	332,000	334,608	407,170	443,010	389,531	353,776	313,193
Shares Outstanding	50,079	49,502	49,222	49,110	48,711	48,317	38,503	38,185
Operating Profit Margin %	9.52	9.52	9.14	6.03	7.35	9.05	9.97	9.23
Net Profit Margin %	10.88	10.75	9.88	4.93	6.27	9.70	12.13	12.24
Return on Equity %	3.09	11.43	11.74	5.66	8.10	10.40	15.06	14.52
Return on Assets %	1.39	5.18	5.16	2.42	3.09	3.68	6.87	6.21
Debt/Total Assets %	28.69	26.35	26.80	30.13	29.56	30.58	18.52	19.99
Price Range	59.30-44.79	46.47-32.85	49.50-29.50	39.25-22.50	44.06-21.00	48.31-29.75	44.65-27.20	38.21-26.20
P/E Ratio	18.89-14.26	16.02-11.33	18.97-11.30	33.55-19.23	26.23-12.50	20.73-12.77	18.15-11.06	18.11-12.42
Average Yield %	1.64	2.09	1.84	2.20	2.00	1.59	1.60	1.67

Address: 1500 Country Road B2 West,	Officers: Randall J. Hogan – Chmn., Pres., C.E.O.,	Investor Contact:651–639–5278
St. Paul, MN 55113	David D. Harrison – Exec. V.P., C.F.O., Chief	Institutional Holding
Telephone: (651) 636–7920	Acctg. Officer	No of Institutions: 19
Web Site: www.pentair.com	Transfer Agents:Wells Fargo Bank Minnesota, N.A.	Shares: 272,559 % Held: –

PEOPLE'S BANK

Exchange	Symbol	Price	52Wk Range	Yield	P/E
NMS	PBCT	$31.98 (5/28/2004)	33.27-18.38	3.63	N/A

*7 Year Price Score 127.9   *NYSE Composite Index=100   ***12 Month Price Score 60.3**

TRADING VOLUME (thousand shares)

Interim Earnings (Per Share)

Qtr.	Mar	Jun	Sep	Dec
2002	------------------0.60------------------			
2003	0.18	0.16	0.16	0.18
2004	(0.83)	...	...	...

Interim Dividends (Per Share)

Amt	Decl	Ex	Rec	Pay
0.26Q	10/16/2003	10/29/2003	11/1/2003	11/15/2003
0.26Q	1/15/2004	1/28/2004	2/1/2004	2/15/2004
0.29Q	4/15/2004	4/28/2004	5/1/2004	5/15/2004
3-for-2	4/15/2004	5/17/2004	5/1/2004	5/15/2004

Indicated Div: $1.16 (Div. Reinv. Plan)

Valuation Analysis

Forecast P/E 32.04 (5/24/2004)

Market Cap	$164.6 Million	Book Value	N/A
Price/Book	N/A	Price/Sales	N/A

Dividend Achiever Status

Rank	1	10 Year Growth Rate	43.97%
Total Years of Dividend Growth			10

Business Summary: Commercial Banking (MIC: 8.1 SIC: 6022 NAIC:522110)

People's Bank had assets of $11.67 billion as of Dec 31 2003. Co. is a diversified financial services company providing commercial, consumer, insurance and investment services. In addition, Co. is an international credit card issuer, ranking 19th nationally as a provider of MasterCard and Visa. As of Dec 31 2003, Co. served the entire Connecticut market through a network of 154 branches, with 64 located in Super Stop and Shop stores. Co.'s subsidiaries offer brokerage services through People's Securities, asset management through Olson, Mobeck and Associates, equipment financing and leasing through People's Capital and Leasing, and insurance services through R.C. Knox and Company.

Recent Developments: For the quarter ended Mar 31 2004, Co. reported a loss from continuing operations of $78.1 million versus income of $17.3 million in the comparable prior-year period. Results for 2003 and 2002 included net gains on the sales of residential mortgage loans of $1.0 million and $4.1 million, net security losses of $4.8 million and $4.6 million, and liability restructuring costs of $133.4 million and $1.2 million, respectively. Net interest income rose 4.4% to $73.3 million. Co. reported a credit for loan losses of $100,000 versus a provision of $7.9 million. Total non-interest income fell 15.9% to $34.5 million. Total non-interest expense surged to $227.7 million versus $86.9 million in 2003.

Prospects: Operating results reflect the recent sale of Co.'s credit card business and the prepayment of over $1.00 billion in high-cost wholesale liabilities. Additionally, Co.'s increased equity position is sustaining its capital levels and providing ample room to support continued strong internal loan growth and to pursue potential acquisition opportunities. Meanwhile, Co. continues to focus on its core consumer and commercial banking businesses, including further strengthening of its franchise in Connecticut. Co. also continues to generate solid growth across its lending businesses, particularly its residential mortgage businesses.

Financial Data

(US$ in Thousands)	3 Mos	12/31/2003	12/31/2002	12/31/2001	12/31/2000	12/31/1999	12/31/1998	12/31/1997
Earnings Per Share	(0.33)	0.68	0.60	0.93	1.18	1.20	0.96	1.00
Tang. Book Val. Per Share	11.17	9.55	8.92	8.88	8.23	7.07	7.49	7.73
Dividends Per Share	1.040	1.020	0.940	0.890	0.800	0.680	0.560	0.440
Dividend Payout %	N.M.	99.02	105.18	63.80	45.19	37.93	38.88	29.72
Income Statement								
Total Interest Income	107,200	514,700	614,200	727,100	766,800	666,800	593,100	524,800
Total Interest Expense	33,900	194,300	263,000	373,100	381,700	328,900	305,900	271,800
Net Interest Income	73,300	320,400	351,200	354,000	385,100	337,900	287,200	253,000
Provision for Loan Losses	(100)	48,600	77,700	101,100	59,900	54,500	45,800	39,900
Non–Interest Income	34,500	251,000	247,900	320,500	293,000	300,800	310,500	250,000
Non–Interest Expense	227,700	435,900	441,000	440,500	452,700	413,800	378,500	319,000
Income Before Taxes	(119,800)	86,900	80,400	132,900	165,500	170,400	173,400	144,100
Income from Cont Ops	(78,100)	...	...	86,700	...	...	...	...
Net Income	119,200	63,800	55,400	75,800	108,400	112,000	91,700	92,400
Average Shs. Outstg.	93,750	92,850	92,550	92,400	92,100	93,000	95,805	92,100
Balance Sheet								
Cash & Due from Banks	279,800	343,000	451,900	408,400	373,900	328,800	288,700	241,500
Securities Avail. for Sale	2,063,500	2,554,600	3,334,600	2,895,900	2,437,400	2,197,300	2,052,600	1,446,600
Net Loans & Leases	7,164,600	8,121,800	7,336,200	6,931,000	7,344,700	6,969,600	6,481,100	5,389,600
Total Assets	10,669,100	11,671,600	12,260,600	11,890,600	11,570,900	10,738,100	9,918,700	8,184,000
Total Deposits	8,793,100	8,714,000	8,426,100	7,983,400	7,761,300	7,191,100	6,937,500	5,818,400
Long–Term Obligations	121,700	1,217,200	1,848,400	1,576,500	2,039,600	1,613,600	1,267,000	925,500
Total Liabilities	9,510,400	10,669,500	11,321,000	10,955,600	10,689,100	9,956,400	9,066,400	7,474,100
Net Stockholders' Equity	1,158,700	1,002,000	939,600	935,000	881,800	781,700	852,300	709,900
Shares Outstanding	93,600	93,000	92,550	92,250	91,950	91,650	95,574	91,740
Return on Equity %	N.M	6.36	5.89	9.27	12.29	14.32	10.75	13.01
Return on Assets %	N.M.	0.54	0.45	0.72	0.93	1.04	0.92	1.12
Equity/Assets %	10.86	8.58	7.66	7.86	7.62	7.27	8.59	8.67
Non–Int. Exp./Tot. Inc. %	160.69	56.92	51.15	42.04	42.71	42.76	41.88	41.17
Price Range	30.99–21.70	22.59–16.33	18.60–13.83	18.83–14.01	17.87–11.33	21.29–13.33	27.42–12.75	25.33–12.64
P/E Ratio	N/A	33.23–24.01	31.00–23.06	20.25–15.06	15.15–9.60	17.74–11.11	28.56–13.28	25.33–12.64
Average Yield %	3.78	5.34	5.78	5.59	5.86	3.77	2.59	2.44

Address: 850 Main Street, Bridgeport, CT 06604

Telephone: (203) 338-7171

Web Site: www.peoples.com

Officers: John A. Klein – Chmn., Pres., C.E.O., Jacinta A. Coleman – Exec. V.P., Chief Info. Off.

Transfer Agents: Mellon Investor Services, LLC, Ridgefield Park, NJ

Investor Contact: 203–338–4114

Institutional Holding
No of Institutions: 95
Shares: 11,812,633   **% Held:** –

PEOPLES ENERGY CORP.

Exchange	Symbol	Price	52Wk Range	Yield	P/E
NYS	PGL	$41.42 (5/28/2004)	45.91-38.92	5.21	14.53

*7 Year Price Score 111.2 *NYSE Composite Index=100 *12 Month Price Score 45.5

TRADING VOLUME (thousand shares)

Interim Earnings (Per Share)

Qtr.	Dec	Mar	Jun	Sep
2000-01	1.03	1.76	0.33	(0.38)
2001-02	0.87	1.55	0.04	0.05
2002-03	0.87	1.77	0.22	0.01
2003-04	0.85	1.46	...	...

Interim Dividends (Per Share)

Amt	Decl	Ex	Rec	Pay
0.53Q	8/6/2003	9/18/2003	9/22/2003	10/15/2003
0.53Q	12/5/2003	12/18/2003	12/22/2003	1/15/2004
0.54Q	2/4/2004	3/18/2004	3/22/2004	4/15/2004
0.54Q	6/2/2004	6/18/2004	6/22/2004	7/15/2004

Indicated Div: $2.16 (Div. Reinv. Plan)

Valuation Analysis

Forecast P/E 15.00 (5/24/2004)

Market Cap $1.5 Billion	Book Value	862.6 Million
Price/Book 1.79	Price/Sales	0.70

Dividend Achiever Status

Rank 293	10 Year Growth Rate	1.74%
Total Years of Dividend Growth	20	

Business Summary: Gas Utilities (MIC: 7.4 SIC: 4924 NAIC:221210)

Peoples Energy is a holding company. Income is derived principally from Co.'s subsidiaries, The Peoples Gas Light and Coke Company and North Shore Gas Company. Co. also derives income from its other subsidiaries, Peoples Energy Resources Company, LLC, Peoples Energy Services Corporation, Peoples Energy Production Company, Peoples District Energy Corporation, Peoples Energy Ventures, LLC and Peoples NGV Corp. Through its subsidiaries, Co. operates six business segments: Gas Distribution, Power Generation, Midstream Services, Retail Energy Services, Oil and Gas Production and Other. As of Sep 30 2003, Co. had approximately 1,000,000 electric customers and approximately 150,000 gas customers.

Recent Developments: For the quarter ended Mar 31 2004, net income decreased 13.5% to $54.9 million compared with $63.5 million in the equivalent period of the previous year. The decrease in earnings was largely due to lower natural gas deliveries and higher operating costs in Co.'s gas distribution segment, partially offset by a 22.0% increase in operating income from its diversified energy businesses. Results for 2004 and 2003 included a pre-tax equity investment gain of $1.5 million and loss of $13,000, respectively. Total revenues climbed 2.6% to $927.0 million from $903.8 million in the prior-year quarter. Operating income declined 17.1% to $94.9 million versus $114.5 million in the year-earlier period.

Prospects: In the near-term, Co.'s gas distribution segment income is expected to be lower than anticipated; however, diversified energy results are exceeding original expectations and should produce significant year-over-year growth in fiscal 2004. Notably, Co.'s oil and gas production and retail energy services segments are expected to generate solid results in 2004. The oil and gas production segment is benefiting from higher production volumes and higher net realized commodity prices. Co.'s retail energy services segment is benefiting from customer growth and enhanced gas margin. Meanwhile, Co. continues to expect that earnings will range from $2.70 to $2.85 per share for full-year 2004.

Financial Data

(US$ in Thousands)	6 Mos	3 Mos	09/30/2003	09/30/2002	09/30/2001	09/30/2000	09/30/1999	09/30/1998
Earnings Per Share	2.54	2.85	2.87	2.51	2.74	2.44	2.61	2.25
Cash Flow Per Share	5.64	(1.61)	5.68	9.24	4.78	1.44	5.17	4.49
Tang. Book Val. Per Share	24.17	23.32	23.11	22.73	22.66	21.86	21.66	20.94
Dividends Per Share	2.120	2.110	2.100	2.060	2.020	1.980	1.940	1.900
Dividend Payout %	83.46	74.35	73.17	82.07	73.72	81.14	74.32	84.44
Income Statement								
Total Revenues	1,531,905	604,884	2,138,394	1,482,534	2,270,218	1,417,533	1,194,381	1,138,057
Total Indirect Exp.	176,151	77,107	243,690	234,809	287,894	242,457	214,043	207,293
Costs & Expenses	1,376,812	544,732	1,928,880	1,311,185	2,108,201	1,258,350	1,038,367	1,024,248
Depreciation & Amort.	59,892	28,921	111,825	98,852	95,046	100,935	83,531	77,195
Operating Income	155,093	60,152	209,514	171,349	162,017	159,183	156,014	113,809
Net Interest Inc./(Exp.)	(24,662)	(12,281)	(49,441)	(60,930)	(72,051)	(52,919)	(39,511)	(35,468)
Income from Cont Ops	...	...	...	...	97,054	...	...	...
Net Income	86,255	31,351	103,934	89,071	97,020	86,415	92,636	79,423
Average Shs. Outstg.	37,253	36,976	36,113	35,492	35,439	35,413	35,490	35,276
Balance Sheet								
Net Property	1,895,792	1,888,216	1,838,173	1,773,901	1,753,912	1,645,340	1,519,836	1,446,661
Total Assets	3,162,485	3,184,729	2,928,538	2,723,647	2,994,054	2,501,918	2,100,164	1,904,500
Long-Term Obligations	846,330	846,330	744,345	554,014	644,308	419,663	521,734	516,604
Net Stockholders' Equity	906,574	862,584	847,999	806,324	805,517	777,082	768,730	741,361
Shares Outstanding	37,502	36,985	36,689	35,459	35,544	35,544	35,489	35,402
Statistical Record								
Operating Profit Margin %	10.20	9.90	10.62	11.55	7.13	11.22	13.06	13.92
Net Inc./Net Property %	4.55	1.66	5.65	5.02	5.53	5.25	6.09	5.49
Net Inc./Tot. Capital %	4.92	1.48	5.19	5.12	5.43	5.61	5.82	5.19
Return on Equity %	9.51	3.60	14.34	11.04	12.04	11.12	12.05	16.73
Accum. Depr./Gross Prop. %	38.29	37.82	37.94	36.52	35.12	34.63	34.79	34.53
Price Range	45.91-38.92	42.65-38.92	45.12-31.68	42.62-29.83	46.56-31.81	39.44-26.81	40.00-32.31	39.63-33.13
P/E Ratio	18.07-15.32	14.96-13.66	15.72-11.04	16.98-11.88	16.99-11.61	16.16-10.99	15.33-12.38	17.61-14.72
Average Yield %	5.03	5.16	5.43	5.53	5.20	6.03	5.25	5.22

Address: 130 East Randolph Drive, Chicago, IL 60601-6207	**Officers:** Thomas M. Patrick - Chmn., Pres., C.E.O., William E. Morrow - Exec. V.P.	**Investor Contact:**312-240-7534 **Institutional Holding**
Telephone: (312) 240-4000	**Transfer Agents:**Computershare Investor Services, Chicago, IL	**No of Institutions:** 3
Web Site: www.peoplesenergy.com		**Shares:** 45,906 **% Held:** -

PEPSICO INC.

Exchange	Symbol	Price	52Wk Range	Yield	P/E
NYS	PEP	$53.37 (5/28/2004)	55.07–43.52	1.72	25.91

*7 Year Price Score 113.4   *NYSE Composite Index=100   *12 Month Price Score 52.6

Interim Earnings (Per Share)

Qtr.	Mar	Jun	Aug	Dec
2001	0.34	0.44	0.34	0.35
2002	0.36	0.49	0.54	0.46
2003	0.45	0.58	0.62	0.40
2004	0.46	...	...	...

Interim Dividends (Per Share)

Amt	Decl	Ex	Rec	Pay
0.16Q	7/24/2003	9/10/2003	9/12/2003	9/30/2003
0.16Q	11/21/2003	12/10/2003	12/12/2003	1/2/2004
0.16Q	1/29/2004	3/10/2004	3/12/2004	3/31/2004
0.23Q	5/5/2004	6/9/2004	6/11/2004	6/30/2004

Indicated Div: $0.92 (Div. Reinv. Plan)

Valuation Analysis

Forecast P/E 23.17 (5/24/2004)

Market Cap	$94.6 Billion	Book Value	12.5 Billion
Price/Book	7.28	Price/Sales	3.30

Dividend Achiever Status

Rank	203	10 Year Growth Rate	7.89%
Total Years of Dividend Growth			32

Business Summary: Food (MIC: 4.1 SIC: 2086 NAIC:312111)

PepsiCo is a global snack and beverage company. Co. manufactures, markets and sells a variety of salty, convenient, sweet and grain–based snacks, carbonated and non–carbonated beverages and foods. Co.'s Frito–Lay North America division's brands include *Lay's* potato chips, *Fritos* corn chips, *Quaker Chewy* granola bars and *Rold Gold* pretzels. PepsiCo Beverages North America brands include *Pepsi, Mountain Dew, Sierra Mist, Mug, SoBe, Gatorade, Tropicana Pure Premium* and *Propel*. PepsiCo International brands include *Sabritas* in Mexico, *Walkers* in the UK, and *Smith's* in Australia. Quaker Foods North America's products include *Quaker* oatmeal and *Cap'n Crunch* and *Life* ready–to–eat cereals.

Recent Developments: For the 12 weeks ended Mar 20 2004, net income was $804.0 million compared with $698.0 million in the corresponding year–earlier period. Results for 2003 included merger–related costs of $11.0 million. Net revenue climbed 10.9% to $6.13 billion from $5.53 billion the previous year. Co.'s improved results were fueled by strong volume growth, with total servings of products sold worldwide up 7.0%. Servings of snacks worldwide grew 7.0%, while worldwide servings of beverages rose 8.0%. Operating profit was $1.13 billion, an increase of 9.8% versus the prior–year period.

Prospects: Co.'s near–term outlook is strengthened by recent favorable operating trends that are contributing to higher revenues and operating profits from across its four operating segments. Notably, Co.'s Frito–Lay North America segment is benefiting from increased volume, positive mix, and modest pricing. Meanwhile, PepsiCo Beverages North America is experiencing strong growth from its non–carbonated beverage portfolio. Future results from this segment should also benefit from new products such as *Pepsi Edge*, a cola with 50.0% less calories and sugar than regular cola, that is expected to be launched in the summer of 2004. Accordingly, Co. is now targeting 2004 earnings of about $2.29 per share.

Financial Data

(US$ in Thousands)	3 Mos	12/27/2003	12/28/2002	12/29/2001	12/30/2000	12/25/1999	12/26/1998	12/27/1997
Earnings Per Share	2.06	2.05	1.85	1.47	1.48	1.37	1.31	0.95
Cash Flow Per Share	0.41	2.48	2.58	2.32	2.65	2.02	2.11	2.17
Tang. Book Val. Per Share	4.16	3.81	2.36	2.16	1.91	1.47	N.M	0.71
Dividends Per Share	0.630	0.620	0.590	0.570	0.550	0.530	0.510	0.480
Dividend Payout %	37.95	30.24	31.89	38.77	37.16	38.68	38.93	50.52
Income Statement								
Total Revenues	6,131,000	26,971,000	25,112,000	26,935,000	20,438,000	20,367,000	22,348,000	20,917,000
Total Indirect Exp.	2,193,000	9,811,000	8,885,000	12,160,000	9,270,000	9,351,000	10,434,000	9,730,000
Depreciation & Amort.	32,000	145,000	138,000	165,000	138,000	183,000	222,000	199,000
Operating Income	1,127,000	4,781,000	4,730,000	4,021,000	3,225,000	2,818,000	2,584,000	2,662,000
Net Interest Inc./(Exp.)	(25,000)	(112,000)	(142,000)	(152,000)	(145,000)	(245,000)	(321,000)	(353,000)
Income Taxes	337,000	1,424,000	1,555,000	1,367,000	1,027,000	1,606,000	270,000	818,000
Income from Cont Ops	...	...	...	...	...	...	...	1,491,000
Net Income	804,000	3,568,000	3,313,000	2,662,000	2,183,000	2,050,000	1,993,000	2,142,000
Average Shs. Outstg.	1,736,000	1,739,000	1,789,000	1,807,000	1,475,000	1,496,000	1,519,000	1,570,000
Balance Sheet								
Cash & Cash Equivalents	773,000	820,000	1,638,000	683,000	864,000	964,000	311,000	1,928,000
Total Current Assets	7,152,000	6,930,000	6,413,000	5,853,000	4,604,000	4,173,000	4,362,000	6,251,000
Total Assets	25,503,000	25,327,000	23,474,000	21,695,000	18,339,000	17,551,000	22,660,000	20,101,000
Total Current Liabilities	5,958,000	6,415,000	6,052,000	4,998,000	3,935,000	3,788,000	7,914,000	4,257,000
Long–Term Obligations	1,648,000	1,702,000	2,187,000	2,651,000	2,346,000	2,812,000	4,028,000	4,946,000
Net Stockholders' Equity	12,591,000	11,896,000	9,298,000	8,648,000	7,249,000	6,881,000	6,401,000	6,936,000
Net Working Capital	1,194,000	515,000	361,000	855,000	669,000	385,000	(3,552,000)	1,994,000
Shares Outstanding	1,708,000	1,705,000	1,722,000	1,756,000	1,446,000	1,455,000	1,471,000	1,502,000
Statistical Record								
Operating Profit Margin %	18.38	17.72	18.83	14.92	15.77	13.83	11.56	12.72
Return on Equity %	6.42	30.04	35.65	30.68	30.11	29.79	31.13	21.49
Return on Assets %	3.15	14.08	14.11	12.27	11.90	11.68	8.79	7.41
Debt/Total Assets %	6.46	6.72	9.31	12.21	12.79	16.02	17.77	24.60
Price Range	52.75–45.39	48.71–37.30	53.12–35.50	50.28–41.26	49.75–30.63	41.81–30.25	44.69–27.69	41.06–29.13
P/E Ratio	25.61–22.03	23.76–18.20	28.71–19.19	34.20–28.07	33.61–20.69	30.52–22.08	34.11–21.14	43.22–30.66
Average Yield %	1.28	1.41	1.28	1.24	1.34	1.44	1.36	1.35

Address: 700 Anderson Hill Road, Purchase, NY 10577–1444 **Telephone:** (914) 253–2000 **Web Site:** www.pepsico.com	**Officers:** Steven S. Reinemund – Chmn., C.E.O., Indra K. Nooyi – Pres., C.F.O. **Transfer Agents:** The Bank of New York, New York, NY	**Investor Contact:** 914–253–3035 **Institutional Holding** **No of Institutions:** 44 **Shares:** 1,317,724 **% Held:** –

PFIZER INC

Exchange	Symbol	Price	52Wk Range	Yield	P/E
NYS	PFE	$35.34 (5/28/2004)	38.85−29.55	1.92	294.50

*7 Year Price Score 94.3 *NYSE Composite Index=100 *12 Month Price Score 49.1

Interim Earnings (Per Share)

Qtr.	Mar	Jun	Sep	Dec
2001	0.30	0.29	0.33	0.30
2002	0.37	0.32	0.38	0.40
2003	0.40	(0.49)	0.29	0.02
2004	0.30	...	...	...

Interim Dividends (Per Share)

Amt	Decl	Ex	Rec	Pay
0.15Q	6/26/2003	8/13/2003	8/15/2003	9/4/2003
0.15Q	10/23/2003	11/12/2003	11/14/2003	12/4/2003
0.17Q	12/15/2003	2/11/2004	2/13/2004	3/5/2004
0.17Q	4/22/2004	5/12/2004	5/14/2004	6/4/2004

Indicated Div: $0.68 (Div. Relnv. Plan)

Valuation Analysis

Forecast P/E 16.48 (5/24/2004)

Market Cap	$217.8 Billion	Book Value	68.8 Billion
Price/Book	3.89	Price/Sales	5.45

Dividend Achiever Status

Rank	72	10 Year Growth Rate	15.67%
Total Years of Dividend Growth		36	

Business Summary: Pharmaceuticals (MIC: 9.1 SIC: 2834 NAIC:325412)

Pfizer is a research−based, global pharmaceutical company that discovers, develops, manufactures and markets medicines for humans and animals as well as consumer healthcare products. The products include *Norvasc*, for the treatment of hypertension and angina, *Zyrtec*, an anti−allergy medicine, *Viagra*, an oral medication for the treatment of erectile dysfunction, *Zoloft*, a selective serotonin re−uptake inhibitor for the treatment of depression. The animal health segment includes anti−parasitic, anti−infective and anti−inflammatory medicines, and vaccines. The consumer healthcare segment includes *Nicorette*, for tobacco dependence, *Benadryl* antihistamine for allergies

Recent Developments: For the three months ended Mar 31 2004, income was $2.32 billion, before a gain of $13.0 million from discontinued operations, compared with income of $2.46 billion, before a gain of $2.24 billion from discontinued operations and an accounting change charge of $30.0 million, in the equivalent quarter of the previous year. Results for 2004 and 2003 included pre−tax merger−related costs of $1.20 billion and $91.0 million, respectively. Revenues advanced 46.8% to $12.49 billion, driven by the inclusion of post−acquisition results of legacy Pharmacia products, strong performance across a broad range of products, and the weakening of the U.S. dollar relative to other currencies.

Prospects: Results continue to reflect the strong performance of Co.'s broad product portfolio as well as contributions from the integration of Pharmacia. Co. should continue to benefit from its clinical investments and ongoing partnering initiatives. Meanwhile, Co. continues to forecast revenues of approximately $54.00 billion and diluted earnings per share of $1.55 for 2004, reflecting additional in−process research and development expenses. Moreover, Co. expects merger−related cost synergies in 2004 to be approximately $3.40 billion and plans to spend about $7.90 billion in research and development.

Financial Data

(US$ in Thousands)	3 Mos	12/31/2003	12/31/2002	12/31/2001	12/31/2000	12/31/1999	12/31/1998	12/31/1997
Earnings Per Share	0.12	0.22	1.47	1.22	0.59	0.82	0.49	0.56
Cash Flow Per Share	0.20	1.60	1.58	1.46	0.97	0.79	0.74	0.41
Tang. Book Val. Per Share	1.22	0.85	3.04	2.63	2.26	2.11	2.05	1.71
Dividends Per Share	0.620	0.600	0.520	0.440	0.360	0.300	0.250	0.220
Dividend Payout %	326.32	272.72	35.37	36.06	61.01	37.39	51.70	39.99
Income Statement								
Total Revenues	12,487,000	45,188,000	32,373,000	32,259,000	29,574,000	16,204,000	13,544,000	12,504,000
Total Indirect Exp.	7,564,000	30,666,000	16,680,000	17,088,000	19,254,000	9,170,000	7,892,000	6,952,000
Depreciation & Amort.	1,261,000	2,183,000	28,000	103,000	120,000	43,000	45,000	68,000
Operating Income	3,129,000	6,873,000	11,676,000	10,240,000	5,533,000	4,549,000	3,603,000	3,346,000
Net Interest Inc./(Exp.)	...	76,000	131,000	273,000	172,000	78,000	49,000	9,000
Income Taxes	809,000	1,621,000	2,609,000	2,561,000	2,049,000	1,244,000	642,000	865,000
Income from Cont Ops	2,318,000	1,639,000	9,181,000	7,752,000	3,718,000	3,199,000	1,950,000	...
Net Income	2,331,000	3,910,000	9,126,000	7,788,000	3,726,000	3,179,000	3,351,000	2,213,000
Average Shs. Outstg.	7,586,400	7,286,000	6,241,000	6,361,000	6,368,000	3,884,000	3,945,000	3,909,000
Balance Sheet								
Cash & Cash Equivalents	965,000	1,520,000	1,878,000	1,036,000	1,099,000	739,000	1,552,000	877,000
Total Current Assets	35,389,000	29,741,000	24,781,000	18,450,000	17,187,000	11,191,000	9,931,000	6,820,000
Total Assets	122,289,000	116,775,000	46,356,000	39,153,000	33,510,000	20,574,000	18,302,000	15,336,000
Total Current Liabilities	24,637,000	23,657,000	18,555,000	13,640,000	11,981,000	9,185,000	7,192,000	5,305,000
Long−Term Obligations	7,144,000	5,755,000	3,140,000	2,609,000	1,123,000	525,000	527,000	729,000
Net Stockholders' Equity	69,048,000	65,377,000	19,950,000	18,293,000	16,076,000	8,887,000	8,810,000	7,933,000
Net Working Capital	10,752,000	6,084,000	6,226,000	4,810,000	5,206,000	2,006,000	2,739,000	1,515,000
Shares Outstanding	7,630,536	7,629,000	6,162,000	6,277,000	6,314,000	3,847,000	3,883,000	3,882,000
Statistical Record								
Operating Profit Margin %	25.05	15.20	36.06	31.74	18.70	28.07	26.60	26.75
Return on Equity %	3.35	2.50	46.02	42.37	23.12	35.99	22.13	27.89
Return on Assets %	1.89	1.40	19.80	19.79	11.09	15.54	10.65	14.43
Debt/Total Assets %	5.84	4.92	6.77	6.66	3.35	2.55	2.87	4.75
Price Range	38.85−33.70	36.18−28.56	42.15−25.92	46.13−35.67	48.94−30.44	50.00−31.71	41.98−24.65	25.94−13.62
P/E Ratio	323.75−280.83	164.5−129.8	28.67−17.63	37.81−29.24	82.94−51.59	60.98−38.67	85.67−50.30	46.32−24.33
Average Yield %	1.71	1.88	1.49	1.06	0.87	0.78	0.74	1.18

Address: 235 East 42nd Street, New York, NY 10017−5755	Officers: Henry A. McKinnell − Chmn., Pres., C.E.O., David L. Shedlarz − Exec. V.P., C.F.O.	Institutional Holding
Telephone: (212) 573−2323	Transfer Agents:EquiServe Trust Company, N.A., Jersey City, NJ	No of Institutions: 13
Web Site: www.pfizer.com		Shares: 9,641,163 % Held: −

PIEDMONT NATURAL GAS CO., INC.

Exchange	Symbol	Price	52Wk Range	Yield	P/E
NYS	PNY	$41.01 (5/28/2004)	43.46-37.32	4.19	15.42

*7 Year Price Score 119.1 *NYSE Composite Index=100 ***12 Month Price Score 46.4**

Interim Earnings (Per Share)

Qtr.	Jan	Apr	Jul	Oct
2000–01	1.56	1.23	(0.52)	(0.25)
2001–02	1.26	1.27	(0.27)	(0.37)
2002–03	1.74	0.93	(0.29)	(0.16)
2003–04	2.18	...	...	...

Interim Dividends (Per Share)

Amt	Decl	Ex	Rec	Pay
0.415Q	2/28/2003	3/21/2003	3/25/2003	4/15/2003
0.415Q	5/30/2003	6/20/2003	6/24/2003	7/15/2003
0.415Q	12/12/2003	12/19/2003	12/23/2003	1/15/2004
0.43Q	2/27/2004	3/23/2004	3/25/2004	4/15/2004

Indicated Div: $1.72 (Div. Reinv. Plan)

Valuation Analysis
Forecast P/E 17.14 (5/24/2004)

Market Cap $1.3 Billion	Book Value 871.4 Million
Price/Book 1.67	Price/Sales 1.08

Dividend Achiever Status

Rank	240	10 Year Growth Rate	5.48%
Total Years of Dividend Growth			24

Business Summary: Gas Utilities (MIC: 7.4 SIC: 4924 NAIC:221210)

Piedmont Natural Gas is an energy services company primarily engaged in the distribution of natural gas to 940,000 residential, commercial and industrial customers in North Carolina, South Carolina and Tennessee, including 60,000 customers served by municipalities who are our wholesale customers. Co.'s subsidiaries are invested in joint venture, energy–related businesses, including unregulated retail natural gas and propane marketing, interstate natural gas storage, intrastate natural gas transportation and regulated natural gas distribution. Co. also sells residential and commercial gas appliances in Tennessee.

Recent Developments: For the three months ended Jan 31 2004, net income advanced 28.7% to $74.6 million compared with $58.0 million in the corresponding quarter of the previous year. Earnings growth was primarily attributable to the acquisition of North Carolina Natural Gas on Sep 30 2003. Operating revenues improved 25.4% to $618.8 million from $493.5 million in the year–earlier period. Margin (revenues less the cost of gas) increased 21.5% to $196.5 million from $161.7 million the year before. Operating income jumped 17.8% to $77.3 million versus $65.7 million in the prior–year quarter. System throughput climbed 15.6% to 73,492 dekatherms from 63,589 dekatherms in 2003.

Prospects: Co. is benefiting from strong revenue growth, reflecting the acquisition of North Carolina Natural Gas (NCNG) and internal customer expansion. Accordingly, Co. increased its earnings guidance to range from $2.35 to $2.45 per share, up from its previous guidance of $2.25 to $2.40 per diluted share. This revision includes earnings accretion related to the NCNG acquisition, recent rate case approvals for NCNG and Nashville Gas divisions and the expected negative impact of higher wholesale natural gas prices. Separately, on Jan 20 2004, Co. announced that it and three other utility partners have completed the sale of their interests in Heritage Propane Partners, L.P. for $130.0 million.

Financial Data

(US$ in Thousands)	3 Mos	10/31/2003	10/31/2002	10/31/2001	10/31/2000	10/31/1999	10/31/1998	10/31/1997
Earnings Per Share	2.66	2.22	1.89	2.02	2.01	1.86	1.96	1.79
Cash Flow Per Share	1.68	2.97	3.30	4.94	1.71	1.01	4.01	4.66
Tang. Book Val. Per Share	21.54	17.21	17.81	17.26	16.52	15.71	14.90	13.90
Dividends Per Share	1.660	1.640	1.580	1.520	1.440	1.360	1.280	1.200
Dividend Payout %	62.41	74.09	83.86	75.24	71.64	73.11	65.30	67.31
Income Statement								
Total Revenues	618,785	1,220,822	832,028	1,107,856	830,377	686,470	765,277	775,517
Total Indirect Exp.	26,455	127,667	112,240	110,587	101,630	111,961	112,057	104,017
Costs & Expenses	541,436	1,117,716	741,901	1,013,087	740,677	594,748	674,120	691,531
Depreciation & Amort.	20,453	63,164	57,593	52,060	48,894	44,131	42,175	39,187
Operating Income	77,349	103,106	90,127	93,969	89,700	91,722	91,157	83,986
Net Interest Inc./(Exp.)	(11,211)	(40,197)	(40,604)	(39,414)	(40,272)	(32,371)	(33,187)	(33,996)
Income Taxes	48,595	8,524	9,010	7,300	...	...	...	...
Eqty Earns/Minority Int.	(11)	...	...	...	...	...	...	...
Income from Cont Ops	74,633	...	...	...	...	...	...	...
Net Income	74,622	74,362	62,217	65,485	64,031	58,207	60,313	54,074
Average Shs. Outstg.	34,222	33,503	32,937	32,420	31,779	31,242	30,717	30,229
Balance Sheet								
Net Property	1,816,349	1,813,414	1,159,601	1,115,862	1,071,983	1,046,975	990,640	941,736
Total Assets	2,443,841	2,296,406	1,445,088	1,393,658	1,445,003	1,288,657	1,162,844	1,098,156
Long–Term Obligations	660,000	460,000	462,000	509,000	451,000	423,000	371,000	381,000
Net Stockholders' Equity	871,448	630,195	589,596	560,379	527,372	491,747	458,268	419,826
Shares Outstanding	38,042	33,655	33,090	32,463	31,914	31,294	30,738	30,193
Statistical Record								
Operating Profit Margin %	27.47	8.44	10.83	8.48	10.80	13.36	11.91	10.82
Net Profit Margin %	27.03	7.48	9.64	7.22	7.71	8.47	7.88	6.97
Net Inc./Net Property %	4.10	4.10	5.36	5.86	5.97	5.55	6.08	5.74
Net Inc./Tot. Capital %	4.31	5.81	5.14	5.40	5.69	5.64	6.41	5.96
Return on Equity %	19.19	11.79	10.55	11.68	12.14	11.83	13.16	12.88
Accum. Depr./Gross Prop. %	24.60	24.14	33.07	31.45	30.18	29.14	28.35	27.24
Price Range	43.46-39.54	40.75-32.90	37.95-28.36	39.38-29.44	33.00-23.75	36.13-28.88	36.44-27.19	30.19-22.38
P/E Ratio	16.34-14.86	18.36-14.82	20.08-15.01	19.49-14.57	16.42-11.82	19.42-15.52	18.59-13.87	16.86-12.50
Average Yield %	3.99	4.43	4.55	4.51	5.01	4.14	4.00	4.78

Address: 1915 Rexford Road, Charlotte, NC 28211	Officers: Thomas E. Skains – Chmn., Pres., C.E.O., David J. Dzuricky – Sr. V.P., C.F.O.	Investor Contact:704–731–4438 Institutional Holding
Telephone: (704) 364–3120 Web Site: www.piedmontng.com	Transfer Agents:Wachovia Bank of North Carolina, NA, Boston, MA	No of Institutions: 16 Shares: 115,224 % Held: –

PIER 1 IMPORTS INC.

*7 Year Price Score 148.6 *NYSE Composite Index=100 ***12 Month Price Score 42.5**

Interim Earnings (Per Share)

Qtr.	May	Aug	Nov	Feb
2000–01	0.17	0.18	0.24	0.38
2001–02	0.13	0.14	0.26	0.51
2002–03	0.23	0.23	0.33	0.57
2003–04	0.21	0.20	0.35	0.53

Interim Dividends (Per Share)

Amt	Decl	Ex	Rec	Pay
0.08Q	6/26/2003	8/4/2003	8/6/2003	8/20/2003
0.08Q	9/25/2003	11/3/2003	11/5/2003	11/19/2003
0.08Q	12/4/2003	2/2/2004	2/4/2004	2/18/2004
0.10Q	3/25/2004	5/3/2004	5/5/2004	5/19/2004

Indicated Div: $0.40 (Div. Reinv. Plan)

Valuation Analysis
Forecast P/E 11.76 (5/24/2004)

Market Cap	$1.8 Billion	Book Value	683.6 Million
Price/Book	2.86	Price/Sales	1.05

Dividend Achiever Status

Rank	24	10 Year Growth Rate	22.08%
Total Years of Dividend Growth			12

Business Summary: Retail – Furniture &Home Furnishings (MIC: 5.9 SIC: 5712 NAIC:442110)

Pier 1 Imports is a retailer of decorative home furnishings, furniture, dining and kitchen goods, bath and bedding accessories and other specialty items for the home imported from over 40 countries. As of May 31 2003, Co. operated *Pier 1 Imports®* stores in 50 states, Canada, Puerto Rico, and Mexico; *The Pier®* stores in the U.K.; and *Cargokids®* in six states. Also, Co. supplies merchandise and licenses the Pier 1 Imports name to Sears Mexico and Sears Puerto Rico, which sell Pier 1 merchandise in a "store–within–a–store" format in 17 Sears Mexico stores and in seven Sears Puerto Rico stores.

Recent Developments: For the year ended Feb 28 2004, net income declined 8.8% to $118.0 million compared with $129.4 million the year before. Net sales totaled $1.87 billion, up 6.5% versus $1.75 billion the prior year. Comparable–store sales were down 2.2% year over year. Cost of sales, including buying and store occupancy costs, increased 8.5% to $1.09 billion from $1.00 billion in the previous year. Selling, general and administrative expenses increased 8.4% to $544.5 million from $502.3 million a year earlier. Operating income slid 9.0% to $186.2 million from $204.7 million the year before.

Prospects: Despite business challenges during fiscal year 2004, Co. was able to generate strong operational cash flow and successfully open 120 new Pier 1 stores. Going forward, Co. plans to implement new marketing and key operational initiatives in fiscal 2005 to improve store execution, increase customer traffic and improve sales consistency, while improving profitability. Meanwhile, Co. is encouraged by increased traffic and conversions in stores, and expects comparable–store sales in the first quarter of fiscal 2005 to range from 2.0% to 4.0% and diluted earnings per share of between $0.21 and $0.24. In fiscal 2005, diluted earnings per share are anticipated to range from $1.44 to $1.52 per share.

Financial Data

(US$ in Thousands)	02/28/2004	03/01/2003	03/02/2002	03/03/2001	02/26/2000	02/27/1999	02/28/1998	03/01/1997
Earnings Per Share	1.29	1.36	1.04	0.97	0.75	0.77	0.72	0.47
Cash Flow Per Share	1.93	1.84	2.54	1.12	1.15	0.87	0.94	1.37
Tang. Book Val. Per Share	7.74	7.09	6.26	5.53	4.69	4.13	3.85	3.19
Dividends Per Share	0.300	0.210	0.160	0.150	0.120	0.110	0.080	0.070
Dividend Payout %	23.25	15.44	15.38	15.46	16.00	15.15	12.19	15.13
Income Statement								
Total Revenues	1,868,243	1,754,867	1,548,556	1,411,498	1,231,095	1,138,590	1,075,405	947,091
Total Indirect Exp.	595,463	548,751	490,948	442,939	389,367	365,759	339,734	294,242
Depreciation & Amort.	50,927	46,432	42,821	43,184	39,973	31,130	23,946	19,765
Operating Income	186,157	204,654	158,813	151,516	123,181	134,658	121,734	90,220
Net Interest Inc./(Exp.)	(1,692)	(2,327)	(2,300)	(3,130)	(6,918)	(7,916)	(8,704)	(9,882)
Income Taxes	69,315	75,988	58,788	55,590	43,887	49,253	45,964	32,129
Income from Cont Ops	...	...	...	...	...	...	...	48,209
Net Income	118,001	129,386	100,209	94,650	74,725	80,357	78,047	44,087
Average Shs. Outstg.	91,624	95,305	96,185	97,952	103,297	108,864	112,880	98,284
Balance Sheet								
Cash & Cash Equivalents	225,101	242,114	235,609	46,841	50,376	41,945	80,729	32,280
Total Current Assets	698,151	663,601	605,153	477,066	415,280	381,943	402,381	285,478
Total Assets	1,052,173	967,487	862,672	735,710	670,710	653,991	653,410	570,268
Total Current Liabilities	279,888	243,589	208,396	144,110	175,966	129,832	121,590	110,386
Long–Term Obligations	19,000	25,000	25,356	25,000	25,000	96,008	114,881	111,250
Net Stockholders' Equity	683,631	643,936	585,656	531,879	440,663	403,894	392,731	323,048
Net Working Capital	418,263	420,012	396,757	332,956	239,314	252,111	280,791	175,092
Shares Outstanding	88,306	90,734	93,417	96,160	93,830	97,672	101,854	101,223
Operating Profit Margin %	9.96	11.66	10.25	10.73	10.00	11.82	11.31	9.52
Net Profit Margin %	13.73	16.03	14.06	14.06	14.58	13.19	15.70	15.80	11.87
Return on Equity %	17.26	20.09	17.11	17.79	16.95	19.89	19.87	14.92
Return on Assets %	11.21	13.37	11.61	12.86	11.14	12.28	11.94	8.45
Debt/Total Assets %	1.80	2.58	2.93	3.39	3.72	14.68	17.58	19.50
Price Range	26.19–14.85	23.95–15.20	20.24–8.13	14.00–7.88	12.25–5.38	20.63–6.31	18.63–7.39	8.28–5.33
P/E Ratio	20.30–11.51	17.61–11.18	19.46–7.82	14.43–8.12	16.33–7.17	26.79–8.20	25.87–10.26	17.61–11.35
Average Yield %	1.46	1.08	1.20	1.36	1.52	0.86	0.66	1.02

Address: 301 Commerce Street, Fort Worth, TX 76102
Telephone: (817) 252–8000
Web Site: www.pier1.com

Officers: Marvin J. Girouard – Chmn., C.E.O., Charles H. Turner – Exec. V.P., Fin., C.F.O., Treas.
Transfer Agents: Mellon Investor Services, Ridgefield Park, NJ

Investor Contact: 817–252–7835
Institutional Holding
No of Institutions: 23
Shares: 669,559 **% Held:** –

PINNACLE WEST CAPITAL CORP.

Exchange	Symbol	Price	52Wk Range	Yield	P/E
NYS	PNW	$40.29 (5/28/2004)	40.29-32.96	4.47	15.32

*7 Year Price Score 95.8   *NYSE Composite Index=100   ***12 Month Price Score 48.4**

Interim Earnings (Per Share)

Qtr.	Mar	Jun	Sep	Dec
2001	0.73	0.79	1.91	0.42
2002	0.63	0.89	1.19	(0.18)
2003	0.22	0.60	1.20	0.50
2004	0.33	...	...	...

Interim Dividends (Per Share)

Amt	Decl	Ex	Rec	Pay
0.425Q	7/17/2003	7/30/2003	8/1/2003	9/1/2003
0.45Q	10/22/2003	10/30/2003	11/3/2003	12/1/2003
0.45Q	1/21/2004	1/29/2004	2/2/2004	3/1/2004
0.45Q	3/17/2004	4/29/2004	5/3/2004	6/1/2004

Indicated Div: $1.80 (Div. Reinv. Plan)

Valuation Analysis

Forecast P/E 14.97 (5/24/2004)

Market Cap	$3.4 Billion	Book Value	2.9 Billion
Price/Book	1.25	Price/Sales	1.28

Dividend Achiever Status

Rank	17	10 Year Growth Rate	24.04%
Total Years of Dividend Growth		10	

Business Summary: Electricity (MIC: 7.1 SIC: 4911 NAIC:221121)

Pinnacle West Capital is a holding company whose principal asset is Arizona Public Service (APS). APS is an electric utility that provides retail and wholesale electric service to substantially all of the state of Arizona, with the major exceptions of the Tucson metropolitan area and about one–half of the Phoenix metropolitan area. Through its marketing and trading operation, APS also generates, sells and delivers wholesale electricity. Co.'s other major subsidiaries are Pinnacle West Energy, which owns and operates generating plants; APS Energy Services, which provides commodity–related energy services; and SunCor, which is engaged in real estate development activities.

Recent Developments: For the quarter ended Mar 31 2004, income was $29.8 million, before income from discontinued operations of $388,000, versus income of $20.2 million, before income from discontinued operations of $5.1 million, in the prior–year quarter. Earnings were primarily driven by higher retail sales volumes at APS due to customer growth and favorable weather conditions. Total operating revenue increased 3.9% to $574.4 million. Regulated electricity revenues grew 9.4% to $415.5 million. Marketing and trading revenues fell 24.3% to $88.4 million, while real estate revenues improved 26.8% to $51.6 million. Operating income rose 20.4% to $83.4 million.

Prospects: Going forward Co.'s prospects remains strong, supported by customer growth of 3.4% during the first quarter, about three times the national average. In addition, retail electricity consumption remains at solid levels, with Co. experiencing a 10.3% increase in electric consumption during the first quarter. However, Co. believes that a positive outcome from its rate request is key to its outlook for the coming year. APS has asked the Staff of the Arizona Corporation Commission to approve the requested rate increase by Jul 1 2004. Meanwhile, based on two recent procedural orders, hearings on the rate case should begin no earlier than August 2004.

Financial Data

(US$ in Thousands)	3 Mos	12/31/2003	12/31/2002	12/31/2001	12/31/2000	12/31/1999	12/31/1998	12/31/1997
Earnings Per Share	2.63	2.52	2.53	3.85	3.56	3.17	2.85	2.74
Cash Flow Per Share	2.47	9.86	10.24	6.72	8.23	7.47	7.09	7.41
Tang. Book Val. Per Share	31.19	30.99	29.43	29.46	28.08	26.00	25.50	23.90
Dividends Per Share	1.750	1.720	1.620	1.520	1.420	1.320	1.220	1.120
Dividend Payout %	65.30	68.45	64.22	39.61	40.02	41.79	42.98	41.05
Income Statement								
Total Revenues	574,369	2,817,852	2,637,279	4,551,373	3,690,175	2,423,353	2,130,586	1,995,026
Total Indirect Exp.	148,277	548,413	532,838	528,971	494,190	482,174	496,585	489,831
Costs & Expenses	490,998	2,335,799	2,121,232	3,876,746	3,014,204	1,844,576	1,563,458	1,437,520
Depreciation & Amort.	101,504	438,143	424,886	427,903	394,410	385,568	379,679	368,285
Operating Income	83,371	482,053	516,047	674,627	675,971	578,777	567,128	557,506
Net Interest Inc./(Exp.)	(41,643)	(156,494)	(144,243)	(127,960)	(149,601)	(150,717)	(150,549)	(163,135)
Income Taxes	15,627	105,560	138,100	213,535	223,852	168,065	164,593	150,281
Eqty Earns/Minority Int.	1,185	24,740	...	...	...	...	...	...
Income from Cont Ops	29,768	230,576	215,153	327,367	...	269,772	...	...
Net Income	30,156	240,579	149,408	312,166	302,332	167,887	242,892	235,856
Average Shs. Outstg.	91,376	91,405	84,964	84,930	84,935	85,008	85,345	86,023
Balance Sheet								
Net Property	7,496,976	7,480,090	6,479,398	5,907,315	5,133,193	4,778,515	4,730,563	4,677,568
Total Assets	9,375,392	9,536,378	8,425,806	7,981,748	7,149,151	6,608,506	6,824,546	6,850,417
Long–Term Obligations	2,462,838	2,897,725	2,881,695	2,673,078	1,955,083	2,206,052	2,048,961	2,244,248
Net Stockholders' Equity	2,850,396	2,829,779	2,686,153	2,499,323	2,382,714	2,205,733	2,163,351	2,027,436
Shares Outstanding	91,359	91,287	91,255	84,824	84,824	84,824	84,824	84,825
Operating Profit Margin %	14.51	17.10	19.56	14.82	18.31	23.88	26.61	27.94
Net Inc./Net Property %	0.40	3.21	2.30	5.28	5.88	3.51	5.13	5.04
Net Inc./Tot. Capital %	0.45	3.40	2.20	5.00	5.51	3.00	4.29	4.06
Return on Equity %	1.04	8.14	8.00	13.09	12.68	12.23	11.22	11.63
Accum. Depr./Gross Prop. %	30.23	29.70	34.90	36.38	38.31	38.77	37.30	35.90
Price Range	40.29–37.26	40.24–29.07	46.16–22.49	50.37–38.10	51.88–25.94	42.88–30.44	48.88–39.75	42.50–27.88
P/E Ratio	15.32–14.17	15.97–11.54	18.25–8.89	13.08–9.90	14.57–7.29	13.53–9.60	17.15–13.95	15.51–10.17
Average Yield %	4.52	4.89	4.44	3.44	3.76	3.48	2.81	3.45

Address: 400 North Fifth Street, Phoenix, AZ 85072–3999	Officers: William J. Post – Chmn., C.E.O., Jack E. Davis – Pres., C.O.O	Investor Contact:602–250–5668
Telephone: (602) 250–1000	Transfer Agents:Pinnacle West Capital Corporation, Phoenix, AZ	Institutional Holding
Web Site: www.pinnaclewest.com		No of Institutions: 5
		Shares: 335,939 % Held: –

PITNEY BOWES, INC.

Exchange	Symbol	Price	52Wk Range	Yield	P/E
NYS	PBI	$44.33 (5/28/2004)	44.60-36.73	2.75	20.52

*7 Year Price Score 91.6   *NYSE Composite Index=100   *12 Month Price Score 50.9

Interim Earnings (Per Share)

Qtr.	Mar	Jun	Sep	Dec
2001	0.42	0.76	0.49	0.41
2002	0.53	0.59	0.61	0.08
2003	0.48	0.50	0.50	0.62
2004	0.54	...	...	...

Interim Dividends (Per Share)

Amt	Decl	Ex	Rec	Pay
0.30Q	7/14/2003	8/20/2003	8/22/2003	9/12/2003
0.30Q	11/10/2003	11/19/2003	11/21/2003	12/12/2003
0.305Q	2/2/2004	2/18/2004	2/20/2004	3/12/2004
0.305Q	4/12/2004	5/19/2004	5/21/2004	6/12/2004
Indicated Div: $2.00 (Div. Reinv. Plan)				

Valuation Analysis

Forecast P/E 17.84 (5/24/2004)

Market Cap	$10.6 Billion	Book Value	N/A
Price/Book	N/A	Price/Sales	N/A

Dividend Achiever Status

Rank	148	10 Year Growth Rate	10.31%
Total Years of Dividend Growth	20		

Business Summary: Office Equipment Supplies (MIC: 11.12 SIC: 3579 NAIC:423420)

Pitney Bowes provides integrated mail and document management solutions for organizations of all sizes. Global Mailstream Solutions includes the sale, rental, and financing of postage meters, mailing machines, address hygiene software, manifest systems, letter and parcel scales, mail openers, mailroom furniture, folders, table–top inserters, and postal payment solutions. Global Enterprise Solutions includes facilities management, through Pitney Bowes Management Services, and sales, service and financing of high–speed, software–enabled production mail systems, through Document Messaging Technologies. Capital Services provides large–ticket financing programs for a broad range of products.

Recent Developments: For the quarter ended Mar 31 2004, net income climbed 11.1% to $126.6 million compared with $113.9 million in the corresponding period of the prior year. The improvement in earnings reflected increased demand for Co.'s mailing solutions and services. Results for 2004 and 2003 included restructuring charges of $15.0 million and $21.3 million, respectively. Total revenues advanced 7.4% to $1.17 billion from $1.09 billion a year earlier. Global Mailstream Solutions segment revenues grew 9.2% to $813.6 million, while Global Enterprise Solutions segment revenues advanced 7.5% to $328.6 million. Capital Services segment revenues fell 26.4% to $29.7 million.

Prospects: Co. is expanding its participation in the mail stream and diversifying its customer base with its continued growth in small business solutions, the enlargement of its pre–sort network, and the growing use of its advanced technologies to process consumer originated mail in retail outlets and on the Internet. Also, on Apr 13 2004, Co. announced that it signed a definitive agreement to acquire all of the outstanding shares of Group 1 Software, Inc. for approximately $321.0 million. This acquisition should position Co. to continue to build its customer communication management capability. The transaction is expected to close in the third calendar quarter of 2004.

Financial Data

(US$ in Thousands)	3 Mos	12/31/2003	12/31/2002	12/31/2001	12/31/2000	12/31/1999	12/31/1998	12/31/1997
Earnings Per Share	2.16	2.10	1.81	2.08	2.18	2.42	2.03	1.80
Cash Flow Per Share	1.17	3.60	2.08	4.18	3.37	3.60	2.74	2.40
Tang. Book Val. Per Share	N.M	N.M	0.10	1.04	4.33	5.27	5.26	5.96
Dividends Per Share	1.200	1.200	1.180	1.160	1.140	1.020	0.900	0.800
Dividend Payout %	55.78	57.14	65.19	55.76	52.29	42.14	44.33	44.44
Income Statement								
Total Revenues	1,171,922	4,576,853	4,409,758	4,122,474	3,880,868	4,432,608	4,220,517	4,100,464
Total Indirect Exp.	493,847	1,483,848	1,837,931	1,619,399	1,438,234	1,628,249	1,543,536	1,457,325
Depreciation & Amort.	73,393	288,808	264,250	317,449	321,157	412,104	361,333	300,086
Operating Income	186,021	885,915	798,599	612,460	995,225	1,114,323	1,013,410	1,003,833
Net Interest Inc./(Exp.)	(40,536)	(164,941)	(179,154)	(184,173)	(192,377)	(179,325)	(149,233)	(200,735)
Income Taxes	59,427	226,244	181,739	252,064	239,723	325,413	296,236	277,071
Income from Cont Ops	...	494,847	437,706	514,320	563,125	659,159	567,941	...
Net Income	126,594	498,117	475,750	488,343	622,546	636,212	576,394	526,027
Average Shs. Outstg.	234,747	236,165	241,483	247,615	258,602	272,006	279,656	292,517
Balance Sheet								
Cash & Cash Equivalents	298,711	293,812	315,156	231,588	198,255	254,270	125,684	137,073
Total Current Assets	2,574,103	2,513,175	2,552,625	2,556,608	2,626,708	3,342,574	2,508,963	2,463,515
Total Assets	9,181,932	8,891,388	8,732,314	8,318,471	7,901,266	8,222,672	7,661,039	7,893,389
Total Current Liabilities	2,934,960	2,646,969	3,350,309	3,083,042	2,881,577	2,872,764	2,721,812	3,373,233
Long–Term Obligations	2,691,094	2,840,943	2,316,844	2,419,150	1,881,947	1,997,856	1,712,937	1,068,395
Net Stockholders' Equity	834,354	1,087,362	853,327	891,355	1,284,975	1,625,610	1,648,002	1,872,577
Net Working Capital	(360,857)	(133,794)	(797,684)	(526,434)	(254,869)	469,810	(212,849)	(909,718)
Shares Outstanding	231,127	232,288	235,373	242,028	248,800	264,694	270,378	279,674
Statistical Record								
Operating Profit Margin %	15.87	19.35	18.10	14.85	25.64	25.13	24.01	24.48
Return on Equity %	...	45.50	51.29	57.70	43.82	40.54	34.46	28.09
Return on Assets %	...	5.56	5.01	6.18	7.12	8.01	7.41	6.66
Debt/Total Assets %	29.30	31.95	26.53	29.08	23.81	24.29	22.35	13.53
Price Range	43.27-39.23	42.44-29.90	43.92-28.80	44.40-32.56	53.75-25.50	71.13-41.75	66.06-43.00	45.22-27.19
P/E Ratio	20.03-18.16	20.21-14.24	24.27-15.91	21.35-15.66	24.66-11.70	29.39-17.25	32.54-21.18	25.12-15.10
Average Yield %	2.92	3.26	3.11	3.02	2.94	1.68	1.75	2.23

Address: One Elmcroft Road, Stamford, CT 06926–0700	**Officers:** Michael J. Critelli – Chmn., C.E.O., Karen M. Garrison – Exec. V.P.	**Investor Contact:**203–351–6349
Telephone: (203) 356 5000	**Transfer Agents:**EquiServe Trust Company, N.A., Providence, RI	**Institutional Holding** **No of Institutions:** 2
Web Site: www.pb.com		**Shares:** 5,800 **% Held:** –

POPULAR INC.

Exchange	Symbol	Price	52Wk Range	Yield	P/E
NMS	BPOP	$43.22 (5/28/2004)	48.10-36.65	2.96	12.01

*7 Year Price Score 135.8 ***NYSE Composite Index=100** ***12 Month Price Score 46.3**

Interim Earnings (Per Share)

Qtr.	Mar	Jun	Sep	Dec
2001	0.53	0.55	0.55	0.54
2002	0.63	0.72	0.65	0.61
2003	0.74	0.99	0.96	0.78
2004	0.87	...	...	...

Interim Dividends (Per Share)

Amt	Decl	Ex	Rec	Pay
0.27Q	11/12/2003	12/10/2003	12/12/2003	1/2/2004
0.27Q	2/11/2004	3/10/2004	3/12/2004	4/1/2004
0.32Q	5/12/2004	6/9/2004	6/11/2004	7/1/2004
100%	5/12/2004	7/9/2004	6/18/2004	7/8/2004

Indicated Div: $1.28 (Div. Reinv. Plan)

Valuation Analysis

Forecast P/E N/A

Market Cap	$5.7 Billion	Book Value	2.4 Billion
Price/Book	2.52	Price/Sales	2.25

Dividend Achiever Status

Rank	67	10 Year Growth Rate	16.03%
Total Years of Dividend Growth		11	

Business Summary: Commercial Banking (MIC: 8.1 SIC: 6022 NAIC:522110)

Popular is a diversified holding company incorporated under the laws of the Commonwealth of Puerto Rico. As of Dec 31 2003, Co. had total assets of $36.43 billion. Co.'s principal subsidiary, Banco Popular de Puerto Rico, is a consumer−oriented bank operating 193 branches and over 550 automated teller machines in Puerto Rico. The bank also operates seven branches in the U.S. Virgin Islands, one branch in the British Islands and one branch in New York. Co. has three other principal subsidiaries; Popular Securities, Inc., Popular International Bank, Inc. and GM Group, Inc. Another wholly owned subsidiary, Levitt Mortgage Corporation, is a mortgage loan company with operations in Puerto Rico.

Recent Developments: For the quarter ended Mar 31 2004, net income increased 19.6% to $118.5 million compared with $99.1 million in the corresponding year−earlier period. Net interest income advanced 10.6% to $330.7 million from $299.1 million the previous year. Average earning assets increased 10.9% to $34.83 billion, driven by an increase in the average loan portfolio, primarily in mortgage and commercial loans. Provision for loan losses amounted to $44.7 million versus $48.2 million last year. Total noninterest income rose 1.7% to $145.2 million from $142.8 million the year before. Noninterest income for 2004 and 2003 included gains on the sale of securities of $13.0 million and $1.4 million, respectively.

Prospects: Despite expectations of some deceleration of its residential mortgage business, Co.'s near−term prospects appear reasonably positive. On the plus side, Co.'s results going forward should benefit from a pick up in commercial loans, due in part to the unfolding global economic recovery. Meanwhile, subject to various approvals, Co. expects to complete its pending acquisition of Quaker City Bancorp, Inc. by the third quarter of 2004. Quaker City is a savings and loan holding company for Quaker City Bank, based in Whittier, CA. Quaker City Bank operates 27 retail full service branches in Southern California, including 16 inside Wal−Mart stores.

Financial Data

(US$ in Thousands)	3 Mos	12/31/2003	12/31/2002	12/31/2001	12/31/2000	12/31/1999	12/31/1998	12/31/1997
Earnings Per Share	3.60	3.47	2.61	2.17	1.97	1.84	1.65	1.50
Tang. Book Val. Per Share	19.14	17.67	16.56	14.03	11.85	9.26	9.84	8.64
Dividends Per Share	1.010	0.940	0.800	0.720	0.640	0.580	0.470	0.380
Dividend Payout %	28.06	27.08	30.65	33.17	32.48	31.52	28.48	25.33
Income Statement								
Total Interest Income	518,742	2,034,238	2,023,797	2,095,862	2,150,157	1,851,670	1,651,703	1,491,303
Total Interest Expense	188,028	749,550	843,468	1,018,877	1,167,396	897,932	778,691	707,348
Net Interest Income	330,714	1,284,688	1,180,329	1,076,985	982,761	953,738	873,012	783,955
Provision for Loan Losses	44,678	195,939	205,570	213,250	194,640	148,948	137,213	110,607
Non−Interest Income	147,402	636,224	544,567	487,525	462,868	374,498	287,593	243,664
Non−Interest Expense	279,738	1,113,083	1,029,002	920,137	877,471	837,482	720,354	636,920
Eqty Earns/Minority Int.	...	(435)	(248)	18	1,152	2,454	328	...
Income from Cont Ops	...	...	...	303,852	...	...	...	...
Net Income	118,504	470,915	351,932	304,538	276,103	257,558	232,348	209,565
Average Shs. Outstg.	133,141	132,797	133,915	136,238	135,907	135,585	135,532	134,036
Balance Sheet								
Cash & Due from Banks	737,599	688,090	652,556	606,142	726,051	663,696	667,707	463,151
Securities Avail. for Sale	10,186,374	20,708,277	21,574,152	18,838,988	17,562,029	14,886,510	14,359,519	10,700,313
Net Loans & Leases	22,937,777	21,922,058	18,116,395	16,892,431	14,942,531	13,996,446	12,167,387	10,899,752
Total Assets	38,101,986	36,434,715	33,660,352	30,744,676	28,057,051	25,460,539	23,160,357	19,300,507
Total Deposits	18,602,940	18,097,828	17,614,740	16,370,042	14,804,907	14,173,715	13,672,214	11,749,586
Long−Term Obligations	125,000	7,117,025	4,567,853	4,009,211	1,451,912	2,127,599	1,582,160	1,678,696
Total Liabilities	35,152,230	33,867,173	31,249,473	28,571,858	26,163,407	23,899,553	21,551,244	17,897,415
Net Stockholders' Equity	2,949,756	2,754,417	2,410,879	2,272,818	1,993,644	1,660,986	1,709,113	1,503,092
Shares Outstanding	132,960	132,891	132,439	136,362	135,998	135,585	135,532	135,366
Return on Equity %	4.01	17.09	14.59	13.36	13.84	15.50	13.59	13.94
Return on Assets %	0.31	1.29	1.04	0.98	0.98	1.01	1.00	1.08
Equity/Assets %	7.74	7.55	7.16	7.39	7.10	6.52	7.37	7.78
Non−Int. Exp./Tot. Inc. %	42.13	41.84	40.39	35.92	33.55	37.64	37.07	36.62
Price Range	48.10-43.00	47.57−31.95	35.85−27.50	36.26−25.25	27.94−18.63	37.88−25.44	36.75−23.03	27.94−16.53
P/E Ratio	13.36-11.94	13.71−9.21	13.74−10.54	16.71−11.64	14.18−9.45	20.58−13.82	22.27−13.96	18.63−11.02
Average Yield %	2.25	2.43	2.55	2.41	2.79	1.91	1.53	1.83

Address: Popular Center Building, San Juan, PR 00918	Officers: Richard L. Carrion − Chmn., Pres., C.E.O., Antonion Luis Ferre − Vice−Chmn.	Investor Contact:787−754−1685
Telephone: (787) 765−9800	Transfer Agents:Banco Popular de Puerto Rico, San Juan, Puerto Rico	Institutional Holding
Web Site: www.popularinc.com		No of Institutions: 10
		Shares: 10,440,374 % Held: −

213

PPG INDUSTRIES, INC.

Exchange	Symbol	Price	52Wk Range	Yield	P/E
NYS	PPG	$59.80 (5/28/2004)	64.60–48.83	3.01	19.29

*7 Year Price Score 102.4 *NYSE Composite Index=100 *12 Month Price Score 48.2

Interim Earnings (Per Share)

Qtr.	Mar	Jun	Sep	Dec
2001	0.33	0.92	0.55	0.49
2002	0.25	(2.00)	0.87	0.52
2003	0.49	0.89	0.83	0.71
2004	0.67	...	...	...

Interim Dividends (Per Share)

Amt	Decl	Ex	Rec	Pay
0.43Q	7/17/2003	8/7/2003	8/11/2003	9/12/2003
0.44Q	10/16/2003	11/6/2003	11/10/2003	12/12/2003
0.44Q	1/15/2004	2/12/2004	2/17/2004	3/12/2004
0.45Q	4/15/2004	5/6/2004	5/10/2004	6/11/2004

Indicated Div: $1.80 (Div. Reinv. Plan)

Valuation Analysis

Forecast P/E 16.06 (5/24/2004)

Market Cap	$10.1 Billion	Book Value	3.0 Billion
Price/Book	3.34	Price/Sales	1.11

Dividend Achiever Status

Rank	246	10 Year Growth Rate	5.22%
Total Years of Dividend Growth			32

Business Summary: Chemicals (MIC: 11.1 SIC: 2851 NAIC:325510)

PPG Industries is a supplier of products for manufacturing, construction, automotive, chemical processing and numerous other world industries. Co. is comprised of three basic business segments: coatings, glass and chemicals. Co. is focused on industrial, aerospace, packaging, architectural, automotive original and refinish coatings, flat glass, automotive original and replacement glass, and continuous–strand fiber glass, and chlor–alkali and specialty chemicals. Co. operates manufacturing facilities in countries including Canada, China, England, France, Germany, Ireland, Italy, Mexico, the Netherlands, Portugal, Spain, Taiwan, Argentina, Australia, Malaysia, Thailand, Turkey and the U.S.

Recent Developments: For the three months ended Mar 31 2004, net income jumped 36.9% to $115.0 million compared with income of $84.0 million, before an accounting change charge of $6.0 million, in the same period of 2003. Results benefited from strategic actions taken by Co. to strengthen its coatings segment, increased sales across all of its businesses, and cost–reduction efforts. Results included asbestos settlement charges of $5.0 million in the 2004 and 2003 periods. Results for 2003 also included business restructuring charges of $1.0 million. Net sales climbed 9.3% to $2.26 billion from $2.07 billion the year before. Gross profit increased 12.9% to $823.0 million.

Prospects: Co. is increasingly optimistic about business levels due to improving growth in the economy. Even though Co. is not predicting sharp growth in the near term, it is seeing volume gains in all regions and all of its business segments. Co.'s continuing effort to focus on generating cash and accelerating cost reductions have begun to pay off. Co. does not expect any large acquisitions in the near term, but small acquisitions, particularly in its optical products, and architectural and industrial coatings businesses, are possible, as Co. expects growth from theses businesses to occur over the next five years.

Financial Data

(US$ in Thousands)	3 Mos	12/31/2003	12/31/2002	12/31/2001	12/31/2000	12/31/1999	12/31/1998	12/31/1997
Earnings Per Share	3.10	2.92	(0.36)	2.29	3.57	3.23	4.48	3.94
Cash Flow Per Share	0.75	6.57	5.13	6.29	5.04	5.13	5.27	5.54
Tang. Book Val. Per Share	7.56	7.36	3.47	9.11	8.61	8.29	13.16	21.29
Dividends Per Share	1.740	1.730	1.700	1.680	1.600	1.520	1.420	1.330
Dividend Payout %	56.13	59.24	N.M.	73.36	44.81	47.05	31.69	33.75
Income Statement								
Total Revenues	2,264,000	8,756,000	8,067,000	8,169,000	8,629,000	7,995,000	7,510,000	7,379,000
Total Indirect Exp.	648,000	2,396,000	3,062,000	2,437,000	2,317,000	2,074,000	1,614,000	1,750,000
Depreciation & Amort.	97,000	394,000	398,000	447,000	447,000	415,000	381,000	348,000
Operating Income	198,000	843,000	(28,000)	666,000	1,017,000	973,000	1,294,000	1,175,000
Net Interest Inc./(Exp.)	(23,000)	(97,000)	(119,000)	(154,000)	(165,000)	(125,000)	(98,000)	(97,000)
Income Taxes	69,000	293,000	(7,000)	247,000	369,000	377,000	466,000	435,000
Eqty Earns/Minority Int.	(14,000)	(54,000)	(40,000)	(17,000)	11,000	...	3,000	(16,000)
Income from Cont Ops	...	500,000	(60,000)	...	...	...	...	...
Net Income	115,000	494,000	(69,000)	387,000	620,000	568,000	801,000	714,000
Average Shs. Outstg.	172,700	170,900	169,900	168,300	172,300	175,500	178,700	181,500
Balance Sheet								
Cash & Cash Equivalents	466,000	499,000	117,000	108,000	111,000	158,000	128,000	129,000
Total Current Assets	3,705,000	3,537,000	2,945,000	2,703,000	3,093,000	3,062,000	2,660,000	2,584,000
Total Assets	8,607,000	8,424,000	7,863,000	8,452,000	9,125,000	8,914,000	7,387,000	6,868,000
Total Current Liabilities	2,241,000	2,139,000	1,920,000	1,955,000	2,543,000	2,384,000	1,912,000	1,662,000
Long–Term Obligations	1,329,000	1,339,000	1,699,000	1,699,000	1,810,000	1,836,000	1,081,000	1,257,000
Net Stockholders' Equity	2,972,000	2,911,000	2,150,000	3,080,000	3,097,000	3,106,000	2,880,000	2,509,000
Net Working Capital	1,464,000	1,398,000	1,025,000	748,000	550,000	678,000	748,000	922,000
Shares Outstanding	171,576	170,926	169,442	168,713	168,222	173,988	175,000	117,826
Statistical Record								
Operating Profit Margin %	7.72	9.58	N.M.	7.28	11.33	12.05	18.90	16.69
Return on Equity %	3.09	17.03	N.M	10.25	18.76	17.99	32.18	30.72
Return on Assets %	1.06	5.88	N.M.	3.73	6.36	6.27	12.54	11.22
Debt/Total Assets %	15.44	15.89	21.60	20.10	19.83	20.59	14.63	18.30
Price Range	64.60–55.18	64.42–42.64	62.44–41.41	59.54–40.71	64.38–36.13	69.69–48.06	76.31–50.50	67.19–49.00
P/E Ratio	20.84–17.80	22.06–14.60	N/A	26.00–17.78	18.03–10.12	21.58–14.88	17.03–11.27	17.05–12.44
Average Yield %	2.94	3.31	3.24	3.27	3.39	2.57	2.27	2.29

Address: One PPG Place, Pittsburgh, PA 15272	Officers: Raymond W. LeBoeuf – Chmn., C.E.O., Charles E. Bunch – Pres., C.O.O.	Investor Contact:412–434–2120
Telephone: (412) 434–3131	Transfer Agents:Mellon Investor Services LLC, Ridgefield Park, NJ	Institutional Holding
Web Site: www.ppg.com		No of Institutions: 14
		Shares: 193,580 % Held: –

PRAXAIR, INC.

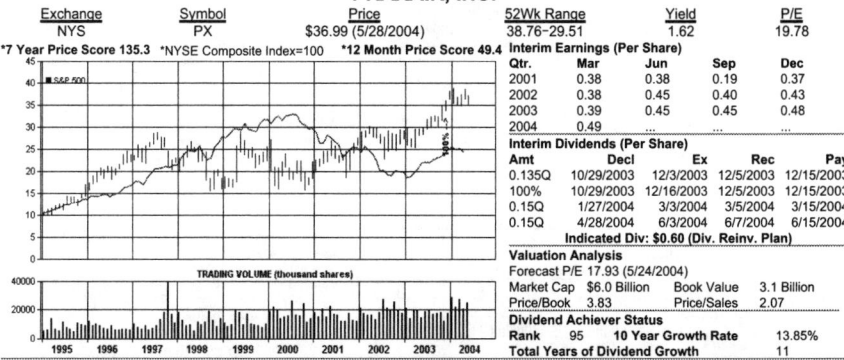

Exchange	Symbol	Price	52Wk Range	Yield	P/E
NYS	PX	$36.99 (5/28/2004)	38.76-29.51	1.62	19.78

*7 Year Price Score 135.3 *NYSE Composite Index=100 *12 Month Price Score 49.4

Interim Earnings (Per Share)

Qtr.	Mar	Jun	Sep	Dec
2001	0.38	0.38	0.19	0.37
2002	0.38	0.45	0.40	0.43
2003	0.39	0.45	0.45	0.48
2004	0.49	...	...	...

Interim Dividends (Per Share)

Amt	Decl	Ex	Rec	Pay
0.135Q	10/29/2003	12/3/2003	12/5/2003	12/15/2003
100%	10/29/2003	12/16/2003	12/5/2003	12/15/2003
0.15Q	1/27/2004	3/3/2004	3/5/2004	3/15/2004
0.15Q	4/28/2004	6/3/2004	6/7/2004	6/15/2004

Indicated Div: $0.60 (Div. Reinv. Plan)

Valuation Analysis

Forecast P/E 17.93 (5/24/2004)

Market Cap	$6.0 Billion	Book Value	3.1 Billion
Price/Book	3.83	Price/Sales	2.07

Dividend Achiever Status

Rank	95	10 Year Growth Rate	13.85%
Total Years of Dividend Growth			11

Business Summary: Chemicals (MIC: 11.1 SIC: 2813 NAIC:325120)

Praxair is one of the largest global suppliers of industrial gases, particularly in North and South America, and has a growing business in Asia and southern Europe. Co.'s primary products are atmospheric gases (oxygen, nitrogen, argon, and rare gases) and process gases (carbon dioxide, helium, hydrogen, electronics gases, and acetylene). Co. also designs, engineers, and builds equipment that produces industrial gases for internal use and external sales. Co.'s surface technology segment supplies wear–resistant and high–temperature corrosion–resistant metallic and ceramic coatings and powders. Co. serves approximately 25 diverse industries.

Recent Developments: For the quarter ended Mar 31 2004, net income rose 26.2% to $164.0 million compared with $130.0 million in the equivalent quarter of 2003. The growth in net income was due to higher sales revenue, higher operating profit and lower interest expense, partially offset by a slightly higher effective tax rate. Sales grew 14.5% to $1.53 billion from $1.34 billion in the prior–year period. Operating profit increased 20.9% to $260.0 million compared with $215.0 million the year before. Sales and operating profit both benefited from strong overall volume growth, higher pricing and currency effects.

Prospects: For the second quarter of 2004, Co. expects sales to grow 11.0% to 13.0% and operating profit to grow 17.0% to 21.0%. Diluted earnings per share for the second quarter are expected to be between $0.48 and $0.52. For full–year 2004, Co. expects sales growth in the range of 9.0% to 13.0% and operating profit growth in the range of 13.0% to 17.0%. Diluted earnings per share for full–year 2004 are expected to be in the range of $1.98 to $2.08. Capital expenditures for full–year 2004 are expected to be about $700.0 million. Separately, on Apr 29 2004, Co. announced that its subsidiary, Praxair Distribution, purchased United Welding Specialties for an undisclosed amount.

Financial Data

(US$ in Thousands)	3 Mos	12/31/2003	12/31/2002	12/31/2001	12/31/2000	12/31/1999	12/31/1998	12/31/1997
Earnings Per Share	1.87	1.77	1.66	1.32	1.12	1.36	1.30	1.26
Cash Flow Per Share	0.54	3.43	3.03	3.11	2.79	2.93	2.86	2.29
Tang. Book Val. Per Share	5.63	6.00	4.02	3.99	3.95	3.70	3.36	2.88
Dividends Per Share	0.500	0.450	0.380	0.340	0.310	0.280	0.250	0.220
Dividend Payout %	26.74	25.84	22.82	25.75	27.55	20.58	19.23	17.39
Income Statement								
Total Revenues	1,531,000	5,613,000	5,128,000	5,158,000	5,043,000	4,639,000	4,833,000	4,735,000
Total Indirect Exp.	364,000	1,368,000	1,223,000	1,211,000	1,100,000	999,000	1,128,000	1,071,000
Depreciation & Amort.	139,000	517,000	483,000	499,000	471,000	445,000	467,000	444,000
Operating Income	260,000	922,000	923,000	800,000	707,000	831,000	856,000	838,000
Net Interest Inc./(Exp.)	(37,000)	(151,000)	(206,000)	(224,000)	(224,000)	(204,000)	(260,000)	(216,000)
Income Taxes	56,000	174,000	158,000	135,000	103,000	152,000	127,000	151,000
Eqty Earns/Minority Int.	(3,000)	(12,000)	(11,000)	(9,000)	(17,000)	(34,000)	(44,000)	(55,000)
Income from Cont Ops	...	...	548,000	432,000	...	441,000	...	416,000
Net Income	164,000	585,000	409,000	430,000	363,000	431,000	425,000	405,000
Average Shs. Outstg.	331,573	330,991	329,490	327,014	322,184	324,444	326,712	328,106
Balance Sheet								
Cash & Cash Equivalents	37,000	50,000	39,000	39,000	31,000	76,000	34,000	43,000
Total Current Assets	1,483,000	1,449,000	1,286,000	1,276,000	1,361,000	1,335,000	1,394,000	1,497,000
Total Assets	8,327,000	8,305,000	7,401,000	7,715,000	7,762,000	7,722,000	8,096,000	7,810,000
Total Current Liabilities	1,066,000	1,117,000	1,100,000	1,194,000	1,439,000	1,725,000	1,289,000	1,366,000
Long–Term Obligations	2,693,000	2,661,000	2,510,000	2,725,000	2,641,000	2,111,000	2,895,000	2,874,000
Net Stockholders' Equity	3,136,000	3,088,000	2,340,000	2,477,000	2,357,000	2,290,000	2,332,000	2,122,000
Net Working Capital	417,000	332,000	186,000	82,000	(78,000)	(390,000)	105,000	131,000
Shares Outstanding	356,383	326,085	324,536	324,285	318,758	318,095	315,142	314,746
Operating Profit Margin %	16.91	16.44	18.77	15.97	14.99	19.57	18.58	19.00
Return on Equity %	5.19	18.97	25.12	18.26	17.33	21.90	19.40	21.75
Return on Assets %	1.95	7.05	7.94	5.91	5.30	6.70	5.76	6.12
Debt/Total Assets %	32.34	32.04	33.91	35.32	34.02	27.33	35.75	36.79
Price Range	38.76-34.70	38.20-25.33	30.30-22.81	27.64-18.65	27.25-15.84	29.06-16.16	26.78-15.69	28.78-20.44
P/E Ratio	20.73-18.56	21.58-14.31	18.25-13.74	20.94-14.13	24.33-14.15	21.37-11.88	20.60-12.07	22.84-16.22
Average Yield %	1.37	1.46	1.37	1.44	1.54	1.26	1.15	0.89

Address: 39 Old Ridgebury Rd., Danbury, CT 06810–5113 **Telephone:** (203) 837–2000 **Web Site:** www.praxair.com	**Officers:** Dennis H. Reilley – Chmn., Pres., C.E.O., Stephen F. Angel – Exec. V.P. **Transfer Agents:**Registrar and Transfer Company, Cranford, NJ	**Investor Contact:**203–837–2210 **Institutional Holding** **No of Institutions:** 12 **Shares:** 32,526 **% Held:** –

PROCTER & GAMBLE CO.

Exchange	Symbol	Price	52Wk Range	Yield	P/E
NYS	PG	$107.82 (5/28/2004)	108.6–86.70	1.85	24.90

*7 Year Price Score 115.0 *NYSE Composite Index=100 *12 Month Price Score 51.8

Interim Earnings (Per Share)

Qtr.	Sep	Dec	Mar	Jun
2000–01	0.82	0.84	0.63	(0.22)
2001–02	0.79	0.93	0.74	0.63
2002–03	1.04	1.06	0.91	0.68
2003–04	1.26	1.30	1.09	...

Interim Dividends (Per Share)

Amt	Decl	Ex	Rec	Pay
0.455Q	10/14/2003	10/22/2003	10/24/2003	11/14/2003
0.455Q	1/13/2004	1/21/2004	1/23/2004	2/17/2004
0.50Q	3/9/2004	4/21/2004	4/23/2004	5/14/2004
100%	3/9/2004	6/21/2004	5/21/2004	6/18/2004

Indicated Div: $2.00 (Div. Reinv. Plan)

Valuation Analysis
Forecast P/E 21.10 (5/24/2004)
Market Cap $140.1 Billion   Book Value 16.8 Billion
Price/Book 8.17   Price/Sales 2.77

Dividend Achiever Status
Rank 132   10 Year Growth Rate   11.45%
Total Years of Dividend Growth   50

Business Summary: Chemicals (MIC: 11.1 SIC: 2841 NAIC:325611)

Procter & Gamble manufactures and markets consumer products. Co. is comprised of five product units. Fabric and Home Care includes laundry detergents, dish care, fabric enhancers and surface cleaners. Beauty Care includes hair care, skin care, cosmetics, fine fragrances, deodorants, tampons, pads and pantiliners. Baby and Family Care includes diapers, wipes, tissue and towels. Health Care includes oral care, personal health care, pharmaceuticals and pet health and nutrition. Snacks and Beverages includes coffee, snacks, commercial services and juice. Co.'s brands include *Always, Ariel, Bounty, Charmin, Crest, Downy, Folgers, Iams, Olay, Pampers, Pantene, Pringles,* and *Tide.*

Recent Developments: For the quarter ended Mar 31 2004, net income increased 20.0% to $1.53 billion from $1.27 billion in the prior–year quarter. Earnings were driven by volume benefits and the completion of Co.'s restructuring program, partially offset by higher marketing investments to support base business growth and new initiatives. Results for 2003 included after–tax restructuring charges of $66.0 million. Net sales climbed 22.3% to $13.03 billion. Unit volume growth increased 20.0% behind double–digit growth in beauty care, health care and developing markets. Gross profit advanced 26.1% to $6.64 billion. Marketing, research, administrative and other expenses grew 31.1% to $4.33 billion.

Prospects: For the fourth quarter of 2004, total sales are expected to grow in the high teens, with foreign exchange increasing sales by 3.0% to 4.0% and the impact of acquisitions and divestitures increasing sales by 7.0% to 8.0%. However, an unfavorable sales mix and lower pricing are expected to reduce sales growth by 2.0% to 3.0%. Co. expects organic volume growth to be about 10.0% with broad–based volume strength across all business units and geographies. Meanwhile, operating margin is expected to decline 75.0 to 125.0 basis points versus prior year core operating margin, largely driven by the inclusion of Wella AG.

Financial Data

(US$ in Millions)	9 Mos	6 Mos	3 Mos	06/30/2003	06/30/2002	06/30/2001	06/30/2000	06/30/1999
Earnings Per Share	4.33	4.15	3.91	3.69	3.09	2.07	2.47	2.59
Cash Flow Per Share	4.96	2.83	1.14	6.20	5.51	4.12	3.27	3.83
Tang. Book Val. Per Share	N.M	N.M	N.M	0.84	N.M	1.55	1.35	2.61
Dividends Per Share	1.770	1.730	1.680	1.640	1.520	1.400	1.280	1.140
Dividend Payout %	40.87	41.68	42.96	44.44	49.19	67.63	51.82	44.01
Income Statement								
Total Revenues	38,445	25,416	12,195	43,377	40,238	39,244	39,951	38,125
Total Indirect Exp.	12,160	7,828	3,673	13,383	12,571	12,406	12,483	10,666
Depreciation & Amort.	1,279	857	407	1,703	1,693	2,271	2,191	2,148
Operating Income	7,688	5,385	2,643	7,853	6,678	4,736	5,954	6,253
Net Interest Inc./(Exp.)	(454)	(290)	(141)	(561)	(603)	(794)	(722)	(650)
Income Taxes	2,263	1,585	781	2,344	2,031	1,694	1,994	2,075
Net Income	5,107	3,579	1,761	5,186	4,352	2,922	3,542	3,763
Average Shs. Outstg.	1,398	1,399	1,398	1,401	1,404	1,405	1,427	1,446
Balance Sheet								
Cash & Cash Equivalents	5,750	5,294	4,049	6,212	3,623	2,518	1,600	2,800
Total Current Assets	17,204	17,165	15,673	15,220	12,166	10,889	10,069	11,358
Total Assets	53,868	53,862	50,496	43,706	40,776	34,387	34,194	32,113
Total Current Liabilities	17,023	17,607	16,812	12,358	12,704	9,846	10,065	10,761
Long–Term Obligations	13,349	12,636	11,993	11,475	11,201	9,792	8,916	6,231
Net Stockholders' Equity	18.292	18,572	17,371	16,186	13,706	12,010	12,287	12,058
Shares Outstanding	1,285	1,292	1,296	1,297	1,300	1,295	1,305	1,319
Statistical Record								
Operating Profit Margin %	19.99	21.18	21.67	18.10	16.59	12.06	14.90	16.40
Return on Equity %	27.92	19.27	10.13	32.04	31.75	24.32	28.82	31.20
Return on Assets %	9.48	6.64	3.48	11.86	10.67	8.49	10.35	11.71
Debt/Total Assets %	24.78	23.45	23.75	26.25	27.46	28.47	26.07	19.40
Price Range	106.0–86.70	99.88–86.70	93.25–86.70	93.00–74.46	94.40–64.47	78.50–54.56	117.8–53.06	102.9–67.00
P/E Ratio	24.48–20.02	24.07–20.89	23.85–22.17	25.20–20.18	30.55–20.86	37.92–26.36	47.67–21.48	39.74–25.87
Average Yield %	1.84	1.86	1.88	1.87	1.89	2.10	1.47	1.30

Address: One Procter &Gamble Plaza, Cincinnati, OH 45202	**Officers:** Alan G. Lafley – Chmn., Pres., C.E.O., Bruce L. Byrnes – Vice–Chmn., Pres., Global Beauty Care & Health Care	**Investor Contact:**rvices,
Telephone: (513) 983–1100		**Institutional Holding**
Web Site: www.pg.com	**Transfer Agents:**The Procter and Gamble Company, Cincinnati, OH	No of Institutions: 32
		Shares: 1,529,927 % Held: –

PROGRESS ENERGY, INC.

Exchange	Symbol	Price	52Wk Range	Yield	P/E
NYS	PGN	$72.50 (5/27/2004)	88.75-69.00	3.17	21.32

*7 Year Price Score 103.8   *NYSE Composite Index=100   ***12 Month Price Score 45.2**

Interim Earnings (Per Share)

Qtr.	Mar	Jun	Sep	Dec
2001	0.77	0.56	1.77	(0.46)
2002	0.62	0.56	0.70	0.65
2003	0.84	0.63	1.42	0.51
2004	0.45	...	...	...

Interim Dividends (Per Share)

Amt	Decl	Ex	Rec	Pay
0.56Q	9/19/2003	10/8/2003	10/10/2003	11/1/2003
0.575Q	12/10/2003	1/8/2004	1/12/2004	2/2/2004
0.575Q	3/17/2004	4/7/2004	4/12/2004	5/1/2004
0.575Q	5/12/2004	7/8/2004	7/12/2004	8/2/2004

Indicated Div: $2.30 (Div. Reinv. Plan)

Valuation Analysis

Forecast P/E 11.91 (5/24/2004)

Market Cap $16.0 Billion	Book Value 7.4 Billion
Price/Book 1.49	Price/Sales 1.27

Dividend Achiever Status

Rank 281	10 Year Growth Rate	3.17%
Total Years of Dividend Growth		15

Business Summary: Electricity (MIC: 7.1 SIC: 4911 NAIC:221121)

Progress Energy is a utility holding company with over 24,000 megawatts of generating capacity as of Dec 31 2003. Co.'s utility segment includes two major electric utilities, Progress Energy Carolinas and Progress Energy Florida. At Dec 31 2003, Co.'s electric utilities served more than 2.8 million customers in North Carolina, South Carolina and Florida. Co.'s Competitive Commercial Operations segment provides non-regulated electricity generation. The Fuels segment is involved in natural gas drilling and production, coal mining and terminal services and fuel delivery. The Rail Services segment engages in rail and railcar services. Other activities include Co.'s telecommunication services.

Recent Developments: For the quarter ended Mar 31 2004, net income declined 47.8% to $108.0 million versus income of $207.0 million, before income from discontinued operations of $11.0 million and an accounting change gain of $1.0 million, in the 2003 quarter. Earnings were adversely affected by lower wholesale sales to other utilities at Progress Carolinas and milder weather at Progress Florida. Total revenues increased 2.1% to $2.23 billion. Utility revenues rose 1.9% to $1.69 billion, while revenues from diversified businesses grew 3.0% to $549.0 million. Operating income decreased 17.1% to $296.0 million from $357.0 million the year before. Comparisons were made with restated results for the previous year.

Prospects: On Apr 27 2004, Co. announced plans to add approximately 500 megawatts of generating capacity to its system by building a fourth phase at its Hines Energy Complex in Polk County. Progress Energy Florida will file a petition with the Florida Public Service Commission to demonstrate the need and will also seek supplemental site certification with the Florida Department of Environmental Protection. Co. expects the unit to be in service by December 2007 to meet the needs of its customer base in Florida, which continues to grow by more than 30,000 annually. Looking ahead to full-year 2004, Co. expects earnings to range from $3.50 to $3.65 per share.

Financial Data

(US$ in Thousands)	3 Mos	12/31/2003	12/31/2002	12/31/2001	12/31/2000	12/31/1999	12/31/1998	12/31/1997
Earnings Per Share	3.01	3.40	2.53	2.64	3.03	2.55	2.75	2.66
Cash Flow Per Share	1.57	7.54	7.32	7.05	5.47	5.60	6.39	5.69
Tang. Book Val. Per Share	13.82	13.78	12.42	10.57	8.59	19.57	19.48	18.62
Dividends Per Share	2.250	2.240	2.180	2.120	2.060	2.000	1.940	1.880
Dividend Payout %	79.40	65.88	86.16	80.30	33.99	...	...	...
Income Statement								
Total Revenues	2,234,000	8,743,000	7,945,120	8,461,459	4,118,873	3,357,615	3,130,045	3,024,089
Total Indirect Exp.	395,000	3,405,000	3,102,174	3,299,322	1,273,133	820,435	636,090	645,424
Costs & Expenses	1,938,000	7,381,000	6,940,637	7,217,684	3,399,315	2,517,072	1,661,115	1,947,234
Depreciation & Amort.	247,000	1,040,000	820,279	1,090,178	740,470	495,670	487,097	481,650
Operating Income	296,000	1,362,000	1,004,483	1,243,775	719,558	840,543	1,468,930	1,076,855
Net Interest Inc./(Exp.)	(162,000)	(614,000)	(618,915)	(662,607)	(235,301)	(169,128)	(164,710)	(139,621)
Income Taxes	1,000	(109,000)	(157,808)	(151,643)	202,774	258,421	257,494	253,048
Eqty Earns/Minority Int.	...	9,000	...	...	...	...	...	...
Income from Cont Ops	...	811,000	552,169	...	...	...	970,657	922,585
Net Income	108,000	782,000	528,386	541,610	478,561	382,255	399,238	388,317
Average Shs. Outstg.	242,000	237,000	218,166	204,683	157,169	148,344	143,941	143,645
Balance Sheet								
Net Property	14,525,000	16,592,000	12,540,505	11,987,961	11,166,360	7,004,795	6,299,540	6,293,176
Total Assets	25,883,000	26,202,000	21,352,704	20,739,791	20,091,012	9,494,019	8,347,406	8,220,394
Long-Term Obligations	9,912,000	9,934,000	9,747,293	9,483,745	5,890,099	3,028,561	2,614,414	2,415,656
Net Stockholders' Equity	7,542,000	7,537,000	6,769,840	6,096,364	5,517,032	3,472,023	3,008,681	2,878,183
Shares Outstanding	246,000	246,000	237,992	218,725	206,089	159,599	151,338	151,340
Operating Profit Margin %	13.24	15.57	12.64	14.69	17.46	25.03	46.92	43.97
Net Profit Margin %	4.92	6.78	2.97	2.81	21.45	26.77	47.46	38.87
Net Inc./Net Property %	0.74	4.71	4.21	4.51	4.28	5.45	6.33	6.17
Net Inc./Tot. Capital %	0.59	4.29	3.02	3.18	3.62	4.69	5.46	5.53
Return on Equity %	1.43	10.76	8.15	8.88	8.67	11.00	32.26	40.84
Accum. Depr./Gross Prop. %	36.09	33.92	49.58	48.05	47.25	42.37	41.65	39.91
Price Range	88.75-69.00	84.25-63.00	79.25-68.00	80.00-65.00	80.00-60.00	93.00-68.00	92.50-76.00	81.25-70.13
P/E Ratio	29.49-22.92	24.78-18.53	31.32-26.88	30.30-24.62	26.40-19.80	36.47-26.67	33.64-27.64	30.55-26.36
Average Yield %	2.74	2.94	3.01	3.01	1.55	N/A	N/A	N/A

Address: 410 South Wilmington Street, Raleigh, NC 27601-1748	Officers: Robert B. McGehee – Chmn., C.E.O., Geoffrey S. Chatas – Exec. V.P., C.F.O.	Investor Contact:919-546-7474
Telephone: (919) 546 6111	Transfer Agents:EquiServe Trust Company, N.A., Providence, RI	Institutional Holding
Web Site: www.progress-energy.com		No of Institutions: 11
		Shares: 306,332 % Held: –

PROGRESSIVE CORP.

Exchange	Symbol	Price	52Wk Range	Yield	P/E
NYS	PGR	$85.77 (5/28/2004)	91.15-64.56	0.12	13.28

*7 Year Price Score 166.2 *NYSE Composite Index=100 *12 Month Price Score 51.3

TRADING VOLUME (thousand shares)

Interim Earnings (Per Share)

Qtr.	Mar	Jun	Sep	Dec
2001	0.38	0.46	0.43	0.55
2002	0.78	0.71	0.80	0.70
2003	1.32	1.29	1.45	1.63
2004	2.09	...	...	...

Interim Dividends (Per Share)

Amt	Decl	Ex	Rec	Pay
0.025Q	8/22/2003	9/10/2003	9/12/2003	9/30/2003
0.025Q	10/3/2003	12/10/2003	12/12/2003	12/31/2003
0.025Q	2/2/2004	3/10/2004	3/12/2004	3/31/2004
0.025Q	4/16/2004	6/9/2004	6/11/2004	6/30/2004
		Indicated Div: $0.10		

Valuation Analysis

Forecast P/E 12.24 (5/24/2004)

Market Cap $18.7 Billion	Book Value 5.5 Billion
Price/Book 3.44	Price/Sales 1.53

Dividend Achiever Status

Rank 267	10 Year Growth Rate	4.14%
Total Years of Dividend Growth		34

Business Summary: Insurance (MIC: 8.2 SIC: 6331 NAIC:524126)

Progressive, through its subsidiaries and affiliates, provides personal automobile insurance and other specialty property–casualty insurance and related services throughout the U.S. Co.'s personal lines business units write insurance for private passenger automobiles and recreation vehicles. Co.'s commercial auto business unit writes insurance for automobiles and trucks owned by small businesses. Co.'s other businesses include writing lenders' collateral protection and directors' and officers' liability insurance and providing insurance–related services, primarily processing business for Commercial Auto Insurance Procedures, which are state supervised plans serving the involuntary market.

Recent Developments: For the quarter ended Mar 31 2004, net income jumped 57.8% to $460.0 million from $291.5 million in the equivalent prior–year quarter. Total revenues increased 20.6% to $3.28 billion from $2.72 billion the previous year. Revenues included net realized investment gains of $59.5 million in 2004 and net realized investment losses of $3.1 million in 2002. Net premiums written grew 13.8% to $3.28 billion. Net premiums earned climbed 19.1% to $3.09 billion versus $2.60 billion a year earlier. Net investment income declined 0.9% to $114.9 million. Losses and loss adjustment expenses rose 13.2% to $1.96 billion.

Prospects: Co. continues to benefit from favorable market conditions in the insurance segment. For example, during the month of March 2004, 47 of the 49 markets in which Co. writes personal lines business were profitable. Meanwhile, policies in force growth remain solid, supported by strong renewals. For instance, in Co.'s personal Lines, 17 markets have year–to–date net premiums written growth of 20.0% or greater. These markets represent 27.0% of the total personal lines premiums. Given Co.'s consistent growth in underwriting profits and current customer retention trends, Co. should be well positioned to produce solid results through the remainder of 2004.

Financial Data

(US$ in Thousands)	3 Mos	12/31/2003	12/31/2002	12/31/2001	12/31/2000	12/31/1999	12/31/1998	12/31/1997
Earnings Per Share	6.46	5.69	2.99	1.82	0.20	1.32	2.03	1.77
Tang. Book Val. Per Share	25.47	23.24	17.28	14.76	13.01	12.55	11.75	9.84
Dividends Per Share	0.100	0.100	0.097	0.093	0.090	0.087	0.083	0.080
Dividend Payout %	1.55	1.75	3.17	5.10	42.73	6.56	4.00	4.51
Income Statement								
Total Premium Income	3,093,500	11,341,000	8,883,500	7,161,800	6,348,400	5,683,600	4,948,000	4,189,500
Other Income	186,800	551,000	410,900	326,400	422,600	440,600	344,400	418,700
Total Revenues	3,280,300	11,892,000	9,294,400	7,488,200	6,771,000	6,124,200	5,292,400	4,608,200
Total Indirect Exp.	41,000	...	...	...	...	...	...	...
Inc. Before Inc. Taxes	678,700	1,859,700	981,400	587,600	31,800	412,200	661,100	578,500
Income Taxes	218,700	604,300	314,100	176,200	(14,300)	117,000	204,400	178,500
Net Income	460,000	1,255,400	667,300	411,400	46,100	295,200	456,700	400,000
Average Shs. Outstg.	216,400	220,500	223,200	225,299	222,900	223,800	224,100	225,900
Balance Sheet								
Cash & Cash Equivalents	23,100	12,100	16,900	11,200	8,900	14,200	18,600	23,300
Premiums Due	2,639,500	2,448,300	2,036,400	1,773,800	1,868,900	2,069,500	1,790,300	1,522,600
Invst. Assets: Total	12,134,100	12,532,300	10,284,300	8,226,300	6,983,300	6,427,700	5,674,300	5,270,400
Total Assets	17,161,900	16,281,500	13,564,400	11,122,400	10,051,600	9,704,700	8,463,100	7,559,600
Long–Term Obligations	1,289,900	1,489,800	1,489,000	1,095,700	748,800	1,048,600	776,600	775,900
Net Stockholders' Equity	5,541,800	5,030,600	3,768,000	3,250,700	2,869,800	2,752,800	2,557,100	2,135,900
Shares Outstanding	217,500	216,400	218,000	220,200	220,500	219,300	217,500	216,900
Statistical Record								
Return on Revenues %	13.39	10.55	7.17	5.49	0.68	4.82	8.62	8.68
Return on Equity %	7.93	24.95	17.70	12.65	1.60	10.72	17.86	18.72
Return on Assets %	2.56	7.71	4.91	3.69	0.45	3.04	5.39	5.29
Price Range	88.00-81.25	83.59-46.55	59.49-46.15	50.28-28.00	36.67-16.40	56.92-23.69	56.69-31.98	39.96-20.67
P/E Ratio	13.62-12.58	14.69-8.18	19.90-15.43	27.63-15.38	183.3-81.98	43.12-17.95	27.92-15.75	22.58-11.68
Average Yield %	0.12	0.15	0.17	0.22	0.31	0.20	0.19	0.27

Address: 6300 Wilson Mills Road, Mayfield Village, OH 44143 **Telephone:** (440) 461 5000 **Web Site:** www.progressive.com	**Officers:** Peter B. Lewis – Chmn., Glenn M. Renwick – Pres., C.E.O. **Transfer Agents:**Corporate Trust Customer Service, National City Bank, Cleveland, OH	**Investor Contact:**440–446–7165 **Institutional Holding** **No of Institutions:** 13 **Shares:** 44,567,540 **% Held:** –

PROTECTIVE LIFE CORP.

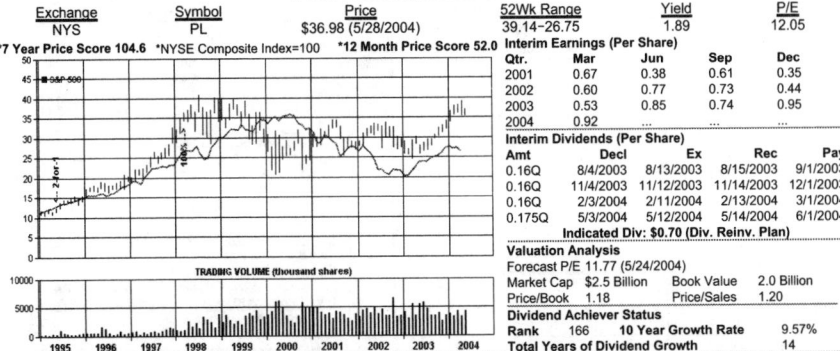

Exchange	Symbol	Price	52Wk Range	Yield	P/E
NYS	PL	$36.98 (5/28/2004)	39.14-26.75	1.89	12.05

*7 Year Price Score 104.6 *NYSE Composite Index=100 *12 Month Price Score 52.0

Interim Earnings (Per Share)

Qtr.	Mar	Jun	Sep	Dec
2001	0.67	0.38	0.61	0.35
2002	0.60	0.77	0.73	0.44
2003	0.53	0.85	0.74	0.95
2004	0.92	...	...	...

Interim Dividends (Per Share)

Amt	Decl	Ex	Rec	Pay
0.16Q	8/4/2003	8/13/2003	8/15/2003	9/1/2003
0.16Q	11/4/2003	11/12/2003	11/14/2003	12/1/2003
0.16Q	2/3/2004	2/11/2004	2/13/2004	3/1/2004
0.175Q	5/3/2004	5/12/2004	5/14/2004	6/1/2004

Indicated Div: $0.70 (Div. Reinv. Plan)

Valuation Analysis
Forecast P/E 11.77 (5/24/2004)

Market Cap	$2.5 Billion	Book Value	2.0 Billion
Price/Book	1.18	Price/Sales	1.20

Dividend Achiever Status

Rank	166	10 Year Growth Rate	9.57%
Total Years of Dividend Growth			14

Business Summary: Insurance (MIC: 8.2 SIC: 6311 NAIC:524113)

Protective Life provides financial services through the administration of insurance and investment products. The Life Marketing segment markets premium term and term-like insurance, universal life, variable universal life insurance products. The Acquisitions segment focuses on acquiring, converting, and servicing policies acquired from other companies. The Annuities segment manufactures, sells, and supports fixed and variable annuity products. The Stable Value Products segment markets investment contracts and other retirement plans. The Asset Protection segment markets extended service contracts and credit life and disability insurance.

Recent Developments: For the quarter ended Mar 31 2004, income was $65.3 million, before an accounting change charge of $10.1 million, compared with net income of $37.7 million in the equivalent period of the previous year. Total revenues increased 9.2% to $518.2 million from $474.6 million in the corresponding 2003 quarter. Net premium and policy fees slipped 1.6% to $194.5 million from $197.7 million, while net investment income grew 2.7% to $264.6 million from $257.7 million the year before. Benefits and settlement expenses were $287.3 million versus $297.3 million a year earlier.

Prospects: Co. is enjoying continued strong life insurance sales, although the pace of sales has moderated somewhat from levels experienced during the fourth quarter of 2003. Moreover, results from both Co.'s Stable Value and Asset Protection businesses are stronger, while the Annuity segment continues to be affected by lower interest rates and increased competition. Meanwhile, Co.'s balance sheet position remains healthy as it continues to look for opportunities for its Acquisition business. Overall, Co. remains optimistic about its outlook for the balance of the year.

Financial Data

(US$ in Thousands)	3 Mos	12/31/2003	12/31/2002	12/31/2001	12/31/2000	12/31/1999	12/31/1998	12/31/1997
Earnings Per Share	3.46	3.07	2.54	2.01	2.32	2.32	2.04	1.78
Tang. Book Val. Per Share	31.09	28.33	24.36	19.72	13.37	10.02	11.50	12.30
Dividends Per Share	0.640	0.630	0.590	0.550	0.510	0.470	0.430	0.390
Dividend Payout %	19.28	20.52	23.22	27.36	21.98	20.25	21.07	21.91
Income Statement								
Total Premium Income	194,457	735,877	783,132	618,669	833,658	761,284	662,795	522,335
Net Investment Income	264,608	1,030,752	1,031,204	884,041	737,284	676,401	636,396	591,376
Other Income	59,129	190,896	106,342	111,507	163,025	96,197	67,224	33,614
Total Revenues	518,194	1,957,525	1,920,678	1,614,217	1,733,967	1,533,882	1,366,415	1,147,325
Total Indirect Exp.	131,479	480,539	491,244	431,997	490,607	413,525	359,926	284,844
Inc. Before Inc. Taxes	99,399	325,412	267,203	209,596	253,795	255,775	220,724	179,373
Income Taxes	34,094	108,362	88,444	68,538	90,858	92,079	77,845	60,987
Eqty Earns/Minority Int.	...	...	...	...	(9,461)	(10,606)	(12,098)	(6,393)
Income from Cont Ops	65,305	...	178,759	141,058	...	153,090	...	...
Net Income	55,177	217,050	177,355	102,943	153,476	151,327	130,781	111,993
Average Shs. Outstg.	70,863	70,644	70,462	69,950	66,281	66,161	64,088	62,850
Balance Sheet								
Cash & Cash Equivalents	114,972	656,117	550,352	363,713	244,655	165,299	225,735	123,588
Premiums Due	2,558,212	2,408,550	2,477,916	2,239,179	1,185,354	940,252	797,164	639,397
Invst. Assets: Total	14,790,126	17,426,151	15,481,501	13,317,678	10,241,409	8,722,009	8,606,610	8,049,420
Total Assets	25,417,656	24,573,991	21,953,004	19,718,824	15,145,633	12,994,164	11,989,495	10,511,635
Long-Term Obligations	701,200	461,329	406,110	376,211	306,125	181,023	152,286	120,000
Net Stockholders' Equity	2,202,165	2,002,144	1,720,702	1,400,144	1,039,058	790,223	814,194	628,197
Shares Outstanding	69,310	68,991	68,675	68,555	64,557	64,502	64,435	61,642
Statistical Record								
Return on Revenues %	12.60	11.08	9.30	8.73	8.85	9.98	9.57	9.76
Return on Equity %	2.96	10.84	10.38	10.07	13.77	17.69	13.85	14.77
Return on Assets %	0.25	0.88	0.81	0.71	1.01	1.17	1.09	1.06
Price Range	38.25-33.84	34.22-24.71	33.75-27.20	34.51-25.55	32.25-20.81	40.00-28.50	40.88-28.63	32.63-18.81
P/E Ratio	11.05- 9.78	11.15-8.05	13.29-10.71	17.17-12.71	13.90-8.97	17.24-12.28	20.04-14.03	18.33-10.57
Average Yield %	1.76	2.16	1.93	1.82	1.90	1.35	1.23	1.61

Address: 2801 Highway 280 South, Birmingham, AL 35223
Telephone: (205) 268-1000
Web Site: www.protective.com

Officers: John D. Johns - Chmn., Pres., C.E.O., Allen W. Ritchie - Exec. V.P., C.F.O.
Transfer Agents:The Bank of New York

Investor Contact:205-268-1000
Institutional Holding
No of Institutions: 2
Shares: 54,496 % Held: -

QUAKER CHEMICAL CORP.

Exchange	Symbol	Price	52Wk Range	Yield	P/E
NYS	KWR	$25.63 (5/28/2004)	30.55-22.44	3.36	16.86

*7 Year Price Score 131.6 *NYSE Composite Index=100 *12 Month Price Score 46.2

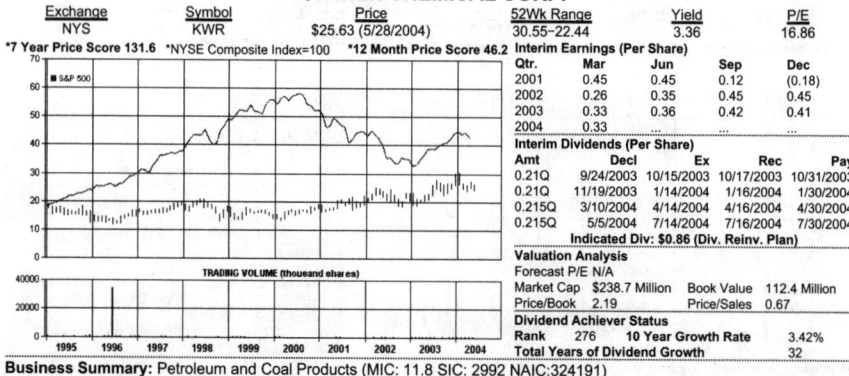

Interim Earnings (Per Share)

Qtr.	Mar	Jun	Sep	Dec
2001	0.45	0.45	0.12	(0.18)
2002	0.26	0.35	0.45	0.45
2003	0.33	0.36	0.42	0.41
2004	0.33	...	...	...

Interim Dividends (Per Share)

Amt	Decl	Ex	Rec	Pay
0.21Q	9/24/2003	10/15/2003	10/17/2003	10/31/2003
0.21Q	11/19/2003	1/14/2004	1/16/2004	1/30/2004
0.215Q	3/10/2004	4/14/2004	4/16/2004	4/30/2004
0.215Q	5/5/2004	7/14/2004	7/16/2004	7/30/2004

Indicated Div: $0.86 (Div. Reinv. Plan)

Valuation Analysis

Forecast P/E N/A

Market Cap	$238.7 Million	Book Value	112.4 Million
Price/Book	2.19	Price/Sales	0.67

Dividend Achiever Status

Rank	276	10 Year Growth Rate	3.42%
Total Years of Dividend Growth	32		

Business Summary: Petroleum and Coal Products (MIC: 11.8 SIC: 2992 NAIC:324191)

Quaker Chemical develops, produces, and markets a wide range of formulated chemical specialty products for various heavy industrial and manufacturing applications and, in addition, offers and markets chemical management services. Co. operates in three segments: metalworking process chemicals, coatings, and other chemical products. Co.'s principal product lines include rolling lubricants, corrosion preventives, hydraulic fluids, machining and grinding compounds, forming compounds, chemical milling maskants, metal finishing compounds, technology for the removal of hydrogen sulfides, construction products and programs to provide chemical management services.

Recent Developments: For the three months ended Mar 31 2004, net income climbed 6.5% to $3.3 million compared with $3.1 million in the equivalent quarter of 2003. Net sales were $98.1 million, up 33.8% from $73.3 million in the prior-year period. Sales growth benefited from foreign exchange rate translations, acquisitions and new chemical management services revenues, as well as double-digit growth in the Asia-Pacific and South American regions. Gross margin as a percentage of sales fell to 33.1% versus 38.7% a year earlier. Operating income increased 3.1% to $5.9 million compared with $5.7 million in the previous year.

Prospects: Looking ahead, Co. expects strong revenue growth for the remainder of 2004 in all of its business segments and in all regions due to its business initiatives as well as an improvement in the global economy. However, Co. also continues to expect to be negatively affected by high crude oil prices as well as the higher selling, general and administrative costs related to these issues and the restoration of performance-based incentive compensation. As a result, Co.'s outlook for 2004 continues to be for a slight improvement in year-over-year earnings. For the second quarter of 2004, Co. expects earnings to be similar to results in 2003.

Financial Data

(US$ in Thousands)	3 Mos	12/31/2003	12/31/2002	12/31/2001	12/31/2000	12/31/1999	12/31/1998	12/31/1997
Earnings Per Share	1.52	1.52	1.51	0.84	1.93	1.74	1.20	1.45
Cash Flow Per Share	(0.19)	0.85	2.57	2.48	2.40	1.58	1.41	1.74
Tang. Book Val. Per Share	7.25	7.22	6.46	7.05	7.63	7.29	7.01	7.01
Dividends Per Share	0.840	0.840	0.830	0.820	0.790	0.760	0.730	0.700
Dividend Payout %	55.27	55.26	55.29	97.61	40.93	43.96	60.83	48.62
Income Statement								
Total Revenues	98,131	340,192	274,521	251,074	267,570	258,461	257,100	241,534
Total Indirect Exp.	26,598	97,259	87,604	86,838	86,892	89,595	98,371	82,822
Depreciation & Amort.	2,265	7,637	6,237	6,380	6,812	6,956	7,111	7,264
Operating Income	5,857	24,115	23,973	14,191	25,148	27,281	17,270	21,148
Net Interest Inc./(Exp.)	(315)	(761)	(790)	(850)	(1,096)	(1,992)	(1,589)	(1,218)
Income Taxes	1,922	7,488	7,782	4,473	8,211	10,860	6,719	7,893
Eqty Earns/Minority Int.	(870)	(1,797)	(2,239)	(2,292)	(1,112)	(640)	572	769
Net Income	3,309	14,833	14,297	7,665	17,163	15,651	10,650	12,611
Average Shs. Outstg.	9,977	9,761	9,474	9,114	8,896	8,975	8,860	8,707
Balance Sheet								
Cash & Cash Equivalents	22,894	21,915	13,857	20,549	16,552	8,677	10,213	18,416
Total Current Assets	152,991	143,524	103,673	92,087	103,181	96,241	96,068	98,126
Total Assets	296,151	287,347	213,858	178,823	188,161	182,213	189,903	170,640
Total Current Liabilities	113,380	105,805	66,144	44,663	50,200	44,657	50,432	47,759
Long-Term Obligations	15,622	15,827	16,590	19,380	22,295	25,122	25,344	25,203
Net Stockholders' Equity	112,444	112,352	88,055	80,899	84,907	81,199	83,735	75,642
Net Working Capital	39,611	37,719	37,529	47,424	52,981	51,584	45,636	50,367
Shares Outstanding	9,624	9,609	9,321	9,137	8,851	8,934	8,894	8,720
Operating Profit Margin %	5.96	7.08	8.73	5.65	9.39	10.55	6.71	9.84
Return on Equity %	2.94	13.20	16.23	9.47	20.21	19.27	12.71	20.13
Return on Assets %	1.11	5.16	6.68	4.28	9.12	8.58	5.60	8.92
Debt/Total Assets %	5.27	5.50	7.75	10.83	11.84	13.78	13.34	14.76
Price Range	30.55-23.96	30.25-18.80	25.05-18.36	22.20-16.40	19.00-13.50	18.06-13.63	21.00-13.19	19.69-15.13
P/E Ratio	20.10-15.76	19.90-12.37	16.59-12.16	26.43-19.52	9.84-6.99	10.38-7.83	17.50-10.99	13.58-10.43
Average Yield %	3.18	3.55	3.78	4.32	4.82	4.81	4.08	4.09

Address: One Quaker Park, Conshohocken, PA 19428-0809	Officers: Ronald J. Naples - Chmn., C.E.O., Joseph W. Bauer - Pres., C.O.O.	Investor Contact:610-832-8500
Telephone: (610) 832-4000	Transfer Agents:American Stock Transfer &Trust Company, New York, NY	Institutional Holding No of Institutions: 47
Web Site: www.quakerchem.com		Shares: 353,764 % Held: -

220

QUESTAR CORP.

Exchange	Symbol	Price	52Wk Range	Yield	P/E
NYS	STR	$36.65 (5/28/2004)	37.00-30.37	2.35	16.81

*7 Year Price Score 139.8 *NYSE Composite Index=100 *12 Month Price Score 49.5

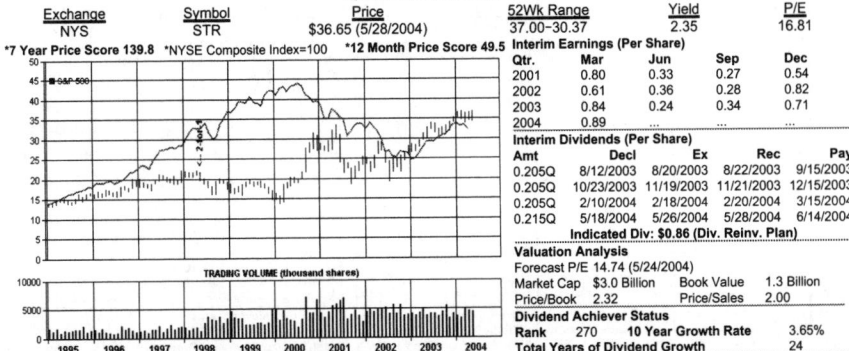

Interim Earnings (Per Share)

Qtr.	Mar	Jun	Sep	Dec
2001	0.80	0.33	0.27	0.54
2002	0.61	0.36	0.28	0.82
2003	0.84	0.24	0.34	0.71
2004	0.89	...	...	...

Interim Dividends (Per Share)

Amt	Decl	Ex	Rec	Pay
0.205Q	8/12/2003	8/20/2003	8/22/2003	9/15/2003
0.205Q	10/23/2003	11/19/2003	11/21/2003	12/15/2003
0.205Q	2/10/2004	2/18/2004	2/20/2004	3/15/2004
0.215Q	5/18/2004	5/26/2004	5/28/2004	6/14/2004

Indicated Div: $0.86 (Div. Reinv. Plan)

Valuation Analysis

Forecast P/E 14.74 (5/24/2004)

Market Cap	$3.0 Billion	Book Value	1.3 Billion
Price/Book	2.32	Price/Sales	2.00

Dividend Achiever Status

Rank	270	10 Year Growth Rate	3.65%
Total Years of Dividend Growth			24

TRADING VOLUME (thousand shares)

Business Summary: Gas Utilities (MIC: 7.4 SIC: 4923 NAIC:221210)

Questar is a natural gas−focused energy company that is involved in a range of natural gas activities through its Market Resources and Regulated Services groups. Market Resources is engaged in gas and oil development and production; cost−of−service gas development; gas gathering and processing; and wholesale gas and hydrocarbon liquids marketing, risk management, and gas storage. Regulated Services, through its two primary subsidiaries, Questar Pipeline Company and Questar Gas Company, conducts interstate gas transmission and storage activities and retail gas distribution services.

Recent Developments: For the quarter ended Mar 31 2004, net income was $76.1 million compared with income of $70.2 million a year earlier. Total revenue advanced 20.0% to $563.6 million. Co.'s results were driven by higher nonregulated natural gas production and commodity prices. Questar Market Resources' (QMR) nonregulated production totaled 25.4 billion cubic feet equivalent, 8.1% higher than the year before. Gas production rose 8.9% to 21.9 billion cubic feet, while oil and natural gas liquids (NGL) production improved 2.6% to 587,000 barrels. QMR's average realized price for natural gas climbed 15.1% to $4.05 per thousand cubic feet. Realized oil and NGL prices increased 19.2% to $29.46 per barrel.

Prospects: Favorable commodity prices, coupled with improving gas and oil and natural gas liquids production, strengthen Co.'s near−term outlook. Significantly, Co. stated that it remains on schedule to grow nonregulated production at least 8.0% in 2004 to approximately 100 billion cubic feet equivalent. Accordingly, Co. now expects full−year 2004 earnings to range from $2.40 to $2.55 per share, an increase of $0.10 from its previous guidance. Co. noted that it has hedged approximately 75.0% of its remaining 2004 natural gas and oil production, which protects against price declines and reduces earnings volatility.

Financial Data

(US$ in Thousands)	3 Mos	12/31/2003	12/31/2002	12/31/2001	12/31/2000	12/31/1999	12/31/1998	12/31/1997
Earnings Per Share	2.18	2.13	2.07	1.94	1.94	1.20	0.93	1.26
Cash Flow Per Share	2.01	5.30	5.62	4.56	3.21	2.60	3.43	2.45
Tang. Book Val. Per Share	14.67	14.12	12.80	12.14	12.00	11.37	10.62	10.29
Dividends Per Share	0.800	0.780	0.720	0.700	0.680	0.670	0.650	0.620
Dividend Payout %	36.70	36.61	35.02	36.34	35.30	55.83	70.16	49.20
Income Statement								
Total Revenues	563,616	1,463,188	1,200,667	1,439,350	1,266,153	924,219	906,256	933,274
Total Indirect Exp.	82,138	296,651	246,413	219,877	192,595	220,168	195,949	158,344
Costs & Expenses	426,826	1,123,358	926,472	1,165,243	1,006,243	794,001	773,475	763,119
Depreciation & Amort.	52,269	192,382	184,952	151,735	141,941	137,744	125,157	124,037
Operating Income	136,790	339,830	274,195	274,107	259,910	130,218	132,781	170,155
Income Taxes	46,005	102,563	91,126	88,270	85,367	47,788	29,030	45,602
Eqty Earns/Minority Int.	1,310	5,008	11,777	159	3,996	(4,356)	2,917	...
Income from Cont Ops	...	179,196	170,893	...	...	...	...	...
Net Income	76,133	173,616	155,596	158,186	156,711	98,830	76,899	104,795
Average Shs. Outstg.	85,168	84,190	82,573	81,658	80,915	82,676	82,817	82,668
Balance Sheet								
Net Property	2,764,581	2,768,529	2,617,798	2,565,098	1,953,993	1,786,914	1,747,641	1,531,220
Total Assets	3,280,817	3,309,055	3,067,850	3,235,711	2,539,045	2,237,997	2,161,281	1,945,017
Long−Term Obligations	950,191	950,189	1,145,180	997,423	714,537	735,043	615,770	541,986
Net Stockholders' Equity	1,315,486	1,261,265	1,138,761	1,080,781	991,066	925,845	877,958	845,778
Shares Outstanding	83,779	83,233	82,053	81,523	80,818	81,418	82,632	82,142
Operating Profit Margin %	24.27	23.22	22.83	19.04	20.52	14.08	14.65	18.23
Net Inc./Net Property %	2.75	6.27	5.94	6.16	8.02	5.53	4.40	6.84
Net Inc./Tot. Capital %	3.34	6.52	5.82	6.53	7.97	5.27	4.54	6.53
Return on Equity %	5.79	14.20	15.00	14.63	15.81	10.67	8.75	12.39
Accum. Depr./Gross Prop. %	39.18	38.51	37.84	37.27	44.86	45.16	43.70	44.15
Price Range	36.85−34.09	35.35−26.66	29.27−19.40	33.51−18.70	31.50−13.81	19.88−14.94	22.31−16.25	22.31−17.25
P/E Ratio	16.90−15.64	16.60−12.52	14.14−9.37	17.27−9.64	16.24−7.12	16.56−12.45	23.99−17.47	17.71−13.69
Average Yield %	2.24	2.49	2.89	2.71	3.21	3.72	3.27	3.15

Address: 180 East 100 South Street, Salt Lake City, UT 84145−0433 **Telephone:** (801) 324−5000 **Web Site:** www.questar.com	**Officers:** Keith O. Rattie − Chmn., Pres., C.E.O., Stephen E. Parks − Sr. V.P., C.F.O. **Transfer Agents:** Questar Corp., Salt Lake City, UT	**Investor Contact:** 801−324−5497 **Institutional Holding No of Institutions:** 16 **Shares:** 1,199,651 **% Held:** −

QUIXOTE CORP.

Exchange	Symbol	Price	52Wk Range	Yield	P/E
NMS	QUIX	$21.00 (5/28/2004)	28.18–19.40	1.62	17.21

*7 Year Price Score 138.6 *NYSE Composite Index=100 *12 Month Price Score 43.7

Interim Earnings (Per Share)

Qtr.	Sep	Dec	Mar	Jun
2000-01	0.29	0.17	0.23	0.66
2001-02	0.16	0.05	0.07	0.45
2002-03	0.22	0.19	0.20	0.56
2003-04	0.27	0.05	0.05	...

Interim Dividends (Per Share)

Amt	Decl	Ex	Rec	Pay
0.16S	11/18/2002	12/4/2002	12/6/2002	1/3/2003
0.17S	5/9/2003	5/30/2003	6/3/2003	7/3/2003
0.17S	11/13/2003	12/3/2003	12/5/2003	1/6/2004
0.17S	5/12/2004	6/3/2004	6/7/2004	7/2/2004

Indicated Div: $0.34

Valuation Analysis

Forecast P/E 13.04 (5/24/2004)			
Market Cap $163.1 Million		Book Value 78.6 Million	
Price/Book N/A		Price/Sales N/A	

Dividend Achiever Status

Rank 251	10 Year Growth Rate	5.14%
Total Years of Dividend Growth		10

Business Summary: Construction – Public Infrastructure (MIC: 3.1 SIC: 1611 NAIC:237310)

Quixote and its subsidiaries develop, manufacture and market highway and transportation safety products to protect, direct and inform motorists and highway workers in both domestic and international markets. These products include energy–absorbing highway crash cushions, flexible post delineators, electronic wireless measuring and sensing devices, weather information systems and forecasting services, variable message signs, highway advisory radios, intelligent intersection control devices and other highway and transportation safety devices. Co.'s two reportable segments, the Protect and Direct segment and Inform segment, are within the highway and transportation safety industry.

Recent Developments: For the three months ended Mar 31 2004, net income totaled $446,000, down 71.3% compared with $1.6 million in the corresponding prior–year quarter. Net sales jumped 43.5% to $36.2 million from $25.2 million a year earlier, driven primarily by the acquisitions of U.S. Traffic Corporation and Peek Traffic Corporation in 2003. Gross profit was essentially unchanged at $10.0 million versus the year before. However, as a percentage of net sales gross profit slipped to 27.6% from 39.9% in 2003, reflecting lower gross margins generated by U.S. Traffic and Peek Traffic. Operating loss totaled $459,000 compared with an operating profit of $2.5 million the previous year.

Prospects: Top–line growth is being negatively affected by sluggish sales volume at U.S. Traffic stemming in part to the absence of new large contracts related to ongoing state and municipal budgetary issues. In addition, results are being hampered by the prolonged delay in the approval of a new federal highway funding bill. Meanwhile, lower sales of truck–mounted attenuators is being partially offset by strong sales of permanent crash cushions and parts. Looking ahead, Co. is targeting fourth–quarter 2004 earnings in the range of $0.30 to $0.35 per share.

Financial Data

(US$ in Thousands)	9 Mos	6 Mos	3 Mos	06/30/2003	06/30/2002	06/30/2001	06/30/2000	06/30/1999
Earnings Per Share	0.93	0.93	0.27	1.17	0.73	1.35	1.10	0.92
Cash Flow Per Share	0.52	0.10	(0.32)	2.00	1.56	1.34	1.03	1.57
Tang. Book Val. Per Share	1.70	1.50	2.62	2.23	3.17	3.36	2.77	2.71
Dividends Per Share	0.340	0.330	0.330	0.320	0.310	0.300	0.280	0.270
Dividend Payout %	36.56	35.48	122.22	27.35	42.46	22.22	25.45	29.34
Income Statement								
Total Revenues	110,847	74,678	39,184	114,310	89,694	93,554	83,770	71,987
Total Indirect Exp.	28,953	18,510	8,667	31,086	26,443	25,051	25,822	21,150
Depreciation & Amort.	4,790	2,985	1,417	3,978	3,539	3,916	3,834	3,425
Operating Income	4,877	5,336	4,109	15,154	9,489	18,887	15,289	12,483
Net Interest Inc./(Exp.)	(1,565)	(982)	(483)	(802)	(1,106)	(1,411)	(901)	(938)
Income Taxes	(133)	1,567	1,305	4,880	3,316	6,645	5,466	4,256
Income from Cont Ops	...	...	...	...	5,897	...	...	7,562
Net Income	3,233	2,787	2,321	9,472	6,824	10,843	8,919	7,802
Average Shs. Outstg.	8,767	8,710	8,679	8,062	8,121	8,049	8,124	8,228
Balance Sheet								
Cash & Cash Equivalents	6,023	1,354	1,169	3,753	1,798	4,118	1,524	2,153
Total Current Assets	69,126	65,159	62,869	67,088	43,094	44,578	34,319	30,797
Total Assets	168,510	164,095	145,608	150,825	100,044	88,029	73,264	71,774
Total Current Liabilities	25,755	26,967	21,039	30,999	12,171	13,542	12,192	12,218
Long–Term Obligations	53,659	50,325	41,493	39,789	24,772	21,526	15,596	11,901
Net Stockholders' Equity	83,910	82,516	78,649	75,555	59,226	50,606	43,116	45,982
Net Working Capital	43,371	38,192	41,830	36,089	30,923	31,036	22,127	18,579
Shares Outstanding	8,696	8,577	8,377	8,305	7,776	7,517	7,388	8,072
Statistical Record								
Operating Profit Margin %	4.39	7.14	10.48	13.25	10.57	20.18	18.25	17.34
Net Profit Margin %	2.67	7.92	12.58	16.82	13.96	25.79	23.69	22.32
Return on Equity %	3.85	3.37	2.95	12.53	9.95	21.42	20.68	16.44
Return on Assets %	1.92	1.69	1.59	6.28	5.89	12.31	12.17	10.53
Debt/Total Assets %	31.84	30.66	28.49	26.38	24.76	24.45	21.28	16.58
Price Range	28.18-20.20	28.00-22.55	28.00-22.55	26.05-14.75	27.83-15.82	28.61-13.00	16.13-11.06	15.50-11.31
P/E Ratio	30.30-21.72	30.11-24.24	103.7-83.52	22.26-12.61	38.12-21.67	21.19-9.63	14.66-10.06	16.85-12.30
Average Yield %	1.42	1.33	1.33	1.72	1.48	1.51	2.00	2.10

Address: 35 East Wacker Drive, Chicago, IL 60601	Officers: Leslie J. Jezuit – Chmn., Pres., C.E.O., Daniel P. Gorey – V.P., C.F.O., Treas.	Investor Contact:312–467–6755
Telephone: (312) 467–6755		Institutional Holding
Web Site: www.quixotecorp.com		No of Institutions: 2
		Shares: 170,847 % Held: –

RAVEN INDUSTRIES, INC.

Exchange	Symbol	Price	52Wk Range	Yield	P/E
NMS	RAVN	$31.78 (5/28/2004)	33.64–19.58	1.38	21.19

*7 Year Price Score 244.5 *NYSE Composite Index=100 ***12 Month Price Score 52.0**

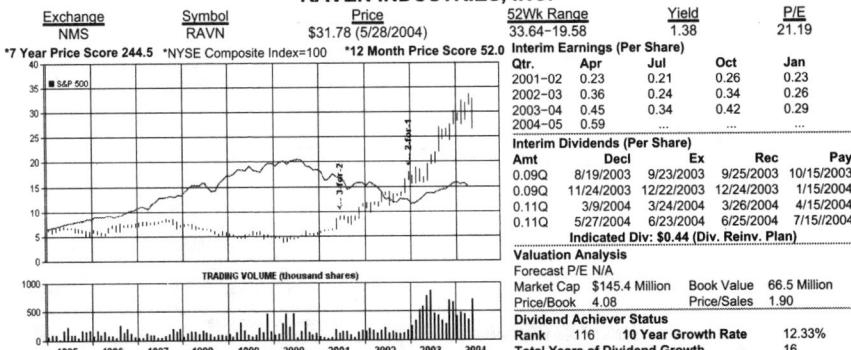

Interim Earnings (Per Share)

Qtr.	Apr	Jul	Oct	Jan
2001–02	0.23	0.21	0.26	0.23
2002–03	0.36	0.24	0.34	0.26
2003–04	0.45	0.34	0.42	0.29
2004–05	0.59	...	...	...

Interim Dividends (Per Share)

Amt	Decl	Ex	Rec	Pay
0.09Q	8/19/2003	9/23/2003	9/25/2003	10/15/2003
0.09Q	11/24/2003	12/22/2003	12/24/2003	1/15/2004
0.11Q	3/9/2004	3/24/2004	3/26/2004	4/15/2004
0.11Q	5/27/2004	6/23/2004	6/25/2004	7/15/2004

Indicated Div: $0.44 (Div. Reinv. Plan)

Valuation Analysis

Forecast P/E N/A

Market Cap $145.4 Million		Book Value 66.5 Million	
Price/Book 4.08		Price/Sales 1.90	

Dividend Achiever Status

Rank 116 10 Year Growth Rate 12.33%
Total Years of Dividend Growth 16

Business Summary: Apparel (MIC: 4.4 SIC: 2399 NAIC:315999)

Raven Industries is a manufacturing company that operates through four core divisions. The Engineered Films division produces rugged reinforced plastic sheeting and high–altitude research balloons for public and commercial research. The Electronics Systems unit provides electronic manufacturing services. The Flow Controls division develops global positioning systems–based control systems, computerized control hardware and software for precision farming, and systems for the precision application of insecticides, fertilizer and road de–icers. Aerostar International Inc. produces custom–shaped advertising inflatables.

Recent Developments: For the first quarter ended Apr 30 2004 net income jumped 29.5% to $5.4 million compared with $4.2 million in the corresponding period of 2003. Results for 2003 included a gain of $9,000 on the sale of businesses and assets. Net sales advanced 4.0% to $38.4 million from $36.9 million a year earlier. Operating income increased 29.1% to $8.5 million from $6.5 million the year before. Overall results benefited from strong sales and earnings growth in Co.'s Flow Controls, Engineered Films and Aerostar segments. Co.'s Electronic Systems Division experienced lower sales and earnings due to its inability to ship in the first quarter.

Prospects: Looking ahead, prospects appear favorable, as Co. believes that the market trends that drove first quarter results should continue. The Flow Controls Division should benefit from increased demand for Co.'s global positioning system–based tractor steering systems. The Engineered Films Division expects to build on the sales momentum of 2003. Meanwhile, Co. expects the Electronic Systems Division to produce significant revenue growth for the full year. Aerostar's decision to exit the commercial outerwear market and focus on higher–margin products is helping to drive growth in operating income. This division should also benefit from the addition of Co.'s high–altitude research balloon business.

Financial Data

(US$ in Thousands)	01/31/2004	01/31/2003	01/31/2002	01/31/2001	01/31/2000	01/31/1999	01/31/1998	01/31/1997
Earnings Per Share	1.50	1.20	0.93	0.62	0.51	0.43	0.55	0.53
Cash Flow Per Share	2.13	1.36	1.94	0.91	0.79	0.74	0.78	0.83
Tang. Book Val. Per Share	6.50	5.66	5.64	5.06	3.87	4.42	4.25	3.78
Dividends Per Share	0.340	0.280	0.250	0.230	0.220	0.200	0.180	0.160
Dividend Payout %	22.66	23.33	27.41	37.63	42.58	47.69	33.93	30.19
Income Statement								
Total Revenues	142,727	120,903	118,515	132,858	147,906	152,798	149,619	139,441
Total Indirect Exp.	12,306	10,271	10,309	6,867	12,761	15,142	14,367	13,316
Depreciation & Amort.	4,145	3,966	3,145	3,667	4,884	5,133	5,137	4,566
Operating Income	21,626	17,065	13,175	10,748	10,577	9,673	10,562	11,971
Net Interest Inc./(Exp.)	(70)	(63)	(129)	(258)	(418)	(474)	(323)	(310)
Income Taxes	7,880	6,069	4,718	4,513	3,741	3,467	4,478	4,227
Net Income	13,836	11,185	8,847	6,411	6,762	6,182	8,062	7,688
Average Shs. Outstg.	9,244	9,347	9,491	10,337	13,116	14,271	14,673	14,265
Balance Sheet								
Cash & Cash Equivalents	14,442	5,217	7,478	10,673	5,707	5,335	2,850	3,439
Total Current Assets	55,710	49,351	45,308	52,236	55,371	60,861	57,831	56,696
Total Assets	79,508	72,816	67,836	65,656	74,047	83,674	82,590	80,662
Total Current Liabilities	11,895	13,167	13,810	13,935	14,702	16,792	19,375	20,016
Long–Term Obligations	57	151	280	2,013	3,024	4,572	1,128	3,181
Net Stockholders' Equity	66,471	58,236	52,032	47,989	54,519	62,293	61,563	56,729
Net Working Capital	43,815	36,184	31,498	38,301	40,669	44,069	38,456	36,680
Shares Outstanding	9,020	9,066	9,211	9,478	14,082	14,082	14,472	14,508
Statistical Record								
Operating Profit Margin %	15.03	14.26	11.42	10.73	7.95	6.33	7.05	8.58
Return on Equity %	20.55	19.51	17.70	20.66	14.57	9.92	13.09	13.55
Return on Assets %	17.18	15.60	13.58	15.10	10.73	7.38	9.76	9.53
Debt/Total Assets %	0.07	0.20	0.41	3.06	4.08	5.46	1.36	3.94
Price Range	30.14–15.68	18.00–9.78	11.75–6.04	6.08–3.71	6.00–4.50	7.50–5.17	8.58–6.54	7.83–5.33
P/E Ratio	20.09–10.45	15.00–8.15	12.63–6.50	9.81–5.98	11.76–8.82	17.44–12.02	15.61–11.89	14.78–10.06
Average Yield %	1.52	2.08	2.94	4.62	4.32	3.20	2.33	2.42

Address: 205 East 6th Street, Sioux Falls, SD 57117–5107
Telephone: (605) 336–2750
Web Site: www.ravenind.com

Officers: Ronald M. Moquist – Pres., C.E.O., Thomas Iacarella – V.P., C.F.O., Treas., Sec.
Transfer Agents: Wells Fargo Bank Minnesota N.A., St. Paul, MN

Investor Contact: 605–336–2750
Institutional Holding
No of Institutions: –
Shares: – **% Held:** –

REGIONS FINANCIAL CORP.

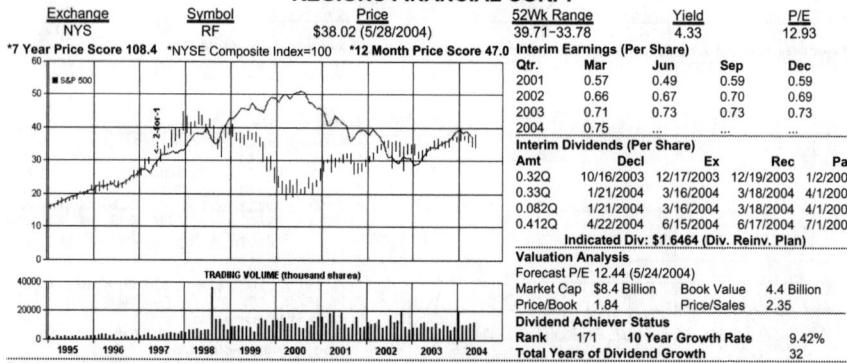

Exchange	Symbol	Price	52Wk Range	Yield	P/E
NYS	RF	$38.02 (5/28/2004)	39.71–33.78	4.33	12.93

*7 Year Price Score 108.4 *NYSE Composite Index=100 *12 Month Price Score 47.0

Interim Earnings (Per Share)

Qtr.	Mar	Jun	Sep	Dec
2001	0.57	0.49	0.59	0.59
2002	0.66	0.67	0.70	0.69
2003	0.71	0.73	0.73	0.73
2004	0.75	...	...	...

Interim Dividends (Per Share)

Amt	Decl	Ex	Rec	Pay
0.32Q	10/16/2003	12/17/2003	12/19/2003	1/2/2004
0.33Q	1/21/2004	3/16/2004	3/18/2004	4/1/2004
0.082Q	1/21/2004	3/16/2004	3/18/2004	4/1/2004
0.412Q	4/22/2004	6/15/2004	6/17/2004	7/1/2004

Indicated Div: $1.6464 (Div. Reinv. Plan)

Valuation Analysis

Forecast P/E 12.44 (5/24/2004)

Market Cap	$8.4 Billion	Book Value	4.4 Billion
Price/Book	1.84	Price/Sales	2.35

Dividend Achiever Status

Rank	171	10 Year Growth Rate	9.42%
Total Years of Dividend Growth		32	

TRADING VOLUME (thousand shares)

Business Summary: Commercial Banking (MIC: 8.1 SIC: 6021 NAIC:522110)

Regions Financial is a regional financial holding company with assets of $48.60 billion as of Dec 31 2003. Co. provides traditional commercial and retail banking services, brokerage and investment services, mortgage banking, insurance brokerage, credit life insurance, commercial accounts receivable factoring and specialty financing. Co.'s banking affiliate, Regions Bank, offers banking services from 681 full–service banking offices in Alabama, Arkansas, Florida, Georgia, Louisiana, North Carolina, South Carolina, Tennessee and Texas. Co. also provides investment and brokerage services, asset management, mutual funds and financial planning from 142 offices of Morgan Keegan & Company, Inc.

Recent Developments: For the three months ended Mar 31 2004, net income increased 6.3% to $168.5 million from $158.6 million in the prior year. Net interest income rose 5.3% to $379.0 million from $359.9 million the year before. Provision for loan losses totaled $15.0 million, down 52.4% compared with $31.5 million the previous year. Total non–interest income advanced 7.0% to $365.5 million from $341.6 million a year earlier. Total non–interest expense grew 9.6% to $491.1 million from $448.2 million in 2003. Income before income taxes climbed 7.5% to $238.4 million from $221.8 million the prior year. At Mar 31 2004, total assets were $48.78 billion, up 0.6% compared with $48.46 billion at Mar 31 2003.

Prospects: On Apr 22 2004, Co. announced that it has entered into a definitive agreement to acquire Evergreen Timberland Investment Management (ETIM), with assets of more than $1.00 billion and approximately 1.0 million acres under management, from Wachovia Corp. Co. plans to rebrand ETIM as Regions Morgan Keegan Timberland Group, a line of businesses within Co.'s trust and asset management division. Terms of the transaction, which is expected to be completed by the end of the second quarter of 2004, were not disclosed. Separately, Co.anticipates that its acquisition of Union Planters Corp. will be completed in mid 2004.

Financial Data

(US$ in Thousands)	3 Mos	12/31/2003	12/31/2002	12/31/2001	12/31/2000	12/31/1999	12/31/1998	12/31/1997
Earnings Per Share	2.94	2.90	2.72	2.24	2.38	2.35	1.88	2.15
Tang. Book Val. Per Share	14.73	20.05	18.87	17.54	15.73	13.89	13.61	13.99
Dividends Per Share	1.240	1.210	1.150	1.110	1.060	0.980	0.890	0.770
Dividend Payout %	42.18	41.72	42.27	49.55	44.53	41.70	47.34	36.04
Income Statement								
Total Interest Income	535,682	2,219,130	2,536,989	3,055,637	3,234,243	2,854,686	2,597,786	1,653,084
Total Interest Expense	156,685	744,532	1,039,401	1,630,144	1,845,446	1,428,831	1,272,968	824,203
Net Interest Income	378,997	1,474,598	1,497,588	1,425,493	1,388,797	1,425,855	1,324,818	828,881
Provision for Loan Losses	15,000	121,500	127,500	165,402	127,099	113,658	60,505	41,773
Non–Interest Income	365,484	1,256,203	1,258,878	981,885	601,210	537,141	474,697	258,553
Non–Interest Expense	491,100	1,827,316	1,747,465	1,524,025	1,121,182	1,064,312	1,103,708	600,341
Income Before Taxes	238,381	911,572	869,240	717,951	741,726	785,026	635,302	445,320
Net Income	168,535	651,841	619,902	508,934	527,523	525,386	421,712	299,692
Average Shs. Outstg.	224,590	225,118	227,639	227,063	221,989	223,967	223,781	139,421
Balance Sheet								
Cash & Due from Banks	970,762	1,255,853	1,577,536	1,239,598	1,210,872	1,393,418	1,619,006	726,059
Securities Avail. for Sale	9,263,908	9,872,935	9,747,683	8,555,005	5,468,406	6,873,308	4,893,410	1,576,648
Net Loans & Leases	32,314,184	31,730,266	30,548,610	30,466,181	30,999,955	27,806,300	24,050,175	16,200,599
Total Assets	48,776,943	48,597,996	47,938,840	45,382,712	43,688,293	42,714,395	36,831,940	23,034,228
Total Deposits	31,425,573	32,732,535	32,926,201	31,548,323	32,022,491	29,989,094	28,350,066	17,750,926
Long–Term Obligations	5,768,131	5,711,752	5,386,109	4,747,674	4,478,027	1,750,861	571,040	400,199
Total Liabilities	44,350,485	44,145,881	43,760,418	41,346,947	40,230,349	39,649,283	33,831,539	21,121,373
Net Stockholders' Equity	4,426,458	4,452,115	4,178,422	4,035,765	3,457,944	3,065,112	3,000,401	1,912,855
Shares Outstanding	218,739	221,967	221,336	230,081	219,769	220,635	220,454	136,696
Return on Equity %	3.80	11.43	14.83	12.61	15.25	17.14	14.05	15.66
Return on Assets %	0.34	1.04	1.29	1.12	1.20	1.22	1.14	1.30
Equity/Assets %	9.07	9.16	8.71	8.89	7.91	7.17	8.14	8.30
Non–Int. Exp./Tot. Inc. %	54.49	52.57	46.03	37.74	29.23	31.37	35.92	31.40
Price Range	39.71–35.70	37.80–30.38	36.20–27.26	32.40–26.19	27.81–18.44	41.00–23.44	44.88–31.12	44.75–25.69
P/E Ratio	13.51–12.14	13.03–10.48	13.31–10.02	14.46–11.69	11.68–7.75	17.45–9.97	23.87–16.55	20.81–11.95
Average Yield %	3.35	3.49	3.42	3.74	4.74	2.83	2.25	2.33

Address: 417 North 20th Street, Birmingham, AL 35203
Telephone: (205) 944–1300
Web Site: www.regionsbank.com

Officers: Carl E. Jones – Chmn., Pres., C.E.O., Richard D. Horsley – Vice–Chmn., C.O.O.
Transfer Agents: EquiServe, Jersey City, NJ

Investor Contact: 205–326–7090
Institutional Holding
No of Institutions: 268
Shares: 65,887,146 **% Held:** 29.80%

REPUBLIC BANCORP, INC.

Exchange	Symbol	Price	52Wk Range	Yield	P/E
NMS	RBNC	$13.29 (5/28/2004)	14.10–11.77	2.86	13.70

*7 Year Price Score 134.2   *NYSE Composite Index=100   *12 Month Price Score 47.2

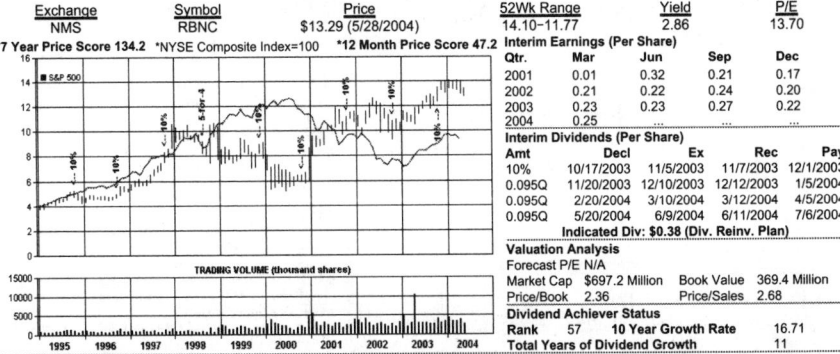

Interim Earnings (Per Share)

Qtr.	Mar	Jun	Sep	Dec
2001	0.01	0.32	0.21	0.17
2002	0.21	0.22	0.24	0.20
2003	0.23	0.23	0.27	0.22
2004	0.25	...	...	...

Interim Dividends (Per Share)

Amt	Decl	Ex	Rec	Pay
10%	10/17/2003	11/5/2003	11/7/2003	12/1/2003
0.095Q	11/20/2003	12/10/2003	12/12/2003	1/5/2004
0.095Q	2/20/2004	3/10/2004	3/12/2004	4/5/2004
0.095Q	5/20/2004	6/9/2004	6/11/2004	7/6/2004

Indicated Div: $0.38 (Div. Reinv. Plan)

Valuation Analysis

Forecast P/E N/A

Market Cap	$697.2 Million	Book Value	369.4 Million
Price/Book	2.36	Price/Sales	2.68

Dividend Achiever Status

Rank	57	10 Year Growth Rate 16.71
Total Years of Dividend Growth		11

Business Summary: Commercial Banking (MIC: 8.1 SIC: 6021 NAIC:522110)

Republic Bancorp, with $5.35 billion in assets as of Dec 31 2003, is the third largest bank holding company headquartered in Michigan and the 82nd largest bank holding company nationwide. Co. provides retail, commercial and mortgage banking products and services through its wholly–owned banking subsidiary, Republic Bank, a state–chartered banking corporation. As of Dec 31 2003, Republic Bank served customers in Michigan, Ohio and Indiana with 93 retail, commercial and mortgage banking offices and 93 ATMs. In addition, Co. performs residential mortgage loan servicing for the benefit of others, including collecting and remitting loan payments and supervising foreclosure proceedings.

Recent Developments: For the quarter ended Mar 31 2004, net income rose 7.6% to $16.3 million compared with $15.2 million in the corresponding period of the prior year. Total interest income increased 3.1% to $67.8 million, while interest expense grew 2.3% to $31.9 million. Net interest income improved 3.9% to $35.9 million from $34.5 million the year before, primarily due to higher average earning assets. Provision for loan losses fell 16.7% to $2.5 million. Total non-interest income declined 27.2% to $10.8 million, primarily due to lower levels of service charges and mortgage banking income. Non-interest expense decreased 13.8% to $21.0 million, principally due to a decline in salaries and employee benefits.

Prospects: Results continue to be fueled by strong growth in consumer loans and core deposits in Co.'s retail banking business line, as well as solid loan growth in Co.'s commercial banking line. Additionally, mortgage banking results continue to reflect lower refinance and closing volumes, while increased application volumes in March 2004 should provide increased closing volume in the second quarter. During the first quarter of 2004, Co. originated $425.0 million in single-family residential mortgages. Meanwhile, Co.'s asset quality remains steady as total non-performing assets decreased $2.3 million, or 5.0%, at Mar 31 2004 compared with Dec 31 2003.

Financial Data

(US$ in Thousands)	12/31/2003	12/31/2002	12/31/2001	12/31/2000	12/31/1999	12/31/1998	12/31/1997	12/31/1996
Earnings Per Share	0.95	0.87	0.71	0.69	0.22	0.59	0.49	0.36
Tang. Book Val. Per Share	5.81	5.26	4.70	3.69	3.00	2.39	1.97	2.17
Dividends Per Share	0.310	0.280	0.250	0.230	0.210	0.190	0.180	0.160
Dividend Payout %	33.49	32.19	35.52	33.59	96.41	33.33	36.82	43.78
Income Statement								
Total Interest Income	265,680	284,704	333,376	348,328	299,662	146,005	118,852	99,147
Total Interest Expense	123,183	137,024	189,767	213,680	171,396	86,364	71,912	62,427
Net Interest Income	142,497	147,680	143,609	134,648	128,266	59,641	46,940	36,720
Provision for Loan Losses	12,000	16,000	8,700	11,650	11,650	4,000	3,031	290
Non–Interest Income	60,779	56,027	59,384	70,838	137,731	137,441	102,515	90,846
Non–Interest Expense	104,654	100,515	132,213	127,641	225,968	157,466	117,742	104,492
Income Before Taxes	86,622	87,192	74,080	71,345	28,379	35,616	28,682	22,784
Income from Cont Ops	...	...	...	...	...	...	...	15,066
Net Income	60,726	62,505	51,565	48,400	17,634	22,890	18,789	14,678
Average Shs. Outstg.	64,171	64,927	66,574	66,416	66,996	38,481	38,389	39,946
Balance Sheet								
Cash & Due from Banks	63,749	75,540	75,270	76,558	74,423	17,627	27,458	33,590
Securities Avail. for Sale	607,450	248,931	364,648	211,860	206,459	47,269	119,881	228,621
Net Loans & Leases	4,117,243	3,620,466	3,429,224	3,743,226	3,346,297	1,201,979	1,088,410	779,919
Total Assets	5,353,688	4,778,195	4,740,605	4,610,641	4,301,615	2,195,612	1,872,893	1,490,365
Total Deposits	2,815,269	2,788,272	2,753,468	2,728,526	2,613,050	1,378,691	1,177,293	1,013,707
Long–Term Obligations	1,616,726	1,321,443	1,314,218	1,431,013	1,219,711	504,068	414,132	183,389
Total Liabilities	4,984,268	4,395,467	4,356,969	4,287,058	4,006,455	2,045,195	1,741,805	1,253,394
Net Stockholders' Equity	369,420	332,728	304,917	294,864	266,441	150,891	132,684	126,711
Shares Outstanding	63,527	63,185	64,330	65,783	66,302	38,254	37,602	37,931
Return on Equity %	16.43	18.78	16.91	16.41	6.61	15.16	14.16	11.89
Return on Assets %	1.13	1.30	1.08	1.04	0.40	1.04	1.00	1.01
Equity/Assets %	6.90	6.96	6.43	6.39	6.19	6.87	7.08	8.50
Non–Int. Exp./Tot. Inc. %	32.05	29.49	32.66	30.45	51.66	55.55	53.18	54.99
Price Range	13.98-10.55	12.69-9.29	12.00-8.08	8.64-5.17	9.43-7.06	10.63-7.45	10.62-5.25	5.59-4.36
P/E Ratio	14.72-11.10	14.58-10.68	16.90-11.38	12.52-7.49	42.86-32.10	18.02-12.63	21.67-10.71	15.54-12.12
Average Yield %	2.55	2.53	2.44	3.60	2.57	2.03	2.63	3.30

Address: 1070 East Main Street, Owosso, MI 48867	**Officers:** Jerry D. Campbell – Chmn., George J. Butvilas – Vice–Chmn.	**Investor Contact:**989–725–7337
Telephone: (989) 725–7337	**Transfer Agents:**EquiServe Trust Company, N.A.,	**Institutional Holding** **No of Institutions:** 22
Web Site: www.republicbancorp.com	Providence, RI	**Shares:** 3,456,166 **% Held:** –

225

RLI CORP.

Exchange	Symbol	Price	52Wk Range	Yield	P/E
NYS	RLI	$35.97 (5/28/2004)	41.25-29.19	1.45	12.62

*7 Year Price Score 156.0 ***NYSE Composite Index=100** ***12 Month Price Score 46.0**

Interim Earnings (Per Share)

Qtr.	Mar	Jun	Sep	Dec
2001	0.31	0.35	0.34	0.37
2002	0.39	0.45	0.28	0.63
2003	0.56	0.60	0.98	0.62
2004	0.65	...	...	...

Interim Dividends (Per Share)

Amt	Decl	Ex	Rec	Pay
0.10Q	9/2/2003	9/26/2003	9/30/2003	10/15/2003
0.11Q	11/24/2003	12/29/2003	12/31/2003	1/15/2004
0.11Q	2/9/2004	3/29/2004	3/31/2004	4/15/2004
0.13Q	5/7/2004	6/28/2004	6/30/2004	7/15/2004

Indicated Div: $0.52 (Div. Reinv. Plan)

Valuation Analysis
Forecast P/E 13.58 (5/24/2004)
Market Cap $714.9 Million   Book Value 576.1 Million
Price/Book 1.70   Price/Sales 1.82

Dividend Achiever Status
Rank 191   10 Year Growth Rate 8.40%
Total Years of Dividend Growth 27

TRADING VOLUME (thousand shares)

1995 1996 1997 1998 1999 2000 2001 2002 2003 2004

Business Summary: Insurance (MIC: 8.2 SIC: 6331 NAIC:524126)

RLI is a holding company that underwrites selected property and casualty insurance through its insurance subsidiaries. Co.'s property segment includes commercial property consisting of excess surplus lines and specialty insurance such as fire and earthquake in the U.S., and homeowners residential property in Hawaii. The casualty segment consists largely of general liability, commercial transportation, commercial and personal umbrella laibility, executive products, special program business and other specialty coverages. The surety segment specializes in writing small to large commercial and small contract surety products, as well as those for the energy, petrochemical and refining industries.

Recent Developments: For the three months ended Mar 31 2004, net income increased 17.4% to $16.9 million compared with $14.4 million in the corresponding quarter of the previous year. Total revenues improved 17.0% to $140.6 million from $120.2 million in the year–earlier period. Net premiums earned climbed 15.3% to $125.9 million from $109.1 million, while net investment income jumped 15.5% to $12.3 million from $10.7 million in the prior–year quarter. Revenues included net realized gains of $2.4 million in 2004 versus $409,000 in 2003. Overall results benefited from the strong performance of Co.'s property segment.

Prospects: Overall sales and earnings are benefiting from favorable market conditions. On a segment basis, Co.'s property segment continues to generate strong growth from gross premiums written, despite lower underwriting profits. Results for the casualty segment are benefiting from a favorable rate environment for general liability and umbrella products. However, Co.'s surety segment continues to be hampered by tighter underwriting standards on contract surety. Looking ahead, net premiums earned should benefit from increased retentions in certain product lines.

Financial Data

(US$ in Thousands)	3 Mos	12/31/2003	12/31/2002	12/31/2001	12/31/2000	12/31/1999	12/31/1998	12/31/1997
Earnings Per Share	2.85	2.76	1.75	1.37	1.35	1.39	1.27	1.56
Tang. Book Val. Per Share	21.83	20.97	17.36	15.36	14.99	13.11	14.12	15.43
Dividends Per Share	0.400	0.380	0.330	0.310	0.290	0.270	0.250	0.230
Dividend Payout %	14.04	13.76	19.14	22.54	21.48	19.35	19.68	14.87
Income Statement								
Total Premium Income	125,898	463,597	348,065	273,008	231,603	195,274	142,324	141,884
Net Investment Income	...	8,578	...	...	...	...	...	...
Other Income	14,751	47,711	34,088	36,346	31,893	30,482	25,790	27,540
Total Revenues	140,649	519,886	382,153	309,354	263,496	225,756	168,114	169,424
Total Indirect Exp.	1,285	3,886	3,505	2,636	3,388	2,091	3,915	4,172
Inc. Before Inc. Taxes	23,780	94,278	48,728	41,018	38,293	43,035	37,721	41,522
Income Taxes	6,837	22,987	12,876	10,771	9,600	11,584	9,482	11,351
Eqty Earns/Minority Int.	1,234	5,548	4,397	2,845	2,979	1,613	1,337	951
Income from Cont Ops	...	...	...	30,247	...	...	...	...
Net Income	16,944	71,291	35,852	31,047	28,693	31,451	28,239	30,171
Average Shs. Outstg.	26,118	25,846	20,512	20,004	19,890	20,444	21,276	18,742
Balance Sheet								
Premiums Due	547,459	639,571	568,004	456,919	406,761	368,794	281,165	248,454
Invst. Assets: Total	1,419,451	1,364,043	1,025,288	814,435	774,159	706,314	690,751	617,472
Total Assets	2,191,585	2,134,364	1,719,327	1,390,970	1,281,323	1,170,363	1,012,685	911,741
Long–Term Obligations	100,000	100,000						
Net Stockholders' Equity	576,112	554,134	456,555	335,432	326,654	293,069	293,959	266,522
Shares Outstanding	25,182	25,165	24,681	19,825	19,607	19,746	20,811	17,268
Return on Revenues %	12.04	13.71	9.38	9.77	10.88	13.93	16.79	17.80
Return on Equity %	2.94	12.86	7.85	9.01	8.78	10.73	9.60	11.31
Return on Assets %	0.77	3.34	2.08	2.17	2.23	2.68	2.78	3.30
Price Range	41.25-36.09	38.10-25.40	29.60-22.25	23.00-19.40	22.34-13.25	19.38-13.97	22.65-15.41	20.05-12.20
P/E Ratio	14.47-12.66	13.80-9.20	16.91-12.71	16.79-14.16	16.55-9.81	13.94-10.05	17.83-12.13	12.85-7.82
Average Yield %	1.03	1.21	1.27	1.48	1.63	1.61	1.28	1.53

Address: 9025 North Lindbergh Drive, Peoria, IL 61615-1499	Officers: Jonathan E. Michael – Pres., C.E.O., Joseph E. Dondanville – Sr. V.P., C.F.O.	Investor Contact:309–693–5880
Telephone: (309) 692-1000	Transfer Agents:Wells Fargo Shareholder Services,	Institutional Holding
Web Site: www.rlicorp.com	St. Paul, MN	No of Institutions: 8
		Shares: 123,312 % Held: –

ROHM & HAAS CO.

Exchange	Symbol	Price	52Wk Range	Yield	P/E
NYS	ROH	$38.54 (5/28/2004)	43.50-30.96	2.59	26.76

*7 Year Price Score 106.2 *NYSE Composite Index=100 *12 Month Price Score 47.1

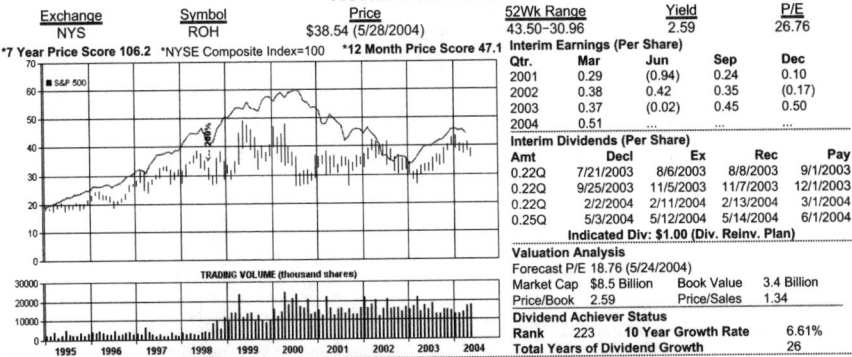

Interim Earnings (Per Share)

Qtr.	Mar	Jun	Sep	Dec
2001	0.29	(0.94)	0.24	0.10
2002	0.38	0.42	0.35	(0.17)
2003	0.37	(0.02)	0.45	0.50
2004	0.51	...	...	...

Interim Dividends (Per Share)

Amt	Decl	Ex	Rec	Pay
0.22Q	7/21/2003	8/6/2003	8/8/2003	9/1/2003
0.22Q	9/25/2003	11/5/2003	11/7/2003	12/1/2003
0.22Q	2/2/2004	2/11/2004	2/13/2004	3/1/2004
0.25Q	5/3/2004	5/12/2004	5/14/2004	6/1/2004

Indicated Div: $1.00 (Div. Reinv. Plan)

Valuation Analysis

Forecast P/E 18.76 (5/24/2004)

Market Cap	$8.5 Billion	Book Value	3.4 Billion
Price/Book	2.59	Price/Sales	1.34

Dividend Achiever Status

Rank	223	10 Year Growth Rate	6.61%
Total Years of Dividend Growth			26

Business Summary: Chemicals (MIC: 11.1 SIC: 2821 NAIC:325211)

Rohm & Haas is a global specialty materials company that operates through six reportable segments: coatings, adhesives and sealants, electronic materials, performance chemicals, salt and monomers. Coatings is Co.'s largest segment in terms of sales, and is comprised of three businesses including architectural functional coatings, powder coatings and automotive coatings. Co. operates over 100 manufacturing and 30 research facilities in 27 countries, and serves several industries, including construction and building, electronics, household products and personal care, packaging, food and retail, and automotive.

Recent Developments: For the three months ended Mar 31 2004, net earnings jumped 39.0% to $114.0 million compared with earnings of $82.0 million, before an accounting change charge of $8.0 million, in the same period of 2003. Earnings benefited from stronger demand in most of Co.'s businesses due to improved global economic conditions and favorable currency exchange rates. Results for 2004 and 2003 included provisions for restructuring and asset impairments of $2.0 million and $5.0 million, respectively. Net sales rose 13.6% to $1.83 billion from $1.61 billion the year before. Gross profit increased 14.5% to $514.0 million compared with $449.0 million a year earlier.

Prospects: For the remainder of the year, Co. expects overall economic conditions to remain positive, which should result in continued growth across all of its businesses. However, higher raw material costs, as well as the uncertainties of currency exchange rates, may temper the full impact of sales growth on Co.'s earnings. Based on current exchange rates, sales per quarter for the remainder of 2004 are expected to be in the range of $1.70 to $1.80 billion. This sales growth, combined with Co.'s focus on tight cost controls and a moderate raw materials environment, should enable it to deliver full-year 2004 earnings per share in the range of $1.95 to $2.10.

Financial Data

(US$ in Thousands)	3 Mos	12/31/2003	12/31/2002	12/31/2001	12/31/2000	12/31/1999	12/31/1998	12/31/1997
Earnings Per Share	1.44	1.30	0.98	(0.31)	1.61	1.27	2.52	2.13
Cash Flow Per Share	0.12	4.49	4.39	3.17	3.49	3.72	3.79	4.11
Tang. Book Val. Per Share	0.53	0.13	N.M	N.M	N.M	N.M	9.06	8.51
Dividends Per Share	0.870	0.860	0.820	0.800	0.780	0.740	0.690	0.630
Dividend Payout %	60.84	66.15	83.67	N.M.	48.44	58.26	27.51	29.73
Income Statement								
Total Revenues	1,832,000	6,421,000	5,727,000	5,666,000	6,879,000	5,339,000	3,720,000	3,999,000
Total Indirect Exp.	312,000	1,400,000	1,385,000	1,567,000	1,490,000	1,337,000	847,000	844,000
Depreciation & Amort.	16,000	67,000	69,000	156,000	159,000	83,000	5,000	6,000
Operating Income	197,000	519,000	432,000	91,000	756,000	628,000	622,000	617,000
Net Interest Inc./(Exp.)	(30,000)	(121,000)	(126,000)	(174,000)	(234,000)	(146,000)	(21,000)	(33,000)
Income Taxes	52,000	127,000	102,000	6,000	227,000	215,000	247,000	201,000
Eqty Earns/Minority Int.	5,000	15,000	15,000	12,000	19,000	7,000	(3,000)	5,000
Income from Cont Ops	...	288,000	218,000	(70,000)	...	...	453,000	...
Net Income	114,000	280,000	(570,000)	395,000	354,000	249,000	440,000	410,000
Average Shs. Outstg.	222,800	222,400	221,900	220,200	220,500	218,981	179,700	192,300
Balance Sheet								
Cash & Cash Equivalents	364,000	196,000	295,000	92,000	92,000	57,000	16,000	40,000
Total Current Assets	2,707,000	2,527,000	2,543,000	2,421,000	2,781,000	2,497,000	1,287,000	1,397,000
Total Assets	9,559,000	9,445,000	9,706,000	10,350,000	11,267,000	11,256,000	3,648,000	3,900,000
Total Current Liabilities	1,818,000	1,797,000	1,621,000	1,624,000	2,194,000	2,510,000	875,000	850,000
Long-Term Obligations	2,475,000	2,468,000	2,872,000	2,720,000	3,225,000	3,122,000	409,000	509,000
Net Stockholders' Equity	3,435,000	3,357,000	3,119,000	3,815,000	3,653,000	3,475,000	1,561,000	1,797,000
Net Working Capital	889,000	730,000	922,000	797,000	587,000	(13,000)	412,000	547,000
Shares Outstanding	222,939	222,453	221,131	220,427	219,937	218,981	154,000	182,700
Operating Profit Margin %	11.02	8.02	7.54	1.60	10.98	11.76	16.72	15.42
Return on Equity %	3.46	8.45	6.98	N.M	9.69	7.16	29.01	22.81
Return on Assets %	1.24	3.00	2.24	N.M.	3.14	2.21	12.41	10.51
Debt/Total Assets %	25.89	26.13	29.58	26.28	28.62	27.73	11.21	13.05
Price Range	43.50-37.35	42.92-26.67	42.27-30.55	38.27-26.12	47.88-26.00	49.13-28.75	38.54-26.75	33.23-23.83
P/E Ratio	30.21-25.94	33.02-20.52	43.13-31.17	N/A	29.74-16.15	38.68-22.64	15.29-10.62	15.60-11.19
Average Yield %	2.17	2.53	2.25	2.35	2.26	1.96	2.09	2.14

Address: 100 Independence Mall West, Philadelphia, PA 19106 **Telephone:** (215) 592-3000 **Web Site:** www.rohmhaas.com	**Officers:** Rajiv L. Gupta – Chmn., C.E.O., J. Michael Fitzpatrick – Pres., C.O.O. **Transfer Agents:** EquiServe Trust Company, N.A., Providence, RI	**Investor Contact:** 215 592-3052 **Institutional Holding** **No of Institutions:** 14 **Shares:** 162,154,220 **% Held:** –

ROPER INDUSTRIES, INC

Exchange	Symbol	Price	52Wk Range	Yield	P/E
NYS	ROP	$52.95 (5/28/2004)	52.95–35.56	0.73	31.15

*7 Year Price Score 131.4 *NYSE Composite Index=100 *12 Month Price Score 51.7

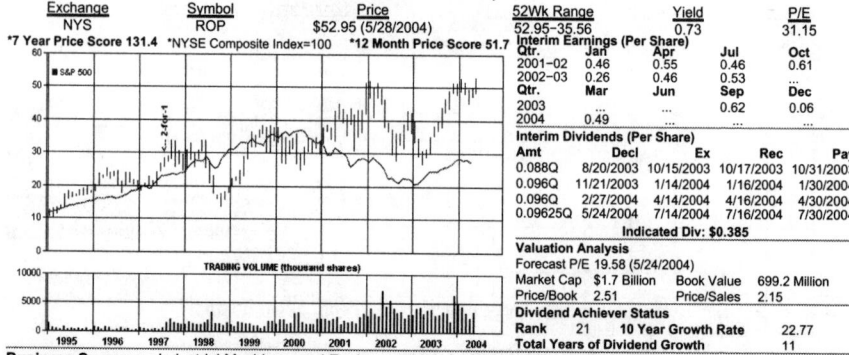

Interim Earnings (Per Share)

Qtr.	Jan	Apr	Jul	Oct
2001–02	0.46	0.55	0.46	0.61
2002–03	0.26	0.46	0.53	...
Qtr.	Mar	Jun	Sep	Dec
2003	...	...	0.62	0.06
2004	0.49	...	...	...

Interim Dividends (Per Share)

Amt	Decl	Ex	Rec	Pay
0.088Q	8/20/2003	10/15/2003	10/17/2003	10/31/2003
0.096Q	11/21/2003	1/14/2004	1/16/2004	1/30/2004
0.096Q	2/27/2004	4/14/2004	4/16/2004	4/30/2004
0.09625Q	5/24/2004	7/14/2004	7/16/2004	7/30/2004

Indicated Div: $0.385

Valuation Analysis

Forecast P/E 19.58 (5/24/2004)

Market Cap	$1.7 Billion	Book Value	699.2 Million
Price/Book	2.51	Price/Sales	2.15

Dividend Achiever Status

Rank	21	10 Year Growth Rate	22.77

Total Years of Dividend Growth 11

TRADING VOLUME (thousand shares)

Business Summary: Industrial Machinery and Equipment (MIC: 11.5 SIC: 3561 NAIC:333911)

Roper Industries is a diversified industrial company. The Instrumentation segment provides equipment and consumables for material analysis, fluid properties testing and industrial leak testing. The industrial technology segment produces industrial pumps, flow measurement and metering equipment, and water meter and automatic meter reading products and systems. The Energy Systems and Controls segment produces control systems, machinery vibration and other non–destructive inspection and measurement products. The Scientific and Industrial Imaging segment produces high–performance digital imaging products and software and handheld computers and software.

Recent Developments: For the first quarter ended Mar 31 2004, net earnings advanced 36.4% to $18.1 million compared with earnings of $13.3 million, before a loss from discontinued operations of $500,000, in the prior–year quarter. Net sales climbed 47.6% to $220.6 million. On a segment basis, Instrumentation sales increased 15.5% to $49.1 million, driven by continued strength in certain petroleum and materials testing markets. Industrial Technology sales surged 131.8% to $93.1 million primarily due to the December 2003 acquisition of Neptune Technology Group Holdings, Inc. Energy Systems & Controls sales grew 15.6% to $32.1 million, while Scientific & Industrial Imaging sales jumped 18.8% to $46.3 million.

Prospects: All business segments are experiencing solid organic growth as Co. continues to benefit from the growth initiatives that it began launching in 2003. Co.'s restructuring actions are now complete and with its high operating leverage, it expects sequentially higher sales in the second quarter of 2004 will further improve both margins and earnings. As a result, Co. expects earnings for the second quarter to range from $0.57 to $0.63 per diluted share. Full–year 2004 earnings are expected in the range of $2.50 to $2.70 per diluted share. Meanwhile, Co.'s focus on working capital velocity and margins should increase operating cash flows by up to two–thirds over 2003.

Financial Data

(US$ in Thousands)	3 Mos	12/31/2003	12/31/2002	10/31/2002	10/31/2001	10/31/2000	10/31/1999	10/31/1998
Earnings Per Share	1.70	1.50	0.04	2.08	1.77	1.58	1.53	1.24
Cash Flow Per Share	0.68	2.22	0.23	2.73	3.25	2.16	1.70	2.40
Tang. Book Val. Per Share	N.M	N.M	N.M	N.M	N.M	N.M	0.55	N.M
Dividends Per Share	0.350	0.350	0.330	0.320	0.290	0.210	0.260	0.240
Dividend Payout %	23.15	23.33	825.00	15.50	16.66	13.29	16.99	24.19
Income Statement								
Total Revenues	220,640	657,356	83,885	627,030	586,506	503,813	407,256	389,170
Total Indirect Exp.	76,466	238,038	36,997	221,490	210,542	170,628	132,548	124,861
Depreciation & Amort.	9,704	16,378	2,620	15,176	27,455	22,298	15,966	14,434
Operating Income	32,972	108,100	4,568	114,829	98,428	88,196	77,955	66,092
Net Interest Inc./(Exp.)	(6,903)	(16,384)	(2,978)	(18,506)	(15,917)	(13,483)	(7,254)	(7,856)
Income Taxes	7,958	18,229	529	29,663	30,600	26,653	24,938	20,300
Income from Cont Ops	...	48,061	1,240	66,023	...	...	...	...
Net Income	18,134	45,239	853	40,053	55,839	49,278	47,346	39,316
Average Shs. Outstg.	37,286	31,992	31,854	31,815	31,493	31,182	30,992	31,717
Balance Sheet								
Cash & Cash Equivalents	82,357	70,234	15,270	12,362	16,190	11,372	13,490	9,350
Total Current Assets	398,841	381,192	247,565	247,622	233,053	213,955	161,819	139,852
Total Assets	1,522,945	1,514,995	824,966	828,973	762,122	596,902	420,163	381,533
Total Current Liabilities	149,779	161,497	121,079	130,237	103,880	84,492	72,243	57,578
Long–Term Obligations	604,160	630,186	308,684	311,590	323,830	234,603	109,659	120,307
Net Stockholders' Equity	699,248	655,781	380,981	376,012	323,506	270,191	231,968	197,033
Shares Outstanding	36,805	36,042	31,370	31,363	30,879	30,599	30,282	30,343
Operating Profit Margin %	14.94	16.44	5.44	18.31	16.78	17.50	19.14	16.98
Return on Equity %	2.59	7.32	0.32	17.55	17.26	18.23	20.41	19.95
Return on Assets %	1.19	3.17	0.15	7.96	7.32	8.25	11.26	10.30
Debt/Total Assets %	39.67	41.59	37.41	37.58	42.49	39.30	26.09	31.53
Price Range	52.75–45.30	51.58–26.84	43.00–36.40	52.00–28.00	45.00–30.00	38.50–25.12	38.38–15.94	33.81–13.75
P/E Ratio	31.03–26.65	34.39–17.89		N.M.	25.00–13.46	25.42–16.95	24.37–15.90	25.08–10.42	27.27–11.09
Average Yield %	0.71	0.89	0.84	0.77	0.77	0.65	0.93	1.01

Address: 2160 Satellite Boulevard, Duluth, GA 30097
Telephone: (770) 495–5100
Web Site: www.roperind.com

Officers: Brian D. Jellison – Chmn., Pres., C.E.O., Martin S. Headley – V.P., C.F.O.
Transfer Agents: Wachovia Bank, N.A., Charlotte, NC

Institutional Holding
No of Institutions: 167
Shares: 28,922,445 **% Held:** 57.60%

ROUSE CO.

Exchange	Symbol	Price	52Wk Range	Yield	P/E
NYS	RSE	$45.65 (5/28/2004)	53.82-37.12	4.12	30.23

*7 Year Price Score 148.7   *NYSE Composite Index=100   *12 Month Price Score 45.7

Interim Earnings (Per Share)

Qtr.	Mar	Jun	Sep	Dec
2001	0.41	0.34	0.37	0.30
2002	0.18	0.76	0.33	(0.12)
2003	0.19	0.41	0.37	0.43
2004	0.30	...	...	...

Interim Dividends (Per Share)

Amt	Decl	Ex	Rec	Pay
0.42Q	5/8/2003	6/12/2003	6/16/2003	6/30/2003
0.42Q	12/4/2003	12/10/2003	12/12/2003	12/23/2003
0.47Q	1/15/2004	3/15/2004	3/17/2004	3/31/2004
0.47Q	5/6/2004	6/14/2004	6/16/2004	6/30/2004

Indicated Div: $1.88 (Div. Reinv. Plan)

Valuation Analysis

Forecast P/E 11.61 (5/24/2004)

Market Cap $4.0 Billion		Book Value 1.6 Billion	
Price/Book 3.42		Price/Sales 4.77	

Dividend Achiever Status

Rank 145	10 Year Growth Rate	10.48%
Total Years of Dividend Growth		11

Business Summary: Property, Real Estate &Development (MIC: 8.3 SIC: 6512 NAIC:531210)

Rouse operates more than 150 properties encompassing retail, office, research and development, and industrial space in 22 states. Co. owns and/or operates 32 regional retail centers and four community centers, with more than 37.7 million square feet. Co. also owns and/or operates six mixed-use projects with 2.2 million square feet of office/industrial space, and 104 office and industrial buildings with 6.8 million square feet located in and around Las Vegas, NV, Columbia, MD and the Baltimore-Washington corridor. Co., through its affiliates, is the developer of the cities of Columbia, MD and Summerlin, NV.

Recent Developments: For the three months ended Mar 31 2004, net earnings more than doubled to $67.1 million versus $24.1 million in the equivalent quarter of 2003. Results for 2004 and 2003 included net gains on the dispositions of interests in operating properties of $36.2 million and $273,000, pension plan settlement losses of $782,000 and $4.5 million, and provision for organizational changes and early retirement costs of $1.0 million and $1.8 million, respectively. Results for 2004 and 2003 also included other one-time charges of $3.3 million and $10.2 million, respectively. Total revenues rose 18.0% to $397.1 million from $336.7 million the year before. Funds from operations grew 16.6% to $89.3 million.

Prospects: Looking ahead, Co. is off to a good start as it continues to improve the quality of its retail portfolio with the completion of the acquisition of Providence Place and the disposition of Westdale Mall in Cedar Rapids, IA. In addition, Co.'s portfolio continues to be well occupied with an average occupancy of 93.0% during the first quarter of 2004. Meanwhile, Co. expects that performance will continue to be very strong for its community development side of the business, as its Columbia, Summerlin, Fairwood and The Woodlands properties are having a solid year. As a result, Co. expects diluted earnings per share in the range of $2.84 to $2.94 for full-year 2004.

Financial Data

(US$ in Thousands)	3 Mos	12/31/2003	12/31/2002	12/31/2001	12/31/2000	12/31/1999	12/31/1998	12/31/1997
Earnings Per Share	1.51	1.40	1.15	1.42	2.21	1.77	1.34	2.59
Cash Flow Per Share	0.76	4.25	4.42	4.17	3.64	2.78	3.84	2.44
Tang. Book Val. Per Share	15.50	14.43	12.79	9.44	9.28	9.03	8.70	6.95
Dividends Per Share	1.260	1.680	1.560	1.420	1.320	1.200	1.120	1.000
Dividend Payout %	40.00	120.00	135.65	100.00	59.72	67.79	83.58	38.61
Income Statement								
Total Revenues	321,336	1,104,866	1,104,734	966,337	633,738	715,657	692,571	916,771
Total Indirect Exp.	55,677	173,280	161,333	125,504	90,307	100,329	84,068	82,944
Depreciation & Amort.	47,910	173,280	161,333	125,504	90,307	100,329	84,068	82,944
Operating Income	102,884	377,810	385,884	337,089	242,708	276,941	250,121	297,985
Net Interest Inc./(Exp.)	(57,701)	(222,766)	(245,321)	(228,765)	(236,744)	(244,515)	(209,564)	(207,490)
Income Taxes	18,616	42,500	(36,543)	(36,727)	(258,858)	284	(24)	(116,066)
Income from Cont Ops	30,676	139,523	112,829	111,813	168,285	141,176	105,176	189,892
Net Income	67,114	260,589	139,851	110,706	170,485	135,297	104,902	167,336
Average Shs. Outstg.	102,116	88,453	84,954	69,694	69,475	71,705	67,874	76,005
Balance Sheet								
Cash & Cash Equivalents	62,732	139,543	73,736	54,280	37,588	49,211	41,950	90,686
Total Current Assets	128,321	193,237	130,663	142,033	82,155	110,435	117,867	204,986
Total Assets	7,007,557	6,639,244	6,386,168	4,880,443	4,175,538	4,427,216	5,154,643	3,589,768
Total Current Liabilities	156,655	179,530	...	...	...	...	...	...
Long-Term Obligations	4,628,983	4,444,492	4,441,477	3,488,820	3,045,769	3,334,419	4,068,459	2,684,140
Net Stockholders' Equity	1,595,332	1,324,964	1,112,084	655,360	630,468	638,580	628,926	465,515
Net Working Capital	(28,334)	13,707	130,663	142,033	82,155	110,435	117,867	204,986
Shares Outstanding	102,878	91,759	86,909	69,354	67,880	70,693	72,225	66,911
Operating Profit Margin %	32.01	34.19	34.93	34.88	38.29	38.69	36.11	32.50
Return on Equity %	1.92	9.93	9.03	14.11	21.92	18.20	13.73	31.49
Return on Assets %	0.43	2.10	1.76	2.29	4.03	3.18	2.04	5.28
Debt/Total Assets %	66.05	66.94	69.54	71.48	72.94	75.31	78.92	74.77
Price Range	53.20-45.81	47.22-30.58	33.35-27.45	30.00-23.86	27.00-19.81	26.03-19.56	31.99-21.73	29.46-22.66
P/E Ratio	35.25-30.34	33.73-21.84	29.00-23.87	21.13-16.80	12.22-8.96	14.71-11.05	23.87-16.22	11.37-8.75
Average Yield %	2.55	4.37	5.07	5.23	5.51	5.31	4.13	3.84

Address: 10275 Little Patuxent Parkway, Columbia, MD 21044-3456	**Officers:** Anthony W. Deering - Chmn., Pres., C.E.O., Thomas J. DeRosa - Vice-Chmn., C.F.O.	**Investor Contact:**410-992-6546
Telephone: (410) 992-6000	**Transfer Agents:** The Bank of New York, New York, NY	**Institutional Holding**
Web Site: www.therousecompany.com		**No of Institutions:** 21
		Shares: 3,496,001 **% Held:** –

229

RPM INTERNATIONAL INC (DE)

Exchange	Symbol	Price	52Wk Range	Yield	P/E
NYS	RPM	$14.71 (5/28/2004)	17.22-12.55	3.81	38.71

*7 Year Price Score 112.2   *NYSE Composite Index=100   *12 Month Price Score 45.6

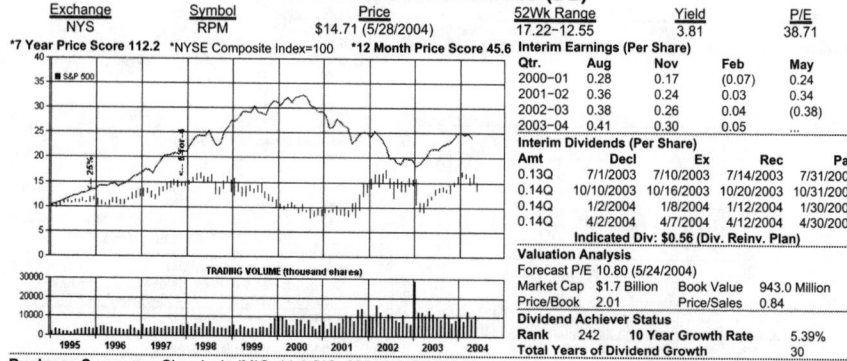

Interim Earnings (Per Share)

Qtr.	Aug	Nov	Feb	May
2000-01	0.28	0.17	(0.07)	0.24
2001-02	0.36	0.24	0.03	0.34
2002-03	0.38	0.26	0.04	(0.38)
2003-04	0.41	0.30	0.05	...

Interim Dividends (Per Share)

Amt	Decl	Ex	Rec	Pay
0.13Q	7/1/2003	7/10/2003	7/14/2003	7/31/2003
0.14Q	10/10/2003	10/16/2003	10/20/2003	10/31/2003
0.14Q	1/2/2004	1/8/2004	1/12/2004	1/30/2004
0.14Q	4/2/2004	4/7/2004	4/12/2004	4/30/2004

Indicated Div: $0.56 (Div. Reinv. Plan)

Valuation Analysis

Forecast P/E 10.80 (5/24/2004)

Market Cap	$1.7 Billion	Book Value	943.0 Million
Price/Book	2.01	Price/Sales	0.84

Dividend Achiever Status

Rank	242	10 Year Growth Rate	5.39%
Total Years of Dividend Growth		30

Business Summary: Chemicals (MIC: 11.1 SIC: 2851 NAIC:325510)

RPM International manufactures and markets high quality specialty paints, protective coatings and roofing systems, sealants and adhesives, focusing on the maintenance and improvement needs of both the industrial and consumer markets. Co.'s family of products includes those marketed under brand CARBOLINE, DAP, DAY-GLO, FLECTO, RUST-OLEUM, STONHARD, TREMCO and ZINSSER. As of May 31, 2003, Co. marketed its products in approximately 130 countries and territories and operated manufacturing facilities in 67 locations in the US, Argentina, Belgium, Brazil, Canada, China, Colombia, Germany, Italy, Mexico, New Zealand, The Netherlands, Poland, South Africa, the United Arab Emirates and the UK.

Recent Developments: For the quarter ended Feb 29 2004, net income climbed 23.2% to $6.0 million compared with $4.9 million in the equivalent 2003 quarter. Net sales grew 10.9% to $480.8 million from $433.6 million a year earlier. The improvement in sales was primarily attributed to organic growth, acquisition activity, and favorable foreign exchange rates. Industrial segment net sales rose 12.6% to $264.8 million from $235.2 million in the prior-year quarter. Consumer segment net sales were $216.0 million, up 8.9% from $198.4 million the year before. Gross profit advanced 13.6% to $210.6 million versus $185.4 million the year before.

Prospects: Looking ahead, Co. continues to expect high single-digit revenue growth, with earnings estimated to increase in the range of 10.0% to 12.0% for full-year 2004. Separately, on Mar 30 2003, Co. announced that it has acquired two businesses in Europe. Ecoloc is a commercial and industrial tile flooring manufacturer and marketer. Compakta/Pactan is a manufacturer and marketer of specialty silicone-based adhesives, joint filler and sealers. These transactions represent Co.'s expanded emphasis on completing acquisitions in Europe, an important part of its growth strategy. Moreover, the acquisitions are expected to be accretive to earnings immediately.

Financial Data

(US$ in Thousands)	9 Mos	6 Mos	3 Mos	05/31/2003	05/31/2002	05/31/2001	05/31/2000	05/31/1999
Earnings Per Share	0.38	0.38	0.38	0.30	0.97	0.62	0.38	0.86
Cash Flow Per Share	0.93	0.56	0.22	1.38	1.82	0.72	0.95	1.05
Tang. Book Val. Per Share	0.12	0.16	N.M	N.M	0.01	N.M	N.M	0.77
Dividends Per Share	0.540	0.530	0.520	0.510	0.500	0.490	0.480	0.460
Dividend Payout %	142.10	139.47	136.84	171.66	51.54	80.24	127.63	54.01
Income Statement								
Total Revenues	1,660,694	1,179,925	590,091	2,083,489	1,986,126	2,007,762	1,954,131	1,712,154
Total Indirect Exp.	593,962	400,466	195,918	879,987	717,628	713,285	678,970	592,666
Depreciation & Amort.	46,784	30,925	15,127	58,674	56,859	81,494	79,150	62,135
Operating Income	158,611	141,513	80,193	74,565	194,588	166,690	175,524	192,378
Net Interest Inc./(Exp.)	(20,761)	(12,994)	(6,283)	(26,712)	(40,464)	(65,203)	(51,793)	(32,781)
Income Taxes	48,937	45,624	26,238	12,526	52,570	38,526	30,769	65,051
Net Income	88,913	82,895	47,672	35,327	101,554	62,961	40,992	94,546
Average Shs. Outstg.	116,593	116,335	116,233	115,986	105,131	102,212	107,384	111,376
Balance Sheet								
Cash & Cash Equivalents	50,868	48,498	47,512	50,725	42,172	23,926	31,340	19,729
Total Current Assets	889,266	930,473	918,742	928,094	801,314	819,420	785,092	705,419
Total Assets	2,223,732	2,261,234	2,234,278	2,247,211	2,036,403	2,078,490	2,099,203	1,737,236
Total Current Liabilities	370,674	391,600	389,029	427,650	364,714	375,768	376,202	302,549
Long-Term Obligations	709,753	721,620	728,367	714,596	707,921	955,399	959,330	582,109
Net Stockholders' Equity	943,049	945,340	901,604	877,008	858,106	639,710	645,724	742,876
Net Working Capital	518,592	538,873	529,713	500,444	436,600	443,652	408,890	402,870
Shares Outstanding	115,952	115,702	115,624	115,496	114,696	102,211	103,134	109,443
Statistical Record								
Operating Profit Margin %	9.55	11.99	13.58	3.57	9.79	8.30	8.98	11.23
Return on Equity %	9.43	8.76	5.28	4.02	11.83	9.84	6.34	12.72
Return on Assets %	4.00	3.66	2.13	1.57	4.98	3.02	1.95	5.44
Debt/Total Assets %	31.92	31.91	32.59	32.25	34.76	45.96	45.69	33.50
Price Range	17.22-12.55	15.15-12.55	14.15-12.55	16.00-9.15	17.68-8.00	10.62-7.88	14.68-9.56	16.51-12.31
P/E Ratio	45.32-33.03	39.87-33.03	37.24-33.03	53.33-30.50	18.23-8.25	17.13-12.71	38.63-25.16	19.20-14.31
Average Yield %	3.70	3.85	3.86	3.83	3.85	5.29	4.14	3.23

Address: P.O. Box 777, Medina, OH 44258	**Officers:** Thomas C. Sullivan – Chmn., Frank C. Sullivan – Pres., C.E.O.	**Investor Contact:** 330-273-8820
Telephone: (330) 273-5090		**Institutional Holding**
Web Site: www.rpminc.com		**No of Institutions:** 257
		Shares: 73,050,845 **% Held:** 63.60%

S & T BANCORP, INC. (INDIANA, PA.)

Exchange	Symbol	Price	52Wk Range	Yield	P/E
NMS	STBA	$29.90 (5/28/2004)	31.42-27.44	3.48	15.33

*7 Year Price Score 120.1 *NYSE Composite Index=100 *12 Month Price Score 47.0

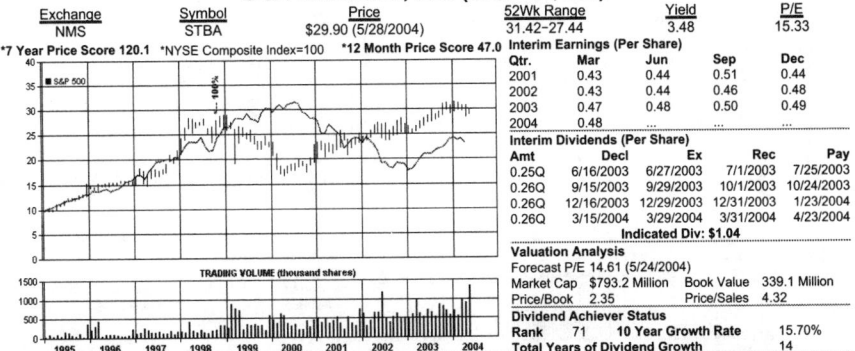

Interim Earnings (Per Share)

Qtr.	Mar	Jun	Sep	Dec
2001	0.43	0.44	0.51	0.44
2002	0.43	0.44	0.46	0.48
2003	0.47	0.48	0.50	0.49
2004	0.48	...	...	...

Interim Dividends (Per Share)

Amt	Decl	Ex	Rec	Pay
0.25Q	6/16/2003	6/27/2003	7/1/2003	7/25/2003
0.26Q	9/15/2003	9/29/2003	10/1/2003	10/24/2003
0.26Q	12/16/2003	12/29/2003	12/31/2003	1/23/2004
0.26Q	3/15/2004	3/29/2004	3/31/2004	4/23/2004

Indicated Div: $1.04

Valuation Analysis

Forecast P/E 14.61 (5/24/2004)
Market Cap $793.2 Million Book Value 339.1 Million
Price/Book 2.35 Price/Sales 4.32

Dividend Achiever Status

Rank	71	10 Year Growth Rate	15.70%
Total Years of Dividend Growth			14

Business Summary: Commercial Banking (MIC: 8.1 SIC: 6022 NAIC:522110)

S&T Bancorp is a bank holding company with assets of $2.90 billion as of Dec 31 2003. Co. has two wholly-owned subsidiaries, S&T Bank and S&T Investment, and owns one-half interest in Commonwealth Trust Credit Life Insurance. S&T Bank offers a variety of services including time and demand deposit accounts, secured and unsecured commercial and consumer loans, letters of credit, discount brokerage services, personal finance planning and credit card services. S&T Investment is an investment holding company, which manages investments previously owned by the bank. Co. operates through a branch network of 49 offices in 10 Pennsylvania counties.

Recent Developments: For the quarter ended Mar 31 2004, net income climbed 3.3% to $13.0 million versus $12.5 million in the same period of 2003. Results benefited from strong growth in Co.'s commercial lending and cash management activities and steady growth in its wealth management, insurance and retail businesses. Results for 2004 and 2003 included security gains of $1.5 million and $1.0 million, respectively. Net interest income slipped 1.2% to $26.1 million. Provision for loan losses dropped 37.5% to $1.5 million from $2.4 million the year before. Total non-interest income grew 8.8% to $8.4 million, while total non-interest expense rose 3.9% to $14.7 million.

Prospects: Co. sees many uncertainties regarding the economy in 2004, and is striving to be well-positioned for changes in both the economy and interest rates, regardless of the timing or direction of these changes. Accordingly, Co.'s balance sheet, capital, liquidity and operations infrastructure are continually assessed in order to be positioned to take advantage of internal or acquisition growth opportunities. Since the majority of revenue comes from the net interest margin, internally generated loan and deposit growth, the mix of that growth is a major factor. Co. will continue to direct its focus and resources in planning for 2004 to improve the generation and retention of low-cost core deposits.

Financial Data

(US$ in Thousands)	3 Mos	12/31/2003	12/31/2002	12/31/2001	12/31/2000	12/31/1999	12/31/1998	12/31/1997
Earnings Per Share	1.95	1.94	1.81	1.82	1.66	1.51	1.35	1.17
Tang. Book Val. Per Share	10.73	10.47	9.47	11.00	10.28	8.87	9.38	9.19
Dividends Per Share	1.020	1.010	0.960	0.900	0.820	0.740	0.630	0.530
Dividend Payout %	52.31	52.06	53.03	49.45	49.39	49.00	46.66	45.29
Income Statement								
Total Interest Income	35,596	151,460	151,160	166,702	176,184	156,727	151,438	141,101
Total Interest Expense	9,506	47,066	56,300	76,713	86,141	69,942	69,156	62,284
Net Interest Income	26,090	104,394	94,860	89,989	90,043	86,785	82,282	78,817
Provision for Loan Losses	1,500	7,300	7,800	5,000	4,000	4,000	10,550	5,000
Non-Interest Income	8,393	34,215	32,680	31,230	22,154	20,100	24,418	16,441
Non-Interest Expense	14,737	60,658	51,766	46,972	45,658	43,490	41,988	43,198
Income Before Taxes	18,246	72,640	67,974	69,247	62,539	59,395	54,162	47,060
Income from Cont Ops	...	...	...	49,185	...	...	...	...
Net Income	12,956	51,777	48,604	47,298	44,973	41,418	37,963	33,414
Average Shs. Outstg.	26,951	26,723	26,784	27,051	27,073	27,366	28,055	28,618
Balance Sheet								
Cash & Due from Banks	44,489	52,361	50,258	52,783	43,665	38,663	48,736	35,951
Securities Avail. for Sale	592,496	1,221,901	1,281,947	1,163,715	1,148,312	1,133,218	1,156,627	1,089,337
Net Loans & Leases	2,151,274	2,069,142	1,968,755	1,615,842	1,577,629	1,469,143	1,339,232	1,253,326
Total Assets	2,956,404	2,900,272	2,823,867	2,357,874	2,310,290	2,194,073	2,069,611	1,920,291
Total Deposits	1,977,330	1,962,253	1,926,119	1,611,317	1,525,332	1,435,065	1,380,063	1,284,658
Long-Term Obligations	116,933	116,933	211,656	251,226	377,997	364,062	240,068	144,218
Total Liabilities	2,617,309	2,567,554	2,517,753	2,064,547	2,033,193	1,954,373	1,809,914	1,660,173
Net Stockholders' Equity	339,095	332,718	306,114	293,327	277,097	239,700	259,637	260,118
Shares Outstanding	26,619	26,652	26,584	26,646	26,947	26,998	27,676	28,282
Return on Equity %	3.82	15.56	15.87	16.76	16.23	17.27	14.62	12.84
Return on Assets %	0.43	1.78	1.72	2.08	1.94	1.88	1.83	1.74
Equity/Assets %	11.46	11.47	10.84	12.44	11.99	10.92	12.54	13.54
Non-Int. Exp./Tot. Inc. %	33.50	32.32	28.15	23.73	23.02	24.59	23.87	27.41
Price Range	31.42-29.51	31.25-25.20	28.30-23.30	25.70-20.31	23.44-16.75	29.00-19.13	29.00-21.19	21.94-14.75
P/E Ratio	16.11-15.13	16.11-12.99	15.64-12.87	14.12-11.16	14.12-10.09	19.21-12.67	21.48-15.69	18.75-12.61
Average Yield %	3.38	3.60	3.76	3.90	4.32	3.01	2.39	2.94

Address: 43 South Ninth Street, Indiana, PA 15701	Officers: Robert D. Duggan – Chmn., James C. Miller – Pres., C.E.O.	Investor Contact:724-465-1466
Telephone: (724) 465-1466	Transfer Agents:American Stock Transfer &Trust Company, New York, NY	Institutional Holding
Web Site: www.stbank.com		No of Institutions: 30
		Shares: 301,628 % Held: –

SARA LEE CORP.

Exchange	Symbol	Price	52Wk Range	Yield	P/E
NYS	SLE	$22.90 (5/28/2004)	23.44-18.36	3.28	15.07

*7 Year Price Score 91.1   *NYSE Composite Index=100   ***12 Month Price Score 52.8**

Interim Earnings (Per Share)

Qtr.	Sep	Dec	Mar	Jun
2000-01	0.27	0.96	0.28	0.36
2001-02	0.30	0.20	31.00	(30.27)
2002-03	0.38	0.42	0.33	0.37
2003-04	0.29	0.39	0.47	...

Interim Dividends (Per Share)

Amt	Decl	Ex	Rec	Pay
0.155Q	1/30/2003	2/27/2003	3/3/2003	4/1/2003
0.155Q	5/8/2003	5/29/2003	6/2/2003	7/1/2003
0.188Q	10/30/2003	11/26/2003	12/1/2003	1/2/2004
0.188Q	4/29/2004	5/27/2004	6/1/2004	7/1/2004

Indicated Div: $0.75 (Div. Reinv. Plan)

Valuation Analysis
Forecast P/E 13.73 (5/24/2004)

Market Cap $17.9 Billion	Book Value	N/A
Price/Book N/A	Price/Sales	N/A

Dividend Achiever Status
Rank   188   10 Year Growth Rate   8.45%
Total Years of Dividend Growth   27

Business Summary: Food (MIC: 4.1 SIC: 2013 NAIC:311613)

Sara Lee is a global manufacturer and marketer of brand-name products for consumers throughout the world. Co. has five reportable segmentsSara Lee Meats, Sara Lee Bakery, Beverage, Household Products, and Intimates and Underwear. Co.'s products and services include fresh and frozen baked goods, processed meats, coffee and tea, beverage systems, intimate apparel, underwear, sportswear, legwear and other apparel, and personal, household and shoe care products. Prominent brands include *Ball Park, Hillshire Farm, Jimmy Dean, Sara Lee, Bryan, Kahn's, Hanes, Hanes Her Way, Playtex, L'eggs, Just My Size, Wonderbra, Lovable, Sanex, Duschdas, Badedas, Radox and Monsavon, Kiwi, Vapona* and *Ridsect*.

Recent Developments: For the 13 weeks ended Mar 27 2004, net income advanced 39.8% to $376.0 million from $269.0 million in the corresponding prior-year period. Results included a pre-tax charge of $6.0 million and a pre-tax gain of $1.0 million in 2004 and 2003, respectively, primarily related to restructuring and business dispositions. Results for 2004 also included a $119.0 million gain stemming from the sale of a business in fiscal 1999. Net sales grew 9.1% to $4.75 billion from $4.35 billion the year before. Cost of sales totaled $2.89 billion, or 60.9% of net sales, up 10.9% versus $2.60 billion, or 59.9% of net sales, a year earlier. Operating income climbed 32.4% to $499.0 million.

Prospects: Results are being positively affected by select price increases that are helping to offset higher raw material costs, improved economic conditions, and favorable foreign currency exchange rates. In addition, increased sales and improved profitability are being driven by new product launches and Co.'s aggressive efforts to control costs. Looking ahead, Co. is targeting earnings of between $0.41 and $0.45 per share for the fourth quarter of fiscal 2004. Near-term results are expected to be negatively affected by continuing challenging market conditions, including higher raw material costs, and competitive pricing in printables.

Financial Data
(US$ in Thousands)

	9 Mos	6 Mos	3 Mos	06/28/2003	06/29/2002	06/30/2001	07/01/2000	07/03/1999
Earnings Per Share	1.52	152	152	1.50	1.23	1.87	1.27	1.26
Cash Flow Per Share	1.72	1.26	0.39	2.24	2.12	1.75	1.68	1.69
Dividends Per Share	0.680	0.650	0.610	0.610	0.590	0.560	0.520	0.490
Dividend Payout %	44.73	42.76	40.13	40.66	47.96	29.94	40.94	38.88
Income Statement								
Total Revenues	14,428,000	9,683,000	4,666,000	18,291,000	17,628,000	17,747,000	17,511,000	20,012,000
Total Indirect Exp.	4,459,000	2,988,000	1,465,000	5,568,000	5,356,000	5,865,000	5,668,000	6,053,000
Depreciation & Amort.	514,000	343,000	170,000	674,000	582,000	599,000	602,000	553,000
Operating Income	1,143,000	757,000	333,000	1,671,000	1,570,000	1,592,000	1,743,000	1,751,000
Net Interest Inc./(Exp.)	(134,000)	(92,000)	(49,000)	(198,000)	(208,000)	(180,000)	(176,000)	(141,000)
Income Taxes	199,000	118,000	50,000	263,000	175,000	248,000	409,000	480,000
Income from Cont Ops	...	...	...	...	...	1,603,000	1,158,000	...
Net Income	918,000	542,000	230,000	1,221,000	1,010,000	2,266,000	1,222,000	1,191,000
Average Shs. Outstg.	798,000	802,000	804,000	812,000	818,000	854,000	912,000	944,000
Balance Sheet								
Cash & Cash Equivalents	703,000	591,000	121,000	942,000	298,000	548,000	314,000	279,000
Total Current Assets	5,987,000	5,781,000	5,231,000	5,953,000	4,986,000	5,083,000	5,974,000	4,987,000
Total Assets	14,978,000	14,908,000	14,224,000	15,084,000	13,753,000	10,167,000	11,611,000	10,521,000
Total Current Liabilities	5,688,000	5,528,000	5,306,000	5,199,000	5,463,000	4,958,000	6,759,000	5,953,000
Long-Term Obligations	4,284,000	4,608,000	4,544,000	5,157,000	4,326,000	2,640,000	2,248,000	1,892,000
Net Stockholders' Equity	2,486,000	2,321,000	1,958,000	1,870,000	1,534,000	899,000	1,007,000	1,034,000
Net Working Capital	299,000	253,000	(75,000)	754,000	(477,000)	125,000	(785,000)	(966,000)
Shares Outstanding	790,335	791,179	790,306	777,347	784,720	781,964	846,331	883,783
Statistical Record								
Operating Profit Margin %	7.92	7.81	7.13	9.13	8.90	8.97	9.95	8.74
Return on Equity %	36.93	23.35	11.74	65.29	65.84	178.30	114.99	115.18
Return on Assets %	6.13	3.63	1.61	8.09	7.34	15.76	9.97	11.32
Debt/Total Assets %	28.60	30.90	31.94	34.18	31.45	25.96	19.36	17.98
Price Range	22.62-18.36	21.24-18.36	19.90-18.42	23.75-16.50	23.04-19.04	25.19-18.44	27.06-13.63	30.69-21.50
P/E Ratio	14.88-12.08	13.97-12.08	13.09-12.12	15.83-11.00	18.73-15.48	13.47-9.86	21.31-10.73	24.36-17.06
Average Yield %	3.36	3.33	3.19	3.05	2.79	2.70	2.54	1.86

Address: Three First National Plaza, Chicago, IL 60602-4260
Telephone: (312) 726-2600
Web Site: www.saralee.com

Officers: C. Steven McMillan - Chmn., Pres., C.E.O., Lee A. Chaden - Exec. V.P., Global Marketing & Sales
Transfer Agents: Sara Lee Corporation, Chicago, IL

Investor Contact: 312-558-8651
Institutional Holding
No of Institutions: 7
Shares: 734,213   **% Held:** -

SBC COMMUNICATIONS, INC.

Exchange	Symbol	Price	52Wk Range	Yield	P/E
NYS	SBC	$23.70 (5/28/2004)	27.59–21.40	5.27	14.36

*7 Year Price Score 63.3   *NYSE Composite Index=100   *12 Month Price Score 47.2

Interim Earnings (Per Share)

Qtr.	Mar	Jun	Sep	Dec
2001	0.55	0.61	0.61	0.37
2002	0.51	0.55	0.53	0.64
2003	0.74	0.42	0.37	0.27
2004	0.59	...	...	...

Interim Dividends (Per Share)

Amt	Decl	Ex	Rec	Pay
0.2825Q	6/27/2003	7/8/2003	7/10/2003	8/1/2003
0.283Q	9/26/2003	10/8/2003	10/10/2003	11/3/2003
0.313Q	12/12/2003	1/7/2004	1/10/2004	2/2/2004
0.313Q	3/26/2004	4/6/2004	4/10/2004	5/3/2004

Indicated Div: $1.25 (Div. Reinv. Plan)

Valuation Analysis

Forecast P/E 16.21 (5/24/2004)

Market Cap $78.7 Billion	Book Value 39.4 Billion
Price/Book 2.04	Price/Sales 1.98

Dividend Achiever Status

Rank 231	10 Year Growth Rate	6.21%
Total Years of Dividend Growth	19	

Business Summary: Communications (MIC: 10.1 SIC: 4813 NAIC:551112)

SBC Communications is a global provider of telecommunications services. Co.'s products and services include local exchange services, wireless communications, long–distance services, internet services, telecommunications equipment, and directory advertising and publishing. Co.'s principal wireline subsidiaries provide telecommunications services in thirteen states: Arkansas, California, Connecticut, Illinois, Indiana, Kansas, Michigan, Missouri, Nevada, Ohio, Oklahoma, Texas, and Wisconsin. As of Dec 31 2003, Co. had 54.7 million network access lines in service and maintained a 60.0% equity interest in Cingular Wireless, which serves more than 24.0 million wireless customers.

Recent Developments: For the quarter ended Mar 31 2004, net income was $1.95 billion compared with income of $2.46 billion in the corresponding year–earlier period. Results for 2003 excluded an accounting change gain of $2.54 billion. Total operating revenues declined 2.4% to $10.13 billion, primarily due to a 9.2% decrease in voice revenue to $5.21 billion. Co.'s consumer retail access line base declined by 305,000 versus declines of 748,000 a year earlier and 424,000 in the quarter ended Dec 31 2003. Meanwhile, Co. added 446,000 digital subscriber lines (DSL) and ended the quarter with nearly 4.0 million DSL lines in service. Operating income fell 17.3% to $1.57 billion versus $1.90 billion the year before.

Prospects: Co.'s outlook appears to be moving in a positive direction, reflecting recent strong digital subscriber line gains, continued long distance growth, increased bundle penetration, and a sharp focus on costs. Meanwhile, Cingular Wireless LLC's proposed acquisition of AT&T Wireless continues to move forward. In addition to approval from AT&T Wireless stockholders, the transaction is subject to review by the U.S. Department of Justice and the Federal Communications Commission. Co. noted that filings with both bodies were made in mid–March 2004. Cingular, which is a joint venture between Co. and BellSouth Corp., expects the transaction to close before year end 2004.

Financial Data

(US$ in Thousands)	3 Mos	12/31/2003	12/31/2002	12/31/2001	12/31/2000	12/31/1999	12/31/1998	12/31/1997
Earnings Per Share	1.65	1.80	2.23	2.14	2.32	1.90	2.05	0.80
Cash Flow Per Share	0.61	4.06	4.54	4.35	4.16	4.79	4.22	3.77
Tang. Book Val. Per Share	11.41	11.08	9.51	8.62	7.37	5.86	4.94	3.60
Dividends Per Share	1.410	1.360	1.060	1.020	1.000	0.960	0.920	0.880
Dividend Payout %	85.45	75.97	47.81	47.78	43.31	50.78	45.12	110.78
Income Statement								
Total Revenues	10,128,000	40,843,000	43,138,000	45,908,000	51,476,000	49,489,000	28,777,000	24,856,000
Total Indirect Exp.	8,558,000	17,721,000	8,578,000	9,077,000	9,748,000	8,553,000	5,177,000	12,198,000
Depreciation & Amort.	1,923,000	7,870,000	8,578,000	9,077,000	9,748,000	8,553,000	5,177,000	4,922,000
Operating Income	1,570,000	6,469,000	8,623,000	10,888,000	10,743,000	11,598,000	6,886,000	3,170,000
Income Taxes	960,000	2,930,000	2,984,000	4,097,000	4,921,000	4,280,000	2,306,000	863,000
Income from Cont Ops	...	5,971,000	7,473,000	7,260,000	...	6,573,000	4,068,000	...
Net Income	1,948,000	8,505,000	5,653,000	7,242,000	7,967,000	8,159,000	4,023,000	1,474,000
Average Shs. Outstg.	3,308,000	3,329,000	3,348,000	3,396,000	3,433,000	3,458,000	1,984,000	1,844,000
Balance Sheet								
Cash & Cash Equivalents	7,081,000	4,806,000	3,567,000	703,000	643,000	495,000	460,000	398,000
Total Current Assets	15,818,000	13,968,000	14,089,000	12,580,000	23,216,000	11,930,000	7,538,000	7,062,000
Total Assets	100,419,000	100,166,000	95,057,000	96,322,000	98,651,000	83,215,000	45,066,000	42,132,000
Total Current Liabilities	13,471,000	14,260,000	14,683,000	23,948,000	30,357,000	19,313,000	9,989,000	10,252,000
Long–Term Obligations	15,854,000	16,060,000	18,536,000	17,133,000	15,492,000	17,475,000	11,612,000	12,019,000
Net Stockholders' Equity	39,409,000	38,248,000	33,199,000	32,491,000	30,463,000	26,726,000	12,780,000	9,892,000
Shares Outstanding	3,311,000	3,305,253	3,318,000	3,354,215	3,386,718	3,395,272	1,959,000	1,837,000
Statistical Record								
Operating Profit Margin %	15.50	15.83	19.98	23.71	20.86	23.43	23.92	12.75
Net Profit Margin %	38.19	28.96	31.15	33.66	34.59	30.57	30.16	12.87
Return on Equity %	4.94	15.61	22.50	22.34	26.15	24.59	31.83	14.90
Return on Assets %	1.93	5.96	7.86	7.53	8.07	7.89	9.02	3.49
Debt/Total Assets %	15.78	16.03	19.49	17.78	15.70	20.99	25.76	28.52
Price Range	27.59–23.71	31.19–19.34	40.17–20.10	52.38–37.38	58.50–35.00	59.19–44.38	54.13–35.78	38.00–25.00
P/E Ratio	16.72–14.37	17.33–10.74	18.01–9.01	24.47–17.47	25.22–15.09	31.15–23.36	26.40–17.45	47.50–31.25
Average Yield %	5.57	5.74	3.46	2.37	2.18	1.83	2.19	2.97

Address: 175 E. Houston, San Antonio, TX 78205–2233	Officers: Edward E. Whitacre – Chmn., C.E.O., William M. Daley – Pres.	Investor Contact:210–351–3990
Telephone: (210) 821 4105	Transfer Agents:EquiServe Trust Company, N.A., Jersey City, NJ	Institutional Holding No of Institutions: 9
Web Site: www.sbc.com		Shares: 18,597,556 % Held: –

SECOND BANCORP, INC.

Exchange	Symbol	Price	52Wk Range	Yield	P/E
NMS	SECD	$32.03 (5/28/2004)	34.42-24.62	2.37	13.29

*7 Year Price Score 121.1 *NYSE Composite Index=100 *12 Month Price Score 49.8

Interim Earnings (Per Share)

Qtr.	Mar	Jun	Sep	Dec
2004	0.29	...	...	...
2001	0.42	0.42	0.43	0.43
2002	0.47	0.43	0.55	0.34
2003	0.89	0.57	0.51	0.44

Interim Dividends (Per Share)

Amt	Decl	Ex	Rec	Pay
0.19Q	6/10/2003	7/11/2003	7/15/2003	7/31/2003
0.19Q	12/9/2003	1/13/2004	1/15/2004	1/30/2004
0.19Q	3/9/2004	4/13/2004	4/15/2004	4/30/2004
0.19Q	5/26/2004	6/25/2004	6/29/2004	7/6/2004

Indicated Div: $0.76 (Div. Reinv. Plan)

Valuation Analysis

Forecast P/E 15.81 (5/24/2004)

Market Cap	$315.9 Million	Book Value	137.0 Million
Price/Book	N/A	Price/Sales	N/A

Dividend Achiever Status

Rank	154	10 Year Growth Rate 10.10%
Total Years of Dividend Growth		16

Business Summary: Commercial Banking (MIC: 8.1 SIC: 6021 NAIC:522110)

Second Bancorp is a one-bank financial holding company with its most significant subsidiary being The Second National Bank of Warren, a Warren, OH based commercial bank. Operating through 33 retail banking centers and five loan production offices as of Dec 31 2003, Second National offers a range of commercial and consumer banking and trust services primarily to business and individual customers in various communities in a nine county area in northeast and east-central Ohio. A second operating subsidiary is Stouffer-Herzog Insurance Agency, which sells a range of property, casualty, life and health insurance products in northeast Ohio. At Dec 31 2003, Co. had total assets of $2.12 billion.

Recent Developments: For the quarter ended Mar 31 2004, net income plunged 68.1% to $2.8 million compared with $8.7 million in the corresponding quarter of 2003. Results for 2004 and 2003 included security gains of $498,000 and $51,000, respectively. Also, results for 2004 included merger costs of $1.1 million, while results for 2003 included a gain on the sale of banking centers of $5.6 million. Net interest income slipped 3.7% to $13.6 million from $14.1 million a year earlier. Provision for loan losses fell 37.9% to $1.4 million. Total non-interest income dropped 54.0% to $6.6 million from $14.3 million in 2003. Total non-interest expense climbed 8.6% $14.8 million from $13.7 million the previous year.

Prospects: The agreement under which Sky Financial will acquire all of Co.'s outstanding shares in a stock-for-stock transaction is on track. Under the agreement, shareholders of Co. will receive 1.26 shares of Sky Financial's common stock for each share held. The acquisition is subject to regulatory approvals and shareholder approval on May 18 2004, and is expected to close on June 30 2004. Meanwhile, Co.'s decline in non-interest income reflects in part slowing secondary market activity in its mortgage lending line of business and higher non-interest expenses.

Financial Data

(US$ in Thousands)	12/31/2003	12/31/2002	12/31/2001	12/31/2000	12/31/1999	12/31/1998	12/31/1997	12/31/1996
Earnings Per Share	2.41	1.79	1.70	0.60	1.51	0.52	1.32	1.26
Tang. Book Val. Per Share	12.34	11.87	10.22	11.05	10.55	11.01	11.24	9.78
Dividends Per Share	0.750	0.710	0.670	0.620	0.550	0.510	0.470	0.420
Dividend Payout %	31.12	39.66	39.41	103.33	36.42	98.07	35.60	33.59
Income Statement								
Total Interest Income	102,562	107,272	112,557	116,298	104,582	106,997	68,247	65,646
Total Interest Expense	46,691	50,812	62,367	66,921	55,310	55,888	33,496	31,785
Net Interest Income	55,871	56,460	50,190	49,377	49,272	51,109	34,751	33,861
Provision for Loan Losses	7,610	6,159	4,718	7,129	3,195	10,579	3,939	4,956
Non-Interest Income	32,948	23,425	19,528	8,275	14,792	12,754	9,204	8,479
Non-Interest Expense	54,763	49,496	41,939	44,213	39,330	46,248	28,591	26,276
Income from Cont Ops	...	...	17,181	...	...	...	...	...
Net Income	23,155	18,000	17,080	6,134	16,178	5,633	8,975	8,552
Average Shs. Outstg.	9,623	10,040	10,271	10,271	10,698	10,742	6,810	6,766
Balance Sheet								
Cash & Due from Banks	40,773	60,822	40,837	35,272	35,238	45,478	24,367	27,934
Securities Avail. for Sale	620,696	523,669	417,496	382,098	367,587	354,415	280,010	231,324
Net Loans & Leases	1,330,946	1,150,196	1,105,197	1,054,872	1,060,493	960,114	559,637	558,437
Total Assets	2,116,761	1,894,715	1,680,356	1,546,290	1,537,278	1,430,233	913,480	867,279
Total Deposits	1,215,342	1,195,112	1,123,131	1,036,135	1,097,589	1,102,590	703,266	669,397
Long-Term Obligations	523,836	365,844	275,152	251,733	200,276	72,782	9,864	26,557
Total Liabilities	1,979,745	1,758,441	1,552,057	1,429,093	1,420,931	1,306,960	834,052	798,042
Net Stockholders' Equity	137,016	136,334	128,299	117,197	116,347	123,273	79,428	69,237
Shares Outstanding	9,471	9,762	9,949	10,057	10,458	10,668	6,800	6,698
Return on Equity %	16.89	13.20	13.39	5.23	13.90	4.56	11.29	12.35
Return on Assets %	1.09	0.95	1.02	0.39	1.05	0.39	0.98	0.98
Non-Int. Exp./Tot. Inc. %	38.80	37.87	31.75	35.49	32.94	38.62	36.91	35.44
Price Range	28.94-21.64	28.32-20.56	22.90-13.75	22.38-12.25	29.88-19.25	37.25-19.75	27.00-15.25	16.50-12.50
P/E Ratio	12.01-8.98	15.82-11.49	13.47-8.09	37.29-20.42	19.78-12.75	71.63-37.98	20.45-11.55	13.10-9.92
Average Yield %	2.89	2.77	3.52	3.85	2.28	1.84	2.20	2.86

Address: 108 Main Ave. S.W., Warren, OH 44482-1311	**Officers:** Rick L. Blossom – Chmn., Pres., C.E.O., Christopher Stanitz – Exec. V.P., Sec.	**Investor Contact:** 330-841-0234
Telephone: (330) 841-0123	**Transfer Agents:** American Stock Transfer & Trust Company, New York, NY	**Institutional Holding**
Web Site: www.secondnationalbank.com		**No of Institutions:** 12
		Shares: 171,092 **% Held:** –

SEI INVESTMENTS CO.

Exchange	Symbol	Price	52Wk Range	Yield	P/E
NMS	SEIC	$29.49 (5/28/2004)	36.09-27.26	0.61	23.04

*7 Year Price Score 126.9 ***NYSE Composite Index=100** ***12 Month Price Score 42.8**

Interim Earnings (Per Share)

Qtr.	Mar	Jun	Sep	Dec
2001	0.25	0.27	0.28	0.29
2002	0.30	0.31	0.32	0.32
2003	0.32	0.32	0.33	0.35
2004	0.37	...	...	...

Interim Dividends (Per Share)

Amt	Decl	Ex	Rec	Pay
0.06S	12/10/2002	12/31/2002	1/3/2003	1/21/2003
0.07S	5/28/2003	6/5/2003	6/9/2003	6/25/2003
0.09S	12/16/2003	1/2/2004	1/6/2004	1/22/2004
0.10S	5/25/2004	6/4/2004	6/8/2004	6/24/2004

Indicated Div: $0.18

Valuation Analysis

Forecast P/E 19.44 (5/24/2004)

Market Cap $3.1 Billion   Book Value 314.3 Million

Price/Book N/A   Price/Sales N/A

Dividend Achiever Status

Rank 18   10 Year Growth Rate   23.11%

Total Years of Dividend Growth   12

Business Summary: Finance Intermediaries &Services (MIC: 8.7 SIC: 6211 NAIC:523120)

SEI Investments is a provider of asset management and investment technology services with operations in five business segments: Private Banking & Trust, which provides investment processing services and investment management programs; Investment Advisors, which provides investment management programs and investment processing services to investors; Enterprises, which provides retirement and treasury business services for corporations; Money Managers, which provides business services to U.S. investment managers and alternative investment managers worldwide; and Investments in New Businesses, which includes Co.'s global businesses. As of Dec 31 2003, Co. operated 22 offices in 11 countries.

Recent Developments: For the quarter ended Mar 31 2004, net income rose 12.3% to $39.4 million from $35.1 million in the corresponding period the year before. Results included a net gain of $2.9 million in 2004 and a net loss of $106,000 in 2003 on investments. Total revenues improved 9.4% to $167.2 million from $152.8 million a year earlier. On a segment basis, Private Banking and Trust revenue slipped 5.7% to $74.6 million, reflecting losses in fund processing revenues and lower investment processing revenues. Investment Advisors revenue climbed 20.2% to $43.2 million, while Enterprises revenue advanced 15.8% to $16.2 million.

Prospects: Co. is optimistic in regard to its future prospects as it has continued to achieve modest increases in revenues, net income and earnings per share, despite significant investment in new products and services to help build long−term sustainable growth. Additionally, Co. is encouraged by the market's interest in its new strategies and an improving business climate. However, the capital markets still face uncertainty, which could lead to further devaluation in the assets Co. manages or administers, continued redemption rates, and prolonged buying decisions among its clients.

Financial Data

(US$ in Thousands)	3 Mos	12/31/2003	12/31/2002	12/31/2001	12/31/2000	12/31/1999	12/31/1998	12/31/1997
Earnings Per Share	1.37	1.32	1.25	1.09	0.87	0.59	0.37	0.23
Cash Flow Per Share	0.39	1.64	1.55	1.51	1.30	0.81	0.87	0.43
Tang. Book Val. Per Share	3.35	3.26	2.54	2.37	1.70	0.59	0.39	0.26
Dividends Per Share	0.160	0.130	0.110	0.090	0.070	0.060	0.050	0.040
Dividend Payout %	15.69	9.84	8.80	8.25	8.42	10.16	13.33	18.56
Income Statement								
Total Revenues	167,161	636,233	620,819	658,013	598,806	456,192	366,119	292,749
Total Indirect Exp.	117,588	146,428	146,968	176,099	171,823	138,482	117,297	98,701
Depreciation & Amort.	4,202	16,788	18,060	19,650	17,305	15,793	15,688	14,068
Operating Income	49,573	206,181	209,819	183,186	147,959	102,494	67,885	45,512
Net Interest Inc./(Exp.)	307	2,060	2,937	4,796	4,126	(90)	(1,017)	(1,505)
Income Taxes	22,409	81,303	82,528	73,380	60,655	42,030	26,904	17,163
Eqty Earns/Minority Int.	9,003	22,461	12,652	10,342	7,533	6,765	3,015	...
Income from Cont Ops	...	...	...	...	...	67,139	42,979	...
Net Income	39,409	142,981	140,520	124,944	98,963	68,431	43,689	26,844
Average Shs. Outstg.	107,449	108,137	112,803	114,810	113,820	113,826	114,756	115,416
Balance Sheet								
Cash & Cash Equivalents	225,690	253,434	175,724	173,685	159,576	73,206	52,980	16,891
Total Current Assets	330,291	352,413	261,435	266,142	249,031	146,992	113,509	83,995
Total Assets	575,318	592,629	464,147	460,916	375,582	253,779	208,772	168,884
Total Current Liabilities	167,754	193,474	134,247	144,343	146,453	138,918	110,794	81,676
Long−Term Obligations	18,556	23,944	33,500	43,055	27,000	29,000	31,000	33,000
Net Stockholders' Equity	376,310	363,773	290,007	270,593	197,421	79,002	59,685	46,410
Net Working Capital	162,537	158,939	127,188	121,799	102,578	8,074	2,715	2,319
Shares Outstanding	104,156	104,869	109,180	109,180	108,560	106,152	107,166	106,602
Operating Profit Margin %	29.65	32.40	33.79	27.83	24.70	22.46	18.54	15.54
Return on Equity %	10.47	39.30	48.45	46.17	50.12	84.98	72.00	57.84
Return on Assets %	6.84	24.12	30.27	27.10	26.34	26.45	20.58	15.89
Debt/Total Assets %	3.22	4.04	7.21	9.34	7.18	11.42	14.84	19.54
Price Range	36.09-30.29	35.92-22.90	45.75-19.30	51.31-27.90	61.72-14.89	21.50-13.23	16.67-6.37	7.37-3.19
P/E Ratio	26.34-22.11	27.21-17.35	36.60-15.44	47.07-25.60	70.94-17.11	36.44-22.42	45.05-17.23	32.07-13.86
Average Yield %	0.48	0.44	0.34	0.23	0.25	0.37	0.43	0.84

Address: 1 Freedom Valley Drive, Oaks, PA 19456−1100	**Officers:** Alfred P. West − Chmn., C.E.O., Carmen V. Romeo − Exec. V.P.	**Investor Contact:**610−676−1000
Telephone: (610) 676−1000	**Transfer Agents:**American Stock Transfer &Trust Co., New York, NY	**Institutional Holding** **No of Institutions:** 202
Web Site: www.seic.com		**Shares:** 58,699,578 **% Held:** 55.9

SERVICEMASTER CO. (THE)

Exchange	Symbol	Price	52Wk Range	Yield	P/E
NYS	SVM	$12.16 (5/28/2004)	12.21-9.40	3.62	N.M.

*7 Year Price Score 77.7   *NYSE Composite Index=100   *12 Month Price Score 50.9

Interim Earnings (Per Share)

Qtr.	Mar	Jun	Sep	Dec
2001	0.08	0.17	0.12	(0.91)
2002	0.10	0.20	0.19	0.07
2003	0.02	0.22	(1.08)	0.09
2004	0.04	...	...	...

Interim Dividends (Per Share)

Amt	Decl	Ex	Rec	Pay
0.105Q	7/18/2003	10/8/2003	10/10/2003	10/31/2003
0.105Q	10/28/2003	1/7/2004	1/9/2004	1/30/2004
0.105Q	3/8/2004	4/6/2004	4/9/2004	4/30/2004
0.11Q	4/30/2004	7/7/2004	7/9/2004	7/30/2004

Indicated Div: $0.44

Valuation Analysis

Forecast P/E 20.10 (5/24/2004)

Market Cap	$3.7 Billion	Book Value	762.2 Million
Price/Book	4.56	Price/Sales	0.97

Dividend Achiever Status

Rank	259	10 Year Growth Rate	4.76%
Total Years of Dividend Growth			33

Business Summary: Accounting &Management Consulting Services (MIC: 12.2 SIC: 8741 NAIC:561110)

ServiceMaster provides outsourcing services to residential and commercial customers. The TruGreen segment provides lawn care services and landscape maintenance services. The Terminix segment includes domestic termite and pest control services. The American Residential Services and American Mechanical Services (ARS/AMS) segment provides plumbing, drain cleaning, heating, ventilation, air conditioning and electrical services. The American Home Shield segment offers warranty contracts on home systems and appliances and home inspection services. The Other Operations segment includes ServiceMaster Clean, Merry Maids and Furniture Medic franchise operations.

Recent Developments: For the quarter ended Mar 31 2004, income from continuing operations surged 136.7% to $11.5 million from $4.8 million in the prior-year quarter. Earnings for 2004 and 2003 excluded losses from discontinued operations of $262.0 million and $168.0 million, respectively. Total revenue increased 6.3% to $756.9 million. On a segment basis, TruGreen revenue climbed 9.8% to $224.7 million, while Terminix revenue rose 4.8% to $236.8 million. American Home Shield revenue grew 9.1% to $102.8 million, and American Residential Services/American Mechanical Services revenue inched up 1.7% to $154.0 million. Other revenue increased 6.7% to $38.7 million. Operating income jumped 23.7% to $31.1 million.

Prospects: On Apr 1 2004, Co. announced that its TruGreen ChemLawn subsidiary has acquired the assets of Greenspace Services Limited from FirstService Corporation. Greenspace Services Limited is Canada's largest professional lawn care service company. The transaction is expected to be marginally accretive to earnings in 2004. Separately, for full-year 2004, Co. expects revenue growth to be in the mid-single digits with earnings per share growing at a somewhat faster rate than revenues. Co. expects the improving economy, consumer confidence and home sales will help to overcome higher insurance, fuel costs and a return to a more normal level of variable compensation.

Financial Data

(US$ in Thousands)	3 Mos	12/31/2003	12/31/2002	12/31/2001	12/31/2000	12/31/1999	12/31/1998	12/31/1997
Earnings Per Share	(0.73)	(0.75)	0.56	(0.54)	0.61	0.55	0.64	0.54
Cash Flow Per Share	0.05	0.95	1.21	1.16	1.31	0.81	1.35	1.24
Dividends Per Share	0.420	0.420	0.410	0.400	0.380	0.360	0.330	31.33
Dividend Payout %	(56.76)	N.M.	73.21	N.M.	62.29	65.45	51.56	...
Income Statement								
Total Revenues	756,891	3,568,586	3,589,089	3,601,429	5,970,615	5,703,535	4,724,119	3,961,502
Total Indirect Exp.	180,732	1,304,306	766,527	1,142,667	857,249	861,326	648,085	559,409
Depreciation & Amort.	1,422	5,917	7,442	126,937	157,691	138,444	104,605	93,062
Operating Income	31,103	(166,243)	341,336	(87,445)	416,899	383,174	396,422	343,933
Income Taxes	7,235	(2,662)	93,468	(29,594)	133,319	122,630	128,786	(54,797)
Income from Cont Ops	11,461	(221,975)	170,098	(171,779)	184,988	...	...	...
Net Income	11,199	(224,687)	156,994	155,033	173,827	173,563	189,992	329,076
Average Shs. Outstg.	296,035	295,610	314,112	311,408	305,518	314,406	298,887	299,640
Balance Sheet								
Cash & Cash Equivalents	235,739	318,701	302,603	483,111	100,917	114,210	120,422	124,124
Total Current Assets	882,933	890,774	919,174	1,150,658	984,759	959,238	670,202	594,084
Total Assets	2,959,897	2,956,426	3,414,938	3,674,739	3,967,668	3,870,215	2,914,851	2,475,224
Total Current Liabilities	859,681	818,240	839,064	814,401	833,414	845,804	753,697	558,177
Long-Term Obligations	792,837	785,490	804,340	1,105,518	1,756,757	1,697,582	1,076,167	1,247,845
Net Stockholders' Equity	762,174	816,517	1,218,700	1,220,961	1,161,588	1,205,716	956,486	524,438
Shares Outstanding	317,451	293,981	299,221	300,531	298,474	307,530	298,030	279,943
Operating Profit Margin %	4.10	N.M.	9.51	N.M.	6.98	6.71	8.39	8.68
Return on Equity %	1.50	N.M	13.95	N.M	15.92	14.39	19.86	62.74
Return on Assets %	0.38	N.M.	4.98	N.M.	4.66	4.48	6.51	13.29
Debt/Total Assets %	26.78	26.56	23.55	30.08	44.27	43.86	36.92	50.41
Price Range	12.01-10.71	11.97-9.05	15.49-9.11	14.10-10.05	14.69-8.75	22.06-10.13	25.38-17.33	19.50-11.00
P/E Ratio	N/A	N/A	27.66-16.27	N/A	24.08-14.34	40.11-18.41	39.65-27.08	36.11-20.37
Average Yield %	3.75	4.06	3.29	3.46	3.43	2.14	1.61	N/A

Address: 3250 Lacey Road, Downers Grove, IL 60515-1700	Officers: Johnathan P. Ward - Chmn. , C.E.O., Ernest J. zek - Pres., C.O.O.	Investor Contact:630-271-1300
Telephone: (630) 663-2000	Transfer Agents:Computershare Investor Services, Chicago, IL	Institutional Holding No of Institutions: 3
Web Site: www. servicemaster.com		Shares: 852,473 % Held: -

SHERWIN-WILLIAMS CO.

Exchange	Symbol	Price	52Wk Range	Yield	P/E
NYS	SHW	$39.30 (5/28/2004)	39.30–26.88	1.73	16.38

*7 Year Price Score 119.2   *NYSE Composite Index=100   ***12 Month Price Score 54.0**

Interim Earnings (Per Share)

Qtr.	Mar	Jun	Sep	Dec
2001	0.23	0.58	0.58	0.29
2002	0.23	0.70	0.73	0.38
2003	0.21	0.75	0.82	0.48
2004	0.35	...	...	...

Interim Dividends (Per Share)

Amt	Decl	Ex	Rec	Pay
0.155Q	7/23/2003	8/20/2003	8/22/2003	9/5/2003
0.155Q	10/24/2003	11/12/2003	11/14/2003	11/28/2003
0.17Q	2/4/2004	2/19/2004	2/23/2004	3/15/2004
0.17Q	4/28/2004	5/26/2004	5/28/2004	6/11/2004

Indicated Div: $0.68 (Div. Reinv. Plan)

Valuation Analysis

Forecast P/E 14.60 (5/24/2004)

Market Cap $5.9 Billion	Book Value 1.2 Billion
Price/Book 4.55	Price/Sales 0.96

Dividend Achiever Status

Rank	169	10 Year Growth Rate	9.51%
Total Years of Dividend Growth			24

Business Summary: Chemicals (MIC: 11.1 SIC: 2851 NAIC:325510)

Sherwin–Williams manufactures, distributes and sells coatings and related products. The Paint Stores' division consists of Co.–operated specialty paint stores in the U.S., Canada, the Virgin Islands, Puerto Rico and Mexico. The Consumer segment manufactures and distributes a variety of paints, coatings and related products to third party customers and the Paint stores segment. Automotive Finishes manufactures and distributes motor vehicle finish products in North and South America, the Caribbean Islands and Europe. International Coatings licenses, and distributes a variety of paints, coatings and related products worldwide. Co.'s brands include *Sherwin–Williams®*, *Dutch Boy®*, and *Krylon®*.

Recent Developments: For the quarter ended Mar 31 2004, net income surged 67.1% to $51.5 million compared with $30.8 million in the corresponding period of the prior year. Net sales advanced 14.9% to $1.32 billion from $1.15 billion the year before. The improvement in sales was primarily attributed to strong domestic architectural paint sales and improving sales and market conditions in domestic industrial maintenance, product finishes and automotive markets. Gross profit climbed 13.9% to $571.6 million from $501.8 million a year earlier. However, operating profit as a percentage of sales declined to 43.3% versus 43.7% in the first quarter of 2003.

Prospects: Co. expects that achieving strong sales and profits as the year progresses will be challenging due to the level of results experienced in the last half of 2003. Going forward, Co. intends to continue launching new products, actively pursuing new customers, opening new stores, enhancing the shopping experience in its stores and increasing the productivity of its operations to grow sales and operating income in all operating segments of its business. Accordingly, Co. now expects annual net sales for 2004 to increase in the mid–to–high single digits over 2003, with diluted net income per common share in the range of $2.54 to $2.62.

Financial Data

(US$ in Thousands)	3 Mos	12/31/2003	12/31/2002	12/31/2001	12/31/2000	12/31/1999	12/31/1998	12/31/1997
Earnings Per Share	2.40	2.26	2.04	1.68	0.10	1.80	1.57	1.50
Cash Flow Per Share	(0.70)	3.80	3.66	3.57	2.83	2.87	2.75	2.52
Tang. Book Val. Per Share	3.02	2.95	3.77	2.59	3.17	2.31	1.76	0.69
Dividends Per Share	0.630	0.620	0.600	0.580	0.540	0.480	0.450	0.400
Dividend Payout %	26.35	27.43	29.41	34.52	540.00	26.66	28.66	26.83
Income Statement								
Total Revenues	1,319,522	5,407,764	5,184,788	5,066,005	5,211,624	5,003,837	4,934,430	4,881,103
Total Indirect Exp.	484,546	1,881,664	1,784,527	1,729,855	2,092,407	1,673,449	1,598,333	1,573,510
Depreciation & Amort.	28,532	116,564	115,648	148,098	160,030	155,744	147,888	139,246
Operating Income	87,081	573,631	554,060	489,774	215,204	575,065	531,638	523,201
Net Interest Inc./(Exp.)	(9,387)	(38,742)	(40,475)	(54,627)	(62,026)	(61,168)	(71,971)	(80,837)
Income Taxes	27,714	190,868	186,463	161,291	127,380	186,258	167,239	166,663
Income from Cont Ops	...	...	310,701	...	...	...	...	...
Net Income	51,468	332,058	127,565	263,158	16,026	303,860	272,864	260,614
Average Shs. Outstg.	145,586	147,005	152,435	156,893	162,695	169,026	173,536	174,032
Balance Sheet								
Cash & Cash Equivalents	103,570	302,813	164,012	118,814	2,896	18,623	19,133	3,530
Total Current Assets	1,682,950	1,715,144	1,505,993	1,506,945	1,551,539	1,597,377	1,547,290	1,532,253
Total Assets	3,651,248	3,682,608	3,432,312	3,627,925	3,750,670	4,052,090	4,065,462	4,035,801
Total Current Liabilities	1,134,566	1,154,170	1,083,496	1,141,353	1,115,243	1,189,862	1,111,973	1,115,663
Long–Term Obligations	503,510	502,992	506,682	503,517	623,587	624,365	730,283	843,919
Net Stockholders' Equity	1,451,341	1,458,857	1,341,890	1,487,764	1,471,864	1,698,532	1,715,940	1,592,180
Net Working Capital	548,384	560,974	422,497	365,592	436,296	407,515	435,317	416,590
Shares Outstanding	142,982	143,406	148,910	153,978	159,558	165,664	171,033	172,907
Operating Profit Margin %	6.59	10.60	10.68	9.66	4.12	11.49	10.77	10.71
Return on Equity %	3.54	22.76	23.15	17.68	1.08	17.88	15.90	16.36
Return on Assets %	1.40	9.01	9.05	7.25	0.42	7.49	6.71	6.45
Debt/Total Assets %	13.79	13.65	14.76	13.87	16.62	15.40	17.96	20.91
Price Range	38.43–33.06	34.74–24.82	33.00–22.06	28.02–20.31	27.00–17.44	32.44–19.00	37.50–20.06	32.69–24.88
P/E Ratio	16.01–13.78	15.37–10.98	16.18–10.81	16.68–12.09	270.0–174.4	18.02–10.56	23.89–12.78	21.79–16.58
Average Yield %	1.81	2.12	2.14	2.42	2.45	1.87	1.51	1.38

Address: 101 Prospect Avenue, N.W., Cleveland, OH 44115–1075 Telephone: (216) 566–2000 Web Site: www.sherwin.com	Officers: Christopher M. Connor – Chmn., C.E.O., Joseph M. Scaminace – Pres., C.O.O. Transfer Agents: The Bank of New York, New York, NY	Investor Contact: 216–566–2000 Institutional Holding No of Institutions: 4 Shares: 308,392 % Held: –

SIGMA-ALDRICH CORP.

Exchange	Symbol	Price	52Wk Range	Yield	P/E
NMS	SIAL	$57.11 (5/28/2004)	58.93–51.65	1.19	19.76

*7 Year Price Score 136.0 *NYSE Composite Index=100 ***12 Month Price Score 47.6**

Interim Earnings (Per Share)

Qtr.	Mar	Jun	Sep	Dec
2001	0.48	0.49	0.45	0.45
2002	0.54	0.58	0.55	0.87
2003	0.68	0.67	0.66	0.67
2004	0.89	...	...	...

Interim Dividends (Per Share)

Amt	Decl	Ex	Rec	Pay
0.16Q	8/12/2003	8/28/2003	9/2/2003	9/15/2003
0.16Q	11/11/2003	11/26/2003	12/1/2003	12/15/2003
0.17Q	2/10/2004	2/26/2004	3/1/2004	3/15/2004
0.17Q	5/4/2004	5/27/2004	6/1/2004	6/15/2004
		Indicated Div: $0.68		

Valuation Analysis
Forecast P/E 17.58 (5/24/2004)

Market Cap	$4.2 Billion	Book Value	N/A
Price/Book	N/A	Price/Sales	N/A

Dividend Achiever Status

Rank	76	10 Year Growth Rate	15.07%
Total Years of Dividend Growth			22

Business Summary: null (MIC: null SIC: 5169 NAIC:424690)

Sigma–Aldrich develops, manufactures and distributes a broad range of biochemicals and organic chemicals. These chemical products and kits are used in scientific and genomic research, biotechnology, pharmaceutical development, the diagnosis of disease, and chemical manufacturing. Co. consists of three business units: Scientific Research, Biotechnology and Fine Chemicals. The Scientific Research unit sells biochemicals, organic chemicals, and reagents. The Biotechnology unit supplies immunochemical, cell culture, molecular biology, cell signaling and neuroscience biochemicals. The Fine Chemicals unit supplies organic chemicals and biochemicals.

Recent Developments: For the three months ended Mar 31 2004, net income rose 27.4% to $62.3 million compared with income from continuing operations of $48.9 million in the equivalent quarter of 2003. Earnings benefited from higher sales from Co.'s Scientific Research, Biotechnology and Fine Chemicals businesses, while currency and process improvements and lower interest costs more than offset increased costs from new sales and marketing initiatives. Results for 2003 excluded gains of $2.6 million from discontinued operations. Net sales climbed 10.0% to $368.1 million from $334.7 million the previous year. Gross profit grew 15.0% to $196.6 million from $171.0 million the year before.

Prospects: Co. expects overall currency adjusted sales growth to continue to improve in the upcoming quarters of 2004 and to achieve a currency adjusted gain for full–year 2004 in the range of 3.0% to 4.0%. Based on currency benefits realized in the first quarter and those expected in upcoming quarters, total sales for full–year 2004 are expected to grow by 7.0% to 10.0%. Separately, on Apr 14 2004, Co. completed the acquisition of Ultrafine, a supplier of contract chemistry services for all phases of drug development. The acquisition enhances Co.'s fine chemicals segment. Terms of the transaction were not disclosed.

Financial Data

(US$ in Thousands)	3 Mos	12/31/2003	12/31/2002	12/31/2001	12/31/2000	12/31/1999	12/31/1998	12/31/1997
Earnings Per Share	2.89	2.68	2.54	1.87	1.66	1.47	1.64	1.62
Cash Flow Per Share	1.15	4.34	4.78	2.11	1.37	2.28	1.60	1.28
Tang. Book Val. Per Share	13.49	12.82	10.89	9.34	9.72	11.88	10.95	9.73
Dividends Per Share	0.580	0.590	0.340	0.330	0.310	0.290	0.280	0.250
Dividend Payout %	20.14	22.01	13.38	17.64	18.67	19.72	17.07	15.43
Income Statement								
Total Revenues	368,100	1,298,146	1,206,982	1,179,447	1,096,270	1,037,945	1,194,290	1,127,084
Total Indirect Exp.	114,700	387,760	299,217	348,230	322,430	354,822	393,836	355,619
Depreciation & Amort.	17,300	69,267	66,326	71,373	67,563	66,919	61,827	48,053
Operating Income	84,100	282,949	285,976	218,175	209,480	203,717	242,590	252,754
Net Interest Inc./(Exp.)	(2,200)	(10,126)	(13,837)	(16,542)	(6,571)	...	...	...
Income Taxes	21,800	82,393	85,404	60,928	63,859	55,112	76,243	86,695
Income from Cont Ops	...	190,400	186,735	...	139,050	148,605	...	...
Net Income	62,300	193,102	130,714	140,705	320,198	172,270	166,347	166,059
Average Shs. Outstg.	69,900	71,126	73,412	75,175	83,585	100,984	101,188	102,804
Balance Sheet								
Cash & Cash Equivalents	125,400	127,628	52,382	37,637	31,058	43,847	24,345	46,228
Total Current Assets	836,700	815,030	694,887	727,311	713,625	774,571	772,681	706,674
Total Assets	1,556,500	1,548,242	1,389,656	1,439,802	1,347,707	1,432,001	1,432,835	1,243,822
Total Current Liabilities	219,300	257,378	265,953	397,563	335,280	105,612	142,372	119,479
Long–Term Obligations	176,300	176,259	176,805	177,700	100,846	205	415	552
Net Stockholders' Equity	1,046,500	999,261	882,174	809,715	859,275	1,259,351	1,216,380	1,060,334
Net Working Capital	617,400	557,652	429,234	329,748	378,345	668,959	630,309	587,195
Shares Outstanding	69,200	69,101	71,253	73,014	76,216	98,292	100,623	100,377
Operating Profit Margin %	22.24	21.79	26.12	18.49	19.10	19.62	20.31	22.42
Return on Equity %	5.74	19.05	24.49	17.37	16.18	11.80	13.67	15.66
Return on Assets %	3.86	12.29	15.54	9.77	10.31	10.37	11.60	13.35
Debt/Total Assets %	11.32	11.38	12.72	12.34	7.48	0.01	0.02	0.04
Price Range	58.93–54.56	57.46–41.17	52.51–39.41	51.21–37.10	40.25–20.75	35.13–25.75	42.75–26.38	39.75–27.50
P/E Ratio	20.39–18.88	21.44–15.36	20.67–15.52	27.39–19.84	24.25–12.50	23.89–17.52	26.07–16.08	24.54–16.98
Average Yield %	1.02	1.15	0.72	0.76	1.00	0.94	0.81	0.76

| **Address:** 3050 Spruce Street, St. Louis, MO 63103 **Telephone:** (314) 771 5765 **Web Site:** www.sigma-aldrich.com | **Officers:** David R. Harvey – Chmn., Pres., C.E.O., Larry S. Blazevich – V.P., Info. Systems **Transfer Agents:**Computershare Investor Services, Chicago, IL | **Investor Contact:**314–286–8004 **Institutional Holding** **No of Institutions:** 25 **Shares:** 776,807 **% Held:** – |

SIMMONS FIRST NATIONAL CORP.

Exchange	Symbol	Price	52Wk Range	Yield	P/E
NMS	SFNC	$24.09 (5/28/2004)	30.00–19.10	2.32	14.60

*7 Year Price Score 140.4 *NYSE Composite Index=100 *12 Month Price Score 46.5

Interim Earnings (Per Share)

Qtr.	Mar	Jun	Sep	Dec
2001	0.32	0.31	0.24	0.28
2002	0.34	0.40	0.40	0.39
2003	0.37	0.45	0.46	0.37
2004	0.37	...	...	...

Interim Dividends (Per Share)

Amt	Decl	Ex	Rec	Pay
0.13Q	8/29/2003	9/11/2003	9/15/2003	10/1/2003
0.14Q	11/24/2003	12/11/2003	12/15/2003	1/2/2004
0.14Q	2/27/2004	3/11/2004	3/15/2004	4/1/2004
0.14Q	5/27/2004	6/11/2004	6/15/2004	7/1/2004

Indicated Div: $0.56

Valuation Analysis

Forecast P/E 15.77 (5/24/2004)

Market Cap	$170.1 Million	Book Value	229.6 Million
Price/Book	1.94	Price/Sales	2.78

Dividend Achiever Status

Rank	86	10 Year Growth Rate	14.36%
Total Years of Dividend Growth			12

Business Summary: Commercial Banking (MIC: 8.1 SIC: 6021 NAIC:522110)

Simmons First National is a bank holding company. Co. owns seven community banks in Arkansas and conducts its operations through 79 offices. Co.'s subsidiaries provide banking services to individuals and businesses throughout the market areas it serves. Services include consumer (credit card, student and other consumer), real estate (construction, single family residential and other commercial) and commercial (commercial, agriculture and financial institutions) loans, checking, savings and time deposits, trust and investment management services, and securities and investment services. As of Dec 31 2003, Co. had total assets of $1.20 billion and deposits of $965.0 million.

Recent Developments: For the quarter ended Mar 31 2004, net income climbed 1.5% to $5.4 million compared with $5.3 million in the corresponding period of 2003. Results benefited from unusually high demand in both mortgage production and investment banking products due to extremely low interest rates in the first quarter of 2004. Net interest income increased 6.5% to $20.1 million from $18.9 million a year earlier. Provision for loan losses declined 2.4% to $2.1 million from $2.2 million in the previous year. Total non–interest income climbed 3.7% to $9.6 million from $9.3 million, while total non–interest expense grew 8.2% to $19.7 million from $18.2 million in 2003.

Prospects: In 2004, Co. has some concerns over the uncertainty of the economy and the effect of foreign imports on the catfish industry in Arkansas. Co. plans to actively monitor the status of the catfish industry in general as it relates to Co.'s loan portfolio specifically and make changes to the allowance for loan losses as necessary. Separately, on Mar 23 2004, Co. completed the acquisition of Alliance Bancorporation and its subsidiary, Alliance Bank of Hot Springs. Alliance Bank will continue its banking operations as a subsidiary of Co. In addition, Alliance Bank will change its name to Simmons First Bank of Hot Springs.

Financial Data

(US$ in Thousands)	3 Mos	12/31/2003	12/31/2002	12/31/2001	12/31/2000	12/31/1999	12/31/1998	12/31/1997
Earnings Per Share	1.65	1.65	1.53	1.15	1.29	1.16	1.13	1.03
Tang. Book Val. Per Share	11.16	11.31	11.60	10.59	9.61	9.03	8.34	6.50
Dividends Per Share	0.520	0.510	0.470	0.430	0.390	0.350	0.310	0.270
Dividend Payout %	31.51	30.90	30.61	37.22	30.23	30.04	27.31	26.08
Income Statement								
Total Interest Income	27,274	107,607	116,142	135,868	136,754	121,490	105,966	78,406
Total Interest Expense	7,159	29,737	40,434	68,463	69,693	56,759	53,732	37,991
Net Interest Income	20,115	77,870	75,708	67,405	67,061	64,731	52,234	40,415
Provision for Loan Losses	2,144	8,786	10,223	9,958	7,531	6,551	7,749	4,013
Non–Interest Income	9,432	38,717	35,303	33,569	30,355	28,277	31,664	27,545
Non–Interest Expense	19,692	73,117	69,013	68,130	62,556	61,929	56,235	46,934
Income Before Taxes	7,926	34,684	31,775	22,886	27,329	24,528	19,914	17,013
Net Income	5,411	23,790	22,078	16,528	18,869	17,168	14,331	11,989
Average Shs. Outstg.	14,540	14,415	14,376	14,324	14,638	14,748	12,632	11,608
Balance Sheet								
Cash & Due from Banks	69,234	78,205	76,452	81,785	77,495	60,324	47,170	58,327
Securities Avail. for Sale	...	...	...	...	...	...	...	160,475
Net Loans & Leases	1,477,409	1,392,967	1,235,357	1,238,288	1,273,553	1,096,550	898,519	781,555
Total Assets	2,394,862	2,235,778	1,977,579	2,016,918	1,912,493	1,697,430	1,464,362	1,326,145
Total Deposits	1,924,802	1,803,468	1,619,196	1,686,404	1,605,586	1,410,633	1,187,913	1,104,501
Long–Term Obligations	115,257	100,916	54,282	42,150	41,681	46,219	49,340	50,281
Total Liabilities	2,165,247	2,025,783	1,779,974	1,834,555	1,739,150	1,538,059	1,332,182	1,214,063
Net Stockholders' Equity	229,615	209,995	197,605	182,363	173,343	159,371	132,180	112,082
Shares Outstanding	14,669	14,101	14,142	14,174	14,361	14,631	12,418	11,452
Statistical Record								
Return on Equity %	2.35	11.20	11.08	8.86	10.73	10.54	10.38	9.74
Return on Assets %	0.22	1.05	1.10	0.80	0.97	0.98	0.93	0.82
Equity/Assets %	9.58	9.39	9.99	9.04	9.06	9.38	9.02	8.45
Non–Int. Exp./Tot. Inc. %	53.33	50.15	45.68	40.42	37.58	41.59	41.29	45.30
Price Range	30.00–25.90	28.90–17.06	21.30–15.64	18.90–11.13	13.75–9.06	20.25–11.50	26.63–16.81	21.00–12.75
P/E Ratio	18.18–15.70	17.52–10.34	13.92–10.22	16.43–9.67	10.66–7.03	17.46–9.91	23.56–14.88	20.39–12.38
Average Yield %	1.89	2.34	2.65	2.87	3.60	2.18	1.41	1.72

Address: 501 Main Street, Pine Bluff, AR 71601	Officers: J. Thomas May – Chmn., Pres., C.E.O., Barry L. Crow – Exec. V.P., C.F.O.	Institutional Holding
Telephone: (870) 541-1000		No of Institutions: 38
Web Site: www.simmonsfirst.com		Shares: 1,527,264 % Held: 21.60%

SJW CORP.

Exchange	Symbol	Price	52Wk Range	Yield	P/E
ASE	SJW	$32.50 (5/28/2004)	38.00-27.25	3.14	19.58

*7 Year Price Score 110.2   *NYSE Composite Index=100   *12 Month Price Score 50.7

Interim Earnings (Per Share)

Qtr.	Mar	Jun	Sep	Dec
2001	0.07	0.45	0.70	0.31
2002	0.19	0.43	0.63	0.30
2003	0.57	0.48	0.65	0.34
2004	0.19	...	...	...

Interim Dividends (Per Share)

Amt	Decl	Ex	Rec	Pay
0.243Q	10/28/2003	11/6/2003	11/10/2003	12/1/2003
0.255Q	1/29/2004	2/5/2004	2/9/2004	3/1/2004
3-for-1	1/29/2004	3/2/2004	2/10/2004	3/1/2004
0.255Q	...	5/10/2004	5/12/2004	6/1/2004
		Indicated Div: $1.02		

Valuation Analysis

Forecast P/E 18.27 (5/24/2004)

Market Cap	$99.0 Million	Book Value	166.4 Million
Price/Book	1.64	Price/Sales	1.83

Dividend Achiever Status

Rank	271	10 Year Growth Rate 3.62%
Total Years of Dividend Growth		37

Business Summary: Water Utilities (MIC: 7.2 SIC: 4941 NAIC:221310)

SJW is a holding company with three subsidiaries. San Jose Water Company is a public utility in the business of providing water service to a population of about 1.0 million people, as of Dec 31 2003, in an area comprising about 138 square miles in the metropolitan San Jose area. SJW Land Company owns and operates parking facilities, which are adjacent to San Jose Water Company's headquarters and the HP Pavilion in San Jose, CA. SJW Land Company also owns commercial buildings and other undeveloped land primarily in the San Jose Metropolitan area. Crystal Choice Water Service LLC is engaged in the sale and rental of water conditioning and purification equipment.

Recent Developments: For the quarter ended Mar 31 2004, net income was $1.8 million compared with $5.3 million a year earlier. Results for 2003 included a net gain of $3.0 million on the sale of non-utility property. Operating revenue climbed 11.1% to $31.1 million. Co. noted that about $2.7 million of the higher revenue was primarily due to cumulative rate increases of 7.0% and higher customer demand of 6.0% as a result of warmer temperatures in March 2004. Total water production costs consisting of purchased water, power and pump taxes grew 18.0% to $10.4 million. Total operating expense, excluding water production costs and income taxes, rose 12.8% to $15.4 million. Operating income fell 1.9% to $4.0 million.

Prospects: Co.'s results going forward may benefit from recent operational enhancements. For instance, during 2003 Co. completed the second phase of a three-year project to improve the Supervisory Control and Data Acquisition (SCADA) system. The project provided for wireless transmission of distribution system data and included installation of additional mobile SCADA terminals in operators' vehicles to improve water system operation and security. Co. noted that it also led to better energy management by automating the system's ability to maximize pumping during off-peak demand hours. Separately, Co.'s new meter reading system provides a platform for improved productivity and customer service.

Financial Data

(US$ in Thousands)	3 Mos	12/31/2003	12/31/2002	12/31/2001	12/31/2000	12/31/1999	12/31/1998	12/31/1997
Earnings Per Share	1.66	2.04	1.55	1.53	1.16	1.73	1.68	1.60
Cash Flow Per Share	1.45	4.58	3.18	2.79	2.63	2.75	2.83	2.51
Tang. Book Val. Per Share	17.38	17.83	16.22	15.75	15.19	15.11	14.42	13.40
Dividends Per Share	0.980	0.970	0.920	0.850	0.820	0.800	0.780	0.760
Dividend Payout %	59.30	47.54	59.35	55.55	70.68	46.24	46.42	47.80
Income Statement								
Total Revenues	31,063	149,732	145,652	136,083	123,157	117,001	106,010	110,084
Total Indirect Exp.	13,153	26,614	23,351	21,064	23,343	22,948	22,800	22,301
Costs & Expenses	27,078	126,778	125,094	116,256	105,232	97,262	87,163	90,770
Depreciation & Amort.	4,393	15,225	14,013	13,240	11,847	10,235	9,594	8,847
Operating Income	3,985	22,954	20,558	19,827	17,925	19,739	18,847	19,314
Net Interest Inc./(Exp.)	(2,382)	(8,471)	(7,803)	(6,737)	(6,434)	(6,552)	(5,629)	(5,695)
Income Taxes	1,244	4,199	4,740	3,946	...	...	...	...
Net Income	1,774	18,667	14,232	14,017	10,665	15,884	16,018	15,216
Average Shs. Outstg.	9,187	9,148	9,135	9,135	9,135	9,164	9,509	9,510
Balance Sheet								
Net Property	440,520	436,353	390,830	367,815	333,475	312,567	291,778	263,650
Total Assets	523,667	511,717	453,223	431,017	391,930	372,427	359,380	323,223
Long-Term Obligations	143,935	139,614	110,000	110,000	90,000	90,000	90,000	75,000
Net Stockholders' Equity	166,696	166,368	153,499	149,354	144,325	143,894	143,149	133,553
Shares Outstanding	9,135	9,135	9,135	9,135	9,135	9,135	9,502	9,510
Operating Profit Margin %	16.83	23.76	20.74	20.00	14.55	16.87	17.77	17.54
Net Inc./Net Property %	0.40	4.28	3.64	3.81	3.19	5.08	5.48	5.77
Net Inc./Tot. Capital %	0.50	5.45	4.88	4.93	4.15	6.11	6.19	6.60
Return on Equity %	1.81	18.81	15.56	14.33	7.38	11.03	11.18	11.39
Accum. Depr./Gross Prop. %	29.25	29.97	29.81	29.51	30.11	30.03	30.45	30.94
Price Range	38.00-29.33	29.90-25.13	29.67-25.42	35.50-23.97	40.58-32.67	40.19-19.08	23.46-16.42	20.17-15.33
P/E Ratio	22.89-17.67	14.66-12.32	19.14-16.40	23.20-15.66	34.99-28.16	23.23-11.03	13.96-9.77	12.60-9.58
Average Yield %	2.93	3.46	3.42	3.01	2.13	2.97	3.95	4.28

Address: 374 West Santa Clara Street, San Jose, CA 95196	**Officers:** w Gibson – Chmn., W. Richard Roth – Pres., C.E.O.	**Institutional Holding** No of Institutions: 8
Telephone: (408) 279 7800		**Shares:** 13,000 **% Held:** –
Web Site: www.sjwater.com		

SLM CORP.

Exchange	Symbol	Price	52Wk Range	Yield	P/E
NYS	SLM	$38.33 (5/28/2004)	42.76-35.70	1.98	12.73

*7 Year Price Score 168.0 *NYSE Composite Index=100 *12 Month Price Score 45.8

Interim Earnings (Per Share)

Qtr.	Mar	Jun	Sep	Dec
2001	0.05	0.56	(0.41)	0.56
2002	0.87	0.26	(0.14)	0.65
2003	0.88	0.80	0.76	0.57
2004	0.64	...	...	...

Interim Dividends (Per Share)

Amt	Decl	Ex	Rec	Pay
0.17Q	7/25/2003	9/3/2003	9/5/2003	9/19/2003
0.17Q	11/14/2003	12/3/2003	12/5/2003	12/19/2003
0.17Q	1/29/2004	3/3/2004	3/5/2004	3/19/2004
0.19Q	5/14/2004	6/2/2004	6/4/2004	6/18/2004
		Indicated Div: $0.76		

Valuation Analysis

Forecast P/E 17.62 (5/24/2004)

Market Cap	$5.9 Billion	Book Value	2.5 Billion
Price/Book	6.90	Price/Sales	4.09

Dividend Achiever Status

Rank	48	10 Year Growth Rate	17.42%
Total Years of Dividend Growth			23

Business Summary: Credit &Lending (MIC: 8.6 SIC: 6141 NAIC:522291)

SLM is a provider of education funding, managing nearly $89.00 billion in student loans for more than seven million borrowers. Co. primarily provides federally guaranteed student loans originated under the Federal Family Education Loan Program, and offers comprehensive information and resources to help guide students, parents and guidance professionals through the financial aid process. Through its subsidiaries and divisions, Co. also provides an array of consumer credit loans, including those for lifelong learning and K−12 education, and business and technical outsourcing services for colleges and universities.

Recent Developments: For the quarter ended Mar 31 2004, net income fell 30.0% to $291.5 million compared with $416.5 million in the corresponding period of the previous year. Earnings included a 19.0% gain in preferred−channel loan originations. Results for 2004 and 2003 included losses from derivative market value adjustments of $116.7 million and $119.1 million, and gains on student loan securitizations of $114.0 million and $305.8 million, respectively. Net interest income slid 7.1% to $321.7 million. Provision for loan losses declined 6.4% to $39.8 million. Total non−interest income dropped 40.7% to $307.7 million. Total operating expenses grew 16.5% to $208.9 million.

Prospects: Co. continues to build market share in a growing student loan market, which is enabling it to further accelerate its privatization and deliver good earnings growth. During the first quarter of 2004, Co.'s preferred−channel loans, loans created by Co.'s owned or affiliated brands and an indicator of future loan acquisition volume, grew 19.0% to more than $5.8 billion year over year. Separately, on Jan 26 2004, Co. signed a definitive agreement to sell its campus−based loan servicing business to JPT Partners. The divestiture was undertaken to comply with federal regulations that prevent schools from contracting with a single entity for servicing Perkins loans.

Financial Data

(US$ in Thousands)	12/31/2003	12/31/2002	12/31/2001	12/31/2000	12/31/1999	12/31/1998	12/31/1997	12/31/1996
Earnings Per Share	3.01	1.64	0.76	0.92	1.02	0.98	0.93	0.70
Tang. Book Val. Per Share	4.18	2.72	3.23	2.53	1.42	1.32	1.22	1.20
Dividends Per Share	0.590	0.280	0.240	0.220	0.200	0.190	0.170	0.160
Dividend Payout %	19.71	17.24	31.79	23.91	19.61	19.39	18.28	22.86
Income Statement								
Total Interest Income	2,348,275	2,211,761	2,997,531	3,478,659	2,808,575	2,587,649	3,283,834	3,449,321
Total Interest Expense	1,021,906	1,202,620	2,124,115	2,836,871	2,114,785	1,924,997	2,526,156	2,582,885
Net Interest Income	1,326,369	1,009,141	873,416	641,788	693,790	662,652	757,678	866,436
Provision for Loan Losses	147,480	116,624	65,991	32,119	34,358	28,619	...	...
Non−Interest Income	1,811,951	1,020,654	517,617	687,632	450,790	476,967	500,872	146,916
Non−Interest Expense	807,871	689,772	707,654	585,710	358,570	360,869	493,767	405,652
Income Before Taxes	2,182,969	1,223,399	617,388	711,591	751,652	750,131	764,783	607,700
Eqty Earns/Minority Int.	...	...	(10,070)	(10,694)	(10,694)	(10,694)	(10,694)	(10,694)
Income from Cont Ops	1,403,589	...	...	...	...	...	511,168	413,508
Net Income	1,533,560	791,996	383,996	465,017	500,831	501,464	507,895	408,716
Average Shs. Outstg.	463,335	474,519	490,200	493,065	489,474	510,198	548,823	586,017
Balance Sheet								
Securities Avail. for Sale	4,573,497	3,537,117	4,053,719	4,244,762	4,396,776	3,306,972	4,549,977	6,833,695
Net Loans & Leases	51,078,136	43,541,720	42,769,017	39,485,817	35,879,327	31,005,649	32,764,280	38,016,342
Total Assets	64,610,651	53,175,005	52,873,959	48,791,788	44,024,784	37,210,009	39,908,797	47,629,890
Long−Term Obligations	39,808,174	22,242,115	17,285,350	14,910,939	4,496,267	8,810,597	14,541,316	22,606,226
Total Liabilities	61,980,605	51,177,055	51,201,497	47,376,452	43,183,870	36,556,383	39,234,225	46,795,943
Net Stockholders' Equity	2,630,046	1,997,950	1,672,462	1,415,336	840,914	653,626	674,572	833,947
Shares Outstanding	447,678	457,740	466,485	492,434	472,729	492,381	550,899	689,802
Return on Equity %	53.36	39.64	22.95	32.85	59.55	76.72	75.77	49.58
Return on Assets %	2.17	1.48	0.72	0.95	1.13	1.34	1.28	0.86
Equity/Assets %	4.07	3.75	3.16	2.90	1.91	1.75	1.69	1.75
Non−Int. Exp./Tot. Inc. %	19.41	21.33	20.13	14.05	11.00	11.77	13.04	11.27
Price Range	42.64-33.85	35.63-26.38	29.13-19.37	22.67-9.44	17.87-13.37	17.00-9.33	15.60-8.56	9.31-6.07
P/E Ratio	14.16-11.24	21.73-16.09	38.33-25.49	24.64-10.26	17.52-13.11	17.35-9.52	16.77-9.20	13.30-8.67
Average Yield %	1.54	0.89	0.95	1.37	1.28	1.44	1.41	2.08

Address: 11600 Sallie Mae Drive, Reston, VA 20193	**Officers:** Edward A. Fox − Chmn., Thomas J. Fitzpatrick − Pres., C.O.O.	**Investor Contact:** 703−810−7751 **Institutional Holding**
Telephone: (703) 810−3000	**Transfer Agents:** The Bank of New York, New York, NY	**No of Institutions:** 25
Web Site: www.salliemae.com		**Shares:** 2,585,516 **% Held:** −

SMITH (A.O.) CORP

Exchange	Symbol	Price	52Wk Range	Yield	P/E
NYS	AOS	$29.45 (5/28/2004)	36.50-27.82	2.04	17.74

*7 Year Price Score 127.2 *NYSE Composite Index=100 ***12 Month Price Score 43.4**

Interim Earnings (Per Share)

Qtr.	Mar	Jun	Sep	Dec
2001	0.36	0.45	0.02	(0.22)
2002	0.50	0.66	0.34	0.36
2003	0.46	0.67	0.20	0.43
2004	0.36	...	...	...

Interim Dividends (Per Share)

Amt	Decl	Ex	Rec	Pay
0.15Q	7/8/2003	7/29/2003	7/31/2003	8/15/2003
0.15Q	10/7/2003	10/29/2003	10/31/2003	11/17/2003
0.15Q	1/15/2004	1/28/2004	1/30/2004	2/17/2004
0.15Q	4/6/2004	4/28/2004	4/30/2004	5/17/2004

Indicated Div: $0.60 (Div. Reinv. Plan)

Valuation Analysis

Forecast P/E 15.49 (5/24/2004)

Market Cap	$589.1 Million	Book Value	592.6 Million
Price/Book	1.01	Price/Sales	0.39

Dividend Achiever Status

Rank	285	10 Year Growth Rate	2.65%
Total Years of Dividend Growth			11

Business Summary: Electrical (MIC: 11.14 SIC: 3621 NAIC:335312)

A.O. Smith is a manufacturer of electric motors and water heating equipment serving residential, commercial and industrial end markets primarily in the United States. The Electric Products segment manufactures hermetic motors, fractional horsepower alternating current and direct current motors, and integral horsepower motors. The Water Systems segment manufactures and markets a line of residential gas and electric water heaters, standard and specialty commercial water heating equipment, high−efficiency copper−tube boilers, and water systems tanks. Co. operates manufacturing facilities in the United States, Canada, Mexico, England, Ireland, Hungary, the Netherlands and China.

Recent Developments: For the first quarter ended Mar 31 2004, net earnings declined 21.2% to $10.8 million versus $13.7 million in the prior−year quarter. Net sales increased 7.4% to $416.5 million from $387.9 million a year earlier. Electrical products segment sales rose 4.9% to $223.6 million, reflecting increased sales of electric motors in all of Co.'s served markets except heating, ventilation and air conditioning. Water Systems segment sales advanced 10.4% to $192.9 million, primarily due to the launch of new products to address regulatory standards changes in the U.S., as well as higher sales volume in China. Gross profit as a percentage of net earnings decreased to 18.8% from 20.2% the year before.

Prospects: Co. has announced price increases to help offset the higher steel costs that it is experiencing in both its electrical products and water systems businesses. The increased prices are scheduled take effect in the latter part of the second quarter of 2004. Separately, Co.'s water systems business is experiencing manufacturing inefficiencies, higher logistics costs and inventory adjustments as a result of multiple conversion programs. Consequently, Co. expects earnings for the second quarter of 2004 to range from $0.50 to $0.54 per share versus the $0.67 per share in the second quarter of 2003. For full−year 2004, Co. expects earnings to range from $1.90 to $2.00 per share.

Financial Data

(US$ in Thousands)	3 Mos	12/31/2003	12/31/2002	12/31/2001	12/31/2000	12/31/1999	12/31/1998	12/31/1997
Earnings Per Share	1.66	1.76	1.86	0.61	1.76	2.11	1.84	1.33
Cash Flow Per Share	(0.39)	0.85	4.05	2.08	3.23	2.00	3.20	2.84
Tang. Book Val. Per Share	9.55	9.07	6.95	6.30	8.64	7.69	10.93	10.68
Dividends Per Share	0.590	0.580	0.540	0.520	0.500	0.480	0.460	0.450
Dividend Payout %	35.54	32.95	29.03	85.24	28.40	22.74	25.36	34.00
Income Statement								
Total Revenues	416,500	1,530,700	1,469,100	1,151,156	1,247,945	1,039,281	917,569	832,937
Total Indirect Exp.	58,600	206,400	206,451	162,066	160,627	110,613	106,622	106,999
Depreciation & Amort.	13,300	200	282	6,956	6,932	37,315	31,173	26,286
Operating Income	19,600	92,300	93,309	40,275	87,497	96,299	80,404	63,711
Net Interest Inc./(Exp.)	(3,200)	(12,200)	(13,926)	(16,418)	(22,102)	(11,429)	(3,059)	1,273
Income Taxes	5,400	26,800	27,045	7,984	23,432	26,822	25,283	21,359
Income from Cont Ops	...	...	...	...	41,656	50,270	...	37,553
Net Income	10,800	52,200	51,345	14,502	29,753	42,422	44,491	153,830
Average Shs. Outstg.	29,912	29,710	27,649	23,914	23,691	23,787	24,184	28,191
Balance Sheet								
Cash & Cash Equivalents	8,100	18,700	32,847	20,759	15,287	14,761	37,666	145,896
Total Current Assets	596,500	547,700	488,251	477,574	406,099	388,627	287,389	365,728
Total Assets	1,327,300	1,279,900	1,224,857	1,293,923	1,059,176	1,063,986	767,432	716,516
Total Current Liabilities	373,200	338,600	261,679	255,950	170,431	168,440	132,157	127,882
Long−Term Obligations	167,900	170,100	239,084	390,385	316,372	351,251	131,203	100,972
Net Stockholders' Equity	592,600	576,200	511,052	451,878	448,395	431,084	401,093	399,705
Net Working Capital	223,300	209,100	226,572	221,624	235,668	220,187	155,232	237,846
Shares Outstanding	29,399	29,246	29,039	23,786	23,549	23,394	23,252	32,550
Operating Profit Margin %	4.70	6.02	6.35	3.49	7.01	9.26	8.76	7.64
Return on Equity %	1.82	9.05	10.04	3.20	9.29	11.66	11.09	9.39
Return on Assets %	0.81	4.07	4.19	1.12	3.93	4.72	5.79	5.24
Debt/Total Assets %	12.64	13.29	19.51	30.17	29.86	33.01	17.09	14.09
Price Range	35.49−28.50	36.50−23.80	32.10−19.15	20.00−14.68	22.63−11.75	31.94−19.00	35.88−15.94	28.58−19.33
P/E Ratio	21.38−17.17	20.74−13.52	17.26−10.30	32.79−24.07	12.86−6.68	15.14−9.00	19.50−8.66	21.49−14.54
Average Yield %	1.87	1.91	2.02	2.96	2.83	1.95	1.68	1.84

Address: P.O. Box 245008,	Officers: Robert J. OToole − Chmn., C.E.O., Paul	Investor Contact:14 359−4009)
Milwaukee, WI 53224−9508	W. Jones − Pres., C.O.O.	Institutional Holding
Telephone: (414) 359−4000	Transfer Agents:Wells Fargo Bank Minnesota,	No of Institutions: 137
Web Site: www.aosmith.com	N.A., St. Paul, MN	Shares: 17,692,136 % Held: 61%

SONOCO PRODUCTS CO.

Exchange	Symbol	Price	52Wk Range	Yield	P/E
NYS	SON	$24.90 (5/28/2004)	25.71-20.64	3.53	16.49

*7 Year Price Score 93.4 *NYSE Composite Index=100 ***12 Month Price Score 49.6**

Interim Earnings (Per Share)

Qtr.	Mar	Jun	Sep	Dec
2001	0.05	0.18	0.45	0.28
2002	0.35	0.39	0.30	0.35
2003	0.30	0.24	0.14	0.75
2004	0.38	...	...	...

Interim Dividends (Per Share)

Amt	Decl	Ex	Rec	Pay
0.21Q	7/16/2003	8/13/2003	8/15/2003	9/10/2003
0.21Q	10/14/2003	11/19/2003	11/21/2003	12/10/2003
0.21Q	2/4/2004	2/18/2004	2/20/2004	3/10/2004
0.22Q	4/21/2004	5/19/2004	5/21/2004	6/10/2004

Indicated Div: $0.88 (Div. Reinv. Plan)

Valuation Analysis

Forecast P/E 17.00 (5/24/2004)

Market Cap $2.4 Billion	Book Value 1.0 Billion
Price/Book 2.27	Price/Sales 0.85

Dividend Achiever Status

Rank	230	10 Year Growth Rate	6.23%
Total Years of Dividend Growth		20	

TRADING VOLUME (thousand shares)

Business Summary: Paper Products (MIC: 11.11 SIC: 2631 NAIC:322130)

Sonoco Products is a manufacturer of industrial and consumer packaging products and provider of packaging services, with 295 locations in 32 countries as of Dec 31 2003. Each of Co.'s operating units has its own sales staff and maintains direct sales relationships with its customers. The industrial packaging segment includes engineered carriers, paper, molded & extruded plastics, wire & cable reels, and protective packaging. The consumer packaging segment includes rigid packaging, closures, printed flexible packaging, packaging services & folding cartons, glass covers & coasters, and artwork management.

Recent Developments: For the quarter ended Mar 28 2004, net income surged 47.9% to $40.4 million compared with income of $27.3 million, before a discontinued operations gain of $1.7 million resulting from the sale of Co.'s High Density Film business in the corresponding period of the prior year. Results for 2004 and 2003 included restructuring charges of $1.3 million and $1.1 million, respectively. Net sales advanced 5.9% to $695.4 million, reflecting favorable foreign exchange and higher average selling prices for recovered paper trade sales, and volume improvements in packaging services and protective packaging.

Prospects: On Apr 29 2004, Co. announced that it has signed a definitive agreement to acquire privately held CorrFlex Graphics LLC, a point-of-purchase display company, for an all-cash purchase price of approximately $250.0 million. The CorrFlex acquisition, which is subject to regulatory approval, is expected to close by the end of the second quarter of 2004. This acquisition is expected to enhance Co.'s consumer segment strategy of being a total products and services provider in the markets it chooses to serve. Co. recently entered into two new separate joint venture agreements with producers in Finland and Italy.

Financial Data
(US$ in Thousands)

	3 Mos	12/31/2003	12/31/2002	12/31/2001	12/31/2000	12/31/1999	12/31/1998	12/31/1997
Earnings Per Share	1.51	1.43	1.39	0.96	1.66	1.83	1.84	...
Cash Flow Per Share	0.23	3.41	2.79	3.80	3.62	2.33	2.18	3.07
Tang. Book Val. Per Share	6.72	6.48	5.25	4.64	5.94	6.37	6.40	7.35
Dividends Per Share	0.840	0.840	0.830	0.800	0.790	0.750	0.700	0.640
Dividend Payout %	55.63	58.74	59.71	83.33	47.59	40.98	38.24	...
Income Statement								
Total Revenues	695,416	2,758,326	2,812,150	2,606,276	2,711,493	2,546,734	2,557,917	2,847,831
Total Indirect Exp.	71,823	339,895	301,320	320,232	277,693	252,917	100,902	750,155
Depreciation & Amort.	36,970	163,234	159,256	158,574	150,816	145,846	145,669	153,524
Operating Income	49,759	158,544	251,040	224,198	326,405	336,712	388,461	115,942
Net Interest Inc./(Exp.)	(8,748)	(50,211)	(52,547)	(48,417)	(55,810)	(47,152)	(48,863)	(52,223)
Income Taxes	5,425	37,698	70,614	82,958	111,999	108,585	153,989	60,111
Eqty Earns/Minority Int.	1,254	7,543	7,437	(1,214)	7,702	6,830	6,387	(991)
Income from Cont Ops	...	78,178	...	...	...	...	191,996	...
Net Income	36,840	138,949	135,316	91,609	166,298	187,805	180,243	2,617
Average Shs. Outstg.	98,181	97,129	97,178	95,807	99,900	102,780	104,275	97,591
Balance Sheet								
Cash & Cash Equivalents	80,398	84,854	31,405	36,130	35,219	36,515	57,249	53,600
Total Current Assets	815,198	755,265	663,267	665,169	695,793	723,081	661,416	873,040
Total Assets	2,565,489	2,520,633	2,390,094	2,352,197	2,212,611	2,297,020	2,082,983	2,176,865
Total Current Liabilities	689,783	679,594	600,027	460,270	437,080	416,631	436,069	434,144
Long-Term Obligations	469,513	473,220	699,346	885,961	812,085	819,540	686,826	696,669
Net Stockholders' Equity	1,038,777	1,014,160	867,425	804,122	801,471	901,220	821,592	848,819
Net Working Capital	125,415	75,671	63,240	204,899	258,713	306,450	225,347	438,896
Shares Outstanding	97,493	97,217	96,640	95,713	95,006	101,448	101,683	95,834
Operating Profit Margin %	7.15	5.74	8.92	8.60	12.03	13.35	19.10	4.07
Return on Equity %	3.54	7.70	15.59	11.39	20.74	21.22	35.58	0.30
Return on Assets %	1.43	3.10	5.66	3.89	7.51	8.32	14.03	0.12
Debt/Total Assets %	18.30	18.77	29.26	37.66	36.70	35.67	32.97	32.00
Price Range	25.15-23.00	24.74-19.58	29.50-19.98	26.45-19.66	23.38-16.81	29.18-20.88	36.78-21.49	30.13-20.92
P/E Ratio	16.66-15.23	17.30-13.69	21.22-14.37	27.55-20.48	14.08-10.13	15.95-11.41	19.99-11.68	N/A
Average Yield %	3.47	3.78	3.25	3.36	3.98	3.01	2.36	2.48

Address: One North Second Street, Hartsville, SC 29551-0160
Telephone: (843) 383-7000
Web Site: www.sonoco.com

Officers: Charles W. Coker - Chmn., Harris E. DeLoach - Pres., C.E.O.
Transfer Agents: EquiServe Trust Company, NA Providence, RI

Investor Contact: 843-383-7524
Institutional Holding
No of Institutions: 211
Shares: 47,928,315 **% Held:** 49.40%

SOUTHTRUST CORP.

Exchange	Symbol	Price	52Wk Range	Yield	P/E
NMS	SOTR	$33.82 (5/28/2004)	34.57-26.83	2.84	15.95

*7 Year Price Score 141.0 *NYSE Composite Index=100 *12 Month Price Score 48.9

Interim Earnings (Per Share)

Qtr.	Mar	Jun	Sep	Dec
2001	0.38	0.40	0.41	0.42
2002	0.44	0.45	0.47	0.49
2003	0.49	0.51	0.53	0.53
2004	0.55	...	...	...

Interim Dividends (Per Share)

Amt	Decl	Ex	Rec	Pay
0.21Q	7/16/2003	8/20/2003	8/22/2003	10/1/2003
0.21Q	10/15/2003	11/19/2003	11/21/2003	1/2/2004
0.24Q	1/21/2004	2/18/2004	2/20/2004	4/1/2004
0.24Q	4/21/2004	5/19/2004	5/21/2004	7/1/2004

Indicated Div: $0.96 (Div. Reinv. Plan)

Valuation Analysis

Forecast P/E 14.83 (5/24/2004)

Market Cap $11.7 Billion	Book Value 4.5 Billion
Price/Book 2.43	Price/Sales 3.65

Dividend Achiever Status

Rank 74	10 Year Growth Rate	15.33%
Total Years of Dividend Growth		33

TRADING VOLUME (thousand shares)

Business Summary: Commercial Banking (MIC: 8.1 SIC: 6021 NAIC:522110)

SouthTrust is a financial holding company. Co. is engaged, through its subsidiary bank, SouthTrust Bank, and its non-banking subsidiaries, in a full range of banking services from 717 banking locations in Alabama, Florida, Georgia, Mississippi, North Carolina, South Carolina, Tennessee, Texas and Virginia. Co. generates revenues from retail and commercial lending, depository services, cash management, and international and commercial leasing services. In addition, Co. provides trust, brokerage, investment, and insurance services. Consolidated total assets as of Dec 31 2003 amounted to $51.92 billion.

Recent Developments: For the three months ended Mar 31 2004, net income increased 6.8% to $183.0 million from $171.3 million in the corresponding prior-year period. Net interest income slipped 1.3% to $412.8 million from $418.1 million the year before. Provision for loan losses declined 6.4% to $27.5 million from $29.4 million the previous year. Non-interest income, excluding securities transactions, slid 0.5% to $163.4 million from $164.3 million a year earlier. Non-interest expense was down 4.3% to $285.4 million from $298.0 million in 2003. Total deposits amounted to $35.51 billion, up 9.9% compared with $32.31 billion the prior year.

Prospects: Earnings are benefiting from improved efficiencies stemming from Co.'s efforts to control expenses, as well as from technology investments to help improve customer service. In addition, results are being positively affected by strong credit quality and increased loan demand, especially in the commercial and real-estate construction segments, reflecting improving economic conditions. Meanwhile, non-interest income growth is being constrained by a decrease in mortgage banking income stemming from reduced refinancing activity due to higher interest rates. Separately, Co. anticipates completing its acquisition of FloridaFirst Bancorp, Inc. during the second quarter of 2004.

Financial Data

(US$ in Thousands)	3 Mos	12/31/2003	12/31/2002	12/31/2001	12/31/2000	12/31/1999	12/31/1998	12/31/1997
Earnings Per Share	2.12	2.06	1.85	1.61	1.43	1.31	1.12	1.01
Tang. Book Val. Per Share	11.22	10.78	11.03	9.19	8.19	6.74	6.36	7.14
Dividends Per Share	0.840	0.800	0.650	0.540	0.480	0.420	0.360	0.320
Dividend Payout %	39.44	38.83	35.13	33.85	33.91	32.31	32.74	31.85
Income Statement								
Total Interest Income	565,028	2,367,085	2,665,411	3,170,760	3,394,088	2,906,447	2,557,462	2,232,252
Total Interest Expense	155,070	713,776	960,327	1,642,658	2,008,351	1,539,538	1,386,256	1,186,079
Net Interest Income	409,958	1,653,309	1,705,084	1,528,102	1,385,737	1,366,909	1,171,206	1,046,173
Provision for Loan Losses	27,522	124,550	126,732	118,293	92,827	141,249	94,796	90,613
Non-Interest Income	152,148	679,712	660,996	571,029	505,683	443,557	386,094	270,507
Non-Interest Expense	285,354	1,179,849	1,276,851	1,153,368	1,087,196	1,010,501	914,443	748,216
Income Before Taxes	263,456	1,028,622	962,497	827,470	711,397	658,716	547,809	477,851
Income from Cont Ops	...	...	...	...	...	...	368,862	...
Net Income	182,957	705,186	649,871	554,468	482,330	443,173	368,610	306,708
Average Shs. Outstg.	335,251	342,498	350,937	345,294	337,812	337,556	328,296	302,016
Balance Sheet								
Cash & Due from Banks	1,393,577	1,061,502	1,005,327	1,159,236	959,750	874,999	970,778	877,885
Securities Avail. for Sale	11,290,620	11,493,045	10,700,990	10,062,158	7,049,966	5,130,509	3,875,933	2,975,830
Net Loans & Leases	35,390,879	34,778,985	33,739,078	32,939,475	30,945,808	31,255,498	26,939,981	22,159,314
Total Assets	52,672,916	51,924,888	50,570,856	48,754,548	45,146,531	43,262,512	38,133,774	30,906,445
Total Deposits	35,514,939	34,746,597	32,945,406	32,634,111	30,702,539	27,739,345	24,839,892	19,586,584
Long-Term Obligations	6,637,266	6,087,721	6,652,838	5,484,485	4,178,092	4,655,807	3,935,277	3,888,798
Total Liabilities	48,175,705	47,565,050	45,943,275	44,792,173	41,794,071	40,335,083	35,395,508	28,711,804
Net Stockholders' Equity	4,497,236	4,359,838	4,627,581	3,962,375	3,352,460	2,927,429	2,738,266	2,194,641
Shares Outstanding	329,820	330,242	346,924	346,272	338,106	335,810	334,422	307,328
Return on Equity %	4.06	16.17	14.04	13.99	14.38	15.13	13.47	13.97
Return on Assets %	0.34	1.35	1.28	1.13	1.06	1.02	0.96	0.99
Equity/Assets %	8.53	8.39	9.15	8.12	7.42	6.76	7.18	7.10
Non-Int. Exp./Tot. Inc. %	39.01	38.72	38.38	30.82	27.87	30.16	31.06	29.89
Price Range	34.57-31.49	32.75-24.70	27.50-20.84	26.90-19.56	20.34-10.50	21.31-16.47	22.47-14.19	21.15-11.50
P/E Ratio	16.31-14.85	15.90-11.99	14.86-11.26	16.71-12.15	14.23-7.34	16.27-12.57	20.06-12.67	20.94-11.39
Average Yield %	2.52	2.80	2.57	2.29	3.39	2.22	1.85	2.18

Address: 420 North 20th Street, Birmingham, AL 35203
Telephone: (205) 254 5000
Web Site: www.southtrust.com

Officers: Wallace D. Malone - Chmn., C.E.O., Thomas H. Coley - Vice-Chmn.
Transfer Agents: American Stock Transfer &Trust Company, New York, NY

Investor Contact: 205-254-5187
Institutional Holding
No of Institutions: 45
Shares: 2,741,676 **% Held:** -

244

THE ST PAUL TRAVELERS COMPANIES INC

Exchange	Symbol	Price	52Wk Range	Yield	P/E
NYS	STA	$40.01 (3/31/2004)	43.35–34.30	2.20	13.89

*7 Year Price Score N/A   *NYSE Composite Index=100   ***12 Month Price Score N/A**

TRADING VOLUME (thousand shares)

Interim Earnings (Per Share)
Qtr.	Mar	Jun	Sep	Dec
2001	0.90	0.41	(2.86)	(3.29)
2002	0.67	(1.07)	0.29	1.17
2003	0.75	0.89	0.98	0.26
2004	1.34	...	...	...

Interim Dividends (Per Share)
Amt	Decl	Ex	Rec	Pay
0.29Q	8/5/2003	9/26/2003	9/30/2003	10/17/2003
0.29Q	11/4/2003	12/29/2003	12/31/2003	1/16/2004
0.29Q	2/3/2004	3/29/2004	3/31/2004	4/16/2004
0.22Q	4/28/2004	6/8/2004	6/10/2004	6/30/2004

Indicated Div: $0.88

Valuation Analysis
Forecast P/E N/A
Market Cap $9.1 Billion	Book Value 6.2 Billion
Price/Book 1.47	Price/Sales 1.02

Dividend Achiever Status
Rank 244	10 Year Growth Rate 5.26%
Total Years of Dividend Growth	17

Business Summary: Insurance (MIC: 8.2 SIC: 6331 NAIC:524130)

St. Paul Companies is a management company principally engaged in two industry segments: commercial property–liability insurance and nonlife reinsurance products and services. Co. also has a presence in the asset management industry through its 77.0% majority ownership of Nuveen Investments, Inc. As a management company, Co. oversees the operations of its subsidiaries and provides those subsidiaries with capital, management and administrative services. The primary business of Co. is underwriting, which produced 95.4% of consolidated revenues in 2002.

Recent Developments: For the quarter ended Mar 31 2004, net income climbed 72.7% to $587.2 million from $340.0 million in the prior-year quarter. Results were fueled by higher premium rates and improved investment returns. Total revenues increased 14.6% to $4.13 billion from $3.60 billion the previous year. Revenues included net realized investment losses of $41.9 million in 2004 and realized investment gains of $6.5 million in 2003. Premiums increased 12.1% to $3.34 billion. Net investment income advanced 35.8% to $618.9 million, while fee income grew 26.5% to $172.4 million. Results for the prior year reflect Travelers Property Casualty Corp. only, as Travelers is treated as the accounting acquirer.

Prospects: On Apr 1 2004, Co. completed the acquisition of Travelers Property Casualty Corp. The combined company is now known as St. Paul Travelers. The combined company should benefit from considerable financial strength, depth and breadth of product offerings, strong distribution presence with enhanced geographic coverage across the U.S., greater efficiencies and economies of scale and enhanced growth opportunities, with greater diversity and stability of earnings. Going forward, Co. expects the combination of current rate levels and anticipated loss trends to continue to generate significant margins in all of Co.'s businesses.

Financial Data
(US$ in Thousands)	3 Mos	12/31/2003	12/31/2002	12/31/2001	12/31/2000	12/31/1999	12/31/1998	12/31/1997
Earnings Per Share	3.47	2.88	1.06	(4.84)	4.32	3.19	0.32	4.19
Tang. Book Val. Per Share	23.46	22.26	20.58	21.02	30.54	26.41	25.79	25.08
Dividends Per Share	1.160	1.160	1.150	1.110	1.070	1.030	0.980	0.920
Dividend Payout %	33.33	40.27	108.49	N.M.	24.76	32.28	307.81	22.05
Income Statement								
Total Premium Income	3,338,500	7,039,000	7,390,000	7,296,000	5,898,000	5,290,000	6,944,575	4,616,456
Net Investment Income	...	1,120,000	1,169,000	1,217,000	1,616,000	1,557,000	1,584,982	886,213
Other Income	789,000	695,000	359,000	430,000	1,094,000	722,000	578,844	716,604
Total Revenues	4,127,500	8,854,000	8,918,000	8,943,000	8,608,000	7,569,000	9,108,401	6,219,273
Total Indirect Exp.	1,065,600	1,266,000	1,184,000	1,306,000	1,306,000	1,140,000	1,624,758	833,749
Inc. Before Inc. Taxes	817,400	836,000	176,000	(1,431,000)	1,453,000	1,017,000	(46,287)	1,018,733
Income Taxes	226,600	137,000	(73,000)	(422,000)	440,000	238,000	(135,635)	245,510
Eqty Earns/Minority Int.	(3,600)	...	...	...	...	...	...	...
Income from Cont Ops	...	699,000	249,000	(1,009,000)	1,013,000	779,000	...	773,223
Net Income	587,200	661,000	218,000	(1,088,000)	993,000	834,000	89,348	705,473
Average Shs. Outstg.	437,200	240,000	227,000	212,000	233,000	246,000	238,682	184,522
Balance Sheet								
Cash & Cash Equivalents	139,700	150,000	315,000	151,000	83,000	210,000	226,668	152,863
Premiums Due	18,660,800	9,792,000	11,127,000	10,569,000	8,661,000	7,185,000	6,404,548	3,544,672
Invst. Assets: Total	39,062,200	20,471,000	20,581,000	20,025,000	25,835,000	24,879,000	26,240,231	14,766,281
Total Assets	65,069,900	39,563,000	39,920,000	38,321,000	41,075,000	38,873,000	38,322,708	21,500,657
Long–Term Obligations	2,675,100	3,750,000	2,713,000	2,130,000	1,647,000	1,466,000	1,260,392	782,825
Net Stockholders' Equity	12,673,800	6,225,000	4,857,000	4,221,000	6,890,000	6,047,000	6,133,687	4,419,710
Shares Outstanding	437,300	228,393	226,798	207,624	218,308	224,830	233,750	167,456
Statistical Record								
Return on Revenues %	13.34	7.89	2.79	N.M.	11.76	10.29	0.98	12.43
Return on Equity %	4.34	11.22	4.33	N.M	14.01	12.03	1.34	16.71
Return on Assets %	0.84	1.76	0.62	N.M.	2.46	2.00	0.23	3.59
Price Range	43.35–39.20	39.65–29.33	50.12–24.20	52.12–35.50	56.38–21.63	36.75–25.56	47.06–29.00	42.66–28.94
P/E Ratio	12.49–11.30	13.77–10.18	47.28–22.83	N/A	13.05–5.01	11.52–8.01	147.1–90.63	10.18–6.91
Average Yield %	2.80	3.30	2.99	2.41	2.71	3.23	2.49	2.48

Address: 385 Washington Street, Saint Paul, MN 55102 Telephone: (651) 310–7911 Web Site: www.stpaul.com	Officers: Jay S. Fishman – Chmn., Pres., C.E.O., John A. MacColl – Vice–Chmn., Gen. Couns. Transfer Agents:Wells Fargo Bank, Minnesota, N.A., St. Paul, MN	Institutional Holding No of Institutions: 405 Shares: 206,910,671 % Held: 90.80%

STANLEY WORKS (THE)

Exchange	Symbol	Price	52Wk Range	Yield	P/E
NYS	SWK	$43.55 (5/28/2004)	45.55-27.37	2.39	38.20

*7 Year Price Score 98.1   ***NYSE Composite Index=100**   ***12 Month Price Score 56.8**

Interim Earnings (Per Share)

Qtr.	Mar	Jun	Sep	Dec
2001	0.54	0.58	0.62	0.07
2002	0.56	0.72	0.62	0.20
2003-04	0.22	0.14	0.51	0.27
2004-05	0.70	...	...	...

Interim Dividends (Per Share)

Amt	Decl	Ex	Rec	Pay
0.26Q	7/15/2003	8/28/2003	9/2/2003	9/23/2003
0.26Q	10/15/2003	11/19/2003	11/21/2003	12/31/2003
0.26Q	1/23/2004	3/4/2004	3/8/2004	3/30/2004
0.26Q	4/23/2004	6/2/2004	6/4/2004	6/29/2004

Indicated Div: $1.04 (Div. Reinv. Plan)

Valuation Analysis

Forecast P/E 14.87 (5/24/2004)

Market Cap $3.7 Billion	Book Value	858.6 Million
Price/Book 3.56	Price/Sales	1.14

Dividend Achiever Status

Rank	263	10 Year Growth Rate		4.39%

Total Years of Dividend Growth   36

Business Summary: Metal Products (MIC: 11.4 SIC: 3423 NAIC:332212)

Stanley Works is a worldwide producer of tools and door products for professional, industrial and consumer use. The Tools segment manufactures and markets carpenters', mechanics', pneumatic and hydraulic tools as well as tool sets. The Doors segment manufactures and markets automatic doors as well as closet doors and systems, home decor, door locking systems, commercial and consumer hardware, security access control systems and patient monitoring devices. A substantial portion of Co.'s products are sold through home centers and mass merchant distribution channels in the U.S.

Recent Developments: For the first quarter ended Apr 3 2004, earnings from continuing operations more than tripled to $58.5 million compared with $19.0 million in the equivalent quarter of 2003. Results benefited from stronger demand from home center and mass merchant customers, improved industrial tool demand, higher revenues from security services and favorable currency translation. Results for 2003 included restructuring charges of $3.1 million. Results for 2004 and 2003 excluded earnings of $95.0 million and $200,000, respectively, from discontinued operations. Net sales rose 23.2% to $778.6 million from $632.2 million in the previous year. Operating profit was $106.9 million versus $45.6 million in 2003.

Prospects: Co. expects diluted earnings per share from continuing operations for the second quarter of 2004 to be between $0.63 to $0.67 versus $0.11 from the same period of 2003. Moreover, Co. expects diluted earnings per share from continuing operations for full-year 2004 to be between $2.75 to $2.85 versus $1.14 for full-year 2003. Also, Co. expects free cash flow from operations for full-year 2004 to approximate $250.0 million to $300.0 million. Separately, on Apr 9 2004, Co. completed the acquisition of Frisco Bay Industries, an international provider of security systems and equipment for financial institutions, government agencies and major industrial corporations.

Financial Data

(US$ in Thousands)	3 Mos	01/03/2004	12/28/2002	12/29/2001	12/30/2000	01/01/2000	01/02/1999	01/03/1998
Earnings Per Share	1.62	1.14	2.10	1.81	2.22	1.67	1.53	(0.47)
Cash Flow Per Share	0.62	5.47	3.23	2.53	2.69	2.47	0.62	2.69
Tang. Book Val. Per Share	1.19	2.64	5.05	9.59	8.46	8.07	7.31	6.56
Dividends Per Share	1.030	1.030	0.990	0.940	0.900	0.870	0.830	0.770
Dividend Payout %	35.69	90.35	47.14	51.93	40.54	52.09	54.24	N.M.
Income Statement								
Total Revenues	778,600	2,678,100	2,593,000	2,624,400	2,748,900	2,751,800	2,729,100	2,669,500
Total Indirect Exp.	216,700	691,000	547,200	666,100	656,600	681,700	684,700	866,200
Depreciation & Amort.	24,400	86,500	71,200	82,900	83,300	85,600	79,700	72,400
Operating Income	84,800	201,800	288,600	257,000	340,800	256,200	251,600	19,900
Net Interest Inc./(Exp.)	(8,000)	(28,300)	(24,500)	(25,600)	(27,100)	(27,900)	(23,100)	(16,600)
Income Taxes	26,300	36,300	87,500	78,400	99,300	80,800	77,600	23,300
Income from Cont Ops	58,500	96,700	...	...	...	...	...	...
Net Income	153,500	107,900	185,000	158,300	194,400	150,000	137,800	(41,900)
Average Shs. Outstg.	83,392	84,839	88,246	87,467	87,667	89,886	90,193	89,469
Balance Sheet								
Cash & Cash Equivalents	192,500	204,400	121,700	115,200	93,600	88,000	110,100	152,200
Total Current Assets	1,275,200	1,200,700	1,190,400	1,141,400	1,094,300	1,091,000	1,086,400	1,005,300
Total Assets	2,808,800	2,423,800	2,418,200	1,839,500	1,724,400	1,722,400	1,755,900	1,679,700
Total Current Liabilities	940,200	753,500	680,900	825,500	707,300	693,000	702,100	622,700
Long-Term Obligations	547,300	534,500	564,300	196,800	248,700	290,000	344,800	283,700
Net Stockholders' Equity	1,004,100	858,600	983,800	832,300	736,500	735,400	669,400	607,800
Net Working Capital	335,000	447,200	509,500	315,900	387,000	398,000	384,300	382,600
Shares Outstanding	81,659	81,276	86,835	84,658	85,188	88,945	88,772	88,788
Operating Profit Margin %	8.05	7.53	11.12	9.79	12.39	9.31	9.21	0.74
Net Profit Margin %	11.43	6.32	13.88	12.00	14.29	11.32	10.73	0.17
Return on Equity %	3.62	11.26	18.80	19.01	26.39	20.39	20.58	N.M.
Return on Assets %	1.29	3.98	7.65	8.60	11.27	8.70	7.84	N.M.
Debt/Total Assets %	19.48	22.05	23.33	10.69	14.42	16.83	19.63	16.88
Price Range	43.53-36.50	37.87-21.00	51.98-28.38	46.60-28.50	31.19-19.25	33.81-22.13	56.38-24.50	47.19-31.75
P/E Ratio	26.87-22.53	33.22-18.42	24.75-13.51	25.75-15.75	14.05-8.67	20.25-13.25	36.85-16.01	N/A
Average Yield %	2.65	3.57	2.48	2.46	3.45	3.08	2.01	1.87

Address: 1000 Stanley Drive, New Britain, CT 06053	**Officers:** John F. Lundgren – Chmn., C.E.O., James M. Loree – Exec. V.P., C.F.O.	**Investor Contact:**860-827-3833
Telephone: (860) 225 5111		**Institutional Holding**
	Transfer Agents: EquiServe Limited Partnership, Boston, MA	**No of Institutions:** 250
Web Site: www.stanleyworks.com		**Shares:** 55,218,112 **% Held:** 64.50%

STATE AUTO FINANCIAL CORP.

Exchange	Symbol	Price	52Wk Range	Yield	P/E
NMS	STFC	$30.75 (5/28/2004)	30.86–21.10	0.52	16.62

*7 Year Price Score 158.7   *NYSE Composite Index=100   ***12 Month Price Score 54.5**

Interim Earnings (Per Share)

Qtr.	Mar	Jun	Sep	Dec
2001	0.36	0.24	0.18	(0.26)
2002	0.33	(0.04)	0.15	0.49
2003	0.53	0.21	0.38	0.46
2004	0.80	...	...	...

Interim Dividends (Per Share)

Amt	Decl	Ex	Rec	Pay
0.04Q	8/15/2003	9/11/2003	9/15/2003	9/30/2003
0.04Q	11/21/2003	12/17/2003	12/19/2003	12/31/2003
0.04Q	3/5/2004	3/17/2004	3/19/2004	3/31/2004
0.04Q	5/28/2004	6/11/2004	6/15/2004	6/30/2004

Indicated Div: $0.16 (Div. Reinv. Plan)

Valuation Analysis

Forecast P/E 15.42 (5/24/2004)

Market Cap	$1.2 Billion	Book Value	586.3 Million
Price/Book	1.65	Price/Sales	0.91

Dividend Achiever Status

Rank	149	10 Year Growth Rate 10.22%
Total Years of Dividend Growth		12

Business Summary: Insurance (MIC: 8.2 SIC: 6331 NAIC:524126)

State Auto Financial, through its principal insurance subsidiaries, State Auto Property and Casualty Insurance, Milbank Insurance, Farmers Casualty Insurance and State Auto Insurance, provides personal and commercial insurance. Co.'s principal lines of business include personal and commercial auto, homeowners, commercial multi–peril, workers' compensation, general liability and fire insurance. As of Dec 31 2003, Co. marketed its products through about 22,400 independent insurance agents associated with 3,400 agencies in 26 states and the District of Columbia. Co.'s products are marketed primarily in the central and eastern U.S., excluding New York, New Jersey and the New England States.

Recent Developments: For the quarter ended Mar 31 2004, net income climbed 53.6% to $32.4 million from $21.1 million in the equivalent prior–year quarter. Total revenue grew 7.8% to $273.1 million from $253.3 million the previous year. Revenue for 2004 and 2003 included net realized investment gains of $5.4 million and $3.8 million, respectively. Net premiums written increased 6.9% to $252.8 million. Earned premiums rose 7.1% to $248.8 million from $232.4 million a year earlier. Net investment income improved 11.5% to $17.5 million. Co.'s combined ratio improved 5.6 percentage points to 89.6% from 95.2% the year before.

Prospects: Co. continues the trend of profitable results, with both the standard and nonstandard business segments contributing nicely to results for the first quarter of 2004. Moreover, Co. continues to improve the loss ratio of its homeowners line due to ongoing underwriting diligence and greater rate adequacy. These improvement in the homeowners line is also due to relatively light catastrophe loss experience and a reduction in large loss frequency. Going forward, Co.'s underwriting and cost–based pricing strategy, absent of any unusual catastrophe experience, should allow for solid results throughout 2004.

Financial Data

(US$ in Thousands)	3 Mos	12/31/2003	12/31/2002	12/31/2001	12/31/2000	12/31/1999	12/31/1998	12/31/1997
Earnings Per Share	1.85	1.58	0.93	0.52	1.21	1.03	0.87	0.91
Tang. Book Val. Per Share	14.76	13.70	11.89	10.22	9.95	8.22	8.06	6.14
Dividends Per Share	0.150	0.140	0.130	0.090	0.110	0.130	0.090	0.060
Dividend Payout %	8.11	9.17	14.24	17.78	9.50	12.62	10.63	6.86
Income Statement								
Total Premium Income	248,800	960,568	896,595	555,207	397,967	392,058	356,210	254,682
Other Income	24,300	81,128	70,884	68,065	64,807	48,813	45,849	34,326
Total Revenues	273,100	1,041,696	967,479	623,272	462,774	440,871	402,059	289,008
Total Indirect Exp.	8,600	291,823	264,348	167,207	119,569	111,772	104,224	74,213
Inc. Before Inc. Taxes	46,000	83,277	37,790	17,976	61,444	56,985	49,605	47,084
Income Taxes	13,600	19,655	795	(2,639)	13,730	14,169	12,108	13,125
Net Income	32,400	63,622	36,995	20,615	47,714	42,816	37,497	33,959
Average Shs. Outstg.	40,500	40,153	39,743	39,681	39,120	41,526	42,901	37,314
Balance Sheet								
Cash & Cash Equivalents	52,000	40,005	96,048	30,016	21,305	24,560	32,605	23,918
Premiums Due	15,600	14,474	23,035	15,468	9,335	10,807	22,667	12,050
Invst. Assets: Total	1,619,000	1,570,312	1,272,316	1,138,656	750,870	627,305	579,966	404,179
Total Assets	1,928,900	1,836,667	1,592,995	1,367,496	898,106	759,945	709,778	493,151
Long–Term Obligations	...	161,220	75,500	45,500	45,500	45,500	...	...
Net Stockholders' Equity	586,300	542,291	463,769	400,193	386,059	317,687	340,824	225,479
Shares Outstanding	39,700	39,559	39,001	38,937	38,554	38,321	42,027	36,684
Return on Revenues %	10.28	6.10	3.82	3.30	10.31	9.71	9.32	11.75
Return on Equity %	4.79	11.73	7.97	5.15	12.35	13.47	11.00	15.06
Return on Assets %	1.45	3.46	2.32	1.50	5.31	5.63	5.28	6.88
Price Range	25.81–22.68	26.82–15.33	17.19–13.10	17.67–12.50	18.00–7.19	13.81–8.88	19.88–11.63	16.13–8.38
P/E Ratio	13.95–12.26	16.97–9.70	18.48–14.09	33.98–24.04	14.88–5.94	13.41–8.62	22.84–13.36	17.72–9.20
Average Yield %	0.62	0.66	0.84	0.58	0.99	1.16	0.59	0.56

Address: 518 East Broad Street, Columbus, OH 43215–3976	**Officers:** Robert H. Moone – Chmn., Pres., C.E.O., Mark A. Blackburn – Sr. V.P.	**Investor Contact:**614–464–5373 **Institutional Holding**
Telephone: (614) 464–5000	**Transfer Agents:**National City Bank, Cleveland, OH	**No of Institutions:** 46
Web Site: www.stateauto.com		**Shares:** 4,818,652 **% Held:** 12%

STATE STREET CORP.

Exchange	Symbol	Price	52Wk Range	Yield	P/E
NYS	STT	$48.42 (5/28/2004)	56.37–38.85	1.24	19.45

*7 Year Price Score 114.0 *NYSE Composite Index=100 ***12 Month Price Score 46.7**

Interim Earnings (Per Share)

Qtr.	Mar	Jun	Sep	Dec
2001	0.36	0.50	0.51	0.53
2002	0.54	0.54	0.56	1.46
2003	0.29	(0.07)	0.60	1.33
2004	0.63	...	...	...

Interim Dividends (Per Share)

Amt	Decl	Ex	Rec	Pay
0.14Q	6/19/2003	6/27/2003	7/1/2003	7/15/2003
0.14Q	9/18/2003	9/29/2003	10/1/2003	10/15/2003
0.15Q	12/18/2003	12/30/2003	1/2/2004	1/15/2004
0.15Q	3/18/2004	3/30/2004	4/1/2004	4/15/2004

Indicated Div: $0.60 (Div. Reinv. Plan)

Valuation Analysis

Forecast P/E 17.71 (5/24/2004)

Market Cap $15.7 Billion	Book Value 5.9 Billion
Price/Book 2.96	Price/Sales 3.52

Dividend Achiever Status

Rank 70	10 Year Growth Rate	15.76%

Total Years of Dividend Growth 23

Business Summary: Commercial Banking (MIC: 8.1 SIC: 6022 NAIC:522110)

State Street, is a bank holding company with $87.53 billion in assets as of Dec 31 2003, that conducts business worldwide principally through its subsidiary, State Street Bank and Trust Company. Co. has two lines of business: investment servicing and investment management. Investment Servicing includes primarily accounting, custody and other services for large pools of assets. Investment management offers index and active equity strategies, short–term investment funds and fixed income products. As of Dec 31 2003, Co. had $1.10 trillion in assets under management.

Recent Developments: For the quarter ended Mar 31 2004, net income more then doubled to $217.0 million compared with $96.0 million in the corresponding period the year before. Results for 2004 and 2003 included pre–tax merger and integration costs of $18.0 million and $37.0 million, and net gains on the sales of available–for–sale investment securities of $3.0 million and $26.0 million, respectively. Total fee revenue grew 28.2% to $1.01 billion. Servicing fees rose 26.7% to $555.0 million and management fees grew 17.6% to $147.0 million. Net interest revenue slid 0.5% to $203.0 million, primarily due to a change in the applicable state tax rate. Total operating expenses increased 8.9% to $908.0 million.

Prospects: Co. continues to win a significant amount of new business, both from new clients and from clients with whom it has long–term relationships. Moreover, Co. is beginning to see additional large wins in its investment management outsourcing business and its equity execution business is growing at a very encouraging pace. Separately, Co. remains on schedule with the integration of the Global Securities Services business, which has strengthened its position in Europe. Looking ahead, Co. believes it is well positioned for 2004, based on its first–quarter operating performance.

Financial Data

(US$ in Thousands)	3 Mos	12/31/2003	12/31/2002	12/31/2001	12/31/2000	12/31/1999	12/31/1998	12/31/1997
Earnings Per Share	2.49	2.15	3.10	1.90	1.81	1.89	1.33	1.16
Tang. Book Val. Per Share	12.13	11.64	12.91	11.87	10.08	8.30	7.19	5.96
Dividends Per Share	0.560	0.540	0.460	0.390	0.330	0.290	0.250	0.210
Dividend Payout %	22.49	25.11	14.83	20.52	18.18	15.34	18.79	18.10
Income Statement								
Total Interest Income	384,000	1,539,000	1,974,000	2,855,000	3,256,000	2,437,000	2,237,000	1,755,000
Total Interest Expense	181,000	729,000	995,000	1,830,000	2,362,000	1,656,000	1,492,000	1,114,000
Net Interest Income	203,000	810,000	979,000	1,025,000	894,000	781,000	745,000	641,000
Provision for Loan Losses	...	...	4,000	10,000	9,000	14,000	17,000	16,000
Non–Interest Income	1,013,000	3,248,000	3,121,000	2,414,000	2,278,000	2,231,000	1,708,000	1,428,000
Non–Interest Expense	908,000	3,622,000	2,841,000	2,867,000	2,644,000	2,336,000	2,068,000	1,734,000
Income Before Taxes	311,000	1,112,000	1,555,000	930,000	906,000	968,000	657,000	564,000
Net Income	217,000	722,000	1,015,000	628,000	595,000	619,000	436,000	380,000
Average Shs. Outstg.	342,129	335,326	327,477	330,492	328,088	327,502	327,854	327,578
Balance Sheet								
Cash & Due from Banks	2,379,000	3,376,000	1,361,000	1,651,000	1,618,000	2,930,000	1,365,000	2,411,000
Securities Avail. for Sale	347,000	405,000	29,055,000	21,775,000	14,744,000	15,489,000	10,072,000	10,580,000
Net Loans & Leases	4,968,000	4,960,000	4,113,000	5,283,000	5,216,000	4,245,000	6,225,000	5,479,000
Total Assets	92,896,000	87,534,000	85,794,000	69,896,000	69,298,000	60,896,000	47,082,000	37,975,000
Total Deposits	53,512,000	47,516,000	45,468,000	38,559,000	37,937,000	34,145,000	27,539,000	24,878,000
Long–Term Obligations	2,244,000	2,222,000	1,270,000	1,217,000	1,219,000	921,000	922,000	774,000
Total Liabilities	86,954,000	81,787,000	81,007,000	66,051,000	66,036,000	58,244,000	44,771,000	35,980,000
Net Stockholders' Equity	5,942,000	5,747,000	4,787,000	3,845,000	3,262,000	2,652,000	2,311,000	1,995,000
Shares Outstanding	335,425	334,474	324,927	323,670	323,422	319,180	321,390	334,446
Statistical Record								
Return on Equity %	3.60	0.80	14.93	6.76	6.37	11.80	6.36	6.76
Return on Assets %	0.23	0.05	0.83	0.37	0.30	0.51	0.31	0.35
Equity/Assets %	6.39	6.56	5.57	5.50	4.70	4.35	4.90	5.25
Non–Int. Exp./Tot. Inc. %	64.99	75.66	55.76	54.41	47.77	50.04	52.42	54.47
Price Range	56.37–50.35	53.40–30.37	57.60–32.38	61.50–25.62	66.75–31.69	47.33–27.84	36.14–24.26	30.82–15.70
P/E Ratio	22.64–20.22	24.84–14.13	18.58–10.45	32.37–13.48	36.88–17.51	25.04–14.73	27.17–18.24	26.56–13.53
Average Yield %	1.05	1.28	1.00	0.78	0.63	0.78	0.79	0.89

Address: 225 Franklin Street, Boston, MA 02110 **Telephone:** (617) 786–3000 **Web Site:** www.statestreet.com	**Officers:** David A. Spina – Chmn., C.E.O, John R. Towers – Vice Chmn. **Transfer Agents:** EquiServe Trust Company, N.A., Providence, RI	**Investor Contact:** 617–664–3477 **Institutional Holding** **No of Institutions:** 5 **Shares:** 4,778,310 **% Held:** –

STEPAN CO.

Exchange	Symbol	Price	52Wk Range	Yield	P/E
NYS	SCL	$24.25 (5/28/2004)	26.11–21.70	3.18	37.89

*7 Year Price Score 96.2   *NYSE Composite Index=100   *12 Month Price Score 46.6

TRADING VOLUME (thousand shares)

Interim Earnings (Per Share)

Qtr.	Mar	Jun	Sep	Dec
2001	0.36	0.61	0.44	0.18
2002	0.45	0.84	0.58	0.18
2003	0.23	0.49	0.12	(0.39)
2004	0.42	...	...	...

Interim Dividends (Per Share)

Amt	Decl	Ex	Rec	Pay
0.19Q	8/12/2003	8/27/2003	8/29/2003	9/15/2003
0.193Q	11/10/2003	11/25/2003	11/28/2003	12/15/2003
0.193Q	2/10/2004	2/25/2004	2/27/2004	3/15/2004
0.193Q	4/27/2004	5/26/2004	5/28/2004	6/15/2004
		Indicated Div: $0.77		

Valuation Analysis

Forecast P/E N/A

Market Cap $214.9 Million	Book Value 151.2 Million
Price/Book 1.33	Price/Sales 0.26

Dividend Achiever Status

Rank	226	10 Year Growth Rate	6.53%
Total Years of Dividend Growth			37

Business Summary: Chemicals (MIC: 11.1 SIC: 2843 NAIC:325613)

Stepan Company produces specialty and intermediate chemicals. Co. operates in three segments: surfactants, polymers, and specialty products. Surfactants are a principal ingredient in cleaning products such as detergents, shampoos, lotions, toothpastes and cosmetics. Other applications include lubricating ingredients and emulsifiers for agricultural products, plastics and composites. Polymer products include phthalic anhydride, polyols and polyurethane foam systems, which are used in plastics, building materials and refrigeration industries, as well as for coating adhesive, sealant and elastomer applications. Specialty products include chemicals used in food, flavoring and pharmaceuticals.

Recent Developments: For the first quarter ended Mar 31 2004, net income advanced 76.1% to $4.0 million versus $2.3 million in the prior–year quarter. Earnings in 2004 benefited from improved sales mix from higher–margin specialty products. Earnings improved in the Surfactant, Polymer and Specialty products segments. Net sales increased 18.3% to $221.4 million from $187.1 million a year earlier primarily due to an overall increase in sales volume, higher selling prices due to increased raw material costs and a favorable currency translation effect. Gross profit climbed 18.1% to $29.7 million from $25.1 million the year before. Operating income jumped 63.7% to $8.0 million from $4.9 million in the previous year.

Prospects: Co. recently entered into a joint venture agreement with Sinopec, Jinling Petrochemical Corporation in Nanjing, China to manufacture aromatic polyester polyols for the domestic Chinese market. Separately, Co. is optimistic that the overall economy is improving and that opportunities exist for additional growth of its businesses in 2004. Surfactant volume in Europe is strong and benefiting from higher value–added products in North America. Meanwhile, Polymers are well–positioned for improved volume and earnings in 2004. However, as a result of increasing raw material costs, Co. has increased surfactant and polymer prices effective Apr 1 2004.

Financial Data

(US$ in Thousands)	3 Mos	12/31/2003	12/31/2002	12/31/2001	12/31/2000	12/31/1999	12/31/1998	12/31/1997
Earnings Per Share	0.64	0.45	2.05	1.59	1.47	2.08	2.12	1.86
Cash Flow Per Share	(0.62)	5.01	4.69	5.28	5.22	4.76	5.32	5.73
Tang. Book Val. Per Share	14.73	14.31	13.98	15.40	15.46	14.28	13.24	12.16
Dividends Per Share	0.760	0.760	0.730	0.700	0.660	0.610	0.560	0.510
Dividend Payout %	121.43	169.44	35.97	44.49	45.06	29.44	26.53	27.55
Income Statement								
Total Revenues	221,387	784,855	748,539	711,517	698,937	666,784	610,451	581,949
Total Indirect Exp.	21,649	93,943	88,596	76,004	79,998	79,167	66,172	59,801
Depreciation & Amort.	10,105	41,426	40,117	39,972	39,277	39,452	37,347	35,281
Operating Income	8,003	9,796	33,930	31,225	32,028	41,778	45,423	44,370
Net Interest Inc./(Exp.)	(2,061)	(8,061)	(7,388)	(7,168)	(8,328)	(8,376)	(7,453)	(7,595)
Income Taxes	1,896	360	10,139	9,774	9,395	12,700	15,312	14,464
Net Income	4,030	4,911	20,129	16,152	15,008	22,129	23,454	20,410
Average Shs. Outstg.	9,698	9,086	9,802	10,133	10,236	10,632	11,043	10,959
Balance Sheet								
Cash & Cash Equivalents	3,188	4,235	3,188	4,224	3,536	3,969	983	5,507
Total Current Assets	233,327	204,460	185,112	185,194	177,213	166,660	149,758	146,482
Total Assets	490,111	464,217	439,667	435,488	415,049	414,576	404,361	374,936
Total Current Liabilities	138,965	132,939	105,017	109,730	108,341	98,045	87,944	82,693
Long–Term Obligations	112,002	92,004	104,304	109,588	96,466	107,420	107,708	94,898
Net Stockholders' Equity	165,767	162,067	158,829	159,729	154,176	155,064	147,984	137,598
Shares Outstanding	8,949	8,933	8,880	9,420	9,024	9,487	9,693	9,692
Statistical Record								
Operating Profit Margin %	3.61	1.24	4.53	4.38	4.58	6.26	7.44	7.62
Return on Equity %	2.43	3.03	12.67	10.11	9.73	14.27	15.84	14.83
Return on Assets %	0.82	1.05	4.57	3.70	3.61	5.33	5.80	5.44
Debt/Total Assets %	22.85	19.81	23.72	25.16	23.24	25.91	26.63	25.31
Price Range	26.11–21.70	26.80–21.55	29.21–23.55	26.38–17.80	25.00–18.50	26.63–22.25	32.13–23.13	32.25–18.00
P/E Ratio	40.80–33.91	59.56–47.89	14.25–11.49	16.59–11.19	17.01–12.59	12.80–10.70	15.15–10.91	17.34–9.68
Average Yield %	3.12	3.11	2.75	3.02	3.06	2.52	1.97	2.20

Address: Edens &Winnetka Road, Northfield, IL 60093 Telephone: (847) 446–7500 Web Site: www.stepan.com	Officers: F. Quinn Stepan – Chmn., C.E.O., F. Quinn Stepan – Pres., C.O.O. Transfer Agents:Computershare Investor Services, LLC, Chicago, IL	Investor Contact:847–501–2164 Institutional Holding No of Institutions: 43 Shares: 3,082,934 % Held: 34.30%

STERLING BANCSHARES, INC.

Exchange	Symbol	Price	52Wk Range	Yield	P/E
NMS	SBIB	$13.13 (5/28/2004)	14.22–11.12	1.52	23.87

*7 Year Price Score 115.8 *NYSE Composite Index=100 *12 Month Price Score 47.3

Interim Earnings (Per Share)

Qtr.	Mar	Jun	Sep	Dec
2001	0.16	0.19	0.18	0.18
2002	0.19	0.21	0.18	0.24
2003	0.21	0.14	0.17	0.12
2004	0.12	...	...	...

Interim Dividends (Per Share)

Amt	Decl	Ex	Rec	Pay
0.045Q	7/29/2003	8/6/2003	8/8/2003	8/22/2003
0.045Q	10/27/2003	11/5/2003	11/7/2003	11/21/2003
0.05Q	1/26/2004	2/4/2004	2/6/2004	2/20/2004
0.05Q	4/26/2004	5/5/2004	5/7/2004	5/21/2004

Indicated Div: $0.20

Valuation Analysis

Forecast P/E N/A
Market Cap $576.2 Million   Book Value 292.6 Million
Price/Book 2.08   Price/Sales 3.03

Dividend Achiever Status

Rank   47   10 Year Growth Rate   17.61%
Total Years of Dividend Growth   10

Business Summary: Commercial Banking (MIC: 8.1 SIC: 6022 NAIC:522110)

Sterling Bancshares is a bank holding company that provides commercial and retail banking services primarily in the Houston, Dallas and San Antonio metropolitan areas through the banking offices of Sterling Bank. Co.'s commercial and consumer banking services include demand, savings and time deposits; commercial, real estate and consumer loans; merchant credit card services; letters of credit; and cash and asset management services. In addition, Co. facilitates sales of brokerage, mutual fund, alternative financing and insurance products through third party vendors. As of Dec 31 2003, Co. had total assets of $3.20 billion and deposits of $2.42 billion.

Recent Developments: For the quarter ended Mar 31 2004, Co. reported net income of $5.2 million compared with income from continuing operations of $9.5 million in the corresponding period the year before. Earnings for 2003 included a net gain of $3.4 million on the sale of banking offices and excluded a gain of $1.7 million from discontinued operations. Net interest income declined 7.0% to $33.0 million from $35.5 million the previous year. Provision for credit losses was $3.5 million versus $4.5 million in 2003. Total noninterest income fell 36.0% to $7.2 million, while total noninterest expense rose 3.5% to $29.1 million.

Prospects: Co. continues to focus on improving its asset quality as non–performing asset measures are in–line with its expectations and are moving to an acceptable level. As a result, Co.can aim its efforts toward loan growth, the further development of its new and existing customer base, as well as the redeployment of its capital. Separately, Co. recently completed the integration of the acquired assets of South Texas Capital Group, expanding its franchise in the San Antonio market to eight offices. This is part of Co.'s strategy to grow within the greater Houston, Dallas, and San Antonio, TX area. Looking ahead, Co. is encouraged by an improving economy and hopes to further grow its assets.

Financial Data

(US$ in Thousands)	12/31/2003	12/31/2002	12/31/2001	12/31/2000	12/31/1999	12/31/1998	12/31/1997	12/31/1996
Earnings Per Share	0.64	0.82	0.71	0.66	0.54	0.47	0.40	0.38
Tang. Book Val. Per Share	5.09	3.67	3.26	3.89	3.28	2.94	2.52	3.20
Dividends Per Share	0.180	0.160	0.140	0.130	0.120	0.100	0.090	0.080
Dividend Payout %	28.12	19.51	20.66	19.99	22.22	22.53	24.04	21.70
Income Statement								
Total Interest Income	171,383	176,391	173,053	156,430	123,621	103,031	79,268	53,413
Total Interest Expense	26,769	29,719	50,052	58,109	35,132	29,681	24,785	16,727
Net Interest Income	144,614	146,672	123,001	98,321	88,489	73,350	54,483	36,686
Provision for Loan Losses	17,698	14,018	11,684	9,100	8,643	5,892	2,945	2,113
Non–Interest Income	29,561	94,510	66,171	39,567	29,268	20,086	9,419	7,648
Non–Interest Expense	117,603	172,352	130,677	89,927	78,026	62,344	41,618	27,134
Income Before Taxes	42,391	54,812	46,811	38,861	31,088	25,695	19,659	15,403
Eqty Earns/Minority Int.	6,188	6,758	6,989	3,420	3,020	3,467	1,839	316
Income from Cont Ops	28,354	36,673	...	...	...	...	...	10,924
Net Income	49,110	36,551	30,401	26,580	21,423	17,304	13,083	10,654
Average Shs. Outstg.	44,648	44,756	43,044	39,832	39,505	36,484	32,407	27,765
Balance Sheet								
Cash & Due from Banks	136,764	139,209	148,295	108,172	91,139	136,089	110,479	78,442
Securities Avail. for Sale	522,936	251,165	276,804	238,117	399,961	123,328	97,088	4,170
Net Loans & Leases	2,126,317	1,882,944	1,643,861	1,213,288	1,111,390	851,790	660,541	450,120
Total Assets	3,204,405	3,582,745	2,778,090	1,925,131	1,959,480	1,416,312	1,182,877	790,073
Total Deposits	2,418,369	2,532,902	2,268,980	1,577,735	1,415,551	1,251,685	1,022,220	717,413
Long–Term Obligations	46,533	...	...	...	...	...	...	...
Total Liabilities	2,831,809	3,253,418	2,503,221	1,737,247	1,796,187	1,276,053	1,074,143	730,666
Net Stockholders' Equity	212,596	169,327	159,869	130,384	105,793	82,759	51,234	59,407
Shares Outstanding	44,642	43,982	43,769	39,345	39,045	35,814	30,960	17,923
Return on Equity %	9.69	14.70	19.01	20.38	20.24	20.90	25.53	18.38
Return on Assets %	0.88	1.02	1.09	1.38	1.09	1.22	1.10	1.38
Equity/Assets %	9.13	6.95	7.82	8.26	6.86	7.87	6.76	7.51
Non–Int. Exp./Tot. Inc. %	57.51	63.62	54.62	54.62	51.03	50.43	46.75	44.20
Price Range	14.00–11.12	15.30–10.60	16.15–10.83	13.42–5.81	10.04–6.83	12.17–7.96	9.78–5.43	5.59–3.33
P/E Ratio	21.88–17.38	18.66–12.93	22.74–15.26	20.33–8.81	18.60–12.65	25.89–16.93	24.44–13.56	14.72–8.77
Average Yield %	1.46	1.21	1.12	1.54	1.46	0.99	1.19	1.86

Address: 2550 North Loop West, Houston, TX 77092	**Officers:** George Martinez – Chmn., J. Downey Bridgwater – Pres., C.E.O.	**Investor Contact:**888–577–7242 **Institutional Holding**
Telephone: (713) 466–8300	**Transfer Agents:**American Stock Transfer &Trust Company, New York, NY	**No of Institutions:** 4
Web Site: N/A		**Shares:** 132,464 **% Held:** –

STERLING FINANCIAL CORP. (PA)

Exchange	Symbol	Price	52Wk Range	Yield	P/E
NMS	SLFI	$25.19 (5/28/2004)	28.95–18.48	2.38	18.66

*7 Year Price Score 130.4 *NYSE Composite Index=100 ***12 Month Price Score 51.0**

TRADING VOLUME (thousand shares)

Interim Earnings (Per Share)

Qtr.	Mar	Jun	Sep	Dec
2001	0.24	0.26	0.25	0.28
2002	0.27	0.28	0.29	0.33
2003	0.31	0.32	0.35	0.37
2004	0.35	...	...	...

Interim Dividends (Per Share)

Amt	Decl	Ex	Rec	Pay
0.144Q	11/18/2003	12/11/2003	12/15/2003	1/2/2004
25%	1/27/2004	2/23/2004	2/6/2004	2/20/2004
0.15Q	2/24/2004	3/11/2004	3/15/2004	4/1/2004
0.15Q	5/24/2004	6/11/2004	6/15/2004	7/1/2004

Indicated Div: $0.60 (Div. Reinv. Plan)

Valuation Analysis

Forecast P/E 16.11 (5/24/2004)
Market Cap $425.1 Million   Book Value 220.0 Million
Price/Book 2.24   Price/Sales 2.78

Dividend Achiever Status

Rank	179	10 Year Growth Rate	8.94%
Total Years of Dividend Growth			16

Business Summary: Commercial Banking (MIC: 8.1 SIC: 6021 NAIC:522110)

Sterling Financial is a multi-bank financial holding company with $2.34 billion in assets as of Dec 31 2003. Co. provides a broad range of financial services to individuals and businesses through its banking and nonbanking subsidiaries, including personal and business banking, leasing, insurance and wealth management. As of Dec 31 2003, Co. operated 57 branch banking offices in south central Pennsylvania and northern Maryland through its subsidiary banks, Bank of Lancaster County, N.A., Bank of Hanover and Trust Company, and First National Bank of North East.

Recent Developments: For the three months ended Mar 31 2004, net income climbed 15.2% to $7.6 million from $6.6 million in the corresponding prior-year period. Results included securities gains of $517,000 and $4,000 in 2004 and 2003, respectively. Net interest income advanced 9.7% to $22.6 million from $20.6 million the previous year. Provision for loan losses totaled $714,000, down 31.0% compared with $1.0 million a year earlier. Non-interest income grew 15.5% to $13.2 million from $11.4 million the year before. Non-interest expense rose 14.0% to $25.0 million from $21.9 million in 2003.

Prospects: Results are being positively affected by sharply higher trust and investment management income and brokerage fees and commissions, which is being driven by the acquisitions of Church Capital Management LLC and Bainbridge Securities, Inc. in the fourth quarter of 2003. Meanwhile, Co. is taking steps to expand into new geographic regions such as Berks County, PA, Carroll County, MD, and New Castle County, DE. Separately, Co. is experiencing higher expenses stemming from its market expansion and from new and enhanced financial services products that are being offered to customers, including brokerage services and registered investment advisor consultation.

Financial Data

(US$ in Thousands)	12/31/2003	12/31/2002	12/31/2001	12/31/2000	12/31/1999	12/31/1998	12/31/1997	12/31/1996
Earnings Per Share	1.35	1.17	1.03	0.84	0.94	0.91	0.81	0.76
Tang. Book Val. Per Share	8.49	8.44	7.78	7.10	6.45	6.46	5.86	5.42
Dividends Per Share	0.550	0.520	0.490	0.470	0.450	0.410	0.390	0.330
Dividend Payout %	40.88	44.21	47.53	56.43	47.56	45.27	48.21	43.42
Income Statement								
Total Interest Income	127,074	123,591	115,916	113,319	67,714	60,066	56,499	52,558
Total Interest Expense	41,156	48,617	57,274	58,501	29,797	27,925	25,326	22,823
Net Interest Income	85,918	74,974	58,642	54,818	37,917	32,141	31,173	29,735
Provision for Loan Losses	3,697	2,095	1,217	605	420	896	1,129	580
Non-Interest Income	49,721	44,806	43,925	37,508	29,497	14,187	11,930	10,572
Non-Interest Expense	92,568	85,922	75,172	70,203	48,831	30,188	28,082	26,769
Income Before Taxes	39,374	31,763	26,178	21,518	18,163	15,244	13,892	12,958
Net Income	29,059	24,745	20,334	16,567	13,239	11,601	10,401	9,811
Average Shs. Outstg.	21,448	21,028	19,656	19,619	13,960	12,652	12,727	12,786
Balance Sheet								
Cash & Due from Banks	64,996	82,208	68,926	61,287	47,674	34,089	34,292	31,339
Securities Avail. for Sale	540,049	551,696	490,955	435,296	207,183	177,878	121,474	79,375
Net Loans & Leases	1,481,369	1,283,075	1,087,102	1,021,499	654,834	526,591	503,907	466,032
Total Assets	2,343,517	2,156,309	1,861,439	1,726,138	1,059,374	919,264	845,488	764,072
Total Deposits	1,778,587	1,702,302	1,535,649	1,420,300	892,432	781,383	718,661	647,036
Long-Term Obligations	195,762	155,478	121,093	113,850	34,291	...	...	...
Total Liabilities	2,123,506	1,959,476	1,709,328	1,586,791	969,356	837,951	771,501	694,893
Net Stockholders' Equity	220,011	196,833	152,111	139,347	90,018	81,313	73,987	69,179
Shares Outstanding	21,717	21,125	19,549	19,603	13,955	12,578	12,612	12,755
Return on Equity %	13.20	12.57	13.36	11.88	14.70	14.26	14.05	14.18
Return on Assets %	1.24	1.14	1.09	0.95	1.24	1.26	1.23	1.28
Equity/Assets %	9.38	9.12	8.17	8.07	8.49	8.84	8.75	9.05
Non–Int. Exp./Tot. Inc. %	52.35	51.02	47.02	46.54	50.23	40.65	41.03	42.40
Price Range	23.54–17.38	21.44–14.40	16.19–9.68	19.84–9.04	23.17–15.87	26.50–15.24	15.60–12.19	13.93–11.64
P/E Ratio	17.44–12.88	18.32–12.31	15.72–9.40	23.62–10.76	24.65–16.89	29.12–16.75	19.26–15.05	18.33–15.32
Average Yield %	2.72	2.88	3.60	4.10	2.47	2.07	3.08	2.62

Address: 101 North Pointe Boulevard, Lancaster, PA 17601–4133	Officers: John E. Stefan – Chmn., J. Roger Moyer – Pres., C.E.O.	Investor Contact:717–735–5602
Telephone: (717) 581–6030	Transfer Agents:American Stock Transfer and Trust Company, New York, NY	Institutional Holding
Web Site: www.sterlingfi.com		No of Institutions: 12
		Shares: 219,830 % Held: –

STRYKER CORP.

Exchange	Symbol	Price	52Wk Range	Yield	P/E
NYS	SYK	$50.85 (5/28/2004)	51.38–33.67	0.14	54.68

*7 Year Price Score 177.9 *NYSE Composite Index=100 *12 Month Price Score 57.3

Interim Earnings (Per Share)

Qtr.	Mar	Jun	Sep	Dec
2001	0.32	0.32	0.30	(0.27)
2002	0.40	0.42	0.36	(0.33)
2003	0.51	0.53	0.53	(0.46)
2004	0.33	...	...	...

Interim Dividends (Per Share)

Amt	Decl	Ex	Rec	Pay
0.05A	12/21/2001	12/27/2001	12/31/2001	1/31/2002
0.06A	12/3/2002	12/27/2002	12/31/2002	1/31/2003
0.07A	12/2/2003	12/29/2003	12/31/2003	1/30/2004
2-for-1	4/21/2004	5/17/2004	5/3/2004	5/14/2004

Indicated Div: $0.07

Valuation Analysis

Forecast P/E 36.24 (5/24/2004)

Market Cap $10.0 Billion		Book Value 2.3 Billion	
Price/Book 7.76		Price/Sales 4.65	

Dividend Achiever Status

Rank	18	10 Year Growth Rate	23.11%
Total Years of Dividend Growth		11	

Business Summary: Medical Instruments &Equipment (MIC: 9.6 SIC: 3841 NAIC:339112)

Stryker develops, manufactures and markets specialty surgical and medical products. Operations are divided into two reportable business segments: Orthopaedic Implants and MedSurg Equipment. The Orthopaedic Implants segment includes orthopaedic reconstructive (hip, knee and shoulder), trauma and spinal implants, bone cement and the bone growth factor osteogenic protein−1. The MedSurg Equipment segment includes powered surgical instruments, endoscopic products, hospital beds and stretchers and micro implant and surgical navigation systems. Co. also provides outpatient physical and occupational rehabilitative services in the U.S.

Recent Developments: For the three months ended Mar 31 2004, net income advanced 30.5% to $135.9 million compared with $104.1 million in the corresponding quarter of the previous year. Net sales increased 22.2% to $1.04 billion. Sales of Orthopaedic Implants improved 23.4% to $633.1 million the year before, due to higher shipments of reconstructive, trauma, spine and micro implant systems and bone cement. Sales of MedSurg Equipment jumped 21.3% to $341.6 million, reflecting higher shipments of powered surgical instruments and endoscopic products. Sales of Physical Therapy Services climbed 16.2% to $60.4 million, due to higher revenue from existing physical therapy centers and new centers.

Prospects: Co. continues to be optimistic regarding the markets it participates in and the underlying growth rates in orthopaedic procedures. Meanwhile, Co. expects diluted net earnings for 2004 to be $1.40 per share. The estimate for 2004 includes net sales growth of approximately 18.0% as a result of strong growth in shipments of Orthopaedic Implants and MedSurg Equipment, favorable foreign currency exchange rate movements and higher revenue from Physical Therapy Services. Moreover, Co. anticipates a favorable impact on net sales in the second quarter and full−year 2004 of approximately $30.0 million and $110.0 million, respectively, if foreign currency exchange rates hold at current levels.

Financial Data

(US$ in Thousands)	3 Mos	12/31/2003	12/31/2002	12/31/2001	12/31/2000	12/31/1999	12/31/1998	12/31/1997
Earnings Per Share	0.93	1.11	0.85	0.67	0.55	0.05	0.10	0.32
Cash Flow Per Share	0.14	1.59	1.23	1.15	0.82	0.71	0.39	0.23
Tang. Book Val. Per Share	3.33	2.97	1.42	0.64	0.03	N.M	N.M	1.47
Dividends Per Share	0.070	0.060	0.050	0.040	0.033	0.030	0.027	0.025
Dividend Payout %	7.49	2.69	2.94	2.98	2.95	30.00	13.75	3.90
Income Statement								
Total Revenues	1,035,100	3,625,300	3,011,600	2,602,300	2,289,400	2,103,700	1,103,208	980,135
Total Indirect Exp.	473,700	1,641,600	1,352,900	1,166,500	1,041,500	966,400	575,509	398,395
Depreciation & Amort.	12,800	45,400	28,900	38,400	34,700	33,900	37,596	33,264
Operating Income	193,200	716,700	576,400	510,400	467,400	181,500	55,626	183,974
Net Interest Inc./(Exp.)	(1,400)	(22,600)	(40,300)	(67,900)	(96,600)	(122,600)	...	...
Income Taxes	58,200	199,000	161,100	133,900	113,900	10,400	20,390	70,000
Income from Cont Ops	...	...	...	271,800	...	...	...	...
Net Income	135,900	453,500	345,600	267,000	221,000	19,400	39,570	125,320
Average Shs. Outstg.	409,100	406,800	407,600	406,000	402,200	397,200	392,520	392,528
Balance Sheet								
Cash & Cash Equivalents	48,900	65,900	37,800	50,100	54,000	80,000	124,951	154,027
Total Current Assets	1,458,500	1,397,600	1,151,300	993,100	997,000	1,110,400	1,311,843	756,608
Total Assets	3,231,700	3,159,100	2,815,500	2,423,600	2,430,800	2,580,500	2,885,852	985,075
Total Current Liabilities	798,300	850,500	707,500	533,400	617,400	669,600	699,455	303,011
Long−Term Obligations	5,400	18,800	491,000	720,900	876,500	1,181,100	1,487,971	4,449
Net Stockholders' Equity	2,287,900	2,154,800	1,498,200	1,056,200	854,900	671,500	652,075	612,775
Net Working Capital	660,200	547,100	443,800	459,700	379,600	440,800	612,388	453,597
Shares Outstanding	400,200	399,400	396,200	393,400	391,800	388,800	386,160	384,236
Operating Profit Margin %	18.66	19.76	19.13	19.61	20.41	8.62	5.04	18.77
Return on Equity %	5.93	21.04	23.06	25.73	25.85	2.88	6.06	20.45
Return on Assets %	4.20	14.35	12.27	11.21	9.09	0.75	1.37	12.72
Debt/Total Assets %	0.16	0.59	17.43	29.74	36.05	45.77	51.56	0.45
Price Range	46.69–42.08	42.45–30.21	33.62–22.23	30.75–22.00	27.75–13.19	17.89–11.17	13.38–7.81	11.10–6.16
P/E Ratio	50.20–45.25	38.24–27.21	39.55–26.15	45.90–32.84	50.45–23.98	357.8–223.4	133.8–78.10	34.67–19.23
Average Yield %	0.16	0.17	0.17	0.15	0.15	0.21	0.20	0.23

Address: 2725 Fairfield Road, Kalamazoo, MI 49002 **Telephone:** (269) 385−2600 **Web Site:** www.stryker.com	**Officers:** John W. Brown − Chmn., C.E.O., Stephen P. MacMillan − Pres., C.O.O. **Transfer Agents:** National City Bank, Cleveland, OH	**Investor Contact:** 616−385−2600 **Institutional Holding** **No of Institutions:** 32 **Shares:** 276,883,031 **% Held:** −

SUNTRUST BANKS, INC.

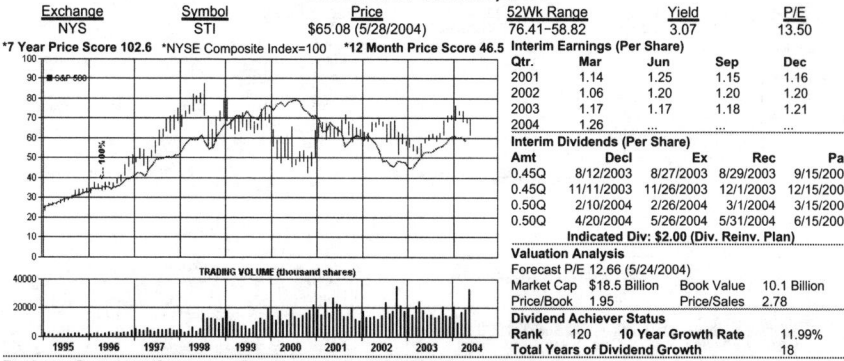

Exchange	Symbol	Price	52Wk Range	Yield	P/E
NYS	STI	$65.08 (5/28/2004)	76.41–58.82	3.07	13.50

*7 Year Price Score 102.6 *NYSE Composite Index=100 *12 Month Price Score 46.5

Interim Earnings (Per Share)

Qtr.	Mar	Jun	Sep	Dec
2001	1.14	1.25	1.15	1.16
2002	1.06	1.20	1.20	1.20
2003	1.17	1.17	1.18	1.21
2004	1.26	...	...	...

Interim Dividends (Per Share)

Amt	Decl	Ex	Rec	Pay
0.45Q	8/12/2003	8/27/2003	8/29/2003	9/15/2003
0.45Q	11/11/2003	11/26/2003	12/1/2003	12/15/2003
0.50Q	2/10/2004	2/26/2004	3/1/2004	3/15/2004
0.50Q	4/20/2004	5/26/2004	5/31/2004	6/15/2004

Indicated Div: $2.00 (Div. Reinv. Plan)

Valuation Analysis

Forecast P/E 12.66 (5/24/2004)

Market Cap	$18.5 Billion	Book Value	10.1 Billion
Price/Book	1.95	Price/Sales	2.78

Dividend Achiever Status

Rank	120	10 Year Growth Rate	11.99%

Total Years of Dividend Growth   18

Business Summary: Commercial Banking (MIC: 8.1 SIC: 6021 NAIC:522110)

SunTrust Banks, through its primary subsidiary, SunTrust Bank, provides deposit, credit, trust and investment services to a broad range of retail, business and institutional clients. Other subsidiaries provide mortgage banking, credit–related insurance, asset management, brokerage and capital market services. Co. operates 1,201 traditional and in–store branches and 2,225 ATMs located in Florida, Georgia, Maryland, Tennessee, Virginia and the District of Columbia. In addition, Co. provides customers with a full range of technology–based banking channels including Internet, personal computer and telephone banking. At Dec 31 2003, Co. had total assets of $125.39 billion.

Recent Developments: For the three months ended Mar 31 2004, net income totaled $358.5 million, up 9.3% compared with $327.8 million in the corresponding prior–year period. Net interest income climbed 3.5% to $851.6 million from $822.5 million the previous year. Provision for loan losses fell 26.5% to $59.4 million from $80.8 million a year earlier. Total non–interest income grew 8.7% to $595.1 million from $547.7 million in 2003, while total non–interest expense increased 8.7% to $889.7 million from $818.2 million the prior year. Total assets amounted to $125.24 billion as of Mar 31 2004, up 4.3% versus $120.06 billion on Mar 31 2003.

Prospects: On Apr 13 2004, Co. announced that its subsidiary, Trusco Capital Management, Inc., has signed a definitive agreement to acquire Seix Investment Advisors, a major institutional fixed–income manager with more than $17.00 billion in assets under management. Terms of the transaction were not disclosed. Meanwhile, earnings are benefiting from higher net interest income, continued solid fee income growth and Co.'s efforts to reduce expenses, partially offset by sluggish commercial loan demand. Meanwhile, non–interest income growth is being driven by increased retail investment services and higher trust and investment fees.

Financial Data

(US$ in Thousands)	3 Mos	12/31/2003	12/31/2002	12/31/2001	12/31/2000	12/31/1999	12/31/1998	12/31/1997
Earnings Per Share	4.82	4.73	4.66	4.70	4.30	3.50	3.04	3.13
Tang. Book Val. Per Share	29.69	28.42	26.55	26.66	25.07	23.24	22.98	23.37
Dividends Per Share	1.850	1.800	1.720	1.600	1.480	1.380	1.000	0.920
Dividend Payout %	38.38	38.05	36.90	34.04	34.41	39.42	32.89	29.55
Income Statement								
Total Interest Income	1,173,864	4,768,842	5,135,197	6,279,574	6,845,419	5,960,208	5,675,900	3,650,739
Total Interest Expense	322,216	1,448,539	1,891,488	3,026,974	3,736,981	2,814,752	2,746,779	1,756,373
Net Interest Income	851,648	3,320,303	3,243,709	3,252,600	3,108,438	3,145,456	2,929,121	1,894,366
Provision for Loan Losses	59,388	313,550	469,792	275,165	133,974	170,437	214,602	117,043
Non–Interest Income	595,086	2,303,001	2,391,675	2,155,823	1,773,625	1,660,031	1,716,173	934,238
Non–Interest Expense	889,744	3,400,616	3,342,268	3,113,538	2,828,533	2,939,393	2,932,386	1,685,595
Income Before Taxes	497,598	1,909,138	1,823,324	2,019,720	1,919,556	1,695,657	1,498,306	1,025,966
Income from Cont Ops	...	...	...	1,369,219	...	1,123,952	...	...
Net Income	358,477	1,332,297	1,331,809	1,375,537	1,294,100	1,326,600	971,017	667,253
Average Shs. Outstg.	283,523	281,434	286,052	291,584	300,956	317,079	319,711	213,480
Balance Sheet								
Cash & Due from Banks	3,364,176	3,931,653	4,455,776	4,229,074	4,110,489	3,909,687	4,289,889	2,991,263
Securities Avail. for Sale	28,261,946	26,051,796	25,162,956	20,999,993	19,752,165	18,576,844	17,798,708	178,434
Net Loans & Leases	78,270,277	79,790,399	72,237,821	68,092,163	71,365,273	65,131,508	60,596,089	39,383,675
Total Assets	125,244,472	125,393,153	117,322,523	104,740,644	103,496,380	95,389,968	93,169,932	57,982,736
Total Deposits	80,869,594	81,189,519	79,706,628	67,536,422	69,533,337	60,100,529	59,033,283	38,197,528
Long–Term Obligations	16,809,810	15,313,922	10,229,820	11,010,580	7,895,430	4,967,346	4,757,869	3,171,832
Total Liabilities	115,154,049	115,661,987	108,553,027	96,381,076	95,257,172	87,763,106	84,991,288	52,783,354
Net Stockholders' Equity	10,090,452	9,731,166	8,769,496	8,359,568	8,239,208	7,626,862	8,178,644	5,199,382
Shares Outstanding	282,331	281,923	270,843	283,040	296,266	293,543	321,124	209,909
Return on Equity %	3.55	13.69	15.18	16.37	15.70	14.73	11.87	12.83
Return on Assets %	0.28	1.06	1.13	1.30	1.25	1.17	1.04	1.15
Equity/Assets %	8.05	7.76	7.47	7.98	7.96	7.99	8.77	8.96
Non–Int. Exp./Tot. Inc. %	50.29	48.08	44.40	36.91	32.81	38.57	39.66	36.76
Price Range	76.41–68.57	71.55–51.56	70.00–51.79	71.81–58.10	68.81–42.56	79.81–62.25	87.44–54.94	74.94–44.38
P/E Ratio	15.85–14.23	15.13–10.90	15.02–11.11	15.28–12.36	16.00–9.90	22.80–17.79	28.76–18.07	23.94–14.18
Average Yield %	2.58	2.96	2.71	2.48	2.80	2.01	1.38	1.56

Address: 303 Peachtree Street, NE, Atlanta, GA 30308	**Officers:** L. Phillip Humann – Chmn., Pres., C.E.O., John W. Spiegel – Vice–Chmn., C.F.O.	**Investor Contact:**404–658–4879
Telephone: (404) 588–7711	**Transfer Agents:**SunTrust Bank Atlanta, Atlanta, GA	**Institutional Holding**
Web Site: www.suntrust.com		**No of Institutions:** 469
		Shares: 136,966,850 **% Held:** 48.90%

SUPERIOR INDUSTRIES INTERNATIONAL, INC.

Exchange	Symbol	Price	52Wk Range	Yield	P/E
NYS	SUP	$32.65 (5/28/2004)	45.91-31.45	1.90	13.55

*7 Year Price Score 117.2   *NYSE Composite Index=100   ***12 Month Price Score 38.6**

Interim Earnings (Per Share)

Qtr.	Mar	Jun	Sep	Dec
2001	0.61	0.51	0.41	0.57
2002	0.65	0.78	0.65	0.83
2003	0.83	0.66	0.40	0.84
2004	0.51	...	...	...

Interim Dividends (Per Share)

Amt	Decl	Ex	Rec	Pay
0.138Q	7/28/2003	10/1/2003	10/3/2003	10/17/2003
0.138Q	11/5/2003	1/7/2004	1/9/2004	1/23/2004
0.138Q	3/23/2004	4/6/2004	4/9/2004	4/23/2004
0.155Q	5/10/2004	6/30/2004	7/2/2004	7/16/2004
			Indicated Div: $0.62	

Valuation Analysis

Forecast P/E 14.57 (5/24/2004)

Market Cap	$860.9 Million	Book Value	598.8 Million
Price/Book	1.59	Price/Sales	1.10

Dividend Achiever Status

Rank	53	10 Year Growth Rate	16.92%
Total Years of Dividend Growth		18

TRADING VOLUME (thousand shares)

1995 1996 1997 1998 1999 2000 2001 2002 2003 2004

Business Summary: Automotive (MIC: 15.1 SIC: 3714 NAIC:336399)

Superior Industries International designs and manufactures automotive parts and accessories for original equipment manufacturers (OEMs). Co. supplies cast and forged aluminum wheels to automobile and light truck manufacturers, with wheel manufacturing facilities in the U.S., Mexico and Hungary. The OEM cast aluminum road wheels, Co.'s primary product, are sold to General Motors and Ford, which together accounted for 85.0% of 2003 sales, as well as to DaimlerChrysler, Audi, BMW, Isuzu, Jaguar, Land Rover, Mazda, MG Rover, Mitsubishi, Nissan, Subaru, Toyota and Volkswagen. Co. also manufactures aluminum suspension and underbody components.

Recent Developments: For the first quarter ended Mar 31 2004, net income declined 38.6% to $13.7 million compared with $22.3 million in the corresponding prior–year quarter. Results for 2004 were negatively affected by the difficult global pricing environment and unusual expenses and inefficiencies at several of Co.'s recently expanded manufacturing facilities. Net sales advanced 10.7% to $234.2 million from $211.5 million a year earlier. Unit wheel shipments climbed 10.2% versus the 2003 first quarter. Cost of sales jumped 20.4% to $209.6 million from $174.1 million the year before. Income from operations dropped 40.9% to $18.7 million from $31.6 million in 2003.

Prospects: Despite the intense global competitive environment and adverse operating issues at several of Co.'s recently expanded plants, continuing growth in both revenue and unit wheel shipments bodes well for its future. Co. recently made progress toward resolving the operating issues that have affected its recent results with the implementation of focused improvement programs at several manufacturing facilities. Going forward, pricing pressures will remain Co.'s biggest challenge. Co. is responding with programs to increase efficiency and productivity though automation, employee training and the implementation of best practices throughout its organization.

Financial Data

(US$ in Thousands)	3 Mos	12/31/2003	12/31/2002	12/31/2001	12/31/2000	12/31/1999	12/31/1998	12/31/1997
Earnings Per Share	2.41	2.73	2.91	2.10	3.04	2.62	1.88	1.96
Cash Flow Per Share	0.30	2.83	3.56	2.24	3.64	3.21	2.86	2.64
Tang. Book Val. Per Share	22.45	22.12	19.96	17.30	15.45	13.34	11.42	10.30
Dividends Per Share	0.530	0.520	0.470	0.420	0.380	0.340	0.300	0.260
Dividend Payout %	22.21	19.23	16.15	20.00	12.50	12.97	15.95	13.26
Income Statement								
Total Revenues	234,191	840,349	782,599	643,395	644,899	571,782	539,431	549,131
Total Indirect Exp.	5,882	22,902	30,843	29,249	20,716	20,310	19,758	19,986
Depreciation & Amort.	...	33,577	32,605	28,388	26,920	28,523	26,698	26,917
Operating Income	18,689	100,889	109,467	76,106	121,505	105,208	80,346	88,184
Net Interest Inc./(Exp.)	591	2,727	3,519	4,048	7,323	5,451	4,287	2,170
Income Taxes	7,198	39,695	42,134	28,835	42,573	37,710	28,482	30,819
Eqty Earns/Minority Int.	2,183	8,655	6,260	3,941	...	...	...	...
Net Income	13,667	73,720	78,250	55,354	79,937	70,808	52,319	55,389
Average Shs. Outstg.	26,978	27,033	26,907	26,361	26,255	27,056	27,818	28,221
Balance Sheet								
Cash & Cash Equivalents	137,591	156,847	96,145	106,839	93,503	108,081	86,566	73,693
Total Current Assets	410,956	388,510	368,941	280,271	245,579	263,740	235,886	199,846
Total Assets	734,199	703,205	645,796	540,838	491,664	460,468	427,430	382,679
Total Current Liabilities	107,396	83,621	97,123	71,137	75,022	86,847	91,111	65,415
Long–Term Obligations	...	...	...	...	...	340	673	1,344
Net Stockholders' Equity	598,757	592,206	530,431	448,741	399,319	353,086	312,034	287,416
Net Working Capital	303,560	304,889	271,818	209,134	170,557	176,893	144,775	134,431
Shares Outstanding	26,667	26,768	26,573	25,932	25,840	26,454	27,312	27,902
Operating Profit Margin %	7.98	12.00	13.98	11.82	18.84	18.40	14.89	16.05
Net Profit Margin %	11.98	18.21	20.76	17.56	25.59	25.57	20.25	21.31
Return on Equity %	2.28	12.44	14.75	12.33	20.01	20.05	16.76	19.27
Return on Assets %	1.86	10.48	12.11	10.23	16.25	15.37	12.24	14.47
Debt/Total Assets %	...	...	...	...	...	0.07	0.15	0.35
Price Range	43.67-34.20	45.91-33.89	53.12-36.20	44.62-29.40	35.31-23.50	29.06-22.81	33.50-20.19	29.38-22.50
P/E Ratio	35.53-14.19	16.82-12.41	18.25-12.44	21.25-14.00	11.62-7.73	11.09-8.71	17.82-10.74	14.99-11.48
Average Yield %	1.38	1.26	1.06	1.13	1.28	1.29	1.10	1.01

Address: 7800 Woodley Avenue, Van Nuys, CA 91406 Telephone: (818) 781–4973 Web Site: www.supind.com	Officers: Louis L. Borick – Chmn., C.E.O., Steven J. Borick – Pres., C.O.O. Transfer Agents:Registrar and Transfer Company, Cranford, NJ	Institutional Holding No of Institutions: 10 Shares: 11,573,062 % Held: –

254

SUPERVALU INC.

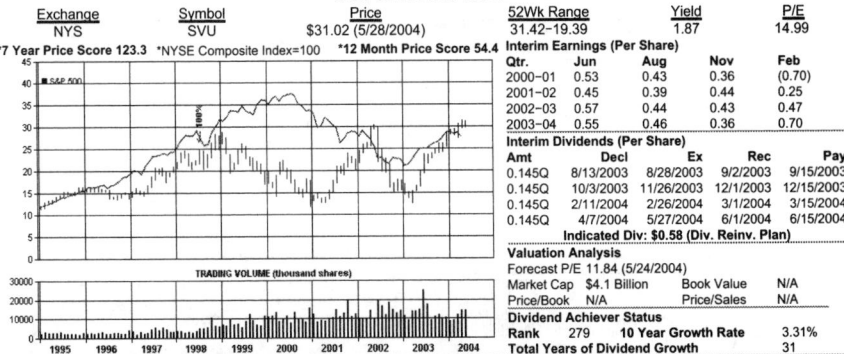

Exchange	Symbol	Price	52Wk Range	Yield	P/E
NYS	SVU	$31.02 (5/28/2004)	31.42-19.39	1.87	14.99

*7 Year Price Score 123.3   ***NYSE Composite Index=100**   ***12 Month Price Score 54.4**

Interim Earnings (Per Share)

Qtr.	Jun	Aug	Nov	Feb
2000-01	0.53	0.43	0.36	(0.70)
2001-02	0.45	0.39	0.44	0.25
2002-03	0.57	0.44	0.43	0.47
2003-04	0.55	0.46	0.36	0.70

Interim Dividends (Per Share)

Amt	Decl	Ex	Rec	Pay
0.145Q	8/13/2003	8/28/2003	9/2/2003	9/15/2003
0.145Q	10/3/2003	11/26/2003	12/1/2003	12/15/2003
0.145Q	2/11/2004	2/26/2004	3/1/2004	3/15/2004
0.145Q	4/7/2004	5/27/2004	6/1/2004	6/15/2004

Indicated Div: $0.58 (Div. Reinv. Plan)

Valuation Analysis

Forecast P/E 11.84 (5/24/2004)

Market Cap	$4.1 Billion	Book Value	N/A
Price/Book	N/A	Price/Sales	N/A

Dividend Achiever Status

Rank	279	10 Year Growth Rate	3.31%
Total Years of Dividend Growth			31

Business Summary: Retail – Food &Beverage (MIC: 5.3 SIC: 5141 NAIC:424410)

Supervalu is a major food retailer and distributor to independently–owned retail food stores. As of Feb 28 2004, Co. operated 1,225 Save–A–Lot extreme value stores, including 821 licensed Save–A–Lot locations, 280 Co.–owned stores and 124 Deals–Nothing Over a Dollar general merchandise stores; 258 regional supermarkets under the Cub Foods, Shop 'n Save, Shoppers Food Warehouse, bigg's, Farm Fresh, Scott's Foods, and Hornbacher's banners. Additionally, Co. is the primary supplier to approximately 2,500 retail grocery stores, as well as Co.'s 258 regional supermarkets, while serving as a secondary supplier to about 660 stores.

Recent Developments: For the 53 weeks ended Feb 28 2004, net earnings climbed 9.0% to $280.1 million from $257.0 million in the corresponding 52–week period the year before. Results included after–tax restructuring and other charges of $9.8 million and $1.8 million in fiscal 2003 and fiscal 2002, respectively. Net sales grew 5.5% to $20.21 billion from $19.16 billion a year earlier. Retail food net sales advanced 7.1% to $10.55 billion from $9.85 billion the previous year, while food distribution net sales rose 3.7% to $9.66 billion from $9.31 billion in the prior year. Operating earnings totaled $194.0 million, up 32.6% compared with $146.3 million the year before.

Prospects: Co. is targeting earnings per share in the range of $2.75 to $2.90 for the current fiscal year, including a net gain of approximately $0.40 per share from the sale of Co.'s interest in WinCo Foods. Meanwhile, comparable store sales for fiscal 2004 are projected to increase 1.0% to 2.0% based on a recovering economy, planned in–market store expansion, and a modest inflationary environment. Capital expenditures in the current fiscal year are expected to range between $400.0 million and $425.0 million, including about $60.0 million in capital leases. During fiscal 2004, Co. plans to open between 110 and 140 new food combination stores and between eight and 10 new regional banner stores.

Financial Data

(US$ in Thousands)	02/28/2004	02/22/2003	02/23/2002	02/24/2001	02/26/2000	02/27/1999	02/28/1998	02/22/1997
Earnings Per Share	2.07	1.91	1.53	0.62	1.87	1.57	1.82	1.30
Cash Flow Per Share	6.14	4.25	5.87	4.90	2.62	4.59	3.10	2.44
Tang. Book Val. Per Share	4.84	3.23	2.90	1.63	1.58	6.09	5.79	6.05
Dividends Per Share	0.570	0.560	0.550	0.540	0.530	0.520	0.510	0.490
Dividend Payout %	27.77	29.58	36.27	87.90	28.60	33.43	27.94	...
Income Statement								
Total Revenues	20,209,679	19,160,368	20,908,522	23,194,279	20,339,079	17,420,507	17,201,378	16,551,902
Total Indirect Exp.	2,235,852	2,023,028	2,084,071	2,213,523	1,481,275	1,382,212	1,365,327	1,286,121
Depreciation & Amort.	301,589	297,056	340,750	343,779	277,062	233,523	230,082	232,071
Operating Income	601,398	569,943	516,477	345,192	582,846	418,168	405,409	380,532
Net Interest Inc./(Exp.)	(146,518)	(161,939)	(172,774)	(190,835)	(135,392)	(101,907)	(113,993)	(120,695)
Income Taxes	174,742	150,962	138,168	72,392	204,513	124,923	154,023	105,468
Eqty Earns/Minority Int.	...	...	...	...	...	...	93,364	20,675
Net Income	280,138	257,042	205,535	81,965	242,941	191,338	230,757	175,044
Average Shs. Outstg.	135,418	134,877	133,978	132,829	130,090	121,961	126,550	134,510
Balance Sheet								
Cash & Cash Equivalents	291,956	29,188	12,171	10,396	10,920	7,608	6,100	6,539
Total Current Assets	2,037,092	1,647,366	1,604,027	2,091,676	2,177,639	1,582,527	1,612,060	1,600,799
Total Assets	6,152,938	5,896,245	5,824,782	6,407,172	6,495,353	4,265,949	4,093,010	4,283,326
Total Current Liabilities	1,871,972	1,525,307	1,701,489	2,341,170	2,509,620	1,521,907	1,457,160	1,369,078
Long–Term Obligations	1,633,721	2,019,658	1,875,873	2,008,474	1,953,741	1,246,269	1,260,728	1,420,591
Net Stockholders' Equity	2,209,524	2,009,240	1,916,693	1,793,495	1,821,479	1,305,639	1,201,905	1,307,423
Net Working Capital	165,120	122,059	(97,462)	(249,494)	(331,981)	60,620	154,900	231,721
Shares Outstanding	134,760	133,688	132,889	132,374	134,662	120,109	120,368	133,764
Operating Profit Margin %	2.97	2.97	2.47	1.48	3.67	2.40	2.35	2.29
Return on Equity %	12.67	12.79	10.72	4.57	22.32	14.65	19.19	13.38
Return on Assets %	4.55	4.35	3.52	1.27	6.25	4.48	5.63	4.08
Debt/Total Assets %	26.55	34.25	32.20	31.34	30.07	29.21	30.80	33.16
Price Range	29.43–12.60	30.50–14.32	24.68–12.80	22.50–11.75	26.13–16.19	28.75–20.31	24.28–14.31	16.31–13.63
P/E Ratio	14.22–6.09	15.97–7.50	16.13–8.37	36.29–18.95	13.97–8.66	18.31–12.94	13.34–7.86	12.55–10.48
Average Yield %	2.52	2.60	2.88	3.22	2.47	2.16	2.72	3.27

Address: 11840 Valley View Road, Eden Prairie, MN 55344
Telephone: (952) 828–4000
Web Site: www.supervalu.com

Officers: Jeffrey Noddle – Chmn., Pres., C.E.O., David L. Boehnen – Exec. V.P.
Transfer Agents: Wells Fargo Shareowner Services, St. Paul, MN

Investor Contact:952–828–4000
Institutional Holding
No of Institutions: 13
Shares: 370,545   **% Held:** –

SUSQEHANNA BANCSHARES, INC

Exchange	Symbol	Price	52Wk Range	Yield	P/E
NMS	SUSQ	$24.27 (5/28/2004)	27.80–22.58	3.63	15.56

*7 Year Price Score 123.0 *NYSE Composite Index=100 ***12 Month Price Score 43.7**

Interim Earnings (Per Share)

Qtr.	Mar	Jun	Sep	Dec
2001	0.32	0.36	0.36	0.37
2002	0.37	0.39	0.40	0.39
2003	0.40	0.41	0.40	0.35
2004	0.40	...	...	...

Interim Dividends (Per Share)

Amt	Decl	Ex	Rec	Pay
0.22Q	7/16/2003	7/28/2003	7/30/2003	8/20/2003
0.22Q	10/15/2003	10/28/2003	10/30/2003	11/20/2003
0.22Q	1/21/2004	1/29/2004	2/2/2004	2/20/2004
0.22Q	4/21/2004	4/29/2004	5/3/2004	5/20/2004

Indicated Div: $0.88 (Div. Reinv. Plan)

Valuation Analysis
Forecast P/E 14.60 (5/24/2004)
Market Cap $961.3 Million Book Value 559.6 Million
Price/Book 1.82 Price/Sales 2.65

Dividend Achiever Status
Rank 207 10 Year Growth Rate 7.69%
Total Years of Dividend Growth 33

TRADING VOLUME (thousand shares)

1995 1996 1997 1998 1999 2000 2001 2002 2003 2004

Business Summary: Commercial Banking (MIC: 8.1 SIC: 6021 NAIC:522110)
Susquehanna Bancshares is a financial holding company that provides a wide range of retail and commercial banking and financial services through its subsidiaries in the mid–Atlantic region. Co. operates eight commercial banks, a trust and investment company, an asset management company, a property and casualty insurance brokerage company and a vehicle company. Co.'s depository institution subsidiaries provide commercial and retail banking services in Pennsylvania, Maryland, and New Jersey. As of Dec 31 2003, Co. had total assets of $5.95 billion, net loans and leases of $4.22 billion and total deposits of $4.13 billion.

Recent Developments: For the three months ended Mar 31 2004, net income slipped 0.9% to $15.9 million compared with $16.1 million in the equivalent period of 2003. Results for 2004 and 2003 included gains on the sale of loans and leases of $3.7 million and $2.5 million, and net gains on securities of $563,000 and $90,000, respectively. Net interest income declined 1.3% to $46.7 million versus $47.3 million the year before. Provision for loan lease losses dropped 37.2% to $1.7 million from $2.7 million a year earlier. Total non–interest income rose 6.2% to $27.1 million from $25.5 million and total non–interest expense climbed 5.4% to $49.3 million from $46.8 million the year before.

Prospects: On Apr 21 2004, Co. announced that its shareholders approved the transaction under which Co. will acquire Patriot Bank, a $1.00 billion financial holding company with 20 offices in eastern Pennsylvania. Shareholders of Patriot Bank have also approved the merger. Final consummation is expected to occur on or about June 10 2004, granted necessary regulatory approvals. Once completed, the combination will increase Co.'s assets to over $7.00 billion and will enhance its presence in the high–growth counties of Berks, Chester, Lehigh, Montgomery and Northampton. Co. will merge Patriot Bank into Equity Bank, a wholly–owned subsidiary of Co.

Financial Data

(US$ in Thousands)	3 Mos	12/31/2003	12/31/2002	12/31/2001	12/31/2000	12/31/1999	12/31/1998	12/31/1997
Earnings Per Share	1.56	1.56	1.55	1.41	1.40	1.17	1.26	1.20
Tang. Book Val. Per Share	12.44	12.13	11.95	12.54	11.56	10.92	10.90	10.24
Dividends Per Share	0.870	0.860	0.810	0.770	0.700	0.620	0.570	0.540
Dividend Payout %	55.77	55.12	52.25	54.60	50.00	52.99	45.23	45.55
Income Statement								
Total Interest Income	69,587	286,020	316,713	341,295	353,416	299,770	292,766	264,100
Total Interest Expense	22,906	99,014	129,473	169,051	188,464	138,848	138,576	118,447
Net Interest Income	46,681	187,006	187,240	172,244	164,952	160,922	154,190	145,653
Provision for Loan Losses	1,700	10,222	10,664	7,310	3,726	7,200	5,247	4,557
Non–Interest Income	27,074	101,750	94,150	84,166	74,010	39,979	30,921	23,754
Non–Interest Expense	49,303	189,430	181,663	167,763	155,581	131,882	113,206	106,028
Income Before Taxes	22,752	89,104	89,063	81,337	79,655	61,819	66,658	58,822
Net Income	15,926	62,373	61,721	55,716	54,962	43,397	45,574	40,202
Average Shs. Outstg.	40,182	40,037	39,932	39,593	39,365	37,137	36,179	33,495
Balance Sheet								
Cash & Due from Banks	137,500	176,240	156,320	149,233	129,101	144,548	105,263	97,341
Securities Avail. for Sale	1,056,929	1,062,844	1,174,866	1,107,878	941,320	896,647	949,101	615,426
Net Loans & Leases	4,186,663	4,220,600	3,791,282	3,481,800	3,396,423	2,957,919	2,738,379	2,535,063
Total Assets	6,049,768	5,953,107	5,544,647	5,051,092	4,792,856	4,310,606	4,064,827	3,524,887
Total Deposits	4,345,898	4,134,467	3,831,344	3,484,331	3,249,013	3,180,520	3,124,332	2,851,217
Long–Term Obligations	622,794	743,850	723,166	675,580	467,954	467,414	370,160	181,888
Total Liabilities	5,490,172	5,405,725	5,010,821	4,557,556	4,339,419	3,906,216	3,673,631	3,178,149
Net Stockholders' Equity	559,596	547,382	533,855	493,536	453,437	404,390	391,196	346,738
Shares Outstanding	39,868	39,861	39,638	39,344	39,221	37,022	35,857	33,832
Return on Equity %	2.84	11.39	11.56	11.28	12.12	10.73	11.64	11.59
Return on Assets %	0.26	1.04	1.11	1.10	1.14	1.00	1.12	1.14
Equity/Assets %	9.24	9.19	9.62	9.77	9.46	9.38	9.62	9.83
Non–Int. Exp./Tot. Inc. %	51.00	48.85	44.21	39.43	36.39	38.81	34.97	36.83
Price Range	26.89–24.51	27.80–20.20	25.97–18.41	22.80–15.75	17.50–12.25	20.69–15.03	26.00–16.38	25.50–14.56
P/E Ratio	17.24–15.71	17.82–12.95	16.75–11.88	16.17–11.17	12.50–8.75	17.68–12.85	20.63–13.00	21.25–12.13
Average Yield %	3.40	3.60	3.60	4.00	4.97	3.50	2.51	2.97

Address: 26 North Cedar St., Lititz, PA 17543 **Telephone:** (717) 626–4721 **Web Site:** www.susqbanc.com	**Officers:** William J. Reuter – Chmn., Pres., C.E.O., Gregory A. Duncan – Exec. V.P., C.O.O. **Transfer Agents:** The Bank of New York, New York, NY	**Investor Contact:** 717–625–6305 **Institutional Holding** **No of Institutions:** 113 **Shares:** 13,144,976 **% Held:** 33.20%

SWS GROUP, INC.

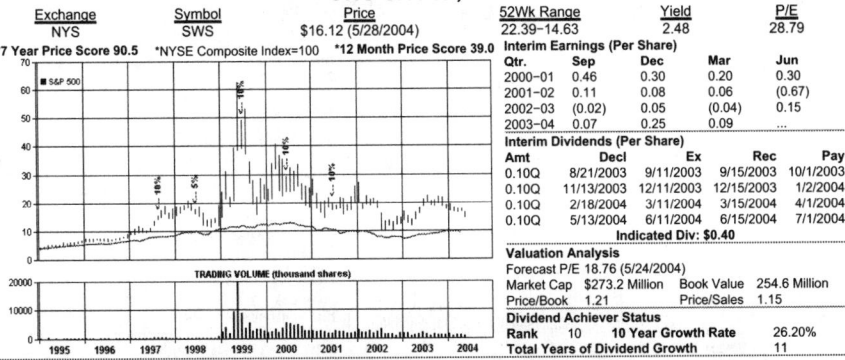

Exchange	Symbol	Price	52Wk Range	Yield	P/E
NYS	SWS	$16.12 (5/28/2004)	22.39-14.63	2.48	28.79

*7 Year Price Score 90.5 *NYSE Composite Index=100 *12 Month Price Score 39.0

Interim Earnings (Per Share)

Qtr.	Sep	Dec	Mar	Jun
2000–01	0.46	0.30	0.20	0.30
2001–02	0.11	0.08	0.06	(0.67)
2002–03	(0.02)	0.05	(0.04)	0.15
2003–04	0.07	0.25	0.09	...

Interim Dividends (Per Share)

Amt	Decl	Ex	Rec	Pay
0.10Q	8/21/2003	9/11/2003	9/15/2003	10/1/2003
0.10Q	11/13/2003	12/11/2003	12/15/2003	1/2/2004
0.10Q	2/18/2004	3/11/2004	3/15/2004	4/1/2004
0.10Q	5/13/2004	6/11/2004	6/15/2004	7/1/2004
			Indicated Div: $0.40	

Valuation Analysis

Forecast P/E 18.76 (5/24/2004)

Market Cap $273.2 Million	Book Value 254.6 Million
Price/Book 1.21	Price/Sales 1.15

Dividend Achiever Status

Rank 10	10 Year Growth Rate	26.20%
Total Years of Dividend Growth		11

Business Summary: Finance Intermediaries &Services (MIC: 8.7 SIC: 6211 NAIC:523110)

SWS Group is a full–service securities and banking firm delivering a range of investment, commercial banking and related financial services to its clients, which include individual and institutional investors, broker/dealers, corporations, governmental entities and financial intermediaries. Co. provides clearing services to 227 correspondent broker/dealers and over 400 independent registered representatives, as well as full–service and limited on–line brokerage services to individual investors. Also, Co. offers full–service, traditional and Internet banking through First Savings Bank, FSB, in Arlington, TX, and asset management services through SWS Capital Corporation.

Recent Developments: For the three months ended Mar 31 2004, Co. reported net income of $1.5 million compared with a net loss of $710,000 in the corresponding year–earlier period. Results for 2004 included an after–tax liability of $2.0 million related to inquiries by the SEC regarding certain mutual fund trading practices, and a gain of $1.0 million on the sale of loans. Total revenues improved 17.6% to $69.7 million from $59.3 million the previous year, primarily due to increases in commission revenue, investment banking, advisory and administrative fees, and net gains on principal transactions.

Prospects: The outlook for Co.'s businesses remains positive. For instance, Co.'s Southwest Securities division is beginning to see significant results from its investment banking presence, which Co. expects to be an important contributor to its bottom line. Moreover, Co. is encouraged by the operating performance of its retail brokerage business, which is being driven by the recent expansion of that business and improved market conditions. In addition to increased commission revenue, margin balances are growing well, reflecting an upswing in investor confidence.

Financial Data

(US$ in Thousands)	9 Mos	6 Mos	3 Mos	06/27/2003	06/28/2002	06/29/2001	06/30/2000	06/25/1999
Earnings Per Share	0.56	0.43	0.23	0.14	(0.42)	1.26	5.35	2.00
Tang. Book Val. Per Share	14.92	14.46	14.30	14.28	14.80	17.36	16.65	20.19
Dividends Per Share	0.400	0.400	0.400	0.400	0.380	0.310	0.250	0.200
Dividend Payout %	71.42	93.02	173.91	285.71	N.M.	24.72	4.68	9.98
Income Statement								
Total Interest Income	71,154	48,142	24,403	97,304	125,119	249,427	265,664	147,006
Total Interest Expense	24,595	16,592	8,169	39,885	65,807	171,578	178,084	99,951
Net Interest Income	46,559	31,550	16,234	57,419	59,312	77,849	87,580	47,055
Non–Interest Income	134,333	87,646	39,367	166,177	207,031	221,275	323,422	190,264
Non–Interest Expense	168,434	110,323	53,491	218,581	273,728	262,722	273,097	196,799
Income Before Taxes	12,458	8,873	2,110	5,015	(7,385)	36,402	137,905	...
Eqty Earns/Minority Int.	(820)	(521)	(300)	(1,551)	(1,151)	(2,384)	(793)	...
Income from Cont Ops	...	...	...	2,423	...	22,213	...	...
Net Income	7,020	5,539	1,283	2,868	(7,184)	19,339	94,234	26,219
Average Shs. Outstg.	17,227	17,228	17,206	16,997	17,215	17,500	17,603	13,022
Balance Sheet								
Securities Avail. for Sale	9,694	10,551	8,640	5,599	3,932	9,687	46,283	172,928
Net Loans & Leases	420,947	380,944	362,350	366,008	345,538	319,949	247,958	...
Total Assets	4,983,530	4,614,371	4,671,812	4,092,084	3,363,653	3,784,757	5,229,035	4,293,274
Total Deposits	522,607	529,792	632,757	528,515	265,370	336,281	265,804	...
Long–Term Obligations	29,642	29,138	27,096	57,169	167,253	122,045	100,368	50,000
Total Liabilities	4,726,646	4,359,716	4,420,613	3,842,311	3,108,368	3,485,318	4,937,895	4,030,990
Net Stockholders' Equity	254,551	254,625	251,199	249,773	255,285	299,439	291,140	262,284
Shares Outstanding	17,056	17,051	17,020	16,957	17,240	17,247	17,481	12,986
Statistical Record								
Return on Equity %	2.76	2.17	0.51	0.97	N.M.	7.41	32.36	9.99
Return on Assets %	0.14	0.12	0.02	0.05	N.M.	0.58	1.80	0.61
Equity/Assets %	5.11	5.51	5.37	6.10	7.58	7.91	5.56	6.10
Non–Int. Exp./Tot. Inc. %	81.96	81.24	83.88	82.95	82.41	55.81	46.35	58.35
Price Range	22.39-16.45	22.39-17.66	22.39-18.75	21.25-10.00	26.93-15.90	33.58-14.73	53.26-15.74	62.61-11.66
P/E Ratio	39.98-29.38	52.07-41.07	97.35-81.52	151.8-71.43	N/A	26.65-11.69	9.96-2.94	31.30-5.83
Average Yield %	2.07	1.99	1.97	2.79	1.89	1.35	0.86	0.90

Address: 1201 Elm Street, Dallas, TX 75202	Officers: Don A. Buchholz – Chmn., William D. Felder – Pres.	Institutional Holding
Telephone: (214) 859–1800	Transfer Agents:Computershare Trust Company, Inc., Lakewood, CO	No of Institutions: 26
Web Site: www.southwestsecurities.com		Shares: 118,959 % Held: –

SYNOVUS FINANCIAL CORP.

Exchange	Symbol	Price	52Wk Range	Yield	P/E
NYS	SNV	$25.75 (5/28/2004)	29.04–21.35	2.69	19.51

*7 Year Price Score 109.4 *NYSE Composite Index=100 *12 Month Price Score 46.3

Interim Earnings (Per Share)

Qtr.	Mar	Jun	Sep	Dec
2001	0.25	0.26	0.27	0.27
2002	0.28	0.29	0.31	0.33
2003	0.30	0.32	0.33	0.33
2004	0.34	...	...	...

Interim Dividends (Per Share)

Amt	Decl	Ex	Rec	Pay
0.165Q	8/20/2003	9/17/2003	9/19/2003	10/1/2003
0.165Q	11/20/2003	12/17/2003	12/19/2003	1/2/2004
0.173Q	2/26/2004	3/17/2004	3/19/2004	4/1/2004
0.173Q	5/19/2004	6/16/2004	6/18/2004	7/1/2004

Indicated Div: $0.6932 (Div. Reinv. Plan)

Valuation Analysis

Forecast P/E 18.17 (5/24/2004)

Market Cap $7.6 Billion	Book Value	2.4 Billion
Price/Book 3.10	Price/Sales	2.94

Dividend Achiever Status

Rank	35	10 Year Growth Rate	19.67%
Total Years of Dividend Growth			27

TRADING VOLUME (thousand shares)

Business Summary: Commercial Banking (MIC: 8.1 SIC: 6021 NAIC:522110)

Synovus Financial, with assets of $21.63 billion as of Dec 31 2003, is a registered bank holding company. Co. provides financial services including commercial and retail banking, financial management, insurance, mortgage and leasing services through affiliate banks and other offices in Georgia, Alabama, South Carolina, Florida and Tennessee. Co. also owns 81.0% of Total System Services, Inc.®(TSYS), which provides electronic payment processing services including consumer, debit, commercial, retail and stored value card processing and related services, as well as student loan processing.

Recent Developments: For the three months ended Mar 31 2004, net income increased 15.8% to $104.2 million from $89.9 million in the corresponding period of the prior year. Net interest income grew 11.7% to $202.7 million from $181.6 million the year before. Provision for loan losses declined 22.6% to $15.7 million from $20.3 million the previous year. Total non–interest income was up 15.9% to $377.1 million from $325.3 million in 2003, while total non–interest expense rose 15.7% to $393.3 million from $340.0 million a year earlier. Total assets were $22.29 billion, up 8.2% compared with $20.60 billion the prior year.

Prospects: Looking ahead, Co. anticipates full–year 2004 earnings per share growth of between 8.0% and 10.0%. This projection is based on expected loan growth in the range of 10.0% to 12.0%, a stable net interest margin in a flat rate environment, continued improvement in credit quality, and net income growth at TSYS of between 5.0% and 7.0%. Meanwhile, Co. continues to expand into new markets that are expected to provide strong growth. Co. entered Savannah, GA with the opening of a Sea Island Bank branch during the first quarter of 2004. In addition, Co. plans to open its first de novo bank, Synovus Bank of Jacksonville, Florida, in the second quarter of 2004.

Financial Data

(US$ in Thousands)	3 Mos	12/31/2003	12/31/2002	12/31/2001	12/31/2000	12/31/1999	12/31/1998	12/31/1997
Earnings Per Share	1.32	1.28	1.21	1.05	0.92	0.80	0.70	0.62
Tang. Book Val. Per Share	5.58	6.49	6.39	5.75	4.97	4.34	3.96	3.43
Dividends Per Share	0.660	0.640	0.570	0.490	0.420	0.340	0.270	0.220
Dividend Payout %	49.62	50.19	47.10	46.90	45.65	42.91	39.99	36.91
Income Statement								
Total Interest Income	269,691	1,061,492	1,055,040	1,130,888	1,097,805	888,007	769,248	725,673
Total Interest Expense	66,944	298,428	337,536	501,097	535,473	374,713	328,722	313,284
Net Interest Income	202,747	763,064	717,504	629,791	562,332	513,294	440,526	412,389
Provision for Loan Losses	15,724	71,777	65,327	51,673	44,341	34,007	26,660	32,296
Non–Interest Income	377,090	1,366,838	1,240,539	935,975	832,732	738,563	560,674	489,269
Non–Interest Expense	393,284	1,422,143	1,299,470	1,005,963	923,274	856,549	673,648	601,293
Income Before Taxes	164,541	611,501	563,880	489,993	411,735	349,315	291,632	258,903
Net Income	104,162	388,925	365,347	311,616	262,557	225,307	187,108	165,236
Average Shs. Outstg.	306,812	304,928	301,197	295,850	286,882	283,355	269,151	265,665
Balance Sheet								
Cash & Due from Banks	622,896	696,030	741,092	648,179	558,054	466,543	348,365	388,134
Securities Avail. for Sale	2,621,576	2,529,257	2,237,725	2,088,287	1,807,039	1,716,678	1,514,054	1,325,036
Net Loans & Leases	16,776,772	16,238,855	14,264,068	12,247,148	10,604,020	8,940,681	7,301,170	6,506,822
Total Assets	22,286,347	21,632,629	19,036,246	16,657,947	14,908,092	12,547,001	10,498,009	9,260,331
Total Deposits	16,214,308	15,941,609	13,928,834	12,146,198	11,161,710	9,440,087	8,542,798	7,707,927
Long–Term Obligations	1,641,852	1,575,777	1,336,200	1,052,943	840,859	318,620	127,015	7,188
Total Liabilities	19,927,923	19,387,590	16,995,393	14,963,001	13,490,921	11,320,332	9,426,408	8,237,689
Net Stockholders' Equity	2,358,424	2,245,039	2,040,853	1,694,946	1,417,171	1,226,669	1,070,601	903,656
Shares Outstanding	304,436	302,090	300,397	294,673	284,642	282,014	270,218	262,808
Statistical Record								
Return on Equity %	4.41	17.21	18.18	18.28	18.47	18.26	17.35	18.28
Return on Assets %	0.46	1.78	1.94	1.86	1.75	1.78	1.76	1.78
Equity/Assets %	10.58	10.37	10.72	10.17	9.50	9.77	10.19	9.75
Non–Int. Exp./Tot. Inc. %	60.81	58.56	56.60	48.67	47.82	52.65	50.65	49.49
Price Range	28.92–22.67	29.04–17.31	31.74–16.81	34.45–23.02	27.19–14.50	25.00–17.50	25.83–18.06	22.21–13.11
P/E Ratio	21.91–17.17	22.69–13.52	26.23–13.89	32.81–21.92	29.55–15.76	31.25–21.88	36.90–25.80	35.82–21.15
Average Yield %	2.61	2.79	2.32	1.75	2.15	1.63	1.20	1.30

Address: 901 Front Avenue, Columbus, GA 31902	Officers: James D. Yancey – Chmn., Pres., C.O.O., Richard E. Anthony – Pres.	Investor Contact: 706–649–5220
Telephone: (706) 649–2401	Transfer Agents: State Street Bank and Trust Company, Boston, MA	Institutional Holding
Web Site: www.synovus.com		No of Institutions: 26
		Shares: 4,023,382 % Held: –

SYSCO CORP.

Exchange	Symbol	Price	52Wk Range	Yield	P/E
NYS	SYY	$37.50 (5/28/2004)	40.90-28.75	1.39	28.41

*7 Year Price Score 153.8   *NYSE Composite Index=100   *12 Month Price Score 51.0

Interim Earnings (Per Share)

Qtr.	Sep	Dec	Mar	Jun
2000-01	0.43	0.21	0.21	0.03
2001-02	0.24	0.24	0.23	0.30
2002-03	0.28	0.28	0.26	0.36
2003-04	0.32	0.34	0.30	...

Interim Dividends (Per Share)

Amt	Decl	Ex	Rec	Pay
0.11Q	9/12/2003	10/1/2003	10/3/2003	10/24/2003
0.13Q	11/7/2003	12/30/2003	1/2/2004	1/23/2004
0.13Q	2/13/2004	3/31/2004	4/2/2004	4/23/2004
0.13Q	5/14/2004	6/30/2004	7/2/2004	7/23/2004

Indicated Div: $0.52 (Div. Reinv. Plan)

Valuation Analysis

Forecast P/E 23.12 (5/24/2004)

Market Cap $24.9 Billion	Book Value N/A
Price/Book N/A	Price/Sales N/A

Dividend Achiever Status

Rank	34	10 Year Growth Rate	20.18%

Total Years of Dividend Growth 27

Business Summary: Retail – Food &Beverage (MIC: 5.3 SIC: 5141 NAIC:424410)

Sysco, acting through its subsidiaries and divisions, is a distributor of food and food related products to the foodservice or "food–prepared–away–from–home" industry. Co. provides its products and services to restaurants, healthcare and educational facilities, lodging establishments and other foodservice customers. Co.'s Broadline companies segment distributes food products and non–food products to both Co.'s traditional and chain restaurant customers. SYGMA companies distribute food products and non–food products to some of Co.'s chain restaurant customer locations.

Recent Developments: For the 13 weeks ended Mar 27 2004, net earnings totaled $195.8 million, up 16.3% compared with $168.4 million in the corresponding prior–year period. Sales climbed 9.9% to $7.03 billion from $6.40 billion a year earlier. Broadline sales increased 7.6% to $5.65 billion from $5.25 billion in 2003, while sales for SYGMA, Co.'s chain restaurant distribution subsidiary, advanced 22.4% to $873.3 million from $713.3 million the previous year. Cost of sales $5.68 billion, or 80.9% of sales, versus $5.14 billion, or 80.4% of total sales, the year before. Earnings before income taxes climbed 16.7% to $318.4 million from $272.7 million the prior year.

Prospects: Results are benefiting from lower food costs and more efficient distribution. Meanwhile, Co. continues to aggressively expand its operations. During the third quarter, Co. opened a new broadline distribution "fold–out" facility, or foodservice distribution center, in Fargo, ND. In addition, Co. has new fold–out facilities in Post Falls, ID and Oxnard, CA under construction and anticipates capital expenditures of approximately $500.0 million during the current fiscal year. Subsequent to the end of the third quarter, Co. completed its acquisition of Overton Distributors Inc., a produce distribution company with locations in Raleigh and Charlotte, NC, and Nashville, TN.

Financial Data

(US$ in Thousands)	9 Mos	6 Mos	3 Mos	06/28/2003	06/29/2002	06/30/2001	07/01/2000	07/03/1999
Earnings Per Share	1.32	1.28	1.22	1.18	1.01	0.88	0.68	0.54
Cash Flow Per Share	1.14	0.55	0.28	2.07	1.61	1.43	1.05	0.86
Tang. Book Val. Per Share	1.71	1.86	1.81	1.68	1.85	2.07	1.89	1.70
Dividends Per Share	0.460	0.440	0.420	0.400	0.320	0.260	0.220	0.190
Dividend Payout %	34.84	34.37	34.26	33.89	31.68	29.54	32.35	35.18
Income Statement								
Total Revenues	21,196,386	14,170,801	7,134,281	26,140,337	23,350,504	21,784,497	19,303,268	17,422,815
Total Indirect Exp.	3,029,682	2,021,189	1,024,336	3,836,507	3,467,379	3,232,827	2,843,755	2,547,266
Depreciation & Amort.	209,054	138,679	69,679	273,142	278,251	248,240	220,661	205,005
Operating Income	1,059,346	726,446	356,178	1,324,274	1,160,962	1,038,532	809,962	667,689
Net Interest Inc./(Exp.)	(50,744)	(35,007)	(18,631)	(72,234)	(62,897)	(71,776)	(70,832)	(72,839)
Income Taxes	392,021	269,682	130,719	482,099	421,083	369,746	283,979	231,616
Income from Cont Ops	...	...	...	...	...	...	453,629	...
Net Income	626,616	430,792	208,811	778,288	679,787	596,909	445,588	362,271
Average Shs. Outstg.	662,482	660,127	657,274	661,535	673,445	667,949	669,555	673,594
Balance Sheet								
Cash & Cash Equivalents	172.695	232,595	221,544	337,447	230,439	135,743	159,128	149,303
Total Current Assets	3,690,550	3,738,789	3,776,173	3,629,534	3,185,289	2,984,882	2,733,215	2,408,767
Total Assets	7,326,832	7,305,577	7,214,194	6,936,521	5,989,753	5,468,521	4,813,955	4,096,582
Total Current Liabilities	2,853,881	2,734,868	2,790,506	2,701,129	2,239,357	2,089,895	1,782,935	1,427,540
Long–Term Obligations	1,420,139	1,395,981	1,195,282	1,249,467	1,176,307	961,421	1,023,642	997,717
Net Stockholders' Equity	2,269,048	2,365,824	2,324,594	2,197,531	2,132,519	2,147,520	1,761,568	1,427,196
Net Working Capital	836,669	1,003,921	985,667	928,405	945,932	894,987	950,280	981,227
Shares Outstanding	637,972	642,204	644,779	643,657	653,540	665,137	662,969	659,344
Statistical Record								
Operating Profit Margin %	4.99	5.12	4.99	5.06	4.97	4.76	4.19	3.83
Return on Equity %	27.62	18.20	8.98	35.41	31.87	27.79	25.75	25.38
Return on Assets %	8.55	5.89	2.89	11.22	11.34	10.91	9.42	8.84
Debt/Total Assets %	19.38	19.10	16.56	18.01	19.63	17.58	21.26	24.35
Price Range	40.90-28.75	36.84-28.75	33.99-28.75	32.34-21.81	30.15-22.22	30.03-19.59	21.69-13.63	15.75-10.09
P/E Ratio	30.98-21.78	28.78-22.46	27.86-23.57	27.41-18.48	29.85-22.00	34.13-22.27	31.89-20.04	29.17-18.69
Average Yield %	1.33	1.34	1.36	1.39	1.17	1.02	1.23	1.42

Address: 1390 Enclave Parkway, Houston, TX 77077-2099	**Officers:** Richard J. Schnieders – Chmn., C.E.O., Thomas E. Lankford – Pres., C.O.O.	**Investor Contact:** 281–584–1458
Telephone: (281) 584–1390	**Transfer Agents:** EquiServe Trust Company, N.A., Providence, RI	**Institutional Holding**
Web Site: www.sysco.com		**No of Institutions:** 14
		Shares: 1,927,072 **% Held:** –

T ROWE PRICE GROUP INC.

Exchange	Symbol	Price	52Wk Range	Yield	P/E
NMS	TROW	$48.16 (5/28/2004)	55.78–35.95	1.58	23.61

*7 Year Price Score 125.6 ***NYSE Composite Index=100** ***12 Month Price Score 50.5**

TRADING VOLUME (thousand shares)

Interim Earnings (Per Share)
Qtr.	Mar	Jun	Sep	Dec
2001	0.38	0.40	0.39	0.35
2002	0.41	0.40	0.34	0.37
2003	0.31	0.42	0.51	0.53
2004	0.58	...	...	...

Interim Dividends (Per Share)
Amt	Decl	Ex	Rec	Pay
0.17Q	6/5/2003	6/18/2003	6/20/2003	7/7/2003
0.17Q	9/4/2003	9/24/2003	9/26/2003	10/10/2003
0.19Q	12/11/2003	12/23/2003	12/26/2003	1/9/2004
0.19Q	3/9/2004	3/19/2004	3/23/2004	4/6/2004

Indicated Div: $0.76

Valuation Analysis
Forecast P/E N/A
Market Cap $5.9 Billion	Book Value 1.4 Billion
Price/Book 4.77	Price/Sales 6.24

Dividend Achiever Status
Rank 31	10 Year Growth Rate	20.54%

Total Years of Dividend Growth 17

Business Summary: Wealth Management (MIC: 8.8 SIC: 6282 NAIC:523930)

T. Rowe Price Group is a financial services holding company with total assets under management of $190.00 billion as of Dec 31 2003. Through its subsidiaries, Co. is engaged in providing investment advisory services to individual and institutional investors through the sponsored T. Rowe Price mutual funds and other investment portfolios. Co.'s assets under management are sourced approximately 20.0% to 30.0% from each of the following: individual U.S. investors, U.S. defined contribution retirement plans, third–party distributors in the U.S. and internationally, and institutional investors in the U.S. and foreign countries.

Recent Developments: For the quarter ended Mar 31 2004, net income jumped 99.5% to $77.3 million compared with $38.8 million in the equivalent 2003 quarter. Net revenues climbed 39.7% to $305.7 million from $218.7 million a year earlier. Investment advisory fees rose 49.0% to $245.0 million driven by an improvement in assets under management. Net operating income leapt 90.6% to $122.9 million versus $64.4 million the year before. Net non–operating income was $821,000 versus a loss of $2.1 million in 2003. Assets under management jumped 43.6% to $201.00 billion, reflecting growing equity markets and $6.40 billion of net investor inflows, including mutual fund net inflows of over $4.70 billion.

Prospects: Co. imposed a 2.0% fee on international fund shares redeemed within 90 days to deter improper trades. Separately, Co. expects second quarter and full–year 2004 advertising and promotion expenditures will be up $4.0 million year over year and up in the range of 20.0% to 25.0% versus 2003, respectively. If the economy generates further gains in employment and there are no large external shocks caused by geopolitics, monetary developments, or other factors, Co. should experience satisfactory growth in the second half of 2004. Meanwhile, a high level of investor interest in the equity markets, may translate to gains for Co.'s managed U.S. equity portfolios through third party distribution.

Financial Data
(US$ in Thousands)	3 Mos	12/31/2003	12/31/2002	12/31/2001	12/31/2000	12/31/1999	12/31/1998	12/31/1997
Earnings Per Share	2.04	1.77	1.52	1.52	2.08	1.85	1.34	1.13
Cash Flow Per Share	0.67	2.31	2.10	2.25	2.49	2.29	1.78	1.54
Tang. Book Val. Per Share	5.96	5.40	3.81	3.34	2.41	6.41	5.11	4.11
Dividends Per Share	0.700	0.680	0.640	0.600	0.520	0.400	0.340	0.260
Dividend Payout %	34.48	38.41	42.10	39.47	25.00	21.62	25.37	23.00
Income Statement								
Total Revenues	306,476	998,855	925,829	1,027,496	1,212,327	1,036,379	886,142	754,957
Total Indirect Exp.	182,790	630,527	602,991	709,599	763,856	621,609	573,328	490,198
Depreciation & Amort.	10,128	45,289	50,578	28,921	11,879	32,628	32,615	29,034
Operating Income	122,861	365,040	320,511	330,589	458,192	414,770	312,814	264,759
Net Interest Inc./(Exp.)	(332)	(1,699)	(2,634)	(12,692)	(9,721)	...	...	...
Income Taxes	46,343	138,029	115,350	135,078	174,818	155,166	118,676	101,208
Eqty Earns/Minority Int.	...	...	...	357	(14,345)	(20,200)	(19,998)	(19,154)
Net Income	77,339	227,487	194,254	195,868	269,029	239,404	174,140	144,397
Average Shs. Outstg.	133,777	128,289	127,706	129,045	129,234	129,200	129,952	128,073
Balance Sheet								
Cash & Cash Equivalents	306,919	236,533	111,418	79,741	80,526	358,472	283,838	200,409
Total Current Assets	439,824	357,828	208,205	183,742	211,567	480,109	384,540	287,204
Total Assets	1,634,023	1,546,577	1,370,433	1,313,115	1,469,459	998,039	796,784	646,067
Total Current Liabilities	214,071	121,221	99,402	105,979	154,819	149,919	129,814	109,557
Long–Term Obligations	...	...	55,899	103,889	312,277	17,716	...	...
Net Stockholders' Equity	1,419,952	1,329,080	1,133,840	1,077,825	991,065	770,184	614,304	486,673
Net Working Capital	225,753	236,607	108,803	77,763	56,748	330,190	254,726	177,647
Shares Outstanding	126,484	122,648	122,648	123,088	122,439	120,107	120,183	118,195
Operating Profit Margin %	40.19	36.54	34.61	32.17	37.79	40.02	35.30	35.06
Net Profit Margin %	55.62	50.41	45.89	45.35	51.03	53.04	46.43	45.93
Return on Equity %	5.45	17.11	17.13	18.17	27.14	31.08	28.34	29.67
Return on Assets %	4.73	14.70	14.17	14.91	18.30	23.98	21.85	22.35
Debt/Total Assets %	...	...	4.07	7.91	21.25	1.77	...	...
Price Range	55.78–47.41	47.41–24.30	41.99–21.45	42.69–25.70	48.63–30.19	40.88–26.44	42.44–22.75	36.75–18.56
P/E Ratio	27.34–23.24	26.79–13.73	27.63–14.11	28.08–16.91	23.38–14.51	22.09–14.29	31.67–16.98	32.52–16.43
Average Yield %	1.34	1.89	1.98	1.73	1.29	1.16	1.00	0.98

Address: 100 East Pratt Street, Baltimore, MD 21202	**Officers:** George A. Roche – Chmn., Pres., Interim C.F.O., James S. Riepe – Vice–Chmn., V.P.	**Investor Contact:**410–345–2124
Telephone: (410) 345–2000	**Transfer Agents:**Wells Fargo Bank Minnesota, N.A., St. Paul, MN	**Institutional Holding** No of Institutions: 283
Web Site: www.troweprice.com		**Shares:** 70,267,878 **% Held:**57.6

TANGER FACTORY OUTLET CENTERS, INC.

Exchange	Symbol	Price	52Wk Range	Yield	P/E
NYS	SKT	$38.82 (5/28/2004)	46.78-32.44	6.44	36.62

*7 Year Price Score 141.9 *NYSE Composite Index=100 *12 Month Price Score 45.2

Interim Earnings (Per Share)

Qtr.	Mar	Jun	Sep	Dec
2001	0.06	0.12	0.17	0.35
2002	0.12	0.13	0.20	0.35
2003	0.19	0.26	0.33	0.39
2004	0.08	...	...	...

Interim Dividends (Per Share)

Amt	Decl	Ex	Rec	Pay
0.615Q	7/10/2003	7/29/2003	7/31/2003	8/15/2003
0.615Q	10/9/2003	10/29/2003	10/31/2003	11/14/2003
0.615Q	1/15/2004	1/28/2004	1/30/2004	2/16/2004
0.625Q	4/15/2004	4/28/2004	4/30/2004	5/14/2004

Indicated Div: $2.50 (Div. Reinv. Plan)

Valuation Analysis

Forecast P/E 10.47 (5/24/2004)

Market Cap $311.7 Million	Book Value	167.4 Million
Price/Book 2.61	Price/Sales	3.59

Dividend Achiever Status

Rank	61	10 Year Growth Rate	16.47%
Total Years of Dividend Growth			10

Business Summary: Property, Real Estate &Development (MIC: 8.3 SIC: 6798 NAIC:525930)

Tanger Factory Outlet Centers is a fully–integrated, self–administered and self–managed real estate investment trust, focusing exclusively on developing, acquiring, owning, operating and managing factory outlet centers. As of Dec 31 2003, Co. had ownership interests in or management responsibilities for 40 centers with a total gross leasable area of approximately 9.3 million square feet. These centers were approximately 96.0% occupied, contained over 2,000 stores and represented over 400 store brands. Co.'s factory outlet centers and other assets are held by, and all of its operations are conducted by, Tanger Properties Limited Partnership.

Recent Developments: For the three months ended Mar 31 2004, net income totaled $1.0 million compared with income of $2.2 million, before a $5,000 gain from discontinued operations, in the corresponding quarter the previous year. Total revenues advanced 59.8% to $45.8 million from $28.7 million a year earlier. Revenues from base rentals increased 66.2% to $32.1 million from $19.3 million the year before, while revenues from expense reimbursements climbed 46.1% to $12.1 million from $8.3 million the prior year. Operating income was $16.5 million, up 75.9% versus $9.4 million in 2003.

Prospects: Revenue growth is being fueled by Co.'s aggressive development activity. Co. expects to complete the expansion of its outlet center in Myrtle Beach, SC during the summer of 2004. Meanwhile, Co. has started the early development and leasing of sites located in Pittsburgh, PA and Deer Park, NY. Completion of the initial phase of the Pittsburgh site is expected in late 2005 or early 2006, while the initial phase of the Deer Park site will likely be completed in late 2006 or early 2007. Looking ahead, Co. is targeting full–year 2004 earnings of between $0.62 and $0.70 per share. In addition, Co. estimates funds from operations to range from $3.68 to $3.76 per share for 2004.

Financial Data

(US$ in Thousands)	12/31/2003	12/31/2002	12/31/2001	12/31/2000	12/31/1999	12/31/1998	12/31/1997	12/31/1996
Earnings Per Share	1.17	0.80	0.70	0.31	1.77	1.28	1.54	1.46
Tang. Book Val. Per Share	12.91	10.00	9.63	11.47	13.68	14.43	17.39	16.75
Dividends Per Share	2.450	2.440	2.430	2.420	2.410	2.350	2.170	2.060
Dividend Payout %	210.04	305.93	348.21	783.06	136.44	183.59	140.90	...
Income Statement								
Rental Income	84,229	79,313	78,089	74,710	72,321	69,274	59,444	52,613
Total Income	121,972	113,167	111,068	108,821	104,016	97,766	85,271	75,500
Total Indirect Exp.	78,920	130,985	131,710	124,137	111,185	104,685	84,523	73,480
Depreciation	29,124	28,754	28,572	26,218	24,824	22,154	18,439	16,458
Interest Expense	26,486	28,460	30,134	27,565	24,239	22,028	16,835	13,998
Eqty Earns/Minority Int.	(3,701)	(2,014)	(2,136)	(956)	(5,374)	(3,944)	(4,756)	(4,425)
Income from Cont Ops	12,865	8,628	7,356	11,293	11,696	11,165	...	11,593
Net Income	12,849	11,007	7,112	4,312	15,588	11,827	12,827	11,191
Average Shs. Outstg.	10,283	8,514	7,948	7,922	7,872	8,009	7,140	6,402
Cash & Cash Equivalents	9,836	1,072	515	634	503	6,330	3,607	2,585
Total Assets	987,347	477,675	476,272	487,408	490,069	471,795	416,014	332,138
Long–Term Obligations	540,319	345,005	358,195	346,843	329,647	302,485	229,050	178,004
Total Liabilities	820,019	387,040	399,901	396,531	382,305	357,756	279,365	221,481
Net Stockholders' Equity	167,418	90,635	76,371	90,877	107,764	114,039	136,649	110,657
Shares Outstanding	12,960	9,061	7,929	7,918	7,876	7,897	7,854	6,603
Net Inc.+Depr./Assets %	4.25	8.23	7.49	6.30	8.25	7.20	7.52	8.32
Return on Equity %	7.68	9.51	9.63	12.42	10.85	9.79	9.38	10.47
Return on Assets %	1.30	1.80	1.54	2.31	2.38	2.36	3.08	3.49
Price Range	42.36-28.85	31.20-20.85	23.31-19.81	24.88-18.50	26.44-18.81	31.75-18.94	30.94-23.75	27.13-22.88
P/E Ratio	36.21-24.66	39.00-26.06	33.30-28.30	80.24-59.68	14.94-10.63	24.80-14.79	20.09-15.42	18.58-15.67
Average Yield %	7.14	8.99	11.24	11.16	10.47	8.55	7.87	8.46

Address: 3200 Northline Avenue,	Officers: Stanley K. Tanger – Chmn., C.E.O.,	Investor Contact:336–292–3010
Greensboro, NC 27408	Steven B. Tanger – Pres., C.O.O.	Institutional Holding
Telephone: (336) 292–3010	Transfer Agents:EquiServe Trust Company. NA,	No of Institutions: 12
Web Site: www.tangeroutlet.com	Providence, RI	Shares: 379,669 % Held: –

TARGET CORP

Exchange	Symbol	Price	52Wk Range	Yield	P/E
NYS	TGT	$44.70 (5/28/2004)	45.63-36.99	0.63	21.18

*7 Year Price Score 126.8 *NYSE Composite Index=100 *12 Month Price Score 51.0

Interim Earnings (Per Share)

Qtr.	Apr	Jul	Oct	Jan
2000	0.26	0.28	0.24	0.60
2001	0.28	0.30	0.20	0.73
2002	0.38	0.38	0.30	0.75
2003	0.38	0.39	0.33	0.91
2004	0.48	...	...	...

Interim Dividends (Per Share)

Amt	Decl	Ex	Rec	Pay
0.07Q	6/12/2003	8/18/2003	8/20/2003	9/10/2003
0.07Q	9/11/2003	11/18/2003	11/20/2003	12/10/2003
0.07Q	1/15/2004	2/18/2004	2/20/2004	3/10/2004
0.07Q	4/11/2004	5/18/2004	5/20/2004	6/10/2004

Indicated Div: $0.28 (Div. Reinv. Plan)

Valuation Analysis

Forecast P/E 16.66 (5/24/2004)

Market Cap $40.6 Billion	Book Value 11.1 Billion
Price/Book 3.16	Price/Sales 0.73

Dividend Achiever Status

Rank	216	10 Year Growth Rate	6.91%
Total Years of Dividend Growth			32

TRADING VOLUME (thousand shares)

Business Summary: Retail – General (MIC: 5.2 SIC: 5331 NAIC:452990)

Target is a diversified general merchandise retailer. As of May 13 2004, Co. operated 1,577 stores in 47 states including 1,249 Target stores, 266 Mervyn's stores and 62 Marshall Field's stores. Target is a national discount store chain offering low prices with stores selling hardlines and fashion softgoods; Mervyn's is a moderate–priced department store chain specializing in active and casual apparel and home softlines. Marshall Field's (including stores formerly named Dayton's and Hudson's) is a full–service, full–line department store chain offering moderate to better merchandise.

Recent Developments: For the three months ended May 1 2004, net earnings totaled $438.0 million, up 25.4% compared with $349.0 million in the corresponding quarter a year earlier. Total revenues climbed 12.3% to $11.59 billion from $10.32 billion the previous year. Revenues from Target stores advanced 14.0% to $10.05 billion from $8.82 billion the year before. Revenues from Mervyn's slipped 1.4% to $793.0 million from $804.0 million the prior year, while revenues from Marshall Field's grew 4.0% to $614.0 million from $590.0 million a year earlier. Total comparable–store sales increased 6.6% year over year, driven by comparable–store sales growth of 7.3% at Target stores.

Prospects: Results are being positively affected by strong top–line growth, which is being driven primarily by comparable–store sales growth at Co.'s Target stores and the contribution of sales from new stores opened during the past year. Meanwhile, earnings are benefiting from fewer merchandise markdowns and a decline in delinquencies and write–offs from Co.'s credit card operations. Separately, Co. continues to evaluate strategic alternatives for its Mervyn's and Marshall Field's department store operations, including the possible sale of one or both of these businesses to existing retailers or other qualified buyers. Looking ahead, Co. is projecting second–quarter 2004 earnings of $0.47 per share.

Financial Data

(US$ in Thousands)	01/31/2004	02/01/2003	02/02/2002	02/03/2001	01/29/2000	01/30/1999	01/31/1998	02/03/1997
Earnings Per Share	2.01	1.81	1.51	1.38	1.27	1.02	0.85	0.50
Cash Flow Per Share	3.44	1.73	2.18	2.08	2.41	1.99	1.93	1.66
Tang. Book Val. Per Share	12.13	10.37	8.68	7.15	6.42	6.12	4.77	4.05
Dividends Per Share	0.260	0.240	0.220	0.210	0.200	0.180	0.160	0.150
Dividend Payout %	12.93	13.25	14.56	15.21	15.74	17.64	19.41	30.66
Income Statement								
Total Revenues	48,163,000	43,917,000	39,888,000	36,903,000	33,702,000	30,951,000	27,757,000	25,371,000
Total Indirect Exp.	12,854,000	11,393,000	9,962,000	9,130,000	8,344,000	6,363,000	5,695,000	5,518,000
Depreciation & Amort.	1,320,000	1,212,000	1,079,000	940,000	854,000	780,000	693,000	650,000
Operating Income	3,519,000	3,264,000	2,680,000	2,478,000	2,329,000	1,954,000	1,742,000	1,225,000
Net Interest Inc./(Exp.)	(559,000)	(588,000)	(464,000)	(425,000)	(393,000)	(398,000)	(416,000)	(442,000)
Income Taxes	1,119,000	1,022,000	842,000	789,000	751,000	594,000	524,000	309,000
Income from Cont Ops	...	...	1,374,000	...	1,185,000	962,000	802,000	474,000
Net Income	1,841,000	1,654,000	1,368,000	1,264,000	1,144,000	935,000	751,000	463,000
Average Shs. Outstg.	917,100	914,000	909,800	913,000	931,400	934,600	927,400	922,400
Balance Sheet								
Cash & Cash Equivalents	716,000	758,000	499,000	356,000	220,000	255,000	211,000	201,000
Total Current Assets	12,928,000	11,935,000	9,648,000	7,304,000	6,483,000	6,005,000	5,561,000	5,440,000
Total Assets	31,392,000	28,603,000	24,154,000	19,490,000	17,143,000	15,666,000	14,191,000	13,389,000
Total Current Liabilities	8,314,000	7,523,000	7,054,000	6,301,000	5,850,000	5,057,000	4,556,000	4,111,000
Long–Term Obligations	10,217,000	10,186,000	8,088,000	5,634,000	4,521,000	4,452,000	4,425,000	4,808,000
Net Stockholders' Equity	11,065,000	9,443,000	7,860,000	6,519,000	5,862,000	5,311,000	4,460,000	3,790,000
Net Working Capital	4,614,000	4,412,000	2,594,000	1,003,000	633,000	948,000	1,005,000	1,329,000
Shares Outstanding	911,808	909,802	905,165	911,682	911,682	823,618	875,600	868,000
Operating Profit Margin %	7.30	7.43	6.71	6.71	6.91	6.31	6.27	4.82
Net Profit Margin %	8.46	8.42	7.66	7.70	7.97	6.94	6.66	4.30
Return on Equity %	16.63	17.51	17.48	19.38	20.21	18.11	17.98	12.50
Return on Assets %	5.86	5.78	5.68	6.48	6.91	6.14	5.65	3.54
Debt/Total Assets %	32.54	35.61	33.48	28.90	26.37	28.41	31.18	35.91
Price Range	41.54-26.06	45.72-26.15	44.41-26.68	38.63-22.75	37.88-27.63	31.88-16.88	18.42-9.47	9.97-6.12
P/E Ratio	20.67-12.97	25.26-14.45	29.41-17.67	27.99-16.49	29.82-21.75	31.25-16.54	21.67-11.14	19.94-12.25
Average Yield %	0.72	0.66	0.60	0.69	0.62	0.80	1.14	1.81

Address: 1000 Nicollet Mall, Minneapolis, MN 55403 Telephone: (612) 304–6073 Web Site: www.target.com	Officers: Robert J. Ulrich – Chmn., C.E.O., Gerald L. Storch – Vice–Chmn. Transfer Agents:EquiServe, Jersey City, NJ	Investor Contact:612–370–6736 Institutional Holding No of Institutions: 7 Shares: 869,205 % Held: –

TCF FINANCIAL CORP.

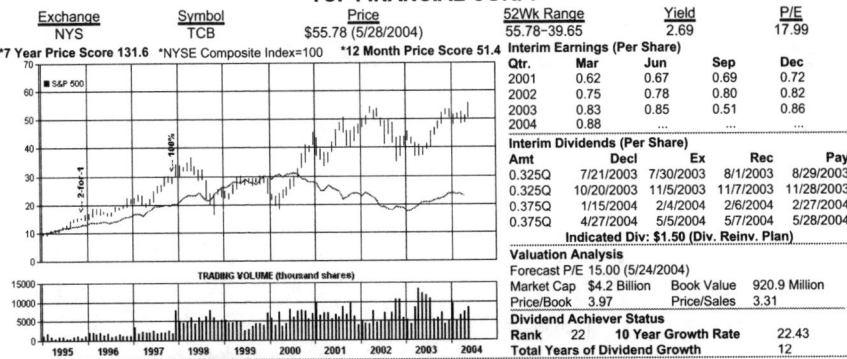

Exchange	Symbol	Price	52Wk Range	Yield	P/E
NYS	TCB	$55.78 (5/28/2004)	55.78-39.65	2.69	17.99

*7 Year Price Score 131.6   *NYSE Composite Index=100   *12 Month Price Score 51.4

Interim Earnings (Per Share)

Qtr.	Mar	Jun	Sep	Dec
2001	0.62	0.67	0.69	0.72
2002	0.75	0.78	0.80	0.82
2003	0.83	0.85	0.51	0.86
2004	0.88	...	...	...

Interim Dividends (Per Share)

Amt	Decl	Ex	Rec	Pay
0.325Q	7/21/2003	7/30/2003	8/1/2003	8/29/2003
0.325Q	10/20/2003	11/5/2003	11/7/2003	11/28/2003
0.375Q	1/15/2004	2/4/2004	2/6/2004	2/27/2004
0.375Q	4/27/2004	5/5/2004	5/7/2004	5/28/2004
Indicated Div: $1.50 (Div. Reinv. Plan)				

Valuation Analysis

Forecast P/E 15.00 (5/24/2004)

Market Cap	$4.2 Billion	Book Value	920.9 Million
Price/Book	3.97	Price/Sales	3.31

Dividend Achiever Status

Rank	22	10 Year Growth Rate	22.43
Total Years of Dividend Growth			12

Business Summary: Commercial Banking (MIC: 8.1 SIC: 6021 NAIC:522110)

TCF Financial, with $11.32 billion in assets as of Dec 31 2003, is the holding company for two national banks. As of Dec 31 2003, Co. operated more than 400 banking offices, including 240 full-service supermarket branches, in Illinois, Indiana, Michigan, Minnesota, Wisconsin and Colorado. Co.'s primary focus is lower- and middle-income customers and small- to medium-sized businesses in its markets. Co.'s branches are typically open 12 hours a day, seven days a week and on holidays. Co.'s products include commercial, consumer and residential mortgage loans and deposit and equipment finance, discount brokerage and investment and insurance sales products.

Recent Developments: For the quarter ended Mar 31 2004, net income rose 0.9% to $60.7 million versus $60.1 million in the corresponding period of the year before. Results for 2004 and 2003 included net gains of $12.7 million and $21.1 million, respectively, on sales of securities available for sale. Results for 2003 also included losses of $6.6 million on the termination of debt. Net interest income slid 3.2% to $118.5 million as a result of a decrease in average interest earning assets. Net interest margin improved to 4.52% from 4.45% in 2003. Provision for credit losses fell 57.2% to $1.2 million. Non-interest income grew 3.4% to $115.2 million. Non-interest expense rose 1.4% to $140.7 million.

Prospects: Co. continues to report solid earnings, reflecting healthy growth in its Power Asset lending operations, strong consumer home equity originations, and sound credit quality. Meanwhile, Co.'s new branch expansion continues with 4 branches opened during the first quarter of 2004 and 24 more branches planned to open during the remainder of the year. Separately, in Mar 2004, TCF Leasing acquired VGM Leasing, a leasing company specializing in home medical equipment financing. The acquisition included 40 leasing professionals in Waterloo, IA and approximately $82.0 million of new portfolio balances as of Mar 31 2004.

Financial Data

(US$ in Thousands)	12/31/2003	12/31/2002	12/31/2001	12/31/2000	12/31/1999	12/31/1998	12/31/1997	12/31/1996
Earnings Per Share	3.05	3.15	2.70	2.35	2.00	1.76	1.69	1.21
Tang. Book Val. Per Share	10.18	10.30	9.90	9.28	7.77	7.74	7.93	7.35
Dividends Per Share	1.300	1.150	1.000	0.820	0.720	0.610	0.460	0.350
Dividend Payout %	42.62	36.50	37.03	35.10	36.25	34.80	27.73	28.93
Income Statement								
Total Interest Income	641,519	733,363	826,609	826,681	752,101	748,894	682,614	582,861
Total Interest Expense	160,374	234,138	345,387	388,145	327,888	323,160	289,018	242,721
Net Interest Income	481,145	499,225	481,222	438,536	424,213	425,734	393,596	340,140
Provision for Loan Losses	12,532	22,006	20,878	14,772	16,923	23,280	17,795	19,820
Non-Interest Income	463,624	416,880	351,625	312,384	288,909	256,174	200,839	145,094
Non-Interest Expense	560,109	538,369	501,996	462,528	452,798	428,700	361,562	341,070
Income Before Taxes	327,783	357,692	329,834	302,838	273,091	265,249	240,907	137,047
Net Income	215,878	232,931	207,322	186,245	166,039	156,179	145,061	85,663
Average Shs. Outstg.	70,770	73,940	76,842	79,388	83,071	88,916	86,134	70,684
Balance Sheet								
Cash & Due from Banks	370,054	416,397	386,700	392,007	429,262	420,477	297,010	238,670
Securities Avail. for Sale	1,533,288	2,426,794	1,584,661	1,403,888	1,521,661	1,677,919	1,430,192	1,003,464
Net Loans & Leases	8,271,159	8,044,120	8,169,174	8,480,030	7,839,988	7,061,165	6,986,605	4,925,213
Total Assets	11,319,015	12,202,069	11,358,715	11,197,462	10,661,716	10,164,594	9,744,660	7,090,862
Total Deposits	7,611,749	7,709,988	7,098,958	6,891,824	6,584,835	6,715,146	6,907,310	4,977,630
Long-Term Obligations	1,536,413	2,268,244	2,303,166	2,098,925	2,073,888	2,093,766	1,614,708	1,200,086
Total Liabilities	10,398,157	11,225,049	10,441,682	10,287,242	9,852,734	9,319,092	8,790,980	6,541,356
Net Stockholders' Equity	920,858	977,020	917,033	910,220	808,982	845,502	953,680	549,642
Shares Outstanding	70,474	73,855	76,931	80,289	81,941	85,569	92,822	69,514
Return on Equity %	23.44	23.84	22.60	20.46	20.52	18.47	15.21	15.58
Return on Assets %	1.90	1.90	1.82	1.66	1.55	1.53	1.48	1.20
Equity/Assets %	8.13	8.00	8.07	8.12	7.58	8.31	9.78	7.75
Non-Int. Exp./Tot. Inc. %	50.68	46.80	42.60	40.60	43.49	42.65	40.92	46.85
Price Range	53.56-37.05	54.39-35.21	50.70-33.70	45.31-18.50	30.25-22.00	36.75-16.56	34.13-19.31	22.50-15.00
P/E Ratio	17.56-12.15	17.27-11.18	18.78-12.48	19.28-7.87	15.13-11.00	20.88-9.41	20.19-11.43	18.60-12.40
Average Yield %	2.91	2.43	2.36	2.77	2.65	2.13	1.83	1.92

Address: 200 Lake Street East, Wayzata, MN 55391-1693 Telephone: (612) 661-6500 Web Site: www.tcfexpress.com	Officers: William A. Cooper – Chmn., C.E.O., Lynn A. Nagorske – Pres., C.O.O. Transfer Agents:EquiServe Trust Company, N.A., Providence, RI	Investor Contact:952-745-2755 Institutional Holding No of Institutions: 16 Shares: 3,774,944 % Held: –

TELEFLEX INCORPORATED

Exchange	Symbol	Price	52Wk Range	Yield	P/E
NYS	TFX	$46.47 (5/28/2004)	54.82–42.00	1.89	17.08

*7 Year Price Score 111.4 *NYSE Composite Index=100 ***12 Month Price Score 45.8**

Interim Earnings (Per Share)

Qtr.	Mar	Jun	Sep	Dec
2001	0.77	0.79	0.56	0.74
2002	0.77	0.84	0.66	0.88
2003	0.74	0.80	0.45	0.74
2004	0.73	...	...	...

Interim Dividends (Per Share)

Amt	Decl	Ex	Rec	Pay
0.20Q	8/4/2003	8/21/2003	8/25/2003	9/15/2003
0.20Q	11/4/2003	11/21/2003	11/25/2003	12/15/2003
0.20Q	2/9/2004	2/23/2004	2/25/2004	3/15/2004
0.22Q	4/30/2004	5/21/2004	5/25/2004	6/15/2004

Indicated Div: $0.88 (Div. Reinv. Plan)

Valuation Analysis

Forecast P/E 14.89 (5/24/2004)

Market Cap $1.8 Billion	Book Value 1.1 Billion
Price/Book 1.82	Price/Sales 0.83

Dividend Achiever Status

Rank 102	10 Year Growth Rate	13.24%

Total Years of Dividend Growth 26

Business Summary: Medical Instruments &Equipment (MIC: 9.6 SIC: 3841 NAIC:339112)

Teleflex operates in three segments. Commercial Products designs and manufactures proprietary mechanical and electrical/electronic controls for the automotive market; mechanical, electrical and hydraulic controls, and electronics for the marine market; and proprietary products for fluid transfer and industrial applications. Medical Products manufactures and distributes a broad range of invasive disposable and reusable devices for selected medical care markets. Aerospace Products designs and manufactures cargo handling systems and containers for aviation, and provide surface treatments, repair services and manufactured components for the aerospace and turbine engine markets.

Recent Developments: For the three months ended Mar 28 2004, net income climbed 0.8% to $29.5 million compared with $29.2 million in the corresponding quarter of 2003. Results for 2003 included gains from asset sales of $3.1 million. Revenues rose 16.8% to $638.0 million from $546.2 million the previous year. Sales of commercial products grew 17.0% to $350.8 million, while sales of medical products rose 27.5% to $150.6 million. Sales of aerospace products climbed 6.5% to $136.6 million due to higher volumes in manufactured components and repair services. Operating profit increased 8.3% to $54.3 million compared with $50.1 million the year before.

Prospects: Co. is benefiting from higher revenues from all three of its business segments and improved operating profit in both the commercial and medical segments. This trend should continue in the near–term as business activity appears to be picking up, evidenced by a 23.0% increase in overall orders for Co. in the first quarter of 2004. Looking ahead, Co. will continue its focus on improving productivity, reducing working capital and generating cash flow from operations. Co. expects earnings per share for full–year 2004 in the range of $3.10 to $3.20, with accelerated earnings growth in the second half of the year.

Financial Data

(US$ in Thousands)	3 Mos	12/28/2003	12/29/2002	12/30/2001	12/31/2000	12/26/1999	12/27/1998	12/28/1997
Earnings Per Share	2.72	2.73	3.15	2.86	2.83	2.47	2.15	1.86
Cash Flow Per Share	0.45	5.63	5.04	4.79	4.90	3.48	3.42	2.14
Tang. Book Val. Per Share	19.92	19.41	16.60	19.98	18.00	15.84	14.20	12.49
Dividends Per Share	0.800	0.780	0.710	0.660	0.580	0.500	0.440	0.380
Dividend Payout %	29.41	28.57	22.53	23.07	20.49	20.44	20.69	20.83
Income Statement								
Total Revenues	638,005	2,282,435	2,076,229	1,905,004	1,764,482	1,601,069	1,437,578	1,145,773
Total Indirect Exp.	119,870	416,892	394,900	404,061	352,852	320,166	300,214	259,023
Depreciation & Amort.	28,622	104,352	95,117	92,401	77,417	67,389	60,105	47,940
Operating Income	47,708	177,828	172,488	159,695	158,214	142,756	124,760	106,405
Net Interest Inc./(Exp.)	(6,775)	(26,337)	(25,023)	(28,465)	(20,787)	(17,732)	(17,054)	(14,435)
Income Taxes	11,461	42,388	47,222	47,384	48,990	47,536	42,210	36,333
Net Income	29,472	109,103	125,266	112,311	109,224	95,220	82,550	70,072
Average Shs. Outstg.	40,457	39,942	39,786	39,280	38,633	38,525	38,425	37,661
Balance Sheet								
Cash & Cash Equivalents	62,898	56,580	44,494	46,900	45,139	29,040	66,689	30,702
Total Current Assets	1,053,357	1,006,187	837,895	747,477	662,038	604,940	616,942	566,477
Total Assets	2,141,430	2,110,613	1,813,384	1,635,020	1,401,288	1,263,444	1,215,917	1,079,165
Total Current Liabilities	618,358	612,671	498,483	495,426	383,872	329,412	311,479	294,907
Long–Term Obligations	222,872	229,882	240,123	228,180	220,557	246,191	275,581	237,562
Net Stockholders' Equity	1,087,727	1,062,302	912,281	778,143	690,422	602,564	534,450	463,753
Net Working Capital	434,999	393,516	339,412	252,051	278,166	275,528	305,463	271,570
Shares Outstanding	40,115	39,795	39,398	38,932	38,344	38,018	37,615	37,118
Operating Profit Margin %	7.47	7.79	8.30	8.38	8.96	8.91	8.67	9.28
Net Profit Margin %	8.21	8.49	10.58	10.87	11.74	11.88	11.61	12.45
Return on Equity %	2.71	10.27	13.73	14.43	15.81	15.80	15.44	15.10
Return on Assets %	1.38	5.16	6.90	6.86	7.79	7.53	6.78	6.49
Debt/Total Assets %	10.40	10.89	13.24	13.95	15.73	19.48	22.66	22.01
Price Range	54.82–47.68	49.95–34.24	58.57–40.92	50.98–35.71	44.69–26.94	50.38–29.69	45.50–30.00	39.38–23.38
P/E Ratio	20.15–17.53	18.30–12.54	18.59–12.99	17.83–12.49	15.79–9.52	20.39–12.02	21.16–13.95	21.17–12.57
Average Yield %	1.61	1.83	1.44	1.49	1.67	1.23	1.13	1.21

Address: 630 West Germantown Pike, Plymouth Meeting, PA 19462	Officers: Lennox K. Black – Chmn., John J. Sickler – Vice–Chmn.	Investor Contact:610–834–6362
Telephone: (610) 834–6301	Transfer Agents: American Stock Transfer &Trust Company, New York, NY	Institutional Holding No of Institutions: 35
Web Site: www.teleflex.com		Shares: 633,895 % Held: –

TELEPHONE AND DATA SYSTEMS, INC.

Exchange	Symbol	Price	52Wk Range	Yield	P/E
ASE	TDS	$71.65 (5/28/2004)	74.43-48.10	0.92	41.90

*7 Year Price Score 86.6 ***NYSE Composite Index=100** ***12 Month Price Score 51.9**

TRADING VOLUME (thousand shares)

Interim Earnings (Per Share)

Qtr.	Mar	Jun	Sep	Dec
2001	0.52	(5.77)	0.89	1.49
2002	0.23	(16.24)	(0.33)	(0.51)
2003	(0.09)	0.35	0.61	0.41
2004	0.34	...	...	...

Interim Dividends (Per Share)

Amt	Decl	Ex	Rec	Pay
0.155Q	8/6/2003	9/12/2003	9/16/2003	9/30/2003
0.155Q	11/14/2003	12/11/2003	12/15/2003	12/30/2003
0.165Q	2/27/2004	3/15/2004	3/17/2004	3/31/2004
0.165Q	5/10/2004	6/14/2004	6/16/2004	6/30/2004

Indicated Div: $0.66 (Div. Reinv. Plan)

Valuation Analysis

Forecast P/E 38.08 (5/24/2004)

Market Cap	$3.7 Billion	Book Value	N/A
Price/Book	N/A	Price/Sales	N/A

Dividend Achiever Status

Rank	232	10 Year Growth Rate	6.19%
Total Years of Dividend Growth			29

Business Summary: Communications (MIC: 10.1 SIC: 4812 NAIC:517212)

Telephone and Data Systems is a diversified telecommunications service company with wireless telephone and wireline telephone operations. At Dec 31 2003, Co. served approximately 5.5 million customers in 36 states, including 4.4 million wireless customers and 1.1 million wireline telephone equivalent access lines. Co. conducts substantially all of its wireless operations through its 82.1%–owned subsidiary, United States Cellular Corporation. Co. conducts its wireline telephone operations through its wholly owned subsidiary, TDS Telecommunications Corporation.

Recent Developments: For the three months ended Mar 31 2004, net income was $19.7 million compared with a loss of $4.0 million a year earlier. Results for 2003 included a loss of $21.6 million related to the difference between the fair value and book value of U.S. Cellular's Florida and Georgia assets that were exchanged with AT&T Wireless. Total operating revenues increased 6.8% to $870.5 million from $815.3 million the previous year. U.S. Cellular operating revenues advanced 8.9% to $657.7 million, while TDS Telecom operating revenues improved to $212.9 million versus $211.5 million the year before.

Prospects: Co.'s results are benefiting from a combination of solid growth from its U.S. Cellular operations and improved bottom–line results from TDS Telecom. For instance, for the quarter ended Mar 31 2004, U.S. Cellular posted net wireless customer additions of 196,000. Additionally, postpay churn, or the rate of customers moving between carriers, improved to 1.3% from 1.4% a year earlier despite continued competition and the availability of wireless local number portability. Meanwhile, Co. expects its TDS Telecom operation to experience continued healthy demand going forward for its digital subscriber line and long distance services.

Financial Data

(US$ in Thousands)	3 Mos	12/31/2003	12/31/2002	12/31/2001	12/31/2000	12/31/1999	12/31/1998	12/31/1997
Earnings Per Share	1.71	1.28	(16.85)	(2.87)	2.39	5.02	1.03	(0.19)
Cash Flow Per Share	1.93	15.90	13.53	9.30	12.45	7.64	5.84	3.42
Tang. Book Val. Per Share	35.10	15.66	14.78	37.29	47.16	21.70	11.85	7.54
Dividends Per Share	0.620	0.620	0.580	0.540	0.50	0.456	0.430	0.410
Dividend Payout %	41.61	48.43	N.M.	N.M.	20.92	9.08	42.71	N.M.
Income Statement								
Total Revenues	870,512	3,445,216	2,985,366	2,588,542	2,326,856	1,963,098	1,805,725	1,471,533
Total Indirect Exp.	485,809	1,946,787	...	1,263	10,258	12,927	34,207	...
Depreciation & Amort.	155,452	595,732	510,445	1,263	10,258	12,927	11,395	301,556
Operating Income	73,167	315,544	386,355	436,155	420,066	370,393	(20,904)	(3,702)
Net Interest Inc./(Exp.)	(46,821)	(171,391)	(132,224)	(103,710)	(100,559)	(99,984)	(126,360)	(89,744)
Income Taxes	20,105	79,892	(577,000)	(44,908)	149,481	228,176	69,297	28,559
Eqty Earns/Minority Int.	(3,508)	(23,612)	(9,068)	(42,419)	(61,683)	(12,927)	(11,395)	...
Income from Cont Ops	...	74,888	(987,737)	(168,248)	145,527	314,151	...	...
Net Income	19,732	61,490	(984,371)	(198,055)	2,237,002	229,961	64,408	(9,549)
Average Shs. Outstg.	57,424	57,875	58,644	58,661	60,636	62,736	60,982	60,211
Balance Sheet								
Cash & Cash Equivalents	1,054,520	937,651	1,298,936	140,744	99,019	111,010	50,083	51,008
Total Current Assets	1,600,847	1,504,946	1,948,012	674,356	527,100	508,008	405,439	408,284
Total Assets	10,137,598	10,171,238	9,602,028	8,046,792	8,634,609	5,375,828	5,527,545	4,971,601
Total Current Liabilities	675,241	696,945	1,167,166	816,216	984,411	369,672	623,379	905,885
Long–Term Obligations	3,669,310	1,994,913	1,641,624	1,507,764	1,172,987	1,279,877	1,553,096	1,264,218
Net Stockholders' Equity	3,128,074	3,108,019	3,059,577	3,526,366	3,943,894	2,492,106	2,263,893	1,999,106
Net Working Capital	925,606	808,001	780,846	(141,860)	(457,311)	138,336	(217,940)	(497,601)
Shares Outstanding	62,751	62,722	58,678	58,569	58,688	61,133	61,177	60,585
Statistical Record								
Operating Profit Margin %	8.42	9.15	12.94	16.84	18.05	18.86	N.M.	N.M.
Net Profit Margin %	6.90	6.81	N.M.	N.M.	19.10	39.24	10.61	3.23
Return on Equity %	0.63	2.40	N.M	N.M	3.68	12.60	2.34	N.M.
Return on Assets %	0.19	0.73	N.M.	N.M.	1.68	5.84	0.95	N.M.
Debt/Total Assets %	36.19	19.61	17.09	18.73	13.58	23.80	28.09	25.42
Price Range	74.43-62.15	63.92-35.96	91.90-44.45	111.2-87.00	126.4-82.95	135.4-44.44	49.69-31.06	48.50-34.63
P/E Ratio	43.53-36.35	49.94-28.09	N/A	N/A	52.88-34.71	26.97-8.85	48.24-30.16	N/A
Average Yield %	0.89	1.21	0.84	0.55	0.57	0.58	1.02	1.02

Address: 30 North Lasalle Street, Chicago, IL 60602	**Officers:** Walter C.D. Carlson – Chmn., LeRoy T. Carlson – Pres., C.E.O.	**Investor Contact:**312–630–1900
Telephone: (312) 630–1900	**Transfer Agents:**ComputerShare Investor Services, Chicago, IL	**Institutional Holding** **No of Institutions:** 1
Web Site: www.teldta.com		**Shares:** 1,364 **% Held:** –

TENNANT CO.

Exchange	Symbol	Price	52Wk Range	Yield	P/E
NYS	TNC	$38.00 (5/28/2004)	45.10–34.95	2.21	24.36

*7 Year Price Score 104.4 ***NYSE Composite Index=100** ***12 Month Price Score 45.7**

Interim Earnings (Per Share)

Qtr.	Mar	Jun	Sep	Dec
2001	0.02	0.14	0.32	0.04
2002	(0.15)	0.32	0.30	0.44
2003	0.28	0.36	0.36	0.56
2004	0.28	...	...	...

Interim Dividends (Per Share)

Amt	Decl	Ex	Rec	Pay
0.21Q	8/13/2003	8/27/2003	8/29/2003	9/15/2003
0.21Q	11/6/2003	11/25/2003	11/28/2003	12/15/2003
0.21Q	2/18/2004	2/25/2004	2/27/2004	3/15/2004
0.21Q	5/6/2004	5/26/2004	5/28/2004	6/15/2004

Indicated Div: $0.84 (Div. Reinv. Plan)

Valuation Analysis

Forecast P/E 21.08 (5/24/2004)

Market Cap $340.9 Million	Book Value	166.2 Million
Price/Book 2.14	Price/Sales	0.77

Dividend Achiever Status

Rank 284	10 Year Growth Rate	2.76%
Total Years of Dividend Growth		31

Business Summary: Purpose Machinery (MIC: 11.13 SIC: 3589 NAIC:333319)

Tennant is a manufacturer of nonresidential floor maintenance and outdoor cleaning equipment, floor coatings and related offerings. Co.'s products include scrubbers, sweepers, extractors, buffers and other specialized floor cleaning equipment and supplies, plus an array of industrial floor coatings. Co. has manufacturing operations in Holland, Michigan and United Kingdom, The Netherlands. Co. sells its products directly in ten countries and through distributors in 50 others.

Recent Developments: For the quarter ended Mar 31 2004, net income increased 4.0% to $2.6 million compared with $2.5 million in the equivalent 2003 quarter. Results for 2003 included a net unusual benefit of $600,000. Net sales grew 5.3% to $119.1 million from $113.1 million a year earlier. Net sales for 2004 included previously deferred revenues of $6.4 million resulting from the amendment of a contract. Gross profit advanced 9.6% to $48.0 million, or 40.3% as a percentage of net sales, versus $43.8 million, or 38.7%, in 2003. Results benefited from continued recovery in equipment sales to industrial customers and from favorable foreign currency translation. Operating income rose 2.4% to $4.3 million.

Prospects: Prospects are mixed. On one hand, Co. is seeing signs of recovering demand within the industrial customer sector. Also, Co. continues to benefit from the extension of its patented foam–scrubbing technology system, $FaST^{TM}$, to more of its cleaning equipment. Conversely, Co. continues to face difficult economic conditions in Europe and the adverse impact of higher costs for steel. Furthermore, Co. expects steel cost increases to continue throughout 2004, which it may not be able to fully offset through price increases and cost reductions. Nevertheless, Co. reaffirmed that it expects to report 2004 net earnings of between $1.55 and $1.85 per share.

Financial Data

(US$ in Thousands)	3 Mos	12/31/2003	12/31/2002	12/31/2001	12/31/2000	12/31/1999	12/31/1998	12/31/1997
Earnings Per Share	1.56	1.56	0.91	0.52	3.09	2.15	2.67	2.41
Cash Flow Per Share	0.93	3.36	2.12	3.70	4.25	4.19	4.51	4.17
Tang. Book Val. Per Share	15.75	16.43	15.18	15.17	15.16	13.06	12.67	12.12
Dividends Per Share	0.840	0.840	0.820	0.800	0.780	0.760	0.740	0.720
Dividend Payout %	53.85	53.84	90.10	153.84	25.24	35.34	27.71	29.87
Income Statement								
Total Revenues	119,102	453,962	424,183	422,970	454,044	429,407	389,388	372,428
Total Indirect Exp.	43,724	159,002	154,247	134,546	139,665	142,747	128,450	120,948
Depreciation & Amort.	3,376	13,879	16,947	18,507	18,391	18,667	17,550	17,468
Operating Income	4,292	22,675	15,576	13,416	43,524	31,262	37,349	36,088
Net Interest Inc./(Exp.)	88	608	510	340	807	(1,097)	1,479	2,678
Income Taxes	1,852	8,328	6,633	8,945	15,794	10,893	13,767	13,425
Net Income	2,557	14,155	8,265	4,804	28,250	19,693	25,325	24,205
Average Shs. Outstg.	9,192	9,064	9,048	9,203	9,135	9,140	9,500	10,032
Balance Sheet								
Cash & Cash Equivalents	19,852	24,587	16,356	23,783	21,512	14,928	17,693	16,279
Total Current Assets	173,476	176,370	162,901	152,387	171,628	165,093	150,868	143,105
Total Assets	263,551	258,873	256,237	246,619	263,285	257,533	239,098	233,870
Total Current Liabilities	67,961	59,507	70,349	55,648	67,255	74,999	60,809	57,149
Long–Term Obligations	1,513	6,295	5,000	10,000	10,000	16,003	23,038	20,678
Net Stockholders' Equity	166,239	165,616	154,145	154,328	154,948	135,915	131,267	134,086
Net Working Capital	105,515	116,863	92,552	96,739	104,373	90,094	90,059	85,956
Shares Outstanding	9,007	8,994	8,981	9,036	9,052	8,989	9,123	9,699
Statistical Record								
Operating Profit Margin %	3.60	4.99	3.67	3.17	9.58	7.28	9.59	9.68
Net Profit Margin %	5.25	6.78	5.07	5.36	13.17	9.65	13.57	13.70
Return on Equity %	1.54	8.54	5.36	3.11	18.23	14.48	19.29	18.05
Return on Assets %	0.97	5.46	3.22	1.94	10.72	7.64	10.59	10.34
Debt/Total Assets %	0.57	2.43	1.95	4.05	3.79	6.21	9.63	8.84
Price Range	44.50–38.44	45.10–29.20	44.00–26.65	48.63–33.00	52.56–30.12	42.88–32.00	44.94–33.00	39.63–26.50
P/E Ratio	158.9–137.3	28.91–18.72	48.35–29.29	93.52–63.46	17.01–9.75	19.94–14.88	16.83–12.36	16.44–11.00
Average Yield %	2.06	2.30	2.24	2.01	2.57	2.18	1.85	2.22

Address: 701 North Lilac Drive, Minneapolis, MN 55440 Telephone: (763) 540–1208 Web Site: www.tennantco.com	Officers: Janet M. Dolan – Pres., C.E.O., Eric A. Blanchard – V.P., Gen. Couns., Sec. Transfer Agents: Wells Fargo Bank Minnesota, N.A., St. Paul, MN	Investor Contact: 763–540–1553 Institutional Holding No of Institutions: 4 Shares: 7,296 % Held: –

TEPPCO PARTNERS, L.P.

Exchange	Symbol	Price	52Wk Range	Yield	P/E
NYS	TPP	$37.40 (5/28/2004)	42.00–34.07	7.09	24.13

*7 Year Price Score 131.2 *NYSE Composite Index=100* ***12 Month Price Score 45.1**

TRADING VOLUME (thousand shares)

Interim Earnings (Per Share)

Qtr.	Mar	Jun	Sep	Dec
2001	0.55	0.89	0.35	0.39
2002	0.46	0.39	0.48	0.46
2003	0.43	0.43	0.36	0.30
2004	0.46	...	...	...

Interim Dividends (Per Share)

Amt	Decl	Ex	Rec	Pay
0.625Q	7/16/2003	7/29/2003	7/31/2003	8/8/2003
0.65Q	10/17/2003	10/29/2003	10/31/2003	11/7/2003
0.65Q	1/16/2004	1/28/2004	1/30/2004	2/6/2004
0.663Q	4/16/2004	4/28/2004	4/30/2004	5/7/2004
			Indicated Div: $2.65	

Valuation Analysis

Forecast P/E 21.80 (5/24/2004)

Market Cap $1.9 Billion		Book Value	1.1 Billion
Price/Book 2.31		Price/Sales	0.60

Dividend Achiever Status

Rank	187	10 Year Growth Rate 8.46%
Total Years of Dividend Growth		11

Business Summary: Oil and Gas (MIC: 14.2 SIC: 4613 NAIC:486910)

TEPPCO Partners operates through three segments. The downstream segment includes transportation and storage of refined products, liquefied petroleum gases and petrochemicals. The upstream segment includes gathering, transportation, marketing and storage of crude oil, and distribution of lubrication oils and specialty chemicals. The midstream segment includes natural gas gathering services, fractionation of natural gas liquids (NGLs) and transportation of NGLs. Texas Eastern Products Pipeline Co., a subsidiary of Duke Energy Field Services (DEFS), serves as the general partner of TPP. Certain assets of the midstream segment are managed and operated by DEFS under an agreement with Co.

Recent Developments: For the three months ended Mar 31 2004, net income increased 19.2% to $40.4 million compared with $33.9 million in the same period a year earlier. Total operating revenues advanced 19.9% to $1.32 billion from $1.10 billion the previous year. Operating income rose 5.1% to $53.9 million. Co.'s results were driven by its upstream operations, which posted operating profits of $10.0 million versus $3.6 million in the prior-year period, primarily due to the benefits of its Nov 1 2003 purchase of assets from Genesis Pipeline Texas, L.P. and increased volumes on Seaway Crude Pipeline.

Prospects: Co. has reaffirmed its full-year 2004 earnings estimate of between $1.55 and $1.85 per unit. Meanwhile, on Apr 26 2004, Co. announced an additional project to expand delivery capacity of liquefied petroleum gases to the Northeast by 8,000 to 10,000 barrels per day. The project is scheduled for completion in October 2004. This Phase II expansion includes construction of three pump stations between Coshocton and Greensburg, PA, and two stations from Greensburg, to Watkins Glen, NY. Additional work on the pipeline segment between Greensburg and Philadelphia, PA, is expected to increase delivery rates to the Philadelphia area.

Financial Data

(US$ in Thousands)	3 Mos	12/31/2003	12/31/2002	12/31/2001	12/31/2000	12/31/1999	12/31/1998	12/31/1997
Earnings Per Share	1.55	1.52	1.79	2.18	1.89	1.91	1.61	1.95
Cash Flow Per Share	0.68	4.00	4.77	4.30	3.21	2.28	1.24	...
Dividends Per Share	2.550	2.500	2.350	2.150	2	1.850	1.750	1.550
Dividend Payout %	163.46	164.47	131.28	98.62	105.82	96.85	108.69	79.48
Income Statement								
Total Revenues	1,318,061	4,255,832	3,242,163	3,556,413	3,087,941	1,934,883	429,638	222,093
Total Indirect Exp.	85,527	4,059,476	3,071,916	3,405,424	2,979,916	1,834,793	349,672	130,543
Depreciation & Amort.	27,820	100,728	86,032	45,899	35,163	32,656	26,938	23,772
Operating Income	53,901	192,408	170,247	150,989	108,025	100,090	79,966	91,550
Net Interest Inc./(Exp.)	(19,595)	(84,250)	(66,192)	(62,057)	(44,423)	(29,430)	(28,989)	(32,229)
Eqty Earns/Minority Int.	5,651	16,863	11,980	16,598	11,425	(736)	(544)	(625)
Income from Cont Ops	...	...	...	...	...	...	53,341	...
Net Income	40,433	125,769	117,862	109,131	77,376	72,120	(19,426)	61,300
Average Shs. Outstg.	62,999	59,765	49,202	39,258	33,594	45,058	74,933	29,000
Balance Sheet								
Cash & Cash Equivalents	3,145	29,469	30,968	25,479	27,096	32,593	47,423	43,961
Total Current Assets	494,329	452,818	360,567	283,480	363,397	263,009	188,576	91,159
Total Assets	2,989,031	2,940,992	2,770,642	2,065,348	1,622,810	1,041,373	914,969	673,909
Total Current Liabilities	515,220	475,591	366,783	686,842	358,271	243,492	148,225	53,875
Long-Term Obligations	1,361,849	1,339,650	1,377,692	730,472	835,784	455,753	427,722	309,512
Net Stockholders' Equity	1,095,018	1,109,321	891,842	543,181	315,057	229,767	227,186	302,967
Net Working Capital	(20,891)	(22,773)	(6,216)	(385,362)	5,126	19,517	40,351	37,284
Shares Outstanding	62,998	62,998	53,809	40,500	32,700	29,000	29,000	29,000
Operating Profit Margin %	93.51	4.61	5.25	4.24	3.49	5.17	18.61	41.22
Return on Equity %	111.32	11.69	13.21	20.09	24.55	31.38	23.47	20.23
Return on Assets %	40.78	4.41	4.25	5.28	4.76	6.92	5.82	9.09
Debt/Total Assets %	45.56	45.55	49.72	35.36	51.50	43.76	46.74	45.92
Price Range	41.97–36.40	41.15–27.75	33.00–26.10	35.90–24.75	26.63–19.31	27.94–18.00	30.50–24.25	27.88–20.13
P/E Ratio	27.08–23.48	27.07–18.26	18.44–14.58	16.47–11.35	14.09–10.22	14.63–9.42	18.94–15.06	14.29–10.32
Average Yield %	6.43	7.26	7.80	7.32	8.72	7.79	6.35	6.56

Address: 2929 Allen Parkway, Houston, TX 77252–2521 **Telephone:** (713) 759 3636 **Web Site:** www.teppco.com	**Officers:** Jim W. Mogg – Chmn., Barry R. Pearl – Pres., C.E.O., C.O.O. **Transfer Agents:** ChaseMellon Shareholder Services, L.L.C., Ridgefield Park, NJ	**Investor Contact:** 800–659–0059 **Institutional Holding** **No of Institutions:** 3 **Shares:** 258 % Held: –

TOOTSIE ROLL INDUSTRIES INC

Exchange	Symbol	Price	52Wk Range	Yield	P/E
NYS	TR	$34.10 (5/28/2004)	37.61-28.74	0.82	26.64

*7 Year Price Score 99.5 *NYSE Composite Index=100 ***12 Month Price Score 48.7**

TRADING VOLUME (thousand shares)

Interim Earnings (Per Share)

Qtr.	Mar	Jun	Sep	Dec
2001	0.22	0.25	0.49	0.30
2002	0.23	0.22	0.49	0.31
2003	0.20	0.23	0.50	0.33
2004	0.22	...	...	...

Interim Dividends (Per Share)

Amt	Decl	Ex	Rec	Pay
0.068Q	12/9/2003	12/17/2003	12/19/2003	1/6/2004
0.068Q	2/17/2004	2/27/2004	3/2/2004	4/1/2004
3%	2/17/2004	2/27/2004	3/2/2004	4/14/2004
0.07Q	5/24/2004	6/11/2004	6/15/2004	7/16/2004
		Indicated Div: $0.28		

Valuation Analysis

Forecast P/E 25.89 (5/24/2004)

Market Cap $1.2 Billion		Book Value 538.1 Million	
Price/Book 2.31		Price/Sales 3.14	

Dividend Achiever Status

Rank 68	10 Year Growth Rate	16.02%
Total Years of Dividend Growth		40

Business Summary: Food (MIC: 4.1 SIC: 2064 NAIC:311340)

Tootsie Roll Industries is primarily engaged in the manufacture and sale of candy products. The majority of Co.'s products are sold under the following registered trademarks: *Tootsie Roll, Tootsie Roll Pops, Caramel Apple Pops, Child's Play, Charms, Blow Pop, Blue Razz, Cella's* chocolate covered cherries, *Mason Dots, Mason Crows, Junior Mints, Charleston Chew, Sugar Daddy, Sugar Babies, Andes* and *Fluffy Stuff* cotton candy. Co. has manufacturing facilities in Illinois, New York, Tennessee, Massachusetts, Wisconsin, Maryland and Mexico. Co.'s principal markets are in the U.S., Canada and Mexico.

Recent Developments: For the first thirteen weeks ended Apr 3 2004, net income increased 5.4% to $11.5 million compared with $10.9 million in the corresponding period of the prior year. The improvement in earnings was primarily attributed to more favorable ingredient costs and higher sales, partially offset by higher trade promotions and discounts, which were accounted for as a reduction in net sales. Net sales climbed 5.9% to $80.0 million from $75.6 million a year earlier. The improvement in sales was primarily attributed to effective marketing programs as well as the timing of the quarter end reporting period.

Prospects: Co. is employing marketing programs as well as trade promotions and discounts, to help further leverage its position in the highly competitive domestic candy business. Meanwhile, ingredient and packaging costs continue to have a major influence on profit margins. Accordingly, Co. continues to seek competitive bids to leverage the high volume of annual purchases it makes of these items and to lower per unit costs. In addition, Co. has the flexibility to change the size of certain of its products, which are usually sold at standard prices, to help offset significant changes in raw material costs. This should give Co. more control over its expenses.

Financial Data

(US$ in Thousands)	3 Mos	12/31/2003	12/31/2002	12/31/2001	12/31/2000	12/31/1999	12/31/1998	12/31/1997
Earnings Per Share	1.28	1.26	1.25	1.26	1.48	1.41	1.36	2.50
Tang. Book Val. Per Share	7.99	8.18	7.79	7.53	6.68	6.91	6.26	10.81
Dividends Per Share	0.330	0.268	0.260	0.250	0.230	0.190	0.150	0.120
Dividend Payout %	25.78	21.27	20.80	19.84	15.54	13.48	11.03	4.80
Income Statement								
Total Revenues	80,046	392,656	393,185	423,496	427,054	396,750	388,659	375,594
Total Indirect Exp.	18,670	77,756	75,751	112,895	109,225	99,670	99,777	97,194
Depreciation & Amort.	3,416	13,913	12,354	3,778	3,420	2,706	2,706	2,706
Operating Income	16,060	92,353	96,669	93,944	110,729	104,519	101,265	90,087
Net Interest Inc./(Exp.)	...	4,292	5,244	6,200	6,770	6,996	6,178	5,281
Income Taxes	5,842	32,933	34,300	35,100	42,071	40,137	38,537	34,679
Net Income	11,493	65,014	66,388	65,687	75,737	71,310	67,526	60,682
Average Shs. Outstg.	52,596	51,784	53,078	51,964	50,917	50,443	49,492	24,248
Balance Sheet								
Cash & Cash Equivalents	52,942	84,084	105,507	106,532	60,882	88,504	80,744	60,433
Total Current Assets	240,815	243,705	224,948	246,096	203,211	224,532	228,539	206,961
Total Assets	671,513	665,297	646,080	618,676	562,442	529,416	487,423	436,742
Total Current Liabilities	66,290	62,887	63,096	57,846	57,446	56,109	53,384	53,606
Long-Term Obligations	7,500	7,500	7,500	7,500	7,500	7,500	7,500	7,500
Net Stockholders' Equity	538,087	536,581	526,740	508,461	458,696	430,646	396,457	351,163
Net Working Capital	174,525	180,818	161,852	188,250	145,765	168,423	175,155	153,355
Shares Outstanding	52,578	51,171	52,480	51,917	50,496	49,966	49,271	24,099
Statistical Record								
Operating Profit Margin %	20.06	23.52	24.58	22.18	25.92	26.34	26.05	23.98
Net Profit Margin %	28.95	33.33	34.33	32.08	37.43	38.20	37.20	34.62
Return on Equity %	2.14	12.11	12.60	12.91	16.51	16.55	17.03	17.28
Return on Assets %	1.71	9.77	10.27	10.61	13.46	13.46	13.85	13.89
Debt/Total Assets %	1.11	1.12	1.16	1.21	1.33	1.41	1.53	1.71
Price Range	37.61-34.75	35.86-25.73	45.22-27.82	46.76-32.10	43.76-25.71	41.54-26.49	40.76-24.99	27.17-15.35
P/E Ratio	29.38-27.15	28.46-20.42	36.17-22.25	37.11-25.48	29.56-17.37	29.46-18.79	29.97-18.38	10.87-6.14
Average Yield %	0.92	0.87	0.73	0.64	0.71	0.56	0.46	0.59

Address: 7401 South Cicero Avenue, Chicago, IL 60629	**Officers:** Melvin J. Gordon – Chmn., C.E.O., Ellen R. Gordon – Pres., C.O.O.	**Investor Contact:**800-851-9677
Telephone: (773) 838-3400	**Transfer Agents:**Mellon Investor Services, L.L.C., Ridgefield Park, NJ	**Institutional Holding**
Web Site: www.tootsie.com		**No of Institutions:** 143
		Shares: 12,300,560 **% Held:** 22.80%

TRANSATLANTIC HOLDINGS, INC.

Exchange	Symbol	Price	52Wk Range	Yield	P/E
NYS	TRH	$88.04 (5/28/2004)	91.86–69.12	0.45	14.09

*7 Year Price Score 121.8 *NYSE Composite Index=100 ***12 Month Price Score 52.7**

TRADING VOLUME (thousand shares)

Interim Earnings (Per Share)

Qtr.	Mar	Jun	Sep	Dec
2001	0.96	0.76	(1.49)	0.13
2002	1.00	1.16	1.16	(0.11)
2003	1.19	1.43	1.53	1.60
2004	1.69	...	...	...

Interim Dividends (Per Share)

Amt	Decl	Ex	Rec	Pay
0.11Q	12/4/2003	3/3/2004	3/5/2004	3/19/2004
0.11Q	3/25/2004	6/2/2004	6/4/2004	6/18/2004
25%	5/20/2004	7/19/2004	6/25/2004	7/16/2004
0.10Q	5/20/2004	9/1/2004	9/3/2004	9/17/2004

Indicated Div: $0.40

Valuation Analysis

Forecast P/E 13.35 (5/24/2004)

Market Cap	$4.6 Billion	Book Value	2.4 Billion
Price/Book	1.78	Price/Sales	1.23

Dividend Achiever Status

Rank	105	10 Year Growth Rate	12.93%
Total Years of Dividend Growth		13	

Business Summary: Insurance (MIC: 8.2 SIC: 6331 NAIC:524126)

Transatlantic Holdings, through its wholly-owned subsidiaries Transatlantic Reinsurance Company, Trans Re Zurich and Putnam Reinsurance Company, offers reinsurance capacity for a full range of property and casualty products on a treaty and facultative basis, directly and through brokers, to insurance and reinsurance companies, in both the domestic and international markets. Co.'s principal lines of reinsurance include auto liability, other liability, medical malpractice, ocean marine and aviation, accident and health and surety and credit in the casualty lines, along with fire, homeowners multiple peril and auto physical damage in the property lines.

Recent Developments: For the three months ended Mar 31 2004, net income jumped 42.7% to $89.7 million from $62.8 million in the corresponding prior-year period. Total revenues advanced 28.4% to $972.4 million from $757.3 million the previous year. Revenues included realized net capital gains of $7.2 million and $538,000 in 2004 and 2003, respectively. Net premiums written increased 18.1% to $907.5 million from $768.1 million the year before. Net premiums earned climbed 29.0% to $893.1 million from $692.2 million a year earlier. Total expenses were $857.0 million, up 26.4% versus $678.1 million the prior year.

Prospects: Prospects appear favorable as worldwide market conditions are expected to remain strong during 2004. Results are benefiting from strong growth in net premiums written in Co.'s domestic and international operations, driven by rate increases, along with increased coverage provided and favorable foreign currency exchange rates. Higher domestic net premiums written are being driven by significant increases in specialty casualty, principally medical malpractice, directors' and officers' and other professional liability, as well as property and aviation lines. Meanwhile, higher international net premiums written are being fueled by property, specialty casualty and auto liability lines.

Financial Data

(US$ in Thousands)	3 Mos	12/31/2003	12/31/2002	12/31/2001	12/31/2000	12/31/1999	12/31/1998	12/31/1997
Earnings Per Share	6.25	5.75	3.21	0.36	4.03	3.58	4.73	3.56
Tang. Book Val. Per Share	46.36	45.29	38.78	35.32	35.58	31.53	30.96	26.16
Dividends Per Share	0.430	0.420	0.390	0.370	0.340	0.310	0.280	0.250
Dividend Payout %	6.88	7.30	12.21	103.33	8.59	8.75	5.91	7.11
Income Statement								
Total Premium Income	893,147	3,171,226	2,369,452	1,790,339	1,631,536	1,484,634	1,380,570	1,259,251
Net Investment Income	72,048	270,972	252,026	240,083	234,485	230,739	222,000	207,646
Total Revenues	972,444	3,442,198	2,621,478	2,030,422	1,866,021	1,715,373	1,602,570	1,466,897
Total Indirect Exp.	239,931	807,139	662,579	526,962	373,564	250,972	140,029	270,899
Inc. Before Inc. Taxes	115,486	386,674	188,320	(34,107)	267,982	236,097	323,351	234,726
Income Taxes	25,833	83,030	19,002	(52,999)	56,344	48,735	75,828	49,226
Net Income	89,653	303,644	169,318	18,892	211,638	187,362	247,523	185,500
Average Shs. Outstg.	52,973	52,762	52,755	52,736	52,476	52,323	52,297	52,126
Balance Sheet								
Cash & Cash Equivalents	154,484	182,887	127,402	124,214	129,246	104,017	70,589	70,737
Premiums Due	1,452,987	1,277,942	1,167,802	1,254,216	778,501	777,086	658,027	590,981
Invst. Assets: Total	6,490,299	6,684,278	5,460,128	4,880,217	4,261,980	4,229,445	4,258,244	3,921,782
Total Assets	9,298,467	8,707,758	7,286,525	6,741,303	5,522,672	5,480,198	5,253,249	4,834,980
Net Stockholders' Equity	2,435,847	2,376,587	2,030,767	1,846,010	1,856,365	1,642,517	1,610,139	1,356,659
Shares Outstanding	52,541	52,468	52,360	52,255	52,160	52,091	52,000	51,844
Return on Revenues %	9.08	8.53	6.68	0.94	13.11	15.74	22.98	14.89
Return on Equity %	3.62	12.35	8.63	1.03	13.18	16.44	22.88	16.10
Return on Assets %	0.95	3.37	2.40	0.28	4.43	4.92	7.01	4.51
Price Range	87.46–80.55	80.80–61.48	91.00–60.55	92.00–63.18	70.58–45.96	53.42–46.12	62.92–46.37	50.42–34.06
P/E Ratio	13.99–12.89	14.05–10.69	28.35–18.86	255.6–175.5	17.51–11.40	14.92–12.88	13.30–9.80	14.16–9.57
Average Yield %	0.51	0.59	0.51	0.48	0.60	0.62	0.54	0.58

Address: 80 Pine Street, New York, NY 10005	**Officers:** M. R. Greenberg – Chmn., Robert F. Orlich – Pres., C.E.O.	**Investor Contact:**212–770–2040
Telephone: (212) 770–2000	**Transfer Agents:**American Stock Transfer &Trust Company, New York, NY	**Institutional Holding** **No of Institutions:** 6
Web Site: www.transre.com		**Shares:** 118,096 **% Held:** –

269

TRUSTMARK CORP.

Exchange	Symbol	Price	52Wk Range	Yield	P/E
NMS	TRMK	$27.75 (5/28/2004)	30.60-25.40	2.74	13.54

*7 Year Price Score 124.5 *NYSE Composite Index=100 *12 Month Price Score 45.4

Interim Earnings (Per Share)

Qtr.	Mar	Jun	Sep	Dec
2001	0.40	0.41	0.45	0.46
2002	0.48	0.50	0.49	0.47
2003	0.41	0.53	0.55	0.51
2004	0.46	...	...	...

Interim Dividends (Per Share)

Amt	Decl	Ex	Rec	Pay
0.165Q	7/15/2003	8/27/2003	9/1/2003	9/15/2003
0.19Q	10/21/2003	11/26/2003	12/1/2003	12/15/2003
0.19Q	1/20/2004	2/26/2004	3/1/2004	3/15/2004
0.19Q	4/20/2004	5/27/2004	6/1/2004	6/15/2004
		Indicated Div: $0.76		

Valuation Analysis

Forecast P/E 13.40 (5/24/2004)

Market Cap $1.7 Billion	Book Value 718.6 Million
Price/Book 2.53	Price/Sales 3.37

Dividend Achiever Status

Rank	100	10 Year Growth Rate	13.68%
Total Years of Dividend Growth			30

Business Summary: Commercial Banking (MIC: 8.1 SIC: 6021 NAIC:522110)

Trustmark is the holding company for Trustmark National Bank, along with its wholly-owned subsidiaries Trustmark Securities, Inc., Trustmark Investment Advisors, Inc. and The Bottrell Insurance Agency, Inc. Co. also provides banking services through its wholly-owned subsidiary, Somerville Bank & Trust Company. Co. provides a full range of financial products and services to individuals and small-business customers through 144 offices in Mississippi, Tennessee and Florida. Co. also provides trust and fiduciary services, brokerage services, insurance services, as well as credit card and mortgage services. In addition, Co. operates a proprietary mutual fund family, The Performance Funds.

Recent Developments: For the quarter ended Mar 31 2004, net income totaled $26.8 million, up 9.3% compared with $24.5 million in the prior year. Earnings for 2004 and 2003 included pre-tax gains on the sale of loans of $1.7 million and $3.9 million and security gains of $13,000 and $8.1 million, respectively. Net interest income slipped 1.2% to $70.5 million from $71.4 million the year before. Provision for loan losses declined 64.9% to $1.1 million from $3.0 million the previous year. Total non-interest income slid 21.0% to $32.5 million from $41.2 million in 2003, while total non-interest expense fell 14.7% to $59.5 million from $69.7 million a year earlier.

Prospects: Earnings are being negatively affected by decreased mortgage refinancing activity due to rising interest rates, partially offset by lower salary and employee benefits expenses. Going forward, results should benefit from Co.'s efforts to expand its operations into new markets.On Mar 12 2004, Co. acquired five branches of Allied Houston Bank, which reported approximately $148.1 million in assets and $161.7 million of deposits and other liabilities, for a $10.0 million deposit premium. The acquisition will expand Co.'s operations into Texas with branches located in the Houston market.

Financial Data

(US$ in Thousands)	3 Mos	12/31/2003	12/31/2002	12/31/2001	12/31/2000	12/31/1999	12/31/1998	12/31/1997
Earnings Per Share	2.05	2.00	1.94	1.72	1.53	1.36	1.14	0.98
Tang. Book Val. Per Share	9.24	8.96	9.25	8.92	8.69	8.38	8.29	7.60
Dividends Per Share	0.710	0.680	0.610	0.550	0.510	0.440	0.350	0.290
Dividend Payout %	34.47	34.25	31.70	32.26	33.33	32.35	30.92	29.84
Income Statement								
Total Interest Income	88,607	359,388	405,952	477,820	488,759	448,509	420,100	376,892
Total Interest Expense	20,248	89,558	113,766	209,242	255,196	205,079	191,900	172,887
Net Interest Income	68,359	269,830	292,186	268,578	233,563	243,430	228,200	204,005
Provision for Loan Losses	1,052	9,771	14,107	13,200	10,401	9,072	7,771	4,682
Non-Interest Income	32,524	157,543	141,870	131,990	124,540	101,943	89,060	75,555
Non-Interest Expense	59,482	236,120	233,841	215,941	189,377	187,071	180,391	167,915
Income Before Taxes	40,349	181,482	186,108	171,427	158,325	149,230	129,098	106,963
Income from Cont Ops	...	...	...	...	104,201	...	...	...
Net Income	26,751	118,530	121,140	111,281	101,737	97,994	83,314	71,064
Average Shs. Outstg.	58,587	59,244	62,416	64,876	67,928	71,921	72,946	72,785
Balance Sheet								
Cash & Due from Banks	340,114	333,096	357,427	328,779	298,651	279,957	312,527	292,555
Securities Avail. for Sale	1,958,767	1,933,993	1,262,570	1,061,495	1,120,633	783,220	776,049	610,570
Net Loans & Leases	5,124,117	4,845,776	4,542,595	4,448,832	4,078,083	3,949,085	3,636,168	2,919,555
Total Assets	8,090,463	7,914,321	7,138,706	7,180,339	6,886,988	6,743,404	6,355,190	5,545,158
Total Deposits	5,574,888	5,089,459	4,686,090	4,613,365	4,058,418	3,924,796	3,946,397	3,818,949
Long-Term Obligations	...	531,035	475,000	225,000	250,000	...	...	...
Total Liabilities	7,371,838	7,224,748	6,459,172	6,494,895	6,257,347	6,087,648	5,703,314	4,951,533
Net Stockholders' Equity	718,625	689,573	679,534	685,444	629,641	655,756	651,876	593,625
Shares Outstanding	58,280	58,246	60,516	63,705	64,755	70,423	72,531	72,740
Return on Equity %	3.72	17.18	17.82	16.23	16.54	14.94	12.78	11.97
Return on Assets %	0.33	1.49	1.69	1.54	1.51	1.45	1.31	1.28
Equity/Assets %	8.88	8.71	9.51	9.54	9.14	9.72	10.25	10.70
Non-Int. Exp./Tot. Inc. %	49.10	45.67	42.68	35.41	30.87	33.98	35.42	37.11
Price Range	30.60-28.64	29.82-22.74	26.90-20.49	24.70-19.56	21.61-15.31	24.06-18.38	25.75-15.38	23.50-12.13
P/E Ratio	14.93-13.97	14.91-11.37	13.87-10.56	14.36-11.37	14.12-10.01	17.69-13.51	22.59-13.49	23.98-12.37
Average Yield %	2.38	2.60	2.51	2.46	2.72	1.99	1.66	1.98

Address: 248 East Capitol Street, Jackson, MS 39201	Officers: Richard G. Hickson – Chmn., Pres., C.E.O., Louis E. Greer – Chief Acctg. Officer	Investor Contact:601-949-6898
Telephone: (601) 208-5111	Transfer Agents:Trustmark National Bank, Jackson, MS	Institutional Holding
Web Site: www.trustmark.com		No of Institutions: 17
		Shares: 3,537,235 % Held: -

UGI CORP. (NEW)

Exchange	Symbol	Price	52Wk Range	Yield	P/E
NYS	UGI	$32.09 (5/28/2004)	34.90-28.93	3.90	14.79

*7 Year Price Score 157.9 *NYSE Composite Index=100 ***12 Month Price Score 45.8**

Interim Earnings (Per Share)

Qtr.	Dec	Mar	Jun	Sep
2000-01	0.66	1.11	(0.10)	(0.41)
2001-02	0.58	1.28	0.09	(0.15)
2002-03	0.86	1.62	(0.05)	(0.14)
2003-04	0.88	1.48	...	...

Interim Dividends (Per Share)

Amt	Decl	Ex	Rec	Pay
0.285Q	7/29/2003	8/27/2003	8/29/2003	10/1/2003
0.285Q	10/28/2003	11/25/2003	11/28/2003	1/1/2004
0.285Q	1/27/2004	2/25/2004	2/27/2004	4/1/2004
0.313Q	4/27/2004	5/26/2004	5/28/2004	7/1/2004

Indicated Div: $1.25 (Div. Reinv. Plan)

Valuation Analysis

Forecast P/E 14.50 (5/24/2004)

Market Cap $884.6 Million	Book Value 608.6 Million
Price/Book 2.40	Price/Sales 0.46

Dividend Achiever Status

Rank	287	10 Year Growth Rate	2.53%
Total Years of Dividend Growth			16

Business Summary: Gas Utilities (MIC: 7.4 SIC: 4924 NAIC:221210)

UGI is a holding company that operates propane distribution, gas and electric utility, energy marketing and related businesses through subsidiaries. Co.'s majority-owned subsidiary AmeriGas Partners, L.P. conducts a retail propane distribution business. UGI Utilities, Inc. owns and operates a natural gas distribution utility and an electricity distribution utility in eastern Pennsylvania. UGI Enterprises, Inc., conducts domestic and international energy-related businesses through subsidiaries. Additionally, Enterprises owns FLAGA GmbH, which is engaged in the distribution of propane in Austria, the Czech Republic, and Slovakia.

Recent Developments: For the quarter ended Mar 31 2004, net income declined 3.9% to $67.1 million from $69.8 million in the prior-year quarter. Results for 2004 included a loss of $5.9 million related to the settlement of contracts associated with Co.'s purchase of the remaining 80.5% ownership interests of AGZ Holding. Results for 2003 included a one-time charge of $3.0 million. Total revenues grew 15.9% to $1.32 billion. By segment, earnings for AmeriGas Propane grew 11.2% to $30.8 million. Gas utility earnings slid 16.1% to $25.6 million. Electric utility earnings rose 3.0% to $3.4 million, while Energy services earnings climbed 22.9% to $4.3 million. International propane earnings fell 46.3% to $2.9 million.

Prospects: On Mar 31 2004, a subsidiary of Co. completed its acquisition of the remaining 80.5% ownership interests of AGZ Holding, the parent company of Antargaz, one of the four largest retail distributors of propane and butane in France. Going forward, Co. will continue to seek selective energy distribution businesses that grow its earnings and diversify cash flows. For the full fiscal year 2004, Co. reaffirmed its earnings per share guidance in the range of $2.10 to $2.20. The range includes a projected loss of about $0.25 per share from both the dilutive effects of the purchase of Antargaz and the estimated seasonal loss from Antargaz for the spring and summer months of April through September.

Financial Data

(US$ in Thousands)	6 Mos	3 Mos	09/30/2003	09/30/2002	09/30/2001	09/30/2000	09/30/1999	09/30/1998
Earnings Per Share	2.17	2.31	2.29	1.80	1.26	1.09	1.16	0.81
Cash Flow Per Share	2.33	0.30	5.76	5.90	4.95	3.24	2.95	3.59
Dividends Per Share	1.140	1.130	1.120	1.070	1.040	1.000	0.970	0.960
Dividend Payout %	52.53	48.91	48.90	59.72	82.23	92.22	83.90	118.44
Income Statement								
Total Revenues	2,210,300	893,700	3,026,100	2,213,700	2,468,100	1,761,700	1,383,600	1,439,700
Total Indirect Exp.	408,700	183,100	719,700	668,100	597,900	522,000	510,500	500,100
Costs & Expenses	1,920,400	785,400	2,723,800	1,961,100	2,240,700	1,570,500	1,207,700	1,269,500
Depreciation & Amort.	55,800	27,500	103,000	93,500	105,200	97,500	89,700	87,800
Operating Income	289,900	108,300	302,300	252,600	227,400	191,200	175,900	170,200
Net Interest Inc./(Exp.)	(53,400)	(26,700)	(109,200)	(109,100)	(104,800)	(98,500)	(84,600)	(84,400)
Income Taxes	64,900	24,300	60,700	46,900	45,400	40,100	43,200	34,400
Eqty Earns/Minority Int.	12,600	4,200	5,300	8,500				
Income from Cont Ops	...	...	...	...	52,000	...	...	...
Net Income	105,900	38,800	98,900	75,500	56,500	44,700	55,700	40,300
Average Shs. Outstg.	44,625	43,947	43,236	41,907	41,059	40,882	48,024	49,684
Balance Sheet								
Net Property	1,884,800	1,360,300	1,336,800	1,271,900	1,268,000	1,073,200	1,084,100	999,000
Total Assets	4,358,900	3,027,000	2,781,700	2,614,400	2,550,200	2,278,800	2,135,900	2,074,600
Long-Term Obligations	1,609,700	1,161,600	1,158,500	1,127,000	1,196,900	1,029,700	989,600	890,800
Net Stockholders' Equity	894,500	608,600	569,800	297,300	235,600	227,200	229,200	347,100
Shares Outstanding	50,770	42,906	42,699	41,551	40,944	40,490	40,905	49,234
Statistical Record								
Operating Profit Margin %	13.12	12.72	10.64	12.19	10.08	12.38	13.92	12.70
Net Inc./Net Property %	5.62	2.85	7.39	5.93	4.45	4.16	5.13	4.03
Net Inc./Tot. Capital %	4.22	1.78	4.69	3.89	2.97	2.71	3.39	2.41
Return on Equity %	11.84	7.26	20.83	29.27	28.71	28.96	29.09	14.43
Accum. Depr./Gross Prop. %	31.15	37.82	37.59	36.16	33.73	35.04	32.20	31.78
Price Range	34.35-28.93	34.05-28.93	34.90-23.47	24.43-17.73	19.39-14.46	16.17-12.17	16.79-10.62	19.87-13.87
P/E Ratio	15.83-13.33	14.74-12.52	15.24-10.25	13.57-9.85	15.39-11.47	14.83-11.16	14.48-9.16	24.54-17.13
Average Yield %	3.52	3.54	3.88	5.20	6.18	6.95	6.82	5.45

Address: 460 North Gulph Road, King of Prussia, PA 19406

Telephone: (610) 337-1000

Web Site: www.ugicorp.com

Officers: Lon R. Greenberg - Chmn., Pres., C.E.O., Anthony J. Mendicino - Sr. V.P., Fin., C.F.O.

Transfer Agents: Mellon Investor Services, LLC

Investor Contact: 610-337-1000

Institutional Holding
No of Institutions: 2
Shares: 74,400 % Held: -

UNITED BANKSHARES, INC.

Exchange	Symbol	Price	52Wk Range	Yield	P/E
NMS	UBSI	$31.20 (5/28/2004)	31.53-28.35	3.21	16.86

*7 Year Price Score 115.5   *NYSE Composite Index=100   *12 Month Price Score 47.2

Interim Earnings (Per Share)

Qtr.	Mar	Jun	Sep	Dec
2001	0.46	0.47	0.48	0.49
2002	0.50	0.51	0.52	0.53
2003	0.53	0.54	0.55	0.23
2004	0.53	...	...	...

Interim Dividends (Per Share)

Amt	Decl	Ex	Rec	Pay
0.25Q	8/28/2003	9/10/2003	9/12/2003	10/1/2003
0.25Q	11/24/2003	12/10/2003	12/12/2003	1/2/2004
0.25Q	2/23/2004	3/10/2004	3/12/2004	4/1/2004
0.25Q	5/17/2004	6/9/2004	6/11/2004	7/1/2004

Indicated Div: $1.00 (Div. Reinv. Plan)

Valuation Analysis

Forecast P/E 14.08 (5/24/2004)

Market Cap $1.3 Billion	Book Value 625.7 Million
Price/Book 2.10	Price/Sales 3.34

Dividend Achiever Status

Rank 200	10 Year Growth Rate	8.07%
Total Years of Dividend Growth		22

Business Summary: Commercial Banking (MIC: 8.1 SIC: 6021 NAIC:522110)

United Bankshares is a bank holding company with assets of $6.38 billion as of Dec 31 2003. Co., through its subsidiaries, United National Bank and United Bank, engages primarily in community banking and mortgage banking and additionally offers most types of business permitted by law and regulation. Included among the banking services offered are the acceptance of deposits in checking, savings, and money market accounts; the making of personal and student loans; and the making of real estate loans. Co. also owns nonbank subsidiaries that engage in mortgage banking and asset management. As of Dec 31 2003, Co. operated 91 offices in West Virginia, Virginia, Maryland, Ohio, and Washington.

Recent Developments: For the quarter ended Mar 31 2004, net income rose 4.3% to $23.5 million from $22.5 million in the corresponding period of the prior year. Interest and fees income slid 4.0% to $76.6 million, while total interest expense fell 25.8% to $22.0 million. Net interest income improved 8.8% to $54.6 million, reflecting an increase in average earning assets due to the Sequoia Bancshares acquisition, and lower funding costs resulting from decreased interest rates. Provision for loan losses declined 6.7% to $1.4 million. Total non–interest income declined 15.0% to $20.1 million, primarily due to decreased mortgage banking activity. Total non–interest expense decreased 0.9% to $37.2 million.

Prospects: Recently, Co. prepaid $156.5 million of Federal Home Loan Bank (FHLB) long–term advances with a low weighted–average interest rate. The early termination of these advances has resulted in an immediate positive impact on the net interest margin. Net interest margin for the first quarter of 2004 grew to 3.86% from 3.76% for the fourth quarter of 2003, primarily due to the savings in funding costs resulting from the prepayment of these FHLB advances. Meanwhile, Co. continues to benefit from the acquisition of Sequoia Bancshares of Bethesda, MD, which expanded Co.'s presence in the Northern Virginia, Washington, D.C. and suburban Maryland market.

Financial Data

(US$ in Thousands)	3 Mos	12/31/2003	12/31/2002	12/31/2001	12/31/2000	12/31/1999	12/31/1998	12/31/1997
Earnings Per Share	1.85	1.85	2.06	1.90	1.40	1.61	1.02	1.35
Tang. Book Val. Per Share	10.50	10.19	10.73	11.79	10.31	9.31	9.74	9.32
Dividends Per Share	1.000	1.000	0.930	0.890	0.840	0.810	0.720	0.660
Dividend Payout %	54.05	54.05	45.14	46.84	60.00	50.31	70.58	48.88
Income Statement								
Total Interest Income	74,074	297,508	339,478	360,610	377,847	354,665	325,647	190,252
Total Interest Expense	21,972	104,151	132,557	175,507	197,766	174,402	155,354	84,499
Net Interest Income	52,102	193,357	206,921	185,103	180,081	180,263	170,293	105,753
Provision for Loan Losses	1,357	7,475	7,937	12,833	15,745	8,800	12,156	3,100
Non–Interest Income	20,057	103,316	73,479	62,205	33,786	51,078	41,752	19,732
Non–Interest Expense	37,226	176,678	144,130	115,745	110,422	117,519	137,964	59,949
Net Income	23,504	78,755	88,933	79,991	58,976	70,248	44,402	40,939
Average Shs. Outstg.	44,258	42,620	43,113	42,064	42,260	43,722	43,461	30,272
Balance Sheet								
Cash & Due from Banks	157,303	217,229	162,261	156,058	142,801	131,091	124,591	80,447
Securities Avail. for Sale	1,224,206	1,266,635	1,022,314	1,147,280	865,266	1,207,363	565,165	273,868
Net Loans & Leases	4,156,383	4,045,587	3,525,774	3,454,926	3,151,962	3,130,497	2,613,202	2,028,693
Total Assets	6,433,296	6,378,999	5,792,019	5,631,775	4,904,547	5,069,160	4,567,899	2,699,790
Total Deposits	4,152,631	4,182,372	3,900,848	3,787,793	3,391,449	3,260,985	3,493,058	2,106,047
Long–Term Obligations	884,850	858,174	679,712	736,455	706,512	953,347	345,867	142,695
Total Liabilities	5,807,555	5,763,808	5,250,480	5,125,246	4,473,677	4,673,230	4,146,368	2,420,352
Net Stockholders' Equity	625,741	615,191	541,539	506,529	430,870	395,930	421,531	279,438
Shares Outstanding	43,627	43,689	42,031	42,926	41,765	42,487	43,256	29,968
Statistical Record								
Return on Equity %	3.75	12.80	16.42	15.79	13.68	17.74	10.53	14.65
Return on Assets %	0.36	1.23	1.53	1.42	1.20	1.38	0.97	1.51
Equity/Assets %	9.72	9.64	9.34	8.99	8.78	7.81	9.22	10.35
Non–Int. Exp./Tot. Inc. %	39.54	44.07	34.90	27.37	26.82	28.96	37.55	28.54
Price Range	31.31–29.40	31.53–26.97	32.01–26.24	28.86–20.19	23.88–16.44	27.25–22.81	34.13–21.50	24.19–16.13
P/E Ratio	16.92–15.89	17.04–14.58	15.54–12.74	15.19–10.63	17.05–11.74	16.93–14.17	33.46–21.08	17.92–11.94
Average Yield %	3.28	3.38	3.16	3.57	4.25	3.23	2.74	3.29

Address: 300 United Center, Charleston, WV 25301 **Telephone:** (304) 424–8800 **Web Site:** www.ubsi-wv.com	**Officers:** Richard M. Adams – Chmn., C.E.O., Steven E. Wilson – C.F.O., Chief Acctg. Officer **Transfer Agents:**Mellon Investor Services LLC, Ridgefield Park, NJ	**Investor Contact:**304–424–8704 **Institutional Holding** **No of Institutions:** 15 **Shares:** 2,460,051 **% Held:** –

272

UNITED DOMINION REALTY TRUST, INC.

Exchange	Symbol	Price	52Wk Range	Yield	P/E
NYS	UDR	$19.94 (5/28/2004)	19.94-16.90	5.87	398.80

*7 Year Price Score 132.2 *NYSE Composite Index=100 ***12 Month Price Score 49.0**

Interim Earnings (Per Share)
Qtr.	Mar	Jun	Sep	Dec
2001	(0.03)	0.20	0.07	0.03
2002	0.07	0.07	0.03	0.04
2003	0.05	0.01	(0.06)	0.05
2004	0.05	...	...	...

Interim Dividends (Per Share)
Amt	Decl	Ex	Rec	Pay
0.285Q	9/25/2003	10/15/2003	10/17/2003	10/31/2003
0.285Q	12/5/2003	1/14/2004	1/16/2004	2/2/2004
0.293Q	3/18/2004	4/14/2004	4/16/2004	4/30/2004
0.293Q	5/11/2004	7/14/2004	7/16/2004	8/2/2004

Indicated Div: $1.17 (Div. Reinv. Plan)

Valuation Analysis
Forecast P/E 12.76 (5/24/2004)
Market Cap	$2.1 Billion	Book Value	903.7 Million
Price/Book	2.73	Price/Sales	4.06

Dividend Achiever Status
Rank	252	10 Year Growth Rate	5.08%
Total Years of Dividend Growth			18

Business Summary: Property, Real Estate &Development (MIC: 8.3 SIC: 6798 NAIC:525930)

United Dominion Realty Trust is a self–administered real estate investment trust that owns, develops, acquires, renovates, and manages middle–market apartment communities nationwide. At Dec 31 2003, Co.'s apartment portfolio included 264 communities located in 55 markets, with a total of 76,244 completed apartment homes. In addition, Co. had three apartment communities under development. Co. focuses on the broad middle–market segment of the apartment that generally consists of young professionals, blue–collar families, single parent households, older singles, immigrants, non–related parties and families renting while waiting to purchase a home.

Recent Developments: For the quarter ended Mar 31 2004, Co. reported income of $13.2 million compared with income of $10.2 million in the prior–year quarter. Results for 2004 and 2003 excluded income from discontinued operations of $2.1 million and $3.2 million, respectively. Rental income grew 7.0% to $154.9 million. On a same–community basis, rental income slipped 0.6% to $142.3 million from $143.1 million a year earlier. Rental expenses climbed 10.2% to $76.5 million. Other expenses rose 1.8% to $76.5 million. Funds from operations amounted to $54.8 million, up 11.6% from $49.1 million the year before.

Prospects: During the quarter, Co. acquired four apartment communities with 1,115 homes for a total purchase price of $105.0 million. These properties were acquired at an average cap rate of 7.0% and a reserve for capital expenditures that ranged from $450.00 to $470.00 per home. Going forward, Co. will continue to seek available communities to buy at prices at or below replacement costs. Co. noted that it remains on track in achieving its goal of $500.0 million in acquisitions for the full year. For the second quarter of 2004, Co. expects funds from operations in the range of $0.39 to $0.40. For the full year, Co. narrowed its projections for funds from operations to a range of $1.50 to $1.58.

Financial Data
(US$ in Thousands)	3 Mos	12/31/2003	12/31/2002	12/31/2001	12/31/2000	12/31/1999	12/31/1998	12/31/1997
Earnings Per Share	0.05	0.05	0.21	0.27	0.41	0.54	0.49	0.60
Tang. Book Val. Per Share	7.07	7.28	6.48	7.10	7.91	8.58	9.10	9.00
Dividends Per Share	1.140	1.130	1.100	1.070	1.060	1.050	1.040	0.990
Dividend Payout %	N.M.	N.M.	525.00	399.07	260.36	195.83	212.24	166.25
Income Statement								
Rental Income	154,874	603,367	594,314	618,590	616,825	618,749	478,718	386,672
Total Income	155,269	604,435	596,120	623,183	622,151	620,691	482,100	387,795
Total Indirect Exp.	105,431	187,088	175,608	187,897	176,805	159,302	128,963	87,247
Depreciation	42,867	165,070	156,265	155,327	157,361	126,152	103,233	78,772
Interest Expense	28,905	117,185	130,956	144,379	156,040	153,748	106,238	79,004
Eqty Earns/Minority Int.	(524)	(982)	(2,914)	(4,192)	(4,386)	(5,679)	(1,541)	(278)
Income from Cont Ops	13,220	51,603	50,058	65,299	75,784	92,695	72,470	70,199
Net Income	15,312	70,404	53,229	61,828	76,615	93,622	72,332	70,149
Average Shs. Outstg.	127,953	115,648	106,952	101,037	103,208	103,639	100,062	87,339
Balance Sheet								
Cash & Cash Equivalents	9,441	12,364	14,925	31,471	55,248	64,647	76,886	17,580
Ttl Real Estate Inv.	3,429,680	3,409,883	3,165,870	3,212,213	3,252,103	3,204,684	3,362,582	2,080,932
Total Assets	3,605,208	3,543,643	3,276,136	3,348,091	3,453,957	3,688,317	3,762,940	2,313,725
Long–Term Obligations	2,234,887	2,132,037	2,057,640	2,064,197	1,992,330	2,127,305	2,117,749	1,156,226
Total Liabilities	2,463,431	2,616,771	2,585,265	2,615,766	2,645,271	2,805,977	2,818,819	1,510,368
Net Stockholders' Equity	1,141,777	1,163,436	1,001,271	1,042,725	1,218,892	1,310,212	1,374,121	1,058,357
Shares Outstanding	127,752	127,295	106,605	103,133	102,219	102,740	103,639	89,168
Net Inc.+Depr./Assets %	1.61	6.60	6.30	6.60	6.80	5.90	4.70	4.70
Return on Equity %	1.34	4.43	4.99	6.26	6.21	7.07	5.27	6.63
Return on Assets %	0.42	1.45	1.52	1.95	2.19	2.51	1.92	3.03
Price Range	19.65–18.04	19.37–15.22	16.70–13.95	14.72–10.75	11.75–9.44	11.94–9.31	14.75–10.06	16.00–13.50
P/E Ratio	393.0–360.8	387.4–304.4	79.52–66.43	54.52–39.81	28.66–23.02	22.11–17.25	30.10–20.54	26.67–22.50
Average Yield %	6.03	6.52	7.16	8.04	10.14	9.79	8.11	6.77

Address: 1745 Shea Center Dr., Highlands Ranch, CO 80129	**Officers:** Robert C. Larson – Chmn., James D. Klingbeil – Vice–Chmn.	**Institutional Holding**	
Telephone: (720) 283–6120	**Transfer Agents:** ChaseMellon Shareholder	**No of Institutions:** 24	
Web Site: www.udrt.com	Services, L.L.C., Pittsburg, PA	**Shares:** 2,623,165 **% Held:** –	

UNITED MOBILE HOMES INC

Exchange	Symbol	Price	52Wk Range	Yield	P/E
ASE	UMH	$13.25 (5/28/2004)	17.50–12.48	7.09	11.23

*7 Year Price Score 135.2   ***NYSE Composite Index=100**   ***12 Month Price Score 39.6**

Interim Earnings (Per Share)

Qtr.	Mar	Jun	Sep	Dec
2001	0.19	0.21	0.23	0.11
2002	0.24	0.20	0.19	0.22
2003	0.23	0.25	0.29	0.25
2004	0.39	...	...	...

Interim Dividends (Per Share)

Amt	Decl	Ex	Rec	Pay
0.228Q	6/19/2003	8/13/2003	8/15/2003	9/15/2003
0.23Q	10/1/2003	11/13/2003	11/17/2003	12/15/2003
0.233Q	1/14/2004	2/12/2004	2/17/2004	3/15/2004
0.235Q	4/1/2004	5/13/2004	5/17/2004	6/15/2004

Indicated Div: $0.94 (Div. Reinv. Plan)

Valuation Analysis

Forecast P/E N/A

Market Cap $101.1 Million	Book Value 42.4 Million
Price/Book 3.08	Price/Sales 3.67

Dividend Achiever Status

Rank 142	10 Year Growth Rate	10.78%
Total Years of Dividend Growth		13

Business Summary: Property, Real Estate &Development (MIC: 8.3 SIC: 6798 NAIC:525930)

United Mobile Homes, a real estate investment trust (REIT), is engaged in the ownership and operation of manufactured home communities located in New Jersey, New York, Ohio, Pennsylvania and Tennessee. As of Dec 31 2003, Co. owned 26 manufactured home communities containing 6,129 sites. Co.'s primary business is leasing manufactured home spaces on a month-to-month basis to private manufactured home owners. Co. also leases manufactured homes to residents, and through its wholly-owned taxable REIT subsidiary, sells homes to residents and prospective residents of its communities.

Recent Developments: For the three months ended Mar 31 2004, net income was $3.3 million compared with $1.8 million in the corresponding year-earlier period. Total revenues increased 22.1% to $9.5 million from $7.8 million the previous year, due primarily to a net gain on securities available for sales transactions of $1.8 million versus a net gain of $194,516 in the year-ago period. Rental and related income rose 3.8% to $5.3 million, due to the acquisitions of new communities during 2003 and 2004 and rental increases. Sales of manufactured homes grew 3.1% to $1.5 million.

Prospects: Co.'s near-term outlook appears satisfactory. For the quarter ended Mar 31 2004, Co.'s funds from operations (FFO) improved to $4.1 million versus $2.5 million a year earlier. FFO is defined as net income excluding gains (or losses) from sales of depreciable assets, plus depreciation. Looking ahead, Co.'s results should benefit from its historic ability to obtain annual rent increases of approximately 3.0% to 4.0%. Also, Co.'s recent acquisitions, including its Mar 1 2004 acquisition of a manufactured home community in Somerset Township, PA, should provide additional opportunities for growth. As a result of this latest acquisition, Co. now owns 27 communities containing 6,268 sites.

Financial Data

(US$ in Thousands)	3 Mos	12/31/2003	12/31/2002	12/31/2001	12/31/2000	12/31/1999	12/31/1998	12/31/1997
Earnings Per Share	1.18	1.02	0.85	0.74	0.71	0.63	0.60	0.63
Tang. Book Val. Per Share	5.06	4.78	3.87	3.70	3.08	2.92	3.20	3.03
Dividends Per Share	0.910	0.900	0.860	0.800	0.756	0.750	0.730	0.700
Dividend Payout %	77.54	88.72	101.76	108.44	106.50	119.04	122.91	111.11
Income Statement								
Total Income	9,466	33,791	29,424	26,882	20,645	18,807	17,193	15,664
Total Indirect Exp.	1,766	13,244	12,775	11,195	9,809	8,362	6,907	5,762
Depreciation	796	3,018	2,923	2,772	2,708	2,530	2,509	2,159
Interest Expense	740	3,190	3,314	2,826	2,625	2,106	1,506	1,123
Net Income	3,278	8,127	6,512	5,550	5,189	4,556	4,202	4,197
Average Shs. Outstg.	8,355	7,942	7,677	7,496	7,341	7,267	7,060	6,679
Balance Sheet								
Cash & Cash Equivalents	2,420	34,341	35,124	27,486	16,894	13,519	8,585	3,739
Ttl Real Estate Inv.	...	40,842	39,866	40,681	38,418	39,193	36,252	35,293
Total Assets	93,064	94,310	89,027	80,335	62,946	58,575	50,047	43,599
Long–Term Obligations	47,886	44,223	43,322	38,652	32,056	30,419	21,412	20,111
Total Liabilities	50,691	55,210	59,290	52,370	40,106	37,184	26,834	22,769
Net Stockholders' Equity	42,373	39,100	29,736	27,965	22,839	21,391	23,213	20,831
Shares Outstanding	8,371	8,164	7,671	7,542	7,394	7,312	7,246	6,865
Net Inc.+Depr./Assets %	327,767	812,706	651,221	555,049	518,937	455,614	420,169	419,726
Return on Equity %	7.74	20.78	21.89	19.84	22.72	21.29	18.10	20.14
Return on Assets %	3.52	8.61	7.31	6.90	8.24	7.77	8.39	9.62
Price Range	17.46–15.61	17.50–12.86	13.75–11.80	12.40–9.63	9.88–7.06	10.75–8.00	12.50–9.69	13.50–11.13
P/E Ratio	14.80–13.23	17.16–12.61	16.18–13.88	16.76–13.01	13.91–9.95	17.06–12.70	20.83–16.15	21.43–17.66
Average Yield %	5.45	5.94	6.72	7.31	8.81	8.12	6.69	5.88

Address: Juniper Business Plaza, Freehold, NJ 07728 **Telephone:** (732) 577–9997 **Web Site:** www.umh.com	**Officers:** Eugene W. Landy – Chmn., C.E.O., Samuel A. Landy – Pres.	**Institutional Holding** **No of Institutions:** 15 **Shares:** 3,157,403 **% Held:** –

274

UNITED TECHNOLOGIES CORP.

Exchange	Symbol	Price	52Wk Range	Yield	P/E
NYS	UTX	$84.61 (5/28/2004)	97.50-69.24	1.65	17.52

*7 Year Price Score 132.4   ***NYSE Composite Index=100**   ***12 Month Price Score 47.2**

Interim Earnings (Per Share)

Qtr.	Mar	Jun	Sep	Dec
2001	0.86	1.16	1.12	0.69
2002	0.92	1.23	1.21	1.06
2003	1.00	1.26	1.27	1.16
2004	1.14	...	...	...

Interim Dividends (Per Share)

Amt	Decl	Ex	Rec	Pay
0.27Q	6/11/2003	8/20/2003	8/22/2003	9/10/2003
0.35Q	9/10/2003	11/12/2003	11/14/2003	12/10/2003
0.35Q	2/3/2004	2/18/2004	2/20/2004	3/10/2004
0.35Q	4/14/2004	5/19/2004	5/21/2004	6/10/2004

Indicated Div: $1.40 (Div. Reinv. Plan)

Valuation Analysis

Forecast P/E 15.78 (5/24/2004)

Market Cap $39.9 Billion	Book Value N/A
Price/Book N/A	Price/Sales N/A

Dividend Achiever Status

Rank	163	10 Year Growth Rate	9.69%
Total Years of Dividend Growth			10

TRADING VOLUME (thousand shares)

Business Summary: Aviation (MIC: 1.1 SIC: 3724 NAIC:336412)

United Technologies provides high technology products and services to the building systems and aerospace industries. Co.'s products include Otis elevators, escalators and automated people movers; Carrier HVAC systems and equipment, refrigeration equipment, aftermarket service and components; Chubb electronic security, fire detection and suppression, monitoring and rapid response systems and security personnel services; Pratt & Whitney commercial, general aviation and military aircraft engines, parts, service, industrial gas turbines and space propulsion; Flight Systems aerospace products and aftermarket services and commercial/military helicopters, aftermarket helicopter and aircraft parts.

Recent Developments: For the quarter ended Mar 31 2004, net income climbed 15.3% to $579.0 million from $502.0 million the previous year. Results included restructuring and related charges of $259.0 million and $11.0 million in 2004 and 2003, respectively. Results for 2004 also included a one-time gain of $250.0 million related to a cash payment from DaimlerChrysler stemming from its sale of MTU Aero Engines GMBH. Revenues increased 29.0% to $8.65 billion from $6.70 billion a year earlier, reflecting increased revenues across all of Co.'s business segments and $703.0 million in revenues from Chubb plc, which was acquired in July 2003. Operating profit rose 15.1% to $963.0 million from $837.0 million a year ago.

Prospects: Earnings growth is being fueled by strong operating profitability at Otis and Carrier, as well as improvement in the commercial aerospace aftermarket and improved results from Co.'s military aerospace operations. In addition, results are benefiting from growth in China and favorable foreign currency exchange rates. Looking ahead, Co. is targeting full-year 2004 earnings in the range of $5.00 and $5.30 per share and revenues of about $35.00 billion. Separately, on Apr 23 2004, Co. announced that it has entered into a definitive agreement to acquire Automated Logic Corporation, a manufacturer of automation and control systems for heating, ventilation, and air conditioning applications.

Financial Data

(US$ in Millions)	3 Mos	12/31/2003	12/31/2002	12/31/2001	12/31/2000	12/31/1999	12/31/1998	12/31/1997
Earnings Per Share	4.83	4.69	4.42	3.83	3.55	1.65	2.52	2.10
Cash Flow Per Share	1.55	5.71	5.64	5.70	5.17	4.55	5.07	4.19
Tang. Book Val. Per Share	5.00	4.62	2.92	3.31	1.89	3.11	5.84	7.84
Dividends Per Share	1.240	1.130	0.980	0.900	0.820	0.760	0.690	0.620
Dividend Payout %	25.67	24.20	22.17	23.49	23.23	46.06	27.52	29.45
Income Statement								
Total Revenues	8,646	31,034	28,212	27,897	26,583	24,127	25,715	24,713
Total Indirect Exp.	1,413	4,681	4,394	4,577	4,473	4,425	4,272	4,102
Depreciation & Amort.	262	799	727	905	859	844	854	848
Operating Income	963	3,845	3,657	3,233	3,140	1,517	2,167	1,959
Income Taxes	245	941	887	755	853	325	623	573
Income from Cont Ops	...	...	...	...	...	841	...	...
Net Income	579	2,361	2,236	1,938	1,808	1,531	1,255	1,072
Average Shs. Outstg.	508	502	505	505	508	506	494	508
Balance Sheet								
Cash & Cash Equivalents	1,731	1,623	2,080	1,558	748	957	550	755
Total Current Assets	13,372	12,364	11,751	11,263	10,662	10,627	9,355	9,248
Total Assets	35,928	34,648	29,090	26,969	25,364	24,366	18,375	16,719
Total Current Liabilities	11,216	10,295	7,903	8,371	9,344	9,215	7,735	7,311
Long-Term Obligations	4,261	4,257	4,632	4,237	3,476	3,086	1,575	1,275
Net Stockholders' Equity	12,085	11,707	8,355	8,369	7,662	7,117	4,378	4,574
Shares Outstanding	513	514	469	472	470	474	450	458
Operating Profit Margin %	11.13	12.38	12.96	11.58	11.81	6.28	8.42	7.92
Net Profit Margin %	12.36	13.67	14.21	12.35	13.21	6.17	9.72	8.97
Return on Equity %	4.79	20.16	26.76	23.15	23.59	11.81	28.66	23.43
Return on Assets %	1.61	6.81	7.68	7.18	7.12	3.45	6.82	6.41
Debt/Total Assets %	11.85	12.28	15.92	15.71	13.70	12.66	8.57	7.62
Price Range	97.50-84.05	95.54-54.15	77.25-49.19	87.21-41.64	79.75-48.06	74.81-52.31	55.88-34.25	43.63-32.81
P/E Ratio	20.19-17.40	20.37-11.55	17.48-11.13	22.77-10.87	22.46-13.54	45.34-31.70	22.17-13.59	20.77-15.63
Average Yield %	1.35	1.55	1.55	1.29	1.32	1.21	1.54	1.61

Address: United Technologies	Officers: George David – Chmn., Pres., C.E.O.,	Investor Contact:800–881–1914
Building, Hartford, CT 06103	Stephen F. Page – Vice-Chmn., C.F.O.	Institutional Holding
Telephone: (860) 728-7000	Transfer Agents:EquiServe Trust Company, N.A. of	No of Institutions: 6
Web Site: www.utc.com	Providence, RI	Shares: 86,988 % Held: –

UNIVERSAL CORP.

Exchange	Symbol	Price	52Wk Range	Yield	P/E
NYS	UVV	$47.06 (5/28/2004)	53.01-40.78	3.31	9.03

*7 Year Price Score 128.1   *NYSE Composite Index=100   ***12 Month Price Score 50.8**

Interim Earnings (Per Share)

Qtr.	Sep	Dec	Mar	Jun
2000-01	0.89	1.01	1.31	0.87
2001-02	1.04	1.09	1.26	0.61
2002-03	1.09	1.04	0.94	1.27
2003-04	1.37	1.48	1.09	...

Interim Dividends (Per Share)

Amt	Decl	Ex	Rec	Pay
0.36Q	5/1/2003	7/10/2003	7/14/2003	8/11/2003
0.39Q	12/4/2003	1/9/2004	1/13/2004	2/9/2004
0.39Q	2/5/2004	4/7/2004	4/12/2004	5/10/2004
0.39Q	5/6/2004	7/8/2004	7/12/2004	8/9/2004

Indicated Div: $1.56 (Div. Reinv. Plan)

Valuation Analysis
Forecast P/E 12.16 (5/24/2004)

Market Cap $1.2 Billion	Book Value	683.6 Million
Price/Book 1.60	Price/Sales	0.38

Dividend Achiever Status

Rank	253	10 Year Growth Rate	5.05%
Total Years of Dividend Growth			33

Business Summary: Trusts &Holding Entities (MIC: 8.9 SIC: 6719 NAIC:551112)

Universal is a holding company. Through its primary subsidiaries, Co. is a major independent leaf tobacco merchant and has operations in agri−products and the distribution of lumber and building products. Co.'s tobacco business includes the selecting, buying, shipping, processing, packing, storing, and financing of leaf tobacco for sale to manufacturers of tobacco products. Co.'s agri−products business involves selecting, buying and processing a number of products, including tea, rubber, sunflower seeds, nuts, dried fruit, and canned and frozen foods. Co. is also engaged in lumber and building products distribution and processing in the Netherlands, Belgium, and other countries in Europe.

Recent Developments: For the three months ended Mar 31 2004, net income was $27.8 million compared with $23.8 million a year earlier. Results for 2003 included restructuring costs of $1.3 million. Sales and other operating revenues rose 15.1% to $683.5 million, aided by the January acquisition of JeWe, a producer and distributor of lumber and building products in the Netherlands. Tobacco segment operating profit declined 2.9% to $52.4 million, and included the benefit of a one−time shift in the allocation of fixed factory overhead associated with the change in Co.'s fiscal year end to March 31. Excluding the effect of this change, tobacco operating profit would have fallen 8.5% to $49.4 million.

Prospects: Co.'s near−term outlook is tempered by a number of factors. First, Co. noted that worldwide flue−cured production is forecast to increase by 15.0%, due to a very large Brazilian crop, and burley crops are expected to be up by more than 6.0%. However, due to adverse weather, the Brazilian crop has not produced as much ripe leaf as normal, which may make it difficult for Co. to provide all of the leaf qualities and styles needed to meet some customers' requirements. Second, African leaf volumes continue to be depressed following a four−year decline in Zimbabwean crops as a result of instability in that country. Lastly, U.S. volumes continue to drop, reflecting non−competitive leaf prices.

Financial Data

(US$ in Thousands)	6 Mos	3 Mos	06/30/2003	06/30/2002	06/30/2001	06/30/2000	06/30/1999	06/30/1998
Earnings Per Share	5.06	4.62	4.34	4.00	4.08	3.77	3.80	3.99
Cash Flow Per Share	4.25	2.09	(1.75)	6.38	5.83	5.88	9.93	3.76
Tang. Book Val. Per Share	...	20.66	19.55	17.64	15.76	13.04	12.47	11.71
Dividends Per Share	1.440	1.420	1.400	1.320	1.260	1.220	1.160	1.090
Dividend Payout %	28.45	30.73	32.25	33.00	30.88	32.36	30.52	27.31
Income Statement								
Total Revenues	1,587,612	786,601	2,636,776	2,500,078	3,017,579	3,401,969	4,004,903	4,287,204
Total Indirect Exp.	163,560	79,939	330,336	292,844	292,522	364,088	355,928	335,210
Depreciation & Amort.	28,000	12,684	53,504	54,987	56,399	52,022	52,762	51,071
Operating Income	136,151	59,654	207,815	200,507	238,782	233,924	254,556	278,394
Net Interest Inc./(Exp.)	(23,274)	(11,076)	(45,270)	(47,831)	(61,576)	(56,869)	(56,837)	(63,974)
Income Taxes	41,318	18,847	53,094	59,821	66,336	68,221	75,963	98,659
Net Income	71,795	34,428	110,594	106,662	112,669	113,805	127,276	141,258
Average Shs. Outstg.	25,110	25,135	25,499	26,680	27,645	30,205	33,477	35,388
Balance Sheet								
Cash & Cash Equivalents	135,793	57,183	44,659	58,003	109,540	61,395	92,784	79,835
Total Current Assets	1,469,142	1,503,072	1,374,997	1,105,037	1,132,646	1,088,150	1,170,325	1,430,289
Total Assets	2,379,952	2,395,170	2,243,074	1,844,415	1,782,373	1,748,104	1,823,123	2,056,705
Total Current Liabilities	729,856	952,352	824,281	673,431	581,765	883,234	898,500	1,101,521
Long−Term Obligations	775,358	609,939	614,994	435,592	515,349	223,262	221,545	263,140
Net Stockholders' Equity	683,643	648,800	620,278	587,995	552,129	497,779	539,036	547,867
Shares Outstanding	24,983	24,983	24,920	26,224	27,184	28,146	32,090	34,866
Statistical Record								
Operating Profit Margin %	8.57	7.58	7.88	8.02	7.91	6.87	6.35	6.49
Net Profit Margin %	9.72	9.16	8.22	9.05	8.13	7.35	6.97	7.89
Return on Equity %	10.50	5.30	17.82	18.13	20.40	22.86	23.61	25.78
Return on Assets %	3.01	1.43	4.93	5.78	6.32	6.51	6.98	6.86
Debt/Total Assets %	32.57	25.46	27.41	23.61	28.91	12.77	12.15	12.79
Price Range	44.28-40.78	43.85-41.20	43.01-31.81	43.05-31.74	41.30-20.63	31.00-13.56	38.75-23.88	48.50-31.75
P/E Ratio	8.75- 8.06	9.49- 8.92	9.91-7.33	10.76-7.94	10.12-5.06	8.22-3.60	10.20-6.28	12.16-7.96
Average Yield %	3.36	3.34	3.73	3.61	3.91	5.28	3.64	2.81

Address: 1501 North Hamilton Street, Richmond, VA 23230 Telephone: (804) 359 9311 Web Site: www.universalcorp.com	Officers: Allen B. King − Chmn., Pres., C.E.O., C.O.O., Hartwell H. Roper − V.P., C.F.O. Transfer Agents:Wells Fargo Bank Minnesota, N.A., St. Paul, MN	Investor Contact:804−359−9311 Institutional Holding No of Institutions: 5 Shares: 202,380 % Held: −

UNIVERSAL HEALTH REALTY INCOME TRUST

Exchange	Symbol	Price	52Wk Range	Yield	P/E
NYS	UHT	$27.57 (5/28/2004)	34.00–24.82	7.15	11.82

*7 Year Price Score 128.7   *NYSE Composite Index=100   ***12 Month Price Score 42.9**

Interim Earnings (Per Share)

Qtr.	Mar	Jun	Sep	Dec
2001	0.46	0.44	0.42	0.42
2002	0.53	0.44	0.43	0.44
2003	0.48	0.45	0.45	0.69
2004	0.74	...	...	...

Interim Dividends (Per Share)

Amt	Decl	Ex	Rec	Pay
0.49Q	6/2/2003	6/12/2003	6/16/2003	6/30/2003
0.49Q	9/4/2003	9/12/2003	9/16/2003	9/30/2003
0.495Q	12/2/2003	12/15/2003	12/17/2003	12/31/2003
0.495Q	3/10/2004	3/17/2004	3/19/2004	3/31/2004

Indicated Div: $1.98 (Div. Reinv. Plan)

Valuation Analysis

Forecast P/E N/A

Market Cap $244.6 Million	Book Value 152.2 Million
Price/Book 2.35	Price/Sales 12.64

Dividend Achiever Status

Rank 294	10 Year Growth Rate	1.68%
Total Years of Dividend Growth		16

Business Summary: Property, Real Estate &Development (MIC: 8.3 SIC: 6798 NAIC:525930)

Universal Health Realty Income Trust is an organized Maryland real estate investment trust (REIT). As of Dec 31 2003, Co. had investments in 44 facilities located in 15 states consisting of investments in healthcare and human service related facilities including acute care hospitals, behavioral healthcare facilities, rehabilitation hospitals, sub–acute care facilities, surgery centers, pre–school and childcare centers and medical office buildings. Six of Co.'s hospital facilities and three medical office buildings are leased to subsidiaries of Universal Health Services, Inc. (UHS). As of Dec 31 2003, UHS owned 6.6% of Co.'s outstanding shares.

Recent Developments: For the three months ended Mar 31 2004, net income decreased 11.0% to $5.0 million compared with $5.7 million in the corresponding quarter of the previous year. Results for 2003 included a gain of $365,000 on the sale of real property from equity in income of limited liability company investments. Total revenues were essentially unchanged at $7.2 million versus the prior–year period. Base rental revenues declined 1.5% to $5.9 million from $6.0 million, while bonus rental revenues increased 4.5% to $1.3 million from $1.2 million in the year–earlier period. Funds from operations climbed 5.0% to $7.8 million versus $7.4 million in the prior–year quarter.

Prospects: Co. continues to experience lower revenues due to a decrease in base rentals from Universal Health Services' facilities likely due to lease renewals at a lower annual base rental rate. Also, Co.'s revenues are being hampered by lower base rental and tenant reimbursements reflecting an increase in the vacancy rate. Moreover, Co. is experiencing the effects of the tight labor market, including a shortage of nurses, which may continue to cause an increase in salaries, wages and benefits expense. In addition, due to unfavorable pricing and availability trends, the cost of commercial professional and general liability insurance coverage may continue to rise.

Financial Data

(US$ in Thousands)	12/31/2003	12/31/2002	12/31/2001	12/31/2000	12/31/1999	12/31/1998	12/31/1997	12/31/1996
Earnings Per Share	2.07	1.84	1.74	1.81	1.56	1.76	1.56	1.58
Tang. Book Val. Per Share	12.96	12.72	12.84	11.05	11.08	11.31	11.46	11.61
Dividends Per Share	1.950	1.910	1.880	1.840	1.800	1.740	1.700	1.695
Dividend Payout %	94.20	103.80	80.45	126.79	115.38	98.86	108.97	107.28
Income Statement								
Rental Income	28,313	28,429	27,574	27,315	23,584	23,123	22,180	21,172
Interest Income	...	...	...	...	281	111	584	751
Total Income	28,313	28,429	27,574	27,315	23,865	23,234	22,764	21,923
Total Indirect Exp.	9,375	9,109	8,956	8,614	6,860	6,944	6,299	5,829
Depreciation	4,536	4,431	4,401	4,461	3,857	3,879	3,775	3,636
Interest Expense	2,497	2,403	3,896	6,114	4,004	3,490	2,943	2,565
Eqty Earns/Minority Int.	7,974	4,923	3,610	1,774	2,554	1,537	445	629
Net Income	24,425	21,623	18,349	16,256	13,972	14,337	13,967	14,158
Average Shs. Outstg.	11,779	11,750	10,536	9,003	8,977	8,974	8,967	8,960
Balance Sheet								
Cash & Cash Equivalents	628	598	629	294	852	572	1,238	137
Ttl Real Estate Inv.	130,789	134,886	139,215	143,108	141,367	129,838	133,486	139,434
Total Assets	194,291	185,117	187,904	183,658	178,821	169,406	146,755	148,566
Long–Term Obligations	...	...	1,446	1,359	1,289	1,216	1,147	1,082
Total Liabilities	42,093	36,255	37,870	84,401	79,146	68,058	44,063	44,584
Net Stockholders' Equity	152,198	148,862	150,034	99,257	99,675	101,348	102,692	103,982
Shares Outstanding	11,736	11,698	11,678	8,980	8,990	8,955	8,954	8,952
Statistical Record								
Net Inc.+Depr./Assets %	14.90	14.10	12.10	11.30	10.00	10.80	12.10	12.00
Return on Equity %	16.04	14.52	12.22	16.37	14.01	14.14	13.60	13.61
Return on Assets %	12.57	11.68	9.76	8.85	7.81	8.46	9.51	9.52
Price Range	30.55–25.30	28.50–22.69	25.70–18.94	19.88–14.31	20.50–14.63	22.50–18.06	22.38–18.50	20.50–17.50
P/E Ratio	14.76–12.22	15.49–12.33	14.77–10.88	10.98–7.91	13.14–9.38	12.78–10.26	14.34–11.86	12.97–11.08
Average Yield %	7.15	7.55	6.33	13.56	9.65	8.68	8.43	6.66

Address: Universal Corporate Center, King of Prussia, PA 19406–0958

Telephone: (610) 265–0688

Web Site: www.uhrit.com

Officers: Alan B. Miller – Chmn., Pres., C.E.O., Charles F. Boyle – V.P., C.F.O., Contr.

Transfer Agents: EquiServe Trust Company, N.A., Providence, R.I.

Institutional Holding
No of Institutions: 73
Shares: 3,510,095   % Held: 30%

UNIZAN FINANCIAL CORP

Exchange	Symbol	Price	52Wk Range	Yield	P/E
NMS	UNIZ	$25.78 (5/28/2004)	26.68-16.55	2.09	30.69

*7 Year Price Score 116.2 *NYSE Composite Index=100 ***12 Month Price Score 54.7**

Interim Earnings (Per Share)

Qtr.	Mar	Jun	Sep	Dec
2001	0.41	0.35	0.33	0.36
2002	(0.08)	0.40	0.40	0.56
2003	0.32	0.30	0.31	0.12
2004	0.11	...	...	...

Interim Dividends (Per Share)

Amt	Decl	Ex	Rec	Pay
0.135Q	8/22/2003	9/12/2003	9/16/2003	9/30/2003
0.135Q	11/21/2003	12/15/2003	12/17/2003	12/31/2003
0.135Q	2/20/2004	3/15/2004	3/17/2004	3/31/2004
0.135Q	5/25/2004	6/3/2004	6/7/2004	6/21/2004

Indicated Div: $0.54 (Div. Reinv. Plan)

Valuation Analysis
Forecast P/E N/A
Market Cap $569.3 Million   Book Value 306.7 Million
Price/Book 1.76   Price/Sales 3.29

Dividend Achiever Status
Rank 172   10 Year Growth Rate 9.39%
Total Years of Dividend Growth 19

Business Summary: Commercial Banking (MIC: 8.1 SIC: 6021 NAIC:522110)

Unizan Financial is a holding company with total assets of $2.73 billion at Dec 31 2003. Through its subsidiaries, Co. offers full-service banking through 45 banking offices in Ohio. Co.'s services include loan, deposit, trust and miscellaneous products and services, as well as ATM access, safe deposit boxes, night deposits, U.S. savings bonds, traveler's checks, money orders and cashier checks, and electronic and on-line banking services. Additionally, Co. offers investment and funds management services through Unizan Financial Services and Unizan Financial Advisors; consumer finance through Unizan Banc Financial Services and title insurance through Unizan Title Services.

Recent Developments: For the quarter ended Mar 31 2004, net income plunged 65.7% to $2.4 million compared with $7.0 million in the equivalent 2003 quarter. Results for 2004 included $3.6 million in relation to the exercise of certain stock options and $1.2 million from an additional expense for merger-related professional fees. Total interest income fell 13.6% to $32.3 million, while total interest expense dropped 16.0% to $13.5 million. Net interest income was $18.8 million versus $21.3 million the year before. Provision for loan losses fell 21.2% to $1.0 million versus $1.3 million in 2003. Total other income rose 0.9% to $7.0 million, while total other expenses climbed 28.2% to $21.4 million.

Prospects: Co.'s pending acquisition by Huntington Bancshares Incorporated is progressing as scheduled. Co. and Huntington Bancshares announced the signing of the definitive agreement on Jan 27, 2004. Under the terms of the transaction, Co.'s shareholders will receive 1.1424 shares of Huntington common stock, on a tax-free basis, for each share of Co., which values the transaction at approximately $587.0 million. The transaction is expected to close promptly following the end of the second quarter, pending customary regulatory approvals, as well as Co. shareholder approval.

Financial Data

(US$ in Thousands)	3 Mos	12/31/2003	12/31/2002	12/31/2001	12/31/2000	12/31/1999	12/31/1998	12/31/1997
Earnings Per Share	0.84	1.05	1.28	1.45	1.35	1.28	0.94	0.76
Tang. Book Val. Per Share	9.04	8.86	8.61	7.97	7.04	6.26	6.06	6.15
Dividends Per Share	0.540	0.540	0.520	0.500	0.480	0.470	0.360	0.320
Dividend Payout %	64.29	51.43	40.63	34.48	35.55	36.71	38.82	42.76
Income Statement								
Total Interest Income	32,279	138,860	146,720	81,184	80,676	68,878	66,005	63,362
Total Interest Expense	13,487	62,129	65,510	38,194	42,740	31,440	30,583	30,322
Net Interest Income	18,792	76,731	81,210	42,990	37,936	37,438	35,422	33,040
Provision for Loan Losses	1,000	4,833	7,893	2,818	1,046	2,425	2,748	2,929
Non-Interest Income	7,014	30,602	25,620	15,469	12,627	14,061	10,934	7,197
Non-Interest Expense	20,784	68,169	60,693	32,349	27,704	27,487	27,018	23,505
Income Before Taxes	3,392	34,331	38,244	23,292	21,813	21,587	16,590	13,803
Income from Cont Ops	...	...	26,505	15,344	...	...	...	...
Net Income	2,412	23,223	25,113	15,330	14,270	14,055	10,900	9,006
Average Shs. Outstg.	21,972	22,205	20,778	10,604	10,608	10,981	11,638	11,786
Balance Sheet								
Securities Avail. for Sale	484,760	471,775	446,301	...	...	...	...	...
Net Loans & Leases	1,944,624	1,943,873	1,881,103	865,969	859,255	761,646	660,261	620,768
Total Assets	2,761,184	2,727,249	2,691,902	1,096,842	1,053,947	970,529	868,743	826,313
Total Deposits	1,946,143	1,975,792	1,931,615	819,488	827,641	764,234	685,494	649,481
Long-Term Obligations	423,729	365,472	331,911	114,818	61,188	54,332	41,571	35,650
Total Liabilities	2,454,498	2,424,426	2,387,612	1,011,474	978,019	899,855	797,041	749,793
Net Stockholders' Equity	306,686	302,823	304,290	85,368	75,928	70,674	71,702	76,520
Shares Outstanding	21,754	21,682	22,070	10,440	10,436	10,752	11,098	11,568
Statistical Record								
Return on Equity %	0.79	7.66	8.71	17.97	18.79	19.88	15.20	11.76
Return on Assets %	0.09	0.85	0.98	1.39	1.35	1.44	1.25	1.08
Equity/Assets %	11.10	11.10	11.30	7.78	7.20	7.28	8.25	9.26
Non-Int. Exp./Tot. Inc. %	52.89	40.22	35.21	33.46	29.69	33.14	35.11	33.31
Price Range	26.68-20.25	21.67-16.50	21.50-17.25	19.98-11.69	16.00-12.13	21.25-13.00	21.50-19.56	20.50-15.00
P/E Ratio	31.76-24.11	20.64-15.71	16.80-13.48	13.78-8.06	11.85-8.98	16.60-10.16	22.87-20.81	26.97-19.74
Average Yield %	2.22	2.78	2.01	3.02	3.67	2.61	1.79	1.75

Address: 220 Market Avenue South, Canton, OH 44702 **Telephone:** (330) 438-1118 **Web Site:** www.unizan.com	**Officers:** Gary N. Fields - Chmn., Edward . Cohn - Exec. V. P. **Transfer Agents:** United National Bank &Trust Co., Canton, OH	**Investor Contact:** 330-438-1118 **Institutional Holding** **No of Institutions:** 63 **Shares:** 748,687 **% Held:** -

VALLEY NATIONAL BANCORP

Exchange	Symbol	Price	52Wk Range	Yield	P/E
NYS	VLY	$25.51 (5/28/2004)	28.54–24.63	3.53	16.46

*7 Year Price Score 126.9 *NYSE Composite Index=100 *12 Month Price Score 44.7

Interim Earnings (Per Share)

Qtr.	Mar	Jun	Sep	Dec
2001	0.26	0.31	0.33	0.35
2002	0.36	0.38	0.38	0.37
2003	0.38	0.38	0.40	0.38
2004	0.39	...	...	...

Interim Dividends (Per Share)

Amt	Decl	Ex	Rec	Pay
0.214Q	11/25/2003	12/3/2003	12/5/2003	1/2/2004
0.214Q	2/26/2004	3/4/2004	3/8/2004	4/1/2004
5%	4/7/2004	4/29/2004	5/3/2004	5/17/2004
0.225Q	5/20/2004	6/2/2004	6/4/2004	7/1/2004

Indicated Div: $0.90 (Div. Reinv. Plan)

Valuation Analysis

Forecast P/E N/A

Market Cap	$2.4 Billion	Book Value	652.8 Million
Price/Book	4.20	Price/Sales	4.67

Dividend Achiever Status

Rank	162	10 Year Growth Rate	9.72
Total Years of Dividend Growth			12

Business Summary: Commercial Banking (MIC: 8.1 SIC: 6021 NAIC:522110)

Valley National Bancorp, with $9.88 billion in assets as of Dec 31 2003, is a bank holding company. Co.'s principal subsidiary is Valley National Bank (VNB). VNB is a national banking association, which provides a full range of commercial and retail banking services through 129 branch offices located in 83 communities serving 11 counties throughout northern New Jersey and Manhattan. These services include the acceptance of demand, savings and time deposits; extension of consumer, real estate, small business administration and other commercial credits; title insurance; investment services; and full personal and corporate trust, as well as pension and fiduciary services.

Recent Developments: For the quarter ended Mar 31 2004, net income rose 1.2% to $38.4 million compared with $38.0 million in the corresponding period of the year before. Net interest income grew 1.1% to $90.2 million from $89.2 million a year earlier. Provision for loan losses dropped 43.2% to $1.8 million.Total non-interest income declined 10.3% to $23.0 million, primarily as a result of lower gains on the sale of residential mortgage loans. Total non-interest expense decreased 2.0% to $53.1 million, largely due to lower employment expenses, partially offset by an increase in depreciation.

Prospects: Although Co.'s earnings remain strong, low interest rates continue to negatively affect operating performance. However, Co.'s business development group and small business initiative, which started in January 2004, are showing positive momentum. As a result, Co. expects higher commercial loan growth throughout 2004. Co. also anticipates opening an additional 12 to 15 branches within the next 18 months. Meanwhile, Co. is positioning itself for long-term profitability by enhancing its balance sheet and daily operations through several initiatives, which include expanding its customer call center to a seven day, 24 hour level, and the addition of Sunday branch hours at 21 locations.

Financial Data

(US$ in Thousands)	12/31/2003	12/31/2002	12/31/2001	12/31/2000	12/31/1999	12/31/1998	12/31/1997	12/31/1996
Earnings Per Share	1.54	1.49	1.25	1.20	1.19	1.15	1.31	1.15
Tang. Book Val. Per Share	6.62	6.32	6.43	6.27	6.72	6.61	7.38	6.82
Dividends Per Share	0.830	0.790	0.740	0.700	0.650	0.580	0.510	0.460
Dividend Payout %	54.23	52.96	59.26	58.01	54.83	51.16	39.09	40.00
Income Statement								
Total Interest Income	497,498	517,419	553,486	460,853	427,535	389,656	368,318	324,284
Total Interest Expense	148,922	157,723	218,653	202,756	169,177	160,104	155,977	145,522
Net Interest Income	348,576	359,696	334,833	258,097	258,358	229,552	212,341	178,762
Provision for Loan Losses	7,345	13,644	15,706	6,130	9,120	12,370	12,250	2,446
Non–Interest Income	89,755	74,146	64,912	50,528	44,720	41,655	40,163	25,498
Non–Interest Expense	216,278	207,994	188,248	141,013	137,946	134,757	123,228	101,168
Income from Cont Ops	145,428	...	...	...	...	...	...	...
Net Income	153,415	154,616	135,204	106,773	106,324	97,348	84,992	67,495
Average Shs. Outstg.	99,223	103,274	107,547	88,426	88,711	84,488	64,677	58,533
Balance Sheet								
Cash & Due from Banks	218,166	243,923	311,850	186,720	161,561	175,794	148,175	162,872
Securities Avail. for Sale	1,809,932	2,140,366	2,171,695	1,305,769	1,005,419	929,073	1,017,225	950,192
Net Loans & Leases	6,107,759	5,698,401	5,268,004	4,607,679	4,499,632	3,927,982	(46,372)	(41,154)
Total Assets	9,880,740	9,134,674	8,583,765	6,425,837	6,360,394	5,541,207	1,468,323	1,509,510
Total Deposits	7,162,968	6,683,387	6,306,974	5,123,717	5,051,255	4,674,689	4,402,954	4,176,206
Long–Term Obligations	1,547,221	1,119,642	975,728	591,808	564,881	...	...	...
Total Liabilities	9,227,951	8,302,936	7,705,390	5,880,763	5,806,894	4,985,420	4,615,296	4,290,138
Net Stockholders' Equity	652,789	431,738	478,375	545,074	553,500	555,787	475,359	396,522
Shares Outstanding	98,605	99,802	105,381	86,876	82,264	83,970	64,361	58,075
Return on Equity %	22.27	35.81	28.26	19.58	19.20	17.51	17.87	17.02
Return on Assets %	1.47	1.69	1.57	1.66	1.67	1.75	5.78	4.47
Non–Int. Exp./Tot. Inc. %	35.70	34.74	30.26	27.55	29.05	31.14	30.00	28.85
Price Range	28.54–21.77	26.25–22.18	23.91–17.72	23.15–14.23	19.29–15.51	22.25–15.75	20.18–12.12	14.15–10.80
P/E Ratio	18.53–14.14	17.62–14.88	19.13–14.18	19.29–11.86	16.21–13.04	19.35–13.69	15.41–9.25	12.30–9.39
Average Yield %	3.25	3.19	3.60	3.92	3.76	3.07	3.51	3.72

Address: 1455 Valley Road, Wayne, NJ 07470	**Officers:** Gerald H. Lipkin – Chmn., Pres., C.E.O., Peter Crocitto – Exec. V.P.	**Investor Contact:**973–305–8800 **Institutional Holding**
Telephone: (973) 305–8800	**Transfer Agents:**American Stock Transfer &Trust Company, New York, NY	**No of Institutions:** 9
Web Site: www.valleynationalbank.com		**Shares:** 346,108 **% Held:** –

VALSPAR CORP.

Exchange	Symbol	Price	52Wk Range	Yield	P/E
NYS	VAL	$47.68 (5/28/2004)	51.35-41.28	1.51	21.48

*7 Year Price Score 124.4 *NYSE Composite Index=100 *12 Month Price Score 48.5

Interim Earnings (Per Share)

Qtr.	Jan	Apr	Jul	Oct
2001	0.10	0.44	0.51	0.05
2002	0.25	0.67	0.74	0.68
2003	0.30	0.62	0.77	0.48
2004	0.35	...	...	...

Interim Dividends (Per Share)

Amt	Decl	Ex	Rec	Pay
0.15Q	8/14/2003	9/29/2003	10/1/2003	10/15/2003
0.18Q	12/10/2003	12/29/2003	12/31/2003	1/15/2004
0.18Q	2/25/2004	3/30/2004	4/1/2004	4/15/2004
0.18Q	5/31/2004	6/29/2004	7/1/2004	7/15/2004

Indicated Div: $0.72 (Div. Reinv. Plan)

Valuation Analysis
Forecast P/E 17.00 (5/24/2004)
Market Cap $2.4 Billion   Book Value 897.0 Million
Price/Book   2.77   Price/Sales 1.09

Dividend Achiever Status
Rank   143   10 Year Growth Rate   10.55%
Total Years of Dividend Growth   25

Business Summary: Chemicals (MIC: 11.1 SIC: 2851 NAIC:325510)

Valspar is a global paint and coatings manufacturer. Co. manufactures and distributes a portfolio of products, including: Industrial coatings for factory application by industrial customers and original equipment manufacturers; Architectural paints, varnishes and stains for the do-it-yourself and professional markets; Packaging coatings and inks for rigid containers, particularly food and beverage cans; Automotive refinish and other specialty coatings, including high performance floor coatings; and Specialty polymers, composites and colorants for use by coatings manufacturers and others, including Co.

Recent Developments: For the quarter ended Jan 30 2004, net income climbed 17.7% to $18.4 million compared with $15.6 million in the equivalent 2003 quarter. Net sales grew 7.0% to $501.6 million from $469.0 million a year earlier, reflecting favorable foreign currency exchange and continuing strength in Co.'s Paints segment and progressive improvement in its coatings segment. Gross profit increased 8.8% to $156.4 million versus $143.6 million the year before. Gross profit as a percentage of net sales was 31.2% in 2004 and 30.6% in 2003. Operating income advanced 8.4% to $40.3 million versus $37.1 million the year before.

Prospects: In January 2004, Co. acquired De Beer Lakfabrieken B.V., a manufacturer and distributor of automotive refinish coatings based in The Netherlands. Co. expects De Beer to add approximately $50.0 million in annualized sales. The acquisition is also expected to be slightly accretive to earnings for the balance of 2004. Meanwhile, Co. is focused on cost reduction initiatives to counter raw material cost pressures. Co. should be well positioned to take advantage of a recovery in the industrial economy and to participate in consolidation opportunities as they occur.

Financial Data

(US$ in Thousands)	3 Mos	10/31/2003	10/25/2002	10/26/2001	10/27/2000	10/29/1999	10/30/1998	10/31/1997
Earnings Per Share	2.22	2.17	2.34	1.10	2.00	1.87	1.63	1.49
Cash Flow Per Share	(0.41)	4.81	4.18	4.23	2.16	2.90	2.56	1.20
Tang. Book Val. Per Share	N.M	N.M	N.M	N.M	5.38	4.07	5.42	6.75
Dividends Per Share	0.630	0.600	0.560	0.540	0.520	0.460	0.420	0.360
Dividend Payout %	28.37	27.64	23.93	49.09	26.00	24.59	25.76	...
Income Statement								
Total Revenues	501,591	2,247,926	2,126,853	1,920,970	1,483,320	1,387,677	1,155,134	1,017,271
Total Indirect Exp.	116,100	478,279	447,064	413,114	280,118	282,271	230,152	206,834
Depreciation & Amort.	14,388	4,463	4,863	29,283	10,675	39,800	30,742	25,771
Operating Income	40,252	227,503	249,605	160,922	163,935	145,011	121,742	111,963
Net Interest Inc./(Exp.)	(10,390)	(45,843)	(48,711)	(72,559)	(21,989)	(19,089)	(10,707)	(5,294)
Income Taxes	11,269	68,960	78,427	39,650	55,280	52,944	46,658	43,300
Net Income	18,386	112,514	120,121	51,500	86,466	82,142	72,130	65,877
Average Shs. Outstg.	52,602	51,924	51,370	46,657	43,195	43,835	44,319	44,232
Balance Sheet								
Cash & Cash Equivalents	38,854	41,589	22,715	20,139	20,935	33,189	14,990	11,113
Total Current Assets	750,470	738,831	701,788	661,494	533,864	514,928	426,069	356,847
Total Assets	2,564,260	2,496,524	2,419,552	2,226,070	1,125,030	1,110,720	801,680	615,470
Total Current Liabilities	524,210	531,063	503,895	475,067	334,288	374,712	267,984	259,420
Long-Term Obligations	790,885	749,199	885,819	1,006,217	300,300	298,874	164,768	35,844
Net Stockholders' Equity	896,990	869,317	737,253	654,565	437,571	393,756	340,188	295,065
Net Working Capital	226,260	207,768	197,893	186,427	199,576	140,216	158,085	97,427
Shares Outstanding	51,053	50,730	50,104	49,481	42,481	42,983	43,418	43,678
Statistical Record								
Operating Profit Margin %	8.02	10.12	11.73	8.37	11.05	10.44	10.53	11.00
Net Profit Margin %	8.15	11.14	13.02	6.80	13.28	13.54	14.32	14.98
Return on Equity %	2.05	12.94	16.29	7.86	19.76	20.86	21.20	22.32
Return on Assets %	0.72	4.50	4.96	2.31	7.68	7.39	8.99	10.70
Debt/Total Assets %	30.84	30.00	36.61	45.20	26.69	26.90	20.55	5.82
Price Range	49.70-47.26	47.95-37.69	49.91-33.21	37.49-25.45	43.06-20.60	39.56-28.06	42.00-26.31	32.94-24.00
P/E Ratio	22.39-21.29	22.10-17.37	21.33-14.19	34.08-23.14	21.53-10.30	21.16-15.01	25.77-16.14	22.11-16.11
Average Yield %	1.30	1.37	1.33	1.69	1.55	1.33	1.20	1.23

Address: 1101 Third Street South, Minneapolis, MN 55415 Telephone: (612) 332-7371 Web Site: www.valspar.com	Officers: Richard M. Rompala – Chmn., C.E.O., William L. Mansfield – Exec. V.P., C.O.O. Transfer Agents:Mellon Investor Services LLC, Ridgefield Park, NJ	Investor Contact:612-332-7371 Institutional Holding No of Institutions: 3 Shares: 101,532 % Held: –

VECTREN CORP

Exchange	Symbol	Price	52Wk Range	Yield	P/E
NYS	VVC	$24.00 (5/28/2004)	26.00–22.30	4.75	15.29

*7 Year Price Score 95.5   ***NYSE Composite Index=100**   ***12 Month Price Score 46.5**

Interim Earnings (Per Share)

Qtr.	Mar	Jun	Sep	Dec
2001	0.61	(0.15)	0.07	0.48
2002	0.67	0.21	0.21	0.59
2003	0.82	0.06	0.10	0.59
2004	0.72	...	...	...

Interim Dividends (Per Share)

Amt	Decl	Ex	Rec	Pay
0.275Q	7/22/2003	8/13/2003	8/15/2003	9/2/2003
0.285Q	10/31/2003	11/12/2003	11/14/2003	12/1/2003
0.285Q	1/28/2004	2/11/2004	2/13/2004	3/1/2004
0.285Q	4/28/2004	5/12/2004	5/14/2004	6/1/2004

Indicated Div: $1.14 (Div. Reinv. Plan)

Valuation Analysis

Forecast P/E 14.10 (5/24/2004)

Market Cap	$1.6 Billion	Book Value	1.1 Billion
Price/Book	1.74	Price/Sales	1.17

Dividend Achiever Status

Rank	268	10 Year Growth Rate 3.96%
Total Years of Dividend Growth		28

Business Summary: Electricity (MIC: 7.1 SIC: 4932 NAIC:221210)

Vectren is an energy and applied technology holding company. At Dec 31 2003, Co. supplied natural gas service to 972,230 Indiana and Ohio customers, including 887,891 residential, 80,292 commercial, and 4,047 industrial and other customers. In addition, at Dec 31 2003, Co. supplied electric service to 135,098 Indiana customers, including 117,868 residential, 17,054 commercial, and 176 industrial and other customers. Co. is also involved in nonregulated activities in four primary business areas: Energy Marketing and Services, Coal Mining, Utility Infrastructure Services, and Broadband.

Recent Developments: For the quarter ended Mar 31 2004, net income slid 1.5% to $54.8 million compared with $55.7 million in the corresponding period of the prior year. The decline in earnings was primarily attributed to the weather, which was 10.0% warmer than the prior year, partially offset by continued growth in Co.'s non-regulated businesses. Total operating revenues grew 3.0% to $645.4 million from $626.3 million a year earlier. Operating income slid 6.4% to $88.6 million versus $94.7 million the year before. Total other income surged 46.8% to $11.2 million from $7.7 million in 2002. Interest expense grew 2.5% to $19.3 million.

Prospects: Electric sales to large volume customers are improving, suggesting the beginning of an economic recovery in Co.'s service territory. In addition, Co.'s non-regulated group continues to grow its contribution to earnings. Accordingly, Co. expects fiscal 2004 earnings to be between $1.60 and $1.75 per share. The targeted range is based on several factors, including normal weather conditions, continued growth from Co.'s complementary non-regulated businesses, continued cost control measures and securing rate relief at Co.'s regulated gas distribution operations.

Financial Data

(US$ in Thousands)	3 Mos	12/31/2003	12/31/2002	12/31/2001	12/31/2000	12/31/1999	12/31/1998
Earnings Per Share	1.47	1.57	1.68	1.01	1.17	1.48	1.40
Cash Flow Per Share	2.87	2.50	4.30	2.74	0.66	2.42	2.93
Tang. Book Val. Per Share	11.92	11.46	9.83	9.68	8.68	11.57	...
Dividends Per Share	1.120	1.110	1.070	1.030	0.740	...	...
Dividend Payout %	75.68	70.70	63.69	101.98	63.24	...	...
Income Statement							
Total Revenues	645,300	1,587,700	1,804,300	2,170,000	1,648,690	1,068,417	997,706
Total Indirect Exp.	123,800	419,400	394,500	435,900	384,407	306,530	290,745
Costs & Expenses	556,700	1,388,300	1,593,000	2,030,400	1,517,769	907,645	849,169
Depreciation & Amort.	32,500	128,700	119,600	123,700	105,661	86,998	81,558
Operating Income	88,600	199,400	211,300	139,600	130,921	160,772	148,537
Net Interest Inc./(Exp.)	(19,300)	(66,500)	(68,100)	(82,600)	(57,133)	(42,862)	(40,301)
Income Taxes	25,700	37,700	38,900	18,600	34,232	45,708	42,328
Eqty Earns/Minority Int.	16,900	12,100	8,600	13,500	16,550	10,722	11,682
Income from Cont Ops	...	...	...	67,400	...	...	...
Net Income	54,800	111,200	114,000	63,600	72,040	90,748	86,600
Average Shs. Outstg.	75,800	70,800	67,900	66,900	61,380	61,430	61,578
Balance Sheet							
Net Property	2,244,300	2,226,000	1,876,100	1,776,700	1,659,238	1,400,807	...
Total Assets	3,259,100	3,353,400	2,926,500	2,856,800	2,888,189	1,940,025	...
Long–Term Obligations	1,072,800	1,072,800	954,200	1,014,000	631,954	486,726	...
Net Stockholders' Equity	1,110,100	1,071,500	869,600	848,100	723,608	701,564	...
Shares Outstanding	75,900	75,600	67,900	67,700	61,419	61,305	...
Operating Profit Margin %	13.73	12.55	11.71	6.43	7.94	15.04	14.88
Net Inc./Net Property %	2.44	4.99	6.07	3.57	4.34	6.47	...
Net Inc./Tot. Capital %	2.26	4.67	5.63	3.07	4.46	6.33	...
Return on Equity %	4.93	10.37	13.10	7.94	9.72	12.58	...
Accum. Depr./Gross Prop. %	38.34	38.36	45.73	45.06	44.21	43.56	...
Price Range	25.72–24.19	26.00–20.01	25.87–18.69	24.19–19.90	26.50–15.75	35.88–22.56	36.56–27.31
P/E Ratio	17.50–16.46	16.56–12.75	15.40–11.13	23.95–19.70	22.65–13.46	24.24–15.24	26.12–19.51
Average Yield %	4.52	4.81	4.49	4.70	3.54	N/A	N/A

Address: 20 N.W. Fourth Street, Evansville, IN 47708 Telephone: (812) 491–4000 Web Site: www.vectren.com	Officers: Niel C. Ellerbrook – Chmn., Pres., C.E.O., Jerome A. Benkert – Exec. V.P., C.F.O. Transfer Agents:National City Bank, Cleveland, OH	Investor Contact:800–227–8625 Institutional Holding No of Institutions: 4 Shares: 2,340 % Held: –

VF CORP.

Exchange	Symbol	Price	52Wk Range	Yield	P/E
NYS	VFC	$46.98 (5/28/2004)	48.43–33.91	2.21	12.66

*7 Year Price Score 106.1   ***NYSE Composite Index=100**   ***12 Month Price Score 51.3**

Interim Earnings (Per Share)

Qtr.	Mar	Jun	Sep	Dec
2001	0.67	0.60	0.90	(0.98)
2002	0.69	0.79	1.15	0.61
2003	0.83	0.68	1.14	0.96
2004	0.93	...	...	...

Interim Dividends (Per Share)

Amt	Decl	Ex	Rec	Pay
0.25Q	9/5/2003	9/9/2003	9/9/2003	9/19/2003
0.26Q	10/23/2003	12/5/2003	12/9/2003	12/19/2003
0.26Q	2/11/2004	3/5/2004	3/9/2004	3/19/2004
0.26Q	4/27/2004	6/9/2004	6/11/2004	6/21/2004

Indicated Div: $1.04 (Div. Reinv. Plan)

Valuation Analysis

Forecast P/E 11.79 (5/24/2004)

Market Cap $5.2 Billion	Book Value 2.1 Billion
Price/Book 2.41	Price/Sales 0.95

Dividend Achiever Status

Rank	248	10 Year Growth Rate	5.17%
Total Years of Dividend Growth			31

Business Summary: Apparel (MIC: 4.4 SIC: 2329 NAIC:315228)

VF designs, manufactures and markets branded jeanswear, sportswear, intimate apparel, occupational apparel, knitwear, outdoor apparel and equipment, and other apparel. Co. manages its business through over 25 marketing units that support specific brands. Marketing units with similar products have been grouped together into four reportable segments: consumer apparel, occupational apparel, outdoor apparel and equipment, and all other. Co.'s principal brands include: *Lee®, Rustler®, Wrangler®, Riders®, Vanity Fair®, Vassarette®, Bestform®, Lily of France®, Lee Sport®, Healthtex®, JanSport®, Eastpak®, Red Kap®, Nautica®* and *The North Face®*.

Recent Developments: For the three months ended Apr 3 2004, net income rose 12.8% to $103.9 million compared with $92.1 million in the equivalent quarter of 2003. Results benefited from foreign currency translations. Net sales rose 14.6% to $1.43 billion from $1.25 billion in the prior–year period. Sales benefited from strong performances in Co.'s outdoor businesses, solid growth in jeanswear and intimates, and the acquisition of Nautica Enterprises, which contributed $146.0 million to sales for the quarter. Operating income increased 13.0% to $172.6 million compared with $152.8 million the year before.

Prospects: On Apr 27 2004, Co. signed a definitive agreement to acquire Vans for $396.0 million in cash. The total transaction is valued at about $396.0 million, which includes the cashout of stock options. The acquisition would launch Co. into the large and growing action sports market. The transaction is expected to close in the third quarter of 2004. Separately, on Apr 14 2004, Co. entered into an agreement to acquire Green Sport Monte Bianco, a designer and marketer of casual outdoor apparel under the Napapijri®brand. The acquisition is expected to be completed by the end of June 2004. Both of the acquisitions are expected to be neutral to earnings per share in 2004 and slightly accretive in 2005.

Financial Data

(US$ in Thousands)	3 Mos	01/03/2004	01/04/2003	12/29/2001	12/30/2000	01/01/2000	01/02/1999	01/03/1998
Earnings Per Share	3.71	3.61	3.24	1.19	2.27	2.99	3.10	2.70
Cash Flow Per Share	0.38	4.92	5.74	5.97	3.78	3.46	3.46	3.50
Tang. Book Val. Per Share	10.14	8.61	10.91	9.97	12.55	10.08	9.33	8.68
Dividends Per Share	1.020	1.010	0.970	0.930	0.890	0.850	0.810	0.770
Dividend Payout %	27.49	27.97	29.93	78.15	39.20	28.42	26.12	28.51
Income Statement								
Total Revenues	1,432,669	5,207,459	5,083,523	5,518,805	5,747,879	5,551,616	5,478,807	5,222,246
Total Indirect Exp.	368,477	1,268,576	1,207,591	1,372,725	1,395,435	1,241,864	1,207,952	1,176,562
Depreciation & Amort.	29,003	118,376	107,398	168,972	173,422	167,432	161,385	156,252
Operating Income	172,559	644,889	621,924	347,246	509,993	652,632	684,169	605,073
Net Interest Inc./(Exp.)	(16,781)	(49,912)	(63,928)	(86,516)	(81,032)	(62,490)	(55,871)	(25,877)
Income Taxes	53,511	200,573	197,300	124,971	164,417	229,334	243,292	234,938
Income from Cont Ops	...	...	364,428	...	267,116	...	...	...
Net Income	103,874	397,933	(154,540)	137,830	260,334	366,242	388,306	350,942
Average Shs. Outstg.	111,515	110,323	112,336	114,764	117,218	122,258	124,995	129,720
Balance Sheet								
Cash & Cash Equivalents	551,688	514,785	496,367	332,049	118,891	79,861	63,208	124,094
Total Current Assets	2,297,530	2,208,531	2,074,540	2,031,420	2,110,096	1,877,416	1,848,152	1,601,466
Total Assets	4,392,921	4,245,552	3,503,151	4,103,016	4,358,156	4,026,514	3,836,666	3,322,782
Total Current Liabilities	804,714	871,857	874,844	813,833	1,006,200	1,113,473	1,033,006	765,908
Long–Term Obligations	956,731	956,383	602,287	904,035	905,036	517,834	521,657	516,226
Net Stockholders' Equity	2,128,127	1,921,320	1,620,946	2,067,165	2,143,330	2,112,274	2,011,964	1,810,428
Net Working Capital	1,492,816	1,336,674	1,199,696	1,217,587	1,103,896	763,943	815,146	835,558
Shares Outstanding	109,457	108,170	108,525	109,998	86,807	116,204	119,466	121,225
Operating Profit Margin %	12.04	12.38	12.23	6.29	8.87	11.75	12.48	11.58
Net Profit Margin %	14.72	15.34	14.93	7.02	10.36	14.85	15.96	15.71
Return on Equity %	4.88	20.39	21.98	6.66	12.46	17.33	19.29	19.38
Return on Assets %	2.36	9.37	10.40	3.35	6.12	9.09	10.12	10.56
Debt/Total Assets %	21.77	22.52	17.19	22.03	20.76	12.86	13.59	15.53
Price Range	47.11–42.36	44.05–32.85	45.33–32.09	41.99–28.61	36.56–22.00	54.25–28.00	53.81–34.00	47.88–32.63
P/E Ratio	12.70–11.42	12.20–9.10	13.99–9.90	35.29–24.04	16.11–9.69	18.14–9.36	17.36–10.97	17.73–12.08
Average Yield %	2.31	2.64	2.43	2.56	3.38	2.13	1.73	1.90

Address: 105 Corporate Center Boulevard, Greensboro, NC 27408

Telephone: (336) 424 6000

Web Site: www.vfc.com

Officers: Mackey J. nald – Chmn., Pres., C.E.O., Robert K. Shearer – V.P., Fin., C.F.O.

Transfer Agents: First Chicago Trust Company of New York, Jersey City, NJ

Institutional Holding
No of Institutions: 53
Shares: 499,036,355   % Held: –

VULCAN MATERIALS CO.

Exchange	Symbol	Price	52Wk Range	Yield	P/E
NYS	VMC	$44.76 (5/28/2004)	50.12–36.62	2.32	19.29

*7 Year Price Score 105.4 *NYSE Composite Index=100   ***12 Month Price Score 47.5**

Interim Earnings (Per Share)

Qtr.	Mar	Jun	Sep	Dec
2001	0.06	0.78	0.90	0.43
2002	0.11	0.64	0.75	0.36
2003	0.01	0.65	0.91	0.61
2004	0.15	...	...	...

Interim Dividends (Per Share)

Amt	Decl	Ex	Rec	Pay
0.245Q	7/11/2003	8/25/2003	8/27/2003	9/10/2003
0.245Q	10/10/2003	11/24/2003	11/26/2003	12/10/2003
0.26Q	2/13/2004	2/25/2004	2/27/2004	3/10/2004
0.26Q	5/14/2004	5/26/2004	5/28/2004	6/10/2004

Indicated Div: $1.04 (Div. Reinv. Plan)

Valuation Analysis
Forecast P/E 16.86 (5/24/2004)

Market Cap	$4.5 Billion	Book Value	1.8 Billion
Price/Book	2.66	Price/Sales	1.65

Dividend Achiever Status

Rank	180	10 Year Growth Rate	8.84%
Total Years of Dividend Growth			11

TRADING VOLUME (thousand shares)

Business Summary: Earth &Rock Mining (MIC: 14.5 SIC: 1422 NAIC:212312)

Vulcan Materials and its subsidiaries are engaged in the production, distribution and sale of construction materials and industrial and specialty chemical, including chloralkali. Co.'s construction materials business consists of the production and sale of construction aggregates and other construction materials and related services. Construction aggregates include crushed stone, sand and gravel, rock asphalt, recrushed concrete, and are employed in virtually all types of construction, including highway construction and maintenance. Other Construction Materials products and services include asphalt mix and related products and ready–mixed concrete.

Recent Developments: For the quarter ended Mar 31 2004, earnings from continuing operations totaled $15.7 million versus income of $2.1 million, before an accounting change charge of $18.8 million, in the comparable prior–year period. Earnings for 2004 and 2003 excluded losses on discontinued operations of $707,000 and $882,000, respectively. Total revenues rose 8.9% to $617.5 million. On a segment basis, Construction Materials sales grew 10.2% to $431.9 million, due to increased volumes in key products and higher aggregates shipments in most markets resulting from better weather conditions and stronger construction activity. Chemicals sales rose 1.8% to $129.2 million due to higher sales prices for chlorine.

Prospects: Looking ahead, earnings for 2004 in Co.'s Construction Materials segment are expected to range from $415.0 million to $445.0 million, supported by a sustained recovery in construction activity. Co. anticipates both highway construction and private nonresidential construction to increase modestly in 2004. Meanwhile, although demand for chlorine and chlorinated products are improving, Co.'s Chemicals segment continues to be negatively affected by considerably weakened caustic soda prices. As a result, Co. expects a segment loss of $5.0 million to $15.0 million in 2004. Overall, Co. anticipates earnings per share to range from $2.45 to $2.65 for the full year.

Financial Data

(US$ in Thousands)	3 Mos	12/31/2003	12/31/2002	12/31/2001	12/31/2000	12/31/1999	12/31/1998	12/31/1997
Earnings Per Share	2.32	2.18	1.86	2.17	2.16	2.35	2.50	2.03
Cash Flow Per Share	0.90	5.05	4.50	4.97	4.09	3.94	3.54	3.36
Tang. Book Val. Per Share	11.96	12.01	11.04	10.02	9.00	8.62	11.46	9.81
Dividends Per Share	0.990	0.980	0.940	0.900	0.840	0.780	0.690	0.620
Dividend Payout %	45.02	44.95	50.53	41.47	38.88	33.19	27.73	30.82
Income Statement								
Total Revenues	617,462	2,892,186	2,796,577	3,019,990	2,491,744	2,355,778	1,776,434	1,678,581
Total Indirect Exp.	54,307	202,458	248,328	279,032	243,198	228,357	206,807	195,558
Depreciation & Amort.	63,494	277,091	267,676	278,209	232,365	207,108	137,792	120,624
Operating Income	31,765	353,116	292,664	370,422	340,489	358,094	342,863	283,570
Net Interest Inc./(Exp.)	(11,285)	(49,592)	(51,469)	(56,836)	(43,409)	(44,246)	(128)	(3,724)
Income Taxes	7,187	87,971	67,247	101,373	92,345	111,868	118,936	91,356
Income from Cont Ops	15,702	223,454	190,413	...	...	...	...	...
Net Income	14,995	194,952	169,876	222,680	219,893	239,693	255,908	209,145
Average Shs. Outstg.	103,425	102,710	102,515	102,497	102,012	102,190	102,177	102,849
Balance Sheet								
Cash & Cash Equivalents	436,987	416,689	170,728	100,802	55,276	52,834	180,568	128,566
Total Current Assets	1,072,361	1,050,242	789,688	729,952	694,504	624,724	576,381	487,132
Total Assets	3,656,261	3,636,860	3,448,221	3,398,224	3,228,574	2,839,493	1,658,611	1,449,246
Total Current Liabilities	543,863	542,952	297,709	344,495	572,231	386,642	211,462	207,697
Long–Term Obligations	609,148	607,654	857,757	906,299	685,361	698,862	76,533	81,931
Net Stockholders' Equity	1,801,741	1,802,836	1,696,986	1,604,274	1,471,496	1,323,653	1,153,700	991,497
Net Working Capital	528,498	507,290	491,979	385,457	122,273	238,082	364,919	279,435
Shares Outstanding	102,104	101,811	101,557	101,320	101,043	100,734	100,596	101,061
Operating Profit Margin %	5.14	12.20	10.46	12.26	13.66	15.20	19.30	16.89
Net Profit Margin %	4.87	13.80	11.61	14.08	16.23	19.67	27.79	23.34
Return on Equity %	0.87	12.39	11.22	13.88	14.94	18.10	22.18	21.09
Return on Assets %	0.42	6.14	5.52	6.55	6.81	8.44	15.42	14.43
Debt/Total Assets %	16.66	16.70	24.87	26.66	21.22	24.61	4.61	5.65
Price Range	50.12–45.93	48.25–29.06	49.55–32.37	55.10–38.15	48.50–36.69	50.50–34.88	44.06–31.62	34.44–18.46
P/E Ratio	21.60–19.80	22.13–13.33	26.64–17.40	25.39–17.58	22.45–16.98	21.49–14.84	17.62–12.65	16.96–9.09
Average Yield %	2.08	2.56	2.23	1.91	1.95	1.84	1.86	2.38

Address: 1200 Urban Center Drive, Birmingham, AL 35242 **Telephone:** (205) 298–3000 **Web Site:** www.vulcanmaterials.com	**Officers:** Donald M. James – Chmn., C.E.O., Mark E. Tomkins – Sr. V.P., C.F.O., Treas. **Transfer Agents:**The Bank of New York., New York, NY	**Investor Contact:**205–298–3220 **Institutional Holding** **No of Institutions:** 255 **Shares:** 70,289,533 **% Held:** 68.90%

WALGREEN CO.

Exchange	Symbol	Price	52Wk Range	Yield	P/E
NYS	WAG	$35.01 (5/28/2004)	37.15-29.05	0.49	28.46

*7 Year Price Score 111.0 *NYSE Composite Index=100 ***12 Month Price Score 48.5**

Interim Earnings (Per Share)

Qtr.	Nov	Feb	May	Aug
2000–01	0.15	0.29	0.21	0.21
2001–02	0.18	0.32	0.25	0.24
2002–03	0.22	0.36	0.29	0.27
2003–04	0.25	0.42	...	...

Interim Dividends (Per Share)

Amt	Decl	Ex	Rec	Pay
0.043Q	7/9/2003	8/18/2003	8/20/2003	9/12/2003
0.043Q	10/8/2003	11/13/2003	11/17/2003	12/12/2003
0.043Q	1/14/2004	2/17/2004	2/19/2004	3/12/2004
0.043Q	4/14/2004	5/19/2004	5/21/2004	6/12/2004

Indicated Div: $0.1725 (Div. Reinv. Plan)

Valuation Analysis

Forecast P/E 26.59 (5/24/2004)

Market Cap	$35.9 Billion	Book Value	7.4 Billion
Price/Book	4.26	Price/Sales	0.93

Dividend Achiever Status

Rank	210	10 Year Growth Rate	7.60%
Total Years of Dividend Growth		28	

Business Summary: Retail – Miscellaneous (MIC: 5.11 SIC: 5912 NAIC:446110)

Walgreen is engaged in the operation of retail drugstores. Co.'s drugstores are engaged in the retail sale of prescription and non–prescription drugs and carry additional product lines such as general merchandise, cosmetics, toiletries, household items, food and beverages. Customer prescription purchases can be made at the drugstores as well as through the mail, by telephone and on the Internet. The total number of stores at Aug 31 2003 was 4,224 stores located in 44 states and Puerto Rico. In addition, Co. operates three mail service facilities.

Recent Developments: For the three months ended Feb 29 2004, net earnings climbed 16.9% to $433.5 million from $370.9 million in the corresponding prior–year period. Results for 2004 and 2003 included after–tax gains of $7.9 million and $200,000, respectively, from litigation settlements. Net sales totaled $9.78 billion, up 15.8% compared with $8.45 billion the previous year. Comparable–store sales increased 11.5% year over year. Prescription sales, which accounted for approximately 60.0% of sales in the second quarter of fiscal 2004, advanced 19.0%. Prescription sales in comparable stores rose 15.5%. Earnings before income taxes increased 16.4% to $693.7 million from $595.8 million the year before.

Prospects: Results are being positively affected by stronger demand for prescription drugs and increased customer traffic levels, partially offset by a decline in the number of new generic prescription drug introductions. Meanwhile, results should continue to benefit from Co.'s ongoing store expansion program. During the first half of the current fiscal year, Co. has opened 109 net new stores. Co. anticipates a fiscal 2004 net increase of about 365 stores after closing and relocations. In May 2004, a new distribution center in Southern California is expected to be operational, which will help support Co.'s aggressive growth in this region.

Financial Data

(US$ in Thousands)	6 Mos	3 Mos	08/31/2003	08/31/2002	08/31/2001	08/31/2000	08/31/1999	08/31/1998
Earnings Per Share	1.23	1.17	1.14	0.99	0.86	0.76	0.62	0.53
Cash Flow Per Share	0.61	0.12	1.44	1.42	0.69	0.95	0.61	0.56
Tang. Book Val. Per Share	7.56	7.19	7.02	6.07	5.10	4.18	3.47	2.85
Dividends Per Share	0.160	0.150	0.149	0.144	0.139	0.134	0.129	0.123
Dividend Payout %	13.00	12.82	13.04	14.52	16.13	17.59	20.76	23.13
Income Statement								
Total Revenues	18,503,000	8,720,800	32,505,400	28,681,100	24,623,000	21,206,900	17,838,800	15,307,000
Total Indirect Exp.	3,923,700	1,895,100	6,950,900	5,980,800	5,175,800	4,516,900	3,844,800	3,332,000
Depreciation & Amort.	...	...	346,100	307,300	269,200	230,100	210,100	189,000
Operating Income	1,082,000	405,000	1,848,300	1,624,200	1,398,300	1,224,100	1,015,400	835,000
Net Interest Inc./(Exp.)	6,800	2,800	10,800	6,900	2,300	5,700	11,900	5,000
Income Taxes	413,100	152,900	713,000	618,100	537,100	486,400	403,200	340,000
Income from Cont Ops	...	...	...	...	...	...	...	537,000
Net Income	688,400	254,900	1,175,700	1,019,200	885,600	776,900	624,100	511,000
Average Shs. Outstg.	1,032,200	1,032,200	1,031,580	1,032,270	1,028,946	1,019,888	1,014,281	1,005,692
Balance Sheet								
Cash & Cash Equivalents	1,107,200	868,100	1,017,100	449,900	16,900	12,800	141,800	144,000
Total Current Assets	7,032,100	6,937,100	6,358,100	5,166,500	4,393,900	3,550,100	3,221,700	2,623,000
Total Assets	12,229,600	12,097,000	11,405,900	9,878,800	8,833,800	7,103,700	5,906,700	4,902,000
Total Current Liabilities	3,677,400	3,883,200	3,420,500	2,955,200	3,011,600	2,303,700	1,923,800	1,580,000
Net Stockholders' Equity	7,743,100	7,374,700	7,195,700	6,230,200	5,207,200	4,234,000	3,484,300	2,849,000
Net Working Capital	3,354,700	3,053,900	2,937,600	2,211,300	1,382,300	1,246,400	1,297,900	1,043,000
Shares Outstanding	1,024,259	1,024,532	1,024,908	1,024,908	1,019,425	1,010,818	1,004,022	996,488
Statistical Record								
Operating Profit Margin %	5.84	4.64	5.68	5.66	5.67	5.77	5.69	5.45
Return on Equity %	8.89	3.45	16.33	16.35	17.00	18.34	17.91	18.84
Return on Assets %	5.63	2.10	10.30	10.31	10.02	10.93	10.56	10.95
Price Range	37.15-30.57	36.81-30.57	35.96-27.35	40.24-30.98	45.63-31.43	35.25-22.75	33.06-19.25	24.47-12.81
P/E Ratio	30.20-24.85	31.46-26.13	31.54-23.99	40.65-31.29	53.05-36.55	46.38-29.93	53.33-31.05	46.17-24.17
Average Yield %	0.46	0.45	0.45	0.39	0.33	0.46	0.45	0.68

Address: 200 Wilmot Road, Deerfield, IL 60015	Officers: David W. Bernauer – Chmn., C.E.O., Jeffrey A. Rein – Pres., C.O.O.	Investor Contact:847–914–2972
Telephone: (847) 940–2500	Transfer Agents:Computershare Investor Services, Chicago, IL	Institutional Holding No of Institutions: 37
Web Site: www.walgreens.com		Shares: 1,634,938 % Held: –

WAL-MART STORES, INC.

Exchange	Symbol	Price	52Wk Range	Yield	P/E
NYS	WMT	$55.73 (5/28/2004)	61.05-50.74	0.93	26.29

*7 Year Price Score 119.3   *NYSE Composite Index=100   *12 Month Price Score 46.2

Interim Earnings (Per Share)

Qtr.	Apr	Jul	Oct	Jan
2000-01	0.30	0.36	0.31	0.43
2001-02	0.30	0.36	0.33	0.50
2002-03	0.37	0.46	0.41	0.57
2003-04	0.41	0.52	0.46	0.64
2004-05	0.50	...	...	...

Interim Dividends (Per Share)

Amt	Decl	Ex	Rec	Pay
0.13Q	3/2/2004	3/17/2004	3/19/2004	4/5/2004
0.13Q	3/2/2004	5/19/2004	5/21/2004	6/7/2004

Indicated Div: $0.52 (Div. Reinv. Plan)

Valuation Analysis

Forecast P/E 20.40 (5/24/2004)			
Market Cap	$246.0 Billion	Book Value	N/A
Price/Book	N/A	Price/Sales	N/A

Dividend Achiever Status

Rank	39	10 Year Growth Rate 18.75%
Total Years of Dividend Growth		22

Business Summary: Retail – General (MIC: 5.2 SIC: 5331 NAIC:452990)

Wal–Mart Stores operated 1,478 discount department stores, 1,471 Supercenters, 538 Sam's Clubs and 64 Neighborhood Markets in the U.S. as of Jan 31 2004. Co. also operated 623 Wal–Mart stores in Mexico, 267 in the U.K., 235 in Canada, 92 in Germany, 53 in Puerto Rico, 25 in Brazil, 15 in South Korea, and eleven in Argentina. Co. also operated 34 stores in China under joint venture agreements. Co.'s supercenters combine food, general merchandise, and services including pharmacy, dry cleaning, portrait studios, photo finishing, hair salons, and optical shops. In addition, Co. owns a 37.8% interest in Seiyu, Ltd., which operates over 400 stores throughout Japan.

Recent Developments: For the three months ended Apr 30 2004, net income totaled $2.17 billion, up 18.4% versus income of $1.83 billion, before a $31.0 million gain from discontinued operations, a year earlier. Net sales increased 14.2% to $64.76 billion from $56.72 billion the year before. Total U.S. comparable–store sales were up 6.4% year over year, reflecting a 5.9% same–store increase at Wal–Mart stores and an 8.8% comparable–store gain for Sam's Club locations. Cost of sales totaled $49.97 billion, or 77.2% of net sales, compared with $43.92 billion, or 77.4% of net sales, the previous year. Income before income taxes climbed 18.0% to $3.40 billion from $2.88 billion the prior year.

Prospects: Results are being positively affected by increased consumer spending on electronics and apparel, due primarily to improving economic conditions and larger income tax refunds in 2004. However, sharply higher gasoline prices and health care expenses are hampering profitability and could hurt consumer spending levels. Meanwhile, Co. is targeting second–quarter 2004 earnings of between $0.60 and $0.62 per share, and comparable–store sales growth in the range of 4.0% to 6.0%. Looking ahead, Co. anticipates full–year 2004 earnings per share of between $2.35 and $2.39.

Financial Data

(US$ in Thousands)	01/31/2004	01/31/2003	01/31/2002	01/31/2001	01/31/2000	01/31/1999	01/31/1998	01/31/1997
Earnings Per Share	2.03	1.81	1.49	1.40	1.25	0.99	0.78	0.66
Cash Flow Per Share	3.65	2.81	2.28	2.14	1.83	1.69	1.57	1.29
Tang. Book Val. Per Share	7.82	6.78	5.95	4.98	3.68	4.17	4.12	3.75
Dividends Per Share	0.360	0.300	0.280	0.240	0.200	0.150	0.130	0.100
Dividend Payout %	17.73	16.57	18.79	17.14	16.00	15.65	17.30	15.78
Income Statement								
Total Revenues	258,681,000	246,525,000	219,812,000	193,295,000	166,809,000	139,208,000	119,299,000	106,146,000
Total Indirect Exp.	44,909,000	41,043,000	36,173,000	31,550,000	27,040,000	22,363,000	19,358,000	16,788,000
Depreciation & Amort.	3,852,000	3,432,000	3,290,000	2,868,000	2,375,000	1,872,000	1,634,000	1,463,000
Operating Income	15,025,000	13,644,000	12,077,000	11,490,000	10,105,000	8,120,000	6,503,000	5,695,000
Net Interest Inc./(Exp.)	(832,000)	(925,000)	(1,326,000)	(1,374,000)	(1,022,000)	(797,000)	(784,000)	(845,000)
Income Taxes	5,118,000	4,487,000	3,897,000	3,692,000	3,338,000	2,740,000	2,115,000	1,794,000
Eqty Earns/Minority Int.	(214,000)	(193,000)	(183,000)	(129,000)	(170,000)	(153,000)	(78,000)	...
Income from Cont Ops	8,861,000	...	...	...	5,575,000	...	...	...
Net Income	9,054,000	8,039,000	6,671,000	6,295,000	5,377,000	4,430,000	3,526,000	3,056,000
Average Shs. Outstg.	4,373,000	4,446,000	4,481,000	4,484,000	4,474,000	4,485,000	4,533,000	4,592,000
Balance Sheet								
Cash & Cash Equivalents	5,199,000	2,758,000	2,161,000	2,054,000	1,856,000	1,879,000	1,447,000	883,000
Total Current Assets	34,421,000	30,483,000	28,246,000	26,555,000	24,356,000	21,132,000	19,352,000	17,993,000
Total Assets	104,912,000	94,685,000	83,451,000	78,130,000	70,349,000	49,996,000	45,384,000	39,604,000
Total Current Liabilities	37,418,000	32,617,000	27,282,000	28,949,000	25,803,000	16,762,000	14,460,000	10,957,000
Long–Term Obligations	20,099,000	19,608,000	18,732,000	15,655,000	16,674,000	9,607,000	9,674,000	10,016,000
Net Stockholders' Equity	43,623,000	39,337,000	35,102,000	31,343,000	25,834,000	21,112,000	18,503,000	17,143,000
Net Working Capital	(2,997,000)	(2,134,000)	964,000	(2,394,000)	(1,447,000)	4,370,000	4,892,000	7,036,000
Shares Outstanding	4,311,000	4,395,000	4,453,000	4,470,000	4,457,000	4,448,000	4,482,000	4,570,000
Operating Profit Margin %	5.80	5.53	5.49	5.94	6.05	5.83	5.45	5.36
Net Profit Margin %	7.38	6.90	6.58	7.07	7.34	7.11	6.50	6.25
Return on Equity %	20.31	20.43	19.00	20.08	21.58	20.98	19.05	17.82
Return on Assets %	8.44	8.49	7.99	8.05	7.92	8.86	7.76	7.71
Debt/Total Assets %	19.15	20.70	22.44	20.03	23.72	19.21	21.31	25.29
Price Range	60.08-46.74	63.75-44.60	59.98-44.00	63.56-43.25	69.75-40.19	43.00-20.41	20.88-11.63	14.13-10.19
P/E Ratio	29.60-23.02	35.22-24.64	40.26-29.53	45.40-30.89	55.80-32.15	43.43-20.61	26.76-14.90	21.40-15.44
Average Yield %	0.66	0.55	0.53	0.45	0.40	0.49	0.77	0.81

Address: 702 S.W. Eighth Street, Bentonville, AR 72716 Telephone: (479) 273–4000 Web Site: www.wal–mart.com	Officers: S. Robson Walton – Chmn., Thomas M. Coughlin – Vice–Chmn. Transfer Agents:EquiServe Trust Company, N.A., Providence, RI	Institutional Holding No of Institutions: 9 Shares: 3,970,827 % Held: –

WASHINGTON FEDERAL INC.

Exchange	Symbol	Price	52Wk Range	Yield	P/E
NMS	WFSL	$23.91 (5/28/2004)	26.36-20.69	3.35	13.74

*7 Year Price Score 130.7 **NYSE Composite Index=100* ***12 Month Price Score 45.5**

Interim Earnings (Per Share)

Qtr.	Dec	Mar	Jun	Sep
2000–01	0.35	0.35	0.38	0.38
2001–02	0.45	0.46	0.46	0.48
2002–03	0.52	0.49	0.47	0.40
2003–04	0.46	0.41	...	...

Interim Dividends (Per Share)

Amt	Decl	Ex	Rec	Pay
0.20Q	9/22/2003	10/1/2003	10/3/2003	10/17/2003
0.20Q	12/22/2003	1/7/2004	1/9/2004	1/23/2004
10%	1/21/2004	2/4/2004	2/6/2004	2/20/2004
0.20Q	3/22/2004	3/31/2004	4/2/2004	4/16/2004

Indicated Div: $0.80

Valuation Analysis

Forecast P/E 13.85 (5/24/2004)			
Market Cap $1.5 Billion		Book Value	1.1 Billion
Price/Book 1.82		Price/Sales	4.63

Dividend Achiever Status

Rank	190	10 Year Growth Rate	8.43%
Total Years of Dividend Growth			20

TRADING VOLUME (thousand shares)

1995 1996 1997 1998 1999 2000 2001 2002 2003 2004

Business Summary: Other Depository Banking (MIC: 8.5 SIC: 6035 NAIC:522120)

Washington Federal is a non–diversified unitary savings and loan holding company with total assets of $7.54 billion, as of Sep 30, 2003. Co. conducts its operations through its federally insured savings and loan association subsidiary, Washington Federal Savings and Loan Association. Co.'s business consists primarily of attracting savings deposits from the general public and investing these funds in loans secured by first mortgage liens on single–family dwellings, including loans for the construction of such dwellings, and loans on multi–family dwellings. As of Sep 30 2003, Co. operated 119 offices located in eight states in the western United States.

Recent Developments: For the quarter ended Mar 31 2004, net income fell 13.7% to $32.5 million compared with $37.7 million in the same period a year earlier. Co. attributed the decline in earnings to a slowdown in loan prepayments and a one–time pretax gain of $3.4 million on the sale of real estate in 2003. Net interest income decreased 8.5% to $59.3 million from $64.8 million the previous year. Provision for loan losses amounted to nil versus $150,000 last year. Other income dropped 65.3% to $1.9 million versus $5.6 million the year before, primarily due to the aforementioned 2003 gain of $3.4 million on the sale of real estate.

Prospects: Co.'s near–term outlook is tempered by the slowdown in the mortgage market due to rising interest rates, as well as the possibility of intensified price competition. However, Co.'s decision to invest cautiously over the past year due to historically low interest rates and an increase in short–term assets now appears prudent. For instance, as of Mar 31 2004, Co.'s cash and cash equivalents totaled $1.18 billion. Consequently, with interest rates higher and seemingly poised to increase further, Co. should have an opportunity to invest at more favorable rates.

Financial Data

(US$ in Thousands)	6 Mos	3 Mos	09/30/2003	09/30/2002	09/30/2001	09/30/2000	09/30/1999	09/30/1998
Earnings Per Share	1.74	1.82	1.88	1.85	1.46	1.36	1.40	1.31
Tang. Book Val. Per Share	...	14.17	12.71	12.03	11.97	9.40	8.84	9.47
Dividends Per Share	0.790	0.780	0.770	0.730	0.690	0.650	0.590	0.540
Dividend Payout %	45.40	42.85	40.97	39.39	47.41	48.00	42.79	41.53
Income Statement								
Total Interest Income	205,364	102,682	450,185	507,317	536,410	498,027	455,577	460,604
Total Interest Expense	87,462	44,056	194,884	234,941	320,120	299,511	244,490	252,233
Net Interest Income	117,902	58,626	255,301	272,376	216,290	198,516	211,087	208,371
Provision for Loan Losses	...	...	1,500	7,000	1,850	...	684	740
Non–Interest Income	4,918	2,848	14,823	8,206	10,137	11,309	12,779	11,270
Non–Interest Expense	21,882	10,779	44,059	51,228	49,113	46,646	46,101	45,116
Income Before Taxes	100,938	50,695	224,565	222,354	175,464	163,179	177,081	173,785
Net Income	65,342	32,822	145,544	143,954	113,614	105,679	114,286	111,836
Average Shs. Outstg.	79,211	71,931	77,255	77,575	77,507	77,473	81,706	85,144
Balance Sheet								
Securities Avail. for Sale	940,840	741,309	1,608,372	1,837,552	2,159,792	2,356,928	2,339,834	1,528,376
Net Loans & Leases	4,758,358	4,666,904	4,606,726	4,292,003	4,207,769	4,949,235	4,378,728	4,143,525
Total Assets	7,543,092	7,544,844	7,535,975	7,392,441	7,026,743	6,719,841	6,163,503	5,637,011
Total Deposits	4,509,026	4,524,690	4,520,051	4,452,250	4,251,113	3,375,036	3,291,857	3,071,175
Long–Term Obligations	1,750,000	1,750,000	1,650,000	1,650,000	1,637,500	1,209,000	1,454,000	1,356,500
Total Liabilities	6,450,752	6,474,644	6,480,379	6,431,723	6,152,734	5,960,676	5,413,480	4,869,839
Net Stockholders' Equity	1,092,340	1,070,200	1,055,596	960,718	874,009	759,165	750,023	767,172
Shares Outstanding	78,498	71,281	78,290	76,884	70,012	76,310	79,401	75,322
Statistical Record								
Return on Equity %	5.98	3.06	13.78	14.98	12.99	13.92	15.23	14.57
Return on Assets %	0.87	0.43	1.93	1.94	1.61	1.57	1.85	1.98
Equity/Assets %	14.48	14.18	14.00	12.99	12.43	11.29	12.16	13.60
Non–Int. Exp./Tot. Inc. %	10.41	10.22	9.47	9.93	8.99	9.17	9.84	9.56
Price Range	26.36-22.91	26.29-22.91	24.01-17.07	22.65-16.53	20.77-13.53	16.22-10.20	17.46-14.09	18.80-13.82
P/E Ratio	15.15-13.17	14.45-12.58	12.77-9.08	12.24-8.93	14.22-9.27	11.93-7.50	12.47-10.06	14.35-10.55
Average Yield %	3.13	3.13	3.73	3.63	3.78	4.99	3.75	3.16

Address: 425 Pike Street, Seattle, WA 98101
Telephone: (206) 624–7930
Web Site: www.washingtonfederal.com

Officers: Guy C. Pinkerton – Chmn., Roy M. Whitehead – Vice Chmn., Pres., C.E.O.
Transfer Agents: ChaseMellon Shareholder Services, LLC, Ridgefield Park, NJ

Investor Contact:206–624–7930
Institutional Holding
No of Institutions: 13
Shares: 480,672 **% Held:** –

WASHINGTON MUTUAL INC.

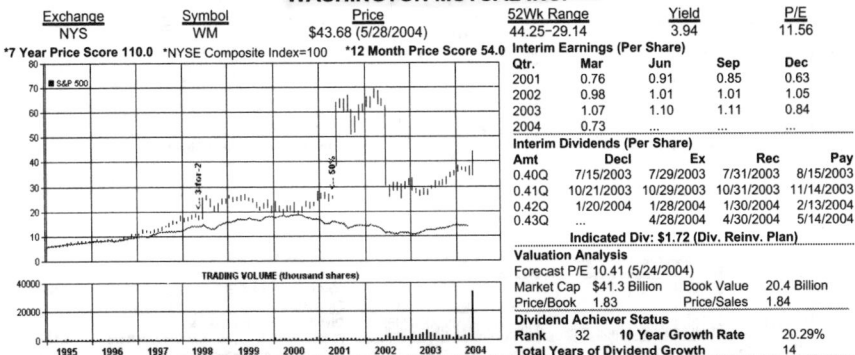

Exchange	Symbol	Price	52Wk Range	Yield	P/E
NYS	WM	$43.68 (5/28/2004)	44.25–29.14	3.94	11.56

*7 Year Price Score 110.0   *NYSE Composite Index=100   *12 Month Price Score 54.0

Interim Earnings (Per Share)

Qtr.	Mar	Jun	Sep	Dec
2001	0.76	0.91	0.85	0.63
2002	0.98	1.01	1.01	1.05
2003	1.07	1.10	1.11	0.84
2004	0.73	...	...	...

Interim Dividends (Per Share)

Amt	Decl	Ex	Rec	Pay
0.40Q	7/15/2003	7/29/2003	7/31/2003	8/15/2003
0.41Q	10/21/2003	10/29/2003	10/31/2003	11/14/2003
0.42Q	1/20/2004	1/28/2004	1/30/2004	2/13/2004
0.43Q		4/28/2004	4/30/2004	5/14/2004

Indicated Div: $1.72 (Div. Reinv. Plan)

Valuation Analysis

Forecast P/E 10.41 (5/24/2004)

Market Cap	$41.3 Billion	Book Value	20.4 Billion
Price/Book	1.83	Price/Sales	1.84

Dividend Achiever Status

Rank	32	10 Year Growth Rate	20.29%
Total Years of Dividend Growth			14

Business Summary: Other Depository Banking (MIC: 8.5 SIC: 6036 NAIC:522120)

Washington Mutual is a holding company for both banking and nonbanking subsidiaries. Co.'s primary banking subsidiaries are Washington Mutual Bank, FA, Washington Mutual Bank and Washington Mutual Bank fsb. These organizations provide consumer banking, mortgage lending, commercial banking, consumer finance and financial services. Co. operates in two segments: consumer group, which offers products and services to consumers and manages activities and operations affecting consumers; and commercial group, which offers a full array of commercial banking products and services. As of Dec 31 2003, Co. and its subsidiaries had assets of $275.18 billion and operated more than 2,400 offices nationwide.

Recent Developments: For the quarter ended Mar 31 2004, Co. reported income from continuing operations of $648.0 million versus income of $978.0 million in the comparable prior–year period. Earnings for 2004 and 2003 excluded gains from discontinued operations of $399.0 million and $19.0 million, respectively. Net interest income declined 13.1% to $1.73 billion, resulting from the downward repricing of assets in the early part of 2003. Provision for loan and lease losses dropped 36.4% to $56.0 million. Total non–interest income slid 4.5% to $1.24 billion, while total non–interest expense grew 14.1% to $1.89 billion.

Prospects: Co. has made considerable progress in its efforts to reduce costs and streamline initiatives. For instance, non–interest expense for the first quarter of 2004 decreased by $221.0 million, or 11.0%, from the fourth quarter of 2003. Additionally, Co.'s efficiency ratio improved to 63.34% compared with 65.51% for the fourth quarter of 2003. Looking ahead, Co. believes it is well positioned to keep 2004 non–interest expense essentially flat with the 2003 level, while executing its targeted growth and expansion plans in 2004. Co.'s expansion plans include the opening of 250 more financial center stores to its nationwide network of approximately 1,800 in 2004.

Financial Data

(US$ in Thousands)	3 Mos	12/31/2003	12/31/2002	12/31/2001	12/31/2000	12/31/1999	12/31/1998	12/31/1997
Earnings Per Share	3.78	4.12	4.05	3.15	2.36	2.10	1.70	0.82
Tang. Book Val. Per Share	10.02	7.87	9.02	6.29	9.95	8.40	8.84	7.97
Dividends Per Share	1.530	1.400	1.060	0.890	0.760	0.650	0.540	0.470
Dividend Payout %	35.33	33.98	26.17	28.46	32.20	31.01	32.03	56.98
Income Statement								
Total Interest Income	2,721,000	12,163,000	14,247,000	15,065,000	13,783,000	12,062,198	11,221,468	6,810,964
Total Interest Expense	989,000	4,534,000	5,906,000	8,189,000	9,472,000	7,610,408	6,929,743	4,154,491
Net Interest Income	1,732,000	7,629,000	8,341,000	6,876,000	4,311,000	4,451,790	4,291,725	2,656,473
Provision for Loan Losses	56,000	42,000	595,000	575,000	185,000	167,076	161,968	207,139
Non–Interest Income	1,237,000	5,850,000	4,790,000	2,627,000	1,984,000	1,508,997	1,577,019	750,892
Non–Interest Expense	1,880,000	7,408,000	6,382,000	4,617,000	3,126,000	2,909,551	3,337,319	2,299,100
Income Before Taxes	1,033,000	6,029,000	6,154,000	4,311,000	2,984,000	2,884,160	2,369,457	901,126
Income from Cont Ops	648,000	3,793,000	...	2,732,000	...	...	...	...
Net Income	1,047,000	3,880,000	3,896,000	3,114,000	1,899,000	1,817,064	1,486,932	481,778
Average Shs. Outstg.	886,467	921,757	960,152	864,700	804,694	861,829	867,843	555,851
Balance Sheet								
Securities Avail. for Sale	12,565,000	74,795,000	43,972,000	58,349,000	42,159,000	82,391,631	65,355,712	21,585,393
Net Loans & Leases	186,202,000	174,394,000	145,875,000	131,587,000	118,612,000	112,703,721	106,544,357	66,454,441
Total Assets	280,768,000	275,178,000	268,298,000	242,506,000	194,716,000	186,513,630	165,493,281	96,981,099
Total Deposits	160,981,000	153,181,000	155,516,000	107,182,000	79,574,000	81,129,768	85,492,141	50,986,017
Long–Term Obligations	72,186,000	63,813,000	65,634,000	73,758,000	67,785,000	63,297,250	45,198,121	22,991,325
Total Liabilities	260,385,000	255,436,000	247,269,400	228,341,000	184,550,000	177,460,951	156,148,881	91,672,028
Net Stockholders' Equity	20,383,000	19,742,000	20,134,000	13,961,000	10,166,000	9,052,679	9,344,400	5,309,071
Shares Outstanding	868,953	880,985	944,046	873,089	809,783	857,383	890,112	579,510
Return on Equity %	6.85	35.77	32.34	19.42	18.67	20.07	15.91	9.07
Return on Assets %	0.49	2.56	2.42	1.12	0.97	0.97	0.89	0.49
Equity/Assets %	7.25	7.17	7.50	5.79	5.22	4.85	5.64	5.47
Non–Int. Exp./Tot. Inc. %	39.93	34.80	29.47	26.09	19.82	21.43	26.07	30.40
Price Range	38.25–35.82	36.15–26.27	69.25–25.30	66.75–24.31	27.95–18.50	28.65–19.72	26.70–15.95	18.35–10.65
P/E Ratio	10.12– 9.48	8.77–6.38	17.10–6.25	21.19–7.72	11.84–7.84	12.79–9.39	15.70–9.38	22.37–12.99
Average Yield %	4.14	4.55	2.31	1.83	3.47	2.70	2.55	3.47

Address: 1201 Third Avenue, Seattle, WA 98101	**Officers:** Kerry K. Killinger – Chmn., Pres., C.E.O., William A. Longbrake – Vice–Chmn.	**Investor Contact:** 206–461–3186	
Telephone: (206) 461–2000	**Transfer Agents:** Mellon Investor Services, L.L.C., Ridgefield Park, NJ	**Institutional Holding** **No of Institutions:** 21	
Web Site: www.wamu.com		**Shares:** 1,421,530 **% Held:** –	

287

WASHINGTON REAL ESTATE INVESTMENT TRUST

Exchange	Symbol	Price	52Wk Range	Yield	P/E
NYS	WRE	$28.27 (5/28/2004)	32.76–25.80	5.55	25.24

*7 Year Price Score 133.4 *NYSE Composite Index=100 ***12 Month Price Score 43.8**

Interim Earnings (Per Share)

Qtr.	Mar	Jun	Sep	Dec
2001	0.30	0.33	0.43	0.19
2002	0.32	0.30	0.30	0.30
2003	0.28	0.29	0.28	0.28
2004	0.27	...	...	...

Interim Dividends (Per Share)

Amt	Decl	Ex	Rec	Pay
0.373Q	8/7/2003	9/12/2003	9/16/2003	9/30/2003
0.373Q	11/19/2003	12/15/2003	12/17/2003	12/31/2003
0.373Q	2/19/2004	3/15/2004	3/17/2004	3/31/2004
0.393Q	5/5/2004	6/14/2004	6/16/2004	6/30/2004

Indicated Div: $1.57 (Div. Reinv. Plan)

Valuation Analysis

Forecast P/E 13.52 (5/24/2004)

Market Cap	$1.1 Billion	Book Value	378.7 Million
Price/Book	3.10	Price/Sales	7.18

Dividend Achiever Status

Rank	250	10 Year Growth Rate	5.15%

Total Years of Dividend Growth 42

Business Summary: Property, Real Estate &Development (MIC: 8.3 SIC: 6798 NAIC:525930)

Washington Real Estate Investment Trust is a self–administered qualified equity real estate investment trust. Co.'s business consists of the ownership and operation of income–producing real estate properties principally in the Greater Washington, D.C.–Baltimore, MD area. Upon the purchase of a property, Co. begins a program of improving the real estate to increase the value and to improve the operations, with the goals of generating higher rental income and reducing expenses. As of Mar 12 2004, Co. owned a diversified portfolio of 67 properties consisting of 11 retail centers, 29 office buildings, nine multifamily buildings and 18 industrial/flex properties.

Recent Developments: For the three months ended Mar 31 2004, net income inched up to $11.3 million compared with $11.2 million in the corresponding quarter of the previous year. Total revenue advanced 13.8% to $44.4 million from $39.1 million in the year–earlier period. Revenue growth was attributable to an increase in real estate rental revenue, which increased 13.9% to $44.4 million from $39.0 million. Other income decreased 39.8% to $65,000 from $108,000 in the prior–year quarter. Funds from operations climbed 9.8% to $21.2 million from $19.3 million the year before. As of Mar 31 2004, Co.'s properties were 90.0% occupied versus 89.3% occupied on Mar 31, 2003.

Prospects: Co. is experiencing increased activity at its commercial properties, which is being driven largely by improvement in the business and economic climate. Meanwhile, the performance of Co.'s multifamily sector continues to be flat; however, Co. anticipates higher levels of occupancy and rental rate growth before year end, provided continued job growth in its hey markets. Separately, on Mar 12 2003, Co. acquired 8880 Gorman Road in Laurel, MD for $11.5 million. The property is 100% occupied by a single tenant and is anticipated to produce a first year return on investment of 8.8%.

Financial Data

(US$ in Thousands)	3 Mos	12/31/2003	12/31/2002	12/31/2001	12/31/2000	12/31/1999	12/31/1998	12/31/1997
Earnings Per Share	1.12	1.13	1.22	1.25	1.13	1.24	1.15	0.90
Tang. Book Val. Per Share	9.02	9.10	8.32	8.33	7.23	7.19	7.10	7.06
Dividends Per Share	1.470	1.450	1.030	1.310	1.230	1.150	1.110	1.070
Dividend Payout %	131.25	130.08	113.93	104.80	108.84	93.34	96.52	188.88
Income Statement								
Rental Income	44,376	163,405	152,929	148,424	134,732	118,975	103,597	79,429
Total Income	44,441	163,819	153,609	148,424	134,732	118,975	103,597	79,429
Total Indirect Exp.	14,711	115,671	103,178	47,050	43,397	33,061	28,969	21,051
Depreciation	9,872	35,755	29,200	26,735	22,723	19,590	15,399	10,911
Interest Expense	8,575	30,040	27,849	27,071	25,531	22,271	17,106	9,691
Eqty Earns/Minority Int.	...	...	...	(32,835)	(30,256)	(25,763)	(21,957)	(15,154)
Income from Cont Ops	...	...	48,080	48,057	41,572	36,392	34,300	...
Net Income	11,302	44,887	51,836	52,353	45,139	44,301	41,064	30,116
Average Shs. Outstg.	41,820	39,600	39,281	37,951	35,872	35,700	35,700	33,400
Balance Sheet								
Cash & Cash Equivalents	6,064	5,486	13,076	26,441	6,426	4,716	4,595	7,908
Ttl Real Estate Inv.	887,366	878,794	706,790	651,961	597,607	578,296	530,573	448,300
Total Assets	938,028	927,129	755,997	707,935	632,047	608,480	558,707	468,571
Long–Term Obligations	516,752	517,182	351,951	359,726	351,260	297,038	238,912	107,461
Total Liabilities	561,171	548,381	429,820	384,328	373,391	351,291	304,974	216,483
Net Stockholders' Equity	376,857	378,748	326,177	323,607	258,656	257,189	253,733	252,088
Shares Outstanding	41,764	41,607	39,168	38,829	35,740	35,721	35,692	35,678
Statistical Record								
Net Inc.+Depr./Assets %	2.26	8.70	10.20	11.20	10.70	10.50	10.10	8.80
Return on Equity %	2.99	3.92	6.20	14.85	16.07	14.14	13.51	11.95
Return on Assets %	1.20	1.60	2.67	6.78	6.57	5.98	6.13	6.43
Price Range	32.45–28.39	31.04–24.10	30.15–21.96	25.45–21.27	25.00–14.31	18.63–14.00	18.63–15.56	19.38–15.88
P/E Ratio	28.97–25.35	27.47–21.33	24.71–18.00	20.36–17.02	22.12–12.67	15.02–11.29	16.20–13.53	21.53–17.64
Average Yield %	4.87	5.25	3.94	5.59	6.89	7.07	8.11	4.67

Address: 6110 Executive Boulevard, Rockville, MD 20852–3927	Officers: Edmund B. Cronin – Chmn., Pres., C.E.O., George F. McKenzie – Exec. V.P., Real Estate	Institutional Holding
Telephone: (301) 984–9400	Transfer Agents:EquiServe Trust Company N.A.,	No of Institutions: 32
Web Site: www.writ.com	Providence, RI	Shares: 1,200,667 % Held: –

WEBSTER FINANCIAL CORP (WATERBURY, CONN)

Exchange	Symbol	Price	52Wk Range	Yield	P/E
NYS	WBS	$46.84 (5/28/2004)	51.65-36.48	1.96	13.16

*7 Year Price Score 136.9 *NYSE Composite Index=100 *12 Month Price Score 48.1

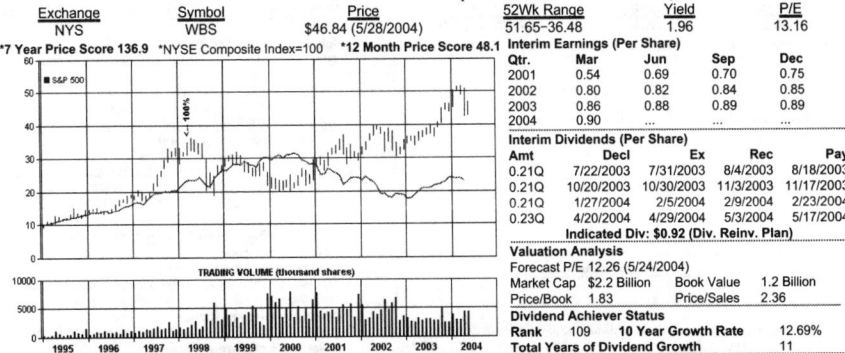

Interim Earnings (Per Share)

Qtr.	Mar	Jun	Sep	Dec
2001	0.54	0.69	0.70	0.75
2002	0.80	0.82	0.84	0.85
2003	0.86	0.88	0.89	0.89
2004	0.90	...	...	...

Interim Dividends (Per Share)

Amt	Decl	Ex	Rec	Pay
0.21Q	7/22/2003	7/31/2003	8/4/2003	8/18/2003
0.21Q	10/20/2003	10/30/2003	11/3/2003	11/17/2003
0.21Q	1/27/2004	2/5/2004	2/9/2004	2/23/2004
0.23Q	4/20/2004	4/29/2004	5/3/2004	5/17/2004

Indicated Div: $0.92 (Div. Reinv. Plan)

Valuation Analysis

Forecast P/E 12.26 (5/24/2004)

Market Cap	$2.2 Billion	Book Value	1.2 Billion
Price/Book	1.83	Price/Sales	2.36

Dividend Achiever Status

Rank	109	10 Year Growth Rate	12.69%
Total Years of Dividend Growth			11

Business Summary: Other Depository Banking (MIC: 8.5 SIC: 6035 NAIC:522120)

Webster Financial is a holding company with $14.57 billion in assets as of Dec 31 2003. Through its subsidiaries, Co. is engaged in providing financial services to individuals, families and businesses, primarily in Connecticut and equipment financing, asset-based lending, mortgage origination and financial advisory services to public and private companies throughout the U.S. Co. provides business and consumer banking, mortgage origination and lending, trust and investment services and insurance services through 119 banking and other offices, 233 ATMs and its Internet website.

Recent Developments: For the quarter ended Mar 31 2004, net income grew 6.0% to $42.3 million compared with $39.9 million in the corresponding prior-year period. Total interest income dropped 3.1% to $164.3 million. Total interest expense fell 9.7% to $58.5 million versus $64.8 million the year before. Net interest income climbed 1.1% to $105.8 million due to loan portfolio growth. Provision for loan losses in 2004 and 2003 was $5.0 million. Total noninterest income advanced 3.0% to $54.7 million from $53.1 million a year ago. Total noninterest expense declined 0.7% to $92.1 million from $92.8 million the year before. At Mar 31 2004, net loans were $9.41 billion, and deposits amounted to $8.64 billion.

Prospects: Co. completed the sale of its majority interest in Duff & Phelps, LLC, a Chicago-based financial advisory services and investment banking firm. The sale frees up Co. to focus more closely on growing its retail and commercial banking, investment and insurance businesses in southern New England. On Apr 21 2004, Co. announced that its principal subsidiary, Webster Bank, completed its conversion to a national bank charter. With $15.10 billion in assets, Co. is the largest Connecticut-based bank, and with its expansion into the Rhode Island and Massachusetts markets via its pending acquisition of FirstFed America Bancorp, Co. should be one of the largest independent banks in southern New England.

Financial Data

(US$ in Thousands)	12/31/2003	12/31/2002	12/31/2001	12/31/2000	12/31/1999	12/31/1998	12/31/1997	12/31/1996
Earnings Per Share	3.52	3.31	2.68	2.55	2.10	1.83	1.22	1.39
Tang. Book Val. Per Share	17.76	16.17	13.96	11.52	10.98	12.76	12.20	10.21
Dividends Per Share	0.820	0.740	0.670	0.620	0.470	0.430	0.390	0.340
Dividend Payout %	23.29	22.35	25.00	24.31	22.38	23.49	31.96	24.37
Income Statement								
Total Interest Income	658,718	692,034	757,235	738,911	645,792	622,453	445,848	265,534
Total Interest Expense	245,199	286,306	389,756	412,395	342,279	377,018	253,923	149,745
Net Interest Income	413,519	405,728	367,479	326,516	303,513	245,435	191,925	115,789
Provision for Loan Losses	25,000	29,000	14,400	11,800	9,000	6,800	15,835	4,000
Non-Interest Income	223,993	176,530	152,934	120,266	84,738	74,163	35,990	25,530
Non-Interest Expense	377,082	328,323	308,932	267,130	244,461	197,789	158,547	97,249
Income from Cont Ops	...	160,012	136,815	...	...	...	...	...
Net Income	163,248	152,732	133,188	118,291	95,350	70,465	33,798	25,608
Average Shs. Outstg.	46,362	48,392	42,742	46,427	45,393	38,571	27,656	18,326
Balance Sheet								
Cash & Due from Banks	209,234	266,463	218,908	265,035	245,783	173,863	122,267	85,163
Securities Avail. for Sale	4,128,255	4,119,245	3,999,133	3,143,327	2,700,585	2,969,822	2,290,254	573,616
Net Loans & Leases	9,091,135	7,795,835	6,869,911	6,819,209	6,022,236	4,993,509	3,824,602	2,525,543
Total Assets	14,568,690	13,468,004	11,857,382	11,249,508	9,931,744	9,033,917	7,019,621	3,917,600
Total Deposits	8,372,135	7,606,122	7,066,471	6,941,522	6,191,091	5,651,273	4,365,756	3,095,876
Long-Term Obligations	3,044,255	2,289,029	2,531,179	2,380,074	1,714,441	1,774,560	1,071,620	407,734
Total Liabilities	13,406,218	12,301,714	10,691,338	10,159,557	9,096,500	8,279,461	6,487,858	3,711,304
Net Stockholders' Equity	1,143,318	904,626	846,890	690,797	436,090	355,302	232,609	206,296
Shares Outstanding	46,276	45,625	49,149	48,939	45,243	37,327	27,306	15,852
Statistical Record								
Return on Equity %	14.15	15.45	13.59	13.28	14.99	12.69	8.84	12.41
Return on Assets %	1.12	1.18	1.15	1.05	0.96	0.78	0.48	0.65
Non-Int. Exp./Tot. Inc. %	42.41	37.41	33.60	30.78	33.10	28.39	32.90	33.41
Price Range	46.50-33.93	39.96-30.65	37.06-26.44	29.63-20.13	32.00-21.88	36.25-18.88	33.38-17.56	19.09-13.38
P/E Ratio	13.21-9.64	12.07-9.26	13.83-9.86	11.62-7.89	15.24-10.42	19.81-10.31	27.36-14.40	13.74-9.62
Average Yield %	2.11	2.09	2.15	2.68	1.70	1.45	1.62	2.19

Address: Webster Plaza, Waterbury, CT 06702	Officers: James C. Smith – Chmn., C.E.O., William T. Bromage – Pres., C.O.O.	Investor Contact:203-578-2318
Telephone: (203) 753-2921	Transfer Agents:American Stock Transfer &Trust Co, New York, NY	Institutional Holding No of Institutions: 4
Web Site: www.websteronline.com		Shares: 118,322 % Held: –

WEINGARTEN REALTY INVESTORS

Exchange	Symbol	Price	52Wk Range	Yield	P/E
NYS	WRI	$30.97 (5/28/2004)	35.26–26.73	5.36	26.25

*7 Year Price Score 138.6   *NYSE Composite Index=100   ***12 Month Price Score 45.7**

Interim Earnings (Per Share)

Qtr.	Mar	Jun	Sep	Dec
2001	0.30	0.28	0.30	0.34
2002	0.30	0.30	0.30	0.26
2003	0.30	0.26	0.31	0.29
2004	0.32	...	...	...

Interim Dividends (Per Share)

Amt	Decl	Ex	Rec	Pay
0.39Q	10/27/2003	11/26/2003	12/1/2003	12/15/2003
0.415Q	2/23/2004	3/3/2004	3/5/2004	3/15/2004
50%	2/23/2004	3/31/2004	3/16/2004	3/30/2004
0.415Q	...	6/2/2004	6/4/2004	6/15/2004

Indicated Div: $1.66 (Div. Reinv. Plan)

Valuation Analysis
Forecast P/E 12.22 (5/24/2004)
Market Cap $1.6 Billion   Book Value 926.6 Million
Price/Book 4.43   Price/Sales 9.36

Dividend Achiever Status
Rank 256   10 Year Growth Rate 4.97%
Total Years of Dividend Growth 15

Business Summary: Property, Real Estate &Development (MIC: 8.3 SIC: 6798 NAIC:525930)

Weingarten Realty Investors is a self–administered and self–managed real estate investment trust that acquires, develops and manages real estate, primarily anchored neighborhood and community shopping centers and, to a lesser extent, industrial properties. As of Dec 31 2003, Co. owned or operated under long–term leases interests in 327 developed income–producing real estate projects. Co. owned 266 shopping centers located in the Houston metropolitan area and in other parts of Texas and in California, Louisiana, Arizona, Nevada, Arkansas, New Mexico, Oklahoma, Tennessee, Kansas, Colorado, Missouri, Illinois, Florida, North Carolina, Utah, Georgia, Mississippi and Maine.

Recent Developments: For the three months ended Mar 31 2004, net income was $28.4 million compared with income of $28.8 million, before a gain of $1.1 million from discontinued operations, in the corresponding quarter of the previous year. Results for 2004 and 2003 included pre–tax gains of $317,000 and $9,000, respectively, on the sale of properties. Total revenues increased 20.7% to $117.8 million from $97.6 million in the prior–year period. Revenue growth was primarily due to a 20.5% increase in rental income. Operating income fell 3.3% to $27.7 million versus $28.6 million in 2003. Funds from operations jumped 18.6% to $53.6 million from $45.2 million the year before.

Prospects: During the quarter, Co. purchased seven shopping centers totaling 1.5 million square feet with a total investment of $230.4 million and a projected return of slightly over 8.0%. Co. has a number of potential acquisitions in various stages of due diligence, and, combined with these first quarter acquisitions, Co. believes that it will achieve its 2004 acquisition plan of $400.0 million. Meanwhile, Co. will continue to maximize the potential of its existing portfolio, assess acquisition and development opportunities and evaluate alternative financing opportunities. Moreover, Co. should continue to benefit from strong leasing activity and expects occupancy to continue to increase.

Financial Data

(US$ in Thousands)	3 Mos	12/31/2003	12/31/2002	12/31/2001	12/31/2000	12/31/1999	12/31/1998	12/31/1997
Earnings Per Share	1.18	1.16	1.16	1.22	0.97	1.27	0.92	0.91
Tang. Book Val. Per Share	10.82	10.03	11.94	11.91	10.39	10.74	8.88	6.50
Dividends Per Share	1.580	1.560	1.480	1.400	1.330	1.260	1.190	1.130
Dividend Payout %	133.89	134.48	126.85	114.48	136.99	99.30	128.83	124.87
Income Statement								
Rental Income	116,001	410,490	359,044	309,457	264,552	225,244	194,624	169,041
Interest Income	276	1,594	1,054	1,167	5,638	1,888	...	2,487
Total Income	117,848	419,160	365,410	314,892	273,374	227,853	196,547	174,512
Total Indirect Exp.	117,896	338,701	265,725	225,775	191,991	151,819	140,836	117,852
Depreciation	26,663	94,108	78,481	68,316	58,518	49,612	41,946	37,976
Interest Expense	27,733	88,871	65,863	54,473	45,545	33,186	33,654	22,110
Eqty Earns/Minority Int.	1,286	2,020	490	5,072	(8,041)	2,616	1,920	...
Income from Cont Ops	...	109,781	110,611	...	...	96,320	61,757	...
Net Income	28,409	116,280	131,867	108,542	79,001	96,130	60,365	54,966
Average Shs. Outstg.	86,281	81,574	80,040	72,553	60,594	60,502	60,455	60,234
Balance Sheet								
Cash & Cash Equivalents	34,455	20,255	27,420	12,434	14,825	5,842	16,623	15,099
Total Assets	3,169,175	2,923,794	2,423,889	2,095,747	1,646,011	1,309,396	1,107,043	946,793
Long–Term Obligations	1,947,070	1,810,706	1,330,369	1,070,835	869,627	594,185	516,366	507,366
Total Liabilities	2,242,505	2,102,231	1,490,476	1,174,675	1,016,144	663,494	573,864	556,807
Net Stockholders' Equity	926,670	821,563	933,413	921,072	629,867	645,902	533,179	389,986
Shares Outstanding	85,578	81,888	78,114	77,280	60,572	60,063	60,014	59,985
Statistical Record								
Net Inc.+Depr./Assets %	...	7.19	7.80	8.40	8.40	11.10	9.40	7.80
Return on Equity %	3.07	13.36	11.85	11.78	12.54	15.26	11.28	14.09
Return on Assets %	0.90	3.75	4.56	5.17	4.79	7.36	5.43	5.80
Price Range	34.60–29.57	30.70–23.80	25.76–20.57	22.40–17.80	19.89–15.42	20.28–16.61	20.61–16.25	20.11–17.39
P/E Ratio	108.1–92.40	26.47–20.52	22.21–17.73	18.36–14.59	20.50–15.89	15.97–13.08	22.40–17.66	22.10–19.11
Average Yield %	4.88	5.59	6.26	6.97	7.45	7.05	6.25	6.01

Address: 2600 Citadel Plaza Drive, Houston, TX 77292–4133
Telephone: (713) 866–6000
Web Site: www.weingarten.com

Officers: Stanford Alexander – Chmn., Martin Debrovner – Vice–Chmn.
Transfer Agents: Mellon Investor Services, LLC, Ridgefield Park, NJ

Investor Contact: 713–866–6050
Institutional Holding
No of Institutions: 7
Shares: 423,186   **% Held:** –

WELLS FARGO & CO.

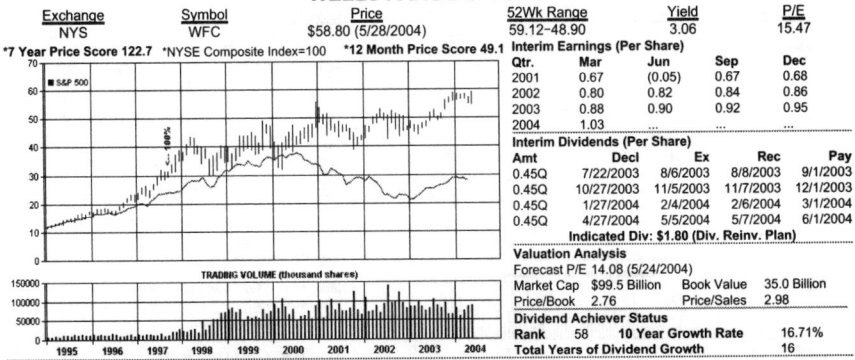

Exchange	Symbol	Price	52Wk Range	Yield	P/E
NYS	WFC	$58.80 (5/28/2004)	59.12–48.90	3.06	15.47

*7 Year Price Score 122.7   *NYSE Composite Index=100   ***12 Month Price Score 49.1**

Interim Earnings (Per Share)

Qtr.	Mar	Jun	Sep	Dec
2001	0.67	(0.05)	0.67	0.68
2002	0.80	0.82	0.84	0.86
2003	0.88	0.90	0.92	0.95
2004	1.03	...	...	...

Interim Dividends (Per Share)

Amt	Decl	Ex	Rec	Pay
0.45Q	7/22/2003	8/6/2003	8/8/2003	9/1/2003
0.45Q	10/27/2003	11/5/2003	11/7/2003	12/1/2003
0.45Q	1/27/2004	2/4/2004	2/6/2004	3/1/2004
0.45Q	4/27/2004	5/5/2004	5/7/2004	6/1/2004

Indicated Div: $1.80 (Div. Reinv. Plan)

Valuation Analysis

Forecast P/E 14.08 (5/24/2004)

Market Cap	$99.5 Billion	Book Value	35.0 Billion
Price/Book	2.76	Price/Sales	2.98

Dividend Achiever Status

Rank	58	10 Year Growth Rate 16.71%
Total Years of Dividend Growth		16

Business Summary: Commercial Banking (MIC: 8.1 SIC: 6021 NAIC:522110)

Wells Fargo is the fifth largest bank holding company in the U.S., based on total assets of $387.80 billion as of Dec 31 2003. Through its subsidiaries, Co. engages in banking and a variety of related financial services businesses. Retail, commercial and corporate banking services are provided through banking stores in 23 states. Other financial services are engaged in various businesses, principally wholesale banking, mortgage banking, consumer finance, equipment leasing, agricultural finance, commercial finance, securities brokerage and investment banking, insurance agency services, computer services, trust services, mortgage-backed securities servicing and venture capital investment.

Recent Developments: For the quarter ended Mar 31 2004, net income improved 18.4% to $1.77 billion from $1.49 billion in the corresponding period of the year before. Results included net gains of $95.0 million in 2004 and net losses of $98.0 million in 2003 from equity investments. Results for 2004 and 2003 also included net gains of $33.0 million and $18.0 million on debt securities available for sale. Net interest income climbed 5.2% to $4.05 billion due to strong growth in loans and deposits. Provision for loan losses slid 1.7% to $404.0 million. Total non-interest income grew 9.3% to $3.10 billion, while total non-interest expense rose 1.8% to $4.03 billion.

Prospects: Co. continues to perform well, with revenue outpacing expenses more than expected. Additionally, Co.'s credit quality remains healthy with continued declines in nonperforming assets and net charge-offs despite an increase in loans. Meanwhile, the substantial growth in fee income in Co.'s non-mortgage banking activities continues to reflect improved business conditions and broad-based growth across Co., with particular strength in deposit service fees and insurance income. Moreover, given the strength of the equity markets and actions Co. has taken to write down its equity portfolios, Co. is encouraged by the quality of the portfolio and expects additional gains going forward.

Financial Data

(US$ in Thousands)	3 Mos	12/31/2003	12/31/2002	12/31/2001	12/31/2000	12/31/1999	12/31/1998	12/31/1997
Earnings Per Share	3.80	3.65	3.32	1.97	2.33	2.23	1.17	1.75
Tang. Book Val. Per Share	10.48	9.69	9.00	6.11	5.90	5.15	4.89	5.35
Dividends Per Share	1.650	1.500	1.100	1.000	0.900	0.780	0.700	0.610
Dividend Payout %	43.42	41.09	33.13	50.76	38.62	35.20	59.82	35.14
Income Statement								
Total Interest Income	4,858,000	19,418,000	18,832,000	19,201,000	18,725,000	14,375,000	14,055,000	6,697,400
Total Interest Expense	808,000	3,411,000	3,977,000	6,741,000	7,860,000	5,020,000	5,065,000	2,664,000
Net Interest Income	4,050,000	16,007,000	14,855,000	12,460,000	10,865,000	9,355,000	8,990,000	4,033,400
Provision for Loan Losses	404,000	1,722,000	1,733,000	1,780,000	1,329,000	1,045,000	1,545,000	524,700
Non-Interest Income	3,097,000	12,382,000	9,641,000	7,690,000	8,843,000	7,420,000	6,427,000	2,962,300
Non-Interest Expense	4,029,000	17,190,000	13,909,000	12,891,000	11,830,000	9,782,000	10,579,000	4,421,300
Income Before Taxes	2,714,000	9,477,000	8,854,000	5,479,000	6,549,000	5,948,000	3,293,000	2,049,700
Income from Cont Ops	...	...	5,710,000	...	...	...	...	...
Net Income	1,767,000	6,202,000	5,434,000	3,423,000	4,026,000	3,747,000	1,950,000	1,351,000
Average Shs. Outstg.	1,721,200	1,697,500	1,718,000	1,726,900	1,718,400	1,665,200	1,641,800	750,059
Balance Sheet								
Cash & Due from Banks	13,972,000	15,547,000	17,820,000	16,968,000	16,978,000	13,250,000	12,731,000	4,912,100
Securities Avail. for Sale	65,714,000	32,953,000	27,947,000	40,308,000	38,655,000	38,518,000	31,997,000	3,598,600
Net Loans & Leases	260,325,000	249,182,000	192,772,000	168,738,000	157,405,000	116,294,000	104,860,000	41,287,700
Total Assets	397,354,000	387,798,000	349,259,000	307,569,000	272,426,000	218,102,000	202,475,000	88,540,200
Total Deposits	248,369,000	247,527,000	216,916,000	187,266,000	169,559,000	132,708,000	136,788,000	55,457,100
Long-Term Obligations	73,390,000	63,642,000	7,459,903	36,095,000	32,046,000	23,375,000	19,709,000	12,766,700
Total Liabilities	361,912,000	353,329,000	279,040,903	280,355,000	245,938,000	195,971,000	181,716,000	81,518,000
Net Stockholders' Equity	35,442,000	34,469,000	30,358,000	27,214,000	26,488,000	22,131,000	20,759,000	7,022,200
Shares Outstanding	1,697,181	1,698,109	1,685,906	1,695,494	1,714,645	1,626,849	1,644,057	758,619
Statistical Record								
Return on Equity %	4.98	17.99	18.63	12.65	15.41	17.00	7.82	19.23
Return on Assets %	0.44	1.59	1.62	1.11	1.49	1.72	0.80	1.52
Equity/Assets %	8.91	8.88	8.69	8.84	9.72	10.14	10.25	7.93
Non-Int. Exp./Tot. Inc. %	50.64	54.05	49.03	47.85	47.85	44.80	53.23	45.77
Price Range	58.89-56.28	58.94-44.15	53.21-42.63	53.94-38.85	55.75-31.94	49.25-32.75	43.44-29.75	38.88-21.63
P/E Ratio	15.50-14.81	16.15-12.10	16.03-12.84	27.38-19.72	23.93-13.71	22.09-14.69	37.13-25.43	22.21-12.36
Average Yield %	2.87	2.97	2.26	2.17	2.11	1.92	1.86	2.12

Address: 420 Montgomery Street, San Francisco, CA 94104 **Telephone:** (800) 333-0343 **Web Site:** www.wellsfargo.com	**Officers:** Richard M. Kovacevich – Chmn., Pres., C.E.O., Howard I. Atkins – Exec. V.P., C.F.O. **Transfer Agents:** Wells Fargo Shareowners Services, St. Paul, MN	**Investor Contact:** 415-396-0523 **Institutional Holding** **No of Institutions:** 23 **Shares:** 7,026,576 **% Held:** –

WESBANCO, INC.

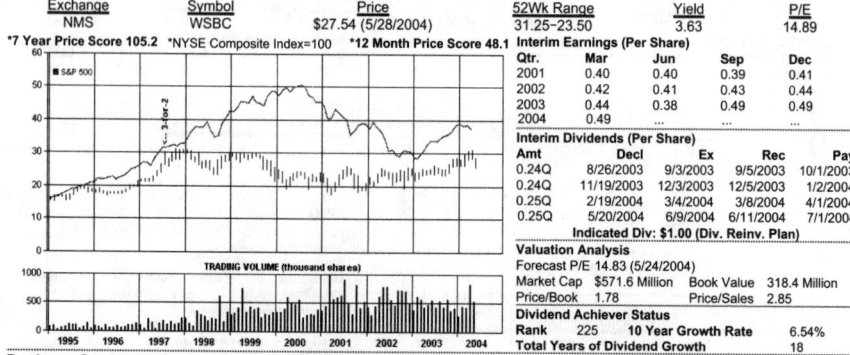

Exchange	Symbol	Price	52Wk Range	Yield	P/E
NMS	WSBC	$27.54 (5/28/2004)	31.25-23.50	3.63	14.89

*7 Year Price Score 105.2   ***NYSE Composite Index=100**   ***12 Month Price Score 48.1**

Interim Earnings (Per Share)

Qtr.	Mar	Jun	Sep	Dec
2001	0.40	0.40	0.39	0.41
2002	0.42	0.41	0.43	0.44
2003	0.44	0.38	0.49	0.49
2004	0.49	...	...	...

Interim Dividends (Per Share)

Amt	Decl	Ex	Rec	Pay
0.24Q	8/26/2003	9/3/2003	9/5/2003	10/1/2003
0.24Q	11/19/2003	12/3/2003	12/5/2003	1/2/2004
0.25Q	2/19/2004	3/4/2004	3/8/2004	4/1/2004
0.25Q	5/20/2004	6/9/2004	6/11/2004	7/1/2004

Indicated Div: $1.00 (Div. Reinv. Plan)

Valuation Analysis

Forecast P/E 14.83 (5/24/2004)

Market Cap $571.6 Million	Book Value 318.4 Million
Price/Book 1.78	Price/Sales 2.85

Dividend Achiever Status

Rank	225	10 Year Growth Rate	6.54%

Total Years of Dividend Growth — 18

Business Summary: Commercial Banking (MIC: 8.1 SIC: 6021 NAIC:522110)

WesBanco is a bank holding company. Through its subsidiary, WesBanco Bank, Inc., Co. offers a range of financial services including retail banking, corporate banking, personal and corporate trust services, brokerage, mortgage banking and insurance through 72 offices located in West Virginia, central and eastern Ohio and western Pennsylvania. Co. also offers services through its non-banking affiliates. WesBanco Insurance Services is a multi-line insurance agency specializing in property, casualty and life insurance. WesBanco Securities is a full service broker-dealer. Co. also serves as investment adviser to a family of mutual funds under the name WesMark Funds.

Recent Developments: For the three months ended Mar 31 2004, net income climbed 9.8% to $9.8 million versus $8.9 million in the corresponding quarter of 2003. Results for 2004 and 2003 included net securities gains of $661,000 and $1.0 million, and merger-related expenses from the acquisition of American Bancorporation of $8,000 and $92,000, respectively. Net interest income grew 6.0% to $26.3 million from $24.8 million the year before, primarily due to growth in earnings assets and a lower cost of funds on interest bearing liabilities. Provision for loan losses slipped 9.1% to $1.8 million. Total non-interest income rose 6.2% to $8.8 million, while total non-interest expense climbed 5.4% to $21.1 million.

Prospects: On Apr 1 2004, Co. announced a definitive agreement to purchase Western Ohio Financial, a savings and loan holding company. Under the terms of the agreement, shareholders of Western Ohio can elect to receive 1.18 shares of Co.'s common stock or $35.00 in cash for each share held. The total transaction is valued at $65.2 million. Once the transaction is completed, the combination of the two banking companies will create a financial services company with about $3.90 billion in total assets and with 80 branch banking locations in Ohio, West Virginia and Pennsylvania. The acquisition is subject to regulatory approvals and is expected to be completed in the fourth quarter of 2004.

Financial Data

(US$ in Thousands)	12/31/2003	12/31/2002	12/31/2001	12/31/2000	12/31/1999	12/31/1998	12/31/1997	12/31/1996
Earnings Per Share	1.80	1.70	1.60	1.41	1.37	1.36	1.40	1.38
Tang. Book Val. Per Share	13.20	13.01	14.46	12.31	13.62	14.35	15.58	14.41
Dividends Per Share	0.950	0.930	0.910	0.890	0.870	0.830	0.770	0.700
Dividend Payout %	53.05	54.70	57.18	63.12	63.50	61.02	55.23	50.47
Income Statement								
Total Interest Income	165,516	176,155	163,939	163,079	155,861	162,718	124,530	112,938
Total Interest Expense	62,512	72,555	76,354	79,552	69,231	73,925	55,774	48,218
Net Interest Income	103,004	103,600	87,585	83,527	86,630	88,793	68,756	64,720
Provision for Loan Losses	9,612	9,359	5,995	3,225	4,295	4,392	4,314	4,336
Non-Interest Income	33,230	27,852	24,588	23,376	24,581	25,715	14,693	12,273
Non-Interest Expense	81,810	76,647	64,894	64,483	67,813	68,308	48,704	43,152
Income Before Taxes	44,812	45,446	41,284	39,195	39,103	41,808	30,431	29,505
Net Income	36,130	34,826	29,002	26,924	27,638	28,313	22,274	21,161
Average Shs. Outstg.	20,056	20,459	18,123	19,092	20,229	20,867	15,867	15,253
Balance Sheet								
Cash & Due from Banks	88,021	80,101	81,563	72,796	67,166	62,989	56,446	58,828
Securities Avail. for Sale	766,883	694,735	517,517	350,287	354,675	465,705	342,510	276,201
Net Loans & Leases	1,905,562	1,791,081	1,513,387	1,568,281	1,493,941	1,344,640	1,005,747	1,010,842
Total Assets	3,445,006	3,297,231	2,474,454	2,310,137	2,269,726	2,242,712	1,789,295	1,677,771
Total Deposits	2,482,082	2,399,956	1,913,458	1,870,361	1,814,001	1,787,642	1,414,254	1,342,820
Long-Term Obligations	217,754	175,634	172,242	159,317	41,588	22,194	...	...
Total Liabilities	3,126,570	2,972,060	2,216,263	2,051,631	2,000,062	1,946,229	1,539,745	1,450,239
Net Stockholders' Equity	318,436	325,171	258,201	258,506	269,664	296,483	249,550	227,532
Shares Outstanding	19,741	20,461	17,854	20,996	19,789	20,660	16,015	15,783
Statistical Record								
Return on Equity %	11.34	10.71	11.23	10.41	10.24	9.54	8.92	9.30
Return on Assets %	1.04	1.05	1.17	1.16	1.21	1.26	1.24	1.26
Equity/Assets %	9.24	9.86	10.43	11.19	11.88	13.21	13.94	13.56
Non-Int. Exp./Tot. Inc. %	41.16	37.57	34.42	34.58	37.58	36.25	34.98	34.46
Price Range	28.74-21.99	25.86-19.42	26.10-17.69	26.00-19.13	30.25-21.69	31.00-23.38	31.25-21.33	21.67-17.17
P/E Ratio	15.97-12.22	15.21-11.42	16.31-11.05	18.44-13.56	22.08-15.83	22.79-17.19	22.32-15.24	15.70-12.44
Average Yield %	3.81	4.00	4.19	3.91	3.11	3.02	2.98	3.78

Address: 1 Bank Plaza, Wheeling, WV 26003	Officers: Edward M. George – Chmn., Paul M. Limbert – Pres., C.E.O.	Investor Contact:304-234-9000
Telephone: (304) 234 9000		**Institutional Holding** No of Institutions: 54
Web Site: www.wesbanco.com		**Shares:** 389,399 **% Held:** –

WESCO FINANCIAL CORP.

Exchange	Symbol	Price	52Wk Range	Yield	P/E
ASE	WSC	$376.95 (5/28/2004)	429.8-298.5	0.37	36.11

*7 Year Price Score 111.7 *NYSE Composite Index=100 *12 Month Price Score 52.0

Interim Earnings (Per Share)

Qtr.	Mar	Jun	Sep	Dec
2001	2.78	2.12	1.57	0.91
2002	2.03	2.09	2.12	1.16
2003	1.76	6.45	1.00	1.28
2004	1.71	...	...	...

Interim Dividends (Per Share)

Amt	Decl	Ex	Rec	Pay
0.335Q	7/17/2003	8/4/2003	8/6/2003	9/4/2003
0.335Q	9/18/2003	11/3/2003	11/5/2003	12/3/2003
0.345Q	12/10/2003	2/2/2004	2/4/2004	3/3/2004
0.345Q	3/11/2004	5/3/2004	5/5/2004	6/2/2004

Indicated Div: $1.38

Valuation Analysis

Forecast P/E N/A

Market Cap	$2.7 Billion	Book Value	N/A
Price/Book	N/A	Price/Sales	N/A

Dividend Achiever Status

Rank	272	10 Year Growth Rate	3.61%
Total Years of Dividend Growth			32

TRADING VOLUME (thousand shares)

Business Summary: Engineering Services (MIC: 12.1 SIC: 5051 NAIC:423510)

Wesco Financial is engaged in three principal businesses: the insurance business, through Wesco–Financial Insurance Company, which engages in the property and casualty insurance business, and The Kansas Bankers Surety Company, which provides specialized insurance coverages for banks; the furniture rental business, through CORT Business Services Corporation, a provider of rental furniture, accessories and related services; and the steel service center business, through Precision Steel Warehouse, Inc. Co.'s operations also include, through MS Property Company, the ownership and management of commercial real estate property, and the development and liquidation of foreclosed real estate.

Recent Developments: For the three months ended Mar 31 2004, net income totaled $12.2 million, down 2.4% compared with $12.5 million in the corresponding prior–year period. Results for 2003 included a pre–tax realized investment gain of $811,000. Total revenues, including the aforementioned investment gain, slid 17.7% to $128.2 million from $155.8 million the previous year. Furniture rental segment revenues slipped 8.2% to $85.7 million from $93.4 million, while revenues in the insurance segment fell 44.7% to $26.8 million from $48.4 million a year earlier. Industrial segment revenues advanced 19.5% to $14.7 million from $12.3 million in 2003.

Prospects: Sales and rentals of furniture are being negatively affected by unfavorable economic conditions and reduced advertising of furniture for sale. Meanwhile, results for the industrial segment are benefiting from increased demand for steel due to a slight rise in manufacturing activity and the lack of domestic steel capacity. However, Co. remains concerned about the ongoing weakness in the domestic manufacturing sector, the shift by many manufacturers from domestic to overseas production, along with increased competitive pressures and a trend towards smaller–sized orders.

Financial Data
(US$ in Thousands)

	12/31/2003	12/31/2002	12/31/2001	12/31/2000	12/31/1999	12/31/1998	12/31/1997	12/31/1996
Earnings Per Share	10.49	7.40	7.38	129.56	7.60	10.08	14.30	4.30
Cash Flow Per Share	17.29	26.47	23.11	N/A	3.29	1.85	4.90	3.47
Tang. Book Val. Per Share	254.44	237.64	231.45	241.15	262.20	308.20	243.56	171.36
Dividends Per Share	1.340	1.300	1.260	1.220	1.180	1.140	1.100	1.060
Dividends Payout %	12.77	17.57	17.07	0.94	15.53	11.31	7.69	24.65
Income Statement								
Total Revenues	614,317	575,677	561,079	1,823,964	145,706	176,179	219,051	108,019
Total Indirect Exp.	278,090	288,353	284,188	234,296	10,265	11,156	9,393	10,849
Depreciation & Amort.	44,114	51,914	7,476	6,342	1,995	2,068	2,056	1,672
Operating Income	109,005	82,911	85,497	1,423,627	77,347	105,322	156,088	42,852
Net Interest Inc./(Exp.)	(749)	(1,994)	(4,169)	(5,235)	(2,549)	(3,016)	(3,320)	(3,352)
Income Taxes	34,852	28,199	28,792	495,922	20,655	30,503	50,959	8,881
Eqty Earns/Minority Int.	1,307	...	...	...	...	...	...	...
Income from Cont Ops	73,404	...	...	...	...	...	...	...
Net Income	74,711	52,718	52,536	922,470	54,143	71,803	101,809	30,619
Average Shs. Outstg.	7,119	7,119	7,119	7,119	7,119	7,120	7,120	7,120
Balance Sheet								
Cash & Cash Equivalents	1,807,096	976,580	788,046	987,747	2,281,214	3,098,629	2,235,535	1,556,048
Total Current Assets	2,030,963	1,231,485	1,044,503	1,271,038	2,281,214	3,098,629	2,242,683	1,563,988
Total Assets	2,538,395	2,406,975	2,319,693	2,460,915	2,652,195	3,228,406	2,588,112	1,818,405
Total Current Liabilities	296,172	272,086	262,459	339,056	707,345	920,035	733,848	468,370
Long–Term Obligations	12,679	32,481	33,649	56,035	3,635	33,635	33,635	37,162
Net Stockholders' Equity	2,078,190	1,958,162	1,912,397	1,977,034	1,895,372	2,223,756	1,764,292	1,251,015
Net Working Capital	1,734,791	959,399	782,044	931,982	1,573,869	2,178,594	1,509,195	1,095,618
Shares Outstanding	7,119	7,119	7,119	7,119	7,119	7,120	7,120	7,120
Statistical Record								
Operating Profit Margin %	17.74	14.40	15.23	78.05	53.08	59.78	71.25	39.67
Net Profit Margin %	23.29	18.95	19.62	104.95	65.51	75.38	93.00	44.78
Return on Equity %	3.53	2.69	2.74	46.65	2.85	3.22	5.77	2.44
Return on Assets %	2.89	2.19	2.26	37.48	2.04	2.22	3.93	1.68
Debt/Total Assets %	0.49	1.34	1.45	2.27	0.13	1.04	1.29	2.04
Price Range	370.0-286.0	334.0-298.0	347.9-273.0	290.0-205.0	354.8-241.5	391.0-284.0	339.5-180.0	190.0-155.0
P/E Ratio	35.27-27.26	45.14-40.27	47.14-36.99	2.24-1.58	46.68-31.78	38.79-28.17	23.74-12.59	44.19-36.05
Average Yield %	0.42	0.42	0.41	0.50	0.38	0.33	0.40	0.61

Address: 301 East Colorado Boulevard, Pasadena, CA 91101–1901	Officers: Charles T. Munger – Chmn., C.E.O., Robert H. Bird – Pres.	Institutional Holding
Telephone: (626) 585–6700	Transfer Agents:Mellon Investor Services, South Hackensack, NJ	No of Institutions: 1
Web Site: N/A		Shares: 60,000 % Held: –

WEST PHARMACEUTICAL SERVICES, INC.

Exchange	Symbol	Price	52Wk Range	Yield	P/E
NYS	WST	$38.01 (5/28/2004)	39.40–23.05	2.21	15.90

*7 Year Price Score 112.7 *NYSE Composite Index=100   ***12 Month Price Score 54.6**

Interim Earnings (Per Share)

Qtr.	Mar	Jun	Sep	Dec
2001	0.38	0.22	0.41	0.36
2002	0.45	0.37	(0.16)	0.23
2003	0.26	0.48	0.28	1.17
2004	0.46	...	...	...

Interim Dividends (Per Share)

Amt	Decl	Ex	Rec	Pay
0.20Q	6/17/2003	7/21/2003	7/23/2003	8/6/2003
0.21Q	8/12/2003	10/20/2003	10/22/2003	11/5/2003
0.21Q	10/28/2003	1/16/2004	1/21/2004	2/4/2004
0.21Q	3/25/2004	4/19/2004	4/21/2004	5/5/2004

Indicated Div: $0.84 (Div. Reinv. Plan)

Valuation Analysis

Forecast P/E 18.16 (5/24/2004)

Market Cap $549.7 Million	Book Value 263.1 Million
Price/Book 2.11	Price/Sales 1.09

Dividend Achiever Status

Rank 214	10 Year Growth Rate	7.05%
Total Years of Dividend Growth		11

Business Summary: Rubber Products (MIC: 11.6 SIC: 3069 NAIC:326299)

West Pharmaceutical Services is involved in drug formulation research and development, clinical research and laboratory services, and the design, development, and manufacture of components and systems for dispensing and delivering pharmaceutical, healthcare, and consumer products. Operations are divided into two business segments. The Pharmaceutical Systems segment designs, manufactures and sells stoppers, closures, medical device components and assemblies made from elastomers, metal, and plastics. The Drug Delivery Systems segment identifies and develops drug delivery systems for biopharmaceutical and other drugs to improve therapeutic performance and/or method of administration.

Recent Developments: For the three months ended Mar 31 2004, net income rocketed 84.2% to $7.0 million compared with $3.8 million in the corresponding quarter of the previous year. Results for 2003 included a pre–tax charge of $5.1 million for costs associated with a plant explosion. Net sales increased 13.4% to $133.6 million from $117.8 million in the year–earlier period. Pharmaceutical Systems sales advanced 12.2% to $130.4 million from $116.2 million, while Drug Delivery Systems sales more than doubled to $3.2 million from $1.6 million in the prior–year quarter. Gross profit climbed 11.5% to $40.6 million from $36.4 million in 2003. Operating income soared 66.2% to $10.8 million.

Prospects: Results continue to be significantly affected by the loss of Co.'s Kinston, NC facility. Co. expects to be back to full production capability at the facility by the end of the 2004. Meanwhile, Co. is pleased with sales growth and the impact of product mix on gross margin. Co. is benefiting from strong demand for its Pharmaceutical Systems products in major geographic markets. Co.'s Drug Delivery Systems business continues to grow as a result of higher utilization of the division's clinical research facility. Also, Co. is well–positioned to continue to benefit from solid order backlog, which was $167.0 million at Mar 31 2004. Moreover, Co. continues to expect that sales will grow 5.0% to 7.0% for 2004.

Financial Data

(US$ in Thousands)	3 Mos	12/31/2003	12/31/2002	12/31/2001	12/31/2000	12/31/1999	12/31/1998	12/31/1997
Earnings Per Share	2.39	2.19	0.89	1.37	0.11	2.57	0.40	2.68
Cash Flow Per Share	0.53	4.75	3.16	2.16	3.37	4.61	4.30	4.08
Tang. Book Val. Per Share	14.49	14.29	10.84	10.05	10.64	11.23	11.24	13.64
Dividends Per Share	0.820	0.810	0.770	0.730	0.690	0.650	0.610	0.570
Dividend Payout %	34.31	36.98	86.51	53.28	627.27	25.29	152.50	21.26
Income Statement								
Total Revenues	133,600	490,700	419,700	396,900	430,100	469,100	449,700	452,500
Total Indirect Exp.	30,600	101,900	89,300	73,300	87,900	76,200	97,700	68,000
Depreciation & Amort.	8,300	33,000	33,000	32,000	37,000	35,700	32,300	31,900
Operating Income	10,800	54,500	26,700	41,300	15,200	66,900	35,000	63,000
Income Taxes	2,900	16,700	4,100	8,600	1,500	18,400	21,200	13,300
Income from Cont Ops	...	...	12,800	19,600	...	...	...	...
Net Income	7,000	31,900	18,400	(5,200)	1,600	38,700	6,700	44,400
Average Shs. Outstg.	15,067	14,546	14,434	14,348	14,409	15,048	16,504	16,572
Balance Sheet								
Cash & Cash Equivalents	40,600	37,800	33,200	42,100	42,700	45,300	31,300	52,300
Total Current Assets	194,800	216,700	161,300	158,500	173,100	184,700	159,700	170,700
Total Assets	604,800	623,600	536,800	511,300	557,400	551,800	505,600	477,900
Total Current Liabilities	109,800	118,900	87,700	75,300	79,300	104,000	104,200	58,000
Long–Term Obligations	148,600	167,000	159,200	184,300	195,800	141,500	105,000	87,400
Net Stockholders' Equity	263,100	257,600	201,500	176,800	204,800	231,200	230,100	277,700
Shares Outstanding	14,824	14,632	14,480	14,344	14,310	14,664	15,026	16,568
Operating Profit Margin %	8.08	11.10	6.36	10.40	3.53	14.26	7.78	13.92
Net Profit Margin %	9.58	13.30	5.00	9.27	1.06	16.09	10.91	15.69
Return on Equity %	2.66	12.38	6.35	11.08	0.78	16.73	2.91	15.98
Return on Assets %	1.16	5.11	2.38	3.83	0.28	7.01	1.32	9.29
Debt/Total Assets %	24.57	26.77	29.65	36.04	35.12	25.64	20.76	18.28
Price Range	37.91–33.09	35.60–17.00	32.09–16.55	28.05–22.90	31.69–19.88	40.25–30.88	35.69–25.81	34.94–27.13
P/E Ratio	15.86–13.85	16.26–7.76	36.06–18.60	20.47–16.72	288.1–180.7	15.66–12.01	89.22–64.53	13.04–10.12
Average Yield %	2.28	3.06	3.01	2.86	2.86	1.83	2.04	1.91

Address: 101 Gordon Drive, Lionville, PA 19341–0645	Officers: Donald E. Morel – Chmn., Pres., C.E.O., William J. Federici – V.P., C.F.O.	Investor Contact:610–594–3346
Telephone: (610) 594–2900	Transfer Agents:American Stock Transfer and Trust Company, New York, NY	Institutional Holding No of Institutions: 80
Web Site: www.westpharma.com		Shares: 10,221,481 % Held: 70.70%

WESTAMERICA BANCORPORATION

Exchange	Symbol	Price	52Wk Range	Yield	P/E
NMS	WABC	$49.38 (5/28/2004)	53.28–42.88	2.27	17.03

*7 Year Price Score 129.9 *NYSE Composite Index=100 ***12 Month Price Score 48.3**

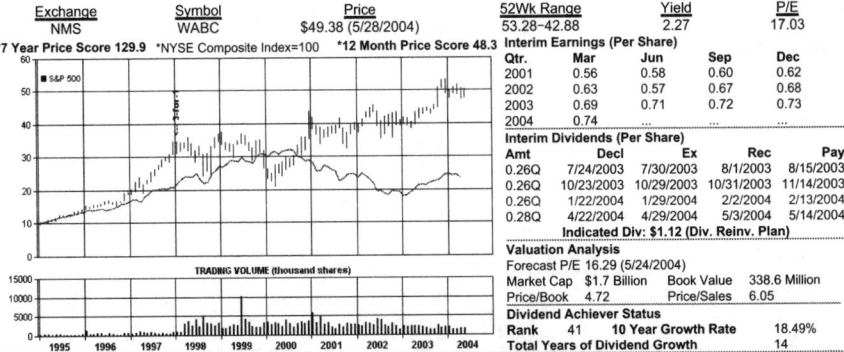

Interim Earnings (Per Share)

Qtr.	Mar	Jun	Sep	Dec
2001	0.56	0.58	0.60	0.62
2002	0.63	0.57	0.67	0.68
2003	0.69	0.71	0.72	0.73
2004	0.74	...	...	...

Interim Dividends (Per Share)

Amt	Decl	Ex	Rec	Pay
0.26Q	7/24/2003	7/30/2003	8/1/2003	8/15/2003
0.26Q	10/23/2003	10/29/2003	10/31/2003	11/14/2003
0.26Q	1/22/2004	1/29/2004	2/2/2004	2/13/2004
0.28Q	4/22/2004	4/29/2004	5/3/2004	5/14/2004

Indicated Div: $1.12 (Div. Reinv. Plan)

Valuation Analysis

Forecast P/E 16.29 (5/24/2004)

Market Cap $1.7 Billion	Book Value 338.6 Million
Price/Book 4.72	Price/Sales 6.05

Dividend Achiever Status

Rank 41   10 Year Growth Rate 18.49%

Total Years of Dividend Growth 14

TRADING VOLUME (thousand shares)

Business Summary: Commercial Banking (MIC: 8.1 SIC: 6021 NAIC:522110)

Westamerica Bancorporation is a bank holding company that provides a full range of banking services to individual and corporate customers in northern and central California through its subsidiary bank, Westamerica Bank. Co. is a regional community bank with 88 branches serving 22 California counties. At Dec 31 2003, Co. had total assets of $4.58 billion and total deposits of $3.46 billion. Co.'s focus is on serving the needs of small businesses. In addition, Co. also owns Community Banker Services Corporation, which is engaged in providing Co. and its subsidiaries data processing services and other support functions.

Recent Developments: For the first quarter ended Mar 31 2004, net income increased 5.7% to $24.3 million versus $23.0 million in the prior-year quarter. Results for 2004 included a loss on debt extinguishment of $1.8 million. Net interest income slipped 1.0% to $48.9 million. Total interest income decreased 4.8% to $54.4 million, while total non-interest expense fell 28.7% to $5.5 million. Provision for loan losses declined 16.7% to $750,000. Non-interest income rose 4.7% to $10.9 million, due to higher gains on the sale of OREO and service charges on deposit accounts, partially offset by lower financial services commissions and merchant credit card income. Non-interest expense decreased 2.1% to $25.0 million.

Prospects: Co. remains focused on improving the long-term profitability of its balance sheet. Co. continues to work to lower the cost of its funding base. For example, low-cost checking accounts now make up approximately 30.0% of its funding. In addition, Co. underwrites loans with a focus on credit quality and a conservative philosophy, which continues to result in low loan losses. Co.'s loan losses declined over the past two years despite the recession of the California economy. Meanwhile, improvements made in Co.'s infrastructure during 2003, should place it in an advantageous position as the economy improves.

Financial Data

(US$ in Thousands)	3 Mos	12/31/2003	12/31/2002	12/31/2001	12/31/2000	12/31/1999	12/31/1998	12/31/1997
Earnings Per Share	2.90	2.85	2.55	2.36	2.16	1.94	1.73	1.10
Tang. Book Val. Per Share	10.65	10.54	10.22	9.18	9.31	8.09	9.25	9.51
Dividends Per Share	1.020	1.000	0.900	0.820	0.740	0.660	0.520	0.360
Dividend Payout %	35.17	35.08	35.29	34.74	34.25	34.02	30.05	32.72
Income Statement								
Total Interest Income	54,411	223,493	237,633	257,056	269,516	257,656	266,820	270,670
Total Interest Expense	5,515	27,197	39,182	68,887	88,614	78,456	86,665	88,054
Net Interest Income	48,896	196,296	198,451	188,169	180,902	179,200	180,155	182,616
Provision for Loan Losses	750	3,300	3,600	3,600	3,675	4,780	5,180	7,645
Non-Interest Income	10,866	30,573	31,496	30,366	28,360	28,045	27,020	27,539
Non-Interest Expense	24,992	101,703	103,323	102,651	100,198	100,133	101,408	137,878
Income Before Taxes	34,020	134,209	128,079	124,573	118,159	114,461	111,732	74,106
Net Income	24,314	95,063	87,138	84,279	79,779	76,088	73,396	48,116
Average Shs. Outstg.	32,662	33,369	34,225	35,748	36,936	39,194	42,524	43,827
Balance Sheet								
Securities Avail. for Sale	3,025,433	1,414,445	948,481	949,504	921,525	982,587	987,911	1,003,484
Net Loans & Leases	2,269,047	2,269,420	2,440,411	2,432,371	2,429,880	2,269,272	2,246,593	2,211,307
Total Assets	4,424,816	4,576,385	4,224,867	3,927,967	4,031,381	3,893,187	3,844,298	3,848,444
Total Deposits	3,447,176	3,463,991	3,294,065	3,234,635	3,236,744	3,065,344	3,189,005	3,078,501
Long-Term Obligations	21,429	129,643	194,607	27,821	31,036	41,500	47,500	52,500
Total Liabilities	4,086,216	4,236,014	3,883,368	3,613,608	3,693,634	3,592,595	3,475,702	3,441,292
Net Stockholders' Equity	338,600	340,371	341,499	314,359	337,747	300,592	368,596	407,152
Shares Outstanding	31,787	32,287	33,411	34,220	36,251	37,125	39,828	42,799
Return on Equity %	7.18	27.92	25.51	26.80	23.62	25.31	19.91	11.81
Return on Assets %	0.54	2.07	2.06	2.14	1.97	1.95	1.90	1.25
Equity/Assets %	7.65	7.43	8.08	8.00	8.37	7.72	9.58	10.57
Non-Int. Exp./Tot. Inc. %	38.28	38.17	37.68	34.24	32.25	33.62	33.28	44.81
Price Range	51.63–47.85	53.28–38.70	45.67–35.57	42.00–32.55	43.75–21.00	37.50–26.63	37.00–24.25	34.67–18.96
P/E Ratio	17.80–16.50	18.69–13.58	17.91–13.95	17.80–13.79	20.25–9.72	19.33–13.72	21.39–14.02	31.52–17.23
Average Yield %	2.05	2.26	2.19	2.16	2.54	2.00	1.62	1.42

Address: 1108 Fifth Avenue, San Rafael, CA 94901	**Officers:** David L. Payne – Chmn., Pres., C.E.O., Robert W. Entwisle – Sr. V.P., Banking Division	**Investor Contact:**707–863–6992
Telephone: (707) 863–8000	**Transfer Agents:**Computershare Investor Services LLC	**Institutional Holding** **No of Institutions:** 25
Web Site: www.westamerica.com		**Shares:** 1,057,005 **% Held:** –

WEYCO GROUP, INC

Exchange	Symbol	Price	52Wk Range	Yield	P/E
NMS	WEYS	$33.10 (5/27/2004)	38.34-27.72	1.33	11.07

*7 Year Price Score 158.3 *NYSE Composite Index=100 ***12 Month Price Score 46.1**

Interim Earnings (Per Share)

Qtr.	Mar	Jun	Sep	Dec
2001	0.39	0.28	0.41	0.56
2002	0.40	0.28	0.78	0.83
2003	0.80	0.60	0.59	0.92
2004	0.88	...	...	...

Interim Dividends (Per Share)

Amt	Decl	Ex	Rec	Pay
50%	7/30/2003	10/2/2003	8/29/2003	10/1/2003
0.10Q	11/3/2003	11/26/2003	12/1/2003	1/2/2004
0.10Q	1/26/2004	3/4/2004	3/8/2004	4/1/2004
0.11Q	4/27/2004	5/27/2004	6/1/2004	7/1/2004

Indicated Div: $0.44

Valuation Analysis

Forecast P/E N/A

Market Cap $94.4 Million	Book Value 103.6 Million
Price/Book 1.48	Price/Sales 0.68

Dividend Achiever Status

Rank 201	10 Year Growth Rate	8.06%
Total Years of Dividend Growth		23

TRADING VOLUME (thousand shares)

1995 1996 1997 1998 1999 2000 2001 2002 2003 2004

Business Summary: Leather and Leather Products (MIC: 4.5 SIC: 3143 NAIC:316213)

Weyco Group is engaged in the distribution of men's footwear. Co.'s products consist of both mid-priced leather dress shoes and lower-priced casual footwear. These shoes are sold under various brand names. The principal brands of shoes sold are *Florsheim, Nunn Bush, Nunn Bush NXXT, Brass Boot, Stacy Adams* and *SAO by Stacy Adams*. Co.'s wholesale division markets footwear through more than 10,000 shoe, clothing and department stores across the U.S. As of Dec 31 2003, the retail division consisted of 30 Company-operated stores in the U.S and three retail stores in Europe.

Recent Developments: For the quarter ended Mar 31 2004, net earnings increased 10.3% to $5.2 million from $4.7 million in the prior-year quarter. Net sales rose 2.3% to $61.7 million from $60.4 million the previous year, with sales in both Co.'s wholesale and retail divisions showing increases. Sales of *Stacy Adams* and *Nunn Bush* brands were up 9.0% and 1.0%, respectively, while Co.'s *Florsheim* brand decreased 11.0%. Gross profit as a percentage of sales improved to 34.4% from 33.4% a year earlier, primarily due to a reduction of closeout sales in Co.'s *Florsheim* division. Operating income amounted to $8.5 million, up 9.6% from $7.7 million the year before.

Prospects: Co.'s Stacy Adams division should continue to enjoy higher sales and licensing revenue, as demand is being supported by an overall market trend towards dressing up. Moreover, Co.'s Nunn Bush division appears poised for future growth due to an improved position in the men's moderate branded footwear market. Meanwhile, despite the recent decline in sales of *Florsheim* products, the outlook for the brand remains strong. Bookings for the fall 2004 season are up and Co. is making good strides in opening new distribution networks that fit with *Florsheim's* updated younger image. Co. remains supportive of its *Florsheim* brand and will continue to invest heavily in both print and outdoor media.

Financial Data

(US$ in Thousands)	3 Mos	12/31/2003	12/31/2002	12/31/2001	12/31/2000	12/31/1999	12/31/1998	12/31/1997
Earnings Per Share	2.99	2.91	2.29	1.64	1.72	1.70	1.38	1.25
Cash Flow Per Share	0.54	4.47	2.48	1.72	1.89	0.40	1.34	1.57
Tang. Book Val. Per Share	16.42	15.62	13.01	13.08	11.97	10.85	9.81	9.30
Dividends Per Share	0.380	0.360	0.330	0.300	0.280	0.250	0.220	0.200
Dividend Payout %	12.71	12.60	14.53	18.69	16.21	14.90	16.42	16.13
Income Statement								
Total Revenues	61,743	215,761	181,200	131,693	148,155	133,498	127,074	127,029
Total Indirect Exp.	12,776	49,184	37,732	24,231	24,586	22,538	22,311	22,674
Depreciation & Amort.	727	2,510	2,231	1,609	1,490	1,242	626	821
Operating Income	8,482	27,261	21,406	13,354	15,972	15,223	13,801	12,646
Net Interest Inc./(Exp.)	(47)	(846)	(436)	726	479	831	1,419	1,475
Income Taxes	3,250	9,555	7,800	5,200	5,850	5,900	5,450	5,065
Net Income	5,153	17,135	13,188	9,501	10,622	11,058	9,805	9,068
Average Shs. Outstg.	5,837	5,878	5,753	5,792	6,162	6,507	7,096	7,237
Balance Sheet								
Cash & Cash Equivalents	11,640	13,298	9,400	20,118	11,210	8,704	13,094	10,684
Total Current Assets	90,148	90,665	95,544	61,720	51,670	53,093	48,051	42,912
Total Assets	151,623	151,186	146,235	97,954	91,943	95,919	92,782	82,204
Total Current Liabilities	39,913	44,254	20,233	20,911	17,758	26,253	26,387	14,643
Long-Term Obligations	...	...	37,802	...	...	...	...	...
Net Stockholders' Equity	103,595	98,846	84,784	73,592	71,345	67,751	65,148	66,677
Net Working Capital	50,235	46,351	75,311	40,810	33,912	26,840	21,664	28,269
Shares Outstanding	5,644	5,630	5,683	5,623	5,959	6,241	6,635	7,162
Statistical Record								
Operating Profit Margin %	13.73	12.63	11.81	10.14	10.78	11.40	10.86	9.95
Net Profit Margin %	18.87	16.79	15.88	15.11	15.06	17.12	16.29	15.11
Return on Equity %	4.97	17.33	15.55	12.91	14.88	16.32	15.04	13.60
Return on Assets %	3.39	11.33	9.01	9.69	11.55	11.52	10.56	11.03
Debt/Total Assets %	...	...	25.85	...	...	...	...	...
Price Range	37.00-30.14	38.34-20.83	27.33-16.90	17.33-15.33	17.75-15.00	17.42-14.42	19.00-14.17	21.33-8.94
P/E Ratio	12.37-10.08	13.18-7.16	11.93-7.38	10.57-9.35	10.32-8.72	10.25-8.48	13.77-10.27	17.07-7.16
Average Yield %	1.13	1.17	1.47	1.86	1.71	1.56	1.32	1.41

Address: 333 West Estabrook Boulevard, Glendale, WI 53212 Telephone: (414) 908-1600 Web Site: www.weycogroup.com	Officers: Thomas W. Florsheim - Chmn., C.E.O., John W. Florsheim - Pres., C.O.O. Transfer Agents:American Stock Transfer &Trust Company, New York, NY	Investor Contact:414-908-1600 Institutional Holding No of Institutions: 8 Shares: 73,700 % Held: -

WGL HOLDINGS, INC.

Exchange	Symbol	Price	52Wk Range	Yield	P/E
NYS	WGL	$27.51 (5/28/2004)	30.28-25.37	4.73	13.82

*7 Year Price Score 103.9 ***NYSE Composite Index=100** ***12 Month Price Score 47.4**

Interim Earnings (Per Share)

Qtr.	Dec	Mar	Jun	Sep
2000-01	1.08	1.44	(0.15)	(0.62)
2001-02	0.62	0.94	(0.29)	(0.47)
2002-03	1.06	1.66	(0.05)	(0.37)
2003-04	0.81	1.60	...	...

Interim Dividends (Per Share)

Amt	Decl	Ex	Rec	Pay
0.32Q	6/25/2003	7/8/2003	7/10/2003	8/1/2003
0.32Q	9/24/2003	10/8/2003	10/10/2003	11/1/2003
0.32Q	12/19/2003	1/7/2004	1/9/2004	2/1/2004
0.325Q	3/2/2004	4/6/2004	4/9/2004	5/1/2004

Indicated Div: $1.30 (Div. Reinv. Plan)

Valuation Analysis

Forecast P/E 15.38 (5/24/2004)

Market Cap $1.3 Billion	Book Value 906.3 Million
Price/Book 1.58	Price/Sales 0.70

Dividend Achiever Status

Rank 295	10 Year Growth Rate	1.65%
Total Years of Dividend Growth		27

TRADING VOLUME (thousand shares)

Business Summary: Gas Utilities (MIC: 7.4 SIC: 4924 NAIC:221210)

WGL Holdings, through its subsidiaries, engages in the sale and distribution of natural gas and other energy–related products and services. Washington Gas Light Company is a regulated natural gas utility serving over 960,000 customers in Washington D.C., Virginia and Maryland as of Sep 30 2003. Hampshire Gas Company is a regulated natural gas storage business, serving Washington Gas Light Company. Washington Gas Energy Services, Inc. sells natural gas and electricity to the Washington D.C. area as well as Baltimore and Richmond. Washington Gas Energy Systems, Inc. designs cost–saving energy systems for the commercial and government markets.

Recent Developments: For the quarter ended Mar 31 2004, net income declined 3.6% to $78.1 million compared with $81.0 million in the equivalent period of the previous year. The decline in earnings was primarily due to increased utility operation and maintenance expenses, partially offset by the favorable impacts of customer growth and positive regulatory decisions. Utility operating revenues decreased 5.1% to $588.6 million. Utility net revenues slipped 2.6% to $231.2 million and utility operating income fell 9.1% to $85.4 million. Non–utility operating revenues rose 18.5% to $273.6 million. Non–utility operating loss was $1.8 million versus $934,000 in 2003.

Prospects: Despite the increase in operation and maintenance expenses in the second quarter, Co. believes the benefits of continued process improvements will help it manage its operating costs going forward. Meanwhile, near–term results should benefit from the addition of nearly 25,000 new customers and Co.'s focus on securing timely, compensatory rates that more accurately reflect the cost of providing service to customers. Looking ahead, Co. expects earnings to range from $1.87 to $1.97 per share for full–year 2004. The projection includes an estimate of the outcome of the pending rate case in Virginia and excludes unusual items.

Financial Data

(US$ in Thousands)	6 Mos	3 Mos	09/30/2003	09/30/2002	09/30/2001	09/30/2000	09/30/1999	09/30/1998
Earnings Per Share	1.99	2.05	2.30	0.80	1.75	1.79	1.47	1.54
Cash Flow Per Share	4.05	0.46	2.94	4.22	1.69	1.90	3.32	2.78
Tang. Book Val. Per Share	18.63	17.32	16.83	15.78	16.23	15.31	14.71	13.82
Dividends Per Share	1.280	1.270	1.270	1.260	1.250	1.230	1.210	1.190
Dividend Payout %	64.32	61.95	55.43	158.12	71.42	68.71	82.31	77.27
Income Statement								
Total Revenues	393,919	162,767	2,064,248	1,569,969	1,933,024	1,247,954	1,112,214	1,040,618
Total Indirect Exp.	(343,225)	(154,800)	923,395	789,371	634,723	339,663	255,363	124,053
Costs & Expenses	257,957	110,383	1,905,012	1,484,008	1,792,980	1,119,009	1,004,457	938,639
Depreciation & Amort.	48,166	25,205	83,549	72,921	68,754	65,514	59,940	54,875
Operating Income	135,962	52,384	159,236	85,961	140,044	128,945	107,757	101,979
Net Interest Inc./(Exp.)	(22,337)	(11,591)	(46,381)	(45,877)	(50,000)	(43,736)	(36,971)	(37,719)
Income Taxes	...	...	68,801	30,427	59,372	49,263	42,519	38,006
Income from Cont Ops	118,258	39,873	...	...	...	...	...	...
Net Income	117,598	39,543	113,662	40,441	83,765	84,574	68,768	68,629
Average Shs. Outstg.	48,836	48,812	48,756	48,563	47,120	46,473	45,984	43,691
Balance Sheet								
Net Property	1,886,740	1,876,280	1,874,923	1,606,843	1,519,747	1,460,280	1,402,742	1,319,501
Total Assets	2,612,316	2,659,952	2,436,052	2,113,664	2,081,113	1,939,840	1,766,724	1,682,433
Long–Term Obligations	617,903	637,610	636,650	667,951	584,370	559,576	506,084	428,641
Net Stockholders' Equity	102,104	814,567	846,391	794,576	816,426	739,669	712,454	636,179
Shares Outstanding	48,647	48,641	48,611	48,564	48,542	46,469	46,473	43,955
Statistical Record								
Operating Profit Margin %	157.27	161.18	11.04	7.41	10.30	14.28	13.51	13.45
Net Inc./Net Property %	6.23	2.10	6.06	2.51	5.51	5.79	4.90	5.20
Net Inc./Tot. Capital %	7.57	2.23	6.60	2.41	5.20	5.75	5.00	5.67
Return on Equity %	15.17	29.64	21.55	8.91	17.53	18.09	15.62	16.76
Accum. Depr./Gross Prop. %	27.70	27.37	26.87	35.25	35.06	34.37	33.64	33.78
Price Range	30.10-26.27	28.32-26.27	28.64-22.38	29.45-20.16	31.44-25.19	29.25-22.63	28.50-21.50	30.94-23.44
P/E Ratio	15.13-13.20	34.96-32.43	12.45-9.73	36.81-25.20	17.96-14.39	16.34-12.64	19.39-14.63	20.09-15.22
Average Yield %	4.57	4.64	4.95	4.80	4.55	4.72	4.76	4.50

Address: 101 Constitution Avenue, N.W., Washington, DC 20080	Officers: James H. DeGraffenreidt – Chmn., C.E.O.,	Investor Contact:202–624–6410
Telephone: (703) 750 4440	Terry D. McCallister – Pres., C.O.O.	Institutional Holding
Web Site: www.wglholdings.com	Transfer Agents:The Bank of New York, New York, NY	No of Institutions: 6
		Shares: 24,921 % Held: –

WHITNEY HOLDING CORP.

Exchange	Symbol	Price	52Wk Range	Yield	P/E
NMS	WTNY	$43.47 (5/28/2004)	43.57-31.94	3.04	17.39

*7 Year Price Score 124.5 *NYSE Composite Index=100 ***12 Month Price Score 51.7**

Interim Earnings (Per Share)

Qtr.	Mar	Jun	Sep	Dec
2001	0.46	0.46	0.48	0.50
2002	0.36	0.59	0.60	0.83
2003	0.58	0.59	0.68	0.59
2004	0.64	...	...	...

Interim Dividends (Per Share)

Amt	Decl	Ex	Rec	Pay
0.30Q	8/27/2003	9/11/2003	9/15/2003	10/1/2003
0.33Q	11/19/2003	12/11/2003	12/15/2003	1/2/2004
0.33Q	2/18/2004	3/11/2004	3/15/2004	4/1/2004
0.33Q	5/26/2004	6/11/2004	6/15/2004	7/1/2004

Indicated Div: $1.32 (Div. Reinv. Plan)

Valuation Analysis
Forecast P/E 16.70 (5/24/2004)

Market Cap $1.7 Billion	Book Value 840.3 Million
Price/Book 1.93	Price/Sales 3.81

Dividend Achiever Status

Rank 51	10 Year Growth Rate	17.25%
Total Years of Dividend Growth	10	

Business Summary: Commercial Banking (MIC: 8.1 SIC: 6021 NAIC:522110)

Whitney Holding, through its principal banking subsidiary, Whitney National Bank, serves the five–state Gulf Coast region stretching from Houston, TX, across southern Louisiana and the coastal region of Mississippi, to central and south Alabama, and into the panhandle of Florida. Co. serves commercial, small business and retail customers, and offers a range of transaction and savings deposit products and cash management services, secured and unsecured loan products, including revolving credit facilities, and letters of credit and similar financial guarantees. Co. also provides trust and investment management services to retirement benefit plans, corporations and individuals.

Recent Developments: For the first quarter ended Mar 31 2004, net income rose 11.5% to $26.2 million compared with $23.5 million in the equivalent period of 2003. Net interest income grew 6.0% to $77.2 million from $72.8 million in the prior–year period due to growth in average earning assets. Results for 2004 included a $2.0 million negative provision for loan losses versus a provision of $500,000 in 2003. Total non–interest income slipped 2.7% to $20.9 million compared with $21.5 million the previous year. Total non–interest expense climbed 4.6% to $62.0 million versus $59.3 million the year before.

Prospects: On Apr 14 2004, Co. agreed to acquire certain assets and assume certain deposits associated with two branches of First National Bank in Fort Walton Beach, FL for a deposit premium of about $2.0 million. The addition of these branches, with deposit accounts totaling about $30.0 million, enhances Co.'s existing operations in the Florida panhandle. The transaction is subject to regulatory approvals and is expected to be completed late in the second quarter of 2004. Separately, a return to a more favorable rate environment in the near term is not anticipated, and both overall production levels and secondary mortgage market fee income in 2004 are expected to be well below 2003 results.

Financial Data

(US$ in Thousands)	12/31/2003	12/31/2002	12/31/2001	12/31/2000	12/31/1999	12/31/1998	12/31/1997	12/31/1996
Earnings Per Share	2.44	2.38	1.90	1.96	1.80	1.49	1.66	1.50
Tang. Book Val. Per Share	18.48	17.53	15.48	15.30	15.46	15.98	15.34	15.02
Dividends Per Share	1.200	1.070	0.990	0.940	0.860	0.780	0.720	0.620
Dividend Payout %	49.18	45.23	52.63	47.95	47.77	52.67	43.59	41.59
Income Statement								
Total Interest Income	338,069	370,909	441,145	417,687	349,813	336,113	291,409	241,706
Total Interest Expense	43,509	75,701	161,349	170,574	124,065	122,981	106,947	89,895
Net Interest Income	294,560	295,208	279,796	247,113	225,748	213,132	184,462	151,811
Provision for Loan Losses	(3,500)	7,500	19,500	10,000	6,000	73	(2,812)	(5,000)
Non–Interest Income	88,349	85,185	91,209	71,625	66,663	60,771	51,035	37,322
Non–Interest Expense	242,923	230,926	239,104	208,903	194,163	195,993	159,630	134,394
Income Before Taxes	144,641	141,967	112,401	99,835	92,248	77,837	78,679	59,739
Net Income	98,542	95,323	75,820	67,028	62,420	52,679	52,218	40,621
Average Shs. Outstg.	40,396	40,121	39,836	34,256	34,636	35,250	31,299	26,973
Balance Sheet								
Cash & Due from Banks	270,387	326,124	271,512	256,825	230,690	214,963	221,318	221,091
Securities Avail. for Sale	2,090,870	1,773,591	1,440,527	456,758	206,932	105,361	103,253	146,972
Net Loans & Leases	4,823,135	4,389,297	4,482,905	4,245,501	3,628,581	3,230,299	2,604,773	2,025,569
Total Assets	7,754,982	7,097,881	7,243,650	6,242,076	5,454,388	5,211,919	4,312,987	3,774,501
Total Deposits	6,158,582	5,782,879	5,950,160	4,960,177	4,309,398	4,256,662	3,510,723	2,861,881
Total Liabilities	6,914,669	6,297,398	6,525,762	5,619,116	4,897,285	4,650,958	3,834,259	3,369,850
Net Stockholders' Equity	840,313	800,483	717,888	622,960	557,103	560,961	478,728	404,651
Shares Outstanding	40,447	40,067	39,667	35,027	33,861	35,089	31,206	26,928
Statistical Record								
Return on Equity %	11.72	11.90	10.56	10.75	11.20	9.39	10.90	10.03
Return on Assets %	1.27	1.34	1.04	1.07	1.14	1.01	1.21	1.07
Equity/Assets %	10.83	11.27	9.91	9.98	10.21	10.76	11.09	10.72
Non–Int. Exp./Tot. Inc. %	56.81	50.63	44.91	42.69	46.62	49.38	46.61	48.16
Price Range	40.99-31.62	38.52-27.98	32.56-24.00	27.79-21.00	27.83-21.46	42.25-23.83	39.83-23.17	23.92-19.67
P/E Ratio	16.80-12.96	16.18-11.76	17.14-12.63	14.18-10.71	15.46-11.92	28.36-16.00	24.00-13.96	15.94-13.11
Average Yield %	3.46	3.27	3.55	4.00	3.45	2.38	2.54	2.95

Address: 228 St. Charles Avenue, New Orleans, LA 70130 Telephone: (504) 586-7272 Web Site: www.whitneybank.com	Officers: William L. Marks – Chmn., C.E.O., R. King Milling – Pres. Transfer Agents:American Stock Transfer &Trust Company, New York, NY	Investor Contact:504–552–4591 Institutional Holding No of Institutions: 15 Shares: 13,709 % Held: –

WILEY (JOHN) & SONS INC.

Exchange	Symbol	Price	52Wk Range	Yield	P/E
NYS	JW A	$31.80 (5/28/2004)	31.80–23.92	0.82	22.88

*7 Year Price Score 133.7 *NYSE Composite Index=100   ***12 Month Price Score 52.9**

Interim Earnings (Per Share)

Qtr.	Jul	Oct	Jan	Apr
2000–01	0.26	0.27	0.27	0.13
2001–02	0.31	0.28	0.34	(0.02)
2002–03	0.32	0.55	0.39	0.12
2003–04	0.35	0.41	0.51	...

Interim Dividends (Per Share)

Amt	Decl	Ex	Rec	Pay
0.065Q	6/19/2003	7/2/2003	7/7/2003	7/17/2003
0.065Q	9/18/2003	9/30/2003	10/2/2003	10/16/2003
0.065Q	12/11/2003	12/23/2003	12/26/2003	1/15/2004
0.065Q	3/10/2004	3/31/2004	4/2/2004	4/16/2004

Indicated Div: $0.26

Valuation Analysis

Forecast P/E N/A

Market Cap	$1.6 Billion	Book Value	427.0 Million
Price/Book	3.13	Price/Sales	1.50

Dividend Achiever Status

Rank	107	10 Year Growth Rate	12.84%
Total Years of Dividend Growth			10

Business Summary: Non–Media Publishing (MIC: 13.3 SIC: 2731 NAIC:511130)

John Wiley & Sons develops, publishes and markets textbooks, reference works, consumer books, periodicals, including journals and other subscription–based products and electronic media products, to colleges and universities, libraries, bookstores, professional groups, industrial organizations, government agencies and individuals in the U.S. and abroad. In addition, Co. imports, adapts, markets and distributes books from other publishers. Co. also develops and markets computer software and electronic databases for educational use and professional research and training.

Recent Developments: For the third quarter ended Jan 31 2004, net income grew 29.4% to $31.3 million compared with $24.2 million in the equivalent 2002 quarter. Revenues climbed 9.6% to $242.4 million from $221.2 million a year earlier. The improvement in earnings and revenues was primarily driven by Scientific, Technical and Medical journals, Professional/Trade books, and Higher Education textbooks and educational materials. In addition, Co.'s results were boosted by the positive effects of operations, the resolution of certain tax matters and favorable foreign exchange rates. Operating margin advanced to 18.1% versus 16.7% the year before.

Prospects: Co. is seeing growing momentum across its core businesses with sales notably higher for its scientific, technical and medical journals, professional/trade books and higher education textbooks and educational materials. Consequently, Co. expects fiscal 2004 revenue growth to approach the high end of its 4.0% to 6.0% guidance, and earnings per share to reach the high end of its mid to high single digit guidance. These projections exclude unusual items and a tax benefit recorded in the third quarter, and are based on nine months results and expectations for the fourth quarter of fiscal 2004.

Financial Data

(US$ in Thousands)	9 Mos	6 Mos	3 Mos	04/30/2003	04/30/2002	04/30/2001	04/30/2000	04/30/1999
Earnings Per Share	1.39	1.27	1.41	1.38	0.91	0.93	0.81	0.60
Cash Flow Per Share	2.81	(0.0084)	(0.23)	2.68	2.22	2.06	2.03	1.77
Dividends Per Share	0.240	0.230	0.210	0.200	0.180	0.160	0.140	0.120
Dividend Payout %	17.26	18.11	14.89	14.49	19.78	17.20	17.59	21.25
Income Statement								
Total Revenues	690,897	448,540	219,660	853,971	734,396	613,790	594,815	508,435
Total Indirect Exp.	344,732	228,204	114,373	442,320	391,125	318,966	310,872	270,798
Depreciation & Amort.	7,382	4,865	2,330	9,620	17,662	17,496	16,447	9,445
Operating Income	113,895	70,045	33,178	120,261	87,763	95,424	89,004	63,654
Net Interest Inc./(Exp.)	(3,092)	(1,872)	(1,260)	(7,964)	(7,480)	(8,025)	(8,390)	(7,322)
Income Taxes	32,011	20,725	10,118	25,284	23,802	31,309	30,243	22,336
Net Income	78,792	47,448	21,800	87,275	57,316	58,918	52,388	39,709
Average Shs. Outstg.	61,800	63,091	62,964	63,086	63,094	63,300	64,825	66,513
Balance Sheet								
Cash & Cash Equivalents	93,051	10,756	8,085	33,241	39,705	52,947	42,299	148,970
Total Current Assets	363,881	300,050	265,923	283,844	275,259	189,535	177,111	255,970
Total Assets	1,045,539	974,588	938,942	955,972	896,145	588,002	569,337	528,552
Total Current Liabilities	330,385	284,020	277,181	323,265	320,393	246,761	254,050	195,100
Long–Term Obligations	200,000	200,000	200,000	200,000	235,000	65,000	95,000	125,000
Net Stockholders' Equity	426,994	399,412	372,866	344,004	276,650	220,023	172,738	162,212
Net Working Capital	33,496	16,030	(11,258)	(39,421)	(45,134)	(57,226)	(76,939)	60,870
Shares Outstanding	62,042	62,140	62,172	61,630	61,701	60,734	60,712	62,382
Statistical Record								
Operating Profit Margin %	16.48	15.61	15.10	14.08	11.95	15.54	14.96	12.51
Return on Equity %	18.45	11.87	5.84	25.37	20.71	26.77	30.32	24.47
Return on Assets %	7.53	4.86	2.32	9.12	6.39	10.02	9.20	7.51
Debt/Total Assets %	19.12	20.52	21.30	20.92	26.22	11.05	16.68	23.64
Price Range	28.20–23.92	28.20–23.92	27.26–23.92	27.32–19.45	27.55–18.66	25.88–17.25	22.86–14.00	23.97–13.13
P/E Ratio	20.29–17.21	22.20–18.83	19.33–16.96	19.80–14.09	30.27–20.51	27.83–18.55	28.22–17.28	39.95–21.89
Average Yield %	0.92	0.88	0.82	0.87	0.80	0.77	0.81	0.68

Address: 111 River Street, Hoboken, NJ 07030	**Officers:** Peter Booth Wiley – Chmn., William J. Pesce – Pres., C.E.O.	**Investor Contact:**201–748–6000
Telephone: (201) 748–6000	**Transfer Agents:**Registrar and Transfer Company, Cranford, NJ	**Institutional Holding** **No of Institutions:** 10
Web Site: www.wiley.com		**Shares:** 359,105 **% Held:** –

WILMINGTON TRUST CORP. (DE)

Exchange	Symbol	Price	52Wk Range	Yield	P/E
NYS	WL	$36.80 (5/28/2004)	38.25-29.14	3.10	17.44

*7 Year Price Score 117.0   *NYSE Composite Index=100   ***12 Month Price Score 49.3**

TRADING VOLUME (thousand shares)

Interim Earnings (Per Share)

Qtr.	Mar	Jun	Sep	Dec
2001	0.46	0.47	0.47	0.48
2002	0.48	0.52	0.52	0.49
2003	0.44	0.49	0.52	0.57
2004	0.53	...	...	...

Interim Dividends (Per Share)

Amt	Decl	Ex	Rec	Pay
0.27Q	7/18/2003	7/30/2003	8/1/2003	8/15/2003
0.27Q	10/17/2003	10/30/2003	11/3/2003	11/17/2003
0.27Q	1/16/2004	1/29/2004	2/2/2004	2/16/2004
0.285Q	4/16/2004	4/29/2004	5/3/2004	5/17/2004

Indicated Div: $1.14 (Div. Reinv. Plan)

Valuation Analysis

Forecast P/E 16.32 (5/24/2004)

Market Cap $2.4 Billion	Book Value 800.8 Million	
Price/Book 2.98	Price/Sales 3.76	

Dividend Achiever Status

Rank 198	10 Year Growth Rate	8.13%
Total Years of Dividend Growth		22

Business Summary: Commercial Banking (MIC: 8.1 SIC: 6022 NAIC:522110)

Wilmington Trust, with assets of $8.82 billion as of Dec 31 2003, is a financial services holding company with offices in California, Delaware, Florida, Georgia, Maryland, Nevada, New York, Pennsylvania, Tennessee, the Cayman and Channel Islands, Dublin, London, and Milan. Co. provides wealth management and specialized corporate services to clients throughout the United States and in more than 50 other countries, and commercial banking services throughout the Delaware Valley region. In addition, Co. is authorized to do business in Luxembourg and the Netherlands.

Recent Developments: For the quarter ended Mar 31 2004, net income rose 21.4% to $35.7 million from $29.4 million in the comparable prior-year period. Net interest income grew 5.1% to $71.8 million from $68.3 million a year earlier. Net interest margin was down 22 basis points to 3.53% as a result of the effects of the continued low interest rate environment and Co.'s asset sensitivity. Provision for loan losses increased 12.2% to $5.5 million compared with $4.9 million in 2003. Non-interest income was up 19.0% to $72.7 million. Non-interest expense increased 3.9% to $18.7 million as a result of business line growth and the completion of two large technology conversion projects.

Prospects: Business development continues to be strong, particularly in Co.'s advisory businesses. Looking ahead, if the financial markets remain at favorable levels, Co. anticipates double-digit growth in fee-based revenue in 2004. Additionally, loan growth in 2004 should remain in the 6.0% to 7.0% range compared with 2003. Moreover, ongoing expenses should reflect continued investment in technology and higher employee benefits costs. For the second quarter of 2004, Co. expects total non-interest expenses to be in the range of $85.0 million to $87.0 million. Co. expects to increase its level of advertising in the next few quarters.

Financial Data

(US$ in Thousands)	12/31/2003	12/31/2002	12/31/2001	12/31/2000	12/31/1999	12/31/1998	12/31/1997	12/31/1996
Earnings Per Share	2.02	2.01	1.88	1.85	1.60	1.67	1.54	1.41
Tang. Book Val. Per Share	8.07	7.30	7.25	6.48	5.17	6.07	7.51	6.85
Dividends Per Share	1.060	1.000	0.940	0.880	0.820	0.760	0.700	0.640
Dividend Payout %	52.72	50.00	50.13	47.83	51.40	45.80	45.77	45.39
Income Statement								
Total Interest Income	368,800	392,871	468,798	530,454	462,176	456,939	430,639	402,850
Total Interest Expense	91,700	116,341	209,985	275,315	216,263	219,242	200,623	188,629
Net Interest Income	277,100	276,530	258,813	255,139	245,913	237,697	230,016	214,221
Provision for Loan Losses	21,600	22,013	19,850	21,900	17,500	20,000	21,500	16,000
Non-Interest Income	265,900	263,412	236,198	223,697	191,453	183,917	157,542	138,237
Non-Interest Expense	312,000	309,892	276,917	264,682	258,204	230,066	207,671	192,339
Income Before Taxes	207,700	206,784	190,049	184,767	161,662	171,548	158,387	144,119
Eqty Earns/Minority Int.	(1,100)	(625)	...	...	...	...	...	...
Income from Cont Ops	...	...	124,040	...	...	...	...	...
Net Income	134,400	133,157	125,170	120,939	107,297	114,325	106,044	97,278
Average Shs. Outstg.	66,536	66,301	65,942	65,360	66,766	68,550	68,932	68,798
Balance Sheet								
Cash & Due from Banks	210,200	248,850	210,104	223,819	225,145	204,579	239,392	231,233
Securities Avail. for Sale	1,875,200	1,343,899	1,264,848	1,440,065	1,686,267	1,298,741	1,316,403	798,519
Net Loans & Leases	6,135,400	5,939,947	5,407,175	5,111,670	4,743,154	4,247,727	3,930,130	3,717,123
Total Assets	8,820,200	8,131,275	7,518,462	7,321,616	7,201,944	6,300,565	6,122,351	5,564,409
Total Deposits	6,577,200	6,337,093	5,590,785	5,286,016	5,369,484	4,536,763	4,169,030	3,913,698
Long-Term Obligations	407,100	160,500	160,500	168,000	168,000	168,000	43,000	43,000
Total Liabilities	8,019,400	7,390,006	6,835,932	6,729,716	6,703,713	5,754,356	5,619,344	5,099,692
Net Stockholders' Equity	800,800	741,269	682,530	591,900	498,231	546,209	503,007	464,717
Shares Outstanding	66,063	65,627	65,400	64,786	64,705	66,658	66,956	67,786
Return on Equity %	16.99	18.13	19.37	21.69	21.53	20.93	21.08	20.93
Return on Assets %	1.54	1.65	1.75	1.75	1.48	1.81	1.73	1.74
Equity/Assets %	9.07	9.11	9.07	8.08	6.91	8.66	8.21	8.35
Non-Int. Exp./Tot. Inc. %	49.15	47.21	39.27	35.09	39.50	35.89	35.30	35.54
Price Range	36.15-26.27	34.63-25.30	33.38-25.68	31.44-20.81	30.21-22.19	32.22-22.23	30.96-17.97	18.77-13.23
P/E Ratio	17.90-13.00	17.23-12.59	17.75-13.66	16.99-11.25	18.88-13.87	19.29-13.31	20.10-11.67	13.31-9.38
Average Yield %	3.45	3.21	3.12	3.57	3.03	2.72	3.06	4.24

Address: Rodney Square North, Wilmington, DE 19890-0001 **Telephone:** (302) 651-1000 **Web Site:** www.wilmingtontrust.com	**Officers:** Ted T. Cecala - Chmn., C.E.O., Robert V. A. Harra - Pres., C.O.O., Treas. **Transfer Agents:** Wells Fargo Shareowner Services, St. Paul, MN	**Investor Contact:** 302-651-8069 **Institutional Holding** **No of Institutions:** 11 **Shares:** 469,986 **% Held:** -

WOLVERINE WORLD WIDE, INC.

Exchange	Symbol	Price	52Wk Range	Yield	P/E
NYS	WWW	$26.35 (5/28/2004)	27.84-18.24	0.99	18.96

*7 Year Price Score 126.6 *NYSE Composite Index=100 *12 Month Price Score 57.5

Interim Earnings (Per Share)

Qtr.	Mar	Jun	Aug	Dec
2001	0.14	0.21	0.34	0.38
2002	0.15	0.21	0.37	0.42
2003	0.18	0.23	0.40	0.46
2004	0.30	...	...	...

Interim Dividends (Per Share)

Amt	Decl	Ex	Rec	Pay
0.055Q	7/10/2003	9/29/2003	10/1/2003	11/3/2003
0.055Q	12/9/2003	12/30/2003	1/2/2004	2/2/2004
0.065Q	2/19/2004	3/30/2004	4/1/2004	5/3/2004
0.065Q	4/23/2004	6/29/2004	7/1/2004	8/2/2004
		Indicated Div: $0.26		

Valuation Analysis

Forecast P/E 17.29 (5/24/2004)

Market Cap	$1.2 Billion	Book Value	430.1 Million
Price/Book	2.25	Price/Sales	1.09

Dividend Achiever Status

Rank	29	10 Year Growth Rate	20.85%
Total Years of Dividend Growth			10

Business Summary: Leather and Leather Products (MIC: 4.5 SIC: 3149 NAIC:316219)

Wolverine World Wide is a designer, manufacturer and marketer of a broad line of casual shoes, rugged outdoor and work footwear, and constructed slippers and moccasins. The products are marketed throughout the world under brand names including *Bates*®, *CAT*®, *Coleman*®, *Harley-Davidson*®, *Hush Puppies*®, *HyTest*®, *Merrell*®, *Sebago*®, *Stanley*®and *Wolverine*®. Co.'s footwear is distributed domestically through 64 Co.-owned retail stores and to numerous accounts including department stores, footwear chains, catalogs, specialty retailers, mass merchants and Internet retailers as of Jan 3 2004. Co.'s products are distributed worldwide in over 140 markets through licensees and distributors.

Recent Developments: For the 12 weeks ended Mar 27 2004, net earnings rose 65.9% to $12.3 million compared with $7.4 million in the corresponding year-earlier period. Revenue advanced 17.4% to $224.9 million, reflecting strong at-once orders, a 3.4% positive effect from foreign currency and $9.8 million of revenue contribution from Co.'s *Sebago* business, which was acquired in November 2003. Gross margin was $85.4 million, or 38.0% of revenue, versus $69.2 million, or 36.1% of revenue, last year. Co. attributed the improvement in gross margin to plant synergies from its *Merrell* business, repositioning efforts in the global *Hush Puppies* wholesale businesses and the effect of the 2003 slipper business realignment.

Prospects: Due to the strength of its first quarter 2004 results, increasing backlog, and anticipated re-order business for the remainder of 2004, Co. has increased its full-year 2004 estimates. Co. noted that its order backlog as of Mar 27 2004 was up approximately 12.0% compared with the previous year, with multiple brands benefiting. Consequently, Co. now expects revenue to range from $960.0 million to $980.0 million, up from its previous estimate of $945.0 million to $965.0 million. Also, Co. expects earnings to range between $1.44 and $1.52 per share, up from its previous estimate of $1.37 to $1.43 per share.

Financial Data

(US$ in Thousands)	01/03/2004	12/28/2002	12/29/2001	12/30/2000	01/01/2000	01/02/1999	01/03/1998	12/28/1996
Earnings Per Share	1.27	1.15	1.07	0.26	0.78	0.97	0.96	1.00
Cash Flow Per Share	2.50	2.11	1.27	1.69	1.13	(0.10)	N.M.	0.34
Tang. Book Val. Per Share	9.83	8.38	8.64	7.77	7.64	6.87	6.19	5.46
Dividends Per Share	0.210	0.170	0.150	0.130	0.110	0.100	0.080	0.060
Dividend Payout %	16.53	15.21	14.48	51.92	15.06	10.74	8.63	6.89
Income Statement								
Total Revenues	888,926	827,106	720,066	701,291	665,576	669,329	665,125	511,029
Total Indirect Exp.	257,600	230,086	195,662	218,771	168,672	157,961	149,827	110,682
Depreciation & Amort.	17,947	16,860	17,621	17,695	14,881	13,036	9,151	7,147
Operating Income	74,462	70,608	68,116	15,111	50,249	61,921	58,909	46,718
Net Interest Inc./(Exp.)	(5,474)	(6,466)	(6,742)	(9,909)	(10,346)	(7,279)	(4,610)	(1,595)
Income Taxes	23,262	23,599	23,307	4,325	17,166	20,157	19,542	14,811
Net Income	51,716	47,912	45,240	10,690	32,380	41,651	41,539	32,856
Average Shs. Outstg.	40,720	41,793	42,448	41,795	41,486	42,952	43,464	43,017
Balance Sheet								
Cash & Cash Equivalents	55,356	27,078	35,820	8,434	1,446	6,203	5,768	8,534
Total Current Assets	386,636	363,345	374,802	325,086	349,301	340,978	303,861	264,628
Total Assets	578,881	531,994	543,678	494,568	534,395	521,478	449,663	361,598
Total Current Liabilities	85,766	80,177	74,521	54,004	48,539	51,268	64,895	69,810
Long-Term Obligations	43,903	57,885	75,818	87,878	134,831	157,089	99,847	41,233
Net Stockholders' Equity	430,094	369,097	374,152	337,238	332,105	300,320	282,430	239,292
Shares Outstanding	39,453	39,970	41,555	41,552	41,300	40,765	42,553	41,698
Operating Profit Margin %	8.37	8.53	9.45	2.15	7.54	9.25	8.85	9.14
Return on Equity %	12.02	12.98	12.09	3.16	9.74	13.86	14.70	13.73
Return on Assets %	8.93	9.00	8.32	2.16	6.05	7.98	9.23	9.08
Debt/Total Assets %	7.58	10.88	13.94	17.76	25.23	30.12	19.98	11.40
Price Range	21.28-14.39	19.24-12.90	19.20-12.56	16.56-8.63	14.00-9.00	30.50-8.44	30.38-19.08	19.33-10.89
P/E Ratio	16.76-11.33	16.73-11.22	17.94-11.74	63.70-33.17	17.95-11.54	31.44-8.70	31.64-19.88	19.33-10.89
Average Yield %	1.13	1.05	0.94	1.18	0.98	0.51	0.33	0.40

Address: 9341 Courtland Drive, Rockford, MI 49351 Telephone: (616) 866-5500 Web Site: www.wolverineworldwide.com	Officers: Geoffrey B. Bloom - Chmn., Timothy J. ODonovan - Pres., C.E.O. Transfer Agents:Computershare Investor Services, Chicago, IL	Investor Contact:616-866-5589 Institutional Holding No of Institutions: 147 Shares: 31,973,038 % Held: 79.9

WPS RESOURCES CORP.

Exchange	Symbol	Price	52Wk Range	Yield	P/E
NYS	WPS	$45.26 (5/28/2004)	48.86-38.55	4.82	13.08

*7 Year Price Score 125.4   *NYSE Composite Index=100   *12 Month Price Score 48.0

Interim Earnings (Per Share)

Qtr.	Mar	Jun	Sep	Dec
2001	0.89	0.41	0.76	0.68
2002	0.89	0.68	0.95	0.90
2003	0.92	0.08	1.04	1.20
2004	1.14	...	...	...

Interim Dividends (Per Share)

Amt	Decl	Ex	Rec	Pay
0.545Q	7/4/2003	8/27/2003	8/29/2003	9/20/2003
0.545Q	9/11/2003	11/25/2003	11/28/2003	12/20/2003
0.545Q	2/12/2004	2/25/2004	2/27/2004	3/20/2004
0.545Q	4/1/2004	5/26/2004	5/28/2004	6/19/2004

Indicated Div: $2.18 (Div. Reinv. Plan)

Valuation Analysis

Forecast P/E 13.53 (5/24/2004)

Market Cap	$1.3 Billion	Book Value	952.1 Million
Price/Book	1.17	Price/Sales	0.26

Dividend Achiever Status

Rank	291	10 Year Growth Rate	2.07%
Total Years of Dividend Growth			45

Business Summary: Electricity (MIC: 7.1 SIC: 4931 NAIC:221121)

WPS Resources operates as a holding company with both regulated utility and non-regulated business units serving an 11,000 square mile service territory in northeastern Wisconsin and an adjacent portion of the Upper Peninsula of Michigan. Co.'s principal wholly-owned subsidiaries are: Wisconsin Public Service Corporation (WPSC), a regulated electric and gas utility in Wisconsin and Michigan; Upper Peninsula Power Company, a regulated electric utility in Michigan; and WPS Energy Service, Inc. and WPS Power Development, Inc., both non-regulated subsidiaries. As of Dec 31 2002, WPSC served 407,696 electric retail and 295,816 gas retail customers.

Recent Developments: For the quarter ended Mar 31 2004, income was $46.4 million, before a loss of $3.0 million from discontinued operations, compared with income of $35.7 million, before a loss of $5.1 million from discontinued operations and an accounting change credit of $3.2 million, in the equivalent period of the previous year. Total revenues climbed 7.1% to $1.37 billion from $1.28 billion in the year-earlier quarter. Nonregulated revenues increased 7.3% to $986.6 million from $919.9 million, largely due to the further expansion of the Canadian retail natural gas business. Utility revenues advanced 6.9% to $386.7 million from $361.9 million, reflecting retail and wholesale electric rate increases.

Prospects: Earnings growth is benefiting from a strong performance by WPS Energy Services and a more favorable sales mix at Wisconsin Public Service. Looking ahead, Co. remains committed to growing earnings through effective management of both risk and costs in its business, execution of its asset management strategy and balanced business expansion between its utility and nonregulated operations. Co.'s long-term basic earnings per share growth target remains at 6.0% to 8.0% on an average annualized basis. Co. expects earnings to range from $2.95 to $3.10 per share for full-year 2004, assuming normal weather, availability of its generating units, its land sales, and the completion of the sales of the Sunbury and Kewaunee plants.

Financial Data

(US$ in Thousands)	12/31/2003	12/31/2002	12/31/2001	12/31/2000	12/31/1999	12/31/1998	12/31/1997	12/31/1996
Earnings Per Share	3.24	3.42	2.74	2.53	2.24	1.76	2.25	2.00
Cash Flow Per Share	1.87	6.11	5.04	5.32	4.31	4.13	5.99	4.86
Tang. Book Val. Per Share	27.39	24.43	22.72	20.21	19.97	19.47	19.99	19.56
Dividends Per Share	2.160	2.120	2.080	2.040	2.000	1.960	1.920	1.880
Dividend Payout %	66.66	61.98	75.91	80.63	89.28	111.36	85.33	94.00
Income Statement								
Total Revenues	4,321,300	2,674,900	2,675,500	1,951,574	1,098,540	1,063,736	878,340	858,254
Total Indirect Exp.	182,200	138,100	122,800	133,641	115,562	118,176	103,989	92,046
Costs & Expenses	4,190,600	2,523,800	2,568,200	1,838,744	978,803	963,692	778,251	759,912
Operating Income	130,700	151,100	107,300	112,830	119,737	100,044	100,089	98,342
Net Interest Inc./(Exp.)	...	(58,100)	(55,800)	(50,780)	(32,768)	(28,637)	(26,403)	(25,000)
Eqty Earns/Minority Int.	...	...	...	...	...	611	797	348
Income from Cont Ops	110,600	...	...	...	62,676	...	...	...
Net Income	97,800	112,500	80,700	70,104	59,565	49,763	56,853	50,866
Average Shs. Outstg.	33,200	31,700	28,300	26,463	26,644	26,511	23,873	23,891
Balance Sheet								
Net Property	1,828,700	1,610,200	1,463,600	1,198,324	1,150,902	1,010,158	886,360	892,851
Total Assets	4,292,300	3,207,900	2,870,000	2,816,142	1,816,548	1,510,387	1,299,602	1,330,664
Long-Term Obligations	871,900	824,400	727,800	72,955	73,585	343,037	304,008	305,788
Net Stockholders' Equity	1,054,300	833,900	767,000	593,945	587,493	568,390	529,023	518,724
Shares Outstanding	36,621	32,040	31,496	26,851	26,851	26,511	23,897	23,897
Operating Profit Margin %	3.02	5.64	4.01	5.78	10.89	9.40	11.39	11.45
Net Inc./Net Property %	5.34	6.98	5.51	5.85	5.17	4.92	6.41	5.69
Net Inc./Tot. Capital %	4.87	6.49	5.15	9.13	7.71	4.81	5.92	5.32
Return on Equity %	10.49	13.49	10.52	11.80	10.66	8.75	10.74	9.80
Accum. Depr./Gross Prop. %	40.60	49.84	51.29	53.59	53.24	54.88	54.33	52.15
Price Range	46.77-37.12	42.45-31.52	36.55-31.82	38.69-22.81	35.50-24.63	37.25-30.25	34.19-23.50	34.13-28.25
P/E Ratio	14.44-11.46	12.41-9.22	13.34-11.61	15.29-9.02	15.85-10.99	21.16-17.19	15.19-10.44	17.06-14.13
Average Yield %	5.27	5.55	6.08	6.89	6.74	5.88	6.89	5.99

Address: 700 North Adams Street, Green Bay, WI 54307-9001 Telephone: (920) 433-4901 Web Site: www.wpsr.com	Officers: Larry L. Weyers - Chmn., Pres., C.E.O., Thomas P. Meinz - Sr. V.P., Public Affairs Transfer Agents:American Stock Transfer &Trust Company, New York, NY	Investor Contact:920-433-1857 Institutional Holding No of Institutions: 7 Shares: 327,449 % Held: -

WRIGLEY (WILLIAM) JR. CO.

Interim Earnings (Per Share)

Qtr.	Mar	Jun	Sep	Dec
2001	0.36	0.44	0.41	0.40
2002	0.38	0.49	0.44	0.47
2003	0.43	0.56	0.50	0.49
2004	0.49	...	...	...

Interim Dividends (Per Share)

Amt	Decl	Ex	Rec	Pay
0.22Q	8/20/2003	10/15/2003	10/15/2003	11/3/2003
0.22Q	10/20/2003	1/13/2004	1/15/2004	2/2/2004
0.235Q	1/28/2004	4/13/2004	4/15/2004	5/3/2004
0.235Q	5/25/2004	7/13/2004	7/15/2004	8/2/2004

Indicated Div: $0.94 (Div. Reinv. Plan)

Valuation Analysis

Forecast P/E 28.32 (5/24/2004)
Market Cap $11.5 Billion   Book Value 1.9 Billion
Price/Book 5.86   Price/Sales 3.38

Dividend Achiever Status

Rank 182   10 Year Growth Rate 8.72%
Total Years of Dividend Growth 23

Business Summary: Food (MIC: 4.1 SIC: 2067 NAIC:311340)

William Wrigley Jr. is a manufacturer and marketer of chewing gum and other confectionery products, both in the U.S. and abroad. Co. has manufacturing facilities in four factories in the U.S. and 11 factories in other countries. Two domestic wholly–owned associated companies, L.A. Dreyfus Company and Northwestern Flavors, LLC, manufacture products other than chewing gum or confectionery products. Co.'s brands are sold in over 150 countries and territories. Brand names include *Doublemint®*, *Wrigley's Spearmint®*, *Big Red®*, *Juicy Fruit®*, *Winterfresh®*, *Extra®*, *Freedent®*, *Hubba Bubba®*, *Orbit®*, *Excel®*, *Eclipse®*, *Airwaves®*, *Alpine®*, *Cool Air®*, and *P.K.*

Recent Developments: For the first quarter ended Mar 31 2004, net income advanced 14.4% to $111.0 million compared with $97.0 million in the corresponding period of the prior year. Net sales increased 20.8% to $812.2 million from $672.4 million the year before. The improvement in sales was primarily attributed to strong volume gains, positive contributions from foreign currency translations and favorable product mix. Gross profit jumped 17.4% to $458.4 million versus $390.4 million a year earlier. Operating income climbed 14.4% to $161.7 million from $141.4 million in 2002. Investment income jumped 63.1% to $2.5 million versus $1.5 million the year before.

Prospects: On Apr 1 2004, Co. announced that it completed the acquisition of certain confectionery businesses of the Joyco Group from Agrolimen, a privately–held Spanish food conglomerate. The purchase price was approximately $260.0 million. This transaction will add *Boomer®*bubble gum and *Pim Pom®*lollipops, and *Solano®*candy to Co.'s product line. In addition, Co. will gain Joyco's sales and production operations in China, India, and Spain, smaller commercial operations in France, Italy and Poland, as well as Cafosa, Joyco's gum base business. This acquisition is expected to reduce earnings in 2004 by less than $0.05 per share, but contribute positively to earnings in 2005.

Financial Data

(US$ in Thousands)	3 Mos	12/31/2003	12/31/2002	12/31/2001	12/31/2000	12/31/1999	12/31/1998	12/31/1997
Earnings Per Share	2.04	1.98	1.78	1.61	1.45	1.33	1.31	1.17
Cash Flow Per Share	0.50	2.86	1.66	1.73	1.97	1.54	1.39	1.26
Tang. Book Val. Per Share	8.25	8.09	6.76	5.67	4.87	4.97	4.98	4.24
Dividends Per Share	0.880	0.860	0.800	0.740	0.700	0.660	0.650	0.580
Dividend Payout %	43.14	43.68	45.22	46.27	48.27	50.00	49.42	50.00
Income Statement								
Total Revenues	812,151	3,069,088	2,746,318	2,429,646	2,145,706	2,079,238	2,023,355	1,954,174
Total Indirect Exp.	296,716	1,142,991	1,011,029	919,236	778,197	779,168	723,094	711,610
Depreciation & Amort.	31,257	120,040	85,568	68,326	57,880	61,225	55,774	50,439
Operating Income	161,669	649,362	585,074	513,356	463,243	445,139	441,494	395,198
Net Interest Inc./(Exp.)	...	...	...	...	...	(709)	(615)	(958)
Income Taxes	52,227	205,647	181,896	164,380	150,370	136,247	136,378	122,614
Net Income	110,983	445,894	401,525	362,986	328,942	308,183	304,501	271,626
Average Shs. Outstg.	224,795	224,963	225,145	225,349	227,036	231,722	231,928	231,928
Balance Sheet								
Cash & Cash Equivalents	514,220	505,217	279,276	307,785	300,599	288,386	214,572	206,627
Total Current Assets	1,350,484	1,290,591	1,006,292	913,843	828,715	803,746	843,172	797,673
Total Assets	2,573,740	2,520,410	2,108,296	1,765,648	1,574,740	1,547,745	1,520,855	1,343,126
Total Current Liabilities	480,199	464,794	386,087	332,324	288,210	251,825	218,626	225,816
Net Stockholders' Equity	1,854,005	1,820,821	1,522,576	1,276,197	1,132,897	1,138,775	1,157,032	985,379
Net Working Capital	870,285	825,797	620,205	581,519	540,505	551,921	624,546	571,857
Shares Outstanding	224,535	224,860	225,056	224,950	232,442	228,992	232,220	231,938
Statistical Record								
Operating Profit Margin %	19.90	21.15	21.30	21.12	21.58	21.40	22.33	20.22
Net Profit Margin %	26.52	27.92	27.86	28.47	29.34	27.92	29.04	26.44
Return on Equity %	5.98	24.48	26.37	28.44	29.03	27.06	27.21	27.56
Return on Assets %	4.31	17.69	19.04	20.55	20.88	19.91	20.70	20.22
Price Range	59.63–55.23	58.11–51.18	58.35–44.52	52.92–43.34	47.91–30.31	50.00–33.66	51.66–36.56	40.81–27.63
P/E Ratio	29.23–27.07	29.35–25.85	32.78–25.01	32.87–26.92	33.04–20.91	37.59–25.31	39.43–27.91	34.88–23.61
Average Yield %	1.54	1.55	1.50	1.53	1.80	1.57	1.53	1.73

Address: 410 North Michigan Avenue, Chicago, IL 60611
Telephone: (312) 644–2121
Web Site: www.wrigley.com

Officers: William Wrigley – Chmn., Pres., C.E.O., Dushan Petrovich – Sr. V.P., Chief Admin. Officer
Transfer Agents: EquiServe Trust Company, N.A., Providence, RI

Investor Contact:800–874–0474
Institutional Holding
No of Institutions: 8
Shares: 9,414,934 **% Held:** –

Canadian Company Reports

AGF MANAGEMENT LTD

Exchange	Symbol	Price	52Wk Range	Yield	P/E
TSX	AGF B	C$18.70 (5/31/2004)	19.87-14.08	2.35	43.49

*7 Year Price Score 104.8 *NYSE Composite Index=100 *12 Month Price Score 49.6

TRADING VOLUME (thousand shares)

Interim Earnings (Per Share) Can$

Qtr.	Feb	May	Aug	Nov
2000–01	0.68	0.63	0.28	0.18
2001–02	0.37	0.40	0.34	0.19
2002–03	0.30	0.21	0.23	(0.27)
2003–04	0.26	...	...	...

Interim Dividends (Per Share) Can$

Amt	Decl	Ex	Rec	Pay
0.075Q	6/25/2003	7/4/2003	7/8/2003	7/18/2003
0.08Q	9/24/2003	10/2/2003	10/6/2003	10/16/2003
0.08Q	12/9/2003	12/17/2003	12/19/2003	1/7/2004
0.11Q	3/31/2004	4/8/2004	4/13/2004	4/23/2004
		Indicated Div: C$0.44		

Valuation Analysis

Forecast P/E 22.23 (5/24/2004)

Market Cap	$80.1 Million	Book Value	N/A
Price/Book	N/A	Price/Sales	N/A

Dividend Achiever Status

Rank	10	5 Year Growth Rate	17.81%
Total Years of Dividend Growth			7

Business Summary: Wealth Management (MIC: 8.8 SIC: 6282 NAIC:523930)

AGF Management is an investment management company with offices across Canada and subsidiaries around the world. Co. serves more than 1.0 million investors and manages about $30.00 billion in total assets. Co.'s products and services include a diversified family of more than 50 mutual funds, AGF Harmony tailored investment program, AGF Private Investment Management and AGF Trust GICs, loans and mortgages. In addition to offices across Canada, Co. has international operations in London, Dublin, Singapore, Tokyo and Beijing. Moreover, Co. has diversified revenue streams from complementary businesses including Unisen, Smith & Williamson and Investmaster Group.

Recent Developments: For the three months ended Feb 29 2004, net income declined 16.2% to C$23.8 million versus C$28.4 million in the equivalent quarter of 2003. Results reflect solid improvement in all areas of Co.'s businesses with strength in the core mutual fund business along with gains in complementary businesses, such as fund administration and trust company operations. Results for 2003 included a gain on the sale of an investment in an associated company of C$12.8 million and the write–down of short–term investments of C$643,000. Revenue was C$159.1 million, up 0.2% from C$158.7 million in the prior–year period. Provision for loan losses jumped 49.0% to C$1.1 million versus C$710,000 the year before.

Prospects: During the first quarter of fiscal 2004, Co. strengthened its high net–worth investment management operations with the acquisition of P.J. Doherty & Associates, an Ottawa–based investment counselling firm for individuals and institutions. This acquisition is strategically in line with Co.'s plans to build a high net–worth investment management presence in key markets across Canada. Meanwhile, Co. believes that it is positioned well to benefit from the growing trend toward international equity funds and enhancements to its Harmony program, an increasingly popular market segment.

Financial Data

(Can$ in Thousands)	9 Mos	6 Mos	3 Mos	11/30/2002	11/30/2001	11/30/2000	11/30/1999	11/30/1998
Earnings Per Share	0.93	1.04	1.23	1.30	1.77	1.07	0.76	0.59
Dividends Per Share	0.280	0.270	0.260	0.250	0.220	0.180	0.150	0.130
Dividend Payout %	30.10	25.96	21.13	19.61	12.42	16.82	19.73	21.84
Income Statement								
Total Revenues	446,926	299,528	158,711	654,103	639,994	508,681	356,703	288,822
Total Indirect Exp.	327,150	217,725	110,660	464,515	463,727	349,368	242,846	195,169
Depreciation & Amort.	116,014	76,606	38,688	147,181	165,645	92,224	70,276	52,717
Operating Income	96,583	66,214	40,265	164,765	151,153	147,839	103,034	82,866
Income Taxes	26,809	18,211	11,893	43,645	(14,867)	59,987	41,324	34,089
Eqty Earns/Minority Int.	...	...	...	(83)	(481)	(36)	...	...
Net Income	69,774	48,003	28,372	119,839	163,754	87,888	61,710	48,777
Average Shs. Outstg.	...	...	91,611	...	...	...	...	...
Balance Sheet								
Cash & Cash Equivalents	27,121	24,202	23,938	28,385	23,466	94,876	56,231	53,244
Total Current Assets	84,200	90,251	83,817	84,296	79,508	127,227	85,622	76,009
Total Assets	1,927,679	1,987,741	1,988,267	1,974,920	1,508,473	1,250,636	628,821	526,168
Total Current Liabilities	79,847	74,699	74,029	102,220	118,954	224,412	44,360	40,961
Long–Term Obligations	150,447	194,929	214,887	225,403	165,481	278,051	72,048	81,422
Net Stockholders' Equity	942,569	927,415	912,492	887,566	764,707	472,048	284,244	233,383
Net Working Capital	4,353	15,552	9,788	(17,924)	(39,446)	(97,185)	41,262	35,048
Shares Outstanding	92,572	92,284	91,611	91,100	89,338	83,046	78,044	77,070
Statistical Record								
Operating Profit Margin %	21.61	22.10	25.37	25.18	23.61	29.06	28.88	28.69
Return on Equity %	7.40	5.17	3.10	13.50	21.41	18.61	21.71	20.89
Return on Assets %	3.61	2.41	1.42	6.06	10.85	7.02	9.81	9.27
Debt/Total Assets %	7.80	9.80	10.80	11.41	10.97	22.23	11.45	15.47
Price Range	17.13–12.11	16.00–12.11	16.00–13.21	28.18–11.75	28.90–18.20	28.20–10.50	14.00–9.03	14.05–6.88
P/E Ratio	13.42–13.02	15.38–11.64	13.01–10.74	21.68–9.04	16.33–10.28	26.36–9.81	18.42–11.88	23.81–11.65
Average Yield %	1.92	1.94	1.76	1.23	0.88	0.95	1.31	1.23

Address: P.O. Box 50, Toronto, ON M5K 1E9 Telephone: (416) 367–1900 Web Site: www.agf.com	Officers: C. Warren Goldring – Chmn., W. Robert Farquharson – Vice–Chmn., Chief Investment. Off. Transfer Agents:Computershare Trust Company of Canada	Institutional Holding No of Institutions: Shares: 4,230,500 % Held: 4.70

ATCO LTD.

Exchange	Symbol	Price	52Wk Range	Yield	P/E
TSX	ACO X	C$48.00 (5/31/2004)	54.00-45.74	2.92	11.65

*7 Year Price Score 115.4 ***NYSE Composite Index=100** ***12 Month Price Score 45.6**

Interim Earnings (Per Share) Can$

Qtr.	Mar	Jun	Sep	Dec
2001	1.40	0.75	0.81	1.16
2002	2.57	0.72	0.87	1.23
2003	1.51	0.67	0.75	1.42
2004	1.28	...	...	...

Interim Dividends (Per Share) Can$

Amt	Decl	Ex	Rec	Pay
0.32Q	7/24/2003	9/11/2003	9/15/2003	9/30/2003
0.32Q	10/21/2003	12/10/2003	12/12/2003	12/31/2003
0.35Q	2/26/2004	3/15/2004	3/17/2004	3/31/2004
0.35Q	5/19/2004	6/14/2004	6/16/2004	6/30/2004
		Indicated Div: $1.40		

Valuation Analysis

Forecast P/E 10.41 (5/24/2004)

Market Cap	$1.3 Billion	Book Value	N/A
Price/Book	N/A	Price/Sales	N/A

Dividend Achiever Status

	16	5 Year Growth Rate	13.49%
Total Years of Dividend Growth		10	

Business Summary: Electricity (MIC: 7.1 SIC: 4911 NAIC:221122)

Atco is a management holding company. Through subsidiaries, Co. operates the following groups: The Power Generation segment includes the supply of electricity. The Logistics & Energy unit includes transportation and supply of natural gas. The Utilities unit includes natural gas, electricity and water services and engineering, procurement and construction services. The Industrial group includes the manufacture and sale of transportable workforce shelters and space rentals products. The Technologies group includes information systems and services, sale of fuel byproducts and manufacture of wood preservation products.

Recent Developments: For the three months ended Mar 31 2004, net earnings declined 16.2% to C$38.2 million compared with C$45.6 million in the corresponding quarter of 2003. Earnings were hampered by a decrease in earnings of 70.0% or C$4.8 million at ATCO Power and ATCO Resources due to lower prices on electricity sold to the Alberta Electric System Operator (AESO) and the related spark spread. Revenues decreased 12.2% to C$1.24 billion from C$1.42 billion in the prior-year period. The decrease in revenues was due to lower prices received for electricity sold to the AESO by ATCO Power and ATCO Resources, lower prices of natural gas purchased for ATCO Midstream's customers and warmer temperatures in ATCO Gas.

Prospects: On Apr 26 2004, Co. reached an agreement to sell its retail energy supply businesses, ATCO Gas and ATCO Electric, to Direct Energy Marketing, a subsidiary of Centrica Plc, a British energy distributor, for C$90.0 million. ATCO Gas and ATCO Electric supply more than one million Alberta, Canada customers with regulated natural gas and electricity. Co. put its retail energy supply business up for sale in 2001, but it has taken a while to close the deal due to taxation policies in Alberta's deregulated utility sector. The deal is expected to close in the near term and C$45.0 million will be payable at closing. The remaining C$45.0 million will be paid after a year.

Financial Data

(Can$ in Thousands)	12/31/2003	12/31/2002	12/31/2001	12/31/2000	12/31/1999	12/31/1998	12/31/1997	12/31/1996
Earnings Per Share	4.35	5.39	4.12	3.75	3.32	2.96	2.68	2.41
Cash Flow Per Share	17.08	12.22	...	...	...	...	...	...
Dividends Per Share	1.250	1.130	1.010	0.890	0.770	0.650	0.530	0.410
Dividend Payout %	28.73	20.96	24.51	23.73	23.19	21.96	19.78	17.01
Income Statement								
Total Revenues	3,929,700	3,196,300	3,754,300	3,076,000	2,374,800	2,071,400	2,045,100	1,937,300
Total Indirect Exp.	3,309,300	2,610,500	3,165,400	2,480,700	1,828,800	1,552,500	1,550,100	1,434,500
Costs & Expenses	3,508,200	2,799,700	3,368,500	2,680,600	2,014,200	1,728,000	1,719,800	1,619,000
Depreciation & Amort.	284,700	257,100	257,500	253,500	241,000	211,000	202,800	195,100
Operating Income	421,500	396,600	385,800	395,400	360,600	343,400	325,300	318,300
Income Taxes	159,800	196,700	174,800	193,100	180,800	187,300	173,200	175,900
Eqty Earns/Minority Int.	158,000	165,000	131,000	126,100	111,200	102,000	100,300	91,800
Income from Cont Ops	...	...	...	...	...	...	...	73,300
Net Income	131,200	163,000	124,400	112,700	100,700	88,900	81,200	80,100
Average Shs. Outstg.	30,172	30,257	29,731	29,723	29,931	30,044	30,261	30,468
Balance Sheet								
Net Property	5,128,400	4,949,200	4,590,800	4,168,200	3,976,600	3,898,400	3,639,400	3,509,100
Total Assets	6,591,200	6,403,300	5,833,700	5,815,600	4,934,900	4,793,700	4,405,100	4,241,600
Long-Term Obligations	2,789,800	2,892,400	2,658,000	2,468,800	2,226,900	2,106,000	1,844,700	1,793,000
Net Stockholders' Equity	1,133,600	1,044,800	911,600	822,300	744,200	681,400	613,000	567,700
Shares Outstanding	29,796	29,816	29,733	29,722	29,791	30,048	30,026	30,475
Statistical Record								
Operating Profit Margin %	10.72	12.40	10.27	12.85	15.18	16.57	15.90	16.43
Return on Equity %	11.57	15.60	13.64	13.70	13.53	13.04	13.24	14.10
Accum. Depr./Gross Prop. %	33.84	33.20	33.13	33.84	33.08	31.83	31.49	30.20
Price Range	49.75-41.15	54.95-41.00	53.00-42.25	47.75-28.40	43.75-32.70	39.00-30.25	34.00-23.60	24.00-17.75
P/E Ratio	11.44-9.46	10.19-7.61	12.86-10.25	12.73-7.57	13.18-9.85	13.18-10.22	12.69-8.81	9.96-7.37
Average Yield %	2.73	2.32	2.13	2.55	1.94	1.85	1.87	2.05

Address: 1400,909 11th Avenue SW, Calgary, AB T2R 1N6	Officers: Ronald D. Southern - Chmn., Nancy C. Southern - Pres., C.E.O.	Investor Contact:800-387-0825
Telephone: (403) 292 7500	Transfer Agents:CIBC Mellon Trust Company, Montreal, Quebec; Toronto, Ontario; Calgary, Alberta; Vancouver, British Columbia	Institutional Holding
Web Site: www.atco.com		No of Institutions: 1
		Shares: 40,100 % Held: -

BANK OF MONTREAL

Exchange	Symbol	Price	52Wk Range	Yield	P/E
NYS	BMO	$53.74 (5/31/2004)	58.77-40.35	2.98	14.56

*7 Year Price Score 136.5 *NYSE Composite Index=100 ***12 Month Price Score 48.7**

Interim Earnings (Per Share) Can$

Qtr.	Jan	Apr	Jul	Oct
2000–01	1.45	1.10	0.83	(0.72)
2001–02	0.71	0.57	0.65	0.75
2002–03	0.75	0.77	0.95	0.97
2003–04	1.00	...	...	...

Interim Dividends (Per Share) Can$

Amt	Decl	Ex	Rec	Pay
0.35Q	8/26/2003	11/7/2003	11/12/2003	11/27/2003
0.35Q	11/25/2003	2/4/2004	2/6/2004	2/26/2004
0.40Q	2/24/2004	5/5/2004	5/7/2004	5/28/2004
0.40Q	5/26/2004	8/4/2004	8/6/2004	8/30/2004

Indicated Div: C$1.60 (Div. Reinv. Plan)

Valuation Analysis

Forecast P/E 12.80 (5/24/2004)

Market Cap	$0.00	Book Value	182.6 Billion
Price/Book	N/A	Price/Sales	N/A

Dividend Achiever Status

Rank	24	5 Year Growth Rate	8.77%
Total Years of Dividend Growth			11

Business Summary: Commercial Banking (MIC: 8.1 SIC: 6029 NAIC:522110)

Bank of Montreal offers a broad range of credit and non–credit products and services to individuals, industry, financial institutions and governments directly and through special–purpose domestic and foreign subsidiaries. Co. operates 970 bank branches in Canada; and operates internationally in 10 other countries. Through the Harris Bank group, Co., operates its own banking business in the U.S. and provides retail banking, private client, personal trust services, corporate and investment banking. Co. also provides a full range of investment dealer services through the BMO Nesbitt Burns group of companies. As of Oct 31 2003, Co.'s total assets amounted to approx. C$265.50 billion.

Recent Developments: For the three months ended Jan 31 2004, net income rose 33.3% to C$532.0 million compared with C$399.0 million in the equivalent quarter of 2003. Net income benefited from better credit performance and Co.'s continued focus on improving productivity. Results included an investment securities gain of C$40.0 million in 2004 and a loss of C$16.0 million in 2003. Net interest income increased 2.0% to C$1.26 billion from C$1.23 billion the year before. Provision for credit losses plunged 90.0% to C$15.0 million versus C$150.0 million a year earlier. Non–interest income grew 10.3% to C$2.35 billion, while non–interest expense slipped 0.8% to C$1.56 billion.

Prospects: On Apr 29 2004, Co. signed an agreement to increase its stake in Fullgoal Fund Management of China to approximately 28.0% from 17.0%. The agreement is with two of the largest shareholders, Haitong Securities and Shenyin & Wanguo Securities, which also increased their stakes by equal amounts. The increase in investment is strategically in line with Co.'s outlook for potential growth in China's asset management marketplace. Co. projects there will be $200.00 billion to $300.00 billion in assets available for management in China within five to ten years. Separately, Co. plans to continue to build on its success in North America by looking for retail banking acquisitions in the midwest.

Financial Data

(Can$ in Millions)	3 Mos	10/31/2003	10/31/2002	10/31/2001	10/31/2000	10/31/1999	10/31/1998	10/31/1997
Earnings Per Share	3.69	3.44	2.68	2.66	3.28	2.36	2.33	2.31
Dividends Per Share	1.340	1.290	1.180	1.090	0.980	0.920	0.880	0.800
Dividend Payout %	36.31	37.50	44.02	40.97	30.03	39.19	37.76	34.63
Income Statement								
Total Interest Income	2,212	8,927	9,135	13,000	14,303	13,174	14,121	11,534
Total Interest Expense	955	4,028	4,306	8,501	10,099	8,895	10,097	7,457
Net Interest Income	1,257	4,899	4,829	4,499	4,204	4,279	4,024	4,077
Provision for Loan Losses	15	455	820	980	358	320	130	225
Non–Interest Expense	1,561	6,542	6,850	6,651	5,659	5,467	4,963	4,888
Income Before Taxes	787	2,577	1,903	2,070	2,914	2,182	2,179	2,170
Eqty Earns/Minority Int.	15	64	62	42	19	21	25	25
Net Income	532	1,825	1,417	1,471	1,857	1,382	1,350	1,305
Average Shs. Outstg.	515	507	499	523	542	545	538	537
Balance Sheet								
Total Assets	265,394	256,494	252,864	239,409	233,396	230,615	222,590	207,838
Total Deposits	178,069	171,551	161,838	154,290	156,697	156,874	143,983	144,212
Long–Term Obligations	2,460	2,856	3,794	4,674	4,911	4,712	4,791	3,831
Total Liabilities	252,458	244,012	240,970	228,727	221,455	219,634	211,982	198,935
Net Stockholders' Equity	12,936	12,482	11,894	10,682	11,941	10,981	10,608	8,903
Shares Outstanding	502	499	492	489	522	534	528	522
Statistical Record								
Return on Equity %	4.11	14.62	11.91	13.77	15.55	12.58	12.72	14.65
Return on Assets %	0.20	0.71	0.56	0.61	0.79	0.59	0.60	0.62
Equity/Assets %	4.87	4.86	4.70	4.46	5.11	4.76	4.76	4.28
Non–Int. Exp./Tot. Inc. %	47.05	73.28	74.98	51.16	39.56	41.49	35.14	42.37
Price Range	58.77–49.33	50.06–38.10	40.30–32.10	44.23–32.80	35.75–21.50	34.65–24.88	43.05–26.35	30.63–19.90
P/E Ratio	15.93–13.37	14.55–11.08	15.04–11.98	16.63–12.33	10.90–6.55	14.68–10.54	18.48–11.31	13.26–8.61
Average Yield %	2.49	3.03	3.24	2.81	3.48	3.12	2.50	3.12

Address: 129 St. Jaques Street, Montreal, QC H2Y 1L6 **Telephone:** (514) 877 7110 **Web Site:** www.bmo.com	**Officers:** F. Anthony Comper – Chmn., C.E.O., William A. Downe – Deputy Chair, C.E.O. of BMO Nesbitt Burns, Head Investment Banking Group **Transfer Agents:** Computershare Trust Company of Canada, Halifax, Montreal, Toronto, Winnipeg, Calgary and Vancouver	**Investor Contact:** 416 867 6785 **Institutional Holding** **No of Institutions:** 64 **Shares:** 198,759,440 **% Held:** 40.50%

BANK OF NOVA SCOTIA (TORONTO, CANADA)

Exchange	Symbol	Price	52Wk Range	Yield	P/E
TSX	BNS	C$34.20 (5/31/2004)	37.15-29.50	3.51	13.90

*7 Year Price Score 149.0 *NYSE Composite Index=100 *12 Month Price Score 49.6

Interim Earnings (Per Share) Can$

Qtr.	Jan	Apr	Jul	Oct
2000-01	0.48	0.50	0.52	0.52
2001-02	0.02	0.55	0.52	0.56
2002-03	0.55	0.56	0.60	0.63
2003-04	0.67			

Interim Dividends (Per Share) Can$

Amt	Decl	Ex	Rec	Pay
0.25Q	12/2/2003	1/2/2004	1/6/2004	1/28/2004
0.25Q	3/1/2004	4/2/2004	4/6/2004	4/28/2004
100%	3/2/2004	4/29/2004	4/6/2004	4/28/2004
0.30Q	6/1/2004	7/1/2004	7/6/2004	7/28/2004

Indicated Div: C$1.00 (Div. Reinv. Plan)

Valuation Analysis

Forecast P/E 12.24 (5/24/2004)

Market Cap $16.8 Billion	Book Value	N/A
Price/Book N/A	Price/Sales	N/A

Dividend Achiever Status

Rank	13	5 Year Growth Rate	16.00%
Total Years of Dividend Growth			12

Business Summary: Commercial Banking (MIC: 8.1 SIC: 6021 NAIC:522110)

Bank of Nova Scotia is a diversified financial services institution, that provides retail, commercial, corporate, investment and international banking services to individuals, small and medium-size businesses, corporations and governments across Canada and around the world. Operations are organized into three main operating segments, including domestic banking, international banking and Scotia Capital. As of Oct 31 2003, Co.'s total assets, assets under management and deposits amounted to C$285.89 billion, C$19.96 billion and C$192.67 billion, respectively. As of Oct 31 2003, Co. maintained a banking network of 1,850 branches and offices, and 3,918 automated teller machines.

Recent Developments: For the quarter ended Jan 31 2004, net income advanced 18.3% to C$704.0 million from C$595.0 million in the corresponding period the year before. Net interest income slipped 4.1% to C$1.48 billion from C$1.54 billion a year earlier. Provision for credit losses dropped 47.7% to C$170.0 million from C$325.0 million the prior year. Total non-interest income rose 0.6% to C$1.04 billion, reflecting stronger gains on the sale of investment securities and a substantial improvement in retail brokerage revenues from higher customer volumes, partially offset by lower securitization revenues. Total non-interest expense grew 3.8% to C$1.41 billion, primarily due to increases in salaries and benefits.

Prospects: Despite the improving economic conditions in many of its markets, Co. remains challenged by margin pressure, the rapid appreciation of the Canadian dollar, and asset growth in business lending. However, Co. is optimistic that its overall strategies will enable it to achieve its performance targets for fiscal 2004. These include building relationships, growing capital and building Co.'s core strengths. Looking ahead, Co. is optimistic about reduced credit losses in 2004. Co. fully intends to keep its capital base strong, which should provide greater flexibility once business opportunities arise.

Financial Data

(Can$ in Millions)	10/31/2003	10/31/2002	10/31/2001	10/31/2000	10/31/1999	10/31/1998	10/31/1997	10/31/1996
Earnings Per Share	2.34	1.65	2.02	1.81	1.46	1.32	1.47	1.02
Dividends Per Share	0.840	0.720	0.620	0.500	0.430	0.400	0.370	0.320
Dividend Payout %	35.82	43.93	30.61	27.62	29.45	30.30	25.17	31.37
Income Statement								
Total Interest Income	13,246	14,368	16,983	15,331	13,471	13,091	10,488	10,622
Total Interest Expense	7,096	7,693	10,783	10,132	8,799	8,714	6,771	7,040
Net Interest Income	6,150	6,675	6,200	5,199	4,672	4,377	3,717	3,582
Non-Interest Expense	5,700	5,737	5,662	5,119	4,756	4,446	4,059	3,217
Income Before Taxes	3,541	2,614	3,184	2,980	2,464	2,194	2,306	1,765
Eqty Earns/Minority Int.	280	216	139	64	46	38	34	31
Net Income	2,477	1,797	2,169	1,926	1,551	1,394	1,514	1,069
Average Shs. Outstg.	1,025	1,025	1,017	1,041	986	981	956	937
Balance Sheet								
Total Assets	285,892	296,380	284,425	253,171	222,691	233,588	195,153	157,261
Total Deposits	192,672	195,618	186,195	173,900	156,618	166,360	138,975	117,894
Long-Term Obligations	2,661	3,878	5,344	5,370	5,374	5,482	5,167	3,251
Total Liabilities	271,278	281,603	269,817	240,196	211,285	222,774	185,755	149,512
Net Stockholders' Equity	14,614	14,777	14,608	12,975	11,406	10,814	9,398	7,749
Shares Outstanding	1,010	1,008	995	995	988	984	980	949
Statistical Record								
Return on Equity %	16.94	12.16	14.84	14.84	13.59	12.89	16.10	13.79
Return on Assets %	0.86	0.60	0.76	0.76	0.69	0.59	0.77	0.67
Equity/Assets %	5.11	4.98	5.13	5.12	5.12	4.62	4.81	4.92
Non-Int. Exp./Tot. Inc. %	43.03	39.92	33.33	33.38	35.30	33.96	38.70	30.28
Price Range	33.36-22.75	27.88-21.27	24.95-19.00	22.60-13.08	18.30-14.35	21.53-11.55	16.99-10.45	10.56-7.19
P/E Ratio	14.26-9.72	16.89-12.89	12.35-9.41	12.49-7.22	12.53-9.83	16.31-8.75	11.56-7.11	10.36-7.05
Average Yield %	2.98	2.91	2.84	2.92	2.63	2.38	2.67	3.92

Address: Scotia Plaza, Toronto, ON M5H 1H1 Telephone: (416) 866 6161 Web Site: www.scotiabank.com	Officers: Richard E. Waugh – Pres., C.E.O., Peter C. Godsoe – Chmn. Transfer Agents:Computershare Trust Company of Canada, Toronto, Ontario; Co-Transfer Agents: Computershare Investor Services PLC, Bristol, United Kingdom; Computershare Trust Company Inc., Colorado, United States	Institutional Holding No of Institutions: 39 Shares: 82,222,442 % Held: –

BMTC GROUP INC.

Exchange	Symbol	Price	52Wk Range	Yield	P/E
TSX	GBT A	C$10.89 (5/31/2004)	13.25-7.89	0.92	12.52

*7 Year Price Score 241.0 *NYSE Composite Index=100 *12 Month Price Score 46.2

Interim Earnings (Per Share) Can$

Qtr.	Mar	Jun	Sep	Dec
2002	0.07	0.29	0.53	(0.09)
2003	0.10	0.44	0.53	(0.16)
2004	0.06	...	...	...

Interim Dividends (Per Share) Can$

Amt	Decl	Ex	Rec	Pay
0.035S	11/22/2002	12/11/2002	12/15/2002	1/3/2003
0.035S	8/20/2003	8/27/2003	8/29/2003	9/4/2003
2-For-1	...	12/9/2003	12/11/2003	12/12/2003
0.05S	...	12/18/2003	12/22/2003	1/5/2004

Indicated Div: C$0.10

Valuation Analysis

Forecast P/E N/A

Market Cap	$242.0 Million	Book Value	N/A
Price/Book	N/A	Price/Sales	N/A

Dividend Achiever Status

Rank	1	5 Year Growth Rate	26.19%
Total Years of Dividend Growth		12	

Business Summary: 001 (MIC: 001 SIC: 5712 NAIC:442110)

BMTC Group is a holding company. Through its subsidiaries, Brault et Martineau Inc. and Ameublements Tanguay, Inc., Co. manages and operates a retail sales network of furniture and household and electronic appliances in Quebec. As of Dec 31 2003, Co.'s network was comprised of twenty stores in Montreal, Quebec City, Laval, Ste–Therese, Ste–Foy, St–Georges, Three Rivers, Sherbrooke, Chicoutimi, Riviere–du–Loup, Rimouski and Gatineau and their surrounding regions. Co.'s network also includes two distribution and administrative centers in Montreal and Quebec City.

Recent Developments: For the three months ended Mar 31 2004, net income declined 4.9% to C$2.3 million compared with C$2.4 million in the corresponding quarter of 2003. Revenues rose 7.0% to C$167.0 million from C$156.1 million the year before. Results from the costs of options had the effect of increasing earnings per share by C$0.03 during the quarter versus a charge of C$0.02 per share in the equivalent quarter of 2003. Income before income taxes climbed to $3.2 million versus $3.2 million in the prior–year period. Earnings per share were C$0.06 compared with C$0.05 in the same period of 2003.

Prospects: Co. announced that its subsidiary, Brault & Martineau, has concluded an agreement with the employees of its distribution center. This settles the labor dispute that started on April 16, 2004. All normal activities of the Montreal distribution center resumed on May 4 2004. Separately, Co. announced its intention to renew its programs to acquire Class A subordinate voting shares in the normal course for the period between June 4 2004 and June 3 2005, at the latest, subject to regulatory approvals. As of May 13 2004, there were 21,473,840 Class A subordinate voting shares and 15,397,060 Class B multiple voting shares issued and outstanding.

Financial Data
(Can$ in Thousands)

	12/31/2003	12/31/2002	12/31/2001
Earnings Per Share	0.91	0.80	0.44
Cash Flow Per Share	2.96	0.73	0.66
Tang. Book Val. Per Share	2.97	3.01	2.48
Dividends Per Share	0.070	0.058	0.050
Dividend Payout %	7.69	7.14	11.36
Income Statement			
Total Revenues	802,870	807,937	642,532
Total Indirect Exp.	746,309	749,462	607,097
Depreciation & Amort.	3,875	3,927	3,389
Operating Income	55,220	57,326	34,193
Income Taxes	18,229	18,884	12,472
Net Income	36,991	38,442	21,721
Average Shs. Outstg.	40,458	47,758	49,416
Balance Sheet			
Cash & Cash Equivalents	57,487	7,875	2,815
Total Current Assets	137,142	145,329	95,008
Total Assets	264,776	260,563	206,289
Total Current Liabilities	150,584	125,490	87,020
Net Stockholders' Equity	113,233	133,808	117,599
Net Working Capital	(13,442)	19,839	7,988
Shares Outstanding	38,000	44,400	47,339
Statistical Record			
Operating Profit Margin %	6.87	7.09	5.32
Return on Equity %	32.66	28.72	18.47
Return on Assets %	13.97	14.75	10.52
Price Range	13.25-6.88	7.75-4.13	4.50-2.00
P/E Ratio	14.56-7.55	9.69-5.16	10.23-4.55
Average Yield %	0.74	0.81	1.71

Address: 8500 Place Marien, Montreal, QC H1B 5W8	**Officers:** Yves Des Groseillers – Pres., C.E.O., Yves Des Groseillers – Chmn.	**Institutional Holding**
Telephone: (514) 648 5757	**Transfer Agents:** National Bank Trust, Inc.	**No of Institutions:** 1
Web Site: www.braultetmartincau.com		**Shares:** 116,721 **% Held:**

BUHLER INDUSTRIES, INC.

Exchange	Symbol	Price	52Wk Range	Yield	P/E
TSX	BUI	C$6.50 (5/28/2004)	7.25-5.48	2.00	12.50

*7 Year Price Score 148.5 *NYSE Composite Index=100 *12 Month Price Score 54.7

TRADING VOLUME (thousand shares)

Interim Earnings (Per Share) Can$

Qtr.	Dec	Mar	Jun	Sep
2000–01	0.11	0.05	0.09	0.05
2001–02	0.13	0.16	0.22	0.07
2002–03	0.09	0.15	0.16	0.11
2003–04	0.09	0.16	...	...

Interim Dividends (Per Share) Can$

Amt	Decl	Ex	Rec	Pay
0.10A	12/15/2000	12/27/2000	12/29/2000	1/29/2001
0.11A	12/3/2001	12/18/2001	12/20/2001	1/28/2002
0.12A	11/29/2002	12/24/2002	12/30/2002	1/29/2003
0.13A	11/10/2003	12/3/2003	12/5/2003	1/14/2004

Indicated Div: C$0.13

Valuation Analysis

Forecast P/E 12.62 (5/24/2004)

Market Cap	N/A	Book Value	N/A
Price/Book	N/A	Price/Sales	N/A

Dividend Achiever Status

Rank	21	5 Year Growth Rate	11.38%
Total Years of Dividend Growth		7	

Business Summary: Machinery Supply Retail (MIC: 12.9 SIC: 5083 NAIC:423820)

Buhler Industries is engaged in the design, manufacturing and distributing of a wide range of agricultural equipment marketed throughout North America under five primary brand names: *Buhler®, Allied®, Farm King®, Inland®* and *Buhler Versatile®*. Co.'s products include augers, belt conveyors, box scrapers, cultivators, discs, drag harrows, front–end loaders, grain cleaners, hammermills, hay rakes, landscape rakes, mounted following harrows, mowers, rear blades, rollermills, rotary tillers, round bale carrier, round baler, snowblowers, square bale carrier, swath rollers, tractors, and wheel loaders.

Recent Developments: For the quarter ended Mar 31 2004, net income increased 17.4% to C$3.9 million compared with C$3.3 million in the corresponding quarter of the previous year. Revenues totaled C$62.6 million, up 28.3% compared with C$48.8 million a year earlier. Tractor sales accounted for the majority of the sales increase; however, Co.'s core products also experienced increases. Gross profit was C$12.0 million, or 19.2% of revenues versus C$11.4 million, or 23.3% of revenues, the year before. Gross margin decreased as a result of the weak U.S. dollar and recent increases in the cost of steel. Operating income slid 0.2% to C$7.3 million. Cash flow grew 12.0% to C$5.6 million.

Prospects: While the farm economy appears to be firming, Co. remains cautious in forecasting future increases in earnings due to reduced gross margins. Steel prices have increased significantly in the past few months and this will continue to have an impact on gross profit. Accordingly, Co. is forecasting fiscal 2004 earnings in the range of $0.50 to 0.52 per share. Meanwhile, Co.'s tractors are continuing to increase in exposure and accessibility as Co. adds more dealers in North America. In addition, Co.'s core products are showing slow and steady increases in sales in spite of the impact of the Mad Cow Disease and the remaining weak U.S. dollar.

Financial Data

(Can$ in Thousands)	3 Mos	09/30/2003	09/30/2002	09/30/2001	09/30/2000	09/30/1999	09/30/1998	09/30/1997
Earnings Per Share	0.51	0.51	0.58	0.30	0.30	0.23	0.28	0.24
Dividends Per Share	0.120	0.120	0.110	0.100	0.090	0.080	0.070	0.060
Dividend Payout %	23.53	23.52	18.96	33.33	30.00	34.78	25.00	25.00
Income Statement								
Total Revenues	42,303	181,162	232,619	187,633	116,700	79,961	89,194	85,375
Total Indirect Exp.	3,598	26,712	29,947	24,462	20,076	16,967	17,183	16,201
Depreciation & Amort.	1,669	6,894	7,339	7,684	5,520	5,126	4,808	4,809
Operating Income	4,993	14,521	19,538	6,948	10,226	9,240	12,060	10,859
Net Interest Inc./(Exp.)	146	703	369	1,032	671	434	458	457
Income Taxes	541	2,647	5,134	(1,313)	2,393	3,131	5,216	4,271
Eqty Earns/Minority Int.	...	267	809	847	903	224	...	...
Net Income	2,093	11,630	13,360	7,115	7,298	5,797	7,113	6,131
Average Shs. Outstg.	...	...	...	...	24,225	24,459	24,968	25,519
Balance Sheet								
Total Current Assets	135,123	132,272	110,455	87,456	99,635	34,403	32,010	28,938
Total Assets	179,918	178,281	156,305	127,531	148,973	74,843	61,139	60,716
Total Current Liabilities	53,889	49,742	49,860	42,239	54,038	14,195	13,004	16,131
Long–Term Obligations	40,530	40,577	42,690	31,850	35,200	1,704	2,770	6,514
Net Stockholders' Equity	69,971	70,868	61,998	53,442	51,659	47,327	44,790	37,497
Net Working Capital	81,234	82,530	60,595	45,217	45,597	20,208	19,006	12,807
Shares Outstanding	23,000	23,000	23,000	23,483	24,225	24,459	24,968	24,121
Statistical Record								
Operating Profit Margin %	11.80	8.01	8.39	3.70	8.76	11.55	13.52	12.71
Return on Equity %	2.99	16.41	21.54	13.31	14.12	12.24	15.88	16.35
Return on Assets %	1.16	6.52	8.54	5.57	4.89	7.74	11.63	10.09
Debt/Total Assets %	22.52	22.76	27.31	24.97	23.62	2.27	4.53	10.72
Price Range	5.94-5.52	5.92-5.20	5.50-3.48	3.60-3.00	3.70-2.65	3.24-2.35	4.10-2.39	2.50-1.70
P/E Ratio	11.65-10.82	11.61-10.20	9.48-6.00	12.00-10.00	12.33-8.83	14.09-10.22	14.64-8.54	10.42-7.08
Average Yield %	2.09	2.16	2.47	2.91	2.94	2.90	1.99	2.83

Address: 1201 Regent Avenue West, Winnipeg, MB R2C 3B2 Telephone: (204) 661–8711 Web Site: www.buhler.com	Officers: John Buhler – Chmn., C.E.O., Craig P. Engel – Pres., C.O.O. Transfer Agents:Computershare Trust Company of Canada, Winnipeg, Manitoba	Institutional Holding No of Institutions: N/A Shares: N/A % Held: N/A

CANADIAN NATIONAL RAILWAY CO.

Exchange	Symbol	Price	52Wk Range	Yield	P/E
TSX	CNR	C$54.00 (5/31/2004)	55.40–42.80	1.44	22.50

*7 Year Price Score 136.5 *NYSE Composite Index=100 *12 Month Price Score 48.7

Interim Earnings (Per Share) Can$

Qtr.	Mar	Jun	Sep	Dec
2001	0.92	0.12	0.84	0.53
2002	0.76	0.69	0.88	(0.45)
2003	0.85	0.60	0.72	0.35
2000	0.73	...	...	...

Interim Dividends (Per Share) Can$

Amt	Decl	Ex	Rec	Pay
0.167Q	10/21/2003	12/4/2003	12/8/2003	12/29/2003
50%	1/28/2004	3/1/2004	2/23/2004	2/27/2004
0.195Q	1/28/2004	3/4/2004	3/8/2004	3/29/2004
0.195Q	4/22/2004	6/7/2004	6/9/2004	6/30/2004

Indicated Div: C$0.78

Valuation Analysis
Forecast P/E 13.53 (5/24/2004)

Market Cap	$10.8 Billion	Book Value	N/A
Price/Book	N/A	Price/Sales	N/A

Dividend Achiever Status

Rank	15	5 Year Growth Rate	13.54%
Total Years of Dividend Growth			7

Business Summary: Rail Transport (MIC: 15.5 SIC: 4011 NAIC:482111)

Canadian National Railway is engaged in the rail transportation business. Co. spans Canada and mid–America, from the Atlantic and Pacific oceans to the Gulf of Mexico, serving the ports of Vancouver, Prince Rupert, B.C., Montreal, Halifax, New Orleans and Mobile, Alabama, and the cities of Toronto, Buffalo, Chicago, Detroit, Duluth, Minnesota/Superior, Wisconsin, Green Bay, Wisconsin, Minneapolis/St. Paul, Memphis, St. Louis and Jackson, Mississippi, with connections to all points in North America. Co.'s movement of goods includes petroleum and chemicals, grain and fertilizers, coal, metals and minerals, forest products, intermodal and automotive.

Recent Developments: For the quarter ended Mar 31 2004, net income grew 2.9% to C$210.0 million compared with income of C$204.0 million, before an accounting change benefit of C$48.0 million, in the equivalent 2002 quarter. The improvement in earnings was primarily attributed to higher freight volumes and lower operating expenses, partially offset by the appreciation of the Canadian dollar relative to the U.S. dollar and lost intermodal revenue caused by the month long Canadian Auto Workers strike. Revenues fell 3.9% to C$1.44 billion. Operating income advanced 5.6% to C$395.0 million. Free cash flow of C$272.0 million, was up 50.3% from C$181.0 million for the same three–month period of 2003.

Prospects: On May 10 2004, Co. completed its acquisition of the rail and marine holdings of Great Lakes Transportation LLC for a purchase price of US$380.0 million. Co. will now integrate the two railroads and a rail switching company into its 17,500–mile North American system. As part of the transaction, Co. has also acquired Great Lakes Fleet, Inc., a non–railroad company with eight Great Lakes vessels transporting bulk commodities, principally for the U.S. steel industry. Meanwhile, for 2004 and the foreseeable future, Co. expects cash flow from operations and from its various sources of financing to meet its debt repayments and future obligations, and to fund anticipated capital expenditures.

Financial Data

(Can$ in Thousands)	12/31/2003	12/31/2002	12/31/2001	12/31/2000	12/31/1999	12/31/1998	12/31/1997	12/31/1996
Earnings Per Share	2.52	1.88	2.41	2.54	2.01	1.61	1.65	0.48
Cash Flow Per Share	5.15	3.85	4.08	3.70	...	4.51	2.59	2.17
Dividends Per Share	0.660	0.570	0.520	0.460	0.400	0.350	0.300	0.260
Dividend Payout %	26.38	30.49	21.54	18.37	19.90	21.90	18.18	54.17
Income Statement								
Total Revenues	5,884,000	6,110,000	5,652,000	5,446,000	5,261,000	4,121,000	4,352,000	4,159,000
Total Indirect Exp.	4,516,000	4,994,000	4,286,000	4,061,000	4,028,000	3,637,000	3,442,000	3,845,000
Depreciation & Amort.	472,000	499,000	463,000	412,000	400,000	316,000	200,000	194,000
Operating Income	1,368,000	1,116,000	1,366,000	1,385,000	1,233,000	418,000	807,000	229,000
Income Taxes	338,000	268,000	392,000	442,000	369,000	74,000	325,000	11,000
Income from Cont Ops	...	...	...	...	...	224,000	421,000	124,000
Net Income	734,000	571,000	727,000	772,000	602,000	266,000	403,000	142,000
Average Shs. Outstg.	290,700	304,200	301,500	304,200	295,950	274,500	255,300	254,700
Balance Sheet								
Cash & Cash Equivalents	130,000	25,000	53,000	19,000	307,000	262,000	365,000	106,000
Total Current Assets	1,092,000	1,163,000	1,164,000	1,125,000	1,527,000	1,038,000	1,549,000	1,161,000
Total Assets	17,150,000	18,924,000	18,788,000	15,196,000	14,757,000	11,952,000	7,075,000	6,236,000
Total Current Liabilities	1,922,000	2,134,000	1,638,000	1,903,000	1,777,000	1,380,000	1,205,000	1,337,000
Long–Term Obligations	4,175,000	5,003,000	5,764,000	3,887,000	3,961,000	3,995,000	1,640,000	1,499,000
Net Stockholders' Equity	6,480,000	6,627,000	6,361,000	5,698,000	5,506,000	5,045,000	3,417,000	2,380,000
Shares Outstanding	284,100	296,250	289,050	285,900	303,600	287,700	256,374	254,835
Statistical Record								
Operating Profit Margin %	23.24	18.26	24.16	25.43	23.43	10.14	18.54	5.50
Return on Equity %	11.32	8.61	11.42	13.54	10.93	5.27	11.79	5.96
Return on Assets %	4.27	3.01	3.86	5.08	4.07	2.22	5.69	2.27
Debt/Total Assets %	24.34	26.43	30.67	25.57	26.84	33.42	23.18	24.03
Price Range	54.99–39.69	56.07–38.61	52.21–28.67	32.97–22.43	46.33–23.07	31.78–21.37	26.28–15.82	18.42–15.92
P/E Ratio	21.82–15.75	29.82–20.54	21.66–11.89	12.98–8.83	18.08–11.48	19.74–13.27	15.93–9.59	38.37–33.16
Average Yield %	1.42	1.18	1.26	1.64	1.35	1.30	1.45	1.50

Address: 935 de La Gauchetiere Street West, Montreal, QC H3B 2M9	Officers: David G.A. McLean – Chmn., E. Hunter Harrison – Pres. &, C.E.O.	Investor Contact:514 399 0052
Telephone: (514) 399 4821	Transfer Agents:Computershare Trust Company of Canada, Montreal, QC; Toronto, ON; Calgary, AB; Vancouver, BC; Computershare Trust Company of New York, New York, NY	Institutional Holding
Web Site: www.cn.ca		No of Institutions: 181
		Shares: 110,888,621 % Held: 57.10%

CANADIAN UTILITIES LTD.

Exchange	Symbol	Price	52Wk Range	Yield	P/E
TSX	CU	C$54.25 (5/31/2004)	64.00–53.15	3.91	13.91

*7 Year Price Score 118.2 *NYSE Composite Index=100* ***12 Month Price Score 45.7**

Interim Earnings (Per Share) Can$

Qtr.	Mar	Jun	Sep	Dec
2001	1.24	0.71	0.65	1.12
2002	2.27	0.67	0.70	1.15
2003	1.34	0.69	0.68	1.36
2004	1.17	...	...	...

Interim Dividends (Per Share) Can$

Amt	Decl	Ex	Rec	Pay
0.215Q	7/24/2003	8/6/2003	8/8/2003	9/1/2003
0.215Q	10/21/2003	11/5/2003	11/7/2003	12/1/2003
0.22Q	1/23/2004	2/9/2004	2/11/2004	3/1/2004
0.22Q	4/23/2004	5/10/2004	5/12/2004	6/1/2004

Indicated Div: $2.12

Valuation Analysis

Forecast P/E 13.55 (5/24/2004)

Market Cap	$2.2 Billion	Book Value	N/A
Price/Book	N/A	Price/Sales	N/A

Dividend Achiever Status

Rank	28	5 Year Growth Rate	4.46%
Total Years of Dividend Growth			21

Business Summary: Electricity (MIC: 7.1 SIC: 4939 NAIC:221121)

Canadian Utilities is a holding company. Through its subsidiaries, Co. is engaged in regulated natural gas and electric energy operations and in related nonregulated operations. Co. has four business groups. *Power Generation* operates power plants. *Utilities* delivers natural gas and electricity to industrial, commercial and residential customers. *Logistics & Energy Services* provides project management and technical services, transmission of natural gas, and natural gas gathering, processing and storage, as well as liquids extraction. *Technologies* provides billing and customer care services, corporate and vacation travel services, and markets coal fuel and wood preservation products.

Recent Developments: For the quarter ended Mar 31 2004, net income dropped 13.3% to C$74.5 million compared with C$85.9 million in the corresponding quarter of the previous year. The decline was due in part to a decrease in ATCO Power's earnings as a result of lower prices on electricity sold to the Alberta Electric System Operator (AESO), and the negative impact of the Alberta Energy and Utilities Board decision in late 2003 on a general tariff application. Revenue fell 13.6% to C$1.19 billion, reflecting lower prices received for electricity sold to AESO by ATCO Power and lower prices of natural gas and electricity purchased for customers on a "no margin" basis by ATCO Gas and ATCO Electric.

Prospects: Co.'s ATCO Power business continues to be affected by lower prices on electricity sold to the Alberta Electric System Operator (AESO). At Mar 31 2004, AESO electricity prices averaged C$48.81 per megawatt hour (MWh), down 41.9% from average prices of C$83.94 per MWh in the equivalent 2003 quarter. Meanwhile, natural gas prices remain relatively strong, and for the three months ended Mar 31 2004 averaged $6.08 per gigajoule (GJ), down 21.7% versus average prices of $7.76 per GJ in the equivalent 2003 quarter. Also, cash flow from operations is relatively stable as the effect of lower earnings is being tempered by increased receipts of deferred availability incentives by Alberta Power.

Financial Data

(Can$ in Thousands)	12/31/2003	12/31/2002	12/31/2001	12/31/2000	12/31/1999	12/31/1998	12/31/1997	12/31/1996
Earnings Per Share	4.07	4.79	3.72	3.58	3.16	3.00	2.85	2.68
Cash Flow Per Share	7.42	5.34	11.71	5.53	6.72	4.00	4.43	5.33
Dividends Per Share	2.040	1.960	1.880	1.800	1.720	1.640	1.560	1.480
Dividend Payout %	50.12	40.91	50.53	50.27	54.43	54.67	54.74	55.22
Income Statement								
Total Revenues	3,742,600	2,975,900	3,500,100	2,923,100	2,207,700	1,945,700	1,927,600	1,816,300
Total Indirect Exp.	3,137,600	2,414,900	2,927,400	2,328,900	1,657,700	1,396,900	1,401,700	1,275,000
Costs & Expenses	3,327,900	2,599,000	3,126,000	2,328,900	1,657,700	1,396,900	1,401,700	1,275,000
Depreciation & Amort.	268,900	244,400	241,700	238,700	229,500	204,100	192,700	186,000
Operating Income	414,700	376,900	374,100	594,200	550,000	548,800	525,900	541,300
Net Interest Inc./(Exp.)	190,300	184,100	198,600	196,000	181,900	173,000	172,700	181,500
Income Taxes	155,700	189,900	164,000	179,400	172,100	180,500	168,100	172,800
Net Income	292,400	323,200	254,100	244,201	215,000	200,600	193,900	180,400
Average Shs. Outstg.	63,665	63,700	63,315	63,328	63,367	63,359	63,714	63,940
Balance Sheet								
Net Property	4,809,400	4,657,000	4,362,900	4,007,000	5,982,900	5,781,800	3,598,600	3,474,500
Total Assets	6,070,500	5,934,400	5,392,300	5,390,100	6,663,800	6,417,000	4,090,700	3,937,400
Long–Term Obligations	2,611,400	2,738,000	2,534,300	2,422,600	2,192,300	2,085,400	1,833,100	1,781,200
Net Stockholders' Equity	2,588,100	2,316,600	1,980,300	1,863,000	1,789,600	1,800,900	1,780,400	1,730,400
Shares Outstanding	63,383	63,412	63,317	63,305	63,349	63,362	63,340	63,971
Statistical Record								
Operating Profit Margin %	11.08	12.66	10.68	20.32	24.91	28.20	27.28	29.80
Return on Equity %	11.29	13.95	12.83	13.10	12.01	11.13	10.89	10.42
Accum. Depr./Gross Prop. %	34.63	33.97	33.73	34.20	33.35	32.08	31.42	30.08
Price Range	58.70–45.10	59.98–48.94	56.05–46.00	51.00–31.40	49.00–33.40	48.70–38.55	41.15–30.45	34.35–25.20
P/E Ratio	14.42–11.08	12.52–10.22	15.07–12.37	14.25–8.77	15.51–10.57	16.23–12.85	14.44–10.68	12.82–9.40
Average Yield %	3.81	3.56	3.67	4.53	3.97	3.65	4.34	5.30

Address: 1500, 909 – 11th Avenue S.W., Calgary, AB T2R 1N6
Telephone: (403) 292 7500
Web Site: www.canadian–utilities.com

Officers: Ronald D. Southern – Chmn., Nancy C. Southern – Pres., C.E.O.
Transfer Agents: CIBC Mellon Trust Company, Montreal, Toronto, Winnipeg, Calgary and Vancouver

Investor Contact: 403 292 7502
Institutional Holding
No of Institutions: 2
Shares: 455,982   **% Held:** –

EMERA INC.

Exchange	Symbol	Price	52Wk Range	Yield	P/E
TSX	EMA	C$17.38 (5/31/2004)	19.80–16.76	5.06	15.80

7 Year Price Score 105.7 *NYSE Composite Index=100 *12 Month Price Score 46.5

Interim Earnings (Per Share) Can$

Qtr.	Mar	Jun	Sep	Dec
2002	0.33	0.16	0.17	0.18
2003	0.47	0.14	0.11	0.44
2004	0.41	...	...	...

Interim Dividends (Per Share) Can$

Amt	Decl	Ex	Rec	Pay
0.215Q	7/4/2003	7/29/2003	7/31/2003	8/15/2003
0.215Q	10/3/2003	10/28/2003	10/30/2003	11/14/2003
0.22Q	1/9/2004	1/29/2004	2/2/2004	2/16/2004
0.22Q	4/8/2004	4/29/2004	5/3/2004	5/17/2004

Indicated Div: $0.88

Valuation Analysis

Forecast P/E 14.81 (5/24/2004)

Market Cap $1.7 Billion		Book Value	N/A
Price/Book N/A		Price/Sales	N/A

Dividend Achiever Status

Rank 30		5 Year Growth Rate	0.96%
Total Years of Dividend Growth			11

Business Summary: Electricity (MIC: 7.1 SIC: 4911 NAIC:221122)

Emera is an energy and services company with two wholly–owned regulated electric utility subsidiaries. Nova Scotia Power supplies over 95.0% of the electric generation, transmission and distribution in Nova Scotia. Co.'s other subsidiary, Bangor Hydro, provides electricity transmission and distribution service to 110,000 customers in eastern Maine. In addition, Co. owns a 12.5% interest in the Maritimes & Northeast Pipeline, which delivers Sable natural gas to markets in Maritime Canada and the northeastern U.S.; Emera Energy Services, which manages energy assets on behalf of third parties; and Emera Fuels, which distributes home heating oil and related products.

Recent Developments: For the quarter ended Mar 31 2004, net earnings fell 14.9% to C$49.8 million from C$58.5 million in the equivalent prior–year quarter. The decrease in earnings was primarily attributed to lower earnings in Nova Scotia Power, reflecting increased pension costs, depreciation expense, amortization and grants in lieu of property taxes. Total revenues decreased 2.2% to C$347.4 million from C$355.2 million the previous year. Electric revenue declined 3.1% to C$305.8 million. Fuel oil revenue fell 10.6% to C$28.6 million, while other revenue jumped 68.8% to C$13.0 million. Operating income was C$115.2 million, down 4.2% from C$120.2 million the year before.

Prospects: Co.'s plan for growth seeks to add energy infrastructure assets to its portfolio. Co. is focused on building on its core electricity business, specifically in regulated transmission and distribution operations, and low risk generation facilities. Co. is concentrating its efforts in northeast North America, which is continuing to develop as an integrated energy market. Meanwhile, Co.'s ability to sell natural gas into a high priced market has sheltered its customers from the impact of higher taxes and other costs for the past several years. However, over the longer term, Co. needs to incorporate these costs into its rate structure, and it will be addressing that in its next rate filing.

Financial Data

(Can$ in Thousands)	12/31/2003	12/31/2002	12/31/2001	12/31/2000	12/31/1999	12/31/1998	12/31/1997	12/31/1996
Earnings Per Share	1.16	0.84	1.16	1.20	1.16	0.99	1.07	1.05
Cash Flow Per Share	1.93	2.60	...	...	...	...	...	...
Dividends Per Share	0.860	0.858	0.850	0.840	0.830	0.820	0.810	0.800
Dividend Payout %	74.13	102.08	73.27	70.00	71.55	82.82	75.70	76.19
Income Statement								
Total Revenues	1,231,300	1,226,900	1,003,900	896,500	824,600	773,100	748,700	741,200
Total Indirect Exp.	451,100	460,300	327,700	298,700	284,500	258,900	245,700	238,600
Costs & Expenses	885,900	970,800	729,000	640,300	575,300	530,200	492,100	477,300
Depreciation & Amort.	145,900	150,800	117,700	117,300	117,900	108,000	100,600	79,900
Operating Income	345,400	256,100	274,500	256,200	249,300	242,900	256,600	263,900
Net Interest Inc./(Exp.)	133,600	145,400	123,500	135,400	136,500	132,700	140,200	148,900
Income Taxes	61,300	4,100	14,800	12,500	7,400	13,600	14,200	11,400
Eqty Earns/Minority Int.	13,200	10,600	12,200	9,900	11,300	11,200	...	...
Net Income	129,200	83,600	114,200	104,400	100,400	85,400	102,200	103,600
Average Shs. Outstg.	123,800	99,000	111,200	87,200	...	...	...	...
Balance Sheet								
Net Property	2,672,800	2,776,400	2,766,800	2,319,700	2,315,000	2,298,400	2,275,500	2,249,600
Total Assets	3,840,900	3,907,900	3,959,400	2,951,000	2,901,200	2,834,100	2,881,200	3,064,700
Long–Term Obligations	1,589,500	1,417,800	1,381,400	1,155,000	1,260,700	1,083,700	1,107,500	1,258,100
Net Stockholders' Equity	1,312,600	1,332,000	1,181,400	977,600	1,173,600	1,111,200	1,092,000	1,062,900
Shares Outstanding	108,260	107,800	98,000	87,350	87,050	86,800	86,500	86,100
Statistical Record								
Operating Profit Margin %	28.05	20.87	27.38	28.57	30.23	31.41	34.27	35.60
Return on Equity %	9.84	6.27	9.66	10.67	8.55	7.68	8.48	8.46
Accum. Depr./Gross Prop. %	38.02	36.12	34.77	34.95	33.51	32.24	30.96	30.11
Price Range	17.94–14.38	17.82–15.65	18.07–15.70	18.20–11.70	19.05–13.20	20.05–14.95	17.40–13.80	14.95–11.75
P/E Ratio	15.47–12.40	21.21–18.63	15.58–13.53	15.17–9.75	16.42–11.38	20.25–15.10	16.26–12.90	14.24–11.19
Average Yield %	5.15	5.10	5.08	5.69	4.93	N/A	N/A	N/A

Address: 1894 Barrington Street, Halifax, NS B3J 2A8 Telephone: (902) 450–0507 Web Site: www.emera.com	Officers: Derek Oland – Chmn., David Mann – Pres., C.E.O. Transfer Agents:Computershare Trust Company of Canada, Halifax, Nova Scotia	Investor Contact:902–428–6999 Institutional Holding No of Institutions: 2 Shares: 2,399,400 % Held: –

EMPIRE CO LTD

Exchange	Symbol	Price	52Wk Range	Yield	P/E
TSX	EMP A	C$25.50 (5/31/2004)	29.50-24.55	1.57	10.00

*7 Year Price Score 141.8   *NYSE Composite Index=100   *12 Month Price Score 46.0

Interim Earnings (Per Share) Can$

Qtr.	Jul	Oct	Jan	Apr
2000–01	7.80	0.33	0.18	0.51
2001–02	0.68	0.61	0.53	0.26
2002–03	0.60	0.59	0.60	0.55
2003–04	0.64	0.56	0.80	...

Interim Dividends (Per Share) Can$

Amt	Decl	Ex	Rec	Pay
0.01Q	6/24/2003	7/11/2003	7/15/2003	7/31/2003
0.01Q	9/10/2003	10/10/2003	10/15/2003	10/31/2003
0.01Q	12/10/2003	1/13/2004	1/15/2004	1/30/2004
0.01Q	3/5/2004	4/13/2004	4/15/2004	4/30/2004

Indicated Div: $0.40

Valuation Analysis
Forecast P/E 10.15 (5/24/2004)

Market Cap	$839.0 Million	Book Value	2.7 Billion
Price/Book	N/A	Price/Sales	N/A

Dividend Achiever Status

Rank	4	5 Year Growth Rate	22.70%
Total Years of Dividend Growth		9	

Business Summary: Retail – Food &Beverage (MIC: 5.3 SIC: 5149 NAIC:424490)

Empire operates principally in three business segments: food distribution, real estate and investments & theater operations. Through its 64.4% owned subsidiary Sobeys Inc., Co. operates a national network of over 1,300 corporate and franchised stores under banners such as IGA, Sobeys and Price Chopper. Co.'s real estate operations are focused on the acquisition, development and management of a portfolio of properties primarily located in Atlantic Canada. In addition, Co. maintains a portfolio of short–term liquid equity investments and operates Empire Theatres Limited, a movie exhibitor in Atlantic Canada.

Recent Developments: For the three months ended Jan 31 2004, net earnings advanced 34.9% to C$53.0 million from C$39.3 million in the corresponding period a year earlier. Results for the recent period included an after–tax capital gain of C$8.8 million, primarily related to the sale of Delhaize Le Lion common stock. Revenue climbed 5.9% to C$2.80 billion from C$2.64 billion the previous year. Food distribution revenue grew 5.6% to C$2.74 billion from C$2.59 billion the year before, while real estate revenue increased 18.0% to C$53.0 million from C$44.9 million the prior year. Operating income totaled C$110.4 million, up 2.6% compared with C$107.6 million in fiscal 2003.

Prospects: On Feb 1 2004, Co.'s subsidiary, Sobeys Inc., completed its acquisition of Commisso's Food Markets Limited and Commisso's Grocery Distributors Limited for about C$61.0 million in cash. Also, on Feb 1 2004, Co.'s subsidiary, Crombie Properties, Limited, completed its purchase of six properties located in Southern Ontario and the Niagara Peninsula for C$42.5 million. Meanwhile, top–line growth is being fueled by increased same–store sales from Co.'s food distribution operations, along with additional sales generated by new retail square footage. Separately, real estate revenue growth is benefiting from increased occupancy levels and higher rental renewal rates.

Financial Data

(Can$ in Thousands)	6 Mos	3 Mos	04/30/2003	04/30/2002	04/30/2001	04/30/2000	04/30/1999	04/30/1998
Earnings Per Share	2.35	2.38	2.34	2.08	8.82	1.12	1.76	1.15
Cash Flow Per Share	1.07	(0.07)	5.40	...	...	...	...	...
Dividends Per Share	0.340	0.330	0.300	0.200	0.120	0.170	0.130	0.120
Dividend Payout %	14.47	13.87	12.98	9.62	1.41	15.55	7.57	10.38
Income Statement								
Total Revenues	5,609,100	2,814,700	10,624,200	9,926,500	11,538,600	11,164,495	6,377,651	3,320,000
Total Indirect Exp.	78,700	38,400	143,600	118,900	117,900	121,416	103,720	70,404
Depreciation & Amort.	78,700	38,400	143,600	118,900	117,900	121,416	103,720	70,404
Operating Income	203,800	101,900	337,100	286,600	202,400	176,435	63,405	45,816
Net Interest Inc./(Exp.)	46,900	24,000	92,900	111,600	142,100	159,511	112,379	76,668
Income Taxes	57,200	30,100	120,400	104,800	148,600	80,543	10,218	32,884
Eqty Earns/Minority Int.	30,300	14,900	67,800	50,000	23,200	38,295	(11,917)	7
Income from Cont Ops	...	...	...	137,200	...	...	...	...
Net Income	79,100	42,300	153,900	195,900	580,000	86,812	134,950	87,782
Average Shs. Outstg.	65,504	65,503	65,781	65,700	65,626	75,572	75,004	73,900
Balance Sheet								
Cash & Cash Equivalents	95,100	253,400	316,800	782,400	556,700	68,090	97,031	184,656
Total Current Assets	1,027,000	1,109,200	1,182,800	1,563,700	1,585,400	1,121,643	1,009,819	486,778
Total Assets	4,474,100	4,515,600	4,516,100	4,312,600	4,254,300	4,171,087	4,023,498	1,907,233
Total Current Liabilities	1,288,700	1,369,800	1,387,500	1,360,800	1,498,700	1,855,772	1,587,151	659,240
Long–Term Obligations	897,100	914,500	923,100	975,000	1,108,300	1,323,700	1,392,435	616,571
Net Stockholders' Equity	1,496,500	1,464,600	1,427,100	1,290,600	1,115,000	602,768	737,682	558,339
Net Working Capital	(261,700)	(260,600)	(204,700)	202,900	86,700	(734,129)	(577,332)	(172,462)
Shares Outstanding	65,804	65,794	65,758	66,607	65,657	65,549	78,266	73,969
Statistical Record								
Operating Profit Margin %	3.63	3.62	3.17	2.88	1.75	1.58	0.99	1.38
Return on Equity %	5.28	2.88	10.78	15.17	52.01	14.40	18.29	15.72
Return on Assets %	1.76	0.93	3.40	4.54	13.63	2.08	3.35	4.60
Debt/Total Assets %	20.05	20.25	20.44	22.60	26.05	31.73	34.60	32.32
Price Range	27.55–23.10	27.55–23.10	33.25–21.80	31.25–15.75	18.13–13.95	16.98–12.33	16.35–12.50	14.20–7.80
P/E Ratio	11.72–9.83	11.58–9.71	14.21–9.32	15.02–7.57	2.05–1.58	15.16–11.00	9.29–7.10	12.35–6.78
Average Yield %	1.31	1.28	1.09	0.99	0.73	1.19	0.93	1.19

Address: 115 King Street, Stellarton, NS B0K 1S0	**Officers:** Donald R. Sobey – Chmn., Paul D. Sobey – Pres., C.E.O.	
Telephone: (902) 755–4440	**Transfer Agents:** Computershare Trust Company of Canada	**Institutional Holding**
Web Site: www.empireco.ca		No of Institutions: 1
		Shares: 72,500 % Held: –

ENBRIDGE INC

Exchange	Symbol	Price	52Wk Range	Yield	P/E
TSX	ENB	C$50.35 (5/31/2004)	54.95-46.25	3.63	12.46

*7 Year Price Score 131.3 *NYSE Composite Index=100 *12 Month Price Score 47.3

Interim Earnings (Per Share) Can$

Qtr.	Mar	Jun	Sep	Dec
2001	0.53	1.69	0.37	0.01
2002	0.65	1.25	(0.03)	0.19
2003	0.63	2.68	0.53	0.16
2004	0.67	...	...	...

Interim Dividends (Per Share) Can$

Amt	Decl	Ex	Rec	Pay
0.415Q	7/30/2003	8/13/2003	8/15/2003	9/1/2003
0.415Q	10/30/2003	11/12/2003	11/14/2003	12/1/2003
0.458Q	1/27/2004	2/11/2004	2/13/2004	3/1/2004
0.458Q	5/5/2004	5/13/2004	5/17/2004	6/1/2004
Indicated Div: $1.83 (Div. Reinv. Plan)				

Valuation Analysis
Forecast P/E 16.64 (5/24/2004)

Market Cap $7.8 Billion	Book Value 4.9 Billion
Price/Book N/A	Price/Sales N/A

Dividend Achiever Status
Rank	25	5 Year Growth Rate	8.19%
Total Years of Dividend Growth		8	

Business Summary: Oil and Gas (MIC: 14.2 SIC: 4619 NAIC:486990)

Enbridge is engaged in the transportation and distribution of energy. Co. operates common carrier and feeder pipelines that transport crude oil and other liquid hydrocarbons in Canada, as well as transmission pipelines that transport natural gas. Co. also has gas utility operations, which serve residential, commercial, industrial and transportation customers, primarily in central and eastern Ontario, and natural gas distribution activities in Quebec, New Brunswick and New York. In addition, Co. has investments in energy transportation and related energy projects outside of Canada and the U.S. At Dec 31 2003, Co. had 1,679,000 active customers.

Recent Developments: For the three months ended Mar 31 2004, net earnings totaled C$121.1 million, up 7.6% compared with C$112.5 million in the corresponding quarter a year earlier. Revenues increased 39.0% to C$1.45 billion from C$1.05 billion the previous year. Gas sales jumped 41.2% to C$969.8 million from C$686.6 million the year before, while transportation revenues advanced 31.3% to C$409.0 million from C$311.6 million the prior year. Energy services revenues climbed 56.3% to C$74.4 million from C$47.6 million in 2003. Operating income totaled C$285.5 million, up 81.6% versus C$157.2 million a year ago.

Prospects: Results are benefiting from strong earnings from Co.'s crude oil pipeline operations, due to Co.'s efforts to expand the system in 2003, partially offset by higher corporate expenses and unfavorable foreign currency exchange rates. In addition, operating performance is also being positively affected by higher ownership interest in the Alliance Pipeline, improved fractionation margins at Co.'s Aux Sable liquids extraction plant, and increased demand for refined products in Spain. Looking ahead, Co. is projecting full-year 2004 earnings of between $3.00 and $3.10 per share.

Financial Data

(Can$ in Thousands)	12/31/2003	12/31/2002	12/31/2001	12/31/2000	12/31/1999	12/31/1998	12/31/1997	12/31/1996
Earnings Per Share	4.00	2.06	2.60	2.54	1.91	1.65	1.57	1.45
Cash Flow Per Share	2.36	5.62	0.84	1.71	...	...	...	...
Dividends Per Share	1.660	1.520	1.400	1.270	1.190	1.120	1.060	1.010
Dividend Payout %	41.50	73.78	53.84	50.00	62.30	67.88	67.52	69.66
Income Statement								
Total Revenues	4,855,300	4,547,500	4,050,100	2,945,000	2,687,700	2,341,700	2,520,000	2,457,900
Total Indirect Exp.	3,963,900	3,938,700	3,334,400	2,290,300	2,108,500	1,849,000	1,948,800	1,877,600
Depreciation & Amort.	443,000	403,900	392,500	453,500	383,800	309,000	274,000	237,000
Operating Income	891,400	608,800	715,700	654,700	579,200	492,700	571,200	580,300
Net Interest Inc./(Exp.)	451,300	422,000	437,100	427,700	380,600	312,900	276,100	271,300
Income Taxes	187,400	102,100	66,700	1,900	87,500	95,300	154,300	138,300
Eqty Earns/Minority Int.	...	...	...	...	...	...	...	22,100
Net Income	700,800	610,100	482,500	410,700	299,800	240,900	217,300	180,300
Average Shs. Outstg.	166,900	162,000	158,800	154,469	150,995	145,448	137,808	124,330
Balance Sheet								
Cash & Cash Equivalents	104,100	40,700	74,000	67,000	53,600	124,900	51,300	13,800
Total Current Assets	2,052,700	1,442,000	2,281,700	1,334,300	1,107,200	1,094,000	797,800	654,000
Total Assets	13,823,300	12,987,400	13,127,700	10,568,200	9,208,200	8,347,200	6,672,200	5,761,100
Total Current Liabilities	2,349,800	1,716,500	3,200,300	1,259,900	910,500	1,286,700	1,372,400	1,005,000
Long-Term Obligations	5,995,500	6,040,300	5,922,800	5,592,700	5,284,800	4,502,300	3,166,400	2,939,000
Net Stockholders' Equity	4,126,000	3,832,400	3,032,100	2,763,400	2,500,600	2,061,400	1,699,400	1,396,000
Net Working Capital	(297,100)	(274,500)	(918,600)	74,400	196,700	(192,700)	(574,600)	(351,000)
Shares Outstanding	171,900	169,700	162,900	161,846	156,308	155,710	148,328	134,980
Statistical Record								
Operating Profit Margin %	18.35	13.38	17.67	22.23	21.55	21.04	22.66	23.60
Return on Equity %	16.98	15.91	15.92	14.99	11.98	11.68	12.78	12.91
Return on Assets %	5.06	4.69	3.67	3.92	3.25	2.88	3.25	3.12
Debt/Total Assets %	43.37	46.50	45.11	52.92	57.39	53.93	47.45	51.01
Price Range	54.14-41.08	49.25-41.20	45.25-34.05	43.70-24.10	36.20-28.65	35.63-29.00	32.70-19.60	20.95-15.94
P/E Ratio	13.54-10.27	23.91-20.00	17.40-13.10	17.20-9.49	18.95-15.00	21.59-17.58	20.83-12.48	14.45-10.99
Average Yield %	3.49	3.37	3.44	3.87	3.64	3.44	4.42	5.70

Address: 3000, 425-1st Street S.W., Calgary, AB T2P 3L8 Telephone: (403) 231 3900 Web Site: www.enbridge.com	Officers: Patrick D. Daniel - Pres., C.E.O., Stephen J.J. Letwin - Group V.P., Gas Strategy & Corp. Devel. Transfer Agents:Computershare Trust Company of Canada, Montreal, Toronto, Winnipeg, Edmonton, and Vancouver	Investor Contact:800 481 2804 Institutional Holding No of Institutions: 37 Shares: 37,759,463 % Held: 23%

GREAT-WEST LIFECO INC.

Exchange	Symbol	Price	52Wk Range	Yield	P/E
TSX	GWO	C$48.47 (5/31/2004)	52.82-38.55	2.67	15.84

*7 Year Price Score 144.2   *NYSE Composite Index=100   ***12 Month Price Score 51.6**

Interim Earnings (Per Share) Can$

Qtr.	Mar	Jun	Sep	Dec
2001	0.43	0.09	0.32	0.52
2002	0.58	0.63	0.64	0.64
2003	0.68	0.70	0.73	0.80
2004	0.83	...	...	...

Interim Dividends (Per Share) Can$

Amt	Decl	Ex	Rec	Pay
0.27Q	5/2/2003	6/12/2003	6/16/2003	6/30/2003
0.293Q	7/30/2003	8/28/2003	9/2/2003	9/30/2003
0.323Q	1/29/2004	3/1/2004	3/3/2004	3/31/2004
0.323Q	...	5/31/2004	6/2/2004	6/30/2004
		Indicated Div: $1.29		

Valuation Analysis

Forecast P/E 16.28 (5/24/2004)

Market Cap $9.0 Billion	Book Value N/A
Price/Book N/A	Price/Sales N/A

Dividend Achiever Status

Rank	7	5 Year Growth Rate	20.65%
Total Years of Dividend Growth			11

Business Summary: Insurance (MIC: 8.2 SIC: 6311 NAIC:524113)

Great-West Lifeco is a financial services holding company with interests in the life insurance, health insurance, retirement savings, and reinsurance businesses. Co. has operations in Canada and internationally through The Great-West Life Assurance Company, London Life Insurance and The Canada Life Assurance Company, and in the United States through Great-West Life & Annuity Insurance and The Canada Life Assurance Company. As of Dec 31 2003, Co. had assets under administration of $112.10 billion in its Canada/Europe segment and $47.10 billion in its United States segment.

Recent Developments: For the three months ended Mar 31 2004, net income jumped 50.6% to C$390.0 million from C$259.0 million in 2003. Results for 2003 included a C$9.0 million pre-tax restructuring charge. Total income amounted to C$5.27 billion, up 21.6% compared with C$4.33 billion the previous year. Premium income increased 15.7% to C$3.41 billion from C$2.95 billion a year earlier. Net investment income advanced 39.7% to C$1.32 billion from C$948.0 million the year before. Fee and other income climbed 22.9% to C$532.0 million from C$433.0 million the prior year.

Prospects: Results are being positively affected by increased demand for Co.'s financial services retirement products and the acquisition of Canada Life Financial Corporation, which was completed during 2003. Meanwhile, lower healthcare premiums are resulting from the sale of the U.S. business group of Co.'s indirect subsidiary, The Canada Life Assurance Company, to Jefferson-Pilot during the first quarter of 2004. The sale of this business, which consists of group life, disability and dental insurance with approximately $340.0 million in annual premiums, should help Co. to focus on growing its core healthcare and retirement services businesses.

Financial Data

(Can$ in Thousands)	9 Mos	6 Mos	3 Mos	12/31/2002	12/31/2001	12/31/2000	12/31/1999	12/31/1998
Earnings Per Share	2.75	2.66	2.59	2.49	1.36	1.72	1.43	1.17
Dividends Per Share	1.030	0.760	0.720	0.945	0.780	0.650	0.530	2.755
Dividend Payout %	48.27	55.03	105.41	36.74	57.35	37.79	37.06	235.47
Income Statement								
Total Premium Income	8,682,000	5,618,000	2,949,000	11,187,000	10,477,000	9,976,000	8,526,000	9,237,000
Total Revenues	7,750,000	8,301,000	4,330,000	16,632,000	16,048,000	15,266,000	13,328,000	13,756,000
Total Indirect Exp.	2,175,000	1,227,000	630,000	2,613,000	2,761,000	2,639,000	2,274,000	2,134,000
Inc. Before Inc. Taxes	1,313,000	784,000	378,000	1,426,000	1,053,000	1,253,000	1,118,000	942,000
Income Taxes	376,000	221,000	106,000	430,000	397,000	451,000	366,000	361,000
Eqty Earns/Minority Int.	72,000	37,000	13,000	34,000	44,000	63,000	123,000	108,000
Net Income	865,000	526,000	259,000	962,000	546,000	674,000	569,000	473,000
Average Shs. Outstg.	394,737	369,836	370,254	372,607	377,364	373,548	373,890	373,000
Balance Sheet								
Premiums Due	...	...	352,000	305,000	410,000	606,000	496,000	378,000
Invst. Assets: Total	59,389,000	35,328,000	36,515,000	36,612,000	35,232,000	32,671,000	32,312,000	32,698,000
Total Assets	99,083,000	57,705,000	59,533,000	60,071,000	59,159,000	55,754,000	53,256,000	54,725,000
Long-Term Obligations	2,999,000	1,547,000	1,568,000	1,012,000	1,075,000	1,032,000	690,000	601,000
Net Stockholders' Equity	8,518,000	4,525,000	4,626,000	4,707,570	4,397,100	4,182,365	3,789,000	3,547,000
Shares Outstanding	448,074	365,463	365,926	366,376	369,459	372,404	374,380	373,000
Statistical Record								
Return on Revenues %	11.16	6.33	5.98	5.78	3.40	4.41	4.26	3.43
Return on Equity %	10.15	11.62	5.59	20.43	12.41	16.11	15.01	13.33
Return on Assets %	0.87	0.91	0.43	1.60	0.92	1.20	1.06	0.86
Price Range	42.30-35.02	42.30-35.02	38.99-35.02	39.80-32.49	40.04-30.95	42.00-16.75	31.00-17.80	27.00-18.00
P/E Ratio	15.38-12.73	15.90-13.17	15.05-13.52	15.98-13.05	29.44-22.76	24.42-9.74	21.68-12.45	23.08-15.38
Average Yield %	2.64	1.99	1.95	2.49	1.64	3.04	2.10	11.87

<table>
<tr><td>

Address: 100 Osborne Street North, Winnipeg, MB R3C 3A5
Telephone: (204) 946-1190
Web Site: www.greatwestlifeco.com

</td><td>

Officers: Robert Gratton - Chmn., Raymond L. McFeetors - Co-Pres., C.E.O.
Transfer Agents: Computershare Trust Company of Canada, Toronto, Ontario; Calgary, Alberta;

</td><td>

Investor Contact: 04-946-7341)
Institutional Holding
No of Institutions: 1
Shares: 1,797,496   **% Held:** -

</td></tr>
</table>

IMPERIAL OIL LTD.

Exchange	Symbol	Price	52Wk Range	Yield	P/E
ASE	IMO	$61.29 (5/31/2004)	64.00-45.55	1.44	13.62

*7 Year Price Score 142.6   *NYSE Composite Index=100   *12 Month Price Score 53.2

Interim Earnings (Per Share) Can$

Qtr.	Mar	Jun	Sep	Dec
2001	0.96	1.04	0.61	0.55
2002	0.29	0.81	0.91	1.18
2003	1.42	1.38	1.01	0.71
2004	1.40	...	...	...

Interim Dividends (Per Share) Can$

Amt	Decl	Ex	Rec	Pay
0.22Q	8/13/2003	8/28/2003	9/2/2003	10/1/2003
0.22Q	11/20/2003	12/1/2003	12/3/2003	1/1/2004
0.22Q	2/18/2004	3/1/2004	3/3/2004	4/1/2004
0.22Q	5/27/2004	6/4/2004	6/8/2004	7/1/2004

Indicated Div: C$0.88 (Div. Reinv. Plan)

Valuation Analysis

Forecast P/E 14.25 (5/24/2004)

Market Cap $23.2 Billion	Book Value 8.9 Billion
Price/Book 1.48	Price/Sales 0.68

Dividend Achiever Status

Rank 29	5 Year Growth Rate	3.14%

Total Years of Dividend Growth 9

Business Summary: Oil and Gas (MIC: 14.2 SIC: 1311 NAIC:211111)

Imperial Oil is an integrated oil company. Co.'s operations are conducted in three main segments: natural resources include the exploration for, and production of, crude oil and natural gas; petroleum products consist of the transportation, refining and blending of crude oil and refined products; and chemicals consist of the manufacturing and marketing of various petrochemicals.In Canada, Co. is a major producer of crude oil and natural gas, and a refiner and marketer of petroleum products. Co. is also a supplier of petrochemicals.As of Dec 31 2003, proved reserves of crude oil and natural gas were 1,670 million barrels and 1,023 billion cubic feet, respectively.

Recent Developments: For the three months ended Mar 31 2004, net income slipped 5.4% to C$509.0 million compared with C$538.0 million the previous year. Results for 2004 included financing costs of C$10.0 million, while results for 2003 included a C$57.0 million financing gain. Total revenues declined 7.5% to C$5.07 billion from C$5.48 billion a year earlier. Expenses from purchases of crude oil and products slid 11.4% to C$2.83 billion from C$3.20 billion the prior year. Earnings before income taxes totaled C$713.0 million, down 9.7% versus C$790.0 million the year before.

Prospects: Earnings are being negatively affected by unfavorable foreign currency exchange rates. However, results are benefiting from higher volumes of crude oil and natural gas, lower effective tax rates in the resources segment, and stronger manufacturing margins for petroleum and chemical products. In March 2004, Co. completed the installation of a new 95−megawatt cogeneration facility at its Sarnia, Ontario manufacturing plant, which should help improve efficiencies and reduce emissions at the plant. Separately, in March 2004, Co. received Alberta government approval for the expansion of its Cold Lake operation, which could boost production of bitumen by 30,000 barrels per day at the facility.

Financial Data

(Can$ in Millions)	12/31/2003	12/31/2002	12/31/2001	12/31/2000	12/31/1999	12/31/1998	12/31/1997	12/31/1996
Earnings Per Share	4.52	3.19	3.16	3.40	1.35	1.26	1.83	1.49
Cash Flow Per Share	5.89	4.42	5.10	5.01	3.42	1.95	...	...
Dividends Per Share	0.860	0.840	0.810	0.780	0.740	0.730	0.730	0.660
Dividend Payout %	19.02	26.33	25.63	22.94	54.81	57.94	39.89	44.30
Income Statement								
Total Revenues	19,208	17,042	17,245	18,053	10,348	9,145	11,122	10,509
Total Indirect Exp.	5,353	5,074	5,076	4,799	4,533	4,456	4,627	4,598
Depreciation & Amort.	750	703	716	724	667	647	685	711
Operating Income	2,362	1,781	1,897	2,321	1,032	747	1,527	933
Income Taxes	680	571	653	901	450	193	680	147
Net Income	1,682	1,210	1,244	1,420	582	554	847	786
Average Shs. Outstg.	372	378	393	417	431	438	462	527
Balance Sheet								
Cash & Cash Equivalents	448	766	872	1,020	674	463	770	582
Total Current Assets	2,628	2,980	2,685	3,476	2,388	2,037	2,428	2,203
Total Assets	12,361	11,868	10,761	11,222	9,687	9,429	10,060	10,524
Total Current Liabilities	3,390	2,743	3,027	3,417	2,239	1,938	2,158	2,375
Long−Term Obligations	859	1,466	906	928	1,239	1,312	1,506	1,544
Net Stockholders' Equity	5,778	5,212	4,429	4,321	4,438	4,180	4,383	4,567
Net Working Capital	(762)	237	(342)	59	149	99	270	(172)
Shares Outstanding	362	378	379	398	431	431	447	476
Statistical Record								
Operating Profit Margin %	12.29	10.45	11.00	12.85	9.97	8.16	13.72	8.87
Return on Equity %	29.11	23.21	28.08	32.86	13.11	13.25	19.32	17.21
Return on Assets %	13.60	10.19	11.56	12.65	6.00	5.87	8.41	7.46
Debt/Total Assets %	6.94	12.35	8.41	8.26	12.79	13.91	14.97	14.67
Price Range	58.22-43.45	49.30-39.50	45.65-34.75	42.25-26.85	35.70-22.00	30.67-21.15	30.67-20.00	21.50-16.00
P/E Ratio	12.88-9.61	15.45-12.38	14.45-11.00	12.43-7.90	26.44-16.30	24.34-16.79	16.76-10.93	14.43-10.74
Average Yield %	1.78	1.89	1.98	2.22	2.53	2.81	3.01	3.53

Address: 111 St. Clair Avenue West, Toronto, ON M5W 1K3 **Telephone:** (416) 968 8145 **Web Site:** www.imperialoil.ca	**Officers:** Tim J. Hearn − Chmn., Pres., C.E.O., Brian J. Fischer − Sr. V.P., Products & Chemicals Div. **Transfer Agents:**CIBC Mellon Trust Company, Toronto, Ontario; Mellon Investor Services LLC, Ridgefield Park, NJ	**Investor Contact:**416 968 8145 **Institutional Holding** **No of Institutions:** 101 **Shares:** 48,371,486 **% Held:** 12.80%

316

IMG Financial Inc.

Exchange	Symbol	Price	52Wk Range	Yield	P/E
TSX	IGI	C$34.90 (5/31/2004)	36.12-27.20	3.15	16.38

*7 Year Price Score 129.1 *NYSE Composite Index=100 ***12 Month Price Score 51.1**

Interim Earnings (Per Share) Can$

Qtr.	Mar	Jun	Sep	Dec
2001	0.30	0.10	0.31	0.33
2002	0.44	0.49	0.47	0.44
2003	0.45	0.48	0.58	0.51
2004	0.56	...	...	...

Interim Dividends (Per Share) Can$

Amt	Decl	Ex	Rec	Pay
0.255Q	7/31/2003	9/26/2003	9/30/2003	10/30/2003
0.255Q	10/30/2003	12/29/2004	12/31/2003	1/30/2004
0.275Q	1/30/2003	3/25/2004	3/29/2004	4/30/2004
0.275Q	...	6/24/2004	6/28/2004	7/30/2004

Indicated Div: $1.10

Valuation Analysis

Forecast P/E N/A

Market Cap $9.2 Billion	Book Value N/A
Price/Book N/A	Price/Sales N/A

Dividend Achiever Status

Rank	5	5 Year Growth Rate	21.67%
Total Years of Dividend Growth		12	

Business Summary: Wealth Management (MIC: 8.8 SIC: 6282 NAIC:523930)

Investors Group provides personal wealth creation and financial planning services. Co. offers financial planning, a family of mutual funds and a comprehensive range of other investment products and financial services, including registered retirement savings plans, registered retirement income funds, deferred profit sharing plans, life and disability insurance, guaranteed investment certificates and mortgages. Co. serves over 1.0 million clients through its network of over 3,300 consultants, working out of 100 financial planning centers across Canada.

Recent Developments: For the quarter ended Mar 31 2004, net income increased 22.5% to C$153.1 million from C$124.9 million in the prior-year quarter. Results were driven by higher mutual fund assets and significantly stronger mutual fund sales. Total fee and net investment income advanced 14.4% to C$520.4 million. Management fees increased 17.6% to C$365.1 million. Administration fees grew 5.6% to C$78.0 million. Distribution fees rose 2.4% to C$34.9 million, while net investment income and other fees improved 15.9% to C$42.4 million. Total mutual fund sales climbed 31.7% to C$3.58 billion. Mutual fund assets under management totaled C$78.10 billion at Mar 31 2004 versus C$64.40 billion at Mar 31 2003.

Prospects: On Apr 30 2004, shareholders approved a change in the name of the company to IGM Financial Inc. This change only affects the name of the public company. Both Investors Group and Mackenzie will continue to operate their businesses under their current names and through their existing brands. Separately, on May 10 2004, Co. acquired a majority interest in IPC Financial Network Inc. in a transaction valued at about C$95.0 million. IPC is a financial planning organization in Canada with C$7.30 billion of client assets under administration and C$1.30 billion of mutual fund assets under management. The acquisition provides Co. with a key presence in the financial planning market.

Financial Data

(Can$ in Thousands)	9 Mos	6 Mos	3 Mos	12/31/2002	12/31/2001	12/31/2000	12/31/1999	12/31/1998
Earnings Per Share	1.95	3.79	1.85	1.84	1.04	1.35	1.12	0.89
Cash Flow Per Share	1.38	0.68	0.25	1.34	...	...	...	...
Dividends Per Share	0.930	0.890	0.860	0.820	0.700	0.580	0.460	0.360
Dividend Payout %	47.69	23.48	46.49	44.66	66.85	42.96	41.07	40.45
Income Statement								
Total Revenues	1,389,411	915,035	454,884	1,940,036	1,784,165	1,197,108	1,014,720	929,481
Total Indirect Exp.	722,521	483,123	246,161	1,032,852	1,112,521	690,875	600,582	605,310
Depreciation & Amort.	164,213	110,691	56,242	230,856				
Operating Income	605,136	389,460	187,792	827,670	598,449	506,233	414,138	324,171
Income Taxes	199,912	130,013	62,870	317,401	252,994	222,208	178,525	135,827
Eqty Earns/Minority Int.	...	...	...	321	492	...	...	...
Income from Cont Ops	...	...	...	509,948	...	...	...	...
Net Income	420,044	259,447	124,922	511,759	272,994	284,025	235,613	188,344
Average Shs. Outstg.	265,099	264,982	264,992	264,873	247,932	210,012	210,854	211,396
Balance Sheet								
Cash & Cash Equivalents	...	...	1,046,279	927,708	1,102,480	1,132,344	948,267	939,584
Total Current Assets	...	...	1,628,221	1,476,677	1,757,574	1,348,126	1,257,180	1,287,742
Total Assets	...	...	6,161,860	5,986,952	6,122,468	1,985,212	1,811,958	1,798,944
Total Current Liabilities	...	...	759,045	709,012	671,248	218,980	306,809	371,628
Long-Term Obligations	...	...	1,484,580	1,386,365	1,362,268	168,435	171,220	262,382
Net Stockholders' Equity	...	...	3,003,884	2,949,955	2,678,244	1,096,285	966,867	850,928
Net Working Capital	...	...	869,176	767,665	1,086,326	1,129,146	950,371	916,114
Shares Outstanding	263,972	263,938	263,845	263,845	263,081	209,742	210,453	211,283
Statistical Record								
Operating Profit Margin %	43.55	42.56	41.28	42.66	33.54	42.28	40.81	34.87
Return on Equity %	13.28	8.44	4.15	17.34	10.19	25.90	24.36	22.13
Return on Assets %	6.72	4.23	2.02	8.54	4.45	14.30	13.00	10.46
Debt/Total Assets %	22.56	23.00	24.09	23.15	22.25	8.48	9.44	14.58
Price Range	29.50-23.60	29.00-23.60	28.17-23.60	32.59-21.90	26.75-18.20	27.85-13.90	26.40-17.15	28.00-17.50
P/E Ratio	15.13-12.10	7.65-6.23	15.23-12.76	17.71-11.90	25.72-17.50	20.63-10.30	23.57-15.31	31.46-19.66
Average Yield %	3.45	3.39	3.34	3.00	3.13	2.90	2.26	1.55

Address: One Canada Centre, Winnipeg, MB R3C 3B6	Officers: Robert Gratton – Chmn., R. Jeffrey Orr – Pres., C.E.O.	Investor Contact:204-956-8532
Telephone: (204) 943-0361		Institutional Holding
Web Site: www.igsecurities.com		No of Institutions: 4
		Shares: 6,640,892 % Held: –

JEAN COUTU GROUP (PJC) INC. (THE)

Exchange	Symbol	Price	52Wk Range	Yield	P/E
TSX	PJC A	C$18.95 (5/31/2004)	19.70-14.41	0.63	19.95

*7 Year Price Score 145.7 *NYSE Composite Index=100 ***12 Month Price Score 54.3**

TRADING VOLUME (thousand shares)

Interim Earnings (Per Share) Can$

Qtr.	Aug	Nov	Feb	May
2000-01	0.11	0.12	0.13	0.13
2001-02	0.14	0.15	0.16	0.17
2002-03	0.17	0.18	0.01	0.36
2003-04	0.19	0.19	0.21	...

Interim Dividends (Per Share) Can$

Amt	Decl	Ex	Rec	Pay
0.03Q	4/16/2003	5/6/2003	5/8/2003	5/22/2003
0.03Q	7/29/2003	8/12/2003	8/14/2003	8/28/2003
0.03Q	1/13/2004	2/10/2004	2/12/2004	2/26/2004
0.03Q	...	5/11/2004	5/13/2004	5/27/2004

Indicated Div: C$0.12

Valuation Analysis

Forecast P/E 18.48 (5/24/2004)

Market Cap	$769.1 Million	Book Value	N/A
Price/Book	N/A	Price/Sales	N/A

Dividend Achiever Status

Rank	5	5 Year Growth Rate	21.67%
Total Years of Dividend Growth		7	

Business Summary: Retail – Miscellaneous (MIC: 5.11 SIC: 5912 NAIC:446110)

Jean Coutu Group is engaged in the distribution and retail sales of pharmaceutical and para–pharmaceutical products. Co.'s franchise network is based mainly in Quebec. As of Nov 30 2003, Co.'s Canadian network was comprised of 275 PJC outlets, 42 PJC Clinic and 2 PJC Santé Beauté, all franchised, in Quebec, New Brunswick and Ontario. In the U.S., Co. also owns and operates 332 Brooks Pharmacy outlets in six northeastern states.

Recent Developments: For the third quarter ended Feb 29 2004, net income grew 14.3% to C$48.5 million from C$42.4 million in the comparable prior-year quarter. Net revenue increased 10.5% to C$1.04 billion from C$938.9 million the previous year. Revenue benefited from higher retail sales volume from both Co.'s Canadian and U.S. outlets, partially offset by unfavorable weather conditions in the northeast states of the U.S. and unfavorable currency translation. U.S. retail sales decreased 11.2% to C$613.6 million, while revenue from Canadian franchising rose 9.7% to C$676.0 million. In terms of comparable stores, the Canadian network's total sales were up 8.3%, while total sales in the U.S. rose by 4.0%.

Prospects: Going forward, Co. will continue its efforts in maintaining success and profitability by forging ahead with the expansion of its Canadian and U.S. networks. On Apr 5 2004, Co signed a definitive agreement with J.C. Penney Company, Inc. to acquire approximately 1,539 Eckerd drugstores and support facilities spread across 13 states of the Northeast and mid-Atlantic U.S., as well as Eckerd's headquarters in Florida, for a total price of US$2.38 billion.The transaction is expected to close in June 2004, subject to government review and approvals. After the closing, Co. will become the fourth largest drugstore chain in North America, with 1,872 stores in the U.S. and 319 in Canada.

Financial Data

(Can$ in Thousands)	6 Mos	3 Mos	05/31/2003	05/31/2002	05/31/2001	05/31/2000	05/31/1999	05/31/1998
Earnings Per Share	0.75	0.74	0.72	0.62	0.49	0.40	0.35	0.30
Cash Flow Per Share	0.66	0.10	0.93	...	...	...	...	...
Dividends Per Share	0.120	0.120	0.120	0.090	0.080	0.055	0.050	0.040
Dividend Payout %	16.00	16.22	16.66	15.32	16.32	14.11	14.18	13.33
Income Statement								
Total Revenues	2,006,943	992,267	4,052,173	3,481,277	2,924,844	2,577,727	2,289,370	1,940,074
Total Indirect Exp.	1,869,620	923,277	3,791,690	3,255,542	2,748,217	2,429,318	2,153,033	1,827,636
Depreciation & Amort.	25,711	12,893	56,293	43,541	47,348	45,993	40,455	33,839
Operating Income	127,714	63,738	234,995	209,592	163,170	133,535	119,457	98,375
Income Taxes	39,701	19,957	71,373	69,713	57,229	47,344	45,150	35,139
Net Income	88,013	43,781	163,622	139,879	105,941	86,191	74,307	63,236
Average Shs. Outstg.	227,935	227,848	227,690	227,267	216,513	211,182	211,035	210,660
Balance Sheet								
Cash & Cash Equivalents	434	...	...	...	163,771	19,400	5,861	12,792
Total Current Assets	799,166	820,838	799,260	778,441	698,162	538,527	444,822	422,919
Total Assets	1,738,024	1,775,117	1,723,567	1,661,605	1,230,805	1,032,671	920,101	851,206
Total Current Liabilities	472,782	437,176	425,233	383,109	266,641	296,155	241,555	317,650
Long–Term Obligations	236,558	258,944	262,981	324,083	124,552	141,700	162,579	82,120
Net Stockholders' Equity	1,064,503	1,065,497	1,019,869	946,059	831,927	588,578	509,465	446,732
Net Working Capital	376,384	383,662	374,027	395,332	431,521	242,372	203,267	105,269
Shares Outstanding	226,923	226,747	209,676	225,717	224,759	211,229	211,167	210,780
Statistical Record								
Operating Profit Margin %	6.36	6.42	5.79	6.02	5.57	5.18	5.21	5.07
Return on Equity %	8.26	4.10	16.04	14.78	12.73	14.64	14.58	14.15
Return on Assets %	5.06	2.46	9.49	8.41	8.60	8.34	8.07	7.42
Debt/Total Assets %	13.61	14.58	15.25	19.50	10.11	13.72	17.66	9.64
Price Range	17.75-14.41	16.58-14.41	19.75-13.25	19.60-12.10	13.75-7.50	9.03-6.75	9.55-4.75	6.30-3.45
P/E Ratio	23.67-19.21	22.41-19.47	27.43-18.40	31.61-19.51	28.06-15.31	22.56-16.88	27.29-13.57	21.00-11.50
Average Yield %	0.74	0.77	0.73	0.60	0.75	0.65	0.69	0.89

Address: 530 Beriault Street, Longueuil, QC J4G 1S8 Telephone: (450) 646–9760 Web Site: www.jeancoutu.com; www.brooks–rx.com	Officers: Jean Coutu – Chmn., C.E.O., Francois J. Coutu – Pres., C.E.O. Transfer Agents:National Bank Trust Inc., Montreal, Quebec	Investor Contact:514–842–1433 Institutional Holding No of Institutions: 3 Shares: 2,108,100 % Held: –

LEON'S FURNITURE LTD.

Exchange	Symbol	Price	52Wk Range	Yield	P/E
TSX	LNF	C$31.73 (5/31/2004)	31.75–26.35	2.52	15.11

*7 Year Price Score 122.9 ***NYSE Composite Index=100** ***12 Month Price Score 50.2**

Interim Earnings (Per Share) Can$

Qtr.	Mar	Jun	Sep	Dec
2001	0.27	0.31	0.49	0.72
2002	0.34	0.35	0.53	0.71
2003	0.23	0.32	0.57	0.82
2004	0.39	...	...	...

Interim Dividends (Per Share) Can$

Amt	Decl	Ex	Rec	Pay
0.12Q	8/21/2003	9/22/2003	9/24/2003	10/24/2003
0.14Q	11/26/2003	12/12/2003	12/16/2003	1/16/2004
0.14Q	2/19/2004	3/3/2004	3/5/2004	4/6/2004
0.20Q	...	6/3/2004	6/7/2004	7/7/2004

Indicated Div: C$0.80

Valuation Analysis
Forecast P/E N/A
Market Cap C$638.5 Million   Book Value N/A
Price/Book N/A   Price/Sales N/A

Dividend Achiever Status
Rank 19   5 Year Growth Rate 12.20%
Total Years of Dividend Growth 7

Business Summary: Chemicals (MIC: 11.1 SIC: 2599 NAIC:337127)

Leon's Furniture is a manufacturer and retailer of furniture and other home furnishings and accessories. Co. sells products through a network of retail stores and corporate–owned franchises located throughout Canada, including Quebec, Ontario, Manitoba, Alberta, Saskatchewan and the Atlantic Provinces. Co.'s product selection includes dining room furniture, bedroom suites, occasional tables, chests, desks, kitchen appliances, washers and dryers, vacuums, and home entertainment. These product lines cover all major design categories including European traditional, contemporary/transitional, American traditional and country/casual designs.

Recent Developments: For the quarter ended Mar 31 2004, net income climbed 63.7% to C$7.5 million from C$4.6 million in the prior–year quarter. Sales increased 13.7% to C$104.5 million from C$91.9 million the previous year. The increase in sales was due to a number of factors, including growth in same store sales, a continuing effort to enhance Co.'s product line and a new vigorous marketing campaign. In addition, Co. also benefited from increased sales from recent new stores and renovated showrooms. Cost of sales, operating, administrative and selling expenses increased 9.6% to C$91.4 million, but decreased as a percentage of sales to 87.5% from 90.8% a year earlier due to productivity improvements.

Prospects: Co.'s prospects are encouraging, supported by continuing efforts to enhance its merchandising line, product margins and marketing strategy. Moreover, during the first quarter there was an improvement in consumer confidence with which Co. was able to combine efficiencies in operations and an increase in sales. Although Co. expects the second quarter to continue to improve, it may not do so at the same pace as in the first quarter due to the volatile nature of the retail environment. Nevertheless, the opening of three new stores this fall, along with the addition of new franchise signings, should enhance Co.'s ability to increase sales and profitability for the balance of the year.

Financial Data

(Can$ in Thousands)	9 Mos	6 Mos	3 Mos	12/31/2002	12/31/2001	12/31/2000	12/31/1999	12/31/1998
Earnings Per Share	1.12	0.55	0.23	1.93	1.79	1.78	1.73	1.27
Cash Flow Per Share	2.04	0.88	0.32	1.81	1.64	...	...	...
Dividends Per Share	0.480	0.480	0.980	0.960	0.400	1.130	0.810	0.270
Dividend Payout %	42.85	87.27	426.08	49.74	22.34	63.48	46.82	21.25
Income Statement								
Total Revenues	319,198	197,924	91,892	449,693	425,687	402,236	370,825	336,895
Total Indirect Exp.	286,186	182,044	85,673	138,074	131,610	122,124	109,782	103,363
Depreciation & Amort.	7,200	4,626	2,247	8,552	7,742	6,933	6,401	5,649
Operating Income	33,012	15,880	6,219	50,354	45,632	45,314	43,398	34,144
Net Interest Inc./(Exp.)	2,659	1,476	661	2,650	4,178	5,041	4,675	4,440
Income Taxes	13,103	6,320	2,313	25,211	26,522	27,301	27,880	21,530
Net Income	22,568	11,036	4,567	38,520	36,323	36,700	36,166	26,406
Average Shs. Outstg.	20,234	20,253	20,280	19,956	20,265	20,575	20,920	20,684
Balance Sheet								
Cash & Cash Equivalents	...	...	84,010	86,014	99,282	103,369	108,124	101,085
Total Current Assets	...	...	154,576	179,845	171,906	167,145	168,556	156,584
Total Assets	...	...	296,838	320,439	295,675	280,656	268,581	245,270
Total Current Liabilities	...	...	62,602	87,605	77,414	78,232	90,232	81,325
Net Stockholders' Equity	...	...	233,866	232,635	218,122	202,345	178,313	163,917
Net Working Capital	...	...	91,974	92,240	94,492	88,913	78,324	75,259
Shares Outstanding	...	19,312	19,490	19,490	19,631	20,228	20,268	20,122
Statistical Record								
Operating Profit Margin %	10.34	8.02	6.76	11.19	10.71	11.26	11.70	10.13
Return on Equity %	...	...	1.95	16.55	16.65	18.13	20.28	16.66
Return on Assets %	...	...	1.53	12.02	12.28	13.07	13.46	11.13
Price Range	31.00–25.50	31.00–25.50	31.00–26.00	34.50–22.20	25.00–19.00	24.25–18.50	24.70–17.00	22.00–16.50
P/E Ratio	27.68–22.77	56.36–46.36	134.8–113.0	17.88–11.50	13.97–10.61	13.62–10.39	14.28–9.83	17.32–12.99
Average Yield %	1.72	1.74	3.42	3.22	1.82	5.60	4.06	1.40

Address: 45 Gordon MacKay Road, Weston, ON M9L 2R8 **Telephone:** (413) 243–7880 **Web Site:** www.leons.ca	**Officers:** Anthony T. Leon – Chmn., Mark J. Leon – V. Chmn., C.E.O. **Transfer Agents:**CIBC Mellon Trust Company, Toronto	**Investor Contact:**416–243–7880 **Institutional Holding** **No of Institutions:** 1 **Shares:** 18,800 **% Held:** –

LOBLAW COS. LTD.

Exchange	Symbol	Price	52Wk Range	Yield	P/E
TSX	L	C$63.25 (5/31/2004)	68.20-58.40	1.20	20.14

*7 Year Price Score 137.2 ***NYSE Composite Index=100** ***12 Month Price Score 45.7**

Interim Earnings (Per Share) Can$

Qtr.	Mar	Jun	Sep	Dec
2001	0.34	0.41	0.50	0.78
2002	0.46	0.53	0.68	0.95
2003	0.55	0.65	0.79	1.06
2004	0.64	...	...	...

Interim Dividends (Per Share) Can$

Amt	Decl	Ex	Rec	Pay
0.15Q	8/27/2003	9/11/2003	9/15/2003	10/1/2003
0.15Q	11/25/2003	12/11/2003	12/15/2003	12/30/2003
0.19Q	2/12/2004	3/11/2004	3/15/2004	4/1/2004
0.19Q	...	6/11/2004	6/15/2004	7/11/2004

Indicated Div: C$0.76

Valuation Analysis

Forecast P/E 17.91 (5/24/2004)

Market Cap	$17.5 Billion	Book Value	N/A
Price/Book	N/A	Price/Sales	N/A

Dividend Achiever Status

Rank	2	5 Year Growth Rate	24.57%
Total Years of Dividend Growth			10

TRADING VOLUME (thousand shares)

Business Summary: Retail – General (MIC: 5.2 SIC: 5399 NAIC:452910)

Loblaw Companies is Canada's largest food distributor. Co. sells a complete line of traditional grocery and other household products. Co.'s food labels include *President's Choice*, *President's Choice Organic*, *Club Pack* and no name. Co. operates stores under various banners including Atlantic SaveEasy, Atlantic Superstore, Dominion, Extra Foods, Fortinos, Loblaws, Lucky Dollar Foods, Maxi, No Frills, Provigo, The Real Canadian Superstore, The Real Canadian Wholesale Club, Shop Easy Foods, SuperValu, Valu–mart, Your Independent Grocer, Zehrs Markets and Cash and Carry.

Recent Developments: For the quarter ended Mar 27 2004, net earnings grew 16.6% to C$176.0 million from C$151.0 million in the prior–year quarter. Sales grew 5.6% to C$5.68 billion due largely to a 2.0% increase in same–store sales and an increase of 2.3 million square feet of net retail square footage from the opening of new stores over the last 12 months. Volumes increased consistently with sales with some minor impact from shifts in product mix. Cost of sales, selling and administrative expenses rose 5.0% to C$5.27 billion. Operating income was C$306.0 million, up 13.3% from C$270.0 million a year earlier.

Prospects: Co. continues to successfully execute its strategic initiatives, improving its cost base and its consumer value proposition and positioning itself for sustainable future growth. Good progress continues on the roll out of non–food categories in conjunction with a solid capital investment program. Going forward, Co. expects sales and profit to grow the rest of the year. However, these increases will likely be constrained by a competitive retail landscape in Canada and food price deflation in some markets. Nevertheless, Co. plans to maintain a solid financial position and good cash flow generation while continuing its planned 2004 capital investment program of approximately C$1.40 billion.

Financial Data

(Can$ in Thousands)	01/03/2004	12/28/2002	12/30/2001	12/30/2000	01/01/2000	01/02/1999	01/03/1998	12/28/1996
Earnings Per Share	3.05	2.62	2.03	1.70	1.37	1.06	0.88	0.72
Cash Flow Per Share	3.72	3.53	...	...	...	...	...	...
Dividends Per Share	0.600	0.460	0.400	0.310	0.220	0.200	0.150	0.120
Dividend Payout %	19.67	17.55	19.70	18.23	...	...	...	...
Income Statement								
Total Revenues	25,220,000	23,082,000	21,486,000	20,121,000	18,783,000	12,497,000	11,008,000	9,848,000
Total Indirect Exp.	393,000	354,000	315,000	283,000	273,000	183,000	147,000	122,000
Depreciation & Amort.	393,000	354,000	315,000	283,000	273,000	183,000	147,000	122,000
Operating Income	1,467,000	1,303,000	1,136,000	976,000	811,000	529,000	426,000	359,000
Net Interest Inc./(Exp.)	196,000	161,000	158,000	143,000	112,000	68,000	44,000	46,000
Income Taxes	426,000	414,000	372,000	317,000	280,000	199,000	169,000	139,000
Net Income	845,000	728,000	563,000	473,000	376,000	261,000	213,000	174,000
Average Shs. Outstg.	277,100	277,900	276,247	276,003	275,076	246,572	242,033	240,631
Balance Sheet								
Cash & Cash Equivalents	996,000	1,127,000	1,001,000	1,050,000	726,000	672,000	776,000	720,000
Total Current Assets	3,485,000	3,526,000	3,086,000	2,916,000	2,415,000	2,249,000	1,681,000	1,553,000
Total Assets	12,177,000	11,110,000	10,008,000	9,025,000	7,979,000	7,105,000	4,013,000	3,531,000
Total Current Liabilities	3,114,000	3,154,000	2,796,000	3,207,000	2,812,000	2,956,000	1,479,000	1,399,000
Long–Term Obligations	3,956,000	3,420,000	3,333,000	2,377,000	1,979,000	1,364,000	915,000	734,000
Net Stockholders' Equity	4,732,000	4,124,000	3,569,000	3,124,000	2,904,000	2,595,000	1,495,000	1,311,000
Net Working Capital	371,000	372,000	290,000	(291,000)	(397,000)	(707,000)	202,000	154,000
Shares Outstanding	274,829	276,018	276,252	276,245	274,910	274,423	242,781	241,341
Statistical Record								
Operating Profit Margin %	5.81	5.64	5.28	4.85	4.31	4.23	3.86	3.64
Return on Equity %	17.85	17.65	15.77	15.14	12.94	10.05	14.24	13.27
Return on Assets %	6.93	6.55	5.62	5.24	4.71	3.67	5.30	4.92
Debt/Total Assets %	32.48	30.78	33.30	26.33	24.80	19.19	22.80	20.78
Price Range	67.85-51.95	63.81-50.50	54.05-46.10	54.50-30.30	41.25-33.00	37.50-24.50	26.85-14.15	14.50-10.29
P/E Ratio	22.25-17.03	24.35-19.27	26.63-22.71	32.06-17.82	30.11-24.09	35.38-23.11	30.51-16.08	20.14-14.29
Average Yield %	1.01	0.80	0.79	0.74	0.59	0.64	0.77	1.02

Address: 22 St. Clair Avenue East, Toronto, ON M4T 2S7	Officers: W. Galen Weston – Chmn., John A. Lederer – Pres.	Investor Contact:
Telephone: (416) 922 8500	Transfer Agents:Computershare Trust Company of Canada, Toronto, Ontario	Institutional Holding
Web Site: www.loblaw.com		No of Institutions: 3
		Shares: 8,130,291 % Held: –

MELCOR DEVELOPMENTS LTD.

Exchange	Symbol	Price	52Wk Range	Yield	P/E
TSX	MRD	C$46.00 (5/31/2004)	48.50–37.50	2.61	8.26

*7 Year Price Score N/A *NYSE Composite Index=100 *12 Month Price Score 49.3

Interim Earnings (Per Share) Can$

Qtr.	Mar	Jun	Sep	Dec
2001	0.19	1.17	1.47	2.38
2002	1.70	1.08	1.65	2.98
2003	1.18	0.71	2.07	1.90
2004	0.89	...	...	...

Interim Dividends (Per Share) Can$

Amt	Decl	Ex	Rec	Pay
0.50S	10/24/2002	12/11/2002	12/13/2002	12/27/2002
0.55S	4/24/2003	6/11/2003	6/15/2003	6/30/2003
0.55S	12/28/2003	12/10/2003	12/13/2003	12/30/2003
0.60S	4/28/2004	6/14/2004	6/16/2004	6/30/2004

Indicated Div: C$1.20

Valuation Analysis

Forecast P/E N/A

Market Cap	$140.3 Million	Book Value	N/A
Price/Book	N/A	Price/Sales	N/A

Dividend Achiever Status

Rank	18	5 Year Growth Rate	12.89%
Total Years of Dividend Growth		8	

Business Summary: Property, Real Estate &Development (MIC: 8.3 SIC: 6552 NAIC:237210)

Melcor Developments is a real estate development company. Co. conducts business through four divisions. The Community Development division is engaged in the acquisition of land for development and sale for residential communities, multi–family sites and commercial sites. Co.'s development is concentrated in Alberta in the regions of Calgary, Edmonton, Red Deer and Lethbridge and the greater Tuscon, AZ area. The Property Development division develops income producing properties, which once completed and 75.0% leased, are transferred to the Investment Property division, which holds the properties as long–term investments. The Golf Courses division owns two public 18–hole golf courses.

Recent Developments: For the first quarter ended Mar 31 2004, net earnings declined 24.1% to C$2.7 million compared with C$3.6 million in the corresponding prior–year quarter. Net revenue declined 25.2% to C$15.6 million from C$20.9 million a year earlier. On a segment basis, Community Development sales fell 30.5% to C$13.3 million, primarily due to lower volume of single–family lots. Recreation Property sales fell 41.1% to C$33,000. Meanwhile, Investment Property sales increased 15.7% to C$2.8 million, primarily due to activity from the Sterling Business Centre acquired in December 2003. Gross profit decreased 17.1% to C$6.1 million from C$7.4 million the year before.

Prospects: Co. recently acquired 160 acres of land in the City of Leduc, Alberta which adjoins one of its existing land holdings. Meanwhile, Co. has received initial planning approvals for a new neighborhood in southwest Edmonton, Alberta. In addition, Co. has agreed to form a new joint venture and to acquire 285 acres of future commercial/industrial lands in the city of Airdrie, Alberta. Separately, Co. is exercising an option to acquire 74 additional acres of land in Lethbridge, Alberta, adjacent to the Paradise Canyon development, which should close during the second quarter of 2004. These actions should drive results going forward as the current real estate market remains strong in Alberta.

Financial Data

(Can$ in Thousands)	12/31/2003	12/31/2002	12/31/2001	12/31/2000	12/31/1999	12/31/1998	12/31/1997	12/31/1996
Earnings Per Share	5.86	7.41	5.21	3.48	2.50	3.08	2.64	1.19
Cash Flow Per Share	5.91	9.00	5.75	...	...	...	...	...
Dividends Per Share	1.100	1.000	0.900	0.800	0.700	0.600	0.500	0.400
Dividend Payout %	18.77	13.49	17.27	...	...	...	18.93	33.61
Income Statement								
Total Revenues	80,035	110,565	82,607	61,221	46,563	57,661	50,589	33,964
Total Indirect Exp.	7,584	8,062	6,838	5,822	5,041	5,234	4,499	3,438
Depreciation & Amort.	1,091	906	832	...	...	...	...	...
Operating Income	23,534	33,343	23,392	16,665	12,454	16,276	14,885	6,879
Net Interest Inc./(Exp.)	2,389	1,716	1,416	1,149	1,658	1,337	621	620
Income Taxes	9,095	12,974	8,871	7,663	6,345	7,863	6,925	3,075
Income from Cont Ops	...	...	...	...	...	9,750	8,581	3,994
Net Income	18,406	23,089	15,971	10,630	7,767	9,659	8,502	3,854
Average Shs. Outstg.	3,139	3,115	3,065					
Balance Sheet								
Cash & Cash Equivalents	5,080	7,105	1,325	1,181	8,404	11,544	12,080	1,905
Total Current Assets	54,320	67,113	47,941	38,088	40,739	47,618	37,622	22,310
Total Assets	251,806	231,795	177,218	158,786	153,350	153,590	128,042	111,229
Total Current Liabilities	9,839	16,410	11,116	7,439	7,109	8,937	7,634	4,200
Long–Term Obligations	74,862	61,539	41,503	37,033	40,479	35,792	26,683	21,567
Net Stockholders' Equity	140,737	126,511	106,718	92,885	85,577	80,963	73,499	67,336
Net Working Capital	44,481	50,703	36,825	30,649	33,630	38,681	29,988	18,110
Shares Outstanding	3,082	3,052	3,045	3,038	3,104	3,134	3,183	3,215
Statistical Record								
Operating Profit Margin %	29.40	30.15	28.31	27.22	26.74	28.22	29.42	20.25
Return on Equity %	13.07	18.25	14.96	11.44	9.07	11.93	11.56	5.72
Return on Assets %	7.30	9.96	9.01	6.69	5.06	6.28	6.64	3.46
Debt/Total Assets %	29.73	26.54	23.41	23.32	26.39	23.30	20.83	19.38
Price Range	48.00–37.00	42.00–26.50	28.50–20.00	20.25–17.00	19.75–16.05	21.25–15.50	18.00–14.25	14.90–10.00
P/E Ratio	8.19–6.31	5.67–3.58	5.47–3.84	5.82–4.89	7.90–6.42	6.90–5.03	6.82–5.40	12.52–8.40
Average Yield %	2.73	2.86	3.72	4.40	3.94	3.30	3.12	3.43

Address: 900, 10310 Jasper Avenue, Edmonton, AB T5J 1Y8	Officers: Timothy C. Melton – Exec. Chmn., Ralph B. Young – Pres., C.E.O.	Institutional Holding
Telephone: (780) 423 6931	**Transfer Agents:**CIBC Mellon Trust Company, Calgary and Toronto	No of Institutions:
Web Site: www.melcor.ca		Shares: % Held:

METRO INC

Exchange	Symbol	Price	52Wk Range	Yield	P/E
TSX	MRU A	C$17.85 (5/31/2004)	22.25-17.31	1.00	10.56

*7 Year Price Score 146.5 *NYSE Composite Index=100 ***12 Month Price Score 42.3**

Interim Earnings (Per Share) Can$

Qtr.	Dec	Mar	Jun	Sep
2000-01	0.24	0.30	0.37	0.27
2001-02	0.29	0.30	0.45	0.37
2002-03	0.35	0.37	0.53	0.42
2003-04	0.38	0.36	...	...

Interim Dividends (Per Share) Can$

Amt	Decl	Ex	Rec	Pay
0.07Q	8/6/2003	8/14/2003	8/18/2003	9/2/2003
0.07Q	9/30/2003	11/6/2003	11/10/2003	12/1/2003
0.085Q	1/27/2004	2/6/2004	2/10/2004	3/3/2004
0.085Q	4/7/2004	4/30/2004	5/4/2004	5/25/2004

Indicated Div: C$0.34

Valuation Analysis
Forecast P/E 10.44 (5/24/2004)

Market Cap	$1.8 Billion	Book Value	N/A
Price/Book	N/A	Price/Sales	N/A

Dividend Achiever Status

Rank	8	5 Year Growth Rate	20.55%
Total Years of Dividend Growth			8

Business Summary: Retail – Food &Beverage (MIC: 5.3 SIC: 5141 NAIC:424410)

Metro is a major Canadian food retailer and distributor with operations concentrated in Quebec and Ontario. Co. is the second largest food retailer in Quebec, where it also holds a substantial position in the food services industry. In addition, Co. is active in the distribution of pharmaceutical products and as the franchisor of Brunet drugstores and Clini–Plus pharmacies. In Ontario, with its Loeb and Super C banners, Co. ranks second in the supermarket segment in Ottawa and northeastern regions of the Province. In 2003, the floor space of Co.'s food retail network totalled more than 9.6 million square feet.

Recent Developments: For the twelve weeks ended Mar 13 2004, net earnings decreased 5.6% to C$35.2 versus C$37.3 million in the equivalent quarter of 2003. Total sales increased 4.2% to C$1.27 billion from C$1.22 billion a year earlier. Food distribution segment sales rose 3.9% to C$1.16 billion, primarily due to expansion of the retail network total floor space as a result of ongoing investment, and to the acquisition of a small–surface store grocery distributor. Pharmaceutical distribution segment sales advanced 7.5% to C$106.4 million, due to continued development of Brunet drugstores and Clini–Plus pharmacies now totaling 177 stores up from 164 in the prior year. Operating income fell 7.6% to C$52.2 million.

Prospects: Co. is confident that, with its ongoing retail investment programs and new merchandising strategies recently implemented, it can maintain its competitive position in the Canadian food market. Co. is continuing with its investment program in the retail network with an objective of investing over C$450.0 million over the next three years to build, expand and remodel stores. Specifically, Co. intends to open new Super C stores in both Québec and Ontario and will further support its expansion in the Ontario market by building, expanding and renovating Loeb supermarkets.

Financial Data

(Can$ in Thousands)	3 Mos	09/27/2003	09/28/2002	09/29/2001	09/30/2000	09/25/1999	09/26/1998	09/27/1997
Earnings Per Share	1.70	1.67	1.41	1.18	0.93	0.72	0.72	0.63
Cash Flow Per Share	0.58	1.97	2.21	...	...	...	...	...
Dividends Per Share	0.280	0.260	0.210	0.170	0.140	0.120	0.100	0.070
Dividend Payout %	73.68	15.86	14.89	14.61	15.59	17.24	14.13	11.90
Income Statement								
Total Revenues	1,348,500	5,567,300	5,146,800	4,868,900	4,657,500	3,995,500	3,653,000	3,432,300
Total Indirect Exp.	1,292,400	64,900	57,600	61,400	52,500	44,300	39,700	39,200
Depreciation & Amort.	15,900	64,900	57,600	61,400	52,500	44,300	39,700	39,200
Operating Income	56,100	249,500	224,500	189,200	167,000	143,000	130,200	115,400
Net Interest Inc./(Exp.)	1,300	2,800	3,000	5,200	9,200	5,900	4,900	5,300
Income Taxes	17,200	80,400	77,800	61,200	60,500	45,700	41,900	43,900
Net Income	37,600	166,300	143,700	122,800	97,300	76,400	65,400	66,200
Average Shs. Outstg.	98,800	99,800	101,900	100,200	100,400	101,800	101,800	102,400
Balance Sheet								
Cash & Cash Equivalents	...	...	...	...	...	400	700	2,400
Total Current Assets	665,900	647,800	556,600	504,500	421,800	382,800	350,500	328,100
Total Assets	1,565,000	1,507,100	1,329,100	1,186,000	1,059,700	996,200	787,500	725,500
Total Current Liabilities	702,400	678,700	568,100	492,100	447,600	425,000	366,400	323,500
Long–Term Obligations	8,200	8,800	25,000	55,300	88,600	144,200	48,600	94,600
Net Stockholders' Equity	784,200	751,900	644,200	558,000	461,700	392,300	342,600	296,200
Net Working Capital	(36,500)	(30,900)	(11,500)	12,400	(25,800)	(42,200)	(15,900)	4,600
Shares Outstanding	97,965	97,812	99,486	100,166	100,416	100,707	101,552	102,088
Statistical Record								
Operating Profit Margin %	4.16	4.48	4.36	3.88	3.58	3.57	3.56	3.36
Return on Equity %	4.79	22.11	22.30	22.00	21.07	19.47	19.08	22.34
Return on Assets %	2.40	11.03	10.81	10.35	9.18	7.66	8.30	9.12
Debt/Total Assets %	0.52	0.58	1.88	4.66	8.36	14.47	6.17	13.03
Price Range	21.33-18.75	20.00-16.10	22.20-16.95	18.50-9.25	9.85-7.48	11.50-8.63	11.00-7.33	8.50-4.63
P/E Ratio	12.55-11.03	11.98-9.64	15.74-12.02	15.68-7.84	10.59-8.04	15.97-11.98	15.28-10.17	13.49-7.34
Average Yield %	1.39	1.41	1.08	1.37	1.57	1.22	1.15	1.06

TRADING VOLUME (thousand shares)

Address: 11011 Maurice–Duplessis Blvd., Montreal, QC H1C 1V6 **Telephone:** (514) 643–1055 **Web Site:** www.metro.ca	**Officers:** Maurice Jodoin – Chmn., Paul Gobeil – Vice–Chmn.	**Investor Contact:** 514–643–1055 **Institutional Holding** **No of Institutions:** 1 **Shares:** 583,700 **% Held:** –

NATIONAL BANK OF CANADA

Business Summary: Commercial Banking (MIC: 8.1 SIC: 6021 NAIC:522110)

National Bank of Canada is an integrated financial group. Co.'s Personal and Commercial segment comprises the branch network, intermediary services, credit cards, insurance, real estate and commercial banking services. Co.'s Wealth Management segment provides full–service retail brokerage, discount brokerage, mutual funds, trust services and portfolio management. Co.'s Financial Markets segment consists of corporate financing and lending, treasury operations, which include asset and liability management, and corporate brokerage. In addition, Co. has securitization operations. As of Oct 31 2003, Co. had assets of C$82.42 billion and total deposits of C$51.46 billion.

Recent Developments: For the first quarter ended Jan 31 2004, net income advanced 12.0% to C$186.0 million compared with C$166.0 million in the corresponding prior–year quarter. Net interest income declined 21.7% to C$278.0 million from C$355.0 million a year earlier. Interest income and dividends fell 12.9% to C$569.0 million, while interest expense decreased 2.3% to C$291.0 million. Provision for credit losses increased 7.3% to C$44.0 million from C$41.0 million the year before. Non–interest income jumped 32.3% to C$635.0 million, while non–interest expense rose 5.7% to C$579.0 million.

Prospects: Co. continues to improve its offering of financial products and investment solutions. For example, National Bank Securities has introduced its Advisor Series which enables independent financial advisors to sell all of its mutual funds. Co. also continues to expand its distribution network by capitalizing on partnerships with distributors and resellers of financial products. Separately, on Mar 2 2004, Co. announced a ten–year outsourcing agreement with INTRIA Items to supply check, bill payment and currency processing for Co. and includes the transfer of processing facilities and nearly 600 employees to INTRIA. The deal should provide continuing quality service while remaining competitive.

Financial Data

(Can$ in Thousands)	3 Mos	10/31/2003	10/31/2002	10/31/2001	10/31/2000	10/31/1999	10/31/1998	10/31/1997
Earnings Per Share	3.47	3.33	1.59	3.10	2.52	2.21	1.67	1.84
Dividends Per Share	1.080	1.040	0.900	0.800	0.740	0.690	0.640	0.550
Dividend Payout %	105.88	31.23	56.60	25.80	29.36	31.22	38.32	29.89
Income Statement								
Total Interest Income	569,000	2,529,000	2,591,000	3,381,000	3,856,000	3,493,000	3,374,000	3,105,000
Total Interest Expense	291,000	1,205,000	1,147,000	2,043,000	2,564,000	2,211,000	2,067,000	1,786,000
Net Interest Income	278,000	1,324,000	1,444,000	1,338,000	1,292,000	1,282,000	1,307,000	1,319,000
Non–Interest Expense	579,000	2,259,000	2,040,000	1,989,000	2,184,000	1,662,000	1,653,000	1,489,000
Income Before Taxes	290,000	926,000	498,000	933,000	816,000	698,000	603,000	596,000
Eqty Earns/Minority Int.	7,000	27,000	30,000	28,000	26,000	32,000	31,000	16,000
Net Income	186,000	624,000	429,000	601,000	509,000	417,000	316,000	342,000
Average Shs. Outstg.	177,008	179,235	187,727	190,815	191,665	178,138	173,615	171,824
Balance Sheet								
Net Loans & Leases	56,408,000	56,312,000	53,679,000	56,324,000	58,332,000	56,460,000	60,674,000	60,271,000
Total Assets	80,812,000	82,423,000	74,611,000	75,763,000	75,827,000	69,801,000	70,663,000	66,235,000
Total Deposits	51,500,000	51,463,000	51,690,000	51,436,000	50,473,000	49,984,000	48,026,000	43,270,000
Long–Term Obligations	1,473,000	1,516,000	1,592,000	1,647,000	1,361,000	1,035,000	966,000	1,069,000
Total Liabilities	76,652,000	78,326,000	70,710,000	71,647,000	71,999,000	66,500,000	67,968,000	63,475,000
Net Stockholders' Equity	4,160,000	4,097,000	3,901,000	4,116,000	3,828,000	3,301,000	2,695,000	2,760,000
Shares Outstanding	173,569	174,619	182,596	190,331	189,474	188,728	171,616	170,461
Statistical Record								
Return on Equity %	4.47	14.62	10.45	12.82	12.56	12.63	11.72	12.39
Return on Assets %	0.23	0.72	0.54	0.69	0.63	0.59	0.44	0.51
Equity/Assets %	5.14	4.97	5.22	5.43	5.04	4.72	3.81	4.16
Non–Int. Exp./Tot. Inc. %	101.75	89.32	78.73	58.82	56.63	47.58	48.99	47.95
Price Range	45.00–40.17	41.19–29.39	34.93–24.12	31.00–23.00	25.25–16.40	26.25–17.15	31.25–20.05	20.35–13.00
P/E Ratio	12.97–11.58	12.37–8.83	21.97–15.17	10.00–7.42	10.02–6.51	11.88–7.76	18.71–12.01	11.06–7.07
Average Yield %	2.56	3.03	2.97	2.90	3.57	3.23	2.56	3.39

Address: National Bank Tower, Montreal, QC H3B 4L2 Telephone: (514) 394 394 8644 Web Site: www.nbc.ca	Officers: Andre Berard – Chmn., C.E.O., Real Raymond – Pres., C.E.O. Transfer Agents:National Bank Trust Inc., Montreal, Quebec	Investor Contact:514–394–6433 Institutional Holding No of Institutions: 4 Shares: 469,113 % Held: –

POWER CORP. OF CANADA

Interim Earnings (Per Share) Can$

Qtr.	Mar	Jun	Sep	Dec
2001	0.77	1.57	0.75	(0.40)
2002	0.74	0.84	0.55	0.63
2003	0.71	0.94	2.97	0.86
2004	0.89	...	...	...

Interim Dividends (Per Share) Can$

Amt	Decl	Ex	Rec	Pay
0.244Q	8/1/2003	9/5/2003	9/9/2003	9/30/2003
0.244Q	11/26/2003	12/8/2003	12/10/2003	12/31/2003
0.244Q	2/20/2004	3/8/2004	3/10/2004	3/31/2004
0.288Q	5/17/2004	6/3/2004	6/7/2004	6/30/2004

Indicated Div: $1.152

Valuation Analysis

Forecast P/E 12.02 (5/24/2004)

Market Cap	$10.5 Billion	Book Value	N/A
Price/Book	N/A	Price/Sales	N/A

Dividend Achiever Status

Rank	12	5 Year Growth Rate	16.47%
Total Years of Dividend Growth		8	

Business Summary: Other Depository Banking (MIC: 8.5 SIC: 6099 NAIC:551112)

Power Corp. of Canada is holding company whose principal asset is a 67.1% interest in Power Financial Corp., which in turn holds controling interests in Great–West Lifeco Inc. (Lifeco) and Investors Group Inc. Lifeco offers a range of life and health insurance, retirement and investment products, as well as reinsurance and specialty general insurance products. Investors Group offers financial planning services and investment products, as well as investment advisory, management and administrative services for mutual funds. Co. also holds interest in Pargesa Holdings S.A., which holds interests in a number of media, specialty minerals, water, waste services and energy companies.

Recent Developments: For the year ended Dec 31 2003, net earnings advanced 96.6% to C$1.27 billion compared with C$645.0 million in the previous year. Total revenues decreased 17.1% to C$15.75 billion from C$19.00 billion a year earlier. Revenues in 2003 were reduced by initial ceded premiums for reinsurance of C$5.37 billion. Gross premium income increased 11.2% to C$12.44 billion, while net investment income climbed 24.3% to C$3.86 billion. Fees and media income slipped 1.9% to C$3.86 billion. Income from operations grew 21.1% to C$2.70 billion from C$2.23 billion the year before.

Prospects: Co.'s goals for its group of financial services companies includes increasing its distribution reach by adding new distribution channels, to lower costs by combining operations and books of business, to focus on the sale and distribution of value–added products with above average growth potential, and to strengthen Co.'s base in Canada while adding significantly to its international earnings. Meanwhile, in Europe, the Pargesa group includes interests in four prominent operating companies with well–established franchises and prospects for continued growth.

Financial Data

(Can$ in Millions)	12/31/2003	12/31/2002	12/31/2001	12/31/2000	12/31/1999	12/31/1998	12/31/1997	12/31/1996
Earnings Per Share	5.48	2.76	2.69	2.93	2.36	1.88	2.99	2.44
Cash Flow Per Share	11.60	8.17	...	...	...	...	...	...
Dividends Per Share	0.938	0.794	0.675	0.575	0.488	0.438	0.400	0.388
Dividend Payout %	16.42	27.62	18.58	19.62	20.66	23.27	13.37	15.90
Income Statement								
Total Revenues	15,747	19,017	18,360	16,906	14,739	15,055	8,615	6,896
Total Indirect Exp.	4,471	4,031	4,391	3,711	3,258	3,049	2,072	1,725
Depreciation & Amort.	142	131	...	...	...	...	...	...
Operating Income	2,698	2,228	1,798	1,741	1,454	1,237	749	647
Income Taxes	837	764	663	755	547	492	121	243
Eqty Earns/Minority Int.	1,404	813	592	582	627	529	305	259
Net Income	1,268	645	618	657	533	420	331	292
Average Shs. Outstg.	226	225	225	220	...	...	...	...
Balance Sheet								
Cash & Cash Equivalents	4,159	3,001	2,590	2,024	1,891	1,978	1,914	1,322
Total Current Assets	4,159	3,001	2,590	2,024	1,891	1,978	1,914	1,322
Total Assets	107,723	70,136	68,730	60,564	57,652	58,925	55,888	32,133
Total Current Liabilities	1,832	1,262	671	219	307	372	488	986
Long–Term Obligations	4,289	2,393	2,544	1,026	985	849	1,068	430
Net Stockholders' Equity	6,042	5,387	4,692	4,502	3,450	3,145	2,640	2,463
Net Working Capital	2,327	1,739	1,919	1,805	1,584	1,606	1,426	336
Shares Outstanding	196	197	196	195	196	197	110	109
Statistical Record								
Operating Profit Margin %	17.13	11.71	9.79	10.29	9.86	8.21	8.69	9.37
Return on Equity %	20.98	11.97	13.17	14.59	15.44	13.35	12.53	11.86
Return on Assets %	1.17	0.91	0.89	1.08	0.92	0.71	0.59	0.90
Debt/Total Assets %	3.98	3.41	3.70	1.69	1.70	1.44	1.91	1.33
Price Range	48.90–35.20	43.85–32.55	39.10–32.00	37.05–19.10	35.10–22.00	37.20–23.25	25.60–13.43	14.50–9.56
P/E Ratio	8.92–6.42	15.89–11.79	14.54–11.90	12.65–6.52	14.87–9.32	19.79–12.37	8.56–4.49	5.94–3.92
Average Yield %	2.20	1.98	1.41	2.45	1.72	1.41	2.24	2.47

Address: 751 Victoria Square, Montreal, QC H2Y 2J3 **Telephone:** (514) 286–7400 **Web Site:** www.powercorporation.com	**Officers:** Paul Desmarais – Chmn., Co–C.E.O., Andre Desmarais – Pres., Co–C.E.O. **Transfer Agents:**Computershare Trust Company of Canada, Toronto, Montreal, and Vancouver	**Investor Contact:** Coun., **Institutional Holding** **No of Institutions:** 4 **Shares:** 2,655,188 **% Held:** –

POWER FINANCIAL CORP

Exchange	Symbol	Price	52Wk Range	Yield	P/E
TSX	PWF	C$54.60 (5/31/2004)	58.60–42.50	2.40	5.31

*7 Year Price Score 144.9 *NYSE Composite Index=100 *12 Month Price Score 52.6

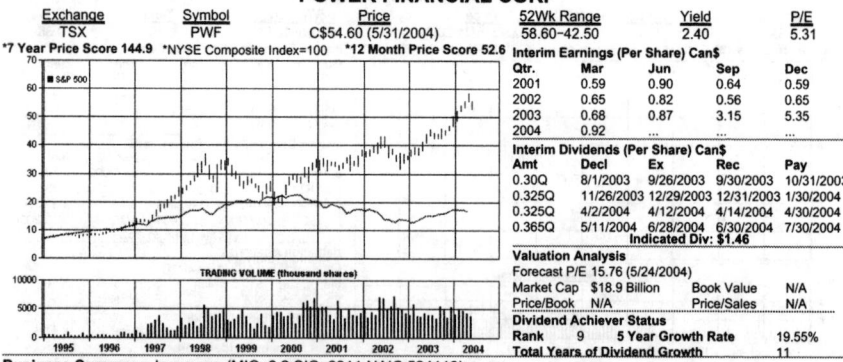

Interim Earnings (Per Share) Can$

Qtr.	Mar	Jun	Sep	Dec
2001	0.59	0.90	0.64	0.59
2002	0.65	0.82	0.56	0.65
2003	0.68	0.87	3.15	5.35
2004	0.92	...	...	...

Interim Dividends (Per Share) Can$

Amt	Decl	Ex	Rec	Pay
0.30Q	8/1/2003	9/26/2003	9/30/2003	10/31/2003
0.325Q	11/26/2003	12/29/2003	12/31/2003	1/30/2004
0.325Q	4/2/2004	4/12/2004	4/14/2004	4/30/2004
0.365Q	5/11/2004	6/28/2004	6/30/2004	7/30/2004

Indicated Div: $1.46

Valuation Analysis

Forecast P/E 15.76 (5/24/2004)

Market Cap $18.9 Billion	Book Value N/A
Price/Book N/A	Price/Sales N/A

Dividend Achiever Status

Rank 9   5 Year Growth Rate   19.55%
Total Years of Dividend Growth   11

Business Summary: Insurance (MIC: 8.2 SIC: 6311 NAIC:524113)

Power Financial is a diversified management and holding company. Through its respective controlling interests of 70.2% and 56.0% in Great–West Lifeco Inc. and Investors Group Inc., Co. holds substantial interests in the financial services industry in Canada and the U.S., as well as in Europe. Together with the Frere group of Belgium, Co. also holds a significant interest in Pargesa Holding SA through Parjointco N.V. The Pargesa group has substantial interests in major media, energy, water, waste services and specialty minerals companies based in Europe. Pargesa's major holdings include Bertelsmann AG, TotalFinaElf, Suez and Imerys S.A.

Recent Developments: For the quarter ended Mar 31 2004, net earnings increased 34.0% to C$339.0 million compared with C$253.0 million in the corresponding year–earlier period. Revenues advanced 21.0% to C$5.80 billion from C$4.79 billion the previous year. Premium income rose 15.7% to C$3.41 billion. Net investment income grew 39.1% to C$1.39 billion. Fee income climbed 18.1% to C$1.00 billion compared with C$847.0 million the year before. Co. attributed the improved operating earnings to a strong increase in contributions from its subsidiaries and affiliate, as well as the additional contribution provided by the shares of Great–West Lifeco acquired in 2003, net of related financing costs.

Prospects: Co.'s outlook appears reasonably positive. Co. has stated that its strategy is to own controlling interests in financial services companies with strong fundamentals that include a low cost structure, competitive and strategically viable distribution channels, value–added products and a size that allows them to invest and develop profitably. In addition, Co. has attempted to maintain a balance between Canadian and non–Canadian earnings, as evidenced by its American and European operations of Great–West Lifeco and its investment in Pargesa, a European–based holding company.

Financial Data

(Can$ in Thousands)	9 Mos	6 Mos	3 Mos	12/31/2002	12/31/2001	12/31/2000	12/31/1999	12/31/1998
Earnings Per Share	4.71	1.54	0.68	2.68	2.72	2.18	2.32	1.87
Dividends Per Share	1.120	1.080	1.040	1.000	0.840	0.690	0.570	0.470
Dividend Payout %	23.77	70.12	152.94	37.31	30.88	...	...	...
Income Statement								
Total Premium Income	3,253,000	5,618,000	2,949,000	11,187,000	10,477,000	9,976,000	8,526,000	9,237,000
Other Income	5,940,000	3,629,000	1,849,000	18,620,000	17,889,000	16,531,000	14,424,000	14,767,000
Total Revenues	9,193,000	9,247,000	4,798,000	18,620,000	17,889,000	16,531,000	14,424,000	14,767,000
Total Indirect Exp.	2,938,000	1,732,000	881,000	3,668,000	4,014,000	3,425,000	2,961,000	2,769,000
Inc. Before Inc. Taxes	2,733,000	1,178,000	541,000	2,198,000	1,953,000	1,756,000	1,704,000	1,449,000
Income Taxes	576,000	351,000	169,000	749,000	642,000	665,000	535,000	483,000
Eqty Earns/Minority Int.	393,000	203,000	123,000	461,000	284,000	305,000	335,000	288,000
Net Income	1,705,000	578,000	253,000	988,000	879,000	786,000	834,000	678,000
Average Shs. Outstg.	351,600	351,500	350,800	351,600	351,700	346,666	346,779	...
Balance Sheet								
Cash & Cash Equivalents	4,520,000	3,075,000	3,236,000	2,437,000	2,120,000	1,831,000	1,622,000	1,670,000
Invst. Assets: Total	83,091,000	50,358,000	51,952,000	52,677,000	52,004,000	49,083,000	48,578,000	50,300,000
Total Assets	106,892,000	66,372,000	68,406,000	68,319,000	67,069,000	59,354,000	56,647,000	58,033,000
Long–Term Obligations	3,612,000	3,151,000	3,242,000	2,313,000	2,437,000	1,026,000	985,000	837,000
Net Stockholders' Equity	7,974,000	6,939,000	7,117,000	6,855,000	5,828,000	4,963,000	3,912,550	4,172,000
Shares Outstanding	348,416	348,416	348,396	346,856	346,701	347,053	346,836	346,580
Statistical Record								
Return on Revenues %	18.54	6.25	5.27	5.30	4.91	4.75	5.78	4.59
Return on Equity %	21.38	8.32	3.55	14.41	15.08	15.83	21.31	16.25
Return on Assets %	1.59	0.87	0.36	1.44	1.31	1.32	1.47	1.16
Price Range	45.90–36.30	45.60–36.30	39.39–36.30	43.25–31.85	38.60–31.00	35.20–19.10	35.40–21.00	36.90–22.88
P/E Ratio	9.75–7.71	29.61–23.57	57.93–53.38	16.14–11.88	14.19–11.40	16.15–8.76	15.26–9.05	19.73–12.23
Average Yield %	2.72	2.70	2.74	2.65	2.47	2.54	2.10	1.59

Address: 751 Victoria Square, Montreal, QC H2Y 2J3 Telephone: (514) 286 7425 Web Site: www.powerfinancial.com	Officers: Paul Desmarais – Chmn., Andre Desmarais – Dep. Chmn. Transfer Agents:Computershare Trust Company of Canada, Toronto, Ontario	Institutional Holding No of Institutions: 3 Shares: 9,002,325 % Held: –

QUEBECOR WORLD INC.

Exchange	Symbol	Price	52Wk Range	Yield	P/E
NYS	IQW	$20.38 (5/28/2004)	28.59-20.89	1.87	N.M.

*7 Year Price Score 77.4   *NYSE Composite Index=100   *12 Month Price Score 49.5

Interim Earnings (Per Share)

Qtr.	Mar	Jun	Sep	Dec
2001	0.38	0.51	0.57	...
2002	0.28	0.40	0.64	0.44
2003	0.12	(0.51)	0.38	(0.49)
2004	0.20	...	...	...

Interim Dividends (Per Share)

Amt	Decl	Ex	Rec	Pay
0.13Q	7/24/2003	8/13/2003	8/15/2003	9/1/2003
0.13Q	10/23/2003	11/12/2003	11/14/2003	12/1/2003
0.13Q	2/6/2004	2/11/2004	2/13/2004	3/1/2004
0.13Q	5/5/2004	5/12/2004	5/14/2004	6/1/2004

Indicated Div: $0.52

Valuation Analysis

Forecast P/E 15.69 (5/24/2004)

Market Cap	N/A	Book Value	3.4 Billion
Price/Book	N/A	Price/Sales	N/A

Dividend Achiever Status

Rank	11	5 Year Growth Rate	16.72%
Total Years of Dividend Growth			13

Business Summary: Printing (MIC: 13.4 SIC: 2759 NAIC:323113)

Quebecor World is engaged in commercial print media services. Co.'s product categories include magazines, retail inserts and circulars, books, catalogs, specialty printing and direct mail, directories, digital pre-media, mail list technologies and other services. As of Dec 31, 2003, Co. had approximately 160 printing and related facilities in the United States, Canada, France, the United Kingdom, Spain, Switzerland, Sweden, Finland, Austria, Belgium, Brazil, Chile, Argentina, Peru, Colombia, Mexico and India.

Recent Developments: For the quarter ended Mar 31 2004, net income was $35.8 million compared with $24.5 million in the corresponding year-earlier period. Results for 2004 included restructuring and other charges of $4.3 million. Revenues rose slightly to $1.55 billion from $1.54 billion last year. Co. noted that excluding the favorable effect of currency, revenues fell 4.0%. North American revenues slid 3.1% to $1.19 billion, primarily due to lower prices. Europe revenues climbed 19.7% to $315.4 million; however, excluding the favorable effect of currency, revenues rose 3.0%. Latin American revenues grew 3.8% to $46.8 million, which Co. also attributed primarily to the positive effect of currency translation.

Prospects: Co.'s outlook is tempered by difficult industry and market conditions that have resulted in overcapacity and negative pricing pressure. As a result, Co. has indicated that it will continue to focus on further reducing costs and improving efficiencies across its global platform. For instance, under its most recent initiative Co. plans to cut 368 employee positions, the majority of which are concentrated in its North American operations. Under this initiative, 331 positions have been eliminated and the remainder will be completed by June 30 2004. Co. noted that this restructuring is in addition to 2,200 plus employee positions that were eliminated as part of its 2003 restructuring.

Financial Data

(US$ in Thousands)	12/31/2003	12/31/2002	12/31/2001	12/31/2000	12/31/1999	12/31/1998	12/31/1997	12/31/1996
Earnings Per Share	(0.50)	1.76	...	1.94	0.56	1.29	1.12	1.09
Cash Flow Per Share	3.39	3.53	4.03	6.24	...	...	...	...
Tang. Book Val. Per Share	N.M	N.M	N.M	N.M	N.M	5.91	7.26	7.26
Dividends Per Share	0.520	0.490	0.460	0.330	0.280	0.240	0.220	0.200
Dividend Payout %	N.M.	27.84	...	17.01	50.00	18.60	19.64	18.34
Income Statement								
Total Revenues	6,391,500	6,242,000	6,320,100	6,521,077	4,952,537	3,808,155	3,483,199	3,110,292
Total Indirect Exp.	970,600	855,900	823,400	804,557	633,885	526,776	478,972	446,641
Depreciation & Amort.	335,900	335,600	337,800	345,079	285,992	239,402	210,729	194,134
Operating Income	232,100	543,200	617,800	724,803	473,245	301,886	267,371	260,533
Net Interest Inc./(Exp.)	221,300	170,200	208,800	231,464	122,177	64,300	65,812	62,540
Income Taxes	39,100	90,900	52,000	137,735	48,161	74,828	69,108	69,083
Eqty Earns/Minority Int.	3,100	2,800	3,200	2,353	12,701	3,198	2,011	2,615
Net Income	(31,400)	279,300	22,400	295,431	80,056	159,560	130,440	126,295
Average Shs. Outstg.	136,000	145,400	143,000	147,041	125,393	115,703	115,567	115,519
Balance Sheet								
Cash & Cash Equivalents	15,100	2,700	85,500	52,732	3,613	309	380	806
Total Current Assets	908,000	967,300	913,200	1,185,274	1,260,977	954,230	958,355	792,598
Total Assets	6,213,800	6,205,500	6,149,900	6,484,660	6,756,252	3,842,116	3,475,538	2,913,410
Total Current Liabilities	1,101,000	1,176,600	1,107,700	1,251,809	1,221,288	710,124	739,046	585,774
Long-Term Obligations	1,985,100	1,783,600	2,075,200	2,121,490	2,762,663	1,199,134	973,290	851,210
Net Stockholders' Equity	2,503,400	2,703,800	2,473,200	2,473,880	2,320,884	1,564,504	1,436,340	1,155,066
Net Working Capital	(193,000)	(209,300)	(194,500)	(66,535)	39,689	244,106	219,309	206,824
Shares Outstanding	131,951	141,145	140,184	146,139	159,675	127,790	115,577	115,535
Statistical Record								
Operating Profit Margin %	3.63	8.70	9.77	11.11	9.55	7.92	7.67	8.37
Return on Equity %	N.M.	10.32	0.90	11.94	3.44	10.19	9.08	10.93
Return on Assets %	N.M.	4.50	0.36	4.55	1.18	4.15	3.75	4.33
Debt/Total Assets %	31.94	28.74	33.74	32.71	40.89	31.21	28.00	29.21
Price Range	37.38-20.89	46.09-32.25	42.60-30.73	39.10-25.60	36.50-31.40	33.85-22.00	27.40-20.35	25.13-21.45
P/E Ratio	N/A	26.19-18.32	...	N/A	20.15-13.20	65.18-56.07	26.24-17.05	24.46-18.17	23.05-19.68
Average Yield %	1.97	1.26	1.25	0.98	0.83	0.89	0.89	0.85

Address: 612 Saint Jacques Street, Montreal, QC H3C 4M8	Officers: Pierre Karl Peladeau – Pres., C.E.O., Claude Heile – Exec. V.P., C.F.O.	Investor Contact:514 877 5118
Telephone: (514) 954 0101	**Transfer Agents:**Computershare Trust of Canada	**Institutional Holding**
Web Site: www.quebecorworld.com		**No of Institutions:** 36
		Shares: 37,799,626 **% Held:** 27%

ROYAL BANK OF CANADA (MONTREAL, QUEBEC)

Exchange	Symbol	Price	52Wk Range	Yield	P/E
TSX	RY	C$59.06 (5/31/2004)	65.59–56.91	3.52	13.18

*7 Year Price Score 132.1   *NYSE Composite Index=100   *12 Month Price Score 46.3

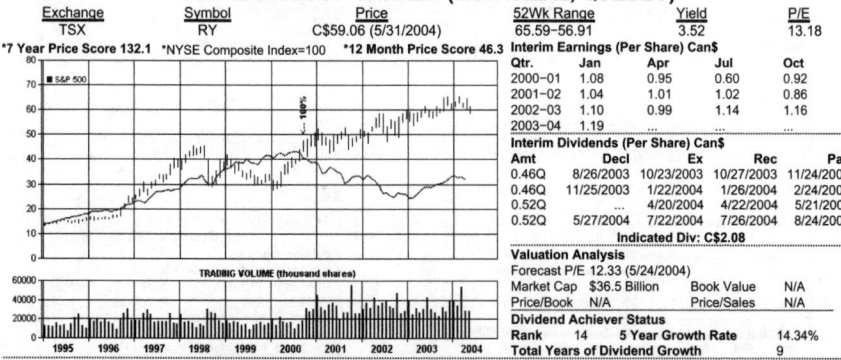

Interim Earnings (Per Share) Can$

Qtr.	Jan	Apr	Jul	Oct
2000–01	1.08	0.95	0.60	0.92
2001–02	1.04	1.01	1.02	0.86
2002–03	1.10	0.99	1.14	1.16
2003–04	1.19	...	...	...

Interim Dividends (Per Share) Can$

Amt	Decl	Ex	Rec	Pay
0.46Q	8/26/2003	10/23/2003	10/27/2003	11/24/2003
0.46Q	11/25/2003	1/22/2004	1/26/2004	2/24/2004
0.52Q	...	4/20/2004	4/22/2004	5/21/2004
0.52Q	5/27/2004	7/22/2004	7/26/2004	8/24/2004

Indicated Div: C$2.08

Valuation Analysis

Forecast P/E 12.33 (5/24/2004)

Market Cap	$36.5 Billion	Book Value	N/A
Price/Book	N/A	Price/Sales	N/A

Dividend Achiever Status

Rank	14	5 Year Growth Rate	14.34%
Total Years of Dividend Growth		9	

Business Summary: Commercial Banking (MIC: 8.1 SIC: 6029 NAIC:522110)

Royal Bank of Canada is engaged in personal and commercial banking (RBC Banking), wealth management (RBC Investments), insurance (RBC Insurance), corporate and investment banking (RBC Capital Markets) and transaction processing (RBC Global Services). In U.S., Co. provides personal and commercial banking, mortgage origination, insurance, full–service brokerage and corporate and investment banking services through RBC Centura and its subsidiaries RBC Mortgage and RBC Builder Finance, as well as through RBC Insurance, RBC Dain Rauscher and RBC Capital Markets. As of Oct 31 2003, Co. had total assets of C$412,591 million, deposits of C$260,518 million and 4,401 automated banking machines.

Recent Developments: For the quarter ended Jan 31 2004, net income rose 3.4% to C$793.0 million compared with C$767.0 million a year earlier. Net interest income fell 3.9% to C$1.65 billion, due in part to a C$60.0 million decline in the translated value of U.S. dollar–denominated net interest income and deposit spread compression in RBC Banking. Non–interest income slid 2.8% to C$2.55 billion. Co. noted that the appreciation of the Canadian dollar relative to the U.S. dollar from the first quarter of 2003 reduced the translated value of non–interest income by C$180.0 million. Recovery of credit losses amounted to C$28.0 million versus a provision for credit losses of C$200.0 million the year before.

Prospects: Co.'s near–term outlook is mixed. On one hand, a lower net interest margin due to significant growth in low interest–yielding assets such as securities, coupled with a decline in RBC Banking's net interest margin could hamper results. However, Co. should continue to benefit from improved credit quality as the North American economic recovery unfolds. Additionally, Co.'s business diversification should continue to result in higher brokerage, underwriting and mutual fund revenues as equity markets strengthen. Lastly, Co. has indicated that it is taking steps to improve returns from its banking operations in the U.S.

Financial Data

(Can$ in Millions)	3 Mos	10/31/2003	10/31/2002	10/31/2001	10/31/2000	10/31/1999	10/31/1998	10/31/1997
Earnings Per Share	4.48	4.39	3.93	3.55	3.40	2.48	2.65	2.50
Dividends Per Share	1.720	1.660	1.480	1.320	1.080	0.930	0.840	0.730
Dividend Payout %	144.53	37.81	37.65	37.18	31.76	37.50	31.88	29.20
Income Statement								
Total Interest Income	3,404	14,053	14,672	17,307	16,109	14,200	14,776	13,307
Total Interest Expense	1,759	7,411	7,514	10,810	10,830	9,083	9,712	8,307
Net Interest Income	1,645	5,921	6,093	5,378	4,588	4,357	4,489	4,620
Provision for Loan Losses	...	721	1,065	1,119	691	760	575	380
Non–Interest Income	2,550	10,776	8,562	8,155	6,680	5,491	4,985	4,279
Non–Interest Expense	3,111	11,047	9,223	8,503	6,624	6,036	5,352	5,116
Income Before Taxes	1,112	4,592	4,235	3,892	3,640	2,707	3,075	2,846
Eqty Earns/Minority Int.	30	127	108	107	20	8	76	77
Net Income	793	3,005	2,762	2,435	2,208	1,725	1,824	1,679
Average Shs. Outstg.	659	669	678	647	609	632	633	618
Balance Sheet								
Net Loans & Leases	182,347	249,211	242,098	246,266	228,925	211,408	212,986	201,502
Total Assets	440,507	403,033	376,956	362,483	294,054	273,298	274,399	244,774
Total Deposits	265,673	259,145	243,486	235,687	206,237	187,897	180,005	173,229
Long–Term Obligations	8,031	6,243	6,614	6,662	5,825	4,596	4,087	4,227
Total Liabilities	422,324	384,658	358,173	344,278	280,757	260,890	262,507	234,384
Net Stockholders' Equity	18,183	18,375	18,783	18,205	13,297	12,408	11,892	10,390
Shares Outstanding	655	656	665	674	602	617	617	616
Statistical Record								
Return on Equity %	4.36	16.35	14.70	13.37	16.60	13.90	15.33	16.15
Return on Assets %	0.18	0.74	0.73	0.67	0.75	0.63	0.66	0.68
Equity/Assets %	4.12	4.55	4.98	5.02	4.52	4.54	4.33	4.24
Non–Int. Exp./Tot. Inc. %	52.25	44.49	39.69	33.39	29.06	30.65	27.08	29.09
Price Range	65.35–60.50	64.90–53.70	58.70–46.56	53.02–42.75	48.30–27.75	41.88–30.15	45.65–29.10	38.00–22.15
P/E Ratio	14.59–13.50	14.78–12.23	14.94–11.85	14.94–12.04	14.21–8.16	16.89–12.16	17.23–10.98	15.20–8.86
Average Yield %	2.74	2.83	2.83	2.73	2.95	2.65	2.13	2.51

Address: 200 Bay Street, Toronto, ON M5J 2J5	Officers: Elisabetta Bigsby – Sr. Exec. V.P., Human Res. & Public Affairs, Peter W. Currie – C.F.O.	Institutional Holding
Telephone: (416) 974 5151	Transfer Agents:Computershare Trust Company of Canada, Montreal, Quebec; The Bank of New York, NY; Computershare Services plc, Bristol, England	No of Institutions: 119
Web Site: www.rbc.com		Shares: 160,956,931 % Held: 24%

TERASEN INC

Exchange	Symbol	Price	52Wk Range	Yield	P/E
TSX	TER	C$48.00 (5/31/2004)	49.85–41.52	3.25	11.82

*7 Year Price Score 135.1 *NYSE Composite Index=100 ***12 Month Price Score 49.1**

Interim Earnings (Per Share) Can$

Qtr.	Mar	Jun	Sep	Dec
2001	1.58	(0.08)	(0.58)	1.27
2002	1.69	0.03	(0.44)	1.15
2003	...	0.16	(0.15)	2.52
2004	1.53	...	...	...

Interim Dividends (Per Share) Can$

Amt	Decl	Ex	Rec	Pay
0.36Q	11/7/2002	11/14/2002	11/18/2002	11/30/2002
0.36Q	2/14/2003	2/20/2003	2/24/2003	2/28/2003
0.39Q	4/25/2003	5/14/2003	5/16/2003	5/31/2003
0.39Q	7/31/2003	8/14/2003	8/18/2003	8/31/2003

Indicated Div: C$1.56

Valuation Analysis

Forecast P/E 16.58 (5/24/2004)

Market Cap	$2.3 Billion	Book Value	N/A
Price/Book	N/A	Price/Sales	N/A

Dividend Achiever Status

Rank	26	5 Year Growth Rate	7.02%
Total Years of Dividend Growth		7	

Business Summary: Gas Utilities (MIC: 7.4 SIC: 4613 NAIC:486910)

Terasen is a provider of energy and utility services. Through Terasen Gas, Co. distributes natural gas to more than 862,000 customers, representing approximately 95.0% of natural gas consumers in British Columbia. Through Terasen Pipelines, Co. provides petroleum transportation services from the Athabasca oil sands to Edmonton, and from Alberta to British Columbia, Washington state, the U.S. Rocky Mountains region and the U.S. midwest. Terasen Utility Services, a subsidiary of Co., is a provider of water treatment services in Western Canada, operating more than 50 water and wastewater treatment systems in British Columbia and Alberta.

Recent Developments: For the three months ended Mar 31 2004, net earnings increased 9.5% to C$82.2 compared with C$75.1 million in the corresponding year–earlier period. Revenues advanced 17.2% to C$651.5 million from C$556.0 million the previous year. Co.'s results were driven by improved petroleum transportation results, reflecting strong throughput volumes from the Trans Mountain mainline and contribution from the Corridor Pipeline, which commenced commercial shipping in May 2003. Petroleum transportation segment earnings climbed 57.8% to C$18.3 million versus C$11.6 million last year. Natural gas distribution segment earnings rose slightly to C$67.4 million from C$67.1 million the year before.

Prospects: On Apr 20 2004, Co. announced that it has entered into an agreement to acquire a 50.0% interest in Fairbanks Sewer and Water Inc. (FSW) for approximately $30.0 million. FSW, which is privately held, provides water and wastewater treatment and water distribution services to Fairbanks, AK. Co. also has an option to acquire the remaining 50.0% at fair market value in 2009. The acquisition expands Co.'s presence in Alaska, where it has been operating the Fairbanks gas distribution system since 2001 under an operating contract with the owner of the gas utility. The transaction is subject to regulatory approvals and is expected to be finalized in the summer of 2004.

Financial Data

(Can$ in Thousands)	12/31/2003	12/31/2002	12/31/2001	12/31/2000	12/31/1999	12/31/1998	12/31/1997	12/31/1996
Earnings Per Share	2.53	2.43	2.19	2.82	2.12	1.85	1.27	2.53
Cash Flow Per Share	5.14	7.29	...	...	...	...	...	...
Dividends Per Share	1.530	1.410	1.300	1.220	1.160	1.090	0.970	0.900
Dividend Payout %	60.47	58.02	59.36	43.43	54.71	58.91	76.37	35.57
Income Statement								
Total Revenues	1,876,600	1,707,200	1,666,300	1,305,600	1,040,600	925,000	933,900	901,400
Total Indirect Exp.	516,900	471,000	367,900	333,600	318,000	326,300	314,700	307,100
Depreciation & Amort.	133,400	115,600	95,100	86,200	82,600	84,600	77,900	78,400
Operating Income	366,400	336,500	295,200	256,600	256,400	260,500	244,000	231,300
Net Interest Inc./(Exp.)	176,000	160,800	148,300	117,500	121,600	121,800	114,700	126,500
Income Taxes	59,000	63,200	55,900	8,900	48,900	62,900	49,600	32,100
Eqty Earns/Minority Int.	...	...	...	4,000	4,700	4,600	5,800	3,900
Net Income	139,400	112,500	91,000	112,700	81,200	71,200	50,800	105,600
Average Shs. Outstg.	52,400	43,600	38,300	38,300	38,300	38,500	40,100	41,800
Balance Sheet								
Cash & Cash Equivalents	1,500	5,100	2,100	22,400	5,600	...	...	29,400
Total Current Assets	577,000	482,900	503,500	631,200	270,700	224,900	188,900	305,200
Total Assets	4,915,100	4,522,400	3,705,700	3,513,100	2,450,500	2,466,100	2,388,100	2,427,100
Total Current Liabilities	1,014,100	878,900	857,700	1,094,400	712,400	858,100	696,700	648,200
Long–Term Obligations	2,301,100	2,123,400	1,928,000	1,561,900	1,001,800	906,700	993,300	1,033,900
Net Stockholders' Equity	1,429,600	1,365,600	840,100	809,500	626,300	590,000	588,200	630,700
Net Working Capital	(437,100)	(396,000)	(354,200)	(463,200)	(441,700)	(633,200)	(507,800)	(343,000)
Shares Outstanding	52,077	51,681	38,343	38,326	38,279	38,266	39,093	41,265
Statistical Record								
Operating Profit Margin %	19.52	19.71	17.71	19.65	24.63	28.16	26.12	25.66
Return on Equity %	9.28	7.74	10.83	13.92	12.96	12.06	8.63	16.74
Return on Assets %	2.69	2.33	2.45	3.20	3.31	2.88	2.12	4.35
Debt/Total Assets %	46.81	46.95	52.02	44.45	40.88	36.76	41.59	42.59
Price Range	48.00–36.35	42.50–32.64	36.40–29.75	33.45–21.50	31.00–21.00	33.95–27.00	27.95–20.25	20.90–15.00
P/E Ratio	18.97–14.37	17.49–13.43	16.62–13.58	11.86–7.62	14.62–9.91	18.35–14.59	22.01–15.94	8.26–5.93
Average Yield %	3.62	3.68	3.92	4.44	4.14	3.60	4.02	5.15

Address: 1111 West Georgia Street, Vancouver, BC V6E 4M4 **Telephone:** (604) 443 6500 **Web Site:** www.terasen.com	**Officers:** John M. Reid – Pres., C.E.O., Richard T. Ballantyne – Pres., Terasen Pipelines Inc. **Transfer Agents:**CIBC Mellon Trust Company, Vancouver, British Columbia	**Investor Contact:**604 443 6559 **Institutional Holding** **No of Institutions:** 2 **Shares:** 912,400 **% Held:** –

THOMSON CORP.

Exchange	Symbol	Price	52Wk Range	Yield	P/E
NYS	TOC	$32.67 (5/28/2004)	47.74-40.05	2.33	25.93

*7 Year Price Score 95.5 *NYSE Composite Index=100 *12 Month Price Score 48.4

Interim Earnings (Per Share)

Qtr.	Mar	Jun	Sep	Dec
2001	0.24	0.18	0.23	0.40
2002	(0.05)	0.14	0.39	0.44
2003	0.10	0.16	0.45	0.60
2004	0.05	...	...	...

Interim Dividends (Per Share)

Amt	Decl	Ex	Rec	Pay
0.18Q	7/31/2003	8/19/2003	8/21/2003	9/15/2003
0.185Q	10/30/2003	11/18/2003	11/20/2003	12/15/2003
0.185Q	2/12/2004	2/20/2004	2/24/2004	3/15/2004
0.19Q	4/27/2004	5/18/2004	5/20/2004	6/15/2004

Indicated Div: $0.76

Valuation Analysis

Forecast P/E 26.30 (5/24/2004)

Market Cap	$29.0 Billion	Book Value	N/A
Price/Book	N/A	Price/Sales	N/A

Dividend Achiever Status

Rank	17	5 Year Growth Rate	12.94%
Total Years of Dividend Growth		9	

TRADING VOLUME (thousand shares)

Business Summary: Non-Media Publishing (MIC: 13.3 SIC: 7375 NAIC:518210)

Thomson provides value-added information, software tools and applications to users in the fields of law, tax, accounting, financial services, higher education, reference information, corporate training and assessment, scientific research and healthcare. Co. organizes its operations into four market groups that are structured on the basis of the customers they serve: Thomson Legal & Regulatory, Thomson Learning, Thomson Financial and Thomson Scientific & Healthcare.

Recent Developments: For the three months ended Mar 31 2004, income was $42.0 million, before a loss of $5.0 million from discontinued operations, compared with income of $36.0 million, before a gain of $11.0 million from discontinued operations, in the equivalent quarter of the previous year. Revenues increased 8.6% to $1.72 billion from $1.58 billion in the year–earlier period. The increase in revenues was primarily attributable to internal growth, contributions from acquisitions and favorable currency translation. Operating income more than doubled to $98.0 million versus $41.0 million in the prior–year quarter.

Prospects: Co. should continue to benefit from significant improvements in its Legal & Regulatory and Learning market groups as well as strong momentum for its Thomson One suite of products in the financial services market. Also, Co. should benefit from growing demand for integrated information solutions in each of its markets and the launch of innovative new products and services . Co. expects full–year 2004 revenue growth to be in the mid–single digits, excluding the effects of currency translation, and driven by continued growth from existing businesses and supplemented by acquisitions. Also, Co. expects to generate strong free cash flow in 2004.

Financial Data

(US$ in Millions)	12/31/2003	12/31/2002	12/31/2001	12/31/2000	12/31/1999	12/31/1998	12/31/1997	12/31/1996
Earnings Per Share	1.31	0.92	1.05	0.92	0.66	0.77	0.91	0.95
Cash Flow Per Share	2.52	2.63	...	...	...	...	...	...
Dividends Per Share	1.150	0.705	0.700	0.680	0.650	0.620	0.590	0.550
Dividend Payout %	88.01	76.63	66.66	74.45	...	...	...	...
Income Statement								
Total Revenues	7,606	7,756	7,237	6,514	5,752	6,269	8,766	7,723
Total Indirect Exp.	6,415	6,526	6,371	5,723	4,947	5,357	7,807	6,941
Depreciation & Amort.	873	830	920	743	602	644	667	554
Operating Income	1,191	1,230	866	791	805	912	959	782
Net Interest Inc./(Exp.)	252	291	236	204	186	252	293	277
Income Taxes	(156)	(192)	(168)	15	105	109	101	93
Eqty Earns/Minority Int.	(13)	(101)	(50)	...	...	...	...	...
Net Income	1,758	1,192	1,406	1,794	941	2,292	1,100	1,138
Average Shs. Outstg.	654	641	628	623	618	612	607	599
Balance Sheet								
Cash & Cash Equivalents	683	709	532	337	329	307	606	375
Total Current Assets	3,044	3,019	2,763	2,528	2,200	2,092	2,680	2,225
Total Assets	18,680	18,542	18,402	15,699	12,558	12,447	13,333	13,173
Total Current Liabilities	3,145	3,202	3,830	2,965	2,477	2,073	2,872	2,393
Long–Term Obligations	3,684	3,487	3,651	2,321	1,909	2,408	4,006	4,594
Net Stockholders' Equity	9,200	8,954	8,220	7,818	6,996	6,745	4,946	4,647
Net Working Capital	(101)	(183)	(1,067)	(437)	(277)	19	(192)	(168)
Shares Outstanding	654	651	630	625	621	616	610	604
Statistical Record								
Operating Profit Margin %	15.65	15.85	11.96	12.14	13.99	14.54	10.93	10.12
Return on Equity %	9.42	6.86	8.32	7.66	6.24	7.44	11.70	12.50
Return on Assets %	4.64	3.31	3.71	3.81	3.47	4.03	4.34	4.41
Debt/Total Assets %	19.72	18.80	19.84	14.78	15.20	19.34	30.04	34.87
Price Range	47.08–37.59	56.70–36.25	57.85–42.70	62.40–38.00	51.00–35.75	45.60–29.05	39.65–26.60	31.05–18.63
P/E Ratio	35.94–28.69	61.63–39.40	55.10–40.67	67.83–41.30	77.27–54.17	59.22–37.73	43.57–29.23	32.68–19.61
Average Yield %	2.75	1.52	1.37	1.30	1.56	1.56	1.84	2.38

Address: Toronto Dominion Bank Tower, Toronto, ON M5K 1A1 Telephone: (416) 360 8700 Web Site: www.thomson.com	Officers: Richard J. Harrington – Pres., C.E.O., Robert D. Daleo – Exec. V.P., C.F.O. Transfer Agents:Computershare Trust Company of Canada, Toronto, Ontario; Capita IRC plc, United Kingdom	Investor Contact:203 328 9470 Institutional Holding No of Institutions: 43 Shares: 26,707,452 % Held: 4.10%

TOROMONT INDUSTRIES LTD.

Exchange	Symbol	Price	52Wk Range	Yield	P/E
TSX	TIH	C$17.40 (5/31/2004)	19.99–11.50	1.49	17.94

*7 Year Price Score 151.6 *NYSE Composite Index=100   ***12 Month Price Score 54.1**

Interim Earnings (Per Share) Can$

Qtr.	Mar	Jun	Sep	Dec
2001	0.09	0.23	0.12	0.26
2002	0.03	0.17	0.13	0.31
2003	0.07	0.21	0.26	0.40
2004	0.10	...	...	...

Interim Dividends (Per Share) Can$

Amt	Decl	Ex	Rec	Pay
0.055Q	10/28/2003	12/15/2003	12/17/2003	1/2/2004
0.065Q	2/18/2004	3/16/2004	3/18/2004	4/1/2004
100%	2/18/2004	4/1/2004	4/5/2004	4/14/2004
0.065Q	4/14/2004	6/14/2004	6/16/2004	7/2/2004

Indicated Div: C$0.26

Valuation Analysis

Forecast P/E 16.84 (5/24/2004)

Market Cap $512.6 Million		Book Value	N/A
Price/Book N/A		Price/Sales	N/A

Dividend Achiever Status

Rank 23	5 Year Growth Rate	10.30%
Total Years of Dividend Growth		14

Business Summary: Purpose Machinery (MIC: 11.13 SIC: 3585 NAIC:333415)

Toromont Industries operates in two segments, the Equipment Group and the Compression Group. The Equipment Group sells, rents and services construction equipment and industrial engines through Co.'s Caterpillar dealership and Battlefield operations. The Compression Group is engaged in manufacturing, encompassing the design, installation and servicing of industrial and recreational refrigeration, carbon dioxide compression, process systems, fuel gas compression and natural gas compression. The Compression Group operates through Toromont Process Systems, Toromont Energy Systems Inc., CIMCO Refrigeration, and Aero Tech Manufacturing.

Recent Developments: For the year ended Dec 31 2003, net income advanced 45.6% to C$60.2 million compared with C$41.4 million the previous year. Revenues jumped 20.7% to C$1.30 billion from C$1.08 billion the year before. Equipment Group revenues climbed 10.0% to C$835.3 million from C$759.7 million, while Compression Group revenues soared 46.3% to C$464.1 million from C$317.3 million a year earlier. Gross profit improved 24.7% to C$271.0 million from C$217.3 million the previous year. Operating income increased 36.5% to C$102.1 million versus C$74.8 million the prior year.

Prospects: Co. is enjoying revenue and earnings momentum, particularly within the Compression Group. Also, Co.'s Equipment Group continues to keep pace with stronger activity levels achieved last year despite the strong Canadian dollar. Also, Co. is seeing new equipment order backlog in both the Compression and Equipment Groups. Looking ahead, the North American economic outlook for 2004 remains positive, while activity in Canada will likely be influenced by foreign exchange fluctuations, the U.S. economy and other global developments. Co. anticipates product and market improvements, combined with increased after-market activity should help Co. weather any short-term weaknesses in the industry.

Financial Data

(Can$ in Thousands)	12/31/2003	12/31/2002	12/31/2001	12/31/2000	12/31/1999	12/31/1998	12/31/1997	12/31/1996
Earnings Per Share	0.94	0.64	0.70	0.54	0.52	0.46	0.41	0.36
Cash Flow Per Share	1.35	1.11	...	...	...	...	...	...
Dividends Per Share	0.200	0.170	0.160	0.150	0.130	0.120	0.090	0.070
Dividend Payout %	21.27	27.73	23.75	28.70	26.19	26.63	22.45	20.13
Income Statement								
Total Revenues	1,299,389	1,076,930	911,005	800,464	723,937	683,482	684,716	542,477
Total Indirect Exp.	168,852	142,455	122,914	103,439	91,935	89,491	92,711	73,964
Depreciation & Amort.	39,423	36,652	...	...	...	...	...	...
Operating Income	102,127	74,829	65,129	59,676	53,770	52,204	46,105	35,258
Net Interest Inc./(Exp.)	13,276	11,366	11,962	10,995	8,366	1,910	2,424	5,213
Income Taxes	31,289	26,318	28,342	23,534	23,487	28,121	43,244	13,173
Eqty Earns/Minority Int.	...	...	...	...	...	...	878	5,033
Income from Cont Ops	...	...	...	...	...	...	59,955	16,872
Net Income	60,230	41,375	43,700	32,345	32,057	38,188	60,833	21,905
Average Shs. Outstg.	64,243	64,866	62,107	57,906	78,688	58,860	58,548	58,404
Balance Sheet								
Cash & Cash Equivalents	...	34,442	35,025	55,450	78,837	28,582	55,954	21,498
Total Current Assets	508,477	483,007	444,268	427,985	385,931	336,242	348,859	249,295
Total Assets	856,176	771,902	720,702	613,787	528,050	442,974	434,341	318,287
Total Current Liabilities	304,900	269,785	226,136	234,579	194,190	190,992	210,651	153,001
Long-Term Obligations	159,694	156,479	171,970	157,187	120,000	60,000	60,000	60,806
Net Stockholders' Equity	376,837	335,316	314,248	218,213	203,062	183,596	155,821	100,305
Net Working Capital	203,577	213,222	218,132	193,406	191,741	145,250	138,208	96,294
Shares Outstanding	63,563	63,455	64,194	57,951	58,576	58,916	58,796	58,536
Statistical Record								
Operating Profit Margin %	7.85	6.94	7.14	7.45	7.42	7.63	6.73	6.49
Return on Equity %	15.98	12.33	13.90	14.82	15.78	20.80	39.04	21.83
Return on Assets %	7.03	5.36	6.06	5.26	6.07	8.62	14.00	6.88
Debt/Total Assets %	18.65	20.27	23.86	25.60	22.72	13.54	13.81	19.10
Price Range	16.62-9.92	13.00-9.32	12.91-7.63	10.38-6.93	9.55-6.88	11.50-7.16	9.19-6.36	6.75-3.63
P/E Ratio	17.68-10.55	20.31-14.57	18.44-10.89	19.21-12.82	18.37-13.22	25.00-15.57	22.41-15.52	18.75-10.07
Average Yield %	1.59	1.59	1.60	1.75	1.56	1.34	1.22	1.58

Address: 3131 Highway 7 West, Concord, ON L4K 1B7
Telephone: (416) 667 5511
Web Site: www.toromont.com

Officers: Robert M. Ogilvie – Exec. Chmn., Hugo T. Sorensen – Pres., C.E.O.
Transfer Agents: CIBC Mellon Trust Company, Toronto, Ontario

Institutional Holding
No of Institutions: 1
Shares: 139,300 **% Held:** –

TORONTO DOMINION BANK

Exchange	Symbol	Price	52Wk Range	Yield	P/E
TSX	TD	$45.40 (5/31/2004)	47.95-35.54	3.00	24.15

*7 Year Price Score 117.7 *NYSE Composite Index=100 *12 Month Price Score 50.1

Interim Earnings (Per Share) Can$

Qtr.	Jan	Apr	Jul	Oct
2002	0.55	0.20	(0.67)	(0.33)
2003	0.50	(0.46)	0.73	0.73
2004	0.88	...	...	...

Interim Dividends (Per Share) Can$

Amt	Decl	Ex	Rec	Pay
0.32Q	8/28/2003	9/16/2003	9/18/2003	10/31/2003
0.32Q	11/26/2003	12/16/2003	12/18/2003	1/31/2004
0.34Q	2/26/2004	3/16/2004	3/18/2004	4/30/2004
0.34Q	5/27/2004	6/15/2004	6/17/2004	7/31/2004

Indicated Div: C$1.36 (Div. Reinv. Plan)

Valuation Analysis
Forecast P/E 12.53 (5/24/2004)

Market Cap	$29.2 Billion	Book Value	N/A
Price/Book	N/A	Price/Sales	N/A

Dividend Achiever Status

Rank	20	5 Year Growth Rate	11.94%
Total Years of Dividend Growth			10

TRADING VOLUME (thousand shares)

Business Summary: Commercial Banking (MIC: 8.1 SIC: 6029 NAIC:522110)

Toronto Dominion Bank is a bank holding company. Through its subsidiaries, Co. offers a full range of financial products and services to approximately 13.0 million customers in Canada and around the world. Co. is organized into three businesses: personal and commercial banking, including TD Canada Trust; wealth management, including the global operations of TD Warehouse, and a wholesale bank, TD Securities, which operates in 20 locations in key financial markets around the world. As of Oct 31 2003, Co.'s total assets were C$273.5 million and its total deposits were C$182.9 million.

Recent Developments: For the three months ended Jan 31 2004, net income soared 73.8% to C$603.0 million compared with C$347.0 million in the corresponding quarter of 2003. Results for 2004 and 2003 included net investment securities gains of C$45.0 million and C$5.0 million, respectively. Net interest income climbed 6.2% to C$1.48 billion from C$1.39 billion a year earlier. Reversal of credit losses amounted to C$104.0 million versus a provision of C$112.0 million the year before. Total non-interest income grew 12.3% to C$1.31 billion compared with C$1.17 billion in the prior-year period. Total non-interest expense slipped 1.6% to C$1.93 billion versus C$1.96 billion in the previous year.

Prospects: Results are benefiting from continued earnings momentum in personal and commercial banking and strong performances in wealth management and wholesale banking. Co.'s ongoing commitment to improving operating efficiencies resulted in an improvement in the efficiency ratio to 58.0%. Meanwhile, the acquisition of 57 retail branches of Laurentian Bank in Ontario and Western Canada added 1.0% to revenue growth and branch integration is on track. Separately, in January 2004, Co. announced an agreement to acquire the Canadian personal property and casualty operations of Liberty Mutual. The acquisition is expected to be slightly accretive to Co.'s earnings in 2004.

Financial Data

(Can$ in Thousands)	10/31/2003	10/31/2002	10/31/2001	10/31/2000	10/31/1999	10/31/1998	10/31/1997	10/31/1996
Earnings Per Share	1.51	(0.25)	2.37	1.77	4.97	1.81	1.77	2.89
Dividends Per Share	1.120	1.120	1.060	0.860	0.700	0.630	0.540	0.480
Dividend Payout %	74.17	N.M.	...	...	...	...	...	16.78
Income Statement								
Total Interest Income	11,202,000	11,751,000	14,471,000	13,675,000	10,874,000	9,997,000	7,826,000	7,360,000
Total Interest Expense	5,586,000	6,451,000	10,080,000	10,070,000	7,893,000	7,056,000	5,004,000	4,855,000
Net Interest Income	5,616,000	5,300,000	4,391,000	3,605,000	2,981,000	2,941,000	2,822,000	2,505,000
Non-Interest Income	...	...	...	...	...	...	...	103,000
Non-Interest Expense	8,550,000	10,677,000	9,376,000	8,465,000	4,785,000	4,406,000	3,743,000	2,806,000
Income Before Taxes	1,490,000	(448,000)	1,462,000	1,540,000	4,127,000	1,732,000	1,729,000	1,410,000
Eqty Earns/Minority Int.	92,000	34,000	45,000	77,000	5,000	...	...	...
Net Income	1,978,000	(320,000)	2,600,000	1,938,000	5,876,000	1,076,000	2,114,000	1,764,000
Average Shs. Outstg.	653,900	646,946	627,047	621,585	599,311	594,040	597,410	597,102
Balance Sheet								
Total Assets	273,532,000	278,040,000	287,838,000	264,818,000	214,417,000	181,831,000	163,852,000	125,644,000
Total Deposits	182,880,000	189,190,000	193,914,000	185,808,000	140,386,000	120,677,000	110,626,000	87,563,000
Long-Term Obligations	5,887,000	4,343,000	4,892,000	4,883,000	3,217,000	3,606,000	3,391,000	2,335,000
Total Liabilities	260,421,000	264,999,000	274,434,000	252,468,000	202,884,000	173,298,000	156,549,000	118,965,000
Net Stockholders' Equity	13,111,000	13,041,000	13,404,000	12,350,000	11,533,000	8,533,000	7,303,000	6,679,000
Shares Outstanding	656,300	645,399	628,451	622,616	620,343	594,238	593,892	605,406
Statistical Record								
Return on Equity %	8.20	N.M.	10.31	8.29	25.84	13.13	14.89	13.68
Return on Assets %	0.39	N.M.	0.48	0.38	1.39	0.61	0.66	0.72
Equity/Assets %	4.79	4.69	4.65	4.66	5.37	4.69	4.45	5.31
Non-Int. Exp./Tot. Inc. %	76.32	90.86	64.79	61.90	44.00	44.07	47.82	37.59
Price Range	43.86-28.35	44.94-25.25	45.27-35.49	46.30-33.20	43.50-21.50	36.50-18.93	25.83-15.68	15.68-11.50
P/E Ratio	29.05-18.77	N/A	19.10-14.97	26.16-18.76	8.75-4.33	20.17-10.46	14.59-8.86	5.42-3.98
Average Yield %	3.14	2.98	2.62	2.30	2.21	2.24	2.68	3.81

Address: P.O. Box 1, Toronto, ON M5K 1A2	Officers: Richard M. Thomson – Chmn., W. Edmund Clark – Pres., C.O.O.	Investor Contact:416–944–5743
Telephone: (416) 982-8222	Transfer Agents:CIBC Mellon Trust Company,	Institutional Holding
Web Site: www.td.com	Toronto; ChaseMellon Shareholder Services LLP,	No of Institutions: 80
	Ridgefield Park, NJ, United States; Mizuho Trust &Banking Co. Ltd, Tokyo, Japan	Shares: 150,091,439 % Held: 23.40%

WEST FRASER TIMBER CO., LTD.

Exchange	Symbol	Price	52Wk Range	Yield	P/E
TSX	WFT	C$42.74 (5/31/2004)	44.89-30.35	1.31	N/A

*7 Year Price Score 118.6 *NYSE Composite Index=100 ***12 Month Price Score 54.2**

Interim Earnings (Per Share) Can$

Qtr.	Mar	Jun	Sep	Dec
2001	(0.09)	1.74	0.82	0.73
2002	0.70	1.90	0.11	0.76
2003	0.29	(0.14)	0.09	0.92
2004	0.71	...	...	...

Interim Dividends (Per Share) Can$

Amt	Decl	Ex	Rec	Pay
0.14Q	6/17/2003	6/25/2003	6/27/2003	7/11/2003
0.14Q	9/16/2003	9/24/2003	9/26/2003	10/10/2003
0.14Q	12/9/2003	12/18/2003	12/22/2003	1/9/2004
0.14Q	2/17/2004	3/24/2004	3/26/2004	4/9/2004
		Indicated Div: C$0.56		

Valuation Analysis

Forecast P/E 438.20 (5/24/2004)

Market Cap	$1.4 Billion	Book Value	N/A
Price/Book	N/A	Price/Sales	N/A

Dividend Achiever Status

Rank	27	5 Year Growth Rate	4.55%
Total Years of Dividend Growth		11	

TRADING VOLUME (thousand shares)

Business Summary: Wood Products (MIC: 11.9 SIC: 2411 NAIC:113310)

West Fraser Timber is an integrated forest products company producing lumber, wood chips, fiberboard, plywood, pulp, linerboard, kraft paper and newsprint. Co. conducts its operations through its subsidiary companies and joint ventures owned directly or indirectly by the Co.'s principal operating subsidiary West Fraser Mills. Most of the forest products manufactured by Co. are sold outside Canada as commodities. Co. operates its facilities in Quesnel and Kitimat in British Columbia; Whitecourt, Edmonton, Slave Lake in Alberta; and West Monroe, LA.

Recent Developments: For the quarter ended Mar 31 2004, net income more than doubled to C$26.5 million compared with C$10.9 million in the corresponding period of the previous year. Results for 2004 included a pre-tax share option expense of C$9.9 million. Net sales increased 11.2% to C$541.1 million from C$486.8 million in the year-earlier quarter. Sales from the lumber segment advanced 19.5% to C$317.2 million from C$265.4 million, while panel segment sales improved 16.5% to C$68.4 million from C$58.7 million in the prior-year period. Pulp and paper segment sales decreased 4.4% to C$155.5 million from C$162.7 million in 2003. Operating income soared to C$41.9 million versus C$2.2 million the year before.

Prospects: Co. continues to benefit from strong revenue growth in its lumber segment, as prices continue to increase on higher demand resulting from stronger housing starts in the U.S. and Canada. Also, Co.'s panels operations are benefiting from increased demand for medium-density fiberboard, although prices have increased only slightly from cyclical lows. Meanwhile, Co.'s pulp and paper businesses is being adversely affected by continued weak prices for linerboard and kraft paper. Looking ahead, Co.'s production levels should benefit from the start-up of its Arkansas sawmill, which recently completed its rebuild activities.

Financial Data

(Can$ in Thousands)	9 Mos	6 Mos	3 Mos	12/31/2002	12/31/2001	12/31/2000	12/31/1999	12/31/1998
Earnings Per Share	0.24	0.15	0.29	3.47	3.20	3.42	3.92	0.04
Cash Flow Per Share	3.44	(0.05)	(1.41)	4.57	...	...	...	...
Dividends Per Share	0.530	0.520	0.500	0.490	0.460	0.450	0.440	0.430
Dividend Payout %	222.72	347.87	175.54	14.32	14.46	13.40	11.36	1
Income Statement								
Total Revenues	1,146,700	764,400	385,400	1,632,239	1,562,306	2,309,440	2,204,115	1,863,399
Total Indirect Exp.	161,300	104,500	56,400	179,605	193,773	196,433	192,898	207,318
Depreciation & Amort.	106,400	71,900	38,900	135,434	123,279	136,961	125,142	127,774
Operating Income	(22,800)	(30,800)	2,200	208,869	187,229	278,822	321,408	118,899
Income Taxes	(13,300)	(15,300)	(2,500)	56,208	34,519	80,509	107,174	21,653
Income from Cont Ops	...	...	...	129,039	108,840	...	...	...
Net Income	8,800	5,700	10,900	137,560	126,488	131,458	147,421	5,625
Average Shs. Outstg.	37,065	37,177	37,264	37,130	33,497	36,707	35,976	35,094
Balance Sheet								
Cash & Cash Equivalents	...	...	118,200	192,916	270,057	...	97,504	...
Total Current Assets	...	...	726,800	693,351	759,015	757,665	793,549	634,611
Total Assets	...	...	2,127,200	2,115,671	2,352,586	2,453,452	2,264,920	2,108,930
Total Current Liabilities	...	...	226,300	212,225	471,224	443,322	449,830	310,067
Long-Term Obligations	...	...	322,900	337,745	359,589	570,633	589,878	718,449
Net Stockholders' Equity	...	...	1,298,000	1,291,762	1,203,410	1,127,331	1,026,273	897,631
Shares Outstanding	36,853	36,848	3,361	36,831	33,396	36,716	36,700	35,174
Statistical Record								
Operating Profit Margin %	N.M.	N.M.	0.57	12.79	11.98	12.07	14.58	6.38
Return on Equity %	...	...	0.83	10.64	10.51	11.66	14.36	0.62
Return on Assets %	...	...	0.51	6.50	5.37	5.35	6.50	0.26
Price Range	39.05-30.01	39.05-30.01	39.05-31.36	40.00-26.36	31.78-21.07	31.82-17.36	33.06-23.97	33.06-16.53
P/E Ratio	162.7-125.0	260.3-200.1	134.7-108.2	11.53-7.60	9.93-6.59	9.30-5.07	8.43-6.11	826.4-413.2
Average Yield %	1.57	1.55	1.45	1.44	1.67	1.73	1.51	1.63

Address: 1000-1100 Melville Street, Vancouver, BC V6E 4A6 **Telephone:** (604) 895 2700 **Web Site:** www.westfraser.com	**Officers:** Henry H. Ketcham - Chmn., Pres., C.E.O., D. Wayne Clogg - V.P., Woodlands **Transfer Agents:**CIBC Mellon Trust Company, Vancouver, British Columbia; Calgary, Alberta;	**Investor Contact:**604-895-2700 **Institutional Holding** **No of Institutions:** 1 **Shares:** 225,000 **% Held:** -

WESTON (GEORGE) LIMITED

Exchange	Symbol	Price	52Wk Range	Yield	P/E
TSX	WN	C$88.45 (5/31/2004)	108.0-88.01	1.64	15.52

*7 Year Price Score 130.7 *NYSE Composite Index=100 *12 Month Price Score 42.9

Interim Earnings (Per Share) Can$

Qtr.	Mar	Jun	Sep	Dec
2001	0.56	0.94	1.08	1.79
2002	0.79	1.17	1.36	1.70
2003	0.96	1.42	1.54	1.86
2004	0.88	...	...	...

Interim Dividends (Per Share) Can$

Amt	Decl	Ex	Rec	Pay
0.30Q	8/28/2003	9/11/2003	9/15/2003	10/1/2003
0.30Q	11/21/2003	12/11/2003	12/15/2003	1/1/2004
0.36Q	2/16/2004	3/11/2004	3/15/2004	4/1/2004
0.36Q	...	6/11/2004	6/15/2004	7/1/2004
		Indicated Div: $1.44		

Valuation Analysis

Forecast P/E 14.93 (5/24/2004)

Market Cap	$11.6 Billion	Book Value	N/A
Price/Book	N/A	Price/Sales	N/A

Dividend Achiever Status

Rank	3	5 Year Growth Rate 24.36%
Total Years of Dividend Growth		8

Business Summary: Food (MIC: 4.1 SIC: 2051 NAIC:311812)

George Weston and its subsidiaries are engaged in the food processing and distribution industry. Co. has three operating segments: Weston Foods, Food Distribution and Fisheries. The Weston Foods segment is primarily engaged in the baking and dairy industries within North America. The Food Distribution segment, which is operated by Loblaw Companies Limited and its subsidiaries, concentrates on food retailing and is increasing its offering of non-food products and services. The Fisheries segment is primarily engaged in the hatching, growing and processing of fresh farmed salmon in North America and Chile.

Recent Developments: For the three months ended Mar 27 2004, net earnings decreased 9.7% to C$121.0 million compared with C$134.0 million in the equivalent period of the previous year. Results for 2004 included pre-tax restructuring and other charges of C$1.0 million. Sales rose 2.9% to C$6.58 billion from C$6.40 billion in the year-earlier quarter. Food Distribution segment sales climbed 5.6% to C$5.68 billion from C$5.38 billion the year before. However, Weston Foods segment sales declined 8.1% to C$1.04 billion from C$1.13 billion, while Fisheries segment sales dropped 26.1% to C$34.0 million from C$46.0 million in 2003. Operating income grew to C$344.0 million versus C$342.0 million in 2003.

Prospects: For the remainder of 2004, Co.'s Food Distribution segment will look to continue its strong growth in sales and net earnings, although constrained by food price deflation in certain markets. Co.will continue to focus on strategic initiatives, improving its cost base and its consumer value proposition and positioning itself for sustainable growth at it Loblaw subsidiary. Conversely, Co.'s Weston Foods segment is being negatively affected by the consumer trend to move away from traditional white flour based bakery products, the difficult food retail environment in the U.S., and the ongoing industry-wide cost pressures from higher commodity, energy and employee related costs.

Financial Data

(Can$ in Millions)	12/31/2003	12/31/2002	12/31/2001	12/31/2000	12/31/1999	12/31/1998	12/31/1997	12/31/1996
Earnings Per Share	5.78	5.02	4.37	3.64	2.67	5.05	5.45	1.73
Cash Flow Per Share	9.69	9.97	...	...	...	...	...	...
Dividends Per Share	1.140	0.920	0.800	0.620	0.420	0.380	0.310	0.280
Dividend Payout %	19.72	18.32	18.30	17.03	15.73	7.52	5.68	16.18
Income Statement								
Total Revenues	29,198	27,446	24,661	22,344	20,851	14,726	13,921	12,709
Total Indirect Exp.	606	507	431	368	357	269	294	257
Depreciation & Amort.	546	507	431	368	357	269	294	257
Operating Income	1,812	1,678	1,440	1,189	969	648	588	500
Net Interest Inc./(Exp.)	266	238	221	171	136	104	72	85
Income Taxes	430	469	435	310	301	208	208	211
Eqty Earns/Minority Int.	324	281	212	175	139	81	64	52
Income from Cont Ops	...	...	...	...	...	670	...	...
Net Income	792	690	582	481	351	773	244	239
Average Shs. Outstg.	132	132	132	132	131	...	...	...
Balance Sheet								
Cash & Cash Equivalents	1,510	1,555	1,261	1,270	1,011	792	651	768
Total Current Assets	4,698	4,705	5,060	3,733	3,170	2,915	2,272	2,236
Total Assets	17,338	16,663	16,277	11,421	10,049	9,036	5,878	5,441
Total Current Liabilities	4,330	4,427	5,653	3,906	3,317	3,325	2,195	2,139
Long-Term Obligations	5,832	5,391	4,908	2,986	2,584	1,984	1,172	1,002
Net Stockholders' Equity	4,462	4,382	3,626	2,904	2,618	2,389	1,756	1,615
Net Working Capital	368	278	(593)	(173)	(147)	(410)	77	97
Shares Outstanding	129	132	131	131	131	132	44	135
Statistical Record								
Operating Profit Margin %	6.20	6.11	5.83	5.32	4.64	4.40	4.22	3.93
Return on Equity %	17.74	15.74	16.05	16.56	13.40	32.35	13.89	14.79
Return on Assets %	4.56	4.14	3.57	4.21	3.49	8.55	4.15	4.39
Debt/Total Assets %	33.63	32.35	30.15	26.14	25.71	21.95	19.93	18.41
Price Range	108.0-89.88	130.7-90.01	105.5-77.00	86.85-45.00	65.50-47.50	59.35-37.67	40.67-22.20	22.28-15.25
P/E Ratio	18.69-15.55	26.03-17.93	24.14-17.62	23.86-12.36	24.53-17.79	11.75-7.46	7.46-4.07	12.88-8.82
Average Yield %	1.15	0.84	0.86	0.97	0.74	0.80	1.04	1.61

Address: 22 St. Clair Avenue East, Toronto, ON M4T 2S7	Officers: W. Galen Weston – Chmn., Pres., Roy R. Conliffe – Sr. V.P., Labor Relations	
Telephone: (416) 922-2500	Transfer Agents:Computershare Trust Company of Canada, Toronto	Institutional Holding
Web Site: www.weston.ca		No of Institutions: 4
		Shares: 1,494,478 % Held: –

Take Advantage of Our Multiple Copy Discount!

Copy or detach and send to:

John Wiley & Sons, PT Journals and Periodicals
989 Market Street, San Francisco, CA 94103-1741

For fastest service:

Call or fax toll-free: Phone 888-378-2537; Fax 888-481-2665

Subscriptions Please _ start _ renew my subscription to *Mergent's Dividend Achievers* at the following rate:

U.S.	_ Individual: $165	_ Institutional: $165
Canada	_ Individual: $165	_ Institutional: $205
All Others	_ Individual: $189	_ Institutional: $239

Subscribe for multiple copies and save!

Bulk subscription discounts for 10 or more copies will save you 25% on each copy. Save more than 40% on subscription orders for 100 copies or more. To learn more about **bulk subscription discounts**, contact our Special Sales representative Jill Gottlieb at 1-201-748-8839.

Also available in single issues!

For information about ordering single copies of this issue, call 1-888-378-2537. **Multiple copy discounts** also exist for single-issue purchases. Call 1-888-378-2537 for details.

$ _____ Total subscriptions. (No sales tax for U.S. subscriptions. Canadian residents, add GST for subscription orders.)

_ Payment enclosed (U.S. check or money order only. All payments must be in U.S. dollars.)

_ VISA _ MC _ Amex # _____ Exp. Date _____

Card Holder Name _____ Card Issue # _____

Signature _____ Day Phone _____

_ Bill Me (U.S. institutional orders only. Purchase order required.)

Purchase order # _____

Federal Tax ID13559302   **GST 89102 8052**

Name _____

Address _____

Phone _____ E-mail _____

_ Yes, I'd like to hear about special discount offers, new products, and more. Place me on the Journals/Periodicals e-mail list.